$$SS_x = \sum_{j=1}^{c} \sum_{i=1}^{n} (\bar{Y}_j - \bar{Y})^2 \quad \text{or} \quad SS_x = \sum_{j=1}^{c} n \, (\bar{Y}_j - \bar{Y})^2$$

$$SS_{error} = \sum_{j=1}^{c} \sum_{i=1}^{n} (Y_{ij} - \bar{Y}_j)^2$$

Y_i = individual observation
$\bar{Y}_j$ = mean for category j
$\bar{Y}$ = mean over the whole sample, or grand mean
Y_{ij} = ith observation in the jth category
c = number of categories of X
n = number of observations in each category
N = total sample size ($= n \times c$)

Measuring the strength of the effects of X on Y:

$$\eta^2 = SS_x/SS_y = (SS_y - SS_{error})/SS_y$$

p. 491: The significance of the overall effect may be tested by

$$F = \frac{SS_x/(c-1)}{SS_{error}/(N-c)} = \frac{MS_x}{MS_{error}}$$

where
MS = Mean square

Chapter 18 Correlation and Regression

p. 513: Product moment correlation:

$$r = \frac{\sum_{i=1}^{n}(X_i - \bar{X})(Y_i - \bar{Y})}{\sqrt{\sum_{i=1}^{n}(X_i - \bar{X})^2 \sum_{i=1}^{n}(Y_i - \bar{Y})^2}}$$

Division of the numerator and denominator by $(n-1)$ gives

$$r = \frac{\displaystyle\sum_{i=1}^{n} \frac{(X_i - \bar{X})(Y_i - \bar{Y})}{n-1}}{\sqrt{\displaystyle\sum_{i=1}^{n} \frac{(X_i - \bar{X})^2}{n-1} \sum_{i=1}^{n} \frac{(Y_i - \bar{Y})^2}{n-1}}}$$

$$= \frac{COV_{xy}}{s_x s_y}$$

p. 517: Expressing r in terms of the decomposition of the total variation:

$$r^2 = \frac{\text{Explained variation}}{\text{Total variation}} = \frac{SS_x}{SS_y}$$

$$= \frac{\text{Total variation} - \text{Error variation}}{\text{Total variation}} = \frac{SS_y - SS_{error}}{SS_y}$$

pp. 521–522: Basic regression equation:

$$Y_i = \beta_0 + \beta_1 X + e_i$$

Estimating the regression parameters:
In most cases, β_0 and β_1 are unknown and are estimated from the sample observations using the equation

$$\hat{Y}_i = a + bX_i$$

The slope, b, may be computed in terms of the covariance between X and Y (COV_{xy}) and the variance of X as

$$b = \frac{COV_{xy}}{s_x^2} = \frac{\sum_{i=1}^{n}(X_i - \bar{X})(Y_i - \bar{Y})}{\sum_{i=1}^{n}(X_i - \bar{X})^2} = \frac{\sum_{i=1}^{n} X_i Y_i - n\bar{X}\bar{Y}}{\sum_{i=1}^{n} X_i^2 - n\bar{X}^2}$$

The intercept, a, may then be calculated using:

$$a = \bar{Y} - b\bar{X}$$

p. 523: Relationship between standardized and nonstandardized regression coefficients:

$$B_{yx} = b_{yx}(s_x/s_y)$$

p. 528: General form of the multiple regression model:

$$Y = \beta_0 + \beta_1 X_1 + \beta_2 X_2 + \beta_3 X_3 + \ldots + \beta_k X_k + e$$

which is estimated by the following equation:

$$\hat{Y} = a + b_1 X_1 + b_2 X_2 + b_3 X_3 + \ldots + b_k X_k$$

pp. 531–532: Coefficient of multiple determination:

$$R^2 = \frac{SS_{reg}}{SS_y}$$

where

$$SS_y = \sum_{i=1}^{n}(Y_i - \bar{Y})^2 \quad \text{and} \quad SS_{reg} = \sum_{i=1}^{n}(\hat{Y}_i - \bar{Y})^2$$

R^2 adjusted for the number of independent variables and the sample size:

$$\text{Adjusted } R^2 = R^2 - \frac{k(1 - R^2)}{n - k - 1}$$

where
n = number of observations
k = number of independent variables

The significance of the overall regression equation can be tested by

$$F = \frac{SS_{reg}/k}{SS_{res}/(n - k - 1)} = \frac{R^2/k}{(1 - R^2)/(n - k - 1)}$$

where

$$SS_{reg} = \sum_{i=1}^{n}(\hat{Y}_i - \bar{Y})^2$$

$$SS_{res} = \sum_{i=1}^{n}(Y_i - \hat{Y}_i)^2$$

The significance of the partial r̄egression coefficient may be tested by

$$t = \frac{b}{SE_b}$$

Where SE_b is the standard

EDITION 4

Basic Marketing Research

Integration of Social Media

NARESH K. MALHOTRA

Nanyang Technological University and Georgia Institute of Technology

PEARSON

Boston   Columbus   Indianapolis   New York   San Francisco   Upper Saddle River
Amsterdam   Cape Town   Dubai   London   Madrid   Milan   Munich   Paris   Montreal   Toronto
Delhi   Mexico City   Sao Paulo   Sydney   Hong Kong   Seoul   Singapore   Taipei   Tokyo

Editorial Director: Sally Yagan
Editorial Project Manager: Meeta Pendharkar
Director of Marketing: Patrice Lumumba Jones
Executive Marketing Manager: Anne Fahlgren
Senior Managing Editor: Judy Leale
Production Project Manager: Kelly Warsak
Senior Operations Supervisor: Arnold Vila
Operations Specialist: Cathleen Petersen
Creative Director: Blair Brown
Senior Art Director: Janet Slowik
Art Director: Steven Frim
Text Designer: Wee Design Group

Cover Designer: Wee Design Group
Manager, Rights and Permissions: Hessa Albader
Media Project Manager: Lisa Rinaldi
Media Assistant Editor: Denise Vaughn
Full-Service Project Management: Jennifer Welsch/
BookMasters, Inc.
Composition: Integra Software Services
Printer/Binder: R.R. Donnelley/Willard
Cover Printer: R.R. Donnelley
Hagerstown
Text Font: 10/12 Times

Credits and acknowledgments borrowed from other sources and reproduced, with permission, in this textbook appear on the appropriate page within text.

Microsoft® and Windows® are registered trademarks of the Microsoft Corporation in the U.S.A. and other countries. Screen shots and icons reprinted with permission from the Microsoft Corporation. This book is not sponsored or endorsed by or affiliated with the Microsoft Corporation.

Many of the designations by manufacturers and sellers to distinguish their products are claimed as trademarks. Where those designations appear in this book, and the publisher was aware of a trademark claim, the designations have been printed in initial caps or all caps.

Library of Congress Cataloging-in-Publication Data
Malhotra, Naresh K.
    Basic marketing research : integration of social media / Naresh K. Malhotra.—4th ed.
      p. cm.
    Includes bibliographical references and index.
    ISBN 978-0-13-254448-1 (hardcover : alk. paper)
1. Marketing research. I. Title.
HF5415.2.M288 2012
658.8'3—dc23
                                                                                    2011019806

10 9 8 7 6 5

ISBN 10: 0-13-254448-2
ISBN 13: 978-0-13-254448-1

To my wife and best friend, Veena, with love.

"A prudent wife is from the LORD."

PROVERBS **19:14**

"Husbands, love your wives, even as Christ also loved the church, and gave himself for it."

EPHESIANS **5:25**

Brief Contents

Contents

Foreword

It is a pleasure to write this foreword. Dr. Naresh K. Malhotra is a very well-known and highly successful author, researcher, and teacher. *Basic Marketing Research: Integration of Social Media,* Fourth Edition, is yet another outstanding textbook that he has written. *Basic Marketing Research* has been a very successful book with several editions and translations. His other book, *Marketing Research: An Applied Orientation,* now in its sixth edition, has also been translated into several languages including Chinese, Spanish, Portuguese, French, Russian, Hungarian, Indonesian, and Japanese. It has been published in several English editions including North American, International, European, Filipino, Indian, and Australian editions.

Basic Marketing Research: Integration of Social Media, Fourth Edition, carries Dr. Malhotra's expertise in marketing research and pedagogical skills even further. With its focus on contemporary issues like international marketing research, social media and new technologies, and ethics, the book effectively captures the current environment. The application of Web-based marketing research is integrated in a pervasive way throughout the book, which reflects the state-of-the-art orientation of the material presented in this text. Particularly noteworthy is the pervasive and innovative emphasis on social media, both as a domain in which to conduct marketing research and as an application of marketing research. This is just one of the ways in which the fourth edition is leading the field of marketing research.

This book is rich in tangible and illustrative examples that bring the student closer to the business world and everyday realities of the marketplace. The opening vignettes, interwoven throughout the respective chapters, further illustrate the marketing research concepts in real-life settings. The Be an MR! and Be a DM!, What Would *You* Do?, and Experiential Learning exercises provide a rich and hands-on experience. The Research in Action examples, case studies, and online video case studies are great learning tools and further reinforce the highly applied and managerial orientation of the text. Particularly noteworthy are the running case, comprehensive critical thinking cases, and several other cases that include questionnaires and real-life data. New to this edition are brief comprehensive Harvard Business School cases that are appropriate for undergraduate students. There are several diagrams, figures, and concept maps in each chapter that truly enhance learning. The lessons are conceptually sound, technically accurate, and communicate the basic research concepts with simplicity and clarity. The book is strong in qualitative concepts and imparts the necessary quantitative knowledge and skills with the use of SPSS, Excel, and other statistical software. The SPSS and Excel demonstration movies, screen captures, step-by-step instructions, and study guide and technology manual provide the greatest resources available anywhere for students to learn these programs.

Basic Marketing Research, Fourth Edition, provides a strong foundation that we believe every student should have in order to be successful. This book is unsurpassed as a basis for undergraduate students to become researchers and intelligent users of marketing research.

Dr. Chuck Chakrapani
Editor, Marketing Research
President, Leger Marketing (Toronto)
Distinguished Visiting Professor, Ryerson University
Ted Rogers School of Management
Toronto, Canada

Preface

The Fourth Edition—Helping Students Learn Marketing Research

Marketing research is an integral part of marketing. The task of marketing research is to assess the information needs and provide management with relevant, accurate, reliable, valid, and current information to aid marketing decision making (see Figure 1.5). Companies use marketing research to stay competitive and to avoid high costs associated with making poor decisions based on unsound information. If you are a marketing major, understanding the various customer groups (consumers, suppliers, channel partners, employees, etc.), competitors, and the environment is the foundation for developing effective marketing programs. Such an understanding is gained by conducting marketing research. This course will help you succeed in your marketing career.

If you are not a marketing major, consider all of the marketing research around you in the form of information available from the Internet, newspapers, magazines, government, commercial firms, and other sources. Any company or organization you work for will be involved in making use of such information for making decisions. It is important to understand how such information is generated and how it should be evaluated to assess its relevance, accuracy, and usefulness. The research process that we describe in this book is very general and can be applied to conduct research in any area of management, not just marketing. Only the context in which we illustrate the research is marketing. Therefore, this course and this book will help you to be more effective in your job, regardless of the specific area in which you work. This knowledge also will provide you with a better understanding of those involved in marketing in the organization where you will work, and it will equip you with better information to function as a consumer.

The fourth edition integrates the use of social media for conducting marketing research in a pervasive way. Since research is best learned by doing it, this book emphasizes a hands-on, do-it-yourself approach. We created *Basic Marketing Research: Integration of Social Media,* Fourth Edition, in part, to help students understand and learn the importance of sound information to make marketing decisions and to see the interaction between marketing research and marketing management decisions. We provide you with several opportunities to experience these interactions through pedagogical tools such as the opening vignette, Be an MR!, Be a DM!; Experiential Learning; What Would *You* Do?; Research in Action; cases; Brief Harvard Business School cases; online video cases; extensive review questions; applied problems; and group discussions. The data-analysis chapters involve a tight integration of SPSS and Excel, illustrating each step in running these programs in detail. We provide four distinct ways in which you can learn these programs on your own. SPSS and Excel files are provided for all data sets; outputs and screen captures are posted on the Web site. This book provides the most extensive help available to marketing research students in learning SPSS and Excel.

We prepared this textbook and all of the additional materials in a way that will best help you to understand the fundamental principles of marketing research and their applications in real-life marketing situations. Students need opportunities to apply concepts to real-life situations. This helps them clearly understand and retain the ideas. As a result, we have prepared a variety of end-of-chapter materials that are designed to help you practice using the concepts. These materials include review questions, applied problems, group discussion questions, cases, Brief Harvard Business School cases, and online video cases. The data-analysis chapters include several real-life data sets where the files have been provided in both SPSS and Excel.

New to the Fourth Edition

While retaining the desirable features of the previous editions, the fourth edition contains major revisions. Several significant changes have been made. These changes were identified by conducting surveys of professors (users and nonusers) and students, and by obtaining critical reviews and detailed evaluations. Major changes include the following:

1. *Integration of Social Media.* The fourth edition features an innovative and pervasive integration of social media. There is a separate section titled "Marketing Research and Social Media" in every chapter, including the data-analysis chapters. In addition, the use of social media is discussed in several other sections of the chapter, including end-of-chapter questions, the Hewlett-Packard running case, and all the online video cases. The major occurrences of social media are highlighted with an icon. We focus on social media both as an application of marketing research and as a domain in which to conduct marketing research. Although we do not expect social media research to replace traditional marketing research, we predict that social media will become an increasingly important domain that complements traditional marketing research.

2. *Comprehensive Brief Harvard Business School Cases.* Four Brief Harvard Business School cases have been added. All these cases are brief and suitable for use at the undergraduate level. All the cases have rich marketing research content and show the interaction between marketing research and marketing management decisions in real-life contexts. All have been written recently. These cases are comprehensive in that marketing research questions have been posed for every chapter, including the data-analysis chapters. These cases are:

   Case 4.1 TruEarth Healthy Foods: Market Research for a New Product Introduction (4065)

   Case 4.2 The Springfield Nor'easters: Maximizing Revenues in the Minor Leagues (2510)

   Case 4.3 Metabical: Positioning and Communications Strategy for a New Weight-Loss Drug (4240)

   Case 4.4 Saxonville Sausage Company (2085)

3. *Updated SPSS and Excel Computerized Demonstration Movies and Screen Captures with Notes.* The fourth edition has computerized demonstration movies and screen captures with notes for IBM SPSS 19 and for Excel 2010. The steps in the book for running every statistical procedure have also been updated to reflect these latest versions. The computerized demonstration movies and screen captures with notes for the earlier versions of SPSS and Excel are also posted on the instructor's as well as students' Web site for the book.

4. *Chapter Modifications.* Each chapter has been modified to present new ideas, update existing materials, or, in some instances, to further clarify concepts. These changes are extensive in most of the chapters. For example, in Chapter 1, a new figure (Figure 1.6) has been added to amplify the decision to conduct marketing research, and the structure of the marketing research industry has been revised to reflect recent changes (revised Figure 1.7 and Table 1.1). A new section titled "Marketing Research and Competitive Intelligence" has been added. Such changes have been made in all the chapters.

5. *New and Updated Examples.* Several new examples have been added, some old ones deleted, and the remaining examples have been updated as appropriate. Thus, the fourth edition reflects the current marketing and research environment.

6. *New and Updated Cases and Online Video Cases.* The Hewlett-Packard running case, the Comprehensive Critical Thinking Cases, Comprehensive Cases with Real Data, and the Online Video Cases have all been updated to reflect the current environment. Online Video Cases 15.1, 16.1, 17.1, and 18.1 have been added for the data analysis chapters.

Integrated Learning Package

We have created several devices that are designed to help you learn the materials in this text. If you take advantage of them, you might find this textbook interesting and even fun. Even those who are not marketing majors may discover that marketing research and all of the activities involved are enjoyable subjects to talk about and study.

- *Lead-In Vignettes.* Each chapter begins with a vignette that is related to the topic being presented. The majority of the vignettes revolve around success stories about companies and products most will recognize, such as Reebok, Gillette, P&G, Olympics, Sears, Spiegel, and United Airlines. The opening vignette is used as a running example throughout the chapter. After discussing the main concepts in each chapter, we refer to the opening vignette to summarize and illustrate the concepts in a section titled "Summary Illustration Using the Opening Vignette."

■ *Integration of Social Media.* The fourth edition features an innovative and pervasive integration of social media. There is a separate section titled "Marketing Research and Social Media" in each chapter, including the data-analysis chapters. In addition, the use of social media is discussed in several other sections of the chapter, including end-of-chapter questions, the Hewlett-Packard running case, and all the online video cases. The major occurrences of social media are highlighted with an icon. We focus on social media both as an application of marketing research and as a domain in which to conduct marketing research. Although we do not expect social media research to replace traditional marketing research, we predict that social media will become an increasingly important domain that complements traditional marketing research.

■ *Stimulating Critical Thinking.* The principles for critical thinking, including Socratic questioning, critical reading and writing, higher order thinking, and assessment, have been embodied in the three comprehensive critical thinking cases, end-of-chapter review questions, applied problems, and group discussions. These materials have been designed based on the guidelines provided by the Foundation for Critical Thinking.

■ *A Hands-On Orientation.* Be an MR!, Be a DM!; Experiential Learning; and What Would *You* Do? require students to actually do some research and make marketing research and marketing management decisions through a hands-on orientation. This hands-on orientation is further reinforced by cases, online video cases, review questions, applied problems, and group discussions.

■ *Interrelationships Among Concepts.* Substantial research shows that concept maps aid in student learning. One or more concept maps have been given in each chapter to illustrate the interrelationships among concepts. These maps have been developed based on the principles and tools provided by the Institute for Human and Machine Cognition. These maps will help you acquire a better understanding of the various concepts. Please be sure to review them!

■ *Real-Life Examples and Illustrations.* Several real-life examples are presented in each chapter and titled "Research in Action." These examples describe in detail the kind of marketing research conducted to address specific managerial problems and the decisions that were based on the findings. Where appropriate, the sources cited have been supplemented by additional marketing research information to enhance the usefulness of these examples. In addition, there are several other examples and illustrations that are blended in the text.

■ *Comprehensive Cases with Real Data.* Each chapter of the book contains the Hewlett-Packard running case (Case 1.1) that features an actual questionnaire and real-life data. The questions for HP appear at the end of each chapter while the case appears toward the end of the book. There are additional comprehensive cases with actual questionnaires and real-life data (Case 3.1 Bank of America, Case 3.2 McDonald's, and Case 3.3 Boeing).

■ *Comprehensive Brief Harvard Business School Cases.* Four Brief Harvard Business School cases have been added to the fourth edition. All these cases are brief and suitable for use at the undergraduate level. All the cases have rich marketing research content and show the interaction between marketing research and marketing management decisions in real-life contexts. All have been written recently. These cases are comprehensive in that marketing research questions have been posed for every chapter, including the data-analysis chapters. These cases have been listed in the previous section.

■ *Online Video Cases with Streaming Video.* Video cases referenced at the end of each chapter are located on the text's companion Web site (www.pearsonhighered.com/malhotra). These online cases include the actual written cases and questions as well as streaming video for students to see the application of chapter concepts to real business situations.

■ *Extensive and Pervasive Internet Coverage.* The Internet has become part and parcel of our lives. The text discusses how the Internet can be integrated in each step of the marketing research process and how it can be used to implement the concepts discussed in each chapter. The coverage of the Internet is so extensive and pervasive that it has not been singled out. Internet applications are ubiquitous. For example, all the Be an MR! exercises require you to research the Internet, including social media.

- *International Focus.* Many of you have traveled to other countries. Most of you interact with students from other countries. Global, international business is all around. This makes understanding international marketing research issues important. Every chapter, except the data-analysis Chapters 16, 17, and 18, has a section titled "International Marketing Research." This section discusses how the concepts of that chapter should be implemented while conducting marketing research in an international setting. Note that data analysis in international marketing research is discussed in Chapter 15.

- *Ethics Focus.* Ethical issues are pervasive in marketing research. Every chapter, except the data-analysis Chapters 16, 17, and 18, has a section titled "Ethics in Marketing Research." This section presents the salient ethical issues involved while implementing the concepts of that chapter. These ethical issues are discussed from the perspectives of the four stakeholders: the client, the marketing research firm, respondents, and the general public. Note that the ethical issues pertinent to data analysis are discussed in Chapter 15.

- *Contemporary Focus.* A contemporary focus has been achieved by illustrating the applications of marketing research to current topics such as customer value, satisfaction, loyalty, customer equity, brand equity and management, innovation, entrepreneurship, return on marketing, relationship marketing, sustainability, and socially responsible marketing throughout the text. These examples cover a diversity of products and companies that are of interest to undergraduate students.

- *Opening Diagrams.* Each chapter, except the first, opens with a diagram that gives the focus of that chapter, its relationship to the previous chapter(s), and its relationship to the marketing research process. This diagram is an excellent way to see the linkages between chapters and to trace the entire marketing research process throughout the book. We also include a diagram that provides an overview of the chapter, showing the major topics and linking them to figures and tables. There is an abundance of diagrams in each chapter.

- *SPSS, Excel, SAS, and Minitab.* Data-analysis procedures are illustrated with respect to SPSS, Excel, SAS, and Minitab, along with other popular computer programs. However, the emphasis is on SPSS and Excel. Detailed, step-by-step instructions are given for running the various statistical procedures using SPSS and Excel. SPSS and Excel files are provided for all data sets, and outputs are provided for the analyses contained in the chapters.

- *SPSS and EXCEL Computerized Demonstration Movies.* We have created computerized demonstration movies illustrating step-by-step instructions for each data-analysis procedure—SPSS and EXCEL—available for downloading from the Web site for this book (see Exhibit 15.2). You can view these movies to promote self-learning.

- *SPSS and EXCEL Screen Captures.* In addition to the demonstration movies, we have also provided screen captures with notes illustrating step-by-step instructions for running each data-analysis procedure presented in the book using SPSS as well as EXCEL. These are on the text Web site for downloading.

- *Conducting a Live Marketing Research Project.* Toward the end of each chapter is a section titled "Live Research: Conducting a Marketing Research Project." These sections show how to implement one or more live marketing research projects in the course. The approach is flexible and can handle a variety of organizations and formats. The entire class could be working on the same project with each team working on all aspects of the project or each team could be assigned a specific responsibility (e.g., a specific component of the problem or a specific aspect of the project like collection and analysis of secondary data). Alternatively, the class could be working on multiple projects with specific teams assigned to a specific project. If your course includes a class project, your instructor will choose the approach that is best for you!

- *Acronyms.* Each chapter contains one or more helpful acronyms that summarize the salient concepts. Acronyms are the most popular mnemonic technique used by undergraduate students. Theoretical and empirical evidence supporting the effectiveness of mnemonic techniques and their usefulness as a pedagogical tool has been discussed in a paper I published in the *Journal of the Academy of Marketing Science* (Spring 1991): 141–150.

You Can Learn SPSS and Excel on Your Own!

Many students complain that they spend a substantial amount of time learning SPSS or Excel. We have addressed this situation. The fourth edition provides four ways in which you can learn SPSS and Excel on your own. Help for running the SPSS and Excel programs used in each chapter is provided in four ways: (1) detailed step-by-step instructions are given in the chapter; (2) you can download (from the Web site for this book) computerized demonstration movies illustrating these step-by-step instructions; (3) you can download screen captures with notes illustrating these step-by-step instructions; and (4) extensive instructions for SPSS and Excel are given in the study guide, a supplement that accompanies this book. Thus, we provide the most extensive help available anywhere to learn SPSS and Excel!

Tips on How to Use This Textbook

We want to offer you a few tips on how to use this book and suggestions on how to master the material presented.

- *Read the Chapter.* Start by reading the chapter. Be sure to look at the learning objectives and opening diagrams, and read the overview so you will know what is in the chapter. Often this is skipped because students don't believe it is important.
- *Review the Key Terms.* It is important read through these new terms to be sure you understand each one. Key terms are often targets of quiz and exam questions.
- *Answer the Review Questions.* Go through the review questions and see if you can answer them without looking in the chapter. When you are finished, go back and check to see if you got each one correct. For the ones you couldn't answer, go back and locate the correct information in the chapter.
- *Do the Applied Problems.* Pick several problems you believe would be interesting. Spend some time thinking about the question and the concepts being explored. You can make these problems fun to do as you analyze the concepts at a deeper level.
- *Have Some Fun with Critical Thinking.* Go to one of the critical thinking cases (2.1 American Idol, 2.2 Baskin-Robbins, and 2.3 Akron Children's Hospital). These cases are comprehensive and contain questions on all the chapters except the data-analysis chapters. Based on the knowledge you have learned in the chapter and the case information, answer the critical thinking questions as well as the technical questions. Doing these cases will help you understand and apply the concepts in real-life situations from a critical thinking perspective.
- *Experience Harvard Business School.* Pick one of the four brief Harvard Business School cases that interest you the most. Answer the marketing research questions that have been posed for each chapter, including the data-analysis chapters. These will help you apply the marketing research concepts to real-life situations and also give you a taste of how they teach at Harvard.

Suggestions for Preparing for Exams

If you have followed the tips provided in the previous section, you will almost be ready for the exam. A brief review of the key terms and a scan of the chapter will be all that you need. But, if you have not followed all of the tips, here is a sequence of activities you can follow that will aid in learning the material.

- Read the chapter.
- Review the concept maps.
- Review the key terms.
- Answer the review questions.
- Read the chapter overview.
- Read the chapter summary.
- Go through the chapter and locate all of the bold and italic words. Read the context of each term to make sure you understand that term.

- Start at the beginning of the chapter and read the topic sentence of each paragraph. These sentences should provide a good summary of that paragraph.
- Re-read the chapter summary.
- Review the key terms.

Congratulations! You are now ready for the exam. Relax—you will do well.

Learning Aids for Students

Companion Web site with Online Video Cases (0132544512)

Housed at www.pearsonhighered.com/malhotra, the companion Web site offers Naresh K. Malhotra's valuable additional resources for *Basic Marketing Research,* Fourth Edition, for instructors as well as students. This site is not password protected so that these materials can be accessed freely. Online Video Cases referenced at the end of each chapter are located on this companion Web site and include the case, questions, and the accompanying streaming video. This site also offers downloads of data files and additional material for use in conjunction with the textbook. Specifically, the Companion Web site contains the following materials:

- Data for Cases 1.1 Hewlett-Packard, 3.1 Bank of America, 3.2 McDonald's, and 3.3 Boeing, given in the book (SPSS and Excel).
- Online video cases for each chapter, including streaming video and questions to help you apply chapter learning objectives.
- Files for all the Experiential Learning exercises.
- Data files for all the Applied Problems (SPSS and Excel).
- Data file for the data set(s) used in each data-analysis chapter (SPSS and Excel).
- Output files for the analysis in each data-analysis chapter (SPSS and Excel)
- SPSS and Excel computerized demonstration movies.
- SPSS and Excel screen captures.
- Additional materials that supplement the topic discussed in the book.

Student Supplements and Value Packs

The book is supported by a useful set of supplements to further enhance your learning.

1. *Student Versions of SPSS.* A student version of SPSS 18 can be obtained as an optional value package with this book.
2. *Study Guide with Technology Manual (0132544563).* A study guide to enhance your learning is available in print format.

Teaching Aids for Instructors

The password protected Instructor Resource Center offers several teaching aids that can be accessed only by instructors. These include:

PowerPoint Presentations (0132544520)

A comprehensive set of PowerPoint slides can be used by instructors for class presentations or by students for lecture preview or review.

Instructor's Manual (0132544504)

A complete instructor's manual, prepared by the author, can be used to prepare lecture or class presentations, find answers to the end-of-chapter application exercises, and even to design the course syllabus. The manual also contains solutions to all the cases (HP Running Case, Comprehensive Critical Thinking Cases, Comprehensive Cases with Questionnaires and Real Data, Comprehensive Brief Harvard Business School Cases) and Online Video Cases.

Test Item File (0132544539)

The test bank for the fourth edition contains multiple-choice and true/false questions for every chapter.

This Test Item File supports Association to Advance Collegiate Schools of Business (AACSB) International Accreditation. Each chapter of the Test Item File was prepared with the AACSB learning standards in mind. Where appropriate, the answer line of each question indicates a category within which the question falls.[1] This AACSB reference helps instructors identify those test questions that support that organization's learning goals.

WHAT ARE AACSB LEARNING STANDARDS?   One of the criteria for AACSB accreditation is the quality of the curricula. Although no specific courses are required, the AACSB expects a curriculum to include learning experiences in such areas as:

- Communication abilities
- Ethical understanding and reasoning abilities
- Analytical skills
- Use of information technology
- Dynamics of the global economy
- Multicultural and diversity understanding
- Reflective thinking skills

These seven categories are AACSB Learning Standards. Questions that test skills relevant to these standards are tagged with the appropriate standard. For example, a question testing the moral questions associated with externalities would receive the ethical understanding and reasoning abilities tag.

HOW CAN I USE THESE TAGS?   Tagged questions help you measure whether students are grasping the course content that aligns with AACSB guidelines. In addition, the tagged questions may help to identify potential applications of these skills. This, in turn, may suggest enrichment activities or other educational experiences to help students achieve these goals.

Other Teaching Aids

The password protected Instructor Resource Center also contains the following:

- Data for cases 1.1 Hewlett-Packard, 3.1 Bank of America, 3.2 McDonald's, and 3.3 Boeing, given in the book (SPSS and Excel)
- Files for all the Experiential Learning exercises
- Data files for all the Applied Problems (SPSS and Excel)
- Data file for the data set(s) used in each data analysis chapter (SPSS and Excel)
- SPSS and Excel Computerized Demonstration Movies
- SPSS and Excel Screen Captures
- SPSS and Excel Output files for data analyses presented in Chapters 15 to 18, and for solutions to all Experiential Learning exercises, Applied Problems, and Cases
- Additional materials that supplement the topic discussed in the book.

---

[1] Please note that not all test questions indicate an AACSB category.

Acknowledgments

Several people have been extremely helpful in writing this textbook. I would like to acknowledge Professor Arun K. Jain (State University of New York at Buffalo), who taught me marketing research in a way I will never forget. My students, especially former doctoral students, as well as several MBA research assistants, have been helpful in many ways. The students in my marketing research courses have provided useful feedback, as the material was class-tested for several years. Michael Baumgardner, President and CEO, Burke Inc., William D. Neal, Founder and Senior Executive Officer of SDR Consulting, Terry Grapentine, Principal at Grapentine Company LLC, and Ken Athaide, Senior Vice President, Market Strategies International, have been very helpful and supportive over the years.

The reviewers have provided many constructive and valuable suggestions. Among others, the help of the following reviewers is gratefully acknowledged.

Reviewers for the First Edition

Dennis B. Arnett
University of Texas at San Antonio

Jerry Katrichis
University of Hartford

Paul L. Sauer
Canisius College

Alan G. Sawyer
University of Florida

Reviewers for the Second Edition

Ronald E. Goldsmith
Florida State University

Manish Kacker
Tulane University

John S. Kakalik
Western Connecticut State University

Alyse Lancaster
University of Miami

Tom Schmidt
Simpson College

Larry Seibert
University of Central Oklahoma

Donald E. Stem, Jr.
Washington State University

R. Greg Surovick
Lehigh University

Reviewers for the Third Edition

Aliosha Alexandrov
University of Wisconsin, Oshkosh

Karen Barr

Nicolet College and Technical Institute

Jacqueline Eastman

Georgia Southern University

Amit Ghosh

Cleveland State University

James Gould

Pace University

Sertan Kabadayi

Fordham University, Rose Hill

Luke Kachersky

Fordham University, Rose Hill

Erika Matulich

The University of Tampa

Norm McElvany

Johnson State College

Paul Young

Liberty University

The team at Prentice Hall provided outstanding support. Special thanks are due to Sally Yagan, editorial director; Meeta Pendharkar, editorial project manager; Anne Fahlgren, senior marketing manager; Kelly Warsak, senior production project manager; and Elisabeth Scarpa, editorial assistant. Special recognition is due to the several field representatives and salespeople who have done an outstanding job.

I want to acknowledge, with great respect, my parents, the late Mr. H. N. Malhotra and Mrs. S. Malhotra. Their love, encouragement, support, and the sacrificial giving of themselves have been exemplary. My heartfelt love and gratitude go to my wife Veena, and my children Ruth and Paul, for their faith, hope, and love.

Most of all, I want to acknowledge and thank my Savior and Lord, Jesus Christ, for the abundant grace and favor He has bestowed upon me. This book is, truly, the result of His favor— "For thou, LORD, wilt bless the righteous; with favor wilt thou compass him as with a shield" (Psalm 5:12). I praise God and give Him all the glory. Undoubtedly, the most significant event in my life was when I accepted the Lord Jesus Christ as my personal Savior and Lord. "For whosoever shall call upon the name of the Lord shall be saved" (Romans 10:13).

Naresh K. Malhotra

About the Author

Dr. Naresh K. Malhotra is Nanyang Visiting Professor, Nanyang Business School, Nanyang Technological University, Singapore and Regents' Professor Emeritus, College of Management, Georgia Institute of Technology, USA. He has been listed in Marquis *Who's Who in America* continuously since the 51st Edition in 1997 and in *Who's Who in the World* since 2000. He received the prestigious Academy of Marketing Science CUTCO/Vector Distinguished Marketing Educator Award in 2005. In 2010, he was selected as a Marketing Legend, and his refereed journal articles will be published in nine volumes by Sage with tributes by other leading scholars in the field. In 2011, he received the Best Professor in Marketing Management, Asia Best B-School Award.

In an article by Wheatley and Wilson (1987 AMA Educators' Proceedings), Professor Malhotra was ranked number one in the country based on articles published in the *Journal of Marketing Research* (JMR) during 1980–1985. He also holds the all-time record for the maximum number of publications in the *Journal of Health Care Marketing*. He is ranked number one based on publications in the *Journal of the Academy of Marketing Science* (JAMS) since its inception through Volume 23, 1995. He is also number one based on publications in JAMS during the 10-year period 1986–1995. (See Tables 6 and 7 of JAMS, Vol. 24, No. 4, Fall 1996, p. 297). In an editorial by Schlegelmilch (JIM, 11(1), 2003), Malhotra was ranked number one based on publications in the *International Marketing Review* (IMR) from 1992–2002. He is also ranked number one based on publications in the *International Marketing Review* since its inception (1983) to 2003. (See Table V, IMR, 22(4) (2005).) He is also ranked number one based on publications in the *International Marketing Review* from 1996–2006 based on a study by Xu et al., published in the *Asia Pacific Journal of Management* (2008) 25: 189–207. In a landmark study by Ford et al. (2010) examining publications in the top four marketing journals (JMR, JM, JAMS, and JCR) over a 25-year period from 1977–2002, Professor Malhotra has three top-three rankings: ranked number three based on publications in all the four journals combined, ranked number three based on publications in JMR, and ranked number one based on publications in JAMS. He has published 10 papers in JMR.

He has published more than 125 papers in major refereed journals, including the *Journal of Marketing Research, Journal of Consumer Research, Marketing Science, Management Science, Journal of Marketing, Journal of Academy of Marketing Science, Journal of Retailing, Journal of Health Care Marketing*, and leading journals in statistics, management science, information systems, and psychology. In addition, he has also published numerous refereed articles in the proceedings of major national and international conferences. Several articles have received best paper research awards.

He was Chairman, Academy of Marketing Science Foundation, 1996–1998; President, Academy of Marketing Science, 1994–1996; and Chairman, Board of Governors, 1990–1992. He is a Distinguished Fellow of the Academy and Fellow, Decision Sciences Institute. He is the founding editor of *Review of Marketing Research* (published by the Emerald Group); served as an associate editor of *Decision Sciences* for 18 years; and has served as section editor, Health Care Marketing Abstracts, *Journal of Health Care Marketing*. Also, he serves on the editorial board of eight journals.

His book titled *Marketing Research: An Applied Orientation*, Sixth Edition, was published by Prentice-Hall, Inc., in 2009. This book has been translated into Chinese, Spanish, Russian, Portuguese, Hungarian, French, Bahasa Indonesia, and Japanese. In addition to the eight translations, this book also has several English editions, including North America, International, Europe, India, and Australia and New Zealand. The book has received widespread adoption at both the graduate and undergraduate levels with more than 144 schools using it in the United States and is being studied in over 75 countries. His book, *Basic Marketing Research: A Decision-Making Approach,* Third Edition, was published by Prentice Hall in 2008 and is likewise a global leader in the field.

Dr. Malhotra has consulted for business, nonprofit, and government organizations in the United States and abroad and has served as an expert witness in legal and regulatory proceedings. He has special expertise in data analysis and statistical methods. He is the winner of numerous awards and honors for research, teaching, and service to the profession, including the Academy of Marketing Science, Outstanding Marketing Teaching Excellence Award, 2003.

Dr. Malhotra is an ordained minister of the Gospel, and a member and Deacon the First Baptist Church, Atlanta. He has been married to Veena for more than 30 years, and they have two children, Ruth and Paul.

Introduction and Early Phases of Marketing Research

Introduction to Marketing Research

LEARNING OBJECTIVES

After reading this chapter, the student should be able to:

1. Define marketing research and distinguish between problem-identification and problem-solving research.

2. Describe a framework for conducting marketing research as well as the six steps of the marketing research process.

3. Understand the nature and scope of marketing research and its role in designing and implementing successful marketing programs.

4. Discuss the role of marketing research in gathering competitive intelligence.

5. Explain how the decision to conduct marketing research is made.

6. Discuss the marketing research industry and the types of research suppliers, including internal, external, full-service, and limited-service suppliers.

7. Describe careers available in marketing research and the backgrounds and skills needed to succeed in them.

8. Explain the role of marketing research in decision support systems in providing data, marketing models, and specialized software.

> **"As a user of marketing research, I gain so much from a well-crafted research project. You can implement marketing programs so much more vigorously when you are confident you understand what is currently important to the customer."**
>
> *Justin Stead*
> *VP International, Fossil, Inc., Richardson, Texas*

How Reebok Fits Shoes

Reebok, which was acquired by Adidas in 2006, designs, markets, and distributes sportswear and athletic footwear and equipment. In order to provide "complete comfort" for athletes and consumers, Reebok invests a lot of effort into its marketing research. Although the slogan belongs to Nike, when it comes to marketing research, Reebok just does it!

Reebok uses "time-use" research to determine how consumers spend their spare time. This type of information enables Reebok to identify opportunities for new products and markets and then design its marketing program to take advantage of them, as illustrated by the recently introduced line of custom-designed Ventilator shoes. The company uses a variety of methods to research time-use trends, including analysis of secondary data (data collected for other purposes, e.g., data available from publications, the Internet, social media, and commercial sources). It also uses qualitative research, such as focus groups (interviews with 8 to 12 people as a group); survey research via telephone, in the malls, and on the Internet; in social media; and interviews at consumers' homes.

Management wanted to identify ways that Reebok could increase its market share. Analysis of secondary data showed that health club memberships had increased more than 10 percent in the early 2000s. Focus groups indicated that a new popular fitness activity was step aerobics (standard aerobics made more intense by the addition of a 3- to 7-inch platform, the "step"). Reebok then conducted a survey to determine the market potential of step aerobics and found that health club members were spending less time in the clubs by an average of 12 percent. The research also showed that the percentage of adults who exercised in the home had grown from 20 percent in 1990 to more than 30 percent in 2010. In response to these results, several research questions were framed around exercising at home.

Based on the results of this research, Reebok redesigned its home–step aerobics line, including home steps, videotapes, aerobic shoes, and body weights. Product research indicated a strong consumer preference for the home–step aerobics line, and the new line was launched nationally. The home–step aerobics line has been very successful, and the popularity of these products has resulted in a Reebok step-workout program on ESPN.

Reebok's in-house marketing research specialists were actively involved in defining and designing the research. However, Reebok contracted data collection and data analysis to external suppliers, who collected and analyzed the data using appropriate statistical techniques. External suppliers can also be used in writing the report, but presentation of the results to the management and assistance in implementation is the responsibility of Reebok's in-house marketing research department. Reebok makes use of full-service suppliers who provide assistance in all the steps of the marketing research process, as well as limited-service suppliers who might handle only one or a few steps of the process. Its in-house marketing research department has helped Reebok introduce many successful products and marketing programs, enabling it to become a premier sportswear and athletic footwear company.

When time-use research revealed in 2010 that women all over the world were spending considerable time, money, and effort in toning and strengthening leg muscles, Reebok designed and marketed its EasyTone shoes as "an innovative footwear solution designed to tone and strengthen key leg muscles with every step."[1]

Overview

Marketing research is one of the most important and fascinating aspects of marketing. As the opening vignette illustrates, marketing research provides a company with valuable information that guides all of its marketing activities. In this chapter, we define and describe the two broad forms of marketing research: (1) research designed to identify problems and (2) research designed to solve problems. We explain the six steps of the marketing research process and take a look at how marketing research fits into the entire marketing decision process. We discuss the role of marketing research in making marketing decisions and gathering competitive intelligence. The marketing research industry consists of a variety of firms, and the field offers exciting career opportunities. We describe the contribution of marketing research to marketing information systems (MIS) and decision support systems (DSS).

The Internet has become integral to conducting marketing research and is used extensively in all phases of the marketing research process. Hence, information on the use of the Internet in marketing research is interwoven into each chapter, rather than discussed in a separate section of the chapter as was done in the earlier editions. Throughout this book, we also discuss applications to contemporary issues of importance in the current marketing and marketing research environment: international marketing research, social media, and ethics. This first chapter provides an introduction to these important application areas; an overview is presented in Figure 1.1. As can

FIGURE 1.1

Introduction to Marketing Research: An Overview

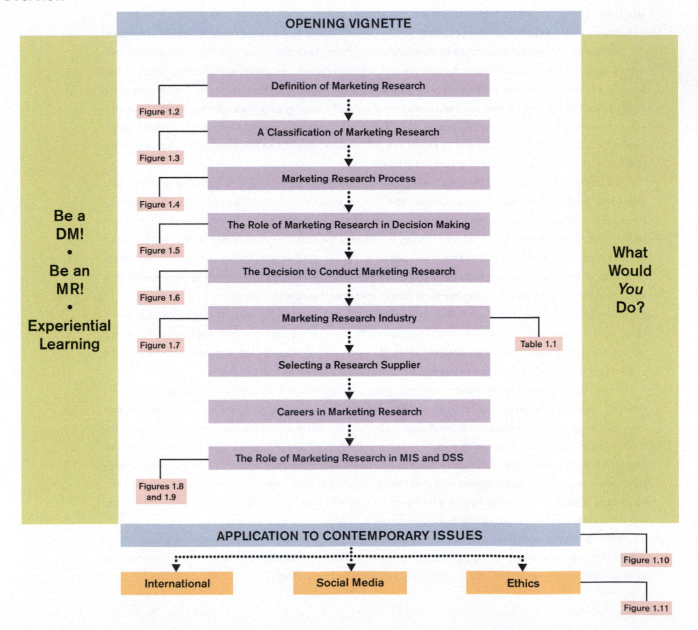

be seen in Figure 1.1, the opening vignette and Application to Contemporary Issues encompass all of the topics discussed in each chapter. We encourage a hands-on approach through the use of "Be an MR!" (Be a Marketing Researcher!) and "Be a DM!" (Be a Decision Maker!) boxes found in each chapter. These hands-on exercises use the Internet and other electronic sources to focus on the interaction between marketing research and marketing decision making. To further highlight this interaction, sometimes the "Be an MR!" box appears first, whereas at other times "Be a DM!" appears first. The research–decision-making interaction also is emphasized in each chapter by the "What Would *You* Do?" situation facing a real company. The situation is described and opportunities are provided to address the marketing research and the marketing management decisions facing the company. This hands-on orientation is further reinforced through the "Experiential Learning" exercises. Thus, we provide a better overall understanding of the key concepts and illustrate how applications can be made in other important areas that are discussed throughout the book.

Definition of Marketing Research

In this book, we emphasize the importance of research in marketing decision making. **Marketing research** is the systematic and objective identification, collection, analysis, dissemination, and use of information that is undertaken to improve decision making related to identifying and solving problems (also known as *opportunities*) in marketing.

   This definition gives marketing research a broad scope, and several aspects of the field are noteworthy. Marketing research involves the identification, collection, analysis, and dissemination of information (see Figure 1.2). Each phase of this process is important. Marketing research begins with the identification or definition of the research problem or opportunity. *Problems* often lead to *opportunities* in business, so from a research perspective, the two words often are used interchangeably. An investigation of each follows the same research process. For example, the discovery that adults were spending less time in health clubs and more time exercising at home represented a problem as well as an opportunity for Reebok. The problem was that when people were spending less time in health clubs, they also were using athletic shoes and equipment to a lesser extent, which resulted in decreased demand. The opportunity was more time spent exercising at home, which represented greater potential for shoes and home exercise equipment.

   The range of data collection methods and the sources used to obtain the data vary in sophistication and complexity. The methods used depend on the specific requirements of the project, including budget and time constraints. The data are then analyzed, and the results are formally presented to the client and used in decision making.

marketing research
The systematic and objective identification, collection, analysis, dissemination, and use of information that is undertaken to improve decision making related to identifying and solving problems (also known as *opportunities*) in marketing.

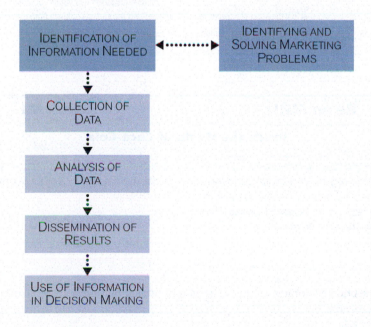

FIGURE 1.2
Definition of Marketing Research

Marketing research is systematic, which means that it follows a predictable path. A marketing research project is planned and documented. It has a scientific basis in that data are collected and analyzed to draw conclusions. The time-use research reported in the Reebok vignette is an example of this. Marketing research obtains its value from its objectivity. It should be conducted impartially, free from the influence of personal or political biases. This is easier said than done, because companies sponsoring the research sometimes pressure the researcher or research firm to generate "support" for a certain desired outcome. However, bending to this sort of pressure is a breach of the ethical codes of conduct that guide the profession. The notion that it provides an unbiased "outside," or objective, opinion gives marketing research its value. Without that objectivity, results cannot be trusted, and the entire discipline is undermined.

The Internet is fast becoming a useful tool in the identification, collection, analysis, and dissemination of information related to marketing research. The Interactive Marketing Research Organization (www.imro.org), which was formed in 2000, is a worldwide association of researchers dedicated to providing an open forum for the discussion of best practices and ethical approaches to research being conducted via the Internet.

Research in Action

A CEO's View of Marketing Research

What does a time-pressed senior executive expect from in-house marketing researchers? Southern Company's (www.southerncompany.com) former chairperson, president, and CEO Allen Franklin offers some valuable insights on this question. Franklin described one manager–researcher exchange of which he was part as follows:

MARKETING RESEARCHER:	"What do you want?"
FRANKLIN (RESPONDING SLOWLY AND FEELING SLIGHTLY EMBARRASSED FOR NOT HAVING A READY ANSWER):	"What do you have?"
MARKETING RESEARCHER:	"I don't have anything, yet. That's why I am here."
FRANKLIN (GROWING INCREASINGLY IRRITATED):	"Well, then, get out of here! You are keeping me from what I need to be doing!"

The implication of this exchange is that the researcher needs to understand the current context for decision makers. Researchers can develop this understanding by scanning the business press, following developing stories, attending conferences within the industry, as well as conducting focused research projects. In short, the researcher needs to be curious and be one of the best learners in the firm. Franklin says it this way: "It is not data that are critical, but the people between the data and the management decision maker. Senior managers will tend to work with those who make the managers more comfortable. Comfort is not increased by 2-hour presentations that leave management saying to itself, 'What are we going to do with that?'"

Here is one way a marketing researcher should approach a senior executive like Allen Franklin:

MARKETING RESEARCHER:	"We know the firm currently has this problem. We can resolve or minimize it by doing this study and acting upon what we learn."

Fortune magazine has named Southern Company the "most admired" electric and gas utility in America, in no small part due to its reliance on marketing research.[2]

Be an MR!	Be a DM!
Inside the World of Coca-Cola	

Social Media

Visit Coca-Cola's Web site at www.coca-cola.com and click on the USA button. How does this site collect marketing research information? How would you improve the Web site in order to collect more or better marketing research information? How could social media be used in this respect?	As the brand manager for Coca-Cola, how would you use information collected on the Web site to market your brand more effectively?

The next section elaborates on this definition of marketing research by classifying the types of marketing research.

A Classification of Marketing Research

Our definition states that organizations engage in marketing research for two reasons: to identify and to solve marketing problems. This distinction serves as a basis for classifying marketing research into problem-identification research and problem-solving research, as shown in Figure 1.3.

Problem-identification research involves going below the surface to identify the underlying problem that the marketing manager is facing. Often these problems are not readily apparent or they are likely to arise in the future. Problem-identification research can be designed to analyze market potential, market share, brand or company image, market characteristics, and sales. It can also be used in short-range forecasting, long-range forecasting, and uncovering business trends. For example, Polo Ralph Lauren might undertake research to determine the size of the market for men's shirts, the projected growth rate of this market, and the market share of major brands. This research might reveal a problem. Say that although Polo's sales of men's shirts have been increasing, they have not been keeping pace with industry growth. Moreover, market research might determine that Polo has been gradually losing market share to competitors, such as Tommy Hilfiger.

Problem identification is the more common of the two forms of research and is undertaken by virtually all marketing firms. This type of research is used to assess the environment and diagnose problems. Information regarding changes in the market provides an initial alert to potential opportunities or problems. A firm that is operating in a growing market but suffering from a declining market share might be dealing with company-specific problems, such as ineffective advertising or high turnover in its sales force. In other instances, problems, such as declining demand, might be common to all the firms in the industry. Considering the economic, social, cultural, or consumer behavior trends can help to identify such problems or opportunities.

Once a problem or opportunity has been identified, a firm undertakes **problem-solving research** to address the problem. Most marketing firms conduct problem-solving research as well. Problem-solving research addresses many topics, including market segmentation and product, pricing, promotion, and distribution. Problem-identification research and problem-solving research go hand in hand, and a given marketing research project can combine both types of research.

problem-identification research
Research undertaken to help identify problems that are not necessarily apparent or that are likely to arise in the future.

problem-solving research
Research undertaken to help solve specific marketing problems.

FIGURE 1.3

A Classification of Marketing Research

Research in Action

The Arch of Marketing Research at the Golden Arches

In the 1960s, McDonald's (www.mcdonalds.com) earned about $170 million domestically; today, the company earns more than that in 2 days. Marketing research has played a vital role in fostering this growth. In 1968, McDonald's formed its marketing research department, which has grown dramatically since its creation. The most prominent aspect of its operation is that 85 percent of all McDonald's are franchises. McDonald's marketing research department actively supports these restaurants by conducting problem-identification and problem-solving research.

In 2005, problem-identification research in the form of customer satisfaction surveys (market characteristics research) revealed that in-store atmosphere and décor were becoming an increasingly important part of the customers' dining experience, even in fast-food restaurants. Based on subsequent problem-solving (segmentation and product) research, in 2006 McDonald's introduced its "Forever Young" brand by remodeling its restaurants, the first major redesign since the 1970s. This was done to keep the brand relevant and appealing to a younger generation of consumers. The new design includes the traditional McDonald's yellow and red colors, but the red is muted to terra cotta, the yellow is now golden for a more "sunny" look, and olive and sage green have been added. The concept consists of a new building design, as well as interior changes, such as recessed lighting,

classical music, and new paint and wall graphics. Re-imaged restaurants attract more customers and enhance perceptions of McDonald's as a place adults, not just kids, enjoy. The company plans to eventually incorporate the new look in all of its 13,700 franchised and company-owned U.S. locations.

As of 2011, the company is the world's leading food service retailer, with more than 32,000 restaurants in 117 countries serving more than 55 million customers each day. McDonald's success is a direct result of the problem-identification and problem-solving research that it undertakes on an ongoing basis.[3]

Classifying marketing research into two main types is useful from a conceptual as well as a practical viewpoint. The McDonald's example illustrates that these two types of research often go hand in hand with problem-identification research leading to problem-solving research. Marketing research discovered that in-store atmosphere and décor were becoming an increasingly important part of the customers' dining experience (problem identification), and the solution was the introduction of the "Forever Young" brand by remodeling restaurants (problem solving). The Reebok vignette also illustrates this point. Problem identification involving analysis of secondary data, focus groups, and a market potential survey revealed that adults were spending less time in health clubs and more time exercising at home. Problem-solving research in the form of product research led to the redevelopment and introduction of the successful home–step aerobics line.

Be a DM!	Be an MR!
Major League Baseball Is Tickled Pink	
As the marketing director of Major League Baseball (MLB), what marketing strategies would you formulate to target female fans?	You have been hired by MLB to devise a marketing strategy for female fans. Visit www.mlb.com and search the Internet—including social media—as well as your library's online databases to obtain information on women's attitudes toward MLB. What kind of marketing research would you recommend?

Social Media

marketing research process
A set of six steps that defines the tasks to be accomplished in conducting a marketing research study: problem definition, developing an approach to the problem, research design formulation, fieldwork, data preparation and analysis, and report preparation and presentation.

Marketing Research Process

The **marketing research process** consists of six steps (see Figure 1.4). This process is a general one and can be followed for conducting research in any functional area (e.g., marketing, finance, accounting, and so forth). Each of these steps is discussed in greater detail in subsequent chapters. We will provide only a brief overview here.

FIGURE 1.4
The Marketing Research Process

Step 1: Defining the Problem

The first step in any marketing research project is to define the problem. Researchers accomplish problem definition through discussions with decision makers, interviews with industry experts, analysis of secondary data including social media, and, perhaps, some qualitative research, such as focus groups. Problem definition involves defining the management-decision problem (what should the management do) and the marketing research problem (what information is needed). In the opening vignette, the management-decision problem was: What should Reebok do to increase its market share? The marketing research problem for Reebok was assessing the market potential for home–step aerobic products. Once the problem has been defined, the research can be designed and conducted properly. (See Chapter 2.)

Step 2: Developing an Approach to the Problem

Developing an approach to the problem includes formulating an analytical framework and models, research questions, and hypotheses. This process is guided by the same tasks performed to define the problem. (See Chapter 2.) In the opening vignette, several research questions were investigated related to exercising at home.

Step 3: Formulating a Research Design

A research design is a framework or blueprint for conducting the marketing research project. It details the procedures needed to obtain the required information. A study might be designed to test hypotheses of interest or to determine possible answers to the research questions, both of which contribute to decision making. Conducting preliminary or exploratory research, defining the variables, and designing appropriate scales to measure them also are part of the research design. The issue of how the data should be obtained from the respondents (e.g., by conducting a survey or an experiment) must be addressed. In the opening vignette, the research design involved analysis of secondary data and focus groups, and a survey was conducted to assess the market potential for home–step aerobic equipment. It also may involve designing a questionnaire and a sampling plan to select respondents for the study. These steps are discussed in detail in Chapters 3 to 13.

Step 4: Doing Fieldwork or Collecting Data

Data collection is accomplished using a staff that operates in the field. Fieldwork involves personal, telephone, mail, or electronic interviewing. Proper selection, training, supervision, and evaluation of the field force are essential to ensure high-quality data collection. Reebok contracted fieldwork or data collection to external suppliers, who analyzed the data using appropriate statistical techniques. (See Chapter 14.)

Step 5: Preparing and Analyzing Data

Data preparation involves data-processing steps leading up to analysis. This includes the editing, coding, and transcribing of collected data. This entire process must then be verified for accuracy. The editing process involves an initial inspection of questionnaires or observation forms for completeness and reasonableness of responses. After this initial inspection, the response to each question is coded to ensure standardized entry into the computer. The data from the questionnaires are transferred onto storage media and then analyzed using different statistical techniques. These results are then interpreted in order to find conclusions related to the marketing research problem. In the opening vignette, Reebok contracted data analysis to external suppliers, who analyzed the data using appropriate statistical techniques. (See Chapters 15 to 18.)

Step 6: Preparing and Presenting the Report

The entire project should be documented in a written report that addresses the specific research questions; describes the approach, the research design, data collection, and data analysis procedures; and presents the results and the major findings. The written report is supplemented by tables, figures, and graphs to enhance clarity and impact and is usually accompanied by a formal presentation. Reebok might use external suppliers in writing the report, but presentation of the results to the management and assistance in implementation are the primary responsibilities of its in-house marketing research department. (See Chapter 19.) Reebok follows a research process that incorporates all six of these steps.

Although we have described the research process as a sequence of steps, it should be noted that these steps are interdependent and iterative. Thus, at each step the researcher should not only look back at the previous steps, but also look ahead to the following steps. As we show, the mar-

Definition of Marketing Research (Figure 1.2)	Marketing Research Process (Figure 1.4)
Identification of information needed	Step 1: Defining the problem
Collection of data	Step 2: Developing an approach to the problem
	Step 3: Formulating a research design
	Step 4: Doing fieldwork or collecting data
Analysis of data	Step 5: Preparing and analyzing data
Dissemination of results	Step 6: Preparing and presenting the report
Use of information	

keting research process (see Figure 1.4) is very consistent with the definition of marketing research presented earlier (see Figure 1.2).

The Internet is very useful for project management. Researchers and clients use e-mail combined with software such as Lotus Notes to communicate with each other and to coordinate the six steps of the marketing research process. The Internet also is being used to disseminate marketing research results and reports, which can be posted on the Web and made available to managers on a worldwide basis.

Be a DM!	Be an MR!
Fossil Goes Fashionable!	

| | As the marketing chief for Fossil, you are considering the introduction of a fashionable wristwatch for men and women priced at $99. What kind of information do you need to help you make this decision? | You've been hired to help Fossil to determine whether to introduce its new wristwatch. Visit www.fossil.com and search the Internet—including social media—as well as your library's online databases to obtain information on consumers' preferences for wristwatches. Describe the six steps of the marketing research process that should be followed. |

The Role of Marketing Research in Marketing Decision Making

The Reebok vignette illustrates only a few applications of marketing research and its role in the marketing decision-making process. Marketing research, indeed, has a broad range of applications and plays a crucial role in the marketing decision-making process. One way to describe the role of marketing research is in light of the basic marketing paradigm given in Figure 1.5.

A major goal of marketing is to identify and then satisfy needs of various customer groups (e.g., consumers, employees, channel members, suppliers). To do this, marketing managers need information about the various customer groups, competitors, and other forces, such as environmental trends in the marketplace. In recent years, timely market information has become even more valuable. For example, the speed of new products entering the marketplace, domestic and international competition, and the increase in demanding and well-informed consumers all contribute to the importance of this type of market data.

The task of marketing research is to assess the information needs and provide management with relevant, accurate, reliable, valid, and current information to aid marketing decision making (see Figure 1.5). Companies use marketing research to stay competitive and to avoid high costs associated with making poor decisions based on unsound information. Sound decisions are not based on gut feeling, intuition, or even pure judgment; they are based on sound information. Without sound information, management cannot make sound decisions. Reebok's successful introduction of the home–step aerobics line was guided by systematic marketing research.

The following example illustrates how Sony improves its products through the use of marketing research. Sony reinforces the fact that management cannot make sound decisions without reliable information provided by marketing research.

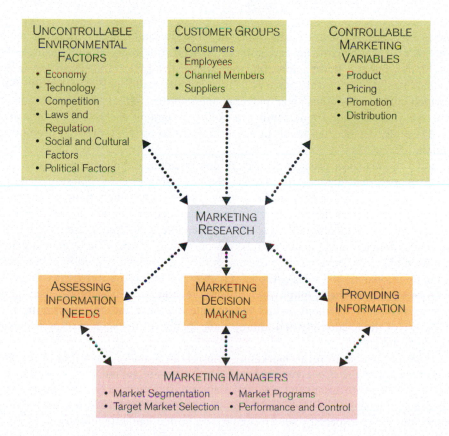

FIGURE 1.5

The Role of Marketing Research in Marketing Decision Making

Research in Action

Sony Gives Santa a Few Tips

The Christmas holiday season is one of the most intensely competitive in terms of gift-giving products. This is true for Sony (www.sony.com) just as much as any other company. However, Sony gains a leg up on its competition by using marketing research to refine its gift products just in time for Christmas.

Sony asks consumers what they would like from Sony's products. It uses descriptive studies of consumer behavior, with actual product-usage information, to refine its offerings. Surveys, focus groups, analysis of social media, interviews, tracking devices, and even syndicated data are all used to gain more knowledge on consumers' perception of Sony products. For example, Sony uses focus groups in which participants get to sample and use a product that might be released for the Christmas season. The participants let Sony know if they like the product, how much they like it, what they would change about it, and whether they would buy it. Sony also uses surveys to determine if there is a current need that could be satisfied by a product that is under development. Tracking devices are used to find out how often and when potential products are put into use by participating "test" consumers.

For instance, focus groups in the United States evaluating a preliminary design for the Sony Reader gave Sony feedback that its electronic book reader had too many buttons and its alkaline battery design was clunky and awkward. Sony engineers modified the design based on the consumers' feedback, including replacing alkaline batteries with rechargeable ones and reducing the number of buttons to ease navigation. The Sony Reader enjoyed high demand throughout the holiday season and beyond.[4]

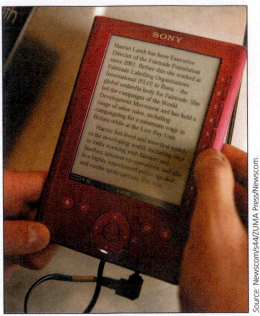

Source: Newscom/s44/ZUMA Press/Newscom.

The Sony example illustrates the numerous strategic and tactical decisions marketing managers face and how marketing research can be helpful in improving the decision-making process. Identifying and finding solutions to customer needs (a primary goal of marketing) requires the integration of a wide range of factors, not just intuition. Figure 1.5 illustrates this range, which includes decisions about potential opportunities, target market selection, market segmentation, planning and implementing marketing programs, marketing performance, and control. These decisions often result in actions related to product, pricing, promotion, and distribution.

To make the decision process even more complicated, a manager must also consider uncontrollable external factors that influence the marketing process. These include general economic conditions (e.g., an economic slowdown or recession), technology (e.g., the impact of new technology, such as the Internet including social media), public policies and laws (e.g., those related to environmental pollution affect automobile companies), the political environment (e.g., Republicans are considered to be pro-business), competition (e.g., many dot.coms have not been able to survive because of competition), and social and cultural changes (e.g., changes in traditional marital roles). Another factor in this mix is the complexity of the various customer groups: consumers, employees, channel members, and suppliers. The marketing manager must attempt to monitor and incorporate all these factors. Marketing research removes some of the uncertainty and improves the quality of decision making in this highly complex environment.

The Internet can be useful to marketing researchers in many ways. Marketing research information related to the client company, its competitors, and the industry, as well as relevant marketing, economic, governmental, and environmental information, can be obtained by conducting a search using any of the popular search engines. Of particular interest is KnowThis (www.knowthis.com), a specialty search engine for a virtual marketing library.

 Social Media

Other important sources of marketing research information on the Internet include bulletin boards, newsgroups, and social media. A *newsgroup* is an Internet site (e.g., groups.google.com)

where people can read and post messages pertaining to a particular topic. *Blogs,* or *Web logs,* can be used to obtain information on a variety of topics and to recruit survey respondents. Although blogs can be located via most search engines, special search engines, such as Blog Search Engine (www.blogsearchengine.com), have been designed for blog searches. The use of social media is discussed in more detail later in the chapter.

Traditionally, a clear distinction existed between the responsibilities of the marketing researchers and those of the marketing manager. However, these roles are beginning to merge as marketing researchers become more involved in decision making and marketing managers become more involved with research. This trend can be attributed to better training of marketing managers, the Internet, advances in technology, and the use of research as an ongoing aspect of the marketing function.

In essence, marketing research must add value to marketing decision making, indeed, to the entire organization.[5] Note that marketing managers do not work in isolation from other functions in the organization. Rather, the marketing orientation embodies a cross-functional perspective to meet consumer needs and attain long-term profitability. Therefore, marketing research should interface with the other functions in the organization, such as manufacturing, research and development, finance, accounting, and other functional areas, as may be relevant in a given project.

Marketing Research and Competitive Intelligence

Competitive intelligence (CI) may be defined as the process of enhancing marketplace competitiveness through a greater understanding of a firm's competitors and the competitive environment. This process is unequivocally ethical. It involves the legal collection and analysis of information regarding the capabilities, vulnerabilities, and intentions of business competitors, conducted by using information databases and other "open sources" and through ethical marketing research inquiry. A heads-up on a new product, information on a rival's costs and prices, and a read on an ally's changing distribution strategy are a few examples of CI.

Competitive intelligence is a crucial part of the emerging knowledge economy. CI enables senior managers in companies of all sizes to make informed decisions about everything from marketing, research and development (R&D), and investing tactics to long-term business strategies. By analyzing rivals' moves, CI allows companies to anticipate market developments rather than merely react to them. Although a variety of methods are used, the Internet, particularly social media, can be mined as a source of CI. Companies are leaking more information than ever into social media channels; one powerful way is through the use of RSS feeds that allow a firm to subscribe anonymously to a competitor's newsletter, Web site, or any other features that are constantly updated (for example, by setting up special Twitter and Facebook accounts). More importantly, the use of social media is a perfectly legal and ethical way because access is public.

Although marketing research plays a central role in the collection, analysis, and dissemination of CI information, CI has evolved into a discipline of its own. The Strategic and Competitive Intelligence Professionals (SCIP) consists of members conducting CI for large and small companies, providing management with early warning of changes in the competitive landscape. For more information on competitive intelligence, go to SCIP's Web page at www.scip.org.

competitive intelligence
The process of enhancing marketplace competitiveness through a greater understanding of a firm's competitors and the competitive environment.

The Decision to Conduct Marketing Research

Although marketing research can be beneficial in a variety of situations, the decision to conduct research is not automatic. Rather, this decision should be guided by a number of considerations including management's attitude toward research, the resources available to conduct the research and to implement the findings, the need for additional information, the importance of the decision, and the costs versus the benefits of conducting the research (see Figure 1.6).

If management does not have a positive attitude toward research, then it is likely that the project report will gather dust if the research is conducted. However, sometimes there are

FIGURE 1.6

The Decision to Conduct Marketing Research

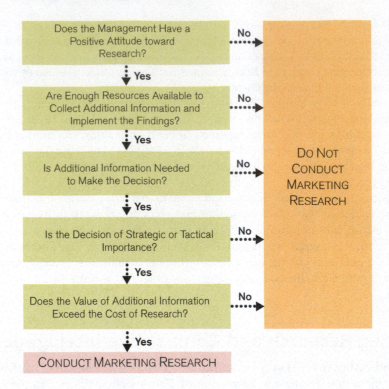

exceptions to this guideline. For example, we conducted a project for a retail chain where the chain management was hostile toward the project, but the research was commissioned and funded by the parent organization. Although the store management was opposed to the findings that reflected negatively on the store chain, the parent company did implement our recommendations.

Resources, especially time and money, are always limited. If either time or money is not available in adequate amounts to conduct a quality project, then that project probably should not be undertaken. It is better to forego a formal project than to undertake one in which the integrity of the research is compromised because of lack of resources. In one instance, we advised Fisher Price not to undertake a formal research project because a go/no-go decision regarding the introduction of a new toy had to be made in just a few days and time was too limited to conduct quality research. Likewise, a firm might lack the resources to implement the recommendations arising from the findings of marketing research. In that case, spending the resources to conduct the research might not be warranted

Other circumstances also might indicate that a particular marketing research project should not be undertaken. If the required information is already available within the organization, the decision for which the research is to be conducted has already been made, or if the research is going to be used for political ends, then the value of the information generated is greatly reduced and the project is generally not warranted.

If the decision to be made is not of strategic or tactical importance, marketing research may not be warranted. In general, marketing research should be undertaken when the expected value of information it generates exceeds the costs of conducting the marketing research project. The more important the decision confronting management and the greater the uncertainty or risk facing them, the greater the value of information obtained. Formal procedures are available for quantifying the expected value as well as the costs of a marketing research project. Although in most instances the value of information exceeds the costs, in some instances the reverse might be true. For example, a pie manufacturer wanted to understand the purchase of pies in convenience stores. We advised against a major marketing research project when we discovered that less than 1 percent of the sales were coming from convenience stores and that this situation was unlikely to change in the next 5 years. However, in many cases, the answer to all the questions of Figure 1.6 is "yes" and marketing research should be conducted.

Be a DM!	Be an MR!	
Solving Estee Lauder's Problem		
As the marketing director of Estee Lauder, would you conduct a formal marketing research project to determine consumer response to a proposed new line of cosmetics? Why or why not?	Visit www.esteelauder.com and search the Internet—including social media—as well as your library's online databases to find information on Estee Lauder's marketing strategy. What type of problem-solving research would you conduct?	Social Media

An Overview of the Marketing Research Industry

The **marketing research industry** consists of suppliers who provide marketing research services. Figure 1.7 broadly categorizes research suppliers as either internal or external. An **internal supplier** is a marketing research department within the firm. Internal research departments can be found in large organizations across a wide range of industries, including automobile companies (e.g., GM and Ford), consumer products firms (e.g., P&G, Colgate Palmolive, Coca-Cola, and Reebok), and banks (e.g., Citigroup and JP Morgan Chase). For these larger companies, the research function often is located at the corporate headquarters, and this one corporate marketing research department caters to all of the firm's research needs. For smaller or decentralized firms that operate independent divisions, the market research function is distributed among the separate divisions. In decentralized organizations, divisions can be structured around products, customers, or geographical regions, with marketing research personnel assigned across the country. Each division (or group based on product line or geographical region) will have its own marketing research operation. Although companies can be found operating under a number of organizational structures, the recent trend has been toward centralization and a trimming of internal marketing research staff.

marketing research industry
The marketing research industry consists of suppliers who provide marketing research services.

internal supplier
Marketing research departments located within a firm.

FIGURE 1.7

Marketing Research Suppliers and Services

TABLE 1.1 Top 10 Global Research Organizations

Rank 2009	Rank 2008	Organization	Headquarters	Parent Country	Web Site (www.)	Number of Countries with Subsidiaries/ Branch Offices	Global Research Revenue (US$, in millions)	Percent of Global Revenue from Outside Home Country
1	1	Nielsen	New York	U.S.	nielsen.com	100	4,628.0	50.3
2	2	Kantar	London & Fairfield, Conn.	U.K.	kantar.com	80	2,823.2	75.0
3	3	IMS Health Inc.	Norwalk, Conn.	U.S.	imshealth.com	75	2,189.7	63.4
4	4	GfK SE	Nuremberg	Germany	gfk.com	59	1,622.8	74.1
5	5	Ipsos Group SA	Paris	France	ipsos.com	64	1,315.0	89.8
6	6	Synovate	London	U.K.	synovate.com	62	816.4	85.0
7	7	SymphonyIRI	Chicago	U.S.	symphonyiri.com	8	706.3	37.5
8	8	Westat Inc.	Rockville, Md.	U.S.	westat.com	1	502.4	—
9	9	Arbitron Inc.	Columbia, Md.	U.S.	arbitron.com	2	385.0	1.5
10	10	INTAGE Inc.	Tokyo	Japan	intage.co.jp	3	368.6	1.7

Source: Reprinted with permission from *Marketing News*, published by the American Marketing Association, Jack Honomichl, "Top 25 Global Research Organizations," (August 30, 2010): 16.

external suppliers

Outside marketing research companies hired to conduct a complete marketing research project or a component of it.

External suppliers are outside firms hired to supply marketing research services. Even firms such as HP and Reebok (see opening vignette) with in-house marketing research departments make at least some use of external suppliers. External suppliers range in size from one- or two-person shops to multinational corporations. Most of the research suppliers are small operations. Table 1.1 lists the top 10 global marketing research suppliers.[6] Many external suppliers form strategic alliances with other firms in the marketing research industry. These alliances enable participating firms to access each other's expertise and resources. Such alliances are formed through mergers, acquisitions, or contractual agreements. For example, Burke, Inc., has partnerships with several marketing research firms in other countries. These partnerships and alliances give Burke, Inc., access to international markets.

full-service suppliers

Companies that offer the full range of marketing research activities.

External suppliers can provide either full or limited service. **Full-service suppliers** offer the entire range of marketing research services, from problem definition, approach development, questionnaire design, sampling, data collection, data analysis, and interpretation to report preparation and presentation. The services of these suppliers can be further broken down into syndicated services, customized services, and Internet/social media services (see Figure 1.7).

syndicated services

Companies that collect and sell common pools of data designed to serve the information needs of multiple clients.

Syndicated services are companies that collect and sell common pools of data designed to serve information needs that are shared by a number of clients. These data are collected primarily through surveys, purchase and media panels, scanners, and audits. For example, Nielsen's national television ratings in the U.S. provides information on audience size and demographic characteristics of households watching specific television programs (www.nielsen.com). The Nielsen Company also provides scanner tracking data, such as that generated by electronic scanners at checkout counters in supermarkets. The NPD Group (www.npd.com), another example of a syndicated service, maintains one of the largest consumer panels in the United States. Syndicated services are discussed in more detail in Chapter 5.

customized services

Companies that tailor research procedures to best meet the needs of each client.

Customized services offer a wide variety of marketing research services customized to suit a client's specific needs. Each marketing research project is designed to meet the client's unique needs. Some of the marketing research firms that offer these services are Synovate, Westat, and Burke, Inc.

Internet services

Companies that specialize in conducting research on the Internet.

Several marketing research firms, including some that have specialized in conducting marketing research on the Internet, offer **Internet services** including social media research. For example, the Toluna Group (www.toluna-group.com), which acquired Greenfield Online and Ciao Surveys in 2009, offers a broad range of customized qualitative and quantitative online marketing research for consumer, business-to-business, and professional markets. Using large,

Source: The Nielsen Company.

The Nielsen Company is the largest marketing research firm in the world with over half its revenue coming from outside the United States.

proprietary databases, studies are conducted within the company's secure Web site. Forrester Research (www.forrester.com), which acquired JupiterResearch in 2008, offers research and consulting services that focus on consumer online behavior and interactive technologies. A special class of Internet services focuses on social media research, and these companies are discussed later in the chapter.

Social Media

Limited-service suppliers specialize in one or a few steps of the marketing research process. Limited-service suppliers specialize in field services, focus groups and qualitative research, technical and analytical services, and other services. **Field services** collect data. They might use the full range of data collection methods (i.e., mail, personal, telephone, and electronic interviewing), or they might specialize in only one method. Some field service organizations maintain extensive interviewing facilities across the country for interviewing shoppers in malls. Many offer qualitative data collection services, such as focus-group interviewing (discussed in Chapter 6). Firms that offer field services include Field Work, Inc. (www.fieldwork.com), Booth Research Services (www.boothresearch.com), and WorldOne (www.worldone.com).

Focus groups and qualitative services provide facilities and recruit respondents for focus groups and other forms of qualitative research, such as one-on-one depth interviews. Some firms might provide additional services, such as moderators, and prepare focus group reports. Examples of such firms include Jackson Associates (www.jacksonassociates.com) and 20|20 Research, Inc. (www.2020research.com).

Technical and analytical services are offered by firms that specialize in design issues and computer analysis of quantitative data, such as those obtained in large surveys. Firms such as SDR of Atlanta (www.sdr-consulting.com) offer sophisticated data analysis using advanced statistical techniques. Sawtooth Technologies (www.sawtooth.com) provides software for research data collection and analysis. Microcomputers and statistical software packages enable firms to perform data analysis in-house. However, the specialized data-analysis expertise of outside suppliers is still in demand. Other services include branded marketing research products and services developed to address specific types of marketing research problems. For example, Survey Sampling International (www.surveysampling.com) specializes in sampling design and distribution. Some firms focus on specialized services, such as research in ethnic markets (i.e., Hispanic, African, multicultural). Two firms that focus on research in ethnic markets are Latin Facts Research, a subsidiary of Facts 'n Figures, Inc. (www.factsnfiguresinc.com) and Multicultural Insights (www.multicultural-insights.com).

A firm without an internal marketing research department or specialists will be forced to rely on external, full-service suppliers. A firm with an internal marketing research staff will make use of both full- and limited-service suppliers. The need for external suppliers arises when the firm does not have the resources or the technical expertise to undertake certain phases of a

limited-service suppliers
Companies that specialize in one or a few steps of the marketing research process.

field services
Companies whose primary service offering is their expertise in collecting data for research projects.

focus groups and qualitative services
Services related to facilities, recruitment, and other services for focus groups and other forms of qualitative research, such as one-on-one depth interviews.

technical and analytical services
Services related to design issues and computer analysis of quantitative data, such as those obtained in large surveys.

particular project. Also, conflict-of-interest issues might necessitate that a project be conducted by an outside supplier, as in the case of Reebok in the opening vignette. At Reebok, data collection and data analysis frequently are contracted to external suppliers. Sometimes Reebok uses full-service suppliers to conduct the entire marketing research project.

Selecting a Research Supplier

When initiating a marketing research study, a firm often will need to hire external suppliers for all or part of the project. The process of selecting an outside supplier can be informal, relying primarily on word-of-mouth endorsements, or it can be very formal, involving a "request for proposal." In the latter case, research suppliers are asked to submit formal proposals for evaluation by the hiring firm. The first step involves compiling a list of prospective suppliers from trade publications, professional directories, Internet sources, and personal contacts. For example, www.greenbook.org can be used to locate marketing research suppliers by region, specialty, and other criteria.

Regardless of the formality of the process, the hiring firm must develop a checklist detailing its selection criteria for outside suppliers. That checklist should go beyond technical requirements, covering the following areas:

- What is the supplier's reputation?
- Does the firm complete projects on schedule? Is it flexible?
- Is it known for maintaining ethical standards?
- Are its research projects of high quality?
- What kind and how much experience does the supplier have?
- Has the firm had experience with projects similar to this one?
- Do the supplier's personnel have both technical and nontechnical expertise? Do they have Professional Researcher Certification offered by the Marketing Research Association (www.mra-net.org)?
- Has the firm formed any strategic alliances? What resources does it have access to?

Reebok International, which subcontracts a great deal of its research to external suppliers, uses a similar checklist. You can also find checklists for qualifying marketing research suppliers at the Web sites of prominent marketing research associations (e.g., www.esomar.org). A checklist helps managers examine the working relationships as well as the project requirements. Because of the importance of most research efforts, compatible working relationships and good communication skills can become primary considerations when hiring an outside firm.

A competitive bidding process usually is used in selecting external suppliers, particularly for large jobs. Often the organization commissioning the research will issue a request for proposal (RFP), a request for information (RFI), a request for application (RFA), an invitation to bid (ITB), or a similar call, inviting suppliers to submit bids. You can locate actual RFPs on the Internet by doing a Google advanced search using "RFP" and "Marketing Research." Some marketing research firms, such as Marketing Research Services, Inc. (www.mrsi.com), will post a RFP form on its Web site that prospective clients can use to issue RFPs. Note that awarding projects based on the lowest price is not a good rule of thumb. The completeness of the research proposal and the selection criteria must all be factored into the hiring decision. Moreover, long-term contracts with research suppliers are preferable to selection on a project-by-project basis.

Be an MR!	Be a DM!
Redesigning Yahoo!	
As the research director for Yahoo!, you are to select a marketing research firm that specializes in researching consumers who shop on the Internet. Visit www.greenbook.org and identify the marketing research firms in your area that conduct Internet-based surveys. Make a list of five such firms. Which firm will you select and why?	As the director of marketing at Yahoo!, how would you use information on consumer shopping on the Internet in redesigning the Yahoo! Web site?

Careers in Marketing Research

Promising career opportunities are available with marketing research firms (e.g., Nielsen, Kantar, Burke, Inc., M/A/R/C). Equally appealing are careers in business and nonbusiness firms and agencies with in-house marketing research departments (e.g., P&G, Coca-Cola, Reebok, the Federal Trade Commission, and the U.S. Census Bureau). Advertising agencies (e.g., BBDO International, McCann Erickson, Ogilvy & Mather, J. Walter Thompson, and Young & Rubicam) also conduct substantial marketing research and employ professionals in this field.

A career in research often begins with a supervisory position in fieldwork or data analysis. With experience, the researcher moves up to project management positions, resulting in director and, eventually, in a vice-president-level position. The most common entry-level position in the marketing research industry for people with bachelor's degrees (e.g., a BBA) is operational supervisor. An operational supervisor is responsible for supervising the day-to-day operations of specific aspects of the marketing research process, ranging from fieldwork to data editing to coding for programming and data analysis. Rather than entering the discipline from the operations side, BBAs with strong organizational skills might start as assistant project managers. An assistant project manager assists in questionnaire design, reviews field instructions, and monitors timing and costs of studies. As research techniques become more sophisticated, there is a growing preference for people with master's degrees. Those with MBA or equivalent degrees are likely to be employed as project managers. In marketing research firms, such as Burke, Inc., the project manager works with the account director in managing the day-to-day operations of a marketing research project.

A researcher entering the profession on the client side would typically begin as a junior research analyst (for BBAs) or research analyst (for MBAs). The junior analyst and the research analyst learn about the particular industry and receive training from a senior staff member, usually the marketing research manager. The junior analyst position includes a training program to prepare individuals for the responsibilities of a research analyst, including coordinating with the marketing department and sales force to develop goals for product exposure. Research analyst responsibilities include checking data for accuracy, comparing and contrasting new research with established norms, and analyzing data for the purpose of market forecasting. As these job titles indicate, careers in marketing research can be highly technical, specializing in the design and the statistical side of the industry, or they can be of a general management nature, with emphasis on client relationships. For descriptions of other marketing research positions and current salaries, visit www.marketresearchcareers.com.

To prepare for a career in marketing research, you should:

- Take all the marketing courses you can.
- Take courses in statistics and quantitative methods.
- Acquire computer and Internet skills.
- Take courses in psychology and consumer behavior.
- Acquire effective written and verbal communication skills.
- Think creatively. Creativity and common sense command a premium in marketing research.

It is important for marketing researchers to be liberally educated in order to better understand the problems managers face and then be able to address them from a broad perspective.[7] A career in marketing research will involve working with other bright, energetic people in a fast-paced, dynamic environment. You will get to work on diverse qualitative and quantitative projects with clients in a variety of industries, including e-commerce, travel, telecommunications, pharmaceuticals, government, and nonprofit. The benefits include ongoing training and career development, a competitive salary, comprehensive health and dental plans, a 401K, the option to wear business casual attire, and excellent advancement opportunities. We present the profile of Merrill Dubrow to showcase a successful career in marketing research.

Social Media

Research in Action

Profile of a Marketing Research Blogger

Merrill Dubrow is president and chief executive officer of M/A/R/C Research (www.marcresearch.com), a 100-person marketing research firm located in Irving, Texas. Prior to taking the leadership role at M/A/R/C, Merrill served as senior vice president of client development at Harris Interactive's Service Bureau. He has also held positions with Elrick & Lavidge, Phone Lab Research, CRC Information, Quick Test, and BizRate.com throughout his more than 25 years in the marketing research industry.

Merrill received a Bachelor of Arts degree from Hofstra University in Long Island, New York, where he took a broad array of courses to prepare him for a career in marketing research.

Merrill also authors The Merrill Dubrow Blog, which he started in August 2006. His topics include the best movies of all time, his painful experience of taking a Bikram Yoga class, and his favorite board games. However, it is not all fun and games; Dubrow's blog also contains discussion of new trends in marketing research, profiles of marketing research industry colleagues, and interesting findings from M/A/R/C's own research.

The power of the blog never ceases to amaze Merrill Dubrow. It hits him every time conference attendees tell him they came to his session because they had read his blog and felt compelled to meet him.[8]

College graduates' lack of awareness of marketing research as a career and a growing demand for marketing researchers in the fields of information technology, pharmaceuticals, financial services, and other booming industries have created a shortage of professionals in the field. Marketing research organizations would like to have more incoming talent in order to have a greater presence in senior management in the future. The need for marketing researchers could not be greater. According to the United States Bureau of Labor and Statistics (www.bls.gov), employment opportunities are expected to grow faster than average for all market research positions through 2015. Job growth will be driven, in part, by retiring workers, shifting of job skills toward computers and quantitative methods, a growing economy, and the need for companies to operate in an increasingly competitive global marketplace. This makes it a career worth pursuing for both the short and the long term. For more information on jobs in marketing research, check out the American Marketing Association's career center at www.marketingpower.com or visit www.marketresearchcareers.com.

Experiential Learning

The World of Marketing Research on the Internet

MarketResearchCareers.com (www.marketresearchcareers.com) offers up-to-date news and information on the market research industry. Here's how to find what you're looking for and get the most out of your visit.

If you're job hunting or hiring, the classifieds section lists jobs in research, marketing, advertising, public relations, and allied professions. The site lists current job openings. Resumes and job listing can be submitted to the site.

The Market Research News section provides company, conference, and product news from the world of market research.

There are many other ways the MarketResearchCareers.com Web site brings the world of marketing research to you. Explore it!

The Role of Marketing Research in MIS and DSS

Earlier, we defined *marketing research* as the systematic and objective identification, collection, analysis, dissemination, and use of information as input in marketing decision making. Combining external market information with internal billing, production, and other records results in a powerful marketing information system (MIS) (see Figure 1.8).

A **marketing information system (MIS)** is a formalized set of procedures for generating, analyzing, storing, and distributing information to marketing decision makers on an ongoing basis. Such systems are differentiated from marketing research in that they are continuously available. Marketing information systems are designed to complement the decision maker's responsibilities, style, and information needs. The power of a MIS is in the access it gives managers to vast amounts of information, combining production, invoice, and billing information

marketing information system (MIS)
A formalized set of procedures for generating, analyzing, storing, and distributing pertinent information to marketing decision makers on an ongoing basis.

FIGURE 1.8

**The Development
of MIS and DSS**

with marketing intelligence, including marketing research, into a centralized data warehouse. MIS offer the potential of much more information than can be obtained from ad hoc marketing research projects. However, that potential often is not achieved when the information is structured so rigidly that it cannot be easily manipulated.

Developed to overcome the limitations of MIS, **decision support systems (DSS)** have built-in flexibility that allows decision makers to interact directly with databases and analysis models. A DSS is an integrated system that includes hardware, a communications network, a database, a model base, a software base, and the DSS user (decision maker) who collects and interprets information for decision making. Information collected by marketing research becomes a part of the DSS, as in the case of Reebok in the opening vignette. Specifically, marketing research contributes research data to the database, marketing models and analytical techniques to the model base, and specialized programs for analyzing marketing data to the software base. Many firms are building huge internal databases as part of the DSS (see database marketing in Chapter 4). The analytical techniques and the software used to analyze these data are discussed later in the text (see Chapters 15 through 18). Decision support systems differ from MIS in that they combine the models and analytic techniques of traditional marketing research with the easy access and retrieval of MIS (Figure 1.9). Well-designed DSS adapt to the decision-making needs of the user with easy interactive processes. In addition to providing easy access to data, DSS can also enhance decision-making effectiveness by using "what-if" analysis. Reebok International makes use of a sophisticated DSS that enables it to assess the impact of introducing new footwear, making a promotional offer, or opening a new facility at a specific location when these projects are still in the planning stage.

MIS and DSS can greatly improve decision making by enabling management to access a wide range of information. An advanced form of DSS, called *expert systems*, uses artificial intelligence procedures to incorporate expert judgment. In addition to crunching numbers and storing and retrieving information, these systems are programmed to reason and make inferences. Thus, the expert systems can actually lead to decisions recommending certain courses of action to the management. All of these systems can greatly enhance the effectiveness of marketing.

decision support system (DSS)

An information system that enables decision makers to interact directly with both databases and analysis models. The important components of a DSS include hardware and a communication network, database, model base, software base, and the DSS user (decision maker).

MIS
- Structured problems
- Use of reports
- Information displaying restricted
- Can improve decision making by clarifying new data

DSS
- Unstructured problems
- Use of models
- Adaptability
- Can improve decision making by using "what-if" analysis

FIGURE 1.9

Marketing Information Systems (MIS) Versus Decision Support Systems (DSS)

Summary Illustration Using the Opening Vignette

To summarize and illustrate the concepts in this chapter, let's return to the opening vignette. Marketing research involves the identification, collection, analysis, dissemination, and use of information about consumers, channel members, competitors, and changes and trends in the marketplace and other aspects of the firm's environment. In the opening vignette, Reebok used "time-use" research in an attempt to discover what consumers do with their spare time. Marketing research can be classified as problem-identification research or problem-solving research. Reebok used problem-identification research involving secondary data analysis, focus groups, and a market potential survey to discover that adults were spending less time in health clubs and more time exercising at home. Problem-solving research, in the form of product research, then led to the development of the successful home–step aerobics line.

The marketing research process consists of six steps, which must be followed systematically. Figure 1.10 provides a concept map for the marketing research process. In this figure, the six steps of the marketing research process are connected, in order, by bold arrows. Each step is described by concepts that are connected to that step by lines with descriptors. Concepts are also linked to other concepts by lines or arrows. Thus, step 1 is defining the problem, which consists of the management decision problem and the marketing research problem. The management decision problem guides the marketing research problem. Reebok follows a very similar marketing research process, and some of these steps were illustrated in the opening vignette.

Marketing research can be conducted internally or purchased from external suppliers. In the case of Reebok, in-house marketing research specialists are actively involved in defining and designing the marketing research project. The in-house specialists also have the primary

FIGURE 1.10

A Concept Map for the Marketing Research Process

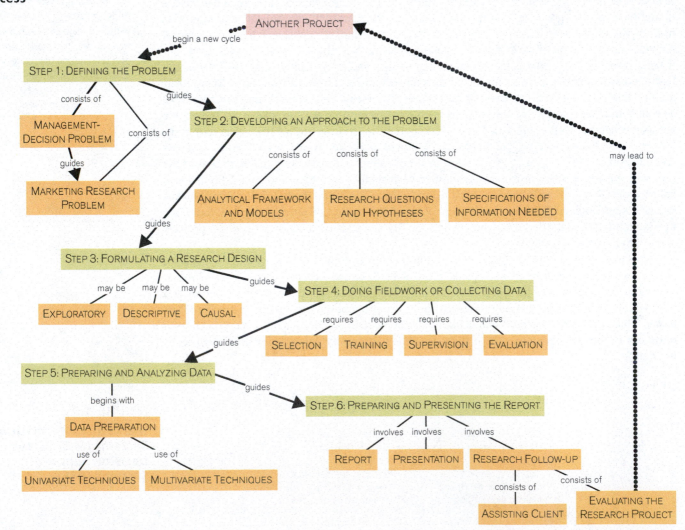

responsibility for presenting the results to management and providing assistance in implementation. Reebok also makes use of full-service suppliers who provide assistance in all the steps of the marketing research process as well as limited-service suppliers who may handle only data collection and analysis and assist in report writing.

The marketing research industry offers a wide range of careers in both corporate (e.g., Reebok) and marketing research organizations. Information obtained using marketing research can stand alone or be integrated into an MIS and DSS, as in the case of Reebok.

Application to Contemporary Issues

Although several contemporary issues are discussed throughout each chapter, we focus special attention on international marketing research, marketing research and social media, and ethics in marketing research. Each of these issues receives a separate section in each chapter of the text (except international marketing research and ethics for the data analysis chapters, Chapters 16 through 18). We show how marketing research principles can be applied when conducting research in an international setting. Because we live in an age of social media, the use of social media as an application and as a domain to conduct marketing research also is discussed. Ethical issues in marketing research are described.

International Marketing Research

The United States accounts for about 40 percent of worldwide marketing research expenditures; another 40 percent is attributable to Western Europe and about 10 percent to Japan. Most of the research in Europe is done in the United Kingdom, Germany, France, Italy, and Spain. Japan is the clear leader in the Asia–Pacific region, followed by Australia, China, South Korea, and Taiwan. Brazil and Mexico lead the Central and South American markets in terms of marketing research expenditures.[9]

With the globalization of markets, marketing research has assumed a truly international character, a trend that is likely to continue. Several U.S.–based market research firms are equipped to conduct international marketing research. They include Nielsen, IMS Health, and SymphonyIRI (see Table 1.1). Foreign-based firms include Kantar (United Kingdom) and GfK (Germany).

International marketing research is much more complex than domestic marketing research. Research of this type should be sensitive to differences in customs, communication, and culture. The environment in the countries or international markets that are being researched influences the way the six steps of the marketing research process should be performed. These environmental factors include marketing, government, legal, economic, structural, informational and technological, and sociocultural factors. When conducted properly, international marketing research can yield high dividends, as demonstrated by the success of Procter & Gamble in China.

Research in Action

Head & Shoulders Stands Head and Shoulders Above Competition in China

As of 2011, Procter & Gamble (P&G) (www.pg.com) markets about 300 products to more than 4 billion consumers in 180 countries. P&G products are the largest daily-use consumer products in China. The company has achieved this status by ignoring popular maxims, instead relying on marketing research.

P&G succeeded because it ignored the standard practices used in marketing to the Chinese consumers. It did not cater to a wealthy audience, although it was told that none other could afford its expensive products. By relying on marketing research, such popular maxims were seen for what they were—misunderstandings. Additionally, by conducting proper cross-cultural research P&G was able to overcome Western biases based on erroneous

Source. AP Wide World Photos/Feng lei sh–Imaginechina/Associated Press.

(*continued*)

beliefs about China, such as that middle-class Chinese could not afford expensive Western products.

Marketing research revealed that dandruff was a major concern, because the Chinese have dark hair, causing dandruff to readily stand out. Furthermore, Chinese shampoos were ineffective in fighting this malady. Research revealed that most Chinese were willing to pay a premium for a shampoo that addressed this problem.

P&G decided to establish its foothold in China by fighting dandruff. P&G targeted a broad segment, rather than just the

wealthy. P&G introduced Head & Shoulders as a premium brand, and within 3 years it was China's leading shampoo. P&G then introduced antidandruff versions of Pert and Pantene. Using careful targeting, both brands performed extremely well. Overall, P&G commands a leading share of the shampoo market in China, even though its products are priced more than 300 percent higher than local brands. This example show that those who overcome their biases and conduct proper research can stand head and shoulders above the competition.[10]

Be an MR!	Be a DM!
Jeans, a Universal Product?	
Visit www.levis.com and search the Internet—including social media—as well as your library's online databases to find information on consumer preferences for jeans. Levi's would like to conduct marketing research to increase its share of the jeans market in the United States and India. How would you conduct marketing research in the two countries?	As Levi's marketing chief, what information would you need to formulate strategies aimed at increasing marketing share?

Marketing Research and Social Media

Social media embody social computing tools commonly referred to as *Web 2.0*. These are Web applications that facilitate interactive information sharing, user-centered design, and collaboration on the World Wide Web. Examples of social media include social-networking sites (e.g., Facebook), video sharing (e.g., YouTube), photo sharing (e.g., Flickr), music sharing (e.g., Last FM), bookmarking (e.g., Delicious), voice networking (e.g., Skype), wikis (e.g., Wikipedia), product and service reviews (e.g., TripAdvisor), virtual worlds (e.g., Second Life), multiplayer games (e.g., Farmville), Web-based communities (e.g., ivillage), blogs (e.g., Direct2Dell), and microblogs (e.g., Twitter). A Web 2.0 site allows its users to interact with other users or to change Web site content, in contrast to noninteractive Web sites where users are limited to the passive viewing of information that is provided to them. Good social media networks use all the tools available to them: discussion, chat, webcast, photo, video, podcasts, animation, surveys, games, and virtual worlds. People interact in different ways, and so it is desirable to give them as many tools as feasible. Moreover, the cost of providing all these tools has become reasonable.

All social media share certain common characteristics that make them very relevant as a domain for conducting marketing research. Social media are marked by user-generated content that is blurring the distinction between professional and amateur content. Key social interactions develop around the user-generated content. Users are able to rate, rank, comment on, review, and respond to the new world of media, a factor that is driving the success of social media. People form online communities by combining one-to-one (e.g., e-mail and instant messaging), one-to-many (Web pages and blogs), and many-to-many (wikis) communication modes.

Marketing researchers can make use of these new social networks, and the open-source social computing tools from which they are built, to extend the boundaries of our research offerings. These social communities open new avenues for understanding, explaining, influencing, and predicting the behaviors of consumers in the marketplace. Thus, they can be used in a variety of marketing research applications including segmentation, idea generation, concept testing, product development, brand launches, pricing, and integrated marketing communications.

Social media are not without limitations. Although the standard for objectivity is high for journalists, expectations about objectivity among bloggers and other social media users are lower. Social media users may not be representative of the target population in many marketing research applications. Social media as a source of samples suffers from at least two biases: first from self-selection in that the respondents can self-select themselves into the sample, and second from advocacy. Yet, as long as these limitations are understood, insights from social media analysis can uncover useful information that can inform marketing decisions. In this book, we advocate the use of social media as an additional domain in which to conduct marketing research to supplement and complement, but not to replace, the traditional ways in which research is conducted. We also discuss social media as an application of marketing research in that we show how the traditional marketing research procedures can be implemented in social media.

A handful of marketing research firms have emerged that specialize in social media conversation mining services. They listen in on online conversations, report on activity, and assess influence. These services charge from a few hundred to a few thousand dollars per month and differ in the features they offer. Nielsen (www.nielsen.com) derives data-driven insights from nearly 100 million blogs, social networks, groups, boards, and other consumer-generated media platforms. The company offers real-time measurement and analysis, balancing investment in text-mining, analytical technologies, and expert analysis. Cymfony (www.cymfony.com), a Kantar Media company, provides market influence analytics by scanning and interpreting voices at the intersection of social and traditional media. The company's Maestro platform identifies the people, issues, and trends impacting businesses. Cymfony offers a range of packaged and custom services to address specific intelligence requirements, such as social media strategy, consumer opinions and trends, customer satisfaction, and reputation management. Attensity's Attensity360 (www.attensity.com) service continuously monitors and analyzes social media conversations and their impact on businesses. It offers real-time analysis and drill-down capabilities to analyze the data in different ways. Client firms can track and analyze the ongoing relevant conversations affecting their businesses, influential opinion leaders and sources, the impact of conversation topics, and topic trends. BrandsEye (www.brandseye.com), developed by Quirk eMarketing, searches the Internet for every mention of a brand and calculates a weighted Reputation Score that companies can use to compare their brands to their competitors. The services of other social media research firms are discussed throughout the book. Here, we illustrate how one firm, namely Starbucks, is using social media to obtain information and connect with consumers in the target market.

Research in Action

Starbucks: The Star of Social Media

Starbucks has a blog, My Starbucks Idea (MSI) (mystarbucksidea.force.com), where it not only connects with customers but also co-creates the company's future with them. Customers can share ideas, vote on ideas others have suggested, discuss ideas with other customers, and view the ideas Starbucks has announced. Starbucks's Idea Partners from different departments within the company take part in answering queries and providing insights to discussions. Starbucks can then get ideas and feedback on how to improve their products to satisfy the needs of customers. Furthermore, the brand takes suggestions posted on the site seriously and publishes implemented suggestions for all to see. It further encourages feedback from customers by providing online incentives in the form of virtual vouchers or purchase points. This enables the brand to interact with its loyal customers. Additionally, Starbucks includes qualitative and quantitative types of survey questions in the form of polls along the sidelines of the blog in a bid to further solicit marketing research data. My Starbucks Idea has a significant impact as, on average, one in three suggestions are implemented. All suggestions are acknowledged and commented on within an hour of uploading; an average of four suggestions are made every hour.

Starbucks has a Facebook page (www.facebook.com/starbucks) that has a total of more than 21 million, and still growing, fans. It uses this site to promote new products and gain the feedback of customers. It also organizes events and uses Facebook's technology to invite customers to attend its events. It has a collection of photos from its products and events, among many others uploaded by fans. Starbucks updates its Facebook page approximately once every 2 days, and every update sees thousands of users responding to it. The company actively comments or replies to its followers' posts or photo tags of them, increasing its presence on social media. Starbucks also uses its Facebook page to develop a target market's profile through descriptive research.

Starbucks also make use of Twitter (www.twitter.com/starbucks) to promote products and connect with customers. The firm uses Twitter to update customers about new products and services with short messages. Tools like retweets allow users to spread messages originally tweeted by Starbucks to others. Starbucks's Twitter account often directs followers to MSI for polls, surveys, or opinions-casting.

Starbucks uses YouTube (www.youtube.com/starbucks) to share videos of its events and special music performances. It is also a way for the company to obtain feedback through the number of views, comments or subscribers, and ratings.

Starbucks is on Flickr (www.flickr.com/starbucks), an image and video-hosting Web site, and has a group (www.flickr.com/groups/starbuckscoffeecompany) where it allows customers to post photos of their experience at the store and have discussions among themselves.

In addition to the official Starbucks blog and social media sites, there are many unofficial Starbucks sites maintained by fans and other

(*continued*)

individuals. An example of one such site, www.starbucksmelody.com, is shown here:

Source: Courtesy of Melody Overton, Starbucksmelody.com.

Being present on many other forms of social media, Starbucks is not absent from MySpace, where it has audio clips uploaded and people discussing issues with one another. It also has a page on Wikipedia, the most popular wiki provider. In addition, Starbucks also makes use of LinkedIn (www.linkedin.com/companies/2271) to present the company profile to others.

An example of how social media have helped Starbucks improve its service is the recurring requests for free wireless and the final move made by Starbucks to officially offer free unlimited wireless to all its customers. Likewise, several members of the MSI community posted ideas requesting fresh fruits to be served at Starbucks. In response, Starbucks began producing a new drink with a fruity touch, alongside its new iced coffee beverage, to help beat the summer heat. From the tropics of the Bahamas to the Forbidden City in Beijing, social media have helped Starbucks to serve its corporate logo alongside freshly brewed coffees in meeting the needs of customers. As of 2011, the brand is represented in more than 55 countries and continues to grow.[11]

Ethics in Marketing Research

Business activities often are discussed from the perspectives of different stakeholders, those individuals or groups who have an interest in or are directly involved in activities related to business. Marketing research activities affect four stakeholders: (1) the marketing researcher, (2) the client, (3) the respondent, and (4) the public. Ethical questions arise when conflict occurs between these stakeholders (Figure 1.11).

In the face of conflict, the behavior of the stakeholders should be guided by codes of conduct. Several organizations, including the Marketing Research Association (MRA) and the American Marketing Association (AMA), provide codes in the area of ethical research behavior. For example, see the respondent bill of rights on the Web site of the Marketing Research Association (www.mra-net.org). Each stakeholder has responsibilities. Neglect of these responsibilities might result in harm to another stakeholder or to the research project. It will always damage the research process and the integrity of the profession.[12]

Ethical issues can arise at each step of the marketing research process. These issues are discussed in more detail in subsequent chapters. Here we give the code of ethics of the Marketing Research Association (MRA). This code is consistent with the ethical guidelines issued by many marketing research and related associations.

FIGURE 1.11

Stakeholders in Marketing Research: An Ethical Perspective

Research in Action

MRA's Ethical Guidelines on the Use of the Internet for Conducting Marketing Research

These *Ethical Guidelines* include:

- Respondent Cooperation Should Be Voluntary
- Researcher's Identity Should Be Disclosed to Respondents
- Respondents' Rights to Anonymity Should Be Safeguarded
- Privacy Policy Statements Should Be Posted Online
- Data Security Should Be Maintained
- Reliability and Validity of Findings Should Be Disclosed to the Public

- Researchers Interviewing Minors Should Adhere to the Children's Online Privacy Protection Act
- Unsolicited E-mail Should Not Be Sent to Those Requesting Not to Receive Any Further E-mail

Source: Code of Ethics of Marketing Research Association (www.mra-net.org). Used with permission.

Experiential Learning

Ethical Guidelines

Compare the ethical guidelines for conducting marketing research posted at the following Web sites:

- CASRO: The Council of American Survey Research Organizations (www.casro.org)
- MRA: Marketing Research Association (www.mra-net.org)
- ESOMAR: European Society for Opinion and Marketing Research (www.esomar.org)

Which organization has the most stringent set of guidelines? Which organization's ethical guidelines are the most complete?

What is missing from the guidelines of all three of the organizations?

WHAT WOULD YOU DO?

Samsonite. Life's a Journey

The Situation

Samsonite is one of the world's largest designers, manufacturers, and distributors of luggage. It sells its products using a number of quality brand names, including Samsonite® and American Tourister®. Samsonite's tagline—"Life's a Journey"—embodies the brand, signifying the role Samsonite continues to play in the multifaceted lives of the global traveler. With net sales of $1.1 billion for its fiscal year ending January 31, 2010, it is a leader in the highly fragmented global luggage industry. Through aggressive product development and marketing, president and chief executive officer Marcello Bottoli hoped to increase the company's market share. Bottoli recognizes the importance of new product development and acknowledges that Samsonite must continually introduce successful new products in the marketplace.

Source: Ross Hailey/MCT/Newscom.

The Marketing Research Decision

1. What type of marketing research should Samsonite undertake? (Check as many as are applicable.)
   a. Product research
   b. Pricing research
   c. Promotion research
   d. Distribution research
   e. All of the above

2. Discuss the role of the type of research you recommend in enabling Marcello Bottoli to increase the market share of Samsonite.

The Marketing Management Decision

1. Marcello Bottoli's aggressive marketing strategy should be built around (check as many as are applicable):
   a. New product development
   b. Price discounts

(continued)

c. International marketing

d. Distribution through flagship stores

e. All of the above

2. Discuss how the marketing management decision action that you recommend to Marcello Bottoli is influenced by the research that you suggested earlier and by the findings of that research.

What Marcello Bottoli Did

Marcello Bottoli unveiled a directional luggage collection by world-renowned designer Alexander McQueen. The collaboration brought together inspiration and

ideas from McQueen's own life experience and travels. The design ethos contrasts fragility and strength, tradition and modernity, resulting in a collection of key travel pieces to appeal to the world's most discerning globe trotters. Underpinning the design features are Samsonite Black Label's contemporary style and luxury, and its values of ultimate performance, function, and durability.

The world of travel is constantly changing, and so is Samsonite. As the brand is taken beyond luggage, Samsonite is constantly seeking opportunities to expand internationally and become present in new distribution channels, leading to the opening of flagship Samsonite Black Label stores in high-end locations in New York, London, Moscow, Berlin, Seoul, Tokyo, Hong Kong, Singapore, Taipei, and Shanghai.[13]

SPSS Windows and Excel

In this book, we feature SPSS programs, not merely as a statistical package, but as an integrative package that can be used in the various stages of the marketing research process. We illustrate the use of SPSS for defining the problem, developing an approach, formulating the research design, data collection, data preparation and analysis, and report preparation and presentation. In addition to the BASE module, we also feature other SPSS programs, such as Decision Time, What If?, Maps, Data Entry, SamplePower Missing Values, TextSmart, and SmartViewer.

The data analyses also are illustrated with three other software packages: Excel, SAS, and Minitab. Detailed, step-by-step instructions are provided for both SPSS Windows and Excel. All the data files are available for both SPSS and Excel. The computerized demonstration movies and screen captures for implementing each and every statistical procedure using SPSS or Excel can be downloaded from the Web site for this book.

Summary

Marketing research assesses information needs and provides relevant information in order to improve the marketing decision-making process. It is a systematic and objective process designed to identify and solve marketing problems. Thus, marketing research can be classified as problem-identification research and problem-solving research. The marketing research process consists of six steps that must be followed systematically. Marketing research provides information about consumers, channel members, competitors, changes and trends in the marketplace, and other aspects of the firm's environment including competitive intelligence. The decision to conduct marketing research should be guided by a number of considerations, including the costs versus the benefits, the resources available to conduct the research, the resources available to implement the research findings, and management's attitude toward research.

A firm can conduct its own marketing research or purchase it from external suppliers. External suppliers might provide full service or specialize in one or more aspects of the process. Full-service suppliers provide the entire range of marketing research services, from problem definition to report preparation and presentation. The services provided by these suppliers can be classified as syndicated services, customized services, or Internet services including social media. Limited-service suppliers specialize in one or a few steps of the marketing research process. These suppliers might offer field services, focus groups and qualitative services, technical and analytical services, and other services such as branded products and services.

The marketing research industry offers a wide range of careers in both corporate and marketing research organizations. Marketing research firms, business and nonbusiness firms, and advertising agencies all employ research professionals. Information obtained using marketing research can stand alone or be integrated into an MIS or DSS. Marketing research contributes to the DSS by providing research data to the database, marketing models and analytical techniques to the model base, and specialized marketing research programs to the software base.

International marketing research is much more complex than domestic research because researchers must consider the environment in the international markets they are researching. Social media are emerging as an important domain in which to conduct marketing research. The ethical issues in marketing research involve four stakeholders: (1) the marketing researcher, (2) the client, (3) the respondent, and (4) the public.

Key Terms and Concepts

Suggested Cases and Video Cases

Running Case with Real Data

1.1 Hewlett-Packard

Comprehensive Critical Thinking Cases

2.1 American Idol   2.2 Baskin-Robbins   2.3 Akron Children's Hospital

Comprehensive Cases with Real Data

3.1 Bank of America   3.2 McDonald's   3.3 Boeing

Comprehensive Brief Harvard Business School Cases

4.1 TruEarth Healthy Foods: Market Research for a New Product Introduction (4065)
4.2 The Springfield Nor'easters: Maximizing Revenues in the Minor Leagues (2510)
4.3 Metabical: Positioning and Communications Strategy for a New Weight-Loss Drug (4240)
4.4 Saxonville Sausage Company (2085)

Online Video Cases

1.1 Burke   2.1 Accenture   3.1 NFL   9.1 P&G   11.1 Dunkin' Donuts
12.1 Motorola   13.1 Subaru   14.1 Intel   19.1 Marriott

Live Research: Conducting a Marketing Research Project

1. Give a background of the client organization.
2. Discuss the client's marketing organization and operations.
3. Explain how the project's result will help the client make specific marketing decisions.
4. Organize the class. This might require the formation of project teams. The entire class could be working on the same project with each team working on all aspects of the project or each team could be assigned a specific responsibility (e.g., a specific component of the problem or a specific aspect of the project, such as collection and analysis of secondary data). Each student should participate in primary data collection. Alternatively, the class could be working on multiple projects with specific teams assigned to a specific project. The approach is flexible and can handle a variety of organizations and formats.
5. Develop a project schedule clearly specifying the deadlines for the different steps.
6. Explain how the teams will be evaluated.
7. One or a few students should be selected as project coordinators.

Acronym

The role and salient characteristics of marketing research can be described by the acronym RESEARCH:

R ecognition of information needs

E ffective decision making

S ystematic and objective

E xodus/dissemination of information

A nalysis of information

R ecommendations for action

C ollection of information

H elpful to managers

Review Questions

1. Define *marketing research.* What are some of the note-worthy aspects of this definition?
2. Describe a classification of marketing research and give examples.
3. Describe the steps in the marketing research process.
4. Describe the task of marketing research and illustrate with an example.
5. What decisions do marketing managers make? How does marketing research help them to make these decisions?
6. Discuss the role of marketing research in gathering competitive intelligence.
7. How would you classify marketing research suppliers?
8. What are syndicated services, and how do they help a firm conduct marketing research?
9. What is the main difference between a full-service and a limited-service supplier?
10. List five guidelines for selecting an external marketing research supplier.
11. What career opportunities are available in marketing research? Are you interested in pursuing such a career? Why or why not?
12. What is a marketing information system (MIS)?
13. How is DSS different from MIS?
14. **Social Media** Discuss the role of social media in conducting marketing research.
15. Who are the stakeholders in marketing research?

Applied Problems

1. Visit the Web site of one of the marketing research firms listed in Table 1.1. Write a report on the types of marketing research conducted by this firm. Classify this firm based on the scheme presented in Figure 1.7.
2. Search the Internet to identify five examples of problem-identification research and five examples of problem-solving research.
3. Describe one marketing research project that would be useful to each of the following organizations:
   a. Your campus bookstore
   b. The public transportation authority in your city
   c. A major department store in your area
   d. A restaurant located near your campus
   e. A zoo in a major city
4. Search the Internet and your library's online databases to identify an innovative new product introduced in the past 12 months and research it. Write a report about the marketing research undertaken to develop this product.
5. Visit the Web sites of the following organizations: MRA (www.mra-net.org), ESOMAR (www.esomar.org), and AMSRS (www.amsrs.com.au). Compare and contrast the information available at these sites. Of the three marketing research associations, which has the most useful Web site? Explain.
6. Visit the U.S. Bureau of Labor Statistics Web site at www.bls.gov and search the Internet to obtain information on the employment potential for marketing researchers.

Group Discussion

As a small group of four or five, discuss the following issues.

1. What type of institutional structure is best for a marketing research department in a large business firm?

2. What is the ideal educational background for someone seeking a career in marketing research?
3. Can ethical standards be enforced in marketing research? If so, how?

Hewlett-Packard Running Case

Review the Hewlett-Packard (HP) case, Case 1.1, and questionnaire given toward the end of the book. Answer the following questions.

1. Discuss the role that marketing research can play in helping HP maintain and build on its leadership position in the personal computers market.
2. What problem-identification research should HP undertake?

3. What problem-solving research should HP undertake?
4. Would you like to pursue a marketing research career with HP? Explain.
5. **Social Media** How can HP make use of social media to obtain marketing research information?

ONLINE VIDEO CASE 1.1

BURKE: Learning and Growing Through Marketing Research

Visit **www.pearsonhighered.com/malhotra** to read the video case and view the accompanying video. Burke: Learning and Growing Through Marketing Research traces the evolution of marketing research and how Burke implements the various steps of the marketing research process. Burke's approach to all the six steps of the marketing research process is highlighted: defining the marketing research problem, developing an approach to the problem, formulating a research design, collecting data, analyzing the data, and preparing and presenting the report. This case can be used to discuss the role of marketing research in marketing decision making and the steps of the marketing research process. Specific marketing research questions are posed in the video case.

2

Defining the Marketing Research Problem and Developing an Approach

Source: AP Wide World Photos/PRNewsFoto/Subaru of America, Inc./Associated Press.

LEARNING OBJECTIVES

After reading this chapter, the student should be able to:

1. Understand the importance of and the process used for defining the marketing research problem.

2. Describe the tasks involved in problem definition, including discussions with decision makers, interviews with industry experts, secondary data analysis, and qualitative research.

3. Discuss the environmental factors affecting the definition of the research problem: past information and forecasts,

resources and constraints, objectives of the decision maker, buyer behavior, legal environment, economic environment, and marketing and technological skills of the firm.

4. Clarify the distinction between the management-decision problem and the marketing research problem.

5. Explain the structure of a well-defined marketing research problem, including the broad statement and the specific components.

6. Discuss in detail the various components of the approach: analytical framework and models, research questions and hypotheses, and specification of information needed.
7. Acquire an appreciation of the complexity involved in defining the problem and developing an approach in international marketing research.

8. **Social Media** Describe how social media can be used to identify and define the marketing research problem and aid in developing an approach.
9. Understand the ethical issues and conflicts that arise in defining the problem and developing the approach.

> "The most challenging part of any research project is defining the problem in the terms management understands and in a way that ensures the desired information is obtained."
>
> *Chet Zalesky*
> *President, CMI, Atlanta, Georgia*

The World's First Sport Utility Wagon

The 2012 Outback Wagon was marketed as having a five-star government crash test rating and received rave reviews from automotive magazines. How was the Outback born?

In the early 1990s, Subaru of America was searching for new ways to penetrate the U.S. automobile market. The marketing research firm hired by the company undertook a comprehensive examination of the marketing situation (a problem audit). The audit enabled the research firm to identify the real problem confronting management (the management-decision problem) as "What can Subaru do to expand its share of the automobile market?" The marketing research problem was defined broadly as determining the various needs of automobile users and the extent to which current product offerings were satisfying those needs. However, for marketing research to be conducted effectively and efficiently, the problem had to be defined more precisely. Subaru's management and the research firm agreed on the following specific problem components:

1. What needs do buyers of passenger cars, station wagons, and sport utility vehicles (SUVs) seek to satisfy?
2. How well do existing automobile product offerings meet these needs?
3. Is there a segment of the automobile market whose needs are not being adequately met?
4. What automobile features does the identified segment desire?
5. What is the demographic and psychographic profile of the identified segment?

The approach to the marketing research problem was developed based on the postulate, or framework, that buyers first decide on the type of car (e.g., station wagon, SUV, passenger car) they want and then select a particular brand. The research firm formulated specific research questions and possible answers (hypotheses) to be tested by collecting survey data.

The research indicated a strong market potential for a vehicle that combined the features of a station wagon and a compact SUV. The needs of a sizable male-dominated segment were not being met by either the station wagon or the SUV, and this segment wanted a hybrid product.

Based on these findings, Subaru of America introduced the 1996 Outback as "the world's first sport utility wagon." Subaru said in a press release that the Outback filled the niche between the SUV and the passenger car. The Outback has several important features that are missing from most SUVs, including an all-wheel-drive system that operates under all road conditions and vehicle speeds, four-wheel independent suspension, antilock brakes, dual air bags, and a side-intrusion protection system. It also has a low door threshold for easy passenger entry and exit and a lower center of gravity for road handling and ride comfort. Inside amenities were also upgraded, and several other features were added.

A TV campaign for Outback featured *Crocodile Dundee*'s Paul Hogan. Viewers liked the ads and, of course, the product. Those taking a test drive were very impressed with the vehicle's capabilities. The result? Sales were triple what Subaru originally expected. Sales of the Outback continued to be strong through the 2012 model year.[1]

Overview

This chapter examines the first two steps of the six steps of the marketing research process described in Chapter 1: defining the marketing research problem and developing an approach to the problem. Figure 2.1 briefly explains the focus of the chapter, the relation of this chapter to the previous one, and on which steps of the marketing research process this chapter concentrates.

In the opening vignette, Subaru's introduction of the Outback to exploit a new market segment demonstrates the crucial importance of correctly defining the marketing research problem. Subaru correctly defined the marketing research problem as determining the various needs of automobile users and the extent to which current product offerings were satisfying those needs. Defining the research problem is the most important aspect of the research process. Only when a problem has been clearly and accurately identified can a research project be conducted properly. This is because problem definition sets the course for the entire project. In this chapter, we will identify the tasks involved and the factors to be considered at this stage and provide guidelines to help the researcher avoid common errors.

The chapter also discusses how to develop an approach to the research problem once it has been identified. The approach lays the foundation for how to conduct the research by specifying the relevant theory and models. It further refines the specific components of the problem by asking more specific questions and formulating the hypotheses that will be tested. The approach also specifies all the information that would need to be collected in the marketing research project. The special considerations involved in defining the problem and developing an approach in international marketing research are discussed. The impact of social media and several ethical issues that arise at this stage of the marketing research process also are considered. Figure 2.2 provides an overview of the topics discussed in this chapter and how they flow from one to the next.

The Importance of Defining the Problem

Although every step in a marketing research project is important, problem definition is the most important step. As mentioned in Chapter 1, marketing researchers consider problems and opportunities confronting management to be interchangeable, because the investigation of each follows the same

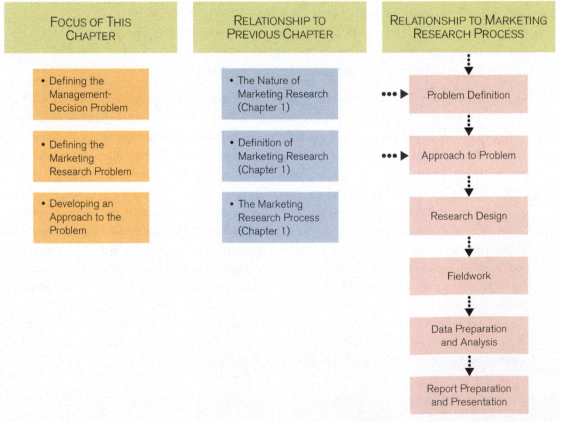

FIGURE 2.1

Relationship of Problem Definition and Approach to the Previous Chapter and the Marketing Research Process

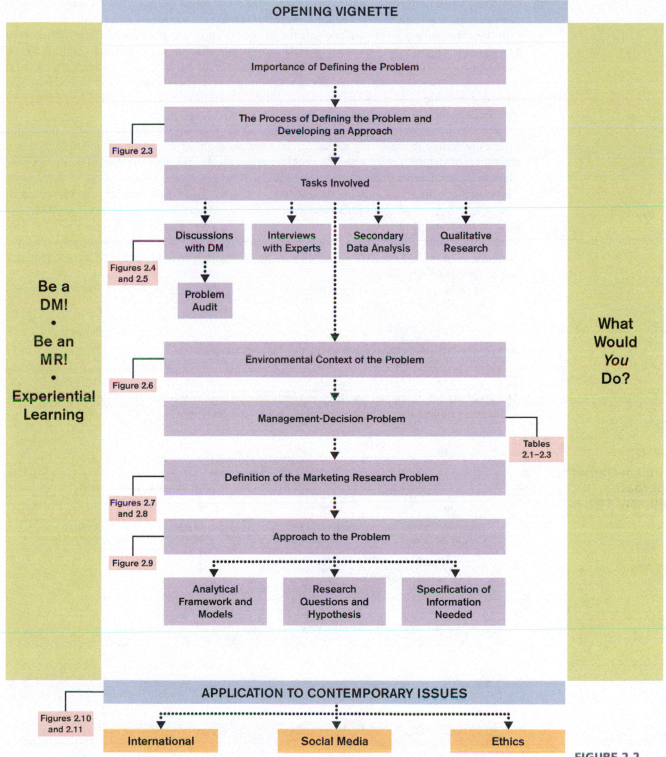

FIGURE 2.2

Defining the Marketing Research Process and Developing an Approach: An Overview

problem definition
A broad statement of the general problem and identification of the specific components of the marketing research problem.

research process. **Problem definition** involves stating the general problem and identifying the specific components of the marketing research problem, as illustrated in the opening vignette.

The opening vignette provided a broad statement of the problem confronting Subaru and identified its five specific components. The researcher and the key decision makers on the client side should agree on the definition of the problem. The *client* is the individual or organization commissioning the research. The client might be an internal person, as in the case of a research director dealing with a decision maker in her or his own organization. Alternatively, the client might be an external entity if the research is being conducted by a marketing research firm. (See Chapter 1.)

Only when both parties have clearly defined and agreed on the marketing research problem can research be designed and conducted properly. Mistakes made at this stage of the process can only mushroom into larger mistakes as the project progresses. As stated by the well-known management expert Peter Drucker, the truly serious mistakes are made not as a result of wrong answers, but rather from asking the wrong questions. Of all the steps in the marketing research process, none is more vital to the ultimate fulfillment of a client's needs than an accurate and adequate definition of the research problem. All the effort, time, and money spent from this point on will be wasted if the problem is not defined properly.

This point is worth remembering. Inappropriate problem definition is one of the major sources of failure in marketing research. The basic message here is that clear identification and definition of the marketing research problem are critical. This was illustrated in the opening vignette. Subaru defined the problem correctly by determining the various needs of automobile users and the extent to which those needs were being satisfied by the current product offerings. The research resulted in an important finding that a substantial segment of the marketplace desired the features of both a station wagon and an SUV, leading to the introduction of a very successful product. Suppose Subaru had incorrectly defined the problem as determining the preferences of the red-hot SUV owners. In such a scenario, it is highly unlikely that the Outback would have been developed.

The problem-definition process provides guidelines on how to correctly define the marketing research problem.

The Process of Defining the Problem and Developing an Approach

The problem-definition and approach development process is illustrated in Figure 2.3. To define a research problem correctly, the researcher must perform a number of tasks.

FIGURE 2.3

The Problem-Definition and Approach Development Process

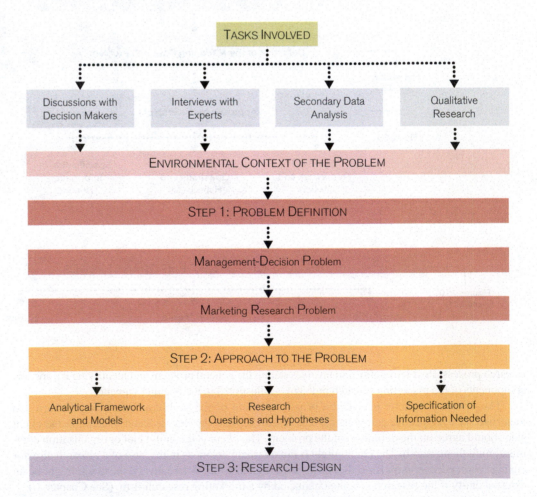

The researcher must discuss the problem with the decision makers in the client organization, interview industry experts and other knowledgeable individuals, analyze secondary data, and sometimes conduct qualitative research. This informal data collection helps the researcher understand the context or environment within which the problem has arisen. A clear understanding of the marketing environment also provides a framework for identifying the management-decision problem: What should the management do? The management-decision problem is then translated into a marketing research problem, the problem that the researcher must investigate. Based on the definition of the marketing research problem, the researcher develops an appropriate approach. Further explanation of the **problem-definition process** follows, with a discussion of the tasks involved.

problem-definition process
The process of defining the management-decision problem and the marketing research problem.

Tasks Involved in Problem Definition

As mentioned earlier, the tasks involved in problem definition include discussions with the decision makers, interviews with industry experts, analysis of secondary data, and qualitative research. The purpose of performing these tasks is to obtain information on the environmental factors that are relevant to the problem and to help define the management-decision problem and the corresponding marketing research problem, as well as to develop an approach. We will discuss and illustrate each of these tasks.

Discussions with Decision Makers

It is essential that the researcher understand the nature of the decision faced by the firm's managers—the management-decision problem—as well as management's expectations of the research. This discussion gives the researcher an opportunity to establish achievable expectations. The decision maker needs to understand the capabilities, as well as the limitations, of the research. Research does not provide automatic solutions to problems; rather, it serves as an additional source of information that the manager should consider in the decision-making process.

To identify the management problem, the researcher must possess considerable skill in interacting with the decision maker and maneuvering through the organization. When the ultimate decision maker is a senior executive, the researcher might have difficulty gaining access to that individual. To complicate the situation even further, several individuals might be involved in the final decision. All individuals responsible for resolving the marketing problem should be consulted in this early phase of the project. The quality of the project will be dramatically improved when the researcher is given the opportunity to interact directly with the key decision makers.

Discussions with the decision maker can be structured around the **problem audit**, which helps to identify the underlying causes of the problem. The problem audit, like any other type of audit, is a comprehensive examination of a marketing problem with the purpose of understanding its origin and nature (see Figure 2.4). The problem audit involves discussions with the decision maker on the following issues, which are illustrated with a problem facing Mars, Inc. (www.mars.com).

problem audit
A comprehensive examination of a marketing problem to understand its origin and nature.

1. *The history of the problem.* This includes an analysis of the events that have led to the decision to act. Mars, the second-leading manufacturer of candies in the United States, with a market share of 25 percent, would like to maintain and increase its share of the market. This problem has come into focus due to recent introductions by Hershey's, the category leader with 42 percent share as of January 1, 2010. Hershey's recent product spin-offs, including Hershey's Goodness and York Pink Patties, are threatening Mars' market share.
2. *The alternative courses of action available to the decision maker.* The set of alternatives might be incomplete at this stage, and qualitative research might be needed to identify the more innovative courses of action. The alternatives available to the management of Mars include introducing new brands of chocolates, reducing the prices of existing brands, expanding channels of distribution, and increasing advertising expenditures.
3. *The criteria that will be used to evaluate the alternative courses of action.* For example, new product offerings might be evaluated on the basis of sales, market share, profitability, return on investment, and so forth. Mars will evaluate the alternatives based on contributions to market share and profits.

FIGURE 2.4

Conducting a Problem Audit

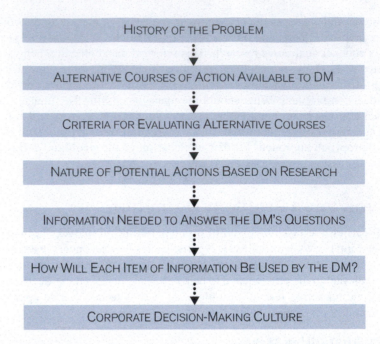

HISTORY OF THE PROBLEM

ALTERNATIVE COURSES OF ACTION AVAILABLE TO DM

CRITERIA FOR EVALUATING ALTERNATIVE COURSES

NATURE OF POTENTIAL ACTIONS BASED ON RESEARCH

INFORMATION NEEDED TO ANSWER THE DM'S QUESTIONS

HOW WILL EACH ITEM OF INFORMATION BE USED BY THE DM?

CORPORATE DECISION-MAKING CULTURE

4. *The nature of potential actions that are likely to be suggested based on the research findings.* The research findings will likely call for a strategic marketing response by Mars.
5. *The information that is needed to answer the decision maker's questions.* The information needed includes a comparison of Hershey's and Mars on all the elements of the marketing mix (product, pricing, promotion, and distribution) in order to determine relative strengths and weaknesses.
6. *The manner in which the decision maker will use each item of information in making the decision.* The key decision makers will devise a strategy for Mars based on the research findings and their intuition and judgment.
7. *The corporate culture as it relates to decision making.* In some firms, the decision-making process is dominant; in others, the personality of the decision maker is more important. A sensitivity to corporate culture in order to identify the individuals who are either responsible for the decision or who have a significant influence over the decision process is essential. In this case, the corporate culture at Mars calls for a committee approach in which key decision makers make the critical decisions.

Conducting a problem audit is essential in order to clarify the problem for the researcher. Not surprisingly, it may serve the same function for the decision maker. Often, the decision maker has only a vague idea of the real problem. For example, the decision maker might know that the firm is losing market share but might not know why. This is because most decision makers focus on the symptoms of a problem rather than its causes. An inability to meet sales forecasts, loss of market share, and a decline in profits are all symptoms. Research that adds value goes beyond the symptoms to address the underlying causes. For example, loss of market share might be caused by a superior promotion by the competition, inadequate distribution of the company's products, lower product quality, price undercutting by a major competitor, or any number of factors (see Figure 2.5).

FIGURE 2.5

Discussion Between the Researcher and the DM

Focus of the DM

SYMPTOMS
• Loss of Market Share

Discussion

Focus of the Researcher

UNDERLYING CAUSES
• Superior Promotion by Competition
• Inadequate Distribution of Company's Products
• Lower Product Quality
• Price Undercutting by a Major Competitor

TABLE 2.1 Problem Definition Based on Symptoms Can Be Misleading

Firm	Symptoms	Problem Definition Based on Symptoms	Problem Definition Based on Underlying Causes
Manufacturer of orange soft drinks	Consumers say the sugar content is too high	Determine consumer preferences for alternative levels of sugar content	Color. The color of the drink is a dark shade of orange giving the perception that the product is too "sugary."
Manufacturer of machine tools	Customers complain prices are too high	Determine the price elasticity of demand	Channel management. Distributors do not have adequate product knowledge to communicate product benefits to customers.

As shown in Table 2.1, a definition of the problem based on symptoms can be misleading. Only when the underlying causes are identified can the problem be successfully addressed, as exemplified by the effort of Nike to stop the loss of market share.

Research in Action

Increased Advertising in the Video Game Industry Puts Nike Back in the Game

Nike (www.nike.com) reported revenues of $19.39 billion for the fiscal year ending May 31, 2010. Although the company was the global and U.S. leader in athletic footwear, it was losing market share. Clearly there was a problem. However, loss of market share was a symptom, and the underlying causes of the problem had to be identified. A problem audit revealed that a major underlying cause of the problem was the amount Nike was spending on advertising, specifically on advertising in the video game industry. Competitor Adidas had increased its advertising in the video game industry and was one of the top brands recalled by gamers in a study conducted by Phoenix Marketing International. Therefore, the problem was defined as whether Nike should increase its advertising budget in the video game industry.

In an effort to answer this problem, an online survey of 540 video gamers was conducted. The results showed that although Nike was popular with gamers age 8 to 17 years, it lagged behind in the 25- to 35-year segment, a segment that was growing in video game use and that also was a massive contributor to sales of athletic shoes.

Based on these findings, Nike decided to increase its advertising budget devoted to the video game industry. This effort yielded good results, and revenues and market share improved. Nike has continued its emphasis on advertising in the video game industry and has maintained its leadership in the U.S. and global athletic footwear markets. Correctly identifying the underlying cause of the problem was a key in this turnaround.[2]

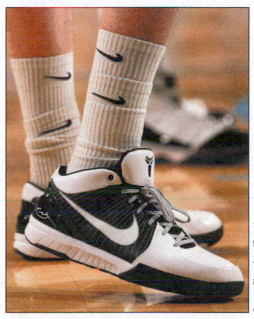

Source: Bloomberg/Getty Images.

The Internet provides several mechanisms that can help the researcher communicate with decision makers. The first and most obvious is e-mail. Researchers can use e-mail to reach decision makers at any place or time. Chat rooms also are good forums for discussion with decision makers. For instance, a chat room discussion with multiple decision makers could be developed around a problem audit. The researcher could introduce the audit issues in the chat, and then the decision makers could respond to the issues and to the each other's responses. Chat rooms can be secured with a password if there is a need to protect the discussion's contents. The use of social media for defining the problem is discussed later in the chapter.

Be a DM!	Be an MR!
Sprite: The Number-Three Soft-Drink Brand	
As the brand manager for Sprite, the third-largest soft-drink brand in the United States, you are concerned about improving the brand's performance. Identify possible symptoms that indicate that Sprite's performance is below expectations.	You are conducting marketing research for Sprite to help improve the brand's performance. Identify possible underlying causes that might be contributing to the brand's lack of performance. Visit www.coca-cola.com and www.sprite.com and search the Internet—including social media—to obtain as much information about Sprite's marketing program as you can.

Interviews with Industry Experts

In addition to discussions with decision makers, interviews with industry experts—individuals knowledgeable about the firm and the industry—can help researchers formulate the marketing research problem. Experts can be found both inside and outside the firm. If the notion of experts is broadened to include people knowledgeable about the general topic being investigated, then the interview also is referred to as an **experience survey** or as the **key-informant technique**. Another variation of this in a technological context is the **lead-user survey**, which involves obtaining information from the lead users of the technology.

Although formal questionnaires normally are not used, a prepared list of topics to be covered during the interview can be often helpful. The order in which these topics are covered and the questions to ask should not be predetermined, but rather decided as the interview progresses. This allows greater flexibility in capturing the experts' insights. The purpose of interviews with experts is to help define the marketing research problem rather than to develop a conclusive solution.

Expert interviews are more commonly used in industrial rather than consumer-research applications. In industrial or highly technical environments, the experts often are more easily identified than in consumer-research settings. This is because consumer settings are more broad and diffused than industrial or technical environments. Expert interviews also are helpful in situations where little information is available from other sources, as in the case of radically new products.

Experts can provide valuable insights in modifying or repositioning existing products, as illustrated by the repositioning of Sears. Once America's number-one retailer, for years, sales at this giant retailer floundered. In 2009, Sears Domestic stores generated $23.7 billion in net sales, down 7.7 percent from the $25.3 billion in sales in 2008, due to an 8.7 percent decrease in comparable store sales. When industry experts were consulted, researchers were able to identify the real problem: lack of image. Traditionally a discount store, Sears had unsuccessfully tried to upgrade its image to a prestigious department store, thereby alienating its loyal customers. Sears finally gave up its attempt to upgrade and re-embraced the image of a discount chain store. Since then, sales and profitability have improved.

Researchers can use the Internet to enhance their ability to obtain information from experts in a specific industry. One approach to finding experts is to use newsgroups. Due to the large amount of information available, searching through the newsgroups for specific information can

experience survey
Interviews with people knowledgeable about the general topic being investigated.

key-informant technique
Interviews with people knowledgeable about the general topic being investigated.

lead-user survey
Surveys that involve obtaining information from the lead users of the technology.

Be an MR!	Be a DM!
Walmart: The Largest Retailer in the World!	
Visit www.walmart.com and search the Internet—including social media—as well as your library's online databases to identify the challenges and opportunities facing Walmart, the largest retailer in the world. Visit groups.google.com and browse retailing newsgroups to identify an expert in online retailing. Interview this expert (via telephone or online) to identify the challenges and opportunities facing Walmart. Alternatively, you can search for and analyze this expert's comments by searching the Internet.	As the CEO of Walmart, what marketing strategies would you formulate to overcome the challenges and capitalize on the opportunities identified by the marketing researcher?

be an arduous task. A good place to start is groups.google.com, which provides categorized lists of newsgroups. Also, you may have access to newsgroups through your ISP (Internet service provider). After finding a relevant newsgroup, access the newsgroup and search for postings about the topic of interest. Surveying postings in a newsgroup is a good starting point for making contacts with the experts in a particular industry.

Secondary Data Analysis

The information that researchers obtain from decision makers and industry experts should be supplemented with available secondary data. **Secondary data** are data collected for some purpose other than the problem at hand, such as data available from trade organizations, the Bureau of Census (www.census.gov), and the Internet. In contrast, **primary data** are originated by the researcher for the specific problem under study, such as survey data. Secondary data include information made available by business and government sources, commercial marketing research firms, and computerized databases. Secondary data are an economical and quick source of background information.

Analyzing available secondary data is an essential step in the problem-definition process and should always precede primary data collection. Secondary data can provide valuable insights into the problem situation and lead to the identification of innovative courses of action. For example, the U.S. Department of Labor says that the median age of the American labor force will increase; by 2030, 23 percent of the U.S. labor force is projected to be age 55 and older, compared with 16 percent in 2005. This is, in part, the result of the maturation of the "baby bust" generation (those born between 1965 and 1976), which will cause a decline in the number of young (age 16 to 24) workers available to fill entry-level positions, with that percentage decreasing from 15 in 2005 to 13 in 2030. This potential shortage of young workers has caused many marketers, particularly those in the service industries, to investigate the problem of consumer response to self-service. Some companies, such as Arby's, have switched from a "high-touch" to a "high-tech" service orientation. By using high-tech equipment, consumers now perform many of the services formerly done by workers, such as placing their own orders by entering them directly into the electronic terminal. Given the tremendous importance of secondary data, this topic will be discussed in detail in Chapters 4 and 5.

secondary data
Data collected for some purpose other than the problem at hand.

primary data
Data originated by the researcher to address the research problem.

Be a DM!	Be an MR!
Wendy's Battling for Market Share	
As the marketing director for Wendy's, what significance do you attach to secondary data showing the aging of the U.S. population? What are the implications of these data for increasing Wendy's market share?	Identify the sources of secondary data including social media that would be helpful in defining the problem of Wendy's increasing its share of the fast-food market. Visit www.wendys.com and search the Internet—as well as your library's online databases—to determine Wendy's market share for the past 3 years.

Social Media

Qualitative and Exploratory Research

Information obtained from decision makers, industry experts, and secondary data might not be sufficient to define the research problem. Sometimes qualitative research must be undertaken to gain a clear understanding of the factors underlying a research problem. **Qualitative research** is unstructured in that the questions asked are formulated as the research proceeds. It is exploratory in nature and based on small samples. It might involve popular qualitative techniques such as focus groups (group interviews) or in-depth interviews (one-on-one interviews that probe the respondents' thoughts in detail). Other exploratory research techniques, such as pilot surveys and case studies, can also be undertaken to gain insights into the phenomenon of interest. **Pilot surveys** tend to be less structured than large-scale surveys in that they generally contain more open-ended questions and the sample size is much smaller. **Case studies** involve an intensive examination of a few selected cases of the phenomenon of interest. The cases could be consumers, stores, firms, or a variety of other units, such as markets, Web sites, and so forth.

qualitative research
An unstructured, exploratory research methodology based on small samples intended to provide insight and understanding of the problem setting.

pilot surveys
Surveys that tend to be less structured than large-scale surveys in that they generally contain more open-ended questions and the sample size is much smaller.

case studies
Involve an intensive examination of a few selected cases of the phenomenon of interest. Cases could be customers, stores, or other units.

The data are obtained from the company, external secondary sources, and by conducting lengthy unstructured interviews with people knowledgeable about the phenomenon of interest. In a project we conducted for a major department chain store, valuable insights into factors affecting store patronage were obtained in a case study comparing the five best stores with the five worst stores of that chain. The role of qualitative research in defining the marketing research problem is further illustrated by Norwegian Cruise Lines.

Once the leader in the Caribbean cruise market, Norwegian Cruise Lines (www2.ncl.com), based in Coral Gables, Florida, had slipped to fourth position. To identify the underlying causes and define the problem, focus groups and pilot (small-scale) surveys were conducted. This qualitative research revealed that one worry that kept people from cruising was the fear of being confined to a boat for a week or more with little to do. This concern was particularly acute among young people. This concern became a major component of the problem, and a large survey was conducted to address it. The survey verified the qualitative research findings.

In response to this information, Norwegian Cruise Lines developed advertising that fought this myth, emphasizing that passengers have the flexibility to make their cruise vacation whatever they want it to be. Its provocative, award-winning print and TV campaigns featured close-ups of young people, often on land, having lots of fun. The campaign helped Norwegian attract new and younger customers and improve its market share and penetration. This success was achieved despite the fact that Norwegian was outspent in advertising two to one by Carnival Cruise Lines and one and one-half to one by Royal Caribbean Cruises.[3] (Exploratory research is discussed in more detail in Chapter 3, and qualitative research techniques are discussed in detail in Chapter 6.)

Although research undertaken at this stage might not be conducted in a formal way, it can provide valuable insights. These insights, together with information obtained from discussions with the decision makers, industry experts, and analysis of secondary data, guide the researcher to an appropriate definition of the problem, as illustrated by P&G for CoverGirl.

Research in Action

P&G's Peep into Privacy Identifies Underlying Causes

P&G decision makers were faced with the problem of increasing the sales and market share of its CoverGirl cosmetics lines. Analysis of internal secondary data showed that the sales to working mothers were stagnating despite the fact that external secondary data revealed that the number of mothers in the workforce was increasing. Past research conducted by P&G as well as interviews with cosmetic experts revealed that the image of CoverGirl was not the problem, as the line was well-thought-of by both the experts and ordinary users.

In an effort to identify the underlying causes, P&G turned to qualitative research. In addition to focus groups, it sent video crews and cameras into households with working mothers, hoping to capture, on tape, life's daily routines and procedures in all their boring glory. A small London research firm, Everyday Lives Ltd. (www.everydaylives.com) ran the program for P&G.

This research revealed that one of the biggest challenges faced by working mothers is their hectic mornings. Between getting the kids off to school and juggling a host of other duties, they still want to make sure they leave the house looking their best. So P&G defined the marketing research problem as determining the potential for multipurpose products that could help this segment of customers by making their makeup routine easier. Subsequent research led to the launch of multipurpose products such as a CoverGirl cosmetic that is a moisturizer, foundation, and sunscreen all rolled into one. This was followed by the introduction in 2010 of "the 3-Minute Facelift Effect," involving CoverGirl & Olay Simply Ageless Serum Primer and Foundation. Working moms were to "first, smooth on the Serum Primer to prep your skin; it hydrates to

help firm skin's appearance. Next, apply the foundation to cover fine lines and wrinkles flawlessly. The results are so amazing everyone will wonder what you did." These products were successful because they met an underlying need of the target segment.[4]

Environmental Context of the Problem

The insights gained from qualitative research, along with discussions with decision makers, interviews with industry experts, and analysis of secondary data, help the researcher understand the environmental context of the problem. The researcher must have a full understanding of the client's firm and industry. Several factors that comprise the **environmental context of the problem** can play an important role in defining the marketing research problem. These factors consist of past information and forecasts pertaining to the industry and the firm, the firm's resources and constraints, decision makers' objectives, buyer behavior, the legal environment, the economic environment, and the firm's marketing and technological skills (see Figure 2.6). Each of these factors is discussed briefly.

Past Information and Forecasts

Past information and forecasts of trends with respect to sales, market share, profitability, technology, population, demographics, and lifestyle are combined to provide the researcher with a fuller picture of the underlying marketing research problem. Not only should the firm's performance and projections be analyzed, but the firm's performance relative to the overall industry should be examined as well. For example, if a firm's sales have decreased but industry sales have increased, the problems will be very different than if industry sales have also decreased. In the former case, the problems are likely to be specific to the firm.

Past information, forecasts, and trends can be valuable in uncovering potential opportunities and problems. For example, pizza restaurants have sought to exploit potential opportunities in the recent trend toward takeout food and home delivery. Pizza Hut has successfully capitalized on this trend by emphasizing takeout and home-delivery services. It opened several takeout-only (with no dine-in service) outlets to better serve this market. As another illustration, in the Subaru vignette, forecasts of future sales of station wagons and SUVs indicated to management that both types of automobiles were not tapping the full market potential.

Past information and forecasts can be especially valuable if resources are limited and there are other constraints on the organization.

Resource Constraints and Objectives

To formulate a marketing research problem of appropriate scope, it is necessary to take into account the resources available, such as money, research skills, and operational capabilities, as well as operational and time constraints. Although adjustments in proposed research expenditure levels are common, proposing a large-scale $100,000 project when only $40,000 has been

environmental context of the problem

Factors that have an impact on the definition of the marketing research problem, including past information and forecasts, resources and constraints of the firm, objectives of the decision maker, buyer behavior, legal environment, economic environment, and marketing and technological skills of the firm.

FIGURE 2.6

Factors to Be Considered in the Environmental Context of the Problem

budgeted will put the research firm at a serious competitive disadvantage. Time constraints also are an important factor in many research projects. A project for Fisher-Price, a major toy manufacturer, involving mall-intercept interviews (conducted with shoppers in malls) in six major cities (Chicago, Fresno, Kansas City, New York, Philadelphia, and San Diego) had to be completed in 4 weeks. Why the rush? The results had to be presented at an upcoming board meeting where a major (go/no-go) decision was to be made about a new product introduction. The time constraint was a major factor that guided the problem definition and the approach adopted.

In formulating the management-decision problem, the researcher must also have a clear understanding of two types of **objectives:** (1) the organizational objectives (the goals of the organization) and (2) the personal objectives of the decision makers. For the project to be successful, it must serve the objectives of the organization and of the decision makers. This may become a challenge when the two are not complementary. For example, a decision maker might wish to undertake research to postpone an awkward decision, to lend credibility to a decision that has already been made, or to get promoted.

It might take skill to get the decision maker to think in terms of objectives that management can act upon (actionable objectives). One effective technique is to confront the decision maker with a number of possible solutions to a problem and ask whether he or she would follow a particular course of action. If the answer is no, further probing might be needed to uncover deeper reasons as to why a particular solution is unsatisfactory.

objectives
Goals of the organization and of the decision maker that must be considered in order to conduct successful marketing research.

Buyer Behavior

buyer behavior
A body of knowledge that tries to understand and predict consumers' reactions based on an individual's specific characteristics.

Buyer behavior is a central component of the environment. It includes the underlying motives, perceptions, attitudes, buying habits, and demographic and psychographic (psychological and lifestyle) profiles of buyers and potential buyers. Most marketing decisions involve a prediction of the buyers' response to a particular marketing action. An understanding of the underlying buyer behavior can provide valuable insights into the problem. Note that in the Subaru vignette, information on the demographic and psychographic characteristics of the automobile segment whose needs were not being met was an important component of the marketing research problem.

Be a DM!	Be an MR!
Timberland Marketing Outdoor Shoes	
As the marketing manager for Timberland, how would your understanding of the consumers' decision-making process affect your decision to sell outdoor shoes on the Internet?	Timberland is a major manufacturer of outdoor footwear. Visit www.timberland.com and search the Internet—including social media—as well as your library's online databases to obtain information on Timberland's marketing program for outdoor shoes. What decision-making process do consumers follow when purchasing outdoor shoes?

 Social Media

In another case, buyer behavior research told ConAgra Frozen Foods that more than 55 percent of Americans pack a lunch and that more and more meals are eaten on the run. However, although consumers increasingly want their food to be portable, they still demand high flavor and good nutrition. Wanting to capitalize on this aspect of buyer behavior, ConAgra further investigated the marketing research problem of consumer preferences for healthy, delicious, and portable food.

The company's answer, based on the findings of this research, was a new entry into the premium-meals category, Healthy Choice Hearty Handfuls frozen sandwiches. As an alternative to many frozen convenience foods, the product targeted an adult taste profile with bakery-style breads, lean meats, and crisp vegetables. True to the name, the sandwiches are both healthy (low in fat and calories) and hearty (at 6 ounces, they are an estimated 35 percent larger than most frozen sandwiches). According to ConAgra, the Hearty Handfuls line exceeded sales expectations, becoming the number-three frozen sandwich brand in its first 6 months.

The increased preference for portable, healthy, and hearty food could be attributed to changes in the sociocultural environment, which includes demographic trends and consumer tastes. The legal, economic, and marketing environment also has a significant impact in some industries.

Legal, Economic, Marketing, and Technological Environments

The **legal environment** includes public policies, laws, government agencies, and pressure groups that influence and regulate various organizations and individuals in society. Important areas of law include patents, trademarks, royalties, trade agreements, taxes, and tariffs. Federal regulation and deregulation has had a huge impact on the marketing process in many industries, such as the airline, banking, and telecommunication industries. The legal and regulatory considerations relevant to a business must be taken into account by the researcher.

Another important component of the environmental context is the **economic environment**, which is composed of purchasing power, gross income, disposable income, discretionary income, prices, savings, credit availability, and general economic conditions. The general state of the economy (rapid growth, slow growth, recession, or stagflation) influences the willingness of consumers and businesses to take on credit and spend on big-ticket items. Thus, the economic environment can have important implications for marketing research problems.

J.C. Penney is one of the largest and most well-known department stores in the United States. In the 1980s, J.C. Penney suffered due to inconsistent sales growth and a drop in the company's image. In the early 2000s, J.C. Penney began a massive overhaul toward a higher-quality image to counter these problems. The company courted famous name brands such as Oshkosh B'Gosh, Levis, and Charles of the Ritz. Unfortunately, J.C. Penney decided to raise prices and go for high-end fashions at a bad time. Price increases coincided with the recession and the economic downturn of 2001 and 2002, and consumers did not have sufficient money to spend. Its most recent attempt in 2011 to recover its image has been to stick with good brand names, to control prices, and to market itself as the store for "middle America." J.C. Penney's lost image has been found by keeping prices competitive and carrying good brand names.

A firm's marketing and technological skills greatly influence which marketing programs and strategies can be implemented. A company's expertise with each element of the marketing mix, as well as its general levels of marketing and production skills, affect the nature and scope of the marketing research project. For example, the introduction of a new product that requires retooling of a manufacturing process or that presumes sophisticated marketing skills might not be a viable alternative if the firm lacks the skills to manufacture or market such a product. However, if the company is able to capitalize on its marketing and technological skills, its products and new introductions are more likely to succeed, as illustrated in the Subaru vignette.

A good understanding of the environmental context of the problem enables the researcher to appropriately define the problem, as illustrated by Gillette.

legal environment
Regulatory policies and norms within which organizations must operate.

economic environment
The economic environment is composed of purchasing power, gross income, disposable income, discretionary income, prices, savings, credit availability, and general economic conditions.

Research in Action

Satin Care for Women Provides a Satin Touch for Gillette

Analysis of past information indicated that most women pamper themselves with products for their beauty regimen and that this trend was likely to continue. Gillette was willing to devote its tremendous financial resources and marketing expertise to capturing a larger share of the women's shaving-products market.

An examination of underlying buyer behavior revealed that women had a strong preference for personal-care products that were rich in moisturizers. Economic and marketing analysis indicated that a substantial segment of this market was not price sensitive and was willing to pay a premium for such products. Accordingly, the marketing research problem was formulated as the investigation of women's preferences and purchase intentions for a shaving preparation rich in moisturizers.

The research showed that women were willing to spend more on shaving products that contained moisturizers. To capitalize on those findings, Gillette introduced Satin Care for Women (www.satincare.com). The product was an innovation in the shaving-products category, because it was the first nonsoap-based shaving preparation and it was infused with seven moisturizers. The product introduction was so successful that Satin Care

Source: HANDOUT/KRT/Newscom.

(continued)

for Women exceeded all expectations in the launch markets of the United States, Canada, and northern Europe. This success reinforced Gillette's understanding of the environmental factors in the shaving-products market. Gillette continued to build on the success of Satin Care for Women by extending the line. As of 2011, the Satin Care line was marketed with the tagline: "Smooth. Sexy. Satin" and included in-shower moisturizers (Dry Skin and Sensitive Skin), shave gel fragrances (Alluring Avocado, Lavender Kiss, Floral Passion, and Radiant Apricot), and shave gel skin formulations (Dry Skin, Sensitive Skin, and Cooling Sensation).[5]

Many of the factors to be considered in determining the environmental context of the problem can be researched via the Internet. Past information and trend forecasts can be found by searching for the appropriate information with the search engines. For company-specific information pertaining to the client or a competitor, the researcher can go to the company's home page.

Gaining an adequate understanding of the environmental context of the problem allows the researcher to define both the management-decision problem and the marketing research problem.

Management-Decision Problem and Marketing Research Problem

management-decision problem
The problem confronting the decision maker. It asks what the decision maker needs to do.

marketing research problem
The marketing research problem asks what information is needed and how it can best be obtained.

The **management-decision problem** asks what the decision maker needs to do, whereas the **marketing research problem** asks what information is needed and how it can best be obtained (see Table 2.2). Research is directed at providing the information necessary to make a sound decision. The management-decision problem is action oriented, framed from the perspective of what should be done. How should the loss of market share be arrested? Should the market be segmented differently? Should a new product be introduced? Should the promotional budget be increased?

In contrast, the marketing research problem is information oriented. Research is directed at providing the information necessary to make a sound decision. The management-decision problem focuses on the symptoms, whereas the marketing research problem is concerned with the underlying causes (see Table 2.2).

In the opening vignette, the management-decision problem was "What can Subaru do to expand its share of the automobile market?" The marketing research problem focused on information about the needs of the buyers of passenger cars, station wagons, and SUVs and on identifying a segment whose needs were not being met. Also, information was to be obtained on the automobile features desired by the identified segment and on the demographic and psychographic characteristics of this segment.

To further illustrate the distinction between the two orientations, consider an illustrative problem: the loss of market share for Unilever's (www.unilever.com) Axe male grooming product line in United States. The decision maker is faced with the problem of how to recover this loss (the management-decision problem). Possible responses include modifying existing products, introducing new products, reducing prices, changing other elements in the marketing mix, and segmenting the market. Suppose the decision maker and the researcher believe that the problem can be traced to market segmentation, in that Axe should be targeted at a specific segment. They decide to conduct research to explore that issue. The marketing research problem would then become the identification and evaluation of different ways to segment or group the market. As the research process progresses, problem definition can be modified to reflect emerging information. Table 2.3 provides additional examples, including that of Subaru from the opening vignette, that further clarify the distinction between the management-decision problem and the marketing research problem.

TABLE 2.2 Management-Decision Problem Versus the Marketing Research Problem

Management-Decision Problem	Marketing Research Problem
Asks what the decision maker needs to do	Asks what information is needed and how it should be obtained
Action oriented	Information oriented
Focuses on symptoms	Focuses on the underlying causes

TABLE 2.3 Management-Decision Problem and the Corresponding Marketing Research Problem

Management-Decision Problem	Marketing Research Problem
Should the advertising campaign be changed?	To determine the effectiveness of the current advertising campaign.
Should the price of the product be changed?	To determine the impact on sales and profits of various levels of price changes.
What can Subaru do to expand its automobile market?	To determine the various needs of the automobile users and the extent to which those needs were being satisfied by the current product offerings.

A good way to link the broad statement of the marketing research problem with the management-decision problem is through the use of a conceptual map.[6] A **conceptual map** involves the following three components:

Management wants to (*take an action*).

Therefore, we should study (*topic*).

So that we can explain (*question*).

conceptual map
A way to link the broad statement of the marketing research problem with the management-decision problem.

The first line states the rationale for the question and the project. This is the management-decision problem. The second line of the conceptual map declares what broader topic is being investigated. The third line implies the question being investigated—the who/how/why that needs to be explained. Thus, the second and third lines define the broad marketing research problem. An example of the conceptual map for AT&T follows:

Management wants to (develop retention programs that will retain 90 percent of heavy users of wireless services and lead to 10 percent higher sales over the next 2 years).

Therefore, we should study (heavy-user loyalty).

So that we can explain (what will be the most important variables in retaining these customers over the next 2 years).

As can be seen, the preceding example provides valuable definitions of the management-decision problem and the broad marketing research problems that are closely linked. The problem is now focused on a segment of customers (heavy users) and one behavior of these customers (staying with the company over the next 2 years). Measurable results, such as "90 percent retention of heavy users," are included, as well as a company goal (10 percent increase in sales over the next 2 years).

Experiential Learning

Kimberly-Clark's Conceptual Map

In an attempt to take market share away from archrival P&G's Pampers, Kimberly-Clark's baby-care division has developed a diaper that remains wet for 2 minutes prior to drying. Called "Wet 'n Act Advanced Trainers," these diapers prompt toddlers to try tinkling in the toilet once they partially wet the diaper. The Huggies team has a keen interest in the primary customer segment it calls "30 & Smart." This segment currently accounts for 15 percent of Pampers and 20 percent of Huggies sales. Members of this segment live primarily in metropolitan areas, are between 30 and 39 years of age, and are well educated.[7]

Visit www.kimberly-clark.com and search the Internet—including social media—as well as your library's electronic databases to obtain information on Kimberly-Clark's and competing diaper brands. Develop a three-level conceptual map from the following elements:

a. Management wants to beat Pampers in the diaper wars.

b. Management wants to successfully introduce a new diaper that will capture an 80 percent market share in the 30 & Smart segment within 12 months after introduction.

c. Therefore, we are studying what will make the best diaper.

d. Therefore, we are studying 30 & Smart evaluations of "Wet 'n Act" in a test market.

e. So that we can explain preferences for competing brands of diapers.

f. So that we can explain the probability of switching to the "Wet 'n Act" diapers within this segment.

Defining the Marketing Research Problem

A general guideline for defining the research problem is that the definition should (1) allow the researcher to obtain all the information needed to address the management-decision problem and (2) guide the researcher in proceeding with the project. Researchers often err by defining the research problem either too broadly or too narrowly (see Figure 2.7).

A broad definition fails to provide clear guidelines for the subsequent steps involved in the project. The following are examples of overly broad marketing research problem definitions: developing a marketing strategy for the brand, improving the competitive position of the firm, or improving the company's image. These definitions are not specific enough to suggest an approach to the problem or a research design.

Focusing the problem definition too narrowly can also be a serious flaw. A narrow focus might inhibit a full examination of plausible options, particularly innovative ones. It might also prevent the researcher from addressing important components of the management-decision problem. For example, a problem will be too narrowly defined if it is confined to how a company should adjust its pricing, given that a major competitor has initiated price changes. The narrow focus on pricing alone leaves out other possible responses (alternative courses of action), such as introducing new brands, changing advertising, or adding new distribution channels.

A narrow definition of the problem could also lead to restrictive sampling, resulting in erroneous conclusions. If Revlon is targeting females age 16 to 29 for its cosmetics line, that is fine for guiding media placement; however, the problem would be too narrowly defined for research measuring advertising effectiveness if the study is restricted to females age 16 to 29. The reason is that TV advertising has a much larger reach. Suppose the advertising turns out to be really effective among women age 30 to 50 instead of 16 to 29. Revlon might have canceled a very effective campaign because it appeared to be failing among the target audience. However, it is possible that Revlon's commercials are working among the age 16-to-29 group, but driving all other age groups away. If we were sampling only the age 16-to-29 segment, we would have overlooked this critical failing. Remember: Always define the problem broadly enough so as not to overlook any relevant aspects.

To minimize the possibility of a wrong decision due to an incorrect definition of the marketing research problem, the researcher should adopt a two-stage process: First, the marketing research problem is stated in broad, general terms; then, it is reduced to its specific components (see Figure 2.8). The **broad statement of the problem** provides perspective on the problem and acts as a safeguard against committing the second type of error. The **specific components of the problem** focus on the key aspects and provide clear guidelines on how to proceed further, avoiding the first type of error.

broad statement of the problem
The initial statement of the marketing research problem that provides an appropriate perspective on the problem.

specific components of the problem
The second part of the marketing research problem definition. The specific components focus on the key aspects of the problem and provide clear guidelines on how to proceed.

FIGURE 2.7

Errors in Defining the Marketing Research Problem

FIGURE 2.8

Proper Definition of the Marketing Research Problem

This process was illustrated in the opening vignette. The broad statement of the problem was to determine the various needs of automobile users and the extent to which current product offerings were satisfying those needs. In addition, five specific components were identified. *Tennis* magazine provides another example of an appropriate marketing research problem definition.

Research in Action

Research Serves *Tennis* Magazine

Tennis magazine (www.tennis.com), a publication of the Miller Publishing Group, wanted to obtain information about its readers. The broad marketing research problem was defined as gathering information about subscribers. The specific components of the problem were as follows:

1. **Demographics**. Who are the men and women who subscribe to the magazine?

2. **Psychological characteristics and lifestyles**. How do subscribers spend their money and their free time? The following lifestyle indicators were examined: fitness, travel, car rental, apparel, consumer electronics, credit cards, and financial investments.

3. **Tennis activity**. Where and how often do subscribers play tennis? What are their skill levels?

4. **Relationship to *Tennis* magazine**. How much time do subscribers spend with the issues? How long do they keep them? Do they share the magazine with other tennis players?

Because the questions were clearly defined, the information provided by this research helped management design specific features on tennis instruction, equipment, famous tennis players, and locations to play tennis to meet readers' specific needs. These changes made *Tennis* magazine more appealing to its readers and resulted in increased circulation and enhanced advertising revenues. As of 2011, the magazine had more than 600,000 subscribers.

Once the marketing research problem has been broadly stated and its specific components identified, as in the case of *Tennis* magazine, the researcher is in a position to develop a suitable approach.

Be a DM!	**Be an MR!**
TiVo: Marketing Innovation	
A TiVo DVR is like a VCR, but without the hassles of videotapes or timers. Browse the TiVo Web site (www.tivo.com) to get a better idea of this innovative product/service. As the marketing manager, you want to increase TiVo's sales. What information do you need in accomplishing this goal?	Broadly define and identify the specific components of the marketing research problem facing TiVo.

Components of the Approach

The tasks performed earlier also help in developing an approach. An approach to a marketing research problem should include the following components: analytical framework and models, research questions and hypotheses, and a specification of the information needed (see Figure 2.3). Each of these components is discussed in the following sections.

objective evidence

Unbiased evidence that is supported by empirical findings.

theory

A conceptual scheme based on foundational statements, which are assumed to be true.

analytical model

An explicit specification of a set of variables and their interrelationships designed to represent some real system or process in whole or in part.

verbal models

Analytical models that provide a written representation of the relationships between variables.

graphical models

Analytical models that provide a visual picture of the relationships between variables.

mathematical models

Analytical models that explicitly describe the relationships between variables, usually in equation form.

Analytical Framework and Models

In general, marketing research should be based on objective evidence and supported by theory. **Objective evidence** (evidence that is unbiased and supported by empirical findings) is gathered by compiling relevant findings from secondary sources. A **theory** guides the collection of this data. It is a conceptual framework based on foundational statements, called *axioms*, which are assumed to be true. Theory may come from academic literature contained in books, journals, and monographs. For example, according to attitude theory, attitude toward a brand, such as Nike sneakers, is determined by an evaluation of the brand on salient attributes (e.g., price, comfort, durability, and style). Relevant theory provides insight regarding which variables should be investigated, which should be treated as dependent variables (those whose values depend on the values of other variables), and which should be treated as independent variables (those whose values affect the values of other variables). Thus, attitude toward Nike will be the dependent variable; price, comfort, durability, and style will be independent variables. The approach should be based on some kind of working theory or framework. This also is helpful in developing an appropriate model.

An **analytical model** consists of a set of variables related in a specified manner to represent all or a part of some real system or process. Models can take many forms. The most common are verbal, graphical, and mathematical structures. In **verbal models**, the variables and their relationships are stated in prose form. These models often are a summary or restatement of the main points of the theory. **Graphical models** are visual and pictorially represent the theory. They are used to isolate variables and to suggest directions of relationships; however, they are not designed to provide numerical results. They are logical, preliminary steps to developing mathematical models. **Mathematical models** explicitly specify the strength and direction of relationships among variables, usually in equation form. Graphical models are particularly helpful in conceptualizing an approach to the problem, as the following jeans purchase model illustrates.

Research in Action

Lee Riveted Rivets Young Consumers with "The Brand That Fits"

According to consumer decision-making theory, the consumer first decides whether to purchase jeans or other casual clothes. If jeans are to be purchased, the consumer will form selection criteria for evaluating alternative brands. The selection criteria consist of factors such as color, price, fit, cut, comfort, and quality. The competing brands of jeans are then evaluated based on the selection criteria to purchase one or more brands. The accompanying graphical model illustrates the decision process for jeans for a consumer considering the purchase of casual clothing.

Lee Riveted jeans (www.lee.com) are targeted at young people, who buy jeans based primarily on fit and cut. Therefore, the marketing theme of Lee Riveted with taglines "the brand that fits" and "cut to be noticed" was based on this model. In 2007, the company expanded its reach by introducing three new lines of fit: Lee Custom Fit, Lee Natural Fit, and Lee Relaxed Fit. In 2010, Lee Jeans introduced Lee Premium Select with the tagline "Comfort where it counts." The line offered softer, stronger, new fits.[8]

FIGURE 2.9

Development of Research Questions and Hypothesis

In the opening vignette, the analytical model postulated that buyers first decide on the type of car they want (e.g., station wagon, SUV, passenger car) and then select a specific brand based on their choice criteria (e.g., features, performance, price, repair and maintenance, gas mileage, and so forth). The verbal, graphical, and mathematical models complement each other and help the researcher identify relevant research questions and hypotheses, as shown in Figure 2.9.

Be an MR!	Be a DM!
GM: Targeting Car Buyers	
Write a report about consumers' perceptions of GM's automobile brands by visiting www.gm.com and searching the Internet, including social media. Develop a graphical model explaining consumers' selection of an automobile brand.	As the marketing chief of GM, how can a graphical model explaining consumers' selection of an automobile brand help you to position GM's various brands?

Research Questions and Hypotheses

Research questions (RQs) are refined statements of the specific components of the problem. A problem component might break into several research questions. Research questions are designed to ask the specific information required to address each problem component. Research questions that successfully address the problem components will provide valuable information for the decision maker.

The formulation of the research questions should be guided, not only by the problem definition, but also by the analytical framework and the model adopted. In the Lee Riveted jeans example, the factors that influenced consumers' selection of jean brands were postulated based on theoretical framework as color, price, fit, cut, comfort, and quality. Several research questions can be posed related to these factors: What is the relative importance of these factors in influencing consumers' selection of jeans? Which factor is the most important? Which factor is the least important? Does the relative importance of these factors vary across consumers?

A **hypothesis** (H) is an unproven statement or proposition about a factor or phenomenon that is of interest to the researcher. It may be a tentative statement about the relationships discussed in the theoretical framework or represented in the analytic model. The hypothesis can also be stated as a possible answer to the research question. Hypotheses are statements about proposed relationships rather than merely questions to be answered. They reflect the researchers' expectation and can be tested empirically. (See Chapter 16.) Hypotheses also play the important role of suggesting variables to be included in the research design. The relationship between the

research questions
Refined statements of the specific components of the problem.

hypothesis
An unproven statement or proposition about a factor or phenomenon that is of interest to the researcher.

marketing research problem, research questions, and hypotheses, along with the influence of the objective/theoretical framework and analytical models, is described in Figure 2.9.

In commercial marketing research, the hypotheses are not formulated as rigorously as they are in academic research. An interesting research question and related hypotheses that could be posed about the need for a hybrid product in the Subaru vignette are as follows:

RQ: Is there an overlap between the features sought by station wagon buyers and buyers of SUVs?

H1: The buyers of station wagons rate certain features of SUVs as important.

H2: The buyers of SUVs rate certain features of station wagons as important.

The following example further illustrates research questions and hypotheses.

Research in Action

"Got Milk?"

Milk consumption had steadily declined for 20 years. Qualitative research indicated that people had misconceptions about milk. Hence, survey research was undertaken to address the following RQ and Hs:

RQ: Do people have misconceptions about milk?
H1: Milk is perceived as fat-laden and unhealthy.
H2: Milk is perceived as an old-fashioned drink.
H3: People believe that milk is meant only for kids.

When the survey data supported these hypotheses, the Milk Processor Education Program launched the well-known "milk mustache" campaign with the "Got Milk?" slogan. This creative advertising was a real attention-getter, showing celebrities ranging from Joan Lunden to Rhea Perlman and Danny DeVito sporting the famous white mustache. The result? Humble milk, until a few years before an also-ran in the advertising race behind soft drinks and juices, became a key beverage-industry player. The decline in milk consumption was arrested and annual milk consumption among children reached 28 gallons in 2002—the highest level in 10 years. Consumption continued to be stable through 2011 (www.gotmilk.com). In 2011, "Got Milk?" ads were touting the health benefits of milk. The advertising campaign included humorous 30-second television spots, a Web site for audiences to visit the imaginary world of Mootopia (www.visitmootopia.com),

and Facebook games. The campaign emphasized interactivity and engagement with audience while promoting the health benefits of milk.[9]

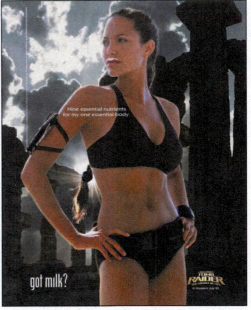

Source: Splash/Newscom.

Social Media

Specification of Information Needed

By focusing on each component of the problem, the analytical framework and models, and the research questions and hypotheses, the researcher can determine what information should be obtained. It is helpful to carry out this exercise for each component of the problem and to make a list specifying all the information that should be collected. We illustrate this process with respect to the opening vignette.

Component 1

- Needs of buyers of passenger cars are operationalized in terms of the attributes or features desired in an automobile.
- Needs of buyers of station wagons are operationalized in terms of the attributes or features desired in an automobile.
- Needs of buyers of SUVs are operationalized in terms of the attributes or features desired in an automobile.

Component 2

- Evaluation of passenger cars on the desired attributes.
- Evaluation of station wagons on the desired attributes.
- Evaluation of SUVs on the desired attributes.

Component 3

- No new information to be collected. The segment can be identified based on information obtained for the first two components.

Component 4

- No new information to be collected. The desired features can be identified based on information obtained for the first two components.

Component 5

- Standard demographic characteristics (e.g., gender, marital status, household size, age, education, occupation, income, and type and number of automobiles owned) and psychographic characteristics. Psychographic characteristics include outdoor and recreational activities, family orientation, and attitude toward daily commuting.

Experiential Learning

Defining the Problem and Developing an Approach

Visit a local business located near your campus. Interview the business owner or manager and identify some of the marketing challenges facing this business. Also, interview an expert in this industry. Search and analyze secondary data pertaining to this business and the industry, and identify the environmental context of the problem.

1. Define the management-decision problem.
2. Define the marketing research problem.
3. Develop a graphical model explaining the consumer-choice process leading to the patronage of this business or its competitors.
4. Develop an appropriate research question and hypothesis.

Summary Illustration Using the Opening Vignette

We can summarize and illustrate the major concepts discussed in this chapter by returning to the opening vignette. The Subaru vignette illustrates the importance of correctly defining the problem and showing how a problem audit can help in the process. The tasks involved in formulating the marketing research problem should lead to an understanding of the environmental context of the problem. In the case of Subaru, forecasts of future sales of station wagons and SUVs indicated that these two types of automobiles were not tapping the market potential. Subaru undertook research to understand the underlying behavior of the consumers and their needs and desires. It capitalized upon its marketing and technological skill to achieve the successful introduction of "the world's first sport utility wagon."

Analysis of the environmental context should help identify the management-decision problem, which should then be translated into a marketing research problem. The management-decision problem asks what the decision maker should do, is action oriented, and focuses on the symptoms. The marketing research problem asks what information is needed and how it should be obtained, is information oriented, and focuses on the underlying causes. In the opening vignette, the management-decision problem was "What can Subaru do to expand its share of the automobile market?" The marketing research problem focused on information about the needs of the buyers of passenger cars, station wagons, and SUVs and identification of a segment whose needs were not being met. Also, information was to be obtained on the automobile features desired by the members of this segment and on their demographic and psychographic characteristics. A broad statement of the problem was given, and specific components were identified. Figure 2.10 provides a concept map for problem definition. In this figure, the major concepts are connected, in order, by bold arrows using descriptors.

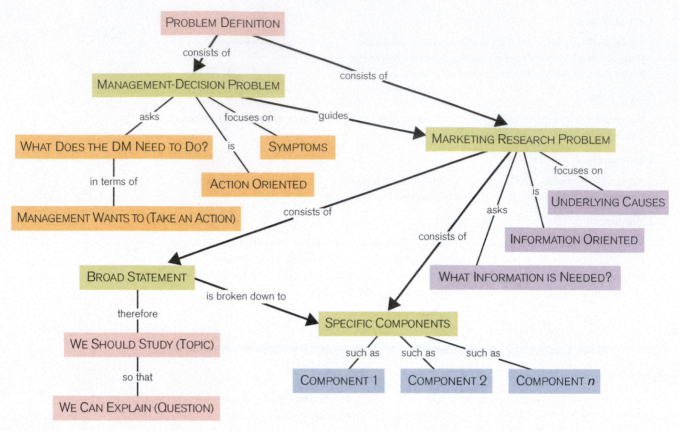

FIGURE 2.10

A Concept Map for Problem Definition

Thus, problem definition consists of defining the management-decision problem and the marketing research problem. The management-decision problem guides the marketing research problem. The marketing research problem consists of a broad statement and specific components. Each major concept is described by minor concepts that are connected to that major concept by lines with descriptors. Thus, the management-decision problem asks what the DM needs to do, is action oriented, and focuses on the symptoms. The rest of the figure can be interpreted similarly.

Developing an approach to the problem is the second step in the marketing research process. The components of an approach consist of an analytical framework and models, research questions and hypotheses, and specification of the information needed. The analytical model postulated that buyers first decide on the type of vehicle (e.g., station wagon, SUV, passenger car) and then decide on a specific brand. Research questions and hypotheses related to the overlap between the features sought by station wagon buyers and buyers of SUVs were formulated. In specifying the information required, the researcher operationalized the needs of automobile buyers in terms of the attributes or features desired. Evaluations of passenger cars, station wagons, and SUVs on the desired attributes had to be obtained. Information on standard demographic characteristics and the identified psychographic characteristics also was needed. Figure 2.11 provides a concept map for developing an approach. The interpretation of this concept map is similar to that for problem definition (see Figure 2.10).

International Marketing Research

Conducting research in international markets often means working within unfamiliar environments. This lack of familiarity with the environmental factors of the country in which the research is being conducted can greatly increase the difficulty of appropriately defining the problem, as illustrated by the Heinz Company in Brazil.

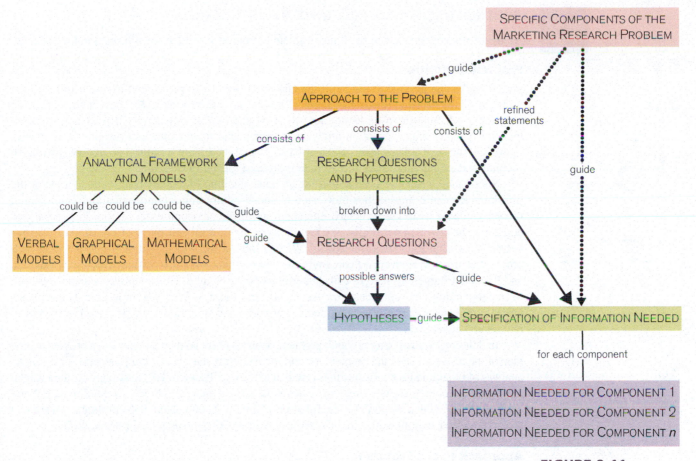

FIGURE 2.11

A Concept Map for Approach to the Problem

Research in Action

Heinz Ketchup Couldn't Catch Up in Brazil

As of 2011, H. J. Heinz Company is one of the world's leading marketers of branded foods to retail and food-service channels. Heinz has number-one or number-two branded businesses in more than 50 world markets. Despite good track records domestically and overseas, H. J. Heinz failed in its initial attempts to penetrate South America's biggest and most promising market. As an entry strategy into Brazil, Heinz entered into a joint venture with Citrosuco Paulista, a giant orange juice exporter, with the future possibility of buying the profitable company. However, the sales of Heinz products, including ketchup, did not take off. Where was the problem?

A post-entry problem audit revealed that the company lacked a strong local distribution system. Heinz had attempted to duplicate a strategy that had been successful in Mexico: distribution through neighborhood shops. However, the problem audit revealed that 75 percent of grocery shopping in Sao Paulo is done in supermarkets, not small, neighborhood shops. Although Mexico and Brazil may appear to have similar cultural and demographic characteristics, consumer behavior was found to vary greatly. A problem audit and an examination of the environmental context of the problem prior to entry in Brazil could have prevented this failure.[10]

Many international marketing efforts fail because a problem audit is not conducted prior to entering the foreign market, and the relevant environmental factors are not taken into account. This leads to an incorrect definition of the marketing research problem and an inappropriate approach, as illustrated in the case of Heinz. While developing theoretical frameworks, models, research questions, and hypotheses, remember that differences in the environmental factors, especially the sociocultural environment, can lead to differences in the formation of perceptions, attitudes, preferences, and choice behavior.

For example, orientation toward time varies considerably across cultures. In Asia, Latin America, and the Middle East, people are not as time conscious as Westerners, which can influence perceptions and preferences for convenience foods, such as frozen foods and prepared dinners. In defining the problem and developing an approach, the researcher must be sensitive to the underlying factors that influence consumption and purchase behavior.

Social Media

Marketing Research and Social Media

Analysis of social media can facilitate problem definition as well as an approach to the problem.

Problem Definition

Social media can be used to aid in all the tasks that need to be performed in order to define the problem. If the decision maker maintains a blog or has a Facebook page, these sources provide additional information in understanding the DM and her/his objectives. It is also possible to identify industry experts, and an analysis of their social media sites can provide insights into their thinking as it relates to problem at hand. Social media are a natural source of qualitative secondary data and qualitative research, as discussed further in Chapters 4, 5, and 6.

Social media can also help in gaining an understanding of the environmental context of the problem. Research approaches built around social computing technologies and open-source thinking enable us to get a richer understanding of the environmental factors in general and consumer behavior in particular. We can analyze the interrelated parts of consumers' various behaviors, within their social networks. We can look at the way consumers interact with each other, over time. Moreover, we can study the environmental context within which they interact, and how environmental changes cause their behavior to change. This adaptive systems approach to understanding consumer behavior has utility, and the new Web 2.0 tools give us the means both to analyze organically arising social networks and to create specific social networks to understand consumers.

In defining the marketing research problem, analysis of social media content can provide a good idea of the broad scope of the problem and aid in identifying the specific components. For example, analysis of blogs and Facebook postings revealed to Hewlett-Packard (HP) that many customers who purchased its computers were having issues with service support. Hence, evaluation of HP and competitors on service support was identified as an important component of the problem. Subsequent research, indeed, confirmed this initial discovery, leading HP to revamp its service function.

Approach to the Problem

An analysis of social media data can also be useful in developing an approach to the problem. With the use of relevant media such as blogs, Facebook, or Twitter, researchers can update consumers on the research that has been ongoing and the actions that have been taken. As such, the use of these media can then further be extended to incorporate feedback from consumers as to whether the researchers are on the right track because the analytical models developed and the research questions as posed by the firm were consistent with and based upon consumer thinking and insights. For instance, Sun Microsystems maintains a blog with its clientele and supporters so as to understand how its marketing efforts can be better suited to its best customers. Researchers can then assess the appropriateness of their models or whether they are asking the right research questions. Furthermore, market researchers can choose to openly discuss their derived hypothesis for feedback among closed social media consumer panels. As illustrated by the opening Subaru vignette, the process of specifying information needed requires the marketing researcher to address multiple consumer segments simultaneously. This process can be aided through the use of social media tools because they allow researchers to customize their interaction with each group of consumers by selectively choosing the platform on which to interact. For example, through the Facebook "fan" pages of a certain brand, marketers are able to solicit opinions from different demographics by filtering user profile data as registered online. Thus, the use of social media facilitates problem definition and the development of an approach, as illustrated by the case of Dell.

Research in Action

From Dell Hell to Tell Dell Through Social Media

In June 2005, Dell saw erosion in its profits and drop in share prices because of public outrage of its products' poor functionality and safety features, from faulty network cards to battery explosions. Popular blogger Jeff Jarvis coined the term "Dell Hell" as consumers regarded the consumption of Dell products as a hellish experience. However, these were but the tip of the iceberg—the symptoms of the underlying problems faced by Dell. Therefore, it was crucial for Dell to identify the problem and develop a research approach.

As negative comments and posts online proliferated, Dell analyzed the secondary data available on social media sites. The analysis of social media data indicated that the underlying problems faced were (1) the poor components of Dell laptops (product fault) and (2) Dell's poor support and response to consumers' complaints. As product fault was more of a technical problem, marketing researchers decided to focus on the other problem of Dell. The management-decision problem was what should Dell do to address consumers' complaints? The broad marketing research problem was to determine the effectiveness of traditional media and social media as platforms for supporting and responding to consumers' complaints. The specific components of the problem were to determine:

1. The effectiveness of the current system in addressing consumers' complaints

2. Whether social media would be an effective support system where consumers' complaints could be addressed

3. Whether there were any other consumer needs that social media could meet

Analysis of social media, along with secondary data from traditional sources, helped Dell to formulate the analytical model shown explaining consumers' choice of a preferred medium to address their complaints.

Based on the graphical model, specific research questions and hypotheses were formulated. When the results of this research favored the use of social media, Dell set up the Online Tech support team to offer assistance to Dell consumers through social media. In July 2006, the Direct2Dell blog was set up to listen to and connect with Dell consumers. Direct2Dell became a moderated medium for Dell to be directly connected to consumers, to hear their complaints, and to provide feedback and support to consumers in the fastest, quickest way.

With the success of Direct2Dell in gathering feedback and control of negative comments, IdeaStorm (www.ideastorm.com) was created in February 2007 as a social media platform that involves the consumers in generating ideas and suggestions. By 2008, Dell had emerged from 2005's public outrage through the use of social media tools as marketing research tools, successfully controlling and reducing unfavorable comments online from 49 percent to 20 percent. In early 2008 Dell stated that as many as 27 product and process innovations had been developed as a direct result of ideas submitted on IdeaStorm by consumers. For example, Dell's offering of the Linux operating system on its desktop computers was motivated by several suggestions posted on IdeaStorm. By 2010, the Dell community had contributed more than 14,000 ideas through IdeaStorm, and 417 ideas had been implemented.[11]

Ethics in Marketing Research

The stakeholders involved in ethical conflicts during the process of defining the problem and developing an approach are likely to be the marketing researcher and the client. Personal interests or hidden agendas of either stakeholder can lead to ethical dilemmas. Ethical issues arise when the personal objectives of the decision maker (e.g., defending a decision) are at variance with the objectives of the client firm. The client should be forthright in disclosing the relevant objectives and the purpose for which the research is being undertaken. Likewise, the researcher should have the best interest of the client at heart.

Suppose that while conducting the problem-definition tasks, a researcher discovers that the problem is a lot simpler than both parties originally thought. Although the reduced scope of the problem will result in substantial savings for the client, it will also cut the revenues for the research firm. Does the researcher continue with the problem definition given in the proposal? Codes of ethics suggest that this situation should be discussed with the client.

Sometimes a client wants to conduct research that, in the opinion of the researcher, is not warranted or needed. Again, the researcher is faced with the ethical dilemma of what to do. Codes of ethics indicate that the researcher should communicate to the client that the research is not necessary. If the client is still insistent, the researcher should feel free to undertake the research.[12]

Likewise, ethical issues might also arise in developing an approach to the problem. Such issues include using models and approaches developed for specific projects for other clients. Researchers who conduct studies for different clients in related industries (e.g., banks and brokerage firms) or in similar research areas (e.g., measuring company image) might be tempted to reuse client-specific models or findings from other projects. However, unless the researcher has obtained client permission, this practice might be unethical.

WHAT WOULD YOU DO?

Kellogg's: From Slumping to Thumping

The Situation

Kellogg's is the world's leading producer of cereal and a leading producer of convenience foods, including cookies, crackers, toaster pastries, cereal bars, frozen waffles, meat alternatives, pie crusts, and cones, with 2010 global sales of about $12.4 billion and a market share of more than 30 percent. David Mackay, CEO of Kellogg's, takes pride in being a part of the Kellogg's company because of the consistency of the decisions that are made within the company to promote the long-term growth of the business, as well as serve the needs of their people and communities.

With such a large market share, one would think that Kellogg's is untouchable. However, Kellogg's faced a slump in the market. Its cereal sales were declining, and it had to face the challenge of getting out of its slump. Kellogg's, therefore, turned to marketing research to identify the problem and develop several solutions to increase cereal sales.

Kellogg's used several tasks to identify the problem. The researchers spoke to decision makers within the company, interviewed industry experts, conducted analysis of available data, and performed some qualitative research. Several important issues came out of this preliminary research. Current products were being targeted to the kids. Bagels and muffins were winning for favored breakfast foods. High prices were turning consumers to generic brands. Some other information also came to light during the research. Adults want quick foods that require very little or no preparation.

The Marketing Research Decision

1. What do you think is the underlying problem facing Kellogg's? Check as many of the following as are applicable:
   a. Kellogg's is targeting the wrong segment: kids.
   b. Competition from bagels and muffins is stiff.
   c. Kellogg's prices are too high.
   d. Kellogg's needs to introduce new products.
   e. Kellogg's needs to change its advertising.
2. Define an appropriate marketing research problem that Kellogg's needs to address.
3. Discuss the role of the type of marketing research problem you have identified in enabling David Mackay to increase Kellogg's sales.

The Marketing Management Decision

1. David Mackay is wondering what changes Kellogg's should make to increase market share. Should Kellogg's (check as many as are applicable):
   a. Introduce new cereals targeted at adults.
   b. Decrease prices.
   c. Increase advertising budget and launch a new campaign.
   d. Launch a sales promotion campaign.
   e. All of the above.
2. Discuss how the marketing management decision action that you recommend to David Mackay is influenced by the research that you suggested earlier and by the findings of that research.

What David Mackay Did

Kellogg's began to introduce flavors more suited to the adult palette. For example, it introduced Honey-flavored Shredded Wheat and Honey Crunch Corn Flakes, both aimed toward the adult market. It also implemented promotions featuring Microsoft software for the entire family instead of the usual toys. Then, it launched an ad campaign aimed at adults called, "Cereal. Eat it for life." This was followed by the launch of the "Be Victorious" Campaign with Special K in January 2010. The campaign encouraged healthy weight management for women with Kellogg's Special K cereals, protein shakes, and meal bars. These efforts were successful and not only arrested the decline in sales but also led to increased sales and profits.[13]

Source: Bloomberg via Getty Images.

Summary

The most important step in a research project is defining the marketing research problem. This task often is made more difficult because of the tendency of managers to focus on symptoms rather than underlying causes. The researcher's role is to help management identify and isolate the problem.

The tasks involved in formulating the marketing research problem include discussions with management, including the key decision makers, interviews with industry experts, analysis of secondary data, and qualitative research. This data-gathering process should lead to an understanding of the environmental context of the problem. Within the environmental context, a number of factors should be analyzed and evaluated. These factors include past information and forecasts about the industry and the firm, the decision maker's objectives, buyer behavior, the firm's resources and constraints, the legal and economic environment, and the firm's marketing and technological skills.

Analysis of the environmental context should help identify the management-decision problem, which should then be translated into a marketing research problem. The management-decision problem asks what the decision maker should do, is action oriented, and focuses on the symptoms. The marketing research problem asks what information is needed and how it should be obtained, is information oriented, and focuses on the underlying causes. The researcher should avoid defining the marketing research problem either too broadly or too narrowly. The researcher can avoid these errors by first defining the research problem using a broad statement and then breaking it down into specific components.

The next step in the marketing research process is to develop an approach to the problem. The components of an approach are the analytical framework and models and research questions and hypotheses. In addition, all the information that needs to be obtained in the marketing research project should be specified. The approach developed should be based on objective or empirical evidence and be grounded in theory. Models are useful for portraying the relationships among variables. The most common kinds of models are verbal, graphical, and mathematical. The research questions are refined statements of the components of the problem that ask what specific information is required with respect to each component. Research questions can be further refined into hypotheses. By focusing on each component of the problem and the analytical framework and models, research questions, and hypotheses, the researcher can determine what information should be obtained.

When defining the problem and developing an approach in international marketing research, the researcher must isolate and examine the impact of cultural factors. Analysis of social media content can facilitate problem definition and the development of an approach. Several ethical issues that have an impact on the client and the researcher can arise at this stage, but they can be resolved by open and honest communication.

Key Terms and Concepts

Problem definition 35	Case studies 42	Broad statement of the problem 48
Problem-definition process 37	Environmental context of the	Specific components of the problem 48
Problem audit 37	problem 43	Objective evidence 50
Experience survey 40	Objectives 44	Theory 50
Key-informant technique 40	Buyer behavior 44	Analytical model 50
Lead-user survey 40	Legal environment 45	Verbal models 50
Secondary data 41	Economic environment 45	Graphical models 50
Primary data 41	Management-decision problem 46	Mathematical models 50
Qualitative research 41	Marketing research problem 46	Research questions 51
Pilot surveys 41	Conceptual map 47	Hypothesis 51

Suggested Cases and Video Cases

Running Case with Real Data

1.1 Hewlett-Packard

Comprehensive Critical Thinking Cases

2.1 American Idol   2.2 Baskin-Robbins   2.3 Akron Children's Hospital

Comprehensive Cases with Real Data

Comprehensive Brief Harvard Business School Cases

Online Video Cases

Live Research: Conducting a Marketing Research Project

1. Invite the client to discuss the project with the class.
2. Have the class (or different teams) analyze the environmental context of the problem: past information and forecasts, resources and constraints, objectives, buyer behavior, legal environment, economic environment, and marketing and technological skills.
3. Jointly with the client, the instructor should make a presentation to the class discussing the management-decision problem and the marketing research problem.

The students should come up with formal definitions of the management-decision problem and the marketing research problem. In conjunction with the client, arrive at consensual definitions.

4. Ask the class or specific teams to develop an approach (analytical framework and models, research questions, hypotheses, and identification of the information needed). Through class discussion, arrive at a consensus.

Acronym

The factors to be considered when analyzing the environmental context of the problem can be summed up by the acronym PROBLEM:

P ast information and forecasts

R esources and constraints

O bjectives of the decision maker

B uyer behavior

L egal environment

E conomic environment

M arketing and technological skills

Review Questions

1. What is the first step in conducting a marketing research project?
2. Why is it important to correctly define the marketing research problem?
3. What are some reasons that management often is not clear about the real problem?
4. What is the role of the researcher in the problem-definition process?
5. What is a problem audit?
6. What is the difference between a symptom and an underlying cause? How can a skillful researcher differentiate between the two and identify the true problem?
7. What are some differences between a management-decision problem and a marketing research problem?

8. What are the common types of errors encountered in defining a marketing research problem? What can be done to reduce the incidence of such errors?
9. How are the research questions related to components of the problem?
10. What are the differences between research questions and hypotheses?
11. What are the most common forms of analytical models?
12. **Social Media** Discuss the role of social media in enabling the researcher to define the marketing research problem and in developing an approach.

Applied Problems

1. Visit www.census.gov and obtain data relating to population trends by age groups. What are some of the marketing implications of these trends?
2. State the marketing research problems for each of the following management-decision problems.
   a. Should a new product be introduced?
   b. Should an advertising campaign, which has run for 3 years, be changed?
   c. Should the in-store promotion for an existing product line be increased?
   d. What pricing strategy should be adopted for a new product?
   e. Should the compensation package be changed to motivate the sales force better?
3. State the management-decision problems for which the following marketing research problems might provide useful information.
   a. Estimate the sales and market share of department stores in a certain metropolitan area.
   b. Determine the design features for a new product that would result in maximum market share.
   c. Evaluate the effectiveness of alternative TV commercials.
   d. Assess current and proposed sales territories with respect to their sales potential and workload.
   e. Determine the prices for each item in a product line so as to maximize total sales for the product line.
4. Identify five symptoms and a plausible cause for each one.
5. **Social Media** Suppose you are conducting research for American Airlines. Identify, from secondary sources including social media, the attributes or factors passengers consider when selecting an airline.
6. You are a consultant to Coca-Cola USA working on a marketing research project for Diet Coke.
   a. Use the online databases in your library to compile a list of articles related to the Coca-Cola Company, Diet Coke, and the soft-drink industry published during the past year.
   b. Visit the Coca-Cola (www.coca-cola.com) and PepsiCo (www.pepsico.com) Web sites and compare the information available at each.
   c. **Social Media** Visit Diet Coke on Facebook (www.facebook.com/DietCoke) and analyze the available information.
   d. Based on the information you have collected, write a report on the environmental context surrounding Diet Coke.
7. Select any firm. Using secondary sources, obtain information on the annual sales of the firm and the industry for the last 5 years. Use a spreadsheet package, such as Excel, or any microcomputer or mainframe statistical package, to develop a graphical model relating the firm's sales to the industry's sales.
8. **Social Media** Visit the Web sites of competing sneaker brands (Nike, New Balance, and Adidas). The URLs are www.nike.com, www.newbalance.com, and www.adidas.com. From an analysis of information available at these sites, as well as a conducting a search in social media, determine the criteria used by consumers in selecting a sneaker brand.

Group Discussion

1. Form a group of five or six people to discuss the following statement: "Correct definition of the marketing research problem is more important to the success of a marketing research project than sophisticated research techniques." Did your group arrive at a consensus?
2. We are all aware that Coca-Cola changed its flagship brand of 99 years to New Coke and subsequently returned to the old favorite, Coca-Cola Classic. Working in a group of four, read as much material as you can on this marketing bungle. Identify the decision problem that Coke management faced. As a team, define the marketing research problem and its specific components.

Hewlett-Packard Running Case

Review the Hewlett-Packard (HP) case, Case 1.1, and the questionnaire provided toward the end of the book.

1. **Social Media** Conduct an Internet and social media search on HP and briefly describe the environmental context of the problem surrounding HP.
2. Define the management-decision problem facing HP as it seeks to maintain and build on its leadership position in the personal computers market.
3. Define an appropriate marketing research problem that corresponds to your definition of the management-decision problem.
4. Present a graphical model describing consumers' selection of a personal computer brand.
5. Describe three research questions, with one or more hypotheses associated with each.

ONLINE VIDEO CASE 2.1

ACCENTURE: The Accent Is in the Name

Visit **www.pearsonhighered.com/malhotra** to read the video case and view the accompanying video. Accenture: The Accent Is in the Name describes the marketing research conducted by Andersen Consulting to change its name, while at the same time maintain the brand equity and the goodwill of its previous name. The case can be used to prompt discussion on the various environmental factors affecting the formulation of a well-defined research problem, as well as discussion on clarifying the distinction between the management decision problem and the marketing research problem. Specific marketing research questions on this and the previous chapter are posed in the video case.

PART

2

Research Design Formulation

3

Research Design

Source: Geralynn Madonna/Spiegel.com.

LEARNING OBJECTIVES

After reading this chapter, the student should be able to:

1. Define research design, classify various research designs, and explain the differences between exploratory and conclusive designs.

2. Compare and contrast the basic research designs: exploratory, descriptive, and causal.

3. Describe the major sources of errors in a research design, including random sampling and nonsampling errors.

4. Discuss managerial aspects of coordinating research projects, particularly budgeting and scheduling.

5. Describe the elements of a marketing research proposal and show how it addresses the steps of the marketing research process.

6. Explain research design formulation in international marketing research.

7. **Social Media** Discuss how the analysis of social media content can facilitate the research design process.

8. Understand the ethical issues and conflicts that arise in formulating a research design.

Marketing Research Helps Spiegel Redesign Its Product Lines

Spiegel (www.spiegel.com) is a leading direct marketer, offering the benefits of home-based shopping via the catalog and the Internet. Private-equity firm and turnaround expert Patriarch Partners acquired Spiegel Brands in June 2009 through a newly formed company named Signature Styles, LLC. The new management realized that a turnaround was needed to regain profits and customers. To achieve this turnaround, the company lowered expenses, reduced inventory, and concentrated on creating an improved Web site to draw in new customers and ultimately boost revenues. Spiegel also wanted to improve its products and marketing programs.

Spiegel conducted extensive marketing research. The marketing research problem was to understand the shopping behavior of potential and current consumers. Several research questions and hypotheses were formulated to examine the unique aspects of consumers' buying behavior. Spiegel used a two-phase research design. The first phase, the exploratory phase, consisted of analysis of secondary data plus 10 focus groups with Spiegel customers. Secondary data provided good background information on current and potential catalog shoppers and vital statistics, such as the size of this segment. Focus groups helped Spiegel understand the values, attitudes, and behavior of its customers as they related to clothing, home furnishings, and shopping. The focus groups revealed that customers wanted variety and quality. They also felt appreciated when a company designed special promotions directed to them. Spiegel came up short on all of these dimensions.

In the second phase, the descriptive phase, the findings of the exploratory phase were tested with a telephone survey of a sample of 1,000 randomly selected Spiegel customers. Efforts were undertaken to control the various sources of non-sampling error. For example, the interviewers were carefully selected and thoroughly trained, and close supervision was exercised to minimize interviewing errors. The results of the survey confirmed the demand for more Spiegel product offerings, and also showed that the Spiegel lines needed more promotion. In the fall of 2010, Spiegel spent millions of dollars in expanding its Signature Collections line and launched a print and social media campaign aimed at revitalizing all of its product lines. Online *Signature Style Magazine* was launched and social networking initiatives were introduced breaking down the Web site into categories like "Wear to Work" and "Favorite Casual Essentials," making shopping simple. Since making these changes, Speigel has experienced growth, which hopefully will lead to success.[1]

Social Media

Overview

As discussed in Chapter 2, defining a marketing research problem and developing a suitable approach are critical to the success of the entire marketing research project. The next step is to formulate a detailed research design to achieve the defined goals. Figure 3.1 gives the relationship of research design to previous chapters and to the marketing research process.

This chapter classifies and describes the basic research designs. At the broad level, the two major types of research designs are exploratory and conclusive designs. Conclusive research designs can be further classified as descriptive or causal. Thus, this classification results in three basic designs: exploratory, descriptive, and causal. These three basic designs are used in different combinations and sequences.

In this chapter, we consider the value of marketing research information within the context of controlling research design errors. We discuss budgeting and scheduling of a proposed research project and present guidelines for writing research proposals. As applications, we consider research design concepts in the context of international marketing research, social media, and ethics in marketing research. Figure 3.2 presents an overview of the chapter's contents.

What Is a Research Design?

research design
A framework or blueprint for conducting the marketing research project that specifies the procedures necessary to obtain the information needed to structure and/or solve the marketing research problem.

The **research design** is a roadmap for conducting the marketing research project. It provides details of each step in the marketing research project. Implementation of the research design should result in all the information needed to structure or solve the management-decision problem. The design process begins by defining the marketing research problem. Next comes the approach: a conceptual framework, research questions, hypotheses, and the information needed (see Chapter 2). The research design is based on the results of these first two steps: the problem definition and the approach (see Figure 3.3).

FIGURE 3.1

Relationship of Research Design to the Previous Chapters and the Marketing Research Process

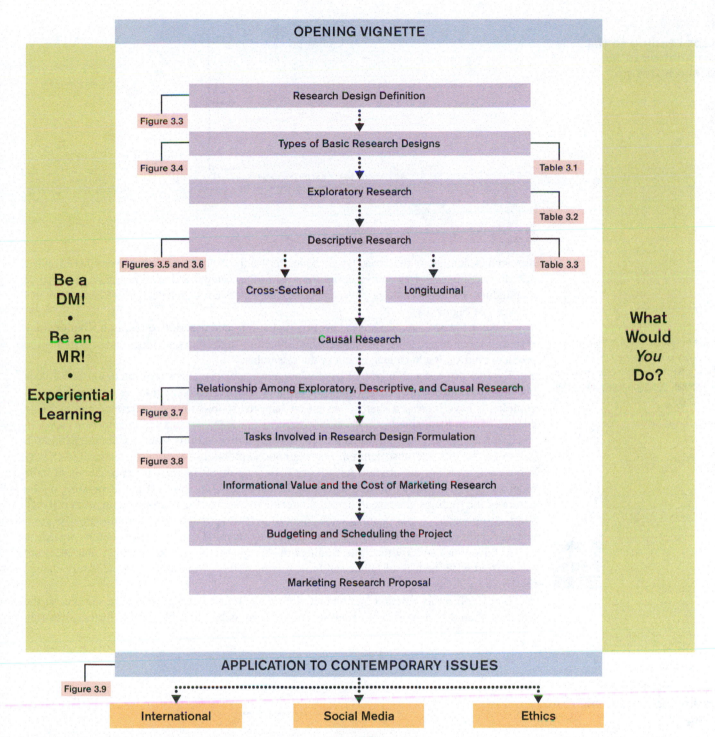

FIGURE 3.2

Research Design: An Overview

Many different designs might be appropriate for a given marketing research problem. A good research design ensures that the information collected will be relevant and useful to management and that all of the necessary information will be obtained. A good design should also help to ensure that the marketing research project will be conducted effectively and efficiently. In this chapter, we will consider the basic types of research designs available. These basic designs can be classified in terms of the research objectives.

FIGURE 3.3

**Steps Leading to the
Formulation of a
Research Design**

Basic Research Designs

Research designs are of two broad types: exploratory and conclusive. Conclusive designs are either descriptive or causal. Descriptive designs can be further categorized as either cross-sectional or longitudinal. Exploratory, descriptive, and causal are the basic research designs we examine in this chapter (see Figure 3.4).

Table 3.1 states the differences between exploratory and descriptive research. **Exploratory research** is conducted to explore the problem situation—that is, to gain ideas and insight into the problem confronting the management or the researcher.

Exploratory research might be used when management realizes a problem exists but does not yet understand why. Perhaps sales are slipping in a particular region, or customer service complaints have increased sharply. As a first step, the problem must be defined and alternate courses of action identified.

Because the information needs are only loosely defined at this stage, exploratory research has to be flexible and unstructured. For example, exploratory research that investigates why some customers are dissatisfied with Ivory bath soap might begin with an analysis of calls recorded on the consumer hotline regarding the nature of complaints. Then, depending on the nature of the findings, the researcher might decide to conduct focus groups with users of Ivory soap. Suppose six focus groups, each involving 10 respondents, are conducted. To get a broader perspective, the researcher then decides to examine social media content posted on blogs, Facebook, and Twitter. The findings of this qualitative research reveal that users are dissatisfied with the lack of lather and moisturizing ability. Should P&G immediately change the Ivory formula?

No! Exploratory research is conducted on a small and nonrepresentative sample, so the findings should be regarded as tentative and be used as building blocks for further research.

exploratory research
A type of research design that has as its primary objective the provision of insights into and comprehension of the problem situation confronting the researcher.

FIGURE 3.4

**A Classification of
Marketing Research
Designs**

TABLE 3.1 Differences Between Exploratory and Conclusive Research

	Exploratory	Conclusive
Objective:	To provide insights and understanding	To test specific hypotheses and examine relationships
Characteristics:	Information needed is defined only loosely	Information needed is clearly defined
	Research process is flexible and unstructured	Research process is formal and structured
	Sample is small and nonrepresentative	Sample is large and representative
	Analysis of primary data is qualitative	Data analysis is quantitative
Findings/Results:	Tentative	Conclusive
Outcome:	Generally followed by further exploratory or conclusive research	Findings used as input into decision making

Typically, more formally defined exploratory research or conclusive research follows. It is dangerous when exploratory research is the only step taken toward developing a solution. The tendency to overlook the limited usefulness of the information, particularly if it confirms preconceived ideas about a problem, can lead management in the wrong direction. Despite these risks, exploratory research can be valuable when researchers are faced with a problem that is not fully understood, for example, why some customers are dissatisfied with a specific brand of bath soap. Exploratory research in the form of depth interviews, examination of social media content, or focus groups could provide valuable insights.

Conclusive research is research designed to assist the decision maker in determining, evaluating, and selecting the best course of action in a given situation. Conclusive research can be used to verify the insights gained from exploratory research. As illustrated in the opening vignette, the findings from secondary data and focus groups (exploratory research) were further tested in a telephone survey (conclusive research). Conclusive research is based on the assumption that the researcher has an accurate understanding of the problem at hand. The information needed for addressing the management-decision problem has been clearly specified. The objective of conclusive research is to test specific hypotheses and examine specific relationships.

Conclusive research is typically more formal and structured than exploratory research. The researcher specifies the detailed steps in the research to be conducted prior to initiating the project. Large, representative samples are used to collect data that are then analyzed with statistical techniques. In the Ivory soap example, a large national survey involving 1,000 randomly selected respondents could be conducted to verify the findings of qualitative research. The survey could be used to obtain consumer evaluations of Ivory soap and competing brands on the important attributes such as mildness, lather, shrinkage, price, fragrance, packaging, moisturizing, and cleaning power.

conclusive research
Research designed to assist the decision maker in determining, evaluating, and selecting the best course of action for a given situation.

Be an MR!	**Be a DM!**
Holiday Inn: All in the Family	
Visit www.ichotelsgroup.com/h/d/hi/1/en/home and write a report about the various hotel brands owned by Holiday Inn. What type of research would you conduct to determine a coherent marketing strategy for the various Holiday Inn hotel brands?	As the vice president of marketing for Holiday Inn, discuss the role that exploratory and conclusive research can play in determining a coherent marketing strategy for the various hotel brands owned by Holiday Inn, such as Holiday Inn Hotels and Resorts, Holiday Inn Select, Holiday Inn SunSpree Resorts, and Holiday Inn Family Suites Resorts.

Exploratory Research

As the name implies, the objective of exploratory research is to explore or search through a problem or situation to gain insights and understanding (see Tables 3.1 and 3.2). For example, Adidas could make use of exploratory research to understand the reasons for its lower market share in the United States as compared to Nike. Exploratory research could be used for any of the following purposes, which are illustrated using Adidas as an example.

1. *To formulate a problem or define a problem more precisely.* Exploratory research might reveal that Adidas has a lower market share because its brand image is not as strong as Nike's.
2. *To identify alternative courses of action.* Alternative courses of action to boost Adidas' image might include improving product quality, increasing the television advertising and social media budget, distributing the product through upscale company-owned stores, increasing the prices of its athletic shoes and apparel, and so forth.
3. *To develop hypotheses.* An interesting hypothesis is that heavy users of athletic shoes are more brand conscious than light users. Another is that heavy users have a weaker image of Adidas as compared to the light users.
4. *To isolate key variables and relationships for further examination.* Celebrity endorsements can have a positive influence on the image of Adidas.
5. *To gain insights for developing an approach to the problem.* Brand image is a composite variable that is influenced by the quality of the product, the pricing strategy, the image of the outlets through which the product is distributed, and the quality and intensity of advertising, social media presence, and promotion.
6. *To establish priorities for further research.* Adidas might want to examine the purchase and consumption behavior of heavy users of athletic shoes.

Exploratory research often is conducted in the beginning stages of a project, as illustrated in the Spiegel vignette. Secondary data provided good background information on Spiegel's customers, whereas focus groups helped Spiegel understand the values, attitudes, and behavior of this segment with regard to clothing and shopping. The results indicated that current and potential customers wanted variety and quality and also appreciated special promotions. However, exploratory research can be used at any point in the research process when the researcher is unclear about the problem situation.

Exploratory research relies heavily on the researcher's curiosity and insight. It is more like a process of informal discovery. Yet the abilities of the researcher are not the sole determinants of good exploratory research. Although the process is highly flexible and relatively informal, exploratory research can benefit from use of the following methods (see Table 3.2):

- Survey of experts/experience surveys (discussed in Chapter 2)
- Pilot surveys (discussed in Chapter 2)
- Case studies (discussed in Chapter 2)
- Qualitative analysis of secondary data, including social media content (discussed in Chapters 4 and 5)
- Qualitative research, such as focus groups, one-on-one depth interviews, social networks, and social media bulletin boards (discussed in Chapter 6)

As discussed in Chapter 2, the Internet offers many resources for marketing research. Newsgroups, list servers, and other bulletin-board-type services can be very useful in the exploratory phase of research. Messages posted to newsgroups can often direct the researcher to other valid sources of information. Newsgroups can be used to set up more formal focus groups with experts or individuals representing the target audience in order to obtain initial information on a subject. In Chapter 6, we discuss the use of the Internet and social media for conducting focus groups in more detail.

Spiegel analyzed secondary data and conducted 10 focus groups as part of its exploratory research to understand the clothing preferences and shopping behavior of its customers. The use of exploratory research in defining the problem and developing an approach was discussed in Chapter 2. The Research in Action feature on the next page provides another application of exploratory research.

TABLE 3.2 A Comparison of Basic Research Designs

	Exploratory	Descriptive	Causal
Objective:	Discovery of ideas and insights	Describe market characteristics or functions	Determine cause-and-effect relationships
Characteristics:	Flexible Versatile Often the front end of total research design	Marked by the prior formulation of specific hypotheses Preplanned and structured design	Manipulation of one or more independent variables Control of other mediating variables
Methods:	Expert/experience surveys Pilot surveys Case studies Secondary data: qualitative Qualitative research	Secondary data: quantitative Surveys Panels Observational and other data	Experiments

Research in Action

Banking on Exploratory Research

As of 2011, Bank of America (www.bankofamerica.com) is one of the world's largest financial institutions. The company serves clients in 175 countries and has relationships with 98 percent of the U.S. *Fortune* 500 and 80 percent of the *Fortune* Global 500 companies. In order to increase its share of a very competitive market, Bank of America (BOA) conducted exploratory research using focus groups of current and potential customers to find out where new branches should be located and what new products should be introduced. Many new product ideas were generated through exploratory research. These ideas were further investigated using descriptive research in the form of customer and non-customer surveys. The research enabled BOA to successfully introduce new products, such as innovative checking, savings, and institutional accounts, and to improve profitability.

Focus groups followed by a telephone survey revealed that a large segment of households wanted interest payments on their checking account balances but were very sensitive to any checking account fees. These consumers maintained large balances in their checking account and were therefore open to a reasonable minimum balance requirement. Accordingly, BOA introduced an interest-paying checking with no fees (monthly or per check) that had a minimum balance requirement of $2,500. Exploratory and descriptive research have helped BOA to become the largest bank in the world with a brand positioning of "Bank of Opportunity."[2]

Note that BOA, like Spiegel, did not rely exclusively on exploratory research. Once new product ideas were identified, they were further tested by descriptive research in the form of surveys.

Be an MR!   Be a DM!

Häagen-Dazs: Ice Cream Indulgence

Visit www.haagendazs.com and search for additional information about the company on the Internet as well as social media. Write a report describing the flavors and products offered by Häagen-Dazs and the company's marketing strategy.

You are conducting a project for Häagen-Dazs to understand consumers' perceptions and preferences for high-quality ice cream. Would you conduct exploratory research? If yes, which methods would you use and why?

As the marketing manager for Häagen-Dazs, how would you use information on consumers' perceptions and preferences for high-quality ice cream to penetrate upper-income U.S. households?

Social Media

Descriptive Research

descriptive research
A type of conclusive research that has as its major objective the description of something—usually market characteristics or functions.

Descriptive research is a type of conclusive research that has as its major objective the description of something—usually market characteristics or functions. Most commercial marketing research is descriptive in nature. Descriptive research is particularly useful when research questions seek to describe a market phenomenon, such as determining purchase frequencies, identifying relationships, or making predictions (see Table 3.2). The following are examples of descriptive research goals:

1. *To develop a profile of a target market.* Levi-Strauss would like to know the age, educational level, income, and media habits of heavy users of jeans in order to make advertising-placement decisions.
2. *To estimate the frequency of product use as a basis for sales forecasts.* Knowing that a "heavy" perfume user buys an average of 1.8 bottles of perfumes per month can help Mary Kay cosmetics predict potential sales for a new perfume brand.
3. *To determine the relationship between product use and perception of product characteristics.* In developing its marketing platform, Motorola would like to determine if and how heavy users of cell phones differ from nonusers in terms of the importance they attach to performance and ease of use.
4. *To determine the degree to which marketing variables are associated.* Microsoft would like to know to what extent Internet usage is related to age, income, and education level.

Descriptive research assumes that the researcher has prior knowledge about the problem situation. This is one of the major differences between descriptive and exploratory research. Descriptive research, in contrast to exploratory research, is based on a clear statement of the problem, specific hypotheses, and specification of the information needed (see Chapter 2). Data are collected in a structured fashion, typically using large, representative samples. The findings are then used to make generalizations about an entire customer group or market. Microsoft, for example, could survey a representative sample of Internet users to determine Internet usage and project the findings to the larger population of Internet users.

Descriptive studies are used to portray market variables. They describe the customer and the market and measure the frequency of behaviors, such as purchasing. Among the major types of descriptive studies are internally or externally focused sales studies, consumer perception and behavior studies, and market characteristic studies (see Figure 3.5).

Sales studies include market potential studies, market share studies, and sales analysis studies. Market potential studies describe the size of the market, the buying power of consumers, and historic growth rates. Market share studies determine the proportion of total sales a company and its competitors receive. Sales analysis studies describe sales by geographic region, product line, and type and size of the account.

Consumer perception and behavior studies include image studies, product usage studies, advertising studies, and pricing studies. Image studies determine consumer perceptions of the

FIGURE 3.5

Major Types of Descriptive Studies

firm and its products. Product usage studies describe consumption patterns. Advertising studies describe media consumption habits and audience profiles for specific television programs and magazines. Pricing studies describe the range and frequency of price changes and the probable consumer response to proposed price changes.

Market characteristic studies include distribution studies and competitive analyses. Distribution studies determine traffic flow patterns and the number and location of distributors. Competitive analyses compare strengths and weaknesses of industry participants.

Say that Swatch would like to determine the size of the market for sports watches, at what rate the market is growing, and the market shares of the leading brands. It might do an analysis of its own sales of Swatch sports watches by type of outlet—jewelry stores, department stores, sporting-goods stores, specialty stores, catalog, Internet operations, and other outlets. Management might ask: How do consumers perceive Swatch? Does the image of Swatch vary between owners and nonowners? Which TV programs do people who buy premium sports watches view? How much of a premium are consumers willing to pay for a high-quality sports watch? Swatch would have to undertake consumer perception and behavior studies to provide management with answers to these questions. Market characteristic studies might examine the following questions: How many distributors does Swatch have for each type of outlet? How does this compare with other competing brands?

These examples demonstrate the range and diversity of descriptive research studies. Descriptive research also uses a variety of data collection techniques, which we discuss in the following chapters. These techniques include:

survey
An interview with a large number of respondents using a predesigned questionnaire.

- Quantitative analysis of secondary data including social media content (Chapters 4 and 5)
- **Surveys** (interviews with a large number of respondents using a predesigned questionnaire) (Chapter 7)
- Panels (Chapters 5 and 7)
- Observational and other data (Chapter 7)

The survey Spiegel conducted in the opening vignette is an example of descriptive research. Descriptive research using these methods can be further classified into cross-sectional and longitudinal research (see Figure 3.4).

Be a DM!	**Be an MR!**
All American!	
As the CEO of American Airlines, how would you use information on the image of your airline versus major competitors to improve your competitive positioning?	Visit www.americanairlines.com and search the Internet—including social media—as well as your library's online databases to obtain information on the competitive positioning of American Airlines. What type of exploratory and descriptive research would you undertake to determine the image of American Airlines versus its major competitors?

Cross-Sectional Designs

A **cross-sectional design,** sometimes called a *sample survey,* can be thought of as a snapshot of the marketplace taken at a specific point in time. In this design, the selected group of respondents is measured only once. The cross-sectional survey is the most frequently used descriptive design in marketing research. Spiegel's survey of 1,000 customers is a cross-sectional design, and so is the Jergens Moisturizer example that follows.

cross-sectional design
A type of research design involving the one-time collection of information from any given sample of population elements.

Research in Action

Jergens Overnight Repair Repairs Consumer Complaints Overnight

The Andrew Jergens Company (www.jergens.com) periodically conducts surveys to measure consumers' perceptions, attitudes, and use of personal-care products. Cross-sectional surveys have helped Jergens develop and introduce many successful products such as the Jergens® Natural Glow Daily Moisturizers, introduced in 2007. A recent cross-sectional survey involving 400 mall-intercept interviews in five major cities showed that many women had complaints about the dryness of their skin. It bothered them when they went to sleep at night. They didn't like the feeling of a dry skin when they woke up in the morning. These findings led to the development of an innovative new product that was introduced in 2010: Jergens Overnight Repair Nightly Restoring Moisturizer. Made with a rich blend of antioxidant vitamins and pure evening primrose extract, Jergens Overnight Repair Nightly Restoring Moisturizer repairs and rejuvenates skin overnight so you can sleep beautifully and wake up to smoother, healthier-looking, revived skin—every morning. The product met with instant success upon introduction.[3]

Longitudinal Designs

longitudinal design
A type of research design involving a fixed sample of population elements that is measured repeatedly. The sample remains the same over time, providing a series of pictures that, when viewed together, portray both the situation and the changes that are taking place.

The typical cross-sectional design offers a snapshot at a single point in time. In contrast, a **longitudinal design** provides a series of pictures, which track the changes that take place over time. In longitudinal designs, a fixed sample from the population is measured repeatedly on the same variables. In other words, two or more measurements on the same variables are obtained from a given group of respondents at different points in time (see Figure 3.6).

A cross-sectional design would be used to ask the question, "How did the American people rate the performance of President Barack Obama immediately following the midterm elections in 2010?" A longitudinal design would be used to address the question, "How did the American people change their view of Obama's performance before and after his first year in office?"

panel
A panel consists of a sample of respondents, generally households that have agreed to provide information at specified intervals over an extended period.

Sometimes, the term *panel* or *true panel* is used interchangeably with the term *longitudinal design*. A **panel** consists of a sample of respondents, generally households that have agreed to provide information at specified intervals over an extended period. Because of the long-term commitment needed for participation on a panel, its members are compensated with gifts, coupons, information, or cash. Panel data are typically collected by commercial research organizations known as *syndicated firms*. NPD (www.npd.com) is one such firm that tracks changes in consumer purchase patterns and then sells the data to other businesses or interested groups for a flat subscription price. The following Tylenol example illustrates longitudinal design. Panels are discussed in more detail in Chapters 5 and 7.

FIGURE 3.6

Cross-Sectional Versus Longitudinal Designs

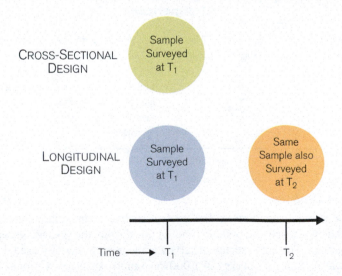

Research in Action

Longitudinal Research Leads to Rapid Success for Tylenol Rapid Release Gels

Tylenol (www.tylenol.com), marketed by Johnson & Johnson, conducts longitudinal surveys with consumer panels to determine how respondents feel about new products prior to their introduction into the marketplace. The company also uses the panel after the product has been in the market for a while to find out information about the product's performance and image in the marketplace. A recent example of the use of panels by Tylenol to ensure the success of a new product is the Rapid Release Gels line of pain relievers.

Tylenol first formed a panel of prospective consumers for the new line of pills it was introducing, making sure that the respondents not only thought well of the product, but would buy it as well. This panel was administered a survey questionnaire and revealed that the speed of the medicine was a key point that should be emphasized. Everyone wanted pain relief, but the quickest product to deliver the relief would definitely sell the best. Tylenol's Extra Strength Rapid Release Gels have gel caps with specially designed holes to release powerful medicine fast. Rapid release equates to rapid relief. The color of the pill was established based on feedback from the panel as blue and red, which the majority of the panelists found "soothing" and related to comfort and care. The introductory advertising campaign featured NASCAR drivers for marketing the product as a sign of the speedy recovery from illness by consuming the tablet. They even had testimonials to prove that this new Tylenol has the power to act as a fast pain reliever and yet be gentle on the stomach.

Tylenol reconvened the panel at 3, 6, and 9 months after the product launch. Each time, the same panelists were administered the same questionnaire used earlier and asked about the advertising, how well the product actually worked, the color scheme, how their friends felt about the product, and if it was better than the products produced by some of Tylenol's competitors. They were also asked the brand of pain reliever they purchased last and when the purchase was made.

Based on the feedback, Tylenol determined that the use of celebrities and sports stars in its ads was not beneficial in the marketing campaign. Most people wanted a simple, down-to-earth message about the new pain reliever's attributes. They wanted to know that it was one of the most preferred pain relievers on the market and that brand loyalty was high.

In response to this feedback, Tylenol changed the advertising campaign and started advertising to the common man, using common people. The new marketing campaign focused on everyday situations requiring a fast pain reliever. Tylenol revised the home page of its Web site to show an employee who has been working in the company for 3 years, just like her grandfather did for 30 years, who promises people that she will put as much care into making Tylenol as her grandfather did. The Web site also offered links so visitors could hear more from the people who make Tylenol. This type of marketing was aimed at connecting with the people.

The use of a longitudinal design using a panel gave Tylenol valuable insight into the direction it should take with its new product line, leading to its success in the marketplace.[4]

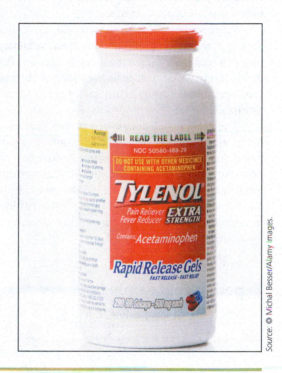

Source: © Michal Besser/Alamy images.

Cross-Sectional Versus Longitudinal Designs

The relative advantages and disadvantages of longitudinal versus cross-sectional designs are summarized in Table 3.3. Because in most situations the researcher is interested in obtaining a picture of the marketplace at one point in time, cross-sectional designs are far more commonly used than longitudinal designs.

Cross-sectional studies cost less. It is relatively simple to select a representative sample, a group of respondents whose characteristics of interest are a reflection of the entire population. Because different respondents are selected each time a survey is conducted, bias due to the same set of respondents answering multiple surveys is eliminated.

A major advantage of longitudinal designs is the ability to detect change as a result of repeated measurements of the same variables on the same respondents. This is illustrated in the Tylenol example. Because the same individuals provide data on the same variables repeatedly, it

TABLE 3.3 Relative Advantages and Disadvantages of Longitudinal and Cross-Sectional Designs

Evaluation Criteria	Cross-Sectional Design	Longitudinal Design
Detecting change	−	+
Large amount of data collection	−	+
Accuracy	−	+
Representative sampling	+	−
Response bias	+	−

Note: A "+" indicates a relative advantage over the other design.
   A "−" indicates a relative disadvantage.

is possible to compare the brand of pain reliever an individual purchases at any given time with the brand purchased in the preceding time period. Thus, the researcher can determine whether an individual is engaging in repeat purchase or brand switching.

Panel research also has an advantage over cross-sectional research in terms of the amount of data that can be collected as well as the accuracy of that data. A typical cross-sectional survey requires recall of past purchases and behavior. Panel data, which rely on continuous recording of purchases in a diary, place less reliance on the respondent's memory. A comparison of panel and cross-sectional survey estimates of retail sales indicates that panel data give more accurate estimates.

The main disadvantage of panels is that they might not be representative of the population of interest. This might happen because of refusals to participate and high dropout rates for panel participants. Bias is introduced when participants try to give the "right" answer or become bored or fatigued and make incomplete diary or Internet entries. In addition, longitudinal designs are more expensive to implement because of the expenses associated with maintaining a panel. In light of these limitations, longitudinal designs are used only when it is necessary to examine changes over time, such as in studies of repeat purchases, brand switching, and brand loyalty.

Experiential Learning

Exploratory and Descriptive Research

Visit www.gallup.com and examine some of the recent projects conducted by the Gallup organization. Read through some of the reports posted on this Web site. What type of exploratory research was conducted in these projects? Which methods were used?

What type of descriptive research was conducted in these projects? Which methods were used? In which project was the research design most appropriate? Why?

Causal Research

causal research
A type of conclusive research whose major objective is to obtain evidence regarding cause-and-effect (causal) relationships.

causal design
A design in which the causal or independent variables are manipulated in a relatively controlled environment.

Like descriptive research, **causal research** requires a planned and structured design. Although descriptive research can determine the degree of association between variables, it is generally not very appropriate for examining causal relationships. Causal relations are those that involve cause-and-effect variables.

The hypothesis that a promotional campaign will lead to (*cause*) an increase in sales is an example. To examine this hypothesis, a researcher would need a **causal design**—a design in which the causal or independent variables are manipulated in a relatively controlled environment. A relatively controlled environment is one in which the other variables that might affect the dependent variable are controlled or checked as much as possible. The effect of this manipulation on one or more dependent variables is then measured to infer causality.

The main method of causal research is an experiment. Experiments can take place either in a laboratory or in a natural setting. An experiment can be designed to test the causal relationship that promotion causes brand sales. Here, the independent variable that will be manipulated is promotion and the dependent variable is brand sales. Variables other than promotion, which also affect sales, such as product quality, price, and distribution need to be controlled. Participants in a laboratory study might be told to imagine they are on a shopping trip. Various promotional offers, as manipulated by the researcher, will be displayed, with each group of respondents seeing only one offer. The purchases of the respondents in this simulated shopping experience would be measured and compared across groups. The experimenter creates and controls the setting so that product quality, price, and distribution are held constant. In a field experiment, the same study would occur in a natural setting, such as retail stores. Various promotional offers would be displayed in stores, with each group of respondents seeing only one offer. The resulting brand sales would be monitored.

In the opening vignette, Spiegel did not make use of causal research. However, it could have, for example, in testing three alternative depictions of its product lines in its catalog. Each of the three versions of the catalog could be mailed to a distinct group of customers. The purchases of Spiegel products by each group could be monitored and compared to determine the depiction that resulted in the highest sales. Causal research is appropriate for the following purposes, illustrated in the context of examining the effect of a promotional campaign on the sales of Mercedes cars:

1. *To understand which variables are the causes (independent variables) and which are the effects (dependent variables) of a phenomenon.* In other words, if an independent variable is manipulated, a change should be detected in the dependent variable. The independent variables will be the dollar amount spent on advertising and the dollar amount spent on sales promotion during a given time period. The dependent variable will be the sales of Mercedes (measured in units and dollars).

2. *To determine the extent of the relationship between the predicted effect and the causal variables.* The relationship between sales promotion and advertising expenditures and the sales of Mercedes is likely to be nonlinear: As more and more is spent on advertising, sales of Mercedes will increase less and less due to the saturation effect.

The implementation of a causal design is further illustrated by Microsoft's experiment with Windows 7.

A causal design is needed for examining the effect of a promotional campaign on the sales of Mercedes cars.

Source: © Mark Richardson/Alamy Images.

Research in Action

Windows 7: A Window into the Hearts of Computer Users

The key to the success (high awareness and high sales) of Windows 7 (www.microsoft.com) was that the product was carefully designed and tested. In a controlled experiment, one group of computer users was asked to work with Windows 7. Two other carefully matched groups worked with the previous versions of Windows: one with Windows Vista and the other with Windows XP. All three groups rated the operating system on ease of use, power, capabilities, and the ability to enhance a computer user's experience. Windows 7 was rated significantly better than the previous versions on all factors, leading to the introduction of this operating system.[5]

Source: Robyn Beck/AFP/Getty Images/Newscom.

In the Microsoft experiment, the causal (independent) variable was the operating system, which was manipulated to have three levels: Windows 7, Windows Vista, and Windows XP. The effect (dependent) variables were ease of use, power, capabilities, and ability to enhance a computer user's experience. The influence of the user's background was controlled by carefully matching the three groups on relevant demographic and computer-usage characteristics.

Due to its complexity and importance, the topic of causal designs and experimental research will be fully explained in a separate chapter (see Chapter 8). In that chapter, we discuss the conditions for causality, validity in experimentation, and specific types of experimental designs.

Be a DM!	Be an MR!
Taco Bell: Thinking Outside the Bun	
As the advertising manager for Taco Bell, how would you determine whether the advertising budget for the next year should be increased, decreased, or remain the same as the current budget?	Visit www.tacobell.com and search the Internet—including social media—as well as your library's online databases to obtain information on Taco Bell's advertising. Write a brief report. Design an experiment to determine whether the advertising budget for Taco Bell for the next year should be increased, decreased, or remain the same as the current budget. Identify the independent, dependent, and the control variables.

Social Media

Relationships Among Exploratory, Descriptive, and Causal Research

Although the preceding example distinguished causal research from other types of research and showed the benefits of causal research, causal research should not be viewed in isolation. Rather, exploratory, descriptive, and causal designs should be used to complement each other. A given problem might lend itself to exploratory, descriptive, or causal research. Consider the loss of market share:

Exploratory Research:	Why are we losing market share?
Descriptive Research:	How do consumers evaluate our brand compared to competing brands?
Causal Research:	By how much will our sales increase if we decrease the price by 5, 10, or 15 percent?

FIGURE 3.7

Some Alternative Research Designs

As mentioned earlier, a given project may incorporate more than one basic research design, depending on the nature of the problem and the approach. We offer the following general guidelines for choosing research designs:

1. When little is known about the problem situation, it is desirable to begin with exploratory research. For example, exploratory research is suitable for generating alternative courses of action, research questions, or hypotheses. Exploratory research can then be followed by descriptive or causal research, as in the Spiegel vignette (see Figure 3.7(a)).
2. It is not necessary to begin every research design with exploratory research. If the researcher has a good understanding of the problem situation, descriptive or causal research might be a more appropriate initial step (see Figure 3.7(b)). Quarterly consumer-satisfaction surveys are an example of research that does not need to begin with or include an exploratory phase.
3. Exploratory research can be used at any point in a study. For example, when descriptive or causal research leads to results that are unexpected or difficult to interpret, the researcher may turn to exploratory research for insight (see Figure 3.7(c)).

Suppose an image study is conducted for a supermarket chain such as Kroger to identify its strengths and weaknesses relative to competing supermarkets. Exploratory research, including secondary data analysis and focus groups, is first conducted to define the problem and to develop a suitable approach. This is followed by a descriptive study consisting of a survey in which a questionnaire is constructed and administered by telephone interviews.

Suppose the image study is to be repeated after one year to determine if any changes had taken place. At that point, exploratory research would probably be unnecessary, and the research design could begin with the descriptive study.

Assume that the survey is repeated a year later and that some unexpected findings are obtained. Kroger management wonders why its supermarkets' ratings on in-store service have declined when the supermarket staff has increased. Exploratory research in the form of focus groups might be undertaken to probe these unexpected findings. The focus groups might reveal that although the store clerks are present, they are not very helpful. This would suggest the need for training the store clerks.

This example illustrates how exploratory and descriptive research can be integrated. Exploratory and descriptive designs are frequently used in commercial marketing research; causal research is not as popular. Another example of the use of exploratory and conclusive research is provided by Kellogg's.

Research in Action

Kellogg's: Smart and Special with Exploratory and Descriptive Research

With 2010 sales of $12.4 billion, Kellogg's (www.kelloggs.com) is the world's leading producer of cereal and a leading producer of convenience foods, including cookies, crackers, toaster pastries, cereal bars, fruit snacks, frozen waffles, and veggie foods. As of 2011, its products were manufactured in 19 countries worldwide and sold in more than 180 countries.

(continued)

Introducing new products, brand extensions, and making changes to existing brands has been a core element of the company's marketing strategy. By undertaking exploratory research followed by conclusive research, Kellogg's understands what new products should be developed and how existing products could be extended into a series of variants that keep the core product strong, but grow the brand as a whole.

Exploratory research in the form of focus groups revealed that consumers wanted cereals and snacks that were natural and healthy and yet tasted great. Conclusive research in the form of descriptive surveys verified demand for such products. Therefore, Kellogg's has developed numerous products that contain whole grains or provide fiber, such as the Smart Start brand, which can help to lower both high blood pressure and cholesterol. It also introduced products that can help consumers watch their weight, such as Special K, and products that are lower in fat and sodium. Kellogg's also has introduced innovative packaging that provides the benefits of portion control. The company introduced a number of new products in 2009/2010, including *Kellogg's FiberPlus*™ Berry Yogurt Crunch cereal, *Kellogg's FiberPlus* Cinnamon Oat Crunch cereal, and *Kellogg's Corn Flakes*® Simply Cinnamon cereal.

As a result of Kellogg's effort to create products that are natural and encourage a healthy diet, *CR Corporate Responsibility Magazine* named Kellogg's one of the 100 best corporate citizens.[6]

Tasks Involved in Formulating a Research Design

In formulating a research design, in most cases the researcher must perform the following tasks (see Figure 3.8):

1. Specify the information needed (Chapter 2).
2. Design the exploratory, descriptive, and/or causal phases of the research (Chapters 4 through 8).
3. Specify the measurement and scaling procedures (Chapters 9 and 10).
4. Construct and pretest a questionnaire (interview form) or an appropriate form for data collection (Chapter 11).

FIGURE 3.8

Tasks Involved in a Research Design

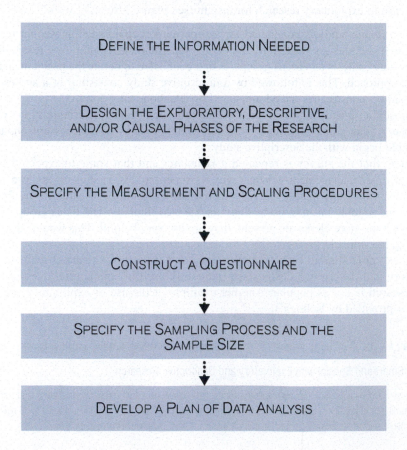

DEFINE THE INFORMATION NEEDED

DESIGN THE EXPLORATORY, DESCRIPTIVE, AND/OR CAUSAL PHASES OF THE RESEARCH

SPECIFY THE MEASUREMENT AND SCALING PROCEDURES

CONSTRUCT A QUESTIONNAIRE

SPECIFY THE SAMPLING PROCESS AND THE SAMPLE SIZE

DEVELOP A PLAN OF DATA ANALYSIS

5. Specify the sampling process and sample size (Chapters 12 and 13).
6. Develop a plan of data analysis (Chapter 15).

Chapter 2 described how to specify the necessary information. As noted, we will discuss in detail the rest of the tasks involved in a research design in subsequent chapters.

Research Design and the Value of Marketing Research

Research is conducted to help reduce management error in decision making. The key word here is *reduce*. Research is not designed to "prove" assumptions, but rather to provide management with an assessment of the degree of risk associated with making decisions based on tested assumptions. As the cost of making the wrong decision increases, typically the formality and structure of a study design increase as well. The research design has a major impact on the cost and value of the marketing research project. Ultimately, the cost of any project must be weighted against the reduced risk of making the decision with additional information.

Before committing funds to a study, management must assess, either formally or informally, the value of the additional information obtained by marketing research. For example, suppose the brand manager for Dannon yogurt is faced with a proposal to spend $50,000 to conduct a causal study regarding the effect of using various promotional offers. The manager must decide whether the value of a decision based on current knowledge could be improved by more than $50,000 with the help of research. If the various promotional offers involved coupons versus free trials, the difference in expenses associated with the two approaches (not to mention the difference in consumer response) could far exceed the $50,000 cost of research. In that case, the high cost of making the wrong decision makes it easier to justify the cost of the research.

The information value of research must also be discounted by the degree of error inherent in a study. No research design, no matter how sophisticated, can eliminate all risk from a decision, because no research is completely error-free. Several potential sources of error can affect a research design. Estimating the level of error in a study is complicated by the fact that, typically, only random sampling error is quantified. A **random sampling error** is an error resulting from the particular sample selected being an imperfect representation of the population of interest. Total error is made up of both sampling and nonsampling errors. In formulating the research design, the researcher should attempt to control the total error, not just the sampling error.

Nonsampling errors, as would be expected, can be attributed to sources other than sampling. They result from a variety of causes, including errors in problem definition, approach, scales, questionnaire design, survey methods, interviewing techniques, and data preparation and analysis. These nonsampling errors can be attributed to the researcher, the interviewer, or the respondent. A good research design attempts to control the various sources of error, as illustrated in the opening vignette, where Spiegel made an effort to control the sampling and nonsampling errors. Random sampling errors were controlled by having a large sample (1,000) that was randomly selected. Spiegel also controlled various sources of nonsampling errors, including interviewer and respondent errors, by careful selection, training, and supervision of the interviewers. These errors are discussed in great detail in subsequent chapters.

random sampling error
The error due to the particular sample selected being an imperfect representation of the population of interest.

nonsampling errors
Errors that can be attributed to sources other than sampling; they can be random or nonrandom.

Budgeting and Scheduling the Project

Once a research design has been specified, the researcher should prepare a detailed budget and schedule. **Budgeting and scheduling** help to ensure that the marketing research project is completed with the available resources: money, time, personnel, and others. The budget process allows the researcher and the decision maker to compare the estimated value of the information

budgeting and scheduling
Management tools needed to help ensure that the marketing research project is completed within the available resources.

with the projected costs. Additionally, the project schedule will help to ensure that the information is obtained in time to address the management-decision problem.

Marketing Research Proposal

marketing research proposal
Contains the essence of the project and serves as a contract between the researcher and management.

Once the research design has been formulated and the budgeting and scheduling of the project has been accomplished, the researcher should prepare a written research proposal. The **marketing research proposal** contains the essence of the project and serves as a contract between the researcher and management. The proposal covers all phases of the marketing research process, including cost and schedules. The format of a research proposal can vary considerably depending on the nature of the problem and the relationship of the client to the research supplier. Most proposals present a detailed research design and contain some or all of the following elements:

1. *Executive summary.* The proposal should begin with an overview of the entire project, a summary of the major points from each of the other sections.
2. *Background.* The background to the problem, including the environmental context, should be described.
3. *Problem definition/research objectives.* Normally, a statement of the problem should be presented. If this statement has not been developed (as in the case of exploratory research), then the objectives of the marketing research project should be clearly specified.
4. *Approach to the problem.* A review of the relevant academic and trade literature, along with some kind of an analytical model, should be included. If research questions and hypotheses have been identified, these should be included in the proposal.
5. *Research design.* The type of research design, whether exploratory, descriptive, causal, or a combination, should be specified. Information should be provided on the following components: (a) the kind of information to be obtained, (b) the method of administering the questionnaire (i.e., mail, telephone, personal, or electronic interviews), (c) scaling techniques, (d) the nature of the questionnaire (i.e., type of questions asked, length, average interviewing time), and (e) the sampling plan and sample size. This section often forms the heart of the proposal.
6. *Fieldwork/data collection.* The proposal should discuss how the data will be collected and who will collect it. If the fieldwork is to be subcontracted to another supplier, this should be stated. Control mechanisms to ensure the quality of data collected should be described.
7. *Data analysis.* The kind of data analysis that will be conducted, and how the results will be interpreted, should be described.
8. *Reporting.* The proposal should specify the nature and number of intermediate reports. The form of the final report, including whether a formal presentation of the results will be made, also should be stated. Industry professionals refer to this part of the report as the "deliverables." The proposal writer must specify what information (specifically, which documents) will be given to the client. Sometimes, the client will want a formal report that is more comprehensive and narrative than a PowerPoint presentation and discussion that might cover many projects. At the least, an executive summary of one to two single-spaced pages should be provided to explain what insights have been gained by the research and what these results mean for the client firm's managers.
9. *Cost and time.* The cost of the project and a schedule, broken down into phases, should be presented. A payment schedule should be worked out in advance, especially for large projects. Conventional industry practice is to have a project paid in three parts: the first payment is due after the proposal is accepted, the second at the project midpoint, and the

third at the conclusion of the project. The schedule developed for the proposal becomes an important coordinating document between the client and the research agency as the project is conducted.

10. *Project personnel.* All personnel who will be working on the project should be identified. The job, duration, responsibility, and authority of each person should be stated.

11. *Appendices.* Any statistical or other information that is of interest to only a few people should be presented in appendices.

The research proposal represents the contract between management and the researcher. It ensures that there is agreement regarding the objectives of the project, and it helps sell the project to management. Therefore, a research proposal should always be prepared, even when repeating a project for a repeat client.

Experiential Learning

Crafting a Research Proposal

Go to the textbook's Web site and download the following file: Meteor Proposal.doc. Meteor Motorcycle Company is one of the industry's leading manufacturers of customized, high-performance bikes in the luxury cruiser class. It is one of the only custom motorcycle makers equipped with full-service design, engineering, manufacturing, paint and polishing, and administrative teams.

The company produces four different kinds of bikes. They are all individually branded under Meteor X, Meteor Y, Meteor Z, and the Comet Chopper brand names and represent the company's varied product offerings, ranging in price from $23,000 to $100,000 or more. The company has seen tremendous growth—from approximately 27 bikes sold in 2000 to an impressive 5,000 in 2010. Comet Chopper, the brainchild of Jeff Branson, the creative force behind Meteor, currently accounts for nearly 55 percent of the company's annual sales of approximately $135 million.

1. Open Meteor Proposal.doc and read about an actual study done for one of the exciting heavyweight cruiser motorcycle companies. The names have been changed here. How well does this proposal correspond to the recommendations about proposals just discussed?

2. If you were the head of the marketing team for the Meteor Motorcycle Company, what would you like to be made clearer in this proposal?

Summary Illustration Using the Opening Vignette

The research design in the opening vignette described how a project was conducted for Spiegel. Research designs can be broadly classified as exploratory or conclusive, whereas conclusive research can be either descriptive or causal. Typically, the project begins with exploratory research, which is followed by descriptive (or causal) research. As seen in the opening vignette, in order to understand the problem situation, Spiegel analyzed secondary data and conducted 10 focus groups. This exploratory research helped Spiegel to identify and understand the unique aspects of its customers' shopping behavior and clothing needs. The findings of exploratory research were treated as tentative and were further verified by descriptive research consisting of telephone interviews with a randomly selected sample of 1,000 customers.

Typically, as in the case of Spiegel, a research project begins with exploratory research. However, other combinations of the basic designs are possible. Exploratory research can be conducted at any point in the project or it might not be undertaken at all. A well-formulated research design will attempt to control the random sampling as well as the nonsampling errors, as demonstrated in the opening vignette. A large and randomly selected sample was used to measure and control random sampling error. Efforts also were made to control the various sources of nonsampling error. For example, the interviewers were carefully selected and thoroughly trained, and close supervision was exercised to minimize interviewing errors attributed to the interviewers and respondents. Figure 3.9 provides a concept map for

FIGURE 3.9
A Concept Map for Research Design

research design. In this figure, the major concepts are connected by bold arrows using descriptors. Thus, research design basic types are exploratory, descriptive, and causal.

Descriptive design may be cross-sectional or longitudinal. Each major concept is described by minor concepts that are connected to that major concept by lines with descriptors. Thus, the methods of exploratory design are expert/experience surveys, pilot surveys, case studies, secondary data: qualitative, and qualitative research. The rest of the figure can be interpreted similarly.

International Marketing Research

The various methods associated with implementing each step of the research design discussed in this chapter must be reassessed within the context of cultural differences before they can be used internationally. Given environmental and cultural differences, a research design appropriate for one country might not be suitable for another. Consider the problem of determining household attitudes toward major appliances in the United States and Saudi Arabia. When conducting exploratory research in the United States, it is appropriate to conduct focus groups jointly with male and female heads of household. It would not be appropriate to conduct such focus groups in Saudi Arabia. As a result of their traditional culture, wives are unlikely to participate freely in the presence of their husbands. It would be more useful to conduct one-on-one depth interviews with both male and female heads of households included in the sample. Procter & Gamble (P&G) encountered a similar situation in Japan.

Research in Action

P&G: Exploring and Wooing Japanese Women

The consumer market in Japan is one of the toughest, most competitive, fastest-moving markets in the world. Japan represents the cutting edge of worldwide technology in many product categories. When P&G started business in Japan, it conducted a detailed study of market characteristics and market profile. The target market for P&G was homemakers, who were largely responsible for the consumption of several products, such as diapers, household cleaners, soaps, and detergents. Exploratory research followed by descriptive research was undertaken for this purpose. Whereas focus groups are most popular in the

United States, one-on-one, depth interviews were used because of the Japanese cultural tendency to not disagree openly in group settings. The descriptive surveys were fielded using in-home personal interviews.

Results showed that the average Japanese homemaker was uncompromising in her demands for high quality, value, and service. She was a paragon of conservation and efficiency in the management of the household. About half the adult women in Japan were employed, but they generally worked outside of the home only before marriage and after their children were raised. Child rearing was the number-one priority for Japanese mothers.

When it came to foreign versus domestic brands, Japanese women preferred foreign name-brand products that had style and status, such as fashionable clothing, French perfumes, wines, liquors, and designer bags. They did not prefer functional products made in foreign countries because these products usually did not meet their exacting and demanding standards.

Japanese women greatly preferred commercials that conserved traditional social and family values and roles, rather than the typical Western examples. P&G initially made a few mistakes in misjudging nuances of Japanese culture before this study was conducted. For example, the introductions of Camay bath soap and Pampers diapers were supported with Western-style advertising that was not well received by Japanese women. However, based on the market profile study, the advertising was changed to stress traditional social and family values, thereby increasing its effectiveness. As of 2010, P&G was using a Japanese actress to endorse its new shampoo line in Japan. This had greater appeal to Japanese women, who use more shampoo on average (6.4 times a week) as compared to American women (who shampoo hair 4.4 times a week). P&G opened an information site exclusively for mobile phones in Japan. This site features information on a variety of topics, including beauty, culture, and fashion, in addition to introducing new products. The decision to open this site was based on the heavy usage of cell phones as a shopping medium by Japanese women as determined by exploratory and descriptive research.[7]

Source: AP Wide World Photos/Shizuo Kambayashi.

In developing countries, consumer panels often are not available, which makes it difficult to conduct descriptive longitudinal research. In many countries, such as Sierra Leone in Africa, the marketing support infrastructure—retailing, wholesaling, advertising, and promotion development—is often lacking, which makes it difficult to implement a causal design involving a field experiment. In formulating a research design, considerable effort is required to ensure the equivalence and comparability of secondary and primary data obtained from different countries. In the context of collecting primary data, qualitative research, survey methods, scaling techniques, questionnaire design, and sampling considerations are particularly important. We discuss these topics in more detail in subsequent chapters.

Be an MR!	Be a DM!

Unilever: Soap Opera(tions)

Visit www.unilever.com and search the Internet—including social media—as well as your library's online databases to find information on consumer preferences for bathing soaps. Unilever, PLC, would like to determine consumer preferences for Lux bath soap in the United States, the United Kingdom, and China. Discuss the similarities and differences in the research design that should be adopted in each country.

As the global marketing manager for Unilever, PLC, how would you use information on consumer preferences for Lux in the United States, the United Kingdom, and China to formulate the marketing strategy for the brand in each of these countries?

Social Media

Marketing Research and Social Media

Social media can be appropriate for conducting exploratory, descriptive, and causal research. One reason why social networks can be suitable for conducting marketing research is that they eliminate the onerous cost of building and maintaining traditional panels. For example, there are more than 100,000 members of various Starbucks communities on Facebook and none of them are sponsored by the coffee retailer. Such panels based on brand communities may not be suitable for all kinds of marketing research. Nevertheless, such panels could be useful for investigating a host of marketing research issues, such as developing new products targeted at core users of the brand. The key is to analyze the characteristics of each social network and choose the network that most closely matches your research objectives. For instance, MySpace is heavily slanted toward the under-20 audience. In contrast, 40 percent of Facebook members are over 35 years old, and the Facebook community tends to be more affluent and better educated than MySpace users.

These network communities can be used to recruit marketing research panels and are distinguished by some key characteristics. Membership is voluntary and reputations are earned by winning the trust of other members. The community's mission and governance is defined by the community's members themselves. Thus, these social media communities are in sharp contrast to traditional marketing research panels in which users' roles are determined by the researcher and governed by well-defined regulations. The respondent's relationship with the researcher is one of dependence, and there are no relationships between respondents. The respondents or panel members have no relationship with the client in traditional panels.

Online communities range from being open to public—Facebook, MySpace—to completely private, closed, by invitation only. Private communities are primarily built for discovery and insight purposes and are called *MROCs* (Marketing Research Online Communities). Unlike public communities with no limit on the number of members, MROCs generally restrict membership. Marketers can assemble a private online community that will function like a traditional market research panel of yesteryear or traditional focus group, but with some key differences. Rather than just posing questions in a focus group, marketers can observe what is happening and how the group interacts to move ideas forward. The invisibility of private panels on the open Internet means the insights are safeguarded from the prying eyes of competitors. Also, a community of customers can help a business with issues of loyalty and usability, while a demographic community (say, teenagers) can show what marketing will work best with targeted segments. This leads to a term in the marketing world called *co-creation with customers*, in which firms employ the help of their consumers in the creative process while simultaneously providing the firms valuable research information. Online community tools include discussions/forums, polls and surveys, blogs, online chat, photo and video uploads, collaboration tools, member personalization, entertainment, and offline activities.

Disney set up the Walt Disney Moms Panel featuring moms who answer questions about the company's theme parks and vacation resorts from prospective visitors. In 2008, Disney launched the Mickey Moms Club, a gated community capped at 10,000 members. This community has become one of the most frequently visited of all Disney sites. Visitors spend an average of 8 to 10 minutes per visit, which is more than they spend on any other Disney site. Site visitors also spend more on their Disney vacations than nonmembers. Moreover, Disney uses the information collected at this site to longitudinally monitor visitors' reaction and feedback about its theme parks and vacation resorts. The use of public panels to conduct exploratory and conclusive research is illustrated by 3M Canada.

Research in Action

3M Canada: Scotch Shoe Becomes a Shoo-In

3M has a history since the 1950s, when it introduced the first transparent tape, known as Scotch Tape—which became synonymous with the product category it stands for. However, Scotch Tape became such an intrinsic part of consumers' daily lives that it became almost invisible. 3M had the sales and market share, but the problem was making the consumers passionate about the product. As a result, 3M Canada wanted to revitalize the brand in 2008.

3M came up with a new product that targeted women. It was a red tape dispenser called *Scotch Shoe* that looked like a heeled Mary Jane shoe. Budget constraints led the company to use

Facebook for its first product launch and testing; they used Facebook to do a comprehensive campaign in October 2008. Facebook was Canada's top social networking site, with more than 8.63 million active Canadian users. More than half were women, which was the target segment.

3M carried out exploratory research followed by conclusive (descriptive) research through a Facebook page. The objective of exploratory research was to find out the strengths and weaknesses of the product. The objectives of the descriptive phase were to quantify the findings of the exploratory phase and to develop an advertising strategy for Scotch Shoe.

Exploratory Research

Through the use of Facebook, the demographic and psychographic data of consumers were accessed by 3M. 3M held focus groups in the format of discussion-board posts that appealed to "shoe-aholics." Through these discussion boards, 3M was able to gather opinions and insights about existing products and about the new product from the images and videos posted. At the same time, 3M also initiated conversations with selected users (one-on-one) to further understand the strengths of the brand that could help increase brand passion and loyalty.

3M also launched two contests: one offering a $100 gift card and one offering a chance to win the new Scotch Shoe tape dispenser. In order to be eligible for the Scotch Shoe contest, fans had to post wall comments, whether positive or negative, about the new product. Through this contest, 3M gained further insights into the strengths and weaknesses of the new product.

Conclusive (Descriptive) Research

Insights gained from exploratory research were used to develop a survey questionnaire. The Scotch Shoe contest required users to complete a brief survey after posting their wall entries, and the survey helped 3M collect quantitative, descriptive data. In addition, 3M also used surveys on the Facebook page, after obtaining qualitative data, for all users to generate quantitative feedback.

The results of this campaign were successful: It generated more than 2,000 fans and close to 200 wall comments. 3M used the results of the survey to design an appealing and engaging advertising campaign. The engagement ads that 3M designed after collecting feedback delivered more than 1.5 million impressions and 300,000 clicks. The new product itself, the Scotch Shoe, sold out in stores immediately after the launch. Besides using the consumers' data for this campaign, the company retained consumer data and interests to cultivate further relationships for future prizes and contests, and to initiate new topics of discussion. The campaign's success was due to 3M conducting good exploratory and descriptive research using a low-cost platform like Facebook.[8]

Ethics in Marketing Research

The choice of a research design has ethical overtones for both the client and the research firm. For example, if Maxwell House is interested in examining brand switching in coffee purchases, a longitudinal design is the only appropriate way to assess changes in an individual respondent's choice of coffee brands. A research firm that justifies the use of a cross-sectional design simply because it has no experience in conducting longitudinal studies is behaving unethically.

Researchers must ensure that the research design will provide the information needed to address the marketing research problem. The client should have the integrity not to misrepresent the project, should describe the constraints under which the researcher must operate, and should not make unreasonable demands. If customer contact has to be restricted, or if time is an issue, the client should make these constraints known at the start of the project. It would be unethical for a client to extract details from a proposal submitted by one research firm and pass them to another who actually would do the project for the client. A proposal is the property of the research firm that prepared it, unless the client has paid for it. The client should not take advantage of the research firm by making false promises of future research contracts in order to solicit concessions for the current project.

Research in Action

Just Business Versus Unethical Concessions

Ethical dilemmas can arise due to the strong desire of marketing research firms to become suppliers to large businesses that are heavy users of marketing research. For example, Visa, Delta Airlines, Coca-Cola, and Ford Motor Company have large marketing research budgets and regularly hire external marketing research suppliers. These large clients can manipulate the price for the current study or demand unreasonable concessions in the research design (e.g., more focus groups, a larger sample, or additional data analyses) by suggesting the potential for the marketing research firm to become a regular supplier. This might be considered just business, but it becomes unethical when there is no intention to follow up with a larger study or to use the research firm in the future. Marketing research firms should be aware of such unethical practices and must discern the intent of the client firms before offering concessions to gain future business.[9]

Equally important, responsibilities to respondents must not be overlooked. The researcher should design the study so as not to violate the respondents' right to safety, privacy, or choice. Furthermore, the client must not violate the anonymity of the respondents. (Respondent-related issues are discussed in more detail in Chapters 4 through 7.)

WHAT WOULD YOU DO?

NASCAR: Changing the Redneck Image

The Situation

The sound of roaring engines, screaming fans, and beating hearts—the excitement of NASCAR! The National Association of Stock Car Auto Racing (NASCAR) is a company unlike any other. Although NASCAR generates excitement in fans across the nation, it had been stereotyped as only appealing to low-income Southerners who work in laborer-type jobs. Brian France, chair and CEO of NASCAR, wanted to increase NASCAR's audience and remake its stereotyped image.

NASCAR conducted exploratory research to identify ways to penetrate the non-race market, reach younger fans, and build its brand image across the nation. Extensive focus groups revealed that (1) NASCAR had a rural sports image, (2) this image was not necessarily negative, and (3) companies that supported sports were viewed positively.

The Marketing Research Decision

1. Do you think the research design adopted by NASCAR was appropriate? Why or why not?

2. Which of the following research designs would you recommend?
   a. Exploratory research: focus groups
   b. Exploratory research: depth interviews
   c. Exploratory research followed by a descriptive survey
   d. Exploratory research followed by causal research
   e. Descriptive survey followed by exploratory research

3. Discuss the role of the type of research design you recommend in enabling Brian France to change the image of NASCAR.

The Marketing Management Decision

1. Brian France realizes that it is crucial for NASCAR to project the right image. However, he wonders what that image is. Is it (check as many as are applicable):
   a. A rural sports image
   b. An urban sports image
   c. Southern heritage
   d. Blue-collar sports
   e. A national sport for all lifestyles

2. Discuss how the course of action you recommend to Brian France is influenced by the research that you suggested earlier and by the findings of that research.

What Brian France Did

Brian France attempted to position NASCAR as a national sport for all lifestyles. He took several initiatives to involve minorities in the sport, which was expanded both by Sprint's national sponsorship and by moving races from the South to speedways across the country. NASCAR also targeted the nontraditional demographic segments, including families, children, and minorities. To further reinforce the national image, Brian France appointed non-Southerners to key positions in the company. As of 2011, NASCAR featured three national series (the NASCAR Sprint Cup Series, NASCAR Nationwide Series, and NASCAR Camping World Truck Series), four regional series, and one local grassroots series, as well as two international series. NASCAR sanctioned more than 1,200 races at 100 tracks in more than 30 U.S. states, Canada, and Mexico.[10]

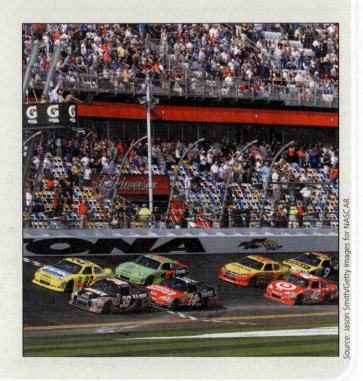

Source: Jason Smith/Getty Images for NASCAR.

Summary

A research design is the roadmap for conducting the marketing research project. It specifies the details of how the project should be conducted. Research designs can be broadly classified as exploratory or conclusive. The primary purpose of exploratory research is to provide insights into the problem. Conclusive research is used to test hypotheses and examine specific relationships. Conclusive research can be either descriptive or causal and is used as input into managerial decision making.

The major objective of descriptive research is to describe market characteristics or functions. Descriptive research can be further classified into cross-sectional and longitudinal designs. Cross-sectional designs involve the collection of information from a sample drawn from a population at a single point in time. In contrast, longitudinal designs entail repeated measurements on a fixed sample at different points in time. Causal research is designed to obtain evidence about cause-and-effect (causal) relationships via an experiment.

In evaluating a research proposal, management must discount the value of the information by the level of error inherent in the study. Error can be associated with any of the six components of the research design. Managers should prepare a written marketing research proposal that includes all the elements of the marketing research process.

The various methods associated with implementing each step of the research design must be reassessed within the context of cultural differences before they can be used internationally. Social media and the Internet can facilitate the implementation of exploratory, descriptive, or causal research. In addition to ethical aspects that concern researchers and clients, the rights of respondents must be respected when formulating the research design.

Key Terms and Concepts

Research design   66
Exploratory research   68
Conclusive research   69
Descriptive research   72
Survey   73

Cross-sectional design   73
Longitudinal design   74
Panel   74
Causal research   76
Causal design   76

Random sampling error   81
Nonsampling errors   81
Budgeting and scheduling   81
Marketing research proposal   82

Suggested Cases and Video Cases

Running Case with Real Data

1.1 Hewlett-Packard

Comprehensive Critical Thinking Cases

2.1 American Idol   2.2 Baskin-Robbins   2.3 Akron Children's Hospital

Comprehensive Cases with Real Data

3.1 Bank of America   3.2 McDonald's   3.3 Boeing

Comprehensive Brief Harvard Business School Cases

4.1 TruEarth Healthy Foods: Market Research for a New Product Introduction (4065)
4.2 The Springfield Nor'easters: Maximizing Revenues in the Minor Leagues (2510)
4.3 Metabical: Positioning and Communications Strategy for a New Weight-Loss Drug (4240)
4.4 Saxonville Sausage Company (2085)

Online Video Cases

3.1 NFL   4.1 Mayo Clinic   5.1 eGO   8.1 AFLAC   9.1 P&G
10.1 Nivea   13.1 Subaru   14.1 Intel   19.1 Marriott

Live Research: Conducting a Marketing Research Project

1. Each team should present to the class the type of research design they think is appropriate. Normally, the teams will end up with similar research designs, unless they are working on different projects.
2. As a class, discuss and select the research design for this project.
3. It is helpful to invite the client to this session.
4. Prepare a formal proposal, as described in this chapter, and obtain client approval.

Acronym

The components of a research design may be summarized by the acronym Design:

D ata analysis plan

E xploratory, descriptive, causal design

S caling and measurement

I nterviewing forms: questionnaire design

G enerating the needed information

N umber: Sample size and plan

Review Questions

1. Define *research design* in your own words.
2. How does formulating a research design differ from developing an approach to a problem?
3. Differentiate between exploratory and conclusive research.
4. What are the major purposes for which descriptive research is conducted?
5. Compare and contrast cross-sectional and longitudinal designs.
6. Discuss the advantages and disadvantages of panels.
7. What is a causal research design? What is its purpose?
8. What is the relationship among exploratory, descriptive, and causal research?
9. List the major components of a research design.
10. **Social Media** How can exploratory and descriptive research be implemented in social media?
11. Discuss the ethical issues involved in formulating an appropriate research design?

Applied Problems

1. Sweet Cookies is planning to launch a new line of cookies and wants to assess the size of the market. The cookies have a mixed chocolate-pineapple flavor and will be targeted at the premium end of the market. Discuss the type of research design that could be used.
2. Welcome, Inc., is a chain of fast-food restaurants located in major metropolitan areas in the South. Sales have been growing very slowly for the last 2 years. Management has decided to add some new items to the menu; however, first they want to know more about their customers and their preferences.
   a. List two hypotheses.
   b. What kind of research design is appropriate? Why?
3. Visit Toluna (www.toluna.com).
   a. What are the surveys currently being conducted?
   b. How are the respondents being recruited for these surveys?
   c. Discuss the different type of errors likely to arise given the way the respondents are being recruited.
4. Visit the Web page of three of the marketing research firms listed in Table 1.1. What types of research designs have these firms implemented recently?
5. You are conducting an image study for Carnival Cruise Lines. As part of exploratory research, analyze the messages posted to the newsgroup rec.travel.cruises to determine the factors that consumers use in evaluating cruise companies. This newsgroup can be located at http://groups.google.com.

Group Discussion

1. Discuss the following statement: "If the research budget is limited, exploratory research can be dispensed with."
2. Discuss the following statement: "The researcher should always attempt to develop an optimal design for every marketing research project."
3. "There are many potential sources of error in a research project. It is impossible to control all of them. Hence, marketing research contains many errors, and we cannot be confident of the findings." Discuss these statements as a group. Did your group arrive at a consensus?

Hewlett-Packard Running Case

Review the Hewlett-Packard (HP) case, Case 1.1, and the questionnaire given toward the end of the book.

1. How can HP make use of exploratory research to understand how household consumers buy personal computers and related equipment?

2. Describe one way in which HP can make use of descriptive research.

3. Describe one way in which HP can make use of causal research.

4. HP would like to determine consumer response to a new lightweight tablet PC that it has developed. What research design would you recommend? Discuss how social media can be used in implementing this design.

ONLINE VIDEO CASE 3.1

NATIONAL FOOTBALL LEAGUE: The King of Professional Sports

Visit www.pearsonhighered.com/malhotra to read the video case and view the accompanying video. National Football League: The King of Professional Sports highlights the NFL's use of marketing research to foster immense goodwill and influence to make a difference to the community. The description of focus groups and consumer perception and attitudinal surveys in the video can stimulate discussion of the three basic research designs (exploratory, descriptive, and causal) and their role in helping the NFL's various social initiatives and programs. Specific marketing research questions on this and the previous chapters are posed in the video case.

LOCALLY OWNED SINCE 1869

The Vindicator

WEDNESDAY
MARCH 9, 2011
50¢

IN HIS STATE OF THE STATE ADDRESS, GOV. KASICH SAID HE IS ASKED ...

'Why do you go to Youngstown?'

GOVERNOR'S SPEECH

Valley references

Gov. John Kasich mentioned the Mahoning Valley several times during his first State of the State address.

Here are a few of them:

◆ **On the Lordstown General Motors plant:**
"We cannot let Lords-

By DAVID SKOLNICK
skolnick@vindy.com

COLUMBUS

DURING HIS FIRST STATE of the State address, Gov. John Kasich spoke of nearly every part of Ohio, with several references to the Mahoning Valley.

Most state legislators from the Valley appreciated the various shout-outs to Youngstown, Lordstown and the region. But many say they've heard it before

Ohio St. suspends and fines Tressel

Buckeyes football coach apologizes for violations

Associated Press

COLUMBUS

Ohio State suspended football coach Jim Tressel for two games and fined him $250,000 for violating NCAA rules by failing to notify the school about information he received involving two players and questionable activities involving Buckeye memorabilia.

Tressel also will receive a public reprimand and must make a

Tressel

IN SPORTS

Reaction to Tressel's pun-

LEARNING OBJECTIVES

After reading this chapter, the student should be able to:

1. Define the nature and scope of secondary data and distinguish secondary data from primary data.

2. Analyze the advantages and disadvantages of secondary data and their uses in the various steps of the marketing research process.

3. Evaluate secondary data using specifications, error, currency, objectives, nature, and dependability criteria.

4. Identify the different sources of secondary data and classify them as internal or external.

5. Explain how internal secondary data involve data warehousing, data mining, customer relationship management, and database marketing.

6. **Social Media** Describe in detail the different sources of external secondary data, including business/nongovernment, government, social media, and syndicated services.

7. Discuss the merging of internal and external secondary data with applications to geo-demographic coding and geo-visual mapping.

> **"Open-source information—also called secondary data—is the foundation for any competitive intelligence effort and can be very significant if properly analyzed."**
>
> *Paul Dishman*
> *President, Society of Competitive Intelligence Professionals (SCIP), 2002 to 2003*

Secondary Data Vindicate the *Vindicator*!

The *Vindicator* (www.vindy.com), a small-sized Youngstown, Ohio, newspaper, wanted to increase its advertising revenues. Management set forth a 1-year goal for its 14 retail and four classified salespeople to substantially increase the number of advertisers, and thus total ad revenue. To be able to increase ad revenues, the sales force needed to pinpoint what they could specifically do to recruit more advertisers to the newspaper or to increase the amount that existing advertisers were spending. From past experience, many on the sales force knew that recruiting advertisers required proving to these advertisers, with hard facts, that their money spent in the *Vindicator* would be an excellent investment. For this purpose, the internally available data routinely collected by the *Vindicator* on the number of customers, duration of subscription, renewals/nonrenewals, and so forth would be insufficient. Additional data would have to be obtained by conducting marketing research.

In this case, the *Vindicator* decided that it needed information on the market potential in advertising readership and how these numbers compared to the potential of other advertising media that the advertisers could use instead of the *Vindicator*. Although the sales force could commission marketing research to obtain primary data, such a project would be quite expensive and time-consuming. Hence, that course of action was not taken. Instead, the *Vindicator* decided to search for secondary research that could be used to obtain the answers it sought. Because the *Vindicator* is a medium-sized newspaper with limited staff resources, it turned to an outside supplier. Inland Research Corp., a small company in Erie, Pennsylvania, was commissioned to conduct a secondary research study.

Inland Research Corp. compiles data from about 40 different sources. Half of its data come from general business sources, such as the Audit Bureau of Circulations (www.accessabc.com), and the other half come from state and federal agencies, such as the U.S. Census Bureau (www.census.gov) and the Bureau of Labor Statistics (www.bls.gov). In addition to print publications, Inland Research also searches several online and Internet databases. Inland Research evaluates all secondary data by examining the methodology, accuracy, timeliness, and nature of the data. Only data from dependable sources are used.

Inland Research receives requests for data from a client who needs to solve a specific problem. It then begins an exhaustive search of its data warehouse to obtain information that is pertinent to the client's needs. In about 4 to 6 weeks, Inland Research produces a report addressing the client's problem. In the case of smaller firms like the *Vindicator*, this represents a fraction of the time it would take for the client to do the research in-house. Inland's biggest selling point is the low price it charges for its research services. Prices range from $3,595 for a newspaper with a circulation of up to 14,900 to $8,445 for a newspaper with a circulation of 60,000 or more. According to Inland Research president and CEO Jerry Szorek, "No other company produces similar reports for newspapers," which makes the information it provides to firms like the *Vindicator* extremely valuable.

For the *Vindicator*, Inland Research focused on obtaining data reports on topics such as the advertising effectiveness of and penetration for different forms of media. For example, data on the relationship between advertising frequency in different media and the resulting effectiveness were collected. Using Inland Research results and secondary data available internally within the organization, *Vindicator* sales representatives were able to persuade some current advertisers to increase the frequency at which their ads were run. They accomplished this in a number of ways utilizing the Inland reports.

For instance, one Inland Research chart demonstrated that advertisement readership grows from 53.5 percent with one ad per week to 81.3 percent with five ads per week. This gave advertisers a reason to increase the frequency of their advertising.

In an attempt to wean advertisers' dollars away from radio, *Vindicator* sales representatives were able to use Inland data indicating that each of the city's seven biggest radio stations had fewer than 8,000 listeners during an average quarter hour, whereas internal secondary data showed that the *Vindicator* had a daily circulation of 62,100 and 87,000 on Sundays, as of 2011. To reduce advertising spending on television, the sales representatives used the following statistics on viewer activity during commercials: 33.6 percent got up and left the viewing room, 29.6 percent talked with others, 9.2 percent switched channels, and 5.9 percent muted the television. Furthermore, secondary data revealed that only 21.7 percent watched the TV commercial. Such selling tactics by the sales force were successful. *Vindicator* management discovered that using secondary research during sales calls strengthened the sales pitches with hard data that could sway advertisers toward spending more on advertising in the Vindicator.[1]

Overview

Chapter 1 discussed the Internet as a source of marketing research information. As mentioned in Chapter 2, analysis of secondary data helps to first define the marketing research problem and then to develop an approach to that problem. Also, as part of formulating the research design (Chapter 3), researchers analyze the relevant secondary data, as illustrated by the *Vindicator* vignette. The relationship of secondary data to the research issues presented in the previous chapters is shown in Figure 4.1.

This chapter discusses the distinction between primary and secondary data, as well as the advantages, disadvantages, and criteria for evaluating secondary data, which can be generated

FIGURE 4.1

Relationship of Secondary Data to the Previous Chapters and the Marketing Research Process

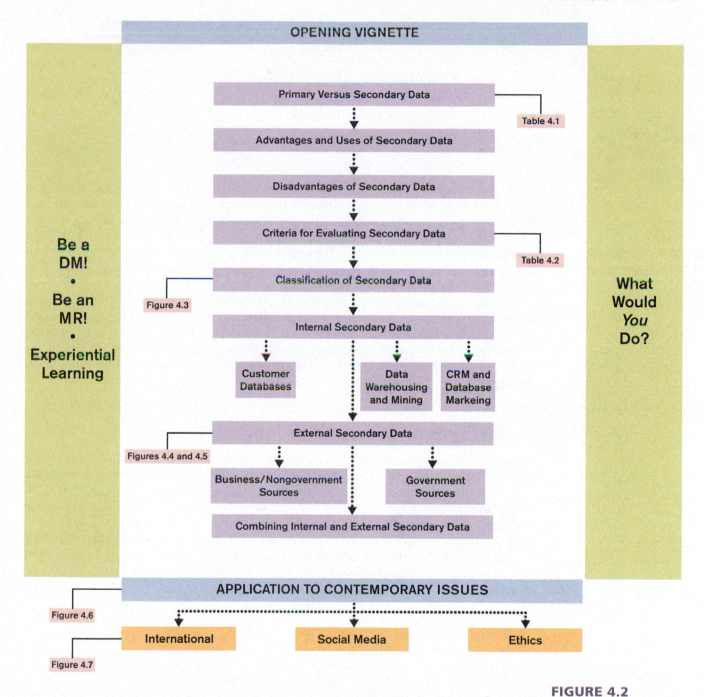

OPENING VIGNETTE

Primary Versus Secondary Data

Table 4.1

Advantages and Uses of Secondary Data

Disadvantages of Secondary Data

Criteria for Evaluating Secondary Data

Table 4.2

Classification of Secondary Data

Figure 4.3

Internal Secondary Data

Customer Databases

Data Warehousing and Mining

CRM and Database Markeing

External Secondary Data

Figures 4.4 and 4.5

Business/Nongovernment Sources

Government Sources

Combining Internal and External Secondary Data

Be a DM!
•
Be an MR!
•
Experiential Learning

What Would *You* Do?

APPLICATION TO CONTEMPORARY ISSUES

Figure 4.6

Figure 4.7

International

Social Media

Ethics

FIGURE 4.2

Secondary Data: An Overview

both internally and externally. The chapter also includes discussion of the practice of merging internal and external secondary data. Additionally, the chapter discusses the collection of international secondary data, the impact of social media, and ethical questions related to secondary data. Figure 4.2 presents an overview of this chapter.

Secondary data can best be distinguished from primary data when the purpose of the original data collection is considered.

Primary Versus Secondary Data

An early outcome of the research process is to define the marketing research problem and to identify specific research questions and hypotheses (Chapter 2). When data are collected to address a specific marketing research problem, they are referred to as **primary data.** Obtaining primary data can be expensive and time-consuming because it involves all six steps of the marketing research process (see Figure 4.1).

primary data
Data originated by the researcher for the specific purpose of addressing the research problem.

TABLE 4.1 A Comparison of Primary and Secondary Data

	Primary Data	Secondary Data
Collection purpose	For the problem at hand	For other problems
Collection process	Very involved	Rapid and easy
Collection cost	High	Relatively low
Collection time	Long	Short

secondary data
Data collected for some purpose
other than the problem at hand.

Before initiating primary data collection, a researcher should remember that the problem under study might not be unique. It is possible that someone else has investigated the same or a similar marketing research problem. A search through existing data might lead to relevant information. **Secondary data** represent any data that have already been collected for purposes other than the problem at hand. Relative to primary data collection, these data can be located quickly and inexpensively, as in the case of the *Vindicator*. The differences between primary and secondary data are summarized in Table 4.1.

It is easy to overlook the many sources of secondary data when developing a formal research design. Once a secondary data search is initiated, however, the volume of existing information can be overwhelming. In order to cost-effectively browse through this mountain of information, it is important that the researcher be familiar with various sources of secondary data, including marketing research firms that specialize in secondary data, such as Inland Research in the opening vignette.

Advantages and Uses of Secondary Data

The main advantages of secondary data are the time and money they can save. This was evident from the low-cost secondary research provided by the Inland Research Corp. in the opening vignette. Additionally, the collection of some secondary data, such as those provided by the U.S. Census Bureau, would not be feasible for individual firms such as Inland Research or the *Vindicator*. Although it is rare for secondary data to provide all the answers to a nonroutine research problem, analysis of secondary data should always be the first step taken toward solving a research problem. Secondary data provided the *Vindicator* with a better understanding of advertising effectiveness and penetration for different forms of media. Such data can help the researcher to:

1. Identify the problem.
2. Better understand and define the problem.
3. Develop an approach to the problem.
4. Formulate an appropriate research design (e.g., by identifying the key variables).
5. Answer certain research questions and test some hypotheses.
6. Interpret primary data with more insight.

Additionally, secondary data also are useful for estimating demand, monitoring the environment, developing business intelligence systems, segmenting and targeting, and a variety of other applications.

Given these advantages and uses of secondary data, we state a basic rule of research:

Examine available secondary data first. The research project should proceed to primary data collection only when the secondary data sources have been exhausted or yield marginal returns.

In the opening vignette, the *Vindicator* exemplifies the rich dividends obtained by following this rule. Another example involves Frost National Bank.

Research in Action

Bank "Zips" Up the Market

From its inception as a small downtown San Antonio bank in 1868, Frost Bank (www.frostbank.com) has grown into a multibillion-dollar, full-service financial institution with more than $13.3 billion in assets at the beginning of 2010. It offers a full range of banking and financial services to retail and commercial customers throughout Texas. The bank was considering modifying its Young Leaders Club (YLC) account to enhance its appeal to San Antonians between the ages of 21 and 35. The YLC offered members a checking account with enhancements such as life insurance, discount movie tickets, store coupons, tours, and social events, all for a monthly membership fee.

Extensive analysis of secondary data was conducted. Using internal secondary data on transactions and addresses, club members were evaluated by zip code and account activity. The results of zip code analysis helped attract advertising and discount coupons from merchants in areas of San Antonio where large numbers of YLC members lived. External secondary data available on this age group provided additional insights for redeveloping the YLC package. Census information related to population, age, and income allowed Frost National Bank to estimate the size of the potential market for the YLC. This secondary data analysis was followed by focus groups and survey research. After completing its

market research, which began with the examination of secondary data, Frost National Bank was able to significantly increase the number of YLC accounts in the target market.

As of 2011, the YLC members enjoyed access via text to all of their Frost deposit and loan accounts—checking, savings, money market accounts, CDs, and business and personal loans. "Our customers live highly mobile lifestyles, and Frost Mobile text messaging offers them versatility and freedom to manage their finances on their busy schedules," said Bobby Berman, Frost executive vice president of e-commerce.[2]

Source: MWarts/Shutterstock.

This example shows that analysis of secondary data can provide valuable insights and lay the foundation for conducting more formal research, such as focus groups and surveys. The researcher should be cautious when using secondary data, however, because there are some disadvantages.

Be an MR!	Be a DM!
Nike: Celebrating Celebrity Endorsement	
Search the Internet—including social media—as well as your library's online databases to obtain information on the use of celebrity endorsements in marketing. You are conducting a marketing research project to determine the effectiveness of celebrity endorsements in Nike's advertising. What type of secondary data would you examine?	As the marketing director of Nike, how would you use secondary data on celebrity endorsements to determine whether you should continue to contract celebrities to endorse the Nike brand?

Social Media

Disadvantages of Secondary Data

The value of secondary data is typically limited by their degree of fit with the current research problem and by concerns regarding data accuracy. The objectives, nature, and methods used to collect secondary data might not be compatible with the current situation. Also, secondary data might be lacking in terms of accuracy, compatibility of units of measurement, or time frame. Before using secondary data, it is important to evaluate them using the criteria in Table 4.2. The Inland Research Corp. used similar criteria in the opening vignette.

TABLE 4.2 Criteria for Evaluating Secondary Data

Criteria	Issues	Remarks
Specifications/Methodology	Data collection method Response rate Quality of data Sampling technique Sample size Questionnaire design Fieldwork Data analysis	Data should be reliable, valid, and generalizable to the problem at hand.
Error/Accuracy	Examine errors in: approach, research design, sampling, data collection, data analysis, reporting	Assess accuracy by comparing data from different sources.
Currency	Time lag between collection and publication Frequency of updates	Census data are periodically updated by syndicated firms.
Objective	Why were the data collected?	The objective will determine the relevance of data.
Nature	Definition of key variables Units of measurement Categories used Relationships examined	Reconfigure the data to increase their usefulness, if possible.
Dependability	Expertise, credibility, reputation, and trustworthiness of the source	Data should be obtained from an original rather than an acquired source.

Criteria for Evaluating Secondary Data

The criteria used for evaluating secondary data consist of specifications, error, currency, objective, nature, and dependability.

Specifications: Methodology Used to Collect the Data

The research design specifications—that is, the methodology used to collect the data—should be examined to identify possible sources of bias. Factors that are important in identifying potential error, as well as relevance of the data, include the size and nature of the sample, response rate and quality, questionnaire design and administration, procedures used for fieldwork, and data analysis and reporting procedures. One reason it is advantageous to use data from the originating source is that a description of the research design is typically provided as a part of the original published study.

Error: Accuracy of the Data

Both secondary and primary data can have errors, stemming from the research approach, research design, sampling, data collection, analysis, and reporting stages of the project. Moreover, it is difficult to evaluate the accuracy of secondary data when the researcher has not directly participated in the research.

Secondary data can be obtained either directly from the source that originated the data or from a secondary source that secured the data from someone else. The further removed one is from the originating data source, the greater the possibility of problems with accuracy. An original source is likely to be more accurate and complete than a nonoriginating source. Always use the originating source if it is available.

One approach to controlling accuracy problems is to find multiple sources of data and compare those using standard statistical procedures. The accuracy of secondary data can also be

Research in Action

Population Dynamics and the Accuracy of Secondary Data

The International Council of Shopping Centers (www.icsc.org) conducted a study to evaluate the consistency of market profiles provided by private vendors of secondary demographic information. Several vendors (e.g., CACI, www.caci.com; Nielsen, www.nielsen. com; and Infogroup, www.infogroup.com) participated in the research. Three markets were analyzed: Baltimore, Detroit, and Phoenix. The vendors supplied the Council with statistics and demographic data for each market area. The Council then analyzed the differences among the vendors' reports using standard statistical procedures.

The results indicated that there was little variation in the data from different sources when the population was relatively stable. However, the vendor-supplied demographic data varied considerably in areas with rapidly changing population. In such cases, the Council recommends that users verify vendor data findings with field investigations of their own.[3]

verified by conducting field investigations, as recommended by the International Council of Shopping Centers.

As this example indicates, the accuracy of secondary data can vary, particularly if they relate to highly volatile market conditions. Moreover, data obtained from different sources might not agree. In these cases, the researcher should verify the accuracy of secondary data by conducting pilot studies or by other appropriate methods. With a little creativity, this can often be accomplished with little expense and effort.

Currency: When the Data Were Collected

Secondary data might not be current. A time lag might exist between data collection and publication, as with census data. Additionally, the data might not be updated frequently enough to answer questions related to the problem at hand. Marketing research requires current data; therefore, the value of secondary data is diminished as they become dated. For instance, although the data from the 2010 census are comprehensive, they might not be applicable to a metropolitan area whose population has changed rapidly during the last few years. Thus, such data might not be current enough for use by Home Depot in predicting potential demand for the year 2015. Fortunately, several marketing research firms update census data periodically and make the current information available for a fee.

Objective: The Purpose for the Study

Understanding why secondary data were originally collected can sensitize the researcher to the limitations of using them for the current marketing problem. Suppose *Sports Illustrated* surveyed its renewing subscriber base regarding readership of its articles and recall of its advertising. One objective of this study would be to use the information to sell advertising space. With that in mind, the results of the study would be made available to advertising managers, who would likely make decisions regarding advertising placement. This type of secondary information might be relevant to the question of where to place future advertising. The results of this survey from *Sports Illustrated* would be biased, however, in that they would reflect the behavior of its renewing subscribers, a group that might be more involved with the magazine than the general subscribers. To accurately interpret this secondary data, the advertising manager would have to understand how closely the *Sports Illustrated* renewing segment represents its total subscribing population.

Nature: The Content of the Data

The *nature*, or *content*, of the data should be examined with special attention to the definition of key variables, the units of measurement, the categories used, and the relationships examined. One of the most frustrating limitations of secondary data comes from differences in definition, units of measurement, the time frame examined, or questionable assumptions regarding the relationships of key variables. If the key variables have not been defined or are defined in a manner inconsistent with the researcher's definition, then the usefulness of the data is limited.

Consider, for example, secondary data related to retail sales. As the researcher interprets the information, questions might arise regarding whether the sales are defined net of returned items or whether they represent cash and credit sales. For example, if Visa decides to investigate the sale of credit card services, this level of distinction becomes critical. Visa spends millions of dollars in marketing the card to retailers and in advertising the card to consumers. The 2012 Olympic Games mark the 26th year of Visa's sponsorship. In order to determine the effectiveness of its Olympic advertising and sponsorships, Visa needs secondary data with relevant content.

Secondary data might be measured in units that are inappropriate for the current problem. For example, income can be measured by individual, family, household, or spending unit, and it can be reported as gross or net after taxes and deductions. If income categories reported in secondary sources are different from those required by the research, the information might not be usable. If Mercedes is interested in high-income consumers with gross annual household incomes of more than $90,000, then secondary data with income categories less than $15,000, $15,001 to $35,000, $35,001 to $50,000, and more than $50,000 will not be of much use.

Finally, we must consider the variables of interest to the researcher. For example, if the researcher is interested in actual purchase behavior, then information on attitudes that only imply behavior might have limited usefulness.

Dependability: How Dependable Are the Data?

An overall indication of the dependability of the data can be obtained by examining the expertise, credibility, reputation, and trustworthiness of the source. This information can be obtained by checking with others who have used information from this source. Data published to promote sales, to advance specific interests, or to carry on propaganda should be viewed with suspicion. The same can be said of data published anonymously or in a form that attempts to hide the details of the data collection methodology and process. In contrast, secondary data published by reputable organizations, such as the U.S. Census Bureau, are very dependable and of high quality.

Be a DM!	Be an MR!
Gallup Polls: On a Gallup	
As the CEO of Home Depot, you come across a Gallup poll reporting that an increasing number of women are shopping for home improvement products and services. How will you use this information to improve the competitiveness of Home Depot?	Visit www.gallup.com. Examine the information on how Gallup conducts its polls. By applying the criteria we have considered, evaluate the quality of Gallup polls. Search the Internet—including social media—to obtain insights into women's role in purchasing home improvement products.

Classification of Secondary Data

As represented in Figure 4.3 and discussed earlier in this chapter, the two primary sources of secondary data are internal and external data.

internal data
Data available within the organization for which the research is being conducted.

external data
Data that originate external to the organization.

Internal data are data generated within the organization for which the research is being conducted. **External data** are data generated by sources outside the organization. In the opening vignette, the data on circulation obtained from the *Vindicator*'s records were internal data. However, data obtained from Inland Research on advertising effectiveness and penetration for different forms of media were external data. Internal secondary data may be available in a ready-to-use form or may require further processing to extract the information needed. Important forms of internal secondary data include customer databases, data warehousing and data mining, and customer relationship management and database marketing. External sources of information include general business/nongovernment, government, and syndicated services. Social media can be a source of both internal and external secondary data and are discussed later in this chapter. Internal sources are discussed next, followed by external data. Given their importance and specialized nature, syndicate sources are given greater coverage and discussed in Chapter 5.

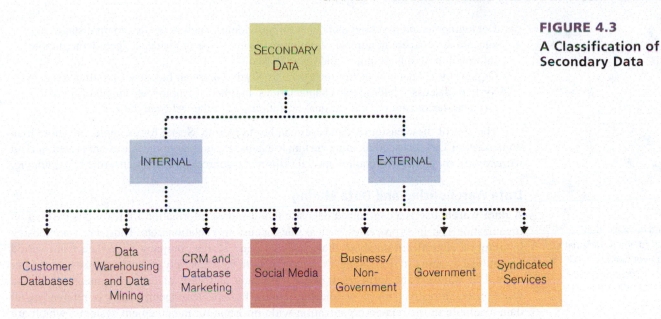

FIGURE 4.3

A Classification of Secondary Data

Internal Secondary Data

Before collecting external secondary data, it is always useful to analyze internal secondary data. Internal data are typically generated as part of the ongoing process of doing business. These data can come from accounting records, sales reports, production or operation reports, social media such as the company's blogs, Facebook, or Twitter accounts, or internal experts. In the opening vignette, the *Vindicator* routinely collects data on the number of customers, the duration each customer has been a subscriber, renewals/nonrenewals, and so on. Although it is possible that internal secondary data might be available in usable form, it is more typical that considerable processing effort will be required before such data can be used. For example, cash register receipts of a department store might contain a wealth of information, such as sales by product line, sales by specific stores, sales by geographical region, sales by cash versus credit purchases, sales in specific time periods, sales by size of purchase, and so on. To derive this information, however, data must be transcribed from the paper-based sales receipts to a computer database and analyzed extensively. Many organizations are building sophisticated internal databases as platforms for their marketing efforts. Of special interest to us are customer databases.

Social Media

Customer Databases

For many companies, the first step in creating a customer database is to transfer raw sales information, such as that found on sales call reports or invoices, to a personal computer. Customer information also is obtained from other sources, such as warranty cards and loyalty programs (e.g., frequent flier programs of airlines). This is augmented with demographic and psychographic information about the customers obtained from external secondary sources. **Psychographics** refer to quantified psychological profiles of individuals. Several companies in this business, including R. R. Donnelley (www.rrdonnelley.com), Experian (www.experian.com), R. L. Polk (www.polk.com), and others, have compiled household lists that include names, addresses, and a great deal of individual-specific data. The elements of a customer database include the following:

psychographics
Quantified psychological profiles of individuals.

- A unique ID or match code
- Name and title of the individual organization
- Mailing address
- Telephone number(s)
- E-mail address
- Source of referral, inquiry, or order
- Complete transaction history by date, frequency, purchase amounts, and products
- Credit history and rating score

■ Demographic and psychographic data for individuals, such as gender, marital status, age, education, occupation, number of children, income, type of residence, geo-demographic information, psychographics, and lifestyle data

■ Organizational data for institutions, such as North American Industry Classification System (discussed later in this chapter), sales, number of employees, length of time in business, headquarters, international operations, and other relevant data

The size of these customer databases can be staggering. Sears, for example, has more than 75 percent of U.S. households in its customer database. Such large databases are stored in *data warehouses;* their analysis requires special skills and resources and has been termed *data mining.*

Data Warehousing and Data Mining

data warehouse
A centralized database that consolidates company-wide data from a variety of operational systems.

A **data warehouse** is a centralized database that captures information from various parts of an organization's business processes, such as sales or customer relations, etc. Thus, data warehousing is simply a centralized database that condenses and stores company-wide data from varied operational systems so that the data are easy to retrieve. Generally, what businesses want from their data warehousing infrastructures is efficiency and ease of use. This means that data warehousing infrastructures (or architecture) should be capable of incorporating or referencing all data available in the related organization-wide information management systems, which are usually specially designed to suit the organization's corporate database management needs. Some databases are even equipped with advanced analytical features or are compatible with data-analysis software so as to facilitate the process of data mining.

data mining
Technique involving the use of powerful computers and advanced statistical and other software to analyze large databases in order to discover hidden patterns in the data.

Data mining involves the use of powerful computers with advanced statistical packages and other software to analyze large databases in order to discover hidden patterns in the data. The term derives its meaning from the exercise of digging through a lot of "coal" (seemingly valueless data) to discover "golden nuggets" (invaluable marketing information). The process of data mining usually consists of five major components:

■ Extract, transform, and load transaction data onto the data warehouse system.
■ Store and manage the data in a multidimensional database system.
■ Provide data access to business analysts and information technology professionals.
■ Analyze the data by application software.
■ Present the data in a useful format, such as a graph or table to display the patterns in the data.

The patterns discovered can be very useful for targeting marketing effort. For example, data mining revealed that husbands tend to buy additional life insurance immediately after the birth of their first child. Therefore, Allstate's (www.allstate.com) slogan, "You're in good hands," is particularly appropriate for targeting first-time fathers with life insurance products. Customer databases and data mining are the building blocks for customer relationship management systems.

Customer Relationship Management and Database Marketing

customer relationship management (CRM) system
A decision support system that is used for managing the interactions between an organization and its customers.

A **customer relationship management (CRM) system** is a decision support system (see Chapter 1) that is used for managing the interactions between an organization and its customers. CRM is a widely used strategy for managing a company's interactions with customers, clients, and sales prospects. It uses technology to organize, automate, and synchronize business processes including those for marketing, customer service, and technical support. It helps the firm to find, attract, and win new clients, nurture and retain those the company already has, entice former clients back into the fold, and reduce the costs of marketing and client service. CRM is a company-wide business strategy embracing all client-facing departments and beyond. In an effective CRM, people, processes, and technology work together to enhance customer satisfaction, increase profitability, and reduce operational costs.

database marketing
The practice of using CRM databases to develop relationships and highly targeted marketing efforts with individuals and customer groups.

Database marketing is the practice of using CRM databases to develop relationships and highly targeted marketing efforts with individuals and customer groups. The CRM databases can be analyzed in terms of a customer's activity over the life of the business relationship. Signs of change in the usage relationships (e.g., a heavy user decreases usage) or significant "customer life cycle" events (e.g., anniversaries) can be identified and addressed. These databases provide the essential tool needed to nurture, expand, and protect the customer relationship and can also serve as a foundation for developing marketing programs.

Organizations that bill their customers for services or that provide statements of customer activities are in a particularly strong position to use their internal secondary data. Utilities, cable television systems, banks, department stores, and health care providers are all examples of organizations that use database marketing.

Research in Action

General Electric: Electrifying Marketing with a Customer Database

As of 2011, General Electric (GE; www.ge.com) operates in more than 100 countries around the world with more than half its revenues coming from outside the United States. In the United States, the company has built a huge customer database of more than 60 million households, which it uses effectively for target marketing. GE has combined demographic, psychographic, media consumption, and purchasing data available externally with internal customer transaction records to pinpoint a customer's appliance ownership and history.

Using this database, GE can determine, for example, which customers are typically ready to replace their washing machines: those who bought the washing machine 6 years ago and have large families. The company can then direct marketing efforts in the form of gift certificates, discounts, and special deals for washing machines at these customers. The database has electrified GE's marketing, resulting in increased market share and profitability.[4]

Source: Kevork Djansezian/AP Images

As the GE example illustrates, database marketing can lead to quite sophisticated and targeted marketing programs. Most large organizations have intranets, which greatly facilitate the search for and access to internal secondary data. Procter & Gamble (P&G), for example, has developed powerful intranet applications that enable its managers worldwide to search for past and current research studies and a wide variety of marketing-related information on the basis of keywords. Once located, the information can be accessed online. Sensitive information can be secured electronically with user names and passwords.

Be a DM!	Be an MR!
An Apple for Every Household	
As the marketing director for Apple, how would you use database marketing to increase the penetration of Apple computers in U.S. households?	Visit www.apple.com and search the Internet—including social media—to obtain information on Apple's marketing strategy. Identify the variables available internally within Apple as well as from external sources that you would use to build a database to help Apple increase its penetration of U.S. households.

Social Media

External Secondary Data

External secondary data sources have grown dramatically over the past 20 years. This growth has been stimulated, in part, by the introduction of personal computers into the workplace, which gives employees easy access to commercial databases. Therefore, it is useful to classify them.

As shown in Figure 4.3, external sources include business/nongovernment, government, and syndicated services. Social media as a source of external secondary data are discussed later in the chapter. The following section provides an overview of some of the business sources of external secondary data.

Business/Nongovernmental Data

Business/nongovernment sources are used as a broad category and encompass nonprofit organizations (e.g., chambers of commerce), trade and professional organizations, commercial publishers, investment brokerage firms, and for-profit firms. Most of this data can be conveniently accessed over the Internet. To enable you to sort through the overwhelming amount of secondary data, we begin our discussion with a classification of business/nongovernment sources of secondary data. These sources include guides, directories, indices, and statistical data (see Figure 4.4).

Businesses publish a great deal of information in the form of books, periodicals, journals, newspapers, magazines, reports, and trade literature. The Audit Bureau of Circulations, cited in the opening vignette, is a general business source that provides data on audits of media, such as newspapers, consumer magazines, trade shows, and the Web. Moody's (www.moodys.com) and Standard & Poor's (www.standardandpoors.com) provide information on U.S. and foreign companies. Another useful source for industrial brand and trade information is ThomasNet (www.thomasnet.com). Valuable marketing and marketing research information can be obtained from SecondaryData.com (www.secondarydata.com).

A variety of business-related sites can provide sales leads, mailing lists, business profiles, and credit ratings for U.S. businesses. Many sites supply information on businesses within a specific industry. For example, all of the American Marketing Association's publications can be searched by keywords at www.marketingpower.com. Encyclopedia Britannica provides free online access to its entire 32-volume set (www.britannica.com). Data on U.S. manufacturers and key decision makers can be obtained from Harris InfoSource, a division of D&B, (www.harrisinfo.com). Another good source is Infogroup (www.infogroup.com).

Guides, indices, and directories can help in locating information available from general business sources. Sources also are available for identifying statistical data. A brief description of each of these resource categories follows.

GUIDES Standard or recurring information is summarized in guides. Guides provide a path to other sources of secondary data contained in directories or published by professional or trade associations. Because guides can open the door to other sources of data, they are one of the first sources a researcher should consult. For example, *Encyclopedia of Business Information Source* (www.gale.cengage.com) identifies live, print, and electronic sources of information listed under alphabetically arranged subjects—industries and business concepts and practices. Listings are arranged by type of resource (directories, databases, newsletters, indices, research centers, etc.) within each subject. @BRINT (www.brint.com) is a guide to business technology management and knowledge management sites with editorial comments.

INDICES AND BIBLIOGRAPHIES Bibliographies, which are organized alphabetically by topic, are another good place to start external secondary research. Current or historic discussion of a particular topic of interest will be indexed in these references, leading the researcher to a number of authors.

FIGURE 4.4

A Classification of Business/Nongovernment Sources

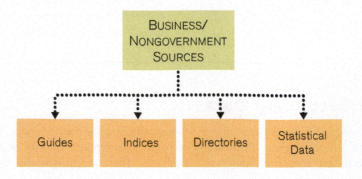

Several indices are available for referencing both academic and business topics. *Business Periodicals Index* (www.hwwilson.com/newdds/wp.cfm), produced by The H.W. Wilson Company, is a bibliographic database that cites articles of at least one column in length from English-language periodicals published in the United States and elsewhere. *Social Sciences Citation Index®*, accessed via *Web of Science®* (www.thomsonreuters.com), provides you with quick, powerful access to the bibliographic and citation information you need to find research data, analyze trends, and locate journals and researchers. Several newspapers, for example *The Wall Street Journal* (www.wsj.com), have an index to conduct a guided search. *CI Resource Index* (www.bidigital.com/ci) features sites for competitive intelligence information.

The Web site "ipl2: information you can trust" (www.ipl.org) was launched in January 2010, merging the collections of resources from the Internet Public Library (IPL) and the Librarians' Internet Index (LII) Web sites. ipl2 is a public service organization and features "Ask an ipl2 Librarian" service and is a useful source for indexes and bibliographies.

DIRECTORIES   Directories provide brief descriptions of companies, organizations, or individuals. They are helpful for identifying manufacturers operating in a particular market, for compiling names and addresses of associations in a sales territory, or for verifying names and addresses of prospective customers who carry a specific job title. *Standard & Poor's Corporate Descriptions* is an example of a directory database that provides summary data on publicly held U.S. corporations. A secondary researcher wanting to compile information on a competitor or prospective customer can obtain data related to the growth of the organization, the size of its workforce, and its financial performance.

Firmographics are the business equivalent of demographics. They include variables such as market share, corporate location, industry classification, and employment size. D&B (www.dnb.com) provides this type of data. The national electronic *Yellow Pages* (www.yellowpages.com) is the largest database of U.S. companies. This database contains more than 10 million records compiled from the nation's 4,800 telephone books. The names, addresses, phone numbers, and NAIC codes for manufacturers, wholesalers, retailers, professionals, and service organizations are available through this source. *Gale Directory of Online, Portable, and Internet Databases* (library.dialog.com/bluesheets/html/bl0230.html) provides detailed information on publicly available databases and database products.

BUSINESS/NONGOVERNMENTAL STATISTICAL DATA   Business research often involves compiling statistical data reflecting market or industry factors. A historic perspective of industry participation and growth rates can provide a context for market share analysis. Market statistics related to population demographics, purchasing levels, television viewership, and product usage are just some of the types of nongovernmental statistics available from secondary sources.

Standard & Poor's Data Services (www.standardandpoors.com) provides several databases and/or data sets including the Compustat® North America and Global databases. Several commercial firms specialize in conducting information searches over the Internet and obtaining data from other secondary sources. Infogroup/ORC (www.infogroup.com) provides customized research and analysis related to market and industry profiles, business and competitive intelligence, benchmarking, new business opportunities, and other applications.

Government Sources

The U.S. government is the largest source of secondary data in this country and in the world. The data the government collects could not feasibly be collected by private industry. Its value ranges from use in developing sales forecasts and market potential estimates to simply locating specific retailers, wholesalers, or manufacturers. The breadth and accuracy of government sources make it a rich source of secondary data. In the opening vignette, Inland Research obtained data from government sources such as the U.S. Census Bureau and the Bureau of Labor Statistics. Government sources can be divided into census data and other types.

CENSUS DATA   Census data are useful in a variety of marketing research projects. The demographic data collected by the U.S. Census Bureau include information about household types, sex, age, marital status, and race. Consumption detail related to automobile ownership, housing characteristics, work status, and practices as well as occupations are just a few of the categories of information available. What makes this demographic information particularly valuable to marketers is that these data can be geographically categorized at various levels of detail. These data can be summarized at various levels: city block, block group, census tract, Metropolitan Statistical Area (MSA), Consolidated Metropolitan Statistical Area (CMSA), region (Northeast, Midwest, South, and West), or they can be aggregated for the nation as a whole. Figure 4.5 shows the geographic subdivision of an MSA. Census tracts have a population of more than 4,000 and are defined by local communities. In urban areas, MSAs have a population of at least 50,000 and comprise counties containing or surrounding a central city. In addition, census data are available by civil divisions, such as wards, cities, counties, and states.

In general, the quality of census data is quite high, and the data often are extremely detailed. To facilitate business analysis, this information is available in multiple forms. One can purchase computer tapes, diskettes, or CD-ROMs from the U.S. Census Bureau or download from the Internet for a nominal fee and recast this information into the desired format. Important census data include Census of Housing, Census of Manufacturers, Census of Population, Census of Retail Trade, Census of Service Industries, and Census of Wholesale Trade. Nielsen (www.nielsen.com) has created a number of research tools using census and other lifestyle data. Integrating enhanced census data with internal company databases is a useful application of multiple secondary sources. This integration of secondary data is discussed later in the chapter.

Experiential Learning

U.S. Census Bureau

The 2010 census of the United States provides insight into the demographic profile of not only the United States in full, but also smaller U.S. regions, such as states and MSAs. Go to the home page for the U.S. Census Bureau (www.census.gov) and do the following:

1. Find the population clocks on the U.S. Census Bureau's home page. What is the current population estimate for the United States? For the world?

2. Compare your home state's "population percentage change from 2000 to 2010" with that of the United States in full. Which grew faster?

3. Find out how many "singles without children living at home" were counted in your zip code in the 2010 census.

OTHER GOVERNMENT SOURCES   In addition to the census, the federal government collects and publishes a great deal of statistical data, much of it relevant to business. The United States, Mexico, and Canada have created a new common classification system to replace the previous

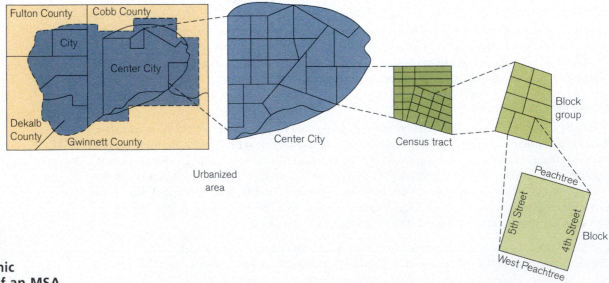

FIGURE 4.5

The Geographic Subdivision of an MSA

classification of each country. The 4-digit Standard Industrial Classification Code (SIC) of the United States has been replaced by a 6-digit North American Industry Classification System (NAICS). The two extra digits in the NAICS accommodate a larger number of sectors and are more flexible in designating subsections. NAICS is organized in a hierarchical structure, much like the SIC. The new codes will be reviewed every 5 years.

Other useful government publications include *County and City Data Book, Statistical Abstract of the United States, Health, United States, State and Metropolitan Area Data Book,* and *World Factbook*. Several U.S. government sources can be accessed at FedWorld (www.fedworld.gov). Extensive business statistics can be obtained from FedStats (www.fedstats.gov). FedStats compiles statistical information from more than 100 agencies. The U.S. Department of Commerce can be reached at www.doc.gov. Bureau of Census information can be accessed via the Department of Commerce Web site or directly at www.census.gov. The Bureau of Labor Statistics provides useful information, especially Consumer Expenditure Surveys (www.bls.gov). A wide range of economic statistics can be obtained from the Bureau of Economic Analysis (www.bea.gov). Information about public companies can be obtained from the EDGAR Database of Corporate Information, which contains SEC filings (www.sec.gov/edgar.shtml). Information about small businesses can be obtained at www.sbaonline.sba.gov. The U.S. Government Printing Office has launched the federal digital system (fdsys) that provides free online access to official federal government publications at www.gpo.gov/fdsys. These government sites can provide valuable information to the marketing researcher, as exemplified by the efforts of Greensboro, North Carolina, to attract young people.

Research in Action

Over the Hill for Greensboro

For years, officials in Greensboro, North Carolina (www.greensboro-nc.gov) have been worried about the lack of young people in the community. The population of certain age groups, namely those ages 15 to 19, 20 to 24, and 25 to 34, has been shrinking. A comparison of the 2000 census data with information in the 2005 American Community Survey showed that Greensboro's average age had increased 2.8 years, from 33.0 to 35.8 years of age, drastically higher than nearby North Carolina cities that were studied for comparison purposes. Raleigh had an age increase of 1.7 years, and Durham had an age increase of 1.5 years. This either meant older people were arriving for retirement, younger people were leaving, or both! A comparison of the 2005 population with that of 2000 by age group revealed that both were true.

This analysis not only confirmed officials' worries but also pointed to a dwindling working population, the group that pays taxes and effectively provides revenue for the city. In business terms, Greensboro was losing sales. The growth in the active-retiree-age population (ages 55 to 59 and 60 to 64) was likely to continue: The first Baby Boomers had turned 60, and North Carolina, with its mountains, beaches, moderate climate, golf courses, and military bases, likely will remain among the nation's leading destinations for retirees.

Based on the analysis of secondary data, Greensboro is putting its marketing energy into attracting younger people, namely professionals aged 20 to 39. An example of this can be seen in the revitalization of and increased activity in the downtown area to give Greensboro more of an urban feel and, hopefully, to attract target "consumers." The city has undertaken several projects like the installation of WiFi on South Elm Street and in Center City Park to program-based initiatives with the goal of advancing leadership opportunities, voice, and quality of life for all young professionals in the Greensboro community. On May 11, 2010, council member Danny Thompson nominated Greensboro as the Best Community for Young People.[5]

In concluding this section, we describe a general procedure for conducting an online search.

How to Conduct an Online Search for External Secondary Data

The following is a general search procedure for locating relevant external secondary data by conducting an online search.

1. Search the online database(s) of your library using key words. Your library provides access to a rich set of databases, and this should be the starting point for your search.
2. Run the search in Google (www.google.com), Yahoo! (www.yahoo.com), Ask.com, Bing (www.bing.com), and possibly other search engines. Use the advanced search option to conduct a more specific search and narrow the list.

3. For industry and company financial information, search financial Web sites such as Google Finance (finance.google.com), CNNMoney (money.cnn.com), Yahoo! Finance (finance.yahoo.com), Bloomberg (www.bloomberg.com), wikinvest (www.wikinvest.com), or similar sites. For information on a specific company, it is helpful to use the trading symbol to get a quote on the stock price. The stock price information contains links to other financial data. Each of the financial Web sites listed here has a provision for obtaining the trading symbol for a specific company.

4. Conduct a search of the social media, if appropriate.

   a. Blogs can be searched by using blog search engines: Technorati (www.technorati.com), IceRocket (www.icerocket.com), Bloglines (www.bloglines.com), or Google Blog Search (blogsearch.google.com). Blogpulse (www.blogpulse.com) is powered by Nielsen and tracks well over 100 million blogs.

   b. Search Facebook and MySpace. Facebook is focusing on the development of analytical tools for page owners, advertisers, and platform developers. IceRocket has dedicated searches for MySpace.com.

   c. Conduct a Twitter search. A prominent set of social media trends is Twitter's Trending Topics (www.twitter.com). These are the words most used in tweets.

   d. Search YouTube (www.youtube.com) for videos and Flickr (www.flickr.com) to locate relevant photos. If photos are of particular interest, search other photo-sharing sites such as Snapfish (www.snapfish.com), Shutterfly (www.shutterfly.com), Photobucket (www.photobucket.com), and Kodak Gallery (www.kodakgallery.com).

   e. If podcasts are of interest, search Apple's iTunes (www.apple.com/itunes), the Who's Who of podcasting. Search engine Podnova (www.podnova.com) lists 90,000 podcast programs in its directory and Podcast Alley (www.podcastalley.com) has more than 37,000 programs.

   f. Search social-bookmarking sites like delicious (www.delicious.com), Digg (www.digg.com), Mixx (www.mixx.com), Chipmark (www.chipmark.com), Linkroll (www.linkroll.com), and StumbleUpon (www.stumbleupon.com).

   g. Web-based news aggregators (such as Bloglines) make it easy to collect and read information published using RSS (really simple syndication). Use them to aggregate and simplify your search.

5. Marketing research reports may be obtained from Mintel (www.mintel.com) and MarketResearch.com. Other companies provide more specialized reports. For example, Packaged Facts (www.packagedfacts.com) compiles marketing research related to the food, beverage, consumer packaged goods, and demographic sectors. General news sites such as Dow Jones Factiva (www.factiva.com) also contain useful information.

6. Vertical search engines are available for searching specific industries. For example, ChemIndustry.com searches articles about the chemical industry, Ebuild (www.ebuild.com) contains information about the construction industry, ThomasNet (www.thomasnet.net) searches industrial parts, and Lawyers.com and Findlaw.com mine legal information.

7. Reports and information are also available for purchase from syndicated firms as described in Chapter 5.

Combining Internal and External Secondary Data

The usefulness of secondary data can be greatly enhanced when internally generated data are merged with data obtained from external sources. By using both internal and external secondary sources, marketing researchers can overlay demographic, economic, or business statistics on proprietary customer files containing transaction data. These data can then be used to develop market assessments or profiles of various customer groups or simply to educate the sales force. The combination of internal and external data results in inexpensive and valuable information that can be used for a variety of purposes, including database marketing, discussed earlier. The following sections describe the merging of internal and external secondary data with applications to geo-demographic coding and geo-visual mapping.

Geo-Demographic Coding

Geo-demographic coding involves merging internal customer data with external geographic, demographic, and lifestyle data on the same customers. Some **syndicated services,** which typically offer their information databases by subscription, have developed demographic and psychographic databases at the household level, along with many products based on these data.

Consider a cable television operator, such as Comcast, that maintains a computerized database of its cable subscribers. This internal database contains customer information on the number of cable services subscribed to, the length of service, changes in subscribed services over time, and the billing history for the past 3 years. Imagine that the president of the cable company has ambitious plans to increase penetration and market share over the next year. He is looking for a recommendation regarding which geographic markets to target. He wants the geographic market potential, profitability of various customer segments, and current cable operating restrictions to be incorporated into this analysis.

In response to this request, the director of marketing research decides to supplement the internal customer database with external secondary data. To expand the internal customer file, the director reviews several outside sources of geographic, demographic, and lifestyle data and then selects The Nielsen Company.

Nielsen (www.nielsen.com) combines data from a number of sources, including the U.S. Census and commercial marketing research firms, such as Arbitron (www.arbitron.com), Experian Simmons (www.experian.com), and GfK MRI (www.gfkmri.com). One of its products, PRIZM (Potential Rating Index for Zip Markets), seems highly appropriate for this research problem. PRIZM is a target marketing system that describes every U.S. neighborhood in terms of 62 distinct lifestyle types called *clusters*. Geographic matching of the internal customer database with PRIZM files begins with a zip code match followed by street address.

These external data are overlaid on the customer file in a process called *geo-coding*. The researcher can use the geo-coded information to develop demographic and lifestyle profiles of customer types in terms of cable subscription levels or any other relevant variable. For example, the analysis of geo-coded data might reveal that heavy users of cable television can be described as midscale families with children at home. This group falls into the lifestyle cluster PRIZM has named "pools and patios." The PRIZM profiles provide a colorful description of customer segments in terms of income, education, and family size as well as lifestyles. Combining profiles with customer profit history helps the researcher formulate the cable company's expansion plans. Based on this information, the cable company can target direct selling efforts and direct-mail campaigns and also design an appropriate advertising campaign to reach heavy users of cable television.

Be an MR!	Be a DM!
A Subway on Every Subway!	
Visit www.subway.com and search the Internet—including social media—as well as your library's online databases to obtain information on Subway's marketing program. Write a report about the PRIZM product and its appropriateness for determining Subway restaurant locations.	As Subway's marketing chief, how will you use geo-demographic information to enhance your market share?

Social Media

Geo-Visual Databases

Another factor to consider before beginning a marketing campaign for our Comcast example is the physical coverage of the cable system's wire. It is pointless to launch a full-scale effort in geographic areas where cable services are not currently available. This pitfall can be avoided by making use of geo-visual databases. **Geo-visual databases** are created by combining internal customer databases with geographic data, as from the U.S. Census Bureau, and making use of appropriate computer mapping software. **Computer mapping** generates thematic maps for solving marketing problems by electronically combining geographic and demographic information and a company's sales data or other proprietary information.

---

geo-demographic coding
Involves merging internal customer data with external geographic, demographic, and lifestyle data on the same customers.

syndicated services
Information services offered by marketing research organizations that provide information from a common database to firms that subscribe to their services.

geo-visual databases
Databases created by combining internal customer databases with geographic data, as from the U.S. Census Bureau, and making use of appropriate computer mapping software.

computer mapping
Maps that solve marketing problems are called *thematic maps*. They combine geography with demographic information and a company's sales data or other proprietary information and are generated by a computer.

The U.S. Census Bureau has introduced a geo-visual product called *TIGER* (Topologically Integrated Geographic Encoding and Referencing), which provides digital street maps of the entire United States. These mapping files contain data on street locations, highways, railroads, pipelines, power lines, and airports. Overlaying the maps of current neighborhoods wired for cable with customer geo-demographic information results in a powerful targeting tool. Such information is very useful in target-market selection and in *micromarketing,* tailoring the marketing mix (the four Ps: product, price, promotion, and place/distribution) to local neighborhoods. Geo-demographic and geo-visual databases can also aid in competitive intelligence (see Chapter 1).

Research in Action

Competitive Intelligence: The Broad Way to Broadband for AT&T

AT&T realized that cable TV companies could become competitors in the emerging field of cable telephony and broadband service. Thus, a competitive intelligence effort was undertaken that combined both primary research as well as both internal and external secondary data. This competitive intelligence task force was called "Project Pronto." Its mission was to understand the extent and capability of potential competition from cable TV companies.

In the primary research stage, members of Project Pronto used tips from AT&T's sales representatives and outside plant technicians to identify the network components of cable TV companies, such as fiber networks, repeaters, and fiber nodes, which could provide two-way cable services with cable modems. Actual field surveys were then used to validate these reports about cable TV network deployment. Next, the knowledge obtained in the first stage was merged with secondary data. Using geo-visual mapping software, routes of these cable TV components were overlaid onto maps with the types and locations of current AT&T customers. In this way, firm leaders were able to see the extent and capability of potential competition from cable TV companies.

These insights gained through Project Pronto shaped the strategic direction of the firm. Based on this knowledge, AT&T directed several billion dollars to the deployment of broadband services and led the way for the company to become the largest provider of broadband DSL (digital subscriber line) services. To further solidify its leadership position, in 2007 AT&T started offering satellite-based non–DSL broadband services in several rural markets for customers who cannot receive traditional high-speed Internet services. As of 2010, AT&T offered three networks to provide customers with speed and mobility 24/7: wired residential broadband, Wi-Fi, and wireless.[6]

Source: US Census Bureau.

Summary Illustration Using the Opening Vignette

In this section, we summarize and illustrate secondary data by returning to the chapter's opening vignette. In contrast to primary data, which are collected for a specific research problem, secondary data have been generated for reasons other than the research problem at hand. The data on advertising effectiveness and penetration for different forms of media provided by the Inland Research Corp. and used by the *Vindicator* are an example of secondary data. The cost and speed advantages of secondary data must be weighed against their limited applicability and accuracy. In evaluating secondary data, factors such as specifications, error, currency, objectivity, nature, and dependability should be considered, as was done by Inland Research.

Internally generated information can represent a gold mine for a marketing researcher. Any department that touches the final consumer in some way might be a source of valuable market data. The *Vindicator* generates data on the number of customers, subscription duration, and renewals/nonrenewals as a normal business operation. The internally generated data can be supplemented with data available from external sources to produce a rich database that can target customers and guide marketing efforts. In the opening vignette, external data on advertising effectiveness and penetration for different forms of media were combined with internal data on circulation to stress the comparative advantages of the *Vindicator* over other media (i.e., radio and television).

FIGURE 4.6

A Concept Map for Secondary Data

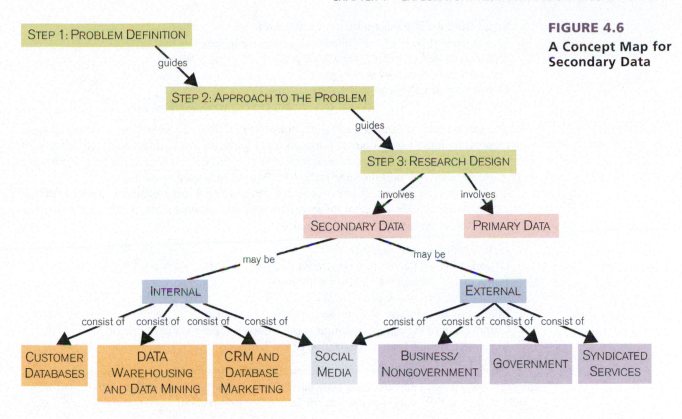

External data are generated by sources outside the organization. These data exist in the form of social media, business/nongovernment, government, or information made available by syndicated services. Inland Research obtains secondary data from all of these sources. Figure 4.6 features a concept map for secondary data. In this figure, the major concepts are connected, in order, by bold arrows using descriptors. Thus, Step 1: Problem Definition guides Step 2: Approach to the Problem, which in turn guides Step 3: Research Design. The rest of the figure can be interpreted similarly.

International Marketing Research

Secondary international data are available from both domestic government and nongovernment sources (see Figure 4.7).

The following are some of the most important government sources:

- Department of Commerce (www.commerce.gov)
- Agency for International Development (www.usaid.gov)

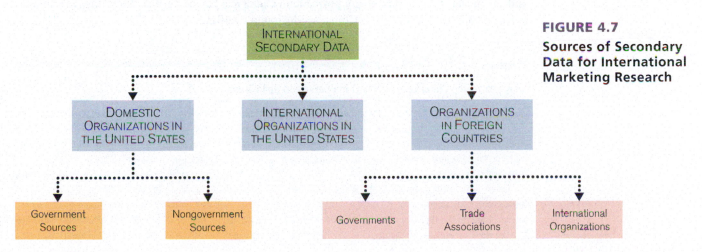

FIGURE 4.7

Sources of Secondary Data for International Marketing Research

- Small Business Administration (www.sba.gov)
- Export–Import Bank of the United States (www.exim.gov)
- Department of Agriculture (www.usda.gov)
- Department of State (www.state.gov)
- Department of Labor (www.dol.gov)
- Port Authority of New York and New Jersey (www.panynj.gov)

The Department of Commerce offers a number of publications as well as a variety of other services, such as the foreign buyer program, matchmaker events, trade missions, an export contact list service, the foreign commercial service, and the custom statistical service for exporters. Another very useful source is the CIA World Factbook (www.cia.gov).

Nongovernment organizations, including international organizations located in the United States, are another source of information about international markets. These data sources include the following international organizations:

- United Nations (www.un.org)
- Organization for Economic Cooperation and Development (www.oecd.org)
- International Monetary Fund (www.imf.org)
- World Bank (www.worldbank.org)
- International Chambers of Commerce (www.iccwbo.org)
- Commission of the European Union to the United States (www.eurunion.org)
- Japanese External Trade Organization (www.jetro.org)

Finally, locally sourced secondary data are available from foreign governments, international organizations located abroad, trade associations, and private services, such as syndicated firms. To illustrate, the following sites provide useful country information:

- Australia (www.nla.gov.au)
- France (www.insee.fr)
- Japan (www.e-stat.go.jp)
- Norway (www.ssb.no)
- South Africa (www.statssa.gov.za)
- United Kingdom (www.statistics.gov.uk)

The problems with data compatibility are even more pronounced when dealing with secondary data from international sources. Differences in units of measurement for such common economic statistics as personal disposable income make comparisons between two countries difficult. The accuracy of secondary data might also vary with the level of industrialization in a country. Data from countries such as the United States are likely to be more accurate than those from developing countries. The taxation structure and the extent of tax evasion affect reported business and income statistics. The measurement frequency of population census data varies considerably. An extreme example is the comparison of the U.S. Census, conducted every 10 years, to the census conducted in the People's Republic of China, where a 29-year gap occurred between the census of 1953 and 1982. However, the situation in China has changed, and secondary data are now easily available in China and can be very useful to firms seeking to enter or establish themselves in China, as illustrated by eBay.

Research in Action

eBay Learns the China Lesson: You Gotta Serve and Build Trust

eBay (www.ebay.com), having successfully established itself in the U.S. e-commerce market, moved on to another big market in 2002—China. While online shopping and auctions in the Chinese market continued to grow, as of 2011, eBay had failed to capture a large share of the market.

Taobao (www.taobao.com), part of the Web portal Alibaba (www.alibaba.com), accounted for 82 percent of total auction transaction value, followed by PaiPai (www.paipai.com) with 10 percent and eBay with 8 percent. How do Taobao and eBay differ? Unlike eBay,

Taobao is a homegrown Chinese company, whereas eBay purchased a Chinese site called *EachNet*. In addition, eBay charges auctioneers a portion of the final sale amount, whereas Taobao charges nothing throughout the auctioning process and is totally free to users.

According to a report published by the China Market Research Group (CMR), a marketing research firm in Shanghai, eBay's listings fees were *not* one of the top five reasons why consumers used Taobao over eBay. In fact, even after eBay offered free listings, it still lost customers to Taobao. CMR found that Chinese consumers like to buy brands from people they "trust" and that offer "over-the-top" customer service. Many consumers disliked eBay because of what they perceived to be bad service and because it did not focus on building trust.

Based on this secondary data from CMR, eBay was able to identify why it was losing market share in China. In response to this information, eBay committed to spending up to $100 million dollars in a massive marketing campaign with a focus on drastically dropping listing fees and repositioning itself in the market to cater to the desires of Chinese consumers. Because of these changes, which were made possible by secondary research, eBay might still succeed in China.[7]

Experiential Learning

When It Comes to Secondary Data, Quirk's Is Not Secondary

One way research professionals stay current with trends and developing marketing research techniques is by reading *Quirk's Marketing Research Review*. The average issue contains more than 100 pages and is printed in full color on glossy paper.

Go to www.quirks.com and click on "Articles" under "Quick Search." To search *Quirk's* article archive, select "Search by Research Topics" under "Market Research Article Quick Search." Click on the drop-down menu to review all of the topics available. Select "International Research." Now click the "Search" button.

Review the available articles about international research, select one that interests you, and read it by double-clicking on the hyperlink.

1. Why were you interested in this particular article?

2. What did you learn about international secondary data by reading this article?

3. What does this article suggest about the complexity of conducting research projects across two or more countries?

Marketing Research and Social Media

As can be seen from Figure 4.3, social media can be a rich source of both internal as well as external secondary data. A company's blog, Facebook page, or Twitter account can generate rich internal secondary data. External social media tools and sites provide a valuable database that researchers can sieve through in a bid to analyze relevant consumer information. The archival information and posts from social media such as blogs or Facebook "fan" pages give an informative account of consumer perception and preference with regard to the problem at hand. Although it is important for researchers to analyze secondary data from typical and traditional sources such as journals, periodicals, and the Internet at large, it is essential that social media not be ignored in light of their significance in representing the true voice of the consumer. Insights from various discussion threads within social media provide credible information that marketing researchers should take into consideration when analyzing secondary data.

Social Media

Social media are relevant to marketing research in that audiences all over the world can be reached in a real-time, controlled, multimedia setting. Social networks, blogs, and other forms of social media have emerged as forums where consumers can discuss their perceptions and preferences and be an avenue where they can be particularly vocal about markets, companies, and their products. Additionally, since these Web sites usually split up and separate the users based on their demographics and interest groups, gathering both internal and external data has become very easy. Companies can tap potential customers based on the sentiments that are expressed online.

Not only are businesses setting up social media sites to collect internal secondary data and to mine external social media sites to obtain valuable information, but nonprofit and government organizations are also doing the same. Recognizing the increase in popularity of social networking sites, in fall 2009 the Department of Justice Criminal Division (Dept. of JCD) began officially mining social media networks, including Facebook, MySpace, Twitter, and LinkedIn, to gather incriminating information about U.S. citizens. Social networking sites allow the department to obtain evidence for criminal cases because these sites are able to reveal personal communications, establish motives and relationships, provide location information, prove or disprove alibis, and establish crime or criminal enterprise. In addition, undercover operations on social networks have enabled the department to gain access to nonpublic information, communicate with suspects, and map social relationships. The Dept. of JCD has also recognized that social media alone should not serve as evidence for any case, but rather provide insights and direction for further investigation. Another, more conventional, example is provided by IBM.

Research in Action

IBM: Using Twitter as a Source of Competitive Intelligence

Generally, IBM obtains secondary data from a wide range of external sources, including journals, publications, reviews from analysts, company annual reports, and the Internet. For instance, they can get professional product reviews from external experts and analysis from various technology and network-server–related magazines like *PCMag*, *Linux* magazine, *Computerworld*, and *Network World*. By gathering information like critiques and opinions on IBM products from these sources, the company is able to get a better evaluation of its products. IBM also uses statistical and economic data gathered from government sources like the U.S. Census Bureau. These data consist of surveys of retail establishments engaged in electronics and appliances, including television, cell phones, computers, radios, and other electrical devices.

With the increasing popularity of social media, IBM set up many Twitter accounts under its different departmental operations. Twitter is a micro-blogging platform that allows users to upload short comments and follow other users. This platform proved to be an invaluable source of external secondary data, which reduces the search cost for information online, as many in the industry, including competitors and experts, use Twitter.

One of IBM's Twitter account is "ibmretail," the global retail operations of IBM, which provides smarter solutions that add business values for retailers. As we can see from the Twitter account, despite having thousands of followers, "ibmretail" follows only 52 users. Like most of IBM's Twitter accounts, the different departmental operations follow one another. A quick browse of "ibmretail" reveals companies like Oracle Retail, Tomax Corporation, Zebra Technologies, and Epicor Retail. Oracle Retail, as described in their Twitter bio, is the number-one provider of

innovative and comprehensive software solutions for retailers. Tomax Corporation provides retail solutions for marketing and merchandising through store operations and workforce management. A quick evaluation shows that these companies are competitors of IBM in the retail solutions business. Being followers of the competitors allows IBM to gather competitive intelligence, a form of secondary data that is external to the company.

"ibmretail" also follows World Retail Congress (WRC), a platform for world retail leaders to meet and discuss issues that are critical to their businesses. WRC acts like the retail industry's association, offering to retail leaders information on brands, audience profiles, and industry newsletters. Therefore, by following WRC, IBM Retail is able to receive updates regarding the retail industry and use secondary data provided by WRC in their marketing research.

The use of social media to collect competitive intelligence and other secondary data has enabled IBM to become a formidable competitor and an industry leader.[8]

Source: Courtesy of IBM.

Ethics in Marketing Research

Researchers sometimes overlook the disadvantages and advantages of secondary data discussed earlier, which raises ethical issues. The research firm has the ethical responsibility to use only secondary data that are relevant and appropriate to the problem. The data used should be evaluated, using the criteria described in this chapter. The researcher should discuss issues surrounding the relevance and accuracy of secondary data with the client.

After a detailed analysis of secondary data has been conducted, the researcher should reexamine the collection of primary data stipulated in the proposal to see if it is still appropriate. Any needed changes in the primary data collection methodology should be discussed with the client. In the extreme case, if primary data are no longer needed, then it is the ethical responsibility of the researcher to disclose this to the client.

In addition to evaluating their quality and completeness, researchers should also evaluate secondary data in terms of moral appropriateness. Data collection might be unethical if the data are generated without the respondents' knowledge or consent and if their use raises ethical questions. When generating secondary data, researchers and syndicate firms should not engage in any questionable or unethical practices, such as abuse of respondents' privacy. Privacy has, indeed, become a burning issue and the debate has gone public. Two main issues are involved. First, consumers feel they should not have to cope with the unsolicited sales pitches that flood their mailboxes, phones, and e-mail addresses. The second issue concerns the sophisticated databases that maintain enormous amounts of information about consumers, ranging from their names to specifics about their lifestyles and product consumption habits. Reputable organizations like the U.S. Census Bureau adhere to strict privacy protection policies.

Research in Action

U.S. Census Bureau: Federal Law Protects Your Information

The Census Bureau is bound by Title 13 of the United States Code. These laws provide strong protection for the information the Bureau collects from individuals and businesses. The following privacy policy is posted on its Web site.

Title 13 Protections

- **Private Information Is Never Published** It is against the law to disclose or publish any private information that identifies an individual or business such as:
  - No names
  - No addresses including GPS coordinates
  - No Social Security numbers
  - No telephone numbers
- **We Collect Information to Produce Statistics** We use your information to produce statistics. Your personal information cannot be used against you by any government agency or court.
- **Sworn for Life to Protect Your Confidentiality** Every person with access to your information is sworn for life to protect your confidentiality.
- **Violating the Law Is a Serious Crime** If anyone violates this law, it is a federal crime; they will face severe penalties, including a federal prison sentence of up to 5 years, a fine of up to $250,000, or both.

Sworn for Life to Protect Confidentiality

We take Title 13 protections seriously. People sworn to uphold Title 13 are legally required to maintain the confidentiality of your data. Every person with access to your data is sworn for life to protect your information and understands that the penalties for violating this law are applicable for a lifetime.[9]

WHAT WOULD YOU DO?

Tommy Hilfiger: Keeping Abreast of the Market to Remain a High Flyer

The Situation

From the blacktop to the golf course, designer Tommy Hilfiger (usa.tommy.com) has the streets covered. His namesake casual wear is worn by rap, rock, teen, and sports stars and fans. These days, many of them are women. Tommy designs, sources, makes, and markets men's and women's sportswear and denim wear, as well as athletic wear, children's wear, and accessories. Through extensive licensing deals (almost 40 product lines), Tommy also offers products such as fragrances, belts, bedding, home furnishings, and cosmetics. The company's clean-cut clothing is sold in major department and specialty stores as well as through 165 Tommy Hilfiger shops and outlets. With such a large empire, it is no wonder that Tommy Hilfiger Corp. CEO Fred Gehring is always busy making sure the company does not forget the most important aspect of its business—satisfying consumers' needs!

Selling apparel will never be an easy job. "Just when you think you've figured out exactly what your customers want, everything changes—sometimes overnight," says apparel expert Richard Romer, executive vice president for The CIT Group/Commercial Services, a New York–based credit protection and lending services provider for apparel manufacturers. "Basically, changes in apparel occur every other year: long skirts to short skirts and back to long." The apparel market's constant state of flux forces catalog retailers and other marketers to constantly reevaluate the market they are targeting and then reinvent their companies, their offerings, and their catalogs.

The Marketing Research Decision

1. What sources of secondary data should Tommy Hilfiger consult to keep informed about apparel fashion trends? (Check all that apply.)
   a. Apparel industry trade association databases
   b. U.S. Bureau of the Census, census of population
   c. University of Michigan, consumer confidence index
   d. United Nations' International database
   e. All of the above

Source: Gaye Gerard/Getty Images for Tommy Hilfiger.

(continued)

2. How would the type of secondary research you recommend enable Fred Gehring and Tommy Hilfiger to keep abreast of apparel trends?

The Marketing Management Decision

1. In order to enhance the appeal of Tommy Hilfiger clothing to the fashion conscious consumer, Fred Gehring should (check all that apply):
   a. Introduce new lines of designer clothing.
   b. Feature supermodels in Tommy Hilfiger's advertising.
   c. Increase the distribution of Tommy Hilfiger clothing through fashion boutiques and other specialty channels.
   d. Lower the prices of Tommy Hilfiger clothing.
   e. Acquire additional brands.
2. How is your marketing management decision influenced by the information in the secondary data sources that you suggested earlier?

What Fred Gehring Did

Tommy Hilfiger Corp. announced that it would begin a search to acquire additional brands. Tommy Hilfiger now says it hopes to develop a multibrand, multichannel business strategy. According to the company, "While we continue to be focused on improving operations in our existing business, we are aggressively seeking opportunities to further diversify our revenue and earnings base."

Bold stripes and high contrast were the visual hallmarks of Tommy Hilfiger's newly designed advertising campaign. Fall fashions were mod-inspired and flaunted by a cast of young, sexy models with tousled hair and smoky eyes, all evoking the iconic imagery of the 1960s. The stripes and bold graphic lines reflect the timeless, universal appeal of the classic Hilfiger designs. Its 2010 campaign was titled "American Stories" and featured America's most celebrated cities, beginning with Los Angeles for spring and ending with Washington, D.C., for fall. The Tommy Hilfiger 2011 collection, celebrating its 25-year heritage, presented an audacious use of color, mixed patterns, and proportion.[10]

Summary

In contrast to primary data that are collected for a specific research problem, secondary data have been generated for reasons other than the current research problem. The cost advantage and speed with which secondary data can be obtained must be weighed against their limited fit to the current research problem and concerns regarding data accuracy. In evaluating secondary data, the researcher should consider factors such as specifications, error, currency, objectivity, nature, and dependability.

Internally generated information can represent a gold mine for a researcher. Any department that touches the final consumer in some way can be a source of valuable market data. The internally generated data can be supplemented with demographic and lifestyle data available from external sources to produce a rich database that can be analyzed via data mining to target customers via database marketing.

External data are generated by sources outside the organization. These data can be obtained from businesses (nongovernment sources), government, social media, and syndicated services. General business data can be located using guides, directories, and indices, and also include statistical data. Government sources can be broadly categorized as census data and other data.

Both internal and external databases yield potentially helpful information. Conducting international research predisposes to problems of data quality, and thus these data should be carefully evaluated. Social media are facilitating the establishment of sophisticated internal databases and are also a rich source of external secondary data. The researcher has the ethical responsibility to use only secondary data that are relevant and appropriate to the problem.

Key Terms and Concepts

Primary data   95
Secondary data   96
Internal data   100
External data   100
Psychographics   101

Data warehouse   102
Data mining   102
Customer relationship management
   (CRM) system   102
Database marketing   102

Geo-demographic coding   109
Syndicated services   109
Geo-visual databases   109
Computer mapping   110

Suggested Cases and Video Cases

Running Case with Real Data

1.1 Hewlett-Packard

Comprehensive Critical Thinking Cases

2.1 American Idol   2.2 Baskin-Robbins   2.3 Akron Children's Hospital

Comprehensive Cases with Real Data

3.1 Bank of America   3.2   McDonald's   3.3 Boeing

Comprehensive Brief Harvard Business School Cases

4.1 TruEarth Healthy Foods: Market Research for a New Product Introduction (4065)
4.2 The Springfield Nor'easters: Maximizing Revenues in the Minor Leagues (2510)
4.3 Metabical: Positioning and Communications Strategy for a New Weight-Loss Drug (4240)
4.4 Saxonville Sausage Company (2085)

Online Video Cases

4.1 Mayo Clinic   5.1 eGO   7.1 Starbucks   8.1 AFLAC
9.1 P&G   11.1 Dunkin' Donuts 12.1 Motorola   13.1 Subaru
14.1 Intel   19.1 Marriott

Live Research: Conducting a Marketing Research Project

1. Assign one, some, or all teams the responsibility of collecting and analyzing secondary data.
2. If this work is divided, one or some teams could search the library's electronic database; others could search government sources; and yet other teams could visit the library and work with a reference librarian to identify relevant sources.

Acronym

The criteria used for evaluating secondary data can be described by the acronym SECOND:

  S pecifications: methodology used to collect the data

  E rror: accuracy of the data

  C urrency: when the data were collected

  O bjective: purpose for which data were collected

  N ature: content of the data

  D ependability: overall, how dependable are the data

Review Questions

1. How do primary and secondary data differ?
2. Why is it important to obtain secondary data before primary data?
3. What are the advantages of secondary data?
4. What are the disadvantages of secondary data?
5. What criteria are used to evaluate secondary data?
6. How do internal and external secondary data differ?
7. What are the various sources of published secondary data?

8. Is it useful to combine internal and external secondary data? Why or why not?
9. What is geo-coding? Give an example.
10. Describe a geo-visual database.
11. What is database marketing?
12. **Social Media** Discuss the use of social media as a source of secondary data.

Applied Problems

1. Select an industry of your choice. Using external published sources, obtain industry sales and the sales of the major firms in that industry for the past year. Estimate the market share of each major firm. Use a computerized database to obtain information on the market shares of these same firms. Do the two estimates agree? Was it easier to obtain the information from published sources or from a computerized database?
2. Determine total e-commerce sales for the past year from each of the following sources: Forrester Research (www.forrester.com), ComScore (www.comscore.com), Nielsen (www.nielsen.com), and the U.S. Commerce Department (www.commerce.gov). Do these four estimates agree?
3. You are enhancing Dell's internal household customer data with externally available information. Visit the Equifax Web site (www.equifax.com) to determine what

demographic and psychographic data are available that would be useful to Dell for targeting the household computer market.
4. Visit the NAICS Association Web site (www.naics.com). Find the NAICS codes for "Computers, manufacturing" and "Hospitals, general medical and surgical." Discuss the significance and usefulness of these codes.
5. Visit www.dnb.com and write a report about the type of information on businesses available from D&B.
6. Visit the Web site of the U.S. Census Bureau (www.census.gov). Write a report about the secondary data available from the Bureau that would be useful to a fast-food firm such as McDonald's for the purpose of formulating a domestic marketing strategy.
7. Visit www.census.gov. Use State Rankings and Vital Statistics to identify the top six states for marketing products to the elderly.

Group Discussion

1. Discuss the significance and limitations of U.S. Census data as a major source of secondary data.

2. Discuss the growing use of computerized databases.

Hewlett-Packard Running Case

Review the Hewlett-Packard (HP) case, Case 1.1, and questionnaire given toward the end of the book.

1. Search the Internet to find information on the latest U.S. market share of HP and other PC marketers.
2. **Social Media** Search the Internet including social media to obtain information on HP's marketing strategy.

Do you agree with HP's marketing strategy? Why or why not?
3. Visit the U.S. Census Bureau at www.census.gov. As HP seeks to increase its penetration of U.S. households, what information available from the U.S. Census Bureau is helpful?

ONLINE VIDEO CASE 4.1

THE MAYO CLINIC: Staying Healthy with Marketing Research

Visit **www.pearsonhighered.com/malhotra** to read the video case and view the accompanying video. The Mayo Clinic: Staying Healthy with Marketing Research describes how the Mayo Clinic has been able to build and maintain its strong brand management efforts by relying on marketing research (i.e., operating as a clearinghouse for external perceptions of the clinic as well as providing physicians with an understanding of their brand). The case can be used to discuss the sources of secondary data that would be helpful in determining consumer preferences for health care facilities. Specific marketing research questions on this and the previous chapters are posed in the video case.

Exploratory Research Design: Syndicated Sources of Secondary Data

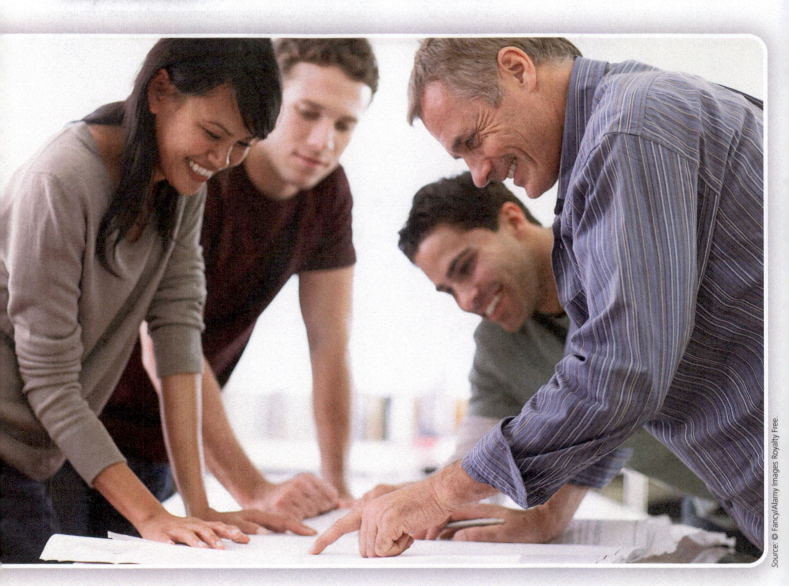

Source: © Fancy/Alamy Images Royalty Free.

LEARNING OBJECTIVES

After reading this chapter, the student should be able to:

1. Explain how syndicated data differ from other types of secondary data.

2. Describe how syndicated data are classified.

3. Discuss the major methods of obtaining syndicated data from households/consumers.

4. Understand how syndicated data are collected from institutions.

5. Explain why multiple sources of secondary data should be used and what is meant by *single-source data*.

6. Describe what syndicated data are available for conducting international marketing research.

7. **Social Media** Discuss how social media can enhance the usefulness of syndicated data.

8. Identify the ethical issues involved in the use of syndicated data.

" As competition intensifies, companies increasingly want marketplace metrics to gauge their performance relative to the competition. For many, syndicated data is what they use. **"**

Kris Baker
Vice President, Group Client Director, The Nielsen Company, Lewisville, Texas

A Casual Affair

Even though clothing designers seem to be defining fashion as dressy, most Americans seem to be opting for a more casual approach to their fashion needs. Today, companies are saying goodbye to three-piece suits, wingtips, and high heels and welcoming a more casual dress style. The West Coast dot.com companies have definitely contributed to the trend in casual dress. More recently, consulting firms, law firms, and investment companies on the East Coast have joined this trend as well. A recent survey reported that a remarkable 87 percent of responding companies have a casual Friday or an everyday casual policy at their place of business. Companies such as Coca-Cola, Ford, J.P. Morgan, and Accenture have implemented full-time casual dress policies. At many companies today, when someone wears a suit to work, the question immediately asked is, "Are you going on a job interview?"

According to data from syndicated marketing research firms, the "business casual" segment is growing. As discussed in Chapter 1, syndicated data are made available for purchase by multiple clients on a subscription basis. For example, according to a recent survey by the NPD Group, a well-known source of syndicated services, almost 90 percent of U.S. workers said they were dressing down at least some of the time. The NPD study revealed that although sales in many categories of tailored clothing, including dresses and men's suits, were down, sales of casual apparel, such as no-iron cotton slacks and sweaters, were on the rise. Several marketers of casual clothing have built their strategies based on these findings.

Haggar Clothing Co. (www.haggar.com) is out to convince its male customers that the company can do everything from tailored to casual. Based on syndicated data, Haggar realized that the trend is not in the direction of tailored suits, where for years the company has been the market leader. The company responded by introducing its "City Casuals" line. Its wrinkle-free cotton trousers have been the line's biggest success.

Haggar's internal research showed that Enron and WorldCom were not the only ones in corporate America allegedly tinkering with numbers. It seems most men do not like to admit their true waist size and end up buying pants that are too small. The product born of this realization was Comfort Fit, a cotton khaki introduced in 2002 that expands up to 3 inches through hidden elastic embedded in the waistline. The pant also appeals to more economically conservative men who, even if they have gained several pounds, hate to throw out pants that are in good condition. In keeping with this trend, Haggar adopted a new theme and in 2008 was marketing its clothing with the slogan, "Making things right," emphasizing shrink-resistant fabric, unbreakable buttons and zippers, unbustable seams, and bigger, unrippable pockets. As of 2011, Haggar was marketing "Work-to-Weekend Khakis" as its most versatile pant.

In an effort to capitalize on this trend toward casual clothing, Levi Strauss (www.levistrauss.com) is pushing its Levi's, Dockers, Signature, and dENiZEN lines, all of which were being marketed in 2011. Although 90 percent of U.S. offices permit employees to wear jeans, some employees are still reluctant to wear them to work because they consider them to be too casual. The company has had huge success with the Dockers trouser line, which has become standard wear for the casual business dresser. The success of Haggar's Comfort Fit has not been lost on Dockers, which introduced its own expandable version, called Individual Fit. On September 14, 2010, Levi Strauss announced the global launch of the Levi's® Digital Fitting Experience, an interactive destination for women to explore and buy their perfect-fitting jeans online based on their shape, not size. This sort of cross-pollination is going on throughout the industry, and the time seems near when consumers will be able to purchase virtually any garment in a stain-free, wrinkle-free, expandable variant.[1]

As this vignette illustrates, even competing firms such as Haggar and Levi Strauss are able to make use of the same data available from syndicate firms such as the NPD Group to formulate their marketing strategies.

Overview

Chapters 1 and 4 introduced the concept of syndicated sources of information. In this chapter, we explain syndicated data in detail and distinguish them from other external sources of secondary data. As shown in Figure 5.1, this chapter relates to marketing research suppliers and services discussed in Chapter 1, tasks involved in problem definition and developing an approach covered in Chapter 2, exploratory and descriptive research designs described in Chapter 3, and secondary data presented in Chapter 4. Thus, this chapter is related to the first three steps of the marketing research process.

This chapter describes the three major methods of collecting syndicated data related to consumers and households: surveys, panels, and electronic scanner services. Syndicated data also are collected from institutions via retail and wholesale audits and institutional services. The chapter also includes a discussion of single-source data. As the name indicates, single-source data combine data from various sources to create a unified database that contains information on consumer purchases, demographic and psychographic variables, and marketing management variables. Finally, the applications of syndicated data to international marketing research, the impact of social media on syndicated data, and the ethics of collecting and using such data are presented. Figure 5.2 provides an overview of the topics discussed in this chapter and how they flow from one to the next.

The Nature of Syndicated Data

In addition to data available from general business/nongovernment, government, and social media, syndicated sources constitute the other major source of external secondary data (see Figure 4.3 in Chapter 4). **Syndicated sources**, also referred to as *syndicated services*, are companies that collect and sell common pools of data of known commercial value, designed to serve information needs shared by a number of clients, including competing firms in the same industry. This was illustrated in the opening vignette. Survey data collected by the NPD Group

syndicated sources
Companies that collect and sell common pools of data designed to serve information needs shared by a number of clients, including competing firms in the same industry.

FIGURE 5.1

Relationship of Syndicated Sources to the Previous Chapters and the Marketing Research Process

Focus of This Chapter	Relationship to Previous Chapters	Relationship to Marketing Research Process
• Syndicated Sources of Secondary Data	• The Marketing Research Suppliers and Services (Chapter 1)	Problem Definition
	• Tasks Involved in Problem Definition and Developing an Approach (Chapter 2)	Approach to Problem
	• Exploratory Research Design (Chapter 3)	Research Design
	• Descriptive Research Design (Chapter 3)	Fieldwork
		Data Preparation and Analysis
	• Secondary Data (Chapter 4)	Report Preparation and Presentation

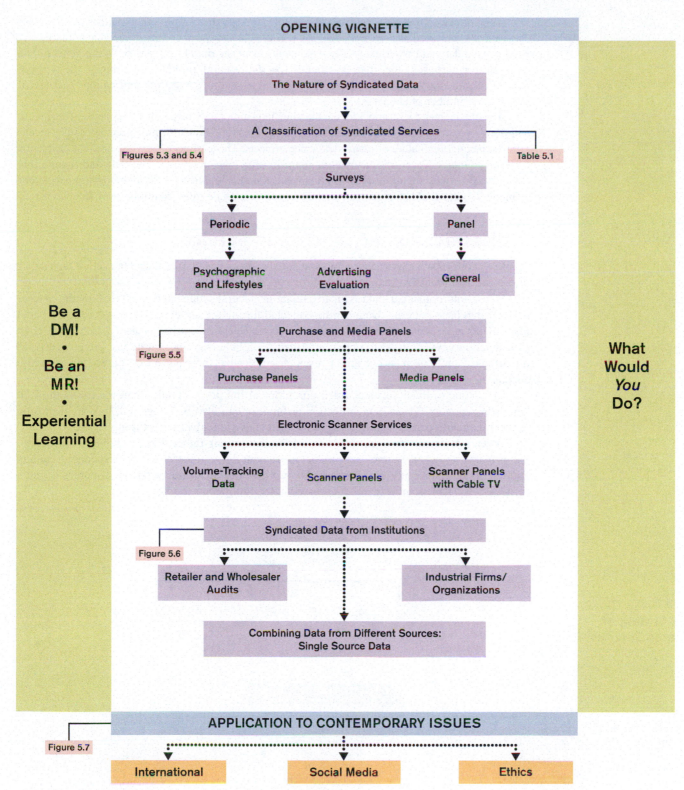

FIGURE 5.2

Syndicated Sources to Secondary Data: An Overview

were useful to Haggar Apparel and Levi Strauss. These data differ from primary data in that the research objective guiding the study is common to several client firms. Syndicated firms make their money by collecting data and designing research products that fit the information needs of more than one organization. Often, syndicated data and services are designed for use by multiple clients from multiple industries.

Although classified as secondary data, syndicated data differ from other sources of secondary data in that syndicated data are collected because they have known commercial value to marketers. Both census data and other externally generated secondary data (see Chapter 4) are general data collected for purposes other than the client's specific research problem. In contrast, the types of data syndicated services collect have very specific marketing research applications that are of interest to a number of clients.

Any client, even two competitors in the same industry (e.g., Coca-Cola Company and PepsiCo), can purchase the same syndicated data, typically through a subscription process. This process reflects the ongoing nature of many syndicated projects. These projects provide data that enable the tracking of change over time as well as point-in-time measurements. The data and reports that syndicated services supply to client companies can be personalized to fit their specific needs. For example, reports could be organized on the basis of the client's sales territories or product lines.

A Classification of Syndicated Services

Figure 5.3 presents a classification of syndicated sources based on either a household/consumer or institutional unit of measurement.

Household/consumer data typically relate to general values and lifestyles, media use, or product-purchase patterns. Data can be collected through a survey process, recorded by panel respondents in diaries (paper or electronic), or captured electronically via scanners (see Figure 5.4). Consumer surveys are used to obtain information on beliefs, values, attitudes, preferences, and intentions. Panels used in consumer research emphasize information on purchases or media consumption.

Electronic scanner services track purchases at the point of sale or in the home through handheld scanners. These data collection techniques can also be integrated, linking electronic scanner data with panels, survey data, or targeted television advertising through cable.

When syndicated services obtain data from institutions rather than households/consumers, the primary subjects they track are product movement through the distribution channel (retailers and wholesalers) or corporate statistics. An overview of the various syndicated sources is given in Table 5.1. These sources will be discussed in the following sections.

FIGURE 5.3

A Classification of Syndicated Services

FIGURE 5.4

A Classification of Syndicated Services: Household Consumers

TABLE 5.1 Overview of Syndicated Services

Type	Characteristics	Advantages	Disadvantages	Uses
Surveys	Surveys conducted at regular intervals	Most flexible way of obtaining data; information on underlying motives	Interviewer errors; respondent errors	Market segmentation; advertising theme selection; advertising effectiveness
Purchase Panels	Households provide specific information regularly over an extended period of time; respondents asked to record specific behaviors as they occur	Recorded purchase behavior can be linked to the demographic/psychographic characteristics	Lack of representativeness; response bias; maturation	Forecasting sales, market share, and trends; establishing consumer profiles and brand loyalty and switching; evaluating test markets, advertising, and distribution
Media Panels	Electronic devices automatically record behavior, supplemented by a diary	Same as purchase panels	Same as purchase panels	Establishing advertising rates; selecting media program or air time; establishing viewer profiles
Scanner Volume-Tracking Data	Household purchases are recorded through electronic scanners in supermarkets	Data reflect actual purchases; timely data; less expensive	Data may not be representative; errors in recording purchases; difficult to link purchases to elements of marketing mix other than price	Price tracking; modeling; assessing effectiveness of in-store promotion
Scanner Panels with Cable TV	Scanner panels of households that subscribe to cable TV	Data reflect actual purchases; sample control; ability to link panel data to household characteristics	Data may not be representative; quality of data limited	Promotional-mix analyses; copy testing; new-product testing; positioning
Audit Services	Verification of product movement by examining physical records or performing inventory analysis	Relatively precise information at the retail and wholesale levels	Coverage may be incomplete; matching of data on competitive activity may be difficult	Measuring consumer sales, market share, and competitive activity; analyzing distribution patterns; tracking of new products
Firm Syndicated Services	Data banks on industrial establishments through direct inquiries of companies, clipping services, and corporate reports	Important source of information on industrial firms; particularly useful in initial phases of the marketing research process	Data is lacking in terms of content, quantity, and quality	Determining market potential by geographic area; defining sales territories; allocating advertising budget

Syndicated Data from Households/Consumers

We discuss the data obtained from households/consumers via surveys, purchase and media panels, and various forms of scanner data.

Surveys

We will begin our discussion with general surveys. The survey by the NPD Group discussed in the opening vignette is an example. The two types of general surveys are periodic and panel surveys.

PERIODIC SURVEYS **Periodic surveys** collect data on the same set of variables at regular intervals, each time sampling a new group of respondents from the target population. Like longitudinal research, periodic surveys track change over time. However, the change due to variation in the respondent pool is not controlled in the way it is for true longitudinal studies. A new sample of respondents is chosen with each survey. Once analyzed, the data are made available to subscribers.

periodic surveys
Surveys that collect data on the same set of variables at regular intervals, each time sampling from a new group of respondents.

panel surveys
Surveys that measure the same group of respondents over time, but not necessarily on the same variables.

PANEL SURVEYS   Syndicated **panel surveys** measure the same group of respondents over time, but not necessarily on the same variables. A large pool of respondents is recruited to participate on the panel. From this pool, different subsamples of respondents might be drawn for different surveys. Any survey technique can be used, including telephone, personal, mail, or electronic interviewing. The content and topics of the surveys vary and cover a wide range. Also known as *omnibus panels*, these panels are used to implement different cross-sectional designs at different points in time, generally for different surveys. For example, Synovate (www.synovate.com), a marketing research firm, offers a number of different omnibus surveys. Its eNation survey involves five weekly online surveys of a sample of 1,000 people that is nationally representative of the American adult population. Another Synovate omnibus service is TeleNation, which involves two national telephone surveys each week that total 2,000 interviews.[2] Both surveys are conducted using Synovate Global Opinion Panels. Omnibus panels are different from panels that use longitudinal designs, which were discussed in Chapter 3. Recall that in a longitudinal design repeated measurements on the same variables are made on the same sample. Such panels are sometimes referred to as *true panels* to distinguish them from omnibus panels.

Panel surveys are used primarily because of their lower cost compared to random sampling. These savings result due to streamlining of the data collection process, enhanced response rates, and readily available sample frames, which can be precisely targeted. Comprehensive demographic, lifestyle, and product-ownership data are collected only once as each respondent is admitted into the panel. The panel is used as a respondent pool from which the research organization can draw either representative or targeted samples based on the relevant background characteristics of the panel members. Response rates to panel surveys, including mail panels, are substantially improved over the random sampling process because of the commitment panel members make to participate in surveys.

Whether the surveys are periodic or panel, the bulk of the survey deals with questions of general interest to the client group. These general questions are typically supplemented with proprietary questions from each participating client. Responses to the general interest questions are available to the entire group, whereas the answers to proprietary questions are held in confidence and provided only to the appropriate client. This way, syndicated research organizations can offer customized reports to their clients, as illustrated by GfK Custom Research North America.

Research in Action

GfK Custom Research North America: Customization via Syndication

GfK Roper OmniTel (www.gfkamerica.com) is a syndicated service offering customized survey reports. GfK's public opinion research service collects data on a broad range of social, economic, political, and consumer issues every 5 weeks. The organization conducts telephone interviews with a national sample of 1,000 adults ages 18 and older. In addition to the standard questions that are common across clients, clients can add customized, proprietary questions. Thus, Ford Motor Company can purchase the general survey results related to automobiles. Ford can also request proprietary questions about its models, such as Taurus, to determine why sales are lagging behind major competitors, such as Toyota's Camry and Honda's Accord.

According to the GfK Custom Research North America, the ability to add proprietary questions along with customized report generation offers a unique combination of frequency, speed of report delivery, quality, low cost, large sample size, and extensive demographic breaks. This ability to customize surveys and reports has been a major factor in the popularity of the OmniTel survey.

Be an MR!	Be a DM!
Samsung: Increasing the Flat Sales of Flat-Panel TV Sets	
Visit www.gfkamerica.com and write a brief report about the company's GfK Roper OmniTel Telephone Survey. How can you use the OmniTel Telephone Survey to obtain information that will help Samsung increase the penetration of flat-panel television sets in the United States?	What marketing strategies should Samsung adopt to increase the penetration of flat-panel television sets in the United States?

Surveys can be broadly classified on the basis of their content as psychographics and lifestyles, advertising evaluation, or general surveys (see Figure 5.4).

PSYCHOGRAPHICS AND LIFESTYLES   The term **psychographics** refers to psychological profiles of individuals and to psychologically based measures of lifestyle, such as brand loyalty and risk taking. The term **lifestyle** refers to the distinctive modes of living within a society or some of its segments, such as the DINKs (Double Income No Kids) lifestyle characterized as being money rich and time poor. Together, these measures are generally referred to as *activities, interests,* and *opinions,* or simply as AIOs. The firm of Yankelovich Research and Consulting Services provided the Yankelovich Monitor, a survey that contained information on lifestyles and social trends. In 2008, Yankelovich joined WPP and merged with Henley Centre HeadlightVision to form The Futures Company (www.thefuturescompany.com). The new company launched the Global MONITOR insight service that assesses changes in consumer attitudes and brand behaviors.

As another example, Strategic Business Insights (www.strategicbusinessinsights.com) conducts an annual survey of consumers that is used to classify persons into VALS (values and lifestyles) types for segmentation purposes. Information on specific aspects of consumers' lifestyles also is available. GfK Custom Research North America conducts an annual survey of 5,000 consumers who participate in leisure sports and recreational activities. Several firms conduct surveys to compile demographic and psychographic information at the household, sub-zip (e.g., 30306-3035), and zip code level, which is then made available on a subscription basis. Such information is particularly valuable for client firms seeking to enhance internally generated customer data for database marketing.

ADVERTISING EVALUATION   The purpose of these surveys is to measure the size and profile of the advertising audience and to assess the effectiveness of advertising using print and broadcast media. A well-known survey is the Gallup and Robinson Magazine Impact Research Service (MIRS) (www.gallup-robinson.com).

psychographics
Quantified psychological profiles of individuals.

lifestyle
A distinctive pattern of living that is described by the activities people engage in, the interests they have, and the opinions they hold of themselves and the world around them (AIOs).

Research in Action

Magazine Impact Research Service

In the Magazine Impact Research Service (MIRS) by Gallup and Robinson (www.gallup-robinson.com), ads are tested using an at-home, in-magazine context among widely dispersed samples. Interviewers screen respondents for eligibility, door-to-door, and ask them to read a current issue magazine as they normally would at home. The issue they receive contains a test ad. The following day they are recontacted and measurements are made on core variables such as intrusiveness, persuasion, brand rating, and ad liking, without looking at the magazine. Next, the entire sample is asked to look at the test ad before they are administered diagnostic questions, which can be both standardized and customized. This information is very useful to companies that advertise heavily in print media, such as American Airlines, Gucci, and GM, for evaluating the effectiveness of their advertising. MIRS has become an industry standard for magazine ad testing.[3]

Source: Bloomberg/Getty Images.

Evaluation of effectiveness is even more critical in the case of television advertising. Television commercials are evaluated using either the recruited-audience method or the in-home viewing method. In the recruited-audience method, respondents are brought to a theater or mobile viewing laboratory. After viewing a series of advertisements, they are surveyed regarding product knowledge, attitudes, and preferences, as well as their reaction to the advertisements. With the in-home viewing method, consumers evaluate commercials in their normal viewing environment. New commercials can be pretested at the network level or in local markets. Audience reaction to the advertisements is recorded along with respondent demographics. Gallup & Robinson, Inc., offers testing of television commercials using both of these methods. These methods also are used for testing the effectiveness of advertising in other media, such as magazines, radio, newspapers, and direct mail. Experian Simmons (www.experian.com) conducts four different surveys with a large sample of respondents to monitor magazine, TV, newspaper, and radio media. GfK MRI (www.gfkmri.com) is another firm that makes available information on the consumption of media, products, and services by households.

GENERAL SURVEYS Surveys also are conducted for a variety of other purposes, including examination of purchase and consumption behavior. Gallup (www.gallup.com) surveys a random sample of 1,000 households by telephone about a variety of topics. The weekly Harris Poll by Harris Interactive (www.harrisinteractive.com) also is based on a nationally representative telephone survey of 1,000 adults ages 18 or over. Again, a wide range of topics is considered. Another example of general surveys is provided by BIGresearch.

Research in Action

BIGresearch Syndicated Surveys Lead to Big Decisions

BIGresearch's (www.bigresearch.com) syndicated Consumer Intentions and Actions (CIA) survey monitors the pulse of more than 8,600 consumers each month. The survey is conducted online and is based on a representative sample. It delivers fresh, demand-based information on where retail consumers are shopping and their changing behavior. In the context of automobile purchase, the survey is predictive of automotive sales at the national level 3 months in advance.

BIGresearch calculates Consumer Equity Share by subtracting the average percentage of those considering a brand first choice or second choice from the current percentage of ownership of the same brand. According to BIGresearch's Consumer Intentions and Actions (CIA) Survey of April 2009, Chevrolet, Dodge, and ill-fated Pontiac all took a hit in Consumer Equity Share among consumers planning to buy a new vehicle. Chevrolet lost more than five and a half points in Consumer Equity Share over last year and Dodge dropped into the negative. In addition, BIGresearch surveys showed that Chrysler was losing market share to Ford.

Based on these findings, Chrysler made some strategic adjustments to build off its historic strengths, but not rely too much on them so as to be at a competitive disadvantage. The Chrysler Group added a more robust customer and brand focus while continuing to stress product leadership. It decided to continue the product offensive through 2011. For example, the all-new 2011 Chrysler 200 had stiffened body mounts and softer ride rate, improved suspension geometry, a new rear sway bar, and new tires and an extensively upgraded treatment for the reduction of noise, vibration, and harshness.[4]

Source: Stan Honda/AFP/Getty Images/Newscom.

USES OF SURVEYS Surveys that are designed to collect psychographic and lifestyle data can be used for market segmentation, developing consumer profiles, or determining consumer preferences, as with casual clothing in the opening vignette. Surveys also are useful for determining product image or positioning and for conducting price-perception analysis and advertising research.

ADVANTAGES AND DISADVANTAGES OF SURVEYS Surveys are the primary means of obtaining information about consumers' motives, attitudes, and preferences. The flexibility of surveys is reflected in the variety of questions that can be asked and the visual aids, packages, products, or other props that can be used during the interviews. Additionally, the sampling process enables targeting of respondents with very specific characteristics.

Because survey researchers rely primarily on respondents' self-reports, data gathered in this way can have serious limitations. What people say is not always what they actually do. Errors might occur because respondents remember incorrectly or feel pressured to give the "right" answer. Furthermore, samples might be biased, questions poorly phrased, interviewers not properly instructed or supervised, and results misinterpreted.

Although surveys remain popular for both primary and secondary research, panels do a much better job of tracking consumer behavior.

Be a DM!	Be an MR!
J.D. Power: Powering Ford Vehicles	
As the CEO of Ford Motor Company, what marketing strategies would you adopt to increase the dependability and image of Ford vehicles?	Visit the J.D. Power Web site at www.jdpower.com and write a brief report about its latest vehicle-dependability study findings and methodology. How can you make use of the J.D. Power vehicle-dependability study and other secondary data—including social media—to help Ford increase the image of its vehicles?

Purchase and Media Panels

Purchase and media panels are composed of a group of individuals, households, or organizations that record their purchases and behavior in a diary or on the Internet over time. Households are continually being recruited and added to the panel as respondents drop out of the study or are removed in order to rotate respondents. The makeup of the panel is designed to be representative of the U.S. (target) population in terms of demographics. Panel members are compensated for their participation with gifts, coupons, information, or cash.

Although panels also are maintained for conducting surveys, the distinguishing feature of purchase and media panels is that the respondents or electronic devices record specific behaviors (e.g., product purchases or media consumption) as they occur. This makes the information more accurate. Previously, behavior was recorded in a diary, and the diary was returned to the research organization every 1 to 4 weeks. Paper diaries have been gradually replaced by electronic diaries. Now, most of the panels are online, and the behavior is recorded electronically, either entered online by the respondents or recorded automatically by electronic devices. Based on the type of information recorded, these panels can be classified as either purchase panels or media panels. Media panels are further characterized by the type of media consumption recorded as television, radio, Internet, mobile, or social media (see Figure 5.5).

However, it should be mentioned that survey, purchase, and media panels are not mutually exclusive categories. Some panels may well combine two or even all three types. For example, TNS Global (www.tnsglobal.com) (a member of Kantar Group) uses a digital panel that combines survey information with clickstream data that passively measures actual behavior to

FIGURE 5.5

Classification of Purchase and Media Panels

purchase panels
A data-gathering technique in which respondents record their purchases in a diary.

media panels
A data-gathering technique that involves samples of respondents whose television viewing behavior is automatically recorded by electronic devices, supplementing the purchase information recorded in a diary.

obtain a more accurate and complete picture of both what consumers are doing and why. We discuss purchase panels first, followed by media panels.

PURCHASE PANELS   Survey data can often be complemented with data obtained from **purchase panels**, in which respondents record their purchases in a diary or on the Internet. The NPD Group (www.npd.com) is a leading provider of market information collected and delivered online for a wide range of industries and markets. The NPD Group combines information obtained via surveys with that recorded by respondents about their behaviors to generate reports on consumption behaviors, industry sales, market share, and key demographic trends. Consumer information is collected from its online panel of more than 1.8 million registered adults and teens on a wide range of product categories, including fashion, food, fun, house and home, technology, and automobile classifications. Respondents provide detailed information regarding the brand and amount purchased, the price paid, whether any special deals were involved, the point of purchase, and the product's intended use. The composition of the panel is representative of the U.S. population as a whole. Information provided by the panel is used by soft-drink firms, such as the Coca-Cola Company, to determine brand loyalty and brand switching and to profile heavy users of various brands.

MEDIA PANELS   In **media panels**, electronic devices automatically record the media consumption behavior of members, supplementing a diary. As shown in Figure 5.5, we classify media panels as measuring television, radio, Internet, mobile, and social media consumption. Again, these classifications are not mutually exclusive, and a panel may well be set up to monitor consumption of multiple media so that client companies can determine the optimal media mix. This is becoming all the more relevant as some forms of entertainment are consumed over multiple media. For example, television programming can be viewed over a TV set, mobile handset, or the Internet using a computer. In the following section we discuss television, radio, mobile, and Internet measurement panels. Social media panels are covered in a later section.

Television Measurement   Perhaps the most familiar television panel is by The Nielsen Company (www.nielsen.com). Nielsen tracks a program's minute-to-minute audiences as well as second-by-second, measuring how long consumers spend with a program and how often they return. This type of information enables television stations to cultivate relationships, maximize programming effectiveness, and establish advertising rates. Nielsen TV Audience Measurement data provide a richer view of TV audiences because of the breadth of their panel as well as the census methodologies they employ. Nielsen TV panels include the following:

- **National sample.** For national audience measurement, they provide data from a statistically selected sample of more than 9,000 households, containing more than 18,000 people who have agreed to participate.
- **Local sample.** Nielsen measures 210 local television markets, which they call DMA® (Designated Market Area) regions. Of these, the 56 largest are measured by meter technology. The remaining smaller markets are measured by paper diaries only.

Households in the national sample and larger local markets have an electronic device, called a *storage instantaneous peoplemeter*, attached to their television sets. The peoplemeter continuously monitors television-viewing behavior, including when the set is turned on, what channels are viewed, and for how long. These data are stored in the peoplemeter and transmitted via telephone lines to a central computer. The data collected by the peoplemeter are supplemented with diary panel records, called *audilogs*. The audilog contains information on who was watching each program, so that audience size and demographic characteristics can be calculated.[5] This type of audience measurement is useful to firms such as AT&T, Kellogg, J.C. Penney, Pillsbury, and Unilever, who are looking for advertising media that are reaching their target markets. Nielsen has also developed a passive peoplemeter that recognizes when a person enters or leaves the room and keeps track of the person's activities as he or she watches television.

Radio Measurement   One of the best-known syndicate services for measuring radio audience is Arbitron (www.arbitron.com). The company produces *Radio Today,* the industry's comprehensive annual review of radio listening trends across America. Along with their popular format-by-format reviews, *Radio Today* also offers insights on the consumer behaviors among 16 radio formats (e.g., country, pop, classic rock, etc.).

The Arbitron Portable People Meter™ (PPM) System measures listening behavior in several major metro areas. This information is combined with diary-based data. The PPM detects listening in two distinct locations—"at home" and "away from home"—while diary-based methodology discerns specific out-of-home locations such as "in-car," "at work," or "other" location. Such information can help marketers understand, target, and reach customers more effectively and improve media strategy by identifying what media the target consumers use.

Internet Measurement   Syndicated services are making use of the growing popularity of the Internet. Nielsen, through its Nielsen Online service, tracks and collects Internet usage in real time from home and work users. It reports site and e-commerce activity, including the number of visits to properties, domains, and unique sites; rankings by site and by category; time and frequency statistics; traffic patterns; and e-commerce transactions. It also reports on banner advertising, including audience response to banners, creative content, frequency, and site placement. On September 27, 2010, Nielsen announced the development of Nielsen Online Campaign Ratings, which will for the first time provide audience data comparable to Nielsen's television ratings. Another leader in the field is ComScore Networks (www.comscore.com). It has built a massive cross-section of more than 2 million global Internet users who have given ComScore explicit permission to confidentially capture their Web-wide browsing, buying, and other transaction behavior, including offline purchasing.

Mobile Measurement   Several services measure mobile media consumption. Nielsen Mobile, the mobile arm of Nielsen, measures billing activity through an opt-in panel of more than 50,000 U.S. mobile subscribers. From the billing data, Nielsen reports on many things, from how many text messages they send to what ringtones and games they download. As of the second quarter, 2008, the report shows that a typical U.S. mobile user sends or receives 357 text messages per month. In comparison, only 204 phone calls were placed or received. More importantly for Coca-Cola, the number of text messages was up 450 percent from just 2 years ago, suggesting consumers' affinity for text-messaging. Encouraged by the data, Coca-Cola implemented the mobile version of My Coke Rewards, which allows people to instantly key in their codes directly from their mobile phones. By the third quarter, 2008, 1.1 million customers were actively text-messaging with Coca-Cola as part of their My Coke Rewards program.[6]

USES OF PURCHASE AND MEDIA PANELS   Purchase panels provide information that is useful for forecasting sales, estimating market shares, assessing brand-loyalty and brand-switching behavior, establishing profiles of specific user groups, measuring promotional effectiveness, and conducting controlled store tests. Media panels yield information helpful for establishing advertising rates by radio and TV networks, selecting appropriate programming, and profiling viewer or listener subgroups. Advertisers, media planners, and buyers find panel information to be particularly useful.

ADVANTAGES AND DISADVANTAGES OF PURCHASE AND MEDIA PANELS   The advantages of panel data over survey data relate to data accuracy and the generation of longitudinal data. Repeated measurement of the same variables from the same group of respondents classifies this as a form of longitudinal data. Longitudinal data enables manufacturers to measure changes in brand loyalty, usage, and price sensitivity over time. Involvement in a purchase panel represents a commitment on the part of the respondent. That commitment is thought to enhance the accuracy, and therefore the quality, of panel data. Purchase panels that record information at the time of purchase also eliminate recall errors. Information recorded by electronic devices is even more accurate, because the devices eliminate human errors.

The disadvantage of panel data can be traced to the fact that panel members might not be representative of the larger population and to increased response errors uniquely associated with the process of maintaining a panel. Recruiters for purchase and media panels attempt to mirror the population in the panel makeup. However, certain groups tend to be underrepresented, such as minorities and those with low education levels. The time commitment necessary to participate on panels contributes to the relatively high level of refusal and dropout rates. Additionally, response biases can occur because simply being on the panel might alter a panel member's behavior. Because some purchase or media data are entered by hand, recording errors also are possible.

Experiential Learning

Nielsen Online

Nielsen Online reports on more than 90 percent of the world's Internet usage to give a broad view of the online world. Go to the Nielsen home page www.nielsen.com. On the top menu bar, select "Measurement" and then select "Online." (If this has changed, search the Nielsen site for online measurement.) Answer the following questions.

1. Describe Nielsen's online measurement methodology.

2. How does Nielsen recruit online panel members?

3. Under "Featured News & Insights" given at the bottom of the page, identify and discuss a recent application of Nielsen's online measurement.

Electronic Scanner Services

scanner data
Data obtained by passing merchandise over a laser scanner that reads the UPC code from the packages.

We now describe various forms of scanner data and discuss their uses, advantages, and disadvantages. **Scanner data** are obtained by using electronic scanners at the cash register that read the Universal Product Code (UPC) from consumer purchases. Among the largest syndicated firms specializing in this type of data collection are Nielsen (www.nielsen.com) and SymphonyIRI Group (www.symphonyiri.com). These companies compile and sell data, which tell subscribers how well their products are selling relative to the competition. This analysis can be conducted for each item with a unique UPC—that is, brand, flavor, and package size. Scanner-based companies represent formidable competition for both purchase panels and physical audit services. The accuracy and speed with which product movement at the retail level can be recorded using electronic scanners have reshaped the marketing research industry. Three types of scanner data are available: volume-tracking data, scanner panels, and scanner panels with cable TV.

volume-tracking data
Scanner data that provide information on purchases by brand, size, price, and flavor or formulation.

VOLUME-TRACKING DATA **Volume-tracking data** are routinely collected by supermarkets and other outlets with electronic checkout counters. When the consumers' purchases are scanned, the data are automatically entered into a computer. These data provide information on purchases by brand, size, price, and flavor or formulation based on sales data collected from the checkout scanner tapes. However, this information cannot be linked to consumers' background characteristics, because their identities are not recorded when their purchases are scanned. This information is collected nationally from a sample of supermarkets with electronic scanners. Scanner services providing volume-tracking data include Nielsen and SymphonyIRI Group (InfoScan). The InfoScan Syndicated Store Tracking service monitors more than 34,000 supermarket, drugstore, and mass-merchandiser outlets. An example of the type of information available from SymphonyIRI Group follows.

Research in Action

Supersizing the Supermarket

SymphonyIRI Group's (www.symphonyiri.com) *Times & Trends*, available at the company's Web site, highlights the consumer packaged goods (CPG) industry's year-end review. *Times & Trends* is a valuable report for busy executives who need a summary insight into today's economic and general business conditions but who also need a detailed insight into CPG trends and retail marketing conditions. For example, a recent report highlighted that at 60-percent household penetration, Walmart Supercenters grab 10 percent of shopper spending. Expanding Supercenter distribution enables Walmart to grab a larger share of the faster growing dinner-solution market. About 25 percent of Walmart Supercenters' shopper spending is for the most challenged meal occasion of the day, the dinner meal. Frozen dinners and entrees are the fifth-most purchased food-and-beverage category item by Walmart Supercenter shoppers, with frozen poultry at number nine. Such information has enabled Walmart to further expand its line of frozen dinners and entrees and open additional Supercenters. Walmart operated 2,772 Supercenters at the end of 2010, an additional 160 locations from 2009, which were primarily from conversions of Walmart Discount Stores.[7]

SCANNER PANEL DATA   With **scanner panels**, each household member is given an ID card that can be read by the electronic scanner at the cash register. Scanner panel members simply present the ID card at the checkout counter each time they shop. In this way, the consumer's identity is linked to product purchases as well as the time and day of the shopping trip. This enables the firm to build a shopping record for that individual. Alternatively, some firms provide handheld scanners to panel members. These members scan their purchases once they are home.

Nielsen's global consumer panel records the purchases of more than 250,000 households across 25 countries. The consumer scans the bar codes on purchases with a handheld scanner, which records the price, promotions, and quantity of each item. The information in the handheld scanner is then transmitted to Nielsen. Nielsen uses the information from the scanner and additional information gathered from the consumer to determine such things as consumer demographics, quantity and frequency of purchases, percentage of households purchasing, shopping trips and expenditures, price paid, and usage information. In recent years, Nielsen has also started providing Nielsen Online service that measures the relationship between online marketing activity and offline purchasing behavior as it acknowledges the role of the Internet in the daily life of a consumer. It directly tracks what sites the panel member visits and quantifies the sites' significance to the overall sales volume. Members of the Nielsen's consumer panel record their offline buying behavior with the scanners; meanwhile, patented Nielsen Online software monitors their Internet use and behavior.

> **scanner panels**
> Scanner data collected from panel members who are issued an ID card that enables their purchases to be linked to their identities.

Research in Action

Tracking Cereal Purchases

Kellogg's (www.kelloggs.com) uses Nielsen's consumer panel, discussed earlier in this chapter, to answer a variety of questions:

- In what areas of the country are Kellogg's cereals purchased most frequently?
- What promotions were offered at the time of purchase?
- What is the number and size of the cereal boxes the typical consumer purchases?
- What are the demographic characteristics of heavy cereal users?

Kellogg's uses this information to better target its products to consumers. The information also is used to design sales promotions, such as coupons and point-of-sale displays, to better meet consumers' needs. For example, larger families of Hispanic origin in California tend to be heavy users of Kellogg's Cornflakes. Kellogg's has attempted to cultivate and retain the patronage of these users by directing coupons and promotional offers to them.[8]

SCANNER PANELS WITH CABLE TV   An even more advanced use of scanning technology, **scanner panels with cable TV**, combines scanner panels with new technologies that have grown out of the cable TV industry. Households on these panels subscribe to one of the cable TV systems in their market. By means of a cable TV "split," the researcher targets various commercials into panel members' homes. For example, half the households might see test commercial A during the 6 PM newscast, while the other half views test commercial B. This enables marketing researchers to conduct fairly controlled experiments in a relatively natural environment. The technology also offers a way to target marketing effort. For example, it is possible to transmit a Dannon yogurt commercial only to Yoplait consumers to determine whether they can be induced to switch brands. SymphonyIRI Group's BehaviorScan system contains such a panel.

Systems have been developed to allow transmission of advertising into participating households without the use of a cable TV system. Because these panels can be selected from all available TV households, not just those with cable TV, the bias of cable-only testing is eliminated. Using this type of system, General Mills, for example, can test which one of four test commercials for Total cereal results in the highest sales. Four groups of panel members are selected, and each receives a different test commercial. These households are monitored via scanner data to determine which group purchased the most Total cereal. Scanner services incorporate advanced marketing research technology, which results in some advantages over survey and purchase panel data.

> **scanner panels with cable TV**
> The combination of a scanner panel with manipulations of the advertising that is being broadcast by cable TV companies.

USES OF SCANNER DATA Scanner data are useful for a variety of purposes. National volume-tracking data can be used for tracking sales, prices, and distribution and for modeling and analyzing early warning signals. Scanner panels with cable TV can be used for testing new products, repositioning products, analyzing promotional mix, and making advertising and pricing decisions. These panels provide marketing researchers with a unique, controlled environment for the manipulation of marketing variables.

ADVANTAGES AND DISADVANTAGES OF SCANNER DATA Given that the major grocery chains have largely completed the conversion to electronic scanning, and drugstores are following suit, electronic data collection is likely to continue to grow. The prompt feedback about point-of-sale product activity enables managers to evaluate existing marketing programs as well as to formulate new ones.

Scanner data are not only available more quickly, but they are also typically more accurate than data collected through either surveys or purchase panels. The response bias that plagues manual data collection is lessened, because the respondents are much less conscious of their role as members of a scanner panel. Errors due to failures in recall also are eliminated with electronic data collection. Scanners also offer the ability to study very short time periods of sales activity.

Another advantage of scanners is that in-store variables, such as pricing, promotions, and displays, also are recorded. Finally, a scanner panel with cable TV provides a highly controlled test environment for alternate promotional messages.

A major weakness of scanner data is its lack of representativeness. Only retailers equipped with scanners are included in the research. Entire retail categories, such as food warehouses and mass merchandisers, might be excluded. Likewise, the availability of scanners might be lacking in certain geographical areas.

The quality of scanner data is only as good as the scanning process itself and can be limited by several factors. All products might not be scanned. For example, a clerk might use the register to ring up a heavy item to avoid lifting it. If an item does not scan on the first try, the clerk might key in the price and ignore the bar code. Sometimes a consumer purchases many flavors of the same item, but the clerk scans only one package and then rings in the number of purchases. Thus, the transaction is recorded inaccurately. Although scanner data provide behavioral and sales information, they do not provide information on underlying attitudes, preferences, and reasons for specific choices.

Be a DM!	Be an MR!
Scanning the Right Price of Lay's Potato Chips	
As the marketing manager for Lay's potato chips, how would you determine the right price?	Visit Nielsen at www.nielsen.com and write a brief report about its retail measurement service. How can you use Nielsen's retail measurement service to determine the optimal price for Lay's potato chips?

Syndicated Data from Institutions

We have already discussed syndicated data collected from consumers and households. Parallel electronic and manual systems also are used to collect institutional and industrial data. As Figure 5.6 shows, syndicated data are available for retailers and wholesalers as well as industrial firms/organizations.

Retailer and Wholesaler Audits

audit
A data collection process derived from physical records or inventory analysis. Data are collected personally by the researcher or by representatives of the researcher, and the data are based upon counts, usually of physical objects.

Collecting product-movement data for wholesalers and retailers is referred to as an **audit**. These periodic audits can be a physical count of the inventory or managed through a link to the scanning process. These audits track inventory flow, current inventory levels, and the impact of both promotional and pricing programs on inventory levels.

A physical audit is a formal examination and verification of product movement carried out by examining physical records or analyzing inventory. An example of the traditional audit is the

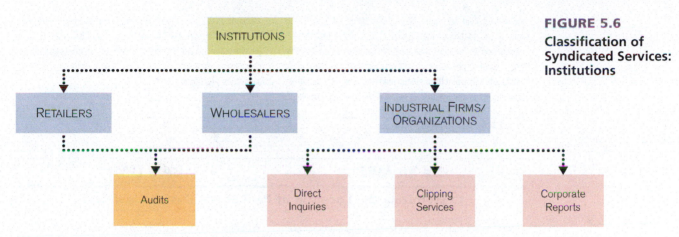

FIGURE 5.6

Classification of Syndicated Services: Institutions

National Retail Census by GfK Retail and Technology USA, (www.gfkrt.com/usa), which provides updated measurements of product distribution in all types of retail and service outlets. Conducted annually since its inception in 1953, it is based on a national probability sample of approximately 30,000 outlets of all kinds throughout the country in more than 500 different geographic areas. The audit is conducted by personal store visits, making GfK's Retail Census the largest annual product availability measurement in the United States. For high speed and accuracy, these in-store audits use handheld computers to capture UPC information electronically. Retail audit data can be useful to consumer product firms. For example, say that Colgate Palmolive is contemplating introducing a new toothpaste brand. A retail audit can help determine the size of the total market and distribution of sales by type of outlet and by different regions.

Wholesale audit services, the counterpart of retail audits, monitor warehouse withdrawals. Participating operators, which include supermarket chains, wholesalers, and frozen-food warehouses, typically account for more than 80 percent of the volume in this area. Audits are now being increasingly conducted by using scanner data and electronic records rather than by physical examination and verification.

USES OF AUDIT DATA   Standardized as well as customized reports are available to help subscribers manage their brands. These reports provide information that can be used to (1) determine market size and share for both categories and brands by type of outlet, region, or city; (2) assess competitive activity; (3) identify distribution problems, including shelf-space allocation and inventory issues; (4) develop sales potentials and forecasts; and (5) develop and monitor promotional allocations based on sales volume. Scanners are now used to collect data that cross the wholesale, retail, and customer levels. The information they offer has had a profound impact on the marketing process.

ADVANTAGES AND DISADVANTAGES OF AUDIT DATA   Audits provide relatively accurate information on the movement of many products at the wholesale and retail levels. Furthermore, this information can be broken down by a number of important variables, such as brand, type of outlet, and size of market.

A major disadvantage of physical audits, however, is the limited retail coverage and delay associated with compiling and reporting inventory data. Typically, a 2-month gap exists between the completion of the audit cycle and the publication of reports. Another disadvantage of physical audits is that, unlike scanner data, audit data cannot be linked to consumer characteristics. In fact, it can be difficult to relate audit data to advertising expenditures and other marketing efforts.

Research in Action

Hispanic Small Food Store Audit

The Hispanic Small Food Store Audit is a bimonthly audit conducted by GfK Audits & Surveys (www.gfkrt.com/usa). Marketers targeting the burgeoning Hispanic segment in the United States can now measure the results of their campaigns through the Hispanic Small Food Store Sales Index. A measurement of sales in a channel for which there is little sales data, this study is conducted through personal visits to 360 stores in high-density Hispanic markets. Manual audits are conducted by trained bilingual

(continued)

local-market field personnel. Store participation on an ongoing basis is secured through the payment of cooperation fees to each individual outlet. Inventory measurements are taken on a bimonthly basis, six times per year (January–February, March–April, etc.); invoice and other purchase memoranda might be recorded more frequently, as jointly determined with the store owners/managers.

The audit tracks the following: sales, brand shares, distribution, inventories, and pricing. Marketers, such as P&G, attempting to penetrate the Hispanic market can make use of the audit findings to determine distribution outlets, product mix, inventories, advertising campaigns, and prices.[9]

Be an MR!	Be a DM!

Customizing the Location of Paul Stuart Custom Jewelers

Social Media

Visit the GfK Audits & Surveys Web site at www.gfkauditsandsurveys.com and write a brief report about the firm's audit services. How can you make use of retail audit data to determine new store locations for Paul Stuart Custom Jewelers? How can social media help you make a better determination?

As the marketing chief for Paul Stuart Custom Jewelers, how would you determine the best store locations?

Industrial Firms/Organizations

Industrial Firms/Organizations
Secondary data derived from industrial firms and organizational sources and intended for industrial or institutional use.

Industrial firms/organizations provide syndicated data about industrial firms, businesses, and other institutions including nonprofit organizations. Financial, operating, and employment data also are collected by these syndicated research services for almost every North American Industry Classification System (NAICS) category. These data are collected by making direct inquiries from clipping services that monitor newspapers, the trade press, or broadcasts, and from corporate reports. The range and sources of syndicated data available for institutional firms are more limited than those available to consumer goods firms. D&B can provide reports of businesses located in the United States and abroad.

The D&B (www.dnb.com) global commercial database provides one-click access to more than 106 million active public/private companies located around the world. After locating a business, you can get key business data, including full address information, NAIC/line of business details, business size (sales, net worth, employees), names of key principals, and identification of this location's headquarters, domestic parent company, and/or global parent company.

These data are very useful in developing business-to-business sales plans and direct-marketing lists, estimating market potential and share within industries, and devising overall marketing strategies. Business statistics related to annual sales, geographic coverage, supplier relationships, and distribution channels are just a few of the categories of information available to business-to-business market planners. These secondary sources also serve as a source for sampling frames when conducting business-to-business research.

USES OF INDUSTRY SERVICES Information provided by institutional services is useful for sales management decisions, including identifying prospects, defining territories, setting quotas, and measuring market potential by geographic areas. It can also aid in advertising decisions, such as targeting prospects, allocating advertising budgets, selecting media, and measuring advertising effectiveness. This kind of information also is useful for segmenting the market and designing custom products and services for segments in the target markets.

ADVANTAGES AND DISADVANTAGES OF INDUSTRY SERVICES Published institutional information provides a valuable first step in business-to-business marketing. The information is typically limited to publicly traded firms, however, and dissemination of that data is typically controlled by the reporting firm itself. A researcher has to be wary of the completeness of reported data as well as the bias introduced by this form of respondent self-report. These data are limited in the nature, content, quantity, and quality of information.

Combining Information from a Variety of Sources: Single-Source Data

As discussed in Chapter 4, combining data from different sources can enhance the value of secondary data. This practice in syndicated services is referred to as *single-source research*. Single-source research tracks the full marketing process from initial advertising communication through product purchase. The process links a person's demographic and psychographic information with television, reading, and shopping habits. A combination of surveys, diaries, and electronic scanners is used to integrate such information. Manufacturer pricing and promotional activities are overlaid on this consumer data as well. Thus, **single-source data** provide integrated information on household variables, such as media consumption and purchases, and on marketing variables, such as product sales, price, advertising, promotion, and in-store marketing effort.

SymphonyIRI Group collects consumer purchase information from a nationally representative household panel of approximately 70,000 recruited households with coverage at the regional, national, and individual market level. It is designed to supply strategic direction to marketers by focusing on the consumer dynamics that drive brand and category performance. Complete multi-outlet purchase information on these households is tracked electronically. Panel households use a simple in-home scanning device, called a ScanKey, to record their purchases from all outlets. Panelists are not required to record any causal information except for manufacturer coupons. Price reductions are recorded by scanner, and features and displays are captured by SymphonyIRI Group's in-store personnel, ensuring an accurate and unbiased record of sales. Other examples of single-source data include CACI Consumer Insights by GfK MRI (www.gfkmri.com) and PRIZM by Nielsen (www.nielsen.com). PRIZM, discussed in Chapter 4, combines census data, consumer surveys about shopping and lifestyles, and purchase data to identify segments. The following example illustrates Campbell Soup Company's application of single-source data.

single-source data
An effort to combine data from different sources by gathering integrated information on household and marketing variables applicable to the same set of respondents.

Research in Action

General Hospital Too General for V8

The Campbell Soup Company (www.campbell.com) used single-source data to target its advertising for V8 juice (www.v8juice.com). By obtaining single-source data on product consumption, media consumption, and demographic characteristics, Campbell found that demographically similar TV audiences consume vastly different amounts of V8. For example, on an index where 100 was the average household's V8 consumption, *General Hospital* viewers had a below-average index of 80. These results were surprising, because the *General Hospital* audience actually had a higher percentage of women 25 to 54 years old, the demographic group most predisposed to buy V8, and so would have been expected to be a better medium to reach V8 drinkers. Using this information, Campbell rearranged its advertising schedule to raise the average index by moving advertising dollars away from *General Hospital*, despite the fact that this soap was one of the third most popular for the week ending October 9, 2010 (www.soapcentral.com), to other TV programs that had an above-average index. In 2010, Campbell introduced the V8 V-Fusion + Tea Beverage, a blend of vegetable, fruit juice, and the natural goodness of green tea, and advertised it on its new schedule.[10]

Source: AP Wide World Photos/Mike Derer.

Summary Illustration Using the Opening Vignette

Syndicated research firms specialize in designing research systems that collect data of commercial interest to multiple users. This was seen in the opening vignette, where the results of the NPD survey were used by multiple firms in the same industry: Haggar and Levi Strauss.

Syndicated sources can be classified based on the unit of measurement (households/consumers or institutions). Syndicated data from households can be obtained via surveys, purchase or media panels, or electronic scanner systems. Although a survey was used in the opening vignette, data on purchases of business casual clothing can also be collected using purchase panels and electronic scanners (or similar systems) installed in department stores. When institutions are the unit of measurement, the data can be obtained from retailers, wholesalers, or institutional firms. It is desirable to combine information obtained from different secondary sources to get a more complete picture of the marketplace. Thus, one could combine data on casual clothing obtained from consumers with data from retailers (e.g., Macy's, Sears, etc.) and manufacturers (e.g., Haggar, Levi Strauss, etc.) to get a better understanding of the casual clothing market. Figure 5.7 offers a concept map for syndicated data. In this figure, the major concepts are connected by bold arrows using descriptors. Thus, syndicated data can be classified based on unit of measurement as obtained from either household/consumers or institutions. The rest of the figure can be interpreted similarly.

FIGURE 5.7

A Concept Map for Syndicated Data

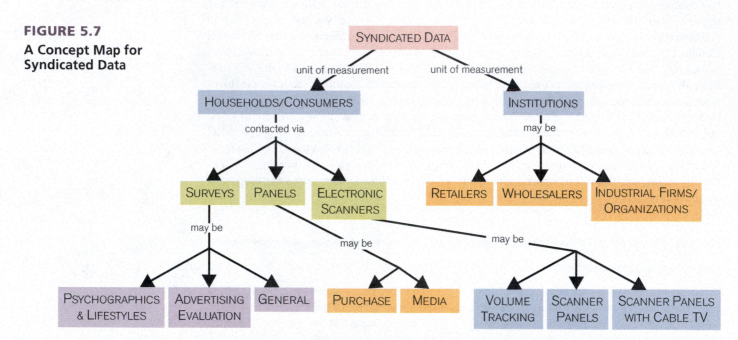

Experiential Learning

Syndicated Firms

Identify and describe syndicated firms, other than those listed in this chapter, that offer the following services. Briefly describe each service. Cite all URLs and references.

a. Lifestyle surveys

b. Advertising evaluation surveys

c. Omnibus panels

d. Purchase panels

e. Media panels (TV, radio, Internet, mobile)

f. Scanner data (volume tracking)

g. Scanner panels

h. Audits

i. Information on business firms

International Marketing Research

U.S. syndicated research firms are an important source of information on overseas consumer and institutional markets. For companies considering expansion internationally or managing existing international ventures, one of the first steps toward understanding and monitoring these markets can be through syndicated sources. The need for relatively inexpensive, comprehensive data related to international markets, consumer and social trends, as well as existing market structures creates a built-in demand for international syndicated services. Many of the same major syndicated firms operating in the United States have invested heavily in creating data collection systems to support their internationally operating clients. Gallup International is just one of the U.S. syndicated firms that have expanded its services to include international research.

Research in Action

Euroconsumers Go for Spending Splash

Gallup (www.gallup.com), which specializes in survey research obtaining both lifestyle and psychographic data, recently conducted interviews with more than 22,500 adults across the European Union. The results point to an exploding consumer durable market, particularly for convenience items such as remote-control TVs, microwave ovens, Blu-ray and DVD players, and cell phones. The educational level and the standard of living among this consumer group are generally improving. Europeans also are displaying higher levels of discretionary purchasing, demonstrated in growing demand for travel packages, which picked up after the recession of 2008–2009 and continued to be strong through 2011. In the personal care market, the number of European women using perfume is declining, offset by growing demand for deodorants.

Such syndicated data are useful to marketers such as Motorola, GE, and AT&T, which are looking to further develop European markets. For example, when renting an apartment in Germany, the renter must install all the major appliances and lighting fixtures. GE has developed value packages offering significant savings on appliances and lighting fixtures that are carefully targeted at apartment renters.[11]

Like Gallup, Nielsen has made huge investments in European markets over the past 30-plus years, introducing scanner and tracking services at the retail level. With international operations a little larger than in the United States, 50.3 percent of Nielsen's business is outside the United States (see Table 1.1 in Chapter 1). Of that overseas business, 50 percent is in Europe.

The global category of the Nielsen Wire blog contains international and regional insights in more than a hundred countries. An example of a post that is found here would be "Social Media Dominates Asia–Pacific Internet Usage." The article highlights the important findings of Nielsen's Asia–Pacific Social Media Report. Social media usage has grown tremendously and is now one of the most critical trends in the online sector. Social media is starting to impact consumers' purchasing decisions. Online product reviews emerged as the third-most-trusted source of information when making purchasing decisions, following behind family and friends. The findings also show that Koreans are most likely to share positive product experiences, while the Chinese would most likely share negative ones. Other key findings include blogging being popular in Japan, China's social networks being attracted by grassroots, Okut's share in India being challenged by Facebook, high percentages of Koreans engaging in social media, and Australians spending large amounts of time in online forums. Reports such as these highlight the different trends in different countries, prompting firms to embrace new policies and strategies that cater to the different markets in order to remain relevant.

Marketing Research and Social Media

The emergence of social media has greatly increased syndicated firms' ability to reach out to the once-unreachables and hear conversations that used to be restricted among neighborhoods and personal physical social networks. Rapid advances in technology have created a new source of information and communication for firms like Nielsen. Social media are rich in qualitative and quantitative data that traditional methods may not be able to collect or that gathering them could have been a more time-consuming and costly process. Information gathered from social media is used by syndicated firms to understand the market, answer clients' concerns, connect to consumers and potential participants, and conduct online research and publicize reports and company information.

Nielsen has an active presence on various forms of social media. The Nielsen Wire is Nielsen's social media platform, which aims to reach out to the Internet-savvy generation of the twenty-first century. Launched in 2008, the blog features important information from its mass of publications and research units, covering the latest daily updates in consumer behavior, media, and marketing trends. The user-friendly blog is divided into six subcategories: consumers, featured insights, global, media and entertainment, online and mobile, and reports and downloads.

Nielsen offers various social media products and services on a syndicated basis. On September 22, 2009, in New York, Nielsen announced its strategic alliance with Facebook to use Nielsen products to help marketers better measure online advertising impact and realize a greater return on investment. This alliance combined Facebook's global reach to consumers and Nielsen's marketing research expertise, thus providing better insights and more information to marketers around the world. It provides a better understanding of how Web content and online advertising affect consumer behavior.

Nielsen BrandLift, the first product of this collaboration, is designed to provide marketers with effectiveness measurement for Facebook advertising. BrandLift uses opt-in polls on Facebook's home page to measure consumer attitudes and purchase intent from display advertising that has appeared on the site. Nielsen BrandLift measures aided awareness, ad recall, message association, brand favorability, and purchase consideration via a set of short, specially designed one- or two-question surveys. The surveys collect the information that marketers need as a seamless part of the Facebook user experience. The frequency of the surveys is carefully controlled to avoid any one user from being asked to participate too often. No personally identifiable information is collected as part of this program. The surveys appear on Facebook's home page in the same space where people see sponsored messages today, with a look, feel, and functionality that fit neatly into the existing Facebook experience.

Advances have also been made in measuring consumer-generated content (CGM). As a result of its existence and ability to thrive on the Internet, online word-of-mouth leaves a "digital trail," allowing content to be located, categorized, analyzed, and then understood. Nielsen BuzzMetrics is a prime example of a tool by a syndicated research firm to "follow" this trail. BuzzMetrics collects and analyzes content from a wide range of CGM/social media sources, including blogs, user groups, discussion boards, social networking sites, and micro-blogging sites such as Twitter. Online content of traditional media sources such as newspapers are also within the radar of this intelligent program. It has the potential to scour for data from different geographical locations and translate foreign languages using its global language capabilities. It is also able to execute consumer segmentation viewable by interest group and demographic type.

BuzzMetrics basically leverages a range of Web technologies that include tagging, probing, and ad collection to gather and analyze large volumes of data. Subsequently, these data are translated into meaningful information in report form and are then sold to companies that subscribe to it. Sony Online Entertainment employed BuzzMetrics to do research on gaming.

Research in Action

Sony Gaming with Social Media

Sony Online Entertainment, the game development arm of Sony, creates massively popular multiplayer online (MMO) games that are played on the Internet by millions of paying subscribers all over the world. To complement the online gaming experience, the company also hosts community forums where gamers and the community managers, people hired by Sony to manage the forums, can communicate. Community managers participate actively in the forums, in most cases working to correct misinformation and sway players' negative perceptions of the brand, which has not always been a success. Sony began to suspect that the negativity was not just confined to the forums. So in 2005, Sony hired Nielsen to track player sentiment across the entire spectrum of social media to see how far-reaching the negative buzz about the brand went. Nielsen employed its BuzzMetrics tool and produced results that were rather displeasing.

As expected, negative player sentiment had spread throughout the Web. In fact, Nielsen found that the consensus among the players was that Sony was only concerned about making money and did not care about them. Through Nielsen's research, Sony was able to locate the main hubs of information and, more importantly, the key social media "influencers," people whose posts were often referred to by other players. To solicit input and help in disseminating correct information about the brand, Sony now invites the top 20 influencers twice every year to its corporate headquarters. According to Sony, the program has been successful so far, due in large part to Nielsen's capability to cast a wider net in social media than Sony ever could internally. Through BuzzMetrics, Sony was able to track true player sentiment in a timely fashion beyond the confines of its own community forums.[12]

Finally, mention must be made of the Nielsen and McKinsey & Company joint venture, NM Incite (www.nmincite.com), which dwells on advancing social media intelligence. NM Incite provides solutions like Social Media Intelligence Strategy that helps companies embed social media intelligence across a range of functional business units. Other solutions include Optimize New Product Innovation, Optimizing Your Marketing, Building Advocacy and Increasing Customer Value, Managing Brand Health and Threat Tracking, and Understanding Your Customers. With all the products and solutions offered by NM Incite, leveraging the Social Media Intelligence, marketing managers can propel their businesses.

Ethics in Marketing Research

Ethical issues in formulating a research design, which were discussed in Chapter 3, also are relevant in collecting syndicated data. Respondents' rights, particularly their privacy, are another salient issue. Obtaining data from respondents without their full knowledge or consent is an invasion of privacy. Consider, for example, the frequent shopper cards that supermarkets issue. These cards provide a variety of services, such as check-cashing identification, special notification of sales, and cash discounts or rebates, at no apparent cost to the cardholders. Although this might sound like a good deal, many cardholders are unaware of the hidden costs involved.

When applying for a card, each shopper provides data on demographic and shopping-related variables and is assigned a UPC code. The shopper's card, which contains the UPC code, is scanned before the grocery purchases are scanned. Thus, a shopper's purchases are linked to that shopper's demographic and shopping-related data collected at the time of card application. This information results in a database that contains rich information on shoppers, including a demographic profile, when they shop, how much they spend, how they pay for purchases, and what products they buy. As discussed in Chapter 4, this database can be used to target consumers and formulate effective marketing strategies. Often, these data are sold to syndicated firms, who in turn sell them to multiple clients, resulting in much wider dissemination and use. Most consumers, however, are unaware that the supermarket has all this information about them simply because they are cardholders.

The supermarkets and other firms engaging in this practice of collecting data without the respondent's direct knowledge or consent are violating the ethical principle of informed consent. According to this principle, researchers have the ethical responsibility to avoid both uninformed and misinformed participation by respondents in market research projects. On a positive note, syndicated firms are playing a significant role in researching ethical issues and sensitizing marketing firms, the marketing research industry, and the general public about these concerns.

Research in Action

Reaching Kids But Alienating Adults: Ethical Repercussions

According to a recent survey by GfK Roper Public Affairs & Corporate Communication, a syndicated marketing division of GfK Custom Research North America (www.gfkamerica.com), the general public is skeptical about advertising aimed at children. Eight of 10 adults agree that business marketing and advertising exploit children by convincing them to buy things that are bad for them or that they do not need.

Adults do not necessarily object to all advertising, only to that they perceive to be harmful to children. Eight of 10 adults say it is "all right" to advertise products such as toys, cereal, and clothing on television during children's programming. Adults are more likely to object to commercials that "sell" sex and poor nutrition, such as PG-13 movies and candy bars. Thus, marketers who engage in such practices in an attempt to reach children run the risk of alienating adults. In 2010, The Center for Science in the Public Interest (a nutrition watchdog group) threatened to sue McDonald's, the giant U.S. restaurant chain, for using toys to sell its fast-food meals to children. The Center claimed that the popular toys illegally lure children into eating habits that threaten their health. It was unfair for McDonald's to bypass parents and market directly to little children.

Several syndicated firms, including GfK Roper Public Affairs & Corporate Communication, are playing a significant role in addressing ethical issues in marketing research by sensitizing researchers, clients, and the general public to such issues and providing reasonable solutions.[13]

WHAT WOULD YOU DO?

Boston Market: Sizing the Market

The Situation

George Michel, president and CEO of Boston Market (www.bostonmarket.com), is well aware of the fact that, according to syndicated data, home meal replacement (HMR) will be the family dining business of the century. HMR is portable, high-quality food that is meant for takeout, and it is the fastest growing and most significant opportunity in the food industry today. According to Nielsen's consumer panel data, 55 percent of respondents purchased a meal for at-home consumption several times a month. Convenience and type of food were the two most influential factors when purchasing an HMR. Also, 77 percent of these respondents preferred their meals be ready to eat.

Another recent study by the NPD Group (www.npd.com) projected that between 2010 and 2015, virtually all growth in food sales will come from food service, defined as food prepared at least partially away from home. Estimates of total HMR market size, as well as future potential, vary widely. Numbers ranging from $50 billion to $150 billion have been given for the year 2015. Sara Lee projections show HMR accounting for as much as 80 percent of food industry growth by 2015. Findings by McKinsey & Company support that premise from two perspectives: (1) the fact that virtually all foods sales growth by the year 2015 will come from food service and (2) that by 2015 many Americans will never have cooked a meal from scratch. HMR is the most important trend to hit the food industry since the advent of frozen food.

Boston Market is now the HMR leader. As of 2011, Boston Market had about 500 company-owned restaurants in 28 states, with more than 13,000 employees. George Michel wants to capitalize on the HMR trend. Boston Market is testing new HMR products that could be introduced in 2012. The products being tested include prepackaged "take-and-go" lunch boxes, expanded catering services, enhanced drive-through operations, and call-ahead pick-up services.

The Marketing Research Decision

1. Given the wide estimates of $50 billion to $150 billion for HMR potential sales for 2015, how can Boston Market get a more reasonable estimate? What sources of syndicated data should be consulted? (Check all that apply.)
   a. SymphonyIRI Group
   b. Nielsen
   c. McKinsey & Company
   d. NPD Group
   e. All of the above

2. How will the type of research you recommend enable George Michel to size the HMR market and determine what new products and services Boston Market should introduce?

The Marketing Management Decision

1. What new products and services should George Michel introduce? (Check all that apply.)
   a. Opening of new restaurant concepts
   b. Expanded catering services
   c. Enhanced drive-through operations
   d. Launching of a new advertising campaign
   e. All of the above

2. Discuss how the marketing management-decision action that you recommend to George Michel is influenced by the syndicated sources of data that you suggested earlier and by the information they provide.

What George Michel Did

Boston Market worked with Arnold Worldwide of Boston to produce a new advertising campaign. In an effort to energize its brand, Boston Market reminded consumers that the restaurant fulfills their need for quick, convenient, wholesome meals. Portraying real-life, recognizable situations Americans often encounter concerning dinner, the tagline was "Time for something good," which was later replaced by "A real meal at a great price…AND time for my life."[14]

Summary

Syndicated research firms specialize in designing research systems that collect data of commercial interest to multiple users. Collecting data to serve a known commercial purpose is one of the primary differentiators when comparing syndicated services to other types of secondary data (discussed in Chapter 4). Syndicated data are timely and cost-effective. Given the need for an impartial monitor of market-wide trends, as well as consumer reactions or behaviors, syndicated researchers provide a unique and valuable service.

Syndicated sources can be classified based on the unit of measurement (households/consumers or institutions). Syndicated data from households can be obtained via surveys, purchase or media panels, or electronic scanner systems. When institutions are the unit of measurement, the data can be obtained from retailers, wholesalers, or industrial firms/organizations. It is desirable to combine information from different sources, resulting in single-source data.

U.S. syndicated research firms are an important source of information on overseas consumer and institutional markets. Social media play an important role in helping syndicated firms to collect data from new sources, develop new products and services, and stay connected with clients and the market. A major ethical issue in collecting syndicated data is the invasion of privacy of the respondents by obtaining data without their full knowledge or consent.

Key Terms and Concepts

Syndicated sources 122
Periodic surveys 125
Panel surveys 126
Psychographics 127
Lifestyle 127

Purchase panels 130
Media panels 130
Scanner data 132
Volume-tracking data 132
Scanner panels 133

Scanner panels with cable TV 133
Audit 134
Industrial firms/organizations 136
Single-source data 137

Suggested Cases and Video Cases

Running Case with Real Data

1.1 Hewlett-Packard

Comprehensive Critical Thinking Cases

2.1 American Idol   2.2 Baskin-Robbins   2.3 Akron Children's Hospital

Comprehensive Cases with Real Data

3.1 Bank of America   3.2 McDonald's   3.3 Boeing

Comprehensive Brief Harvard Business School Cases

4.1 TruEarth Healthy Foods: Market Research for a New Product Introduction (4065)
4.2 The Springfield Nor'easters: Maximizing Revenues in the Minor Leagues (2510)
4.3 Metabical: Positioning and Communications Strategy for a New Weight-Loss Drug (4240)
4.4 Saxonville Sausage Company (2085)

Online Video Cases

5.1 eGO   8.1 AFLAC   9.1 P&G   11.1 Dunkin' Donuts
12.1 Motorola   13.1 Subaru   19.1 Marriott

Live Research: Conducting a Marketing Research Project

1. Visit the Web sites of syndicated firms to identify the relevant information, some of which can be obtained without cost.
2. If the project is supported by a budget, then relevant information can be purchased from syndicated sources.
3. **Social Media** One, a few, or all of the teams can be assigned the responsibility of collecting and analyzing data from the Internet and social media.
4. Encourage students to visit relevant Web sites of the client and its competitors and to conduct a thorough online search using search engines.

Acronym

The salient characteristics of syndicated data may be described by the acronym SYNDICATED:

S   urveys

Y   ield data of known commercial value

N   umber of clients use the data

D   iary panels

I   nstitutional services

C   ost is low

A   udits

T   imely and current

E   lectronic scanner services

D   ata combined from different sources: single-source data

Review Questions

1. How do syndicated data and data available from other secondary sources differ?
2. List and describe the various syndicated sources of secondary data.
3. What is the nature of information collected by surveys?
4. How can surveys be classified?
5. Explain what a panel is. How do purchase panels and media panels differ?
6. What are the relative advantages of purchase panels over surveys?
7. What kinds of data can be gathered through electronic scanner services?
8. Describe the uses of scanner data.
9. What is an audit? Discuss the uses, advantages, and disadvantages of audits.
10. Describe the information provided by institutional and industrial services.
11. Why is it desirable to use multiple sources of secondary data?
12. Explain what is meant by single-source data.
13. **Social Media** How are syndicated firms using social media?

Applied Problems

1. Visit www.npd.com and write a description of a panel maintained by NPD.
2. Visit www.nielsen.com and write a report about the various services offered by Nielsen.
3. Visit www.symphonyiri.com and write a report about the products and services offered by SymphonyIRI Group.
4. Visit www.gallup.com and write a report about Gallup's syndicated services.
5. Visit www.arbitron.com and write a report about Arbitron's syndicated services.
6. Select an industry of your choice. Contact one of the syndicated firms to obtain industry sales and the sales of the major firms in that industry for the past year. Estimate the market shares of each major firm. From a published source, obtain information on the market shares of these same firms. Do the two estimates agree?

Group Discussion

Discuss how the Nielsen TV ratings can affect the price that advertisers pay for a commercial broadcast during a particular time.

Hewlett-Packard Running Case

Review the Hewlett-Packard (HP) case, Case 1.1, and questionnaire given toward the end of the book. Answer the following questions.

1. What information available from syndicated firms would be useful to HP as it seeks to increase its penetration of U.S. households?

2. How can HP make use of lifestyle information available from syndicated services?

3. **Social Media** What information is available on consumer social media usage from syndicated firms? How can HP make use of this information?

4. What information available from www.nielsen.com can help HP evaluate the effectiveness of its Web site?

ONLINE VIDEO CASE 5.1

eGO: Reinventing Wheels

Visit **www.pearsonhighered.com/malhotra** to read the video case and view the accompanying video. eGO: Reinventing Wheels highlights eGO's various strategies and initiatives such as marketing research, customer feedback, direct marketing, and online sales in order to establish a strong market image for its product. The description of secondary data analysis efforts includes the need for eGO to understand consumer price sensitivity, tastes, and local restrictions in various countries. The case can be used to discuss the sources of syndicated data that would be useful to eGO in projecting future demand for its vehicles. Specific marketing research questions on this and the previous chapters are posed in the video case.

6 Exploratory Research Design: Qualitative Research

Source: Stockbyte/Thinkstock.

LEARNING OBJECTIVES

After reading this chapter, the student should be able to:

1. Explain the difference between qualitative and quantitative research in terms of objectives, sampling, data collection and analysis, and outcomes.

2. Understand the various forms of qualitative research, including direct procedures such as focus groups and depth interviews, and indirect methods such as projective techniques.

3. Describe focus groups in detail, with emphasis on planning and conducting focus groups.

4. Explain how focus groups are used, and their advantages and disadvantages.

5. Discuss depth interview techniques in detail.

6. Discuss the applications of depth interviews and their advantages and disadvantages.

> **"I have degrees in mathematics, but have become an enthusiastic user of qualitative research because of the rich insights I have gained with well done qualitative research."**
>
> *Mary Klupp*
> *Director, Ford Credit Global Consumer Insights, Ford Motor Company, Dearborn, Michigan*

Gillette Supports Equal Rights for Women: A Close Shave

Gillette successfully introduced Venus Embrace disposables in 2010. It was the first disposable women's razor to have five blades instead of the typical three. This new product idea was inspired by the successful introduction of Sensor for Women earlier.

How was Sensor for Women developed? After being given the job of redesigning Gillette's feminine razor, Jill Shurtleff relied heavily on qualitative research. She used one-on-one or individual depth interviews with 30 women she chose based on her own judgment from different segments of the potential target market. Individual depth interviews were selected over focus groups because shaving is a rather personal experience for women. This technique allowed for extensive probing of the respondent's feelings in a more personal setting and thus provided deeper insights into the shaving experience.

The depth interviews showed that women shave very differently from men. The American woman shaves much more surface area than a man but only shaves two or three times per week. She changes the blade about once a month. Whereas men usually shave in front of a well-lit mirror, women generally prefer to shave in the shower, which is often dimly lit, and they must shave areas that they cannot see well, such as their underarms and the backs of their legs. The research indicated that shaving was a personal experience for women that evoked feelings of anticipation and acceptance.

The research also showed that most women did not like so-called women's razors and opted instead for men's razors or cheap disposables. Women preferred razors with a firm grip and those that gave a clean, smooth shave. Typically, men's razors have a much sharper blade than women's. Although a woman was more likely to nick herself with a man's razor, the shaving quality with a man's razor was better than traditional women's razors. These findings were substantiated in a survey of women using in-home personal interviews. A representative sample of 500 women was selected for this purpose.

With information on the current state of affairs under her belt, Shurtleff began her product design. She first tossed out the T-shaped design used for men's razors, which gives men the sensitive control they need but puts women at risk due to shifting blade angles. Shurtleff settled on a wafer-like design for the handle, white with an aqua insert in the center. The colors were different from the typical pink for women's razors and evoked a clean, watery feeling. The aqua insert was clear plastic and had wavy ridges to help prevent slippage. The razor head was nearly the same as that used by the Sensor (men's razor) and was angled at 46 degrees, a compromise between the ideal underarm and leg-shaving angles.

The finishing touch was the name. The name Lady Sensor was declined because it seemed condescending and many women did not like it. The company settled on the name Sensor for Women, because it seemed straightforward, honest, and elicited the most favorable response in a word-association test examining several possible names. Word association was also used to select the Venus Embrace name.

Shurtleff used qualitative research to develop a successful product. The Sensor for Women quickly and easily displaced the market leader, Personal Touch, and garnered 60 percent of the market share. Moreover, Sensor for Women provided a strong launching pad for the Venus line. When qualitative research in the form of focus groups and depth interviews revealed that women wanted the convenience of a shave gel and razor combined in a single system, and quantitative research estimated a definite demand for such a product, in 2007 Gillette introduced a new two-in-one razor and shave gel bars. In 2007, Gillette was marketing the New Venus Breeze as the "only razor with built-in shaving gel bars. Just wet and shave." This was followed by the introduction of Venus Embrace (refillable) in 2008. The Venus line has been a tremendous success. Sales from Gillette's women's products amounted to more than $1 billion dollars by the year 2011.[1]

Overview

In Chapter 3, marketing research was classified as exploratory or conclusive. Secondary data analysis, discussed in Chapters 4 and 5, is one aspect of exploratory research. The other major exploratory technique, qualitative research, is the subject of this chapter. Figure 6.1 presents the focus of the chapter, the relation of this chapter to the previous ones, and the steps of the marketing research process on which this chapter concentrates.

As demonstrated in Figure 6.1, qualitative research is part of the marketing research process presented in Chapter 1, is one of the tasks involved in problem definition and development of an approach covered in Chapter 2, and is one of the exploratory research design techniques discussed in Chapter 3.

Often, qualitative research follows a review of internal and external sources of secondary data. It is typically used to define the problem more precisely, to formulate hypotheses, or to identify or clarify key variables to be investigated in the quantitative phase. The opening vignette illustrated this. The findings of depth interviews regarding how women shaved were further investigated by conducting an in-home personal survey (quantitative research).

Unlike secondary data, which are generated for purposes other than the specific marketing research problem at hand, qualitative research generates primary data. The definition of the marketing research problem guides qualitative data collection.

FIGURE 6.1

Relationship of Qualitative Research to the Previous Chapters and the Marketing Research Process

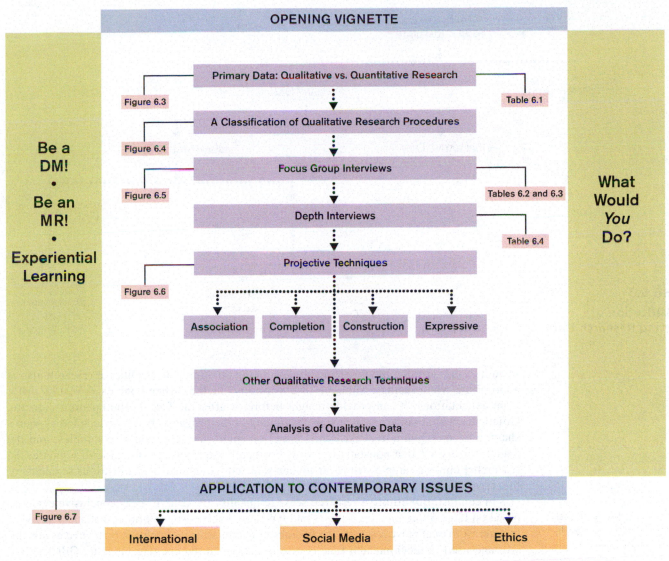

FIGURE 6.2
Qualitative Research: An Overview

This chapter presents the differences between qualitative and quantitative research and the role of each in the marketing research project. We provide a classification of qualitative research techniques, as well as an overview of the major qualitative techniques used in the industry. These techniques include focus groups, depth interviews with individuals, and projective techniques. The chapter then moves to discussion of the application of qualitative research in international marketing research, the use of social media, and ethical issues. Figure 6.2 offers an overview of the topics discussed in this chapter and how they flow from one to the next.

Primary Data: Qualitative Versus Quantitative Research

Even though qualitative research is exploratory in nature, it results in primary data because the research is carried out for the specific purpose of addressing the problem at hand. Therefore, both qualitative and quantitative research can generate primary data, as shown in Figure 6.3. The distinction between qualitative and quantitative research closely parallels the distinction between exploratory and conclusive research discussed in Chapter 3 (see Table 3.1). The differences between the two research methodologies are summarized in Table 6.1. Note that Table 6.1 is similar to Table 3.1.

Qualitative research provides insight into and understanding of the problem setting. It explores the problem with few preconceived notions about the outcome of that exploration.

qualitative research
An unstructured, exploratory research methodology based on small samples that provides insights and understanding of the problem setting.

FIGURE 6.3

A Classification of Marketing Research Data

In addition to defining the problem and developing an approach, qualitative research also is appropriate when facing a situation of uncertainty, such as when conclusive results differ from expectations. It can provide insight before or after the fact. In the opening vignette, Gillette used qualitative research at the beginning of the project to better understand women's shaving needs. Qualitative research is based on small, nonrepresentative samples, and the data are analyzed in a nonstatistical way. For depth interviews in the Gillette vignette, the researcher chose a sample size of 30 women selected judgmentally from various segments of the target market.

quantitative research
A research methodology that seeks to quantify the data and typically applies some form of statistical analysis.

In contrast, **quantitative research** seeks to quantify the data. It seeks conclusive evidence based on large, representative samples and typically involves some form of statistical analysis. In contrast to qualitative research, the findings of quantitative research can be treated as conclusive and used to recommend a final course of action. In the opening vignette, Gillette used quantitative (survey) research based on a representative sample of 500 women to substantiate the findings of qualitative research (depth interviews).

The approach to data collection can vary along a continuum from highly structured to completely unstructured. In a highly structured approach, the researcher predetermines the wording of the questions asked and the range of responses available. Thus, the researcher assumes full understanding of the range of possible response options. A multiple-choice question is an example of a highly structured question. Typically, a formal questionnaire is used. This is in contrast to an unstructured data collection approach in which neither the questions nor the

TABLE 6.1 Qualitative Versus Quantitative Research

	Qualitative Research	Quantitative Research
Objective	To gain a qualitative understanding of the underlying reasons and motivations	To quantify the data and generalize the results from the sample to the population of interest
Sample	Small number of nonrepresentative cases	Large number of representative cases
Data collection	Unstructured	Structured
Data analysis	Nonstatistical	Statistical
Outcome	Develop a richer understanding	Recommend a final course of action

possible responses are predetermined. The respondent is encouraged to talk freely about the subject of interest. Qualitative or exploratory research lies at the unstructured end of this continuum, whereas quantitative research is highly structured.

Whenever a new marketing research problem is addressed, quantitative research must be preceded by appropriate qualitative research, as Gillette did. Sometimes qualitative research is undertaken to explain the findings obtained from quantitative research. The findings of qualitative research are misused, however, when they are regarded as conclusive and are used to make generalizations to the population of interest. For example, if 20 of the 30 women in the depth interviews said they preferred men's razors to women's razors, it would not be appropriate to conclude that 66.7 percent of the women in the general population have the same preference. Quantitative data from a large, representative sample should be collected using a survey, as in the opening vignette, if the sample results are to be projected to the population. It is a sound principle of marketing research to view qualitative and quantitative research as complementary rather than competitive parts of the research process.

The danger of ignoring qualitative research when the research problem is not fully understood and directly proceeding to quantitative research is illustrated by Coca-Cola's decision to change Coke to New Coke. The decision to change the formulation of the flagship soft-drink brand was based on extensive quantitative taste tests without the benefit of appropriate qualitative research. The results clearly indicated that consumers preferred the taste of the new formulation. However, when the change was made and New Coke replaced Coke, there was a strong consumer backlash. Coke's loyal consumers reacted because their favorite soft drink had been changed. The quantitative research conducted was misguided because it asked the wrong questions. The researchers were focusing on taste rather than the emotional attachment consumers had forged with the brand, which was actually a more significant variable guiding brand preference and loyalty than taste.

These types of mistakes can be avoided by conducting qualitative research. Had the researchers first used qualitative techniques to explore why people purchased Coke, rather than assuming they knew why, the quantitative research conducted would have been different, leading management to a different decision. This classic marketing mistake also points out that the researcher must obtain an adequate understanding of the problem situation before formulating a research design. Qualitative researchers can be located through the Qualitative Research Consultants Association (www.qrca.org), which is the largest body of independent qualitative research consultants in the world.

Be a DM!	Be an MR!
Go West, Young Woman!	
As the marketing manager, what marketing strategies would you formulate in helping Nine West increase its penetration of the women's shoe market?	Visit www.ninewest.com and search the Internet—including social media—as well as your library's online databases to obtain information on Nine West's marketing strategy. How would you use qualitative and quantitative research in helping Nine West increase its penetration of the women's shoe market?

A Classification of Qualitative Research Procedures

A classification of qualitative research procedures is presented in Figure 6.4. These procedures are classified as either direct or indirect, based on whether the respondents know the true purpose of the project. A **direct approach** is not disguised. The purpose of the project is disclosed to the respondents or is otherwise obvious from the questions asked. Focus groups and depth interviews are the major direct techniques. In contrast, research that takes an **indirect approach** disguises the true purpose of the project. Projective techniques are the most commonly used indirect approach. A discussion of each of these techniques follows, beginning with focus groups.

direct approach
A type of qualitative research in which the purposes of the project are disclosed to the respondent or are obvious given the nature of the interview.

indirect approach
A type of qualitative research in which the purposes of the project are disguised from the respondents.

FIGURE 6.4

A Classification of Qualitative Research Procedures

Focus-Group Interviews

A **focus group** is an interview with a small group of respondents conducted by a trained moderator who leads the discussion in a nonstructured and natural manner. The main purpose of a focus group is to gain insights on issues of interest to the researcher by listening to a group of people from the appropriate target market. The value of the technique lies in the rich findings that can be obtained from a free-flowing group discussion.

Focus groups are the most important qualitative research procedure. They are so popular that many marketing research practitioners consider this technique to be synonymous with qualitative research. Several hundred facilities around the country now conduct focus groups several times a week. The typical focus group costs the client about $4,000. Given their importance and popularity, the procedure for conducting focus groups is described in detail.

Conducting a Focus Group

The process of conducting a focus group, as with any research effort, involves careful planning. This chapter discusses considerations related to the environment for focus groups, the selection of participants, and the moderator. It also covers the development of a discussion guide, how the group interview is conducted, and the format for summarizing the results (see Figure 6.5).

FIGURE 6.5

Procedure for Conducting a Focus Group

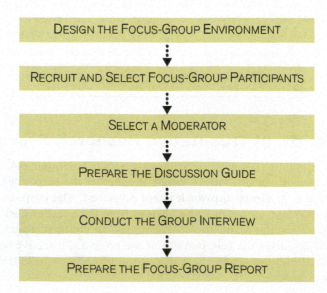

TABLE 6.2 Characteristics of Focus Groups

Group size	8 to 12 participants
Group composition	Homogeneous; respondents prescreened
Physical setting	Relaxed, informal atmosphere
Time duration	1 to 3 hours
Recording	Use of audio- and video-recording
Moderator	Observational, interpersonal, and communication skills of the moderator are critical

DESIGNING THE ENVIRONMENT   Focus-group sessions typically are held in facilities specially equipped to comfortably accommodate and record a group discussion. In most instances, the setting is an informal conference room equipped with a one-way mirror and with microphones throughout the room. Behind the one-way mirror is a viewing room for management.

Most focus groups are scheduled to last 1 to 3 hours (see Table 6.2). This amount of time is needed to establish rapport with the participants and to explore in depth their beliefs, feelings, ideas, attitudes, and insights regarding the topics of concern. Focus groups are either audio- or video-recorded to preserve the comments for analysis. Video recording has the advantage of recording facial expressions and body movements, but it can increase the costs significantly.

Frequently, clients observe the session from an adjacent room using a one-way mirror. Clients can also use video-transmission technology to observe the focus-group session live from a remote location.

RECRUITING AND SELECTING FOCUS-GROUP PARTICIPANTS   The major characteristics of a focus group are summarized in Table 6.2. A focus group usually has 8 to 12 members. The advantages that come from the group dynamics are often lost to groups larger than this. Smaller groups of four or five respondents might be used if the session is highly exploratory and if extensive, unstructured probing is necessary.

A focus group should be homogeneous in terms of product usage, demographics, and socio-economic characteristics. This commonality among group members avoids interactions and conflicts on side issues. Suppose a focus group is conducted to evaluate the appeal of a line of frozen foods. It might not be desirable to include professional women and homemakers in the same group. It is clear that these two subgroups have strong differences of opinion regarding the role of women in the family. If they are included in the same group, the conversation could deviate into a discussion of the role of women in the family rather than the appeal of the frozen foods. If so, the researcher would not gain any insights relevant to the objective of assessing the product's basic appeal.

Not only should the group be homogeneous in terms of demographic and socioeconomic characteristics, but group members should also have a common base of experience or involvement

Layout of the focus-group room and viewing room

Viewing room looking into the focus-group room through a one-way mirror

Source: Photos, compliments of Campos Inc. (Market Research and Strategic Marketing Consulting) Pittsburgh, PA, www.campos.com.

with the object or issue being discussed. Thus, heavy users and nonusers of the product should not be included in the same group. Finally, people who have participated in multiple focus groups become familiar with the process to the point that their responses might be biased by their exposure to the technique. These so-called professional respondents should be screened out of the group. To ensure that the focus-group respondents are homogeneous in terms of experience, demographics, and other relevant variables, potential respondents are prescreened. A questionnaire covering demographic characteristics, attitudes, product use, and experience of the respondent is typically deve-loped and administered to potential respondents to select only those who meet the qualifications.

SELECTING A MODERATOR   The moderator plays a key role and must be well trained. General group management skills as well as a background in psychology and marketing typically suffice in most focus-group situations. The moderator must be able to establish rapport with the participants, keep the discussion moving forward, and probe the respondents to elicit insights. In addition, this individual might also play a central role in the analysis and interpretation of the data. Therefore, the moderator should possess knowledge of the discussion topic and an understanding of the nature of group dynamics in order to appropriately interpret focus-group responses. Despite the importance of the moderator, at present, no central body certifies or trains focus-group moderators. This lack of standardization in qualifications is one of the problems to be overcome in this type of research. This limitation can be minimized by preparing a detailed moderator discussion guide.

PREPARING THE DISCUSSION GUIDE   Regardless of the moderator's skills or qualifications, any focus group will flounder without an outline of the topics to be covered. The discussion guide should reflect the objectives of qualitative research. The objectives, in turn, should be derived from the definition of the marketing research problem, approach, and the research design adopted. A moderator's discussion guide can reduce some of the reliability problems inherent in focus groups, such as the lack of consistency in topics covered from group to group.

Most group discussions can be broken into three phases, the first being a preamble and introduction to establish rapport, relax the group, and describe the process. The bulk of the group session revolves around discussion of the research topic. In the closing phase, the moderator summarizes the comments and attempts to get a final read on the strength of the group's commitment to the statements made. The questions are typically kept fairly general to allow the moderator to pursue important ideas when participants mention them. To be effective, the moderator must understand the client's business, the focus-group objectives, and how the findings will be used. The following is a sample discussion guide for focus groups on purchase motivations and the buying process for smartphones.

Research in Action

Focus-Group Discussion Guide for Smartphones

Preamble (5 minutes)

- Thanks and welcome
- Nature of a focus group (informal, multiway, all views acceptable, disagree)
- There are no right or wrong answers—all about finding out what people think
- Audio- and video-recording
- Colleagues viewing
- Help self to refreshments
- Going to be talking about smartphones
- Questions or concerns?

Introductions and Warm-Up (5 minutes)

I'd like to go around the room and have you introduce yourselves:

- First name
- Best thing about having a smartphone
- Worst thing about having a smartphone

Smartphone Usage (15 minutes)

I'd like to understand a bit about how you typically use your smartphone:

- How many times a day do you use it?
- What are some of the most common types of things you use it for?

Briefly Explore

- If we were to take away your smartphone from you, what difference would that make to your life?

Briefly Explore

Past Smartphone Purchase (15 minutes)

Thinking now about your current smartphone, I'd like to talk about two different things:

- How did you actually go about the process of choosing the smartphone?
- Did you have any criteria for the smartphone itself?

Past Smartphone Selection Process

- Thinking first only about *how* you went about choosing your smartphone, *not* any features you wanted, how did you go about choosing one?

Explore Process
Past Smartphone Criteria

- Now tell me what you actually looked for in a smartphone.

Explore
Usage of Smartphone Features (20 minutes)

- Thinking now about Smartphone features, I'd like to start by making a list of all the features you can think of—anything the smartphone can do, any settings you can change, etc.
- We'll talk in a minute about which features you actually use, but I want to start with a list of everything your smartphone could do.

Flipchart

- Which features have you ever used, even if only once?

Flipchart

- Are there any settings you only changed once, but are really glad you could change?
- Why?

Explore

- Which features do you use regularly?
- Why?

Explore
Desired Features (10 minutes)

- Are there any features your smartphone doesn't have but that you wish it did?

Explore
Motivations for Buying (20 minutes)
You've all been invited here because you own a smartphone.

- What motivated you to buy your smartphone?

Explore

- What do you think are some of the reasons that people would buy smartphones?

Explore

- What were *all* the factors involved in that decision?
- What was the single biggest reason?

Explore
Closing Exercise (10 minutes)

- Finally, I'd like your creativity for a few minutes in coming up with ideas.
- Don't worry about whether it's a good idea or a bad idea.
- The only word I'm going to ban is "free"!
- Supposing a smartphone manufacturer wanted to encourage you to buy tomorrow. What could they do?
- Just call out anything at all that occurs to you—obvious, profound, serious, silly, whatever.

Explore and Refine

- Thank the respondents and close the session

CONDUCTING THE GROUP INTERVIEW   During the interview, the moderator must (1) establish rapport with the group, (2) state the rules of group interaction, (3) set objectives, (4) probe the respondents and provoke intense discussion in the relevant areas, and (5) attempt to summarize the group's response to determine the extent of agreement.

The number of focus groups conducted depends on (1) the nature of the issue, (2) the number of distinct market segments, (3) the number of new ideas generated by each successive group, and (4) the time and cost. Ideally, groups should be conducted until the moderator becomes familiar enough with the range of responses and can anticipate what will be said. This usually happens after three or four groups. It is recommended that a minimum of two groups be conducted.[2]

PREPARING THE FOCUS-GROUP REPORT   Following the focus-group session, the moderator and the managers who viewed the session will often engage in an instant interpretation. This free exchange has value in that it captures the impressions of the group and might be a good source of information for additional brainstorming. The danger is that the emotional power of the group's comments can cloud important points, which may be lost unless a detailed review of the focus-group video recording is conducted. Hence, no conclusions should be drawn until either the moderator or an analyst reviews and analyzes the results and a complete report has been prepared.

Due to the small number of participants, frequencies and percentages are not usually reported in a focus-group summary. Instead, reports typically include expressions such as "most participants thought" or "participants were divided on this issue." The report should not only present the findings based on the verbal comments but should also analyze consistent responses, new ideas, and concerns suggested by facial expressions and body language. Meticulous documentation and interpretation of the session lays the groundwork for the final step, taking action. This usually means doing additional research. A topline report that gives preliminary results, usually showing responses to a few key questions, is prepared first, followed by a more detailed report. We illustrate a topline report in the case involving Mall of the Boondocks (the actual name has been disguised).

Research in Action

Mall of the Boondocks Focus-Group Topline Report

Focus-Group Objectives
The latest in a quarterly series, Mall of the Boondocks focus groups were conducted to understand shopping-mall expectations of the student segment, to determine this group's perceptions of a recent weekend visit, and to analyze the perceived brand identity of the mall based on the individual's experience.

Method and Procedures
Reactions were solicited for the Mall of the Boondocks experience from 20 student visitors (8 males and 12 females) who attended the mall on the weekend prior to the group discussion (i.e., Labor Day Weekend). Two focus groups were conducted, each with 10 respondents. A variety of ages, life stages, and previous work experience was represented within the groups. The current focus groups were conducted at Good Stuff's videoconference facility on September 10, 2010. Students were given $30 and instructed to visit the mall between September 4 and 5; however, no other instructions or explanations were given to the students. They were not aware that they would be participating in a discussion group when they visited the mall.

Summary of Findings
Mall-Visit Experience

- For entertainment, participants typically engage in movies (theater and rental), sports (spectator and participatory), drinks, or just "hanging out" with friends. They typically need only 3 or 4 hours to experience the mall and try to hold cost to under $30, except for a special occasion.
- Examples of special occasions include dinner, concerts, theater, museums, and theme malls. Most often, the theme mall is a destination like Mall of America, Universal Studios, or Sea World. Many have visited Mall of the Boondocks more than once, and a few have been Mall of the Boondocks "Crown Customers," who shop at the Mall of the Boondocks loyally.
- Visitors were pleasantly surprised and delighted with the mall's entertainment, the surprisingly short lines in the children's area, the first-class magic show, and winning a large stuffed animal.
- When asked to describe feelings surrounding the experience, most were very positive—"excited to go," "feel like a kid again," "didn't feel like I should have to go to work tomorrow," and "friendly, fun to share the experience with others in attendance." The only negatives were "tired," "hot," and "yucky."

- On the other hand, visitors were frustrated to find a lack of signage and maps, a "deserted" feeling resulting from the lack of hosts or guides, and the dry, dirty look of some areas in the mall.
- Visitors were asked to suggest necessary changes in the mall.

  - **Crowds.** Can be daunting, and there must be a way to make them more palatable, such as drinking fountains, benches, water misters, ceiling fans that work, or entertainment. Made comparisons to Mall of America, which respondents said had more space and better-groomed patrons.
  - **Dress code.** There were complaints that many people were showing a lot of skin but hardly anyone looked like Britney Spears or Ricky Martin. Who wants the bowling-alley crowd to dress this way? Several agreed there should be a "no shirt, no shoes, no service" policy.
  - **Information.** Booths placed in visible spots throughout the mall would be helpful. Visitors agreed that maps were very hard to find and that handing them out in line at the entrance of the mall might help.

Brand Identity Versus Mall of America
General Personality

- **Mall of the Boondocks.** Definitely male, but surprisingly, not teenaged. Middle-aged or older, a little tired, moody. Blue-collar worker, not very smart, wearing "gimme" T-shirt and cap, maybe with a beer logo (e.g., Budweiser). Drives a big old American car, may have money problems. A follower rather than a leader.
- **Mall of America.** Both female and male, perhaps that loving, indulgent aunt and uncle who shower you with experiences you don't get at home. Dressed classically in khakis and a polo shirt. Nurturing, approachable, well-rounded, and affluent. Like this person better than the Mall of the Boondocks personality because it's more fun.

Brand Value
To many, Mall of the Boondocks was described as "just a bunch of shops and rides." Other malls, such as Mall of America, encompass a complete entertainment experience. Several "long-timers" remember a time when Mall of the Boondocks

included the experience of regional history and of other cultures. What made it unique in the past is gone now, as the specific areas have become less distinct and not associated with as much meaning. As a result, there was a general feeling that the value had declined.

Implications

In general, the results of this latest in the series of focus groups—focusing upon student perceptions—are similar to those from previous focus groups with nonstudents. Respondents view the Mall of the Boondocks as more of a "working person's" mall. The student respondents' perceptions of the Mall of the Boondocks were markedly more negative when compared to the Mall of America than the perceptions of any other segment of customers included in this series of quarterly focus groups begun 3 years ago. Perhaps Mall of America's recently completed remodeling has become more salient in the minds of the Mall of the Boondocks student customers because of students' higher use of informal "buzz" (word-of-mouth). More research on this topic using a large sample survey is needed.

Source: © David L. Moore–Washington/Alamy Images.

Advantages and Disadvantages of Focus Groups

Focus groups are popular because of their many advantages. The immediacy and the richness of the comments, which come from real customers, make this technique highly useful. The group interaction produces a wider range of information, insights, and ideas than do individual interviews. The comments of one person can trigger unexpected reactions from others, leading to snowballing with participants responding to each other's comments. The responses are generally spontaneous and candid, providing rich insights. Ideas are more likely to arise out of the blue in a group than in an individual interview and are likely to be unique and potentially creative.[3]

However, some of the qualities that make focus groups so strong also create some of their more serious limitations. The disadvantages of focus groups should not be overlooked. The clarity and conviction with which group members often speak lead to a tendency for researchers and managers to regard findings as conclusive rather than as exploratory. Focus groups also are difficult to moderate. The quality of the results depends heavily on the skills of the moderator; unfortunately, moderators who possess all of the desirable skills are rare. Further, the unstructured nature of the responses makes coding, analysis, and interpretation difficult.

Experiential Learning

Gatorade: From a Sports Drink to a Lifestyle Drink

Management would like to transform Gatorade from a sports drink to a lifestyle drink. Visit www.gatorade.com and search the Internet—including social media—as well as your library's online databases to obtain information on the marketing strategy of Gatorade energy drinks.

1. Prepare a focus-group discussion guide to determine why people consume Gatorade drinks and what would lead them to consume more Gatorade.

2. Conduct a focus group of 8 to 12 students using your discussion guide.

3. Prepare a focus-group topline report for Gatorade management.

Social Media

Online Focus Groups

Online focus groups are becoming increasingly popular because of their greater convenience, cost-effectiveness, and faster turnaround as compared to traditional focus groups. Using Internet technologies, marketing research companies have created virtual focus-group facilities consisting of waiting rooms, focus-group rooms, and client rooms. Respondents are prerecruited, generally from an online list of people who have expressed an interest in participating. Some are recruited through e-mail lists, Web intercepts, banner ads, or traditional methods (phone or mail). A screening questionnaire is administered online to qualify the respondents. Those who qualify are invited to participate in a focus group and receive a time, a URL, a room name, and a password via e-mail. Generally, four to six people participate in the online group. An online focus group has fewer participants than a face-to-face meeting because too many respondents can cause confusion.

Before the focus group begins, participants receive information about the focus group that covers such things as how to express emotions when typing. Emotions are indicated by using keyboard characters and are standard in their use on the Internet. For example, :-) and :-(represent smiling and sad faces, respectively. The emotion indicators usually are inserted into the text at the point where the emotion is meant. Emotions can also be expressed using a different font or color. The participants can also preview information about the focus-group topic by visiting a Web site and reading information or downloading and viewing an actual TV ad on their PCs. Then, just before the focus group begins, participants visit a Web site where they log on and get some last-minute instructions.

When it is time for the group, they move into a Web-based chat room. They go to the focus-group location (a URL) and click on the "Enter Focus Room" item. To enter, they must supply the room name, user name, and password that was e-mailed to them earlier. The moderator signs on early and administers a rescreening questionnaire as the respondents enter the waiting room to verify their identities. Once in the focus-group chat room, the moderator and the participants type to each other in real time. The general practice is for the moderators to pose their questions in all capital letters, and the respondents are asked to use upper- and lowercase. The respondents also are asked to always start their response with the question number, so the moderator can quickly tie the response to the proper question. This makes it fast and easy to transcribe a focus-group session. The group interaction lasts for about 60 to 90 minutes. A raw transcript is available as soon as the group is completed, and a formatted transcript is available within 48 hours. The whole process is much faster than the traditional method. Examples of companies that provide online focus groups include comScore (www.comscore.com), Harris Interactive (www.harrisinteractive.com), and Burke (www.burke.com).

New forms of online focus groups continue to emerge. For example, online bulletin board focus groups involve the moderator and the respondents over an extended period of time, from a few days to a few weeks. Thus, respondents can think and respond at their own convenience. An example is comScore's FocusSite for holding an in-depth discussion among 25 or more participants over an extended period of time. Participants enter the discussion several times over 1 to 2 days, depending on the research objectives. The extended time period allows respondents to react to and build on each other's ideas in a way that often is not possible during a typical 2-hour focus-group session. Other forms of online qualitative research also have emerged, including blogs, message boards, online communities, and other social media sites and are discussed in a later section. Some of the useful insights gained from these procedures are illustrated by Del Monte.

Research in Action

Del Monte: Understanding the Love of Dog Lovers

Since its inception during the California Gold Rush of 1849, Del Monte (www.delmonte.com) has been leading the food industry in innovative marketing practices. The company generated approximately $3.7 billion in net sales in fiscal 2010. Recently, the Pet Products Division of Del Monte Foods needed to connect with dog owners in a new way in order to get closer to them, gain fresh perspectives on their attitudes and behaviors, and drive true innovation. The company used MarketTools (www.markettools.com) to bring together three important sources of insight:

- **Analysis.** The key topics consumers are discussing and their overall sentiment and engagement levels are discovered by identifying and analyzing relevant content from more than 50 million blogs, message boards, and media sites.

- **Online community interaction.** Clients gain an online environment through online communities built by MarketTools. Through these communities, clients can observe and interact with a targeted audience to gain an understanding of their attitudes, behaviors, and preferences.
- **Quantitative survey research.** Clients can qualify trends and validate the potential of new concepts and ideas through MarketTools' on-demand survey platform and large consumer panel.

After identifying dog lovers as the key target segment, Del Monte Foods and MarketTools created a custom Insight Network. One of the first activities provided by the Insight Network was "Text Analysis," in which relevant content from more than 50 million blogs was collected and analyzed to evaluate current topics of discussion among the target consumers.

First, the analysis revealed that of the topics dog lovers are most interested in, doggie daycare, travel with dogs, and even pet entertainment were some of the most popular. Compared to other topics, dog care proved to be a high-involvement topic that generated repeated mentions among bloggers who were in the target group. Dog care engagement was higher, for example, than holiday cookie-baking, an online topic used to benchmark engagement level.

The text analysis also revealed that although each age group has a dog-lover segment, this segment is most prominent in the Baby Boomer demographic. Older dog owners seem to prize the companionship their dog provides at a proportionately higher level, whereas Gen X tends to be more concerned with on-the-go issues such as daycare and travel. Gen Y tends not to concern itself as much with the responsibility-oriented themes—daycare, grooming, and so on. Their focus is on companionship, dog care, and apparel.

To refine these insights, MarketTools created the "I Love My Dog" online community, which gave members and Del Monte a place to interact and collaborate. This was followed by an online survey to quantify and statistically validate the qualitative insights. Based on the results, Del Monte formulated a number of targeted marketing strategies. For example, the premium brands in its product line (Kibbles 'n Bits, Gravy Train, and Nature's Recipe, as well as dog snack brands such as Milk-Bone, Snausages, and Meaty Bone) were targeted at the Baby Boomer dog lovers given their greater attachment to and love for their dogs. This effort resulted in increased sales and market share.[4]

Advantages of Online Focus Groups

People from all over the country or even the world can participate in online focus groups, and the client can observe the group from the convenience of home or office. Geographical constraints are removed, and time constraints are lessened. Unlike traditional focus groups, online groups offer the unique opportunity for recontacting group participants at a later date to either revisit issues or to introduce them to modifications in material presented in the original focus group. The Internet enables the researcher to reach segments that are usually hard to recruit, such as doctors, lawyers, other professional people, working mothers, and others who lead busy lives and are typically not interested in taking part in traditional focus groups.

Moderators might also be able to carry on side conversations with individual respondents, probing deeper into interesting areas. People are generally less inhibited in their responses and are more likely to fully express their thoughts online. A lot of online focus groups go well past their allotted time because so many responses are expressed. Finally, because there is no travel, videotaping, or facilities to arrange, the cost is much lower than for traditional focus groups. Firms are able to keep costs between one-fifth and one-half the costs of traditional focus groups. Online groups can also be conducted more quickly than traditional focus groups.

Disadvantages of Online Focus Groups

Only people who have and know how to use a computer can be interviewed online. Because the name of an individual on the Internet often is private, actually verifying that a respondent is a member of a target group is difficult. This is illustrated in a cartoon in *The New Yorker,* where two dogs are seated at a computer and one says to the other "On the Internet, nobody knows you are a dog!" To overcome this limitation, traditional methods, such as telephone calls, are used for recruitment and verification of respondents. Body language, facial expressions, and tone of voice cannot be obtained online, and electronic emotion indicators obviously do not capture as full a breadth of emotion as does videotaping.

Another factor that must be considered is the lack of general control over the respondent's environment and his or her potential exposure to distracting external stimuli. Because online focus groups could potentially have respondents scattered all over the world, the researchers and moderators have no idea what else the respondents might be doing while participating in the group. Only audio and visual stimuli can be tested. Products cannot be touched (e.g., clothing) or smelled (e.g., perfumes). It is difficult to get the clients as involved in online focus groups as they are in observing traditional focus groups. Table 6.3 presents a comparison of online and traditional focus groups.

TABLE 6.3 Online Versus Traditional Focus Groups

Characteristic	Online Focus Groups	Traditional Focus Groups
Group size	4 to 6 participants	8 to 12 participants
Group composition	Anywhere in the world	Drawn from the local area
Time duration	1 to 1.5 hours	1 to 3 hours
Physical setting	Researcher has little control	Under the control of the researcher
Respondent identity	Difficult to verify	Easily verified
Respondent attentiveness	Respondents can engage in other tasks.	Attentiveness can be monitored.
Respondent recruiting	Easier. Can be recruited online, by e-mail, or by traditional means (telephone, mail).	Recruited by traditional means (telephone, mail).
Group dynamics	Limited	Synergistic, snowballing (bandwagon) effect
Openness of respondents	Respondents are more candid due to lack of face-to-face contact.	Respondents are candid, except for sensitive topics.
Nonverbal communication	Body language cannot be observed. Emotions expressed by using symbols.	Easy to observe body language and emotions.
Use of physical stimuli	Limited to those that can be displayed on the Internet.	A variety of stimuli (products, advertising, demonstrations, and so on) can be used.
Transcripts	Available immediately	Time-consuming and expensive to obtain
Observers' communication with moderator	Observers can communicate with the moderator on a split screen.	Observers can manually send notes to moderator in the focus-group room.
Unique moderator skills	Typing, computer usage, familiarity with chat room slang	Observational
Turnaround time	Can be set up and completed in a few days.	Takes many days for set up and completion.
Client travel costs	None	Can be expensive
Client involvement	Limited	High
Basic focus-group costs	Much less expensive	More expensive due to facility rental, food, audio- and video-recording, and transcript preparation.

Applications of Focus Groups

Focus groups, whether traditional or online, can be used in almost any situation that requires preliminary understanding or insight into the problem. The range of research topics relevant for focus-group investigation includes research designed to do any of the following:

1. Understand consumer perceptions, preferences, and behavior concerning a product category (e.g., how consumers select a cellular service provider and their perceptions of AT&T, Verizon, and Sprint Nextel).
2. Obtain impressions of new product concepts (e.g., consumer response to Sony's world's smallest 3D camera).

3. Generate new ideas about older products (e.g., new packaging and positioning for Tide detergent).
4. Develop creative concepts and copy material for advertisements (e.g., a new campaign for Pepsi).
5. Secure price impressions (e.g., the role of price in consumer selection of luxury cars, such as Cadillac, Lexus, Mercedes, and BMW).
6. Obtain preliminary consumer reaction to specific marketing programs (e.g., General Mills' instant coupons for Cheerios).
7. Interpret previously obtained quantitative results (e.g., the reasons for the 5.6-percent sales decline of Vanderbilt perfume).

Research in Action

Intel: Inside the Health Care Industry

Intel conducts exploratory research such as customer focus groups to find out what consumers think the future will hold. Intel became extremely interested in the health care industry because focus groups showed that health care professionals, including doctors, nurses, and hospital staff, are increasingly recognizing the benefits of information technology (IT). More and more doctors were interested in using IT to help organize and integrate patient records in a more efficient and modern way. In addition, increasing computational abilities of medical research platforms and devices will inevitably save costs and accelerate medical research. This is different from the traditional trend of health care being slow to adopt IT due to the high amount of person-to-person contact in the industry.

These findings led Intel to create a digital health division. This division works directly with hospitals and health care professionals to innovate new products for the industry. Through the use of exploratory research through focus groups, Intel was able to discover an industry untapped by the technological market segment. For example, Intel is developing technologies that will allow for greater and better data storage and management efficiency to deal with increasing data volumes and MPOC (mobile point of contact) technologies that will provide health care workers with greater information access and sharing at the point of decision making. This way, health care workers will be able to make more precise decisions that might save the lives or improve the health of patients.

As of 2011, the digital health division was growing and contributing significantly to Intel's revenues. A focus on customers' needs through qualitative and quantitative research has enabled Intel to become one of the top-10 most valuable brands in the world.[5]

Despite broad applicability, focus groups are only one of the personal interviewing techniques used to collect qualitative data. One-on-one depth interviews are another technique.

Depth Interviews

Depth interviews are loosely structured conversations with individuals drawn from the target audience. Like focus groups, depth interviews are an unstructured and direct way of obtaining information. Unlike focus groups, however, depth interviews are conducted on a one-on-one basis. These interviews typically last from 30 minutes to more than an hour. They attempt to uncover underlying motives, prejudices, or attitudes toward sensitive issues.

Conducting Depth Interviews

As with focus groups, the interviewer prepares a discussion outline to guide the interview. However, the purpose of depth interviews is to uncover hidden issues that might not be shared in a group setting. Therefore, substantial probing is done to surface underlying motives, beliefs, and attitudes. This was illustrated in the opening vignette in which Gillette used depth interviews to understand the underlying motives and attitudes of women toward shaving. The depth interviews showed that women shave much more surface area than men do, that they do this only two or three times a week, that they often shave in a dimly lit shower, and that they must shave areas they cannot see well. Furthermore, shaving tends to be a personal experience for women that evokes feelings of anticipation and acceptance. Probing is necessary to understand these findings and feelings. Probing is done by asking such questions as "Why do you say that?" "That's interesting, can you tell me more?" or "Would you like to add anything else?" (Probing is discussed in detail in Chapter 14.) As the interview progresses, the type of questions asked, the probes used, and the wording of the questions depend on the answers received.

depth interview
An unstructured, direct personal interview in which a single respondent is probed by a highly skilled interviewer to uncover underlying motivations, beliefs, attitudes, and feelings on a topic.

To illustrate the technique, suppose an interviewer is conducting depth interviews with working men and women who are frequent Internet shoppers. The objective is to understand how these shoppers view the Internet shopping experience. The interview may go something like this:

INTERVIEWER: "How do you feel about shopping through the Internet?" *The interviewer then encourages the subject to talk freely about attitudes and feelings about Internet shopping. After asking the initial question, the direction of the interview is determined by the respondent's initial reply.*

RESPONDENT: "I sometimes like to relax with a cup of coffee, surfing Internet shopping sites at the end of the day. It's fun and relaxing."

INTERVIEWER: "Why is it fun and relaxing?" *If the answer is not very revealing (e.g., "It lets my mind wander."), the interviewer might ask further probing questions (e.g., "Why is it fun to let your mind wander?").*

RESPONDENT: "I have to think logically all day long. When I sit down to surf Internet shopping sites, I can fantasize about how I will look in certain clothing or how my living room will look with a piece of furniture. And, there is no pressure to do anything!"

INTERVIEWER: "Why is it important to have no pressure to do anything?"

RESPONDENT: "My whole day is pressure. In my job, I have to constantly react to pressure someone else is putting on me. Home is the one place where I can control the pressure, even eliminate it."

As this example indicates, probing is effective in uncovering underlying or hidden information. In this case, the respondent finds Internet shopping relaxing and a form of low-stress escape (the need to feel "no pressure to do anything").

As with focus groups, the success of depth interviews rests with the skill of the interviewer. The interviewer should (1) avoid appearing superior and put the respondent at ease; (2) be detached and objective, yet personable; (3) ask questions in an informative manner; (4) not accept brief "yes" or "no" answers; and (5) probe the respondent.

Depth interviews can be used to create an environment that fosters a more candid and comprehensive discussion of an issue than can be done in a group. The resulting data provide insight into motivation, beliefs, attitudes, and perceived consequences of behavior. Also, because depth interviews are conducted one-on-one, the comments can be traced directly to individual respondents. This might be particularly relevant in business-to-business research where a decision maker's comments can be evaluated within the context of that individual's personal and corporate background.

Advantages of Depth Interviews

Depth interviews can uncover deeper insights about underlying motives than focus groups can. Also, depth interviews attribute the responses directly to the respondent, unlike focus groups, where it is often difficult to determine which respondent made a particular response. Depth interviews result in a free exchange of information that might not be possible in focus groups, where there is sometimes social pressure to conform. As a result of probing, it is possible to get at real issues when the topic is complex. This was illustrated in the opening vignette in which Gillette used depth interviews to understand the shaving needs of women.

Disadvantages of Depth Interviews

The disadvantages of focus groups are magnified in individual depth interviews. Skilled interviewers capable of conducting depth interviews are expensive and difficult to find. The lack of structure makes the results susceptible to the interviewer's influence, and the quality and completeness of the results depend heavily on the interviewer's skills. The data obtained are difficult to analyze and interpret; the services of skilled psychologists are typically required for this purpose. The length of the interview combined with high costs means that only a small number of depth interviews can be conducted in a project.

TABLE 6.4 Focus Groups Versus Depth Interviews

Characteristic	Focus Groups	Depth Interviews
Group synergy and dynamics	+	−
Peer pressure/group influence	−	+
Client involvement	+	−
Generation of innovative ideas	+	−
In-depth probing of individuals	−	+
Uncovering of hidden motives	−	+
Discussion of sensitive topics	−	+
Interviews with respondents who are competitors	−	+
Interviews with respondents who are professionals	−	+
Scheduling of respondents	−	+
Amount of information	+	−
Bias in moderation and interpretation	+	−
Cost per respondent	+	−

+ indicates a relative advantage over the other procedure

− indicates a relative disadvantage over the other procedure

Despite these disadvantages, depth interviews do have applications, particularly in business-to-business marketing where it is often difficult to assemble a group of executives for a focus-group session. They are also useful in advertising research where it is important to understand the feelings and emotions the advertisement evokes. A relative comparison of focus groups and depth interviews is given in Table 6.4.

Applications of Depth Interviews

As with focus groups, the primary use of depth interviews is for exploratory research to gain insight and understanding. Unlike focus groups, however, depth interviews are used infrequently in marketing research. Nevertheless, depth interviews can be employed effectively in special problem situations, such as those requiring the following:

1. Detailed probing of the respondent (e.g., automobile purchase)
2. Discussion of confidential, sensitive, or embarrassing topics (e.g., personal finances, loose dentures)
3. Situations where strong social norms exist and the respondent might be easily swayed by the group's response (e.g., attitude of college students toward sports)
4. Detailed understanding of complicated behavior (e.g., department-store shopping)
5. Interviews with professional people (e.g., industrial marketing research)
6. Interviews with competitors, who are unlikely to reveal the information in a group setting (e.g., travel agents' perceptions of airline package travel programs)
7. Situations where the product consumption experience is sensory in nature, affecting mood states and emotions (e.g., shaving experience, as in the opening vignette)

Research with children is an example for which depth interviews might be productive. Mars, Inc., used depth interviews to uncover an effective advertising approach.

Research in Action

Mission from Mars

As of 2011, Mars (www.mars.com) is a global business whose products are consumed in more than 150 countries. Perhaps more surprisingly, and unusual for a business of this magnitude, the company is still privately owned, making it one of the largest "small family businesses" in the world.

Most children have a very active and colorful fantasy life. Recognizing this characteristic in their target audience, Mars decided to use depth interviews to uncover childhood fantasies that might be relevant to the company's promotional efforts. Mars conducted depth interviews with schoolchildren and found that a

(continued)

majority of these fantasies revolve around extraterrestrial beings, wars, and exciting action. Previously, the candy manufacturer had never fully developed its extraterrestrial images, although they seemed natural given product names such as Mars and Milky Way. In response to the depth interview findings, it decided to introduce extraterrestrial characters from the planet Mars.

The company developed an imaginative story involving the Mars' Minister of Candy. He directed four Martians to bring back the "best candy in the universe" in order to eliminate the suffering Martians had endured for many years. Moreover, this advertising was linked to a promotional campaign that included back-to-school sweepstakes offering a grand prize of $100,000, 50 trips to Disney World, and other prizes. The four extraterrestrial

heroes made appearances at malls and children's hospitals across the country. This successful multimillion-dollar campaign was shaped by the fantasies of children, uncovered by using depth interviews.[6]

Source: © Christine Whitehead/ Alamy Images.

grounded theory
An inductive and more structured approach in which each subsequent depth interview is adjusted based on the cumulative findings from previous depth interviews with the purpose of developing general concepts or theories.

Research with children is an example for which depth interviews might be productive. Mars used depth interviews to uncover an effective advertising approach. This example illustrates the value of depth interviews in uncovering the hidden responses that underlie the clichés elicited in ordinary questioning (e.g., "It's good" or I like it"). Like focus groups, depth interviews can be conducted online. A special way in which depth interviews are used is grounded theory. **Grounded theory** uses an inductive and more structured approach in which each subsequent depth interview is adjusted based on the cumulative findings from previous depth interviews with the purpose of developing general concepts or theories. Sometimes historical records also are analyzed. This approach is useful in designing new products or modifying existing products and developing advertising and promotion strategies.

Be an MR!	Be a DM!
More People Go with Visa	
Social Media — Search the Internet—including social media—as well as your library's online databases to obtain information on why people use credit cards. Conduct two depth interviews for determining why people use credit cards.	As the marketing manager for Visa, how would you use information about why people use credit cards to increase your market share?

Projective Techniques

projective technique
An unstructured and indirect form of questioning that encourages respondents to project their underlying motivations, beliefs, attitudes, or feelings regarding the issues of concern.

Both focus groups and depth interviews are direct approaches in which the true purpose of the research is disclosed to the respondents or is otherwise obvious to them. **Projective techniques** are different from these techniques in that they attempt to disguise the purpose of the research. They are used in marketing research situations in which the respondent is unable or unwilling to answer a question directly. To get around this problem, the interviewer presents the respondent with a series of vague or incomplete pictures, statements, or scenarios. The underlying assumption is that when asked to respond to these prompts, the individual will reveal personal information that is perhaps held subconsciously.

Projective techniques are unstructured, indirect forms of questioning that require respondents to describe vague and ambiguous stimulus situations. In describing these situations, respondents indirectly project their own motivations, beliefs, attitudes, or feelings into the situation. The underlying information about respondents is uncovered by analyzing their responses. As an example, respondents might be asked to interpret the behavior of others rather than describe their own behavior. In doing so, respondents indirectly project their own motivations, beliefs, attitudes, or feelings into the situation. In a landmark study, the U.S. Postal Service (USPS) made use of this technique to determine why most boys ages 8 to 13 years did not collect stamps as a hobby. A sample of boys was shown a picture on a screen of a 10-year-old boy fixing stamps in his album and asked to describe the scene and characterize the boy.

Most respondents described the boy in the picture as a "sissy." After these findings were confirmed with survey research, the Postal Service undertook a successful advertising campaign directed at 8- to 13-year-olds to dispel the belief that stamp collecting was for "sissies."

Projective techniques used in marketing research can be classified as association, completion, construction, or expressive techniques.

Association Techniques

With **association techniques**, the individual is presented with a list of words or images and asked to respond with the first thing that comes to mind. Word association is the best known of these techniques. With **word association**, respondents are presented with a list of words, one at a time, and asked to respond to each with the first word that comes to mind. The words of interest, called *test words,* are interspersed throughout the list, which also contains some neutral, or filler, words to disguise the purpose of the study. For example, in a retailing study some of the test words might be *location, parking, shopping, quality,* and *price.* The subject's response to each word is recorded verbatim, and responses are timed. Respondents who hesitate or reason out a response (defined as taking longer than 3 seconds to reply) are identified.

In analyzing these data, the researcher looks at the frequency with which a response is given, the amount of hesitation before responding, and the number of instances when no response is given. Patterns in responses are analyzed, as are the response times. It often is possible to classify the associations as favorable, unfavorable, or neutral. The longer an individual hesitates before answering, the higher the assumed level of involvement with the subject. A nonresponse is thought to indicate the highest level of emotional involvement, because these people are too involved to be able to respond in a short time. Gillette used word association to help it name the Sensor for Women shaver (see opening vignette). A sample of women was presented with several different names for the new feminine razor, including Sensor for Women and Lady Sensor, and asked to write down the first word that came to mind. Because Sensor for Women elicited the most favorable responses, the company selected this name. Gillette also used word association to select the Venus Embrace name.

Completion Techniques

Completion techniques are a natural extension of association techniques, generating more detail about the individual's underlying feelings and beliefs. The respondent is asked to complete a sentence, a paragraph, or a story. With **sentence completion**, respondents are given incomplete sentences and asked to finish them. Generally, they are asked to use the first word or phrase that comes to mind, as in the following example.

> **association techniques**
> A type of projective technique in which the respondent is presented with a stimulus and asked to respond with the first thing that comes to mind.

> **word association**
> A projective technique in which respondents are presented with a list of words, one at a time. After each word is presented, respondents are asked to give the first word that comes to mind.

> **completion technique**
> A projective technique that requires the respondent to complete an incomplete stimulus situation.

> **sentence completion**
> A projective technique in which respondents are presented with a number of incomplete sentences and asked to complete them.

Research in Action

Tommy Hilfiger Is a High Flyer in Men's Shirts

In order to determine men's underlying attitudes toward Tommy Hilfiger shirts, sentence completion could be used as follows:

> A person who wears Tommy Hilfiger shirts is _____.
> As compared to Polo, Gant, and Eddie Bauer, Tommy Hilfiger shirts are _____.
> Tommy Hilfiger shirts are most liked by _____.
> When I think of Tommy Hilfiger shirts, I _____.

Using such techniques, Tommy Hilfiger (www.tommy.com) discovered that men preferred shirts that were less formal and that had a nontraditional cut. Men preferred to buy these shirts at upscale department stores, such as Macy's. These findings, after they were confirmed by survey research, formed the platform for Tommy Hilfiger's successful marketing strategy. The New York–based lifestyle brand's Spring/Summer 2011 global advertising campaigns for all collections epitomized the classic, cool, American style for which the Tommy Hilfiger brand is known.

A variation of sentence completion is paragraph completion, in which the respondent finishes a paragraph that begins with the stimulus phrase. An expanded version of sentence completion and paragraph completion is **story completion**. With story completion, respondents are given part of a story, enough to direct attention to a particular topic, but not enough to hint at the ending. They are required to give the conclusion in their own words.

> **story completion**
> A projective technique in which respondents are provided with part of a story and required to give the conclusion in their own words.

Construction Techniques

construction technique

A projective technique in which the respondent is required to construct a response in the form of a story, dialogue, or description.

picture-response technique

A projective technique in which the respondent is shown a picture and asked to tell a story describing it.

cartoon tests

Cartoon characters are shown in a specific situation related to the problem. The respondents are asked to indicate the dialogue that one cartoon character might make in response to the comment(s) of another character.

Construction techniques follow the same logic as other projective techniques, requiring the respondent to construct a response to a picture or cartoon. These techniques provide even less initial structure than verbally oriented association or completion techniques. Picture-response and cartoon tests are two of the well-known projective techniques. With **picture-response techniques**, persons or objects are depicted in pictures, and respondents are asked to write a descriptive story, dialogue, or description. The responses are analyzed in an attempt to identify themes reflecting the individual's perceptual interpretation of the pictures. The USPS example given earlier illustrated the use of this technique. In a variation of this technique—Zaltman's Metaphor Elicitation Technique—respondents are asked to bring 12 to 15 pictures of their choice to the interview and then are asked to describe the salient content of each picture. The picture descriptions reveal respondents' underlying values, attitudes, and beliefs. In another variation, called *photo sort*, respondents are provided with a photo deck portraying different types of people. Respondents sort the photos to connect the people in the photos with the brands that they would use. A photo sort for Visa revealed that the credit card had a middle-of-the road, female image. Therefore, Visa renewed its relationship with the National Football League through the 2014 season to attract more males. Another variation of this technique requires the respondents to draw pictures or drawings to express their feelings about the brand or object being investigated.

In **cartoon tests**, highly stylized stick characters are used to eliminate references to clothing, facial expressions, and even gender. The respondents are asked to complete the conversation they would attribute to the cartoon characters. These techniques typically ask for verbal responses from the cartoon characters and for unspoken thoughts. This tends to maximize the candid nature of the response. Because cartoon tests are simpler to administer and analyze than picture-response techniques, they are the most commonly used construction technique. An example is shown in Figure 6.6.

In marketing research applications, construction techniques are used to evaluate attitudes toward the topic under study and to build psychological profiles of the respondents, as illustrated by Porsche.

Research in Action

Taxonomy of a Porsche Buyer

Porsche (www.porsche.com) sells sports cars; the lowest-priced unit costs more than $40,000. The demographics of Porsche owner are well known: male, mid-40s, college graduate, with average earnings exceeding $200,000 per year. Traditional advertising had focused on the car's performance and how good the car makes the owner look.

In an attempt to learn more about customers' motivations and their psychological profile, Porsche hired a group of researchers to find out why its buyers bought the car. Among other techniques, the researchers used picture responses. Current and potential buyers were shown pictures of Porsche owners with their cars and asked to describe the owners. The results were surprising and revealed that Porsche had been using the wrong advertising approach.

According to the results, most Porsche owners did not care if people saw them in their Porsche. To better direct advertisements to potential buyers, researchers produced five psychographic profiles:

1. **Top Guns.** Driven, ambitious types. Power and control matter to these people, and they expect to be noticed.

2. **Elitists.** Old money, blue bloods. To them, a car is just a car, not an extension of their personality;

3. **Proud Patrons.** Their car is a trophy earned for hard work, and they are not concerned with whether they are seen in it or not.

4. **Bon Vivants.** Worldly jet setters and thrill seekers. Their car adds excitement to their passionate lives.

5. **Fantasists.** Their car is a fantasy escape. They are not trying to impress anyone and, in fact, are a little embarrassed about owning a Porsche.

After survey research confirmed these findings, marketing and advertising were directed at these psychographic segments. As a result of this research and after years of poor sales, Porsche's sales in the United States increased significantly and sales continued to progress through 2011. The 2011 Cayenne Turbo had a performance of 500 horsepower at 6,000 rpm, 0 to 60 mph in 4.4 seconds, top track speed of 172 mph, and was priced (MSRP) at $104,800.[7]

FIGURE 6.6
A Cartoon Test

Expressive Techniques

In **expressive techniques**, respondents are presented with a verbal or visual situation and asked to relate, not their own feelings or attitudes, but those of others. The two main expressive techniques are role playing and the third-person technique. In **role playing**, respondents are asked to play the role or assume the behavior of someone else. The researcher assumes that the respondents will project their own feelings into the role.

In the **third-person technique**, the respondent is presented with a verbal or visual situation and asked to relate the beliefs and attitudes of a third person rather than directly expressing personal beliefs and attitudes. This third person might be a friend, a neighbor, a colleague, or a "typical" person. Again, the researcher assumes that the respondent will reveal personal beliefs and attitudes while describing the reactions of a third party. Asking the individual to respond in the third person reduces the social pressure to give an acceptable answer, as the following example shows.

expressive techniques
Projective techniques in which the respondent is presented with a verbal or visual situation and asked to relate the feelings and attitudes of other people to the situation.

role playing
Respondents are asked to play the role or assume the behavior of someone else.

third-person technique
A projective technique in which the respondent is presented with a verbal or visual situation and asked to relate the beliefs and attitudes of a third person to the situation.

Research in Action

What Will the Neighbors Say?

A study was performed for a commercial airline to understand why some people do not fly. When the respondents were asked, "Are you afraid to fly?" very few people said "yes." The major reasons given for not flying were cost, inconvenience, and delays caused by bad weather. It was suspected, however, that the answers were heavily influenced by the need to give socially desirable responses.

Therefore, a follow-up study was done using the third-person technique. In the second study, the respondents were asked, "Do you think your neighbor is afraid to fly?" The answers indicated that most of the neighbors who traveled by some other means of transportation were afraid to fly. Thus, the third-person technique was able to uncover the true reason for not flying: fear of flying.[8]

Note that in the example, asking the question in the first person ("Are you afraid to fly?") did not elicit the true response. Phrasing the same question in the third person ("Do you think your neighbor is afraid to fly?") lowered the respondents' defenses and resulted in truthful answers. In another popular version of the third-person technique, the researcher presents the respondent with a description of a shopping list and asks for a characterization of the purchaser, thus gaining data on shopping behavior.

Suppose the researcher is interested in determining attitudes toward prepared dinners. Two otherwise identical grocery shopping lists are prepared, except that one list contains prepared dinners.

Respondents would be asked to characterize the purchaser identified with each list. The differences in the characteristics of the two purchasers reveal attitudes toward prepared dinners. For example, as compared to the other purchaser, the purchaser of prepared dinners may be described as lazy and disorganized. This would reveal that respondents think that lazy and disorganized people purchase prepared dinners.

We conclude our discussion of projective techniques by describing their advantages, disadvantages, and applications.

Advantages of Projective Techniques

Projective techniques have a major advantage over the unstructured direct techniques (i.e., focus groups and depth interviews): They may elicit responses that subjects would be unwilling or unable to give if they knew the purpose of the study. At times, in direct questioning, the respondent might intentionally or unintentionally misunderstand, misinterpret, or mislead the researcher. In these cases, projective techniques can increase the validity of responses by disguising the purpose. This is particularly true when the issues to be addressed are personal, sensitive, or subject to strong social norms. Projective techniques also are helpful when underlying motivations, beliefs, and attitudes are operating at a subconscious level.

Disadvantages of Projective Techniques

Projective techniques suffer from many of the disadvantages of unstructured direct techniques, but to a greater extent. These techniques generally require personal interviews with highly trained interviewers and require skilled interpreters to analyze the responses. Hence, they tend to be expensive. Furthermore, interpretation bias is a serious risk. With the exception of word association, all techniques are open-ended, making analysis and interpretation difficult and subjective.

Some projective techniques, such as role playing, require respondents to engage in unusual behavior. For example, to assess a company's image, respondents might be asked to play the role of a person that best describes the company. It is possible that respondents who agree to participate are themselves unusual in some way. Therefore, they might not be representative of the population of interest. As a result, it is desirable to compare findings generated by projective techniques with the findings of the other techniques that permit a more representative sample.

Application of Projective Techniques

With the exception of word association, projective techniques are used much less frequently than either focus groups or depth interviews. Word association is commonly used for testing brand names and, occasionally, to measure attitudes about particular products, brands, packages, or advertisements. Like focus groups, depth interviews and virtually all the projective techniques discussed can be implemented over the Internet. For example, various companies and marketing researchers are using the picture-response technique effectively. Coca-Cola can provide a picture on a Web site and ask respondents to write a story about it. The demographic data of the person coupled with the story can provide valuable insights into the respondent's psychographic profile and consumption patterns. The success of conducting qualitative research over the Internet lies in the respondents having access to and being comfortable with the Internet.

Experiential Learning

Online Qualitative Research Experiential Learning

The following Web sites illustrate the types of qualitative research that can be conducted online.

1. To experience the steps involved in designing and analyzing online bulletin board research, go to www.2020research.com, click "Technology Products," and then select "QualBoard."

To advance this overview, use the buttons at the bottom of the screen.

2. If you would like to join a panel of respondents who can earn prizes and other rewards for participating in online discussions, visit Toluna (www.toluna.com)

or 20/20 Research, Inc.'s Web site (www.2020research.com) and follow the instructions provided for joining a panel.

3. To experience how a sponsor of an online focus group monitors the actual focus group as if one was behind the one-way mirror in the back room of the focus-group facility, go to www.activegroup.net. Click "products," select "ActiveGroup," and then take the "Client Lounge Demo." You will have to provide an e-mail address and a one-word user name to activate the streaming video.

As the examples have shown, projective techniques can be used in a variety of situations. The usefulness of these techniques is enhanced when the following guidelines are observed:

1. Projective techniques are used when the sensitivity of the subject matter is such that respondents might not be willing or able to answer honestly to direct questions.
2. Projective techniques are used to uncover subconscious motives, beliefs, or values, providing deeper insights and understanding as part of exploratory research.
3. Projective techniques are administered and interpreted by trained interviewers who understand their advantages and limitations.

Given these guidelines, projective techniques, along with other qualitative techniques, can yield valuable information.

Be a DM!	Be an MR!
Projecting Cosmetic Usage	
As the brand manager for Clinique, how would you use information about the reasons why women use cosmetics to formulate marketing strategies that would increase your market share?	Visit www.clinique.com and search the Internet—including social media—as well as your library's online databases to obtain information on the underlying reasons why women use cosmetics. Which, if any, of the projective techniques would you use to determine why women use cosmetics?

 Social Media

Other Qualitative Research Techniques

There are also other qualitative research techniques that are used sometimes. These include:

- *Friendship pairs and triads.* Two or three people who know each other are interviewed together. The benefit is that the presence of a familiar person keeps the discussion open, and directs it away from the interviewer's lead.
- *Conflict groups.* Two sides of a debate are gathered and observed on how they prompt and provoke discussion in each other.
- *Affinity groups.* These groups are the opposite of conflict groups, in that like-minded people come together to discuss a certain topic while the moderator may act as a devil's advocate. This method leads to more authentic responses.
- *House-Tree-Person (HTP) Test.* The respondents provide drawings of a house, a tree, and a person. This serves as a basis for the researcher to infer the inclusion, exclusion, and characteristics of each part of the drawing, along with other features of the drawings that reflect the target market's self-image, conflicts, and perceptions toward various issues.
- *Personification.* Respondents are required to name an animal or object that symbolizes the product, brand, or company, thereby revealing its attributes.
- *The Friendly Martian.* The friendly Martian is a projective technique in which respondents are asked—individually or in a group—to advise a friendly Martian who has no knowledge on the subject, covering all the things he should do, what he should avoid, and so on. This method allows the respondents to express their views in a less self-conscious manner.

Given the limited evidence on the validity of these techniques, they should not be used as stand-alone procedures but in conjunction with focus groups, depth interviews, or the standard projective techniques.

Analysis of Qualitative Data

Sophisticated computer programs are available for processing large volumes of qualitative data and conducting complex analyses efficiently. The data are transmitted into text using a word processor. The data are then coded. Codes are labels assigned by the researcher to data segments to facilitate organization of the data. Thus, the computer can recall and print all the material belonging to a particular code. The source of each data segment is identified so that the researcher can see from where it was extracted. The computer program can perform complex searches, such as listing data segments pertaining to code "scary rides in theme parks," as described by teenagers. The program also enables the researcher to examine relationships between data segments such as the relationship between "scary rides in theme parks" and "fun and excitement in the park." Popular software programs include XSight (www.qsrinternational.com), Atlas/Ti (www.atlasti.com), HyperResearch (www.researchware.com), and NVivo 9 (www.qsrinternational.com).

Experiential Learning

Galaxy of Rides: A Joy Ride?

One type of qualitative research involves participation. Here, researchers actually involve themselves in the consumer behavior of interest. For example, a set of researchers was hired to better understand the experience of consumers visiting the Galaxy of Rides amusement park. Go to the textbook Web site and download "Five Narratives.doc." Read the narratives provided by the five participant observers.

1. Which participant helped you understand the consumer experience at Galaxy of Rides the best? Why?

2. Which participant helped you understand the consumer experience at Galaxy of Rides the least? Why?

These narratives could serve as the foundation for a thematic analysis.

1. What themes emerge across the narratives?

2. How do these themes help organize your insights about what could be done by the owners and managers of Galaxy of Rides to improve the consumer experience?

Qualitative Research Software

The objective of qualitative research is to perform induction—to go from the specific details to the general organizing idea explaining the data. In other words, qualitative researchers must sift and resift data in order to detect important patterns in the data and make an interpretation, if possible. This is difficult mental work. The process is lengthy, and it is easy to become "lost" in the details of the project.

Once interviews begin, qualitative researchers begin to accumulate an enormous amount of textual data when transcripts of interviews are made. In today's media-rich environment, researchers can also collect photo images, vocal recordings, illustrations, and drawings by respondents, as well as artifacts such as physical prototypes of improved products created by respondents in model form. With any data that can be put in digital form, software is now available for archiving, hyperlinking, and analyzing all such data from qualitative research endeavors.

One of the new tools enabling qualitative researchers to obtain more powerful perspectives on their data is QSR International's XSight software. With XSight, project artifacts and transcripts can be imported and coded. Simple frequency counts can be made of words. Queries can be made about where words are located in the text and what demographic variables are associated with respondents using such focal words. For example, in an extensive qualitative research project about cell-phone usage, researchers could use XSight to query how many times the word "security" occurs. Because XSight allows researchers to list the respondents' demographic profiles, researchers could also use XSight to query how many of those mentioning "security" comprise teenage girls. In this way, analysis can continue so that meaningful patterns can be identified.

The accompanying screen capture is from an actual marketing research project focused on cell-phone usage. The Project Explorer in XSight comprises the far left-side of the screen. Project

Source: Xsight is developed by QSR International Pty. Ltd., XSight is a trademark or registered trademark of QSR International. www.qsrinternational.com.

Explorer acts like a frame for a Web page that is always accessible to the user as subsequent navigation using hyperlinks occurs. In this way, Project Explorer offers an overview of the project structure. Such a structure is developed interactively between the user and XSight. Project Explorer offers nine frameworks for accessing the data under the heading "Analysis Frameworks." Among these frameworks are "Relationship with Cell Phones," "Core Values of NX (a brand)," and "Response to Club Ad," among others. Additionally, seven navigational buttons underneath the analysis frameworks are hyperlinked to important parts of the investigator's notes, such as "Documents" and "Interpretations."

In this example, "Relationship with Cell Phones" is the analysis framework selected, so the details of this "analysis framework" are presented to the right of Project Explorer. Here, the "Group 1 CF 18–22 (Chicago Females 18–22 years old)" sample is chosen as well as the "Availability" heading. On the right side of the screen, one can see the commentaries in the data about availability for this sample. The first and third commentaries represent notes made by the investigator at an earlier stage in the analysis of the data. The rest of the commentaries are actual quotes from the respondents. In this way, the investigator is able to select different samples and make comparison of the raw data that the investigator has previously coded as being related to availability. Thus, the XSight software allows powerful movement back and forth through the hyperlinked data. This provides the investigator with the ability to make comparisons across samples in pursuit of identifying new themes (headings).

For a Web-based product tour of QSR International's XSight software, go to www.qsr.com.au/products/productoverview/XSight.htm.

Summary Illustration Using the Opening Vignette

Qualitative research is appropriate when a company is faced with an uncertain situation or is presented with conclusive results that differ from expectations. This type of research can provide insight either before or after the fact. Qualitative research methods tend to be much less structured than quantitative methods and are based on small, nonrepresentative samples. In the opening vignette, Gillette used qualitative research at the beginning of the project to understand the shaving needs of women.

In contrast, quantitative research seeks conclusive evidence that is based on large, representative samples and that typically involves some form of statistical analysis. This was

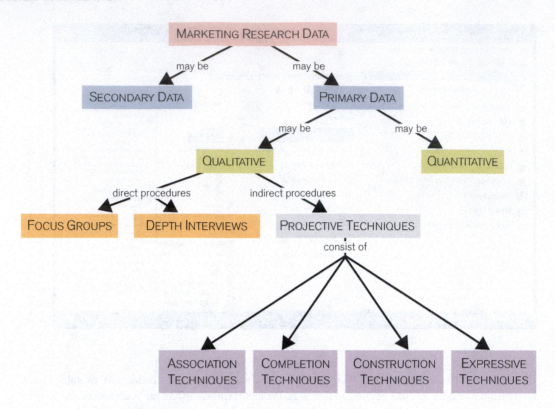

FIGURE 6.7

A Concept Map for Qualitative Research

seen in the opening vignette in which Gillette used quantitative research involving a survey of a representative sample of 500 women to substantiate the findings of qualitative research (depth interviews).

Focus groups, the most frequently used qualitative technique, are conducted in a group setting, whereas depth interviews are conducted one-on-one. In the opening vignette, Gillette chose depth interviews over focus groups because shaving is a rather personal experience for women, and their personal feelings could be tapped much better in a one-on-one setting than in a group environment.

Projective techniques aim to project the respondent's motivations, beliefs, attitudes, and feelings onto ambiguous situations. Projective techniques can be classified as association, completion, construction, or expressive techniques. Gillette used word association to select an appropriate name for the new razor. Using word association to select names for new products is quite common. Figure 6.7 provides a concept map for qualitative research. In this figure, the major concepts are connected by bold arrows using descriptors. Thus, marketing research data may be secondary or primary.

Primary data may be qualitative or quantitative. The rest of the figure can be interpreted similarly.

International Marketing Research

When a company is unfamiliar with the nuances of foreign markets, decisions that appear on the surface to be harmless and logical from a strategic business perspective might fail because the company did not fully understand the culture. This is why qualitative research is crucial in international marketing research. In the initial stages, qualitative research can provide insights into the problem and help in developing an approach by generating relevant models, research questions, and hypotheses. Thus, qualitative research might reveal the differences between foreign and domestic markets.

Focus groups can be used in many settings, particularly in industrialized countries. However, professional standards and practices might vary from those in the United States. For example, in Mexico it is considered acceptable for recruiters to invite family and friends to participate in a focus group. In some countries, such as India and Bolivia, due to lack of proper facilities, focus groups are held in hotels with closed-circuit monitoring. The moderator should not only be trained in focus-group methodology, but should also be familiar with the language, culture, and patterns of social interaction prevailing in that country. The focus-group findings should be derived not only from the verbal contents, but also from nonverbal cues, such as voice intonations, inflections, expressions, and gestures. In some countries, such as those in the Middle and Far East, people are hesitant to discuss their feelings in a group setting. In these cases, depth interviews should be used. The use of projective techniques should be carefully considered, because the responses that these techniques generate can reflect deeply rooted cultural influences. When used appropriately, however, as in the following example, qualitative techniques can play a crucial role in the success of the marketing research project.

Research in Action

Spanish Expansion

The Spanish airline Iberia (www.iberia.com) was faced with the problem of expanding the number of routes from Europe to South and Central America. Amid a multitude of airlines operating over the Atlantic, the question was how to differentiate Iberia from its many competitors. Focus groups provided some initial answers by revealing several insights: (1) International travelers saw Iberia as "the gateway to South America"; (2) providing several days' layover in Miami would attract a number of passengers, particularly tourists; and (3) the pairing of destinations, such as Miami and Cancun, in travel packages would promote more business. When subsequent survey research confirmed the focus-group findings, Iberia chose to make Miami a hub for its flights to South America. These findings also were used to design travel packages, make changes in services, and differentiate the airline. In 2011, Iberia was offering free additional services, such as hotel stays, lunches, and tours, at transfer destinations for customers using new transatlantic routes between Europe and destinations in the Americas and vice versa, further strengthening the airline's position.[9]

Be an MR!	Be a DM!
Johnson's Baby	
Visit the Johnson & Johnson Web site at www.jnj.com and search the Internet—including social media—as well as your library's online databases to obtain information on how consumers select baby-product brands in the United States. Obtain similar information for France. What qualitative research techniques would you use to determine how consumers select baby-product brands in France?	As the brand manager for Johnson & Johnson, how would you use information on how consumers select baby-product brands to formulate marketing strategies that would increase your market share in France?

Marketing Research and Social Media

Social networks are defined by the relationships between members. These relationships go by various names, such as friends, followers, connections, etc. On some networks, these relationships are created by mutual consent as "friends" in Facebook or "connections" in LinkedIn. Other networks, such as Twitter, permit unilateral relationships unless blocked by the other member. Relating to friends is a key appeal of social networks. Groups are another element of many social networks. These groups are an evolution of the early online discussion forums and are self-organized collections of members with common interests. They feature discussion forums and may also include photo-, video-, and music-sharing. Google Groups (www.groups.google.com) has also simplified online group communication as people can discuss issues more easily with others on this platform. There are various features on the Web site that facilitate discussion and uploading of files for the perusal of the people in the group.

Marketing researchers can tap into these social networks for conducting qualitative research.

Focus Groups

Social networks provide you with a large audience eager to talk for free. Companies have very cleverly come up with ways to carry out a form of focus group and other forms of qualitative research using social media. Just being a part of different types of social media and analyzing what people are talking about can yield a basic understanding of customers, but if you really want something constructive to take shape from all that talking, you need to listen to the right people. For this reason—besides increasing their presence on varying social networks—companies are creating private online communities, which can play the role of extended focus groups. The members are carefully recruited, and membership is only by invitation. Expert facilitators engage the members regularly to build familiarity and a pattern as the customers start to view the community as their own. A lively, friendly place is designed to assist customers in engaging in insightful conversations. Enterprise-class software that excavates deeply to get the most out of every conversation is also a part of the community. JCPenney presents a case study of successfully using a private online community to conduct an extended form of focus group.

Research in Action

JCPenney: Using Social Bodies to Design Body Lingerie

JCPenney, one of America's leading retailers, launched a private online community called the *Ambrielle Team*, which was dedicated to consumers of the JCPenney lingerie line. This team aimed at learning more about the Ambrielle customer and her fit concerns. This was a type of focus group that was conducted through forming a private community. The sample size was small, and the information was collected in a natural and unstructured manner. The product team played the role of moderators and facilitated conversations in the right direction. Team members were handpicked and limited in number. JCPenney also gathered lifestyle, demographic, and psychographic information about members, so as to make sure that the firm had a reasonably complete picture of each member. The Ambrielle team had a series of online discussions within the community so as to help JCPenney figure out the basic fit and quality issues of women. This was followed by a "wear" test to give a more definite focus to the feedback regarding specific products. After the "wear" test, members were again asked to express their views via the private discussion board, an online activity, and live online chats with the product team.

Based on this customer alliance and consumer response, JCPenney made substantial product changes to the lingerie bands, straps, and overall sizing so that customer needs were better satisfied. These changes were posted in the community to make the team realize that the company had inculcated their insights and feedback into the product. Store sales of Ambrielle products soon increased.[10]

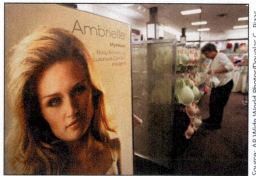

Source: AP Wide World Photos/Douglas C. Pizac.

Another way to conduct a focus-group type of research involves participant blogs. The general approach is to define a specific topic and then recruit participants to blog about that topic. Each participant is given his or her own blog to maintain. The number of participants typically ranges from 8 to 60. Blog projects tend to last from 1 to 4 weeks. Qualitative analyses of the blogs' content results in rich insights.

Depth Interviews

Burger King conducted a form of depth interview using social media. Burger King customers were secretly filmed after being told that the company's signature Whopper sandwich was being discontinued. A 1-minute funny TV commercial was developed using this episode. However, an 8-minute video called *Whopper Freakout* was posted on a companion Web site. Visitors viewing the video were encouraged to post their comments, and follow-up one-on-one interviews were held online with select respondents. The analysis of these comments and interviews revealed a consistent theme. When customers were confronted with the idea that they could no longer order a Whopper, they immediately recalled their childhood memories of Whoppers. Remarks such as "The people in this video are still eating at Burger King today because their parents brought them there as kids" were obtained. This led Burger King to build a marketing campaign for the Whopper based on childhood memories and nostalgia.

Projective Techniques

Several projective techniques can be easily implemented using social media communities. The unstructured and indirect form of questioning on social media has consumers willing to project their underlying thoughts, motivations, and feelings regarding the issues of concern.

SENTENCE COMPLETION GlaxoSmithKline Consumer Healthcare used Communispace (www.communispace.com) social network groups to closely define the customer base for its new line of Alli weight-loss products. The research company used sentence completion online when it was trying to investigate self-image issues with overweight people. Community members were asked to complete sentences like, "When you talk to yourself, you refer to yourself as _____." Members were also asked to post photos showing what they most regretted about their obesity. Analysis of sentence completion and photos indicated that people were frustrated about being excluded from everyday activities. However, they were willing to take responsibility for their own weight loss. They were also willing to accept slow progress in return for long-term results. Alli was targeted at this segment, and Glaxo sold $155 million worth of Alli in the first 6 weeks after introduction.

PICTURE-RESPONSE TECHNIQUES Online photo-sharing sites include Flickr (a leader in this category), PhotoBucket, Shutterfly, Smugmug, and Snapfish. Many people communicate better with photos than they do with words. Concepts such as beauty, color, aesthetics, emotions, and feelings can be captured visually and investigated by analyzing photo-sharing sites. When analyzing these photos, look for *tags*, descriptive labels applied by photographers to their own work as well as the work of others. Analyses of tags can identify perceptions, emotions, and beliefs that may be quite revealing and relevant. During March 2010, Tropicana posted pictures on their Facebook photo page. The album was named "Tropicana Juicy Rewards," which was part of the advertising campaign for Tropicana. The picture-post on Facebook gave consumers a brand new look at their advertising slogan, packaging, and pictures that Tropicana was going to use. Feedback on the pictures gathered 47 "likes" and a majority of the consumers commenting "Yummy!" or "Slurp!" This feedback, along with the posted comments, helped shape the advertising campaign for Tropicana.

ROLE PLAYING Procter & Gamble (P&G, www.pg.com) used role playing in social media to determine consumer reaction and build upon its "Talking Stain" commercial aired during the 2008 Super Bowl. The company set up a profile on YouTube and invited comments and submissions of commercials that would build upon the Super Bowl commercial. Thus, consumers were asked to play the role of a TV commercial producer. The winning entry was to be aired on prime-time television. More than 100 entries were received. Through this research, P&G was able to tap into consumer feedback and innovative thinking that served as the basis for future commercials. In addition, the company was able to sustain the Super Bowl commercial long after its 30 seconds of fame ended.

Limitations

Using social media to conduct qualitative research is not without drawbacks. Often the amount of information generated can be voluminous, drowning the company and its marketing research personnel in weeks of work. General Motors' Chevy Apprentice research effort, in which visitors contributed TV commercials assembled from video clips on a Web site, logged about 22,000 submissions. That amounted to a lot of video to view and to analyze.

Ethics in Marketing Research

Respondents' rights and privileges must be respected when conducting qualitative research. Some of the salient ethical issues relate to misleading or deceiving respondents, not maintaining their anonymity, and embarrassing or harming the respondents. An additional issue with wider ramifications is the use of research results in an unethical manner.

Some qualitative researchers allow their clients to be present at focus-group discussions by introducing them as co-researchers. Nonetheless, many participants are able to discern that the co-researcher is in fact the client. This deception raises ethical concerns and generates mistrust that has an adverse impact on the quality of the data and the integrity of marketing research.

As mentioned earlier, focus-group discussions often are recorded using hidden video cameras. Whether or not they are initially told of the hidden camera, the respondents should be informed about the recording at the end of the meeting. The purpose of the video, including who will be able to view it, should be disclosed. In particular, if the client will have access to it, this should be made known as well. Each respondent should be asked to sign a written statement granting permission to use the recording. Participants should be given the opportunity to refuse signing, in which case the recording should be edited to completely omit the identity and comments of the respondents who refuse.

Social Media

With the use of social media panels, panelists are enrolled and told of the objective and their duties. However, ethical issue arise when the consumers are not told that the very objects, items, or even words that they use online could be monitored without their knowledge. To continue the use of social media monitoring techniques without adverse impact, consumers should be adequately informed about such stealthy activities. Moreover, firms can act ethically by extracting only the keywords that they are looking for without looking for more than necessary information. Firms should also consider donations or being involved in a community cause to defray the negative association of such techniques.

The researcher has an obligation to make the respondents feel comfortable. If a respondent is experiencing discomfort or stress, the interviewer should show restraint and should not aggressively probe any further. At the end of the interview, respondents should be allowed to reflect on all they have said and be allowed to ask questions. This helps reduce their stress and return them to their preinterview emotional state.

The ethical issues involved in social media research are very similar except that the need to protect the privacy of respondents assumes greater importance. A final issue relates to the ethics of using qualitative research results for questionable purposes, as in the presidential campaigns profiled here.

Research in Action

Focus (Groups) on Mudslinging

The ethics of negative or "attack" ads has been debated for some time. The focus, however, has shifted from the ads themselves to the ethics of employing marketing research techniques to design the ad message. Nowhere is this phenomenon more prevalent than in political "mudslinging" campaigns. The pronounced use of negative ads goes back to the George H.W. Bush campaign against Michael Dukakis in the 1988 U.S. presidential election and, unfortunately, has remained in force since.

Before designing negative ads about Dukakis, Bush campaign leaders tested negative information about Dukakis in focus groups. The idea was to develop some insight into how the American public would react if this negative information was released in the form of advertisements. Negative issues that

elicited very negative emotions about Dukakis from the focus groups were chosen for Bush's political advertising. The result? Partly because he was painted "as an ineffectual, weak, liberal, do-gooder lacking in common sense," Dukakis lost the election by a wide margin.

This misuse of qualitative research was observed in the 1992 and 1996 presidential elections that Bill Clinton won, in part, by negatively attacking the Republicans. In the 2000 presidential election, Al Gore unfairly attacked George W. Bush as lacking in experience after data culled from focus groups and surveys revealed that experience was an important criterion for voters. The 2004 presidential election also was noted for negative attacks by both parties, particularly by John Kerry on

George W. Bush, again based on focus-group and survey findings.

Similar (mis)use of qualitative research was attributed to Clinton and Barack Obama in the hotly contested 2008 Democratic primaries and by Obama in the 2008 presidential elections. When Obama discovered through focus groups, analysis of social media, and survey research that President George W. Bush had low approval ratings, he linked John McCain closely with Bush. By linking McCain to Bush, the Obama campaign successfully undercut McCain's image as an independent maverick. For example, the Obama ad called "Two Faces" that targeted Hispanic voters featured two lines in the script:

> "John McCain and his Republican friends have two faces. One tells lies to get our votes. The other, even worse, follows the failed policies of George Bush, putting the interests of powerful groups ahead of working families."

> "John McCain: more of the same Republican deceit."

The rest is history. Obama became the first African-American president of the United States.[11]

Source: K2 images/Shutterstock.

WHAT WOULD YOU DO?

Lotus Development Corporation: Developing Its Web Site

The Situation

Mike Rhodin is the CEO of Lotus Software (www.ibm.com), which is one of the brands of the IBM Software group. Lotus is a company that recognizes the need for individuals and businesses to work together. Therefore, it redefines the concept of conducting business through practical knowledge management, e-business, and other groundbreaking ways of connecting the world's ideas, thinkers, buyers, sellers, and communities via the Internet. As of 2011, Lotus marketed its products in more than 80 countries worldwide through direct and extensive business partner channels. The company also provides numerous professional consulting, support, and education services through the Lotus Professional Services organization. To help Lotus stay ahead of its competitors, Mike Rhodin wishes to increase the number of Web site visitors and for Lotus to maintain a Web site that is going to best meet the needs of its customers.

Lotus conducts focus groups of customers and business partners every 4 months to determine users' reactions to its Web site. This routine recognizes the fact that Web sites have very short lifecycles and need ongoing attention to keep them up-to-date. The focus groups evaluate Lotus' Web site and those of other companies. Some objectives for the focus groups include identifying factors that lead Internet users to visit a Web site, identifying what factors entice visitors to return often to a Web site, and identifying users' technological capabilities.

The use of focus groups enables Lotus to actively collect some information that is not collected passively. Passive counters can keep track of the number of visitors to a Web site as well as the number of visitors who actually use the site. For example, Lotus can monitor the number of visitors who use its chat rooms that pertain to specific products. Just knowing that the number of visitors is changing, however, does not provide a company with insights concerning why there is a decrease or increase in visitors. Focus groups can be used to gain those insights.

From focus groups, Lotus learned that customers wanted improved navigation and a higher level of consistency. In the past, the emphasis was on making sure that information was delivered quickly to customers. Focus groups revealed that the company needed to further develop the site to make it easier for Web site visitors to navigate through all of the information.

The Marketing Research Decision

1. Do you think that Lotus adopted the right research design? Which one of the following types of research designs would you recommend and why?
   a. Focus groups
   b. Depth interviews
   c. Survey research
   d. Projective techniques
   e. Focus groups followed by survey research

2. Discuss the role of the type of research you recommend in enabling Mike Rhodin to design an effective Web site.

The Marketing Management Decision

1. What should Mike Rhodin do to increase traffic to the Web site and enhance the user experience?
   a. Redesign the Web site.

(continued)

    b. Upgrade the existing Web site, making only the necessary changes.

    c. Engage in aggressive banner advertising.

    d. Engage in aggressive print advertising.

    e. Offer price discounts to customers on the Web site.

2. Discuss how the marketing management-decision action that you recommend to Mike Rhodin is influenced by the research design that you suggested earlier and by the findings of that research.

What Mike Rhodin Did

Mike Rhodin redesigned the Lotus Web site completely to improve navigation and enhance the efficiency with which visitors could search and download the information they wanted. He also engaged in aggressive print and banner advertising. IBM launched Lotus Workplace with print advertising in the *Wall Street Journal,* the *New York Times,* and the *Boston Globe.* In addition, banner advertising was launched on a wide variety of Web sites, including eWeek, Information Week, BusinessWeek, and Forbes. These ads were all part of the "Can You See It" ad campaign that demonstrated how IBM Software enables on-demand business and invited readers to the Web site.[12]

Source: Reprint Courtesy of International Business Machines Corporation, © International Business Machines Corporation.

Summary

Qualitative and quantitative research should be viewed as complementary. Qualitative research methods tend to be much less structured and are based on small, nonrepresentative samples. The various qualitative options vary in terms of how directly they ask questions of the respondent. Direct methods, such as focus groups and depth interviews, do not attempt to disguise the purpose of the research. Focus groups, the most frequently used qualitative technique, are conducted in a group setting, whereas depth interviews are done one-on-one.

Indirect techniques make a deliberate attempt to disguise the true purpose of the research. They are called projective techniques because they seek to project the respondent's motivations, beliefs, attitudes, and feelings onto ambiguous situations. Projective techniques can be classified as association, completion, construction, or expressive techniques. Projective techniques are particularly useful when respondents are unwilling or unable to provide the required information by direct methods.

In the international context, qualitative research can reveal differences between foreign and domestic markets. Social media have enhanced both the quality and quantity of qualitative research. Ethical issues in qualitative research relate to respecting respondents' rights and privileges.

Key Terms and Concepts

Suggested Cases and Video Cases

Running Case with Real Data

1.1 Hewlett-Packard

Comprehensive Critical Thinking Cases

2.1 American Idol   2.2 Baskin-Robbins   2.3 Akron Children's Hospital

Comprehensive Cases with Real Data

3.1 Bank of America   3.2 McDonald's   3.3 Boeing

Comprehensive Brief Harvard Business School Cases

4.1 TruEarth Healthy Foods: Market Research for a New Product Introduction (4065)
4.2 The Springfield Nor'easters: Maximizing Revenues in the Minor Leagues (2510)
4.3 Metabical: Positioning and Communications Strategy for a New Weight-Loss Drug (4240)
4.4 Saxonville Sausage Company (2085)

Online Video Cases

6.1 Nike   7.1 Starbucks   9.1 P&G   10.1 Nivea   11.1 Dunkin' Donuts
12.1 Motorola   13.1 Subaru   14.1 Intel   19.1 Marriott

Live Research: Conducting a Marketing Research Project

1. For most projects, it will be important to conduct some form of qualitative research.
2. **Social Media** Different teams can be assigned different responsibilities (e.g., interviewing key decision makers, interviewing industry experts, conducting depth interviews with consumers, doing a focus group, analyzing social media content, and so forth). Alternatively, all the teams can work on these tasks.
3. If possible, have at least one team use the qualitative research software discussed in this chapter and make a presentation to the class.

Acronyms

The key characteristics of a focus group may be described by the acronym FOCUS GROUPS:

F ocused on a particular topic

O utline prepared for discussion

C haracteristics of the moderator

U nstructured

S ize: 8 to 12 participants

G roup composition: homogeneous

R ecorded: audio- and video-recording

O bservation: one-way mirror

U ndisguised

P hysical setting: relaxed

S everal sessions needed: 1 to 3 hours each

The main features of a depth interview may be summarized by the acronym DEPTH:

D epth of coverage

E ach respondent individually interviewed

P robe the respondent

T alented interviewer required

H idden motives may be uncovered

Review Questions

1. What are the primary differences between qualitative and quantitative research techniques?
2. What is qualitative research, and how is it conducted?
3. What are the differences between direct and indirect qualitative research? Give an example of each.
4. Why is the focus group the most popular qualitative research technique?
5. Why is the focus-group moderator so important in obtaining quality results?
6. What are some key qualifications of focus-group moderators?
7. Why should one safeguard against professional respondents?
8. What are two ways in which focus groups can be misused?
9. What is a depth interview? Under what circumstances is it preferable to focus groups?
10. What are the major advantages of depth interviews?
11. What are projective techniques? What are the four types of projective techniques?
12. What is the word-association technique? Give an example of a situation in which this technique is especially useful.
13. When should projective techniques be employed?
14. **Social Media** How can social media be used to conduct qualitative research?

Applied Problems

1. Following the methods outlined in the text, develop a plan for conducting a focus group to determine consumers' attitudes toward and preferences for imported automobiles. Specify the objectives of the focus group and write a screening questionnaire.
2. Suppose Baskin-Robbins wants to know why some people do not eat ice cream regularly. Develop a cartoon test for this purpose.
3. The Coca-Cola Company has asked you to conduct Internet focus groups with heavy users of soft drinks. Explain how you would identify and recruit potential respondents.
4. Could a depth interview be conducted via the Internet? What are the advantages and disadvantages of this procedure over conventional depth interviews?
5. Visit the Web site of Qualitative Research Consultants Association (www.qrca.org). Write a report about the current state-of-the-art in qualitative research.
6. *Tennis* magazine would like to recruit participants for online focus groups. How would you make use of a newsgroup to recruit participants? Visit http://groups.google.com and then navigate the site to select "Recreation—Sports—Tennis."

Group Discussion

1. In a group of five or six, discuss whether qualitative research is scientific.
2. Discuss the following statement in a small group: "If the focus-group findings confirm prior expectations, the client should dispense with quantitative research."
3. Discuss the following statement in a small group: "Quantitative research is more important than qualitative research because it results in statistical information and conclusive findings."

Hewlett-Packard Running Case

Review the Hewlett-Packard (HP) case, Case 1.1, and questionnaire given toward the end of the book.

1. In gaining an understanding of the consumer decision-making process for personal computer purchases, would focus groups or depth interviews be more useful? Explain.
2. Develop a focus-group discussion guide for understanding the consumer decision-making process for personal computer purchases.
3. Can projective techniques be useful to HP as it seeks to increase its penetration of U.S. households? Which project technique(s) would you recommend?
4. Devise word-association techniques to measure consumer associations that might affect attitudes toward personal computer purchases.
5. Design sentence completion techniques to uncover underlying motives for personal computer purchases.
6. **Social Media** How can HP make use of social media to conduct qualitative research?

ONLINE VIDEO CASE 6.1

NIKE: Associating Athletes, Performance, and the Brand

Visit **www.pearsonhighered.com/malhotra** to read the video case and view the accompanying video. Nike: Associating Athletes, Performance, and the Brand highlights Nike's use of marketing research to build its brand into one of the most well-known and easily recognized brands in the world. In terms of qualitative research, the particular use of focus groups is described in the video. The case can be used to discuss the future use of qualitative research in order to strengthen Nike's image. Specific marketing research questions on this and the previous chapters are posed in the video case.

Descriptive Research Design: Survey and Observation

Source: © Tony Hobbs/Alamy Images.

LEARNING OBJECTIVES

After reading this chapter, the student should be able to:

1. Discuss and classify survey methods and describe the various telephone, personal, mail, and electronic interviewing methods.

2. Identify the criteria for evaluating survey methods, compare the different methods, and evaluate which is best suited for a particular research project.

3. Explain how survey response rates can be improved.

4. Describe how observation differs from the survey method and the procedures that are available for observing people and objects.

5. Discuss the relative advantages and disadvantages of observational methods as compared to survey methods.

> **"** Much of the insights about consumers' future behavior are gained by simply asking consumers about their attitudes and intentions. **"**

Surjya Roy
Senior Project Manager, Market Strategies, Inc., Livonia, Michigan

Procter & Gamble's New Marketing Platform: Everyday Low Pricing and Brand Extensions

As part of its ongoing marketing research, Procter & Gamble (P&G) routinely analyzes scanner data and conducts consumer surveys. Scanner-panel data from The Nielsen Company (see Chapter 5) revealed that a typical, brand-loyal family spent $725 each year on P&G products. In comparison, a family that bought similar products as private-label or low-priced brands spent less than $500. In a time when value-consciousness dominated, this premium-pricing strategy presented a problem to P&G. This led P&G to create a new marketing platform for its products.

At the base of the new platform was the concept of value. The platform was designed to recognize that P&G had been overcharging for many of its products, including Tide detergent, Crest toothpaste, Pampers disposable diapers, Vick's cough syrup, and Head & Shoulders shampoo. Focus groups and depth interviews conducted by P&G revealed that customers were no longer willing to pay for non–value-added costs. Furthermore, surveys using mail panels indicated that customers loyal to P&G preferred prices that were consistently low rather than price discounts and special deals. A computer-assisted telephone survey of a randomly selected representative sample resulted in similar findings for the general population. The concept developed from these findings is known as *everyday low pricing* (EDLP). This concept was the exact opposite of P&G's previous platform of maintaining high list prices offset by frequent and irregular discounts.

Another problem that led P&G to reformulate its platform had to do with new-product development. Previous research indicated that P&G brands enjoyed considerable equity in that they were well known and preferred by a large segment of the market. In 2000, P&G decided to drop the word "Oil" from Oil of Olay, its line of skin-care products and cosmetics, in an effort to make the line more appealing to younger women. This led to the strategy of brand extensions (BE), the practice of using a successful brand name to launch a new or modified product. An example is Olay Beauty Bar, a brand extension of Olay lotion. The beauty bar was developed as a response to the growing consumer demand for a product that would keep skin feeling soft and young, not only on the face, but all over, as well. The bar was specially engineered with a synthetic cleansing system and light Olay moisturizers that help the skin to hold moisture better than soap does. In addition to the special formulation, the bar was designed to stay firm during use and not melt away like most other beauty bars.

Prior to its introduction, the Olay Beauty Bar was tested in mall-intercept interviews. In these interviews, respondents actually washed their hands and face with the bar in a test area located in the mall before responding to a survey. Because the results of these mall-intercept interviews were quite positive, three types of bars were introduced: pink and white with different scents and an unscented hypoallergenic version for sensitive skin. The Olay Beauty Bar has been a great success and won one of *Marketing News'* Edison Best New Products Awards. P&G continued this strategy of brand extension, launching other extensions of the Olay line, such as the Olay Regenerist line that consists of an eye-lifting serum, a daily regenerating serum, and an anti-aging lip treatment. In 2009, Consumer Survey of Product Innovation gave their "Product of the Year Award" to Olay Body Wash plus Spa. As of 2010, Carrie Underwood was the new face of Olay.

The strategies of EDLP and BE continue to pay dividends for the company. The company's sales and market share continued to improve through 2011, strengthening its position as a world leader in consumer products, with P&G brands serving consumers in more than 180 countries.[1]

Overview

The marketing research process begins by defining the research problem and then formulating an approach and a research design. As discussed in Chapter 3 the major types of research designs are exploratory and conclusive. Exploratory designs rely primarily on secondary data analysis (Chapters 4 and 5) and qualitative research (Chapter 6). Conclusive research designs can be classified as causal or descriptive. Causal designs are explained in Chapter 8. This chapter discusses survey and observation methods, the quantitative techniques typically used to collect descriptive research data. Figure 7.1 briefly explains the focus of the chapter, the relation of this chapter to the previous ones, and the steps of the marketing research process on which this chapter concentrates.

Survey data do much more than merely report behavior. Surveys can provide insights into who the consumers are, how they behave, and why they behave in certain ways. Respondents' reports of their conscious motives, values, or beliefs provide some insight into consumer behavior. This was illustrated in the opening vignette in which P&G used different types of surveys to understand consumers' preferences for everyday low prices versus discounts and special sales.

Surveys can be classified in terms of how the data are collected: telephone interviews, computer-assisted telephone interviews, in-home interviews, mall-intercept interviews, computer-assisted personal interviews, mail interviews, mail panels, and electronic surveys (e-mail and Internet). In this chapter, each of these methods is described and the criteria used to select an appropriate method for a particular project are discussed.

The chapter also presents the major observational methods of personal observation and mechanical observation. It discusses the advantages and disadvantages of observation compared to survey methods, as well as the role of survey and observation methods in international marketing research. The use of social media for descriptive research is discussed, and several ethical issues that arise in survey research and observation methods are identified. Figure 7.2 gives an overview of the topics discussed in this chapter and how they flow from one to the next.

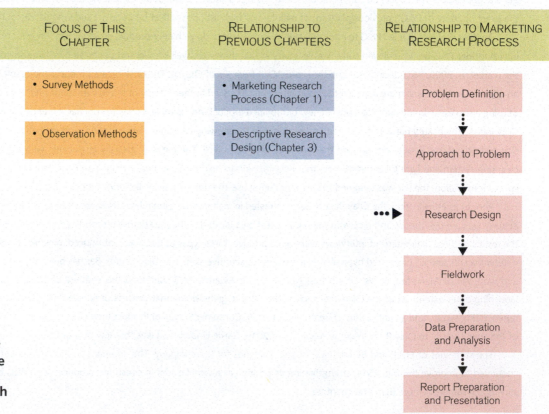

FIGURE 7.1

Relationship of Survey and Observation to the Previous Chapters and the Marketing Research Process

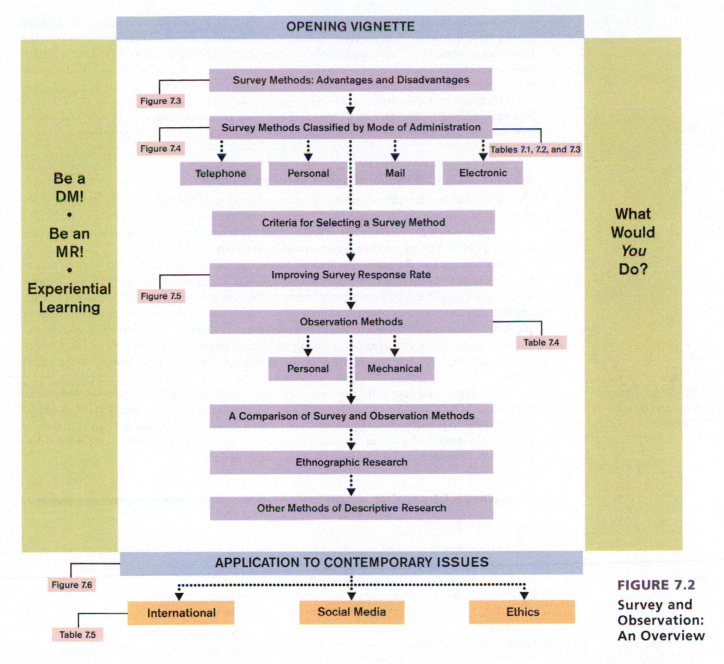

FIGURE 7.2

Survey and Observation: An Overview

Survey Methods

The **survey method** is one of the two main ways of obtaining quantitative descriptive data (see Figure 7.3). It is based on questioning respondents. Surveys are used when the research involves sampling a large number of people and asking them a series of questions. Surveys can be conducted in person, by telephone, through a mailed questionnaire, or electronically via the computer.

survey method

A structured questionnaire given to a sample of a population and designed to elicit specific information from respondents.

FIGURE 7.3

Methods of Obtaining Quantitative Data in Descriptive Research

QUANTITATIVE DESCRIPTIVE RESEARCH

SURVEY
Information Obtained by Questioning Respondents

OBSERVATION
Information Obtained by Observing Behavior or Phenomena

Perhaps the biggest issue researchers must tackle is how to motivate respondents to candidly answer their questions. The uninvited intrusion of telemarketers and direct marketers into the home has resulted in an increasing number of consumers shutting the door to anyone trying to make contact. The challenges of controlling this nonresponse problem are discussed later in the chapter.

The range of topics that can be investigated using surveys is as varied as the research problems businesses face. Questions regarding behavior, intentions, attitudes, beliefs, awareness, motivations, and demographic and lifestyle characteristics all lend themselves to survey research.

Advantages and Disadvantages of Survey Research

The survey method has the advantages of ease, reliability, and simplicity. Questionnaires are relatively easy to administer. Using fixed-response (multiple-choice) questions reduces variability in the results, which can be caused by differences among interviewers, and enhances the reliability of the responses. It also simplifies coding, analysis, and interpretation of data.

Disadvantages of the survey method are that respondents might be unable or unwilling to provide the desired information. For example, consider questions about motivational factors. Respondents might not be consciously aware of the real reasons they prefer one brand over another. The subconscious nature of their motives might make it impossible for them to answer questions accurately. Respondents might be unwilling to respond if the information requested is sensitive or personal. For example, consider questions about religious beliefs. Some respondents might view this topic as very personal and might be unwilling to answer any questions related to it.

structured data collection
Use of a formal questionnaire that presents questions in a prearranged order.

Also, **structured data collection** involving a questionnaire with fixed-response choices can result in loss of validity for certain types of data, such as beliefs and feelings. Finally, it can be quite difficult to properly phrase questions (see Chapter 11 on questionnaire design). Yet, despite these disadvantages, the survey approach is by far the most common method of primary data collection in marketing research, particularly quantitative data.

Experiential Learning

Surveys and You

The Council of American Survey Research Organizations (CASRO) is the trade association of survey-research businesses, representing more than 200 companies and research operations in the United States, Canada, and Mexico. CASRO communicates the importance of survey research in the public realm and helps educate those in the research industry about standards for ethics and performance. Go to the CASRO Web site (www.casro.org) and click "Surveys and You" under "For Public/Media." Here you will find a user-friendly overview to survey research entitled "Surveys and You." Read this short overview and then answer the following questions:

1. Of the questions posed in "Surveys and You," which one helped you learn the most?

2. What did you learn as a result of this question?

3. What did you learn about the importance of surveys?

Survey Methods Classified by Mode of Administration

Figure 7.4 illustrates the various methods of collecting survey data, broadly classified as telephone, personal, mail, or electronic interviews. Telephone interviewing can be further broken down in terms of whether computers are used in the interview process. Personal interviews can be conducted in the home, as mall-intercept interviews, or as computer-assisted personal interviews (CAPI). The third major method, mail interviewing, takes the form of ordinary mail surveys or surveys conducted using mail panels.

Electronic interviews are generally administered over the Internet or by using e-mail. Of these methods, telephone interviews are the most popular in the United States, followed by personal interviews. The popularity of electronic surveys is increasing quickly. Mail interviews are the least popular.

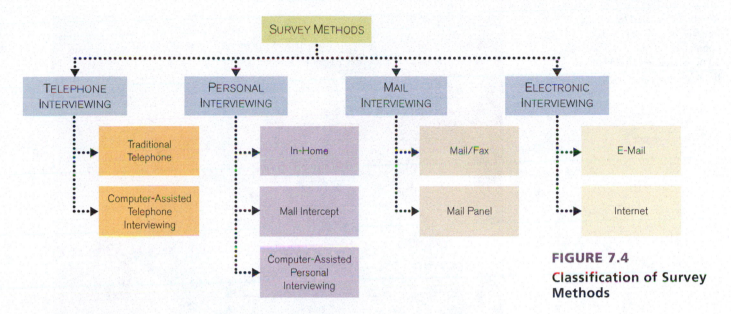

FIGURE 7.4

Classification of Survey Methods

Telephone Methods

As stated earlier, telephone interviews vary in terms of the degree of computer assistance supporting the interview.

TRADITIONAL TELEPHONE INTERVIEWS   Traditional telephone interviews involve phoning a sample of respondents and asking them a series of questions. The interviewer uses a paper questionnaire and records the responses with a pencil. Telephone interviews are generally conducted from centrally located research facilities. Telephone research centers are specifically equipped to accommodate large groups of interviewers. These facilities have proliferated because of the cost and control advantages they offer. The low cost of telecommunication services has made nationwide telephone interviewing from a central location practical.

Additionally, field service supervisors can closely monitor the telephone conversations. This monitoring helps to control interviewer bias that results from variation in the way in which the questions are asked and the responses are recorded. Data quality is enhanced with on-the-spot review of completed questionnaires. Finally, the research budget, both in terms of labor costs and time restrictions, can be more easily managed when the interviewers are assembled in one location.

COMPUTER-ASSISTED TELEPHONE INTERVIEWING   Computer-assisted telephone interviewing (CATI) uses a computerized questionnaire administered to respondents over the telephone. The interviewer sits in front of a computer screen and wears a headset. The computer screen replaces a paper and pencil questionnaire, and the headset substitutes for a telephone. CATI from a central location is now much more popular than the traditional telephone method. More than 95 percent of all telephone interviews in the United States are conducted using a CATI system.

Upon command, the computer dials the telephone number to be called. When contact is made, the interviewer reads the questions posed on the computer screen and records the respondent's answers directly into the computer memory bank. CATI combines the interview with the editing and data-entry steps to produce a highly efficient and accurate survey process. Because the responses are entered directly into the computer, interim and update reports can be compiled instantaneously as the data are being collected.

CATI software has built-in logic, which also enhances data accuracy. The program will personalize questions and control for logically incorrect answers, such as percentage answers that do not add up to 100 percent. The software has built-in branching logic, which will skip questions that are not applicable or will probe for more detail when warranted. For example, if a respondent answered "yes" to the question, "Have you ever purchased Nike athletic shoes?" an entire series of questions related to the experience with Nike shoes would follow. If, however, the respondent answered "no," that line of questioning would be skipped. An application of CATI was illustrated in the opening vignette, where P&G used this method to survey a randomly selected sample, asking questions related to pricing preferences.

Computer-assisted telephone interviewing (CATI) uses a computerized questionnaire administered to respondents over the telephone, as shown.

Source: © OJO Images/SuperStock.

sample control

The ability of the survey mode to effectively and efficiently reach the units specified in the sample.

response rate

The percentage of the total attempted interviews that are completed.

ADVANTAGES AND DISADVANTAGES OF TELEPHONE INTERVIEWING Telephone interviewing, in a computer-assisted format, remains one of the most popular survey methods. This popularity can be traced to several factors. Interviews can be completed quickly, because the travel time associated with personal interviews is eliminated. **Sample control,** or the ability to reach the units specified in the sample, is good when proper sampling and callback procedures are followed. Control of the field force is good, because the interviewers can be supervised from a central location. The control is even better in CATI, because these systems allow the supervisor to monitor an interview without the interviewer or the respondent being aware of it. The **response rate,** the percentage of total attempted interviews that are completed, also is good. Moreover, telephone surveys are not very expensive.

However, telephone interviews do have some inherent disadvantages (see Table 7.1). The questioning is restricted to the spoken word. Interviewers cannot use physical stimuli, such as visual illustrations or product demonstrations, and they cannot ask complex questions. This limits the applicability of telephone techniques for certain types of research, such as new product or advertising research.

TABLE 7.1 Relative Advantages of Different Survey Methods

Method	Advantages	Disadvantages
Telephone	Fast	No use of physical stimuli
	Good sample control	Limited to simple questions
	Good control of field force	Low quantity of data
	Good response rate	
	Moderate cost	
In-Home	Complex questions can be asked	Low control of field force
	Good for physical stimuli	High social desirability
	Very good sample control	Potential for interviewer bias
	High quantity of data	Most expensive
	Very good response rate	Some samples (e.g., high-crime areas) may be difficult to access
	Longer interviews can be done	May take long to collect the data

TABLE 7.1 Continued

Method	Advantages	Disadvantages
Mall Intercept	Complex questions can be asked Very good for physical stimuli Very good control of environment Very good response rate	High social desirability Potential for interviewer bias Moderate quantity of data High cost
CAPI	Complex questions can be asked Very good for physical stimuli Very good control of environment Very good response rate Low potential for interviewer bias	High social desirability Moderate quantity of data High cost
Mail	No field-force problems No interviewer bias Moderate/high quantity of data Low social desirability Low cost	Limited to simple questions Low sample control for cold mail No control of environment Low response rate for cold mail Low speed
Mail Panel	No field-force problems No interviewer bias High quantity of data Low social desirability Low/moderate cost Good sample control	Limited to simple questions No control of environment Low/moderate speed
Electronic: E-mail	No interviewer bias Low cost Low social desirability High speed Contact hard-to-reach respondents	Low sample control No control of environment Low response rate Moderate quantity of data Security concerns
Electronic: Internet	No interviewer bias Low cost Low social desirability Very high speed Visual appeal and interactivity Personalized, flexible questioning Contact hard-to-reach respondents	Low sample control No control of environment Low response rate Moderate quantity of data

Personal rapport and commitment are difficult to establish due to lack of face-to-face interaction between the interviewer and the respondent. Respondents can easily escape the interview process, either by cutting the interview short or simply hanging up the phone. This results in less tolerance for lengthy interviews over the phone and limits the quantity of data that can be collected.

Research in Action

Telephone Calling Makes Pizza Hut the One to Call

As of 2011, Pizza Hut was the largest pizza restaurant company in the world. It had more than 11,600 outlets in about 100 countries and territories and served more than 1.5 million pizzas every day to approximately 4 million customers worldwide. Pizza Hut, which initiated a customer satisfaction survey in January 1995, currently conducts 50,000 interviews a week. Data are collected through an outbound telephone survey (i.e., Pizza Hut initiates the telephone call). Selected customers in Pizza Hut's delivery and carryout database are called within 24 hours of their purchases. The outbound interviews are limited to 4 minutes, and customers are given a 60-day breather before they are called again.

(continued)

The company also has an interactive 800-number inbound survey of randomly selected dine-in customers (the customer initiates the call). One of every 20 to 30 dine-in customers receives a coupon at the bottom of the receipt and a toll-free number to call to participate in the interactive survey. Tracking results show that 67 percent of the surveys are completed within 1 day of the visit, fulfilling a desire by management for the inbound survey results to be fresh.

The survey focuses only on issues that unit managers can control. The questions deal with service, food, and problems during the customer's most recent visit. The survey results have been very useful. For example, customers rushed to buy the new Stuffed Crust Pizza, but there was no subsequent rise in loyalty. Survey results showed that because of service problems, new customers were not making return trips. The survey helped Pizza Hut identify problems, and it now has a better understanding of how to handle the next major product launch. Half of the unit manager's quarterly bonus is linked to the survey results. As a result, customer satisfaction is at an all-time high.[2]

Source: © Najlah Feanny/Corbis.

Personal Methods

Personal interviewing methods can be categorized as in-home, mall-intercept, or computer-assisted interviews.

PERSONAL IN-HOME INTERVIEWS   In personal in-home interviews, respondents are interviewed face-to-face in their homes. The interviewer's task is to contact the respondents, ask the questions, and record the responses. In recent years, the use of personal in-home interviews has declined. Nevertheless, they are still used, particularly by syndicated firms (see Chapter 5).

Be a DM	Be an MR!
Is Delta American?	
Social Media — As the marketing manager for Delta Airlines, how would you use information on consumers' airline preferences for domestic travel to formulate marketing strategies that would increase your market share?	Visit www.delta.com and search the Internet—including social media—as well as your library's online databases to obtain information on consumers' preferences for selecting an airline for domestic travel. What would be the advantages and disadvantages of using telephone interviewing to conduct a survey to obtain information on consumers' airline preferences for domestic travel? Would you recommend this method to Delta Airlines?

ADVANTAGES AND DISADVANTAGES OF IN-HOME INTERVIEWING   In-home interviewing offers many advantages. It enables the interviewer to provide clarifications to the respondent, allowing for complex questions. It permits the use of physical stimuli, such as visual aids, charts, and maps, and it allows the interviewer to display or demonstrate the product. It provides very good sample control as well, because homes can be selected without generating a list of all the homes in a given area. The homes can be selected by instructing the interviewer to start at a given location, travel in a certain direction, and select every nth (e.g., every eighth) home. A large quantity of data can be collected because the respondents are interviewed in their own homes, and they might be more willing to participate for a longer period of time. The response rate is very good, particularly if respondents have been prenotified.

In-home interviewing has lost favor due to social, labor, control, and cost factors. Changes in the family, particularly related to the dominance of two-income earners, leaves few people at home during the day. Interviewer supervision and control is difficult, because the interviewers are traveling door to door. Consequently, problems with the questionnaire or with the style of the interviewer become more difficult to detect and correct. **Social desirability,** the tendency of respondents to give answers that are socially desirable but incorrect, is high when there is face-to-face contact between the interviewer and the respondent. This factor also leads to a high potential for **interviewer bias.** Interviewers can influence the

social desirability
The tendency of the respondents to give answers that might not be accurate but that might be desirable from a social standpoint.

interviewer bias
The error due to the interviewer not following the correct interviewing procedures.

answers by facial expressions, intonations, or simply by the way they ask the questions. This method also is the most expensive.

Despite their value, personal in-home interviews are being largely replaced by mall intercepts.

MALL-INTERCEPT PERSONAL INTERVIEWS   In mall-intercept personal interviews, respondents are approached and interviewed in shopping malls. The process involves stopping the shoppers, screening them for appropriateness, and either administering the survey on the spot or inviting them to a research facility located in the mall to complete the interview. For example, in a survey for a cell-phone manufacturer, a shopper is intercepted and asked about his or her age, education, and income. If these characteristics match the client's target population, the individual is then questioned on product usage. Some usage of cell phones is a prerequisite for inclusion in the sample. Only those who have experience with cell phones are invited to a test facility located in the mall to evaluate several new prototype designs under consideration.

Although the sample is composed only of individuals who shop in that retail mall, this is not a serious limitation. Though not representative of the population in general, shopping mall customers do constitute a major share of the market for many products.

ADVANTAGES AND DISADVANTAGES OF MALL INTERCEPTS   A major advantage of mall-intercept interviews is that it is more efficient for the respondent to come to the interviewer than for the interviewer to go to the respondent. The popularity of this method is evidenced by the several hundred permanent mall-research facilities located across the country. Complex questions can be asked when there is face-to-face contact. Mall intercepts are especially appropriate when the respondents need to see, handle, or consume the product before they can provide meaningful information. This was illustrated in the opening vignette, when P&G used this technique to determine consumers' responses to Olay Beauty Bar prior to introduction. Mall-intercept interviewing was chosen because it conveniently allowed the respondents to use the beauty bar in a test area in the mall before they responded to the survey. The researcher has very good control of the environment in which the data are being collected, and the response rate is very good.

The main disadvantages are the potential for social desirability and interviewer bias due to face-to-face contact in the interviewing process. The quantity of data that can be collected is only moderate, because people are generally in a hurry while shopping. The cost of mall-intercept interviewing is high.

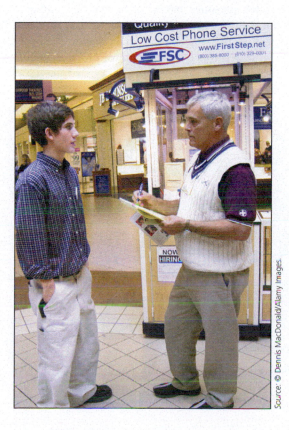

Source: © Dennis MacDonald/Alamy Images.

In mall-intercept personal interviews, respondents are approached and interviewed in shopping malls, as shown.

Research in Action

Altamonte Mall Relies on Mall Intercepts

Altamonte Mall (www.altamontemall.com) in Altamonte Springs, Florida, regularly surveys its customers. In a recent mall-intercept survey, 300 consumers were surveyed regarding what changes might convince them to visit the mall more often or for a longer period of time. The results indicated that 36 percent wanted a children's play area; 60 percent, a movie theater; and 50 percent, a casual dining establishment. Other survey results showed that consumers preferred book superstores to small book outlets; that they wanted additional, specific retailers, such as Hollister and Gymboree; and they wanted additional parking that was easy to access.

Altamonte Mall took the survey results to heart and put $28 million into constructing new niceties for visitors. A luxurious $232,000 play space for children was constructed; an AMC 18-screen movie theater was built. An 8,500-square-foot casual dining establishment was opened, and a second parking deck was built. Furthermore, Barnes & Noble responded to the marketing research as well and removed its small B. Dalton bookstore located in Altamonte and set up a 26,000-square-foot Barnes & Noble book superstore. These moves resulted in increased patronage of the mall and enhanced customer loyalty.[3]

COMPUTER-ASSISTED PERSONAL INTERVIEWING In computer-assisted personal interviewing (CAPI), the third form of personal interviewing, the respondent sits in front of a computer terminal and answers a questionnaire on the screen by using the keyboard or a mouse. Several user-friendly electronic packages can aid in designing easy and understandable questions. Help screens and courteous error messages also are provided. The colorful screens and on- and off-screen stimuli add to the respondent's interest and involvement in the task. This method has been classified as a personal-interview technique, because an interviewer is usually present to serve as a host and to guide the respondent as needed.

This approach is used in shopping malls, preceded by the intercept and screening process described earlier. It also is used to conduct business-to-business research at trade shows or conventions. For example, UPS could measure its image and test the effectiveness of its slogan, "We Love Logistics," by administering a CAPI survey at the expedited package delivery trade show. The process of interacting with the computer is simplified to minimize respondent effort and stress. Thus, the use of open-ended questions that require typing is minimized.

ADVANTAGES AND DISADVANTAGES OF CAPI CAPI seems to hold respondent interest and has several advantages. Complex questions can be asked, and the computer automatically performs skip patterns and conducts logic checks. Interviewer bias is reduced, because the computer administers the interview. Like mall intercepts, CAPI can be useful when the survey requires the use of physical stimuli. It also offers excellent control of the data collection environment and results in a very good response rate.

In computer-assisted personal interviewing (CAPI), the respondent is positioned in front of a computer and answers a questionnaire on the screen, as shown.

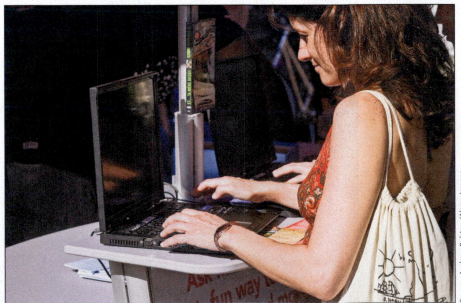

Source: Andrew Rubtsov/Alamy Images.

Its main disadvantages, which are shared with mall-intercept interviews, are the effects of high social desirability, moderate quantity of data, and high cost.

Be an MR!	Be a DM!
ESPN: Widening Its Reach	
Visit www.espn.com and search the Internet—including social media—as well as your library's online databases to obtain information on consumers' perceptions of ESPN. What are the advantages and disadvantages of personal interviews in conducting a survey to obtain information on consumers' perceptions of ESPN? Which, if any, method of personal interviewing would you recommend for administering the survey?	As the marketing manager for ESPN, how would you use information on consumers' perceptions of ESPN to formulate marketing strategies that would increase your audience?

Social Media

Mail Methods

Mail interviews, the third major form of survey administration, can be conducted with independently compiled mailing lists or by using a mail panel.

MAIL INTERVIEWS   The traditional mail interview is a "cold" mail survey that is sent to individuals who meet a specified demographic profile but who have not been precontacted to participate in the survey. A typical mail interview package consists of the outgoing envelope, cover letter, questionnaire, postage-paid return envelope, and possibly an incentive. Those individuals motivated to do so complete and return the questionnaire through the mail. There is no verbal interaction between the researcher and the respondent. Individuals are selected for cold surveys through mailing lists the client maintains internally or has purchased commercially. Commercial mailing lists typically contain some demographic and psychographic information that assists in the targeting process. Regardless of its source, a mailing list should be current and closely related to the population of interest.

The researcher must also make decisions about the various elements of the mail interview package (see Table 7.2). The type of envelope, the cover letter, the length of the questionnaire, and the incentive, if one is offered, all affect response rates.

The time involved and the response rate can be improved by faxing the questionnaire instead of mailing it. In a **fax survey,** the questionnaire is transmitted by a fax machine to respondents. The respondents can then return the completed questionnaire by faxing it to a designated (toll-free) number or, sometimes, by mail. Fax surveys share many characteristics with mail surveys; however, they can provide faster, and often higher, response rates. Greater urgency is associated with fax correspondence, and people are more likely to respond and do so sooner than they would to mail correspondence. Although the image quality of the fax transmission does not match that of a mailed questionnaire, this does not reduce the quality of the data. Fax numbers can be programmed into computers and the documents (cover letter and questionnaire) sent directly by the computer to the fax machine. This not only saves paper and printing costs, but labor as well, because there is no need to type addresses, print labels, stuff envelopes, and so on. Because many households do not have fax machines, this method is not suitable for household surveys. It can be used in a variety of surveys with commercial and other institutional respondents, however.

fax survey
A survey for which the questionnaire is transmitted by a fax machine to respondents. The respondents can then return the completed questionnaire by faxing it to a designated (toll-free) number or, sometimes, by mail.

MAIL PANELS   In contrast to a cold mail interview, a **mail panel** consists of a large and nationally representative sample of individuals who have agreed to participate in periodic survey research (see Chapters 3 and 5). Incentives in the form of cash or gifts are often offered to the individuals who agree to participate. Once the individuals have been admitted to the panel, detailed demographic and lifestyle data are collected on each household. The researcher uses this information to select targeted mailing lists within the panel based on client needs.

mail panel
A large and nationally representative sample of households that have agreed to periodically participate in mail questionnaires, product tests, and survey research.

TABLE 7.2 Some Decisions Related to the Mail Interview Package

Outgoing Envelope
Size, color, and return address for envelope
Postage
Method of addressing

Cover Letter
Sponsorship
Signature
Personalization
Postscript
Type of appeal

Questionnaire
Length
Layout
Content
Color
Size
Format
Reproduction
Respondent anonymity

Return Envelope
Type of envelope
Postage

Incentives
Monetary vs. Nonmonetary
Prepaid vs. Promised

TNS (www.tnsglobal.com), a Kantar Group company, is an example of a marketing research organization that maintains mail panels. Mail panels can be used to reach a general as well as a targeted sample. In the opening vignette, P&G used mail panel surveys to target consumers loyal to P&G and determine their pricing preferences. In a longitudinal design, the purchases of these customers for P&G and competing brands were monitored over time to identify the loyal customers.

ADVANTAGES AND DISADVANTAGES OF MAIL SURVEYS Mail surveys are an economical and efficient way to reach consumers. Cold mail surveys have a low cost, and the cost of mail panels is only moderately higher. The problems of interviewer bias and the expense of field staff management are eliminated. Social desirability is low, because there is no personal contact with the respondent during data collection. A moderate amount of data can be collected through cold mail surveys, whereas mail panels permit the collection of large quantities of data.

These clear advantages are offset, however, by problems regarding lack of control of the interviewing process. Unlike telephone and personal interviewing, there is no personal contact, and the respondent might feel less compelled to either participate or candidly complete the questionnaire. This problem is particularly acute with cold mail interviews. With cold mail interviews, the researcher has little control over who answers the questionnaire, how they answer it, and how quickly they return it. This results in low sample control, low speed, and no control over the data collection environment. Thus, it is difficult to assess the quality and validity of the data.

nonresponse bias
Bias that arises when actual respondents differ from those who refuse to participate in ways that affect the survey results.

Finally, response rates to cold mail surveys are low, and nonresponse introduces a serious bias in the data. Those individuals who choose not to participate in mail interviews might have very different demographic and psychographic profiles than responders, resulting in **nonresponse bias.** Individuals with higher income and educational levels, or individuals inexperienced or uninterested in the research topic, all tend to have lower response rates. Mail panels are successful in boosting response rates, and the problem of nonresponse bias also is reduced.

Despite its shortcomings, the relative ease and low cost of mail interviews continue to make this a viable research option.

Research in Action

Kick the Can: Canned Soup, That Is

In a mail survey, respondents were asked to make canned or dry soups at home and then respond to a questionnaire. The findings indicated a strong desire for a fresh alternative to canned and dry soups. Guided by these results, Stockpot Soups, a subsidiary of Campbell Soup (www.campbellfoodservice.com), developed Stockpot Classic Soups Soup Concentrate. Packed in resealable pouches, these soups are sold in the refrigerated dairy case as an alternative to canned and dry soups. Each 10-ounce pouch makes four bowls of hearty home-style soup with ingredients such as fresh-cut vegetables, real dairy products, and premium meats and seafood. This new product has been a success, because it was born of consumer desire discovered via a mail survey. As of 2011, Campbell Soup was the leader in fresh-refrigerated soups, and the food-service industry leader.[4]

Be a DM!	**Be an MR!**
Outback Wants to Be In!	
As the marketing manager for Outback, how would you use information on consumers' preferences for casual restaurants to formulate marketing strategies that would increase your sales and market share?	Visit www.outback.com and search the Internet—including social media—as well as your library's online databases to obtain information on consumers' preferences for casual restaurants. What are the advantages and disadvantages of using mail, a mail panel, or fax in conducting a survey to obtain information on consumers' preferences for casual restaurants? Which, if any, of these methods would you recommend for conducting a survey for Outback?

Social Media

Electronic Methods

Electronic surveys can be conducted via electronic mail (e-mail), if the respondents' addresses are known, or by posting the survey to a Web site.

E-MAIL SURVEYS   E-mail surveys are questionnaires distributed through electronic mail. If the addresses are known, the survey can simply be mailed electronically to respondents included in the sample. E-mail usage in the United States is very high, particularly in business firms where virtually everyone has access to e-mail. Using batch-type e-mail, researchers send e-mail surveys to potential respondents who use e-mail. Respondents key in their answers and send an e-mail reply. Typically, a computer program is used to prepare the questionnaire and the e-mail address list and to prepare the data for analysis.

E-mail surveys are simple to prepare and can be distributed quickly. They also are convenient for the respondent, because they show up in the e-mail box and catch the respondent's attention. As compared to regular mail (snail-mail) surveys, e-mail surveys offer time and cost advantages and more flexibility. Respondents are also more willing to answer open-ended questions in e-mail surveys.

Some e-mail systems can handle color and graphics, whereas others are limited to plain text. Respondent anonymity is difficult to maintain, because a reply to an e-mail message includes the sender's address. Security and privacy issues can also be a concern.

E-mail surveys are especially suited to projects for which the e-mail lists are readily available, such as surveys of employees, institutional buyers, and consumers who frequently contact the organization via e-mail (e.g., frequent fliers of an airline). E-mail letters can also be used to ask respondents to participate in an Internet survey and provide them with a link and password to the Web site where the survey is posted.

INTERNET SURVEYS   An Internet survey is a questionnaire posted on a Web site that is self-administered by the respondent. The questions are displayed on the screen, and the respondents provide answers by clicking an icon, keying an answer, or highlighting a phrase. Web survey systems are available for constructing and posting Internet surveys. They consist of a questionnaire designer, a Web server, a database, and a data-delivery program. The questionnaire is constructed with a user-friendly editor that uses a visual interface. The Web server distributes the questionnaire and files responses in a database. At any time, the researcher can obtain survey completion statistics, descriptive statistics of the responses, and graphical display of the data. As compared to e-mail surveys, Internet surveys offer more flexibility, greater interactivity, personalization, automatic skip patterns, and visual appeal. The Qualtrics (www.qualtrics.com) software distributed with this book will also enable you to design electronic surveys.

Internet panels are gaining in popularity and can be an efficient source of obtaining Internet samples (as discussed in more detail in Chapter 12). In fact, many marketing research suppliers and syndicated firms have replaced their traditional mail panels with Internet panels. Internet panels take less time and cost less to build and maintain as compared to mail panels. Several companies offer Internet panels that can be used by other researchers—for a fee—to draw Internet samples. Such firms include Harris Interactive (www.harrisinteractive.com) and Survey Sampling International (www.surveysampling.com). The advantages and disadvantages of electronic surveys relative to the other methods are discussed in more detail in the next section.

ADVANTAGES AND DISADVANTAGES OF ELECTRONIC METHODS   Both e-mail and Internet methods survey thousands of potential respondents simultaneously and quickly. Of the two, Internet surveys can be conducted more quickly; the data collected can be analyzed speedily, almost in real time. The incremental cost of reaching additional respondents is marginal, and hence, much larger samples can be accommodated as compared to the other methods.

Both methods are cost-effective. The cost savings as compared to the other methods can be dramatic for large samples. Moreover, both methods are good for contacting hard-to-reach respondents, because the survey can be answered at a time and place convenient to each respondent. Thus, high-income professionals, such as doctors, lawyers, and CEOs, can be reached. These groups are well represented online.

Internet surveys, and to some extent e-mail surveys, can be readily personalized. In addition to personalizing the name, the questions themselves can be personalized based on the respondent's answers to the previous questions; for example, "If your favorite brand of toothpaste, Crest, was not available, which brand would you buy?" Internet surveys can be programmed to automatically perform skip patterns (if the answer to question 3 is "no," go to question 9). Internet surveys are interactive and can utilize color, sound, graphics, and animation, much like computer-assisted personal interviewing.

Callbacks are easier to make in e-mail surveys and Internet surveys that draw respondents from a panel. The computer software can automatically send e-mail reminders to respondents who have not answered the survey. The electronic methods share many of the advantages of the mail methods, including the absence of field-force problems and interviewer bias. They also have low social desirability.

Both methods have some disadvantages as well. Both suffer from respondent-selection bias in that only people with access to e-mail or the Internet can be included in the sampling frame. This bias is further accentuated by the fact that heavy users of these media have a higher probability of being included in the sample. These individuals might differ from the target population in ways that might bias the results. Another potential problem is that if no controls are imposed, the same respondent can answer over and over again. In addition, some Internet users might consider e-mail surveys to be a form of spam.

The electronic methods also share many of the disadvantages of mail surveys. Only simple questions can be asked; sample control is low; the data collection environment cannot be controlled; and response rates are low. Only moderate quantities of data can be obtained. Even though these disadvantages exist, the Internet holds tremendous promise that is increasing with the increased penetration of the Internet in homes.

ELECTRONIC SURVEYS SOFTWARE AND SITES   Software is available for designing surveys administered over the Internet or through other modes (e.g., telephone, personal interviews, or mail). Although the following describes the use of software for constructing Internet surveys, the functions are essentially similar for surveys constructed by other modes. The software will help in the development and dissemination of the survey and, in many cases, retrieve and analyze the collected data and prepare a report. The software can automatically perform a variety of tasks, including:

- *Personalization.* The respondent's name and personal responses are automatically inserted into key questions.
- *Incorporate complex skip patterns.* The software can check many conditions and responses to determine which question should be asked next.
- *Randomize response choices.* The order of presentation of response options in multiple-choice questions can be randomized for each respondent to control for order bias.
- *Consistency checks.* Consistency checks can be programmed to identify inconsistent responses while the interview is still in progress so that corrective action can be taken, if necessary.
- *Add new response categories as the interviewing progresses.* If many respondents give a particular response to the "Other, please specify" category, that response will be automatically converted into a check-off category and added to the set of prespecified response options.

In addition, most programs have a variety of features that facilitate survey construction including question list, question libraries, survey appearance, preview, publish, and notification.

As each respondent completes the survey, the data are transferred over the Web to the data file on the host server. The data can be downloaded and analyzed at any time, even when the survey is running. Thus, results can be examined in real time. Some commonly used survey software includes Qualtrics (www.qualtrics.com), SurveyPro 5 (www.apian.com), Vovici (www.vovici.com), and SSI Web by Sawtooth Software (www.sawtoothsoftware.com). With this book you have access to Qualtrics, which will enable you to electronically design surveys.

FREE/LOW COST SURVEY SITES Several Web sites allow users to create and file their own surveys for free or at a low cost. Zoomerang (www.zoomerang.com) by MarketTools (www.markettools.com), SurveyMonkey (www.surveymonkey.com), PollDaddy (www.polldaddy.com), Kwik Surveys (www.kwiksurveys.com), FreeOnlineSurveys.com (freeonlinesurveys.com), eSurveyspro (www.esurveyspro.com), FreePollKit (www.freepollkit.com), and Impressity (www.impressity.com) are some of the firms offering free basic plans that allow anyone to create and administer online surveys. The survey firm distributes the survey, monitors participation and participants, and then collects and analyzes the data, all for free, because it is sponsored by Web advertising. However, the firm does not provide respondents. Users do this at their discretion. For instance, they can create a Web page and have the survey as a link from the Web page or send out an e-mail with the link, asking people to participate in the survey. Low cost Web-based services include CreateSurvey (www.createsurvey.com), SurveyGizmo (www.surveygizmo.com), and Checkbox (www.checkbox.com).

Some Other Survey Methods

Researchers have developed a number of variations based on the basic survey methods just described. The more popular of these other methods are presented in Table 7.3.

Experiential Learning

Internet Surveys

The following Web sites demonstrate Internet surveys for respondents as well as researchers.

1. To experience what an Internet survey is like, go to Web Online Surveys at www.web-online-surveys.com. Select "Sample," and take the short "Website Survey."

2. If you would like to join a panel of respondents who can earn prizes and other rewards for completing online surveys, sign up at Lightspeed Research's MySurvey.com (www.mysurvey.com) and/or www.zoomerang.com.

3. To examine actual Internet surveys (and some results) fielded by firms in their research programs, go to www.createsurvey.com and click any of the hyperlinks under "Demo."

4. To get a feel for building your own electronic survey, access the Qualtrics (www.qualtrics.com) software made available with this book and go through the demo/tutorials.

TABLE 7.3 Additional Survey Methods

Method	Advantages/ Disadvantages	Comment
Completely automated telephone surveys (CATS)	Same as CATI	Useful for short, in-bound surveys initiated by respondent.
Wireless phone interview (voice-based format)	Same as CATI	Useful for point-of-purchase survey if respondent cooperation is obtained.
Wireless phone interview (text-based format)	Same as e-mail	Useful for point-of-purchase survey if respondent cooperation is obtained.
In-office interview	Same as in-home interview	Useful for interviewing busy managers.
Central location interview	Same as mall-intercept interview	Examples include trade shows, conferences, exhibitions, purchase intercepts.
Kiosk-based computer interview	Same as CAPI	See www.intouchsurvey.com for more information.
Fax interview	Same as mail survey, except higher response rate	Useful in some business surveys.
Drop-off survey	Same as mail survey, except higher cost and higher response rate	Useful for local-market surveys.

Criteria for Selecting a Survey Method

When evaluating the various survey methods within the context of a specific research project, one has to consider the salient factors relevant to data collection. Often, certain factors dominate, leading to a particular survey method as the natural choice. For example, if a new perishable food product has to be tested, respondents would have to taste the product before answering the questionnaire. This would involve interviewing at central locations, leading to mall intercept or CAPI as the natural choices. If no method is clearly superior, the choice must be based on an overall consideration of the advantages and disadvantages of the various methods. We offer the following guidelines:

1. If complex and diverse questions have to be asked, one of the personal methods (in-home, mall intercept, or CAPI) is preferable. Internet surveys are an option as well, but the other self-administered methods (mail, mail panels, and e-mail) might not be appropriate because it is not possible to clarify respondent questions in an interactive manner. Telephone surveys are limited, because the respondent cannot see the questionnaire and the interviewer–respondent contact is not face-to-face.
2. From the perspective of the use of physical stimuli, personal methods (in-home, mall intercept, or CAPI) are preferable.
3. If sample control is an issue, cold mail (but not mail panel), fax, and electronic methods might not be appropriate.
4. Control of the data collection environment favors the use of central location (mall intercept and CAPI) interviewing.
5. High quantity of data favors the use of in-home and mail panels and makes the use of telephone interviewing inappropriate.
6. Low response rates make the use of cold mail and electronic methods disadvantageous.
7. If social desirability is an issue, mail, mail panel, fax, and Internet surveys are best.
8. If interviewer bias is an issue, the use of mail (cold and panels), fax, and electronic interviewing (e-mail and Internet) is favored.
9. Speed favors Internet, e-mail, telephone, and fax methods.
10. Costs favor cold mail, fax, electronic (e-mail and Internet), mail panels, telephone, mall intercept, CAPI, and in-home methods, in that order (most favorable to least favorable).

Often, these methods are combined to enhance the quality of data in a cost-effective manner. This is likely when the research project is large in scope, as in the case of P&G formulating its new marketing platform in the opening vignette. Note that P&G used scanner panels to monitor household expenses of P&G and competing brands and used mail panels to target consumers loyal to P&G. It used CATI to reach a representative sample of all households and used mall intercepts to determine consumer response to the Olay Beauty Bar prior to introduction. However, caution should be exercised when using different methods in the same domestic marketing research project, which is referred to as using mixed-mode surveys. The method used can affect the responses obtained, and hence responses obtained by different methods might not be comparable. The results of studies examining the effect of survey methods on respondents are not very consistent. The Microsoft examples illustrate the selection of survey modes.

Research in Action

Microsoft: Accessibility Technology in Computing

Microsoft hired Forrester Research to conduct a study to determine the market potential for a new accessibility technology. This new technology would enable people to adjust their computers to meet their particular visual, hearing, dexterity, cognitive, and speed needs. The goal of the study was to identify cognitive and physical abilities among working-age adults and current computer users in the United States and the range of impairments limiting activity.

The selection of a survey method was based on the relative advantages and disadvantages of the different methods as well as the survey's subject matter. Because physical impairments can limit computer usage, electronic survey methods, such as e-mail and Internet surveys, were not considered suitable. Given the potential for high social desirability (i.e., inhibition of admitting impairment) and the high cost, in-home and mall-intercept interviews were not favored. Mail and telephone methods were selected. A mail survey was considered to be the best way to survey people with a hearing impairment, and telephone interviews were viewed as the best option for those with visual impairments. Therefore, the research involved a nationwide phone and mail survey of 15,000 people. The sample included 10,464 respondents who were members of a mail panel managed by GfK Custom Research North America (www.gfkamerica.com); 5,013 respondents were contacted by phone through random

digital dial. People were asked a range of questions designed to assess a variety of difficulties and impairments experienced by individuals who use computers. The survey examined multiple types of impairments and difficulties, and people were asked about their daily tasks, impairments, and problems with employment. Additionally, they were asked demographic and lifestyle questions.

The findings showed that 27 percent of respondents had a visual difficulty or impairment, 26 percent had a dexterity difficulty or impairment, 21 percent had a hearing impairment, 20 percent had cognitive difficulty, and 4 percent had speech impairment. Thus, the majority of working-age adults are likely to benefit from the use of an accessibility technology. The average age of computer users is rising. Difficulties and impairments increase with age, indicating a clear need for accessibility technologies that can be used by an aging population.

As of 2010, among computer users in the United States, 27 percent had a vision impairment and 20 percent had hearing impairment. Microsoft has used these findings to create new products with accessibility technologies in order to meet consumers' needs. It is building accessibility options into its products as well as developing specialty hardware and software products that help individuals interact with their computers.[5]

Improving Survey Response Rates

Regardless of the survey method chosen, researchers should attempt to improve response rates. This can be done through prior notification, incentives, follow-up, and other methods (see Figure 7.5).

Prior Notification

Prior notification consists of sending a letter or e-mail or making a telephone call to potential respondents, notifying them of the imminent mail, telephone, personal, or electronic survey. Prior notification increases response rates for samples of the general public because it reduces surprise and uncertainty and creates a more cooperative atmosphere.

Incentives

Offering monetary as well as nonmonetary incentives to potential respondents can increase response rates. Monetary incentives can be prepaid or promised. A **prepaid incentive** is included with the survey or questionnaire. A **promised incentive** is sent to only those respondents

prepaid incentive
Coupons, money, or some other incentive to participate that is included with the survey or questionnaire.

promised incentive
Coupons, money, or some other incentive to participate that is sent only to those respondents who complete the survey.

FIGURE 7.5

Improving Response Rates

who complete the survey by the specified deadline. The most commonly used nonmonetary incentives are premiums and rewards, such as pens, pencils, books, and offers of survey results.

Prepaid incentives have been shown to increase response rates to a greater extent than promised incentives. The amount of incentive can vary from $0.25 to $50.00 or more, with a dollar being the most common in consumer surveys. The amount of the incentive has a positive relationship with response rate, but the cost of large monetary incentives might outweigh the value of the additional information obtained.

Follow-Up

Follow-up, or contacting nonrespondents periodically after the initial contact, is particularly effective in decreasing refusals in mail surveys. The researcher might send a postcard or letter to remind nonrespondents to complete and return the questionnaire. Two or three mailings might be needed in addition to the original one. With proper follow-up, the response rate in mail surveys can be increased to 80 percent or more. Follow-up can also be done by telephone, e-mail, or personal contact.

Other Facilitators of Response

Personalization, or sending letters addressed to specific individuals, is effective in increasing response rates. The example that follows describes the procedure that *Bicycling* magazine used to increase its response rate.

Research in Action

Bicycling Magazine's Procedure for Increasing Response to Mail Surveys

As of 2011, *Bicycling* magazine (www.bicycling.com) was owned by Rodale, a global content company in health and wellness. Rodale reaches more than 70 million people around the world each month through its category-leading media properties and integrated marketing solutions and is one of the largest direct-to-consumer businesses. *Bicycling* magazine conducts a semiannual survey of individual bicycle dealers throughout the United States. The following procedure is used to increase the response to the survey.

1. An "alert" letter is sent to advise the respondent that a questionnaire is coming.

2. A questionnaire package is mailed 5 days after the alert letter. The package contains a cover letter, a 5-page questionnaire, a new $1 bill, and a stamped return envelope.

3. A second package, containing a reminder letter, a questionnaire, and a stamped return envelope, is mailed 5 days after the first package.

4. A follow-up postcard is mailed a week after the second package.

5. A second follow-up postcard is mailed a week after the first.

In a recent survey, 1,000 questionnaires were mailed to bicycle dealers, and 68 percent of these were returned after follow-up. This represents a good response rate for a mail survey.

Be a DM!	Be an MR!
Harley Goes Whole Hog	
As the marketing manager for Harley-Davidson, how would you use information on consumers' image of motorcycle brands to formulate marketing strategies that would increase your sales and market share?	Visit www.harley-davidson.com and search the Internet—including social media—as well as your library's online databases to obtain information on consumers' images of motorcycle brands. If a survey is to be conducted for Harley-Davidson to determine consumers' image for motorcycle brands, which method do you recommend for administering the survey and why? How would you improve the response rate?

Observation Methods

Observation methods are the second type of methodology used in descriptive research. **Observation** involves recording the behavioral patterns of people as well as data on objects and events in a systematic manner to obtain information about the phenomenon of interest. The observer does not question or communicate with the people being observed. Information can be recorded as the events occur or from records of past events. The major observation methods are personal observation and mechanical observation.

Personal Observation

In **personal observation**, a trained observer collects the data by recording behavior exactly as it occurs. The observer does not attempt to control or manipulate the phenomenon being observed, but simply records what takes place. For example, a researcher might record traffic counts and observe traffic flows in a department store. This information could aid in determining store layouts, the location of individual departments, shelf locations, and merchandise displays. **Humanistic inquiry** is a special form of personal observation in which the researcher is immersed in the system under study. This is in contrast to the traditional scientific method in which the researcher is a dispassionate observer. In yet another application, called *on-site observation*, observers are positioned in supermarkets and presented as shoppers who need advice from another shopper in making purchase decisions.

The main advantage of personal observation is that it is a highly flexible method, because the observer can record a wide variety of phenomena (see Table 7.4). It also is highly suitable for use in natural settings. For example, the sales manager of General Motors can observe the attitudes of dealers toward a new inventory policy at one of the regular sales meetings.

The main disadvantage is that the method is unstructured in that an observation form is generally not used for recording the behavior as it occurs. Rather, the observer records the phenomenon after completing the observation in a free, unstructured format. This leads to high observation bias. Also the data and their interpretation are highly subjective, leading to high analysis bias.

observation
The recording of behavioral patterns of people, objects, and events in a systematic manner to obtain information about the phenomenon of interest.

personal observation
An observational research strategy in which human observers record the phenomenon being observed as it occurs.

humanistic inquiry
A special form of personal observation in which the researcher is immersed in the system under study.

TABLE 7.4 Relative Advantages and Disadvantages of Observation Methods

Method	Advantages	Disadvantages
Personal observation	Most flexible Highly suitable in natural settings	High observation bias High analysis bias
Mechanical observation	Low observation bias Low-to-medium analysis bias	Can be intrusive Not always suitable in natural settings

Research in Action

Identifying High-Potential Starbucks' Locations by Personal Observation

China is the most important, and potentially largest, market for Starbucks outside North America. Since the opening of the first Starbucks in Taiwan in 1998, in China in 1999, in Hong Kong in 2000, and in Macau in 2002, the growing appreciation and interest in coffee and the Starbucks experience by Chinese consumers have produced steady store expansion throughout China. To determine the location of its stores, Starbucks used a variety of methods, including a heavy reliance on personal observation.

A team of researcher observers with handheld counting devices were sent to monitor pedestrians outside a potential Starbucks store site, tallying likely customers. By doing this, they were able to tally the number of potential customers who would patronize the store. One such example was a woman in her 50s; although normally she would have been passed off as a normal pedestrian, researchers for Starbucks included her based on the

fact she had looked into a nearby boutique store. This was seen as a sign of a person who loves adventure and experience.

The other method that Starbucks uses to determine where to set up stores is sending a team of "hot-spot" seekers to trace paths that link the places where potential customers live, work, and play. Starbucks can use this method to effectively locate stores in areas where its sales would definitely go up.

In 2010, Starbucks launched a new lineup of locally relevant "black" beverages and food in China such as the Black Sesame Green Tea and the Frappuccino blended crème. For the third quarter of 2010, comparable store sales in Chinese stores surged by double-digit percentage points.[6] As of 2011, Starbucks has more than 375 stores in mainland China, in 26 cities, including Beijing, Tianjin, Shanghai, Guangzhou, and Shenzhen.

Mechanical Observation

mechanical observation
An observational research strategy in which mechanical devices, rather than human observers, record the phenomenon being observed.

Mechanical observation, as one would expect, involves the use of a mechanical device to record behavior. These devices might or might not require respondents' direct participation. Such devices are particularly useful for recording continuous behavior, such as traffic flow in a grocery store. Nielsen's peoplemeter (see Chapter 5) is an example of indirect observational devices in use today. Respondents do not need to change their behavior in any way to be involved in this type of observational study. The peoplemeter is attached to a television and continually records not only the channels the television is tuned to, but also who is watching. Arbitron has developed the portable peoplemeter, a wearable device that measures what television and radio programming a person watches or listens to during their waking hours. The PreTesting Group (www.pretesting.com) uses the PeopleReader, which unobtrusively records reading material and reader's eye movements to determine the reader's habits as well as the stopping power and the brand recall associated with different size ads.

Other common examples of indirect mechanical observation include turnstiles that record the number of people entering or leaving a building and traffic counters placed across streets to determine the number of vehicles passing certain locations. On-site cameras (still or video) are increasingly used by retailers to assess the impact of package designs, counter space, floor displays, and traffic-flow patterns. The Universal Product Code (UPC) is a built-in source for mechanical observation. For those retailers equipped with optical scanners, the UPC system allows for the automatic collection of consumer purchase information, classifying it by product category, brand, store type, price, and quantity (see Chapter 5).

The scanner data that P&G used in the opening vignette is an example of mechanical observation. The data revealed that a typical brand-loyal family spent $725 annually on P&G products. In comparison, a family that bought similar products as private-label or low-priced brands spent less than $500.

The Internet can be a very good source for observation and can provide valuable information. The observations can be made in a variety of ways. The primary observations can be made by the number of times the Web page is visited. The time spent on the page can also be measured through more advanced techniques, such as a timer that starts when a person visits a page and clicks on a certain icon and then stops when the person clicks the next icon. Further, various other links can be provided by the researcher on the Web page, and the researcher can observe which links are accessed more often. This will provide the researcher with important data about the information needs of the individuals and also the interests of the target segment. Analysis of the links that direct a person to a company's Web site provides the marketing researcher with important information regarding consumers' related interests, and an in-depth analysis of the link sites will provide information on advertising, competitors, consumers, and target market demographics and psychographics.

Web-based tracking of Internet users is an exciting and controversial electronic observation technique. Web surfers are served cookies. The cookie is a group of letters and numbers stored in a Web surfer's browser that identify the user. It is a sophisticated means by which a Web site can collect information on visitors. Often this process takes place without the Web surfer's knowledge. Companies and individuals that host Web sites use cookies to collect marketing research information on visitors. Cookies follow the traveler through the Web site and record the pages accessed by the visitor and the number of minutes spent on each page. The user's name, address, phone number, and access site can be collected by the cookie and saved into a database if the visitor enters any additional information. During a follow-up visit, the cookie accesses this information and has the ability to repeat it to the visitor. In essence, the cookie collects data on the user during every visit to the site. Google's online advertising company DoubleClick (www.google.com/doubleclick) uses information obtained from cookies to target advertising. For example, if a user visits an airline site and then a hotel site, that individual will be targeted with Delta Airlines and Marriott advertisements. Such practices are controversial because they raise issues of consumer privacy.

When it comes to developing new products, some smart companies, such as HP, Motorola, and Steelcase, are observing their customers rather than just listening to what they say. Traditional research, relying exclusively on questioning, can produce bland products. New Coke did well in taste tests, yet was a dismal failure. People said they wanted low-calorie burgers, but would not buy McDonald's McLean. The movie *Junior* did great in screenings, but made only $36 million. Baseball players said they loved the pump baseball glove, but would not pay the increased cost. This is why it is important to combine questioning with observation methods and why mechanical observation is gaining ground.

Research in Action

Steelcase Makes the Case for Mechanical Observation

Steelcase (www.steelcase.com) is a global company with fiscal 2010 revenue of approximately $2.3 billion and nearly 13,000 employees around the world. The firm offers a comprehensive portfolio of workplace products, furnishings, and services. The company used mechanical observation when it designed a furniture line for work teams. It set up hidden video cameras at various companies to observe what really goes on during the workday, looking for information on behavior and routines people might not even know they exhibited.

The company found that teams function best when members can work collectively some of the time and independently at others. The results of this study led to the very successful introduction of modular office furniture. This furniture can be quickly and easily assembled or reassembled to allow office workers to work in a large team area or in individual work spaces.[7]

Although the Steelcase study did not require the direct involvement of the participants, many mechanical observation devices do. Physical responses to sights, sounds, smells, or any sensory stimuli are an important area of observational research. Advertising or other promotional changes, such as special sales, can elicit a physical response in consumers that cannot be observed by merely looking at them. Specialized equipment designed to monitor heart and breathing rates, skin temperature, and other physiological changes is used in these situations. Because these measurements cost more than verbal reports of the respondent's reaction, they are only used when it is assumed that the respondent cannot, or will not, respond accurately to questioning. All of the physiological measurement devices operate on the assumption that the cognitive and emotional responses to stimuli elicit predictable differences in physical response. This assumption has not yet been clearly demonstrated, however.

The main advantage of mechanical observation is low observation bias, because the behavior is recorded mechanically and not by an observer. Likewise, the data are analyzed according to prespecified norms and guidelines, resulting in low analysis bias. The main disadvantages are that some of these methods can be intrusive or expensive and might not be suitable in natural settings, such as the marketplace.

EyeTracking, Inc.

1. What are the ethical issues of employing such personal observations in retail stores? Visit EyeTracking, Inc. (www. eyetracking.com). Under "solutions" locate "Consumer Marketing." Examine the descriptions and case studies and then write a report about the eye-tracking solutions offered by this research firm for TV commercials, online advertising, and package design.

2. What steps would need to be taken to collect these mechanical observations in an ethical manner?

3. What role can survey research play in enhancing the solutions offered by eye tracking?

A Comparison of Survey and Observation Methods

With the exception of scanner data and certain types of media panels, marketing research is seldom conducted solely with observational methods. However, observational data do offer some unique advantages. When combined with survey techniques, observation can deliver excellent results.

Relative Advantages of Observation

Observational data collection methods offer several advantages. First, many of these methods do not require conscious respondent participation, which minimizes nonresponse errors. Although ethical questions surround the practice of observation without consent, even conscious participation requires less effort from the respondent than that required with other research techniques.

Interviewer bias resulting from interaction with the respondent or subjective interpretation of the questionnaire is minimized, because the observer only has to record what is occurring. Additionally, the errors inherent in self-reported behavior are eliminated given that the observer records only actual behavior; the observer does not have to ask any questions of the respondent.

Data regarding product preferences or reactions to marketing materials from children or pets can best be collected using observational techniques. Observation also is useful in situations investigating unconscious behavior patterns or behaviors that individuals might be unwilling to discuss honestly.

Observational techniques are best applied to phenomena that occur frequently or are of short duration. In these types of applications, observational methods might cost less and be faster than survey methods.

Relative Disadvantages of Observation

Observational data provide insight into what behavior is occurring, but not why. Attitudes, motivations, and values are all lost to the observational method. Additionally, highly personal behaviors related to personal hygiene or intimate family interactions are not available for observation.

Individuals have a tendency to selectively observe only what they want to, and that might cause an observer to overlook important aspects of behavior. This perceptual difference among observers threatens the integrity of the approach.

Finally, observational techniques can be adopted for only frequent behaviors of short duration. Behaviors occurring infrequently or spanning a long period of time (e.g., individual car purchases over time) are too expensive to record using this technique.

To sum up, observation can potentially provide valuable information when properly used. From a practical standpoint, it is best to view observation as a complement to survey methods rather than as being in competition with them.

Ethnographic Research

ethnographic research
The study of human behavior in its natural context that involves observation of behavior and setting along with depth interviews.

Ethnographic research is the study of human behavior in its natural context and involves observation of behavior and setting along with depth interviews. Sometimes, audio and visual recordings also are obtained. Thus, both the questioning and observation methods are combined to understand the behavior of consumers. The following example illustrates this method.

Research in Action

PortiCo Documents with Documentaries

PortiCo Research (www.porticoresearch.com) specializes in observing individuals, questioning them in depth, recording them on videos, and selling these tapes for tens of thousands of dollars to its major clients, such as Honda, Delta, Lipton, and Procter & Gamble. They have fine-tuned the method of collecting ethnographic data and turned it into a very profitable business.

PortiCo's specialty is total immersion in the lives of consumers in an effort to document how they make purchasing decisions. Research teams of anthropologists, social psychologists, and ethnographers (professionals who comparatively study people) go into the subjects' homes with videographers. The teams tape the subjects in their homes and also take shopping trips with them to watch what they buy and to get feedback on the reasons for their purchases. After filming, employees of PortiCo transcribe the findings of the videos and analyze them for their clients. The analysis is based on the research problem that the client must gather more information about or solve. For example, PortiCo did a large study for Lipton to find out people's attitudes toward tea. With the results of the study,

Lipton would be able to determine whether to invest more in advertising, to develop new flavors, or to market more iced tea instead of hot tea. The findings showed that Americans do not drink very much hot tea, especially because of the presence of decaffeinated coffee in the marketplace. If and when they do drink hot tea, it is normally flavored herbal tea. Most of Lipton's hot tea is not in special flavors. Lipton has recently begun to bring herbal teas to market, however. The study did find that American consumers like iced tea. As a result of the findings, Lipton has initiated a number of creative developments in the iced-tea arena. It pushed the marketing of Brisk Iced Tea in a can, which is now the number-one selling brand of ready-to-drink iced tea. Lipton also created a Cold Brew Blend tea bag in both family and single size; users may make a whole pitcher or a single glass for one serving. This tea bag allows iced tea to be brewed with cold water instead of boiling water. Therefore, consumers can enjoy their tea faster with much less hassle. These marketing efforts, guided by the findings of PortiCo Research, have resulted in increased sales and market share for Lipton.[8]

Other Methods of Descriptive Research

In addition to ethnographic research, a variety of other methods combine the use of questioning and observation. One such method that is commonly used is mystery shopping. Trained observers pose as consumers and shop at the company's stores or those of competitors to collect data about customer–employee interaction and other marketing variables, such as prices, displays, layout, and so forth. The mystery shoppers question the store employees, mentally take note of the answers, and observe the variables of interest. IntelliShop (www.intelli-shop.com) is a firm that specializes in mystery shopping. For more information on mystery shopping, visit www.mysteryshop.org.

Be a DM!	Be an MR!
Planned Versus Unplanned Purchases	
As the marketing manager for Kroger, how would you use information on consumer behavior related to supermarket shopping to formulate marketing strategies that would increase your market share?	Visit www.kroger.com and search the Internet—including social media—as well as your library's online databases to obtain information on consumer behavior related to supermarket shopping. Kroger wants to determine to what extent consumers plan their product and brand purchases before entering the store. How will you combine the survey and observation methods to obtain this information?

Social Media

Summary Illustration Using the Opening Vignette

Surveys involve the administration of a questionnaire and can be classified as traditional telephone interviews, computer-assisted telephone interviews (CATI), in-home personal interviews, mall-intercept interviews, computer-assisted personal interviews (CAPI), mail surveys, mail panels, or electronic surveys administered by e-mail or Internet. These data collection methods should not be considered mutually exclusive. Often, it is possible to employ them productively in combination, as illustrated in the opening vignette. P&G used the CATI method to survey the general population, a mail panel to determine the pricing preferences of consumers loyal to P&G brands, and mall-intercept interviews to assess reaction to the Olay Beauty Bar prior to introduction.

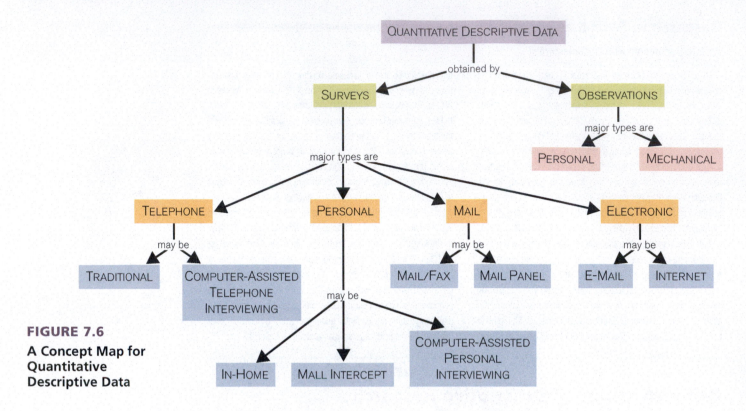

FIGURE 7.6

A Concept Map for Quantitative Descriptive Data

CATI is very suitable for surveying a representative sample of households, because telephone numbers can be randomly generated using computer programs. A mail panel allows repeated measurements on the same respondents; thus, brand-loyal users can be identified (respondents who purchased P&G brands repeatedly). Mall-intercept interviews are very conducive to showing a new product to respondents before questioning them. Thus, this method was appropriate for assessing consumer response to P&G's brand extension (Olay Beauty Bar). Electronic methods, especially Internet surveys, can obtain information from large samples of respondents quickly and at a low cost.

In contrast to direct questioning in surveys, observation methods simply observe people and objects. The major observational methods are personal observation and mechanical observation. Certain types of data are best obtained through observation. An example would be consumers' purchases of various brands in supermarkets. P&G used scanner-panel data (mechanical observation) to determine that a typical brand-loyal family spent $725 each year on P&G products. In comparison, a family that bought similar products as private-label or low-priced brands spent less than $500. Figure 7.6 provides a concept map for quantitative descriptive data. In this figure, the major concepts are connected by bold arrows using descriptors. Thus, quantitative descriptive data are obtained from surveys and observations. The rest of the figure can be interpreted similarly.

International Marketing Research

Selecting appropriate interviewing methods for international marketing research is much more difficult because of the challenges of conducting research in foreign countries. Given the differences in the economic, structural, informational, technological, and sociocultural environments, the feasibility and popularity of the different interviewing methods vary widely. Table 7.5 provides an illustration of how cultural and environmental factors can impact survey method selection.

In the United States and Canada, nearly all households have telephones. As a result, telephone interviewing is the dominant mode of administering questionnaires. This is also true in some European countries, such as Sweden. In many other European countries, however, not all households have telephones. In some developing countries, only a few households have them.

TABLE 7.5 The Impact of Cultural and Environmental Factors on the Selection of Survey Methods

- A survey that takes 20 minutes in the United States could take more than twice as long in Germany. The German language is not as concise as English, and Germans like to talk more than Americans do. For similar reasons, the interviewing time could be longer in other countries as well, such as in Brazil.

- Telephone directories are unreliable in some countries (e.g., some African nations, such as Sierra Leone), because they are updated infrequently.

- The incidence of unlisted telephones can vary widely across countries and across segments. For example, in Colombia, the numbers of some members of the elite and upper classes are never listed.

- In some countries, such as Japan, China, Thailand, Malaysia, and those in Southeast Asia, telephone interviews are considered rude. In contrast, in some South American countries, such as Argentina and Peru, the response rates to telephone surveys are high given the low levels of telemarketing and the element of surprise in receiving an unexpected long-distance or local call.

- Traditional personal interviewing methods remain popular in some European countries (e.g., Switzerland, Sweden, France), Asian countries (e.g., China, India, Hong Kong), African countries (e.g., Nigeria, Kenya), and South American countries (e.g., Colombia, Mexico) due to the prevalence of face-to-culture.

- Low literacy rates and/or the lack of a reliable postal system in rural areas might make mail surveys infeasible in some countries (e.g., Ghana, Ivory Coast, El Salvador, Uruguay, Paraguay).

- Mall interviews are limited due to the lack of shopping malls in many developing countries and some developed countries (e.g., Germany). In addition, domestic laws might prohibit or make it more difficult to interview people while shopping.

- Telephone penetration is low in some countries, particularly in rural areas. In some countries, such as Cambodia, multiple families might share a phone line because of high phone rates.

- In countries with high cellular/mobile phone penetration and low hard/wired-line penetration (e.g., Thailand, Malaysia), the use of traditional phone surveys is unappealing.

- Poor access to computers and the Internet make the use of electronic interviewing infeasible in some countries (e.g., rural populations in Africa, Asia, and South America).

In-home personal interviews are the dominant mode of collecting survey data in many European countries, such as Switzerland, and in newly industrialized countries (NICs) or developing countries. Although mall intercepts are being conducted in some European countries, such as Sweden, they are not popular in other European countries or in developing countries. In contrast, central location/street interviews constitute the dominant method of collecting survey data in France and The Netherlands.

Due to their low cost, mail interviews continue to be used in most developed countries where literacy is high and the postal system is well developed. Some examples are the United States, Canada, Denmark, Finland, Iceland, Norway, Sweden, and The Netherlands. In Africa, Asia, and South America, however, the use of mail surveys and mail panels is low because of illiteracy and the large proportion of the population living in rural areas. Mail panels are used extensively only in a few countries outside the United States, such as Canada, the United Kingdom, France, Germany, and The Netherlands. However, the use of panels might increase with the advent of new technology. Likewise, although a Web site can be accessed from anywhere in the world, access to the Web or e-mail is limited in many countries, particularly developing countries. Hence, the use of electronic surveys is not feasible, especially for interviewing households in rural areas. European marketing research firms have been slower to adopt electronic interviewing, because Internet penetration in Europe has lagged that in the United States.

Different incentives are more or less effective in improving response rates in different countries. In Japan, it is more appropriate to use gifts with business surveys rather than cash as incentives. The same is true for household surveys in Mexico. Some methods are more reliable in some countries than others. When collecting data from different countries, it is desirable to use survey methods with equivalent levels of reliability rather than necessarily using the identical method. However, the use of panels can substantially overcome this limitation as in the Nation Brands Index.

Research in Action

Proud to be an American!

Conducted annually with GfK Roper (www.gfkamerica.com), the Anholt-GfK Roper Nation Brands Index (NBI) measures the image of 50 nations. Each year, approximately 20,000 adults ages 18 and up are interviewed online in 20 core panel countries, both developed and developing, all across the world. Results from the 2010 NBI survey show the United States holding the top spot for the second year in a row as the country with the best overall brand.

Among the top 10 nations, Southern Europe has seen several changes from 2009, with Spain no longer part of the top 10, and Italy overtaken by Canada. France was ranked lower than Germany. Such results can be very useful to marketing managers in the United States, not only to those who are in the tourism and travel industries but also to those in other industries who wish to emphasize American in the marketing.[9]

Anholt-GfK Roper Nation Brands Index
Overall Brand Ranking (Top 10 of 50 Nations)

	2010	2009
1	United States	United States
2	Germany	France
3	France	Germany
4	United Kingdom	United Kingdom
5	Japan	Japan
6	Canada	Italy
7	Italy	Canada
8	Switzerland	Switzerland
9	Australia	Australia
10	Sweden	Spain, Sweden (tie)

Source: 2010 and 2009 Anholt-GfK Roper Nation Brands IndexSM. Used with permission from GFK.

As in the case of surveys, the selection of an appropriate observation method in international marketing research should also take into account the differences in the economic, structural, informational, technological, and sociocultural environment.

Marketing Research and Social Media

Social media can be used to conduct surveys as well as observations.

Surveys

Many social sites today present an excellent platform for allowing researchers the widespread ability to disseminate questionnaires and thereby retrieve quantitative feedback on a large scale. The use of social media overcomes the need to manually solicit attention from the public and this helps keep costs low, thus allowing greater sample size per dollar invested. Furthermore, when implemented correctly, the collection of survey data through social media sites can not only be automated, but also allow the researcher to customize reach to various segments of consumers. Research questions can be varied conveniently with little restrictions. Moreover, online surveys conducted through social media platforms encourage committed and credible feedback due to the inherent relevance and anonymity for the consumer. Should this fail, the virtual nature of these tools also allows subtle motivational factors to be used when soliciting quantitative data via the use of electronic coupons where consumers can be given freebies as they leave the survey site after completing the survey. Coupled with the simplicity with which electronic content can be created and implemented, we see that conducting surveys through social media avenues becomes highly viable and cost-effective and offers several advantages.

ADVANTAGES OF SOCIAL MEDIA FOR CONDUCTING SURVEYS   Social media offer the following advantages for conducting surveys:

- Wider coverage through the virtual nature of outreach
- Simplicity in implementing surveys due to easy-to-use social media tools
- Ability to field more complex questions with aid from interactive multimedia computing
- Responses are more candid due to the veil of anonymity and lack of physical interaction, thus encouraging honest feedback.
- Improved accessibility: The nature of the Internet allows tags and URLS to be linked to other sites of interest; thus, content of surveys is more accessible.
- Lower cost of research: There is no need to maintain large field forces of interviewers and supervisors.
- Ability to use multiple survey methods: For example, social media worlds such as Second Life allow one-to-one Internet phone surveys to be made.
- No interviewer bias
- Low social desirability
- High-speed, instantaneous results of polling

Nonetheless, the limitless boundaries of the World Wide Web do have inherent spillover effects in the use of social media, and these may be detrimental to conducting surveys in the following ways.

DISADVANTAGES OF SOCIAL MEDIA FOR CONDUCTING SURVEYS   Social media offer the following disadvantages for conducting surveys:

- Surveys do not address the responses from nonusers of social media, especially the older consumers.
- Survey administration is difficult to control and content may be accessible to competitors.
- Response rates may be low because of the clutter involved through the use of virtual communities. Surveys may be dismissed as spam.
- Confidentiality is an issue to consumers because of the relatively insecure features of virtual media, thus discouraging the release of sensitive information.

Short surveys can be administered on the social media site itself, e.g., a Facebook page. For longer surveys, a link can be provided on the site that directs the user to the survey site, as in the survey conducted by the Captura Group.

Research in Action

Captura Group: Expectations of the U.S. Government

The Captura Group (www.capturagroup.com) is a specialist marketing research firm that primarily targets the American Hispanic online market. In 2008, Captura Group implemented and fielded a social media survey with the objective of understanding how the public viewed access to U.S. government information. This survey was commissioned due to rising volumes of negative public sentiment concerning the organization of government departments and agencies in the post-9/11 climate. With the enactment of the U.S.A. Patriot Act and various other laws, America in the late 2000s found itself creating more agencies to overcome lapses in security. As of 2009, there were more than 1,000 individual departments or agencies in the federal government, and that number continues to grow. As a result, U.S. citizens faced increasing red tape whenever they had to obtain information regarding state and government matters, because many departments and agencies had overlapping degrees of jurisdiction.

The survey was conducted as follows:

Duration:	October 22, 2008, to January 5, 2009
Respondent Facts:	• Average age of 42
	• 501 people started the survey, with 385 completing (78.5%)
	• 50/50 male: female ratio
	• 58 percent of respondents were familiar with the U.S. government
Social Media Platforms Accessible:	11, including MySpace, blogs, Twitter, Yahoo! Answers, etc.

(continued)

Analysis of the survey results revealed the following trends:

- The majority of respondents are interested in accessing government information via social media.
- Credibility of government information online is critical for respondents.
- Facebook is the preferred social media tool among respondents.
- Respondents are very interested in having conversations with the government.

- Relevant and timely content is critical; the channel used is secondary.
- 60 percent of respondents are interested in government information on nongovernment sites.

After viewing the results, the Obama administration admitted that the current governmental organization was overly complex and still flawed, having many loopholes. It has since strived to revamp the organization of its departments and agencies in lieu of the post-9/11 climate so as to make government more accessible and less complicated to the average citizen.[10]

Observation

In a real sense, the comments, photos, videos, audio, and other stimuli posted voluntarily by consumers on their social media sites are traces of their behaviors. An analysis of these constitutes a form of observation known as *trace analysis*. Some researchers consider participant blogs and online research communities to be examples of e-ethnography or netnography (ethnographic research online). It is also possible to more directly observe the behavior of interest to the researcher in the virtual world, as done by Starwood for Aloft Hotels.

When Starwood Hotels & Resorts considered launching a new range of design hotels under the brand name "Aloft," it decided to first build the hotel virtually within Second Life. This helped the company obtain vital consumer feedback on the desired hotel design and concept. Consumers were invited on Second Life to interact in the virtual Aloft Hotel. Marketing researchers mechanically observed their behaviors and preferences. They were able to observe how the avatar moved through spaces and what areas and furniture were more popular in Second Life. Thus, they were able to obtain feedback from the consumers and ideas that they could implement in the real hotel. This social media tool was crucial to Aloft Hotels since it did not have to spend money in physically constructing the Aloft Hotel prototype. The results provided the company with a better understanding of which features might be important for users. The findings led to several design changes, including the decision to build radios in the guest rooms' showers. Aloft hotels were opened in 2008. They offer a harmony of modern elements to the

Aloft Hotel was first built and tested in Second Life using observation methods.

Source: Courtesy Starwood Hotels & Resorts Worldwide, Inc.

classic American tradition to both business and leisure travelers. As of 2010, Aloft had 65 hotels all around the world including Asia, Europe, and the Middle East, as well as Central and South America, and they are still expanding.

Ethics in Marketing Research

Surveys often are used as a cover for a targeted sales effort. The real purpose is not to obtain information to address a marketing research problem, but to sell a product. This practice, called *sugging* in the trade language, is unethical. A similar unethical practice is *frugging* and involves fund-raising under the guise of research. To illustrate, assume you get a call from a company stating that they are conducting research on consumer attitudes. After asking a few diagnostic questions, the company tries to sell you one of its products (sugging) or asks for a donation (frugging).

Respondents' anonymity, discussed in the context of qualitative research in Chapter 6, is also an important issue in survey as well as observational research. Researchers have an ethical obligation to not disclose the identities of respondents to anyone outside the research organization, including the client. Only when researchers notify respondents in advance and obtain their consent prior to administering the survey can an exception be made and the respondents' identities revealed to the client. Even in such cases, prior to disclosing identification information the researcher should obtain an assurance from the client that the respondents' trust will be kept and their identities will not be used for sales effort or misused in other ways. Ethical lapses in this respect by unscrupulous researchers and marketers have resulted in a serious backlash for marketing research.

The researcher has the responsibility to use an appropriate survey method in an ethical and legal way. For instance, federal legislation prohibits unsolicited faxed surveys. In many states, totally automated outgoing (initiated by the researcher) telephoning is illegal.

Researchers often observe people's behavior without their consent, arguing that informing the respondents might alter their behavior. This can be considered an invasion of the respondents' privacy. One guideline proposed to resolve this problem is that research observation should only be conducted in places where people would expect to be observed by the public. Public places such as malls or grocery aisles, places where people observe other people routinely, are fair game. Nonetheless, notices stating that these areas are under observation for marketing research purposes should be posted at the sites. After observing their behavior, the researcher is still obligated to obtain the necessary permission from the subjects.[11]

It should also be mentioned that the common practice of serving cookies on the Internet raises ethical concerns. Many users do not realize it, but they have been served a cookie or two while on the Internet. A cookie is not a culinary delight in this case. It is a sophisticated means by which a Web site can collect information on visitors. Often this process takes place without the Web surfers' knowledge and is an invasion of their privacy and right to consent.

Research in Action

Have a Cookie!

Wired (www.wired.com), a Web site devoted to technology and culture, offers dynamic online tools, such as search engines, that provide people with important information. Wired uses cookies to collect information about Web site traffic by tracking an individual's preference for hotel choice, airline travel, and other interests. Wired uses this information to target customers with advertisements by promoting discounts and specials using the individual's preferred choices. In addition, the information helps marketing personnel collect demographics on the reader. Also, the company can monitor "hits" on particular topics and gain valuable feedback on user interest. For example, using cookies, Wired might find out that after

visiting its Web site, a particular respondent then visits Travelocity (www.travelocity.com) for flight and hotel information pertaining to Jamaica. The next time that same visitor visits wired.com, a pop-up Web advertisement will alert that visitor of special airfare and hotel packages to Jamaica offered by Wired.

This technique enables Wired to monitor use patterns and to eliminate socially acceptable response bias. Information collected in this manner has been used to modify editorial content and the site's format to make the site more appealing. Although this information is helpful to Wired, the use of cookies in this way raises several ethical issues.[12]

WHAT WOULD YOU DO?

Microsoft: Small Businesses Represent a Big Market

The Situation

Statistics from the U.S. Small Business Administration show that as of 2011 small businesses contributed about 50 percent of the nonfarm private gross domestic product and also employed about 50 percent of the U.S. private-sector employees. Microsoft Corp. is impressed with these statistics, because they indicate that small businesses might represent a big market for its products. It wonders whether the needs of small businesses are different than those of large businesses. Steve Ballmer, Microsoft CEO, would like to develop specialized products for the small businesses. Some of these products could include the following: a Web site just for small businesses, the Microsoft Small Business Council (which provides information to help small businesses use technology), the Microsoft Small Business Technology Partnership Board (an educational resource), the BackOffice Small Business Server (for a more direct route to small businesses), and a small business edition of Microsoft Works.

The Marketing Research Decision

1. To survey small businesses' preferences for software products, which survey method would you recommend and why?
   a. CATI
   b. On-site personal interviews
   c. Mail
   d. Internet
   e. E-mail
2. Discuss the role of the type of research you recommend in enabling Steve Ballmer to determine small businesses' preferences for software products.

The Marketing Management Decision

1. Which of the following should Microsoft do to effectively meet the needs of small businesses?
   a. Develop a specific Web site for small businesses.
   b. Develop new products for small businesses.
   c. Customize existing products (e.g., Microsoft Office).
   d. Give price discounts to small businesses.
   e. Develop an advertising campaign specifically directed at small businesses.

2. Discuss how the marketing-decision action that you recommend to Steve Ballmer is influenced by the type of survey that you suggested earlier and by the findings of that survey.

What Steve Ballmer Did

Steve Ballmer decided to develop a dedicated Web site for small businesses (www.microsoft.com/smallbusiness/hub.mspx). Small businesses can use this site to access tech support, security, products, and a learning center, all designed specifically for small businesses. As of 2011, the company was providing Microsoft Cloud Services that allow small businesses access to the latest technology from a state-of-the-art data center. Subscribing to software delivered over the Web can enable small businesses to take advantage of enterprise-class software without the burden or cost of managing the technology. Small businesses do not have to buy computing infrastructure up front, which is often a very large expense. Products are available on a pay-as-you-need subscription basis.[13]

Source: Used with permission from Microsoft.

Summary

Surveys and observations are the two primary methods of conducting quantitative, descriptive research. Surveys involve the direct questioning of respondents, whereas respondent behavior is simply recorded in observation.

Surveys involve the administration of a questionnaire and can be classified based on the method or mode of administration as traditional telephone interviews, computer-assisted telephone interviews (CATI), in-home personal interviews, mall-intercept interviews, computer-assisted personal interviews (CAPI), mail surveys, mail panels, or electronic surveys administered by e-mail or Internet. Of these methods, telephone interviews (CATI) are the most popular in the United States. However, each method has some general advantages and disadvantages. Although these data collection methods are usually thought of as distinct and competitive, they should not be considered mutually exclusive. It is possible to employ them productively in combination.

The major observational methods are personal observation and mechanical observation. As compared to surveys, the relative advantages of observational methods are (1) they permit measurement of actual behavior; (2) there is no reporting bias; and (3) there is less potential for interviewer bias. Also, certain types of data can be obtained best, or only, by observation. The relative disadvantages of observation are (1) very little can be inferred about motives, beliefs, attitudes, and preferences; (2) there is potential for observer bias; (3) most methods are time-consuming and expensive; (4) it is difficult to observe some forms of behavior; and (5) there is potential for unethical behavior. With the exception of scanner data and certain types of media panels, observation is rarely used as the sole method of obtaining primary data, but it can be usefully employed in conjunction with survey methods.

An important consideration in selecting the methods of administering surveys internationally is to ensure equivalence and comparability across countries. Social media have added a new dimension to survey as well as observation research, constituting an important domain in which both can be implemented. Misuse of surveys as a guise for selling, failing to maintain the anonymity of respondents, and observing behavior without respondents' knowledge or consent are major ethical issues in implementing survey and observation methods.

Key Terms and Concepts

Survey method   185
Structured data collection   186
Sample control   188
Response rate   188
Social desirability   190
Interviewer bias   190

Fax survey   193
Mail panel   193
Nonresponse bias   194
Prepaid incentive   199
Promised incentive   199
Observation   201

Personal observation   201
Humanistic inquiry   201
Mechanical observation   202
Ethnographic research   204

Suggested Cases and Video Cases

Running Case with Real Data

1.1 Hewlett-Packard

Comprehensive Critical Thinking Cases

2.1 American Idol   2.2 Baskin-Robbins   2.3 Akron Children's Hospital

Comprehensive Cases with Real Data

3.1 Bank of America   3.2 McDonald's   3.3 Boeing

Comprehensive Brief Harvard Business School Cases

4.1 TruEarth Healthy Foods: Market Research for a New Product Introduction (4065)
4.2 The Springfield Nor'easters: Maximizing Revenues in the Minor Leagues (2510)
4.3 Metabical: Positioning and Communications Strategy for a New Weight-Loss Drug (4240)
4.4 Saxonville Sausage Company (2085)

Online Video Cases

7.1 Starbucks   9.1 P&G   10.1 Nivea   11.1 Dunkin' Donuts
12.1 Motorola   13.1 Subaru   14.1 Intel   19.1 Marriott

Live Research: Conducting a Marketing Research Project

As a class, discuss the various survey methods and select one that is appropriate for the project. In addition to the criteria given in this chapter, certain practical constraints might have to be considered if the students must collect data. Examples include the following:

1. A budget for making long-distance calls should be supplied if a telephone survey is to be done beyond the local calling area.

2. If a CATI system is not available, the telephone method can be limited to traditional telephone.

3. Students will not be allowed to conduct mall-intercept interviews unless permission is obtained from the mall management. Some malls have signed exclusive contracts with marketing research firms for data collection.

4. It might not be practical to do in-home personal interviews covering a large geographic area, or even in a local region.
5. There might not be enough time for a mail survey, and a mail panel might be prohibitively expensive.
6. E-mail addresses might not be available or might be very difficult to get.

7. **Social Media** As students have personal social media sites (e.g., Facebook accounts), a social media survey may be a possibility, especially as a preliminary survey.
8. Mechanical observation devices can be impractical to obtain and use.

The survey/data collection method selected should be discussed and approved by the client.

Acronym

The classification of survey methods by mode of administration may be described by the acronym METHODS:

M   ail panels

E   lectronic interviews

T   elephone interviews

H   ome (in-home personal) interviewing

O   n-site mall interviews

D   irect-mail interviews

S   oftware for CATI/CAPI

Review Questions

1. Explain briefly how the topics covered in this chapter fit into the framework of the marketing research process.
2. Name the major modes for obtaining information via a survey.
3. What are the relevant factors for evaluating which survey method is best suited to a particular research project?
4. What would be the most appropriate survey method for a project in which control of field force and cost are critical factors?

5. **Social Media** How would you use a Facebook account to conduct a survey? When might such a survey be appropriate?
6. Name the types of mechanical observation, and explain how they work.
7. What are the relative advantages and disadvantages of observation?

Applied Problems

1. Describe a marketing research problem in which both survey and observation methods could be used for obtaining the information needed.
2. The campus food service would like to determine how many people eat in the student cafeteria. List the ways in which this information could be obtained. Which method is best?
3. Locate and answer an Internet survey for which you would qualify as a respondent. How would you evaluate this survey based on the discussion in this chapter?

4. Locate an Internet survey and examine the content of the questionnaire carefully. What are the relative advantages and disadvantages of administering the same survey using CATI or mall-intercept interviewing?
5. Design an e-mail survey to measure students' attitudes toward credit cards. E-mail the survey to 10 students. Summarize, in a qualitative way, the responses received. Are student attitudes toward credit cards positive or negative?

Group Discussion

1. As a small group, discuss the ethical issues involved in disguised observation. How can such issues be addressed?

2. "With advances in technology, observation methods are likely to become popular." Discuss this statement as a small group.

Hewlett-Packard Running Case

Review the Hewlett-Packard (HP) case, Case 1.1, and questionnaire given toward the end of the book.

1. The HP survey was administered by posting it on a Web site and sending an e-mail invitation to respondents. Evaluate the advantages and disadvantages of this method. Do you think that this was the most effective method?

2. **Social Media** Compare the various survey methods for conducting the HP survey. Could HP have used social media? If yes, how?

3. Can HP make use of the observation method to determine consumers' preferences for PCs and notebook computers? If yes, which observation method would you recommend and why?

4. Visit a store selling PCs and notebooks (e.g., Best Buy, Office Depot, etc.). If this store wants to conduct a survey to determine consumer preferences for PCs and notebook computers, which survey method would you recommend and why?

ONLINE VIDEO CASE 7.1

STARBUCKS: Staying Local While Going Global Through Marketing Research

Visit www.pearsonhighered.com/malhotra to read the video case and view the accompanying video. Starbucks: Staying Local While Going Global Through Marketing Research describes how Starbucks has gathered useful feedback and marketing research information from customers, leading to the introduction of several successful new products and penetration into new global markets. The case can be used to discuss the various benefits and limitations of descriptive research and particularly the use of both survey and observation methods. Specific marketing research questions on this and the previous chapters are posed in the video case.

8

Causal Research Design: Experimentation

Source: B2M Production/Stone/Getty Images.

LEARNING OBJECTIVES

After reading this chapter, the student should be able to:

1. Explain the concept of causality in marketing research, and how one distinguishes between the ordinary meaning and the scientific meaning of causality.

2. Discuss the conditions for causality, and whether a causal relationship can be demonstrated conclusively.

3. Understand the two types of validity, internal and external, and how they differ.

4. Describe the various types of experimental designs, and the differences among pre-experimental, true experimental, quasi-experimental, and statistical designs.

5. Compare and contrast the use of laboratory versus field experimentation and experimental versus nonexperimental designs in marketing research.

6. Explain test marketing, and how it involves experimentation.

> "Marketing research—and marketing—would be much better off if researchers conducted more experiments. Well-done experiments are and have always been the 'gold standard' of evidence in science."
>
> *Larry Gibson*
> *Senior Associate, Eric Marder and Associates, Minneapolis, Minnesota*

Muzak: An Uncommon Remedy for the Common Cold

Once referred to as "background music," in the business world Muzak (www.muzak.com) is now referred to as "audio architecture." As of 2011, Muzak provides media-based solutions, and more than 100 million people hear its harmonic convergences each day. The company offers music, sound systems, videos and TV, and messaging at 200 sales and service locations across the United States.

Muzak has now moved into audio marketing in supermarkets. In a time of increasing competition, more store advertising at the point of purchase might be just what is needed. Research shows that few customers come to the grocery store with a specific brand in mind. Most consumers know what items they need and choose brands or sizes only when they reach the store. So audio advertising, such as that provided by Muzak, seems to hold promise.

An experiment was designed to test the effectiveness of Muzak advertising. Twenty randomly selected supermarkets were assigned to one of two groups, each group containing 10 supermarkets. One group of supermarkets, randomly selected, was the experimental group and the other was the control group. Muzak ads for selected products were run in the experimental group supermarkets for a period of 10 weeks. These ads were informational, telling consumers of the benefits of the advertised products. The price and other factors (e.g., shelf space) affecting the sale of these items were kept the same in both the experimental and control group stores. The sales of the advertised products were monitored for both the experimental and control groups. The results showed an increase in the sales of advertised items, with cold/allergy/sinus-relief products recording the highest increase of 29.8 percent (see the table). Thus, there might be an expanding market for Muzak in the near future.[1]

Product	Percent Sales Increase in Experimental Stores
Potato chips	3.5
Condensed milk	7.1
Tea bags	13.7
Cold cereal	12.2
Juice	14.5
Laundry detergent	27.4
Toothpaste	28.9
Cold/allergy/sinus relief	29.8

Overview

Chapter 3 introduced two broad categories of conclusive research: causal and descriptive research designs. Descriptive designs were discussed in Chapter 7. This chapter concentrates on causal research designs. Figure 8.1 briefly explains the focus of the chapter, its relation to the previous ones, and the steps of the marketing research process on which this chapter concentrates. Experimentation is the primary method employed to collect data in causal research designs. The opening vignette illustrates an experiment conducted to determine the effect of in-store Muzak advertising on the sales of selected items.

This chapter presents experimentation in detail. The concepts of causality, research validity and threats to that validity are discussed. A classification of experimental designs is provided as well as consideration of specific designs, along with the relative merits of laboratory versus field experiments. The applications of experimentation in international marketing research and the impact of social media on experimentation are discussed. The chapter ends with a discussion of ethical issues in experimentation. Figure 8.2 gives an overview of the different topics discussed in this chapter and how they flow from one to the next.

The Concept of Causality

A causal inference relates to whether a change in one marketing variable produces a change in another variable. Marketing managers often are faced with decisions in which they attempt to infer causal relationships. For example, will a 10-percent price reduction in Maxwell House coffee result in an increase in sales to a level that will at least cover the revenues lost due to the price reduction? In evaluating this question, the marketing manager is drawing a causal inference that price influences the sale of Maxwell House coffee. In the opening vignette, the inference was that Muzak advertising leads to (i.e., causes) increased sales. **Causality** means something very different to the average person on the street than it means to a scientist. Take, for example, the statement "X causes Y."

causality
When the occurrence of X increases the probability of the occurrence of Y.

FIGURE 8.1

Relationship of Experimentation to the Previous Chapters and the Marketing Research Process

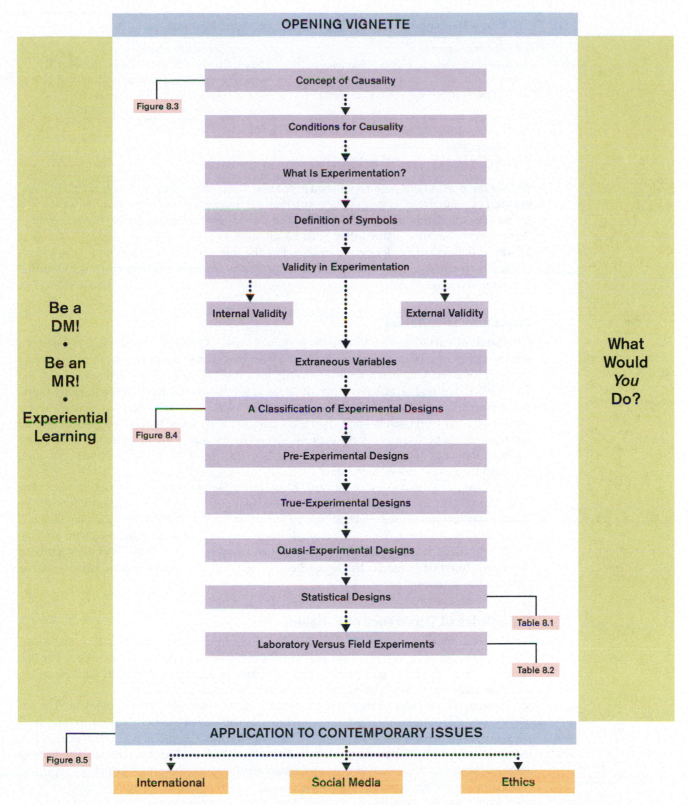

FIGURE 8.2

Experimentation: An Overview

The scientific meaning of causality is more appropriate to marketing research because it is sensitive to the limitations that surround the data collection process and the causal inferences that can legitimately be drawn. In the opening vignette, experimenters realized that in-store advertising was only one cause of sales. Other causes, such as prices and shelf displays, also affected sales and consequently had to be controlled.

Ordinary Meaning	Scientific Meaning
X is the only cause of Y.	X is only one of a number of possible causes of Y.
X must always lead to Y. (X is a deterministic cause of Y.)	The occurrence of X makes the occurrence of Y more probable. (X is a probabilistic cause of Y.)
It is possible to prove that X is a cause of Y.	We can never prove that X is a cause of Y. At best, we can infer that X is a cause of Y.

Conditions for Causality

At least three conditions must be satisfied in order to justify the inference of a causal relationship between two variables: (1) concomitant variation, (2) time order of occurrence of variables, and (3) absence of other possible causal factors. These conditions are necessary but not sufficient to demonstrate causality; that is, they must be satisfied to justify drawing a causal inference. However, their presence does not guarantee that the true variables responsible for the effects being observed have been isolated. These conditions are explained in more detail in the following sections.

Concomitant Variation

concomitant variation
A condition for inferring causality that requires that a cause, *X*, and an effect, *Y*, occur together or vary together as predicted by the hypothesis under consideration.

Concomitant variation occurs when the presumed cause (X) and presumed effect (Y) are both present and both vary in a manner predicted by the hypothesis. Suppose a regional marketing manager for a fast-food outlet wants to identify the causes of variation in food sales across the 20 outlets in her region. After visiting all 20 sites, she has concluded that the monthly outlet performance scores (X)—which reflect factors such as average wait time during peak hours, cleanliness, and food quality—directly impact sales (Y). Given that hypothesis, outlets that are scoring high on performance measurements should be recording the highest sales levels. Her analysis indicates that this relationship does, in fact, hold. Can she conclude that high performance scores "cause" high sales?

The answer to that question is "no." Many other factors might be impacting sales. For example, the outlet location, the presence of competition, and the concentration of the surrounding residential area might all have an impact on sales, even though they are not included in the outlet performance score. This example illustrates the limitations associated with drawing causal inferences. It is not possible to conclude that the cause of fast-food-outlet sales has been identified from this research. The researcher can only say that an association exists between performance scores and sales.

Time Order of Occurrence of Variables

Another requirement in determining a causal relationship relates to when the variables occur; that is, the occurrence in time of the presumed cause relative to the presumed effect. For one variable to hypothetically cause another, it must precede or occur simultaneously with the effect; it cannot occur afterwards. This is referred to as the *time order of variables*.

Although time order of variables seems like an intuitively obvious requirement, it is not always easy to determine time order in a marketing situation. For example, customers who shop frequently in a department store are more likely to have the credit card for that store. Also, customers who have a department store's credit card are likely to shop there frequently. The time order of these variables—credit card ownership and frequent shopping—is not obvious. Did credit card ownership precede frequent shopping or did frequent shopping precede credit card ownership? An understanding of the underlying phenomena associated with department store shopping might be necessary to accurately identify time order.

Absence of Other Possible Causal Factors

As can be seen in the previous examples, both time order and concurrent variation conditions might be satisfied, but the relevant cause-and-effect relationship might remain unidentified. The presence of additional or extraneous variables that impact the effect (i.e., dependent) variable must be controlled in order to draw causal inferences. To illustrate, in-store service might be a cause of sales if it is possible to ensure that changes in all other factors that affect sales—such as pricing, advertising, level of distribution, product quality, competition, and so on—were held constant or otherwise controlled. Ruling out other possible causal factors is seldom an easy task. The point-of-purchase buying example shows the difficulty of establishing a causal relationship.

Research in Action

POP Buys

Recent statistical data indicate that consumers make as much as 80 percent of their buying decisions at the point-of-purchase (POP). POP buying decisions have increased concurrently with increased advertising efforts in stores. These include radio advertisements as well as ads on shopping carts, floor space, grocery bags, ceiling signs, and shelf displays. It is difficult to separate the cause from the effect of POP advertising and POP buying. It is possible that these variables might be both causes and effects in this relationship. In other words, there is more POP advertising because there is more POP buying, and there is more POP buying because there is more POP advertising.[2]

Source: © Ken Welsh/Alamy Images.

If, as the POP example indicates, it is difficult to establish cause-and-effect relationships, what is the role of evidence obtained in experimentation?

Role of Evidence

The combination of evidence of causality in the form of concomitant variation, time order of occurrence of variables, and elimination of other possible causal factors does not guarantee a causal relationship. However, an accumulation of consistent evidence increases the confidence that a causal relationship exists. Controlled experiments can provide strong evidence of all three conditions.

Be a DM!	Be an MR!
Internet Use and Information Availability	
As the head of the Federal Trade Commission, what are your concerns about the increased availability of information on the Internet?	Search the Internet—including social media—as well as your library's online databases to obtain information on Internet usage by consumers. What conditions are necessary for you to conclude that increased use of the Internet by consumers is increasing the availability of information on the Internet?

Social Media

What Is Experimentation?

Experimentation is the research technique used in causal research (see Figure 8.3). It is the primary method for establishing cause-and-effect relationships in marketing (see Chapter 3). Experiments can be described in terms of independent, dependent, and extraneous variables; test units; and random assignment to experimental and control groups. To conduct an **experiment**,

experiment
The process of manipulating one or more independent variables and measuring their effect on one or more dependent variables, while controlling for the extraneous variables.

FIGURE 8.3

Experimentation as Conclusive Research

the researcher manipulates one or more independent variables and then observes the effects that those manipulated variables have on the dependent variables, while controlling the influence of outside or extraneous variables. In this section, these concepts are defined and illustrated using the example from the opening vignette.

Independent Variables

independent variables
Variables that are manipulated by the researcher and whose effects are measured and compared.

Independent variables are variables or alternatives that are manipulated (i.e., the researcher changes their levels) and whose effects are measured and compared. These variables, also known as *treatments,* might include price levels, package designs, and advertising themes. In the opening vignette, the independent variable was Muzak advertising, and the treatments consisted of Muzak advertising versus no advertising.

Test Units

test units
Individuals, organizations, or other entities whose response to independent variables or treatments is being studied.

Test units are individuals, organizations, or other entities whose response to the independent variables or treatments is being examined. Test units might include consumers, stores, or geographic areas. In the opening vignette, the test units were supermarkets.

Dependent Variables

dependent variables
Variables that measure the effect of the independent variables on the test units.

Dependent variables are the variables that measure the effect of the independent variables on the test units. These variables might include sales, profits, and market shares. The dependent variables in the opening vignette were the sales of specific products.

Extraneous Variables

extraneous variables
Variables, other than the independent variables, that influence the response of the test units.

Extraneous variables are all variables other than the independent variables that affect the response of the test units. These variables can confound the dependent variable measures in a way that weakens or invalidates the results of the experiment. Extraneous variables include store size, store location, and competitive effort. In the opening vignette, the extraneous variables would be other variables—such as price, amount of shelf space, and so on—that would affect the sales of the selected products.

Random Assignment to Experimental and Control Groups

random assignment
Involves randomly assigning test units to the experimental and control groups. It is one of the most common techniques used to control for the effect of extraneous variables on the dependent variable.

Random assignment involves randomly assigning test units to the experimental and control groups and is one of the most common techniques used to control for the effect of extraneous variables on the dependent variable. Random assignment to experimental and control groups attempts to minimize the influence of extraneous factors such as age, income, or brand preference by spreading them equally across the groups under study.

experimental group
The group exposed to the manipulated independent variable.

When an experiment is being conducted, at least one group will be exposed to the manipulated independent variable. This is called the **experimental group**. The results of this experimental group might be compared to another experimental group at a differing level of manipulation or to a control group. The **control group** is not exposed to the independent variable manipulation. It provides a point of comparison when examining the effects of these manipulations on the dependent variable. In the opening vignette, the supermarket stores were randomly assigned to the two groups. One group was randomly chosen to be the experimental group (that was exposed to Muzak advertising), and the other served as the control group (that received no advertising).

control group

The control group is not exposed to the independent variable manipulation. It provides a point of comparison when examining the effects of these manipulations on the dependent variable.

Experimental Design

An **experimental design** is a set of procedures specifying (1) the test units and how these units are to be divided into homogeneous subsamples, (2) what independent variables or treatments are to be manipulated, (3) what dependent variables are to be measured, and (4) how the extraneous variables are to be controlled.

experimental design

The set of experimental procedures specifying (1) the test units and sampling procedures, (2) independent variables, (3) dependent variables, and (4) how to control the extraneous variables.

In the opening vignette, the test units were stores that were randomly assigned to two groups. The independent variable to be manipulated was Muzak advertising versus no advertising, and the dependent variables were the sales of specific products. Extraneous variables such as price and shelf space were kept at the same levels in both the experimental and control group supermarkets by exercising managerial control.

As a further illustration of these definitions, consider the following example.

Research in Action

Taking Coupons at Face Value

An experiment was conducted to test the effects of coupon value on redemption. Personal interviews were conducted in New York with 280 shoppers who were entering or leaving a supermarket. Two levels of the independent variable (coupon value) were used, one offering 15 cents off and the other 50 cents off. Shoppers were randomly assigned to these two coupon value levels.

Brand usage was presumed to be an extraneous variable. Four brands—Tide detergent, Kellogg's Corn Flakes, Aim toothpaste, and Joy liquid dishwashing detergent—were used. The respondents answered questions about which brands they used so that the effect of this extraneous variable could be controlled during analysis. Respondents also were asked how likely they were to cash coupons of the given face value the next time they shopped. An interesting finding was that higher face value

coupons produced a greater likelihood of redemption among infrequent or nonbuyers of the promoted brand but had little effect on regular buyers.[3]

Source: JohnKwan/Shutterstock.

In the coupon experiment, the independent variable was the value of the coupon (15 cents versus 50 cents). The dependent variable was the likelihood of cashing the coupon. The extraneous variable that was controlled was brand usage. The experimental design required the random assignment of shoppers to two experimental groups. A control group was not used in this design.

Definition of Symbols

To help in our discussion of extraneous variables and specific experimental designs, we will use a set of symbols commonly used in marketing research.

X = the exposure of a group to an independent variable, treatment, or event, the effects of which are to be determined

O = the process of observation or measurement of the dependent variable on the test units or group of units

R = the random assignment of test units or groups to separate treatments

In addition, the following conventions are adopted:

- Movement from left to right indicates movement through time.
- Horizontal alignment of symbols implies that those symbols refer to a specific treatment group.
- Vertical alignment of symbols implies that those symbols refer to activities or events that occur simultaneously.

For example, the symbolic arrangement

$$X \quad O_1 \quad O_2$$

means that a given group of test units was exposed to the treatment variable (X), and the response was measured at two different points in time, O_1 and O_2.

Likewise, the symbolic arrangement

$$R \quad X_1 \quad O_1$$
$$R \quad X_2 \quad O_2$$

means that two groups of test units were randomly assigned (R) to two different treatment groups at the same time (X_1 and X_2), and the dependent variable was measured in the two groups simultaneously (O_1 and O_2).

Validity in Experimentation

In conducting an experiment, a researcher has two goals. The first is to draw valid conclusions about the effect of the independent variables on the dependent variables. This is referred to as *internal validity*. The second goal is to make valid generalizations from the specific experimental environment to a larger population. This goal is satisfied when external validity is achieved.

Internal Validity

internal validity
A measure of accuracy of an experiment. It measures if the manipulation of the independent variables, or treatments, actually caused the effects on the dependent variable(s).

Internal validity refers to whether the manipulation of the independent variables or treatments actually caused the observed effects on the dependent variables. Internal validity is threatened when the influences of extraneous variables are mixed with the independent variables. Without proper control of the extraneous variables, the researcher is unable to isolate the effect of the independent variable and thus cannot establish internal validity. In the opening vignette, to claim internal validity the researcher had to show that the increase in sales of the products in the experimental group supermarkets was in fact due to (i.e., caused by) Muzak advertising. Thus, the researcher had to show that price and other extraneous variables (e.g., shelf space) affecting the sale of these products were kept the same in both the experimental and control group stores.

External Validity

external validity
A determination of whether the cause–effect relationships found in the experiment can be generalized.

External validity refers to whether the cause-and-effect relationships found in the experiment remain the same when replicated in a larger population. In other words, can the results be generalized beyond the experimental situation? If so, to what populations, settings, times, independent variables, and dependent variables can the results be projected? In the opening vignette, to claim external validity the researcher must show that the sample of 20 supermarkets was representative, no peculiar conditions were encountered, and the results are generalizable to all supermarkets.

Threats to external validity arise when the experiment is conducted in an unrealistic manner, limiting the ability to generalize. This occurs when the experimental conditions do not account for factors likely to be encountered in the real world. Experiments conducted in a laboratory environment are more likely to lack external validity than field experiments. This is because laboratory experiments are conducted in artificial, highly controlled environments.

Marketing researchers often have to make decisions to trade off one form of validity in order to gain another. However, internal validity must be protected in order to produce results that are meaningful enough to generalize. Extraneous variables threaten both the internal and external validity.

Extraneous Variables

The need to control extraneous variables in order to establish internal and external validity has already been discussed. In this section, extraneous variables are classified into the following categories: history, maturation, testing, instrumentation, statistical regression, selection bias, and mortality.

History

Contrary to what the name implies, **history** (H) does not refer to the occurrence of events before the experiment. Rather, *history* refers to specific events that are external to the experiment but occur at the same time as the experiment. For example, general economic conditions might decline during the experiment, thereby contaminating the posttreatment observation. The longer the time interval between observations, the greater the possibility that history will confound an experiment.

history
Specific events that are external to the experiment but that occur at the same time as the experiment.

Maturation

Maturation (MA) is similar to history except that it refers to changes in the test units themselves. These changes are not caused by the impact of independent variables or treatments, but occur with the passage of time. In an experiment involving people, maturation takes place as people become older, more experienced, tired, bored, or uninterested. Tracking and marketing studies that span several months are vulnerable to maturation, because it is difficult to know how respondents are changing over time.

maturation
An extraneous variable attributable to changes in the test units themselves that occurs with the passage of time.

Testing Effects

Testing effects are caused by the experimentation process. Typically, these are the effects on the experiment of taking a measure on the dependent variable before and after the presentation of the treatment. For example, the respondents try to maintain consistency between their pre- and posttreatment attitudes. As a result of the testing effect, posttreatment attitudes might be influenced more by pretreatment attitudes than by the treatment itself.

Instrumentation

Instrumentation (I) refers to changes in the measuring instrument, in the observers, or in the scores themselves. Sometimes, measuring instruments are modified during the course of an experiment. Consider an experiment in which dollar sales are being measured before and after exposure to an in-store display (treatment). If there is a nonexperimental price change between measurements, this results in a change in instrumentation, because dollar sales will be measured using different unit prices. Instrumentation effects are likely when interviewers make pre- and posttreatment measurements. The effectiveness of interviewers can differ at different times.

instrumentation
An extraneous variable involving changes in the measuring instrument or in the observers or scores themselves.

Statistical Regression

Statistical regression (SR) effects occur when test units with extreme scores move closer to the average score during the course of the experiment. In the advertising experiment, suppose that some respondents had either very favorable or very unfavorable attitudes. On posttreatment measurement, their attitudes might have moved toward the average. People's attitudes change continuously. Those with extreme attitudes have more room for change, so variation is more likely. This has a confounding affect on the experimental results, because the observed effect (change in attitude) might be attributable to statistical regression rather than to the treatment (test commercial).

statistical regression
An extraneous variable that occurs when test units with extreme scores move closer to the average score during the course of the experiment.

Selection Bias

Selection bias (SB) refers to the improper assignment of test units to treatment conditions. This bias occurs when selection or assignment of test units results in treatment groups that differ on the dependent variable before the exposure to the treatment condition. If test units self-select their own groups or are assigned to groups on the basis of the researchers' judgment, selection bias is possible. For example, consider a merchandising experiment in which two different

selection bias
An extraneous variable attributable to the improper assignment of test units to treatment conditions.

merchandising displays (old and new) are assigned to different department stores. The stores in the two groups might not be equivalent to begin with. They might vary with respect to a key characteristic, such as store size. Store size is likely to affect sales regardless of which merchandising display was assigned to a store.

Mortality

mortality
An extraneous variable attributable to the loss of test units while the experiment is in progress.

Mortality (*MO*) refers to the loss of test units while the experiment is in progress. This happens for many reasons, such as test units refusing to continue in the experiment. Mortality confounds results because it is difficult to determine if the lost test units would respond to the treatments in the same manner as those that remain. Consider again the merchandising display experiment. Suppose that during the course of the experiment three stores in the new display treatment condition drop out. The researcher could not determine whether the average sales for the new display stores would have been higher or lower if these three stores had continued in the experiment.

Controlling Extraneous Variables

Extraneous variables represent alternative explanations of experimental results. They pose a serious threat to the internal and external validity of an experiment. Unless they are controlled, they affect the dependent variable and thus confound the results. For this reason, they also are called *confounding variables*. Extraneous variables can be controlled in four ways: randomization, matching, statistical control, and design control.

Randomization

randomization
A method of controlling extraneous variables that involves randomly assigning test units to experimental and control groups by using random numbers. Treatment conditions also are randomly assigned to experimental groups.

Randomization refers to the random assignment of test units to experimental and control groups by using random numbers. Treatment conditions also are randomly assigned to experimental groups. For example, respondents are randomly assigned to one of three experimental groups. One of the three versions of a test commercial, selected at random, is administered to each group. As a result of random assignment, extraneous factors can be represented equally in each treatment condition. It is possible to check whether randomization has been effective by measuring the possible extraneous variables and comparing them across the experimental and control groups. Therefore, randomization is the preferred method for controlling extraneous variables.

Matching

matching
A method of controlling extraneous variables that involves matching test units on a set of key background variables before assigning them to the treatment conditions.

Matching involves comparing test units on a set of key background variables before assigning them to the treatment conditions. In the merchandising display experiment, stores could be matched on the basis of annual sales, size, or location. Then one store from each matched pair would be assigned to each experimental group. Matching has two drawbacks. First, test units can be matched on only a few characteristics, so the test units might be similar on the variables selected but unequal on others. Second, if the matched characteristics are irrelevant to the dependent variable, then the matching effort has been futile.

Statistical and Design Control

statistical control
A method of controlling extraneous variables by measuring the extraneous variables and adjusting for their effects through statistical methods.

design control
A method of controlling extraneous variables that involves using specific experimental designs.

Statistical control involves measuring the extraneous variables and adjusting for their effects through statistical analysis. **Design control** involves the use of experiments designed to control specific extraneous variables. A classification of experimental designs is described in the next section.

A Classification of Experimental Designs

pre-experimental designs
Designs that do not control for extraneous factors by randomization.

The four broad categories of experimental designs are pre-experimental, true experimental, quasi-experimental, and statistical designs (see Figure 8.4). **Pre-experimental designs** do not use randomization to control for extraneous factors. Thus, they suffer from many threats to internal and external validity. However, with a proper note of their limitations, they can add value when used in an exploratory fashion. Three examples of this design are the one-shot case study, the one-group pretest–posttest design, and the static group. These designs, along with the others that follow, are discussed in detail later.

In **true experimental designs**, the researcher can randomly assign subjects and experimental groups. Therefore, these designs provide a larger degree of control over extraneous variables. Included in this category are the pretest–posttest control group design and the posttest-only control group design.

Quasi-experimental designs result when the researcher is unable to fully manipulate the independent variables or treatments but can still apply part of the apparatus of true experimentation. These designs are typically employed in natural environments, enabling some degree of experimental control in a natural setting. Two such designs are time series and multiple time series designs.

Statistical designs are series of basic experiments that allow for statistical control and analysis of external variables. Statistical designs are classified on the basis of their characteristics and use. Statistical designs include factorial designs.

We will illustrate the various experimental designs in the context of measuring the effectiveness of PepsiCo advertising. Pepsi makes heavy use of celebrities in its advertising. Pepsi ads have included stars such as Beyoncé Knowles, the Osbourne family, Shakira, Enrique Iglesias, Britney Spears, Mariah Carey, Christina Aguilera, the Spice Girls, Pink, Puff Daddy, Mary J. Blige, and The All-American Rejects. Pepsi FIFA World Cup 2010 advertising featured soccer stars Lionel Messi, Thierry Henry, Ricardo Kaká, Frank Lampard, Andrei Arshavin, and Didier Drogba.

Should Pepsi continue to feature celebrities in its advertising? Is this advertising effective? Experimental research that measures advertising effectiveness can provide useful information. We begin our discussion with the pre-experimental designs.

FIGURE 8.4

A Classification of Experimental Designs

true experimental designs
Experimental designs distinguished by the fact that the researcher can randomly assign test units to experimental and control groups and also randomly assign treatments to experimental groups.

quasi-experimental designs
Designs that apply part of the procedures of true experimentation, while lacking full experimental control.

statistical designs
Designs that allow for the statistical control and analysis of external variables.

The effectiveness of Pepsi advertising that makes use of celebrities can be assessed by using appropriate experimental designs.

Source: Adam Nemser/PHOTOlink/PHOTOlink/Newscom.

Pre-Experimental Designs

Pre-experimental designs are characterized by an absence of randomization. This section describes three specific designs: the one-shot case study, the one-group pretest–posttest design, and the static group.

One-Shot Case Study

one-shot case study
A pre-experimental design in which a single group of test units is exposed to a treatment X, and then a single measurement on the dependent variable is taken.

Also known as the *after-only design,* the **one-shot case study** can be represented symbolically as

$$X \quad O_1$$

A single group of subjects is exposed to a treatment (X), and then a single measurement on the dependent variable is taken (O_1). This type of design is constructed using a nonrandom sampling process in which the subjects are self-selected or selected arbitrarily by the researcher. Without randomization, the observed dependent variables are subject to the influences of several extraneous variables.

Additionally, the design lacks a control group. Without a control group, there is no point of comparison for the results. Due to lack of randomization and the absence of a control group, this design is clearly weak in terms of internal validity. It does not control for history, maturation, selection, or mortality. For these reasons, the one-shot case study is more appropriate for exploratory rather than conclusive research.

Research in Action

One Shot at Pepsi Advertising

To assess the effectiveness of Pepsi advertising featuring celebrities, telephone interviews would be conducted with respondents who report watching the particular TV program on which the commercial was aired the previous night (X). The dependent variables (Os) are unaided and aided recall and attitudes toward the advertisement, the brand, and the celebrity. First, unaided recall would be measured by asking the respondents whether they recall seeing a commercial for a soft drink. If they recall the Pepsi commercial, details about commercial content and execution would be solicited. Respondents who do not recall the test commercial would be asked if they saw a Pepsi commercial (aided recall). For those who have an unaided or aided recall of the commercial, attitudes toward the commercial, the brand advertised, and the celebrity featured would be measured. The results of these experimental measures can be compared with normal scores for these types of questions in order to assess the effectiveness of the advertising and the celebrity featured.

One-Group Pretest–Posttest Design

one-group pretest–posttest design
A pre-experimental design in which a group of test units is measured twice, once before and once after the treatment.

The **one-group pretest–posttest design** can be symbolized as

$$O_1 \quad X \quad O_2$$

In this design, a group of subjects is measured once before the experimental treatment (O_1) and once after (O_2). Again, this design lacks a control group for comparison. The treatment effect is computed as $O_2 - O_1$. Although this design is considered better than a case study, the validity of conclusions is questionable, because extraneous variables are largely uncontrolled due to lack of randomization and the lack of a control group. History, maturation, testing, instrumentation, selection, mortality, and regression could possibly be present. The following example shows how this design is used.

Research in Action

Can Pepsi Perform in a Theater?

Firms such as GfK Custom Research North America (www.gfkamerica.com) commonly use the one-group pretest–posttest design to measure the effectiveness of test commercials. Respondents are recruited to central theater locations in various test cities. The respondents are interviewed, and their attitudes toward Pepsi advertising, the brand, and the celebrity (O_1) are measured.

Then they watch a TV program containing the Pepsi commercial (X) and other filler commercials. After viewing the TV program, the respondents are again interviewed regarding their attitudes toward Pepsi advertising, the brand, and the celebrity (O_2). The effectiveness of the test commercial is determined by the difference between O_2 and O_1.

Static Group Design

The **static group** is a two-group experimental design in which one of the groups acts as a control group (CG). Only one group, the experimental group (EG), receives the experimental treatment. The subjects are not assigned randomly, and measurements are made on both groups following the treatment (posttest). This design is expressed symbolically as:

$$\text{EG:} \quad X \quad O_1$$
$$\text{CG:} \quad \quad O_2$$

static group

A pre-experimental design in which there are two groups: the experimental group (EG), which is exposed to the treatment, and the control group (CG). Measurements on both groups are made only after the treatment, and test units are not assigned at random.

The treatment effect would be measured as the difference between the control and experimental group ($O_1 - O_2$). The lack of randomization leaves the experiment open to some extraneous effects. The two groups might differ before the treatment, leading to selection bias. Mortality effects might be present, because more test units might withdraw from the experimental group than the control group.

In practice, the control group often is defined as the group receiving the current level of marketing activity, rather than as a group that receives no treatment at all. In many cases, it is impossible to reduce marketing input (e.g., price) to zero.

Research in Action

Is Pepsi Advertising Static?

A static group comparison to measure the effectiveness of a Pepsi commercial would be conducted as follows. Two groups of respondents would be recruited on the basis of convenience. Only the experimental group would be exposed to the TV program that contains the Pepsi commercial (X). Attitudes toward Pepsi advertising, the brand, and the celebrity would then be measured in both the experimental (O_1) and the control group (O_2). The effectiveness of the Pepsi commercial would be measured as the difference between the test and control group ($O_1 - O_2$).

Be an MR!	Be a DM!

Fox News Format: A Foxy Business

Visit www.foxnews.com and search the Internet—including social media—as well as your library's online databases to obtain information on consumers' preferences for network news channels. Fox News wants to determine which one of three new formats it should implement. Would you recommend a pre-experimental design? If so, which one would you recommend?

As the marketing manager of Fox News, how would you use information on consumers' preferences for network news channels to formulate marketing strategies that would increase your audience and market share?

Social Media

True Experimental Designs

True experimental designs are differentiated from pre-experimental designs by the fact that subjects are randomly assigned to groups. Treatment conditions also are randomly assigned to groups. For example, respondents are randomly assigned to one of three experimental groups. One of the three versions of a test commercial, selected at random, is administered to each group. As a result of random assignment, extraneous factors can be represented equally in each group or treatment condition. Randomization is the preferred procedure for ensuring the prior equality of experimental groups. However, randomization might not be effective when the sample size is small, because it merely produces groups that are equal on average. It is possible, though, to check whether randomization has been effective by measuring the possible extraneous variables and comparing them across the experimental groups.

True experimental designs include the pretest–posttest control group design and the posttest-only control group design.

Pretest–Posttest Control Group Design

pretest–posttest control group design

A true experimental design in which the experimental group is exposed to the treatment but the control group is not. Pretest and posttest measures are taken on both groups. Test units are randomly assigned.

In the **pretest–posttest control group design**, subjects are randomly assigned to either the experimental or the control group. A pretreatment measure is taken on each group. Thus, each group is measured prior to administering the treatment to the experimental group. Then, posttest measures are taken on both groups. This design is symbolized as:

$$\text{EG:} \quad R \quad O_1 \quad X \quad O_2$$
$$\text{CG:} \quad R \quad O_3 \qquad O_4$$

The treatment effect (TE) is measured as:

$$(O_2 - O_1) - (O_4 - O_3)$$

The use of a control group and randomization in this design controls for most extraneous variables. The extraneous effects are presumed to be represented equally in both the control and experimental groups. The difference between the control and experimental groups is thought to reflect only the treatment. With the use of a pretest measure in this design, the posttest measurement is susceptible to **interactive testing effects**, which means that a prior measurement affects the test unit's response to the independent variable.

interactive testing effect

An effect in which a prior measurement affects the test unit's response to the independent variable.

Research in Action

Pepsi Pre- and Postmortem

An experiment for measuring the effectiveness of Pepsi's advertising using a pretest–posttest control group design would be conducted as follows. A sample of respondents would be distributed randomly, half to the experimental group and half to the control group. A pretest questionnaire would be administered to the respondents in both groups to obtain a measurement on attitudes toward Pepsi advertising, the brand, and the celebrity. Only the respondents in the experimental group would be exposed to the TV program containing the Pepsi commercial. Then, a questionnaire would be administered to respondents in both groups to obtain posttest measures on attitudes toward Pepsi advertising, the brand, and the celebrity.

As this example shows, the pretest–posttest control group design involves two groups and two measurements on each group. A simpler design is the posttest-only control group design.

Posttest-Only Control Group Design

posttest-only control group design

A true experimental design in which the experimental group is exposed to the treatment but the control group is not and no pretest measure is taken. Posttest measures are taken on both groups. Test units are randomly assigned.

The **posttest-only control group design** does not involve any premeasurement. It can be symbolized as:

$$\text{EG:} \quad R \quad X \quad O_1$$
$$\text{CG:} \quad R \qquad O_2$$

The treatment effect is the difference between the experimental and control group measurements.

$$\text{TE} = O_1 - O_2$$

The simplicity of this design offers time, cost, and sample-size advantages. For these reasons, it is the most popular experimental design in marketing research. However, this design is not without limitations. Although randomization is used to equalize groups, without a pretest, there is no way to verify group similarity. Selection bias and mortality might be present. Without a pretest, researchers also are unable to examine changes in individual subjects over the course of the study. Note that, except for premeasurement, the implementation of this design is very similar to that of the pretest–posttest control group design. The opening vignette provided an application. The supermarket stores were randomly assigned to the experimental group and the control group. No premeasurements were taken. Only the stores in the experimental group were exposed to Muzak advertising. Measurements on the sales of advertised items were obtained in the experimental group (O_1) and control group (O_2) stores. The increase in sales due to Muzak advertising was determined as ($O_1 - O_2$).

Experiential Learning

Determining Price Sensitivity for Canon's Advanced Digital Camera

Canon wants to determine consumers' price sensitivity for its new advanced digital camera and hires you as a consultant.

1. Visit www.bestbuy.com and identify the price ranges of the digital cameras by Canon and other brands.

2. Search the Internet—including social media—as well as your library's online databases to obtain information on consumers' price sensitivity for digital cameras.

3. Canon wants to determine consumers' price sensitivity for its new advanced digital camera. Design an appropriate experiment. Would you recommend a true experimental design? If yes, which one?

4. As the marketing manager of Canon cameras, how would you use information on consumers' price sensitivity for digital cameras to formulate pricing strategies that would increase your market share?

Social Media

Quasi-Experimental Designs

Quasi-experimental designs are appropriate when researchers are faced with situations where they are unable to randomize or control the scheduling of experimental treatments. The experimenters might, however, be able to control when and on whom experimental measurements are taken. Quasi-experimental designs are faster and less expensive than other experimental designs and, in some natural research settings, might be the only avenue open for data collection. However, because full experimental control is lacking researchers must take into account the specific variables that are not controlled. Popular forms of quasi-experimental designs are time series and multiple time series designs.

Time Series Design

The **time series design** involves the use of periodic measurements of a group or individuals. At some point during the measurement, an experimental manipulation occurs naturally or is artificially introduced. Additional measurement follows. A time series experiment can be symbolized as:

$$O_1\ O_2\ O_3\ O_4\ O_5\ X\ O_6\ O_7\ O_8\ O_9\ O_{10}$$

This is a quasi experiment because the researcher lacks control in terms of randomization of the subjects to treatments. Additionally, the researcher may have no control over the timing of treatment presentation, as well as which subjects are exposed to the treatment. Multiple measurements might create a testing effect, causing a change in measured behavior simply because the respondents know they are being measured. History is not controlled. Nevertheless, time series designs are useful, particularly when evaluating behavior occurring in a natural setting.

time series design
A quasi-experimental design that involves periodic measurements on the dependent variable for a group of test units. Then, the treatment is administered by the researcher or occurs naturally. After the treatment, periodic measurements are continued in order to determine the treatment effect.

Research in Action

Time Will Tell the Effectiveness of Pepsi Advertising: Time Series Design

The effectiveness of a Pepsi commercial (X) could be examined by broadcasting the commercial into a series of markets a predetermined number of times. The test units or respondents are members of a panel. Although the marketer can control the scheduling of the test commercial, it is not possible to control when or if panel members are exposed to it. The marketer will examine panel members' attitudes toward Pepsi advertising, the brand, and the celebrity, as well as purchases before, during, and after the campaign to determine whether the test commercial had a short-term effect, a long-term effect, or no effect.

multiple time series design
A time series design that includes another group of test units to serve as a control group.

The **multiple time series design** is similar to time series except that it adds a control group that also is repeatedly measured. This group is not subject to the experimental treatment. If the control group is carefully selected, this design can be an improvement over the simple time series experiment.

Statistical Designs

Statistical designs consist of a series of basic experiments that allow for statistical control and analysis of external variables. In other words, several basic experiments are conducted simultaneously. Thus, statistical designs are influenced by the same sources of invalidity that affect the basic designs being used. Statistical designs offer the following advantages:

1. The effects of more than one independent variable can be measured.
2. Specific extraneous variables can be statistically controlled.
3. Economical designs can be formulated when each subject is measured more than once.

The most common statistical designs are the factorial designs.

Factorial Design

factorial design
A statistical experimental design used to measure the effects of two or more independent variables at various levels and to allow for interactions between variables.

A **factorial design** is used to measure the effects of two or more independent variables at various levels. It allows for the measurement of interactions between variables. An interaction is said to take place when the simultaneous effect of two or more variables is different from the sum of their separate effects. For example, an individual's favorite drink might be coffee and her favorite temperature level might be cold, but she might not prefer cold coffee, leading to an interaction.

A factorial design can also be thought of as a table. In a two-factor design, each level of one variable represents a row, and each level of another variable represents a column. Factorial designs involve a cell for every possible combination of treatment variables, as in the example that follows.

Research in Action

Factoring Humor and Information in Pepsi Commercials

Suppose that in the Pepsi case the researcher is interested in examining the effect of humor and the effect of various levels of brand information on advertising effectiveness. Three levels of humor (no humor, some humor, and high humor) are to be examined. Likewise, brand information is to be manipulated at three levels (low, medium, and high). The resulting table would be three rows (levels of information) by three columns (levels of humor), producing nine possible combinations or cells, as laid out in Table 8.1. The respondents would be randomly assigned to one of the nine cells. Respondents in each cell would receive a specific treatment combination. For example, respondents in the upper-left corner cell would view a commercial that had no humor and low brand information. After exposure to a treatment combination, measures would be obtained on attitudes toward Pepsi advertising, the brand, and the celebrity from respondents in each cell.

TABLE 8.1 An Example of a Factorial Design

Amount of Brand Information	Amount of Humor		
	No Humor	Medium Humor	High Humor
Low			
Medium			
High			

Statistical procedures such as analysis of variance (discussed in Chapter 17) are used to analyze the treatment effects and interactions. The main disadvantage of a factorial design is that the number of treatment combinations increases multiplicatively with an increase in the number of variables or levels. However, this is often not a serious limitation as the researcher can control both the number of variables and the levels.

Selecting an Experimental Design

Selecting an experimental design often involves a trade-off in terms of control. Designs that offer the greatest degree of internal validity typically are conducted in highly artificial environments that can threaten the generalizability or external validity of the experimental results.

One solution to finding the optimum combination of internal and external validity might be to use differing experimental designs at differing points in the study. For example, designs that offer tight internal validity (i.e., laboratory experiments) could be used during the early stages of the research effort. In this way, a more reliable measure of the true treatment effect could be secured. During later stages of the study, more natural settings (i.e., field experiments) could be used to enable generalization of results.

The following section discusses the distinction between laboratory and field experimentation in more detail.

Laboratory Versus Field Experiments

A **laboratory environment** is an artificial one, which affords the greatest amount of control over the crucial factors involved in the study. Advertising testing and test kitchens in central-location theaters are examples of laboratory experiments used in marketing research. Because the environments are highly contrived, questions of external validity are raised. Compared to field experiments, the artificial nature of laboratory environments might cause reactive error in that the respondents react to the situation itself rather than to the independent variable. Also, laboratory environments can cause **demand artifacts**, a phenomenon in which the respondents attempt to guess the purpose of the experiment, modifying their responses accordingly. On the positive side, laboratory experiments do allow for more complex designs than field experiments. Hence, the researcher can control for more factors or variables in the laboratory setting, which increases internal validity.

A **field environment** involves measurement of behavior, attitudes, or perceptions in the environment in which they occur. The researcher has much less control over extraneous variables that might impact internal validity. However, if internal validity can be maintained, the results can be generalized more easily than those obtained in a laboratory setting. The opening vignette presents an example of a field experiment. The use of scanner panels to conduct field experiments was discussed in Chapter 5. The differences between the two environments are summarized in Table 8.2.

laboratory environment
An artificial setting for experimentation in which the researcher constructs the desired conditions.

demand artifacts
Responses given because the respondents attempt to guess the purpose of the experiment and respond accordingly.

field environment
An experimental location set in actual market conditions.

TABLE 8.2 Laboratory Versus Field Experiments

Factor	Laboratory	Field
Environment	Artificial	Realistic
Control	High	Low
Reactive error	High	Low
Demand artifacts	High	Low
Internal validity	High	Low
External validity	Low	High
Time	Short	Long
Number of units	Small	Large
Ease of implementation	High	Low
Cost	Low	High

The Internet can provide a mechanism for controlled experimentation in a laboratory-type environment. Continuing with the example of testing the effectiveness of Pepsi's advertising, various Pepsi advertisements or commercials can be posted at various Web sites. Matched or randomly selected respondents can be recruited to visit these sites, with each group visiting only one site. If any pretreatment measures have to be obtained, the respondents answer a questionnaire posted on the site. They are then exposed to a particular Pepsi advertisement or a commercial at that site. After viewing the advertisement or commercial, the respondents answer additional questions providing posttreatment measures. Control groups can be implemented in a similar way. All of the experimental designs that we have considered can be implemented in this manner.

Internet experiments can also be used to test the effectiveness of alternative Web designs. Visitors are randomly exposed to different Web designs and their purchases are tracked over time, keeping the other marketing variables constant. Thus, the most effective design can be determined and implemented on the company's Web site.

Experiential Learning

Factorial Experimental Design

A local pizza maker is considering changing its cheese from mozzarella to a provolone/mozzarella cheese mix in a 1:2 ratio or a 2:1 ratio. This pizza maker also is considering holding the price for pizza the same, increasing the price 10 percent, or reducing the price 10 percent.

Social Media

1. Search the Internet—including social media—as well as your library's online databases to obtain information on consumers' preferences for and consumption of pizza.

2. Design a marketing experiment that will determine which formulation customers prefer. Your experimental design and format should consist of the following parts:
   a. Independent variables: The things that you changed.
   b. Dependent variable(s): What changed as a result of the manipulated variables, such as rating the formulation of cheese and price.

c. Extraneous variables: Everything else that did not change during the experiment, such as location of the test, the crust, and so forth.
   d. Control group: Did you use one? Why or why not?

3. Would it be better to use a laboratory or a field experiment to conduct your research? Explain.

4. Thirty respondents would be needed in each cell to accurately test your results. If each respondent receives $20 to participate, how much would the incentives cost in your experiment?

5. Describe how you would change your experiment to make it less costly. How might these changes affect your results?

6. How can the pizza maker use this information to increase its market share?

Limitations of Experimentation

Although experimentation is becoming increasingly important in marketing research, it does have limitations: time, cost, and administration of an experiment.

Time

Many types of field experiments become increasingly accurate with time. For example, to observe the long-term effect of a promotional campaign or a product introduction, purchase behavior must be observed over multiple purchase cycles. The accuracy of such behavioral information tends to increase with the passage of time. This added precision must be weighted against the costs of delaying a product rollout or the launch of a new advertising campaign.

Cost

New-product research in field environments can be extremely expensive. It is much more expensive than laboratory experiments, which typically occur on a small scale and use a limited number of subjects. In order to field test a new product, management must consider more than just the direct costs of data collection and analysis. Production must be initiated on a limited scale; point-of-sale promotional campaigns as well as mass advertising must be developed and introduced on a limited basis. Limited distribution channels might also have to be opened. Test market experiments can easily cost millions of dollars.

Administration

Controlling the effects of extraneous variables is an essential aspect of experimental research. Achieving the desired level of control becomes increasingly difficult as the research moves from the laboratory to the field. Field experiments often interfere with a company's ongoing operations, and obtaining cooperation from the retailers, wholesalers, and others involved can be difficult. Also, competitors might deliberately contaminate the results of a field experiment.

Application: Test Marketing

Test marketing is an example of a controlled field experiment conducted in limited but representative parts of a market. The research sites are called **test markets**. In a test market experiment, a national marketing program is replicated on a small scale. The two major objectives of test marketing are (1) to determine market acceptance of the product and (2) to test alternative levels of marketing mix variables. The independent variables being manipulated in such studies typically include elements of the marketing mix. The researcher can manipulate factors such as promotional investments, pricing, product modifications, or distribution elements. Observed consumer reactions represent the dependent variables, measured in terms of purchase behavior (i.e., sales) and/or attitudes or reactions to the marketing manipulations being studied. Test marketing is being practiced by both consumer-product and industrial-product companies.

Designing a standard market test involves deciding what criteria to use for selecting test markets, how many test markets to use, and the duration of the test.[4] Among all of the criteria considered in selecting a test market, representativeness is perhaps the most important. For example, information gathered from a new-product test can be used to predict ultimate market acceptance of that product and will govern the go/no-go decision regarding full market rollout. The test market must also be self-contained in terms of media coverage if mass-market advertising is planned to support the test. This prevents wasting promotional dollars. Additionally, the promotion of new products that are available in only a limited area can create negative consumer reaction toward future rollouts.

Test marketing runs the risk of revealing strategies, new product developments, or modified product positioning to the competition. Therefore, the strength of competition in a particular test site is another important consideration. Some commonly used test markets are Charlotte, North Carolina; Indianapolis, Indiana; Kansas City, Missouri; Nashville, Tennessee; Rochester, New York; and Sacramento and Stockton, California. These cities are desirable test markets because each is considered to be fairly representative of a large segment of the U.S. population.

In general, the more test markets that can be used, the better. If resources are limited, at least two test markets should be used for each program variation to be tested. However, when external validity is important, at least four test markets should be used. Despite its limitations in terms of time demands, costs, and competitive responses, test marketing can be very beneficial to a product's successful introduction.

test marketing
An application of a controlled experiment done in limited, but carefully selected, test markets. It involves replicating the planned national marketing program for a product in the test markets.

test markets
Carefully selected parts of the marketplace that are particularly suitable for test marketing.

Summary Illustration Using the Opening Vignette

Three conditions must be satisfied before causal inferences can be made that X is a cause of Y: (1) concomitant variation, which implies that X and Y must vary together in a hypothesized way; (2) time order of occurrence of variables, which implies that X must precede or occur simultaneously with Y; and (3) elimination of other possible causal factors, which implies that competing explanations must be ruled out. Thus, for Muzak advertising to be a cause of sales, sales of advertised products must be higher in stores with Muzak than in stores without Muzak; Muzak advertising must occur before or simultaneously with an increase in sales (it cannot occur afterwards); and the sales increase must not be attributable to other factors, such as price, shelf space, and so forth.

Experiments provide the most convincing evidence of all three conditions. An experiment is formed when the researcher manipulates one or more independent variables (presence or absence of Muzak advertising) and measures their effect on one or more dependent variables (sales of advertised products), controlling for the effect of extraneous variables (price, shelf space, and so forth).

In designing an experiment, it is important to consider internal and external validity. Internal validity refers to whether the manipulation of the independent variables actually caused the effects on the dependent variables. External validity refers to the generalizability of experimental results. In the opening vignette, to claim internal validity the researcher must show that Muzak advertising was, in fact, the cause of the increase in sales of the products in the experimental group of supermarkets. Thus, the researcher must show that price and other extraneous variables (e.g., shelf space) affecting the sale of these products were kept the same in both the experimental and control group stores. To claim external validity, the researcher must show that the sample of 20 supermarkets selected was representative, that no peculiar conditions were encountered, and that the results are generalizable to all supermarkets.

Experimental designs can be classified as pre-experimental, true experimental, quasi-experimental, and statistical designs. The design selected in the opening vignette was a true experimental design, because the supermarkets were randomly selected and assigned to the two groups, and one of the groups was randomly chosen as the experimental group. The specific design adopted was the posttest-only control group. An experiment can be conducted in a laboratory environment or under actual market conditions in a real-life setting, as in the opening vignette. Figure 8.5 provides a concept map for experiments. In this figure, the major concepts are connected by bold arrows using descriptors. Thus, primary quantitative data may be descriptive obtained through surveys and observations or they may be causal obtained through experiments. The rest of the figure can be interpreted similarly.

International Marketing Research

Field experiments pose even greater challenges in international markets than those faced in the United States. The researcher might be faced with market differences in terms of marketing support systems, economics, structural differences, information availability, and the technological environment. For example, in many countries, television stations are owned and operated by the

FIGURE 8.5

A Concept Map for Experiments

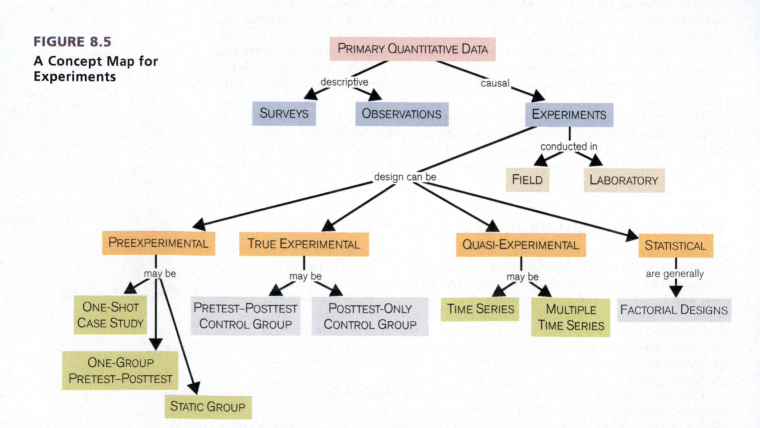

government, with severe restrictions on television advertising. This makes field experiments manipulating advertising levels extremely difficult, because the researcher might lack the flexibility to vary advertising content and expenditures.

Differential levels of infrastructure development and differing practices associated with retailing also plague test market feasibility. In some African countries, for example, the limited availability of supermarkets makes it difficult for Procter & Gamble to conduct experiments to determine the effect of in-store promotions on the sales of its detergents. In emerging countries in Asia, Africa, and South America, achieving adequate distribution of products to the rural populations is difficult because of the lack of basic infrastructures, such as roads, transportation, and warehouses.

Thus, the internal and external validity of field experiments conducted overseas is generally lower than in the United States. While pointing to the difficulties of conducting field experiments in other countries, we do not wish to imply that such causal research cannot or should not be conducted. To the contrary, as the following example indicates, creatively designed field experiments can result in rich findings.

Research in Action

Pepsi: Experimenting in Europe

In 2010, in order to counter sluggish sales in the domestic U.S. market, Pepsi International emphasized its advertising in global markets. PepsiCo International and Microsoft partnered for a new global soccer (known as *football* in most of the world) campaign focused on the World Cup 2010. The new campaign was served to football fans through Microsoft advertising. PepsiCo International's global football campaign was offered on no less than 14 markets worldwide, including Europe, the Middle East, and South America. PepsiCo and Microsoft put together an integrated brand engagement campaign, featuring ad content from Pepsi as well as a new Web site hosted on MSN.

The new strategy was decided in favor of previous advertising based on experiments conducted in several international markets. Respondents were randomly assigned and asked to evaluate either the new or the previous campaign. The new campaign resulted in more favorable evaluations. The new campaign resulted in increased sales in 2010.[5]

Marketing Research and Social Media

Both the virtual and real social worlds can be used for marketing research purposes. In virtual worlds, one can use Second Life (www.secondlife.com) as a tool to conduct standard marketing research projects at a lower cost. Incentives in the form of Linden dollars can be given to gain residents' cooperation and improve response rates. The researcher can also give nonmonetary incentives such as free virtual products and services like clothing or scripts that add certain features to avatars. The French market research firm Repères (www.reperes.net) is one of the leading providers within this domain. According to this firm, the cost for a virtual qualitative focus group is about 33 percent lower, and quantitative surveys can be conducted at half the cost of a comparable real-life project. Laboratory-type experiments can also be conducted in virtual space. In the virtual world, it is a lot simpler and much less costly to manipulate the independent variable and control for mediating variables than it is in the real world. All of the experimental designs that we have discussed in this chapter can be implemented within the context of virtual world. This is also true of test marketing. However, opinions, tastes, and preferences in virtual worlds may not be the same as in a real setting. Therefore, each new idea generated within virtual worlds needs to be subject to a thorough reality test before actually being implemented.

All of the experimental designs that we have discussed in this chapter can also be implemented within the context of the real social world. As compared to the field, experimentation in social media offers the advantages of ease of implementation and lower cost. The internal validity may be satisfactory in most cases as extraneous variables can generally be controlled. However, external validity will not be a high as that of field experiments. A study conducted by The Nielsen Company provides an illustration of using social media for experimentation.

Research in Action

The Three Faces of Facebook Ads

The Nielsen Company undertook research to determine the effectiveness of advertising on Facebook. To that end, Nielsen took a close look at 14 Facebook ad campaigns that incorporated the "Become A Fan" button. The ads were classified into three experimental groups by each of the types of ads available on Facebook: (1) a standard home-page ad, (2) home-page ads with social context, and (3) organic ads—newsfeed stories that are sent to friends of users who engage with advertising on a brand. These three different types of ads serve as independent variables in the experiment.

Nielsen's case study involved serving one of three Facebook ads to 99 percent of the users who fit the defined targeting criteria, while 1 percent of that audience was randomly assigned to serve as a control group. The control group consisted of users who were within the target segment and would have been shown an ad during the course of the campaign, but were prevented from seeing that ad. The three experimental groups consisted of those exposed to (1) Engagement Ad (Ad 1), (2) Ad with Social Context (Ad 2), and (3) those exposed to Engagement Ad (Ad 1) Plus Organic Ad Impression (Ad 3). A day after ad exposure, the three experimental groups and the control group were served Nielsen Brand Lift polls, and the impact of the ad campaign was measured. In the analysis, three dependent variables important to brand advertisers were examined: ad recall, awareness, and purchase intent.

The experiment showed that consumers who were exposed to an Engagement Ad (Ad 1) on the Facebook home page (experimental group 1) had 10 percent higher ad recall, 4 percent higher brand awareness, and 2 percent higher purchase intent than consumers who were not exposed (control group). When a Facebook home page featured the Ad with Social Context (Ad 2) (i.e., the ad includes a list of people on the viewer's "friend list" who are registered fans of the brand or product; experimental group 2), the increase in recall, awareness, and purchase intent compared to nonexposed consumers was substantially higher at 16 percent, 8 percent, and 8 percent, respectively, for the three measures. Nielsen suggests that this may be a result of consumers trusting their friends and peers more than anyone else when making a purchasing decision. Those users exposed to both the Engagement Ad (Ad 1) plus the Organic Ad Impression (Ad 3) (experimental group 3) exhibited the highest effectiveness with an increase in 30 percent for ad recall, 13 percent for brand awareness, and 8 percent for purchase intent versus the control group.

This case study clearly shows that the use of social media, particularly an engagement ad combined with the organic ad impression, causes an increase in metrics of concern to marketers: ad recall, awareness, and purchase intent. This drives home the message that marketers should not disregard Facebook in their marketing mix but instead realize that, with the right advertising, positive outcomes can be achieved.[6]

1: Engagement Ad

This is How to Fly

Everyone deserves to be happy. In-Flight WiFi, movies, music, on-demand food and more. Climb Aboard.

51,930 people are fans of Virgin America.

Become a Fan

2: Ad with Social Context

This is How to Fly

Everyone deserves to be happy. In-Flight WiFi, movies, music, on-demand food and more. Climb Aboard.

Meg, Ryan, and 6 other friends are fans of Virgin America.

Become a Fan

3: Organic Ad Impression

Alex and Libby become fans of Virgin America about an hour ago. Become a Fan

Ethics in Marketing Research

In experimentation, oftentimes the researcher deliberately attempts to disguise the purpose of the research, arguing that disguise is needed to produce valid results. Consider the earlier example of determining the effectiveness of Pepsi commercials. The respondents are recruited and brought to a central facility. They are told that they will be watching a television program on food and then will be asked some questions. Interspersed in the program is the commercial for Pepsi (test commercial) as well as commercials for some other products (filler commercials). After viewing the program and the commercials, the respondents are administered a questionnaire. The questionnaire obtains evaluations on the program content, the test commercial, and some of the filler commercials. The evaluations of the program content and the filler commercials are not of interest but are obtained to reinforce the nature of the disguise. If the respondents knew that the true purpose was to determine the effectiveness of the Pepsi commercial, their responses might be biased. However, disguising the purpose of the research does not have to, and should not, lead to deception.

One solution to this problem would be to tell respondents about the existence of disguise at the start of the experiment and allow them to inquire about it at the conclusion of the experiment. Thus, at the beginning, the researcher should explain the general nature of the experiment, including that the purpose of the experiment will be disguised but will be fully explained at the end, and the role of the respondents. The respondents should know that they are free to discontinue the experiment at any time and withdraw the information they have provided.

Explaining the purpose and details at the conclusion of the experiment is called **debriefing**. Debriefing should include procedures for reducing experimental stress. In the Pepsi example, the respondents could find it discouraging that they had spent their time evaluating a soft-drink commercial. The researcher should address this issue and ease the respondents' discomfort by explaining the true purpose and importance of the experiment, as well as the experimental procedures.

debriefing
After the experiment, the process of informing test subjects what the experiment was about and how the experimental manipulations were performed.

It is the researcher's responsibility to use the most appropriate experimental design for the problem at hand. The researcher should disclose to the client any problems that arise during the course of the experiment, and the research firm and the client should jointly work out a solution, as in the following example.

Research in Action

Pepsi Advertising: Shooting the Star

The effectiveness of Pepsi advertising featuring Brazilian soccer ace Ronaldinho is investigated using a one-group pretest–posttest design. Respondents' attitudes toward Pepsi advertising, Pepsi, and Ronaldinho are obtained prior to respondents being exposed to a food program and several commercials, including the one for Pepsi. Attitudes are again measured after respondents have viewed the program and the commercials. By observing the first few subjects, it is discovered that strongly held prior attitudes about Ronaldinho are affecting the measurement of attitudes toward Pepsi and Pepsi advertising. This problem should be disclosed immediately to the client, and corrective action should be determined jointly. For example, the client and the researcher might decide that a more sophisticated statistical design is needed that explicitly controls for attitude toward Ronaldinho. If the researcher chooses to ignore this problem and continue with the experiment, a serious ethical breach takes place. In this case, the researcher discovers that the research design adopted is inadequate, but this knowledge is withheld from the client.

Source: Photo-montage for Pepsi via Getty Images.

WHAT WOULD YOU DO?

Levi's: Fading Jeans and Market Share

The Situation

Levi's has a long history, with more than 150 years in the clothing business. Although one might think that this long history can only result in good things, Levi's heritage has been its worst enemy. John Anderson, president and CEO for Levi Strauss & Company, had to work to revamp Levi's antique image and make the brand appealing to younger generations in efforts to boost its declining sales. In the last few years, Anderson saw worldwide sales drop, losing market share to Gap, Calvin Klein, Tommy Hilfiger, and Diesel. Another problem for Anderson was store-brand jeans, such as JCPenney's Arizona brand jeans, and Gap's in-house brand, which have changed their image and launched an assault on big brand names like Levi's. These store-brand jeans, along with other store-label jeans, now target the teenage market with "cutting edge" advertising. Trade publication *Brand Strategy* estimated that the Levi's brand had lost about 50 percent of the younger consumer market share worldwide in the early 2000s.

To compete with these brands and maintain leadership, Levi's, the market leader, is considering introducing its own line of private-label jeans to capture a larger portion of the teenage market. Anderson wonders how powerful a national brand like Levi's is when compared to an in-house brand such as Gap or a store brand such as JCPenney's Arizona jeans.

The Marketing Research Decision

1. If you were John Anderson, what type of research would you want to be conducted to help arrive at an answer? Which one of the following types of research would be most appropriate?
   a. Secondary data analysis
   b. Focus groups
   c. Descriptive cross-sectional survey
   d. Descriptive longitudinal survey
   e. Causal research

2. Explain how you would implement the type of research you have recommended.

(continued)

3. Discuss the role of the type of research you recommend in enabling John Anderson to determine the power of a national brand like Levi's compared to an in-house brand like Gap or a store brand like JCPenney's Arizona jeans.

The Marketing Management Decision

1. What should John Anderson do to compete with in-house and store brands of jeans?
   a. Discount the price of Levi's.
   b. Introduce a new brand of lower-priced jeans.
   c. Sell Levi's through discount stores, such as Walmart and Target.
   d. Increase the advertising budget for Levi's.
   e. Establish a presence in social media.

2. Discuss how the marketing management-decision action that you recommend to John Anderson is influenced by the research that you suggested earlier and by the findings of that research.

What John Anderson Did

John Anderson introduced a new line of cheaper jeans and clothing to mark its first foray into the discount market. The new Signature brand was made available through Walmart stores in the United States and is a key feature in Levi's drive to reverse years of declining market share. Levi's established its presence on Facebook and as of 2011 had more than half-a-million fans. The company regularly posts updates, photos, and competitions that fans can view, comment on, and be a part of. *Unzipped* is a blog maintained by Levi Strauss & Co.

Social Media

Readers get a "behind-the-seams" look and hear from a variety of voices, from both inside and outside the company.[7]

Source: Bloomberg/Contributor.

Summary

The scientific notion of causality implies that the condition where X causes Y cannot be proven. At best, it can only be inferred that X is one of the causes of Y, in that it makes the occurrence of Y probable. Three conditions must be satisfied before causal inferences can be made: (1) concomitant variation, which implies that X and Y must vary together in a hypothesized way; (2) time order of occurrence of variables, which implies that X must precede Y or at least occur simultaneously; and (3) elimination of other possible causal factors, which implies that competing explanations must be ruled out. Experiments provide the most convincing evidence of all three conditions. An experiment is formed when a researcher manipulates one or more independent variables and measures their effect on one or more dependent variables, controlling for the effects of extraneous variables.

In designing an experiment, it is important to consider internal and external validity. Internal validity refers to whether the manipulation of the independent variables actually caused the effects on the dependent variables. External validity refers to the generalizability of experimental results. For the experiment to be valid, the researcher must control the threats that extraneous variables pose.

Experimental designs can be classified as pre-experimental, true experimental, quasi-experimental, and statistical designs. An experiment might be conducted in a laboratory environment or under actual market conditions in a real-life setting.

Although experiments have limitations in terms of time, cost, and administration, they are becoming increasingly popular in marketing. Test marketing is an important application of experimental design. Field experiments pose even greater challenges in international markets than those faced in the United States. Using social media, such as virtual reality, the researcher can create an environment that represents the field (marketplace) and yet exercise the degree of control possible only in a laboratory setting. Disguising the purpose of the research should not lead to deception, and debriefing should be used to reduce experimental stress.

Key Terms and Concepts

Suggested Cases and Video Cases

Running Case with Real Data

1.1 Hewlett-Packard

Comprehensive Critical Thinking Cases

2.1 American Idol   2.2 Baskin-Robbins   2.3 Akron Children's Hospital

Comprehensive Cases with Real Data

3.1 Bank of America   3.2 McDonald's   3.3 Boeing

Comprehensive Brief Harvard Business School Cases

4.1 TruEarth Healthy Foods: Market Research for a New Product Introduction (4065)
4.2 The Springfield Nor'easters: Maximizing Revenues in the Minor Leagues (2510)
4.3 Metabical: Positioning and Communications Strategy for a New Weight-Loss Drug (4240)
4.4 Saxonville Sausage Company (2085)

Online Video Cases

8.1 AFLAC   9.1 P&G   12.1 Motorola
13.1 Subaru   19.1 Marriott

Live Research: Conducting a Marketing Research Project

If an experiment is to be conducted, an experimental design should be chosen based on class discussion. The choice of an experimental design might have to be tempered by several considerations:

1. It might not be possible to control for certain extraneous variables.
2. There might be only limited flexibility to manipulate the independent variables (e.g., advertising or sales effort cannot be reduced to the zero level).

3. Random assignment of test units to the treatment conditions might not be possible.
4. The choice of dependent variables might be limited by measurement considerations.

The experimental design selected should be discussed and approved by the client.

Acronym

The salient characteristics of experiments may be described by the acronym EXPERIMENT:

E xtraneous variables

X independent variable or treatment

P re-experimental, true experimental, quasi-experimental, and statistical designs

E ffect or dependent variable

R andom assignment

I nternal validity

M easurement or observation

E xternal validity

N eutral or control group

T est units

Review Questions

1. What are the requirements for inferring a causal relationship between two variables?
2. Differentiate between internal and external validity.
3. What key characteristic distinguishes true experimental designs from pre-experimental designs?
4. List the steps involved in implementing the posttest-only control group design. Describe the design symbolically.
5. What is a time series experiment? When is it used?
6. How does a multiple time series design differ from a basic time series design?
7. What advantages do statistical designs have over basic designs?
8. Compare laboratory and field experimentation.
9. What is test marketing?
10. Social Media How can social media be used to conduct an experiment?

Applied Problems

1. A prolife group wants to test the effectiveness of an anti-abortion commercial. Two random samples, each of 250 respondents, are recruited in Chicago. One group is shown the anti-abortion commercial. Then, attitudes toward abortion are measured for respondents in both groups.
   a. Identify the independent and dependent variables in this experiment.
   b. What type of design was used?
2. In the anti-abortion commercial experiment just described, suppose the respondents had been selected by convenience rather than randomly. What type of design would result?
3. Identify the type of experiment being conducted in the following situations:
   a. A major distributor of office equipment is considering a new sales presentation program for its salespeople. The largest sales territory is selected, the new program is implemented, and the effect on sales is measured.
   b. Procter & Gamble wants to determine if a new package design for Tide detergent is more effective than the current design. Twelve supermarkets are randomly selected in Denver. In six of them,

randomly selected, Tide is sold in the new packaging. In the other six, the detergent is sold in the old package. Sales for both groups of supermarkets are monitored for 3 months.

4. Describe a specific situation for which each of the following experimental designs is appropriate. Defend your reasoning.
   a. One-group pretest–posttest design
   b. Pretest–posttest control group design
   c. Posttest-only control group design
   d. Time series design
   e. Factorial design
5. Design an experiment for determining the effectiveness of online coupons based on relevant information obtained from www.coupons-online.com.
6. Coca-Cola has developed three alternative package designs for its flagship product, Coke. Design an Internet-based experiment to determine which, if any, of these new package designs is superior to the current one.
7. Microsoft has developed a new version of its Excel spreadsheet, but is not sure what the user reaction will be. Design an Internet-based experiment to determine user reaction to the new and previous versions of Excel.

8. Explain how you would implement a posttest-only control group design on the Internet to measure the effectiveness of a new print ad for Toyota Camry.

9. Explain how you would implement a posttest-only control group design in social media to measure the effectiveness of a new print ad for Hilton hotel.

Group Discussion

"Because one cannot prove a causal relationship by conducting an experiment, experimentation is unscientific for examining cause-and-effect relationships." Discuss this statement as a small group.

Hewlett-Packard Running Case

Review the Hewlett-Packard (HP) case, Case 1.1, and questionnaire given toward the end of the book.

1. **Social Media** Is causal research necessary in this case? If yes, which experimental designs would you recommend and why? If not, describe a scenario in which it would be. Can the latter experimental design be implemented in social media? If yes, how?

2. If a mall-intercept interview is used and HP conducts causal research without randomizing respondents, which pre-experimental design would you recommend?

3. Can you think of any way in which the static group design can be randomized to increase its validity?

ONLINE VIDEO CASE 8.1

AFLAC: Marketing Research Quacks a Duck

Visit **www.pearsonhighered.com/malhotra** to read the video case and view the accompanying video. AFLAC: Marketing Research Quacks a Duck describes the crucial role of marketing research in designing the right advertising campaign and the resulting impact on brand recognition for AFLAC. In particular, the AFLAC duck commercials were tested against alternatives in experimental design situations. This case can be used to discuss the use of alternative experimental designs in evaluating advertising effectiveness. Specific marketing research questions on this and the previous chapters are posed in the video case.

9 Measurement and Scaling: Fundamentals and Comparative Scaling

Source: AP Wide World Photos/Eric Gay.

LEARNING OBJECTIVES

After reading this chapter, the student should be able to:

1. Explain what is meant by measurement and scaling, and how scaling can be considered a part of measurement.

2. Describe the basic scale characteristics and how they relate to the levels of measurement.

3. Discuss the primary scales of measurement, and how they differ.

4. Understand how scaling techniques are classified, and the various comparative scaling techniques.

5. Explain how measurement and scaling relate to the various steps of the marketing research process.

6. Discuss the considerations involved in implementing the primary scales of measurement in an international setting.

7. **Social Media** Explain how social media can be used to implement measurement and scaling.

8. Describe the ethical issues involved in selecting scales of measurement.

" In every survey project, researchers have to decide what type of scales will be used to measure the variables. You really have to know what these scale types can give you. **"**

James C. Fink
CEO, Worldwide Marketing Research, Opinion Research Corporation, Princeton, New Jersey

Scaling the Olympics

Tens of thousands of teens swarmed Beijing, China, for the 2008 Olympics and were looking to do the same in London for the 2012 Olympics. The games also are very popular among teen television watchers. In fact, the Olympics are the single most popular televised sporting event (ranked number one) among teenage boys (71 percent) and girls (62 percent), according to The New World Teen Study. The BrainWaves Group (www.brainwavecc.com), a New York global consulting and trends company, conducted this survey of 6,500 teens in 26 countries. Elissa Moses, managing director of The BrainWaves Group, says, "The Olympics are young people's favorite athletic package because in the global teen culture sport is a dominant theme, with both boys and girls being active participants and spectators."

Globally, the Olympics enjoys its highest popularity rating in the Middle East, where it is the favorite televised sporting event of 85 percent of teen boys and girls. Australia, host of the 2000 Olympic Games, is third, where the games are the favorite of 84 percent of teen males and 80 percent of teen females. The United States is lower in the ranking: Only 71 percent of teen girls and 68 percent of teen boys named the Olympics their favorite televised sports competition.

However, any similarity between the tastes of teen boys and girls ends with the Olympics. A majority of teen boys (63 percent) cite basketball as their favorite sport, followed by soccer (58 percent). Teen girls voted gymnastics their most popular sport (57 percent), followed by basketball (51 percent). Only 17 percent of the boys voted gymnastics their favorite spectator sport. In fact, on a global basis of both boys and girls, teens' favorite spectator sport is basketball. Note that each respondent could name more than one sport as his or her favorite.

The BrainWaves Group developed a complete ranking of the popularity of all sports in terms of the percentage of teenagers who indicated each sport as their favorite. Information of this type can be used by marketers of global brands, such as Levi's, in their attempts to penetrate the teen market. For example, Levi's would do well to air its commercials on televised basketball and soccer games in order to reach teenage boys. However, to reach teenage girls, Levi's should replace soccer advertising with gymnastics.[1]

Overview

After developing the research design (Chapters 3 through 8), the researcher is ready to move to the next phase of research. The researcher must decide how to measure information and which types of scales to use. In the opening vignette, scales were designed to measure the popularity of various sports and sporting events.

This chapter describes the concepts of scaling and measurement. Figure 9.1 briefly explains the focus of the chapter, the relation of this chapter to the previous ones, and the steps of the marketing research process on which this chapter concentrates.

This chapter discusses the fundamental scale characteristics of description, order, distance, and origin. Four primary scales of measurement are reviewed: nominal, ordinal, interval, and ratio. Comparative and noncomparative scaling techniques are presented, and comparative techniques are explained in detail. (Noncomparative techniques are discussed in more depth in Chapter 10.) The applications of primary scales and comparative scaling in international marketing research are discussed. The impact of social media on scaling and ethical issues that arise in measurement and scaling also are covered. Figure 9.2 provides an overview of the topics discussed in this chapter and how they flow from one to the next.

Measurement and Scaling

measurement
The assignment of numbers or other symbols to characteristics of objects according to certain prespecified rules.

Measurement is assigning numbers or other symbols to characteristics of objects being measured, according to predetermined rules. Characteristics of the item are measured, rather than the item directly. Thus, this means that consumers are not measured, only their perceptions, attitudes, preferences, or other relevant characteristics. In the opening vignette, teenagers' preferences for various sports and sporting events were measured.

In marketing research, numbers usually are assigned for one of two reasons:

- To permit statistical analysis of the generated data
- To help communicate information about the results

The most important aspect of measurement is deciding how to assign numbers to the characteristics being studied. In the opening vignette, numbers had to be assigned to measure

FIGURE 9.1

Relationship of Comparative Scaling to the Previous Chapters and the Marketing Research Process

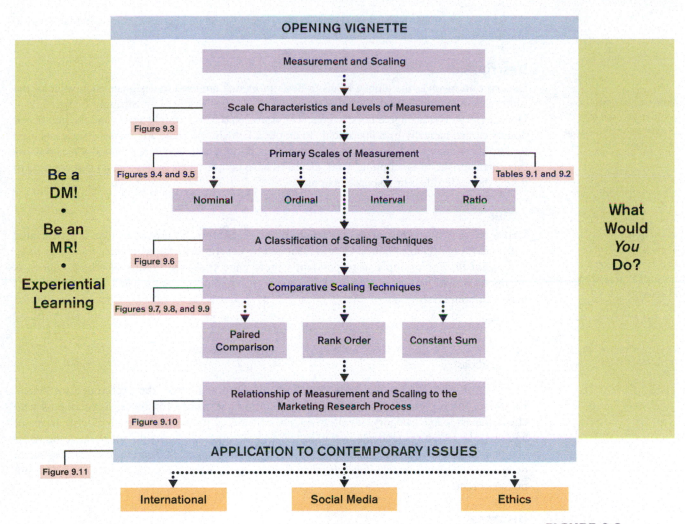

FIGURE 9.2

Fundamentals and Comparative Scaling: An Overview

the popularity of different sports in terms of the percentage of respondents who mentioned each sport as their favorite (most preferred). In developing the assignment process, a one-to-one correspondence must exist between the numbers and the characteristics being measured. Only then can the numbers be associated with specific characteristics of the object being measured. For example, the same dollar figures are assigned to products that are priced the same. In addition, the rules for assigning numbers should be applied in a standard way. They must not change over objects or time.

Scaling can be considered a part of measurement. Scales place the objects being measured along a continuum. To illustrate, suppose you wanted to measure consumers in terms of their attitude toward Wrigley chewing gum. Based on the response, each consumer would be assigned a number indicating an unfavorable attitude (measured as 1), a neutral attitude (measured as 2), or a favorable attitude (measured as 3). Measurement is the actual assignment of 1, 2, or 3 to each respondent using a scale that ranges from one to three. In this example, scaling is the process of placing consumer response along an attitudinal spectrum from unfavorable, to neutral, to favorable. The scale is the set of values ranging from one to three. In the opening vignette, measurement was the actual assignment of a number from 0 to 100 to each sport given its preference (as favorite sport) for teenage boys and girls. Scaling was the process of placing each sport along a preference continuum from 0 to 100 percent.

scaling
The generation of a continuum upon which measured objects are located.

Scale Characteristics and Levels of Measurement

All the scales used in marketing research can be described in terms of four basic characteristics. These characteristics are description, order, distance, and origin, and together they define the level of measurement of a scale. The level of measurement denotes what properties of an object the scale is, or is not, measuring. An understanding of the scale characteristics is fundamental to understanding the primary type of scales.

Description

description
Refers to the unique labels or descriptors that are used to designate each value of the scale. All scales possess description.

Description involves the unique labels or descriptors that are used to designate each value of the scale. Some examples of descriptors are 1 = Female, 2 = Male; 1 = Strongly disagree, 2 = Disagree, 3 = Neither agree nor disagree, 4 = Agree, and 5 = Strongly agree; and the number of dollars earned annually by a household. To amplify, Female and Male are unique descriptors used to describe values 1 and 2 of the gender scale. It is important to remember that all scales possess this characteristic of description. Thus, all scales have unique labels or descriptors that are used to define the scale values or response options.

Order

order
The relative sizes or positions of the descriptors; it is denoted by descriptors such as *greater than, less than,* and *equal to.*

Order refers to the relative sizes or positions of the descriptors. No absolute values are associated with order, only relative values. Order is denoted by descriptors such as *greater than, less than,* and *equal to.* For example, a respondent's preference for three brands of athletic shoes is expressed by the following order, with the most preferred brand being listed first and the least preferred brand last.

> Nike
>
> Asics
>
> Adidas

For this respondent, the preference for Nike is greater than the preference for Asics. Likewise, the preference for Adidas is less than the preference for Asics. Respondents who check the same age category, say 35 to 49, are considered to be equal to each other in terms of age and older than respondents in the 20-to-34 age group. All scales do not possess the order characteristic. In the gender scale (1 = Female, 2 = Male) considered earlier, it is not possible to determine whether a female is greater than or less than a male. Thus, the gender scale does not possess order.

Distance

distance
The absolute differences between the scale descriptors are known and can be expressed in units.

The characteristic of **distance** means that absolute differences between the scale descriptors are known and can be expressed in units. The disagree-agree scale considered earlier (1 = Strongly disagree, 2 = Disagree, 3 = Neither agree nor disagree, 4 = Agree, and 5 = Strongly agree) has the characteristic of distance. Note that "Strongly agree (5)" expresses one more unit of agreement than "Agree (4)," which in turn expresses one more unit of agreement than the neutral category of "Neither agree nor disagree (3)."

Notice that a scale that has distance also has order. We know five units are greater than four units. Likewise, three units are less than four units. Thus, distance implies order, but the reverse might not be true.

Origin

origin
A unique or fixed beginning or true zero point of a scale.

The **origin** characteristic means that the scale has a unique or fixed beginning or true zero point. Thus, an exact measurement of income by a scale such as:

> What is the annual income of our household before taxes? $ _____

has a fixed origin or a true a zero point. An answer of zero would mean that the household has no income at all. A scale that has origin also has distance (and order and description). Many scales used in marketing research do not have a fixed origin or true zero point, as in the disagree-agree scale considered earlier. Notice that such a scale was defined as 1 = Strongly disagree, 2 = Disagree, 3 = Neither agree nor disagree, 4 = Agree, and 5 = Strongly agree. However, 1 is an arbitrary starting point. This scale could just as easily have been defined as 0 = Strongly disagree, 1 = Disagree, 2 = Neither agree nor disagree, 3 = Agree, and 4 = Strongly agree, with 0 as the origin. Alternatively, shifting the origin to –2 will result in an equivalent scale: –2 = Strongly disagree, –1 = Disagree, 0 = Neither agree nor disagree, 1 = Agree, and 2 = Strongly agree. These

FIGURE 9.3

An Illustration of Scale Characteristics

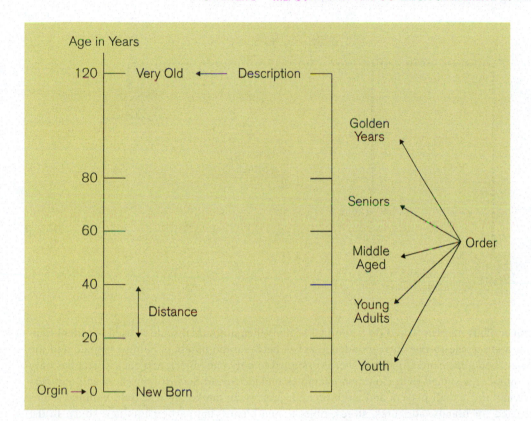

three forms of the agree-disagree scale, with the origin at 1, 0, or –2, are equivalent. Thus, this scale does not have a fixed origin or a true zero point and consequently does not possess the characteristic of origin.

Note that description, order, distance, and origin represent successively higher-level characteristics, with origin being the highest-level characteristic. Description is the most basic characteristic that is present in all scales. If a scale has order, it also has description. If a scale has distance, it also has order and description. Finally, a scale that has origin also has distance, order, and description. Thus, if a scale has a higher-level characteristic, it also has all the lower-level characteristics. However, the reverse might not be true; that is, if a scale has a lower-level characteristic, it might or might not have a higher-level characteristic.

Figure 9.3 is an illustration of scale characteristics in measuring age. The scale descriptors New Born and Very Old are examples of description. The age categories of Golden Years, Seniors, Middle Aged, Young Adults, and Youth denote order, from the oldest to the youngest. The difference between 40 years and 20 years represents distance. Finally, 0 age, denoting a newborn child, represents a fixed origin reflecting distance. With an understanding of scale characteristics, let's now discuss the primary type of scales.

Primary Scales

The word *primary* means "basic" or "fundamental." The four primary scales of measurement are nominal, ordinal, interval, and ratio scales (see Figure 9.4).

The nominal scale is the most limited, followed by the ordinal, the interval, and the ratio scale. As the measurement level increases from nominal to ratio, scale complexity increases. For the respondents, nominal scales are the simplest to use, whereas ratio scales are the most complex. These scales are illustrated in Figure 9.5. Their properties are summarized in Table 9.1 and are discussed in the following sections.

Nominal Scale

A **nominal scale** uses numbers as labels or tags for identifying and classifying objects. The only characteristic possessed by these scales is description. For example, teenagers participating in the sports survey discussed in the opening vignette might each be assigned a

nominal scale
A scale whose numbers serve only as labels or tags for identifying and classifying objects. When used for identification, there is a strict one-to-one correspondence between the numbers and the objects.

FIGURE 9.4

A Classification of Primary Scales of Measurement

number. This number would be a nominal scale. When a nominal scale is used for identification, a strict one-to-one correspondence exists between the numbers being assigned and the objects being measured. Each number is assigned to only one object, and each object has only one number assigned to it. Common examples include Social Security numbers and numbers assigned to football players and worn on their jerseys. In marketing research, nominal scales are used for brands, attributes, stores, objects, and identifying participants in a study. In the opening vignette, numbers could be used to denote the various spectator sports: 1. tennis, 2. hockey, 3. soccer, 4. basketball, and so on, resulting in a nominal scale. Note that the numbers merely identify the sports and do not denote any characteristic of the sport. Thus, a 1 denotes tennis and a 3 denotes soccer, but these numbers do not tell us whether tennis is more or less popular than soccer.

Nominal scales are used for classification purposes. They serve as labels for classes or categories. The classes are mutually exclusive and collectively exhaustive. *Mutually exclusive* means that there is no overlap between classes; every object being measured falls into only one class. The objects in each class are viewed as equivalent in terms of the characteristic represented by the nominal scale. All objects in the same class have the same number, and no two classes have the same number. *Collectively exhaustive* means that all the objects fall into one of the classes. For example, the numbers 1 and 2 can be used to classify survey respondents based on gender, with 1 denoting female and 2 denoting male. Each respondent will fall into one of these two categories.

FIGURE 9.5

An Illustration of Primary Scales of Measurement

SCALE					
Nominal	Numbers Assigned to Runners	17	21	13	Finish
Ordinal	Rank Order of Winners	Third Place	Second Place	First Place	
Interval	Performance Rating on a 0 to 100 Scale	74	90	97	
Ratio	Time to Finish, in Seconds	16.1	14.0	13.2	

TABLE 9.1 Primary Scales of Measurement

Primary Scale	Basic Description	Scale Characteristics	Common Examples	Marketing Examples	Permissible Statistics
Nominal	Numbers identify and classify objects	Description	Social Security numbers, numbering of football players	Brand numbers, store types, gender classification	Percentages, mode
Ordinal	Numbers indicate the relative positions of the objects but not the magnitude of differences between them	Description, order	Quality rankings, rankings of teams in a tournament	Preference rankings, market position, social class	Percentile, median
Interval	Differences between objects can be compared; zero point is arbitrary	Description, order, distance	Temperature (Fahrenheit, Celsius)	Attitudes, opinions, index numbers	Range, mean, standard deviation
Ratio	Zero point is fixed; ratios of scale values can be computed	Description, order, distance, origin	Length, weight	Age, income, costs, sales, market shares	Geometric mean, all statistics

The numbers assigned in a nominal scale do not reflect relative amounts of the characteristic being measured. For example, a high Social Security number does not imply that the person is in some way superior to those with lower Social Security numbers or vice versa. The same applies to numbers assigned to classes. By assigning 1 to female and 2 to male, the researcher does not imply that either sex is superior to the other in any way. The numbers in a nominal scale can only be counted. Therefore, the only statistics that are useful when using a nominal scale are those based on frequency counts. These include percentage, mode, and chi-square (see Chapter 16). It is not meaningful to compute an average Social Security number or the average gender of the respondents in a survey. The following example on nominal scale illustrates this limitation.

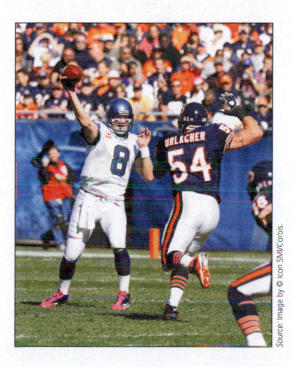

Source: Image by © Icon SMI/Corbis.

A common example of a nominal scale is numbers assigned to football players.

Research in Action

Nominal Scale

In a study to measure consumer preferences for jeans, numbers 1 through 10 were assigned to the 10 brands being considered (see Table 9.2). Thus, brand number 9 referred to Old Navy. Brand number 6 was assigned to Jordache. This did not imply that Old Navy was in any way superior or inferior to Jordache. Any reassignment of the numbers, such as switching the numbers assigned to Old Navy and Jordache, would have no effect on the results. The numbers did not reflect any characteristics of the brands.

It is meaningful to make statements such as, "Thirty-five percent of the respondents had purchased Levi jeans, or brand number 8." The *mode*, defined as the number with the highest frequency, denotes the brand preferred by the largest number of respondents, for example, Guess? However, although the average of all the assigned numbers, 1 to 10, is 5.5, it is not meaningful to state that the number of the average brand of jeans is 5.5.

Ordinal Scale

ordinal scale
A ranking scale in which numbers are assigned to objects to indicate the relative extent to which some characteristic is possessed. Thus, it is possible to determine whether an object has more or less of a characteristic than some other object.

An **ordinal scale** is a ranking scale. In an ordinal scale, numbers are assigned to objects, which allows researchers to determine whether an object has more or less of a characteristic than some other object. However, we cannot determine how much more or less from this type of scale. Objects ranked first have more of the characteristic being measured than objects ranked second; however, it is not possible to determine whether the object ranked second is a close second or a distant second. Thus, ordinal scales possess description and order characteristics, but not distance (or origin). Common examples of ordinal scales include quality rankings, rankings of teams in a tournament, and educational levels (less than high school, high school, some college, and so on).

In marketing research, ordinal scales are used to measure relative attitudes, opinions, perceptions, and preferences. Measurements of this type ask the respondent to make "greater than" or "less than" judgments. Asking respondents to rank-order the various sports in terms of their preference, as in the opening vignette, is an example of an ordinal scale.

Ordinal scales are like nominal scales in that equivalent objects receive the same rank. Any series of numbers can be assigned as long as they preserve the ordered relationships between the objects. Because of this quality, ordinal scales can be transformed in any way as long as the basic ordering of the objects is maintained. In ordinal scales, numbers differ only in terms of their order, not in terms of their magnitude; there is no magnitude associated with numbers on an ordinal scale (see the following example on ordinal scale). For these reasons, in addition to the counting operation allowable for nominal scale data, ordinal scales also permit the use of statistics based on centiles. This means that it is meaningful to calculate percentile, median, or other summary statistics from ordinal data (see Chapter 16).

TABLE 9.2 An Illustration of Primary Scales of Measurement

Nominal Scale		Ordinal Scale	Interval Scale		Ratio Scale
No.	Jean Brand	Preference Rankings	Preference Ratings 1–7	11–17	Price in Dollars ($)
1.	Bugle Boy	7 79	5	15	30
2.	Calvin Klein	2 25	7	17	48
3.	Diesel	8 82	4	14	27
4.	Gap	3 30	6	16	32
5.	Guess?	1 10	7	17	34
6.	Jordache	5 53	5	15	35
7.	Lee	9 95	4	14	30
8.	Levi	6 61	5	15	33
9.	Old Navy	4 45	6	16	29
10.	Wrangler	10 115	2	12	24

Source: Fuse/Getty Images.

A consumer's selection of jeans illustrates all of the primary scales of measurement.

Research in Action

Ordinal Scale

Table 9.2 gives one respondent's preference rankings. Respondents ranked 10 brands of jeans in order of preference by assigning a 1 to the most preferred brand, a 2 to the second most preferred brand, and so forth. Note that Guess? (ranked 1) is preferred to Calvin Klein (ranked 2). However, it is not possible to determine how much more it is preferred. Also, it is not necessary to assign numbers from 1 to 10 to obtain a preference ranking. The second ordinal scale, which assigns a number 10 to Guess?, 25 to Calvin Klein, 30 to Gap, and so on, is an equivalent scale. The two scales result in the same ordering of the brands according to preference. This illustrates an important property of ordinal scales: Any series of numbers can be assigned as long as they preserve the ordered relationships between the objects.

Note that the ordinal scale does not replace the nominal scale, but merely supplements it. One could say that brand number 5 receives the highest preference ranking—rank 1 on the first ordinal scale—and identify it as Guess?

Be a DM!	Be an MR!
Enhancing Customer Satisfaction with Sears	
As the marketing director for Sears, what marketing strategies would you formulate to enhance satisfaction with Sears?	Visit www.sears.com and search the Internet—including social media—as well as your library's online databases to obtain information on customer satisfaction with department stores. How would you use nominal and ordinal scales to measure customer satisfaction with the major department stores, such as Sears?

Social Media

Interval Scale

In an **interval scale,** numerically equal distances on the scale represent equal values in the characteristic being measured. An interval scale contains all the information of an ordinal scale. In addition, it allows you to compare the differences between objects. The difference between 1 and 2 is same as the difference between 2 and 3, which is the same as the difference between 5 and 6. The distance between descriptors is known. The interval scales possess the characteristics of description, order, and distance. In marketing research, data on attitudes (e.g., attitude toward sports) obtained from rating scales (1 = do not like at all, 7 = like very much) often are treated as interval data. In the opening vignette, interval data would be obtained if the respondents were asked to rate each sport in terms of preference using a 7-point scale with ratings of 1 = not at all preferred and 7 = greatly preferred. Note that in an interval scale two objects can be assigned the same number if they each contain the characteristic being measured to the same extent. Scales of this type are discussed further in Chapter 10.

In an interval scale, the location of the zero point is not fixed. Both the zero point and the units of measurement are arbitrary; that is, these scales do not possess the origin characteristic. This is illustrated in the measurement of temperature. The Fahrenheit scale uses different zero points and smaller units of measurement than the Celsius scale. However, both are used to measure the same characteristic: temperature. Any positive linear transformation of the form $y = a + bx$ will preserve the properties of the scale. Here, x is the original scale value, y is the transformed scale value, b is a positive constant, and a is any constant. Two interval scales that rate women's handbag brands Coach, Dooney & Burke, Vende, and Gucci as 1, 3, 3, and 5, or as 22, 26, 26, and 30 are equivalent. Note that the latter scale can be derived from the former by using $a = 20$ and $b = 2$ in the transforming equation. Their equivalence can also be seen as follows.

$$\text{Poor} \quad 1 \quad 2 \quad 3 \quad 4 \quad 5 \quad \text{Excellent}$$

or

$$\text{Poor} \quad 22 \quad 24 \quad 26 \quad 28 \quad 30 \quad \text{Excellent}$$

Because the zero point is not fixed, it is not meaningful to take ratios of scale values. Thus, it is not meaningful to say that it is 1.5 times as hot in Phoenix (temperature = 90 degrees Fahrenheit) as it is in Buffalo (temperature = 60 degrees Fahrenheit). When the temperatures are converted to a Celsius scale, the ratio is no longer 1.5 to 1. In the handbag example, the ratio of Gucci to Dooney & Burke is 5:3 using the first scale. It becomes 15:13 when the scale is transformed.

All the statistical techniques and measures of central tendency (mode and median) that apply to nominal and ordinal data can also be applied to interval scale data. In addition, the arithmetic mean, standard deviation (see Chapter 16), and other statistics commonly used in marketing research are permitted. However, certain specialized statistics, such as geometric means, are not meaningful on interval scale data. The jeans example gives a further illustration of an interval scale.

Research in Action

Interval Scale

In Table 9.2, a respondent's preferences for the 10 brands in the jeans study are expressed on a 7-point rating scale. We can see that although Gap received a preference rating of 6 and Wrangler a rating of 2, this does not mean that Gap is preferred three times as much as Wrangler. When the ratings are transformed to an equivalent 11 to 17 scale by adding 10 (next column), the ratings for these brands become 16 (6 + 10) and 12 (2 + 10), and the ratio is no longer 3 to 1. This example becomes clearer when you realize that an interval scale has an arbitrary origin or zero point.

Ratio Scale

A **ratio scale** possesses all the properties of the nominal, ordinal, and interval scales. In addition, a zero point is specified; that is, the origin of the scale is fixed. Thus, ratio scales possess the characteristic of origin (and distance, order, and description). When measurement is taken using ratio scales, the researcher can identify or classify objects, rank the objects, and compare intervals or differences. Unlike interval data, it is meaningful to compute ratios of scale values. Not only is the difference between 2 and 5 the same as the difference between 14 and 17, but 14 is seven times as large as 2 in an absolute sense. Common examples of ratio scales include height, weight, age, and income. In marketing, sales, costs, market share, and number of customers are variables measured on a ratio scale. In the opening vignette, ratio data would be obtained if the teenagers were asked to state the amount of time they spent watching each sport on TV during the Olympics.

Ratio scales can be transformed using proportions. The transformation formula is $y = bx$, where b is a positive constant. Note that the a of the interval-scale-transformation formula is missing here. One cannot transform a ratio scale by adding an arbitrary constant (a), as in the case of an interval scale. An example of a ratio transformation is provided by the conversion of yards to feet ($b = 3$). Comparisons between measurements are identical, whether made in yards or feet.

All statistical techniques can be applied to ratio data. These include specialized statistics, such as the geometric mean. An illustration of the use of a ratio scale in the context of the jeans example follows.

Research in Action

Ratio Scale

The ratio scale illustrated in Table 9.2 gives the prices of the 10 brands of jeans. Note that because the price of Calvin Klein is $48 and the price of Wrangler is $24, Calvin Klein costs the buyer twice as much as Wrangler. In dollar terms, the zero point is fixed.

A price of zero dollars means that the item is free. Additionally, multiplying these prices by 100 to convert dollars to cents results in an equivalent scale, illustrating the fact that the ratio scale has an absolute zero or a fixed origin.

Be an MR!	Be a DM!

Coaching Consumer Preferences for Coach

Visit www.coach.com and search the Internet—including social media—as well as your library's online databases to obtain information on consumer preferences for leather goods. How would you use interval and ratio scales to measure consumer preferences for leather goods?

As the marketing director for Coach, how would you use information on consumer preferences for leather goods to increase your market share?

Social Media

Selecting a Level of Measurement

A variable of interest can be measured using different types of primary scales. We illustrate this in the context of measuring annual household income.

Nominal Scale

In the past year, who made a contribution to your household income?

1. Male head of the household
2. Female head of the household
3. Both male and female head of the household

Ordinal Scale

In the past year, what was your annual household income before taxes?

1. Less than $20,001
2. $20,001 to $50,000
3. $50,001 to $100,000
4. $100,001 to $150,000
5. More than $150,000

Interval Scale

In the past year, what was your annual household income before taxes?

Much Below Average			Average		Much Above Average	
1	2	3	4	5	6	7

Ratio Scale

In the past year, what was your annual household income before taxes? $ _____

Which type of primary scale should be selected to measure the variable of interest (i.e., income)? The amount of information obtained increases from nominal to ordinal to interval to ratio scale. However, the cognitive load imposed on the respondents while obtaining information also increases in that order. So a trade-off has to be made. The general rule is to select the lowest level of measurement that will enable the researcher to obtain the needed information and conduct the appropriate statistical analyses. Suppose the researcher is merely interested in cross-tabulating the level of income with consumer purchases to see if the level of income has an effect on the amount purchased. To meet this objective, measuring income at an ordinal level would be sufficient. More than one type of primary scale is used in a typical survey, as the following example illustrates.

Research in Action

Primary Scales in Online Surveys

CustomInsight (www.custominsight.com) provides Web-based survey software and tools that make creating and deploying online surveys quick and painless. CustomInsight's software guides users through the creation of surveys and allows for the use of all of the scales of measurement. Surveys can easily be designed for employee or customer satisfaction, group feedback, organizational effectiveness, and various other applications. A sample employee satisfaction survey includes questions using the following measurement scales:

1. Job function: nominal scale

2. Employee level: nominal scale

3. Years of service: ratio scale

4. Empowerment assessment: interval scale

5. Compensation assessment: interval scale

6. Ranking of management efficiency: ordinal scale

Surveys of this type have been used to develop better human resource programs to attract and retain the best employees.

A Classification of Scaling Techniques

comparative scales
Scaling techniques in which there is direct comparison of stimulus objects with one another.

The scaling techniques commonly used in marketing research can be classified into comparative and noncomparative scales (see Figure 9.6). **Comparative scales** involve the direct comparison of two or more objects. For example, respondents might be asked whether they prefer Coke or Pepsi. A comparative scale gives the marketer data that measure relative differences. It has only ordinal or rank order properties.

Comparative scaling is sometimes referred to as nonmetric scaling. The opening vignette presented an example of comparative scaling when the different sports were ranked in terms of the percentage of respondents mentioning each sport as their favorite. The resulting ordinal scale presented a relative comparison of all the sports. As Figure 9.6 illustrates, comparative scales include paired comparisons, rank order, and constant sum scales.

The major benefit of comparative scaling is that small differences between objects under study can be detected. The comparison process forces respondents to choose between two objects. Respondents asked to perform a ranking task bring the same point of reference to the task. This makes comparative scales easy to understand and apply. They also tend to reduce halo or carryover effects in which early judgments influence later judgments. The major disadvantage of comparative scales is the limitation in terms of analyzing ordinal data. In addition, it is not possible to generalize beyond the objects under study. For instance, say a study was done to

FIGURE 9.6

A Classification of Scaling Techniques

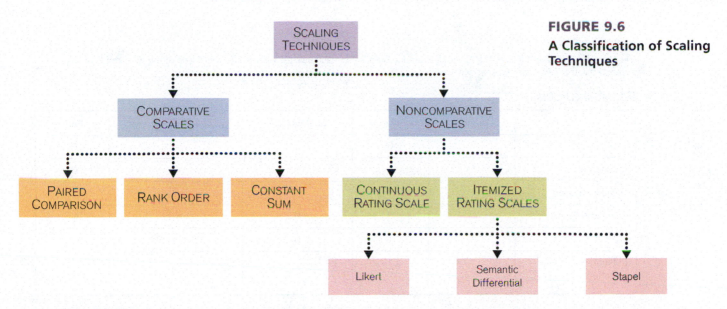

compare Coke and Pepsi. If later these brands were to be compared to RC Cola, the researcher would have to do a new study. These disadvantages are substantially overcome by noncomparative scaling techniques.

In **noncomparative scales**, also referred to as *monadic* or *metric* scales, objects are scaled independently of each other. The resulting data are generally assumed to be interval scaled. For example, respondents might be asked to evaluate Coke on a 1-to-7 preference scale (1 = not at all preferred, 7 = greatly preferred). Similar evaluations would be obtained for Pepsi and RC Cola. In the opening vignette, the use of noncomparative scaling would involve respondents rating each sport, taken by itself, on a 1-to-7 preference scale. As Figure 9.6 illustrates, noncomparative scales comprise continuous rating or itemized rating scales. The itemized rating scales can be further classified as Likert, semantic differential, or Stapel scales.

Noncomparative scaling techniques are the most widely used scaling in marketing research. Chapter 10 is devoted to noncomparative scaling. The rest of this chapter focuses on comparative scaling techniques.

noncomparative scales
Scaling techniques in which each stimulus object is scaled independently of the others.

Comparative Scaling Techniques

We describe the main comparative scaling techniques consisting of paired comparison, rank order, and constant sum scaling (see Figure 9.6).

Paired Comparison Scaling

As its name implies, in **paired comparison scaling** a respondent is presented with a pair of alternatives and asked to select one based on some criterion (see Figure 9.7). Data obtained in this way are ordinal in nature. A consumer involved in a paired comparison study might state that she shops in JC Penney more than in Sears, likes Total cereal better than Kellogg's Product 19, or likes Crest toothpaste more than Colgate. Paired comparison scales are frequently used when the research involves physical products. Coca-Cola is reported to have conducted more than 190,000 paired comparisons before introducing New Coke. Paired comparison scaling is the most widely used comparative scaling technique.

Paired comparison scaling is useful when the number of brands under consideration is limited to no more than five. When a large number of brands is involved, the number of comparisons becomes unwieldy. For example, to evaluate the 10 brands of jeans in Table 9.2, 45 paired comparisons would be involved. The order in which the alternatives are presented might bias the results. Also problematic is the fact that paired comparisons bear little resemblance to the marketplace situation, which involves selection from multiple alternatives. Respondents might prefer one alternative to another; however, that does not imply that they like it in an absolute sense. The GlaxoSmithKline example provides further insights into paired comparison scaling.

paired comparison scaling
A comparative scaling technique in which a respondent is presented with two objects at a time and asked to select one object in the pair according to some criterion. The data obtained are ordinal in nature.

INSTRUCTIONS

We are going to present you with 10 pairs of shampoo brands. For each pair, please indicate which one of the two brands of shampoo in the pair you would prefer for personal use.

RECORDING FORM

	Jhirmack	Finesse	Vidal Sassoon	Head & Shoulders	Pert
Jhirmack		0	0	1	0
Finesse	1[a]		0	1	0
Vidal Sassoon	1	1		1	1
Head & Shoulders	0	0	0		0
Pert	1	1	0	1	
Number of times preferred	3[b]	2	0	4	1

[a] A "1" in a particular box means that the brand in that column was preferred over the brand in the corresponding row. A "0" means that the row brand was preferred over the column brand.

[b] The number of times a brand was preferred is obtained by summing the 1s in each column.

FIGURE 9.7

Paired Comparison Scaling

Research in Action

Looking Good: Dietary Supplements Versus Prescription Weight Loss Drugs

GlaxoSmithKline Consumer Healthcare, maker of over-the-counter weight loss drug Alli, sponsored a study to explore consumer perceptions and experiences with dietary supplements for weight loss. The research was conducted between November 18, 2009, and January 10, 2010, using random-digit dialing that reached 12,599 households. A sample of 3,500 people completed the telephone interview (for a response rate of 27.8%). The respondents were asked a variety of questions about their beliefs and opinions about the safety and effectiveness of weight loss products. Paired comparison scaling was used to obtain respondents' opinions and attitudes about the relative safety and effectiveness of dietary supplements, prescription weight loss drugs, and over-the-counter weight loss drugs.

The research had some interesting findings. Comparative ratings between dietary supplements (for weight loss treatment) and prescription weight loss drugs found that respondents considered supplements to be safer but less effective than the prescription drugs. Also, African Americans (50%) and Hispanics (49%) were more likely than Caucasians (36%) to believe that dietary supplements were safer relative to over-the-counter weight loss drugs or relative to prescription weight loss drugs. The survey, being ordinal in nature, could not determine the magnitude of such perceptions. However, the research was revealing in that it suggests that many adults are confused about the safety and regulation of dietary supplements for weight loss. As another example, more than 60 percent of the 1,444 respondents who had made significant efforts to lose weight mistakenly said that such supplements have been tested and are proven to be safe (65%) and effective (63%); and more than half (54%)

mistakenly believe that these products are approved by the U.S. Food and Drug Administration (FDA).

GlaxoSmithKline used the results of the survey to point to the importance of and need for accurate information on the best programs and products to help people achieve their weight loss goals. As part of its corporate social responsibility, the company launched educational programs about the benefits and risks associated with the myriad of weight loss products available.[2]

Source: Jeff J Mitchell/Getty Images.

Experiential Learning

Which Is It? Coke or Pepsi

Which cola drink would be the most popular among your friends in a taste test? Download the Kit Kat Taste Test from the Web site of this textbook and use it as a guide to develop a script for testing for preference between two cola drinks: Coke and Pepsi. Make sure the drinks are chilled to the same temperature and poured into three groups of identical cups. Each person will select a cup from the first group, taste the cola, eat a cracker, and take a swallow of water. Repeat this when tasting from the second and third groups. (The first group might be Pepsi, the second group Coke, and the third group Pepsi.) After tasting from each of the three cola sample groups, have the respondents complete the survey form you created. To avoid a biasing effect from the order of presentation of the samples, it will be important for half of the respondents to have

a rotated order of presentation: The first group Coke, the second group Pepsi, and the third group Coke. Conduct the taste test on 30 respondents/students.

1. How many respondents correctly identified the two identical samples of cola?

2. Of those who correctly identified the two identical samples of cola, which cola was preferred: Coke or Pepsi?

3. Of those who correctly identified the two identical samples of cola, how many had no preference between Coke and Pepsi?

4. In sum, who would you say is the winner in your taste test: Coke or Pepsi? Or, is it too close to tell?

Rank Order Scaling

After paired comparisons, the most popular comparative scaling technique is rank order scaling. In **rank order scaling**, respondents are simultaneously presented with several alternatives and asked to rank them according to some criterion (see Figure 9.8).

For example, consumers might be asked to rank brands of jeans according to overall preference, as in Table 9.2. These rankings typically are obtained by asking the respondents to assign a rank of 1 to the most preferred brand, 2 to the second most preferred, and so on, until each alternative is ranked down to the least preferred brand. Like paired comparison, this approach is also comparative in nature. However, it is possible that even the brand ranked 1 is not liked in an absolute sense; that is, it might be the least disliked. Rank order scaling also results in ordinal data. See Table 9.2, which uses rank order data to derive an ordinal scale.

Rank order scaling often is used to measure preferences among brands as well as among brand attributes. Rank order scaling forces the respondent to discriminate among alternatives. This type of scaling process comes closer to resembling the shopping environment. It also takes less time than paired comparisons. Another advantage is that it is easily understood, and the results are easy to communicate. The opening vignette showed that the Olympic games are the

rank order scaling
A comparative scaling technique in which respondents are presented with several objects simultaneously and asked to order or rank them according to some criterion.

FIGURE 9.8
Rank Order Scaling

INSTRUCTIONS
Rank the various brands of toothpaste in order of preference. Begin by picking out the one brand that you like most and assign it a rank "1." Then, find the second most preferred brand and assign it a rank "2." Continue this procedure until you have ranked all the brands of toothpaste in order of preference. The least preferred brand should be assigned a rank of "10."

No two brands should receive the same rank number.

The criterion of preference is entirely up to you. There is no right or wrong answer. Just try to be consistent.

BRAND	RANK ORDER
1. Crest	_____
2. Colgate	_____
3. Aim	_____
4. Mentadent	_____
5. Macleans	_____
6. Ultra Brite	_____
7. Close Up	_____
8. Pepsodent	_____
9. Plus White	_____
10. Stripe	_____

single most popular (ranked number one) sporting venue among teenage boys and girls, with basketball as teens' overall favorite spectator sport around the globe. These results are easy to communicate. The major disadvantage of this technique is that it produces only ordinal level data.

Research in Action

The World's Top Football Nations

According to The Fédération Internationale de Football Association (FIFA), as of March 9, 2011, the world's top ranked nation in football (known as soccer in the US) is Spain. A ranking of the top 8 countries follows.

Such information is very helpful to global marketers like Adidas, which advertise using endorsements from soccer stars and teams.[3]

Rank	Country	Points
1	Spain	1880
2	Netherlands	1730
3	Germany	1486
4	Argentina	1412
5	Brazil	1411
6	England	1212
7	Uruguay	1172
8	Croatia	1071

Source: www.fifa.com. Used with permission.

Constant Sum Scaling

constant sum scaling
A comparative scaling technique in which respondents are required to allocate a constant sum of units, such as points, dollars, chits, stickers, or chips, among a set of stimulus objects with respect to some criterion.

In **constant sum scaling**, respondents allocate a constant sum of units, such as points, dollars, or chips, among a set of alternatives according to some specified criterion. Respondents might be asked, for example, to allocate 100 points to eight attributes of bath soap (see Figure 9.9).

The points are allocated to represent the importance attached to each attribute. If an attribute is unimportant, the respondent assigns it zero points. If an attribute is twice as important as some other attribute, the respondent assigns it twice as many points. All the points a respondent assigns must total 100. Hence, the name of the scale: constant sum. A constant sum scale also results whenever percentages are calculated, as in the opening vignette.

Note that the constant sum scale has an absolute zero—10 points are twice as many as 5 points, and the difference between 5 and 2 points is the same as the difference between 57 and 54 points. For this reason, constant sum scale data are sometimes treated as metric. Although this

FIGURE 9.9
Constant Sum Scaling

INSTRUCTIONS
Below are eight attributes of bathing soaps. Please allocate 100 points among the attributes so that your allocation reflects the relative importance you attach to each attribute. The more points an attribute receives, the more important the attribute is. If an attribute is not at all important, assign it zero points. If an attribute is twice as important as some other attribute, it should receive twice as many points.

FORM

AVERAGE RESPONSES OF THREE SEGMENTS			
Attribute	Segment I	Segment II	Segment III
1. Mildness	8	2	4
2. Lather	2	4	17
3. Shrinkage	3	9	7
4. Price	53	17	9
5. Fragrance	9	0	19
6. Packaging	7	5	9
7. Moisturizing	5	3	20
8. Cleaning Power	13	60	15
Sum	100	100	100

might be appropriate in the limited context of the objects scaled, these results are not generalizable or applicable to other objects not included in the study. Hence, strictly speaking, the constant sum should be considered an ordinal scale.

The main advantages of the constant sum scale are that it allows for fine discrimination among alternatives and does not require too much time. However, it has one major disadvantage: Respondents can allocate more or fewer units than those specified. For example, a respondent might allocate 108 or 94 points. If this occurs, the researcher must adjust the data to sum to 100 points or eliminate that respondent from analysis.

Constant sum scales in the form of percentages often are used to present research results. In the opening vignette, the popularity of a spectator sport was measured in terms of the percentage of respondents who reported it as their favorite. As another example, consider the following.

Research in Action

The Malling of America

The number of malls and shopping centers dotting the U.S. landscape in 2011 exceeded 90,000. California had the highest number of shopping centers, followed by Florida, Texas, and Illinois. According to a recent Maritz Ameri-Poll, visiting the local mall has become part of the American lifestyle. The results of this poll indicated that, on average, 23 percent of adults make less than one trip per month, while 40 percent of adults shop at a mall one or two times per month. Another 20 percent shop three or four times per month, and 10 percent make five to seven trips. "Born to shop" is the description applied to people who average eight or more trips each month. According to this poll, 7 percent of the population is "born to shop."

Information conveyed as percentages is an illustration of a constant sum scale. Department store chains use this type of information in planning the number of store locations in malls.

The 23 percent who shop less than once per month represent a segment that needs to be penetrated.[4]

Source: Losevsky Pavel/Shutterstock.

Be a DM!	Be an MR!
Lexus: Luminescence of Luxury	
As the marketing manager for Lexus, how would you use information on consumer purchase intentions for luxury cars to increase your sales?	Visit www.lexus.com and search the Internet—including social media—as well as your library's online databases to obtain information on consumer purchase intentions for luxury cars. Would you use a comparative scaling technique to measure consumer purchase intentions for luxury cars? If yes, which technique?

Social Media

Relationship of Measurement and Scaling to the Marketing Research Process

The relationship of measurement and scaling to the previous and subsequent steps of the marketing research process is described in Figure 9.10. The marketing research problem is defined in Step 1. Based on this definition, an approach to the problem is developed (Step 2). An important component of the approach is specifying the information needed to address the marketing research problem. Measurement and scaling are part of the research design (Step 3). The researcher must identify an appropriate level of measurement (nominal, ordinal, interval, or ratio) for each item of information needed. If the measurement level is ordinal, the researcher generally selects one of the comparative techniques (paired comparison, rank order, or constant sum). If the data are interval, the researcher selects one of the noncomparative techniques (continuous or itemized rating scale: Likert, semantic differential, or Stapel).

FIGURE 9.10

Relationship of Measurement and Scaling to the Marketing Research Process

Likewise, the researcher must select an appropriate scale for an information item that is to be measured on a nominal or ratio level. When designing a questionnaire, also part of the research design (Step 3), the researcher must translate the information needed to appropriate questions using the identified scales. While conducting fieldwork (Step 4), the questions should be administered by the interviewer, the computer, or self-administered by the respondent using the appropriate scales identified by the researcher. When analyzing the data (Step 5), the researcher should use only those statistical techniques that are compatible with the measurement level of the data. For example, regression analysis, discussed in Chapter 18, assumes that the dependent variable is measured using an interval or ratio scale. Thus, regression analysis should not be used when the data have been measured on an ordinal level. Finally, in Step 6, the report should discuss the statistical results and the findings in light of the scales used to measure the variables.

Summary Illustration Using the Opening Vignette

The fundamental scale characteristics are description, order, distance, and origin. Description means that unique labels or descriptors are used to designate each value of the scale. Order means the relative sizes or positions of the descriptors. Order is denoted by descriptors such as *greater than, less than,* and *equal to.* The characteristic of distance means that absolute differences between the scale descriptors are known and can be expressed in units. The origin characteristic means that the scale has a unique or fixed beginning or true zero point. Description is the most basic characteristic that is present in all scales. If a scale has order, it also has description. If a scale has distance, it also has order and description. Finally, a scale that has origin also has distance, order, and description.

The four primary scales of measurement are nominal, ordinal, interval, and ratio. Of these, the nominal scale is the most basic. The numbers are used only for identifying or classifying objects under study. In the opening vignette, numbers could be used to denote the various spectator sports: 1. tennis, 2. hockey, 3. soccer, 4. basketball, and so forth. Although soccer is identified by the number 3 and basketball by the number 4, this does not mean that soccer is either more or less preferred to basketball. In the ordinal scale, the numbers indicate the relative position of the objects, but not the magnitude of difference between them. The ranking of the various sports, with basketball at the top, constitutes an ordinal scale. The interval scale permits a comparison of the differences between the objects. However, it has an arbitrary zero point. Therefore, it is not meaningful to calculate ratios of scale values on an interval scale. Preference ratings for the various spectator sports on a 7-point scale (1 = Not so preferred, 7 = Greatly preferred) would be an interval scale.

Alternatively, this preference scale could go from –3 to +3. The latter scale can be derived from the former by subtracting 4 from each scale unit. The ratio scale in which the zero point is fixed represents the highest level of measurement. The researcher can compute ratios of scale values using this scale. The ratio scale incorporates all the properties of the lower-level scales: nominal, ordinal, and interval. Time or money spent watching each sport would be examples of ratio scales.

Scaling techniques can be classified as comparative or noncomparative. Comparative scaling involves a direct comparison of alternatives. The opening vignette presented an example of comparative scaling when the different sports were ranked in terms of the percentage of respondents mentioning each sport as their favorite. The resulting scale presented a relative comparison of all the sports. In noncomparative scaling, objects are evaluated individually, one at a time. In the opening vignette, the use of noncomparative scaling would involve respondents rating each sport, taken by itself, on a 1-to-7 preference scale. Comparative scales include paired comparisons, rank order, and constant sum. The data obtained by these procedures have only ordinal properties. The opening vignette illustrates the use of rank order scaling by ranking basketball at the top. Figure 9.11 gives a concept map for primary scales. In this figure, the major concepts are connected by bold arrows using descriptors. Thus, primary scales used to identify and classify objects are nominal scales. Each major concept is described by minor concepts that are connected to that major concept by lines with descriptors. Thus, permissible statistics for nominal scales are percentages and mode. The rest of the figure can be interpreted similarly.

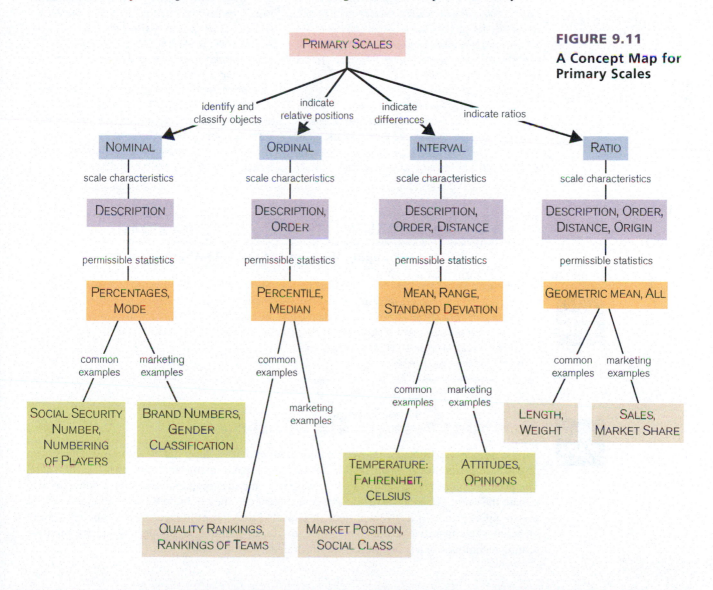

FIGURE 9.11

A Concept Map for Primary Scales

International Marketing Research

The higher levels of education and product experience of respondents in many developed countries enable them to provide responses on interval and ratio scales. In some developing countries, the respondents might have difficulty expressing their opinions in a fashion required by interval and ratio scales. Therefore, consumer preferences in these types of countries are best measured with ordinal scales. In particular, dichotomous scales (such as preferred/not preferred), the simplest type of ordinal scale, are recommended. For example, when measuring preferences for jeans in the United States, Levi Strauss could ask consumers to rate their preferences for wearing jeans on specified occasions using a 7-point interval scale. Consumers in the United States have experience with jeans, which should lead to a wide range of preference levels. However, consumers in rural Papua, New Guinea, could be shown a pair of jeans and simply asked whether they would prefer to wear them for a specific occasion (e.g., when shopping, working, relaxing on a holiday, and so on). In Japan, it is best to use a 100-point scale for measuring performance, because the Japanese commonly use this scale for such purposes. The advantage of matching the primary scales to the profile of the target respondents is well illustrated by the Japanese survey of automobile preferences in Europe.

Research in Action

Car War—Japan Making a Spearhead

Nissan (www.nissan-global.com) formed an alliance with Renault, SA, and was 44.3 percent owned by Renault as of 2011. Recently, European journalists gave their car-of-the-year award to a Japanese model—Nissan's new British-made Micra, a $10,000 subcompact. This came as a blow to European automakers, who had been trying to keep the Japanese off the continent. "They will change the competitive balance," warned Bruce Blythe, Ford of Europe's head of business strategy.

How did the Japanese do it?

Nissan conducted a survey of European consumers' automobiles preferences. Nissan used interval scales to capture the range of differences in preference. For instance, consumers were asked to rate the popular automobile brands and features in terms of preference, using a 7-point scale, with 1 = not at all preferred and 7 = greatly

preferred. The data derived from these interval scales enabled Nissan to compare the differences between automobile brands and features and determine which features were preferred for what brands. The findings revealed distinct consumer preferences. The cars were redesigned to meet consumer preferences and needs.

Nissan also benefited by setting up production plants in Europe to customize its cars to local styling tastes and preferences. On June 29, 2010, the Nissan LEAF became the first electric vehicle to charge up at Portugal's first charging station, which was unveiled to the public. By 2011, the Japanese were producing more than 1 million cars a year in Europe, 75 percent of them in Britain. With a strong focus on consumer preferences measured via interval scales, the Japanese are taking away market share from European manufacturers in the European markets.[5]

Be an MR!	Be a DM!

Plugging the Gap in Casual Clothing

Social Media

Visit www.gap.com and search the Internet—including social media—as well as your library's online databases to obtain information on consumer preferences for casual clothing. Which comparative scaling technique(s) would you use to measure consumer preferences for casual clothing in the United States and in rural Nigeria?

As the marketing manager for Gap, how would you use information on consumer preferences for casual clothing to increase your sales?

Social Media

Marketing Research and Social Media

All the primary scales and all the comparative scales that we have discussed in this chapter can be easily implemented in social media. No additional requirements are imposed by social media. The principles underlying scaling and measurement and the comparative scaling techniques also remain the same. An analysis of social media content can shed light on the level of measurement that is appropriate in a given project. It can also provide guidance on the type of scaling techniques, comparative or noncomparative, to use. In addition, it is convenient to use multiple scaling techniques in a given project, as illustrated by Kraft Foods.

Research in Action

Kraft Uses Primary Type of Scales to Craft a Primary Product

Communispace (www.communispace.com), based in Watertown, Massachusetts, is a research company that specializes in creating private communities of customers and prospects who provide feedback on all kinds of issues. It helped Kraft Foods (www.kraftfoodscompany.com) to conceive and launch its successful line of Nabisco 100 Calorie Packs. Dialogue with customers on Kraft's community network revealed important insights, such as people who want to lose weight valued portion control more than they valued special low-cal ingredients. Communispace used ordinal scales to narrow the domain of discussion by asking community members to rank-order the identified issues. The research company then made use of interval and ratio scales to determine factors like maximum fat and calorie count and the type of snacks to produce. It then distributed samples and showed prototype advertising to the group. Again, interval and ordinal scales were used to obtain feedback. As a result, the Nabisco 100 calorie snack line was conceived and successfully introduced into the marketplace. The items in the line of 100-calorie packs were also determined based on feedback from community members and range from crackers to cookies to candy-covered cookie bits. The new product line rang up $100 million in sales in the first year and, as of 2011, has assumed primary importance in Kraft's snack line.[6]

Finally, some specific measures have been developed to evaluate social media sites based on information that is publicly available. The more commonly used measures include longevity, output (frequency, quantity), inbound links, technorati, bloglines or blogpulse rankings, number of friends or followers, number of comments, and media citations.

Experiential Learning

Qualtrics Question Library and Corresponding Scales

Access to Qualtrics is included with this book. Use the Qualtrics question library to electronically develop the following scales.

1. Gender measured on a nominal scale
2. Age measured on an ordinal scale
3. Age measured on a ratio scale
4. Income measured on an ordinal scale

Design your own question to measure income on an interval scale.

Ethics in Marketing Research

It is the researcher's responsibility to use the appropriate scales to obtain the necessary data to answer the research questions and test the hypotheses. Take, for example, a study Lenovo initiated to measure and explain consumer preferences for different brands of computers (Lenovo, HP, Acer, Gateway, NEC, Apple, and Dell). One way to gain information on consumers' preferences would be to give each respondent several cards, each listing one computer brand. The respondent then ranks the brands (cards) in order of preference. The respondent selects the card for the most preferred brand first, followed by the card for the second most preferred brand, third most preferred brand, and so on, until, last of all, the card for the least preferred brand is selected. This results in ordinal data. Although it will provide rich insight into brand preference by allowing respondents to compare the cards, shuffle them, compare again, and reshuffle, these data cannot be analyzed using popular statistical techniques. To explain preferences for computer brands in terms of the relevant attributes, interval scale data are needed.

Knowingly using inappropriate scales raises ethical questions. It is the obligation of the researcher to obtain the data that are most appropriate given the research questions, as the following example illustrates.

Research in Action

Scaling Ethical Dilemmas

In a study designed to measure ethical judgments of male and female marketing researchers, scale items from a previously developed and tested scale were used. However, after a pretest was conducted on a convenience sample of 65 marketing professionals, it became apparent that some original scale items were worded in a way that did not reflect current usage. Therefore, these items were updated. For example, an item that was gender specific, such as, "He pointed out that . . ." was altered to read, "The project manager pointed out that. . . ."

(continued)

Respondents were asked to show their approval or disapproval of the stated action of a marketing research director with regard to specific ethical dilemmas using the scenario approach. Realizing that a binary or dichotomous scale (disapprove/approve) would be too restrictive, approval or disapproval was indicated by having respondents supply interval level data via 5-point scales with descriptive labels of 1 = Disapprove, 2 = Disapprove somewhat, 3 = Neither approve or disapprove, 4 = Approve somewhat, and 5 = Approve. The results revealed some differences, and female marketing researchers were found to be more ethical than their male counterparts. These differences probably would not have been discovered if the original dichotomous scale (approve, disapprove) had been used. However, the finer discrimination afforded by the 5-point interval scale enabled the researcher to discover these differences. This example illustrates the use of appropriate scaling techniques in examining ethical issues in marketing research.[7]

WHAT WOULD YOU DO?

New Balance: Attaining a Balance in Marketing Strategy

The Situation

The U.S. athletic footwear market is likely to grow slowly from 2010 to 2015, according to a recently published report from Mintel International. This is due to factors such as overly complex manufacturer–retailer relationships that sap brand loyalty and foster excessive bargain hunting, a slow-growth economy, and competition from brown shoe manufacturers, as the previously distinct line between athletic and brown shoes becomes blurred. In addition, weak retail pricing is likely to lead to more of a two-tier market—(1) an upscale shoe market for those most dedicated to athletic shoes (young males) and those with higher levels of discretionary income and (2) a mass market for the rest of the nation. One bright spot revealed by Mintel's consumer research is that respondents overwhelmingly agree that they are willing to "spend money on good sneakers."

Jim Davis, chair of New Balance Athletic Shoe, Inc., is trying to appeal to those consumers identified in Mintel's research. New Balance rose quickly, starting in the mid-1990s to become the third-largest seller of athletic shoes. Its strategy mirrored Nike's in launching the largest possible number of shoe styles and selling primarily through specialty athletic shoe stores and sporting goods stores. A big difference, however, was that New Balance created an upscale brand image that aimed to attract a greater number of 35- to 64-year-olds. Times are changing, however, and New Balance is learning that it must also change to keep improving its market growth and profits.

The Marketing Research Decision

1. New Balance would like to determine consumer preferences for its brand as compared to Nike, Reebok, and Adidas. Which scaling technique should be used?
   a. Paired comparison
   b. Rank order
   c. Constant sum
   d. Continuous rating scales
   e. Itemized rating scales

2. Discuss the role of the type of scaling technique you recommend in enabling Jim Davis to determine consumer preferences for New Balance as compared to Nike, Reebok, and Adidas and increase the market share of New Balance.

The Marketing Management Decision

1. In order to increase the market share of New Balance, Jim Davis should:
   a. Use celebrity endorsements.
   b. Introduce lower-priced shoes.
   c. Enhance the style and color of shoes.
   d. Increase the promotional budget.
   e. Sell New Balance shoes on the Internet.

2. Discuss how the marketing management-decision action that you recommend to Jim Davis is influenced by the scaling technique that you suggested earlier and by the findings of that research.

What Jim Davis Did

Rather than use endorsements, New Balance looked at sponsorships and promotions as a way to gain notoriety for its product. Some of the events included the Chicago Marathon, the title sponsorship for the national indoor track and field championships in New York, various walking organizations, and the U.S. modern pentathlon team. Along the promotional aspect, the company offered The Million Dollar Challenge, a 7-figure prize to the man or woman who broke existing U.S. marathon records. Also, its sponsorship of the Race For the Cure, in partnership with Susan G. Komen (www.komen.org), has raised money and awareness of New Balance among women.

To continue its success, New Balance added style and color to its already available models, but not enough to lose integrity with old customers. This helped New Balance attract new consumers while maintaining the old ones. New Balance also is planning to boost media spending. Most of the increase is allotted for television advertising of men's running and cross-training shoes. New Balance also will run print ads accenting men's and women's running shoes and women's walking shoes, focusing on the Baby-Boomer crowd. In addition, New Balance is looking at other market opportunities, such as lower price points, that would best be accomplished under a different brand name.[8]

Source: Handout/MCT/Newscom.

Summary

Measurement is the assignment of numbers or other symbols to characteristics of objects according to set rules. Scaling involves the generation of a continuum upon which measured objects are located. The fundamental scale characteristics are description, order, distance, and origin. Description means the unique labels or descriptors that are used to designate each value of the scale. Order means the relative sizes or positions of the descriptors. Order is denoted by descriptors such as *greater than, less than,* and *equal to.* The characteristic of distance means that absolute differences between the scale descriptors are known and can be expressed in units. The origin characteristic means that the scale has a unique or fixed beginning or true zero point. Description is the most basic characteristic that is present in every scale. If a scale has order, it also has description. If a scale has distance, it also has order and description. Finally, a scale that has origin also has distance, order, and description.

The four primary scales of measurement are nominal, ordinal, interval, and ratio. Of these, the nominal scale is the most basic and possesses only the description characteristic. The numbers are used only for identifying or classifying the objects under study. In the ordinal scale, the numbers indicate the relative position of the objects but not the magnitude of the difference between them. The ordinal scale possesses description and order characteristics. The interval scale permits a comparison of the differences between the objects and possesses the characteristics of description, order, and distance. However, because it has an arbitrary zero point, it is not meaningful to calculate ratios of scale values on an interval scale. The ratio scale, in which the zero point is fixed, represents the highest level of measurement. The researcher can compute ratios of scale values using this scale. The ratio scale incorporates all the properties of the lower-level scales and possesses all the scale characteristics.

Scaling techniques can be classified as comparative or noncomparative. Comparative scaling involves a direct comparison of alternatives. Comparative scales include paired comparisons, rank order, and constant sum. The data obtained by these procedures have only ordinal properties.

In developed countries, respondents are used to providing responses on interval and ratio scales. However, in developing countries responses are best measured with simple ordinal scales. All of the comparative scales can be implemented in social media. Ethical considerations require that the appropriate type of scales be used in order to get the information needed to answer the research questions and test the hypotheses.

Key Terms and Concepts

Measurement 246	Origin 248	Comparative scales 256
Scaling 247	Nominal scale 249	Noncomparative scales 257
Description 248	Ordinal scale 252	Paired comparison scaling 257
Order 248	Interval scale 254	Rank order scaling 259
Distance 248	Ratio scale 254	Constant sum scaling 260

Suggested Cases and Video Cases

Running Case with Real Data

1.1 Hewlett-Packard

Comprehensive Critical Thinking Cases

2.1 American Idol   2.2 Baskin-Robbins   2.3 Akron Children's Hospital

Comprehensive Cases with Real Data

3.1 Bank of America   3.2 McDonald's   3.3 Boeing

Comprehensive Brief Harvard Business School Cases

4.1 TruEarth Healthy Foods: Market Research for a New Product Introduction (4065)
4.2 The Springfield Nor'easters: Maximizing Revenues in the Minor Leagues (2510)

4.3 Metabical: Positioning and Communications Strategy for a New Weight-Loss Drug (4240)
4.4 Saxonville Sausage Company (2085)

Online Video Cases

9.1 P&G   11.1 Dunkin' Donuts   13.1 Subaru   19.1 Marriott

Live Research: Conducting a Marketing Research Project

1. As a class, discuss the level of measurement (nominal, ordinal, interval, or ratio) that is appropriate for the key variables.
2. Discuss which, if any, of the comparative techniques are appropriate.
3. Consider the practical constraints. For example, if a certain level of measurement has been used to measure a variable in the past (e.g., ordinal preference), the same level might have to be used again to compare the findings with past results.

Acronyms

The four primary types of scales can be described by the acronym FOUR:

F igurative: nominal scale

O rdinal scale

U nconstrained zero point: interval scale

R atio scale

The different comparative and noncomparative scales can be represented by the acronym SCALES:

S emantic differential scale

C onstant sum scale

A rranged in order: rank order scale

L ikert scale

E ngaged: paired comparison scale

S tapel scale

Review Questions

1. What is measurement?
2. What are the primary scales of measurement?
3. Describe the differences between a nominal and an ordinal scale.
4. What are the implications of having an arbitrary zero point in an interval scale?
5. What are the advantages of a ratio scale over an interval scale? Are these advantages significant?
6. What is a comparative rating scale?
7. What is a paired comparison?
8. What are the advantages and disadvantages of paired comparison scaling?
9. Describe the constant sum scale. How is it different from the other comparative rating scales?
10. **Social Media** Can the primary scales of measurement be implemented in social media? Please explain your reasoning.

Applied Problems

1. Identify the type of scale (nominal, ordinal, interval, or ratio) being used in each of the following. Please explain your reasoning.
    a. I like to solve crossword puzzles.

        Disagree   Agree

            1   2   3   4   5

    b. How old are you? _____

    c. Please rank the following activities in terms of your preference by assigning ranks 1 to 5, with 1 being most preferred and 5 being least preferred.
        i. Reading magazines _____
        ii. Watching television _____
        iii. Dating _____
        iv. Shopping _____
        v. Eating out _____
    d. What is your Social Security number?

e. On an average weekday, how much time do you spend doing your homework and class assignments?
   i. Less than 15 minutes _____
   ii. 15 to 30 minutes _____
   iii. 31 to 60 minutes _____
   iv. 61 to 120 minutes _____
   v. More than 120 minutes_____
f. How much money did you spend last month on entertainment? _____

2. Show how intentions to purchase four brands of soft drinks (Coke, Pepsi, Dr. Pepper, and 7-Up) can be measured using ordinal, interval, and ratio scales.

3. Visit the Web sites of two marketing research firms conducting surveys. Analyze one survey from each firm to critically evaluate the primary type of scales being used.

4. **Social Media** Surf the Internet—including social media—to find two examples of each of the four primary types of scales. Write a report describing the context in which these scales are being used.

5. Search the Internet to identify the top five selling automobile brands during the last calendar year. Rank-order these brands according to sales.

6. Target and Walmart are two of the major department stores. Develop a series of paired comparison scales comparing these two stores on store image characteristics. Identify the relevant store image characteristics by visiting the Web sites of these two stores (www.target.com, www.walmart.com).

Group Discussion

1. "A brand could receive the highest median preference rank on a rank order scale of all the brands considered and still have poor sales." Discuss.

2. Select one of the readings from the notes in this chapter and lead a class discussion.

Hewlett-Packard Running Case

Review the Hewlett-Packard (HP) case, Case 1.1, and questionnaire given toward the end of the book.

1. What primary scales of measurement have been employed in the HP questionnaire? Illustrate each type.

2. Access to Qualtrics is included with this book. What primary scales are available using Qualtrics? How can HP make use of these scales?

3. Use the Qualtrics question library to illustrate the use of rank order and constant sum scales in a customer perception survey by HP.

4. **Social Media** Develop an ordinal scale to measure preferences for HP and two other competing brands in social media.

ONLINE VIDEO CASE 9.1

PROCTER & GAMBLE: Using Marketing Research to Build Brands

Visit **www.pearsonhighered.com/malhotra** to read the video case and view the accompanying video. Procter & Gamble: Using Marketing Research to Build Brands presents P&G's strong culture of understanding its consumers by conducting marketing research and innovating to meet their needs and desires. The case can be used to illustrate the use of the primary type of scales in measuring consumer preferences for toothpaste and diaper brands. Specific marketing research questions on this and the previous chapters are posed in the video case.

10 Measurement and Scaling: Noncomparative Scaling Techniques

Source: © AF archive/Alamy Images.

LEARNING OBJECTIVES

After reading this chapter, the student should be able to:

1. Understand how noncomparative scaling techniques differ from comparative scaling, and the distinction between continuous and itemized rating scales.

2. Explain the differences among Likert, semantic differential, and Stapel scales.

3. Describe the decisions involved in constructing itemized rating scales, and the options that should be considered.

4. Discuss the evaluation of scales, and the relationship between reliability and validity.

5. Understand the considerations that are important in implementing noncomparative scales in an international setting.

6. **Social Media** Describe the implementation of noncomparative scaling in social media.

7. Discuss the ethical issues involved in developing noncomparative scales.

Noncomparative Scaling Techniques Result in an Incomparable Hit Movie

The entertainment industry regularly conducts market research to determine audience response to new offerings. For example, film studios routinely conduct prerelease screenings in order to gauge audience reaction. One method of measuring audience reaction is electronic continuous measurement. Audience members are each given a dial and are told to continuously rate their reaction to the film while watching it. They simply turn the dial from positive to negative to record their reactions. Because the recording is continuous, audience reaction to every scene can be measured. This method is particularly useful when the size of the audience is 100 or fewer—that is, when the sample size is relatively small.

When the size of the audience is large, a survey questionnaire is administered at the end of each segment of the movie. These surveys generally employ Likert-type scales that are 5-point scales measuring respondents' degree of agreement or disagreement with the specified statements.

The scales are balanced so that they have an equal number of agree and disagree categories. Moreover, the scales have an odd number of categories, generally five, to allow neutral responses, such as neither agree nor disagree, because many respondents might not like or dislike specific scenes. All the scale categories are labeled to reduce ambiguity. A "no opinion" option is not provided, because it is believed that all respondents should be able to express an opinion, having just seen the movie. Sometimes, both electronic continuous measurement and Likert scales are used to allow an assessment of the validity of the scales by comparing responses from the two methods. For example, the following is a statement designed to measure the response to ending scenes:

	Strongly disagree	Disagree	Neither agree nor disagree	Agree	Strongly agree
I like the ending of the movie.	1	2	3	4	5

Audience reaction and response to the original ending of the movie *Fatal Attraction* was the primary reason its original ending was changed. Although the audience liked the movie in general, electronic continuous measurement and survey responses indicated that the ending was poorly received. With the changes, the movie went on to become one of the blockbuster hits of the last two decades. How was the ending changed?

Fatal Attraction has gone down in history as a major romantic/thriller/slasher-style movie. Michael Douglas stars as a caring husband and father who has a very brief affair with his colleague, Glenn Close. Douglas thinks nothing of the affair, but Close becomes obsessed with Douglas and eventually turns into a psychotic. The original ending of this movie made Douglas out as the villain, and Close as the victim. However, test audiences despised Close's character so much that Paramount spent $1.3 million to switch the ending of the movie to make Close the villain and Douglas the victim. *The Hurt Locker* also made extensive use of continuous measurement and Likert-type scales to adapt the movie to audience reactions, and it won the Best Picture for the 82nd Academy Awards in 2010. In addition, *The Hurt Locker* won five other awards, including Best Director for Kathryn Bigelow, the first woman to win an Academy Award for Best Director.[1]

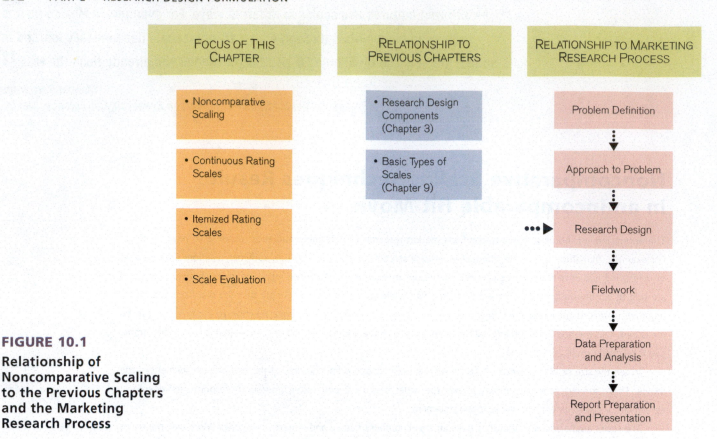

FIGURE 10.1

Relationship of Noncomparative Scaling to the Previous Chapters and the Marketing Research Process

Overview

As discussed in Chapter 9, scaling techniques are classified as either comparative or noncomparative. The comparative techniques discussed in the last chapter consisted of paired comparison, rank order, and constant sum scaling. The subject of this chapter is noncomparative techniques. Figure 10.1 briefly explains the focus of the chapter, the relation of this chapter to the previous ones, and the steps in the marketing research process on which this chapter concentrates.

As discussed in Chapter 9, noncomparative scales are broadly classified as either continuous or itemized. The most popular itemized scales are Likert, semantic differential, and Stapel scales (see Figure 9.6). The opening vignette illustrated the use of both continuous and itemized rating scales to measure audience response to movies prior to release. Continuous scaling was illustrated by the use of handheld dials that the respondents turn while watching the movie. The 5-point Likert scale that was used to measure response to the ending of the movie is an example of an itemized rating scale.

In this chapter, the multi-item rating scales and the importance and meaning of a scale's reliability and validity are briefly described. The chapter also discusses the applications of these scaling techniques in international marketing research, the impact of social media, and several ethical issues that arise in rating-scale construction. Figure 10.2 provides an overview of the topics discussed in this chapter and how they flow from one to the next.

Noncomparative Scaling Techniques

noncomparative scale
One of two types of scaling techniques in which each stimulus object is scaled independently of the other objects in the stimulus set.

A **noncomparative scale** often is called a *monadic scale* because only one object is evaluated at a time. An object is not compared to another object or to some specified ideal, such as "the perfect brand." Respondents using a noncomparative scale apply their own rating standard. This was illustrated in the opening vignette in which the movie *Fatal Attraction* was evaluated

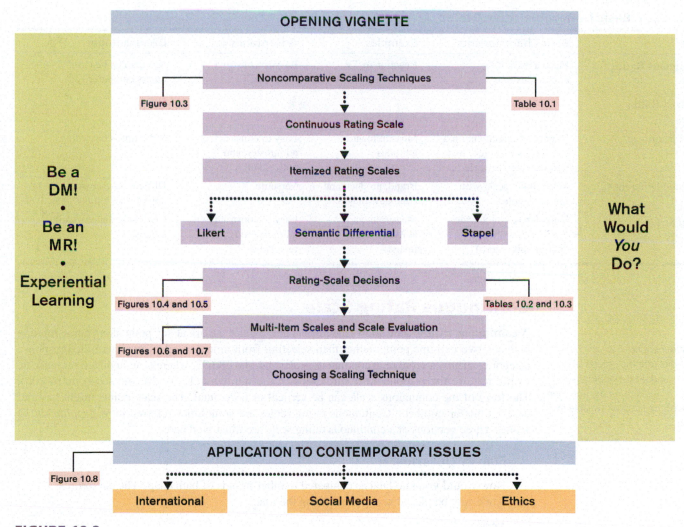

FIGURE 10.2

Noncomparative Scaling Techniques: An Overview

by itself, without comparison to any other movie. The range of noncomparative techniques and their relationship to each other is illustrated in Figure 10.3, which presents a classification of these scales. The basic characteristics of each scale are summarized in Table 10.1 and are discussed later in this chapter. As can be seen from Figure 10.3, noncomparative scales consist of continuous and itemized rating scales. Continuous scales are discussed first followed by itemized scales.

FIGURE 10.3

A Classification of Noncomparative Rating Scales

TABLE 10.1 Basic Noncomparative Scales

Scale	Basic Characteristics	Examples	Advantages	Disadvantages
Continuous Rating Scale	Place a mark on a continuous line	Reaction to TV commercials	Easy to construct	Scoring can be cumbersome unless computerized
Itemized Rating Scales				
Likert Scale	Degree of agreement on a 1 (strongly disagree) to 5 (strongly agree) scale	Measurement of attitudes	Easy to construct, administer, and understand	More time-consuming
Semantic Differential	Seven-point scale with bipolar labels	Brand, product, and company images	Versatile	Difficult to construct appropriate bipolar adjectives
Stapel Scale	Unipolar 10-point scale, −5 to +5, without a neutral point (zero)	Measurement of attitudes and images	Easy to construct and administered over telephone	Confusing and difficult to apply

Continuous Rating Scale

continuous rating scale
A measurement scale in which respondents rate the objects by placing a mark at the appropriate position on a line that runs from one extreme of the criterion variable to the other.

A **continuous rating scale** allows the respondent to place a mark at any point along a line running between two extreme points rather than selecting from among a set of predetermined response categories. Thus, a score on a continuous scale could be 28.637, whereas an itemized rating scale would require the respondent to circle one of the numbers (1, 10, 20, and so on up to 100). The form of the continuous scale can be vertical or horizontal. The scale points might be brief descriptions or numbers. Continuous rating scales are sometimes referred to as *graphic rating scales*. Three versions of a continuous rating scale are illustrated here.

SURVEY QUESTION:

How would you rate Dial as compared to other brands of bath soap? The cursor/tick mark may be placed at any point along the line.

Version 1
Probably   Probably
the worst - - - - - - - | - the best

Version 2
Probably   Probably
the worst - - - - - - | - - - - - - - - - - - - - - - - - - the best
        1 10 20 30 40 50 60 70 80 90 100

Version 3
                Very bad   Neither good   Very good
                                nor bad
Probably   Probably
the worst - - - - - - | - - - - - - - - - - - - - - - - - - the best
        1 10 20 30 40 50 60 70 80 90 100

Once the respondent has provided the ratings or markings on the continuous line, the researcher divides the line into as many categories as desired and assigns scores based on the categories into which the ratings fall. Because the distance between categories is constant and the zero point is arbitrary, this type of scale would produce interval data. Thus, this scale possesses the characteristics of description, order, and distance, as discussed in Chapter 9.

Continuous scales are easy to construct. However, scoring them can be difficult and unreliable unless they are presented on a computer screen, as in computer-assisted personal interviewing or Internet surveys discussed in Chapter 7, or using computerized equipment, as in the opening vignette (see Table 10.1). Continuous rating scales can be easily implemented on the Internet. The cursor can be moved on the screen in a continuous fashion to select the exact position on the scale that best describes the respondent's evaluation. The computer can automatically score the scale values, increasing the speed and accuracy of processing the data.

Continuous scales are being used more frequently as computers, the Internet including social media, and other technologies are used more often in surveys, as illustrated by the opening vignette. Continuous scales are particularly useful for evaluating objects and things, such as movies and TV commercials, continuously over time. An example of a commercial follows.

Research in Action

Scaling Emotional Peaks

The Perception Analyzer® by Dialsmith, LLC (www. perceptionanalyzer. com), is an interactive technology that helps researchers and presenters understand their customers and audiences more clearly. The Perception Analyzer is used around the world to test marketing strategies, advertising campaigns, television programming, political candidates, and public policy issues. Members of focus groups use it to record their emotional response to television commercials, instantly and continuously. Each participant is given a dial and instructed to continuously record his or her reaction to the material being tested. As the respondents turn the dials, the information is fed to a computer. Thus, the researcher can determine the second-by-second response of the respondents as the commercial is run. Furthermore, this response can be superimposed on the commercial to see the respondents' reactions to the various frames and parts of the commercial.

Perception Analyzer was recently used to measure responses to a series of "slice of life" commercials for McDonald's. The researchers found that mothers and daughters had different responses to different aspects of the commercial. Using the emotional-response data, the researchers could determine which commercial had the greatest emotional appeal across mother–daughter segments.[2]

Source: The Perception Analyzer® by Dialsmith, LLC.

Be an MR!	Be a DM!

Developing Hit Movies Is Not a Mickey Mouse Business

Visit www.disney.com and search the Internet—including social media—as well as your library's online databases to obtain information on consumer movie-viewing habits and preferences. How would you measure audience reaction to a new movie slated for release by the Walt Disney Company?	As the marketing director for Disney movies, how would you develop "hit" movies?

Itemized Rating Scales

An **itemized rating scale** has a number of brief descriptions associated with each response category. The categories typically are arranged in some logical order, and the respondents are required to select the categories that best describe their reactions to whatever is being rated, as illustrated in the opening vignette. Itemized rating scales are the most widely used scales in marketing. This section presents the commonly used itemized rating scales—the Likert, semantic differential, and Stapel scales—and examines the major issues surrounding the use of itemized rating scales. All these scales possess the characteristics of description, order, and distance, as discussed in Chapter 9. The data typically are treated as interval because the origin is arbitrary.

itemized rating scale
A measurement scale that has numbers and/or brief descriptions associated with each category. The categories are ordered in terms of scale position.

Likert scale
A measurement scale with five response categories ranging from "strongly disagree" to "strongly agree," which requires the respondents to indicate a degree of agreement or disagreement with each of a series of statements related to the stimulus object.

Likert Scale

Named after its developer, Rensis Likert, the Likert scale is one of the most widely used itemized scales. The end points of a **Likert scale** typically are "strongly disagree" and "strongly agree." The respondents are asked to indicate their degree of agreement by checking one of five response categories. The following example shows how a Likert scale was used in a retailing study.

INSTRUCTIONS

Listed below are different opinions about Macy's. Please indicate how strongly you agree or disagree with each statement by placing an X beside a number from 1 to 5, where:

1 = Strongly disagree
2 = Disagree
3 = Neither agree nor disagree
4 = Agree
5 = Strongly agree

FORM

	Strongly disagree	Disagree	Neither agree nor disagree	Agree	Strongly agree
1. Macy's sells high-quality merchandise.	1	2X	3	4	5
2. Macy's has poor in-store service.	1	2X	3	4	5
3. I like to shop at Macy's.	1	2	3X	4	5
4. Macy's does not offer a good mix of different brands within a product category.	1	2	3	4X	5
5. The credit policies at Macy's are terrible.	1	2	3	4X	5
6. Macy's is where America shops.	1X	2	3	4	5
7. I do not like the advertising done by Macy's.	1	2	3	4X	5
8. Macy's sells a wide variety of merchandise.	1	2	3	4X	5
9. Macy's charges fair prices.	1	2X	3	4	5

When using this approach to determine the total score for each respondent regarding each store, it is important to use a consistent scoring procedure so that a high (or low) score consistently reflects a favorable response. This requires that the categories assigned to the negative statements by the respondents be scored by reversing the scale. Note that for a negative statement, an agreement reflects an unfavorable response, whereas for a positive statement, agreement represents a favorable response. Accordingly, a "strongly agree" response to a favorable statement and a "strongly disagree" response to an unfavorable statement would both receive scores of five.

In the scale shown here, if a higher score is to denote a more favorable attitude, the scoring of items 2, 4, 5, and 7 will be reversed. This can be easily done by subtracting the original scale value from a number that is the highest scale value plus one. Thus, the second item will be scored as follows: $(5 + 1) - 2 = 4$. The respondent in our example has an attitude score of 22. This equals the sum of all nine item scores after scores for the negative items (2, 4, 5, and 7) are reversed. Each respondent's total score for each store is calculated. A respondent will have the most favorable attitude toward the store with the highest score.

The Likert scale has several advantages (see Table 10.1). It is easy for the researcher to construct and administer, and it is easy for the respondent to understand. Therefore, it is suitable for mail, telephone, personal, or electronic interviews. Several versions of the Likert scale that vary the number of scale points (e.g., seven or nine points) as well as the descriptors (e.g., importance, familiarity) and other characteristics discussed later are commonly used in marketing. Consider, for example, a 7-point scale designed to measure the importance of attributes, where 1 = not at all important and 7 = very important.

The major disadvantage of the Likert scale is that it takes longer to complete than other itemized rating scales. Respondents have to read the entire statement rather than a short phrase. Sometimes, it might be difficult to interpret the response to a Likert item, especially if it is an unfavorable statement. In our example, the respondent disagrees with statement number 2 that Macy's has poor in-store service. By reversing the score of this item prior to summing, it is assumed that this respondent would agree with the statement that Macy's has good in-store service. This, however, might not be true; the disagreement merely indicates that the respondent would not make statement number 2. The following example shows another use of a Likert scale in marketing research.

Research in Action

Happiness Is a Ford?

J.D. Power and Associates' (www.jdpa.com) "Automotive Perform-ance, Execution and Layout" (APEAL) survey is based on responses from almost 100,000 new-vehicle owners and measures what excites and delights them about their vehicle's features and design. It comprises eight specific areas of vehicle performance and design, including more than 80 attributes that identify what consumers like and dislike about their new vehicles during the first 90 days of ownership. These areas include the following: vehicle exterior styling; engine and transmission; comfort and convenience; ride, handling, and braking; seats; heating, ventilation, and cooling; cockpit and instrument panel; and sound system.

Carmakers use the results of the J.D. Power survey in advertisements and to check the results of their own consumer satisfaction surveys as well as those of competitors. Thus, they can benchmark their performance.

For the first time since 1997, domestic auto brands, collectively, surpassed import brands as a whole in vehicle appeal, according to the J.D. Power and Associates 2010 Automotive

Performance, Execution and Layout (APEAL) Study.[SM] Ford captured five segment-level awards—more than any other vehicle brand in 2010—for the Expedition, Explorer Sport Trac, Flex, Fusion, and Taurus. Ford used these results in its advertising to convince consumers that its cars are more appealing to own and operate.[3]

Source: © Jim West/Alamy Images.

Semantic Differential Scale

The **semantic differential scale** is a 7-point rating scale on which the end points are adjectives representing opposites. When using a semantic differential, the respondent is typically asked to rate a brand, store, or some other object in terms of these bipolar adjectives, such as "cold" and "warm." This scale is illustrated here by presenting a respondent's evaluation of Macy's on five attributes.

semantic differential scale
A 7-point rating scale with end points associated with bipolar labels that have semantic meaning.

INSTRUCTIONS

This part of the study measures what certain department stores mean to you. We want you to judge the department stores in terms of the following questions. Each question is bounded by bipolar adjectives, which are opposite in meaning. Please mark (X) at the point along the scale that best describes what the store means to you.

Please be sure to mark every scale; do not omit any scale.

FORM

Macy's is:

Powerful	:—:—:—:X:—:—:	Weak
Unreliable	:—:—:—:—:X:—:	Reliable
Modern	:—:—:—:—:—:X:	Old-Fashioned
Cold	:—:—:—:—:X:—:	Warm
Careful	:—:X:—:—:—:—:	Careless

The respondents mark the blanks that best indicate how they would describe the object being rated. Thus, in the Macy's example, Macy's is evaluated as somewhat weak, reliable, very old-fashioned, warm, and careful. To encourage careful consideration of each question, the negative adjective or phrase sometimes appears on the left side of the scale and sometimes on the right. This helps to control the tendency of some respondents, particularly those with very positive or very negative attitudes, to mark the right- or left-hand sides without reading the labels. For an expanded discussion of how to select labels for semantic differential scales, see the referenced work by the author describing the application of this scaling technique to the measurement of self-concepts, person concepts, and product concepts.[4] That scale is described in the following example.

Research in Action

A Semantic Differential Scale for Measuring Self-Concepts, Person Concepts, and Product Concepts

1. Rugged	:—:—:—:—:—:	Delicate	12. Orthodox	:—:—:—:—:—:	Liberal
2. Excitable	:—:—:—:—:—:	Calm	13. Complex	:—:—:—:—:—:	Simple
3. Uncomfortable	:—:—:—:—:—:	Comfortable	14. Colorless	:—:—:—:—:—:	Colorful
4. Dominating	:—:—:—:—:—:	Submissive	15. Modest	:—:—:—:—:—:	Vain
5. Thrifty	:—:—:—:—:—:	Indulgent			
6. Pleasant	:—:—:—:—:—:	Unpleasant			
7. Contemporary	:—:—:—:—:—:	Noncontemporary			
8. Organized	:—:—:—:—:—:	Unorganized			
9. Rational	:—:—:—:—:—:	Emotional			
10. Youthful	:—:—:—:—:—:	Mature			
11. Formal	:—:—:—:—:—:	Informal			

PepsiCo, for example, can make use of such a scale for measuring the self-concept of target consumers, the concept or image of selected celebrities, as well as the concept or image of the Pepsi brand (see Chapter 8 examples). This analysis will help Pepsi determine the brand image that will have the greatest appeal to target consumers. It will also help Pepsi select the right celebrities to endorse the brand so as to achieve the desired image and positioning.

Individual items on a semantic differential scale can be scored on either a -3 to $+3$ or a 1 to 7 scale. The resulting data are typically treated as interval data and analyzed using profile analysis. In profile analysis, means or median values for each item are calculated, plotted, and statistically analyzed. By plotting the results, the researcher can see overall differences and similarities among the objects measured. Differences across respondent groups also can be compared. When the researcher requires an overall comparison of objects, such as to determine store preference, the individual item scores can also be summed to arrive at a total score, as with the Likert scale.

The semantic differential is a highly popular scale in marketing research because of its versatility (see Table 10.1). It is used to compare brand, product, and company images, to develop advertising and promotion strategies, and in new product development studies. The major disadvantage is the difficulty in determining the appropriate bipolar adjectives required to construct the scale. Several modifications of the basic scale have been proposed.

Stapel Scale

The **Stapel scale** was named after its developer, Jan Stapel, and is typically presented vertically, with one adjective appearing at the midpoint of a scale ranging from $+5$ to -5. The respondent is

Stapel scale
A scale for measuring attitudes that consists of a single adjective in the middle of an even-numbered range of values.

not allowed a neutral response, because no zero point is offered. Respondents are asked to indicate how accurately or inaccurately each term describes the object by selecting the appropriate number. The higher the number, the more accurately the adjective describes the object. In the retailing study, evaluations of Macy's would be obtained as follows.

INSTRUCTIONS

Please evaluate how accurately each word or phrase describes each of the department stores. Select a plus number by placing an (X) beside it for the phrases you think describe the store accurately. The more accurately you think the phrase describes the store, the larger the positive number you should choose. You should select a negative number for phrases you think do not describe the store accurately. A large negative number indicates that the phrase does not describe the store at all. You can select any number, from +5 for phrases you think are very accurate, to −5 for phrases you think are very inaccurate.

FORM

Macy's

	Macy's	
+5	+5	+5
+4	+4	+4X
+3	+3	+3
+2	+2	+2
+1	+1	+1
High Quality	**Poor Service**	**Wide Variety**
−1	−1X	−1
−2X	−2	−2
−3	−3	−3
−4	−4	−4
−5	−5	−5

The data obtained from a Stapel scale are treated as interval data, analyzed in much the same way as semantic differential data. Using only one adjective in the Stapel scale has an advantage over semantic differentials, in that no pretest is needed to assure that the adjectives chosen are indeed opposites. The simplicity of the scale also lends itself to telephone interviewing. Some researchers believe the Stapel scale is confusing and difficult to apply, however. It is therefore used the least of the three itemized rating scales discussed here (see Table 10.1). The advantages of this scale warrant wider applications than have been made in the past. For instance, it could be used more widely in telephone interviewing, which is currently the most popular method of administering consumer surveys in the United States.

Be a DM!	Be an MR!

The Diet Craze

Be a DM!	Be an MR!
As the brand manager for Diet Coke, how would you use information on consumer attitudes to segment the market?	Visit www.dietcoke.com and search the Internet—including social media—as well as your library's online databases to obtain information on consumers' attitudes toward diet soft drinks. How would you use each of the three itemized scales to measure consumers' attitudes toward Diet Coke and other diet soft drinks? Which scale do you recommend?

Social Media

Noncomparative Itemized Rating-Scale Decisions

One of the advantages of using noncomparative scales is the flexibility of adapting them to a specific research project. When constructing the itemized scales discussed in this chapter, six factors can be adjusted. These factors, along with recommended guidelines, are described in Table 10.2 and briefly reviewed here.

Number of Scale Categories

From the researcher's perspective, the larger the number of categories contained in a scale, the finer the discrimination between the brands, alternatives, or other objects under study. The **sensitivity** of a scale is the ability to detect subtle differences in the attitude or the characteristic being measured. Increasing the number of scale categories increases sensitivity. The larger the number of categories, however, the greater the information-processing demands imposed on the respondents. Thus, the desire for more information must be balanced against the demands on the respondent. There is a limit to how much information a respondent can process when answering a question. Another important factor is the mode of data collection. Telephone interviews, in which the respondent cannot see the questionnaire, can become very confusing if the number of scale categories is too large. Space limitations on the survey form itself represent another constraint.

Although there is no optimal number, the researcher should strive to balance the need for information with consideration of the demands placed on the respondent and the nature of the data collection task. Traditional guidelines suggest that no fewer than five and no more than nine categories of information should be used. With fewer than five scale categories, not enough discrimination is generated to make the research useful. Beyond nine scale categories, the respondents become confused and fatigued, and the quality of data suffers. The opening vignette illustrated the use of 5-point scales to measure reaction to new films.

Balanced Versus Unbalanced Scale

In a **balanced scale**, the number of favorable and unfavorable categories or scale points is equal. In an unbalanced scale, they are unequal. Examples of balanced and unbalanced scales are given in Figure 10.4. Generally, balanced scales are desirable, ensuring the data collected are objective, as in the opening vignette.

If the researcher suspects that the responses are likely to skew either negatively (i.e., most of the responses will be negative or unfavorable) or positively, an unbalanced scale might be appropriate. Under these conditions, more categories are included in the direction of the skew. For example, customer satisfaction is typically positively skewed because most of the customers are satisfied with the company and its products. Therefore, many researchers prefer to use an unbalanced scale with a larger number of satisfied categories and fewer unsatisfied categories when measuring customer satisfaction. When unbalanced scales are used, the nature and degree of unbalance in the scale should be taken into account in data analysis.

sensitivity
The ability to detect subtle differences in the attitude or the characteristic being measured.

balanced scale
A scale with an equal number of favorable and unfavorable categories.

TABLE 10.2 Summary of Itemized Rating-Scale Decisions

Decision Factor	Guidelines
Number of categories	While there is no single optimal number, traditional guidelines suggest there should be between five and nine categories.
Balanced vs. unbalanced	In general, the scale should be balanced to obtain objective data.
Odd vs. even number of categories	If a neutral or indifferent scale response is possible for at least some of the respondents, an odd number of categories should be used.
Forced vs. nonforced	In situations where the respondents are expected to have no opinion, the accuracy of data may be improved by a nonforced scale.
Verbal description	An argument can be made for labeling all or many scale categories. The category descriptions should be located as close to the response categories as possible.
Physical form	A number of options should be tried and the best one selected.

Balanced Scale	Unbalanced Scale
SURFING THE INTERNET IS	SURFING THE INTERNET IS
_____ Extremely Good	_____ Extremely Good
_____ Very Good	_____ Very Good
_____ Good	_____ Good
_____ Bad	_____ Somewhat Good
_____ Very Bad	_____ Bad
_____ Extremely Bad	_____ Very Bad

FIGURE 10.4

Balanced and Unbalanced Scales

Odd or Even Numbers of Categories

When an odd number of categories are used in a scale, the midpoint typically represents a neutral category. The decision to use a neutral category and its labeling has a significant influence on the response. The Likert scale is an example of a balanced rating scale with an odd number of categories and a neutral point.

The scale should have an odd number of categories if the researcher has reason to believe that a portion of the respondent population is actually neutral on a particular subject. This was illustrated in the opening vignette in which a neutral response was allowed for measuring audience response. It was recognized that many respondents might not like or dislike specific scenes in movies. However, if the researcher wants to force a response or believes that no neutral or indifferent response exists, a rating scale with an even number of categories should be used. A related issue is whether the choice should be forced or nonforced.

Forced or Nonforced Choice

In a **forced rating scale**, the respondents are forced or required to express an opinion, because a "no opinion" option is not provided. When forced rating scales are applied to situations where a significant portion of the response population holds no opinion, the respondents will tend to select an option at the midpoint of the scale. Marking a middle position when, in fact, "no opinion" is the desired response will distort measures of central tendency and variance. In situations where the respondent holds no opinion rather than simply being reluctant to disclose that opinion, a nonforced scale that includes a "no opinion" category can improve the accuracy of data. For example, respondents might not be familiar with some of the brands in a study comparing multiple brands and, therefore, be unable to express an opinion. Otherwise, the use of a "no opinion" category should be avoided, as in the opening vignette. Although the neutral point would be the midpoint of the scale, a "no opinion" option might be better placed at the far right or left of the scale, as shown:

forced rating scale
A rating scale that forces the respondents to express an opinion because a "no opinion" option is not provided.

Strongly Disagree				Strongly Agree	
1	2	3	4	5	No opinion

Nature and Degree of Verbal Description

The way a scale category is described can have a considerable effect on the response. Scale categories can have verbal, numerical, or even pictorial descriptions. They might be provided for each category or only at the end points of the scale. Surprisingly, providing a verbal description for each category may not improve the accuracy or reliability of the data. Yet, an argument can be made for labeling all or many scale categories to reduce scale ambiguity. The category descriptions or labels should be located as close to the response categories (i.e., the scale point numbers) as possible, as illustrated by the Likert scale in the opening vignette.

The strength of the adjectives used to anchor the scale also influences the responses. Suppose respondents are asked to indicate their degree of (dis)agreement with the statement, "The moral values in America are declining." Strong anchors (1 = completely disagree, 7 = completely agree) will result in more responses toward the midpoint of the scale because respondents are hesitant to check extreme responses (1 or 7). By contrast, weak anchors (1 = generally disagree, 7 = generally agree) produce uniform or flat distributions. In such cases, the respondents feel more comfortable in checking the scale end points (1 or 7), because these

FIGURE 10.5

Rating-Scale Configurations

A variety of scale configurations may be employed to measure the comfort of Nike shoes. Some examples follow:

Nike shoes are

1) PLACE AN "X" ON THE APPLICABLE BLANK SPACE:

Very
Uncomfortable _____ _____ _____ _____ _____ _____ Very
Comfortable

2) CIRCLE A NUMBER:

Very   1   2   3   4   5   6   7   Very
Uncomfortable   Comfortable

3) PLACE AN "X" ON THE APPLICABLE BLANK SPACE:

_____ Very Uncomfortable

_____

_____ Neither Uncomfortable nor Comfortable

_____

_____

_____ Very Comfortable

4) PLACE AN "X" ON THE APPLICABLE BLANK SPACE:

_____ _____ _____ _____ _____ _____ _____

Very   Uncomfortable Somewhat   Neither   Somewhat   Comfortable   Very
Uncomfortable   Uncomfortable   Comfortable   Comfortable   Comfortable
                                             nor Uncomfortable

5) CIRCLE A NUMBER:

−3   −2   −1   0   1   2   3
Very   Neither   Very
Uncomfortable   Comfortable   Comfortable
                                         nor Uncomfortable

responses are not that extreme. Knowledge of the distribution of the characteristic being measured along with the objectives of the study can help the researcher select appropriate anchors.

Physical Form or Configuration

The way a scale is presented can vary quite dramatically. Scales can be presented vertically or horizontally. Categories can be expressed by boxes, discrete lines, or units on a continuum and might or might not have numbers assigned to them. If numerical values are used, they may be positive, negative, or both. Several possible configurations are presented in Figure 10.5. Before selecting a configuration, the researcher should try a number of options. Table 10.3 presents

TABLE 10.3 Some Commonly Used Scales in Marketing

Construct	Scale Descriptors				
Attitude	Very Bad	Bad	Neither Bad nor Good	Good	Very Good
Importance	Not at All Important	Not Important	Neutral	Important	Very Important
Satisfaction	Very Dissatisfied	Dissatisfied	Neither Dissatisfied nor Satisfied	Satisfied	Very Satisfied
Purchase Intent	Definitely Will Not Buy	Probably Will Not Buy	Might or Might Not Buy	Probably Will Buy	Definitely Will Buy
Purchase Frequency	Never	Rarely	Sometimes	Often	Very Often

some commonly used scales. Although these particular scales have five categories, the number of categories can be varied based on the researcher's judgment.

Finally, different types of itemized rating scales can be used in a single questionnaire, as the following example illustrates.

Research in Action

Unbalanced Scales Help Advanced Micro Devices Achieve Balance in Customer Satisfaction

MarketTools CustomerSat (www.markettools.com) is a premier provider of Internet-survey research services. It conducted an Internet-based customer satisfaction survey for Advanced Micro Devices (AMD; www.amd.com), a leading manufacturer of integrated circuits. Various types of itemized rating scales were employed. The importance of attributes used to evaluate AMD was measured on 7-point balanced scales (Extremely Important, Very Important, Important, Neutral, Unimportant, Very Unimportant, Extremely Unimportant). However, satisfaction was measured using 5-point unbalanced scales (Excellent, Very Good, Good, Fair, Poor). The use of unbalanced scales to measure satisfaction was justified, because satisfaction levels tend to be positively skewed.

Furthermore, a "Not Applicable (N/A)" option was also allowed when measuring satisfaction with AMD on specific attributes, because not all attributes might be relevant for a particular respondent. The results of this survey helped AMD identify customer concerns affecting satisfaction levels and to take corrective actions. For example, filling the orders accurately and in a timely manner had a very important impact on customer satisfaction. Yet, this was an area where AMD was not up to par. Accordingly, AMD reorganized this function, resulting in improved performance and increased customer satisfaction.

Be an MR!	Be a DM!
Rockport: Leave in Comfort, Arrive in Style	
Visit www.rockport.com and search the Internet—including social media—as well as your library's online databases to obtain information on consumers' preferences for dress shoes. Develop an itemized scale to measure consumers' preferences for dress shoes and to justify your rating-scale decisions.	As the marketing manager for Rockport, how would you use information on consumers' preferences for dress shoes to increase your sales?

Social Media

Multi-Item Scales

A **multi-item scale** consists of multiple items, where an item is a single question or statement to be evaluated. The Likert, semantic differential, and Stapel scales presented earlier to measure attitudes toward Macy's are examples of multi-item scales. Note that each of these scales has multiple items. Developing multi-item rating scales requires considerable technical expertise. The steps involved in constructing a multi-item scale are described in Figure 10.6.

The characteristic to be measured is frequently called a *construct*. The researcher begins by developing the construct of interest. A **construct** is a specific type of concept that exists at a higher level of abstraction than do everyday concepts, such as brand loyalty, product involvement, attitude, satisfaction, and so forth. Next, the researcher must develop a theoretical definition of the construct that states the meaning of the central idea or concept of interest. For this, we need an underlying theory of the construct being measured. A theory is necessary not only for constructing the scale but also for interpreting the resulting scores. For example, "brand loyalty" might be defined as the consistent repurchase of a brand prompted by a favorable attitude toward the brand. The construct must be operationalized in a way that is consistent with the theoretical definition. The operational definition specifies which observable characteristics will be measured and the process of assigning value to the construct. For example, in the context of toothpaste purchases, consumers will be characterized as brand loyal if they exhibit a highly favorable attitude (top quartile) and have purchased the same brand on at least four of the last five purchase occasions. Then, the multi-item scale should be developed. The researcher generates a

multi-item scale
A scale consisting of multiple items, where an item is a single question or statement to be evaluated.

construct
A specific type of concept that exists at a higher level of abstraction than do everyday concepts.

FIGURE 10.6

Developing a Multi-Item Scale

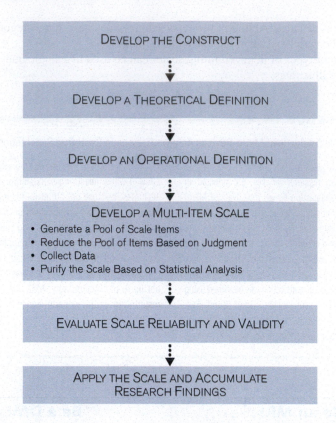

set of questions based on theory, analysis of secondary data, and qualitative research. This initial pool is repeatedly reduced using input from experts and the researcher's qualitative judgment. If the reduced set of items is still too large, quantitative techniques are available for further reduction and "purification." The researcher evaluates the purified scale for reliability and validity and selects a final set of scale items. The final scale is used in a variety of applications so that a wealth of research findings can accumulate.

Experiential Learning

Measuring Satisfaction Using Qualtrics Question Library

Access to Qualtrics is included with this book. Use the Qualtrics question library to electronically develop the following satisfaction scales.

1. Five-point Likert (type) balanced scale
2. Five-point Likert (type) unbalanced scale
3. Seven-point Likert (type) balanced scale
4. Seven-point semantic differential scale
5. Five-point smiling faces scale

systematic error
Systematic error affects the measurement in a constant way and represents stable factors that affect the observed score in the same way each time the measurement is made.

random error
Measurement error that arises from random changes that have a different effect each time the measurement is made.

Scale Evaluation

A multi-item scale should be evaluated for reliability and validity, as shown in Figure 10.7. To understand these concepts, it is useful to think of total measurement error as the sum of systematic error and random error. **Systematic error** affects the measurement in a constant way, that is, in the same way each time the measurement is made. **Random error**, in contrast, arises from random changes and has a different effect each time the measurement is made. Thus,

$$\text{Total measurement error} = \text{Systematic error} + \text{Random error}$$

FIGURE 10.7
Scale Evaluation

Reliability

Reliability refers to the extent to which a scale produces consistent results if repeated measurements are made. Therefore, reliability can be defined as the extent to which measures are free from random error.

Reliability is determined by repeatedly measuring the construct or variable of interest. The higher the degree of association between the scores derived through this repeated measurement, the more reliable the scale. Popular approaches for assessing reliability are test–retest, alternative-forms, and internal-consistency methods.

TEST–RETEST RELIABILITY   In **test–retest reliability**, respondents are administered identical scales at two different times under as nearly equivalent conditions as possible. The retest typically follows the original measurement by 2 to 4 weeks. The degree of similarity between the two measurements is determined by computing a correlation coefficient (see Chapter 18). The higher the correlation coefficient, the greater the reliability.

ALTERNATIVE-FORMS RELIABILITY   In order to test **alternative-forms reliability**, two equivalent forms of the scale are constructed. The same respondents are measured using alternative scale forms. Correlation between the responses to the two equivalent forms of the scale provides a measure of reliability.

INTERNAL-CONSISTENCY RELIABILITY   **Internal-consistency reliability** is used to assess the reliability of a summated scale, or subscale, where scores for several items are summed to form a total score for a construct (e.g., attitude). In a scale of this type, each item measures some aspect of the construct measured by the entire scale. The items should be consistent in what they indicate about the characteristic. This measure of reliability refers to the consistency with which each item represents the construct of interest. Consider the 9-item Likert scale used to measure atti-tudes toward Macy's discussed earlier in this chapter. How consistently do items such as "Macy's sells high-quality merchandise" or "I like to shop at Macy's" measure attitudes toward Macy's?

The simplest measure of internal consistency is **split-half reliability**. In applying this procedure, the scale items are randomly divided into halves, and the resulting half scores are correlated. High correlations between the halves indicate high internal consistency. The correlation between the halves will be affected by how the groups are split.

A popular approach to overcoming this problem is to use the coefficient alpha. The **coefficient alpha**, or Cronbach's alpha, is calculated by averaging the coefficients that result from all possible combinations of split halves.[5] This coefficient varies from 0 to 1, and a value of 0.6 or less generally indicates unsatisfactory internal-consistency reliability.

reliability
The extent to which a scale produces consistent results if repeated measurements are made on the characteristic.

test–retest reliability
An approach for assessing reliability in which respondents are administered identical sets of scale items at two different times under as nearly equivalent conditions as possible.

alternative-forms reliability
An approach for assessing reliability that requires two equivalent forms of the scale to be constructed, and then measures the same respondents at two different times using the alternate forms.

internal-consistency reliability
An approach used to assess the reliability of a summated scale and which refers to the consistency with which each item represents the construct of interest.

split-half reliability
A form of internal-consistency reliability in which the items constituting the scale are divided into two halves, and the resulting half scores are correlated.

coefficient alpha
A measure of internal-consistency reliability that is the average of all possible split-half coefficients resulting from different splittings of the scale items.

Experiential Learning

McCann Erickson and Ad Promises

SPSS Data File

Excel Data File

As of 2011, McCann Erickson Worldwide Advertising (www.mccannerickson.com) is a leading advertising agency and part of McCann Worldgroup (www.mccann.com). Eric Keshin, Regional Director, McCann Erickson North America, has become concerned that viewers might be overcome with the "dazzle" of television ads at the expense of actually learning about the brands featured in them. To address the need for improved measures of viewer response to ads, researchers have developed a set of multi-item scales called Ad Promises.[6] Eight-point Likert type scales were used to measure each of the eight subscales of Ad Promises.

Go to the Web site for this book and download the following files: (10a) McCann Erickson Experiential learning (Word file); (10b) Ad promises not reversed (Excel file); (10c) Ad promises reversed (SPSS file).

1. Read the Word file (10a) to understand the context of Ad Promises.
2. Use the Excel file (10b) to perform the following operations [see detailed instructions in the Word file (10a)]:
   a. Reverse-code the original eight variables into these eight new variables.
   b. Save your Excel file as "Ad Promises Reversed Coded.xls" and then import its contents into SPSS.
3. Use the SPSS file that you have created to perform the following operations [see detailed instructions in the Word file (10a)]:
   a. Create a composite variable representing each of the eight Ad Promise constructs.
   b. Compute Cronbach's Alpha for each of these eight sets of items.

validity
The extent to which differences in observed scale scores reflect true differences among objects on the characteristic being measured, rather than systematic or random errors.

content validity
A type of validity, sometimes called *face validity*, that consists of a subjective but systematic evaluation of the representativeness of the content of a scale for the measuring task at hand.

criterion validity
A type of validity that examines whether the measurement scale performs as expected in relation to other variables selected as meaningful criteria.

construct validity
A type of validity that addresses the question of what construct or characteristic the scale is measuring. An attempt is made to answer theoretical questions of why a scale works and what deductions can be made concerning the theory underlying the scale.

convergent validity
A measure of construct validity that measures the extent to which the scale correlates positively with other measures of the same construct.

discriminant validity
A type of construct validity that assesses the extent to which a measure does not correlate with other constructs from which it is supposed to differ.

Validity

The **validity** of a scale can be defined as the extent to which differences in observed scale scores reflect true differences in what is being measured, rather than systematic or random error. A scale with perfect validity would contain no measurement error—that is, no systematic error and no random error. Researchers can assess validity in different ways: content validity, criterion validity, or construct validity.

CONTENT VALIDITY   Content validity involves a systematic but subjective assessment of how well a scale measures the construct or variable of interest. For a scale to be content valid, it must address all dimensions of the construct. This is a commonsense evaluation of the scale. For example, a scale designed to measure the construct "store image" would be considered inadequate if it omitted any of the major dimensions of image (quality, variety and assortment of merchandise, and so on). Content validity alone is not a sufficient measure of the validity of a scale. It must be supplemented with a more formal evaluation of the scale's validity, namely criterion validity and construct validity.

CRITERION VALIDITY   Criterion validity reflects whether a scale performs as expected given other variables considered relevant to the construct. These variables are called *criterion variables*. They may include demographic and psychographic characteristics, attitudinal and behavioral measures, or scores obtained from other scales. For example, the researcher may measure attitudes toward cereal brands using a multi-item scale administered to members of a scanner panel. Based on attitude levels, future purchases of cereal (criterion variable) are predicted. Scanner data are used to track the actual cereal purchases of the panel members. The predicted and actual purchases are compared to assess criterion validity of the attitudinal scale.

CONSTRUCT VALIDITY   Construct validity addresses the question of what construct or characteristic the scale is, in fact, measuring. In order to assess construct validity, the researcher must have a strong understanding of the theory that provided the basis for constructing the scale. The researcher uses theory to explain why the scale works and what deductions can be drawn from it. As Figure 10.7 shows, construct validity includes convergent, discriminant, and nomological validity. **Convergent validity** is the extent to which the scale correlates positively with other measures of the same construct. **Discriminant validity** is the extent to which a measure does not correlate with other constructs from which it is supposed to differ.

Nomological validity is the extent to which the scale correlates in theoretically predicted ways with measures of different, but related, constructs.

In the opening vignette, construct validity is assessed by measuring audience reaction via continuous measurement using a dial and Likert scales and correlating the measures. We illustrate construct validity in the context of a multi-item scale designed to measure self-concept, the image that consumers have of themselves. This construct is of interest to marketers because consumers prefer products and brands that are consistent with and reinforce their self-concept.

nomological validity
A type of validity that assesses the relationship between theoretical constructs. It seeks to confirm significant correlations between the constructs as predicted by theory.

Research in Action

To Thine Own Self Be True

Following are findings that provide evidence of validity for a multi-item scale to measure self-concept:

- Three experts agree that all the items in the scale are relevant for measuring self-concept (content validity).
- High correlations exist between scales designed to measure self-concept and personality assessments of the same person by their friends (criterion validity).
- High correlations exist with other scales designed to measure self-concepts (convergent validity).
- Low correlations exist with unrelated constructs of brand loyalty and variety seeking (discriminant validity).
- Brands that are congruent with the individual's self-concept are more preferred, as postulated by the theory (nomological validity).
- There is a high level of reliability.

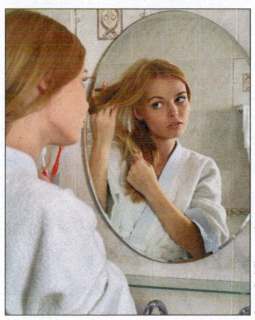

Source: Tassh/Shutterstock.

Notice that a high level of reliability was included as evidence of construct validity in this example. This illustrates the relationship between reliability and validity.

Relationship Between Reliability and Validity

If a measure is perfectly valid, it also is perfectly reliable. In this case, neither systematic nor random error is present. Thus, perfect validity implies perfect reliability. (No measurement error implies no random error.) If a measure is unreliable, it cannot be perfectly valid, because, at a minimum, random error is present. (If random error is present, measurement error is present.) Furthermore, systematic error might also be present. Thus, unreliability implies invalidity. If a measure is perfectly reliable, it might or might not be perfectly valid, because systematic error might still be present. (If there is no random error, measurement error might still be present due to systematic error.) Although lack of reliability constitutes negative evidence for validity, reliability does not in itself imply validity. Reliability is a necessary, but not sufficient, condition for validity.

Choosing a Scaling Technique

In addition to theoretical considerations and evaluation of reliability and validity, the researcher should consider certain practical factors in selecting scaling techniques for a particular marketing research problem. These include the level of measurement desired (nominal, ordinal, interval, or ratio), the experience of the respondents with the research topic, the difficulty of administering the scales, and the context. The general rule is to select the lowest level of measurement that will enable the researcher to obtain the needed information and conduct the appropriate statistical analyses. Additionally, using multiple scale items to measure the same characteristic will improve the accuracy of results. In many situations, it is desirable to use more than one scaling technique, as illustrated in the opening vignette.

Summary Illustration Using the Opening Vignette

Noncomparative rating scales can be either continuous or itemized. Both types were illustrated in the opening vignette. Audience members viewing a movie are each given a dial and are told to continuously rate their reactions to the film from positive to negative by turning the dial in the desired direction, thus recording their response on a continuous scale. The itemized rating scales are further classified as Likert, semantic differential, or Stapel scales. The data from all these three types of scale are typically treated as interval scale data. Thus, these scales possess the characteristics of description, order, and distance, as discussed in Chapter 9.

Large-scale surveys conducted to assess respondents' reactions to movies make use of Likert scales. When using noncomparative itemized rating scales, the researcher must decide on the number of scale categories, balanced versus unbalanced scales, odd or even number of categories, forced versus nonforced scales, nature and degree of verbal description, and the physical form or configuration. The Likert scale in the opening vignette made use of five categories following the traditional guidelines and is balanced to avoid bias in any direction. A neutral response (3) is allowed as it is recognized that many respondents might not like or dislike specific scenes in movies. All the scale categories are labeled in order to reduce ambiguity. A forced scale is used, without a "no opinion" category, because people generally express opinions on movies they have seen.

Multi-item scales consist of a number of rating-scale items. These scales should be evaluated in terms of reliability and validity. Reliability refers to the extent to which a scale produces consistent results if repeated measurements are made. Approaches to assessing reliability include test–retest, alternative forms, and internal consistency. Validity, or accuracy of measurement, can be assessed by evaluating content validity, criterion validity, and construct validity. In the opening vignette, convergent validity is assessed by measuring audience reaction using different methods (continuous measurement using a dial and Likert scales) and then correlating the measures.

The choice of particular scaling techniques in a given situation should be based on theoretical and practical considerations. As a general rule, select the lowest level of measurement that will enable you to obtain the needed information and conduct the appropriate statistical analyses. Also, multiple measures should be obtained, as in the opening vignette. Figure 10.8 provides a concept map for noncomparative scales.

In this figure, the major concepts are connected by bold arrows using descriptors. Thus, basic noncomparative scales consist of continuous rating scales and itemized rating scales. Each major concept is described by minor concepts that are connected to that major concept by lines with descriptors. Thus, the basic characteristic of continuous rating scales is to place a mark on a continuous line. The rest of the figure can be interpreted similarly.

International Marketing Research

Pan-cultural scales, designed to be free of cultural biases, are used in international research. In addition to eliminating cultural biases, it also is essential to accommodate differing levels of education and experience. Of the scaling techniques considered, the semantic differential has been applied with the greatest consistency in results across countries. Rating scales also are used to construct indices used to make global comparisons, as illustrated by the MasterCard Worldwide Centers of Commerce Index.

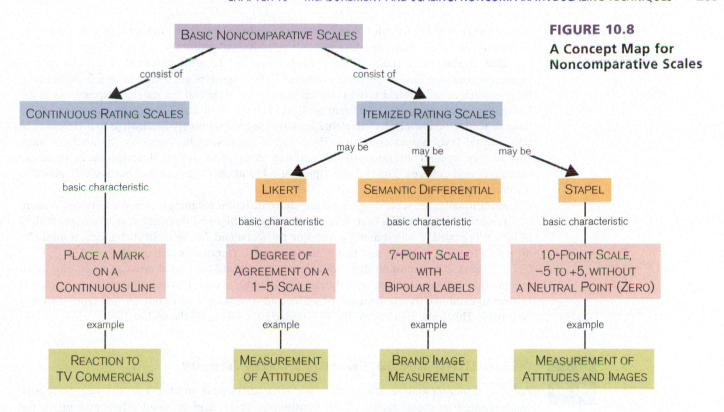

FIGURE 10.8

A Concept Map for Noncomparative Scales

Research in Action

Mastering Global Commerce

Recognizing a need for cutting-edge insights into the evolving global marketplace, the MasterCard Worldwide Centers of Commerce Index, introduced in 2007, ranks the world's top cities in terms of their performance as Centers of Commerce in the global economy. The index is based on six dimensions: (1) legal and political framework, (2) economic stability, (3) ease of doing business, (4) financial flow, (5) business center, and (6) knowledge creation and information flow. Rating scales are used to rate the cities on each of these dimensions and to develop a composite score. The Commerce Index ranks the top 50 Centers of Commerce based on six measurement dimensions. In 2007, it placed London first, followed by New York, Tokyo, Chicago, and Hong Kong. Completing the top 10 were Singapore, Frankfurt, Paris, Seoul, and Los Angeles, in that order.

London beats New York by a narrow margin of only 3.99 in the overall Index value. With a flexible operating environment for business, strong global financial connections, and exceptionally high levels of international trade, travel, and conferences, London secured the top spot. The city outperformed New York in four of the six measurement dimensions and scored significantly higher than other European cities. To maintain its leading position, London must improve its legal and political framework and knowledge creation and information flow—the two dimensions on which New York did better. London with an aggregate score of 79.17 did, indeed, improve and widen its lead over New York with a score of 72.77 in the 2008 Index. Continued efforts along these lines will further fortify London's number-one position and strategic role in global marketplace.[7]

Source: © Russell Kord/Alamy Images.

An alternative approach to developing pan-cultural scales is to use descriptors the respondents create themselves. For example, respondents might be asked to indicate the verbal descriptors for the extreme scale categories (anchors) before positioning an object along the scale. This approach is useful when conducting attitude research related to cultural norms (e.g., attitude towards friends). Suppose the researcher is interested in measuring the influence of friends on the purchase of personal clothing in a cross-cultural study involving students in the United States and India. The question asked is "To what extent should your friends influence your purchase of personal clothing?" The responses are obtained on a 7-point scale. Respondents in India might provide the anchors as 1 = little and 7 = much. Respondents in the United States might provide different anchors: 1 = not at all and 7 = a great deal. Such scales have proven to be universally adaptable because they are relatively insensitive to differences in educational level across countries. However, if the researchers specify the anchors, they should pay special attention to determining equivalent verbal descriptors in different languages and cultures. The end descriptors used to anchor the scale are particularly prone to different interpretations.

Additionally, the scale numbering may have different meanings. In some cultures, a score of 1 might be interpreted as best, whereas in others it might be interpreted as worst, regardless of how it is scaled (1 = best and 7 = worst or 1 = worst and 7 = best). In such cases, it might be desirable to avoid numbers and to just use boxes that respondent can check (worst ☐ ☐ ☐ ☐ ☐ ☐ ☐ best). It is important that the scale end points and the verbal descriptors be employed in a manner that is consistent with the culture. Finally, in international marketing research it is critical to establish the equivalence of scales and measures used to obtain data from different countries. This topic is complex and is discussed elsewhere by the author.[8]

Marketing Research and Social Media

All the noncomparative scales that we have discussed in this chapter can be easily implemented in social media. Even continuous scales can be used efficiently given the computerized nature of measurement. An analysis of social media content can provide guidance on whether continuous or itemized rating scales should be used. It can also aid the researcher in making appropriate rating-scale decisions. Furthermore, it is quite feasible to employ more than one scaling method to measure a given construct so as to obtain evidence on convergent validity. The use of rating scales in social media can yield rich dividends, as exemplified by Future Shop of Canada.

Research in Action

Future Shop Has Social Media in Its Future

Future Shop is Canada's largest consumer electronics retailer. The company is using social media conversations not only to learn about its customers but also to support and sell products. The company was initially built on the high-touch model in which sales associates were taught to be valued customer advisors. Recently, the company has duplicated this real-world experience online. Visitors to the Future Shop Web site (www.futureshop.ca) are greeted by a video image of a sales associate who offers to help guide their experience. Customers can ask questions of the avatar and get answers from a growing database of advice that is contributed by other customers and sales associates. Future Shop has co-developed a rating system with Lithium Technologies, a leading provider of Social CRM solutions (www.lithium.com), that obtains feedback from customers on each other's comments and on the quality of information given by sales associates. The ratings are obtained using balanced, Likert-type scales. Likert scales are chosen for their simplicity and ease of administration online. Customer contributors can earn discounts and status in the community while sales associates can earn cash. Since implementing this system, the Web site traffic has increased dramatically. So has the effectiveness of their in-store selling. "We actually see people walking in (the store) with printouts and asking for specific experts they've met online," said the company.[9]

Ethics in Marketing Research

Because scale construction can influence scale responses, and hence the results of the study, several ethical issues are pertinent. Of particular concern is the researcher's attempt to deliberately bias the results by building that bias into noncomparative scales. This can be done, for example, by using scale descriptors that can be manipulated to bias results in a desired direction (e.g., to generate a positive view of the client's brand or a negative view of a competitor's brand). To project the client's brand favorably, the respondents can be asked to indicate their opinion of the brand on several attributes using 7-point scales anchored by the descriptors "extremely poor" to "good." Note that this scale has a strongly negative descriptor with only a mildly positive one. Respondents will be reluctant to rate the product extremely negatively by rating it as "extremely poor." In fact, respondents who believe the product to be only mediocre will end up responding favorably. Try this yourself. How would you rate Lexus automobiles on the following attributes?

Reliability:	Horrible	1	2	3	4	5	6	7	Good
Performance:	Very poor	1	2	3	4	5	6	7	Good
Quality:	One of the worst	1	2	3	4	5	6	7	Good
Prestige:	Very low	1	2	3	4	5	6	7	Good

Did you find yourself rating Lexus cars positively? The same technique can also be used to negatively bias evaluations of competitors' products by providing a mildly negative descriptor against a strongly positive descriptor.

Thus, it is clearly important to use scales with comparable positive and negative descriptors. This problem emphasizes the need to adequately establish the reliability and validity of scales so that we can be confident that the variables have been accurately measured. The researcher has a responsibility to both the client and respondents to ensure the applicability and usefulness of the scale, as illustrated by the following example.

Research in Action

An Ethical Scale for Measuring Ethics

The theory of moral philosophy was used to develop a scale for measuring ethical evaluations of marketing activities. The resulting scale had 29 7-point bipolar items ranging from fair to unfair and efficient to inefficient. Evaluations of this scale, through its use in evaluating various ethical scenarios, indicated high internal consistency, reliability (measured via Cronbach's alpha), and a strong degree of construct (convergent, discriminant, and nomological) validity. Accordingly, this scale has been useful in a variety of contexts for investigating ethical issues in marketing. In a recent study, this scale was used to classify the firms as ethical or unethical and to examine the variables that differentiated the two groups. It was found that in ethical firms ethics are considered to be important, the leadership is committed to ethical practices, and codes of ethical conduct are enforced. Also, smaller firms tended to be more ethical than larger firms.[10]

WHAT WOULD YOU DO?

Monster: The Monster of Career Networks

The Situation
When you think of the word *monster*, what do you think? Scary creatures under your bed? Elmo and Grover from *Sesame Street*? The Walt Disney movie *Monsters, Inc.*? These days, when one hears the word *monster*, the person is apt to think of the so-named online job-search company that has connected millions of job searchers with employers. Monster (www.monster.com) was founded in 1994 by Jeff Taylor, and Sal Iannuzzi was appointed chairman and CEO in 2007, a position he still held in 2011. It is the leading online global careers network and the world's number-one hiring management resource. As of 2011, its clients included more than 90 of the *Fortune* 100 and approximately 490 of the *Fortune* 500 companies. The company had operations in about 50 countries around the world. No wonder this company has added a whole new meaning to the word *monster*.

Monster makes heavy use of marketing research techniques in a unique way. Instead of companies like Nielsen that conduct marketing research for different companies, Monster researches companies that are in need of employees to fill their positions and provides the service of matching job searchers to these companies. Although Monster is doing well, more and more companies have followed in the company's footsteps and have entered the arena of providing online job-search services. Monster's competitors include Kforce (www.kforce.com) and several smaller organizations. With all of these different services available, the market is becoming saturated with Internet recruiting Web sites. It is important for Monster now more than ever to differentiate itself from the competition.

The Marketing Research Decision
1. Monster's success lies in its ability to match client companies' job specifications with applicants' skills and qualifications. What scaling techniques should Monster use to measure companies' job specifications and job applicants' skills and qualifications?
   a. Ordinal
   b. Likert
   c. Semantic differential

d. Stapel

e. Paired comparison

2. Discuss the role of the type of scaling technique you recommend in enabling Sal Iannuzzi to match companies' job specifications and job applicants' skills and qualifications and thereby increase Monster's market share.

The Marketing Management Decision

1. What should Sal Iannuzzi do to gain market share over competitors?

a. Offer price discounts to client companies.

b. Aggressively recruit job applicants.

c. Develop a more efficient system to match Monster's client companies' job specifications with job applicants' skills and qualifications.

d. Increase the quality of job applicants.

e. Promote Monster more aggressively.

2. Discuss how the marketing management-decision action that you recommend to Sal Iannuzzi is influenced by the scaling technique you suggested earlier and by the findings of that research.

What Sal Iannuzzi Did

Sal Iannuzzi decided to promote Monster more aggressively. Monster planned to invest about $50 million a year into directly marketing itself to consumers. Monster earns money when employers post job openings on its site and when it hires for those openings. Monster wants to make itself a household name in cities across the country; therefore, the more resumes it has on its site, the more willing corporate human resource departments will be to spend money advertising job openings there. As part of raising awareness of Monster in locations across the country, Sal Iannuzzi said he is open to doing something extremely bold to build buzz, such as sitting on a billboard for a month. Monster's Fiddling Beaver Official Super Bowl 2010 ad got rave reviews from the media.[11]

Summary

In noncomparative scaling, each object is scaled independently of the other objects in the stimulus set. Noncomparative rating scales can be either continuous or itemized. The itemized rating scales are further classified as Likert, semantic differential, or Stapel scales. The data from these three types of scales typically are treated as interval scales. These scales possess the characteristics of description, order, and distance, as discussed in Chapter 9. When using noncomparative itemized rating scales, the researcher must decide on the number of scale categories, balanced versus unbalanced scales, odd or even number of categories, forced versus nonforced scales, nature and degree of verbal description, and the physical form or configuration.

Multi-item scales consist of a number of rating-scale items. These scales should be evaluated in terms of reliability and validity. Reliability refers to the extent to which a scale produces consistent results if repeated measurements are made. Approaches to assessing reliability include test–retest, alternative forms, and internal consistency. Validity, or accuracy of measurement, can be assessed by evaluating content validity, criterion validity, and construct validity. The choice of particular scaling techniques for a given situation should be based on theoretical and practical considerations. As a general rule, multiple measures should be taken.

In international marketing research, special attention should be devoted to determining equivalent verbal descriptors in different languages and cultures. Social media can be used for developing, testing, and implementing continuous and itemized rating scales. The misuse of scale descriptors also raises serious ethical concerns. Ethically, the researcher has the responsibility to both the client and respondents to ensure the applicability, usefulness, and honesty of the scales.

Key Terms and Concepts

Noncomparative scale   272
Continuous rating scale   274
Itemized rating scale   275
Likert scale   276
Semantic differential scale   277
Stapel scale   278
Sensitivity   280
Balanced scale   280
Forced rating scale   281

Multi-item scale   283
Construct   283
Systematic error   284
Random error   284
Reliability   284
Test–retest reliability   285
Alternative-forms reliability   285
Internal-consistency reliability   285
Split-half reliability   285

Coefficient alpha   285
Validity   286
Content validity   286
Criterion validity   286
Construct validity   286
Convergent validity   286
Discriminant validity   286
Nomological validity   287

Suggested Cases and Video Cases

Running Case with Real Data

1.1 Hewlett-Packard

Comprehensive Critical Thinking Cases

2.1 American Idol   2.2 Baskin-Robbins   2.3 Akron Children's Hospital

Comprehensive Cases with Real Data

3.1 Bank of America   3.2 McDonald's   3.3 Boeing

Comprehensive Brief Harvard Business School Cases

4.1 TruEarth Healthy Foods: Market Research for a New Product Introduction (4065)
4.2 The Springfield Nor'easters: Maximizing Revenues in the Minor Leagues (2510)
4.3 Metabical: Positioning and Communications Strategy for a New Weight-Loss Drug (4240)
4.4 Saxonville Sausage Company (2085)

Online Video Cases

10.1 Nivea   13.1 Subaru   19.1 Marriott

Live Research: Conducting a Marketing Research Project

1. Continuous measures are generally more difficult to implement.
2. As a class, discuss the type of itemized rating scales (Likert, semantic differential, or Stapel) that are appropriate for the key variables.
3. Discuss multi-item scales and the issues of reliability and validity.
4. Consider the practical constraints. For example, if a certain type of scale has been used to measure a variable in the past (e.g., a 10-point Likert-type scale to measure customer satisfaction), the same scale might have to be used again to allow a comparison of the findings with past results or industry norms (e.g., the American Customer Satisfaction Index).

Acronym

The rating scale decisions may be described by the acronym RATING:

R   esponse option: forced versus nonforced

A   ttractive versus unattractive number of categories: balanced versus unbalanced

T   otal number of categories

I   mpartial or neutral category: odd versus even number of categories

N   ature and degree of verbal description

G   raphics: physical form and configuration

Review Questions

1. What is a semantic differential scale? For what purposes is this scale used? Give an example.
2. Describe the Likert scale. Give an example.
3. What are the differences between the Stapel scale and the semantic differential scale? Which scale is more popular?
4. What are the major decisions involved in constructing an itemized rating scale?
5. How many scale categories should be used in an itemized rating scale? Why?
6. What is the difference between balanced and unbalanced scales? Give an example of each.
7. Should an odd or even number of categories be used in an itemized rating scale? Why? When?
8. What is the difference between forced and nonforced scales? Give an example of each.

9. How does the nature and degree of verbal description affect the response to itemized rating scales?
10. What are multi-item scales? Give an example.
11. What is reliability?
12. What are the differences between test–retest and alternative-forms reliability?
13. Describe the notion of internal-consistency reliability.
14. What is validity?
15. What is criterion validity? How is it assessed?
16. What is the relationship between reliability and validity?
17. How would you select a particular scaling technique?
18. **Social Media** Discuss the use of social media in implementing itemized rating scales.

Applied Problems

1. Develop a Likert, semantic differential, and a Stapel scale for measuring store loyalty.
2. Develop a multi-item scale to measure students' attitudes toward internationalization of the management curriculum. How would you assess the reliability and validity of this scale?
3. Construct a Likert scale for measuring Internet usage. Explain how the rating-scale decisions were made.
4. Design Likert scales to measure the usefulness of Ford Motor Company's Web site. Visit www.ford.com and rate it on the scales that you have developed.
5. Design semantic differential scales to measure the perception of FedEx overnight delivery service and compare it to that offered by UPS. Relevant information can be obtained by visiting the Web sites of these two companies (www.fedex.com, www.ups.com).

6. Visit the Office of Scales Research at Southern Illinois University (http://scaleresearch.siuc.edu).(If this URL has changed, search www.siu.edu to locate it.) Identify one application of the Likert scale and one application of the semantic differential. Write a report describing the context in which these scales have been used.
7. Visit the Web sites of two marketing research firms conducting surveys. Analyze one survey of each firm to critically evaluate the itemized rating scales being used.
8. Surf the Internet to find two examples each of Likert, semantic differential, and Stapel scales. Write a report describing the context in which these scales are being used.

Group Discussion

1. "It really does not matter which scaling technique you use. As long as your measure is reliable, you will get the right results." Discuss this statement as a small group.
2. "One need not be concerned with reliability and validity in applied marketing research." Discuss this statement as a small group.

3. As a small group or as a class, discuss one of the articles listed in the notes to this chapter.

Hewlett-Packard Running Case

Review the Hewlett-Packard (HP) case, Case 1.1, and questionnaire given toward the end of the book. Go to the Web site for this book and download the HP data file.

1. Perform the following operations:
   a. Reverse the scoring of the second and the third items under the Innovativeness scale.
   b. Sum the Market Maven items (q10_1 to q10_4) to form a Total Market Maven Score.
   c. Sum the Innovativeness items (q10_5 to q10_10) to form a Total Innovativeness Score. Note that you will have to reverse the scores for the negatively worded items (q10_6 and q10_7) before summing.
   d. Sum the Opinion Leadership items (q10_11 to q10_13) to form a Total Opinion Leadership Score.
   e. Compute Cronbach's alpha for each of these three sets of items.

2. Design Likert, semantic differential, and Stapel scales to measure consumers' preferences for HP computers.

3. **Social Media** Develop Likert-type scales to measure preferences for HP and two other competing brands in social media.

ONLINE VIDEO CASE 10.1

NIVEA: Marketing Research Leads to Consistency in Marketing

Visit **www.pearsonhighered.com/malhotra** to read the video case and view the accompanying video. Nivea: Marketing Research Leads to Consistency in Marketing describes how Nivea, a large company, had to rely on marketing research to revamp its brand image to keep itself relevant and to appeal to consumers. The company's launch of *Nivea Vital* demonstrates that if researched well, a product line can significantly enhance a company's brand image, even though the product might not be targeted at the core target audience. The case can be used as a backdrop to develop Likert, semantic differential, and Stapel scales for determining consumers' evaluation of skin care products. Specific marketing research questions on this and the previous chapters are posed in the video case.

11

Questionnaire and Form Design

Source: The China Post/picture alliance/ANN/Newscom.

LEARNING OBJECTIVES

After reading this chapter, the student should be able to:

1. Understand the purpose of a questionnaire and its objectives.

2. Discuss the process of designing a questionnaire, the steps that are involved, and the guidelines for each step.

3. Explain how observational forms are designed to most effectively observe behavior.

4. Describe the considerations involved in designing questionnaires for international marketing research.

5. **Social Media** Explain how social media interface with questionnaire design.

6. Discuss the ethical issues involved in questionnaire design.

"Pretesting a questionnaire is absolutely essential for success. All legitimate researchers understand this and won't dare waste the public's time or their own effort with a questionnaire that hasn't been pretested.**"**

Diane Bowers
President, Council of American Survey Research Organizations (CASRO),
Port Jefferson, New York

World Vision Imparts Donors a Vision for Caring

World Vision (WV, www.worldvision.org), one of the leading charities in 2011, is a Christian-based organization that helps relief victims and needy children in nearly 100 countries around the world. World Vision needed at least $800,000 to continue caring for unsponsored children in developing countries. The children, who needed food, shelter, and medical care, had either never been sponsored or had lost their sponsors for various reasons. World Vision designed a questionnaire to determine donors' motivations for giving. The information obtained, and the order in which it was obtained, follows:

1. Priorities and motivations for giving
2. Awareness of the WV organization
3. Perceptions of the organization
4. Communication with donors
5. Demographic information

To increase the willingness of donors and potential donors to participate and complete the questionnaire, the researchers made the context of the survey clear, and minimized the effort required of the respondents by asking them questions that were easy to answer. Only necessary questions were asked, and combined questions were avoided. Most of the questions were structured; the respondents simply had to circle a number on the scale. However, open-ended questions were included where it was felt that the respondents needed the freedom to express underlying motivations for giving.

In deciding on question wording, words with unequivocal meanings that were familiar to the donors were used. Special effort was made to be objective so as not to bias the responses in any direction. The questionnaire was kept simple and detailed, and clear instructions were given because it had to be administered by mail. The questionnaire was divided into parts, with a separate part devoted to each type of information sought. The name and address of the respondents were optional and obtained at the end of the questionnaire. The questionnaire was professionally reproduced to have a neat appearance and was thoroughly pretested.

The results of the mail survey showed that the most important factors motivating donors to sponsor a child were the feelings of warmth and contact with the child they were sponsoring. Based on these findings, the charity decided to target its in-house list of current sponsors to see if they would consider sponsoring additional children. To motivate these already generous supporters, WV designed a warm, interactive mail package to increase the donor's involvement with the organization. The package included a letter from the WV president, a sticker with the sponsored child's name on it, and a small notebook. The letter explained that, in developing nations, paper for schoolchildren is extremely scarce. The recipient was then asked to affix the sticker to the cover of the notebook, sign the inside cover, and mail the book back in an enclosed, postage-paid envelope. The organization would then deliver the notebook to the sponsored child, along with another rarity—a pencil.

With a total budget of $117,796, WV sent 240,893 pieces of direct mail. The response rate in terms of donations received was 46.1 percent, beating the previous campaign by 25.95 percent. The cost per response was a low amount of about a dollar. The total income exceeded the goal by $197,000. Beyond the 46.1 percent who responded by making a donation, more than 80 percent of the respondents returned their notebooks, signifying a much higher level of donor involvement than suggested by the donations. Thus, the campaign was very successful. A properly designed questionnaire that resulted in valuable findings was crucial to this success.[1]

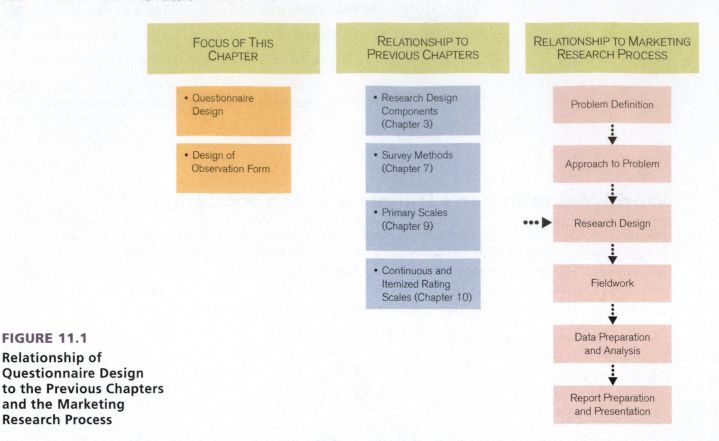

FIGURE 11.1

Relationship of Questionnaire Design to the Previous Chapters and the Marketing Research Process

Overview

The opening vignette illustrates the importance of questionnaires to the research process. The findings obtained by using a questionnaire can assist in the formulation of effective marketing strategies. A well-designed questionnaire enabled WV to discover donors' underlying motivation and design a successful campaign to solicit funds for children in developing countries.

The development of a questionnaire or observational form follows problem definition and approach (see Chapter 2), specification of the type of research design (see Chapters 3 through 8), and selection of the scaling procedures (see Chapters 9 and 10). Figure 11.1 briefly explains the focus of this chapter, the relation of this chapter to the previous ones, and the steps of the marketing research process on which this chapter concentrates.

This chapter describes the importance of a questionnaire and presents the process for developing questionnaires and observational forms. Guidelines are provided for each stage of the questionnaire construction process. The chapter also discusses questionnaires in relation to international marketing, social media, and ethics. Figure 11.2 provides an overview of the topics discussed in this chapter and how they flow from one to the next.

Importance of the Questionnaire

As discussed in Chapter 6, researchers can collect quantitative primary data for descriptive research through surveys or observation. Standardization of the data collection process is essential to ensure internally consistent and coherent data for analysis. Imagine how difficult it would be to analyze the results of a national survey conducted by 40 different interviewers if the questions had not been asked in a standard way (i.e., if the interviewers had asked different questions using different wording and order). A questionnaire ensures standardization and comparability of the data across interviewers, increases speed and accuracy of recording, and facilitates data processing. As illustrated in the opening vignette, a questionnaire also enables the researcher to collect the relevant information necessary to address the management-decision problem.

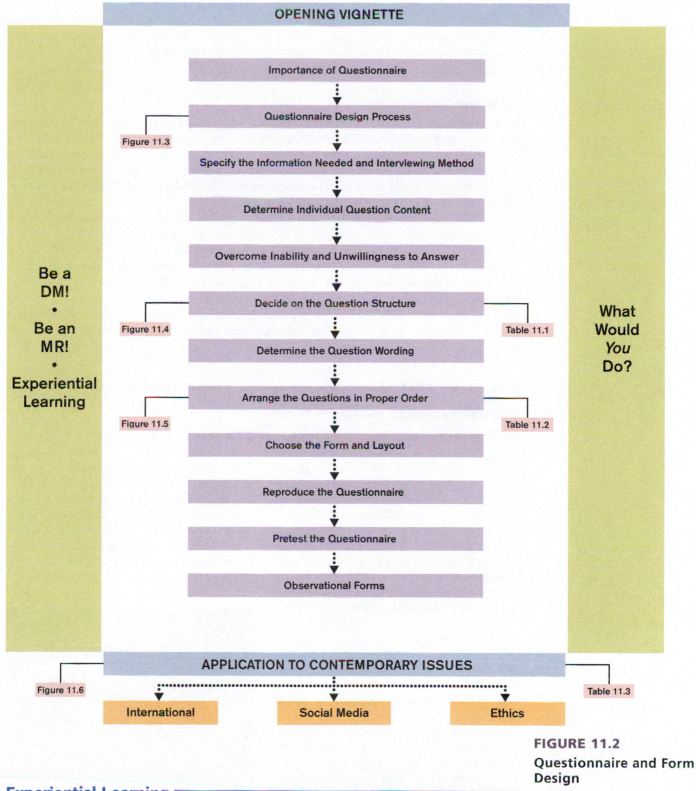

FIGURE 11.2

Questionnaire and Form Design

Experiential Learning

How Important Is a Questionnaire?

Sprite is the third most popular soft-drink brand, behind Coke and Pepsi. College students are heavy users of soft drinks.

1. As the brand manager for Sprite, what information do you need to target this segment?

2. Search the Internet—including social media—as well as your library's online databases to obtain information that will assist the brand manager of Sprite in targeting the student segment.

Social Media

(continued)

3. You and a fellow student each interview a different respondent (another student) to determine preferences for soft drinks, without constructing a questionnaire. How comparable are the data each of you obtained? Develop a formal questionnaire jointly and each of you administer it to another respondent. Are the data you two obtained more comparable than before? What does this teach you about the importance of a questionnaire?

Questionnaire Definition

A **questionnaire** is a formalized set of questions for obtaining information from respondents. It has three specific objectives. The overriding objective is to translate the researcher's information needs into a set of specific questions that respondents are willing and able to answer. Although this may seem straightforward, questions can yield very different and unanticipated responses. For example, how would you answer the following question: "Which state is larger, New York or Texas?" Would you answer based on population or area?

Second, a questionnaire should be written to minimize demands imposed on respondents. It should encourage them to participate in the entire interview, without biasing their responses. Incomplete interviews have limited usefulness, at best. In order to keep a respondent involved throughout a questionnaire, the researcher should attempt to minimize fatigue and boredom.

Third, a questionnaire should minimize response error. These errors can arise from respondents who give inaccurate answers or from researchers incorrectly recording or analyzing their answers. Minimizing the error introduced by the questionnaire itself is an important objective of questionnaire design. The following is an example of how questionnaires can be designed to achieve these objectives.

Research in Action

An Old-Fashioned Approach with Young Respondents

The Family Room (www.familyroomllc.com) is a strategic research firm focused exclusively on toddlers to teens and their families. The objective is to record children's views on favorite snack foods, television shows, commercials, radio, magazines, buzzwords, and movies. The one-on-one interviews conducted in malls are kept short, typically lasting only 8 to 10 minutes.

The Family Room attempts to make questions as clear and meaningful as possible so that kids can understand and answer them. This is done by establishing a context for questions. For example, when asking about a child's radio-listening habits, they ask, "What about when you're in Mom's car, do you listen to the radio?" rather than, "How often do you listen to radio? More than once a day, once a day, more than once a week?" The latter queries are big questions for little children.

A trade-off is made between attempting to cover all possible areas of interest in one study and ensuring that the most important information is of high quality. Given children's limited attention span, minimizing boredom and being sensitive to fatigue becomes more important than asking all possible questions. Thus, The Family Room motivates the kids to complete the questionnaire.

Some clients attempt to meet all of their research objectives with one study. The questionnaires keep going through the approval process and people keep adding questions: "Well, let's ask this question, let's add that question, and why don't we talk about this also?" This results in keeping children 25 minutes in a central mall location, which makes them kind of "itchy." The response error increases and the quality of data suffers. By keeping the questionnaire short and clear, The Family Room also tries to reduce response error. Conducting research on children is not easy, but The Family Room has been successful in designing questionnaires that meet stated objectives. As of 2011, The Family Room clients include Crayola, Kellogg's, McDonald's, and Office of National Drug Control Policy.[2]

Source: Holly Harris/Getty Images.

Questionnaire Design Process

No scientific principles guarantee an optimal or ideal questionnaire. Questionnaire design is as much an art as a science. The creativity, skill, and experience of the researcher play a major role in the end design. However, several guidelines are available to assist researchers in the questionnaire development process and to help them avoid major mistakes.

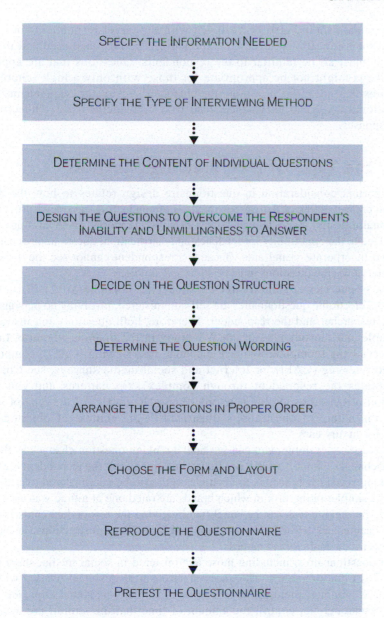

FIGURE 11.3
Questionnaire Design Process

The guidelines to support questionnaire design are shown as a series of 10 steps (see Figure 11.3): (1) specify the information needed, (2) specify the type of interviewing method, (3) determine the content of individual questions, (4) design the questions to overcome the respondent's inability and unwillingness to answer, (5) decide on the question structure, (6) determine the question wording, (7) arrange the questions in proper order, (8) choose the form and layout, (9) reproduce the questionnaire, and (10) pretest the questionnaire. In practice, questionnaire design is an iterative rather than a sequential process. For example, pretesting of a question might reveal that respondents misunderstand the wording, sending the designer back to an earlier step.

Specify the Information Needed

The first step in questionnaire design is to specify the information needed. A continual review of the earlier stages of the research project—particularly the specific components of the problem, the research questions, and the hypotheses—will help keep the questionnaire focused. This was illustrated in the WV study in the opening vignette, which clearly specified the information the questionnaire was to obtain.

Questionnaires should also be designed with the target respondents in mind, taking into account their educational level and experience. The language used and the context of the questions must all be familiar to the respondents. Questions that are appropriate for college students might not be appropriate for those with only a high school education. Questionnaires that fail to keep in mind the characteristics of the respondents, particularly their educational level and experience, lead to a high incidence of "uncertain" or "no opinion" responses.

Specify the Type of Interviewing Method

Another important consideration in questionnaire design relates to how the data will be collected. An understanding of the various methods of conducting interviews provides guidance for questionnaire design (see Chapter 7). For example, personal interviews use face-to-face interaction. Due to the opportunity for feedback and clarification, questionnaires can be lengthy, complex, and incorporate visual aids. Because a respondent cannot see the questionnaire in telephone interviews, the questions must be short and simple.

Any type of interviewer-administered questionnaire should be written in a conversational style. Mail and electronic questionnaires are self-administered, involving no personal interaction between the researcher and the respondent. Therefore, both questions and instructions must be kept simple and thorough, as in the WV study in the opening vignette. In computer-assisted interviewing [computer-assisted telephone interviewing (CATI), computer-assisted personal interviewing (CAPI), or Internet and social media surveys, see Chapter 7], the **Social Media** computer guides the respondent through complex skip patterns and can incorporate randomization of questions to eliminate order bias. The impact of the type of interviewing method on the nature of questions is illustrated in the context of obtaining consumer preferences for luxury cars.

In the luxury car example, you can see how a ranking question changes as the method of interviewing changes. In mail, e-mail, or Internet questionnaires, the respondent records the rank orders. Ranking seven car brands is too complex a task to be administered over the telephone. Therefore, the simpler rating task in which brands are rated one at a time was used. In personal interviewing, the ranking task can be simplified by giving the respondent cards imprinted with the car brand name, and the interviewer is provided with special instructions (in capital letters). The interviewer records the brand names.

Social Media Internet questionnaires, including those administered in social media, share many of the features of CAPI questionnaires. The questionnaire can be designed using a wide variety of stimuli, such as graphics, pictures, advertisements, animations, sound clips, and full-motion video. The researcher can control the amount of time that the stimuli are available to the respondents and the number of times a respondent can access each stimulus. This greatly increases the range and complexity of questionnaires that can be administered over the Internet. As in the case of CATI and CAPI, complicated skip patterns can be programmed into the questionnaire. The questions can be personalized, and answers to previous questions can be inserted into subsequent questions, a process called *variable piping*.

Research in Action

Effect of Interviewing Method on Questionnaire Design

Mail, E-Mail, or Internet (Including Social Media) Questionnaire

Please rank the following luxury cars in order of your preference. Begin by picking out the one car brand that you like most and assign it a number 1. Then find the second most preferred car brand and assign it a number 2. Continue this procedure until you have ranked all the cars in order of preference. The least preferred car brand should be assigned a rank of 7. No two brands should receive the same rank number. The criterion of preference is entirely up to you. There is no right or wrong answer. Just try to be consistent.

Car Brand	Rank Order
1. Acura	_____
2. Cadillac	_____
3. Lexus	_____
4. Lincoln	_____
5. Infiniti	_____
6. Mercedes	_____
7. BMW	_____

Telephone Questionnaire

I will read to you the names of some luxury cars. Please rate them in terms of your preference. Use a 6-point scale, where 1 denotes not so preferred and 6 denotes greatly preferred. Numbers between 1 and 6 reflect intermediate degrees of preference. Remember that the higher the number, the greater the degree of preference. Now, please tell me your preference for (READ ONE CAR BRAND AT A TIME).

Personal Questionnaire

(HAND CAR BRAND CARDS TO THE RESPONDENT.) Here is a set of luxury car names, each written on a separate card. Please examine these cards carefully. (GIVE RESPONDENT TIME.) Now, examine these cards again and pull out the card that has the name of the car brand you like the most, that is, your most preferred car. (RECORD THE CAR NAME AND KEEP THIS CARD WITH YOU.) Now, please examine the remaining six cards. Of these remaining six names, what is your most preferred car brand? (REPEAT THIS PROCEDURE SEQUENTIALLY UNTIL THE RESPONDENT HAS ONLY ONE CARD LEFT.)

	Car Brand	Not So Preferred				Greatly Preferred	
1.	Acura	1	2	3	4	5	6
2.	Cadillac	1	2	3	4	5	6
3.	Lexus	1	2	3	4	5	6
4.	Lincoln	1	2	3	4	5	6
5.	Infiniti	1	2	3	4	5	6
6.	Mercedes	1	2	3	4	5	6
7.	BMW	1	2	3	4	5	6

	Car Rank	Name of the Car
1.	1	_____
2.	2	_____
3.	3	_____
4.	4	_____
5.	5	_____
6.	6	_____
7.	7	_____

The type of interviewing method also influences the content of individual questions.

Determine the Content of Individual Questions

Once the information needed is specified and the type of interviewing method is decided, the next step is to determine question content. In other words, the researcher must determine what should be included in each question.

Is the Question Necessary?

Before including a question, the researcher should ask, "How will I use these data?" Questions that might be nice to know, but that do not directly address the research problem, should be eliminated. There are exceptions to this rule. Filler questions can be added to disguise the purpose or sponsorship of the project. For example, in brand studies a researcher might include questions about the full range of competing brands so the respondents will not know who is sponsoring the study. Early in the interviewing process when the researcher is attempting to build a relationship with respondents and capture their attention, a few easy-to-answer neutral questions can be helpful. At times, certain questions can also be repeated for the purpose of assessing reliability or validity.

Are Several Questions Needed Instead of One?

In some cases, two questions are better than one. However, asking two questions in one is not the solution. Consider the following question:

Do you think Nike Town offers better variety and prices than other Nike stores?

(Incorrect)

A "yes" answer will presumably be clear; however, what if the answer is "no"? Does this mean that the respondent thinks that Nike Town does not offer better variety, that it does not offer better prices, or that it neither offers better variety nor better prices? Such a question is called a **double-barreled question**, because two or more questions are combined into one. To avoid confusion, these questions should be asked separately, as follows:

Do you think Nike Town offers better variety than other Nike stores?
Do you think Nike Town offers better prices than other Nike stores?

(Correct)

double-barreled question
A single question that attempts to cover two issues. Such questions can be confusing to respondents and can result in ambiguous responses.

More than one question is needed to determine the respondents' evaluation of Nike Town.

Source: © Kevin Foy/Alamy images.

Another example of multiple questions embedded in a single question is the "why" question. In marketing research, a primary question of interest to researchers concerns brand selection. This is a "why" question in actuality. In other words, the researcher might be tempted to ask the question this way: "Why did you choose the Ford Explorer?" A typical answer to this question will likely be short. Answers such as "It was the best buy" or "I liked it" do not help the researchers understand much about this brand-choice decision. Instead, a series of questions is needed. For example, "What was your main motivation in choosing the Ford Explorer?" "How does the Ford Explorer compare to other SUV brands?" "What features of the Ford Explorer appealed to you?"

Be a DM!	Be an MR!
Old Navy: Quality and Style Are Never Old	
As the CEO of Old Navy, what would you do to improve consumers' perceptions of the quality of your brand?	Visit www.oldnavy.com and search the Internet—including social media—as well as your library's online databases to obtain information on Old Navy's marketing program. Formulate a double-barreled question to determine consumer perceptions of the quality and style of Old Navy clothing. Then reformulate this question to obtain unambiguous answers.

Social Media

Design the Questions to Overcome the Respondent's Inability to Answer

Respondents might not always be able to answer the questions posed to them. Researchers can help them overcome this limitation by keeping in mind the reasons people typically cannot answer a question: They might not be informed; they might not remember; or they might be unable to articulate certain types of responses.

Is the Respondent Informed?

Respondents often are asked to answer questions they are uninformed about. A husband might not be informed about monthly expenses for groceries and department store purchases if it is the wife who makes these purchases, or vice versa. Despite the fact that they are uninformed, respondents might provide answers, although inaccurate ones, as the following example shows.

Research in Action

Unknown Question Elicits Known Answers

In one study, respondents were asked to express their degree of agreement or disagreement with the following statement: "The National Bureau of Consumer Complaints provides an effective means for consumers who have purchased a defective product to obtain relief." Even with a "don't know" option available, 51.9 percent of the lawyers and 75.0 percent of the general public still expressed an opinion about the National Bureau of Consumer Complaints. Why should these high response rates be problematic? Because there is no such entity as the National Bureau of Consumer Complaints![3]

When the research topic requires specialized experience or knowledge, **filter questions** that measure familiarity, product use, and past experience should be asked before questions about the topics themselves. Filter questions enable the researcher to eliminate from the analysis those respondents who are not adequately informed.

In addition to filter questions, a "don't know" option to a question is helpful. This option has been found to reduce the number of uninformed responses without reducing the overall response rate. If it is suspected that many respondents might be uninformed about the topic, "don't know" should be added to the list of response alternatives.

filter questions
Initial questions in a questionnaire that screen potential respondents to ensure they meet the requirements of the sample.

Can the Respondent Remember?

Many common experiences or practices are difficult to remember. Can you remember the brand name of the shirt you are wearing, what you had for lunch a week ago, or what you were doing a month ago today? Further, do you know how many gallons of soft drink you consumed during the past 4 weeks? When making estimates about product consumption levels, in particular, research has found that consumers dramatically overestimate usage.

People tend to remember events that are personally relevant or unusual or that occur frequently. People remember their wedding anniversary and birthday. Likewise, the more recently the event occurred, the more readily an event will be recalled. For example, you are more likely to remember the purchases you made on your last trip to the grocery store than the purchases you made three shopping trips ago.

Questions can be designed to aid recall or they can be unaided, depending on the research objectives. For example, unaided recall of soft-drink commercials could be measured by questions such as, "What brands of soft drinks do you remember being advertised last night on TV?" A question that employs aided recall attempts to stimulate the respondent's memory by providing cues related to the event of interest. The aided-recall approach would list a number of soft-drink brands and then ask, "Which of these brands were advertised last night on TV?" One of the risks of presenting cues is that they can bias responses and make a respondent unduly sensitive to a topic, thus distorting their answers.

Can the Respondent Articulate?

Respondents might be unable to articulate certain types of responses. This does not mean, however, that they do not have an opinion on that topic. For example, it is difficult to describe the ideal atmosphere of a department store. However, if the respondents are provided with alternative descriptions of store atmosphere, they will be able to indicate the one they like best. When asked to provide answers that are difficult to articulate, respondents are likely to ignore that question and might refuse to complete the questionnaire. Visual aids in the form of pictures, diagrams, or maps, as well as verbal descriptions, can help respondents to articulate responses.

Be an MR!	Be a DM!

Nordstrom: A Leading Fashion Specialty Retailer

Search the Internet—including social media—as well as your library's online databases to obtain information on factors that influence the atmosphere of a department store. Develop four alternative descriptions of store atmosphere. Also, write a description of the ideal atmosphere of a department store.

As the CEO of Nordstrom, what type of atmosphere do you desire to have in your stores? Explain.

Social Media

Design the Questionnaire to Overcome the Respondent's Unwillingness to Answer

Even if respondents are able to answer a particular question, they might be unwilling to do so. Respondents might refuse to answer a question due to a variety of circumstances. The respondent might feel simply too much effort is involved, that the question serves no legitimate purpose, or that the information requested is too sensitive.

Effort Required of the Respondent

Although most individuals are willing to participate in a survey, this sense of cooperation might vanish if the questions require too much effort to answer. Suppose the researcher is interested in determining from which departments in a store the respondent purchased merchandise on the most recent shopping trip. This information can be obtained in at least two ways. The researcher could ask the respondent to list all the items purchased on his or her most recent shopping trip, or the researcher could provide a list of departments and ask the respondent to check those that are applicable. Consider the following examples:

> Please list all the departments from which you purchased merchandise on your most recent shopping trip to a department store.
>
> (Incorrect)

> In the list that follows, please check all the departments from which you purchased merchandise on your most recent shopping trip to a department store.

1. Women's dresses   _____
2. Men's apparel   _____
3. Children's apparel   _____
4. Cosmetics   _____
   .
   .
   .
8. Jewelry   _____
9. Other (please specify)   _____

(Correct)

The second option is preferable because it requires less effort from respondents. In the WV questionnaire in the opening vignette, the effort required of the respondents was reduced by asking easy questions for which the respondents merely had to check one of the response options.

Legitimate Purpose

Respondents also object to questions that do not seem to serve a legitimate purpose. Why should a firm that is marketing cereals want to know their age, income, and occupation? The researcher should anticipate these types of objections and attempt to overcome them by explaining why the data are needed. A statement such as, "To determine how the consumption of cereal and preferences for cereal brands vary among people of different ages, incomes, and occupations, we need information on . . . " can make the request for information seem legitimate. Moreover, the context of the survey should be clearly explained, as in the WV project.

Sensitive Information

It can be difficult to obtain information of a personal or highly sensitive nature from respondents. Examples of sensitive topics include money, family life, political and religious beliefs, and involvement in accidents or crimes. Respondents might be embarrassed to answer such questions, because accurate responses might threaten their prestige or self-image. To increase the likelihood of obtaining sensitive information, such topics should be placed at the end of the questionnaire. By then, rapport has been created and legitimacy of the project established, making respondents more willing to give information. Where appropriate, sensitive information should be obtained in the form of response categories rather than asking for specific figures. Whereas respondents might refuse to answer the question,

What is your household's exact annual income?

(Incorrect)

they might be willing to check the appropriate income category. A better way of obtaining information on income is to ask:

Which one of the following categories best describes your household's annual income?

_____ under $25,001
_____ $25,001 to $50,000
_____ $50,001 to $75,000
_____ $75,001 to $100,000
_____ over $100,000

(Correct)

Decide on the Question Structure

A question can be unstructured or structured. In the following sections, we define unstructured questions and discuss their advantages and limitations. This is followed by a discussion of the popular forms of structured questions: multiple-choice, dichotomous, and scales (see Figure 11.4).

Unstructured Questions

Unstructured questions are open-ended questions that respondents answer in their own words. They are also referred to as free-response or free-answer questions. The following are examples of unstructured questions:

- What is your favorite pastime?
- How would you describe the typical user of Land Rover SUVs?
- Do you intend to travel overseas within the next 6 months?

Open-ended questions are good as first questions on a topic. They enable the respondents to express general attitudes and opinions that can help the researcher interpret their responses to structured questions. Open-ended questions allow respondents to express their atti-tudes or opinions without the bias associated with restricting responses to predefined alternatives. Thus, they can be useful in identifying underlying motivations, beliefs, and attitudes, as in the WV vignette. Analysis of the verbatim comments provides a rich context for interpreting later questions. Unstructured questions are useful in exploratory research (see Table 11.1).

The disadvantages of unstructured questions relate to recording error, data coding, and the added complexity of analysis. In personal or telephone interviews, successfully recording verbatim comments depends entirely on the recording skills of the interviewer. Interviewer bias is introduced as decisions are made regarding whether to record answers verbatim or to write down only the main points. Audio recording should be used if verbatim reporting is important.

unstructured questions
Open-ended questions that respondents answer in their own words.

FIGURE 11.4
Types of Questions

TABLE 11.1 Advantages and Disadvantages of Unstructured and Structured Questions

Question Type	Advantages	Disadvantages	Comments
Unstructured	Good as first questions	Potential for interviewer bias	Useful for exploratory research
	Responses are less biased	Coding is costly and time-consuming	
	Can provide rich insights	Greater weight to articulate respondents	
		Unsuitable for self-administered questionnaires	
Multiple-Choice	Interviewer bias is reduced	Order or position bias	Responses should be mutually exclusive and collectively exhaustive
	Easy to code and analyze	Difficult to design response options	
	Improved respondent cooperation		Useful in large surveys
Dichotomous	Same as multiple-choice	Wording can bias the responses	Use split-ballot technique
Scales	Same as multiple-choice	Difficult to design multi-item scales	Scales should be evaluated for reliability, validity, and generalizability

Categorizing the recorded comments to open-ended questions introduces the second source of bias and another major disadvantage. Implicitly, unstructured questions give extra weight to respondents who are more talkative or articulate. The process of summarizing comments into a format that can be analyzed is both time-consuming and expensive. Unstructured questions also are of limited value in self-administered questionnaires (mail, CAPI, or electronic), because respondents tend to be more brief in writing than in speaking.

Research in Action

Open-Ended Questions Open the Way to a New Opportunity for Nabisco

In an exploratory survey, ConAgra Foods asked a series of open-ended questions related to cookies to identify any consumer needs it was not meeting. The survey included questions like: "What do you like about cookies?" "What do you dislike about cookies?" "What are the health benefits of cookies?" "What are health disadvantages of cookies?"

The findings revealed that the needs of a subset of specialty cookie consumers were not being met by existing "wellness specialty offerings," cookies offering health benefits. These consumers wanted great taste combined with health benefits, so that they could enjoy the cookies without feeling guilty. Seeing this opportunity, Nabisco and ConAgra joined to create and market Healthy Choice (www.healthychoice.com), an adult specialty cookie with an indulgent, yet healthful, profile. Healthy Choice cookies rank among the top-100 specialty cookie/cracker category. The Raspberry Tart ranks 33; the Apricot Tart, 92. According to the company, both were outselling all of key competitor Pepperidge Farms' wellness cookies. This success is

attributed to a focus on unsatisfied consumer needs identified through open-ended questions. As of 2011, Healthy Choice products included a line of frozen meals, fresh mixers, frozen treats, soups, and bread, none of which compromise on taste or nutrition.[4]

Source: © Ian Dagnall/Alamy Images.

In general, open-ended questions are useful in exploratory research and as opening questions. However, in a large survey, the complexity of recording, tabulation, and analysis outweighs their advantages.

Structured Questions

Structured questions specify the set of responses as well as their format. A structured question might offer multiple choices, only two choices (dichotomous question), or a scale (see Figure 11.4).

structured questions
Questions that prespecify the set of response alternatives and the response format. A structured question could be multiple-choice, dichotomous, or a scale.

MULTIPLE-CHOICE QUESTIONS   In multiple-choice questions, the researcher provides a choice of answers, and respondents are asked to select one or more of the alternatives given. Consider the following question:

Do you intend to travel overseas within the next 6 months?

```
_____ Definitely will not travel
_____ Probably will not travel
_____ Undecided
_____ Probably will travel
_____ Definitely will travel
```

Many of the issues associated with constructing itemized rating scales (see Chapter 10) also apply to multiple-choice questions. Two additional concerns in designing multiple-choice questions are (1) the number of alternatives that should be included and (2) order or position bias.

Multiple-choice questions should include choices that cover the full range of possible alternatives. The alternatives should be mutually exclusive and collectively exhaustive. An "other (please specify)" category should be included where appropriate. Instructions should clearly indicate whether the respondent is to choose only one alternative or to select all that apply. (For example, "Please indicate all the brands of soft drinks that you have consumed in the past week.") As the list of choices increases, the questions become more difficult to answer. When the alternative list becomes long, the researcher should consider using more than one question to simplify the respondents' workload.

Order or position bias is the respondents' tendency to check an alternative merely because it occupies a certain position in a list. Alternatives that appear at the beginning and, to a lesser degree, at the end of a list have a tendency to be selected most often. When questions relate to numeric values (quantities or prices), there is a tendency to select the central value on the list. Order bias can be controlled by preparing several forms of the questionnaire with changes in the order of the alternatives from form to form. Each alternative should appear once in each of the extreme positions, once in the middle, and once somewhere in between. If the questionnaire is to be administered in a computer-aided environment (CATI, CAPI, or Internet, see Chapter 7), then the software can randomize the order of the alternatives and keep track of the order for correct analysis later.

order or position bias
A respondent's tendency to choose an alternative merely because it occupies a certain position on the page or in a list.

Multiple-choice questions are easier for respondents to answer. They also are easier to analyze and tabulate than open-ended questions. Interviewer bias also is reduced, given that these types of questions work very well in self-administered conditions. Respondent cooperation in general is improved if the majority of the questions are structured.

Multiple-choice questions are not without disadvantages. It is difficult to develop effective multiple-choice options. Often, exploratory research must be conducted using open-ended questions to identify the appropriate response options. When large numbers of respondents check the "other (please specify)" category, it indicates that the alternative list might be seriously flawed. The list of options itself also introduces bias.

dichotomous question

A structured question with only two response alternatives, such as yes and no.

DICHOTOMOUS QUESTIONS   A **dichotomous question** has only two response alternatives: yes or no, agree or disagree, and so forth. Sometimes, multiple-choice questions can be dichotomous, as in the overseas travel question asked earlier:

Do you intend to travel overseas within the next 6months?

_____ Yes
_____ No

Dichotomous questions should be used when the researcher has reason to believe that the respondent thinks of the topic in yes/no terms. When the respondent is highly involved in a subject or has a great deal of knowledge related to the topic, a multiple-choice question or scale might be more appropriate.

Dichotomous questions have many of the same strengths and weaknesses of multiple-choice questions. They are among the easiest type of questions to code and analyze, as illustrated by the following American Airlines example. They have one serious flaw, however. The direction of question wording can have a significant effect on the responses given. To illustrate this directional bias, the statement, "Individuals are more to blame than social conditions for crime and lawlessness in this country," produced agreement from 59.6 percent of the respondents in a research study. However, on a matched sample that responded to the opposite statement, "Social conditions are more to blame than individuals for crime and lawlessness in this country," 43.2 percent agreed (as opposed to 40.4% expected based on agreement with the opposite statement). To overcome this directional bias, the question should be framed in one direction on one-half of the questionnaires and in the opposite direction on the other half. This is referred to as the *split-ballot technique*. Consider the use of dichotomous questions by American Airlines.

Research in Action

The Use of Dichotomous Questions Is American

American Airlines is one of the largest scheduled passenger airlines in the world. As of 2011, American and its regional airline affiliates, American Eagle and the AmericanConnection airlines, serve 250 cities in more than 40 countries with more than 3,500 daily flights. Naturally, one of the world's largest airlines would need to implement surveys and other methods of feedback in order to continuously improve its service. American Airlines employs Key Survey (www.KeySurvey.com) to conduct customer satisfaction tracking surveys on topics from ticket booking to in-flight meals. The surveys are conducted online. A random sample of about 25,000 people is picked every 2 weeks from American's customer database. The respondents are e-mailed a link to the survey. The survey asks them how their flight was and information about the in-flight service so that American Airlines can get an overview of how well it is performing. The survey questions are structured in such a way so as to ask "did this happen?" For example, survey questions might ask "When you checked in, were you greeted by the agent?" "Were you served a predeparture drink?" and so on. All respondents have to do is answer yes or no for 30 dichotomous questions.

As a result of these surveys, several modifications have been made. Customer insights gathered through surveys revealed that customers felt baffled and confused when trying to use the American Airlines Web site to book a flight. Therefore, the process for booking a flight has been made more transparent and easy for the end user.[5]

SCALES   Scales were discussed in detail in Chapters 9 and 10. Sometimes, multiple-choice questions can alternatively be framed as scales, as in the overseas travel question asked earlier.

Do you intend to travel overseas within the next 6 months?

Definitely will not travel	Probably will not travel	Undecided	Probably will travel	Definitely will travel
1	2	3	4	5

Questions making use of scales are easy to answer and, therefore, are popular, as in the WV opening vignette.

Be a DM!	Be an MR!	
Estee Lauder: The Sweet Smell of Perfume		
As the marketing chief for Estee Lauder perfumes, how would you instill positive consumer attitudes toward your brands?	Search the Internet—including social media—as well as your library's online databases to obtain information on consumers' attitudes toward perfumes. Obtain information on consumers' attitudes toward Estee Lauder perfumes using an unstructured, a multichotomous, a dichotomous, and a scaling question.	

Determine the Question Wording

Translating the information needed into clearly worded questions that are easily understood is the most difficult aspect of questionnaire development. Poorly worded questions can confuse or mislead respondents, leading to nonresponse or response error. Poorly worded questions can also frustrate the respondents to the point that they refuse to answer those questions or items. This is referred to as *item nonresponse* and leads to nonresponse error. If respondents interpret questions differently than intended by the researcher, serious bias can occur, leading to response error.

To avoid problems in question wording, consider the following five guidelines: (1) define the issue, (2) use ordinary words, (3) avoid ambiguous words, (4) avoid leading questions, and (5) use positive and negative statements.

Define the Issue

Questions should always clearly define the issue being addressed. Beginning journalists are told to define the issue in terms of *who*, *what*, *when*, *where*, *why*, and *way* (the six Ws). These—particularly *who*, *what*, *when*, and *where*—can also serve as guidelines for defining the issue in a question. Consider the following question:

Which brand of toothpaste do you use?

(Incorrect)

On the surface, this might seem to be a well-defined question, but a different conclusion can be reached when it is examined under the microscope of *who*, *what*, *when*, and *where*.

The Ws	Defining the Question
Who	**The Respondent**
	It is not clear whether this question relates to the individual respondent or the respondent's total household.
What	**The Brand of Toothpaste**
	It is unclear how the respondent is to answer this question if more than one brand is used.
When	**Unclear**
	The time frame is not specified in this question. The respondent could interpret it as meaning the toothpaste used this morning, this week, or over the past year.
Where	**Not Specified**
	At home, at the gym, on the road?

A more clearly defined question might read:

Which brand or brands of toothpaste have you personally used at home during the past month? In case of more than one brand, please list all the brands that apply.

(Correct)

A well-defined question is needed to determine which brand(s) of toothpaste a person uses.

Source: George Dolgikh/Shutterstock.

Use Simple Words

Simple, ordinary words that match the vocabulary level of the respondent should be used in a questionnaire. When choosing words, keep in mind that the average person in the United States has a high school, not a college, education. For certain respondent groups, the education level is even lower. Simplicity in wording and a conscious effort to avoid technical jargon should guide questionnaire development. As marketing professionals, it also is important to remember that most respondents do not understand marketing terminology. For example, instead of asking,

Is the distribution of snack foods adequate?

(Incorrect)

ask,

Are snack foods readily available when you want to buy them?

(Correct)

Use Unambiguous Words

When selecting words for a questionnaire, the questionnaire designer should choose words with only one meaning. This is not an easy task given that a number of words that appear unambiguous can have different meanings to different people. These include *usually, normally, frequently, often, regularly, occasionally,* and *sometimes.* Consider the following question:

In a typical month, how often do you go to a movie theater to see a movie?

_____ Never
_____ Occasionally
_____ Sometimes
_____ Often
_____ Regularly

(Incorrect)

The categories of this multiple-choice question can have different meanings to different people, leading to response bias. Three respondents who go to movie theaters once a month might check three different categories: occasionally, sometimes, and often. The following is a much better worded question:

In a typical month, how often do you go to a movie theater to see a movie?

_____ Less than once
_____ 1 or 2 times
_____ 3 or 4 times
_____ More than 4 times

(Correct)

This question is less ambiguous because each respondent is answering it from a consistent frame of reference. Response categories have been objectively defined, and respondents are no longer free to interpret them in their own way. Additionally, all-inclusive or all-exclusive words are understood differently by different people. Some examples of such words are *all, always, any, anybody, ever,* and *every.* Such words should be avoided. To illustrate, *any* could mean "every," "some," or "one only" to different respondents, depending on how they look at it.

Avoid Leading or Biasing Questions

A **leading question** is one that clues the respondent to what the answer should be. Some respondents have a tendency to agree with whatever way the question is leading them to answer. This tendency is know as *yea-saying* and results in a bias called **acquiescence bias**. Consider the following question:

Do you think that America should provide financial aid to poor foreign countries when it is not our responsibility to do so?

_____ Yes
_____ No
_____ Don't know

(Incorrect)

leading question
A question that gives the respondent a clue as to what the answer should be.

acquiescence bias
Bias resulting from some respondents' tendency to agree with the direction of a leading question (yea-saying).

This question would lead respondents to a "no" answer. The answer would be unduly biased by the phrase "it is not our responsibility to do so." Therefore, this question would not help determine the preferences of Americans for providing aid to poor foreign countries. A better question would be:

Do you think that America should provide financial aid to poor foreign countries?

_____ Yes
_____ No
_____ Don't know

(Correct)

Words can lead respondents in a particular direction. Identification of the research sponsor can have the same effect. When respondents are made aware of the sponsor, they tend to answer questions about that sponsor in a positive manner. The question,

Is Colgate your favorite toothpaste?

(Incorrect)

is likely to bias the responses in favor of Colgate. A more unbiased way of obtaining this information would be to ask,

What is your favorite brand of toothpaste?

(Correct)

Likewise, the mention of a prestigious or nonprestigious name can bias the response, as in, "Do you agree with the American Dental Association that Colgate is effective in preventing cavities?" Question wording should be objective, as in the WV opening vignette.

Balance Dual Statements

Many questions, particularly those measuring attitudes and lifestyles, are worded as statements to which respondents indicate their degree of agreement or disagreement using Likert scales. The statements in these types of questions can be worded either positively or negatively. Evidence shows that the responses obtained often depend on the direction of the wording of the questions—that is, whether they are stated positively or negatively. Questions of this type should be balanced by dual statements, some of which are positive and some negative. Two different questionnaires that reverse the direction of the questions could also be used to control for any bias introduced by the positive or negative nature of the statements. An example of dual statements was provided in the summated Likert scale in Chapter 10 that was designed to measure attitudes toward Macy's.

Social Media

Be a DM!	Be an MR!
FedEx: The Big Caters to the Small	
As the marketing director for FedEx, how would you penetrate the important small business market for overnight package delivery?	Visit www.fedex.com and search the Internet—including social media—as well as your library's online databases to obtain information on the overnight package delivery market. Write a brief report. Evaluate the wording of the following question asked of small business owners/CEOs: If FedEx were to introduce a new overnight delivery service for small businesses, how likely are you to adopt it?

Arrange the Questions in Proper Order

When arranging questions in a proper order, the researcher should consider the opening questions, the type of information sought, question difficulty, and the effect on subsequent questions. Questions should be arranged in a logical order, organized around topic areas.

Opening Questions

Opening questions set the stage for the remainder of the questionnaire. They serve a variety of purposes. They can introduce the topic, attempt to gain the confidence and cooperation of respondents, or establish the legitimacy of the study. The opening questions should be interesting, simple, and nonthreatening. Questions that ask respondents for their opinions are always good openers, because most people like to express their opinions.

Sometimes opening questions might be asked to simply establish rapport. Some studies require a prescreening of the respondents to ensure that they are eligible to participate in the interview. In these cases, qualifying questions are used as opening questions.

Research in Action

Qualifying Respondents Leads to Unqualified Success for Kellogg's

Looking to expand its share of the ready-to-eat cereal category, Kellogg's conducted a telephone survey of users. The nonusers of ready-to-eat cereals were not relevant for this study and, thus, not part of the target population. The first question was:

How often do you have ready-to-eat cereal for breakfast?

_____ Less than twice a week
_____ Two or three times per week
_____ Four or five times per week
_____ More than five times per week

If the answer was "less than twice a week," that respondent was thanked and the interview terminated. Such respondents were operationally classified as nonusers and excluded from the study.

The results of the survey indicated that consumers were looking for a crunchy, tasty, yet low-fat and healthy cereal. Based on the survey's findings, Kellogg's introduced Kellogg's FiberPlus™ Berry Yogurt Crunch cereal. It contains whole grain wheat and rice flakes with berry and yogurt flavored clusters. This new cereal supplies 40 percent of daily fiber requirements. Kellogg's also introduced Fiber Plus chewy bars. These new products have been a great success in a very competitive market.[6]

Type of Information

Three types of information are obtained from a questionnaire: (1) basic information, (2) classification information, and (3) identification information. **Basic information** relates directly to the research problem. **Classification information** consists of socioeconomic and demographic characteristics. It is used to classify the respondents in order to analyze results across different groups. **Identification information** includes name, postal address, e-mail address, and telephone number. Identification information can be obtained for a variety of purposes, including verifying that the respondents listed were actually interviewed, remitting promised incentives, and so forth. Because basic information is the most important aspect of a study, it should be obtained first, followed by classification and then identification information. Classification and identification information is of a more personal nature. Respondents might resist answering a series of personal questions. Therefore, these types of questions should appear at the end of the questionnaire, as in the WV vignette.

basic information
Information that relates directly to the marketing research problem.

classification information
Socioeconomic and demographic characteristics used to classify respondents.

identification information
A type of information obtained in a questionnaire that includes name, postal address, e-mail address, and phone number.

Difficult Questions

Respondents can perceive questions as difficult for a variety of reasons. They might relate to sensitive issues or be embarrassing, complex, or dull. Questions that could be perceived as difficult should be placed late in the sequence, after a relationship has been established and the respondent is involved in the process. The last question of the classification section is typically income information. The respondent's telephone number is the final item in the identification section for the same reasons.

Effect on Subsequent Questions

Initial questions can influence questions asked later in a questionnaire. As a rule, a series of questions should start with a general introduction to a topic, followed by specific questions related to the topic. This prevents specific questions from biasing responses to the general questions. Consider the following sequence of questions:

Q1: What considerations are important to you in selecting a department store?
Q2: In selecting a department store, how important is convenience of location?

(Correct)

The first question is general, whereas the second is specific. If these questions were reversed, respondents would be more likely to cite convenience of location as the response to the general question. Going from general to specific is called the **funnel approach**, because it begins with broader (more general) questions and then asks narrower (more specific) questions, reflecting the shape of a funnel (see Figure 11.5).[7]

funnel approach
A strategy for ordering questions in a questionnaire in which the sequence starts with the general questions, which are followed by progressively specific questions, in order to prevent specific questions from biasing responses to general questions.

FIGURE 11.5

The Funnel Approach to Ordering Questions

BROAD OR GENERAL QUESTIONS

NARROW OR SPECIFIC QUESTIONS

The funnel approach was illustrated in the opening vignette when general information about motivations for giving was obtained before measuring awareness and perceptions of World Vision. Although the funnel approach is more commonly used, sometimes an inverted funnel approach is used when the respondents do not have clearly formulated views about a topic or when they lack a common frame of reference in responding to general questions on the topic. In this approach, the specific questions are asked first, followed by more general questions.

Logical Order

Questions should be asked in a logical order, organized around topic areas. This was illustrated in the WV vignette. The order in which the questions were asked was as follows: (1) priorities and motivations for giving, (2) awareness of the organization (WV), (3) perceptions of the organization, (4) communication with donors, and (5) demographic information. When switching topics, brief transitional phrases or sentences should be used to help respondents switch their train of thought; for example, "In this section, we ask questions related to your purchase of a new car in the last 6 months."

branching questions
Questions used to guide respondents or interviewers through a survey by directing them to different spots on the questionnaire depending on the answers given.

Branching questions direct respondents or interviewers to different places in the questionnaire based on their response to the question at hand. To avoid confusion, they should be designed carefully. Here is an example of a well-designed question: "If the answer to Question 4 (Have you purchased a new car in the last 6 months?) is 'no,' go to Question 10; skip Questions 5 through 9 related to a new car purchase." Branches enable respondents to skip irrelevant questions or elaborate in areas of specific interest. Skip patterns can become quite complex to the point that they are best administered in computer-aided interviewing environments (CATI, CAPI, or Internet, see Chapter 7). The general order of questions is outlined in Table 11.2 and illustrated in the context of grocery shopping.

Be an MR!	Be a DM!

Is the Flat-Panel TV Market Flat?

Social Media

Search the Internet—including social media—as well as your library's online databases to obtain information on consumers' perceptions, preferences, and purchase intentions for flat-panel television sets. Specify the information needed and the order in which you would obtain information on consumers' perceptions, preferences, and purchase intentions for Sony flat-panel television sets.

As the vice president of marketing, what marketing strategies would you formulate to increase Sony's penetration of the flat-panel television market?

TABLE 11.2 The General Ordering of Questions in a Questionnaire

Question Type	Nature	Function	Example
Qualifying/Screening Questions	Focus on respondent inclusion criteria	To determine if a respondent is eligible to participate in the survey	Who in your household does most of the shopping for groceries?
Introductory Questions/ Warm-Ups	Broad, easy questions	To break the ice and put the respondent at ease	How often do you shop for groceries?
Main Questions: Easy	Related to the information needed but easy to answer	To focus on the survey topic and reassure the respondent that survey is easy	How important is each of the following factors in selecting a supermarket?
Main Questions: More Difficult	Related to the information needed but may be difficult to answer	To obtain the rest of the information needed	How would you rank order the following eight supermarkets in terms of your preference to shop?
Psychographics/Lifestyles	Not relevant in all surveys	To obtain personality-related information	Please indicate your degree of disagreement with the following statements.
Demographics	Personal information	To classify the respondents	What was your household's total annual income last year?
Identification Information	Name, address, telephone	To identify the respondent	Name:_____

Choose the Form and Layout

The physical characteristics of a questionnaire, such as the format, spacing, and positioning, can have a significant effect on the results. This is particularly true for self-administered questionnaires. Experiments on mail questionnaires for the 2010 and earlier census revealed that questions at the top of the page received more attention than those at the bottom. Instructions printed in red made little difference, except that they made the questionnaire appear more complicated to the respondents.

Dividing a questionnaire into sections with separate topic areas for each section is a good practice, as illustrated in the WV project. Several parts might be needed for questions pertaining to the basic information. The questions in each part should be numbered, particularly when branching questions are used. Numbering also makes coding the responses easier. Preferably, the questionnaires should be precoded. In **precoding**, the codes to enter in the computer are printed on the questionnaire. Typically, the code identifies the line number and the column numbers in which a particular response will be entered. Note that when CATI or CAPI are used, the precoding is built into the software. Coding of questionnaires is explained in more detail in Chapter 15 on data preparation. An example of precoding a questionnaire is shown in the residential carpeting survey.

precoding
In questionnaire design, assigning a code to every conceivable response before data collection.

Research in Action

Precoding a Questionnaire

Residential Carpeting Survey

(A)

(Please ignore the CAPITAL LETTERS alongside the answers. They are only to help us in data processing.)

Please answer the following questions pertaining to household carpeting by following the specified directions.

Part A

Q1. Does your household currently own carpeting?

1. _____ Yes   (B)
2. _____ No

(IF YES, GO TO QUESTION Q2; IF NO, GO TO QUESTION Q7.)

Q2. Which of the following styles of carpeting do you have in your home? Please check as many as apply.

a. _____ One Color; Traditional Style   (C)
b. _____ Multicolor; Traditional Style   (D)
c. _____ One Color; Contemporary Style   (E)
d. _____ Multicolor; Contemporary Style (F)
e. _____ Other   (G)

Please indicate your agreement with each of the following statements (Q3 through Q6).

Q3. Carpeting is an important part of my home.

Strongly Disagree   Neutral   Strongly Agree
1 2 3 4 5 6 7   (H)

Q4. Carpeting is a fashion item for the home.

Strongly Disagree   Neutral   Strongly Agree
1 2 3 4 5 6 7   (I)

Q5. Carpeting is a central item in my interior design for my home.

Strongly Disagree   Neutral   Strongly Agree
1 2 3 4 5 6 7   (J)

Q6. It is more important for a carpet to last long than look pretty.

Strongly Disagree   Neutral   Strongly Agree
1 2 3 4 5 6 7   (K)

The next question deals with your likelihood of buying new carpeting.

Q7. How likely is your household to buy new carpeting in the next 3 months?

                    Maybe/
Not so Likely   Maybe Not   Very Likely
1 2 3 4 5 6 7   (L)

In the preceding example, the capital letters denote the columns of a spreadsheet. The questionnaire ID will be entered in column A and the response to Question 1 will be entered in column B, and so on. In general, the questionnaires themselves should be numbered serially, because this enhances control of questionnaires in the field, as well as the coding and analysis. This numbering system alerts the researcher if questionnaires are misplaced or lost. A possible exception to this rule is mail questionnaires. Respondents are promised anonymity, and the presence of a questionnaire identifier might be interpreted as a breach of that promise. Some respondents might refuse to participate or answer differently if they believe the answers can be traced to them. However, recent research suggests that this loss of anonymity has little, if any, influence on the results.

Reproduce the Questionnaire

The quality of the paper and print process used for the questionnaire also influences response. For example, if the questionnaire is reproduced on poor-quality paper or is otherwise shabby in appearance, the respondents might conclude that the project is unimportant, and this perception will be reflected in the quality of the responses. Therefore, the questionnaire should be reproduced on good-quality paper and have a professional appearance, as illustrated in the WV study. Multipage questionnaires should be presented in booklet form rather than simply stapled or clipped. This format is easier for the interviewer to handle and enhances the overall appearance.

Questions should not be continued from one page to the next. In other words, researchers should avoid splitting a question, including its response categories. Respondents might be misled into thinking that a split question has ended at the bottom of a page and base their answers on the incomplete question.

The tendency to crowd questions together to make the questionnaire look shorter should be avoided. Overcrowding leaves little space for responses, which results in shorter answers. It also increases errors in data tabulation. In addition, crowded questionnaires appear more complex, resulting in lower cooperation and completion rates. Although shorter questionnaires are more desirable than longer ones, reduction in size should not be obtained at the expense of crowding.

Experiential Learning

Designing a Survey Questionnaire

Meteor Motorcycle Company is one of the industry's leading manufacturers of customized, high-performance bikes in the luxury cruiser class. Return to Chapter 3's experiential learning, "Crafting a Research Proposal," to review the proposal presented to this company. Go to the textbook Web site and download the following file: Meteor Survey A.doc. This is the draft version of the survey used to fulfill the research objectives listed in the research proposal for the Meteor Motorcycle Company presented in Chapter 3 as Meteor Proposal.doc. Open Meteor Survey A.doc and read the actual draft version of the survey questionnaire done after this proposal was accepted by Meteor.

1. How would you improve this draft of the questionnaire? Hints: Think about what was promised in the proposal.

Think also about the guidelines presented in this chapter.

2. Create an electronic copy of Meteor Survey A.doc titled "Meteor Survey A2.doc." Make your proposed revisions in this new document.

3. How would you make this draft of the survey appear more appealing to the respondent? Hint: Think about the "Form and Layout" and "Reproduce the Questionnaire" sections.

4. Make your proposed revisions in this new document Meteor Survey A2.doc.

5. Using Qualtrics (access is included with this book), develop an online version of your revised survey as given in Meteor Survey A2.doc.

Pretest the Questionnaire

pretesting

The testing of the questionnaire on a small sample of respondents for the purpose of improving the questionnaire by identifying and eliminating potential problems before using it in the actual survey.

Pretesting refers to testing the questionnaire on a small sample of respondents, usually 15 to 30, to identify and eliminate potential problems. Even the best questionnaire can be improved by pretesting. As a general rule, a questionnaire should not be used in the field study without extensive pretesting, as in the WV vignette. All aspects of the questionnaire, including question content, wording, sequence, form and layout, question difficulty, and instructions, should be tested. Additionally, pretesting should be conducted with a subset of the respondent group. The pretest groups should be similar to the survey respondents in terms of their background characteristics, familiarity with the topic, and attitudes and behaviors of interest.[8]

Pretests are best done by personal interviews, even if the actual survey is to be conducted by telephone, mail, or electronically, so that interviewers can observe respondent reactions and attitudes. After the necessary changes have been made, another pretest could be administered using the actual data collection approach, if it is mail, telephone, or electronic. This stage of the pretest will reveal any potential problems in the interviewing method to be used in the actual survey. The pretest should be conducted in an environment and context similar to that of the actual survey.

Based on feedback from the pretest, the questionnaire should be edited, and the ident problems corrected. After each significant revision of the questionnaire, another pretest shou conducted, using a different sample of respondents. Pretesting should be continued until no f changes are needed. As a final step, the responses obtained during the pretest should be cod analyzed. The analysis of pretest responses can serve as a check on the adequacy of the p definition and provide insight into the nature of the data as well as analytic techniques tha required. Table 11.3 outlines the questionnaire design process in the form of a checklist.

TABLE 11.3 Questionnaire Design Checklist

Step 1   Specify the Information Needed

1. Ensure that the information obtained fully addresses all the components of the problem.
2. Have a clear idea of the target population.

Step 2   Specify the Type of Interviewing Method

1. Review the type of interviewing method determined based on considerations discussed in Chapter 7.

Step 3   Determine the Content of Individual Question

1. Is the question necessary?
2. Are several questions needed instead of one to obtain the required information in an unambiguous manner?
3. Do not use double-barreled questions.

Step 4   Overcome the Respondent's Inability and Unwillingness to Answer

1. Is the respondent informed?
2. If respondents are not likely to be informed, filter questions that measure familiarity, product use, and past experience should be asked before questions about the topics themselves.
3. Can the respondent remember?
4. Questions that do not provide the respondent with cues can underestimate the actual occurrence of an event.
5. Can the respondent articulate?
6. Minimize the effort required by the respondents.
7. Make the request for information seem legitimate.
8. Is the information sensitive?

Step 5   Decide on the Question Structure

1. Open-ended questions are useful in exploratory research and as opening questions.
2. Use structured questions whenever possible.
3. In multiple-choice questions, the response alternatives should include the set of all possible choices and should be mutually exclusive.
4. In a dichotomous question, if a substantial proportion of the respondents can be expected to be neutral, include a neutral alternative.
5. Consider the use of the split-ballot technique to reduce order bias in dichotomous and multiple-choice questions.
6. If the response alternatives are numerous, consider using more than one question.

Step 6   Determine the Question Wording

1. Define the issue in terms of who, what, when, where, why, and way (the six Ws).
2. Use ordinary words. Words should match the vocabulary level of the respondents.
3. Avoid ambiguous words: *usually, normally, frequently, often, regularly, occasionally, sometimes,* and so forth.
4. Avoid leading questions that clue the respondent to what the answer should be.
5. Use positive and negative statements.

Step 7   Arrange the Questions in Proper Order

1. The opening questions should be interesting, simple, and nonthreatening.
2. Qualifying questions should serve as the opening questions.
3. Basic information should be obtained first, followed by classification, and, finally, identification information.
4. Difficult, sensitive, or complex questions should be placed late in the sequence.
5. General questions should precede specific questions.
6. Questions should be asked in a logical order.

(Continued)

TABLE 11.3 Continued

Step 8   Choose the Form and Layout

1. Divide a questionnaire into several parts.
2. Number the questions in each part.
3. Precode the questionnaire.
4. Serially number the questionnaires themselves.

Step 9   Reproduce the Questionnaire

1. The questionnaire should have a professional appearance.
2. Use a booklet format for long questionnaires.
3. Reproduce each question on a single page (or double-page spread).
4. Avoid the tendency to crowd questions to make the questionnaire look shorter. Place directions or instructions for individual questions as close as possible to the questions.

Step 10 Pretest the Questionnaire

1. Always pretest.
2. Test all aspects of the questionnaire, including question content, wording, sequence, form and layout, question difficulty, and instructions.
3. Use respondents in the pretest that are similar to those who will be included in the actual survey.
4. Begin the pretest by using personal interviews.
5. Conduct the pretest by mail, telephone, or electronically if those methods are to be used in the actual survey.
6. Use a variety of interviewers for pretests.
7. The pretest sample size should be small, varying from 15 to 30 respondents for the initial testing.
8. After each significant revision of the questionnaire, conduct another pretest, using a different sample of respondents.
9. Code and analyze the responses obtained from the pretest.

Observational Forms

Observational forms are designed to record respondent reaction to new products, advertising, packaging, or some other marketing stimuli. Because there is no questioning of the respondents, the researcher does not need to be concerned with the psychological impact of the questions and the way they are asked. Observational forms are designed primarily for the fieldwork and the tabulation phase, providing a guide for recording information accurately and simplifying coding, entry, and analysis of data.

Observational forms should specify the *who, what, when, where, why,* and *way* of behavior to be observed. Refer to the discussion on descriptive research in Chapter 3 for a similar analysis. Suppose that McDonald's wants to observe consumers' reaction to the deluxe sandwiches to be introduced nationally. An observational form to record customer reaction would include space for all of the information specified in the McDonald's example.

Research in Action

Are McDonald's Deluxe Sandwiches Truly Deluxe?

Who:	Purchasers, adults, parents with children, teenagers
What:	Deluxe sandwiches, other sandwiches and menu items considered/purchased, influence of children or other family members
When:	Day, hour, and date of observation
Where:	At checkout counter, inside the store in the eating area, outside the store upon exit
Why:	Influence of promotion or family members on the purchase
Way:	Personal observer disguised as sales clerk, undisguised personal observer, hidden camera, or obtrusive mechanical device

Source: © mediablitzimages (uk) Limited/Alamy Images.

The same physical design considerations of layout and reproduction apply to both questionnaires and observational forms. A well-designed form guides the observer to appropriately record the details of the observation rather than merely summarize them. Finally, like questionnaires, observational forms also require adequate pretesting.

Be a DM!	Be an MR!
The Joy (and Craziness) of Christmas Shopping	
As the marketing director for Neiman Marcus, develop marketing programs to capitalize upon consumers' Christmas retail shopping for the upcoming season.	Search the Internet—including social media—as well as your library's online databases to obtain information on consumers' Christmas retail shopping behavior. Specify the method and design an observational form to observe the consumers' Christmas retail shopping behavior.

Social Media

Software for Questionnaire Design

Software can greatly facilitate the process of developing a questionnaire. The software discussed in Chapter 7 in the section titled "Electronic Surveys Software and Sites" can also be used for designing questionnaires. With this book you have access to Qualtrics (www.qualtrics.com), which will enable you to electronically design questionnaires.

A number of Web sites housed in universities offer valuable resources, such as scales and question libraries, for constructing questionnaires. Some helpful sites include the Interuniversity Consortium for Political and Social Research at the University of Michigan (www.icpsr.umich.edu); the Roper Center at the University of Connecticut (www.ropercenter.uconn.edu); the Survey Research Library at Florida State University (www.fsu.edu/~survey); and the Odum Institute, which houses the Louis Harris Data Center at the University of North Carolina, Chapel Hill (www.irss.unc.edu).

Summary Illustration Using the Opening Vignette

We summarize and illustrate the questionnaire design process by returning to the opening vignette. Notice that the information obtained for WV and the order in which it was obtained were clearly specified. The questionnaire was kept simple, and detailed instructions were provided, because it had to be administered by mail. Only necessary questions were asked, and combined questions were avoided. To increase the willingness of the donors and potential donors to participate and complete the questionnaire, the context of the survey was made clear, and the effort required of the respondents was minimized. Most of the questions were structured questions, requiring the respondents to simply circle a number on the scale. However, a few open-ended questions were included where it was felt that the respondents needed the freedom to express underlying motivations for giving to charity.

Words with unequivocal meanings but that were familiar to the donors were used. Special effort was made to not bias the responses in any direction. The ordering of the questions was logical, and the funnel approach was used. General questions about priorities and motivations for giving were asked first; questions about awareness and perceptions of WV followed. The questionnaire was divided into parts, with a separate part devoted to each type of information sought. Information on name and address was optional and was obtained at the end of the questionnaire. The questionnaire was professionally reproduced and thoroughly pretested. Figure 11.6 provides a concept map for question wording. In this figure, the major concept (A Question Should) is described by minor concepts that are connected to that major concept by lines with descriptors. Thus, a question should define the issue in terms of who, what, when, where, why and way. The rest of the figure can be interpreted similarly.

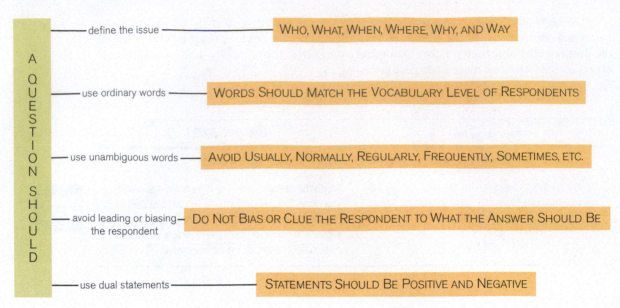

FIGURE 11.6

A Concept Map for Question Wording

International Marketing Research

The questionnaire or research instrument should be designed to be sensitive to cultural differences encountered in international research. Differences in underlying consumer behavior, decision-making processes, psychographics, lifestyles, and demographic variables should all be considered. Questions related to marital status, education, household size, occupation, income, and dwelling unit might have to be modified to be comparable across countries, requiring rewording. For example, household definition and size vary greatly, given the extended family structure in some countries and the practice of two, or even three, families living under the same roof.

Although personal interviewing is the dominant survey method in international marketing research, different interviewing methods might be used in different countries. Therefore, the questionnaire must be adaptable to a variety of administration methods. In countries with lower levels of education or product experience, two or more simple questions rather than a single complex question should be used. The researcher should realize that respondents in some countries, for example, in some African nations, might not be as well informed about the subject matter of the survey as respondents in the United States.

Using unstructured questions might be necessary if the researcher does not fully understand the range of alternatives associated with a response. Using unstructured questions can also minimize the risk of cultural bias. However, unstructured questions are more sensitive to differences in educational levels than are structured questions. They should be used with caution in countries with high illiteracy rates.

In addition to design considerations, the researcher must also pay close attention to translation issues. An equivalent word or phrase might not be available in some languages. For example, it is not easy to translate *self-respect* into German or *macho* into Arabic. Pretesting of the questionnaire is complicated in international research, because the linguistic equivalence must be pretested. Two sets of pretests are recommended. The translated questionnaire should be pretested on respondents who speak only their native language, as well as on bilingual subjects. Multiple languages are spoken in some countries, and a national survey in such a country can require questionnaire translation into different languages. This is true in some large countries such as India, which has 19 major languages and more than 200 dialects. It also is true in some small countries such as Singapore, where the languages spoken include English, Malay, Hokkien, Tamil, Mandarin, and Cantonese. The pretest data from administering the questionnaire in different countries or cultures should be analyzed, and the pattern of responses compared, to detect any cultural biases.

Research in Action

Engaging Respondents About Engagement

A questionnaire dealing with engagement rings was administered to women in seven European countries. The first set of questions used in England was:

1. Are you married?
   If "yes," in what year were you married?
   If "no," are you engaged to be married?
   If married or engaged:

2. Do you own an engagement ring, or did you obtain one or more rings at the time of your engagement?
   If "yes":

3. What type of ring is it/was it?
   _____ No stones
   _____ Single diamond only
   _____ Several diamonds, no other stones
   _____ Diamonds and other stones
   _____ Other stones only

This looks like a very simple list of questions, involving no difficulty of direct or literal translation. Yet, if the questionnaire were literally translated for use in some of the other countries, the results would have been meaningless. The question, "Do you own an engagement ring?" would not have worked in Germany, because many German women receive a plain gold band at the time of engagement, which they later transfer to the other hand and use as a wedding ring. Instead of a single question, a whole battery of questions was needed to obtain information from Germany that was equivalent to that of the other six countries. Thus, the researcher had to translate the meaning rather than do a literal translation (transliteration).

Another modification to ensure comparability concerned the list of precoded ring types. Although pearl rings were relatively unimportant in most countries covered, they were a high proportion of engagement rings in Spain and France. To include pearl rings as a separate category in most of the countries would have unnecessarily complicated the list. However, to exclude them in Spain or France would have resulted not only in the loss of information, but also in confusion arising from the list of type of rings being incomplete. Therefore, the pearl ring was included as a ring type in only the Spanish and French questionnaires.[9]

Marketing Research and Social Media

Analysis of social media can provide a good understanding of the underlying issues pertaining to the problem at hand. Such an understanding can be very valuable in designing an appropriate questionnaire for use in traditional or social media surveys. As we have discussed earlier in this chapter, some of the challenges in questionnaire design involve determining the content, structure, and wording of individual questions. To come up with questions that are appropriate in terms of content, structure and wording, research skills have to be applied from the respondents' viewpoints. The same is true for deciding on the order of questions. Social media are an effective and accessible domain for capturing viewpoints of the target respondents. For questionnaires to be used in surveys to be conducted in social media, the general principles and guidelines remain the same as discussed in the chapter.

Research in Action

Bottled Innovation

Sigg USA (www.mysigg.com) is a manufacturer of eco-friendly aluminum water bottles. The company makes bottles that customers can reuse, instead of throwing plastic bottles into a landfill. Sigg wanted to conduct a survey to determine the consumer's views on eco-friendliness. However, designing a questionnaire was turning out to be a challenge as it was not clear what questions should be asked, and what should be the content, structure, and wording of the questions. So Sigg worked with the Gold Mobile (www.gold-mobile.com), a social media marketing agency, to create a contest called "What Does Eco-Friendly Mean To You?" The agency targeted its promotion to eco-friendly specialty sites like Hugg, a social bookmarking service for eco-enthusiasts. It also sponsored the contest on InHabitat, a community for design and architecture professionals with interest in eco-friendly trends. Ecology bloggers noticed the presence on InHabitat, leading to more than 100 mentions of the contest. Ultimately, more than 160 entries were submitted, providing rich insights into what eco-friendly meant to consumers and more than enough information to design a survey questionnaire. A dominant theme that emerged was that eco-friendliness meant protection of nature, from oceans to the open prairies. The survey findings not only helped Sigg to develop innovative eco-friendly bottle designs but also an effective marketing platform to target the eco-friendly consumers. On July 4, 2009, Sigg launched "Celebrate America," a limited-release collection of their famous bottles. The collection consists of six eco-friendly special Sigg bottle designs by American artists, including Keith Haring and Drew Brophy. The images on the bottles celebrate daily life in the States from coast to coast, from the big surf to the open prairies.[10]

Ethics in Marketing Research

Administering a questionnaire is a substantial intrusion by the researcher. Therefore, several ethical concerns arise pertaining to the researcher–respondent relationship. Ethical issues pertinent to the researcher–client relationship might also have to be addressed.

In consideration of the respondents, questions that are confusing, that exceed the respondents' ability, that are difficult, or that are otherwise improperly worded should be avoided. When asking sensitive questions, researchers should attempt to minimize the respondents' discomfort. It should be made clear at the beginning of the questionnaire that respondents are not obligated to answer any question that makes them uncomfortable. Similarly, overly long questionnaires should be avoided. As a general guideline, the following are considered overly long: a personal, in-home interview lasting more than 60 minutes; a telephone interview more than 30 minutes; a mall-intercept interview more than 30 minutes; and a mail or electronic interview more than 30 minutes. Overly long questionnaires are a burden on the respondents and adversely affect the quality of responses.

The researcher has the ethical responsibility to design a questionnaire that obtains the required data in an unbiased manner. Deliberately biasing the questionnaire in a desired direction—for example, by asking leading questions—cannot be condoned. In deciding the question structure, the most appropriate, rather than the most convenient, option should be adopted, as illustrated by the next example. If the questionnaire is not thoroughly pretested, an ethical breach has occurred.

Research in Action

Questioning International Marketing Ethics

One way to avoid biased questions in the international arena is to use open-ended questions. This is particularly appropriate if the response categories are not known. In a study designed to identify ethical problems in international marketing, a series of open-ended questions was used. The objective of the survey, directed at Australian firms engaged in international marketing activities, was to find the three most frequently encountered ethical problems, in order of priority. After reviewing the results, the researcher tabulated and categorized them into 10 categories that occurred most often: traditional small-scale bribery, large-scale bribery, gifts/favors/entertainment, pricing, inappropriate products/technology, tax evasion practices, illegal/immoral activities, questionable commissions to channel members, cultural differences, and involvement in political affairs. The sheer number of categories indicates that international marketing ethics should probably be questioned more closely! The use of structured questions in this case, although more convenient, would have been inappropriate, raising ethical concerns as the researcher lacked knowledge of the set of possible response options required for multiple-choice questions.[11]

WHAT WOULD YOU DO?

Does Delta Stack Up to the Competition?

The Situation

Richard Anderson has been chief executive officer of Delta Air Lines since 2007. Delta is one of the largest airlines in the world in terms of operating revenue and passengers carried. The airline's innovative developments in the areas of technology and e-commerce have also been widely noted. The annual Wichita State University Airline Quality Rating study named Delta the number-one airline. In addition, *Forbes* ranked Delta number one based on five important customer-service criteria.

Since 2000, the Global Airline Performance (GAP) study teamed up with P. Robert and Partners and the London-based Aviation Information and Research unit of the International Air Transport Association (IATA) to perform a two-part syndicated survey for measuring passenger satisfaction on 22 different airlines in 30 different countries. It samples 240,000 passengers each year and is conducted in seven languages. The interviewers catch the respondents at the most opportune time: while waiting to board the plane. The first part of the survey consists of 20 questions about the airline staff and their willingness to assist; the second part, one that must be sent by mail or fax, asks questions of the boarding process, service on the plane, and comfort. Delta General Manager of Marketing Research Paul Lai agrees that keeping the information fresh in the respondent's mind helps get a clearer view of how the airline can increase customer satisfaction. Another benefit of the survey is that it is ongoing, so responses can be tracked over time. Lai also enjoys receiving the data for other airlines so Delta can conduct comparative analyses and identify areas in which Delta is lagging the competition. The survey revealed to Delta and other airlines that two service issues are most important. One is the operational service, such as arrival/departure times without delays. The second is more subjective and cannot be controlled as easily—airline employee and customer relations. If Richard Anderson remains in tune with the surveys conducted by GAP, Delta should be able to stay ahead of the flight competition.

The Marketing Research Decision

1. Paul Lai would like to improve the effectiveness of Part 2 of the GAP question-naire given in Appendix 11A. This can be done best by (check as many as are applicable):
   a. Eliminating double-barreled questions
   b. Eliminating leading questions
   c. Rearranging the order of questions
   d. Using unstructured questions
   e. Reducing the length of the questionnaire

2. Discuss the role of the questionnaire you recommend in enabling Richard Anderson to determine consumer preferences for airlines and increase Delta's market share.

The Marketing Management Decision

1. Richard Anderson would like to improve Delta's in-flight services. Which of the following should he improve?
   a. The cabin features
   b. The cabin crew
   c. Food and beverages
   d. Onboard amenities/entertainment
   e. All of the above

2. Discuss how the marketing-decision action that you recommend to Richard Anderson is influenced by the questionnaire that you suggested earlier and by the findings of that research.

What Richard Anderson Did

Richard Anderson stepped up the level of food and drinks and in-flight amenities Delta offers. In particular, he sought to overcome the bad connotations associated with the generally sub-par "airplane food." Delta provides "real" food from popular restaurants and bakeries. Therefore, it is now possible to purchase a quality lunch from Gate Gourmet or a favorite sandwich from the Atlanta Bread Company, not to mention the continued availability of kosher and vegetarian meals.

In order to meet the needs of the new technologically savvy business class, Delta has also added e-mail access and full broadband Internet service on several flights. All BusinessElite seats now have a personal telephone and increased console space to serve as a desk. However, if a strict work ethic does not appeal while onboard the fleet's newest member, the Boeing 777, have no fear—television screens at every seat offer a choice of movies and an array of programming. As of 2011, Delta and the Delta Connection carriers offer service to 350 destinations in 70 countries on six continents.[12]

Source: © Bayne Stanley/Alamy Images.

Summary

To collect quantitative primary data, a researcher must design a questionnaire or an observational form. A questionnaire has three objectives. It must (1) translate the information needed into a set of specific questions, (2) motivate respondents to complete the interview, and (3) minimize response error.

Designing a questionnaire is as much an art as it is a science. Development guidelines are available, but no one optimal questionnaire design fits every research need. The process begins by specifying the information needed and the type of interviewing method. The next step is to decide on the content of individual questions.

Questions must be written to overcome the respondents' inability to answer. Respondents might be unable to answer if they are not informed, cannot remember, or cannot articulate the response. When too much effort is required or the research context seems inappropriate, respondents will be unwilling to participate. Questions that attempt to collect sensitive information might also be met with resistance. Questions can be unstructured (open ended) or structured to a varying degree. Structured questions include multiple-choice, dichotomous questions, and scales.

Determining the wording of each question involves defining the issue, using ordinary words, using unambiguous words, and using dual statements. The issue should be clearly defined in terms of *who, what, when,* and *where*. The *why* and *way* might not always be relevant. The researcher should avoid leading questions. Once the questions have been worded, the order in which they will appear in the questionnaire must be decided. Special consideration should be given to opening questions, type of information, question difficulty, and the effect on subsequent questions. The questions should be arranged in a logical order.

The stage is now set for determining the form and layout of the questions. The physical considerations in reproducing the questionnaire include appearance, use of booklets, fitting the entire question on a page, response category format, avoiding overcrowding, placement of directions, color coding, and cost. The effectiveness of all these design decisions must be assessed in a pretest.

The design of observational forms requires explicit decisions about what is to be observed and how that behavior is to be recorded. It is useful to specify the *who, what, when, where, why,* and *way* of the behavior to be observed.

Several software packages are available to facilitate questionnaire design. Several firms provide software and services for designing computer and Internet-administered questionnaires. The questionnaire or research instrument should be adapted to the specific cultural environment and should not be biased in terms of any one culture. Analysis of relevant social media content can be very valuable in designing an appropriate questionnaire for use in traditional or social media surveys. In consideration of the respondents, overly long questionnaires or questions that exceed the respondents' willingness or ability to respond should be avoided. The questionnaire should be designed to obtain information in an unbiased manner.

Key Terms and Concepts

Questionnaire   300
Double-barreled question   303
Filter questions   305
Unstructured questions   307
Structured questions   309
Order or position bias   309

Dichotomous question   310
Leading question   313
Acquiescence bias   313
Basic information   315
Classification information   315
Identification information   315

Funnel approach   315
Branching questions   316
Precoding   317
Pretesting   318

Suggested Cases and Video Cases

Running Case with Real Data

1.1 Hewlett-Packard

Comprehensive Critical Thinking Cases

2.1 American Idol   2.2 Baskin-Robbins   2.3 Akron Children's Hospital

Comprehensive Cases with Real Data

3.1 Bank of America   3.2 McDonald's   3.3 Boeing

Comprehensive Brief Harvard Business School Cases

4.1 TruEarth Healthy Foods: Market Research for a New Product Introduction (4065)
4.2 The Springfield Nor'easters: Maximizing Revenues in the Minor Leagues (2510)
4.3 Metabical: Positioning and Communications Strategy for a New Weight-Loss Drug (4240)
4.4 Saxonville Sausage Company (2085)

Online Video Cases

11.1 Dunkin' Donuts   12.1 Motorola   13.1 Subaru   14.1 Intel   19.1 Marriott

Live Research: Conducting a Marketing Research Project

1. Each team can develop a questionnaire following the principles discussed in the chapter. The best features of each questionnaire can be combined to develop the project questionnaire.

2. Each team should be assigned a few pretest interviews.

3. If a questionnaire has already been prepared, it should be critically evaluated in the class.

4. The resulting questionnaire should be discussed and approved by the client.

Acronyms

The objectives and steps involved in developing a questionnaire may be defined by the acronym QUESTIONNAIRE:

Objectives	Q	uestions that respondents can answer
	U	plift the respondent
	E	rror elimination
Steps	S	pecify the information needed
	T	ype of interviewing method
	I	ndividual question content
	O	vercoming inability and unwillingness to answer
	N	onstructured versus structured questions
	N	onbiased question wording
	A	rrange the questions in proper order
	I	dentify form and layout
	R	eproduction of the questionnaire
	E	liminate bugs by pretesting

The guidelines for question wording may be summarized by the acronym WORDS:

W   ho, what, when, where, why, and way

O   bjective questions: Avoid leading questions

R   egularly, normally, usually, etc., should be avoided

D   ual statements (positive and negative)

S   imple, ordinary words

The guidelines for deciding on the order of questions may be summarized by the acronym ORDER:

O   pening questions: simple

R   udimentary or basic information should be obtained first

D   ifficult questions toward the end

E   xamine the influence on subsequent questions

R   eview the sequence to ensure a logical order

Review Questions

1. What is the purpose of questionnaires and observational forms?
2. Explain how the mode of administration affects questionnaire design.
3. How would you determine whether a specific question should be included in a questionnaire?
4. What is a double-barreled question?
5. What are the reasons that respondents are unable to answer the question asked?
6. Explain the concepts of aided and unaided recall.
7. What are the reasons that respondents are unwilling to answer specific questions?
8. What can a researcher do to make the request for information seem legitimate?
9. What are the advantages and disadvantages of unstructured questions?
10. What are the issues involved in designing multiple-choice questions?
11. What are the guidelines available for deciding on question wording?
12. What is a leading question? Give an example.
13. What is the proper order for questions intended to obtain basic, classification, and identification information?
14. What guidelines are available for deciding on the form and layout of a questionnaire?
15. Describe the issues involved in pretesting a questionnaire.
16. **Social Media** How can social media aid in developing a questionnaire?
17. What are the major decisions involved in designing observational forms?

plied Problems

1. Develop three double-barreled questions related to flying and passengers' airline preferences. Also, develop corrected versions of each question.
2. List at least 10 ambiguous words that should not be used in framing questions.
3. Do the following questions define the issue? Why or why not?
   a. What is your favorite brand of shampoo?
   b. How often do you go on a vacation?
   c. Do you consume orange juice? 1. Yes 2. No
4. Design an open-ended question to determine whether households engage in gardening. Also, develop a multiple-choice and a dichotomous question to obtain the same information. Which form is the most desirable?
5. Formulate three questions that exceed respondents' ability to answer. Then, reformulate these questions correctly.
6. A new graduate hired by the marketing research department of a major telephone company is asked to prepare a questionnaire to determine household preferences for telephone calling cards. The questionnaire is to be administered in mall-intercept interviews. Using the principles of questionnaire design, critically evaluate this questionnaire.

Household Telephone Calling Card Survey

1. Your name _____
2. Age _____
3. Marital status _____
4. Income _____
5. Which, if any, of the following telephone calling cards do you have?
   1. AT&T _____ 2. Verizon _____ 3. Sprint Nextel _____ 4. Others _____
6. How frequently do you use a telephone calling card?

   Infrequently   Very Frequently
      1   2   3   4   5   6   7
7. What do you think of the telephone calling card offered by AT&T?

   _____

   _____

8. Suppose your household were to select a telephone calling card. Please rate the importance of the following factors in selecting a card.

	Not Important				Very Important
a. Cost per call	1	2	3	4	5
b. Ease of use	1	2	3	4	5
c. Rebates and discounts on calls	1	2	3	4	5
d. Quality of telephone service	1	2	3	4	5
e. Quality of customer service	1	2	3	4	5

9. How important is it for a telephone company to offer a calling card?

   Not important   Very Important
      1   2   3   4   5   6   7
10. Do you have children living at home? _____

   Thank You For Your Help!

---

7. Lenovo would like to conduct an Internet survey to determine the image of Lenovo PCs and the image of its major competitors (e.g., Sony, Dell, and HP). Develop such a questionnaire. Relevant information can be obtained by visiting the Web sites of the following companies: www.lenovo.com, www.sony.com, www.dell.com, and www.hp.com.
8. Using an electronic questionnaire design package, such as Qualtrics (included with this book), design a questionnaire to measure consumer preferences for sneakers. Then, develop the same questionnaire manually. Compare your experiences in designing this questionnaire electronically and manually.
9. Visit the Web site of one of the online marketing research firms (e.g., Toluna at www.toluna.com). Locate a survey being currently administered at this site. Critically analyze the questionnaire using the principles discussed in this chapter.

Group Discussion

1. "Because questionnaire design is an art, it is useless to follow a rigid set of guidelines. Rather, the process should be left entirely to the creativity and ingenuity of the researcher." Discuss in a small group.

2. In a small group, discuss the role of questionnaire design in minimizing total research error.

3. Discuss the importance of form and layout in questionnaire construction.

Hewlett-Packard Running Case

Review the Hewlett-Packard (HP) case, Case 1.1, and questionnaire given toward the end of the book.

1. Critically evaluate the HP questionnaire using the principles discussed in this chapter.
2. Draft a questionnaire to measure students' preferences for notebook computers.
3. Evaluate the questionnaire you have developed using the principles discussed in this chapter.
4. Develop a revised questionnaire to measure students' preferences for notebook computers.
5. What did you learn in the questionnaire revision process?
6. **Social Media** Administer your revised questionnaire in social media. You can post the questionnaire or a link to it on your Facebook account and invite your friends to respond.

ONLINE VIDEO CASE 11.1

DUNKIN' DONUTS: Dunking the Competition

Visit **www.pearsonhighered.com/malhotra** to read the video case and view the accompanying video. Dunkin' Donuts: Dunking the Competition highlights the emphasis that Dunkin' Donuts places on using marketing research to make the customers critical stakeholders who provide feedback and insight and help direct the innovation process. The company conducts research using survey questionnaires and taste testing in many different markets. The case can be used as a springboard to develop a questionnaire for assessing consumer preferences for fast coffee shops. Specific marketing research questions on this and the previous chapters are posed in the video case.

Appendix 11A

Global Airline Performance Questionnaire
Part 2—English—211

Welcome on Board

Thank you for agreeing to complete this questionnaire.

Your opinion on today's flight performance is *essential,* because it will allow the airline to improve its performance according to your needs.

Please answer Part 2 after you have landed and collected your luggage (if any). Then mail/fax it back to us.

Thank you for your help.

Unless stated otherwise, all ratings should be provided using the following scale:

Excellent
Very good
Good
Fair
Poor
Did not notice/use

1. Please rate this flight on the following items.

Boarding and Departure
  1 Efficiency of aircraft boarding
  2 Punctuality of flight departure
  3 Information given if flight delayed
Overall rating for boarding and departure

Your Comfort and the Cabin Features
  4 Space to store carry-on hand luggage
  5 Condition of cabin interior
  6 Comfort of seat
  7 Sleeping comfort
  8 Amount of legroom
  9 Cleanliness of your seat and table on departure
  10 Cleanliness of toilets/lavatories
Overall rating for comfort and cabin features

The Cabin Crew
  11 Professional appearance of cabin crew
  12 Responsiveness of cabin crew in serving your needs
  13 Courtesy/helpfulness of cabin crew
  14 Availability of cabin crew throughout the flight
  15 Ability to speak your language
  16 Information provided by cabin crew and pilots
Overall rating for cabin crew

Food and Beverages
  17 Quality of the meal(s) and/or snack(s)
  18 Quantity/sufficiency of the meal(s) and/or snack(s)
  19 Choice of beverages available on board
Overall rating for food and beverages

Onboard Amenities/Entertainment
  20 Choice of newspapers and magazines
  21 Telecommunications services (phone, fax, PC port)
  22 Choice of movies shown

23 Choice of other video programming
24 Quality of the video system (sound, vision)
25 Choice of audio programming
26 Quality of the audio programs (sound)
Overall rating for onboard amenities/entertainment

2. **After leaving this flight, please rate the following items.**
27 Punctuality of flight arrival
28 Efficiency of leaving aircraft
29 Speed of luggage delivery
30 Arrival lounge
Overall rating for postflight

3. **From the specific items you have just rated in Sections 1 and 2, could you please indicate which three items (numbered 1–30) are most in need of improvement for this airline:**
The three items in their order of need of improvement:
1st
2nd
3rd

4. **Your overall judgment of today's flight:**
31 Value for money you received from this flight
32 Your overall rating of this airline's performance today, taking everything into account
33 The airline's performance compared with your expectations
Much better
Little better
Much as expected
Little worse
Much worse

5. **Based on your experience of today's flight, would you select this airline for your next trip on this route?**
Definitely would
Probably would
Might/might not
Probably not
Definitely not

6. **Based on your experience of today's flight, how likely would you be to recommend this airline to a friend or colleague?**
Extremely likely
Very likely
Somewhat likely
Not very likely
Not at all likely

7. **Approximately how many of the seats were occupied in your section of the aircraft?**
Up to half full
Half to three-quarters full
Over three-quarters to nearly full
Full
Completely full

8. **In which class did you sit on this flight?**
First
Business
Economy/coach
Special economy (which)

9. Flight Date: DD MM YY Airline:
Flight No.: LETTERS NUMBERS Name: Mr./Ms.:

Source: Lynne Shulhafer.

LEARNING OBJECTIVES

After reading this chapter, the student should be able to:

1. Understand how a sample differs from a census, and the conditions that favor the use of a sample over a census.

2. Explain the steps involved in the sampling design process.

3. Describe the classification of sampling techniques and the difference between nonprobability and probability sampling techniques.

4. Discuss the various nonprobability sampling techniques and when they are used.

5. Explain the various probability sampling techniques and when they are used.

6. Describe the conditions that favor the use of nonprobability sampling versus probability sampling.

7. Understand how online samples should be selected.

8. Explain how sampling techniques are used in international marketing research.

9. **Social Media** Describe how the representativeness of social media samples can be improved.

10. Discuss the ethical issues involved in sampling design.

" A good sampling design, carefully executed, is a key to obtaining high quality data. Too often this is taken for granted, and the results can be profound. **"**

David Fruend
Director and Manager, Market Research,
Progress Energy, Inc., Raleigh, North Carolina

Old Spice Red Zone Invisible Solid Spices Growth in the Deodorant Market

After spending millions to develop invisible solid and controlled-release scent technologies, Procter & Gamble (P&G, www.pg.com) conducted consumer research on the best way to introduce a new antiperspirant/deodorant—Old Spice Red Zone Invisible Solid—based on these technologies. The sampling procedures played a critical role in revealing important findings that guided the development of the new product and its introduction. The company defined the population of interest, the *target population*, as male heads of households. It then developed a questionnaire to measure preferences for solid deodorants versus other forms, such as sprays and roll-ons, and to compare the invisible solid to conventional solids. The questionnaire was administered via computer-assisted telephone interviewing.

Given the large size of the target population and limited time and money, it was clearly not feasible to interview the entire population, that is, to take a *census*. So a sample was taken, and a subgroup of the population was selected for participation in the research. The basic unit sampled was households, and within the selected households the male heads of households were interviewed. Probability sampling, where each element of the population has a fixed chance of being selected, was chosen, because the results had to be generalizable to the larger population—that is, projectable to all male heads of U.S. households. Simple random sampling was used to select 1,000 households. This sample size was selected based on qualitative considerations, such as the importance of the decision, nature of the research, statistical analyses that would be required, resource constraints, and the sample sizes used in similar studies P&G had conducted on new-product development. Simple random sampling was selected, because efficient computer programs were available to randomly generate household telephone numbers and to minimize waste due to nonexistent household telephone numbers. An initial call was made to recruit the respondents and to explain the study. Those who qualified and agreed to participate were mailed a sample of the new invisible solid deodorant with instructions to use it for 2 weeks. A follow-up telephone interview was then conducted.

The results indicated that 56 percent of men preferred solid deodorants. Moreover, invisible solids were preferred to conventional solids on a variety of attributes: gliding on without dragging, ease of application, and no white residue on the skin or clothing. Based on these findings, P&G introduced Old Spice Red Zone Invisible Solid. The launch was successful, and Old Spice Red Zone Invisible Solid accelerated the retail value growth of the entire antiperspirant/deodorant market. Sound sampling procedures adopted in this research resulted in clear-cut findings that aided in the development and launch of a successful product. As of 2011, Old Spice Red Zone Invisible Solid antiperspirant and deodorant was being marketed in 12 scents including After Hours, Aqua Reef, Artic Force, Pure Sport, and Showtime (www.oldspice.com).[1]

Overview

Sampling design issues are a part of the research design process. By this point in the research process, the researcher has identified the information needs of the study as well as the nature of the research design (exploratory, descriptive, or causal) (Chapters 3 through 8). Furthermore, the researcher has specified the scaling and measurement procedures (Chapters 9 and 10) and has designed the questionnaire (Chapter 11). The next step is to design suitable sampling procedures. Figure 12.1 briefly explains the focus of the chapter, the relation of this chapter to the previous ones, and the steps of the marketing research process on which this chapter concentrates.

Five basic questions are addressed in the sample design phase: (1) Should a sample be taken? (2) If so, what process should be followed? (3) What kind of sample should be taken? (4) How large should it be? (5) What can be done to adjust for incidence—the rate of occurrence of eligible respondents—and completion rates?

This chapter addresses the first three questions of the sample design phase. Chapter 13 addresses the last two questions. The chapter discusses sampling in terms of the qualitative considerations underlying the sampling design process. The question of whether or not to sample is addressed and the steps involved in sampling are described. Next, nonprobability and probability sampling techniques are presented. These issues were introduced in the opening vignette, in which P&G used a probability sampling scheme to select the respondents. Sampling techniques in international marketing research are described. The chapter also discusses sampling in social media and identifies the relevant ethical issues and Internet applications. Figure 12.2 provides an overview of the topics discussed in this chapter and how they flow from one to the next.

element
Objects that possess the information the researcher seeks and about which the researcher will make inferences.

population
The aggregate of all the elements, sharing some common set of characteristics, that comprise the universe for the purpose of the marketing research problem.

Sample or Census

In sampling, an **element** is the object (or person) about which or from which the information is desired. In survey research, the element is usually the respondent. A **population** is the total of all the elements that share some common set of characteristics. Each marketing research project has

FIGURE 12.1

Relationship of Sampling Design to the Previous Chapters and the Marketing Research Process

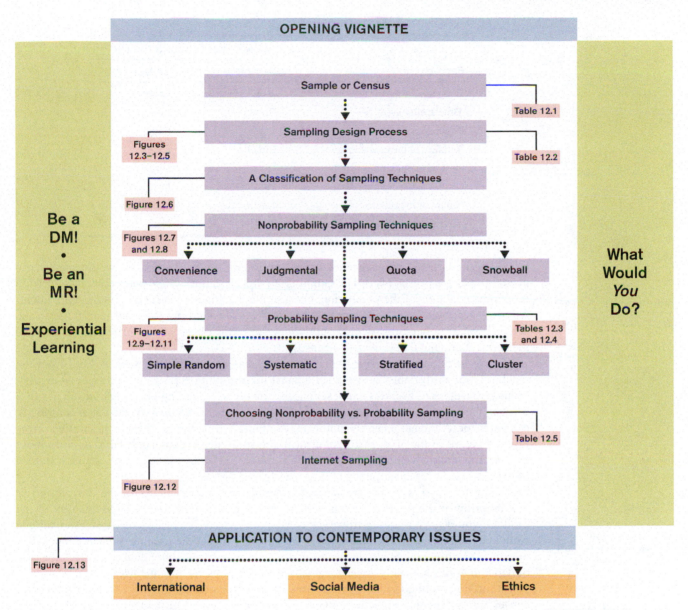

FIGURE 12.2

Sampling Design Procedures: An Overview

a uniquely defined population that is described in terms of its parameters. The objective of most marketing research projects is to obtain information about the characteristics or parameters of a population. The proportion of consumers in the target market that are loyal to a particular brand of toothpaste is an example of a population parameter. In the opening vignette, the percentage of male heads of all U.S. households that preferred a solid deodorant was a population parameter. This parameter was estimated via sampling to be 56 percent. The researcher can obtain information about population parameters by taking either a census or a sample. A **census** involves a complete count of each element in a population. A **sample** is a subgroup of the population. Table 12.1 summarizes the conditions favoring the use of a sample over a census.

The primary considerations favoring a sample are budget and time limits. Conducting a census is costly and time-consuming. In research studies involving large populations, such as users of consumer products, it is generally not feasible to take a census, as illustrated in the opening vignette. Therefore, a sample is the only viable option. However, business-to-business research involving industrial products typically involves a much smaller population. A census becomes not only possible, but often desirable, in such situations. For example, while investigating the use of certain machine tools by U.S. automobile manufacturers, a census would be preferable to a sample, because the population of automobile manufacturers is small. A census also becomes more attractive when there are large variations in the population.

census

A complete enumeration of the elements of a population or study objects.

sample

A subgroup of the elements of the population selected for participation in the study.

TABLE 12.1 Choosing a Sample Versus a Census

	Conditions Favoring the Use of	
Factors	Sample	Census
Budget	Small	Large
Time available	Short	Long
Population size	Large	Small
Variance in the characteristic	Small	Large
Cost of sampling error	Low	High
Cost of nonsampling errors	High	Low
Nature of measurement	Destructive	Nondestructive
Attention to individual cases	Yes	No

For example, large differences in machine-tool usage from Ford to Honda would suggest the need for taking a census instead of sampling. In this case, if a sample was taken, it is unlikely to be representative of the population, because the machine-tool usage of automobile manufacturers not included in the sample is likely to be substantially different than those in the sample. Small populations, which vary widely in terms of the characteristics of interest to the researcher, lend themselves to a census.

The cost of sampling error (e.g., omitting a major manufacturer such as Ford from the machine-tool study) must be weighed against nonsampling error (e.g., interviewer errors). In many business-to-business studies, concerns involving sampling error support the use of a census. In most other studies, however, nonsampling errors are found to be the major contributor to total error. Although a census eliminates sampling errors, the resulting nonsampling errors might increase to the point that total error in the study becomes unacceptably high. In these instances, sampling would be favored over a census. This is one of the reasons the U.S. Bureau of the Census checks the accuracy of its census by conducting sample surveys.[2]

Sampling also is preferable if the measurement process results in the destruction or consumption of the product. In this case, a census would mean that a large quantity of the product would have to be destroyed or consumed, greatly increasing the cost. An example would be product usage tests that result in the consumption of the product, such as a new brand of cereal. Sampling might also be necessary to focus attention on individual cases, as in the case of depth interviews. Finally, other pragmatic considerations, such as the need to keep the study secret (an important consideration for firms such as Coca-Cola), might favor a sample over a census. In the opening vignette, P&G chose sampling over a census because the size of the population of male heads of households in the United States is too large to make a census feasible, particularly given limited time and money. Also, as is generally the case in consumer research, the cost of sampling errors was small as compared to the cost of nonsampling errors. As explained in Chapter 3, sampling error is the error due to the particular sample selected being an imperfect representation of the population of interest. In contrast, nonsampling errors result from a variety of causes, including errors in problem definition, approach, scales, questionnaire design, survey methods, interviewing techniques, and data preparation and analysis. Evidence shows that in consumer research the cost of sampling error is small compared to the cost of nonsampling errors.

Be an MR!	Be a DM!
Boeing: Spreading Its Wings	
Search the Internet—as well as your library's online databases—to determine the population of all airlines operating in the United States. If a survey of airlines is to be conducted to determine their future plans to purchase/lease airplanes, would you take a sample or a census? Explain.	As the CEO of Boeing, how would you use information about the future plans of airlines to purchase/lease airplanes to formulate your marketing strategy?

FIGURE 12.3
Sampling Design Process

The Sampling Design Process

The sampling design process includes five steps, which are shown sequentially in Figure 12.3. Each step is closely related to all aspects of the marketing research project, from problem definition to presentation of the results. Therefore, sample design decisions should be integrated with all other decisions in a research project.

Define the Target Population

Sampling design begins by specifying the target population. The **target population** is the collection of elements or objects that possess the information the researcher is seeking. It is essential that the researcher precisely define the target population if the data generated are to address the marketing research problem. Defining the target population involves translating the research problem into a precise statement of who should and who should not be included in the sample. In the opening vignette, the target population was defined as all male heads of households in the United States.

The target population should be defined in terms of elements, sampling units, extent, and time frame. As stated earlier, an element is the object (or person) about which or from which the information is desired. The respondent is an example. A **sampling unit** might be the element itself, or it might be a more readily available entity containing the element. Suppose that Revlon wanted to assess consumer response to a new line of lipsticks and wanted to sample women over 18 years of age. In this study, Revlon's element would be women over 18 years of age. It might be possible to sample them directly, in which case the sampling unit will be the same as an element. More typically, Revlon would use a sampling unit such as households, interviewing one woman over age 18 in each selected household. Here, the sampling unit and the population element are different. As another illustration, in the opening vignette, the element was male head of household, and the sampling unit was a household.

Extent refers to geographical boundaries. In our example, Revlon is interested only in the domestic U.S. market. The *time frame* is the time period of interest. Revlon may be interested in studying lipstick demand for the upcoming summer market. This target population is defined in Figure 12.4.

Determine the Sampling Frame

A **sampling frame** is a representation of the elements of the target population. It consists of a list or set of directions for identifying the target population. A sampling frame can come from the telephone book, a computer program for generating telephone numbers, an association directory listing the firms in an industry, a mailing list purchased from a commercial organization, a city directory, or a map. If a listing is not readily available, it must be compiled. Specific instructions for identifying the target population should be developed, such as procedures for generating random telephone numbers of households mentioned in the opening vignette.

The process of compiling a list of population elements often is difficult and imperfect, leading to sampling frame error. Elements may be omitted, or the list might contain more than the desired population (see Figure 12.5).

target population
The collection of elements or objects that possess the information the researcher seeks and about which the researcher will make inferences.

sampling unit
The basic unit containing the elements of the population to be sampled.

sampling frame
A representation of the elements of the target population. It consists of a list or set of directions for identifying the target population.

FIGURE 12.4

Defining the Target Population

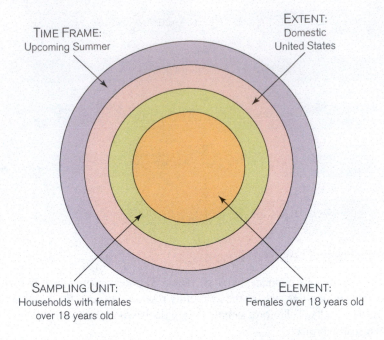

TIME FRAME:
Upcoming Summer

EXTENT:
Domestic
United States

SAMPLING UNIT:
Households with females
over 18 years old

ELEMENT:
Females over 18 years old

FIGURE 12.5

Sampling Frame Error

TARGET POPULATION:
Single-parent households
in Chicago

SAMPLING FRAME:
List supplied by a
commercial vendor

Sampling
Frame Error

For example, the telephone book often is used as a sampling frame for telephone surveys. However, at least three sources of sampling frame error are present in the telephone book: (1) It does not contain unlisted numbers; (2) it does not contain the telephone numbers of people who have moved into the area after the telephone book was published; and (3) it lists the inactive telephone numbers of people who have moved out of the area since the telephone book was published. Small differences between the sample frame and the population can be ignored. In most cases, however, the researcher should recognize and treat the sampling frame error. The researcher has three options:

1. The population can be redefined in terms of the sampling frame. When the telephone book is used as the sampling frame, the population can be defined as households with a correct listing in the telephone book in a given area. This approach is quite simple and eliminates any misinterpretation of the definition of the population under study.[3]
2. The representativeness of the research frame can be verified during the data collection process. Basic demographic, product familiarity, product usage, and other relevant information can be collected to ensure that the elements of the sampling frame satisfy the criteria for the target population. Although inappropriate elements can be identified and eliminated from the sample in this way, this procedure does not correct for elements that have been omitted.
3. The data can be statistically adjusted by weighting under- or overrepresented segments to achieve a more representative sample. Although sample frame error can be minimized through this type of adjustment, it assumes the researcher has accurate knowledge of the makeup of the target population.

FIGURE 12.6

Classification of Sampling Techniques

The researcher can adopt any combination of these adjustments. The important point is to recognize and attempt to eliminate sampling frame error, so that inappropriate population inferences can be avoided.

Select a Sampling Technique

Selecting a sampling technique involves choosing nonprobability or probability sampling (see Figure 12.6). **Nonprobability sampling** relies on the personal judgment of the researcher, rather than chance, in selecting sample elements. The researcher might select the sample arbitrarily, based on convenience, or make a conscious decision about which elements to include in the sample. Examples of nonprobability sampling include interviewing people at street corners, in retail stores, or in malls. Although nonprobability sampling produces good estimates of population characteristic, these techniques are limited. It is not possible to objectively evaluate the precision of the sample results. **Precision** refers to the level of uncertainty about the characteristic being measured. The greater the precision, the smaller the sampling error. Suppose the researcher wanted to determine how much an average household spends on Christmas shopping and surveyed people in the malls. Due to the convenience nature of the sample, there would be no way of knowing how precise the results of this survey are. The probability of selecting one element over another is unknown. Therefore, the estimates obtained cannot be projected to the population with any specified level of confidence.

In **probability sampling**, elements are selected by chance, that is, randomly. The probability of selecting each potential sample from a population can be prespecified. Although every potential sample need not have the same probability of selection, it is possible to specify the probability of selecting a particular sample of a given size. Confidence intervals can be calculated around the sample estimates, and it is meaningful to statistically project the sample results to the population—that is, to draw inferences about the target population. Because projectability of the sample results to the population of all male heads of households was important, P&G used probability rather than nonprobability sampling in the opening vignette. We will discuss the various nonprobability and probability sampling techniques later in this chapter.

Determine the Sample Size

Sample size refers to the number of elements to be included in the study. Determining the sample size involves both qualitative and quantitative considerations. The qualitative factors are discussed in this section; the quantitative factors are discussed in Chapter 13. Important qualitative factors that the researcher should consider in determining the sample size are (1) the importance of the decision, (2) the nature of the research, (3) the number of variables, (4) the nature of the analysis, (5) sample sizes used in similar studies, and (6) resource constraints.

As a general rule, the more important the decision, the more precise the information must be. This implies the need for larger samples. The need for greater precision must be weighed against the increase in cost that comes with the collection of information from each additional element.

The nature of the research also has an impact on the sample size. Exploratory research, such as a focus group, employs qualitative techniques that are typically based on small samples. Conclusive research, such as a descriptive survey, requires large samples. As the number of variables in a study increases, the sample size must grow accordingly. For example, problem identification surveys that measure a large number of variables typically require large samples of 1,000 to 2,500 (see Table 12.2).

nonprobability sampling
Sampling techniques that do not use chance selection procedures, but that instead rely on the researcher's personal judgment and/or convenience.

precision
The level of uncertainty about the characteristic being measured. Greater precision implies smaller sampling error.

probability sampling
A sampling procedure in which each element of the population has a fixed probabilistic chance of being selected for the sample.

sample size
The number of elements to be included in a study.

TABLE 12.2 Samples Sizes Used in Marketing Research Studies

Type of Study	Minimum Size	Typical Range
Problem-identification research (e.g., market potential)	500	1,000–2,500
Problem-solving research (e.g., pricing)	200	300–500
Product tests	200	300–500
Test-marketing studies	200	300–500
TV/radio/print advertising (per commercial or ad tested)	150	200–300
Test-market audits	10 stores	10–20 stores
Focus groups	2 groups	10–15 groups

The type of analysis planned also influences the sample size requirements. Sophisticated analysis of the data using advanced techniques or analysis at the subgroup rather than the total sample level requires larger samples, as in the case of P&G in the opening vignette.

Prior studies can serve as a guide for estimating sample sizes. Table 12.2 gives an idea of sample sizes used in different marketing research studies. These sample sizes have been determined based on experience and can serve as rough guidelines, particularly when nonprobability sampling techniques are used, but they should be applied with caution. Finally, the sample size decisions are guided by money, personnel, and time limitations. In any marketing research project, resources are limited, in turn limiting the sample size. In the opening vignette, the sample size of 1,000 was based on the following considerations: P&G would use the results to make an important decision involving the introduction of invisible solid deodorants; quantitative analysis would be conducted; and this sample size had been adequate in similar studies conducted by P&G in the past.

Execute the Sampling Process

Execution of the sampling process refers to implementing the various details of the sample design. The population is defined, the sampling frame is compiled, and the sampling units are drawn using the appropriate sampling technique needed to achieve the required sample size. If households are the sampling unit, an operational definition of a household is needed. Procedures should be specified for vacant housing units and for callbacks in case no one is home.

Sometimes it is necessary to qualify the potential respondents to make sure they belong to the target population. In such a case, the criteria used to qualify the respondents should be specified, and the qualifying questions should be asked at the beginning of the interview (see Chapter 11). In a survey of heavy users of online services at home, a criterion for identifying heavy users is needed (e.g., those using online services for more than 30 hours per week at home). Detailed information must be provided for all sampling design decisions. This is illustrated by a survey done for the Florida Department of Tourism.

Research in Action

Tourism Department Telephones Birthday Boys and Girls

A telephone survey was conducted for the Florida Department of Tourism related to the travel behavior of in-state residents. The sampling unit was the household. Probability sampling was used. Data were collected using a stratified random sample from three regions: north, central, and south Florida. To participate in the study, respondents had to meet the following qualifying criteria:

- Age 25 years or older
- Live in Florida at least 7 months of the year
- Have lived in Florida for at least 2 years
- Have a Florida driver's license

All household members meeting these four qualifications were eligible to participate in the study. The person with the next birthday in the household was selected. Repeated callbacks were made to reach that person. The following are the components of the sampling design process:

1. Target population: Adults meeting the four qualifications (element) in a household with a working telephone number (sampling unit) in the state of Florida (extent) during the survey period (time)

2. Sampling frame: Computer program for generating random telephone numbers

3. Sampling technique: Probability sampling

4. Sample size: 868

5. Execution: Allocate the sample among the north, central, and southern strata. Use the probability sampling technique

of computerized random-digit dialing. List all members in the household who meet the four qualifications. Select one member of the household using the next-birthday method.[4]

Experiential Learning

The New York Yankees: Targeting Families

The New York Yankees is one of America's favorite baseball teams.

1. As the marketing manager of the N.Y. Yankees, what marketing programs will you design to target families?

2. Search the Internet and social media—as well as your library's online databases—to obtain information that will

assist the marketing manager of the N.Y. Yankees to target families.

3. The N.Y. Yankees want to conduct a telephone survey to determine how to attract more families to the Yankees' games. Design the sampling process.

A Classification of Sampling Techniques

Sampling techniques can be broadly classified as nonprobability or probability (see Figure 12.6). Commonly used nonprobability sampling techniques include convenience sampling, judgmental sampling, quota sampling, and snowball sampling (see Figure 12.7). The important probability sampling techniques are simple random sampling, systematic sampling, stratified sampling, and cluster sampling.

Nonprobability Sampling Techniques

Figure 12.8 presents a graphical illustration of the various nonprobability sampling techniques. The population consists of 25 elements; a sample size of 5 is needed. A, B, C, D, and E represent groups and can also be viewed as strata or clusters.

Convenience Sampling

Convenience sampling, as the name implies, involves obtaining a sample of elements based on the convenience of the researcher. The selection of sampling units is left primarily to the interviewer. Respondents often are selected because they happen to be in the right place at the right time. Examples of convenience sampling are (1) use of students, church groups, and members of social organizations; (2) mall-intercept interviews conducted without qualifying the respondents; (3) department stores using charge account lists; (4) tear-out questionnaires included in a magazine; (5) "people on the street" interviews; and (6) Internet browsers.

Convenience sampling has the advantages of being both inexpensive and fast. Additionally, the sampling units tend to be accessible, easy to measure, and cooperative. Despite these advantages, this form of sampling has serious limitations. Primary among them is that the resulting sample is not representative of any definable target population. This sampling process suffers from selection bias, which means the individuals who participate in a convenience sample might have characteristics that are systematically different than the characteristics that define the target population. Because of these limitations, it is not theoretically meaningful to generalize to any population from a convenience sample.

convenience sampling
A nonprobability sampling technique that attempts to obtain a sample of convenient elements. The selection of sampling units is left primarily to the interviewer.

```
NONPROBABILITY SAMPLING TECHNIQUES
        |           |           |           |
  Convenience   Judgmental     Quota      Snowball
   Sampling     Sampling      Sampling    Sampling
```

FIGURE 12.7
Nonprobability Sampling Techniques

FIGURE 12.8

A Graphical Illustration of Nonprobability Sampling Techniques

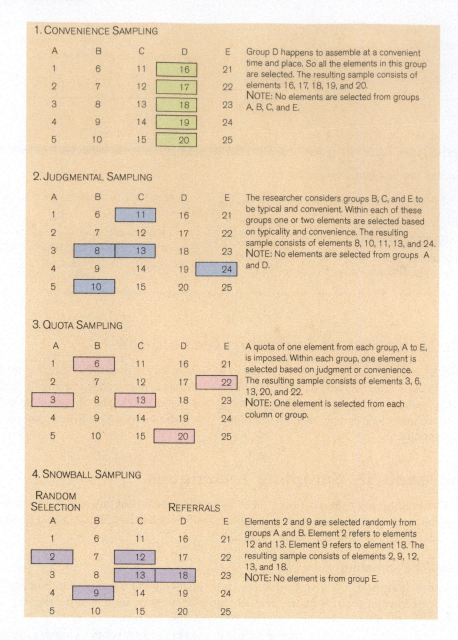

Convenience samples are not appropriate for descriptive or causal research where the aim is to draw population inferences. Convenience samples are useful, however, in exploratory research where the objective is to generate ideas, gain insights, or develop hypotheses. They can be used for focus groups, pretesting questionnaires, or pilot studies. Even in these cases, caution should be exercised in interpreting the results. Despite these limitations, this technique is sometimes used even in large surveys, as in the example that follows.

Research in Action

Starbucks Bucks Up on Ice Cream

When Starbucks wanted to assess the brand equity behind its name in order to consider possible line extensions, researchers used convenience sampling to select a group of people patronizing its various coffee shops and retail outlets. Using convenience sampling in this manner was justified because the core market for the line extensions would consist of existing Starbucks customers.

A survey was administered that obtained information on the respondents' preference and loyalty for Starbucks coffee and for other products they would like to see branded with the Starbucks name.

Results of this survey revealed a tremendous potential to extend the Starbucks name to ice creams. Accordingly, Starbucks leveraged the strong equity of its coffee and loyal customer base to create a line of ice cream based on its coffee. The product is a rich, creamy ice cream that delivers on the intense flavor of Starbucks coffee. According to SymphonyIRI (www.symphonyiri.com) data, it became the nation's number-one brand of coffee ice cream 3 months after it was introduced. As of 20011, Starbucks was selling seven coffee and noncoffee flavors of ice cream: Java Chip, Coffee, Caramel Macchiato, Mocha Frappuccino, Signature Hot Chocolate, Strawberry & Crème Frappuccino, and Vanilla Bean Frappuccino.[5]

Source: Jordan Strauss/Stringer/WireImage.

Judgmental Sampling

Judgmental sampling is a form of convenience sampling in which the population elements are selected based on the researcher's judgment. The researcher chooses the sampling elements because she or he believes they represent the population of interest. Common examples of judgmental sampling include (1) test markets selected to determine the potential of a new product; (2) purchase engineers selected in industrial marketing research because they are considered to be representative of the company; (3) bellwether precincts selected in voting-behavior research; (4) expert witnesses used in court; and (5) department stores selected to test a new merchandising display system.

Judgment sampling has appeal because it is low cost, convenient, and quick. It is subjective, however, relying largely on the expertise and creativity of the researcher. Therefore, generalizations to a specific population cannot be made, usually because the population is not defined explicitly. This sampling technique is most appropriate in research when broad population generalizations are not required. For example, Carl's Jr. test-marketed its Foot-long Cheeseburger in 50 Carl's Jr. restaurants in Southern California and 50 Hardee's units in Indiana. These locations were selected because the researcher felt they would provide a good general indicator of initial response to the new product. Note that Carl's Jr. was only looking to evaluate the initial response to Foot-long Cheeseburger, not to make projections of how much it would sell nationally. An extension of judgment sampling involves the use of quotas.

judgmental sampling
A form of convenience sampling in which the population elements are purposively selected based on the judgment of the researcher.

Quota Sampling

Quota sampling introduces two stages to the judgmental sampling process. The first stage consists of developing control categories, or *quotas*, of population elements. Using judgment to identify relevant categories such as age, sex, or race, the researcher estimates the distribution of these characteristics in the target population. For example, white women ages 18 to 35 years might be considered the relevant control category for a study involving cosmetic purchases. The researcher would then estimate the proportion of the target population falling into this category based on past experience or secondary information sources. Sampling would then be done to ensure that the proportion of white women ages 18 to 35 years in the target population would be reflected in the sample. Quotas are used to ensure that the composition of the sample is the same as the composition of the population with respect to the characteristics of interest.

Once the quotas have been assigned, the second stage of the sampling process takes place. Elements are selected using a convenience or judgment process. Considerable freedom exists in selecting the elements to be included in the sample. The only requirement is that the elements that are selected fit the control characteristics. This technique is illustrated in the following example.

quota sampling
A nonprobability sampling technique that is a two-stage restricted judgmental sampling. The first stage consists of developing control categories or quotas of population elements. In the second stage, sample elements are selected based on convenience or judgment.

Research in Action

How Timely Is *Time* Magazine's Readership?

A readership study was conducted for *Time* magazine using a quota sample. One thousand adults living in a metropolitan area of 500,000 people were selected. Age, sex, and race were used to define the makeup of the sample. Based on the composition of the adult population in that community, the quotas were assigned as follows:

Control Characteristic	Population Composition Percentage	Sample Composition Percentage	Sample Composition Number
Sex			
Male	48	48	480
Female	52	52	520
	100	100	1,000
Age (years)			
18–30	27	27	270
31–45	39	39	390
46–60	16	16	160
Over 60	18	18	180
	100	100	1,000
Race			
White	59	59	590
Black	35	35	350
Other	6	6	60
	100	100	1,000

By imposing quotas proportionate to the population distribution, the researcher was able to select a sample that reflected the composition of the metropolitan area in terms of sex, age and race.

In the preceding example, proportionate quotas were assigned so that the composition of the population in the community was reflected in the sample. In certain situations, however, it is desirable either to under- or oversample elements with certain characteristics. For example, heavy users of a product might be oversampled in order to examine their behavior in greater detail. Although this type of sample is not representative, it might nevertheless be quite relevant.

A number of potential problems are associated with this sampling technique. Relevant characteristics might be overlooked in the quota-setting process, resulting in a sample that does not mirror the population on relevant control characteristics. Because the elements within each quota are selected based on convenience or judgment, many sources of selection bias are potentially present. Interviewers might be tempted to select areas where they believe they will have success in soliciting participants. They might avoid people who look unfriendly, who are not well dressed, or who live in undesirable locations. Quota sampling also is limited in that it does not permit assessment of sampling error.

Quota sampling attempts to obtain representative samples at a relatively low cost. Quota samples are also relatively convenient to draw. With adequate controls, quota sampling obtains results close to those for conventional probability sampling.

Snowball Sampling

snowball sampling
A nonprobability sampling technique in which an initial group of respondents is selected randomly. Subsequent respondents are selected based on the referrals or information provided by the initial respondents. This process may be carried out in waves by obtaining referrals from referrals.

In **snowball sampling**, an initial group of respondents is selected, usually at random. After being interviewed, these respondents are asked to identify others who belong to the target population of interest. This process is continued, resulting in a snowball effect, as one referral is obtained from another. Thus, the referral process effectively produces the sampling frame from which respondents are selected. Although this sampling technique begins with a probability sample, it results in a nonprobability sample. This is because referred respondents tend to have demographic and psychographic characteristics that are more similar to the person referring them than would occur by chance.

Snowball sampling is used when studying characteristics that are relatively rare or difficult to identify in the population. For example, the names of users of some government or social services, such as food stamps, are kept confidential. Groups with special characteristics such as widowed men under 35 years old or members of a scattered minority population might be impossible to locate without referrals. In industrial research, snowball sampling is used to identify buyer–seller pairs.

The major advantage of snowball sampling is that it substantially increases the likelihood of locating the desired characteristic in the population. It also results in relatively low sampling variance and costs. Snowball sampling is illustrated by the following example.

Research in Action

Survey Snowball

To study the demographic profile of marketing research interviewers in Ohio, a sample of interviewers was generated using a variation of snowball sampling. Interviewers were initially contacted by placing classified advertisements in the newspapers of seven major metropolitan areas. These notices asked experienced marketing research interviewers willing to answer 25 questions about their job to write to the author. These responses were increased through a referral system. Each responding interviewer was asked for the names and addresses of other interviewers. Eventually, this process identified interviewers from many communities throughout the state who had not seen the original newspaper notices. Only 27 percent of returned questionnaires resulted from the classified notices; the remainder could be traced to referrals and to referrals from referrals.[6]

In this example, the initial groups of respondents were contacted using a nonrandom selection technique, through classified advertisements. In this instance, the procedure was more efficient than random selection. In other cases, random selection of respondents through probability sampling techniques is more appropriate.

Be a DM!	Be an MR!
Unisex Shirts: Sampling Gender Inequalities Affirmatively	
As the vice president of marketing for Polo Ralph Lauren, what information would you need to determine whether the company should launch nationally a new line of unisex shirts it has developed?	Visit www.polo.com and search the Internet and social media—as well as your library's online databases—to obtain information on Polo Ralph Lauren's marketing strategy. Polo Ralph Lauren would like to determine initial consumer reaction to a new line of unisex shirts it has developed. If nonprobability sampling is to be used, which sampling technique would you recommend and why?

Probability Sampling Techniques

The probability sampling techniques consist of simple random, systematic, stratified, and cluster sampling (see Figure 12.9). Probability sampling techniques vary in terms of sampling efficiency. *Sampling efficiency* is a concept that reflects a trade-off between sampling cost and precision.

FIGURE 12.9
Probability Sampling Techniques

Costs increase with improved precision. The trade-off comes into play as researchers balance the need for greater precision with higher sampling costs. The efficiency of a probability sampling technique can be assessed by comparing it to that of simple random sampling. Figure 12.10 presents a graphical illustration of the various probability sampling techniques. As in the case of nonprobability sampling, the population consists of 25 elements, and a sample size of 5 must be selected. A, B, C, D, and E represent groups and can also be viewed as strata or clusters.

Simple Random Sampling

In **simple random sampling** (SRS), each element in the population has a known and equal probability of selection. Furthermore, each possible sample of a given size *(n)* has a known and equal probability of being the sample actually selected. The implication in a random sampling procedure is that each element is selected independently of every other element. Placing the names in a container, shaking the container, and selecting the names in a lottery-style drawing is

simple random sampling
A probability sampling technique in which each element in the population has a known and equal probability of selection. Every element is selected independently of every other element, and the sample is drawn by a random procedure from a sampling frame.

FIGURE 12.10

A Graphical Illustration of Probability Sampling Techniques

1. SIMPLE RANDOM SAMPLING

Select five random numbers from 1 to 25. The resulting sample consists of population elements 3, 7, 9, 16, and 24.
NOTE: There is no element from group C.

2. SYSTEMATIC SAMPLING

Select a random number between 1 to 5, say 2. The resulting sample consists of population 2, $(2 + 5 = 7)$, $(2 + (5 \times 2) = 12)$, $(2 + (5 \times 3) = 17)$, and $(2 + (5 \times 4) = 22)$.
NOTE: All the elements are selected from a single row.

3. STRATIFIED SAMPLING

Randomly select a number from 1 to 5 for each stratum, A to E. The resulting sample consists of population elements 4, 7, 13, 19, and 21.
NOTE: One element is selected from each column.

4. CLUSTER SAMPLING (TWO-STAGE)

Randomly select 3 clusters, B, D, and E. Within each cluster, randomly select one or two elements. The resulting sample consists of population elements 7, 18, 20, 21, and 23.
NOTE: No elements are selected from clusters A and C.

an example of a random sampling procedure. To draw a simple random sample, the sampling frame is compiled by assigning each element a unique identification number. Random numbers, generated using a computer routine or random number table (see Table 1 in the Appendix of Statistical Tables), are then used to determine which element to select.

In telephone surveys, the random-digit-dialing (RDD) technique often is used to generate a random sample of telephone numbers. RDD consists of randomly selecting all 10 digits of a telephone number (area code, prefix or exchange, suffix). Although this approach gives all households with telephones an approximately equal chance of being included in the sample, not all the numbers generated in this way are working telephone numbers. Several modifications have been proposed to identify and eliminate the nonworking numbers. This makes the use of SRS in telephone surveys quite attractive, as illustrated in the case of P&G in the opening vignette and the following GM example.

Research in Action

GM Refocuses on Hybrid Technology

Lagging behind the global industry leader in hybrid technology (Toyota), GM (www.gm.com) funded a study examining consumers' preferences and thoughts about energy-efficient cars. The poll was conducted by Peter D. Hart Research Associates (www.hartresearch.com) and was carried out as a telephone survey of 1,004 adults nationwide. The respondents were selected using RDD software. The use of RDD resulted in a sample that was representative of automobile buyers. The study had a margin of error of 3.1 percent.

The survey found that Toyota had a 65 percent favorable rating; Honda, 64 percent; GM, 60 percent; Ford, 56 percent; and Chrysler, 47 percent. In addition, among top priorities for automakers, 36 percent of respondents wanted them to improve gas mileage and safety features, and 32 percent urged the industry to find alternatives to gas engines. Encouraged by these findings, GM introduced six hybrid models in 2010 that relied on two innovative technologies to efficiently power the vehicles.[7]

SRS has many benefits. It is easily understood and produces data that are representative of a target population. Most statistical inference approaches assume that random sampling was used. However, SRS suffers from at least four significant limitations: (1) Constructing a sampling frame for SRS is difficult; (2) SRS can be expensive and time-consuming because the sampling frame might be widely spread over a large geographical area; (3) SRS often results in lower precision, producing samples with large standard error; and (4) samples generated by this technique might not be representative of the target population, particularly if the sample size is small. Although samples drawn will represent the population well on average, a given simple random sample might grossly misrepresent the target population. For these reasons, SRS is not widely used in marketing research. Procedures such as systematic sampling are more popular.

Systematic Sampling

In **systematic sampling**, the sample is chosen by selecting a random starting point and then picking every ith element in succession from the sampling frame. The frequency with which the elements are drawn, i, is called the *sampling interval*. It is determined by dividing the population size N by the sample size n and rounding to the nearest integer. For example, suppose there are 100,000 elements in the population and a sample of 1,000 is desired. In this case, the sampling interval, i, is 100. A random number between 1 and 100 is selected. If, for example, this number is 23, the sample consists of elements 23, 123, 223, 323, 423, 523, and so on.[8]

The population elements used in systematic sampling typically are organized in some fashion. If the telephone book is used as the sampling frame, the elements are organized alphabetically. In some cases, this order might be related to some characteristic of interest to the researcher. For example, credit-card customers might be listed in order of outstanding balance or firms in a given industry might be ordered according to annual sales. When the population elements are organized in a manner related to the characteristics under study, systematic sampling can produce results quite different from SRS. Systematic sampling from a list of industrial firms, organized in increasing order by sales, will produce a sample that includes small and large firms. In comparison, a simple random sample might be less representative. For example, only small firms or a disproportionate number of small firms might be drawn in SRS.

systematic sampling
A probability sampling technique in which the sample is chosen by selecting a random starting point and then picking every ith element in succession from the sampling frame.

Sampling frames that are organized in a cyclical pattern tend to be less representative when systematic sampling is used. To illustrate, consider the use of systematic sampling to generate a sample of monthly department-store sales from a sampling frame containing monthly sales for the last 60 years. If a sampling interval of 12 is chosen, the resulting sample would not reflect the month-to-month variation in sales.

Systematic sampling is less costly and easier than SRS because random selection is done only once. Systematic sampling can also be applied without knowledge of the makeup of the sampling frame. For example, every *i*th person leaving a department store or mall can be intercepted. For these reasons, systematic sampling often is employed in consumer mail, telephone, mall-intercept, and Internet surveys, as illustrated by the following example.

Research in Action

Tennis Magazine's Systematic Sampling Returns a Smash

Tennis magazine conducted a mail survey of its subscribers to gain a better understanding of its market. A systematic sample was drawn from the subscription list to produce a sample of 1,472 subscribers. The list was ordered according to the duration of subscription to ensure that recent as well as long-time subscribers would be included. If we assume that the subscriber list had 603,520 names, the sampling interval would be 410 (603,520/1,472). A starting point was selected between 1 and 410. Suppose this was 237. The sample would then be collected by selecting every 410th subscriber, that is, subscribers numbered 237, 647, 1057, 1467, and so on. Systematic sampling was chosen because a convenient sampling frame was available and this procedure is easier to implement than SRS.

An incentive in the form of a brand-new dollar bill was included in the mail survey to boost participation in the study. The respondents were sent an alert postcard a week before the survey. A second, follow-up questionnaire was sent to the entire sample 10 days after the initial questionnaire. Of the 1,472 questionnaires mailed, 76 were returned with no forwarding address, so the net effective mailing was 1,396. Six weeks after the first mailing, 778 completed questionnaires were returned, yielding a response rate of 56 percent.[9]

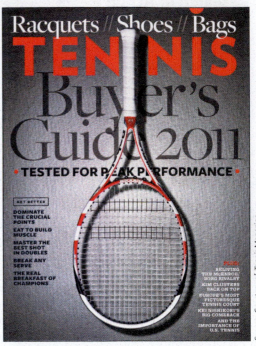

Source: Courtesy of Tennis Magazine.

Be an MR!	Be a DM!
Dell: Targeting *Fortune* 500 Companies	
Visit www.fortune.com and find the list of *Fortune* 500 companies. A systematic random sample of 25 firms is to be selected from the list of *Fortune* 500 firms, numbered from 1 to 500. Determine the sampling interval, and specify the firms that should be selected.	As the marketing director for Dell, how would you target the *Fortune* 500 companies for computers, servers, and storage and networking equipment?

Stratified Sampling

stratified sampling
A probability sampling technique that uses a two-step process to partition the population into subpopulations, or strata. Elements are selected from each stratum by a random procedure.

Stratified sampling involves a two-step sampling process, producing a probability rather than a convenience or judgment sample. First, the population is divided into subgroups called *strata*. Every population element should be assigned to one and only one stratum, and no population elements should be omitted. Second, elements are then randomly selected from each stratum. Ideally, SRS should be used to select elements from each stratum. In practice, however, systematic sampling and other probability sampling procedures can be used.

A major objective of stratified sampling is to increase precision without increasing cost. The population is partitioned using stratification variables. The strata are formed based on four criteria: homogeneity, heterogeneity, relatedness, and cost. The following guidelines should be observed:

- Elements within strata must be similar or homogeneous.
- Elements between strata must differ or be heterogeneous.
- The stratification variables must be related to the characteristic of interest.
- The number of strata usually varies between two and six. Beyond six strata, any gain in precision is more than offset by the increased costs.

Stratification offers two advantages. Sampling variation is reduced when the research follows these listed criteria. Sampling costs can also be reduced when the stratification variables are selected in a way that is easy to measure and apply. Variables commonly used for stratification include demographic characteristics (as illustrated in the example for quota sampling), type of customer (credit-card versus non–credit-card customer), size of firm, or type of industry. Stratified sampling improves the precision of SRS. Therefore, it is a popular sampling technique, as illustrated in the BMW 5 Series survey.

Research in Action

Stratifying the Success of BMW 5 Series

Extensive marketing research went into the design of the BMW 5 Series models (www.bmwusa.com). When a survey of luxury car buyers was conducted to project preferences for specific luxury car features, stratified random sampling was used. This procedure was selected because it includes all the important subpopulations and results in good precision. The variables chosen for stratification were age and income, variables known to correlate with the purchase of luxury cars. The results indicated that luxury car buyers put a premium on performance, handling, engineering, and, of course, luxury.

Based on this feedback, the new 5 Series advanced the concept of a four-door sedan that embodies performance, easy handling, active and passive safety engineering, and luxury. In the U.S. models, the engine was larger, delivering greater torque for more effortless performance. For the first time, automatic climate control was standard in 5 Series models offered in the United States. Extensive innovations and new features were incorporated into virtually every part of the vehicle (e.g., Dynamic Stability Control and Dynamic Brake Control). The results? The models were a roaring success. As of 2011, the new 5 Series was being marketed with an extended line consisting of five Sedan models and four Gran Turismo models (www.bmwusa.com).[10]

Source: Lynne Shulhafer.

Cluster Sampling

In **cluster sampling**, the target population is first divided into mutually exclusive and collectively exhaustive subpopulations, or *clusters*. Then a random sample of clusters is selected based on a probability sampling technique, such as SRS. For each selected cluster, either all the elements are included in the sample or a sample of elements is drawn probabilistically. If all the elements in each selected cluster are included in the sample, the procedure is called *one-stage cluster sampling*. If a sample of elements is drawn probabilistically from each selected cluster, the procedure is *two-stage cluster sampling* (see Figure 12.11). Cluster sampling increases sampling efficiency by decreasing cost.

A number of key differences between cluster and stratified sampling are summarized in Table 12.3.

One common form of cluster sampling is area sampling. **Area sampling** relies on clustering based on geographic areas, such as counties, housing tracts, or blocks. Sampling can be achieved using either one or more stages. *Single-stage area sampling* involves sampling all the elements within a particular cluster. For example, if city blocks were used as the clusters, then all the households within the selected blocks would be included within a single-stage sample. In the case of *two-stage area sampling*, only a portion of the households within each block would be sampled.

cluster sampling
A two-step probability sampling technique. First, the target population is divided into mutually exclusive and collectively exhaustive subpopulations called *clusters*. Then, a random sample of clusters is selected based on a probability sampling technique, such as simple random sampling. For each selected cluster, either all the elements are included in the sample or a sample of elements is drawn probabilistically.

area sampling
A common form of cluster sampling in which the clusters consist of geographic areas, such as counties, housing tracts, blocks, and so forth.

FIGURE 12.11

Types of Cluster Sampling

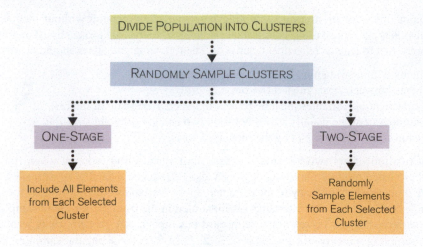

TABLE 12.3 Cluster Sampling Versus Stratified Sampling

Cluster Sampling	Stratified Sampling
Only a sample of the subpopulations (clusters) is selected for sampling.	All of the subpopulations (strata) are selected for sampling.
Within a cluster, elements should be different (heterogeneous), whereas homogeneity or similarity is maintained between different clusters.	Within a strata, elements should be homogeneous with clear differences (heterogeneity) between the strata.
A sampling frame is needed only for the clusters selected for the sample.	A complete sampling frame for the entire stratified subpopulations should be drawn.
Increases sample efficiency by decreasing cost.	Increases precision.

Cluster sampling has two major advantages: feasibility and low cost. Because sampling frames often are available in terms of clusters rather than population elements, cluster sampling might be the only feasible approach. Given the resources and constraints of the research project, it might be extremely expensive, and perhaps infeasible, to compile a list of all consumers in a population. Lists of geographical areas, telephone exchanges, and other clusters of consumers can be constructed relatively easily. Cluster sampling is the most cost-effective probability sampling technique. This advantage must be weighed against several limitations. Cluster sampling produces imprecise samples in which distinct, heterogeneous clusters are difficult to form. For example, households in a block tend to be similar rather than dissimilar. It can be difficult to compute and interpret statistics based on clusters. The strengths and weaknesses of cluster sampling and the other basic sampling techniques are summarized in Table 12.4.

Be a DM!	Be an MR!
Herbal Essences: Introducing New Products Is of the Essence	
As the marketing chief of Herbal Essences, how would you determine which new shampoos should be introduced into the market?	Search the Internet—as well as your library's online databases—to determine the size of the shampoo market in the United States. Herbal Essences would like to determine the demand for a new shampoo. If a survey is to be conducted using probability sampling, which sampling technique should be used and why?

TABLE 12.4 Strengths and Weaknesses of Basic Sampling Techniques

Technique	Strengths	Weaknesses
Nonprobability Sampling		
Convenience sampling	Least expensive, least time-consuming, most convenient	Selection bias, sample not representative, not recommended for descriptive or causal research
Judgmental sampling	Low cost, convenient, not time-consuming	Does not allow generalization, subjective
Quota sampling	Sample can be controlled for certain characteristics	Selection bias, no assurance of representativeness
Snowball sampling	Can estimate rare characteristics	Time-consuming
Probability Sampling		
Simple random sampling(SRS)	Easily understood, results projectable	Difficult to construct sampling frame, expensive, lower precision, no assurance of representativeness
Systematic sampling	Can increase representativeness, easier to implement than SRS, sampling frame not necessary	Can decrease representativeness
Stratified sampling	Includes all important subpopulations, precision	Difficult to select relevant stratification variables, not feasible to stratify on many variables, expensive
Cluster sampling	Easy to implement, cost-effective	Imprecise, difficult to compute and interpret results

Choosing Nonprobability Versus Probability Sampling

Choosing between nonprobability and probability samples is based on considerations such as the nature of the research, the error contributed by the sampling process relative to nonsampling error, variability in the population, and statistical and operational considerations such as costs and time (see Table 12.5). For example, in exploratory research, the findings are treated as preliminary and the use of probability sampling might not be warranted. However, in conclusive research where the researcher wishes to generalize results to the target population, as in estimating market shares, probability sampling is favored. Probability samples allow statistical projection of the results to a target population. For these reasons, P&G decided to use probability sampling as described in the opening vignette.

TABLE 12.5 Choosing Nonprobability Versus Probability Sampling

	Conditions Favoring the Use of	
Factors	Nonprobability Sampling	Probability Sampling
Nature of research	Exploratory	Conclusive
Relative magnitude of sampling and nonsampling errors	Nonsampling errors are larger	Sampling errors are larger
Variability in the population	Homogeneous (low)	Heterogeneous (high)
Statistical considerations	Unfavorable	Favorable
Operational considerations		
Time	Favorable	Unfavorable
Cost	Favorable	Unfavorable

When high levels of sampling accuracy are required, as is the case when estimates of population characteristics are made, probability sampling is preferred. In these situations, the researcher needs to eliminate selection bias and calculate the effect of sampling error. To do this, probability sampling is required. Even with this added sampling precision, probability sampling will not always result in more accurate results. Nonsampling error, for example, cannot be controlled with probability sampling. If nonsampling error is likely to be a problem, then nonprobability sampling techniques, such as judgment samples, might be preferable, allowing greater control over the sampling process.

When choosing between sampling techniques, the researcher must also consider the similarity or homogeneity of the population with respect to the characteristics of interest. For example, probability sampling is more appropriate in highly heterogeneous populations, in which it becomes important to draw a representative sample. Probability sampling also is preferable from a statistical viewpoint, because it is the basis of the most common statistical techniques.

Although probability sampling has many advantages, it is sophisticated and requires statistically trained researchers. It generally costs more and takes longer than nonprobability sampling. In many marketing research projects, it is difficult to justify the additional time and expense, and thus operational considerations favor the use of nonprobability sampling. In practice, the objectives of the study often exert a dominant influence on which sampling method will be used, as illustrated in the following example.

Research in Action

The Alluring Charm of Allure Fragrance

Chanel, Inc. (www.chanel.com) wanted to launch a major new fragrance in department and specialty stores that would reach and sustain at least the sales volume of Chanel No. 5. The target population was defined as women 18 years and older who would appreciate a unique and broadly appealing fragrance. In conducting a survey to determine women's preferences for perfumes, a nonprobability sampling scheme making use of quota sampling was adopted in conjunction with mall-intercept interviews. Quotas were assigned for age, income, and marital status. A nonprobability sampling scheme was chosen because the main objective of this exploratory research was qualitative: to understand what constituted a desirable, classic, yet contemporary, fragrance that women would choose to wear.

The results of the survey indicated a strong preference for a perfume that was fresh, clean, warm, and sexy. Moreover, women were looking for a perfume that would enable them to express themselves. Based on these findings, the company launched Allure, a unique and innovative fragrance created by Chanel perfumer Jacques Polge and packaged in a signature beige carton and sleek bottle. Diversity and individuality were successfully communicated through multi-image ads in a breakthrough print and TV campaign. The advertising portrayed many different women, because every woman expresses Allure in her own way. After its launch, Allure achieved a top-10 ranking in major retail accounts and sales volume equivalent to Chanel No. 5. The success of Allure could be attributed in no small part to the carefully designed sampling procedures that resulted in important survey findings on which the new perfume was developed and marketed. As of 2011, Allure was being marketed as "Clean and sheer, warm and sexy. Difficult to define. Impossible to resist."[11]

Experiential Learning

U.S. Department of Transportation Survey

Enlightened U.S. public-policy makers seek citizen input to the development of the country's infrastructure. One example of this is the requirement for the U.S. Department of Transportation (DOT) to conduct an annual survey about citizen satisfaction with all transportation modes in the country. The Bureau of Transportation Statistics (BTS) is charged with conducting this survey in order to provide insights about citizen satisfaction with travel and transportation to members of Congress, to employees of the U.S. DOT, as well as to U.S. citizens themselves.

Go to the textbook's Web site and download the file U.S.DOT Survey. This is the actual record of how the BTS and Battelle (a research organization hired to assist in the survey) designed and administered a nationally representative study called the Omnibus Survey. Read the first two pages of the Introduction and Background (pages 3 and 4), and then Appendix F: The Final Sampling Plan (pages 124–131 or F1–F8).

1. What was the target population in this study?

2. How was the sampling frame derived in this study?

3. Was a nonprobability or probability sampling technique used?

4. What were the two variables used for stratifying the sample?

5. How many implicit strata were employed in the design of the sample?

6. The study designers wanted to secure 2,000 completed interviews. To obtain this number of completed interviews, how many phone numbers will need to be screened to determine if the phone number is a working residential phone number?

7. What do users of the survey results gain from the BTS using this sampling design instead of using a convenience sample of 2,000?

Internet Sampling

We will discuss the salient issues in online sampling as well as the commonly used online sampling techniques.

Issues in Online Sampling

As discussed in Chapter 7, Internet surveys (and sampling) offer many advantages. The respondents can complete the survey at their convenience. Internet surveys can incorporate automatic skip patterns, consistency checks, and other intelligent features, as is also true for computer-assisted surveys [computer-assisted telephone interviewing (CATI) and computer-assisted personal interviewing (CAPI)]. The data collection can be fast and inexpensive. A major issue related to Internet sampling is representativeness, because many U.S. households do not have computers with Internet access. Internet access is even more restricted in foreign countries. Furthermore, heavy users of the Internet might have a disproportionately higher probability of being included. Unrestricted Internet samples in which any visitor can participate are convenience samples and suffer from self-selection bias in that the respondents can initiate their own selection.

Sampling potential respondents who are surfing the Internet is meaningful if the sample that is generated is representative of the target population. More and more industries are meeting this criterion. In many technical fields, it is rapidly becoming feasible to use the Internet for sampling respondents for quantitative research, such as surveys. For internal customer surveys, where the client's employees share a corporate e-mail system, an intranet survey is practical even if workers have no access to the external Internet. Sampling on the Internet is not yet practical for many non–computer-oriented consumer products. For example, if P&G were to do a survey of housewives to determine their preferences and usage of laundry detergents, an Internet survey would not be a good choice, because an Internet sample is unlikely to be representative of the target population.

To avoid sampling errors, the researcher must be able to control the pool from which the respondents are selected. Also, steps must be taken to ensure that the respondents do not respond multiple times ("stuff the ballot box"). These requirements are met by e-mail surveys, for which the researcher selects specific respondents. Furthermore, the surveys can be encoded

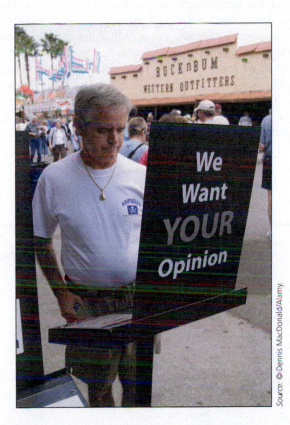

Source: © Dennis MacDonald/Alamy.

In Internet surveys, the researcher must be able to control the pool from which the respondents are selected in order to avoid sampling errors.

to match the returned surveys with their corresponding outbound e-mailings. This can also be accomplished with Web surveys by e-mailing invitations to selected respondents and asking them to visit the Web site where the survey is posted. In this case, the survey is posted in a hidden location on the Web, which is protected by a password. Hence, uninvited Web surfers are unable to access it.

Online Sampling Techniques

The sampling techniques commonly used on the Internet can be classified as online intercept (nonrandom and random), online recruited, and other techniques, as shown in Figure 12.12. Online recruited sampling can be further classified as panel (recruited or opt-in) or nonpanel (opt-in list rentals).

In online intercept sampling, visitors to a Web site are intercepted and given an opportunity to participate in the survey. The interception can be made at one or more Web sites, including high-traffic sites such as Yahoo! In nonrandom sampling, every visitor is intercepted. This can be meaningful if the Web site traffic is low, the survey has to be completed in a short time, and no incentive is being offered. This results in a convenience sample, however. Quotas can be imposed to improve representativeness. In random intercept sampling, the software selects visitors at random and a "pop-up" window asks whether the person wants to participate in the survey. The selection can be made based on simple random or systematic random sampling. If the population is defined as Web site visitors, then this procedure results in a probability sample (simple random or systematic, as the case may be). If the population is other than Web site visitors, then the resulting sample is more similar to a nonprobability sample. Nevertheless, randomization improves representativeness and discourages multiple responses from the same respondent.

Internet panels function in ways similar to non–Internet panels discussed in Chapters 3 and 5, and they share many of the same advantages and disadvantages. In recruited panels, members can be recruited online or even by traditional means (mail, telephone). Based on the researcher's judgment, certain qualifying criteria can be introduced to prescreen the respondents. They are offered incentives for participation, such as sweepstake prizes, redeemable points, and other types of Internet currencies. Members typically provide detailed psychographic, demographic, Internet usage, and product consumption information at the time of joining. Opt-in panels operate similarly except that members choose to opt-in as opposed to being recruited. To select a sample, the online company sends an e-mail message to those panelists who qualify based on sample specifications given by the researcher. All of the sampling techniques can be implemented using both types of Internet panels. The success of probability sampling techniques depends on the extent to which the panel is representative of the target population. Highly targeted samples can be achieved (e.g., teenage girls who shop in malls more than twice a month). For example, respondents for Harris Poll Online (HPOL) surveys are drawn from the multimillion-member HPOL database (www.harrisinteractive.com). E-mail addresses for respondents in the database have been obtained from a number of sources, including the HPOL

FIGURE 12.12

A Classification of Internet Sampling

registration site, HPOL banner advertisements, and Epinion registrations. To maintain the reliability and integrity in the sample, the following procedures are used:

- *Password protection.* Each invitation contains a password that is uniquely assigned to that e-mail address. A respondent is required to enter the password at the beginning of the survey to gain access into the survey. Password protection ensures that a respondent completes the survey only one time.
- *Reminder invitations.* To increase the number of respondents in the survey and to improve overall response rates, up to two additional reminder invitations are typically e-mailed at 2- to 4-day intervals to those respondents who have not yet participated in the survey.
- *Summary of the survey findings.* To increase the number of respondents in the survey and to improve overall response rates, respondents often are provided with a summary of some of the survey responses via the Internet.

Nonpanel recruited sampling methods can also be used, which involves requesting potential respondents to go online to answer a survey. To illustrate, a consumer electronics store, such as Best Buy, might hand its customers a flier that directs them to a password-protected site to respond to a questionnaire. If the population is defined as the company's customers, as in a customer satisfaction survey, and a random procedure is used to select respondents, a probability sample will be obtained. Other nonpanel approaches involve the use of e-mail lists that have been rented from suppliers. Presumably, these respondents opted in or gave permission for their e-mail addresses to be circulated. Offline techniques such as short telephone-screening interviews also are used for recruiting Internet samples. Several companies routinely collect e-mail addresses in their customer relationship databases by obtaining that information from customer telephone interactions, product registration cards, on-site registrations, special promotions, and so on.

A variety of other online sampling approaches also are possible. For example, a survey invitation might pop up every time a visitor makes a purchase. Furthermore, the Internet can be used to order and access samples generated by marketing research suppliers, such as Survey Sampling International (www.surveysampling.com).

Be an MR!	Be a DM!
Is Online Sampling for Amazon?	
Visit www.amazon.com and search the Internet and social media—as well as your library's online databases—to obtain information on consumer Internet shopping behavior. Amazon wants you to conduct an Internet survey to determine customer satisfaction. How would you select the sample?	As the marketing chief for Amazon, what marketing strategies would you adopt to enhance customer satisfaction and loyalty?

Social Media

Summary Illustration Using the Opening Vignette

In the Old Spice Red Zone Invisible Solid antiperspirant/deodorant survey, the target population was defined as male heads of households. Given the large size of the target population and limited time and money, P&G decided to take a sample rather than a census. The sampling unit was households, and the elements or the respondents were male heads of households. The sampling frame consisted of telephone numbers of all U.S. households, randomly generated by computer programs. The researchers chose probability sampling because the results had to be generalizable—that is, projectable to all male heads of households. The technique of simple random sampling was selected because computer programs were available to randomly generate household telephone numbers and to minimize wastage due to nonexistent household telephone numbers. Simple random sampling was used to select 1,000 households. This sample size was selected based on qualitative considerations, such as the importance of the decision, the nature of the research, resource constraints, and the sample sizes used in similar studies

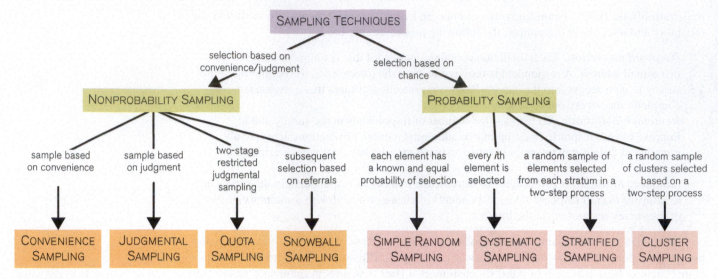

FIGURE 12.13

A Concept Map for Sampling Techniques

conducted by P&G. Figure 12.13 provides a concept map for sampling techniques. In this figure, the major concepts are connected by bold arrows using descriptors. Thus, sampling techniques in which selection is based on judgment/convenience are called *nonprobability sampling*. The rest of the figure can be interpreted similarly.

International Marketing Research

Implementing the sampling design process in international marketing research is seldom an easy task. Several factors should be considered in defining the target population. Identification and access to the relevant sampling elements vary widely across countries. Additionally, a reliable sampling frame might not be available. In many studies, the researcher is interested in analyzing the attitudes and behaviors of the household decision maker. This individual responsible for making or influencing decisions also varies across countries. For example, in the United States, children play an important role in the purchase of children's cereals. In countries with authoritarian child-rearing practices, the mother might be the dominant decision maker for that purchase. For an international researcher, this means the mother, rather than the child, would be the element of interest. Identification of the decision maker and the relevant respondent might have to be done on a country-by-country basis.

Developing an appropriate sampling frame also is a difficult task. In the United States, researchers can rely on government census data or commercially available lists for their sampling frames. These types of high-quality secondary data, however, often are not available in international markets. Government data in many developing countries might be unavailable or highly biased. Population lists might not be available commercially. For example, elections are not held in Saudi Arabia, and there is no officially recognized census of population. Hence, there are no voter registration records or accurate maps of population centers. In such a case, the time and money required to compile this information might be prohibitive. Alternate sampling techniques, such as instructing the interviewers to begin at specified starting points and to sample every nth dwelling, could be used until the specified number of units has been sampled.

Equivalence of samples is a key issue in marketing research studies extending beyond the home country. Researchers must minimize the effects of sample differences that are not relevant to the main purposes of the study. For example, if American Express wanted to compare cultural differences in consumer attitudes toward saving in the United States and Mexico, differences in saving behavior could not be attributed to cultural differences alone if the U.S. respondents averaged 55 years of age while the Mexican respondents averaged 30 years of age. The life stage differs greatly for these two groups. The U.S. group would likely be saving for retirement years, whereas the Mexican group would be saving little in order to establish their households and to pay for the upbringing of their children. Thus, in order to compare the effects of cultural differences, it would be necessary to hold the other variables constant across the two countries.

Given the lack of suitable sampling frames; the inaccessibility of certain respondents, such as women in some cultures; and the dominance of personal interviewing over other survey methods, probability sampling techniques are uncommon in international marketing research. These constraints have led to a reliance on quota sampling for both consumer and industrial surveys.

Likewise, the use of Internet sampling in international marketing research must consider the possibility that Internet availability and use vary markedly across countries. Many countries lack servers, hardware, and software, and this lack of technical infrastructure makes Internet research difficult and expensive. In addition, there may be cultural differences in attitude toward and usage of the Internet. For example, in Latin America the attitude toward Internet research is not positive, due to the respondents missing social interaction with others while participating in the research.

Sampling techniques and procedures vary in accuracy, reliability, and cost from country to country. If the same sampling procedures are used in each country, the results might not be comparable.[12] To achieve comparability in sample composition and representativeness, it might be desirable to use different sampling techniques in different countries, as the following example illustrates.

Research in Action

Achieving Sample Comparability Through Diversity

Research in the United States found that most consumers feel that a purchase is accompanied by a degree of risk when they choose among alternative brands. A study was conducted to compare the U.S. results with those from Mexico, Thailand, and Saudi Arabia. The targeted respondent in each culture was an upper–middle-income woman residing in a major city. Reaching that target respondent presented challenges that required an adjustment in the sampling process across the countries in this study.

In the United States, random sampling from the telephone directory was used. In Mexico, judgmental sampling was used by having experts identify neighborhoods where the target respondents lived. Homes were then randomly selected for personal interviews. In Thailand, judgmental sampling also was used, but the survey took place in major urban centers, and a store-intercept technique was used to select respondents. Finally, in Saudi Arabia, convenience sampling employing the snowball procedure was used, because there were no lists from which sampling frames could be drawn and social customs prohibited spontaneous personal interviews. Comparability in sample composition and representativeness was achieved by adapting the sampling procedures to suit the social customs and information restrictions of each country.[13]

Source: © Novel Creative/Alamy.

Be a DM!	Be an MR!

PC Usage in USA and India

As the global marketing manager for Intel, the computer microprocessor manufacturer, would you adopt the same or different marketing strategies in the United States and India?

Search the Internet and social media—as well as your library's online databases—to obtain information on the usage or nonusage of personal computers by households in the United States and India. Intel wants to conduct cross-cultural research to determine the similarities and differences in the usage or nonusage of personal computers by households in the United States and India. Should the same or different sampling techniques be used in the two countries, and which technique(s) should be used?

Social Media

Social Media

Marketing Research and Social Media

General social media content available in the public domain may not be representative or even appropriate in all cases. The sampling frame is biased and limited in that only consumers who are online and engaged in social media are represented. Even so, consumers who are heavy users of social media have a greater probability of being sampled. Yet, there are ways in which one could improve the representativeness of information gleaned from general social media analysis and monitoring.

- Instead of targeting an entire site, select sections of sites that suit the brand's profile. Careful screening can result in a more targeted and representative sample.
- Narrow your search results by designing search queries that mine social media content with consumer-, category-, or brand-related terms.
- Use text analysis that detects age, gender, geography, or other characteristics that distinguish different types of voices and then filter the results to more accurately reflect your target population. This information may be obtained from publicly available social media profile information of the individuals posting comments.

Research in Action

Simple Random Sampling Results in Sophisticated Market Segmentation

Umbria, now a part of J.D. Power and Associates (www. jdpower.com), used its text-mining technology to segment the market for an apparel client. A large number of comments pertaining to apparel were first collected from a variety of social media sites. Simple random sampling (SRS) was then used to select a manageable but representative subset. SRS was chosen because the sampling frame was readily available and the results were projectable. The selection of a representative sample facilitated a more detailed analysis than might have been possible on all the comments collected. Text-mining was used to analyze the selected comments to arrive at six segments: Fit Finders, Self-Expressives, Bargain Seekers, Label Whores, Style Gurus, and Dissenters. These labels were quite descriptive of the segments. For example, Fit Finders are Generation Xers who want jeans that complement their changing physiques. Self-Expressives want to customize their jeans by distressing them or adding patches and embroidery. The client used these findings to design and market products tailor made for each segment, resulting in a sophisticated segmentation scheme and a successful marketing strategy.[14]

Ethics in Marketing Research

The researcher has the ethical responsibility to formulate a sampling design that is consistent with the objectives of the research and adequately controls the sampling error. Probability sampling techniques should be used whenever the results are to be projected to the population. Projecting findings based on nonprobability sampling to the population is misleading and therefore unethical. As the following example demonstrates, appropriate definitions of the population, sampling frame, and sampling technique are essential if the research is to be conducted and the findings are to be used ethically.

Research in Action

Systematic Sampling Reveals Systematic Gender Differences in Ethical Judgments

In an attempt to explore differences in research ethics judgments between male and female marketing professionals, data were obtained from 420 respondents. The population was defined as marketing professionals (elements), who also comprised the sampling unit. The sampling frame was the American Marketing Association directory, and the extent was the United States. The respondents were selected based on a systematic sampling plan from the directory. Systematic random sampling was chosen over simple random sampling because it was easier to implement. Respondents were asked to indicate the degree of ethicalness of various ethical scenarios and promised a copy of the results in an attempt to boost response rates.

The study revealed that female marketing professionals, in general, demonstrated higher levels of research ethical judgments than did their male counterparts. Similar findings have been obtained in other studies. Thus, the systematic random sampling plan was not only efficient, but resulted in findings that were also generalizable to the target population.[15]

When conducting research with small populations, as in business-to-business marketing or employee research, researchers must be sensitive to preserving the respondents' anonymity. The results should be presented in such a way that respondents cannot be identified or linked to specific comments and findings.

WHAT WOULD YOU DO?

MTV: The World's Most Widely Distributed TV Network

The Situation

As of 2011, MTV (www.mtv.com) sites included favorites such as MTV, MTV Dance, MTV Tr3s, MTV2, MTVU, and other networks around the world. MTV uses a free-flowing corporate culture and a group of power brands to earn big profits for parent Viacom (www.viacom.com).

Tom Freston, CEO of MTV, actually took MTV as a small start-up company and turned it into a cultural behemoth. Judy McGrath was named chair and CEO of MTV Networks in July 2004. Although MTV has become a global icon, with millions of viewers all over the world glued to its programming, MTV is constantly trying to keep up with what is popular and keep its viewers watching.

MTV is always trying to find new ways to engage its target audience, which is 18- to 24-year-olds. This has not always been an easy task. For example, the channel had fading hits with shows like *Beavis & Butt-head* and *The Real World*. Ratings began to slip as users complained that there was no longer music on MTV. Telephone surveys were conducted with the target audience. The sample was selected by choosing households based on computerized random-digit dialing. If the household had multiple 18- to 24-year-olds, one person was selected using the next-birthday method. If no person between these ages resided in the house, a new random number was selected. The results of this survey showed that MTV needed a makeover.

The Marketing Research Decision

1. As trends come and go, it is important for MTV to stay in touch with its audience members and know their wants. Judy McGrath especially wants to keep in touch with the 18- to 24-year-olds through periodic surveys. What sampling technique would you recommend?
   a. Convenience sampling
   b. Quota sampling
   c. Systematic sampling
   d. Stratified sampling
   e. Simple random sampling
2. Discuss the role of the type of sampling technique you recommend in enabling Judy McGrath to keep in touch with the 18- to 24-year-olds.

The Marketing Management Decision

1. What should Judy McGrath do to attract the 18- to 24-year-old audience group to MTV?
   a. Launch music hours shown live from popular places (e.g., Times Square)
   b. Make VeeJays more authentic
   c. Feature more celebrities
   d. Focus more on music programming
   e. All of the above

2. Discuss how the marketing management-decision action that you recommend to Judy McGrath is influenced by the sampling technique suggested earlier and by the findings of that research.

What Judy McGrath Did

MTV launched music hours shown live from Times Square. New shows, such as the animated *Daria*, were created, and the *Video Music Awards* were revamped. VeeJays became more authentic, and not as TV-pretty. The objective was to give MTV a cleaner, more pensive image to keep its viewers happy. The 18-to-24-year-old crowd is important to the network, because younger teens and the 25-to-35-year-old crowd looks to it for image and style ideas.

MTV is still striving to make its programming fresh and hip. TV shows such as *The Osbournes* and *Punk'd* have gotten great reviews. Also, on MTV's detailed Web site (www.mtv.com) viewers can do everything from requesting music videos to chatting with fellow MTV fans. On July 8, 2010, MTV Networks acquired Social Express, a social gaming development company, marking the company's first entry into the social gaming space. MTV is continuing to grow and expand, and with the help of marketing research it should be able to stay hip for generations to come.[16]

Source: Paul Chappells/Newscom.

Summary

Researchers can obtain information about the characteristics of a population by conducting either a sample or a census. Samples tend to be preferred because of budget and time limits, large population sizes, and small variances in the characteristics of interest. Sampling also is preferred when the cost of sampling error is low, the cost of nonsampling error is high, the nature of measurement is destructive, and attention must be focused on individual cases. The opposite conditions favor the use of a census.

Sampling design begins by defining the target population in terms of elements, sampling units, extent, and time. Then the sampling frame should be determined. A sampling frame is a list of the elements of the target population. Directions for constructing the sampling frame should also be included. Sampling techniques are applied to the sample frame to develop the eventual sample. The sample size is determined based on both quantitative and qualitative considerations. Finally, execution of the sampling process requires detailed specifications for each step in the process.

Sampling techniques can be classified as nonprobability and probability techniques. Nonprobability sampling techniques rely on the researcher's convenience and/or judgment. Consequently, they do not permit an objective evaluation of the precision of the sample results, and the estimates cannot be projected to the larger population. The commonly used nonprobability sampling techniques include convenience sampling, judgmental sampling, quota sampling, and snowball sampling.

In probability sampling techniques, sampling units are selected by chance. Each sampling unit has a nonzero chance of being selected, and the researcher can prespecify every potential sample of a given size that could be drawn from the population, as well as the probability of selecting each sample. It also is possible to determine the precision of the sample estimates and inferences and make projections to the target population. Probability sampling techniques include simple random sampling, systematic sampling, stratified sampling, and cluster sampling. The choice between probability and nonprobability sampling should be based on the nature of the research, degree of error tolerance, relative magnitude of sampling and nonsampling errors, variability in the population, and statistical and operational considerations. Nonprobability as well as probability sampling techniques can be implemented on the Internet, with the respondents being prerecruited or tapped online.

When conducting international marketing research, it is desirable to achieve comparability in sample composition and representativeness even though this might require using different sampling techniques in different countries. There are several ways to improve the representativeness of social media samples. It is unethical and misleading to treat nonprobability samples as probability samples and project the results to a target population.

Key Terms and Concepts

Suggested Cases and Video Cases

Running Case with Real Data

1.1 Hewlett-Packard

Comprehensive Critical Thinking Cases

2.1 American Idol   2.2 Baskin-Robbins   2.3 Akron Children's Hospital

Comprehensive Cases with Real Data

3.1 Bank of America   3.2 McDonald's   3.3 Boeing

Comprehensive Brief Harvard Business School Cases

4.1 TruEarth Healthy Foods: Market Research for a New Product Introduction (4065)
4.2 The Springfield Nor'easters: Maximizing Revenues in the Minor Leagues (2510)
4.3 Metabical: Positioning and Communications Strategy for a New Weight-Loss Drug (4240)
4.4 Saxonville Sausage Company (2085)

Online Video Cases

12.1 Motorola   13.1 Subaru   14.1 Intel   19.1 Marriott

Live Research: Conducting a Marketing Research Project

1. A census might be feasible in a business-to-business project where the size of the population is small, but it is infeasible in most consumer projects.
2. Define the target population (element, sampling unit, extent, and time), and discuss a suitable sampling frame.
3. Probability sampling techniques are more difficult and time-consuming to implement, and their use might not be warranted unless the results are being projected to a population of interest.

Acronym

The sampling design process and the steps involved may be represented by the acronym SAMPLE:

S   ampling design process

A   mount: sample size determination

M   ethod: sampling technique selection

P   opulation definition

L   ist: sampling frame determination

E   xecution of the sampling process

Review Questions

1. What is the major difference between a sample and a census?
2. Under what conditions is a sample preferable to a census? When is a census preferable to a sample?
3. Describe the sampling design process.
4. How should the target population be defined?
5. What is a sampling unit? How is it different from the population element?

6. What qualitative factors should be considered in determining the sample size?
7. How do probability sampling techniques differ from nonprobability sampling techniques?
8. What is the least expensive and least time-consuming of all sampling techniques? What are the major limitations of this technique?
9. What is the major difference between judgmental and convenience sampling?
10. What is the relationship between quota sampling and judgmental sampling?
11. What are the distinguishing features of simple random sampling?
12. Describe the procedure for selecting a systematic random sample.
13. Describe stratified sampling. What are the criteria for the selection of stratification variables?
14. Describe the cluster sampling procedure. What is the key distinction between cluster sampling and stratified sampling?
15. What factors should be considered in choosing between probability and nonprobability sampling?
16. Social Media How can the representativeness of social media samples be improved?

Applied Problems

1. Define the appropriate target population and the sampling frame in each of the following situations:
   a. The manufacturer of a new cereal brand wants to conduct in-home product usage tests in Chicago.
   b. A national chain store wants to determine the shopping behavior of customers who have its store charge card.
   c. A local TV station wants to determine households' viewing habits and programming preferences.
   d. The local chapter of the American Marketing Association wants to test the effectiveness of its new-member drive in Atlanta.
2. A manufacturer would like to survey users to determine the demand potential for a new power press. The new press has a capacity of 500 tons and costs $225,000. It is used for forming products from light- and heavyweight steel and can be used by automobile, construction equipment, and major appliance manufacturers.

   a. Identify the population and sampling frame that could be used.
   b. Describe how a simple random sample can be drawn using the identified sampling frame.
   c. Could a stratified sample be used? If so, how?
   d. Could a cluster sample be used? If so, how?
   e. Which sampling technique would you recommend? Why?
3. Ben & Jerry's Homemade Ice Cream would like to conduct a survey of consumer preferences for premium ice cream brands in Los Angeles. Stratified random sampling will be used. Visit www.census.gov to identify information that will be relevant in determining income and age strata.
4. Using a computer program, generate a set of 1,000 random numbers for selecting a simple random sample.
5. Visit Gallup (www.gallup.com). Examine the Internet surveys being conducted. Write a report about the sampling plans being used.

Group Discussion

1. "Given that the U.S. Bureau of the Census uses sampling to check on the accuracy of various censuses, a constitutional amendment should be passed replacing the decennial census with a sample." Discuss as a small group.
2. "Because nonsampling errors are greater in magnitude than sampling errors, it really does not matter which sampling technique is used." Discuss this statement.

Hewlett-Packard Running Case

Review the Hewlett-Packard (HP) case, Case 1.1, and questionnaire given toward the end of the book.

1. As the marketing manager of HP personal computers, what marketing programs will you design to target families?
2. **Social Media** Search the Internet and social media—as well as your library's online databases—to obtain information that will assist you in targeting families.
3. HP wants to conduct a telephone survey to determine how it can attract more families to HP PCs and notebooks. Design the sampling process.
4. **Social Media** Discuss the advantages and disadvantages of HP using social media samples to obtain information on consumers' preferences for notebook computers.

ONLINE VIDEO CASE 12.1

MOTOROLA: Projecting the Moto Lifestyle

Visit **www.pearsonhighered.com/malhotra** to read the video case and view the accompanying video. Motorola: Projecting the Moto Lifestyle highlights the use of marketing research findings to create the Moto campaign, which established Motorola as a chic and aspirational brand that helped it overcome its poor consumer image and branding problems. The case can be used to evaluate the mall-intercept interviewing conducted by Motorola and to design a sampling plan for such survey research. Specific marketing research questions on this and the previous chapters are posed in the video case.

13

Sampling: Final and Initial Sample-Size Determination

Source: Yuri Arcurs/Shutterstock.

LEARNING OBJECTIVES

After reading this chapter, the student should be able to:

1. Understand the key concepts and symbols that are pertinent to sampling.

2. Describe how the sampling distribution, statistical inference, and standard error are relevant to sampling.

3. Explain the statistical approach to determining sample size based on simple random sampling and the construction of confidence intervals.

4. Discuss how formulas can be derived to statistically determine the sample size for estimating means and proportions.

5. Understand how the sample size should be adjusted to account for incidence and completion rates.

6. Explain why it is difficult to statistically determine the sample size in international marketing research.

7. **Social Media** Discuss sample-size determination in social media research.

8. Describe the ethical issues related to sample-size determination, particularly the estimation of population variance.

" Sample size not only is determined by statistical considerations, but also real pressures, such as time and cost. **"**

Chris Bonbright
Manager, Research & Market Analysis,
Tracker Marine Group,
Springfield, Missouri

Sizing the Sample-Size Problem

An article in the *Chicago Tribune* (www.chicagotribune.com) suggested that just as the introduction of television reduced the audiences for both theater and radio, so have online services reduced the audience for television. To support his claim, the author offered survey data about America Online, Inc., which found that online subscribers watch less television than the average U.S. household. An executive at the research company that performed the survey said, "It doesn't matter why people watch less television. It only matters that they do."

The general reader and the general businessperson might read this piece and walk away with the notion that, indeed, increasing online use is directly related to decreasing television viewing. You can almost imagine the buzzing of such discussions at breakfast tables, water coolers, and in carpools: "Hey, I just read in the paper this morning that. . . ."

A more skeptical reader would rightly question much of the study's findings and its application to everyday consumer media preferences. A closer look at the report reveals that the sample size comprised only 262 members of the online service's subscribers. Is this enough to mitigate random sampling error? Is this sample large enough to make such bold claims about television viewing? To make decisions and set policy and strategy? The *confidence level*, which is the level of certainty, was not reported. Only the margin of error as "probably" about 5 percentage points was estimated. Was it 5 percent or not? How confident are we that this conclusion is accurate? What is the confidence level and what is the *confidence interval*—that is, the range likely to contain the true population parameter? Moreover, the completion rate was not reported. Without considering the appropriate sampling specifications, it is not appropriate to draw inferences from the sample about the population. Therefore, based on this study it is not appropriate to conclude that users of online services, in general, watch less television. Such findings continue to be reported in the popular media. For example, a recent study reported that Canadians were switching from television and radio to the Internet. However, the findings of this study also are suspect, because the sample size and the sampling procedures were not reported.[1]

Overview

Chapter 12 discussed the role of sampling in research design formulation, described the sampling process, and presented the various nonprobability and probability sampling techniques. This chapter focuses on the determination of sample size in simple random sampling. Figure 13.1 briefly explains the focus of the chapter, the relation of this chapter to the previous ones, and the steps of the marketing research process this chapter describes.

The opening vignette illustrates the importance of statistically determining the sample size and the random sampling error before generalizing the sample findings to the population. In order to understand and appreciate these issues, the chapter presents definitions of various concepts and symbols and discusses the properties of the sampling distribution. Statistical approaches to sample-size determination based on confidence intervals are presented. In addition, formulas for calculating the sample size with these approaches will be offered and illustrated by examples.

The sample size determined statistically is the final or net sample size that represents the number of interviews or observations that need to be completed. For example, a sample size of 1,000 for a telephone survey means that the interviewers must complete 1,000 interviews. To obtain this final sample size, however, a much larger number of potential respondents must be contacted initially. Thus, to complete 1,000 interviews, it might be necessary to initially contact as many as 3,000 respondents, for example, because only some of the potential respondents might qualify to participate. That is, the incidence rate is generally less than 100 percent. Furthermore, some of those who do qualify might refuse to participate or complete the survey. The completion rate also is less than 100 percent. This chapter will describe the adjustments that need to be made to the statistically determined sample size to account for incidence and completion rates and to calculate the initial sample size. The chapter will also discuss the difficulty of statistically determining the sample size in international marketing research, social media research, and the relevant ethical issues. Figure 13.2 offers an overview of the topics discussed in this chapter and how they flow from one to the next.

Statistical determination of sample size requires knowledge of the normal distribution and the use of normal probability tables. The **normal distribution** is bell-shaped and symmetrical. Its mean, median, and mode are identical (see Chapter 16). Information on the normal

normal distribution
A basis for classical statistical inference that is bell-shaped and symmetrical in appearance. Its measures of central tendency are all identical.

FIGURE 13.1

Relationship of Sample-Size Determination to the Previous Chapters and the Marketing Research Process

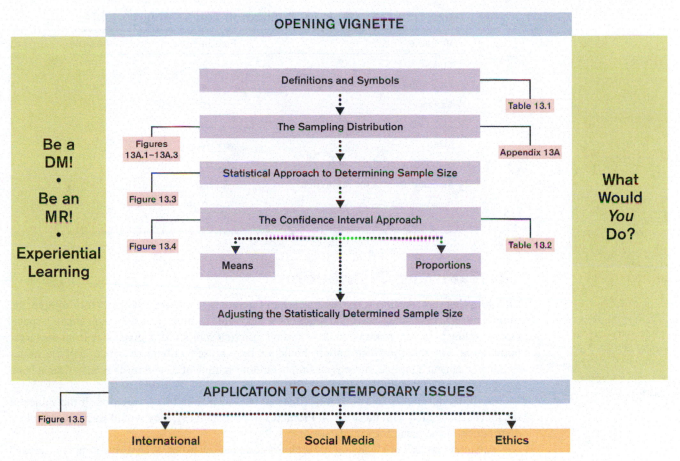

FIGURE 13.2
Final and Initial Sample-Size Determination: An Overview

distribution and the use of normal probability tables is presented in Appendix 13A. We recommend that you also review a statistics textbook.

Definitions and Symbols

The statistical concepts used in sample-size determination are defined in the following list.

- **Parameter:** A summary description of a fixed characteristic or measure of the target population. A parameter denotes the true value that would be obtained if a census (a survey of the complete population), rather than a sample, was undertaken.
- **Statistic:** A summary description of a characteristic or measure of the sample. The sample statistic is used as an estimate of the population parameter.
- **Precision level:** When estimating a population parameter by using a sample statistic, the precision level is the desired size of the estimating interval. This is the maximum permissible difference between the sample statistic and the population parameter.
- **Confidence interval:** The range into which the true population parameter will fall, assuming a given level of confidence.
- **Confidence level:** The probability that a confidence interval will include the population parameter.
- **Random sampling error:** The error that results when the particular sample selected is an imperfect representation of the population of interest (see Chapter 3). Note that this is different from the random error in measurement discussed in Chapter 10.

The symbols used in statistical notation for describing population and sample characteristics are summarized in Table 13.1.

parameter
A summary description of a fixed characteristic or measure of the target population.

statistic
A summary description of a characteristic or measure of the sample that is used as an estimate of the population parameter.

precision level
Precision level is the desired size of the estimating interval and is the maximum permissible difference between the sample statistic and the population parameter.

confidence interval
The range into which the true population parameter will fall, assuming a given level of confidence.

confidence level
The probability that a confidence interval will include the population parameter.

random sampling error
The error due to the particular sample selected being an imperfect representation of the population of interest.

TABLE 13.1 Symbols for Population and Sample Variables

Variable	Population	Sample
Mean	μ	$\overline{X}$
Proportion	π	p
Variance	σ^2	s^2
Standard deviation	σ	s
Size	N	n
Standard error of the mean	$\sigma_{\overline{x}}$	$s_{\overline{x}}$
Standard error of the proportion	σ_p	s_p
Standardized variate (z)	$\dfrac{X - \mu}{\sigma}$	$\dfrac{X - \overline{X}}{s}$

The Sampling Distribution

sampling distribution
The distribution of the values of a sample statistic computed for each possible sample of a given size that could be drawn from the target population under a specified sampling plan.

The **sampling distribution** is the distribution of the values of a sample statistic, for example, the sample mean. These values are computed for each possible sample of a given size. Under a specified sampling plan, it is possible to draw several different samples of a given size from the target population.[2] The sampling distribution should not be confused with the distribution of the values of the elements in a sample. Suppose a simple random sample of 5 steel mills is to be drawn from a population of 20 steel mills. There are $(20 \times 19 \times 18 \times 17 \times 16)/(1 \times 2 \times 3 \times 4 \times 5)$, or 15,504 different samples of 5 steel mills that can be drawn from this population. If the values of the means associated with these 15,504 samples were assembled, they would form the sampling distribution of the mean for sample size $n = 5$.

statistical inference
The process of generalizing the sample results to the population results.

An important task in marketing research is to calculate statistics, such as the sample mean and sample proportion, and to use them to estimate the corresponding true population values. This process of generalizing the sample results to the population results is referred to as **statistical inference**. In practice, a single sample of predetermined size is selected, and the sample statistics (such as means or proportions) are computed. The sample statistics become the basis for making inferences about the population values. This inferential process is possible because sampling distributions enable us to use probability theory to make inferences about the population values. Of direct relevance is the **central limit theorem**, which states that as the sample size increases, the distribution of the sample mean of a randomly selected sample approaches the normal distribution. This holds true regardless of the shape of the original population distribution from which the sample is drawn.

central limit theorem
As the sample size increases, the distribution of the sample mean of a randomly selected sample approaches the normal distribution.

We now describe the important properties of the sampling distribution of the mean and the corresponding properties for the proportion for large samples (30 or more). Please refer to Table 13.1 for a definition of the symbols used in these formulas.

1. The sampling distribution of the mean is a normal distribution (see Appendix 13A). Strictly speaking, the sampling distribution of a proportion is a binomial that approximates the normal distribution in large samples ($n = 30$ or more).
2. The mean (the average) of the sampling distribution of the mean

$$\left(\overline{X} = \left(\sum_{i=1}^{n} X_i \right) / n \right)$$

or of the proportion (p = number of sample elements of interest/n) equals the corresponding population parameter value, μ or π, respectively.

standard error
The standard deviation of the sampling distribution of the mean or proportion.

3. The standard deviation of the sampling distribution is called the **standard error** of the mean or the proportion. This distinction is made to clarify the point that we are talking about a sampling distribution of the mean or the proportion, not about a distribution of elements in a sample or a population. The formula for the standard error of the mean is

$$\sigma_{\overline{x}} = \frac{\sigma}{\sqrt{n}}$$

The formula for the standard error of the proportion is

$$\sigma_p = \sqrt{\frac{\pi(1 - \pi)}{n}}$$

4. Often the population standard deviation, σ, is not known. In these cases, it can be estimated from the sample by using the following formula:

$$s = \sqrt{\frac{\sum_{i=1}^{n}(X_i - \overline{X})^2}{n - 1}}$$

or

$$s = \sqrt{\frac{\sum_{i=1}^{n}X^2_i - \frac{\left(\sum_{i=1}^{n}X_i\right)^2}{n}}{n - 1}}$$

In cases where σ is estimated by s, the standard error of the mean becomes

$$\text{est. } \sigma_{\overline{x}} = s_{\overline{x}} = \frac{s}{\sqrt{n}}$$

The "est." denotes the fact that s has been used as an estimate of σ.

5. Likewise, the standard error of the proportion can be estimated by using the sample proportion p as an estimator of the population proportion, π, as

$$\text{est. } \sigma_p = s_p = \sqrt{\frac{p(1 - p)}{n}}$$

6. The area under the sampling distribution (normal distribution) curve between any two points can be calculated in terms of z values. The **z value** for a point is the number of standard errors that point is away from the mean. The z values may be computed as follows:

z value
The number of standard errors that a point is away from the mean.

$$z = \frac{\overline{X} - \mu}{\sigma_{\overline{x}}}$$

For example, 34.13 percent of the area under one side of the curve lies between the mean and a z value of 1.0. The area from the mean to the z values of 2.0 and 3.0 is equal to 0.4772 and 0.4986, respectively. (See Table 2 in the Appendix of Statistical Tables.) The same percentages of the area under the sampling distribution curve lie between the mean and z values of -1.0, -2.0, and -3.0. This is because the sampling distribution curve is symmetric around the mean. In the case of proportions, the computation of z values is similar.

Statistical Approach to Determining Sample Size

In addition to statistical considerations, several qualitative factors should be considered when determining the sample size (see Chapter 12). These include the importance of the decision, the nature of the research, the number of variables, the nature of the analysis, sample sizes used in similar studies, incidence rates, completion rates, and resource constraints. The statistically determined sample size is the net or final sample size—the sample remaining after eliminating potential respondents who do not qualify or who do not complete the interview. Depending on incidence and completion rates, the initial sample might need to be much larger than the net or final sample requirements. In commercial marketing research, limits on time, money, and expert resources can exert an overriding influence on sample-size determination.

The statistical approach to determining sample size is based on traditional statistical inference using the formulas (equations) presented in the previous section. In this approach, the

FIGURE 13.3

The Confidence Interval Approach to Determining Sample Size

precision level is specified in advance. This approach is based on the construction of confidence intervals around sample means or proportions (see Figure 13.3).

The Confidence Interval Approach

Confidence intervals around sample means or proportions are estimated using the standard error formula. As an example, suppose that a researcher has taken a simple random sample of 300 households to estimate the monthly expenses on department-store shopping and has found that the mean household monthly expense for the sample is $182. Past studies indicate that the population standard deviation, σ, can be assumed to be $55.

We want to find an interval within which a fixed proportion of the sample means would fall. Suppose we want to determine an interval around the population mean that will include 95 percent of the sample means, based on samples of 300 households; that is, we choose 95 percent as the confidence level. The 95 percent could be divided into two equal parts, half below and half above the mean, as shown in Figure 13.4. Calculation of the confidence interval involves determining a distance below $(\overline{X}_L)$ and above $(\overline{X}_U)$ the population mean (μ), which contains a specified area of the normal curve. The z values corresponding to $\overline{X}_L$ and $\overline{X}_U$ can be calculated as

$$z_L = \frac{\overline{X}_L - \mu}{\sigma_{\overline{x}}}$$

$$z_U = \frac{\overline{X}_U - \mu}{\sigma_{\overline{x}}}$$

where $z_L = -z$ and $z_U = +z$. Therefore, the lower value of $\overline{X}$ is

$$\overline{X}_L = \mu - z\sigma_{\overline{x}}$$

and the upper value of $\overline{X}$ is

$$\overline{X}_U = \mu + z\sigma_{\overline{x}}$$

FIGURE 13.4

95% Confidence Interval

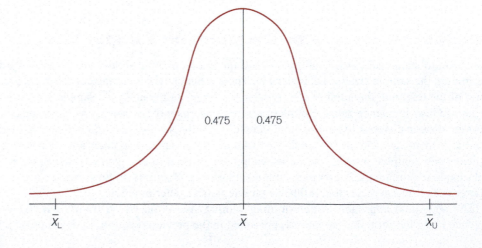

Note that μ is estimated by $\overline{X}$. The confidence interval is given by

$$\overline{X} \pm z\sigma_{\overline{x}}$$

We can now set a 95-percent confidence interval around the sample mean of $182. As a first step, we compute the standard error of the mean:

$$\sigma_{\overline{x}} = \frac{\sigma}{\sqrt{n}} = 55/\sqrt{300} = 3.18$$

From Table 2 in the Appendix of Statistical Tables, we can see that the central 95 percent of the normal distribution lies within $\pm$ 1.96 z values, i.e., $z = 1.96$. The 95-percent confidence interval is given by

$$\overline{X} \pm 1.96\,\sigma_{\overline{x}}$$

$$= 182.00 \pm 1.96(3.18)$$

$$= 182.00 \pm 6.23$$

Thus, the 95-percent confidence interval ranges from $175.77 to $188.23. The probability of finding the true population mean to be within $175.77 and $188.23 is 95 percent. If the confidence interval is not reported, or cannot otherwise be calculated from the information given, we have no way of knowing how precise the sample estimates are. This was illustrated in the opening vignette, in which it was difficult to evaluate the precision of the results of the America Online survey.

Confidence intervals often are associated with scales used to measure customer satisfaction, as illustrated by the American Customer Satisfaction Index.

Research in Action

The American Customer Satisfaction Index

The American Customer Satisfaction Index (ACSI, www.theacsi.org) is a national measure of satisfaction with quality that provides a resource for examining the differences in satisfaction among customers of different industries by their demographic and socio-economic characteristics. The ACSI is based on 42,149 customer interviews and is converted to a scale of 0 to 100.

The first national measure of ACSI gave an index reading of 74.5 with a 95-percent confidence interval of 74.3 to 74.7. This narrow confidence interval is due to the large sample size and indicates that customer satisfaction was measured with a high degree of precision. The ACSI also is broken down by economic sectors and industries. The ACSI is a useful new tool for companies to benchmark their customer satisfaction scores against those of other companies in their own and other industries.[3]

Source: www.theacsi.org. Used with permission from the American Customer Satisfaction Index.

Sample-Size Determination: Means

Confidence interval estimation formulas can be used to determine the sample size that will result in a desired confidence interval. In this case, we use the same formulas but have a different unknown, namely the sample size, n. Suppose the researcher wants to estimate the monthly household expense on department-store shopping so that the estimate will be within plus or minus $5 of the true population value. What should the size of the sample be? The following steps, summarized in Table 13.2, will lead to an answer.

1. *Specify the level of precision.* This is the maximum permissible difference (D) between the sample mean and the population mean. In our example, $D = \pm$ $5.
2. *Specify the level of confidence.* Suppose that a 95-percent confidence level is desired.

3. *Determine the z value associated with the confidence level using Table 2 in the Appendix of Statistical Tables.* For a 95-percent confidence level, the probability that the population mean will fall outside either end of the interval is 0.025 (0.05/2), with an associated z value of 1.96.

4. *Determine the standard deviation of the population.* The standard deviation of the population might be available from secondary sources, estimated from pilot-study data, or based on the researcher's judgment. For example, the range of a normally distributed variable is approximately equal to plus or minus three standard deviations. The standard deviation of sample data can therefore be estimated by dividing the range of that data by six. The researcher can often estimate the range based on knowledge of the phenomenon or knowledge of the scale used. For example, the traditional Likert scale has a range of four (5 through 1).

5. *Determine the sample size using the formula for the standard error of the mean.* Let us use the formula for z and derive the formula for the sample size, n. Recall that

$$z = \frac{\overline{X} - \mu}{\sigma_{\overline{x}}}$$

because $D = \overline{X} - \mu$

$$z = \frac{D}{\sigma_{\overline{x}}}$$

Solving for $\sigma_{\overline{x}}$

$$\sigma_{\overline{x}} = \frac{D}{z}$$

But

$$\sigma_{\overline{x}} = \frac{\sigma}{\sqrt{n}}$$

TABLE 13.2 Sample-Size Determination for Means and Proportions

Steps	Means	Proportions
1. Specify the level of precision.	$D = \overline{X} - \mu = \pm \$5.00$	$D = p - \pi = \pm 0.05$
2. Specify the confidence level (CL).	CL = 95%	CL = 95%
3. Determine the z value associated with the CL.	z value = 1.96	z value = 1.96
4. Determine the standard deviation of the population.	Estimate σ	Estimate π
	$\sigma = 55$	$\pi = 0.64$
	$n = \dfrac{\sigma^2 z^2}{D^2}$	$n = \dfrac{\pi(1 - \pi)z^2}{D^2}$
5. Determine the sample size using the formula for the standard error.	$n = \dfrac{55^2(1.96)^2}{5^2}$	$n = \dfrac{0.64(1 - 0.64)(1.96)^2}{(0.05)^2}$
	$n = 465$	$n = 355$
6. If necessary, reestimate the confidence interval by employing s to estimate σ.	$\overline{X} \pm z s_{\overline{x}}$	$p \pm z s_p$

Therefore,

$$\frac{\sigma}{\sqrt{n}} = \frac{D}{z}$$

Solving for n

$$n = \frac{\sigma^2 z^2}{D^2}$$

In our example,

$$n = \frac{55^2(1.96)^2}{5^2}$$

$$= 464.83$$

$$= 465 \,(\text{rounded to the next higher integer})$$

It can be seen from the preceding formulas that sample size is influenced by three factors. It increases as population variability increases, as greater confidence is required (i.e., as confidence level increases), and as the precision level required of the estimate increases (i.e., size of the estimating interval becomes smaller).

6. *If the population standard deviation, σ, is unknown and an estimate is used, it should be reestimated once the sample has been drawn.* The sample standard deviation, s, is used as an estimate of σ. A revised confidence interval should then be calculated to determine the precision level actually obtained.

Suppose that the value of 55 used for σ was an estimate because the true value was unknown. A sample size (n) of 465 is drawn, and these observations generate a mean ($\overline{X}$) of 180 and a sample standard deviation s of 50. The revised confidence interval then is

$$= \overline{X} \pm z s_{\overline{x}}$$

$$= 180 \pm 1.96(50/\sqrt{465})$$

$$= 180 \pm 4.55$$

or

$$175.45 \leq \mu \leq 184.55$$

Note that the confidence interval obtained is narrower than planned because the population standard deviation was initially overestimated to be 55, compared to the sample standard deviation of only 50.

It is very important to note that the population size, N, does not directly affect the size of the sample. An example will make this point more obvious. Suppose all the population elements are identical on a characteristic of interest. A sample size of one would then be sufficient to estimate the mean perfectly. This would be true regardless of whether there were 50, 500, 5,000, or 50,000 elements in the population. Thus, a probability sample size can be a small percentage of the population size and still be very accurate in that it has little sampling error. The sample size is directly affected by the variability of the characteristic in the population. This variability enters into the sample size calculation by way of population variance σ^2 or sample variance s^2. Also, note that the larger the sample size, the more accurate the parameter estimation (sample mean)—that is, the smaller the error denoted by the precision level for a given level of confidence. This can be seen from the formula in step 5. A larger sample will also result in a narrower confidence interval. This can be seen from the formula for the confidence interval in step 6.

A sample size of 400 is enough to represent China's more than 1.4 billion people or the more than 300 million American people. The sample size is independent of the population size for large populations.

Source: Bartlomiej Magierowski/Shutterstock.

Source: Tyler Olson/Shutterstock.

Be an MR!	Be a DM!

Estimating Average Monthly Household Expenditure for Cellular Services to a T

Social Media

Visit www.att.com and search the Internet—including social media—as well as your library's online databases to obtain information on the average monthly amount U.S. households spend on cellular (cell phone) services. Assuming a confidence level of 95 percent, a precision level of +/−$10, and a standard deviation of $100, what should be the sample size to determine the average monthly household expenditure on cellular services?

As the vice president of marketing for AT&T, how would you use information on the average monthly household expenditure for cellular services to expand your revenues?

Sample-Size Determination: Proportions

Proportions are estimated when the choice is dichotomous, that is, when there are only two categories (e.g., yes or no). The researcher is examining the percentage of elements that is in one of the two categories. If the parameter of interest is a proportion, rather than a mean, the approach to sample-size determination is similar. Suppose that the researcher is interested in estimating the proportion of households possessing a department-store credit card. The researcher should follow these six steps, also summarized in Table 13.2:

1. *Specify the level of precision.* Suppose the desired precision is such that the allowable interval is set as $D = p - \pi = \pm\, 0.05$ (i.e., 5% expressed as a decimal equivalent).
2. *Specify the level of confidence.* Suppose that a 95-percent confidence level is desired.
3. *Determine the z value associated with the confidence level.* As explained in the case of estimating the mean, this will be $z = 1.96$.
4. *Estimate the population proportion, π.* As explained earlier, the population proportion might be estimated from secondary sources or from a pilot study or be based on the judgment of the researcher. Suppose that based on secondary data the researcher estimates that 64 percent of the households in the target population possess a department-store credit card. In this case, $\pi = 0.64$.
5. *Determine the sample size using the formula for the standard error of the proportion.* The derivation of the formula for sample size is similar to that used for means. We know that

$$\sigma_p = \frac{p - \pi}{z}$$

Substituting D for $p - \pi$ we get

$$\sigma_p = \frac{D}{z}$$

We also know that

$$\sigma_p = \sqrt{\frac{\pi(1 - \pi)}{n}}$$

Therefore, setting

$$\frac{D}{z} = \sqrt{\frac{\pi(1 - \pi)}{n}}$$

and solving for n, we get

$$n = \frac{\pi(1 - \pi)z^2}{D^2}$$

In our example,

$$n = \frac{0.64(1 - 0.64)(1.96)^2}{(0.05)^2}$$

$$= 354.04$$

$$= 355 \text{ (rounded to the next higher integer)}$$

6. *If the estimate of π turns out to be poor, the confidence interval will be more or less precise than desired.* Suppose that after the sample has been taken, the proportion p is calculated to have a value of 0.55. The confidence interval is then reestimated by employing s_p to estimate the unknown σ_p as

$$p \pm z s_p$$

where

$$s_p = \sqrt{\frac{p(1-p)}{n}}$$

In our example,

$$s_p = \sqrt{\frac{0.55(1-0.55)}{355}}$$

$$= 0.0264$$

The confidence interval, then, is

$$= 0.55 \pm 1.96(0.0264)$$

$$= 0.55 \pm .052$$

which is wider than the specified precision level. This could be attributed to the fact that the sample standard deviation determined from our actual sample based on $p = 0.55$ is larger than the population standard deviation determined from the researcher's judgment and based on $\pi = 0.64$.

If the resulting confidence interval is too wide, the sample size can be recalculated using the maximum possible variation in the population. Maximum variation occurs when the product $\pi(1 - \pi)$ is at a maximum. This occurs when π is set at 0.5. This result can also be seen intuitively. If a population was evenly divided in terms of one value of a characteristic, more evidence would be required to obtain a valid inference than if the majority of the population possessed that characteristic. In our example, this leads to a sample size of

$$n = \frac{0.5(0.5)(1.96)^2}{(0.05)^2}$$

$$= 384.16$$

$$= 385 \,(\text{rounded to the next higher integer})$$

Thus, in our opening vignette if the proportion of online users is to be estimated with 95-percent confidence level and with a margin of error (allowable interval) not to exceed plus or minus 5 percent, the sample size should have been at least 385. The sample size was only 262, however, falling substantially short of the required size. In the photo example given earlier, we can now understand why a sample size of 400 (it is greater than 385) is enough to represent China's more than 1.4 billion people or the more than 300 million American people.

Research in Action

Small Businesses Have Big Technology Plans

The Hewlett-Packard (HP) Small Business Survey was conducted by Harris Interactive, Inc., among 399 small business owners or senior-level employees age 25 to 64 at companies with fewer than 100 employees. Interviews were conducted by telephone between March 3 and 15, 2010. The sample size was selected based on statistical considerations so that percentage estimates would not differ from the true estimates by more than 5 percent.

Survey respondents believe that technology is essential to the operations and success of their businesses, and 81 percent planned to increase technology spending in a variety of ways (e.g., company Web sites, online services, and blogs) over the next 2 to 3 years. In addition, 68 percent of those surveyed reported that they plan to adopt additional technology products in the coming year. Based on these findings, HP set up a dedicated portion of their Web site (www.hp.com/sbso/index.html) for small businesses. On June 3, 2010, HP launched several technology initiatives aimed at this segment.[4]

Be an MR!	Be a DM!

Wells Fargo: Banking on Online Banking

Visit www.wellsfargo.com and search the Internet—including social media—as well as your library's online databases to obtain information on the proportion of consumers who use online banking. If about 15 percent of the people in a given area are expected to use Internet banking, what should be the sample size for a 95-percent confidence level and 5-percent precision level?	As the vice president of marketing for Wells Fargo, what information would you need to determine whether the bank should expand its online services?

Social Media

Experiential Learning

How the Poll Was Conducted

Credible media sources today, such as the *New York Times* (www.nytimes.com), attempt to make their research methods as transparent as possible to their readers. For example, the *New York Times* routinely runs a sidebar column explaining how a poll was conducted when an accompanying story draws heavily upon the results of such a poll. In one sidebar column titled "How the Poll Was Conducted," the following was used as part of the details describing the research methods:

In theory, in 19 cases out of 20 the results based on such samples will differ by no more than 3 percentage points in either direction from what would have been obtained by seeking out all American adults.

In other words, "19 cases out of 20" would correspond to a 95-percent confidence level. (Remember that the value for z associated with a 95-percent confidence interval would be 1.96.) Also, remember that results showing 50 percent "for" and 50 percent "against" would have the highest amount of variance. Therefore, computations using 0.50 as the proportion (π) would account for the most challenging scenario when designing a sample.

1. Using the equations presented in this chapter, estimate the size of the sample used in this national poll if the most challenging scenario existed.

2. What would the size of the sample have to be if researchers wanted a precision level of +/−1 percent?

3. If the original poll had used a 90-percent confidence interval, what would the sample size have to be?

Adjusting the Statistically Determined Sample Size

The sample size specified by these statistical methods is a final, or net, sample size. It represents the number of returned mail questionnaires or the number of completed interviews. Initial oversampling, in which a much larger number of respondents are originally contacted, is required to achieve the desired net sample. This is due to two factors: the incidence rate and the completion rate.

Incidence Rate

The **incidence rate** refers to the rate of occurrence. It is influenced by the proportion of people in the population with the characteristics under study. When studying a characteristic with a low incident rate, the researcher must initially contact many more people than if the characteristic has a high incidence rate, screening out those who do not meet the study requirements. Suppose a study of jewelry calls for a sample of female heads of households ages 25 to 55 years. Of the women between the ages of 20 and 60 years who might reasonably be approached to see if they qualify, approximately 75 percent are heads of households between age 25 and 55. That is, the incidence rate or the rate of occurrence is 0.75. This means that, on average, 1.33 (1.00/0.75) women must be approached in order to obtain one qualified respondent.

Additional criteria for qualifying respondents (e.g., they must be using a specific product brand) will further decrease the incidence rate and therefore increase the number of contacts. Suppose it is decided that respondents must have worn jewelry in the past week in order to be eligible to participate in the study. It is estimated that 60 percent of the women contacted would meet this criterion of wearing jewelry. Then the incidence rate drops from 75 percent to 45 percent (0.75 × 0.60). To deliver one qualified respondent to the sample, 2.22 individuals (1.00/0.45) must be contacted initially.

incidence rate
The rate of occurrence of persons eligible to participate in the study expressed as a percentage.

Completion Rate

completion rate
The percentage of qualified respondents who complete an interview. It enables researchers to take into account anticipated refusals by people who qualify.

The number of initial contacts must also be increased in anticipation of refusals coming from people qualified to participate. The **completion rate** denotes the percentage of qualified respondents who complete the interview. For example, if the researcher expects an interview completion rate of 80 percent of eligible respondents, the number of contacts should be increased by a factor of 1.25 (1.00/0.80).

Combined Adjustment

Combining the expected incident and completion rates results in a contacted sample that is 2.78 (2.22 × 1.25) times the final sample size requirement. In general,

$$\text{Initial sample size} = \frac{\text{Final sample size}}{\text{Incidence rate} \times \text{Completion rate}}$$

The number of units that must be sampled is equal to the initial sample size. These calculations assume that an attempt to contact a respondent will result in a determination as to whether the respondent is eligible. However, this might not be case. An attempt to contact the respondent might be inconclusive, because the respondent might refuse to answer, not be at home, be busy, and so on. Such instances will further increase the initial sample size. The following example illustrates a variety of variables that can be used to qualify potential respondents. It also shows that as the number of qualifying variables increases, the incidence rate will fall.

Research in Action

Targeting Women's Lips

When Lancôme (www.lancome.com) conducted a survey to determine women's preferences for lip color, it defined the target population very precisely. A respondent had to meet the following screening criteria to be included in the study: (1) female, (2) age 25 to 55 years, and (3) annual household income of at least $30,000. Having three qualifying factors resulted in a highly targeted sample, although it boosted the initial sample size because of a much lower incidence rate. Survey results showed that these women were looking for a lipstick that provided more moisturizing comfort, more even application and coverage, and less caking and feathering.

Based on these findings, Lancôme developed and introduced L'absolu Rouge, an advanced replenishing and reshaping lipcolor, and La Base L'absolu Rouge, a revitalizing

lip treatment. These lipsticks were well received in the marketplace.[5]

Source: AP Photo/Weng lei–Imaginechina.

response rate
The number of completed interviews divided by the number of eligible respondents in the sample.

Another rate that is of interest in surveys is the **response rate**, which is the number of completed interviews divided by the number of eligible respondents in the sample. Thus, it is calculated as follows:

$$\text{Response rate} = \frac{\text{Number of completed interviews}}{\text{Number of eligible respondents in the sample}}$$

Tools such as response rate calculators are available to determine survey response rates (see, for example, www.answersresearch.com).

Online Sampling Adjustments

Social Media

The sample size for online sampling including social media surveys generally exceeds that determined statistically. The reason for this is that the marginal cost of collecting and analyzing larger samples is low. Moreover, larger samples permit a more detailed level of analysis at the subgroup or segment level. Some of the biggest challenges in online research are the abilities to generate a truly random sample that is representative of the target population and to increase the response rate. This is more problematic when conducting consumer surveys as compared to business surveys.

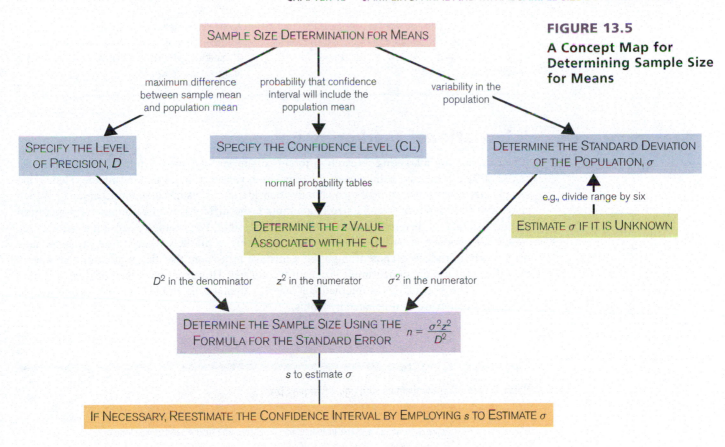

FIGURE 13.5

A Concept Map for Determining Sample Size for Means

Summary Illustration Using the Opening Vignette

The statistical approaches to determining sample size based on confidence intervals can involve estimation of the mean (e.g., mean hours spent watching TV or using online services) or proportion (e.g., proportion of respondents using online services). Statistical calculation of sample size requires specification of the precision level, the confidence level, and the population standard deviation. In the opening vignette, only the precision level (about 5%) was disclosed. Therefore, we could not determine whether the sample size of 262 in the America Online survey was adequate and whether the conclusion reached was warranted. However, we know that the sample size required to estimate a proportion near 0.5 with a 95-percent confidence level and a +/−5-percent precision level is 385. The sample size in the opening vignette falls substantially short of this mark. Figure 13.5 offers a concept map for determining sample size for means. In this figure, the major concepts are connected by bold arrows using descriptors.

Thus, in determining the sample size for means, the maximum difference between the sample mean and the population mean specifies the level of precision. Each major concept is described by minor concepts that are connected to that major concept by lines with descriptors. Thus, when the sample size is determined using the formula for the standard error, and s is used as an estimate of σ, if necessary, reestimate the confidence interval by employing s to estimate σ. The rest of the figure can be interpreted similarly.

Experiential Learning

The Ultimate Rocky Mountain Destination

Skiing is a popular winter sport in the United States.

1. Visit www.ski.com and search the Internet—including social media—as well as your library's online databases to obtain information on the incidence (proportion) of people who ski every season.

2. In a survey of the general population on skiing, what should be the sample size for a 95-percent confidence level and a +/−5-percent precision level? As an estimate of the population proportion, use the proportion you have determined in step 1.

Social Media

3. Using the incidence rate you have determined and a completion rate of 50 percent, what should be the number of initial contacts to achieve a final sample size of 500 skiers?

4. As the director of marketing for Vail Cascade Resort in Colorado, "the ultimate Rocky Mountain destination," what information would you need to formulate marketing strategies to increase your sales?

International Marketing Research

When conducting marketing research in foreign countries, statistical estimation of sample size can be difficult, because estimates of the population variance might be unavailable. Hence, the sample size often is determined by qualitative considerations, as discussed in Chapter 12. When statistical estimation of sample size is attempted, the differences in estimates of population variance should be recognized and factored in, if possible. For example, consumer preferences for certain products might be relatively heterogeneous in markets where those products have been newly introduced. Thus, it might be a mistake to assume that the population variance is the same or to use the same sample size across countries. However, when the goal is to examine differences across countries or international markets, then it is desirable to have the same sample size across countries, as illustrated by Nokia.

Research in Action

Nokia: Determining Inequalities with Equal Sample Sizes

With net sales of EUR 42.45 billion and operating profit of EUR 2.07 billion in 2010, Nokia is the world's largest manufacturer of mobile telephones. But with industry disappointment in its N-Gage series, Nokia intends to revive its mobile gaming market with the new smart mobile phones. A survey was done by a joint effort between Nielsen and Nokia in 2009 of 1,800 mobile gamers in six nations: the United States, Germany, Spain, China, India, and Thailand. They divided the 1,800 respondents into 300 member groups from each nation and region. The sample size was kept constant across countries, because the goal was to compare the findings across nations to determine differences.

The findings revealed several differences across countries. In the U.S. market, over-the-air game distribution from the phone deck was favored by 60 percent of gamers surveyed, and only 27 percent preferred the Internet. Out of the 300 respondents surveyed in this market, 40 percent said they play games every day, as opposed to Germany, where only 21 percent do so. In time spent gaming per session, U.S. gamers (30.6 minutes) were second only to Indian players (38.9 minutes), with Chinese gamers (18.6 minutes) spending the least amount of time on games. Also, according to the survey, Nokia found that 63 percent of those surveyed prefer the more sophisticated designs over older Java and 2D games once they had been trialed. Based on these findings, Nokia developed a customized strategy for penetrating

each country's mobile gaming market with the new smart mobile phones with sophisticated gaming features.[6]

Source: Markuu Ulander/AFP/Getty Images/Newscom.

Marketing Research and Social Media

Social Media

The issues with online sampling in general and social media sampling in particular were discussed in Chapter 12. It is feasible to have large, even very large, sample sizes when conducting marketing research in social media. This is due to the large size of many social media communities, both public and private, and the fact that the marginal cost of increasing the sample size is minimal. Thus, in many social media projects, the sample size can far exceed that required by statistical considerations. It is important to address the issues of the appropriateness and representativeness of social media as outlined in Chapter 12. Once that is done, large samples can be desirable as they result in greater confidence in the findings and allow statistical analysis at a disaggregate or subgroup level, as in the case of Threadless.

Research in Action

Threadless, But Not in Terms of Statistical Significance

Threadless (www.threadless.com) is a clothing manufacturer based in Chicago. The company was founded in 2000 with $1,000 in seed money and was on track to sell more than $20 million worth of T-shirts in 2011. The secret to the company's success is that Threadless conducts continuous marketing research using a social media community of enthusiasts, which serves as a built-in marketing research panel. Every week, six new designs are chosen from about 700 entries submitted by community members. The community votes on the winners with winning designs receiving $2,000 each. The winning designs go into production and between 500 to 1,500 T-shirts are produced for each new design.

The community (panel) size exceeds 400,000 and members are rewarded by monetary and nonmonetary incentives to maintain their interest and involvement in the community. The

Threadless Web site spotlights the weekly winners and the alumni club showcases past winners. Members can upload photos of themselves wearing Threadless products and earn discounts toward merchandise purchase. A weekly newsletter is sent to all the community members. The large size of this community enables Threadless to gather data that are based on large samples, far exceeding the sample sizes required for statistical significance, so that the company can have a great degree of confidence in the findings. In addition, large sample sizes enable the analyses of data at the level of subgroups based on demographic characteristics. So far, the use of social media to conduct marketing research on large samples has paid off handsomely for the company and its products are usually a hit with the target consumers.[7]

Ethics in Marketing Research

The sample size is one of the major determinants of cost in a marketing research project. It might seem that if the sample size is statistically determined, this procedure is free from ethical conflicts. This might not be true, however. As this chapter has emphasized, the sample size is directly proportional to the variance of the variable. Estimates of the population variance are based on small pilot studies, related research, and the researcher's judgment. Because judgment is involved, the researcher has the ethical responsibility to not use large estimates of the population variance simply to increase the cost of the project by inflating the sample size. Using the sample-size formula, we can see that increasing the standard deviation by 20 percent, for example, will increase the sample size by 44 percent. This practice is clearly unethical.

Furthermore, the researcher might be faced with ethical dilemmas when the sample standard deviation varies widely from that which is assumed. In this case, the confidence interval will be larger than required if the actual sample standard deviation turns out to be much larger than that used to estimate the sample size. If this happens, the researcher should disclose the larger confidence interval to the client and jointly arrive at a corrective action. The ethical ramifications of miscommunication of the confidence intervals of survey estimates based on statistical samples are underscored in the case of political polling.

Research in Action

Surveys Serve Up Elections

The release of political polling results during an election has been strongly criticized as manipulative and unethical. Critics have claimed that the general public is misled by these results. Polling results released before an election are thought to discourage voters from casting votes for candidates that are clearly trailing. Prediction of election results on election night has come under even harsher criticism. For example, in the Obama versus McCain 2008 presidential election, polls by some television stations projected the winner in some states

while polling was still open in several West Coast states. Opponents of this practice feel that this predisposes voters to vote for the projected winner or that it might even discourage voter turnout if a race appears to be decided. Not only are the effects of such projections criticized, but, frequently, the accuracy of the projections is questionable as well. Although voters might be told a candidate has a certain percentage of the votes within plus or minus 1 percent, the error denoted by the precision level might be much larger, depending on the sample size.[8]

WHAT WOULD YOU DO?

Procter & Gamble: Taking a Gamble on Core Brands

The Situation

Bob McDonald, CEO of Procter & Gamble (P&G), has refocused P&G on its big brands, including Tide, Pampers, and Crest. McDonald believes there is still tremendous growth in the core brands. He has made one thing clear: P&G's stodgy corporate culture is gone for good.

In May 2001, P&G acquired Moist Mates, "America's first moist bath tissue on a roll." P&G's research had found that 60 percent of consumers used some type of wet cleaning system, such as sprinkling water on dry toilet paper, using baby wipes, or wetting a washcloth. With that in mind, the purchase of Moist Mates became a strategic move in the market. P&G took the product and changed its name to Charmin Fresh Mates to go hand-in-hand with the popular Charmin dry tissue. The biggest problem consumers had experienced was that their makeshift cleaning methods were inconvenient. P&G's marketing research showed that the familiarity of brand name, convenience, and easy-to-use wet tissue on a roll appealed to the consumer. "Together, these products offer consumers a convenient way to choose dry, choose moist, or choose both," said Wayne Randall, global franchise manager for Charmin. As of 2011, the Charmin line consisted of Charmin Ultra Soft and Charmin Ultra Strong, super premium two-ply tissues; Charmin Basic, a one-ply tissue; Charmin Plus with lotion with aloe; and Charmin Freshmates, adult flushable moist wipes. Charmin and other P&G products are available in 180 countries around the world, and the company knows its products are "fresh." Yet some question whether Charmin and Charmin Fresh Mates are perceived as complementary or competing products.

The Marketing Research Decision

1. P&G would like to conduct periodic surveys to determine consumer perceptions and preferences for bath tissues, including Charmin and Charmin Fresh Mates. How should the sample size be determined?
   a. Using the confidence interval approach: means
   b. Using the confidence interval approach: proportions
   c. Based on sample size used in similar studies
   d. Guided by budget constraints
   e. Set at 500
2. Discuss the role of the sample size you recommend in enabling Bob McDonald to determine consumer perceptions and preferences for bath tissues, including Charmin and Charmin Fresh Mates.

The Marketing Management Decision

1. To further increase the market share of Charmin and Charmin Fresh Mates, Bob McDonald should do which of the following?
   a. Package Charmin and Charmin Fresh Mates together.
   b. Lower the prices of Charmin and Charmin Fresh Mates.
   c. Increase advertising expenditures on Charmin and Charmin Fresh Mates.
   d. Offer "buy one, get the other at half price" promotion.
   e. Promote Charmin products aggressively.
2. Discuss how the marketing management-decision action that you recommend to Bob McDonald is influenced by the sample size that you suggested earlier and by the findings of that research.

What Bob McDonald Did

Bob McDonald decided to promote Charmin products aggressively. P&G introduced the Charmin Pottypalooza tour, which provided bathroom facilities with Charmin products. Charmin's in-bathroom marketing reached 30 million consumers in 2002. Research showed a 14-percent increase in Charmin sales among those consumers who used the P&G facilities, leading the company to roll out a second Pottypalooza unit for 2003. The event provided Charmin the ultimate captive audience and integrated marketing opportunity. People who lined up outside the bathrooms were entertained by a Charmin bear and once inside they saw a nonstop loop of TV ads featuring the iconic bear. The aggressive promotion of the Charmin line continued through 2011 with gains in sales and market share.[9]

Source: Lynne Shulhafer.

Summary

The statistical approaches to determining sample size are based on confidence intervals. These approaches can involve the estimation of the mean or proportion. When estimating the mean or the proportion, determination of sample size using the confidence interval approach requires the specification of precision level, confidence level, and population standard deviation. The sample size determined statistically represents the final or net sample size that must be achieved. The initial sample size must be much larger to account for incidence rates and completion rates in order to deliver the final sample size.

The statistical estimation of sample size is even more complicated in international marketing research, because the population variance might differ from one country to the next. It is feasible to have very large sample sizes when conducting marketing research in social media, far exceeding those required by statistical consideration. The preliminary estimation of population variance for the purpose of determining the sample size also has ethical ramifications.

Key Terms and Concepts

Normal distribution 366	Confidence level 367	Standard error 368
Parameter 367	Random sampling error 367	z value 369
Statistic 367	Sampling distribution 368	Incidence rate 377
Precision level 367	Statistical inference 368	Completion rate 378
Confidence interval 367	Central limit theorem 368	Response rate 378

Suggested Cases and Video Cases

Running Case with Real Data

1.1 Hewlett-Packard

Comprehensive Critical Thinking Cases

2.1 American Idol   2.2 Baskin-Robbins   2.3 Akron Children's Hospital

Comprehensive Cases with Real Data

3.1 Bank of America   3.2 McDonald's   3.3 Boeing

Comprehensive Brief Harvard Business School Cases

4.1 TruEarth Healthy Foods: Market Research for a New Product Introduction (4065)
4.2 The Springfield Nor'easters: Maximizing Revenues in the Minor Leagues (2510)
4.3 Metabical: Positioning and Communications Strategy for a New Weight-Loss Drug (4240)
4.4 Saxonville Sausage Company (2085)

Online Video Cases

13.1 Subaru   19.1 Marriott

Live Research: Conducting a Marketing Research Project

1. Discuss the qualitative and statistical considerations involved in determining the sample size.
2. Illustrate the confidence interval approach (mean or proportion) to calculate the sample size of the project, even though the sample size might have been determined based on qualitative considerations.
3. Discuss the expected incidence and completion rates and the initial sample size.
4. The sampling technique and the sample size should be discussed and approved by the client.

Acronym

The statistical considerations involved in determining the sample size can be summarized by the acronym SIZE:

S ampling distribution

I nterval (confidence)

Z value

E stimation of population standard deviation

Review Questions

1. Define the sampling distribution.
2. What is the standard error of the mean?
3. What is a confidence interval?
4. What is the procedure for constructing a confidence interval around a mean?
5. How do the degree of confidence and the degree of precision differ?
6. Describe the procedure for determining the sample size necessary to estimate a population mean given the degree of precision and confidence level and a known population variance. After the sample is selected, how is the confidence interval generated?
7. Describe the procedure for determining the sample size necessary to estimate a population mean when the degree of precision and confidence level are known but the population variance is unknown. After the sample is selected, how is the confidence interval generated?
8. How is the sample size affected when the absolute precision with which a population mean is estimated is doubled?
9. How is the sample size affected when the degree of confidence with which a population mean is estimated is increased from 95 percent to 99 percent?
10. Describe the procedure for determining the sample size necessary to estimate a population proportion given the degree of precision and confidence level. After the sample is selected, how is the confidence interval generated?
11. How can the researcher ensure that the generated confidence interval will be no larger than the desired interval when estimating a population proportion?
12. **Social Media** Discuss the pros and cons of using large sample sizes in social media research.

Applied Problems

1. Using Table 2 of the Appendix of Statistical Tables, calculate the probability that:
   a. z is less than 1.48.
   b. z is greater than 1.90.
   c. z is between 1.48 and 1.90.
   d. z is between −1.48 and 1.90.
2. What is the value of z if:
   a. 60 percent of all values of z are larger.
   b. 10 percent of all values of z are larger.
   c. 68.26 percent of all possible z values (symmetrically distributed around the mean) are to be contained in this interval.
3. The management of a local restaurant wants to determine the average monthly amount spent by households in fancy restaurants. Management wants to be 95-percent confident of the findings and does not want the error to exceed plus or minus $5.
   a. After the survey was conducted, the average expenditure was found to be $90.30 and the standard deviation was $45. Construct a 95-percent confidence interval.
   b. What sample size would have resulted in a standard deviation of $45?
4. To determine the effectiveness of the advertising campaign for a new digital video recorder, management would like to know what percentage of the households is aware of the new brand. The advertising agency thinks that this figure is as high as 70 percent. The management would like a 95-percent confidence interval and a margin of error no greater than plus or minus 2 percent.
   a. What sample size should be used for this study?
   b. Suppose that management wanted to be 99-percent confident, but could tolerate an error of plus or minus 3 percent. How would the sample size change?
5. Assuming that $n = 100$ and $\sigma = 5$, compute the standard error of the mean.
6. Using a spreadsheet software package (e.g., Excel), program the formulas for determining the sample size under the various approaches.
7. Solve Applied Problems 3 through 5, using the programs that you have developed in Applied Problem number 6.
8. Visit the GfK Custom Research North America Web site (www.gfkamerica.com). Identify some of the surveys recently completed by GfK. What were the sample sizes, and how were they determined in these surveys?

Group Discussion

1. "Quantitative considerations are more important than qualitative considerations in determining the sample size." Discuss this statement as a small group. Alternatively, split a group into two smaller subgroups.
One subgroup develops arguments for this statement; the other, against.
2. Discuss the various options available for estimating incidence rates.

Hewlett-Packard Running Case

Review the Hewlett-Packard (HP) case, Case 1.1, and questionnaire given toward the end of the book.

1. **Social Media** Search the Internet—including social media—as well as your library's online databases to obtain information on the proportion of U.S. households that have Internet access at home.
2. In a survey of the general population on Internet usage, what should be the sample size for a 95-percent confidence level and a +/−5-percent precision level? Use the estimate of the population proportion that you determined in step 1.
3. **Social Media** If HP were to conduct a survey in social media to determine consumers' preferences for notebook computers, what should be the sample size? Explain your reasoning.
4. As the director of marketing for HP PCs and notebooks, what information would you need to formulate marketing strategies to increase your sales?

ONLINE VIDEO CASE 13.1

SUBARU: "Mr. Survey" Monitors Customer Satisfaction

Visit **www.pearsonhighered.com/malhotra** to read the video case and view the accompanying video. Subaru: "Mr. Survey" Monitors Customer Satisfaction presents an interesting overview of Joe Barstys's role at Subaru and the importance and utility of surveys in building customer loyalty. About 500,000 mail surveys (with a high response rate) a year plus Internet surveys have helped Subaru get continuous feedback on key parameters that shape customer experience resulting in high brand loyalty. The case can be used to discuss how sample size can be determined for a questionnaire study in measuring consumers' evaluation of Subaru brands. Specific marketing research questions on this and the previous chapters are posed in the video case.

Appendix 13A

The Normal Distribution

In this appendix, we provide a brief overview of the normal distribution and the use of the normal distribution table. The normal distribution is used in calculating the sample size, and it serves as the basis for classical statistical inference. Many continuous phenomena follow the normal distribution or can be approximated by it. The normal distribution can, likewise, be used to approximate many discrete probability distributions.*

The normal distribution has some important theoretical properties. It is bell-shaped and symmetrical in appearance. Its measures of central tendency (mean, median, and mode) are all identical. Its associated random variable has an infinite range ($-\infty < x < +\infty$).

The normal distribution is defined by the population mean, μ, and the population standard deviation, σ. Because an infinite number of combinations of μ and σ exist, an infinite number of normal distributions exist and an infinite number of tables would be required. By standardizing the data, we need only one table, such as Table 2 given in the Appendix of Statistical Tables. Standardization is the process of rescaling data to have a mean of 0 and a standard deviation of 1. Any normal random variable X can be converted to a standardized normal random variable z by the formula:

$$z = \frac{X - \mu}{\sigma}$$

Note that the random variable z is always normally distributed with a mean of 0 and a standard deviation of 1. The normal probability tables are generally used for two purposes: (1) finding probabilities corresponding to known values of X or z and (2) finding values of X or z corresponding to known probabilities. We will discuss each of these uses.

Finding Probabilities Corresponding to Known Values

Suppose Figure 13A.1 represents the distribution of the number of engineering contracts an engineering firm receives per year. Because the data span the entire history of the firm, Figure 13A.1 represents the population. Therefore, the probabilities or proportion of area under the curve must add up to 1.0. The vice president of marketing wishes to determine the probability that the number of contracts received next year will be between 50 and 55. The answer can be determined by using Table 2 of the Appendix of Statistical Tables.

FIGURE 13A.1

Finding Probabilities Corresponding to Known Values

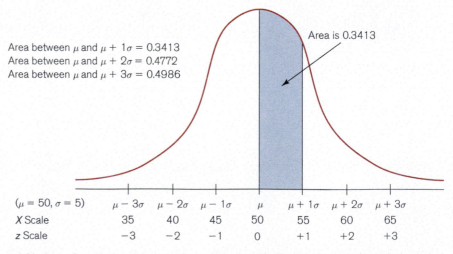

Area between μ and $\mu + 1\sigma$ = 0.3413
Area between μ and $\mu + 2\sigma$ = 0.4772
Area between μ and $\mu + 3\sigma$ = 0.4986

Area is 0.3413

$(\mu = 50, \sigma = 5)$	$\mu - 3\sigma$	$\mu - 2\sigma$	$\mu - 1\sigma$	μ	$\mu + 1\sigma$	$\mu + 2\sigma$	$\mu + 3\sigma$
X Scale	35	40	45	50	55	60	65
z Scale	−3	−2	−1	0	+1	+2	+3

*This material is drawn from Mark L. Berenson, David M. Levine, Timothy Krehbiel, and David F. Stephan, *Basic Business Statistics: Concepts and Applications*, 12th ed. (Upper Saddle River, NJ: Prentice Hall, 2010).

Table 2 of the Appendix of Statistical Tables gives the probability or area under the standardized normal curve from the mean (zero) to the standardized value of interest (z). Only positive entries of z are listed in the table. For a symmetrical distribution with zero mean, the area from the mean to $+z$ (i.e., z standard deviations above the mean) is identical to the area from the mean to $-z$ (i.e., z standard deviations below the mean).

Note that the difference between 50 and 55, which is 5, corresponds to a difference in z values of 1.00 ($1.00 - 0.00$). Note that to use Table 2 all z values must be recorded to two decimal places. To read the probability or area under the curve from the mean to $z = +1.00$, scan down the z column of Table 2 until the z value of interest (in tenths) is located. In this case, stop in the row $z = 1.00$. Then, read across this row until you intersect the column containing the hundredth place of the z value. Thus, in Table 2, the tabulated probability for $z = 1.00$ corresponds to the intersection of the row $z = 1.0$ with the column $z = 0.00$. This probability is 0.3413. As shown in Figure 13A.1, the probability is 0.3413 that the number of contracts received by the firm next year will be between 50 and 55. It can also be concluded that the probability is 0.6826 (2×0.3413), or 68.26 percent, that the number of contracts received next year will be between 45 and 55.

This result could be generalized to show that for any normal distribution the probability is 0.6826 that a randomly selected item will fall within ± 1 standard deviation above or below the mean. Also, it can be verified from Table 2 that there is a 0.9544 probability that any randomly selected normally distributed observation will fall within ± 2 standard deviations above or below the mean and that there is a 0.9973 probability the observation will fall within ± 3 standard deviations above or below the mean.

Finding Values Corresponding to Known Probabilities

Suppose the vice president of marketing wishes to determine how many contracts must come in so that this number represents 5 percent of the contracts expected for the year. If 5 percent of the contracts have come in, 95 percent of the contracts have yet to come. As shown in Figure 13A.2, this 95 percent can be broken down into two parts: contracts above the mean (i.e., 50 percent) and contracts between the mean and the desired z value (i.e., 45 percent). The desired z value can be determined from Table 2, because the area under the normal curve from the standardized mean, zero, to this z must be 0.4500. From Table 2, we search for the area or probability 0.4500.

The closest value is 0.4495 or 0.4505. For 0.4495, we see that the z value corresponding to the particular z row (1.6) and z column (0.04) is 1.64. However, the z value must be recorded as negative (i.e., $z = -1.64$), because it is below the standardized mean of zero. Similarly, the z value corresponding to the area of 0.4505 is -1.65. Because 0.4500 is midway between 0.4495 and 0.4505, the appropriate z value could be midway between the two z

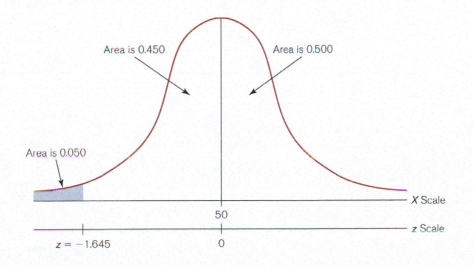

FIGURE 13A.2

Finding Values Corresponding to Known Probabilities

FIGURE 13A.3

Finding Values Corresponding to Known Probabilities: Confidence Interval

values and estimated as −1.645. The corresponding X value can then be calculated from the standardization formula as follows:

$$X = \mu + z\sigma$$

or

$$X = 50 + (-1.645)5 = 41.775$$

Suppose the vice president wanted to determine the interval in which 95 percent of the contracts for next year are expected to lie. As can be seen from Figure 13A.3, the corresponding z values are ±1.96. This corresponds to X values of 50 ± (1.96) 5, or 40.2 and 59.8. This range represents the 95-percent confidence interval.

PART

3

Data Collection, Analysis, and Reporting

14

Fieldwork: Data Collection

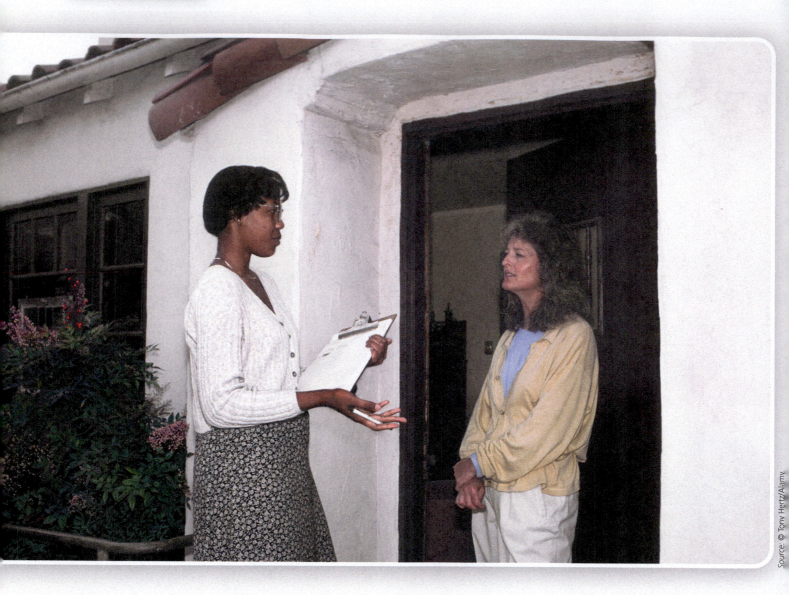

Source: © Tony Hertz/Alamy

LEARNING OBJECTIVES

After reading this chapter, the student should be able to:

1. Understand what is meant by fieldwork and the fieldwork process.

2. Explain how field-workers should be trained in different aspects of interviewing.

3. Describe how the field-workers should be supervised to enhance their effectiveness and efficiency.

4. Discuss how field-workers should be evaluated.

5. Understand how fieldwork should be conducted in international marketing research.

6. **Social Media** Explain fieldwork in relation to social media.

7. Discus the ethical issues involved in fieldwork.

Gallup's Galloping Fieldwork

Now more than ever, Americans are hanging up on interviewers. The primary difficulty of telephone interviewing is declining response rates and, more specifically, increasing refusal rates. Many techniques and procedures have been used to combat this problem, including incentives, aggressive call designs, shorter interviews, and special introductory statements. The most critical variable, however, might be the interviewers themselves.

Refusals are largely a function of interviewing skill. Top interviewers are rarely turned down. The Gallup Organization (www.gallup.com), a prestigious marketing research and consulting firm that specializes in survey research, has identified the following characteristics of an outstanding interviewer:

- **Work orientation.** Works hard and sees work as more than a job, but as an expression of oneself.
- **Teamwork.** Forms good team relationships with others.
- **Aptitude.** Has a natural affinity for telephone research—enjoys collecting opinions via the telephone.
- **Pride.** Is positive, quality-conscious, and likes being recognized for a job well done.
- **Discipline.** Stays focused on a task and completes it.
- **Third ear.** Empathizes with a respondent and tailors presentation accordingly.
- **Command.** "Takes charge"—can turn refusals around by conveying the purpose of the survey and its importance.
- **Woo.** Gets people to like him or her quickly; convinces people to cooperate who might not otherwise respond.
- **Ethics.** Is honest and behaves ethically at all times.

Using this theme, the hiring process for interviewers at The Gallup Organization has become very selective, hiring only 1 out of every 16 candidates. The selected interviewers are carefully trained in all aspects of interviewing, from making the initial contact to terminating the interview. The Council of American Survey Research Organizations' guidelines for effective interviewing are followed. Experienced and qualified supervisors closely monitor the interviewers' work, making sure appropriate procedures are followed and the interviews are being properly conducted.

Validation of fieldwork and the evaluation of interviewers are continuous activities. As a result, The Gallup Organization has not only increased the retention rate of its field-workers, but has significantly increased the productivity and quality of its data collection. Gallup interviews more than 3 million people every year in the United States and has built a worldwide reputation for the high quality of its data collection process. As of 2011, Gallup had operations in 40 countries around the world and employed more than 2,000 professionals.[1]

Overview

Fieldwork is the fourth step in the marketing research process. It follows problem definition and development of the approach (see Chapter 2) and formulation of the research design (see Chapters 3 through 13). Figure 14.1 briefly explains the focus of the chapter, the relationship of this chapter to the previous ones, and the steps of the marketing research process on which this chapter concentrates.

During this phase, the field-workers make contact with the respondents, administer the questionnaires or observation forms, record the data, and turn in the completed forms for processing. Field-workers include a personal interviewer administering questionnaires door-to-door, an interviewer intercepting shoppers in a mall, a telephone interviewer calling from a central location, a worker mailing questionnaires from an office, an observer counting customers in a particular section of a store, and others involved in data collection and supervision of the process. The opening vignette gives the characteristics of outstanding interviewers, who form the backbone of fieldwork.

This chapter describes the nature of fieldwork and the fieldwork/data collection process. This process involves the selection, training, and supervision of field-workers, the validation of fieldwork, and the evaluation of field-workers. Care taken at each of these stages of the fieldwork process can pay big dividends, as illustrated by The Gallup Organization in the opening vignette. The chapter also discusses fieldwork in the context of international marketing research and social media, and identifies the relevant ethical issues. Figure 14.2 gives an overview of the topics discussed in this chapter and how they flow from one to the next.

The Nature of Fieldwork

Those who design the research rarely collect marketing research data. Researchers have two major options for collecting their data: They can develop their own organizations, or they can contract with a fieldwork agency. In either case, data collection involves using some kind of field force. This field force can operate either in the field (personal in-home, mall intercept, computer-assisted personal interviewing, and observation) or from an office (telephone/computer-assisted telephone interviewing, mail/mail panel, and electronic surveys). The field-workers who collect the data typically have little research background or training. Therefore, to ensure high quality the fieldwork/data collection process should be streamlined and well controlled, as discussed in the following section.

FIGURE 14.1

Relationship of Fieldwork to the Previous Chapters and the Marketing Research Process

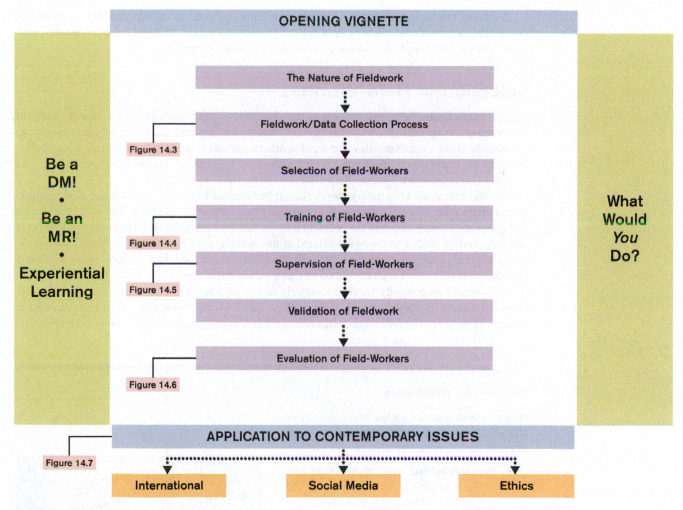

FIGURE 14.2
Fieldwork: An Overview

Fieldwork/Data Collection Process

All fieldwork involves the selection, training, and supervision of those who collect the data. The validation of fieldwork and the evaluation of field-workers also are parts of the process. All of these aspects were seen in the opening vignette, which described how Gallup selected, trained, supervised, monitored, and evaluated its field-workers. Figure 14.3 represents a general framework for the fieldwork/data collection process.

FIGURE 14.3

The FieldWork/Data Collection Process

Although this chapter describes a general process, it should be recognized that the nature of fieldwork varies with the mode of data collection and that the relative emphasis on the different steps will vary for telephone, personal, mail, and electronic interviews.

Selection of Field-Workers

The first step in the fieldwork process is the selection of field-workers. The researcher should (1) develop job specifications for the project, taking into account the mode of data collection; (2) decide what characteristics the field-workers should have; and (3) recruit appropriate individuals. Interviewers' background characteristics, opinions, perceptions, expectations, and attitudes can affect the responses they elicit.

To the extent possible, interviewers should be selected to match respondents' demographic characteristics, because this increases the probability of a successful interview. The job requirements will also vary with the nature of the problem and the data collection method. However, some general qualifications of field-workers were outlined in the opening vignette: work orientation, teamwork, aptitude, pride, discipline, third ear, command, the ability to woo, and ethics. Interviewers with these qualifications will have a high likelihood of being successful in conducting fieldwork.

Field-workers generally are paid an hourly rate or on a per-interview basis. The typical interviewer is a married woman, age 35 to 54, with an above-average education and an above-average household income. The following example illustrates a psychographic breakdown of interviewers.

Research in Action

The Four Faces of Interviewers

Interviewers can be segmented into four distinct psychographic groups, based on an analysis made by M/A/R/C (www.marcresearch.com) for the Marketing Research Association:

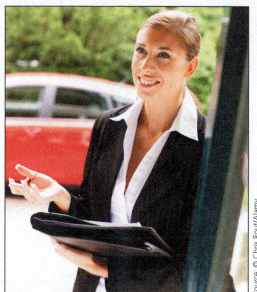

Source: © Chris Rout/Alamy.

- **Dedicated Debbie.** To the Dedicated Debbie, interviewing is not just a job, but something much more important. She interviews because she enjoys it.
- **Independent Inez.** Independent Inez interviews because of the independence it gives her. Interviewing gives her freedom to choose when she wants to work and some freedom on the job as well.
- **Social Sara.** This interviewer enjoys interviewing almost as much as Dedicated Debbie, but she does not feel that interviewing is important. What attracts her is the chance to socialize, to meet interesting people, and to interact with others.
- **Professional Pat.** This is the career-oriented interviewer. She sees the job not only as a means to earn her living, but also as a marketing research career opportunity. Professional Pat considers the two most important attributes of an interviewer to be a detailed mind and exceptional intelligence.

Such an understanding of the psychographic profile of interviewers, along with their demographic characteristics, can greatly assist in identifying and selecting the right interviewers.

Training of Field-Workers

Training field-workers is critical to the quality of data collected. Training can be conducted in person at a central location, or, if the interviewers are geographically dispersed, by mail, Internet, or videoconferencing. Training ensures that all interviewers administer the questionnaire in the same manner so that the data can be collected uniformly. Training should cover all phases of the interviewing process (see opening vignette): making the initial contact, asking questions, probing, recording answers, and terminating the interview (see Figure 14.4).

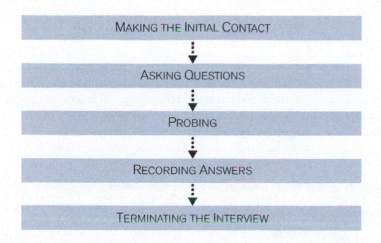

FIGURE 14.4
Training Field-Workers

The initial contact can result in the cooperation or the loss of potential respondents. Interviewers should be trained to make opening remarks that will convince potential respondents that their participation is important. Questions that directly ask permission, such as "May I have some of your valuable time?" or "Would you like to answer a few questions?" should be avoided, because people can answer "no." Interviewers should also be instructed on handling objections and refusals. For example, if the respondent says, "This is not a convenient time for me," the interviewer should respond, "What would be a more convenient time for you? I will call back then."

Asking questions is an art. Even a slight change in the wording, sequence, or manner in which a question is asked can distort its meaning and bias the response. Training in asking questions can yield high dividends by eliminating potential sources of bias. One method used to reduce response bias is to probe respondents. **Probing** is intended to motivate respondents to elaborate, clarify, or explain their answers. Probing also helps respondents focus on the specific content of the interview and provide only relevant information. Probing should not introduce any bias. Commonly used probes include questions such as "Any others?" "Anything else?" and "Could you tell me more about your thinking on that?" Probing can result in rich insights, as illustrated by Whirlpool.

probing
A motivational technique used when asking survey questions to induce the respondents to enlarge on, clarify, or explain their answers and to help the respondents focus on the specific content of the interview.

Research in Action

Probing Enables Whirlpool to Spin Out New Innovations

Whirlpool Corporation (www.whirlpool.com) is the world's leading manufacturer of major home appliances, with annual sales of more than $18.37 billion in 2010. As of 2011, the company markets Whirlpool, Maytag, KitchenAid, Jenn-Air, Amana, Brastemp, Consul, Bauknecht, and other major brand names to consumers in more than 130 countries around the world. Through in-home personal interviews, Whirlpool researched the market and the need for laundry equipment in Brazil. In-home personal interviews were used so that the interviewers could effectively probe respondents to determine their usage and underlying needs for major appliances. Great emphasis was placed on the selection and training of the interviewers.

The research concluded that there was high need for inexpensive equipment, but also showed that laundry equipment is viewed as a status symbol by many Brazilians. Moreover, the respondents expressed a strong desire to "show off" their washers to friends; they want them to be able to see how they work. These findings led Whirlpool to invest $30 million over 18 months to develop inexpensive washing machines in Brazil. These machines sell for less than $200 and feature a clear plastic lid so that people can watch the washer operate.

Emphasis on the quality of fieldwork has resulted in important findings, allowing Whirlpool to be a leader in the appliance industry and to successfully incorporate its new technologies into the marketplace.[3]

Although recording respondent answers seems simple, several mistakes are common. All interviewers should use the same format and conventions to record the interviews and edit completed interviews. Although the rules for recording answers to structured questions vary with each questionnaire, the general rule is to check the box that reflects the respondent's answer. The general rule for recording answers to unstructured questions is to record the responses verbatim.

Before terminating the interview, the interviewer should answer the respondent's questions about the project. The respondent should be left with a positive feeling about the interview. It is important to thank the respondent and express appreciation for his or her participation. The following example shows the importance of well-trained interviewers in the data collection process and the effect this has on new-product development research.

Research in Action

Brushing Interviewers Results in a Successful New Toothbrush Series

When Oral-B (www.oralb.com), a division of Procter & Gamble, was conducting a survey to determine the market potential for a new toothbrush, the company realized that this research would be crucial to the development and introduction of a new product. To obtain high-quality data, the interviewers were carefully trained in all aspects of interviewing. Training in making the initial contact resulted in a much lower refusal rate. The interviewers were instructed to ask the questions as written, to diligently probe the respondents for open-ended questions, and to record the answers fully and accurately. Probing was crucial for questions such as, "Why are you (dis)satisfied with the brands of toothbrush currently available in the market?" Probing and recording answers to open-ended questions were particularly important, because the company was seeking to identify creative solutions to the oral-care problems consumers faced.

One innovative idea that emerged from the survey findings was a toothbrush would clean hard to reach spaces between teeth. Based on this finding, Oral-B developed and launched the Oral-B CrossAction toothbrush series. The CrossAction series' flexing CrissCross bristles are angled just like the angles between teeth, attacking plaque from an optimal 16° in opposing directions, cleaning hard to reach spaces between teeth. The series was positioned as the state-of-the-art choice for people who were serious about oral care.

The launch was a strong success, because the product addressed an unmet consumer need. As of 2011, Oral-B CrossAction manual toothbrushes were available in four varieties: Pro, Vitalizer, Vitalizer Plus, and the basic CrossAction. The manual series was supplemented with CrossAction Power Series of electric toothbrushes. A major factor contributing to the success of the CrossAction series was the careful training of the interviewers that was instrumental in discovering the need for these innovative toothbrushes.[4]

Source: Bill Greenblatt UPI Photo Service/Newscom.

Be a DM!	Be an MR!
Beyond Cosmetic Changes: Selecting and Training Field-Workers	
As the brand manager for Clinique, what information would help you to formulate marketing strategies to increase Clinique's sales?	Visit www.clinique.com and search the Internet—including social media—as well as your library's online databases to obtain information on women's cosmetics usage. How would you select and train field-workers to conduct a mall-intercept survey to determine women's cosmetics usage in a project for Clinique?

Social Media

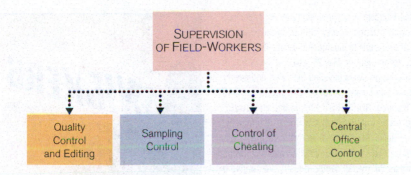

FIGURE 14.5
Supervising Field-Workers

Supervision of Field-Workers

Supervision of field-workers means making sure that they are following the procedures and techniques in which they were trained, as illustrated by The Gallup Organization in the opening vignette. Supervision involves quality control and editing, sampling control, control of cheating, and central office control (see Figure 14.5).

Quality control of field-workers requires checking to see if the field procedures are being properly implemented. If problems are detected, the supervisor should discuss them with the field-workers and provide additional training, if necessary. To understand the interviewers' problems, the supervisors should also conduct some interviews. Supervisors should collect questionnaires and edit them daily. They should examine the questionnaires to ensure that all the appropriate questions have been completed, that unsatisfactory or incomplete answers have not been accepted, and that the writing is legible. Supervisors should also keep a record of hours worked and expenses. This will make it easy to determine the cost per completed interview, whether the job is moving on schedule, and if any interviewers are having problems.

An important aspect of supervision is **sampling control**, which attempts to ensure that the interviewers are strictly following the sampling plan rather than selecting sampling units based on convenience or accessibility. To control these problems, supervisors should keep daily records of the number of calls made, the number of not-at-homes, the number of refusals, the number of completed interviews for each interviewer, and the total for all interviewers under their control.

Cheating involves falsifying part of a question or the entire questionnaire. An interviewer might falsify part of an answer to make it acceptable or might fake answers. The most blatant form of cheating occurs when the interviewer falsifies the entire questionnaire, filling in answers without contacting a respondent. Cheating can be minimized through proper training, supervision, and validation of fieldwork.

Central office control involves tabulating the responses to important demographic characteristics and key questions. It also includes checking on the quotas to make sure they are being met. Supervisors provide quality and cost-control information to the central office so that a progress report can be maintained.

The following example illustrates the importance of close supervision in collecting high-quality data.

sampling control
An aspect of supervision that ensures that the interviewers strictly follow the sampling plan rather than select sampling units based on convenience or accessibility.

Research in Action

Sweet and Savory Is from Mars

Mars, Inc. (www.mars.com) frequently conducts mall-intercept interviews to identify and test new product concepts. Shoppers are intercepted at various locations in the mall and taken to a central facility where they can taste candy bars under development and then respond to surveys. The surveys contain a fair number of open-ended or unstructured questions that require interviewers to probe respondents. Probing provides rich insights into respondents' underlying values, attitudes, and beliefs. Because all such interviews are conducted at a central location, supervision of the interviewers is greatly facilitated. Completed questionnaires are available to the supervisors immediately after the interview for editing and quality control. Sampling control is easily exercised and cheating is eliminated, so there is no need for validation. This procedure also is good for implementing quota sampling, which often is used, and also facilitates other aspects of central office control, such as tabulation of responses to key questions.

A recent mall-intercept survey indicated a strong preference for candy bars with enticing, savory fillings, because such a product would allow people to indulge and escape the stresses of daily routine. Accordingly, on May 25, 2010, at the Sweets & Snacks Expo in Chicago, Mars unveiled the sweet and savory M&M'S® Pretzel Chocolate Candies, SNICKERS® Brand Peanut Butter Squared, SNICKERS® Xtreme Bar, and DOVE® Sugar Free Chocolates with Peanut Butter Crème. Jim Murphy, vice president of Sales, Mars Chocolate North America, said: "According to industry research, peanut butter candy is growing at twice the rate as the overall candy industry. We're giving consumers more delicious options, with the addition of these four new items that contrast the sweet taste of real milk chocolate with enticing, savory fillings." Close supervision of field-workers, made possible by mall-intercept interviewing, facilitated the research responsible for introducing yet other winners for Mars.[5]

Source: Lynne Shulhafer.

Experiential Learning

Feeding Interviewers Chips and Snacks

Consumption patterns for chips and snacks change often. The brand manager for Lay's chips would like to conduct a telephone survey to determine the consumption of chips and snacks.

Social Media

1. Visit www.fritolay.com/lays and search the Internet—including social media—as well as your library's online databases to obtain information on the consumption of chips and snacks. Design an appropriate questionnaire.

2. Train an interviewer (a fellow student) and have her or him conduct the telephone interview with a respondent (another student).

3. How would you supervise this interviewer?

4. As the brand manager for Lay's chips, what information would help you formulate marketing strategies to increase sales?

Validation of Fieldwork

Validation of fieldwork means verifying that field-workers are submitting authentic interviews. To validate the study, the supervisors call 10 to 25 percent of the respondents to inquire whether the field-workers actually conducted the interviews. The supervisors ask about the length and quality of the interview, reaction to the interviewer, and basic demographic data. The demographic information is cross-checked against the information reported by the interviewers on the questionnaires.

Evaluation of Field-Workers

It is important to evaluate field-workers to provide them with feedback on their performance. Evaluation helps identify the more effective field-workers in order to build a better, higher-quality field force. As in the case of The Gallup Organization in the opening vignette, the evaluation of field-workers should be an ongoing process. The evaluation criteria should be clearly communicated to the field-workers during their training. The evaluation of field-workers should be based on the criteria of quantity (cost and time, response rates) and quality (quality of interviewing, quality of data), as shown in Figure 14.6.

Interviewers can be compared in terms of the total cost (salary and expenses) per completed interview. Field-workers should also be evaluated on how they spend their time. Time should be broken down into categories, such as actual interviewing, travel, and administration. It is important to monitor response rates on a timely basis so that corrective action can be taken if

FIGURE 14.6
Evaluating Field-Workers

these rates are too low. Supervisors can help interviewers with an inordinate number of refusals by listening to the introductions they use and providing immediate feedback. When all the interviews are over, different field-workers' percentage of refusals can be compared to identify the better workers.

To evaluate interviewers on the quality of interviewing, the supervisor must directly observe the interviewing process. The supervisor can do this in person, or the field-worker can tape record the interview. The completed questionnaires of each interviewer should be evaluated for the quality of data. Some indicators of quality data are (1) the recorded data are legible; (2) all instructions, including skip patterns (discussed in Chapter 11), are followed; (3) the answers to unstructured questions are recorded verbatim; (4) the answers to unstructured questions are meaningful and complete enough to be coded (discussed in Chapters 11 and 15); and (5) for structured questions item nonresponse occurs infrequently.

Experiential Learning

Vending Fieldwork

What is it like to conduct fieldwork? Go to the textbook Web site and download the following file: Vending Machine Survey.doc. Print five copies of this survey, select a building on campus with vending machines, go there, and conduct separate survey interviews with five different people from that building.

1. How did you feel approaching these respondents?

2. What seemed to be the most challenging part of the survey for the respondents?

3. If other students were employed to collect the data for this survey project, how should they be trained?

4. If other students were employed to collect the data for this survey project, how should their fieldwork be supervised?

5. If other students were employed to collect the data for this survey project, how should their fieldwork be evaluated?

Using the Internet in Fieldwork

The Internet can play a valuable role in all the phases of fieldwork, including the selection, training, supervision, validation, and evaluation of field-workers. As far as selection is concerned, interviewers can be located, interviewed, and hired via the Internet. This process can be initiated, for example, by posting notices of job vacancies for interviewers at the company Web site, bulletin boards, and other suitable locations. Although this would confine the search to only Internet-savvy interviewers, this might well be a qualification for the job.

Similarly, the Internet, with its multimedia capabilities, can be a good supplementary tool for training the field-workers in all aspects of interviewing. Training in this manner can complement personal training programs and add value to the process. Facilitating communication between the supervisors and the interviewers via e-mail and secured chat rooms enhances supervision. By posting progress reports and quality and cost-control information on a secured location at a Web site, it is easily available to all the relevant parties and can strengthen central office control.

Validation of fieldwork, especially for personal and telephone interviews, can be easily accomplished for those respondents who have an e-mail address or access to the Internet. These respondents can be sent a short verification survey by e-mail or be asked to visit a Web site where the survey is posted. The evaluation criteria can be communicated to field-workers during the training stage by using the Internet, and performance feedback can also be provided to them using this medium.

Summary Illustration Using the Opening Vignette

Notice the care The Gallup Organization took in selecting its interviewers, choosing only 1 out of every 16 possible candidates. In selecting interviewers, Gallup looks for the following qualities: work orientation, teamwork, aptitude, pride, discipline, third ear, command, the ability to woo, and ethical behavior. These interviewers are thoroughly trained by following the guidelines on interviewing by the Council of American Survey Research Organizations. Experienced and qualified supervisors closely supervise the interviewers. The interviewers' work is validated and evaluated, and they are continuously provided with feedback on performance. As a result, Gallup has been very successful in cultivating and retaining high-quality field-workers who contribute significantly to the data collection process and the reputation of the organization. Figure 14.7 provides a concept map for the fieldwork/data collection process. In this figure, the major concepts are connected by bold arrows using descriptors.

Thus, the fieldwork/data collection process involves the selection of field-workers. Each major concept is described by minor concepts that are connected to that major concept by lines with descriptors. Thus, to select field-workers, one has to develop job specifications, decide the characteristics of field-workers, and implement a recruitment plan. The rest of the figure can be interpreted similarly.

Research in Action

Interviewing Guidelines by CASRO

The Council of American Survey Research Organizations (www.casro.org) has provided the following guidelines for effective interviewing:

1. Provide his or her full name, if asked by the respondent, as well as a phone number for the research firm.

2. Read each question exactly as written. Report any problems to the supervisor as soon as possible.

3. Read the questions in the order indicated on the questionnaire, following the proper skip sequences.

4. Clarify any question by the respondent in a neutral way.

5. Do not mislead respondents as to the length of the interview.

6. Do not reveal the identity of the ultimate client unless instructed to do so.

7. Keep a tally on each terminated interview and the reason for each termination.

8. Remain neutral in interviewing. Do not indicate agreement or disagreement with the respondent.

9. Speak slowly and distinctly so that words will be understood.

10. Record all replies verbatim, not paraphrased.

11. Avoid unnecessary conversations with the respondent.

12. Probe and clarify for additional comments on all open-end questions, unless otherwise instructed. Probe and clarify in a neutral way.

13. Write neatly and legibly.

14. Check all work for thoroughness before turning it in to the supervisor.

15. When terminating a respondent, do so in a neutral way, such as, "Thank you," or "Our quota has already been filled in this area, but thank you anyway."

16. Keep all studies, materials, and findings confidential.

17. Do not falsify any interviews or any answers to any question.

18. Thank the respondent for participating in the study.

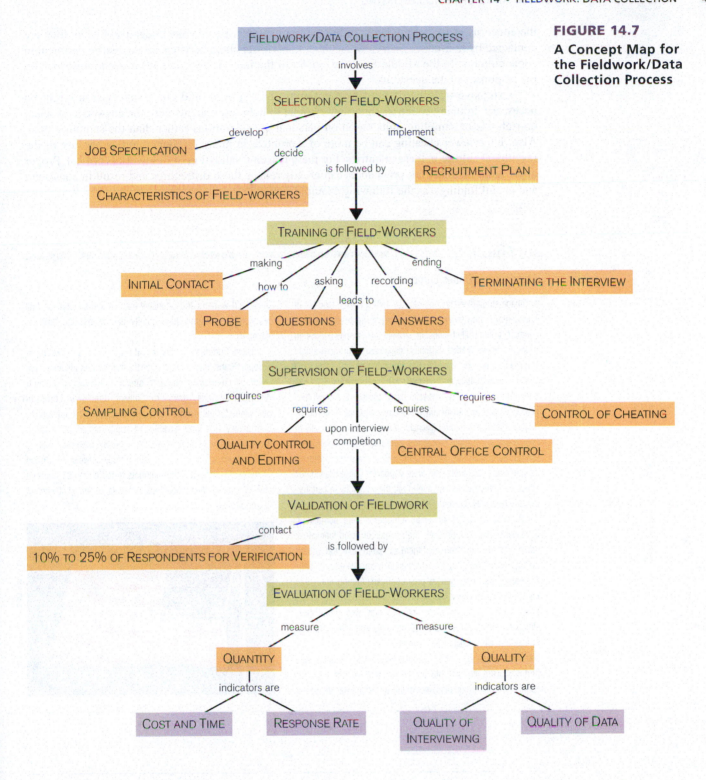

FIGURE 14.7

A Concept Map for the Fieldwork/Data Collection Process

International Marketing Research

The selection, training, supervision, and evaluation of field-workers are critical in international marketing research. Local fieldwork agencies are unavailable in many countries; therefore, it might be necessary to recruit and train local field-workers or import trained foreign workers. Using local field-workers is preferable, however, because they are familiar with the local language and culture and can create an appropriate climate for the interview, being sensitive to the concerns of the respondents. In France, for example, people react negatively when they are contacted by non-native interviewers. Other interviewer characteristics might also be pertinent in some cultures. In the Middle East, the gender of the interviewer can have a strong influence on the responses to the questions.

Extensive training of field-workers might be required, and close supervision might be necessary. In many countries, interviewers tend to help respondents with the answers and select households or sampling units based on personal considerations rather than the sampling plan. Also, interviewer cheating can be more of a problem in many foreign countries because of the lax ethical culture in these countries. For these reasons, validation of fieldwork is critical. Proper application of fieldwork procedures can greatly reduce these difficulties and result in consistent and useful findings, as the following example demonstrates.

Research in Action

Americanism Unites Europeans

An image study recently conducted by TNS Global, a member of The Kantar Group (www.tnsglobal.com), a marketing research company in the United Kingdom, showed that, despite unification of the European market, European consumers still increasingly favor U.S. products. The survey was conducted in Germany, the United Kingdom, Italy, and The Netherlands. In each country, local interviewers and supervisors were used, because it was felt they would be better able to identify with the respondents. However, the field-workers were trained extensively and supervised closely to ensure that appropriate procedures were followed. The validation efforts were doubled: 20 percent, rather than the minimum 10 percent, of the interviews were validated. These procedures ensured quality results and minimized the variability in country-to-country results due to differences in fieldwork.

A total of 6,724 personal interviews were conducted. Europeans gave U.S. products high marks for being innovative; some countries also regarded them as fashionable and of high quality. Interestingly, France, which is often considered to be anti-American, also emerged as pro-American. Among the 1,034 French consumers surveyed, 40 percent considered U.S. products fashionable and 38 percent believed they were innovative, although only 15 percent said U.S. products were of high quality. In addition, when asked what nationality they preferred for a new company in their area, a U.S. company was the first choice. These findings were comparable and consistent across the four countries. A key to the discovery of these findings was the use of local field-workers and extensive training and supervision that resulted in uniformly high-quality data across the different countries.

These findings are very useful for U.S. firms marketing in Europe. "Rather than trying to hide the fact that they are American, we think companies ought to stress or try to exploit their American heritage," says Eric Salaam, director of European operations for the Henley Center, the U.K. economic forecasting consultancy. U.S. firms have, in fact, capitalized on the "made in America" equity. As a result, exports to Europe have been soaring in recent years. As of 2011, bilateral trade between the United States and European Union amounts to more than $1 billion a day, and, jointly, their global trade accounts for almost 40 percent of world trade.[6]

Source: June Marie Sobrito/Shutterstock.

Be a DM!	Be an MR!

GM: Extending Its Field to China

Social Media

As the international marketing manager for General Motors, what information would you like in order to formulate marketing strategies to increase your sales in China?

Visit www.gm.com and search the Internet—including social media—as well as your library's online databases to obtain information on Chinese consumers' preferences for cars. How would you select, train, and supervise field-workers conducting an in-home survey in China to determine consumers' preferences for cars?

Marketing Research and Social Media

Interviewers conducting telephone or personal interviews are generally employed on a part-time or contract basis. However, research staff collecting and analyzing data from social media are normally full-time employees of the research firm. Furthermore, a limited number of operational staff or field-workers, as few as two or three, may be assigned to a social media project. Both of these factors make the selection, training, supervision, validation, and evaluation of field-workers much more streamlined although many of the issues involved are the same as encountered in traditional fieldwork. Another challenge a researcher faces is working closely with the client in making additional fieldwork decisions. When collecting qualitative data, several decisions have to be made, and these should be arrived at jointly by the researcher and the client. These decisions involve determining the type and specification of the social media channels to be monitored; developing a standardization of terms, conversation types, and content types; establishing a standardized coding scheme; and setting benchmarks. Thus, a crucial part of the organization of fieldwork is forming a core nucleus team of people drawn from both the client and research organizations. This is illustrated in the research project undertaken by KDPaine & Partners for Georgia Tech.

Research in Action

Georgia Tech: Using Social Media to Make Social Comparisons

KDPaine & Partners (www.kdpaine.com) provides custom research to measure the effectiveness of social media and traditional public relations. The research firm undertook a project to determine specifically what presence and activity Georgia Tech (www.gatech.edu) and its peer institutions had in social media. The fieldwork was organized as follows: Two senior members of Georgia Tech's communications/marketing team, the CEO of KDPaine & Partners, LLC, the KDPaine Director of Research, and the KDPaine Education team leader formed a nucleus team working together to determine goals, methodology, and the timeline for the project. Following the development of goals and the project vision, the KDPaine Director of Research and the Education team leader finalized coding instructions.

Once instructions were completed the Education team leader conducted training on test items for readers (field-workers) until they reached acceptable reliability standards for all major variables. Then, the KDPaine Director of Research and the Education team leader determined and acquired the desired population and sample sizes. Once the desired sample was achieved and coders trained, official reading of social media sites (data collection) began with intercoder reliability tests being administered intermittently to assure accuracy. Every month, results were compiled and reported on to set a benchmark and examined over time. Team meetings were held regularly between Georgia Tech and KDPaine to discuss the efficacy of the fieldwork methodology and the ensuing results.[7]

Ethics in Marketing Research

High ethical standards should be used when collecting data. Researchers and field-workers should make the respondents feel comfortable by addressing their apprehensions and concerns. This can be done by providing respondents with adequate information about the project, addressing their questions, and clearly stating the responsibilities and expectations of both the field-workers and the respondents at the beginning of the interview. Otherwise, respondents might be unsure about how their answers will be used and might not respond candidly. Researchers and field-workers should respect respondents' time, feelings, privacy, and right to self-determination.

Researchers and fieldwork agencies also are responsible to the clients for following the accepted procedures for the selection, training, supervision, validation, and evaluation of field-workers. Fieldwork procedures should be carefully documented and made available to clients. As illustrated by the following example, ethical codes are available for guiding fieldwork/data collection.

Research in Action

An Ethical Code for Data Collection and Coding

On May 12, 2003, the Marketing Research Association (www.mra-net.org) adopted a new code of marketing research standards that clarifies expectations by delineating specific acceptable practices. Some of the salient ethical responsibilities of fieldwork firms pertaining to respondents are as follows:

Companies Engaged in Data Collection . . .

- Will treat the respondent with respect and not influence a respondent's opinion or attitude.
- Will conduct themselves in a professional manner and ensure privacy and confidentiality.

(continued)

- Will make factually correct statements to secure cooperation and will honor promises made to respondents.
- Will not use information to identify respondents without the permission of the respondent, except to those who check the data or are involved in processing the data.
- Will adhere to and follow these principles when conducting online research:
  - Respondents' rights to anonymity must be safeguarded.
  - Unsolicited e-mail must not be sent to those requesting not to receive any further e-mail.

- Researchers interviewing minors must adhere to the Children's Online Privacy Protection Act (COPPA).
- Data will not be used in any way contrary to the provider's published privacy statement without permission from the respondent.
- Will respect the respondent's right to withdraw or to refuse to cooperate at any stage of the study.
- Will obtain and document respondent consent when personally identifiable information of the respondent might be passed to a third party for legal or other purposes.

WHAT WOULD YOU DO?

Nissan: Taking Xterra to the (E)Xtreme

The Situation

Carlos Ghosn, president and CEO of Nissan Motor Company, is known as the "Icebreaker" for his skill at ignoring local business practices that stand in the way of making money. Ghosn is the troubleshooter charged with reviving Nissan Motor Company. Ghosn is not afraid to take different paths and knows that taking risks to meet consumer demand is what business is all about.

Ghosn was faced with a new dilemma. When Nissan considered launching a new model sport utility vehicle (SUV), marketers wanted to appeal to Generation X. Hence, the Xterra was born. However, Ghosn did not want the Xterra to just be another SUV. He wanted it to fully meet the needs of drivers.

Ghosn decided to let Nissan partner with The Designory Team to determine the target audience for advertising of the new SUV. The Designory Team put together a design team for the Xterra to conduct some observational research, "trying to get to the heart of what it means to be a hardcore SUV owner." The team headed to the woods to observe how these hardcore SUV owners bungee, kayak, and mountain bike. Nissan wanted to know how to market to this younger Generation X market.

Nissan would like to conduct mall-intercept interviews with consumers to determine the type of positioning for Xterra that will appeal to Generation X consumers. The questionnaire is a mix of unstructured and structured questions. Some of the questions require substantial probing of the respondents, and the supervision of the interviewers will be critical to collecting good quality data.

The Marketing Research Decision

1. In what areas should the supervisors be trained to closely monitor the interviewers?
   a. Quality control and editing
   b. Sampling control
   c. Control of cheating
   d. Central office control
   e. All of the above
2. Discuss the role of supervisor training you recommend in enabling Carlos Ghosn to identify the needs of Generation X consumers.

The Marketing Management Decision

1. Carlos Ghosn wants to enhance the appeal of the Xterra to Generation X consumers. What changes should be made?
   a. Change the image of Xterra.

b. Change the features of Xterra.
   c. Lower the price to make it more affordable.
   d. Promote Xterra over the Internet.
   e. All of the above.
2. Discuss how the marketing management-decision action that you recommend to Carlos Ghosn is influenced by the supervisor training that you suggested earlier and by the findings of mall intercept interviews.

What Carlos Ghosn Did

Carlos Ghosn made tremendous adaptations to Xterra in order to enhance its appeal to Generation X. It includes the availability of a supercharged V6, new front-end styling, a new hood, 17-inch wheels and off-road tires, three new exterior colors, new trim colors, a radically revised interior, new dual-stage airbags, new rear child seat anchors, an optional "Enthusiast Package" for dyed-in-the-wool off-roaders, and some changes to option packages in general. Nissan opted for an Eaton M62 roots-type supercharger, which is a first in a compact SUV. This is the same setup offered as part of an option package in Nissan's Frontier pickup truck. However, unlike the Frontier, Nissan offers Xterra drivers supercharger a la carte, very much in keeping with Xterra's motto, "Everything You Need, Nothing You Don't." The new model really does have more of what you need. Whether it is more power, more style, more interior, or more amenities, this Xterra builds upon an already great compact SUV. The 2011 Nissan Xterra had a starting price of $23,850.[8]

Source: eVox Productions LLC/Photolibrary.

Summary

Researchers have two major options for collecting data: developing their own organizations or contracting with fieldwork agencies. In either case, data collection involves the use of a field force. Field-workers should be carefully selected and trained in important aspects of fieldwork, including making the initial contact, asking the questions, probing, recording the answers, and terminating the interview. Supervision of field-workers involves quality control and editing, sampling control, control of cheating, and central office control. Validation of fieldwork can be accomplished by calling 10 to 25 percent of those who have been identified as respondents and inquiring whether the interviews actually took place. Field-workers should be evaluated on the basis of cost and time, response rates, quality of interviewing, and quality of data collection.

Fieldwork can contribute to, and benefit from, quality-control procedures. The selection, training, supervision, and evaluation of field-workers are even more critical in international marketing research, because local fieldwork agencies are not available in many countries. Fieldwork in social media research is more streamlined as compared to traditional fieldwork. Ethical issues include making the respondents feel comfortable in the data collection process so that their experience is positive. Every effort must be undertaken to ensure that the data are of high quality. The Internet can greatly facilitate the fieldwork/data collection process.

Key Terms and Concepts

Probing   395

Sampling control   397

Suggested Cases and Video Cases

Running Case with Real Data

1.1 Hewlett-Packard

Comprehensive Critical Thinking Cases

2.1 American Idol   2.2 Baskin-Robbins

Comprehensive Cases with Real Data

3.1 Bank of America   3.2 McDonald's   3.3 Boeing

Comprehensive Brief Harvard Business School Cases

4.1 TruEarth Healthy Foods: Market Research for a New Product Introduction (4065)
4.2 The Springfield Nor'easters: Maximizing Revenues in the Minor Leagues (2510)
4.3 Metabical: Positioning and Communications Strategy for a New Weight-Loss Drug (4240)
4.4 Saxonville Sausage Company (2085)

Online Video Cases

14.1 Intel   19.1 Marriott

Live Research: Conducting a Marketing Research Project

1. The students conducting fieldwork should be appropriately trained. Follow the guidelines in the chapter.
2. The team leaders can conduct fewer interviews but also act as supervisors. They should be trained in supervision.
3. The callback procedures should be specified (e.g., abandon a telephone number after three callback attempts).
4. If in-home interviews are to be conducted in the local area, each interviewer (student) can be assigned a specific part of a census track.

Acronyms

In the fieldwork/data collection process, the organization VESTS in the field-workers:

V alidation of fieldwork

E valuation of field-workers

S election of field-workers

T raining of field-workers

S upervision of field-workers

The areas in which field-workers should be trained may be summarized by the acronym TRAIN:

T erminating the interview

R ecording the answers

A sking the questions

I nitial contact development

N osy behavior: probing

Review Questions

1. What options are available to researchers for collecting data?
2. Describe the fieldwork/data collection process.
3. What qualifications should field-workers possess?
4. What are the guidelines for asking questions?
5. What is probing?
6. How should the answers to unstructured questions be recorded?
7. How should the field-worker terminate the interview?
8. What aspects are involved in the supervision of field-workers?
9. How can respondent selection problems be controlled?
10. What is validation of fieldwork? How is this done?
11. Describe the criteria that should be used for evaluating field-workers.
12. **Social Media** Compare the fieldwork in social media research to traditional fieldwork.

Applied Problems

1. Write interviewer instructions for in-home personal interviews to be conducted by students.
2. Comment on the following field situations, making recommendations for corrective action.
   a. One of the interviewers has an excessive rate of refusals in in-home personal interviewing.
   b. In a CATI situation, many phone numbers are giving a busy signal during the first dialing attempt.
   c. An interviewer reports that, at the end of the interviews, many respondents asked if they had answered the questions correctly.
   d. While validating the fieldwork, a respondent reports that she cannot remember being interviewed over the telephone, but the interviewer insists that the interview was conducted.
3. Visit the Web sites of three marketing research suppliers. Make a report of all the material related to fieldwork that is posted on these sites.
4. Visit the Marketing Research Association Web site (www.mra-net.org) and examine the ethical codes relating to data collection. Write a brief report.

Group Discussion

1. Discuss the impact of women's changing lifestyles on fieldwork during the last decade.
2. Discuss the notion of interviewer cheating. Why do interviewers cheat? How can cheating be detected and prevented?

Hewlett-Packard Running Case

Review the Hewlett-Packard (HP) case, Case 1.1, and questionnaire given toward the end of the book.

What's it like to shop for notebook computers? Design a questionnaire to determine students' shopping behavior for notebook computers. Administer the survey to five different students on your campus.

1. How did you feel approaching these respondents?
2. What seemed to be the most challenging part of the survey for the respondents?

3. If other students were employed to collect the data for this survey project, how should they be trained?
4. If other students were employed to collect the data for this survey project, how should they be supervised?
5. **Social Media** Administer the questionnaire you designed by posting it or a link to it on your Facebook account and inviting your student friends to participate in the survey. What fieldwork related issues did you encounter?

ONLINE VIDEO CASE 14.1

INTEL: Building Blocks Inside Out

Visit **www.pearsonhighered.com/malhotra** to read the video case and view the accompanying video. Intel: Building Blocks Inside Out demonstrates the critical role that marketing research has played in Intel's phenomenal growth. Marketing research was instrumental in developing the Intel brand, designing the "Intel Inside" campaign, and crafting the new logo with the "Leap ahead" tag line. The case can be used as a springboard for students to create a mall-intercept interview study using a fieldwork process to determine consumer preferences for an ultra-light notebook that uses a newly designed chip. Specific marketing research questions on this and the previous chapters are posed in the video case.

15 Data Preparation and Analysis Strategy

Source: © B. O'Kane/Alamy.

LEARNING OBJECTIVES

After reading this chapter, the student should be able to:

1. Understand the nature and scope of data preparation and the data preparation process.

2. Explain questionnaire checking and editing.

3. Describe how questionnaires should be coded to prepare the data for analysis.

4. Discuss the methods that are available for cleaning the data and treating missing responses.

5. Understand how researchers select the appropriate data-analysis strategy.

6. Explain how data collected in international marketing research projects should be prepared.

7. **Social Media** Describe text coding and categorization and other aspects of data preparation in social media research.

8. Discuss the ethical issues that are important in data preparation and analysis.

" In many projects, editing, coding, cleaning, and preparing the data for analysis accounts for the majority of the time an analyst will spend with the data. **"**

Jim McGee
Global Mapping International,
Colorado Springs, Colorado

Database Awakens a Sleeping Giant

Since its founding, Sears, Roebuck and Company has been a leading department-store retailer of apparel, home products, and automobile products and services. In the late 1990s, Sears tried to lose its reputation as a "hardware and tools" store in order to create a trendier and modern store image for customers. Once held up as a textbook example of a mighty marketer failing to adapt to changing consumer demands, Sears, Roebuck and Company has since become an innovator in the retail world, pulling off a comeback that has even the retailer's harshest critics gushing.

One crucial element in its success was building a high-quality database about its customers and potential customers. By 2011, Sears had built a massive database of more than 75 percent of U.S. households. The data are collected from a variety of primary and secondary sources. One hallmark is the care taken to prepare the data before they become a part of the database. In the case of primary data, completed questionnaires returned from the field are carefully checked and edited for incomplete responses (e.g., questions that are incorrectly skipped) or inconsistent responses (e.g., a respondent reports purchases made on a Sears credit card but does not have one). Any questionnaires with unsatisfactory responses are simply discarded, because the proportion of such respondents is small in relation to the total sample size. The data are coded by following appropriate procedures. To ensure uniformity in coding, Sears has prepared a codebook containing the coding instructions and the necessary information about the variables in the data set. The data are then transcribed from the questionnaires into the computer, using state-of-the-art technology.

Further checks are performed on the data to ascertain their consistency and accuracy. An effort is made to identify data that are out of range (e.g., a response of 8 on a 1-to-7 scale), logically inconsistent (e.g., sum of percentages totaling more or less than 100 percent), or have extreme values (e.g., household size of 11). Missing values are kept to a minimum by proper selection, training, and supervision of field-workers and are treated by following a variety of methods to determine the impact on the results. A similar process is followed for data collected from secondary sources.

This superior database enables Sears to identify the needs of the marketplace and target its marketing efforts accordingly. The company now executes 270 campaigns a month. Based on the findings of a survey of 3,000 randomly selected households from its database, Sears spent $4 billion renovating its stores. It markedly improved store layout, design, cleanliness, and merchandising mix. The move is clearly paying off, with Sears reporting higher sales and revenue per selling square foot than it did prior to the renovation.[1]

Overview

After the researcher has defined the research problem and developed a suitable approach (see Chapter 2), formulated an appropriate research design (see Chapters 3 to 13), and conducted fieldwork (see Chapter 14), she or he can move on to data preparation and analysis, the fifth step of the marketing research process.

Before the raw data contained in the questionnaires can be subjected to statistical analysis, they must be converted into a suitable form. Care exercised in the data preparation phase can substantially improve the quality of the findings, resulting in better managerial decisions, as explained in the Sears opening vignette. In contrast, inadequate attention to data preparation can seriously compromise statistical results, leading to biased findings and incorrect interpretation.

This chapter describes the data preparation process, which begins with checking the questionnaires for completeness. It also discusses the editing of data and provides guidelines for handling illegible, incomplete, inconsistent, ambiguous, or otherwise unsatisfactory responses. Coding, transcribing, and data cleaning are presented, with an emphasis on the treatment of missing responses. The chapter then discusses the selection of a data-analysis strategy, the role of technology, and the ethical issues and Internet applications related to data processing. Figure 15.1 briefly explains the focus of the chapter, the relationship of this chapter to the previous ones, and the steps of the marketing research process on which this chapter concentrates. Figure 15.2 provides an overview of the topics discussed in this chapter and how they flow from one to the next.

Help for running the SPSS and Excel programs used in this chapter is provided in four ways: (1) detailed step-by-step instructions are given later in the chapter, (2) you can download (from the Web site for this book) computerized demonstration movies illustrating these step-by-step instructions, (3) you can download screen captures with notes illustrating these step-by-step instructions, and (4) you can refer to the Study Guide and Technology Manual, a supplement that accompanies this book, which provides more help for SPSS and Excel.

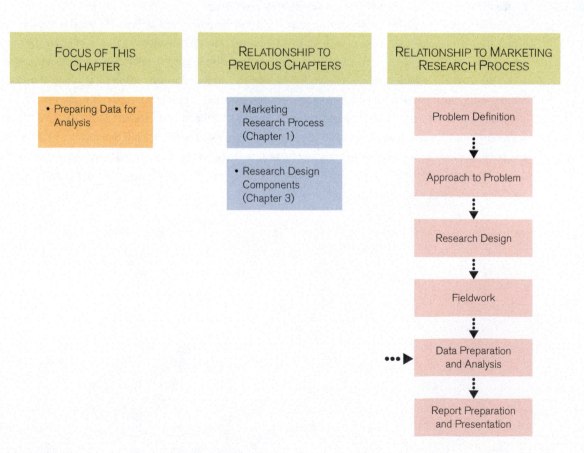

FIGURE 15.1

Relationship of Data Preparation to the Previous Chapters and the Marketing Research Process

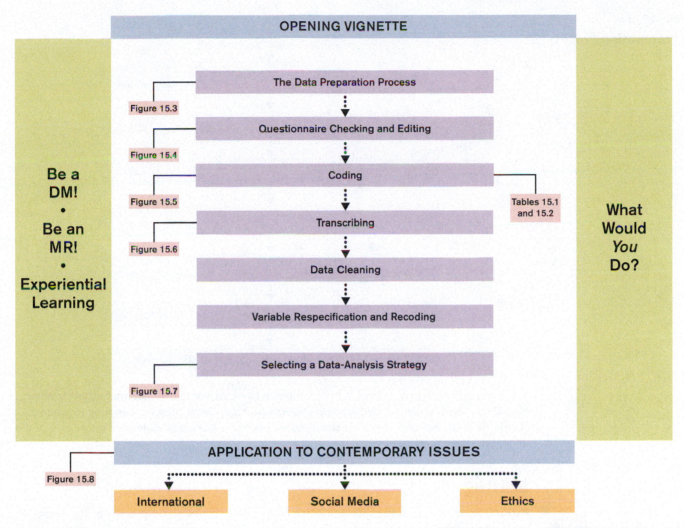

FIGURE 15.2
Data Preparation:
An Overview

The Data Preparation Process

The data preparation process is shown in Figure 15.3. Sears followed a similar process, as explained in the opening vignette. The entire process is guided by the preliminary plan of data analysis that was formulated in the research design phase (see Chapter 3). As the first step, the fieldwork supervisor checks for acceptable questionnaires. This is followed by editing, coding, and transcribing the data, which are all done by the data collection agency as part of fieldwork (see Chapter 14). The researcher cleans the data, performs further checks for consistency, specifies how missing responses will be treated, and respecifies and recodes the variables as needed. The researcher then selects an appropriate data-analysis strategy. The final data-analysis strategy differs from the preliminary plan of data analysis due to the information and insights gained since the preliminary plan was formulated. Data preparation should begin as soon as the first batch of questionnaires is received from the field, while the fieldwork is still taking place. Thus, if any problems are detected, the fieldwork can be modified to incorporate corrective action.

Questionnaire Checking

The initial step in questionnaire checking involves checking for completeness and interviewing quality. This is a continuous process and begins as soon as the first set of questionnaires is returned, while fieldwork is still underway. Therefore, any problems can be detected early on and corrective action can be taken before too many surveys have been completed. A questionnaire returned from the field can be unacceptable for several reasons. For example, parts of the questionnaire might be incomplete, skip patterns might not have been followed (see Chapter 11), one or more pages might be missing, and so forth.

FIGURE 15.3

Data Preparation Process

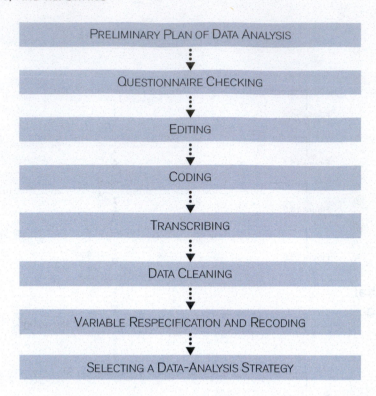

PRELIMINARY PLAN OF DATA ANALYSIS

QUESTIONNAIRE CHECKING

EDITING

CODING

TRANSCRIBING

DATA CLEANING

VARIABLE RESPECIFICATION AND RECODING

SELECTING A DATA-ANALYSIS STRATEGY

If quotas or cell group sizes have been imposed (see Chapter 12), the acceptable questionnaires should be classified and counted accordingly. Any problems in meeting the sampling requirements should be identified and corrective action taken, such as conducting additional interviews in the underrepresented cells.

Editing

editing

A review of the questionnaires with the objective of increasing accuracy and precision.

Editing involves reviewing questionnaires to increase accuracy and precision. It consists of screening questionnaires to identify illegible, incomplete, inconsistent, or ambiguous responses, as in the opening vignette.

Responses might be illegible if they have been poorly recorded, such as answers to unstructured or open-ended questions. Likewise, questionnaires might be incomplete to varying degrees. A few or many questions might be unanswered. At this stage, the researcher makes a preliminary check for consistency. Certain obvious inconsistencies can be easily detected, for example, a respondent who reports an annual income of less than $20,000 yet indicates frequent shopping at prestigious department stores, such as Neiman Marcus. A response is ambiguous, for example, if the respondent has circled both 4 and 5 on a 7-point scale.

Unsatisfactory responses are commonly handled by returning to the field to get better data, by assigning missing values, or by discarding unsatisfactory respondents (see Figure 15.4).

FIGURE 15.4

Treatment of Unsatisfactory Responses

TREATMENT OF UNSATISFACTORY RESPONSES

RETURN TO THE FIELD

ASSIGN MISSING VALUES

DISCARD UNSATISFACTORY RESPONDENTS

Substitute a Neutral Value

Casewise Deletion

Pairwise Deletion

The questionnaires with unsatisfactory responses can be returned to the field so that the interviewers can recontact the respondents to get better/complete data. This approach is particularly attractive for business and industrial marketing surveys, where the sample sizes are small and the respondents are easily identifiable. If returning the questionnaires to the field is not feasible, the editor might assign missing values to unsatisfactory responses. This approach is desirable if (1) the number of respondents with unsatisfactory responses is small, (2) the proportion of unsatisfactory responses for each of these respondents is small, or (3) the variables with unsatisfactory responses are not the key variables.

Alternatively, the respondents with unsatisfactory responses are simply discarded. This approach has merit when (1) the proportion of unsatisfactory respondents is small (less than 10 percent), (2) the sample size is large, (3) the unsatisfactory respondents do not differ from satisfactory respondents in obvious ways (e.g., demographics, product usage characteristics), (4) the proportion of unsatisfactory responses for each of these respondents is large, or (5) responses on key variables are missing (see the opening vignette). However, unsatisfactory respondents might differ from satisfactory respondents in systematic ways, and the decision to designate a respondent as unsatisfactory might be subjective. Both these factors related to unsatisfactory respondents can bias the results. If the researcher decides to discard unsatisfactory respondents, the procedure adopted to identify these respondents and the number of unsatisfactory respondents should be reported by the researcher in the project report, as in the following example.

Research in Action

A Complaint Against Consumer Complaints

In a study examining consumer complaints, 1,000 questionnaires were mailed to households in each of three service categories: automotive repair, medical care, and banking services. The numbers of responses received were automotive repair, 155; medical care, 166; and banking services, 172. The returned questionnaires were carefully checked and edited. Those respondents who did not meet the qualifying criteria (being able to recall a recent dissatisfying experience) and those with a large number of missing values or missing values on key variables were discarded. The usable samples that remained were automotive repair, 116; medical care, 125; and banking services, 104.

The researchers complained that a large number of respondents had to be discarded because of failure to meet the qualifying criteria or a high incidence of missing values. These complaints are justified because discarding such a high proportion of returned questionnaires (25.2% for automotive repair, 24.7% for medical care, and 39.5% for banking services) is not a good research practice. According to the general guidelines, no more than 10 percent of the returned questionnaires should be discarded.[2]

Coding

Coding means assigning a code, usually a number, to each possible response to each question. If the questionnaire contains only structured questions or very few unstructured questions, it is precoded. This means that codes are assigned before fieldwork is conducted. If the questionnaire contains unstructured questions, codes are assigned after the questionnaires have been returned from the field (postcoding). Although precoding was briefly discussed in Chapter 11 on questionnaire design, the next section provides further guidelines on coding structured and open-ended questions.

The respondent code and the record number should appear on each record in the data. The following additional codes should be included for each respondent: project code, interviewer code, date and time codes, and validation code. **Fixed field codes** are highly desirable. This means that the number of records for each respondent is the same and the same data appear in the same column(s) for all respondents. If possible, standard codes should be used for missing data. For example, a code of 9 (or −9) could be used for a single-column variable (responses coded on a 1-to-7 scale), 99 for a double-column variable (responses coded on a 1-to-11 scale), and so forth. The missing value codes should be distinct from the codes assigned to the legitimate responses.

Coding Structured Questions

Coding structured questions is relatively simple, because the response options are predetermined. The researcher assigns a code for each response to each question and specifies the appropriate record and columns in which the response codes are to appear. For example,

coding
The assignment of a code to represent a specific response to a specific question, along with the data record and column position that code will occupy.

fixed field code
A code in which the number of records for each respondent are the same and the same data appear in the same columns for all respondents.

In the last month, have you bought a product or service over the Internet?
1. Yes   2. No (G)

For this question, a "yes" response is coded 1 and a "no" response receives a 2. The number in parentheses indicates that the code assigned will appear in column G for this respondent, for example in an Excel spreadsheet. Because only one response is allowed and there are only two possible responses (1 or 2), a single column is sufficient. In general, a single column is sufficient to code a structured question with a single response.

In questions that permit multiple responses, each possible response option should be assigned a separate column. Such questions include those about brand ownership or usage, television viewing, and magazine readership, as in the magazine readership example.

Research in Action

Reading Magazine Readership

Which magazines have you read during the last 2 months? ("X" as many as apply.)

Time	❏	(D)
Newsweek	❏	(E)
BusinessWeek	❏	(F)
Forbes	❏	(G)
Fortune	❏	(H)
The Economist	❏	(I)
Other Magazines	❏	(J)

Source: © moodboard/Alamy.

Suppose a respondent checked *Time, Newsweek,* and Other Magazines. On the record for this respondent, a 1 will be entered in the columns D, E, and J. All the other columns (F, G, H, and I) will receive a 0.

Coding Open-Ended Questions

Coding unstructured or open-ended questions is more complex. Respondents' verbatim responses are recorded on the questionnaire. Codes are then developed and assigned to these responses by analyzing the data of a few respondents. The following guidelines are suggested for coding unstructured questions and questionnaires in general.

Category codes should be mutually exclusive and collectively exhaustive. Categories are mutually exclusive if each response fits into one, and only one, category code. Categories should not overlap. Categories are collectively exhaustive if every response fits into one of the assigned category codes. This can be achieved by adding an additional category code of "other" or "none of the above." However, only a few (10 percent or less) of the responses should fall into this category. The vast majority of the responses should be classified into meaningful categories.

Data should be coded to retain as much detail as possible. For example, if data on the exact number of trips made on commercial airlines by business travelers have been obtained, they should be coded as such, rather than grouped into two category codes of "infrequent fliers" and "frequent fliers." Obtaining information on the exact number of trips allows the researcher to later define categories of business travelers in several different ways (e.g., fewer than 3 trips per month, 4 to 6 trips per month, 7 to 10 trips per month, 11 to 15 trips per month, and more than 15 trips per month). If the categories were predefined (e.g., infrequent fliers and frequent fliers), the subsequent analysis of data would be limited by those categories. The following illustrates the coding of responses to open-ended questions.

CODING OF OPEN-ENDED QUESTION RESPONSES   Question: Why do you prefer Colgate to Crest toothpaste?

Sample Responses

1. It is a better value.
2. It has a lower price.
3. Tastes better.
4. I like the packaging better.
5. Better buy for my money.
6. I don't like the taste of Crest.
7. It prevents tooth decay.
8. It gives me fresh breath.
9. It has a better-looking package.
10. I like the smell of Colgate.
11. I like Colgate advertising.
12. Crest has a taste disadvantage.
13. Colgate's advertising is creative.
14. Colgate is more effective in fighting cavities.
15. It is better for your health.

Similar responses are grouped, and category codes are developed, as follows.

Category Descriptors	Sample Responses	Category Code
Better value/lower price/better buy	1, 2, 5	1
Tastes better/don't like taste of Crest/Crest's taste disadvantage	3, 6, 12	2
Better packaging/better-looking package	4, 9	3
Prevents tooth decay/fights cavities/better for health	7, 14, 15	4
Fresh breath/like smell	8, 10	5
Like advertising/creative advertising	11, 13	6
Other		7

Developing a Data File

It often is helpful to prepare a **codebook** containing the coding instructions and the necessary information about the variables in the data set (see opening vignette). Data can be entered into a spreadsheet program, such as Excel. Most analysis programs can import data from a spreadsheet. In this case, the data for each respondent for each field is a cell. Typically, each row of the (Excel) spreadsheet contains the data of one respondent or case. The columns will contain the variables, with one column for each variable or response. The use of Excel can be complicated if there are more than 256 variables. Later in this chapter, in an experiential learning situation, we show how the data from an Excel file can be converted to an SPSS file.

    These concepts are illustrated in Table 15.1. This table gives the data from a pretest sample of 20 respondents on preferences for restaurants.

    Each respondent was asked to rate his or her preference to eat in a familiar restaurant (1 = Weak Preference, 7 = Strong Preference) and to rate the restaurant in terms of quality of food, quantity of portions, value, and service (1 = Poor, 7 = Excellent). Annual household income was obtained and coded as: 1 = Less than $20,000, 2 = $20,000 to 34,999, 3 = $35,000 to 49,999, 4 = $50,000 to 74,999, 5 = $75,000 to 99,999, 6 = $100,000 or more. The codebook for coding these data is given in Figure 15.5. Note that in addition to the data of Table 15.1, the codebook also contains information on several other codes that are not shown.

    If the data of Table 15.1 are entered using either Excel or SPSS, the resulting data files will resemble Table 15.1. You can verify this by downloading Excel and SPSS files for Table 15.1 from the student Web site for this book. In Table 15.1, as well as in the corresponding Excel and SPSS files, the columns represent he fields, and the rows represent the records or respondents, because

codebook

A book containing coding instructions and the necessary information about variables in the data set.

SPSS Data File

Excel Data File

TABLE 15.1 Restaurant Preference

ID	Preference	Quality	Quantity	Value	Service	Income
1	2	2	3	1	3	6
2	6	5	6	5	7	2
3	4	4	3	4	5	3
4	1	2	1	1	2	5
5	7	6	6	5	4	1
6	5	4	4	5	4	3
7	2	2	3	2	3	5
8	3	3	4	2	3	4
9	7	6	7	6	5	2
10	2	3	2	2	2	5
11	2	3	2	1	3	6
12	6	6	6	6	7	2
13	4	4	3	3	4	3
14	1	1	3	1	2	4
15	7	7	5	5	4	2
16	5	5	4	5	5	3
17	2	3	1	2	3	4
18	4	4	3	3	3	3
19	7	5	5	7	5	5
20	3	2	2	3	3	3

there is one record per respondent. Notice that there are seven columns. The first column contains the respondent ID, and the second column contains the preference for the restaurant. Columns three to six contain the evaluations of the restaurant on quality of food, quantity of portions, value, and service, respectively. Finally, the seventh column contains the respondent's income, coded as specified in the codebook (Figure 15.5). Each row contains all the data of a single respondent and represents a record. The table has 20 rows, or records, indicating that data for 20 respondents are stored in this data file. Note that Table 15.1 is a 20 × 7 matrix, because there are 20 respondents and 7 variables (including ID). Note that the SPSS data file has two views: the data view and the variable view. The data view gives a listing of the data and resembles Table 15.1.

The variable view gives a listing of the variables showing the type, labels or description, values, and underlying coding for each variable, as shown in Table 15.2. Clicking on the "Values" column of the SPSS file opens a "Value Labels" dialog box. Value labels are unique labels assigned to each possible value of a variable. For example, 1 denotes weak preference and 7 denotes strong preference. If descriptors were used for the other preference values, those other preference values would also be assigned the corresponding "Value Labels." The other columns of Table 15.2 are self-explanatory.

Databases consist of one or more files that are interrelated. For example, a database might contain all the customer satisfaction surveys conducted quarterly for the last 5 years.

Be a DM!	Be an MR!

Are There Any Patriotic Feelings Toward the New England Patriots?

Social Media

As the marketing director for the New England Patriots, what information would help you to formulate marketing strategies to increase the attendance at the Patriots home games?

Visit www.nfl.com and search the Internet—including social media—as well as your library's online databases to obtain information on why people attend professional football games. A survey was administered to attendees at a Patriots home game to determine why they were attending. What guidelines will you follow in checking the questionnaire, editing, and coding?

FIGURE 15.5
A Codebook Excerpt

Column Number	Variable Number	Variable Name	Question Number	Coding Instructions
1	1	ID		1 to 20 as coded
2	2	Preference	1	**Input the number circled** 1 = Weak preference 7 = Strong preference
3	3	Quality	2	**Input the number circled** 1 = Poor 7 = Excellent
4	4	Quantity	3	**Input the number circled** 1 = Poor 7 = Excellent
5	5	Value	4	**Input the number circled** 1 = Poor 7 = Excellent
6	6	Service	5	**Input the number circled** 1 = Poor 7 = Excellent
7	7	Income	6	**Input the number circled** 1 = Less than $20,000 2 = $20,000 to $34,999 3 = $35,000 to $49,999 4 = $50,000 to $74,999 5 = $75,000 to $99,999 6 = $100,000 or more

SPSS Data File

TABLE 15.2 SPSS Variable View of the Data of Table 15.1

Name	Type	Width	Decimals	Label	Values	Missing	Columns	Align	Measure
ID	Numeric	8	0	Respondent Number	None	None	8	Right	Scale
PREFERENC	Numeric	8	0	Restaurant Preference	{1, Weak Preference} . . .	None	11	Right	Scale
QUALITY	Numeric	8	0	Quality of Food	{1, Poor} . . .	None	10	Right	Scale
QUANTITY	Numeric	8	0	Quantity of Portions	{1, Poor} . . .	None	10	Right	Scale
VALUE	Numeric	8	0	Overall Value	{1, Poor} . . .	None	10	Right	Scale
SERVICE	Numeric	8	0	Restaurant Service	{1, Poor} . . .	None	10	Right	Scale
INCOME	Numeric	8	0	Annual Household Income	{1, Less than $20,000} . . .	None	10	Right	Scale

Transcribing

Transcribing data involves transferring the coded data from the questionnaires or coding sheets onto disks or directly into computers by keypunching or other means, as in the opening vignette. If the data have been collected by CATI, CAPI, or Internet surveys, this step is unnecessary, because the data are entered directly into the computer as they are collected. Besides keypunching, the data can be transferred by using optical recognition, digital technologies, bar codes, or other technologies (see Figure 15.6).

Optical character recognition programs transcribe printed text into computer files. Optical scanning is a data transcribing process whereby answers recorded on computer-readable forms are scanned to form a data record. This requires responses to be recorded with a special pencil in a predesignated area coded for that response. A machine can then read the data. A more flexible process is optical mark recognition, whereby a spreadsheet-type interface is used to read and process forms created by users. These marked-sensed forms are then processed by optical scanners, and the data are stored in a computer file. Digital technology has resulted in computerized sensory analysis systems, which automate the data collection process. The questions appear on a computerized grid pad, and responses are recorded directly into the computer using a sensing device. Field interviewers use notebook computers, PDAs, and other handheld devices to record responses, which are then sent via a built-in communication modem, wireless LAN, or cellular link directly to another computer in the field or a remote location. Bar codes involve direct machine reading of the codes and simultaneous transcription. A familiar example is the transcription of Universal Product Code (UPC) data at supermarket checkout counters. Census 2010 used bar codes to identify residents. Companies such as UPS and FedEx use bar codes on labels for expedited packages shipments.

Several other technologies can also be used to transcribe the data. Voice recognition and voice response systems can translate recorded voice responses into data files. For example, Microsoft XP and Windows 7 software include advanced speech recognition functions that can transcribe speech into data. Newer technologies are being developed. It is now possible to integrate visual images, streaming video, and audio data that could well be used for recording a focus group or a survey interview.

When CATI, CAPI, or electronic methods are used, data are verified as they are collected. In the case of inadmissible responses, the computer will prompt the interviewer or respondent. In case of admissible responses, the interviewer or the respondent can see the recorded response on the screen and verify it before proceeding.

The selection of a data transcription method is guided by the type of interviewing method used and the availability of equipment. If CATI, CAPI, or electronic methods are used, the data are entered directly into the computer. Keypunching into a computer is most frequently used for ordinary telephone, in-home, mall-intercept, and mail interviews. However, the use of digital technology in personal interviews is growing with the increasing use of grid pads and handheld computers. Optical scanning can be used in structured and repetitive surveys, and optical mark recognition is used in special cases. Bar codes are used to collect scanner data and in a variety of other applications.

FIGURE 15.6

Data Transcription

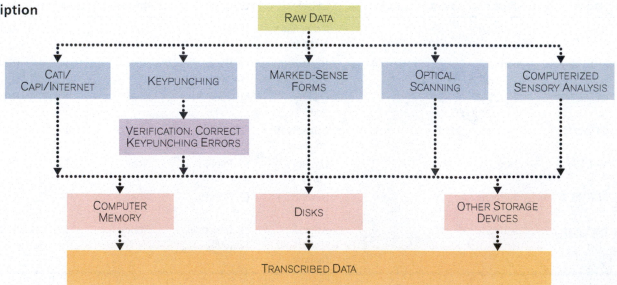

Data Cleaning

Data cleaning includes consistency checks and treatment of missing responses. Although preliminary consistency checks have been made during editing, the checks at this stage are more thorough and extensive because they are made by computer.

Consistency Checks

Consistency checks identify data that are out of range, that are logically inconsistent, or that have extreme values (see the opening vignette). Out-of-range data values are inadmissible and must be corrected. For example, respondents have been asked to express their degree of agreement with a series of lifestyle statements on a 1-to-5 scale. Assuming that 9 has been designated for missing values, data values of 0, 6, 7, and 8 are out of range. These out-of-range responses can arise due to respondent or interviewer errors. Computer packages such as SPSS, SAS, Minitab, and Excel can be programmed to identify out-of-range values for each variable and print out the respondent code, variable code, variable name, and out-of-range value.[3] This makes it easy to check each variable systematically for out-of-range values. The correct responses can be determined by going back to the edited and coded questionnaire.

Responses can be logically inconsistent in various ways. For example, a respondent might indicate that she charges long-distance calls to a calling card, even though she does not have one. Or a respondent might report both unfamiliarity with, and frequent use of, the same product. The necessary information (respondent code, variable code, variable name, and inconsistent values) can be printed to locate these responses and take corrective action.

Extreme values should be closely examined. Not all extreme values result from errors; however, they might point to problems with the data. For example, an extremely low evaluation of a brand might be the result of the respondent indiscriminately circling 1s (on a 1-to-7 rating scale) on all attributes of this brand.

data cleaning
Thorough and extensive checks for consistency and treatment of missing responses.

consistency checks
A part of the data-cleaning process that identifies data that are out of range, logically inconsistent, or that have extreme values. Data with values not defined by the coding scheme are inadmissible.

Research in Action

Apple's iPhone 4: What Does the Buzz Mean?

Despite the buzz on the new product, speculation was running wild as to whether the iPhone 4's sales in the mobile phone market will be able to match that of iPod's success in the digital music market. Markitecture (www.markitecture.com) conducted an online survey of a national sample of 1,300 cell phone owners and users.

Before any analysis was done, the data were thoroughly checked for quality. Any unsatisfactory questionnaires discovered during checking or editing were resolved by recontacting the respondent. A standard coding scheme was used, and because the data were collected using an online survey, subsequent transcription was unnecessary. Several procedural and logical checks were built into the online system so that inconsistencies could be identified and rectified while the data were being collected during the course of the interview. These high-quality data provided Apple with an accurate measurement of what is important to potential iPhone 4 customers, enabling it to effectively address those issues.

Among those familiar with the iPhone 4, overall impressions were positive, although not overwhelming: 41 percent thought the phone was excellent or very good, based on everything they had seen or heard. On the flip side, 21 percent thought it was only fair or poor. Cost was cited as the top reason for not purchasing the iPhone 4: It was an issue for 77 percent of respondents. Based on these findings, Apple decided to diversify in the long term, producing iPhones of different prices, sizes, and capacities, similar to what it now offers with

the iPod, in order to make an impact on the cell-phone market in general.[4]

Source: Ryan Anson/AFP/Getty Images/Newscom.

Treatment of Missing Responses

Missing responses represent values of a variable that are unknown, either because respondents provided ambiguous answers or their answers were not properly recorded. The former cause also is known as *item nonresponse;* it occurs because the respondent refuses, or is unable, to answer specific questions or items because of the content, form, or the effort required. The incidence of missing responses should be minimized by proper selection, training, and supervision of field-workers (see Chapter 14), as illustrated by Sears in the opening vignette. Treatment of missing responses poses problems, particularly if the proportion of missing responses is more than 10 percent. The following options are available for the treatment of missing responses (see Figure 15.4):

1. *Substitute a neutral value.* A neutral value, typically the mean response to the variable, is substituted for missing responses. Thus, the mean of the variable remains unchanged and other statistics, such as correlations, might not be affected much if the proportion of missing values is small. Although this approach has some merit, the logic of substituting a mean value (say 4) for respondents who, if they had answered, might have used either high ratings (6 or 7) or low ratings (1 or 2) is questionable.

2. *Casewise deletion.* In **casewise deletion**, cases or respondents with any missing responses are discarded from the analysis. Suppose 20 percent of the respondents do not respond to the income questions. All of these respondents will be excluded from analysis that involves the income variable, thus reducing the sample size by 20 percent. If several variables are involved in the analysis (e.g., income, education, occupation), respondents with missing values on any of those variables will be excluded. Because many respondents might have missing responses on different variables, this approach could result in a small sample. Throwing away large amounts of data is undesirable, because it is costly and time-consuming to collect data. Furthermore, respondents with missing responses could differ from respondents with complete responses in systematic ways. If so, casewise deletion could seriously bias the results.

3. *Pairwise deletion.* In **pairwise deletion**, instead of discarding all cases with any missing values, the researcher uses only the cases or respondents with complete responses for each calculation. Suppose the researcher is interested in calculating all possible correlations between a set of variables—say awareness, attitude, preference, and purchase intention—all measured on a 1-to-7 scale (see Chapter 18). Then, in calculating the correlation between attitude and preference, all respondents with legitimate responses on the two variables will be included in the analysis, even though these respondents may have missing values on the other two variables, namely awareness and purchase intentions. In contrast, in casewise deletion, respondents with missing values on any of the four variables would be excluded from the analysis.

   Pairwise deletion might be appropriate when (1) the sample size is large, (2) there are few missing responses, and (3) the variables are not highly related. Yet this procedure can produce results that are unappealing, or even infeasible, because different calculations in an analysis might be based on different sample sizes. For example, statistics, such as pairwise correlations (see Chapter 18), might be based on different sample sizes, making comparisons more difficult.

The various procedures for the treatment of missing responses can yield different results, particularly when the responses are not missing at random and the variables are related. The researcher should carefully consider the implications of the various procedures before selecting a particular method for the treatment of nonresponse. It also is recommended that the data be analyzed using different options for handling missing responses to determine the impact on the results, as illustrated by Sears in the opening vignette.

Variable Respecification and Recoding

Variable respecification involves the transformation of data to create new variables or modify existing ones. The purpose of respecification is to create variables that are consistent with the objectives of the study. Respecification often involves summing the items of a Likert-type scale to create a summed score. For example, in Chapter 10 a Likert scale consisting of nine statements was used to measure attitude toward Macy's. These nine statements need to be summed, after reversing the scoring of the negative statements, to arrive at a total attitudinal score. The process of reversing the scoring for the negative statements, as well as the process of summing, involves variable respecification.

Once the data have been coded, transcribed, and cleaned, it might be necessary to redefine the categories of a categorical variable, such as income. For example, if there are too few respondents in the lowest income category, this category can be combined or merged with the next lowest category. This is referred to as *recoding*.

Be an MR!	Be a DM!
Lexus: The Treatment of Luxury	
Visit www.lexus.com and search the Internet—including social media—as well as your library's online databases to obtain information on the criteria buyers use in selecting a luxury car brand. Demographic and psychographic data were obtained in a survey designed to explain the choice of a luxury car brand. What kind of consistency checks, treatment of missing responses, and variable respecification should be conducted?	As the marketing manager for Lexus, what information would you like to have in order to formulate marketing strategies to increase your market share?

Selecting a Data-Analysis Strategy

Selecting a data-analysis strategy should be based on the earlier steps of the marketing research process, known characteristics of the data, properties of statistical techniques, and the background and philosophy of the researcher (see Figure 15.7).

When selecting a data-analysis strategy, the researcher must begin by considering the earlier steps in the process: problem definition (step 1), development of an approach (step 2), and research design (step 3). The researcher should use as a springboard the preliminary plan of data analysis that was prepared as part of the research design. It might be necessary to make changes to the preliminary plan in light of additional information generated in subsequent stages of the research process.

The next step is to consider the known characteristics of the data. The measurement scales used exert a strong influence on the choice of statistical techniques (see Chapter 9). In addition,

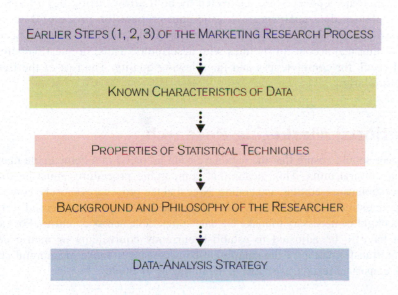

FIGURE 15.7

Selecting a Data-Analysis Strategy

the research design might favor certain techniques. The insights into the data obtained during data preparation can be valuable in selecting a strategy for analysis.

It also is important to take into account the properties of the statistical techniques, particularly their purpose and underlying assumptions. Some statistical techniques are appropriate for examining differences in variables, others for assessing the magnitudes of the relationships between variables, and others are appropriate for making predictions (see Chapters 16, 17, and 18). The techniques also involve different assumptions, and some techniques can withstand violations of the underlying assumptions better than others. The statistical techniques can be broadly classified as univariate or multivariate. **Univariate techniques** are used for analyzing data when there is a single measurement of each element or unit in the sample, or, if there are several measurements of each element, each variable is analyzed in isolation. In contrast, **multivariate techniques** are used for analyzing data when there are two or more measurements on each element and the variables are analyzed simultaneously.

The researcher's background and philosophy affect the choice of a data-analysis strategy. The experienced, statistically trained researcher will employ a range of techniques.

univariate techniques
Statistical techniques appropriate for analyzing data when there is a single measurement of each element in the sample or, if there are several measurements of each element, each variable is analyzed in isolation.

multivariate techniques
Statistical techniques suitable for analyzing data when there are two or more measurements on each element and the variables are analyzed simultaneously. Multivariate techniques are concerned with the simultaneous relationships among two or more phenomena.

Summary Illustration Using the Opening Vignette

While collecting primary data, the completed questionnaires returned from the field are carefully checked and edited for incomplete (e.g., questions that are incorrectly skipped) or inconsistent responses (e.g., a respondent reports purchases made on a Sears credit card but does not have one). Any respondents with unsatisfactory responses are simply discarded, because the proportion of such respondents is small in relation to the total sample size and research by Sears has shown that the unsatisfactory respondents do not differ from satisfactory respondents on the key variables. The data are coded by following the standard procedures given in Sears' codebook. Then, the data are transcribed from the questionnaires into the computer using state-of-the art technology. As part of data cleaning, Sears performs further checks on the data to ascertain their consistency and accuracy. An effort is made to identify data that are out of range (e.g., a response of 8 on a 1-to-7 scale), logically inconsistent (e.g., sum of percentages adding to more or less than 100 percent), or that have extreme values (e.g., household size of 11). Missing values are kept to a minimum by proper selection, training, and supervision of field-workers. In addition, Sears analyzes the data by different procedures for treating missing values, including casewise and pairwise deletion, to determine the impact on the results. A similar process is followed for data collected from secondary sources. This care taken in preparing the data has resulted in a high-quality database that enables Sears to identify the needs of the marketplace and target its marketing efforts accordingly. Figure 15.8 provides a concept map for the data preparation process. In this figure, the major concepts are connected by bold arrows using descriptors. Thus, the preliminary plan of data analysis guides the data preparation process. Data preparation involves questionnaire checking. Each major concept is described by minor concepts that are connected to that major concept by lines with descriptors. Thus, in questionnaire checking, one should check for completeness and interviewing quality. The rest of the figure can be interpreted similarly.

International Marketing Research

The researcher should ensure that the data have been prepared in a comparable manner across countries or cultural units. This means that comparable procedures must be followed for checking questionnaires, editing, and coding. Note that the procedures must be comparable even though the questionnaire itself and, therefore, the coding scheme, could vary. Certain adjustments might be necessary to make the data comparable across countries. For example, the data might have to be adjusted to establish currency equivalents or metric equivalents. Furthermore, transformation of the data might be necessary to make meaningful comparisons and achieve consistent results, as shown in the following example.

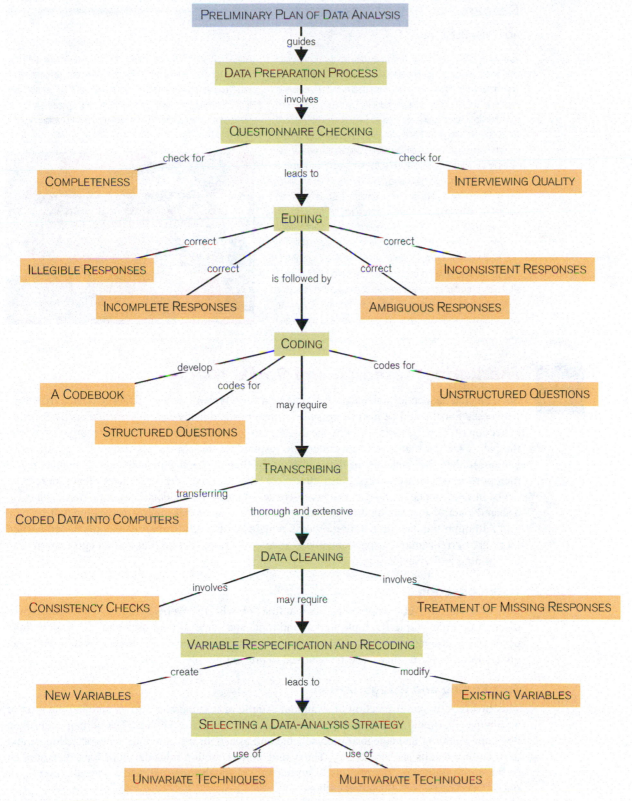

FIGURE 15.8
A Concept Map for the Data Preparation Process

Research in Action

Acer Pulls Out an Ace

As of 2011, Taiwan-based Acer (www.acer.com) has transformed itself from a no-name cloner into one of the most popular branded-PC vendors in the world. The company supports dealers and distributors in more than 100 countries. A crucial factor in Acer's success has been its knowledge of consumer preferences for PCs, which it has obtained by conducting surveys in different countries. Great pains are taken at the data preparation stage to ensure that the data are comparable. For example, the price of PCs in each country is converted to a common unit. This transformation is necessary, because the prices are specified in different local currencies and a common basis is needed for comparison across countries. Also, in each country the premium price is defined in relation to the prices of competing brands in that country.

The care taken at the data preparation stage has resulted in rich findings. For example, Acer found that, even though the relative importance varies from country to country, eight product attributes contribute to brand preference for desktop PCs on a worldwide basis: price, ease of installation and use, service and support, features, performance, reliability, scope of usage, and compatibility on a network. Such findings have enabled Acer to launch global marketing strategies that are responsive to variations in local preferences. On July 26, 2010, Acer successfully launched the new S1 line of ultra-thin, space-saving displays with advanced eco-friendly technology and packaging.[5]

Source: © Thayyilani/Dreamstime.com.

Marketing Research and Social Media

Social media data collection and analysis can be a very dynamic process. Data generated by a large networked panel could be made accessible to members and analyzable for researchers by the right collection of Web 2.0 tools, enabling the discussions to dynamically organize and reorganize within the panel. Unlike traditional data collection, respondents do not merely respond to questions or stimuli. Rather, they generate the data and edit it by their communal participation. They may revise their posts in response to others, irrespective of whether the others are researchers, clients, or respondents. In short, social media respondents co-create, and thus "respondents" become "participants" in a shared enterprise, retaining the rights to set the agenda rather than simply responding to it.

Although the data preparation process remains essentially similar to that discussed earlier, there are certain unique aspects involving data collection, text coding and categorization, and text-mining and visualization.

Data Collection

This involves the Web-scraping process that first "crawls" the Web site to locate and identify the discussion topics, topic ID, topic starter, and topic start date. It then uses topic ID to download posts and messages by the topic. It is important that when storing the messages in a database, quotes in posts from others' text be removed to prevent double counting.

Text Coding and Categorization

This involves human inspection of a random sample of text messages to understand the type of acronyms, shorthand, and terminologies used and get a feel for the data. The human coder then develops a coding and categorization scheme and assists in the computer categorization of text until coding results are satisfactory. The coding and extraction rules developed are then applied to the entire data set. This process is similar to, yet much more extensive than, the coding of open-ended responses illustrated earlier.

Text-Mining and Visualization

The coded text data are interpreted by matching positive or negative comments with overlapping terms that link the positive and negative comments to mentions of the product/ brand. It is helpful to compare discussions when competitor brands are also discussed. If the data set was extracted for a certain period, longitudinal data patterns can be analyzed.

The unique aspects of social media data preparation and analysis are illustrated by the procedure followed by KDPaine & Partners.

Research in Action

KDPaine: Specialists in Social Media Data Collection and Analysis

KDPaine & Partners (www.kdpaine.com) undertook a project to determine specifically what presence and activity Georgia Tech (www. gatech.edu) and its peer institutions had in social media. The relevant aspects of their data collection and preparation were as follows.

Data Collection

The first step was to develop a standardization of collection techniques for Georgia Tech and its competitors. To best achieve these goals, it was decided to observe and explore a predefined range of social media channels for Georgia Tech as well as a small group of peer academic institutions over a 3-month benchmark period. For example, the researchers came up with a total of 50 external blogs and 114 institutional blogs. Articles were pulled manually from the selected blogs and manually imported into a dashboard where readers then coded them. Collection techniques were developed by testing and finalizing a master list of search terms that included all possible social media mentions of Georgia Tech and its peers.

Text Coding and Categorization

For text coding and categorization, a standardization of terms, conversation types, and content types had to be developed.

Ultimately, a final list of 27 conversation types and 19 video types was developed and used for coding purposes to give insights into what people were talking about through the social media channels. Tone was defined as positive, neutral, or negative. Additionally, the researchers examined whether each item contained one or more of the institution's key messages, what subjects were discussed, which departments or colleges were mentioned, and how each item positioned the institution on key issues.

Text-Mining and Visualization

Another obstacle was simply handling the large amounts of mentions found for each school. There were thousands of items to code and organize each month, so KDPaine used a digital dashboard to organize mass amounts of data and conduct data analysis across all variables. The findings varied somewhat by social media channel. For example, Facebook discussions were largely positive or neutral, showing students' loyalty to their institutions. Georgia Tech specifically had no negative mentions and was just under average for share of positive discussions. Based on these findings, several recommendations were made to Georgia Tech to enhance its presence on social media.[6]

Ethics in Marketing Research

Ethical issues can arise during the data preparation and analysis step, particularly in areas where the researcher has to exercise judgment. While checking, editing, coding, transcribing, and cleaning, the researcher can get some idea about the quality of the data. Sometimes it is easy to identify respondents who did not take the questionnaire seriously or who otherwise provided data of questionable quality. Consider, for example, a respondent who checks the "neither agree nor disagree" response to all 30 items measuring attitude toward spectator sports. Decisions about whether such respondents should be discarded—that is, not included in the analysis—can raise ethical concerns. A good rule of thumb is to make such decisions during the data preparation phase before conducting any analysis. Discarding respondents after analyzing the data raises ethical concerns, particularly if this information is not fully disclosed in the written report. Moreover, the procedure used to identify unsatisfactory respondents and the number of respondents discarded should be clearly disclosed, as in the following example.

Research in Action

Ethical Editing of Data

In a study of MBAs' responses to marketing ethics dilemmas, respondents were required to respond to 14 questions regarding ethically ambiguous scenarios by writing a simple sentence regarding what action they would take if they were the manager in those situations. The responses were then analyzed to determine if they were indicative of ethical behavior. However, in the data preparation phase 6 respondents out of the 561 total respondents were eliminated from further analysis because their responses indicated that they did not follow the directions that told them to clearly state their choice of action. This is an example of ethical editing of the data. The criterion for unsatisfactory responses is clearly stated, the unsatisfactory respondents are identified before the analysis, and the number of respondents eliminated is disclosed.[7]

Another ethical concern relates to interpretation of the results, drawing conclusions, and making recommendations. Although interpretations, conclusions, and recommendations necessarily involve the subjective judgment of the researcher, this judgment must be exercised honestly, free from any personal biases or agendas of the researcher or the client. Suppose a survey reveals that 31 percent of the respondents preferred the client's brand, whereas 30.8 percent preferred the closest competing brand, with all the other brands being preferred to a much lesser extent. For the researcher to state that the client's brand is the most preferred brand in the marketplace, without disclosing that a competing brand is a very close second, might be misleading if it conveys the false impression that the client's brand is the dominantly preferred brand.

WHAT WOULD YOU DO?

Banana Republic: Going Bananas over a Makeover

The Situation

For most of its time as a leading retailer, Gap Inc. (www.gapinc.com) has carefully honed its image through its in-house resources, starting from the design of its clothing to the look of its ads. However, that changed as soon as Jack Calhoun, Banana Republic's chief marketing officer, took over in 2003. Calhoun was one of the first marketing hires by former Walt Disney executive Paul Pressler, who took over as Gap Inc. president–CEO, succeeding Millard "Mickey" Drexler. One of Pressler's first acts was to hire Publicis Groupe's Leo Burnett USA, Chicago, to oversee segmentation studies of the Gap brands, including Banana Republic and Old Navy. Calhoun reported to newly hired Banana Republic president Marka Hansen, most recently Gap's head of adult merchandising.

The Banana Republic (bananarepublic.gap.com) makeover will be the second in the history of the chain, which started out as a travel catalog and then opened safari-themed stores with beat-up jeeps in its storefronts. After the chain was purchased by Gap Inc., Drexler, known for his ability to spot fashion trends, remade it into an upscale version of Gap.

In recent months, Banana Republic's buzz has quieted and sales have not recovered at a pace that's up to speed with siblings Old Navy, Gap, and Piperlime. "The challenge for Banana is the repetition of the fashion lines and marginal quality for the price," said Burt Flickinger, managing director, Strategic Resource Group/Flickinger Consulting, New York.

Calhoun said he and Gap management are carefully building a new positioning for Banana Republic, which traditionally had advertising echoing that of the lower-priced Gap. "We want to build an architecturally sound and beautiful house," said Calhoun of the makeover. "We don't want a Cape Cod with a lot of additions."

A telephone survey was conducted to determine consumers' perceptions of the Banana Republic brand and how the brand could be positioned to offer more value to the consumers.

The Marketing Research Decision

1. The telephone survey resulted in a sample size of 1,008. As the data were being prepared for analysis, the researchers realized that 132 respondents had missing values. However, the variables with unsatisfactory responses were not the key variables. How should the missing values be treated?
   a. Return the questionnaires with missing values to the field.
   b. Assign missing values: Substitute a neutral value.
   c. Casewise deletion.
   d. Pairwise deletion.
   e. Discard respondents with missing values.

2. Discuss how the treatment of missing values you recommend influences Jack Calhoun's decision to enhance Banana Republic's image.

The Marketing Management Decision

1. What should Jack Calhoun do to enhance the perceived value of the Banana Republic brand?
   a. Launch new product lines.
   b. Lower the price.
   c. Change advertising.
   d. Make the clothing more trendy and fashionable.
   e. Make the clothing more functional.

2. Discuss how the marketing management decision action that you recommend to Jack Calhoun is influenced by the treatment of missing values that you suggested earlier and by the findings of the telephone survey.

What Jack Calhoun Did

Jack Calhoun launched new product lines. For women, he introduced a new feminine collection with art deco–inspired details that brought a soft, romantic touch to the more structured fall looks, and the men's collection conveyed a sense of confidence. He also changed the advertising. What the change meant in terms of ads and marketing was a shift from narrowly defined, single-concept campaigns such as "work" and "suede" to those that represented a range of sensibilities in dress. The campaign was comprised of black-and-white photos, along with more vibrant color shots, all with a family album feel. The aim of the new campaign was to express the idea of diversity, age, family, and expressions of the customers. The new personality-focused approach also appealed to a more mature customer than Banana Republic has courted in the past; however, Banana Republic was not targeting a new audience, but rather refocusing on its customers. Due to his successful makeover, Jack Calhoun was promoted and as of 2011 was serving as president and CEO of Banana Republic.[8]

Source: © Peter Horree/Alamy.

Software Applications

Major statistical packages, such as SPSS (www.spss.com), Excel (office.microsoft.com/en-us/excel), Minitab (www.minitab.com), and SAS (www.sas.com) have Web sites that can be accessed for a variety of information. Exhibit 15.1 details how to use these packages to make consistency checks. These packages also contain options for handling missing responses and for statistically adjusting the data. In addition, a number of statistical packages can now be found on the Internet. Although some of these programs do not offer integrated data analysis and management, they can be very useful for conducting specific statistical analyses. Although we discuss four statistical packages in this book, special emphasis is placed on SPSS and Excel.

SPSS Modeler (formerly Clementine) is a versatile data-mining workbench that can use a broad range of data, including data stored in operational databases and files, as well as unstructured data such as call center notes, e-mails, Web 2.0 sources, and survey responses. Modeler Premium includes a powerful text-mining workbench for extracting key concepts, sentiments, and relationships from textual or "unstructured" data and converting them to a structured format that can be used to make predictive models more accurate.

SPSS and Excel Computerized Demonstration Movies

We have developed computerized demonstration movies that give step-by-step instructions for running all the SPSS and Excel programs that are discussed in this book. These demonstration movies can be downloaded from the Web site for this book. The instructions for running these demonstration movies are given in Exhibit 15.2.

SPSS and Excel Screen Captures with Notes

The step-by-step instructions for running the various SPSS and Excel programs discussed in this book are also illustrated in screen captures with appropriate notes. These screen captures can be downloaded from the Web site for this book.

EXHIBIT 15.1
Computer Programs for Data Preparation

SPSS

Out-of-range values can be selected using the SELECT IF or PROCESS IF statements. These cases, with the identifying information (subject ID, variable name, and variable value) can then be printed using the PRINT or WRITE commands. As a further check, the LIST command can be used to display the values of variables for each case.

Excel

In Excel, the IF statement can be used to make logical checks and check out-of-range values. The IF statement can be accessed under FORMULAS > INSERT FUNCTION > IF.

Minitab

Minitab features control statements that enable the user to set the order of commands in a macro. The IF command allows implementation of different blocks of commands, including IF, ELSEIF, ELSE, and ENDIF.

SAS

Within BASE SAS the IF, IF-THEN, and IF-THEN ELSE can be used to select cases with missing or out-of-range values. The LIST statement is useful for printing suspicious input lines. SAS Enterprise Guide allows the user to identify missing or out-of-range values with the FILTER DATA tab within the QUERY and FILTER DATA task. The procedures MI and MIANALYZE in SAS/STAT also offer the capability of imputing missing values when a more sophisticated approach is required.

SPSS Windows

Using the base module of SPSS, out-of-range values can be selected using the SELECT IF command. These cases, with the identifying information (subject ID, variable name, and variable value), can then be printed using the LIST or PRINT commands. The PRINT command saves active cases to an external file. If a formatted list is required, the SUMMARIZE command can be used.

IBM® SPSS® DATA COLLECTION is a complete suite of products for survey and marketing research. It enables you to quickly and efficiently acquire and clean data from a range of sources using an array of methods. IBM® SPSS® Modeler is a versatile data and text analytics workbench that helps you build predictive models. It is rather intuitive and does not require programming knowledge.

Detailed Steps: Overview

Detailed step-by-step instructions for running the SPSS programs for the data analysis presented in this chapter can be downloaded from the Web site for this book in two forms: (1) computerized demonstration movies and (2) screen captures. In addition, these steps are illustrated in the following sections. These steps are given for PASW STATISTICS 18 and IBM SPSS STATISTICS 19; they are essentially the same in both these versions. The steps in the earlier versions are about the same with minor differences in the labeling of some of the boxes. The demonstration movies, and screen captures for the earlier versions, have also been posted on the Web site.

Detailed Steps: Variable Respecification

We illustrate the use of the base module in creating a new variable using the data of Table 15.1 (SPSS file). We want to create a variable called *overall evaluation of the restaurant (Overall)* that is the sum of the ratings on quality, quantity, value, and service. Thus,

Overall = Quality + Quantity + Value + Service

These steps are as follows.

1. Select TRANSFORM.
2. Click COMPUTE VARIABLE.
3. Type "overall" into the TARGET VARIABLE box.
4. Click "quality" and move it to the NUMERIC EXPRESSION box.
5. Click the "+" sign.
6. Click "quantity" and move it to the NUMERIC EXPRESSION box.
7. Click the "+" sign.
8. Click "value" and move it to the NUMERIC EXPRESSION box.
9. Click the "+" sign.
10. Click "service" and move it to the NUMERIC EXPRESSION box.
11. Click TYPE & LABEL under the TARGET VARIABLE box and type "Overall Evaluation." Click CONTINUE.
12. Click OK.

Detailed Steps: Variable Recoding

We also want to illustrate the recoding of a variable to create a new variable using the data of Table 15.1. Income category 1 occurs only once and income category 6 occurs only twice. Therefore, we want to combine income categories 1 and 2 and categories 5 and 6 and create a new income variable "rincome" labeled "Recoded Income." Note that rincome has only four categories, which are coded as 1 to 4. We describe how to do this using SPSS WINDOWS.

1. Select TRANSFORM.
2. Select RECODE INTO DIFFERENT VARIABLES.
3. Click income and move it to the INPUT VARIABLE → OUTPUT VARIABLE box.
4. Type "rincome" into the OUTPUT VARIABLE NAME box.
5. Type "Recoded Income" into the OUTPUT VARIABLE LABEL box.
6. Click the OLD AND NEW VAULES box.
7. Under OLD VALUES, on the left, click RANGE. Type 1 and 2 in the range boxes. Under NEW VALUES, on the right, click VALUE and type 1 into the value box. Click ADD.
8. Under OLD VALUES, on the left, click VALUE. Type 3 in the value box. Under NEW VALUES, on the right, click VALUE and type 2 into the value box. Click ADD.
9. Under OLD VALUES, on the left, click VALUE. Type 4 in the value box. Under NEW VALUES, on the right, click VALUE and type 3 in the value box. Click ADD.
10. Under OLD VALUES, on the left, click RANGE. Type 5 and 6 in the range boxes. Under NEW VALUES, on the right, click VALUE and type 4 in the value box. Click ADD.
11. Click CONTINUE.
12. Click CHANGE.
13. Click OK.

Experiential Learning

Data Conversion and Preparation Using SPSS

Go to the textbook Web site and download the following comma-delimited file: Hotelsat. This is an Excel file. You will read this file into the SPSS program and then use the power of the SPSS program to (1) substitute mean values for variables into cells with missing values and (2) clean the file for out-of-range values.

Import into SPSS

Open SPSS
  FILE
    OPEN
      DATA
        OPEN FILE window

SPSS Data File

Excel Data File

FILES OF TYPE window (All Files)
Select Hotelsat. Click OPEN.

Text Import Wizard Step 1—accept default settings. There should be a check beside "READ VARIABLES NAMES FROM THE FIRST ROW OF DATA." —Click OK.

Variable names will be taken from the first row of the spreadsheet.

Note: The earlier versions of SPSS will have more steps in the Text Import Wizard. For each of these steps, accept default settings.

To view data, click the DATA VIEW tab at the bottom of the SPSS window.

Note: Variable names will be at the top of the columns. Click VARIABLE VIEW. In the DECIMALS column, set decimals for all variables to 0, one at a time.

Clean Data

1. Count how many cases have complete sets of responses.

   TRANSFORM
   COMPUTE VARIABLE
   COMPUTE VARIABLE window
   In the TARGET VARIABLE box type "numval"
   In the NUMERIC EXPRESSION box, under FUNCTION GROUP select ALL and then select NVALID. Replace the "?" with "Q3 to Q5". NVALID(Q3 to Q5) will then appear in the NUMERIC EXPRESSION box. This is equivalent to the following expression:
   numval = NVALID(Q3 to Q5)

   Note: Select NVALID(variable,…) under FUNCTIONS. Replace the "?" with "Q3 to Q5". Click OK.

   Note: A new variable "numval" is created. Five of 200 cases have a value of "2" instead of "3," meaning 5 have one missing value.

2. Mean substitution.

   TRANSFORM
   REPLACE MISSING VALUES
   NEW VARIABLE(S) window
   Double-click Q3
   Q3_1 = SMEAN(Q3) appears as new variable.
   Double-click Q4.
   Q4_1 = SMEAN(Q4) appears as new variable.
   Double-click Q5
   Q5_1 = SMEAN(Q5) appears as new variable.
   Click OK.

   Note: Output will show 5 values were replaced for variable Q4_1.

3. Check distributions of the new variables with substituted means for out-of-range values.

   ANALYZE
   DESCRIPTIVE STATISTICS
   FREQUENCIES
   FREQUENCIES window: Select (Q3_1 to Q5_1)
   Note: These variables will appear as SMEAN(Q3) [Q3_1], SMEAN(Q4)[Q4_1], and SMEAN(Q5) [Q5_1].
   STATISTICS
   Select MINIMUM, MAXIMUM, MEAN, STD. DEVIATION
   Click CONTINUE.
   Click OK.

   Note: Q4_1 has 5 cases that received the mean value of 5.8. Q5_1 has 13 cases with the "−9" value. In some data entry plans, such an entry as "−9" is intended to represent a missing value.

4. Convert missing value entries of Q5_1 (those cases with a "−9" representing a missing value during the data-entry phase) into SYSMIS values.

   TRANSFORM
   RECODE INTO DIFFERENT VARIABLES
   RECODE INTO DIFFERENT VARIABLES window
   Select Q5_1. This appears as SMEAN(Q5) [Q5_1]
   In the OUTPUT VARIABLE window, type Q5new in the NAME box.
   Select OLD AND NEW VALUE
   Under OLD VALUE
   Select −9
   Under NEW VALUE
   Select SYSTEM-MISSING (SYSMIS)
   Then, select ADD

   Note: You are recoding "−9" to have a system missing value so that "−9" will now be recognized by SPSS to be "SYSMIS"—a placeholder, for all practical purposes.
   Under OLD VALUE
   Select RANGE 1 thru 7
   Under NEW VALUE
   Select COPY OLD VALUE(S)
   Then, select ADD
   Select CHANGE
   Then select CONTINUE

   Note: You are directing SPSS to copy the old values for any entries with a value of 1 through 7.
   Back at the RECODE INTO DIFFERENT VARIABLES window
   Click OK.
   Check distribution for Q5new by replicating Step 3 and replacing Q5new for Q3_1, Q4_1, and Q5_1 in the FREQUENCIES window step.

   Note: You will see Q5new has no cases with "−9" now, but Q5new now has 13 cases with missing values.

5. Check work.
   ANALYZE
   DESCRIPTIVE STATISTICS
   FREQUENCIES
   FREQUENCIES window: Select Q3_1, Q4_1, and Q5new

   Note: Output for variables Q3_1 has a value of 5 for all 200 cases, and Q5new should now have only values of 1–7, as can be seen for SMEAN(Q3), and Q5new, respectively. Q4_1 should have five cases with 5.8, with the rest being integers from 1–7, as can be seen for SMEAN(Q4).

6. Save your new SPSS system file as follows.
   FILE
   SAVE AS…
   Note: You will now select the location to save this SPSS system file.
   In FILE NAME block of SAVE DATA AS window
   Type in "Hotelsat New."
   In SAVE AS TYPE block
   Select "SPSS STATISTICS (*.sav)" or "PASW STATISTICS (*.sav)"
   Click on SAVE.

   Note: Your new SPSS system file will be named "Hotelsat New."

Excel

Although Excel is an effective spreadsheet program, it lacks the qualities of a relational database that SPSS offers. As a result, distributions of variables cannot be directly produced, and data recoding must be done through if-then statements.

Detailed Steps: Overview

Detailed step-by-step instructions for running the Excel programs for the data analysis presented in this chapter can be downloaded from the Web site for this book in two forms: (1) computerized demonstration movies and (2) screen captures. In addition, these steps are illustrated in the following sections. These steps are given for Excel 2007 and Excel 2010; they are essentially the same in both these versions. The steps in the earlier versions are about the same with minor differences in how "Data Analysis" is accessed and the labeling of some of the boxes. The demonstration movies, and screen captures for the earlier versions, have also been posted on the Web site.

Detailed Steps: Variable Respecification

We illustrate the use of Excel in creating a new variable using the data of Table 15.1. We want to create a variable called *overall evaluation of the restaurant (Overall)* that is the sum of the ratings on quality, quantity, value, and service. Once you open Table 15.1 (Excel file), the steps are as follows.

1. Click on the cell H1.
2. Type "New Variable" in cell H1.
3. Type "=B2+C2+D2+E2" in cell H2.
4. Click on the "Accept formula value" or "Enter" symbol (✓).
5. Next, right click on cell H2. An Excel pop-up menu gets displayed.
6. Select the COPY menu item.
7. Next, select (highlight) cells H3 through H21.
8. Right click in any one of these highlighted cells. An Excel pop-up menu gets displayed.
9. Select the PASTE menu item.
10. The values for the new variable are now displayed in the cells.

Detailed Steps: Variable Recoding

We also want to illustrate the recoding of a variable using Excel to create a new variable using the data of Table 15.1 (Excel file). We will be recoding income into four categories (as explained earlier using SPSS).

1. Click on the cell H1.
2. Type "RINCOME" in cell H1.
3. Carefully type the formula
   "=IF(F2=6,4,IF(F2=5,4,IF(F2=4,3,IF(F2=3,2,IF(F2=2,1,IF(F2=1,1,1))))))"
   correctly in cell H2.
4. Click on the "Accept formula value" or "Enter" symbol (✓).
5. Next, right click on cell H2. An Excel pop-up menu gets displayed.
6. Select the COPY menu item.
7. Next, select (highlight) cells H3 through H21.
8. Right click in any one of these highlighted cells. An Excel pop-up menu gets displayed.
9. Select the PASTE menu item.
10. The recoded values for the new variable are now displayed in the cells.

Excel Data File

Experiential Learning

Data Conversion and Preparation Using Excel

To illustrate Excel's data-recoding features, the following example is provided using the same Hotelsat data set used in Experiential Learning using SPSS. For both Q4 and Q5, the next higher digit to the mean value of each variable will be inserted into any missing or out-of-range value. In this case, the value of 6 will be inserted. The screen captures using Excel for these steps can be downloaded from the Web site for this book.

> Open Hotelsat
>> In column F, type in the variable name "q4new"
>>> In cell F2, type in the following if-then statement:
>>>> = IF(D2<1,6, IF(D2>7,6,D2))

This if-then statement directs Excel to evaluate the current entry in cell D2 in the following manner. If this entry in D2 is less than 1, then enter a value of 6 in cell F2; if this entry in D2 is greater than 7, then enter a value of 6 in cell F2. Otherwise, just enter the current value in D2 in F2.

Click the lower-right corner of cell F2, and drag to cell F201 in order to copy the F2 cell to all cells from F3 to F201. In this way,

you have inserted the value of 6 into any cells with missing or out-of-range values, or simply copied the original values if the cell entries were okay.

> In column G, type in the variable name "q5new."
>> In cell G2, type in the following if-then statement:
>>> = IF(E2<1,6, IF(E2>7,6,E2))

This if-then statement directs Excel to evaluate the current entry in cell E2 in the following manner. If this entry in E2 is less than 1, then enter a value of 6 in cell G2; if this entry in E2 is greater than 7, then enter a value of 6 in cell G2. Otherwise, just enter the current value of E2 in G2.

Click the lower-right corner of cell G2 and drag to cell G201 in order to copy the G2 cell to all cells from G3 to G201. In this way, you have inserted the value of 6 into any cells with missing or out-of-range values or simply copied the original values if the cell entries were okay.

Summary

Data preparation begins with a preliminary check of all questionnaires for completeness and quality. Then, more thorough editing takes place. Editing consists of screening questionnaires to identify illegible, incomplete, inconsistent, or ambiguous responses. Such responses can be handled by returning questionnaires to the field, assigning missing values, or discarding the unsatisfactory respondents.

The next step is coding. A numerical or alphanumeric code is assigned to represent a specific response to a specific question, along with the column position that code will occupy. It often is helpful to prepare a codebook containing the coding instructions and the necessary information about the variables in the data set. The coded data are transcribed onto disks or entered into computers via keypunching. Marked-sense forms, optical scanning, or computerized sensory analysis might also be used.

Cleaning the data requires consistency checks and treatment of missing responses. Options available for treating missing responses include substitution of a neutral value, such as the mean; casewise deletion; and pairwise deletion. Data variables may also need respecification and recoding. The selection of a data-analysis strategy should be based on the earlier steps of the marketing research process, known characteristics of the data, properties of statistical techniques, and the background and philosophy of the researcher.

When analyzing the data in international marketing research, the researcher should ensure that the units of measurement are comparable across countries or cultural units. Although the data preparation process remains essentially similar when conducting research in social media, there are certain unique aspect involving data collection, text coding and categorization, text-mining and visualization. Several ethical issues are related to data processing, particularly the discarding of unsatisfactory respondents, and evaluation and interpretation of results. Major statistical packages, such as SPSS, SAS, Minitab, and Excel, have Web sites that can be accessed for useful information.

Key Terms and Concepts

Editing 412
Coding 413
Fixed field codes 413
Codebook 415

Data cleaning 419
Consistency checks 419
Missing responses 420
Casewise deletion 420

Pairwise deletion 420
Variable respecification 420
Univariate techniques 422
Multivariate techniques 422

Suggested Cases and Video Cases

Running Case with Real Data

1.1 Hewlett-Packard

Comprehensive Cases with Real Data

3.1 Bank of America   3.2 McDonald's   3.3 Boeing

Comprehensive Brief Harvard Business School Cases

4.1 TruEarth Healthy Foods: Market Research for a New Product Introduction (4065)
4.2 The Springfield Nor'easters: Maximizing Revenues in the Minor Leagues (2510)
4.3 Metabical: Positioning and Communications Strategy for a New Weight-Loss Drug (4240)
4.4 Saxonville Sausage Company (2085)

Online Video Cases

15.1 Marriott

Live Research: Conducting a Marketing Research Project

1. The project coordinators should number the questionnaires and keep track of any quotas.
2. The team leaders should be responsible for the initial editing of the questionnaires.
3. Each student should be responsible for coding her or his questionnaires and for data entry. It is recommended that the data be entered into an Excel spreadsheet using the coding scheme developed by the instructor or one of the teams.
4. The project coordinators should assemble all the student files into one data file, conduct the computer checks, and clean up the data.
5. The data-analysis strategy should be specified by the instructor and discussed in the class.

Acronym

The data preparation process may be summarized by the acronym DATA PREP:

D ata consistency checks

A djusting the data for missing values

T ranscribing

A nalysis strategy

P ost fieldwork questionnaire checking

R ecording numerical or alphanumerical values: Coding

E diting

P reliminary plan of data analysis

Review Questions

1. Describe the data preparation process.
2. What activities are involved in the preliminary checking of questionnaires that have been returned from the field?
3. How does one edit a questionnaire?
4. How are unsatisfactory responses discovered in the editing process treated?
5. What is the difference between precoding and postcoding?
6. Describe the guidelines for the coding of unstructured questions.
7. What does transcribing the data involve?
8. What kinds of consistency checks are made in cleaning the data?
9. What options are available for the treatment of missing data?
10. What considerations are involved in selecting a data-analysis strategy?

Applied Problems

1. Shown below is part of a questionnaire used to determine consumer preferences for digital cameras. Set up a coding scheme for the following three questions (Q9, Q10, and Q11). Note that the first eight questions are not included.

   9. Please rate the importance of the following features you would consider when shopping for a new digital camera.

	Not so important				Very important
a. Megapixel	1	2	3	4	5
b. F-stop	1	2	3	4	5
c. Optical zoom	1	2	3	4	5
d. Auto focus	1	2	3	4	5

   10. If you were to buy a new digital camera, which of the following outlets would you visit? Please check as many as apply.
       a. _____ Drugstore
       b. _____ Camera store
       c. _____ Discount/mass merchandiser
       d. _____ Consumer electronics store
       e. _____ Internet stores/shopping sites
       f. _____ Other

   11. Where do you get most of your photo processing done? Please check only one option.
       a. _____ Drugstore
       b. _____ Mini labs
       c. _____ Camera stores
       d. _____ Discount/mass merchandiser
       e. _____ Consumer electronics store
       f. _____ Mail order/Internet
       g. _____ Kiosk/other

2. Explain how you would make consistency checks for the part of the questionnaire given in Applied Problem number 1 using SPSS, SAS, Minitab, or Excel.

3. Use an electronic questionnaire design and administration package, such as Qualtrics, which is distributed with this book, to program the camera-preference questionnaire given in Applied Problem number 1. Add one or two questions of your own. Administer the questionnaire to five students and prepare the data for analysis. Does computer administration of the questionnaire facilitate data preparation?

Group Discussion

1. "Data preparation is a time-consuming process. In projects with severe time constraints, data preparation should be circumvented." Discuss this statement in a small group.

2. "The researcher should always use computer-assisted interviewing (CATI, CAPI or Internet) to collect the data, because these methods greatly facilitate data preparation." Discuss this statement in a small group.

Hewlett-Packard Running Case

Review the Hewlett-Packard (HP) case, Case 1.1, and questionnaire given toward the end of the book. Go to the Web site for this book and download the HP data file.

1. Recode the respondents based on total hours per week spent online (q1) into two groups: 5 hours or fewer (light users) and 6 hours or more (heavy users).

2. Recode the respondents based on total hours per week spent online (q1) into three groups: 5 hours or fewer (light users), 6 to 10 hours (medium users), and 11 hours or more (heavy users).

3. Form a new variable that denotes the total number of things that people have ever done online based on q2_1 to q2_7. Note the missing values for q2_1 to q2_7 are coded as 0.

4. Recode q4 (overall satisfaction) into two groups: Very satisfied (rating of 1), and somewhat satisfied or dissatisfied (ratings of 2, 3, and 4).

5. Recode q5 (would recommend) into two groups: Definitely would recommend (rating of 1), and probably would or less likely to recommend (ratings of 2, 3, 4, and 5).

6. Recode q6 (likelihood of choosing HP) into two groups: Definitely would choose (rating of 1), and probably would or less likely to choose (ratings of 2, 3, 4, and 5).

7. Recode q9_5per into three groups: Definitely or probably would have purchased (ratings of 1 and 2), might or might not have purchased (rating of 3), and probably or definitely would not have purchased (ratings of 4 and 5).

8. Recode q9_10per into three groups: Definitely or probably would have purchased and might or might not have purchased (ratings of 1, 2, and 3), probably would not have purchased (rating of 4), and definitely would not have purchased (ratings of 5).
9. Recode the demographics as follows:
   a. Combine the two lowest education (q11) categories into a single category. Thus, some high school or less and high school graduate will be combined into a single category labeled "High school graduate or less."
   b. Recode age (q12) into four new categories: 18 to 29, 30 to 39, 40 to 49, and 50 or older.
   c. Combine the two lowest income (q13) categories into a single category labeled "Under $30,000."

ONLINE VIDEO CASE 15.1

Visit **www.pearsonhighered.com/malhotra** to read the video case and view the accompanying video. Marriott: Marketing Research Leads to Expanded Offerings suggests that Marriott's sustained vast expansion over the last several decades is due in large part to marketing research. The case can be used as a springboard for students to design a short survey regarding a comparison in consumer perceptions about the overall Marriott brand name—in light of the chapter's objectives, discuss how the survey questionnaire should be coded, how the collected data will be cleaned, and what combination of univariate and multivariate analyses should be investigated. Specific marketing research questions on this and the previous chapters are posed in the video case.

16

Data Analysis: Frequency Distribution, Hypothesis Testing, and Cross-Tabulation

Source: Tim Isbell/Biloxi Sun Herald/MCT.

LEARNING OBJECTIVES

After reading this chapter, the student should be able to:

1. Understand why preliminary data analysis is desirable and the insights that can be obtained from such an analysis.

2. Explain what is meant by frequency counts and what measures are associated with such an analysis.

3. Describe the general procedure for hypothesis testing and the steps involved.

4. Discuss how cross-tabulation analysis should be conducted and the associated statistics.

5. Understand how the chi-square statistic is calculated and the purpose for which it is used.

6. Discuss the other statistics used to test association between two variables and when they are used.

7. Describe the computer programs available for conducting frequency and cross-tabulation analyses.

8. **Social Media** Illustrate the application of basic data analysis to social media.

" Cross-tabulation still remains the most frequently used data analysis technique for marketers. However, cross-tabulation alone leaves a lot of information unexplored and does not exploit the predictive value of research. For that, you need to go beyond cross-tabulation to much more complex and sophisticated multivariate models. "

William Neal
Senior Executive Officer, SDR Consulting, Atlanta, Georgia

Consumers Consume Coupons

More than $331 billion in potential consumer savings were distributed through coupons in 2006, with more than $2.6 billion redeemed. This was a decline in both distribution (–12%) and redemption (–13%) from 2005. Following a leveling-off period from 2006–2008, coupon redemptions grew by 27 percent to 3.3 billion coupon redemptions in 2009 due to the economic recession. A recent Promotional Attitudes and Practices Study surveyed 682 female primary grocery shoppers who were members of the Synovate Panel (www.synovate.com). The survey data were analyzed by calculating frequency counts, percentages, and means. The survey found that 93 percent of the respondents liked coupons, 99 percent had used coupons in the last year, and 95 percent had used a coupon within the last 30 days. The survey also reported that 642 respondents (94%) said coupons were helpful in reducing the cost of groceries, 593 (87%) used coupons for brands they normally bought, and 212 (31%) used coupons to try new products. Despite the growing influence of frequent-customer clubs, frequency counts indicated that most of the respondents did not limit their shopping to a single store. Of the 44 percent who are club members, 19 percent said that their membership makes them more likely to shop at that store, whereas 51 percent shop other stores for specials. The average number of stores shopped was 2.9 per household.

As illustrated here, survey data often are analyzed to obtain *frequency counts* (593 respondents used coupons for brands they normally bought), *percentages* (95% had used a coupon within the last 30 days), and *means* (the average number of stores shopped was 2.9 per household). A *cross-tabulation* of coupon usage with income indicated that households at all income levels were cashing coupons. Furthermore, lower-income households had higher coupon usage as compared to middle- and higher-income households, and this association was statistically significant. Supermarkets can use such findings to target their coupon and promotional strategies. It is clear that supermarkets cannot rely exclusively on frequent customer clubs; coupons and price specials also play a major role in attracting shoppers. This is why supermarkets such as Kroger make heavy use of coupons and price specials in addition to the Kroger Plus Shoppers' card.[1]

Overview

Once the data have been prepared for analysis (see Chapter 15), the researcher should conduct some basic analyses. Often, this involves computing frequency counts, percentages, and averages, as in the opening vignette. This chapter describes basic data analysis techniques, including frequency distribution, hypothesis testing, and cross-tabulation.

First, the chapter describes the frequency distribution of a single variable and explains how it provides an indication of the number of out-of-range, missing, or extreme values, as well as insight into the central tendency and variability of the underlying distribution. Next, hypothesis testing is presented, and a general procedure is provided. The use of cross-tabulation for understanding the associations between variables taken two at a time is then considered. Although the nature of the association can be observed from tables, statistics are available for testing the significance and strength of the association. Figure 16.1 briefly explains the focus of the chapter, the relationship of this chapter to the previous ones, and the steps of the marketing research process on which this chapter concentrates. Figure 16.2 provides an overview of the topics discussed in this chapter and how they flow from one to the next.

Help for running the SPSS and EXCEL programs used in this chapter is provided in four ways: (1) detailed step-by-step instructions are given later in the chapter, (2) you can download (from the Web site for this book) computerized demonstration movies illustrating these step-by-step instructions, (3) you can download screen captures with notes illustrating these step-by-step instructions, and (4) you can refer to the Study Guide and Technology Manual, a supplement that accompanies this book.

Many commercial marketing research projects do not go beyond basic data analysis. These findings often are displayed using tables and graphs, as discussed further in Chapter 19. Although the findings of basic analysis are valuable in their own right, the insights gained from the basic analysis also are invaluable in interpreting the results obtained from more sophisticated statistical techniques. Therefore, before conducting more advanced statistical analysis, it is useful to examine the frequency distributions of the relevant variables.

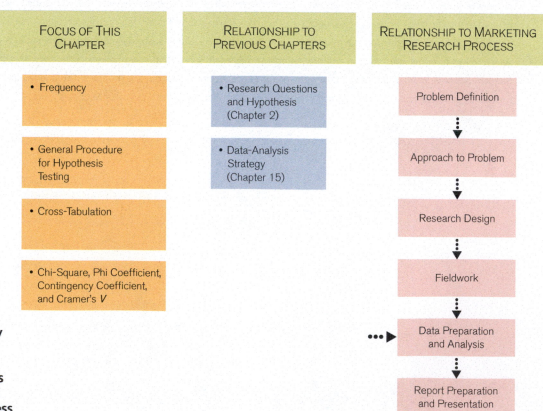

FIGURE 16.1

Relationship of Frequency Distribution, Hypothesis Testing, and Cross-Tabulation to the Previous Chapters and the Marketing Research Process

FOCUS OF THIS CHAPTER
- Frequency
- General Procedure for Hypothesis Testing
- Cross-Tabulation
- Chi-Square, Phi Coefficient, Contingency Coefficient, and Cramer's V

RELATIONSHIP TO PREVIOUS CHAPTERS
- Research Questions and Hypothesis (Chapter 2)
- Data-Analysis Strategy (Chapter 15)

RELATIONSHIP TO MARKETING RESEARCH PROCESS
Problem Definition
Approach to Problem
Research Design
Fieldwork
Data Preparation and Analysis
Report Preparation and Presentation

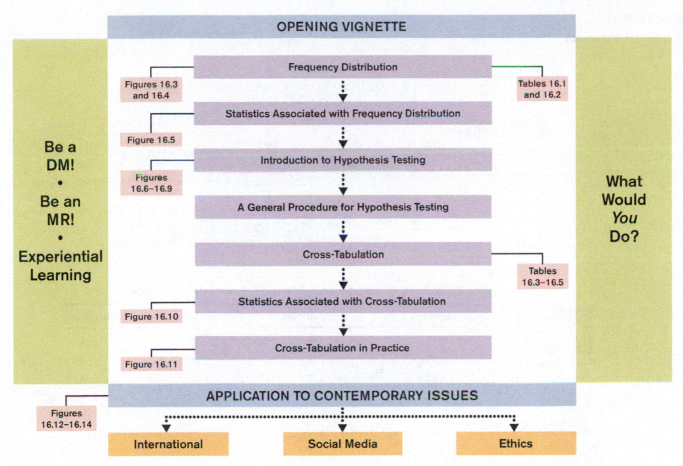

FIGURE 16.2

Frequency Distribution, Hypothesis Testing, and Cross-Tabulation: An Overview

Frequency Distribution

Marketing researchers often need to answer questions about a single variable. For example:

- What is the percentage of shoppers using coupons? (See opening vignette.)
- What percentage of the market consists of heavy users, medium users, light users, and nonusers?
- How many customers are very familiar with a new product offering? How many are familiar, somewhat familiar, and unfamiliar with the brand? What is the mean rating on familiarity with the brand? Is there much variance in the extent to which customers are familiar with the new product?
- What is the income distribution of brand users? Is this distribution skewed toward low-income brackets?

The answers to these kinds of questions can be determined by examining frequency distributions. In a **frequency distribution**, one variable is considered at a time. The objective is to obtain a count of the number of responses associated with different values of the variable. The relative occurrence, or relative frequency, of different values of the variable is expressed in percentages, as in the opening vignette. A frequency distribution for a variable produces a table of frequency counts, percentages, and cumulative percentages for all the values associated with that variable.

The steps involved in conducting frequency analysis are given in Figure 16.3. The frequency procedure is illustrated using the data of Table 16.1, which gives the attitude toward Nike, usage, and gender of a sample of Nike users. Attitude is measured on a 7-point Likert-type scale (1 = very unfavorable, 7 = very favorable). The users have been coded as 1, 2, or 3, representing light, medium, or heavy users. Gender has been coded as 1 for females and 2 for males. This table gives the data for only 45 respondents so that that the calculations of the basic statistics by hand can be shown.

frequency distribution
A mathematical distribution with the objective of obtaining a count of the number of responses associated with different values of one variable and to express these counts in percentage terms.

FIGURE 16.3
Conducting Frequency Analysis

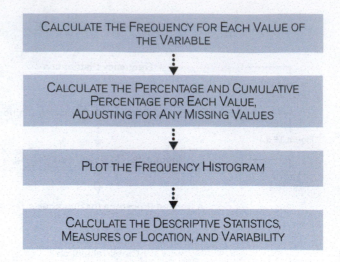

TABLE 16.1 Usage and Attitude Toward Nike Shoes

SPSS Data File

Excel Data File

Number	User Group	Gender	Attitude
1	3.00	2.00	7.00
2	1.00	1.00	2.00
3	1.00	1.00	3.00
4	3.00	2.00	6.00
5	3.00	2.00	5.00
6	2.00	2.00	4.00
7	2.00	1.00	5.00
8	1.00	1.00	2.00
9	2.00	2.00	4.00
10	1.00	1.00	3.00
11	3.00	2.00	6.00
12	3.00	2.00	6.00
13	1.00	1.00	2.00
14	3.00	2.00	6.00
15	1.00	2.00	4.00
16	1.00	2.00	3.00
17	3.00	1.00	7.00
18	2.00	1.00	6.00
19	1.00	1.00	1.00
20	3.00	1.00	5.00
21	3.00	2.00	6.00
22	2.00	2.00	2.00
23	1.00	1.00	1.00
24	3.00	1.00	6.00
25	1.00	2.00	3.00
26	2.00	2.00	5.00
27	3.00	2.00	7.00
28	2.00	1.00	5.00
29	1.00	1.00	9.00
30	2.00	2.00	5.00
31	1.00	2.00	1.00

TABLE 16.1 (Continued)

Number	User Group	Gender	Attitude
32	1.00	2.00	4.00
33	2.00	1.00	3.00
34	2.00	1.00	4.00
35	3.00	1.00	5.00
36	3.00	1.00	6.00
37	3.00	2.00	6.00
38	3.00	2.00	5.00
39	3.00	2.00	7.00
40	1.00	1.00	4.00
41	1.00	1.00	2.00
42	1.00	1.00	1.00
43	1.00	1.00	2.00
44	1.00	1.00	3.00
45	1.00	1.00	1.00

These hand calculations provide the reader a better idea of the basic concepts. In practice, the sample size is much larger. The analysis of such large data sets is illustrated later in the chapter in an Experiential Learning exercise that analyzes the taste-test data for 648 respondents regarding a new reduced-fat version of Nestlé's Kit Kat candy bar.

Table 16.2 provides the frequency distribution of attitude from Table 16.1. In the table, the first column contains the labels assigned to the different categories of the variable. The second column indicates the code or value assigned to each label or category. The third column gives the number of respondents for each value, including the missing values.

For example, of the 45 respondents who participated in the Nike survey, 6 respondents have a value of 2, denoting an unfavorable attitude. One respondent did not answer and has a missing value denoted by 9. The fourth column displays the percentage of respondents checking each value. These percentages are obtained by dividing the frequencies in column 3 by 45. The next column shows percentages calculated by excluding the cases with missing values; in this example, by dividing the frequencies in column 3 by 44 (i.e., 45 − 1). As can be seen, eight respondents (18.2%) have an attitude value of 5. If there were no missing values, columns 4 and 5 would be identical. The last column represents cumulative percentages after adjusting for missing cases. The cumulative percentage for a value denotes the percentage of responses that are less than or equal to that value. The cumulative percentage corresponding to the value of 5 is 70.5 percent. In other words, 70.5 percent of the respondents have a value of 5 or less. The data

TABLE 16.2 Frequency Distribution of Attitude Toward Nike

Value Label	Value	Frequency	Percentage	Valid Percentage	Cumulative Percentage
Very unfavorable	1	5	11.1	11.4	11.4
	2	6	13.3	13.6	25.0
	3	6	13.3	13.6	38.6
	4	6	13.3	13.6	52.3
	5	8	17.8	18.2	70.5
	6	9	20.0	20.5	90.9
Very favorable	7	4	8.9	9.1	100.0
	9	1	2.2	Missing	
Total		**45**	**100.0**	**100.0**	

SPSS

SPSS Output File

Excel

Excel Output File

FIGURE 16.4

Frequency Histogram

SPSS Output File

Excel Output File

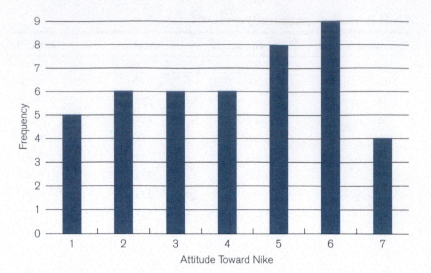

of Table 16.1 as well as the SPSS and Excel outputs, along with explanatory notes, can be downloaded from the Web site for this book.

A frequency distribution helps determine the extent of illegitimate responses. Values of 0 and 8 would be illegitimate responses, or errors. The cases with these values can be identified and corrective action taken. The presence of *outliers*, cases with extreme values, can also be detected. In the case of a frequency distribution of household size, a few isolated families with household sizes of nine or more might be considered outliers. A frequency distribution also indicates the shape of the empirical distribution of the variable. The frequency data can be used to construct a histogram, or a vertical bar chart, in which the values of the variable are portrayed along the x-axis and the absolute or relative frequencies of the values are placed along the y-axis.

Figure 16.4 is a histogram of the attitude data in Table 16.2. From the histogram, one could examine whether the observed distribution is consistent with an expected or assumed distribution. Note that in this case the observed distribution does not look like the standard normal distribution. This might be important in determining what type of statistical test is appropriate. For further illustration, consider the following example.

Research in Action

The Signal Is Green for Yellow-Pages Advertising by Physicians

A census was conducted of every physician's Yellow Pages listing in Atlanta, Georgia; Chicago, Illinois; and Charlotte, North Carolina. The contents of these listings were analyzed to determine the types of ads. The various types of Yellow Pages ads were as follows:

Type of Yellow Pages Ad	Frequency	Percentage
Nondisplay listings: light face	5,454	46
Nondisplay listings: face	1,656	14
Display ads	4,694	40
Total advertisements	**11,804**	**100**

Based on the frequency counts, the study concluded that Yellow Pages listings are a widely used form of physician advertising: 11,804 ads were located in the three areas. The majority of the physicians (46% + 14% = 60%), however, were using nondisplay (light face/face) listings, which are more appropriate

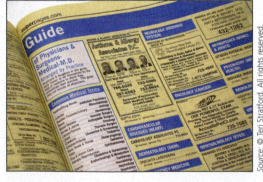

for physicians with established practices who have all the patients they want. Only 40 percent were using the larger display ads that have a much higher likelihood of being seen by potential patients who consult Yellow Pages when looking for a physician. Because a majority of the physicians were looking for new patients, the study concluded that more physicians should use the display rather than nondisplay ads in the Yellow Pages.[2]

Note that the numbers and percentages in the preceding example indicate the extent of advertising. Because numbers are involved, a frequency distribution can be used to calculate descriptive or summary statistics. Some of the statistics associated with frequency distributions are discussed in the next section.

Statistics Associated with Frequency Distribution

As illustrated in the previous section, a frequency distribution is a convenient way of looking at the values of a variable. A frequency table is easy to read and provides basic information, but sometimes this information might be too detailed and the researcher must summarize it by the use of descriptive statistics. The most commonly used statistics associated with frequencies are measures of location (mean, mode, and median) and measures of variability (range and standard deviation).

Measures of Location

The **measures of location** discussed in this section are measures of central tendency, because they tend to describe the center of the distribution (see Chapter 13). If the entire sample is changed by adding a fixed constant to each observation, then the mean, mode, and median change by the same fixed amount. Suppose the number 10 was added to the attitude ratings of all the $(45 - 1 =) 44$ respondents who expressed their attitudes toward Nike in Table 16.1. In this case, the mean, mode, and median will all increase by 10.

measures of location
A statistic that describes a location within a data set. Measures of central tendency describe the center of the distribution.

MEAN The **mean**, or average value, is the most commonly used measure of central tendency or center of a distribution (see the opening vignette). It is used to estimate the average when the data have been collected using an interval or ratio scale (see Chapter 9). The data should display some central tendency, with most of the responses distributed around the mean.

The mean, $\overline{X}$, is given by

$$\overline{X} = \sum_{i=1}^{n} X_i/n$$

mean
The average; that value obtained by summing all elements in a set and dividing by the number of elements.

Where

X_i = Observed values of the variable X

n = Number of observations (sample size)

Generally, the mean is a robust measure and does not change markedly as data values are added or deleted. For the frequency counts given in Table 16.2, the mean value is calculated as follows:

$$\overline{X} = (5 \times 1 + 6 \times 2 + 6 \times 3 + 6 \times 4 + 8 \times 5 + 9 \times 6 + 4 \times 7)/44$$
$$= (5 + 12 + 18 + 24 + 40 + 54 + 28)/44$$
$$= 181/44$$
$$= 4.11$$

MODE The **mode** is the value that occurs most frequently. It represents the highest peak of the distribution. The mode is a good measure of location when the variable is inherently categorical or has otherwise been grouped into categories. The mode in Table 16.2 is 6, because this value occurs with the highest frequency; that is, nine times (see also the histogram in Figure 16.4).

mode
A measure of central tendency given as the value that occurs the most in a sample distribution.

MEDIAN The **median** of a sample is the middle value when the data are arranged in ascending or descending rank order (see Chapter 9). If the number of data points is even, the median is usually estimated as the midpoint between the two middle values—by adding the two middle values and dividing their sum by 2. The middle value is the value where 50 percent of the values are greater than that value, and 50 percent are less. Thus, the median is the 50th percentile. The median is an appropriate measure of central tendency for ordinal data. In Table 16.2, the middle value is the average of the 22nd and 23rd observations when the data are arranged in ascending or descending order. This average is 4, and so the median is 4. The median can be easily

median
A measure of central tendency given as the value above which half of the values fall and below which half of the values fall.

determined by using cumulative percentages in the frequency table. Note that at a value of 4, the cumulative percentage is 52.3 percent, but for a value of 5, it is 70.5 percent, and for a value of 3, it is 38.6 percent. Therefore, the 50-percent point occurs at the value of 4.

As can be seen from Table 16.2, the three measures of central tendency for this distribution are different (mean = 4.11, mode = 6, median = 4). This is not surprising, because each measure defines central tendency in a different way. The three values are equal only when the distribution is symmetric. In a symmetric distribution, the values are equally likely to plot on either side of the center of the distribution, and the mean, mode, and median are equal (see Figure 16.5).

The normal distribution discussed earlier in Chapter 13 is a symmetric distribution, and the three measures of central tendency are equal. An advantage of calculating all three measures of central tendency is that we can determine whether the distribution is symmetric or asymmetric. The asymmetry of the distribution of Table 16.2 can also be seen from the histogram of Figure 16.4.

If the distribution is asymmetric, which measure should be used? If the variable is measured on a nominal scale, the mode should be used. If the variable is measured on an ordinal scale, the median is appropriate. If the variable is measured on an interval or ratio scale, the mode is a poor measure of central tendency. This can be seen from Table 16.2. Although the modal value of 6 has the highest frequency of nine, it represents only 20.5 percent of the sample. In general, for interval or ratio data, the median is a better measure of central tendency than the mode, although it, too, ignores available information about the variable. The actual values of the variable above and below the median are ignored. The mean is the most appropriate measure of central tendency for interval or ratio data. The mean makes

FIGURE 16.5

Skewness of a Distribution

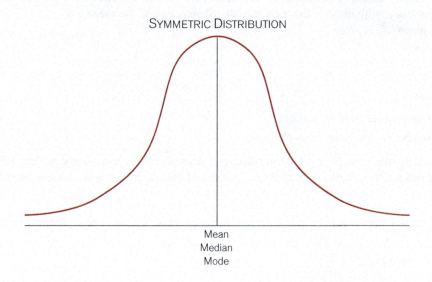

SYMMETRIC DISTRIBUTION

Mean
Median
Mode

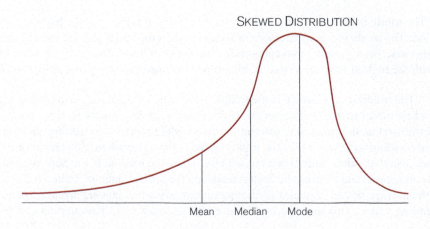

SKEWED DISTRIBUTION

Mean   Median   Mode

use of all the information available, because all of the values are used in computing it. However, the mean is sensitive to isolated cases with outliers, that is, extremely small or extremely large values. When there are outliers in the data, the mean is not a good measure of central tendency, and it is useful to consider both the mean and the median.

Measures of Variability

The **measures of variability** indicate the dispersion of a distribution. The most common, which are calculated on interval or ratio data, are the range, variance, and standard deviation.

measures of variability
Statistics that indicate the distribution's dispersion.

RANGE   The **range** measures the spread of the data. It is simply the difference between the largest and smallest values in the sample. As such, the range is directly affected by outliers.

range
The difference between the smallest and largest values of a distribution.

$$\text{Range} = X_{\text{largest}} - X_{\text{smallest}}$$

If all the values in the data are multiplied by a constant, the range is multiplied by the same constant. The range in Table 16.2 is $7 - 1 = 6$.

VARIANCE AND STANDARD DEVIATION   The difference between the mean and an observed value is called the *deviation from the mean*. The **variance** is the mean squared deviation from the mean, that is, the average of the square of the deviations from the mean for all the values. The variance can never be negative. When the data points are clustered around the mean, the variance is small. When the data points are scattered, the variance is large. The variance helps us to understand how similar or different the data points are. If the data points are similar, the variance is small and their distribution is clustered tightly around the mean. If the data points are very different in value, the variance is large and their distribution is spread more widely around the mean. If all the data values are multiplied by a constant, the variance is multiplied by the square of the constant.

variance
The mean squared deviation of all the values from the mean.

The **standard deviation** is the square root of the variance. Thus, the standard deviation is expressed in the same units as the data, whereas the variance is expressed in squared units. The standard deviation serves the same purpose as the variance in helping us to understand how clustered or spread the distribution is around the mean value.

standard deviation
The square root of the variance.

The standard deviation of a sample, s_x, is calculated as

$$s_x = \sqrt{\sum_{i=1}^{n} \frac{(X_i - \overline{X})^2}{n-1}}$$

We divide by $n - 1$ instead of n, because the sample is drawn from a population and we are trying to determine how much the responses vary from the mean of the entire population. However, the population mean is unknown; therefore, the sample mean is used instead. The use of the sample mean makes the sample seem less variable than it actually is. By dividing by $n - 1$ instead of n, we compensate for the smaller variability observed in the sample. For the data given in Table 16.2, the variance is calculated as follows:

$$\begin{aligned}
\text{Variance} = s_x^2 &= \{5 \times (1 - 4.11)^2 + 6 \times (2 - 4.11)^2 + 6 \times (3 - 4.11)^2 \\
&\quad + 6 \times (4 - 4.11)^2 + 8 \times (5 - 4.11)^2 + 9 \times (6 - 4.11)^2 \\
&\quad + 4 \times (7 - 4.11)^2\}/43 \\
&= (48.36 + 26.71 + 7.39 + 0.07 + 6.34 + 32.15 + 33.41)/43 \\
&= 154.43/43 \\
&= 3.59
\end{aligned}$$

The standard deviation, therefore, is calculated as

$$\begin{aligned}
\text{Standard deviation} = s_x &= \sqrt{3.59} \\
&= 1.90
\end{aligned}$$

Be a DM!	Be an MR!
Wendy's Customers: Who Are the Heavyweights?	
As the marketing director for Wendy's, how would you target heavy users of fast-food restaurants?	Visit www.wendys.com and search the Internet—including social media—as well as your library's online databases to obtain information on the heavy users of fast-food restaurants. In a survey for Wendy's, information was obtained on the number of visits to Wendy's per month. How would you identify the heavy users of Wendy's, and what statistics would you compute to summarize the number of visits to Wendy's per month?

Introduction to Hypothesis Testing

Hypotheses were defined and illustrated in Chapter 2. Recall that hypotheses are unproven statements or propositions of interest to the researcher. Hypotheses are declarative and can be tested statistically. Often, hypotheses are possible answers to research questions. Basic analysis invariably involves some hypothesis testing. The following are examples of hypotheses generated in marketing research:

- The average number of stores shopped for groceries is 3.0 per household (see the opening vignette).
- The department store is being patronized by more than 10 percent of the households.
- The heavy and light users of a brand differ in terms of psychographic characteristics.
- One hotel has a more upscale image than its close competitor.
- Familiarity with a restaurant results in greater preference for that restaurant.

Chapter 13 examined the concepts of the sampling distribution, standard error of the mean or the proportion, and the confidence interval.[3] Because all of these concepts are relevant to hypothesis testing, it would be wise to review them. The next section describes a general procedure for hypothesis testing that can be applied to test a wide range of hypotheses.

A General Procedure for Hypothesis Testing

The following steps are involved in hypothesis testing (see Figure 16.6).

1. Formulate the null hypothesis H_0 and the alternative hypothesis H_1.
2. Select an appropriate statistical test and the corresponding test statistic.
3. Choose the level of significance (α).
4. Determine the sample size and collect the data. Calculate the value of the test statistic.
5. Determine the probability associated with the test statistic calculated from the sample data under the null hypothesis, using the sampling distribution of the test statistic. Alternatively, determine the critical value associated with the test statistic that divides the rejection and nonrejection regions, given the level of significance (α).
6. Compare the probability associated with the test statistic with the level of significance specified. Alternatively, determine whether the test statistic calculated from the sample data falls into the rejection or the nonrejection region.
7. Make the statistical decision to reject or not reject the null hypothesis.
8. Arrive at a conclusion. Express the statistical decision in terms of the marketing research problem.

Step 1: Formulating the Hypothesis

null hypothesis
A statement suggesting no expected difference or effect. If the null hypothesis is not rejected, no changes will be made.

alternative hypothesis
A statement suggesting some difference or effect is expected. Accepting the alternative hypothesis will lead to changes in opinions or actions.

The first step is to formulate the null and alternative hypothesis. A **null hypothesis** is a statement of the status quo, one of no difference or no effect. If the null hypothesis is not rejected, no changes will be made. An **alternative hypothesis** is one in which some difference or effect is expected. Accepting the alternative hypothesis will lead to changes in opinions or actions. Thus, the alternative hypothesis is the opposite of the null hypothesis.

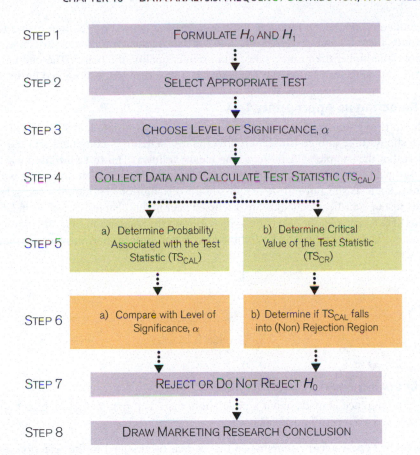

FIGURE 16.6

A General Procedure for Hypothesis Testing

The null hypothesis is always the hypothesis that is tested. The null hypothesis refers to a specified value of the population parameter (e.g., μ, σ, π), not a sample statistic (e.g., $\overline{X}$). (See Table 13.1 in Chapter 13.) A null hypothesis might be rejected, but it can never be accepted based on a single test. A statistical test can have one of two outcomes. One is that the null hypothesis is rejected and the alternative hypothesis accepted. The other outcome is that the null hypothesis is not rejected based on the evidence. However, it would be incorrect to conclude that because the null hypothesis is not rejected it can be accepted as valid. In classical hypothesis testing, there is no way to determine whether the null hypothesis is true.[4]

In marketing research, the null hypothesis is formulated in such a way that its rejection leads to the acceptance of the desired conclusion. The alternative hypothesis represents the conclusion for which evidence is sought. For example, AT&T is considering the introduction of a new servicing plan. The plan will be introduced if it is preferred by more than 40 percent of customers. The appropriate way to formulate the hypotheses is as follows:

$$H_0: \pi \leq 0.40$$

$$H_1: \pi > 0.40$$

If the null hypothesis H_0 is rejected, then the alternative hypothesis H_1 will be accepted and the new service plan introduced. However, if H_0 is not rejected, the new service plan should not be introduced unless additional evidence is obtained.

This test of the null hypothesis is a **one-tailed test** because the alternative hypothesis is expressed directionally: The proportion of customers who express a preference is greater than 0.40. However, suppose the researcher wanted to determine whether the new service plan is different (superior or inferior) from the current plan, which is preferred by 40 percent of customers. Then a **two-tailed test** would be required, and the hypotheses would be expressed as

$$H_0: \pi = 0.40$$

$$H_1: \pi \neq 0.40$$

one-tailed test
A test of the null hypothesis where the alternative hypothesis is expressed directionally.

two-tailed test
A test of the null hypothesis where the alternative hypothesis is not expressed directionally.

In commercial marketing research, the one-tailed test is used more often than a two-tailed test. Typically, there is some preferred direction for the conclusion for which evidence is sought. For example, the higher the profits, sales, and product quality, the better. The one-tailed test is more powerful than the two-tailed test. The power of a statistical test is discussed further in step 3.

Step 2: Selecting an Appropriate Test

To test the null hypothesis, it is necessary to select an appropriate statistical technique. The researcher should take into consideration how the test statistic is computed and the sampling distribution that the sample statistic (e.g., the mean) follows. The **test statistic** measures how close the sample has come to the null hypothesis. The test statistic often follows a well-known distribution, such as the normal, t, or chi-square distribution. Guidelines for selecting an appropriate test or statistical technique are discussed later in this chapter, as well as in Chapter 17.

In our AT&T example, the z statistic, which follows the standard normal distribution, would be appropriate. This statistic would be computed as follows for proportions (see Chapter 13):

$$z = \frac{p - \pi}{\sigma_p}$$

Where

$$\sigma_p = \sqrt{\frac{\pi(1 - \pi)}{n}}$$

test statistic
A measure of how close the sample has come to the null hypothesis. It often follows a well-known distribution, such as the normal, t, or chi-square distribution.

Step 3: Choosing Level of Significance

Whenever an inference is made about a population, there is a risk that an incorrect conclusion will be reached. Two types of error can occur.

TYPE-I ERROR **Type-I error** occurs when the sample results lead to the rejection of the null hypothesis when it is in fact true. In our example, a type-I error would occur if we concluded, based on the sample data, that the proportion of customers preferring the new service plan was greater than 0.40, when in fact it was less than or equal to 0.40. The probability of type-I error (α) also is called the **level of significance**. The type-I error is controlled by establishing the tolerable level of risk of rejecting a true null hypothesis. The selection of a particular risk level should depend on the cost of making a type-I error. The level of significance (α), when expressed as a percentage, is equal to 100 percent minus the confidence level (see Chapter 13).

type-I error
Also known as *alpha* (α) *error*, it occurs when the sample results lead to the rejection of a null hypothesis that is in fact true.

level of significance
The probability of making a type-I error.

TYPE-II ERROR **Type-II error** occurs when, based on the sample results, the null hypothesis is not rejected when it is in fact false. In our example, the type-II error would occur if we concluded, based on sample data, that the proportion of customers preferring the new service plan was less than or equal to 0.40 when, in fact, it was greater than 0.40. The probability of type-II error is denoted by β. Unlike α, which is specified by the researcher, the magnitude of β depends on the actual value of the population parameter (i.e., mean or proportion). The probability of type-I error (α) and the probability of type-II error (β) are shown in Figure 16.7. The complement ($1 - \beta$) of the probability of a type-II error is called the *power of a statistical test*.

type-II error
Also known as *beta* (β) *error*, occurs when the sample results lead to nonrejection of a null hypothesis that is in fact false.

POWER OF A TEST The **power of a test** is the probability ($1 - \beta$) of rejecting the null hypothesis when it is false and should be rejected. Although β is unknown, it is related to α. An extremely low value of α (e.g., 0.001) will result in intolerably high β errors. Thus, it is necessary to balance the two types of errors. As a compromise, α often is set at 0.05; sometimes it is 0.01; other values of α are rare. The level of α, along with the sample size, will determine the level of β for a particular research design. The risk of both α and β can be controlled by increasing the sample size. For a given level of α, increasing the sample size will decrease β, thereby increasing the power of the test.

power of a test
The probability of rejecting the null hypothesis when it is in fact false and should be rejected.

Step 4: Data Collection

Sample size is determined after taking into account the desired α and β errors, incidence and completion rates, and other qualitative considerations, such as budget constraints (see Chapter 13). Then, the required data are collected and the value of the test statistic computed. In our

FIGURE 16.7

Type-I Error (Alpha) and Type-II Error (Beta)

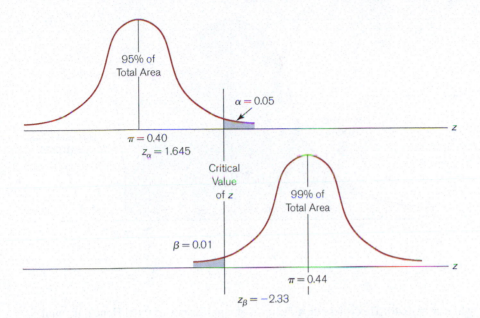

example, suppose 500 customers were surveyed and 220 expressed a preference for the new service plan. Thus, the value of the sample proportion is $p = 220/500 = 0.44$.

The value of σ_p can be determined as follows:

$$\sigma_p = \sqrt{\frac{\pi(1 - \pi)}{n}}$$

$$= \sqrt{\frac{(0.40)(0.6)}{500}}$$

$$= 0.0219$$

The test statistic z can be calculated as follows:

$$z = \frac{p - \pi}{\sigma_p}$$

$$= \frac{0.44 - 0.40}{0.0219}$$

$$= 1.83$$

Step 5: Determining the Probability (Critical Value)

Using standard normal tables (see Table 2 of the Appendix of Statistical Tables), the probability of obtaining a z value of 1.83 or larger can be calculated (see Figure 16.8). The shaded area between $-\infty$ and 1.83 is 0.9664. Therefore, the area to the right of $z = 1.83$ is $1.0000 - 0.9664 = 0.0336$. Most computer programs automatically calculate this value. It also is called the **p value** and is the probability of observing a value of the test statistic as extreme as, or more extreme than, the value actually observed, assuming that the null hypothesis is true.

Alternatively, the critical value of z, which will give an area to the right side of the critical value of 0.05, is between 1.64 and 1.65 and equals 1.645. Note that in determining the critical value of the test statistic, the area to the right of the critical value is either α or $\alpha/2$. It is α for a one-tail test and $\alpha/2$ for a two-tail test.

p value
This is the probability of observing a value of the test statistic as extreme as, or more extreme than, the value actually observed, assuming that the null hypothesis is true.

Steps 6 and 7: Comparing the Probability (Critical Value) and Making the Decision

a. The probability associated with the calculated or observed value of the test statistic calculated from the sample data is 0.0336. This is the probability of getting a p value of 0.44

FIGURE 16.8

Probability of z Value with a One-Tailed Test

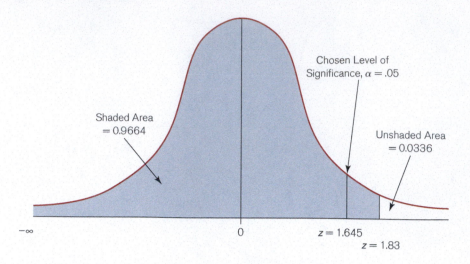

Shaded Area = 0.9664

Chosen Level of Significance, $\alpha = .05$

Unshaded Area = 0.0336

$-\infty$ 0 $z = 1.645$

$z = 1.83$

when $\pi = 0.40$. This is less than the level of significance of 0.05. Hence, the null hypothesis is rejected.

  b. Alternatively, the calculated value of the test statistic $z = 1.83$ lies in the rejection region, beyond the value of 1.645. Again, the same conclusion to reject the null hypothesis is reached.

Note that the two ways of testing the null hypothesis are equivalent but mathematically opposite in the direction of comparison. If the probability associated with the calculated or observed value of the test statistic (TS_{CAL}) is *less than* the level of significance (α), the null hypothesis is rejected. However, if the absolute value of the calculated value of the test statistic (TS_{CAL}) is *greater than* the absolute value of the critical value of the test statistic (TS_{CR}), the null hypothesis is rejected. The **critical value** is the value of the test statistic that divides the rejection and nonrejection regions. The reason for this sign shift is that the larger the absolute value of TS_{CAL}, the smaller the probability of obtaining a more extreme value of the test statistic under the null hypothesis. This sign shift can be easily illustrated as follows:

critical value

The value of the test statistic that divides the rejection and nonrejection regions. If the absolute value of the calculated value of the test statistic is greater than the absolute value of the critical value of the test statistic, the null hypothesis is rejected.

Under (a):

if probability of TS_{CAL} < significance level (α), then reject H_0

Under (b),

if $|TS_{CAL}| > |TS_{CR}|$, then reject H_0

Step 8: Marketing Research Conclusion

The conclusion reached by hypothesis testing must be expressed in terms of the marketing research problem and the managerial action that should be taken. In our example, we conclude that there is evidence that the proportion of customers preferring the new service plan is significantly greater than 0.40. Hence, the recommendation would be to introduce the new service plan. Another illustration of hypothesis testing is provided by the Holiday Inn example.

Hypotheses testing can be related to either an examination of associations or an examination of differences (see Figure 16.9). In tests of associations, the null hypothesis is that there is no association between the variables (H_0: . . . is *not* related to . . .). In tests of differences, the null hypothesis is that there is no difference (H_0: . . . is *not* different from . . .). Tests of differences could relate to means or proportions. First, we discuss hypotheses related to associations in the context of cross-tabulations.

FIGURE 16.9

A Broad Classification of Hypothesis-Testing Procedures

Research in Action

Holiday Inn: The "In" Thing

As of 2011, there were more than 3,300 Holiday Inns in more than 105 countries around the world. This famous hotel chain is owned by InterContinental Hotels Group (IHG). Although IHG (www.ichotelsgroup.com) has a room capacity of 18.8 million rooms, it only holds 3 percent of the market share. In an attempt to increase its market share, IHG was considering opening other hotel chains for middle-class hotel customers that would have more stylish rooms. Management analysis indicated that this would be feasible if more than 20 percent of the target customers preferred stylish rooms. The following hypotheses were formulated:

$$H_0 : \pi \leq 0.20$$
$$H_1 : \pi > 0.20$$

Note that this is a one-tailed test. IHG recruited TNS Landis Strategy & Innovation (www.landis-si.com) to survey 14,000 travelers on three continents. The findings of this study showed that a surprising 40 percent of middle-class hotel customers cared about style and design in their hotel rooms, leading to the rejection of the null hypothesis.

In response to this finding, IHG introduced a few different kinds of "branded" hotels, such as Holiday Indigo, Nickelodeon Family

Suites, Holiday Inn Sunspree Resorts, and Holiday Inn Garden Court. The main aim of these chains is to capitalize on mid-market customers who are willing to spend on luxury and service. Each chain is personalized and unique, fighting against the "sea of sameness" into which the hotel industry has sunk. By conducting hypothesis testing, IHG has discovered the needs of its customers in a changing market. It will be able to cater to these needs and differentiate its hotels to stand above the competition.[5]

Source: Ian Dagnall/Alamy.

Cross-Tabulation

Although answers to questions related to a single variable are interesting, they often raise additional questions about how to link that variable to other variables. To introduce the frequency distribution, we posed several representative marketing research questions. For each of these, a researcher might pose additional questions to relate these variables to other variables. For example:

- What percentage of coupon users has annual household incomes of more than $50,000? (See the opening vignette.)
- Is product use (measured in terms of heavy users, medium users, light users, and nonusers) related to interest in outdoor activities (high, medium, and low)?
- Is familiarity with a new product (unfamiliar, familiar) related to education levels (high school or less, some college, college degree)?
- Is the income (high, medium, and low) of brand users related to the geographic region in which they live (north, south, east, and west)?s

The answers to such questions can be determined by examining cross-tabulations. Whereas a frequency distribution describes one variable at a time, a **cross-tabulation** describes two or more variables simultaneously. Cross-tabulation results in tables that reflect the joint distribution

cross-tabulation
A statistical technique that describes two or more variables simultaneously and results in tables that reflect the joint distribution of two or more variables that have a limited number of categories or distinct values.

SPSS Output File

Excel Output File

TABLE 16.3 A Cross-Tabulation of Gender and Usage of Nike Shoes

Usage	Gender		
	Female	Male	Row Total
Light users	14	5	19
Medium users	5	5	10
Heavy users	5	11	16
Column total	**24**	**21**	**45**

of two or more variables with a limited number of categories or distinct values. The categories of one variable are cross-classified with the categories of one or more other variables. Thus, the frequency distribution of one variable is subdivided according to the values or categories of the other variables. This was illustrated in the opening vignette in which coupon usage was cross-classified with income. The analysis revealed that lower-income households had higher coupon usage as compared to middle- and higher-income households.

Suppose Nike was interested in determining whether gender was associated with the degree of usage of Nike shoes. In Table 16.1, the respondents were divided into three categories of light (denoted by 1), medium (2), or heavy users (3) based on reported wear-time per week. There were 19 light users, 10 medium users, and 16 heavy users. Although data on attitude were missing for one respondent, information on usage and gender was available for all respondents. Gender was coded as 1 for females and 2 for males. The sample included 24 females and 21 males.

The cross-tabulation is shown in Table 16.3. A cross-tabulation includes a cell for every combination of the categories of the two variables. The number in each cell shows how many respondents gave that combination of responses. In Table 16.3, 14 respondents were females and light users. The marginal totals (column totals and row totals) in this table indicate that of the 45 respondents with valid responses on both the variables 19 were light users, 10 were medium users, and 16 were heavy users, confirming the classification procedure adopted.

Furthermore, 21 respondents were males, and 24 were females. Note that this information could have been obtained from a separate frequency distribution for each variable. In general, the margins of a cross-tabulation show the same information as the frequency tables for each of the variables. Cross-tabulation tables also are called **contingency tables**.

contingency table
A cross-tabulation table. It contains a cell for every combination of categories of the two variables.

Cross-tabulation is widely used in commercial marketing research because (1) cross-tabulation analysis and results can be easily interpreted and understood by managers who are not statistically oriented; (2) the clarity of interpretation provides a stronger link between research results and managerial action; and (3) cross-tabulation analysis is simple to conduct and more appealing to less sophisticated researchers. We will discuss cross-tabulation for two variables, the most common form in which this procedure is used.

Cross-tabulation with two variables also is known as *bivariate cross-tabulation*. Consider again the cross-classification of gender and usage of Nike shoes given in Table 16.3. Is usage of Nike shoes related to gender? It might be. We see from Table 16.3 that disproportionately more of the males are heavy users and disproportionately more of the females are light users. Computation of percentages can provide more insights.

Because two variables have been cross-classified, percentages could be computed either column-wise, based on column totals (see Table 16.4), or row-wise, based on row totals (see Table 16.5).

SPSS Output File

Excel Output File

TABLE 16.4 Usage of Nike Shoes by Gender

Usage	Gender	
	Female	Male
Light users	58.4%	23.8%
Medium users	20.8%	23.8%
Heavy users	20.8%	52.4%
Column total	**100.0%**	**100.0%**

TABLE 16.5 Gender by Usage of Nike Shoes

Usage	Gender		Row Total
	Female	Male	
Light users	73.7%	26.3%	100.0%
Medium users	50.0%	50.0%	100.0%
Heavy users	31.2%	68.8%	100.0%

SPSS Output File

Excel Output File

Which of these tables is more useful? The answer depends on which variable will be considered as the independent variable and which as the dependent variable. The general rule is to compute the percentages in the direction of the independent variable, across the dependent variable. In our analysis, gender would be considered as the independent variable and usage as the dependent variable. Therefore, the correct way of calculating percentages is as shown in Table 16.4. Note that although 52.4 percent of the males are heavy users, only 20.8 percent of females are heavy users. This seems to indicate that compared to females, males are more likely to be heavy users of Nike shoes. The recommendation to management might be to promote more heavily to women to increase their usage rate or to promote more heavily to men to prevent brand loyalty erosion. Obviously, additional variables would need to be analyzed before management would act upon such recommendations. Nevertheless, this illustrates how hypotheses tests should be linked to recommended managerial actions.

Note that computing percentages in the direction of the dependent variable across the independent variable, as shown in Table 16.5, is not meaningful in this case. Table 16.5 implies that heavy usage of Nike shoes causes people to be males, which obviously is not meaningful. The corresponding SPSS and Excel outputs for this cross-tabulation with explanatory notes can be downloaded from the Web site for this book. As another example, consider the following study.

Research in Action

Old Is Gold, but Some Marketers Treat It as Dust

A study examined whether older models are depicted in a negative light in TV commercials. Television commercials emanating from the three major networks, one local station, and five cable companies were analyzed by the researchers. The results are below in terms of the number and percentage of models of different age groups that were depicted in a positive or negative light:

Note that as the age of the model increases, the percentages in the negative-depiction column increase. Therefore, the study concluded that older models do tend to be depicted in a negative manner. Thus, some marketers might be pursuing self-defeating strategies by depicting older consumers unfavorably. Marketers should note that older consumers represent a large and growing segment that controls substantial income and wealth.[6]

Source: ampyang/Shutterstock.

Depiction	Age of the Model (years)					
	Under 45		45–64		65 and over	
	No.	%	No.	%	No.	%
Positive	415	83.1	64	66	28	54
Negative	85	16.9	33	34	24	46
Total	500	100	97	100	52	100

Statistics Associated with Cross-Tabulation

This section focuses on the statistics commonly used for assessing the statistical significance and strength of association of cross-tabulated variables. The statistical significance of the observed association is commonly measured by the chi-square statistic. The strength of association, or degree of association, is important from a practical or managerial perspective. Generally, the strength of an association is of interest only if the association is statistically significant. The strength of the association can be measured by the phi correlation coefficient, the contingency coefficient, and Cramer's V.

Chi-Square

The **chi-square statistic** (χ^2) is used to test the statistical significance of the observed association in a cross-tabulation. It can be used in determining whether a systematic association exists between two variables. This is illustrated in the opening vignette where a systematic association exists between coupon usage and income, with lower-income households consuming more coupons than middle- or higher-income households. The null hypothesis, H_0, is that there is no association between the variables. The test is conducted by computing the cell frequencies that would be expected if no association was present between the variables, given the existing row and column totals. These expected cell frequencies, denoted f_e, are then compared to the actual observed frequencies, f_o, found in the cross-tabulation to calculate the chi-square statistic. The greater the discrepancies between the expected and actual frequencies, the larger the value of the statistic. Assume that a cross-tabulation has r rows and c columns and a random sample of n observations. The expected frequency for each cell, f_e, can be calculated by using a simple formula as follows:

$$f_e = \frac{n_r n_c}{n}$$

where

n_r = total number in the row

n_c = total number in the column

n = total sample size

For the data in Table 16.3, the total number in the row, n_r, is 19 for light users, 10 for medium users, and 16 for heavy users. The total number in each column, n_c, is 24 for females and 21 for males. Therefore, the expected cell frequencies for the six cells from left to right and top to bottom are

$$f_e = (19 \times 24)/45 = 10.1 \qquad f_e = (19 \times 21)/45 = 8.9$$

$$f_e = (10 \times 24)/45 = 5.3 \qquad f_e = (10 \times 21)/45 = 4.7$$

$$f_e = (16 \times 24)/45 = 8.5 \qquad f_e = (16 \times 21)/45 = 7.5$$

Generally, the expected cell frequency will be different for each cell, as is the case here. Only when all row totals are the same and all column totals are the same will the expected cell frequency be the same for each cell.

Once the expected cell frequencies are calculated, the value of χ^2 is calculated as follows:

$$\chi^2 = \sum_{\substack{all \\ cells}} \frac{(f_o - f_e)^2}{f_e}$$

For the data in Table 16.3, in which there are six cells, the value of χ^2 is calculated as

$$\chi^2 = \frac{(14 - 10.1)^2}{10.1} + \frac{(5 - 8.9)^2}{8.9}$$

$$+ \frac{(5 - 5.3)^2}{5.3} + \frac{(5 - 4.7)^2}{4.7}$$

$$+ \frac{(5 - 8.5)^2}{8.5} + \frac{(11 - 7.5)^2}{7.5}$$

$$= 1.51 + 1.71 + 0.02 + 0.02 + 1.44 + 1.63$$

$$= 6.33$$

To determine whether a systematic association exists, the probability of obtaining a value of chi-square as large as or larger than the one calculated from the cross-tabulation is estimated (see Figure 16.6, step 5). An important characteristic of the chi-square statistic is the number of degrees of freedom (df) associated with it. In general, the number of degrees of freedom is equal to the number of observations less the number of constraints needed to calculate a statistical term. In the case of a chi-square statistic associated with a cross-tabulation, the number of degrees of freedom is equal to the product of number of rows (r) less one and the number of columns (c) less one. That is, df $= (r - 1) \times (c - 1)$. The null hypothesis (H_0) of no association between the two variables will be rejected only when the calculated value of the test statistic is greater than the critical value of the chi-square distribution with the appropriate degrees of freedom, as shown in Figure 16.10. (See Figure 16.6, step 6).

Unlike the normal distribution, the **chi-square distribution** is a skewed distribution, the shape of which depends solely on the number of degrees of freedom. As the number of degrees of freedom increases, the chi-square distribution becomes more symmetrical. Table 3 in the Appendix of Statistical Tables contains upper-tail areas of the chi-square distribution for different degrees of freedom. In this table, the value at the top of each column indicates the area in the upper portion (the right side, as shown in Figure 16.10) of the chi-square distribution. To illustrate, for 2 degrees of freedom, the critical value of chi-square (χ^2_{CR}) for an upper-tail area of 0.05 is 5.991. This indicates that for 2 degrees of freedom the probability of exceeding a chi-square value of 5.991 is 0.05. In other words, at the 0.05 level of significance with 2 degrees of freedom, the critical value of the chi-square statistic is 5.991.

For the cross-tabulation given in Table 16.3, there are $(3 - 1) \times (2 - 1) = 2$ degrees of freedom. The calculated chi-square statistic had a value of 6.33. Because this is greater than the critical value of 5.991, the null hypothesis of no association is rejected, indicating that the association is statistically significant at the 0.05 level.

The chi-square statistic can also be used in *goodness-of-fit tests* to determine whether certain models fit the observed data. These tests are conducted by calculating the significance of sample deviations from assumed theoretical (expected) distributions and can be performed on cross-tabulations as well as on frequencies (one-way tabulations). The calculation of the chi-square statistic and the determination of its significance is the same as illustrated earlier.

The chi-square statistic should be estimated only on counts of data. When the data are in percentage form, they should first be converted to absolute counts or numbers. In addition, an underlying assumption of the chi-square test is that the observations are drawn independently. This means that respondents do not influence each other's responses in any way. As a general rule, chi-square analysis should not be conducted when the expected or theoretical frequencies in any of the cells is less than five. Low expected frequencies would cause the calculated value of chi-square to be higher than it should be (bias it upward) and make it more likely to commit a type-I error. The issue of cell sizes is directly related to statistical determination of sample size discussed in Chapter 13. When the frequency in any of the cells is low, it is often possible to reduce the size of the table (i.e., reduce the number of rows and/or columns) by combining categories. This was illustrated in Chapter 15 where the RECODE procedure in SPSS was employed to reduce the number of income categories from six to four. In the case of a 2×2 table, the chi-square is related to the phi coefficient.

chi-square distribution
A skewed distribution whose shape depends solely on the number of degrees of freedom. As the number of degrees of freedom increases, the chi-square distribution becomes more symmetrical.

FIGURE 16.10

Chi-Square Test of Association

Phi Coefficient

The **phi coefficient** (ϕ) is used as a measure of the strength of association in the special case of a table with two rows and two columns (a 2 × 2 table). The phi coefficient is proportional to the square root of the chi-square statistic. For a sample of size n, this statistic is calculated as

$$\phi = \sqrt{\frac{\chi^2}{n}}$$

It takes the value of 0 when there is no association, which would be indicated by a chi-square value of 0 as well. When the variables are perfectly associated, phi assumes the value of 1, and all the observations fall just on the main or minor diagonal. (In some computer programs, phi assumes a value of –1 rather than 1 when there is perfect negative association.) In the more general case involving a table of any size, the strength of association can be assessed by using the contingency coefficient.

Contingency Coefficient

The phi coefficient is specific to a 2 × 2 table; the **contingency coefficient** (C) can be used to assess the strength of association in a table of any size. This index is related to chi-square, as follows:

$$C = \sqrt{\frac{\chi^2}{\chi^2 + n}}$$

The contingency coefficient varies between 0 and 1. The 0 value occurs in the case of no association (i.e., the variables are statistically independent), but the maximum value of 1 is never achieved. Rather, the maximum value of the contingency coefficient depends on the size of the table (number of rows and number of columns). For this reason, it should be used only to compare tables of the same size.

Normally, the strength of association is not meaningful and, hence, not calculated when the null hypothesis of no association is not rejected. If there is no relationship between the two variables, there can be no strength. In our case, the null hypothesis was rejected; thus, it is meaningful to calculate the contingency coefficient. The value of the contingency coefficient for Table 16.3 is

$$C = \sqrt{\frac{6.33}{6.33 + 45}}$$
$$= \sqrt{.1235}$$
$$= 0.351$$

This value of C indicates that the association is low to moderate.

Cramer's V

Cramer's V is a modified version of the phi correlation coefficient, ϕ, and is used in tables larger than 2 × 2. When phi is calculated for a table larger than 2 × 2, it has no upper limit. Cramer's V is obtained by adjusting phi for either the number of rows or the number of columns in the table, based on which of the two is smaller. The adjustment is such that V will range from 0 to 1. A large value of V merely indicates a high degree of association. It does not indicate how the variables are associated. As a rule of thumb, values of V below 0.3 indicate low association, values between 0.3 and 0.6 indicate low-to-moderate association, and values above 0.6 indicate strong association. For a table with r rows and c columns, the relationship between Cramer's V and the phi correlation coefficient is expressed as

$$V = \sqrt{\frac{\phi^2}{\min(r-1),(c-1)}}$$

or

$$V = \sqrt{\frac{\chi^2/n}{\min(r-1),(c-1)}}$$

The value of Cramer's V for Table 16.3 is

$$V = \sqrt{\frac{6.33/45}{1}}$$

or

$$V = \sqrt{.01409}$$
$$= 0.375$$

Thus, the association is low to moderate.

Given that the null hypothesis was rejected and we have determined the strength of association as low to moderate, we can interpret the pattern of relation by looking at the percentages in Table 16.4. There is a low-to-moderate association between gender and usage of Nike shoes. Males tend to be heavy users, whereas females tend to be light users.

General Comments on Cross-Tabulation

Although three or more variables can be cross-tabulated, the interpretation can be quite complex. Also, because the number of cells increases multiplicatively, maintaining an adequate number of respondents or cases in each cell can be problematic. As a general rule, each cell should have at least five expected observations for the chi-square statistic used for testing cross-tabulation hypothesis to be reliable. Thus, cross-tabulation is an inefficient way of examining relationships when there are several variables. Note that cross-tabulation examines association between variables, not causation. To examine causation, the causal research design framework should be adopted (see Chapter 8).

Cross-Tabulation in Practice

When conducting cross-tabulation analysis in practice, it is useful to proceed following these steps (see Figure 16.11):

1. Construct the cross-tabulation table.
2. Test the null hypothesis that there is no association between the variables using the chi-square statistic (see the procedure described in Figure 16.6).
3. If you fail to reject the null hypothesis, there is no relationship.
4. If H_0 is rejected, determine the strength of the association using an appropriate statistic (phi coefficient, contingency coefficient, or Cramer's V) as discussed earlier in this chapter.
5. If H_0 is rejected, interpret the pattern of the relationship by computing the percentages in the direction of the independent variable, across the dependent variable. Draw marketing conclusions.

Be an MR!	Be a DM!

Analyzing Cosmetic Usage Is No Cosmetic Effort

Visit www.loreal.com and search the Internet—including social media—as well as your library's online databases to obtain information on the heavy users, light users, and nonusers of cosmetics. How would you analyze the data to determine whether the heavy users, light users, and nonusers of cosmetics differ in terms of demographic characteristics?

As the marketing director for L'Oreal, what marketing strategies would you adopt to reach the heavy users, light users, and nonusers of cosmetics?

Social Media

FIGURE 16.11

Conducting Cross-Tabulation Analysis

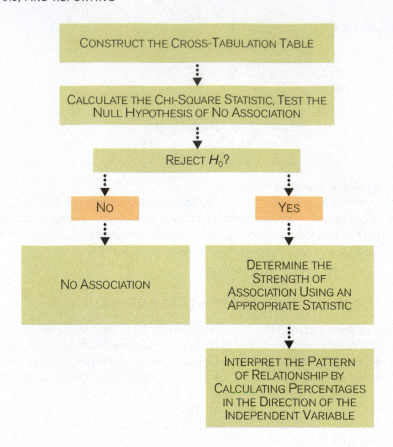

Summary Illustration Using the Opening Vignette

Basic data analysis provides valuable insights, as in the case of the coupon-usage study presented in the opening vignette. A frequency distribution produces a table of frequency counts, percentages, and cumulative percentages for all the values associated with that variable. The mean, mode, and median of a frequency distribution are measures of central tendency. Some of the important statistics and the insights they provided in the opening vignette included frequency counts (593 respondents used coupons for brands they normally bought), percentages (95% had used a coupon within the last 30 days), and means (the average number of stores shopped was 2.9 per household).

Hypotheses are declarative statements. Basic analysis invariably involves some hypothesis testing. Based on the data collected in the opening vignette, one could test the hypothesis that the average number of stores shopped for groceries is 3.0 per household. Cross-tabulations are tables that reflect the joint distribution of two or more variables. The chi-square statistic provides a test of the statistical significance of the observed association in a cross-tabulation. In the opening vignette, a cross-tabulation of coupon usage with income indicated that households at all income levels were cashing coupons. Yet, lower-income households had higher coupon usage as compared to middle- and higher-income households, and this association was statistically significant. Such findings can be used by supermarkets to target their coupon and promotional strategies. Figures 16.12, 16.13, and 16.14 provide concept maps for frequency analysis, hypothesis testing, and cross-tabulation, respectively. In these figure, the major concepts are connected by bold arrows using descriptors. Thus, in Figure 16.12, frequency analysis involves the frequency of each value of the variable. Each major concept is described by minor concepts that are connected to that major concept by lines with descriptors. Thus, the frequency of each value is used to calculate descriptive statistics and plot the frequency histogram. The rest of Figure 16.12, and Figures 16.13 and 16.14, can be interpreted similarly.

Marketing Research and Social Media

Data collected in social media often lend themselves to basic analysis involving frequencies, percentages and cross-tabulations. Although these statistical analyses are basic, they can nevertheless yield valuable insights, as illustrated by the case of The American Idol 2010.

Research in Action

Social Media Predicts The American Idol 2010

This example revolves around the center of America pop culture, The American Idol 2010. Social media research accurately predicted Lee DeWyze as the winner of the 2010 Idol contest, leaving the crowd favorite, Crystal Bowersox, as the loser or first runner-up. The traditional media cried upset, but the researchers at Idolstats spoke otherwise. Idolstats.com, launched by Biz360.com on April 1, 2010, is a tracking tool designed to track and evaluate conversations so as to predict the outcomes of American Idol. Biz360 is the provider of social media monitoring and market intelligence solutions and was acquired by the Attensity Group (www.attensity.com) on April 28, 2010. It has since been known as Attensity360.

Attensity360 aggregated and analyzed social media conversations—including blogs, message boards, forums, micro-blogs, online news media, and social networks—that were then translated into a graphic report indicating the most "talked-about" contestant. This graphic would be updated once a week (in tandem to the stages of the show) to predict the likely winner.

The analysis was based on simple frequency counts and percentages. Idolstats had indicated that Lee DeWyze had more than 60 percent of the contestant conversation, going against media favorite Crystal Bowersox, and predicted him as the winner in their blog. The data indicated that Lee DeWyze was much more popular than Crystal in social media and twice as likely to be talked about online. As far as sentiment goes, Lee had a slight edge over Crystal, with Lee at 66 percent positive and Crystal at 62 percent. In absolute terms, because Lee had more mentions (higher frequency), he had more positive mentions than did Crystal.[7]

This example shows the might of social media in being a proxy for public opinions and its usefulness in predicting an outcome.

— Crystal Bowersox
— Lee DeWyze

Publish Date

This graph shows that Crystal had been a favorite all season long, and most often just ahead of Lee, but in the final weeks, Lee began surging.

Source: Graph from Idol Stats blog used with permission of Attensity.

FIGURE 16.12

A Concept Map for Frequency Analysis

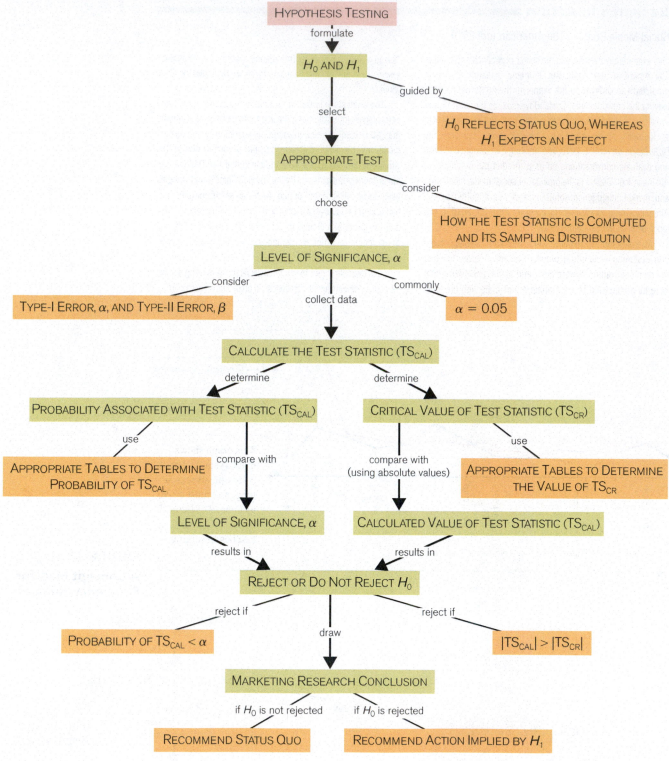

FIGURE 16.13
A Concept Map for Hypothesis Testing

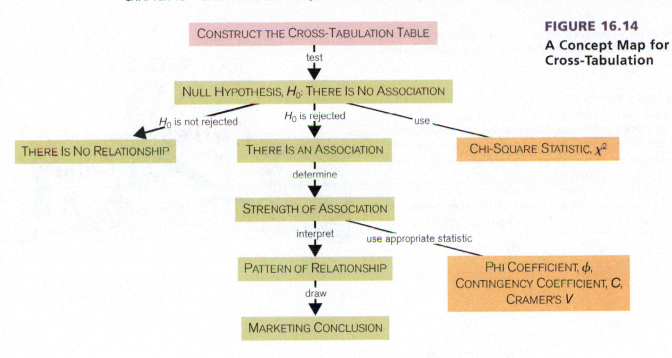

FIGURE 16.14
A Concept Map for Cross-Tabulation

WHAT WOULD YOU DO?

General Mills' Curves Cereal: Helping Women Achieve Their Curves

The Situation

Kendall J. Powell, CEO of General Mills (www.generalmills.com), is constantly faced with the challenge of how to keep up with consumers' changing tastes and preferences. General Mills recently conducted thorough focus groups and survey research on the most important consumers in grocery stores today: women. It is a known fact that three out of every four grocery shoppers in the United States are women, and many of these women are focusing more on their health and the nutritious value of foods. Although there are many cereals on the market with the same amount of valuable vitamins and minerals, such as Total or Kellogg's Smart Start, General Mills decided to design a product specifically for women.

Dietitian Roberta Duyff claims that women do not get enough nutrients such as calcium or folic acid from day to day. According to Duyff, "It is great that a woman can now increase her intake of these important nutrients with a simple bowl of cereal for breakfast, and if you add milk, the vitamin D in milk makes the calcium in both the fortified cereal and milk itself more absorbable." This is one way in which General Mills saw an advantage—convenience for the woman. She can grab a bowl in the morning and start off her day with the nutrients she needs. Not only is the convenience of the product an incentive to market it, but focus group findings also indicated that women like to have a product of their own. In fact, according to Megan Nightingale, assistant marketing manager at General Mills, "Our research has shown that women are looking for something that's nutritious, fast, convenient, and has a good taste."

In 2007, General Mills, in partnership with Curves International, launched Curves Cereal (www.curvesfoods.com). This new cereal of lightly sweetened toasted flakes of whole grain rice and wheat is available in two delicious flavors, Whole Grain Crunch and Honey Crunch. Both have fewer than 200 calories per serving and contain a least 33 percent of the recommended amounts of whole grains and 2 grams of fiber. They also are an excellent source of several important vitamins and minerals.

A telephone survey was conducted to determine the preference for and consumption of Curves and the relative importance that women attached to a cereal being nutritious, fast, convenient, and good tasting.

The Marketing Research Decision

1. What is the relative importance of the four variables (nutritious, fast, convenient, and good taste) in influencing women to buy Curves cereal? What type of analysis should be conducted?
   a. Frequency distribution of the importance attached to the four factors
   b. Mean levels of importance of the four variables
   c. Cross-tabulation of Curves cereal purchases with the importance of the four variables: chi-square analysis
   d. Cross-tabulation of Curves cereal purchases with the importance of the four variables: Cramer's V
   e. All of the above

2. Discuss the role of the type of data analysis you recommend in enabling Kendall J. Powell to understand women's preference for and consumption of Curves cereal.

The Marketing Management Decision

1. Advertising for Curves cereal should stress which of the four factors?
   a. Nutrition
   b. Quick consumption
   c. Convenience
   d. Good taste
   e. All of the above

(continued)

2. Discuss how the management-decision action that you recommend to Kendall J. Powell is influenced by the type of data analysis you suggested earlier and by the findings of that analysis.

What Kendall J. Powell Did

Kendall J. Powell decided to focus on nutrition, quick consumption, and convenience. General Mills markets Curves cereal by using the idea that women do not have the time or patience to remember all the vitamins and minerals they need each day to stay healthy. Curves cereal makes it convenient. Simply pour yourself a bowl of cereal and you will get many of the important nutrients you need. To complement Curves cereal, in 2007 General Mills also launched Curves Chewy Granola bars in Chocolate Peanut and Strawberries and Cream varieties. As of 2011, General Mills was one of the largest food companies in the world.[8]

Software Applications

We describe the programs available in the four statistical packages for conducting frequency analysis followed by cross-tabulations. In SPSS the main program is FREQUENCIES. It produces a table of frequency counts, percentages, and cumulative percentages for the values of each variable and gives all of the associated statistics. DESCRIPTIVES and MEANS procedures can also be used as discussed in Exhibit 16.1. In Excel, the DATA > DATA ANALYSIS > HISTOGRAM function computes the descriptive statistics. The output

EXHIBIT 16.1
Computer Programs for Frequencies

SPSS

The main program in SPSS is FREQUENCIES. It produces a table of frequency counts, percentages, and cumulative percentages for the values of each variable. It gives all of the associated statistics. If the data are interval scaled and only the summary statistics are desired, the DESCRIPTIVES procedure can be used. All of the statistics computed by DESCRIPTIVES are available in FREQUENCIES. However, DESCRIPTIVES is more efficient, because it does not sort values into a frequency table. An additional program, MEANS, computes means and standard deviations for a dependent variable over subgroups of cases defined by independent variables.

Excel

The DATA > DATA ANALYSIS > HISTOGRAM function computes the descriptive statistics. The output produces the mean, standard error, median, mode, standard deviation, variance, range, minimum, maximum, sum, count, and confidence level. Frequencies can be selected under the histogram function. A histogram can be produced in bar format.

Minitab

The main function is STAT > DESCRIPTIVE STATISTICS. The output values include the mean, median, mode, standard deviation, minimum, maximum, and quartiles. A histogram in a bar chart or graph can be produced from the GRAPH > HISTOGRAM selection.

SAS

The SUMMARY STATISTICS task provides summary statistics including basic summary statistics, percentile summary statistics, and more advanced summary statistics including confidence intervals, t statistics, coefficient of variation, and sums of squares. It also provides graphical displays including histograms. The ONE-WAY FREQUENCIES task can be used to generate frequency tables as well as binomial and chi-square tests.

produces all the measures of location and variability that we have discussed. Frequencies can be selected under the HISTOGRAM function and a histogram can be produced in bar format. In Minitab, the main function is STAT > DESCRIPTIVE STATISTICS. The output includes the measures of location and variability. A histogram in the form of a bar chart or graph can be produced from the GRAPH > HISTOGRAM selection. In SAS, SUMMARY STATISTICS task provides summary statistics and also provides graphical displays including histograms. The ONE-WAY FREQUENCIES task can be used to generate frequency tables.

The major cross-tabulation program in SPSS is CROSSTABS (Exhibit 16.2). This program displays the cross-classification tables and provides cell counts, row and column percentages, the chi-square test for significance, and all the measures of the strength of the association that have been discussed. The INSERT > PIVOT TABLE function performs cross-tabulations in Excel. To do additional analysis or customize data, select a different summary function, such as maximum, minimum, average, or standard deviation. The Chi-square test can be accessed under FORMULAS > INSERT FUNCTION > CHITEST. In Minitab, cross-tabulations and chi-square are under the STAT > TABLES function. Each of these features must be selected separately under the TABLES function. In SAS, TABLE ANALYSIS will display the cross-classification table and provide cell counts, row and column percentages, the chi-square test for significance, and all the measures of strength of the association that have been discussed (see Exhibit 16.2).

SPSS and Excel Computerized Demonstration Movies

We have developed computerized demonstration movies that give step-by-step instructions for running all the SPSS and Excel programs that are discussed in this book. These demonstration movies can be downloaded from the Web site for this book. The instructions for running these demonstration movies are given in Exhibit 15.2.

SPSS and Excel Screen Captures with Notes

The step-by-step instructions for running the various SPSS and Excel programs discussed in this book are also illustrated in screen captures with appropriate notes. These screen captures can be downloaded from the Web site for this book.

EXHIBIT 16.2
Computer Programs for Cross-Tabulation

SPSS
The major cross-tabulation program is CROSSTABS. This programs will display the cross-classification tables and provide cell counts, row and column percentages, the chi-square test for significance, and all the measures of the strength of the association that have been discussed.

Excel
The INSERT > PIVOT TABLE function performs cross-tabulations in Excel. To do additional analysis or customize data, select a different summary function, such as maximum, minimum, average, or standard deviation. The Chi-square test can be accessed under FORMULAS > INSERT FUNCTION > CHITEST.

Minitab
In Minitab, cross-tabulations and chi-square are under the STAT > TABLES function. Each of these features must be selected separately under the Tables function.

SAS
The major cross-tabulation task is called TABLE ANALYSIS. This task will display the cross-classification table and provide cell counts, row and column percentages, the chi-square test for significance, and all the measures of strength of the association that have been discussed.

SPSS Windows

The main program in SPSS is FREQUENCIES. It produces a table of frequency counts, percentages, and cumulative percentages for the values of each variable, as well as all of the associated statistics. If the data are interval scaled and only the summary statistics are desired, the DESCRIPTIVES procedure can be used. All of the statistics computed by DESCRIPTIVES are available in FREQUENCIES. DESCRIPTIVES is more efficient, however, because it does not sort values into a frequency table. Moreover, the DESCRIPTIVES procedure displays summary statistics for several variables in a single table and can also calculate standardized values (z scores). The EXPLORE procedure produces summary statistics and graphical displays, either for all cases or separately for groups of cases. Mean, median, variance, standard deviation, minimum, maximum, and range are some of the statistics that can be calculated.

To select these procedures, click the following:

Analyze > Descriptive Statistics > Frequencies . . .

or   Analyze > Descriptive Statistics > Descriptives . . .

or   Analyze > Descriptive Statistics > Explore . . .

The major cross-tabulation program is CROSSTABS. This program will display the cross-classification tables and provide cell counts, row and column percentages, the chi-square test for significance, and all the measures of the strength of the association that have been discussed.

To select this procedure, click the following:

Analyze > Descriptive Statistics > Crosstabs . . .

Detailed Steps: Overview

Detailed step-by-step instructions for running the SPSS programs for the data analysis presented in this chapter can be downloaded from the Web site for this book in two forms: (1) computerized demonstration movies, and (2) screen captures. In addition, these steps are illustrated in the following sections. These steps are given for PASW STATISTICS 18 and IBM SPSS STATISTICS 19; they are essentially the same in both these versions. The steps in the earlier versions are about the same with minor differences in the labeling of some of the boxes. The demonstration movies, and screen captures for the earlier versions, have also been posted on the Web site.

Detailed Steps: Frequencies

Detailed steps are presented for running frequencies on attitude toward Nike (see Table 16.1) and for plotting the histogram (see Figure 16.4).

1. Select ANALYZE on the SPSS menu bar.
2. Click DESCRIPTIVE STATISTICS, and select FREQUENCIES.
3. Move the variable "Attitude toward Nike [attitude]" to the VARIABLE(S) box.
4. Click STATISTICS.
5. Select MEAN, MEDIAN, MODE, STD. DEVIATION, VARIANCE, and RANGE.
6. Click CONTINUE.
7. Click CHARTS.
8. Click HISTOGRAMS, then click CONTINUE.
9. Click OK.

Detailed Steps: Cross-Tabulations

We give detailed steps for running the cross-tabulation of gender and usage of Nike shoes given in Table 16.3 and calculating the chi-square, contingency coefficient, and Cramer's V.

1. Select ANALYZE on the SPSS menu bar.
2. Click DESCRIPTIVE STATISTICS, and select CROSSTABS.

3. Move the variable "User Group [usergr]" to the ROW(S) box.
4. Move the variable "Sex [sex]" to the COLUMN(S) box.
5. Click CELLS.
6. Select OBSERVED under COUNTS, and select COLUMN under PERCENTAGES.
7. Click CONTINUE.
8. Click STATISTICS.
9. Click CHI-SQUARE, PHI, and CRAMER'S *V.*
10. Click CONTINUE.
11. Click OK.

Experiential Learning

Categorical Data Analysis

In this experiential exercise, you will learn how to run frequencies and cross-tabulations using SPSS. Go to the textbook Web site and download the following SPSS system file: KitKat.sav. Also, download the actual taste-test instructions to customers: TasteTest.doc. These files refer to the Nestlé taste test presented in Chapter 9. Here, respondents were asked to taste three different samples of the Kit Kat candy bar. Two of the samples were the currently marketed version of Kit Kat. One of the samples was a new reduced-fat version of the Kit Kat candy bar that had not been put into the market yet. In order to minimize an effect from the presentation order (e.g., respondents might tend to prefer the first or the last one presented), the order of presentation was changed for the different respondents.

1. Read the taste-test instructions of TasteTest.doc.

2. Open KitKat.sav. Double-click the icon.

3. Check data by running frequencies.
   Check distributions for the following variables: rotation, sex, age, differen, and prefer.

Menu Bar
   ANALYZE
      DESCRIPTIVE STATISTICS
         FREQUENCIES
            Transfer each of the five variables in the
   FREQUENCIES window.
            Click OK.
   Check the distribution of the "State" variable.

Menu Bar
   ANALYZE
      DESCRIPTIVE STATISTICS
         FREQUENCIES
            Select "State" in the FREQUENCIES window.
               CHARTS
                  BAR CHARTS
                     CONTINUE
                        OK

4. Analyze results for the taste test using SPSS.

   Refer to the frequency distributions you just created in the preceding check data section to answer the following questions:

   a. Which of these three demographic variables (sex, age, and state) did the designers of this taste test want to have

   equal representation across the possible values of the demographic variables?

   b. What is the mode in the distribution of "state"?

   c. What percentage of the respondents preferred the new reduced-fat version of Kit Kat (the "different sample," in this case)? What percent preferred the currently marketed version of Kit Kat? What percent expressed no preference between the two versions?

5. Do cross-tabulation analysis to determine if a relationship exists between sex and preference for the new version of the Kit Kat candy bar. Before your analysis, write down what are the H_0 and H_1 for cross-tabbing "sex" and "prefer." Conduct the first cross-tabulation analysis as follows:

Menu Bar
   DATA
      SELECT CASES
         ALL CASES
            Click OK.
Menu Bar
   ANALYZE
      DESCRIPTIVE STATISTICS
         CROSSTABS
            Select "prefer" for ROW(S) and "sex" for
   COLUMN(S)
               Click STATISTICS. Select CHI-SQUARE.
   Click CONTINUE.
               Click CELLS. Under PERCENTAGES,
   check COLUMN
                  Click CONTINUE. Then click OK.
   After examining your results, what decision do you make regarding H_0 and H_1 now?

6. What are the H_0 and H_1 for cross-tabulating "sex" and "prefer" when only those stating a preference are considered?

   Conduct the second cross-tabulation analysis as follows:

Menu Bar
   DATA
      SELECT CASES
         IF
            Prefer <= 2
               CONTINUE
                  OK

Menu Bar	Click STATISTICS. Select CHI-SQUARE.
ANALYZE	Click CONTINUE.
DESCRIPTIVE STATISTICS	Click CELLS. Under PERCENTAGES,
CROSSTABS	check COLUMN.
Select "prefer" for ROWS(S) and "sex" for	Click CONTINUE. Then click OK.
COLUMN(S).	What decision do you make regarding H_0 and H_1 now?

Excel

This section gives the detailed steps for running the Excel programs for conducting the analysis discussed in this chapter.

Detailed Steps: Overview

Detailed step-by-step instructions for running the Excel programs for the data analysis presented in this chapter can be downloaded from the Web site for this book in two forms: (1) computerized demonstration movies, and (2) screen captures. In addition, these steps are illustrated in the following sections. These steps are given for Excel 2007 and Excel 2010; they are essentially the same in both these versions. The steps in the earlier versions are about the same with minor differences in how "Data Analysis" is accessed and the labeling of some of the boxes. The demonstration movies, and screen captures for the earlier versions, have also been posted on the Web site.

Detailed Steps: Frequencies

We give detailed steps for running frequencies on attitude toward Nike (see Table 16.1) using Excel.

1. Select DATA tab.
2. In the ANALYSIS group, select DATA ANALYSIS.
3. The DATA ANALYSIS window pops up.
4. Select HISTOGRAM from the DATA ANALYSIS window.
5. Click OK.
6. The HISTOGRAM pop-up window appears on screen.
7. The HISTOGRAM window has two portions:
   a. INPUT
   b. OUTPUT OPTIONS
8. INPUT portion asks for two inputs.
   a. Click in the INPUT RANGE box and select (highlight) all 45 rows under ATTITUDE. $D$2: $D$46 should appear in the input range box.
   b. Do not enter anything into the BIN RANGE box. (Note that this input is optional; if you do not provide a reference, the system will take values based on range of the data set.)
9. In the OUTPUT portion of pop-up window, select the following options:
   a. NEW WORKBOOK
   b. CUMULATIVE PERCENTAGE
   c. CHART OUTPUT
10. Click OK.
11. Note that the default chart output size is very small. Click the histogram diagram and drag it on the corners to view it better.

Detailed Steps: Cross-Tabulations

We show the detailed steps for running the cross-tabulation of sex and usage of Nike shoes given in Table 16.3.

1. Select INSERT (Alt + N).
2. Click on PIVOT TABLE. The PIVOT TABLE window pops up.

3. Select columns A to D and rows 1 to 46. "$A$1:$D$46" should appear in the range box.
4. Select NEW WORKSHEET in the CREATE PIVOT TABLE window.
5. Click OK.
6. Drag variables into the layout on the left in the following format:

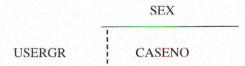

USERGR   CASENO

7. Right click on SUM OF CASENO in the lower-right corner. Select "VALUE FIELD SETTINGS".
8. Under "SUMMARIZE VALUE FIELD BY" select COUNT.
9. Click OK.

Summary

Basic data analysis provides valuable insights and guides the rest of the data analysis as well as the interpretation of the results. A frequency distribution should be obtained for each variable in the data. This analysis produces a table of frequency counts, percentages, and cumulative percentages for all the values associated with that variable. It indicates the extent of out-of-range, missing, or extreme values. The mean, mode, and median of a frequency distribution are measures of central tendency. The variability of the distribution is described by the range and the variance or standard deviation.

The general procedure for hypothesis testing involves eight steps. Formulate the null and the alternative hypotheses, select an appropriate test statistic, choose the level of significance (α), calculate the value of the test statistic, and determine the probability associated with the test statistic calculated from the sample data under the null hypothesis. Alternatively, determine the critical value associated with the test statistic. Compare the probability associated with the test statistic with the level of significance specified or, alternatively, determine whether the calculated value of the test statistic falls into the rejection or the nonrejection region. Accordingly, make the decision to reject or not reject the null hypothesis, and arrive at a conclusion.

Cross-tabulations are tables that reflect the joint frequency distribution of two or more variables. In cross-tabulation, the cell percentages can be computed either column-wise, based on column totals, or row-wise, based on row totals. The general rule is to compute the percentages in the direction of the independent variable, across the dependent variable. The chi-square statistic provides a test of the statistical significance of the observed association in a cross-tabulation. The phi coefficient, contingency coefficient, and Cramer's V provide measures of the strength of association between the variables.

Key Terms and Concepts

Frequency distribution 439	Null hypothesis 446	p value 449
Measures of location 443	Alternative hypothesis 446	Critical value 450
Mean 443	One-tailed test 447	Cross-tabulation 451
Mode 443	Two-tailed test 447	Contingency tables 452
Median 443	Test statistic 448	Chi-square statistic 454
Measures of variability 445	Type-I error 448	Chi-square distribution 455
Range 445	Level of significance 448	Phi coefficient 456
Variance 445	Type-II error 448	Contingency coefficient 456
Standard deviation 445	Power of a test 448	Cramer's V 456

Suggested Cases and Video Cases

Running Case with Real Data

1.1 Hewlett-Packard

Comprehensive Cases with Real Data

3.1 Bank of America   3.2. McDonald's   3.3. Boeing

Comprehensive Brief Harvard Business School Cases

4.1 TruEarth Healthy Foods: Market Research for a New Product Introduction (4065)
4.2 The Springfield Nor'easters: Maximizing Revenues in the Minor Leagues (2510)
4.3 Metabical: Positioning and Communications Strategy for a New Weight-Loss Drug (4240)
4.4 Saxonville Sausage Company (2085)

Online Video Case

16.1. Marriott

Live Research: Conducting a Marketing Research Project

1. Each team can conduct the entire analysis or the data analysis can be split between teams with different teams conducting a different type of analysis. It is helpful to run a frequency count for every variable. This gives a good feel for the data.
2. Calculate the measures of location (mean, median, and mode) and measures of variability (range and standard deviation) for each variable.
3. Relevant associations can be examined by conducting cross-tabulations. Procedures should be specified for categorizing interval or ratio-scaled variables. In this process, it is helpful to examine the frequency distributions.

Acronyms

The statistics associated with frequencies can be summarized by the acronym FREQUENCIES:

F requency histogram
R ange
E stimate of location: mean
Q uotients: percentages
U ndulation: variance
E stimate of location: mode
N umbers or counts
C umulative percentage
I ncorrect and missing values
E stimate of location: median
S hape of the distribution

The salient characteristics of cross-tabulations can be summarized by the acronym TABULATE:

T wo variables at a time
A ssociation and not causation is measured
B ased on expected cell count of at least five
U nderstood easily by managers
L imited number of categories
A ssociated statistics
T wo ways to calculate percentages
E xpected cell frequencies

Review Questions

1. Describe the procedure for computing frequencies.
2. What measures of location are commonly computed for frequencies?
3. What measures of variability are commonly computed for frequencies?
4. What is the major difference between cross-tabulation and frequency distribution?
5. What is the general rule for computing percentages in cross-tabulation?
6. Describe the chi-square distribution.
7. What is meant by the expected cell frequency?
8. How is the chi-square statistic calculated?
9. When is it meaningful to determine the strength of association in a cross-tabulation?
10. What statistics are available for determining the strength of association in cross-tabulation?
11. Discuss the reasons for the frequent use of cross-tabulations. What are some of its limitations?

Applied Problems

1. In each of the following situations, formulate the null and alternative hypotheses.
   a. A new product will be introduced if it is preferred by more than 70 percent of the consumers in the target market.
   b. A new commercial will be aired if the average preference for it exceeds 5.8 on a 7-point scale.
   c. A company will start selling its products online if more than 55 percent of the consumers express a preference for online purchasing.
   d. The average price of a pair of jeans available in the marketplace exceeds $45.
   e. Less than 40 percent of the people approve of the job that President Obama is doing.
   f. The mean familiarity with banks is different from 4.0 on a 7-point scale.
2. In each of the following situations, indicate the statistical analysis you would conduct and the appropriate test or test statistic that should be used.
   a. Respondents in a survey of 1,000 households were classified as heavy, medium, light, or nonusers of ice cream. They also were classified as being in high-, medium-, or low-income categories. Is the consumption of ice cream related to income level?
   b. In a survey using a representative sample of 2,000 households from the Synovate consumer panel, the respondents were asked whether they preferred to shop at Sears. The sample was divided into small and large households based on a median split of household size. Does preference for shopping in Sears vary by household size?
3. The current advertising campaign for a major soft-drink brand would be changed if less than 30 percent of the consumers like it.
   a. Formulate the null and alternative hypotheses.
   b. Discuss the type-I and type-II errors that could occur in hypothesis testing.
4. A major department store chain is having an end-of-season sale on refrigerators. The number of refrigerators sold during this sale at a sample of 10 stores was:

   80   110   0   40   70   80   100   50   80   30

   a. Compute the mean, mode, and median. Which measure of central tendency is most appropriate in this case and why?
   b. Compute the variance and the standard deviation.
   c. Construct a histogram, and discuss whether this variable is normally distributed.
5. In a study measuring households' familiarity with downloading pictures from the Internet, the following results were obtained (1 = not at all familiar, 7 = very familiar).

Level of Familiarity	Number of Households
1	22
2	26
3	34
4	40
5	32
6	28
7	18

   a. Convert the number of household into percentages.
   b. Calculate the cumulative percentages.
   c. Construct a histogram with familiarity on the x-axis and frequency on the y-axis.
   d. Calculate the mean, median, and mode of the distribution.
6. A research project examining the impact of income on the consumption of gourmet foods was conducted. Each variable was classified into three levels of high, medium, and low. The following results were obtained.

		Income		
		Low	Medium	High
Consumption of	Low	25	15	10
Gourmet	Medium	10	25	15
Foods	High	15	10	25

a. Is the relationship between income and consumption of gourmet food significant?
b. Is the relationship between income and consumption of gourmet food strong?
c. What is the pattern of the relationship between income and consumption of gourmet food?
7. A pilot survey was conducted with 30 respondents to examine Internet usage for personal (nonprofessional) reasons. The following table contains the resulting data giving each respondent's sex (1 = male, 2 = female), familiarity with the Internet (1 = very unfamiliar, 7 = very familiar), Internet usage in hours per week, attitude toward Internet and toward technology, both measured on a 7-point scale (1 = very unfavorable, 7 = very favorable), and whether the respondent shopped or banked online (1 = yes, 2 = no).

a. Obtain the frequency distribution of familiarity with the Internet. Calculate the relevant statistics.
b. For the purpose of cross-tabulation, classify respondents as light or heavy users. Those reporting 5 hours or less usage should be classified as light users and the remaining as heavy users. Run a cross-tabulation of sex and Internet usage. Interpret the results. Is Internet usage related to one's sex?

SPSS Data File

Excel Data File

				Internet Usage Data			
Respondent Number	Sex	Familiarity	Internet Usage	Attitude Toward Internet	Attitude Toward Technology	Usage of Internet: Shopping	Usage of Internet: Banking
1	1.00	7.00	14.00	7.00	6.00	1.00	1.00
2	2.00	2.00	2.00	3.00	3.00	2.00	2.00
3	2.00	3.00	3.00	4.00	3.00	1.00	2.00
4	2.00	3.00	3.00	7.00	5.00	1.00	2.00
5	1.00	7.00	13.00	7.00	7.00	1.00	1.00
6	2.00	4.00	6.00	5.00	4.00	1.00	2.00
7	2.00	2.00	2.00	4.00	5.00	2.00	2.00
8	2.00	3.00	6.00	5.00	4.00	2.00	2.00
9	2.00	3.00	6.00	6.00	4.00	1.00	2.00
10	1.00	9.00	15.00	7.00	6.00	1.00	2.00
11	2.00	4.00	3.00	4.00	3.00	2.00	2.00
12	2.00	5.00	4.00	6.00	4.00	2.00	2.00
13	1.00	6.00	9.00	6.00	5.00	2.00	1.00
14	1.00	6.00	8.00	3.00	2.00	2.00	2.00
15	1.00	6.00	5.00	5.00	4.00	1.00	2.00
16	2.00	4.00	3.00	4.00	3.00	2.00	2.00
17	1.00	6.00	9.00	5.00	3.00	1.00	1.00
18	1.00	4.00	4.00	5.00	4.00	1.00	2.00
19	1.00	7.00	14.00	6.00	6.00	1.00	1.00
20	2.00	6.00	6.00	6.00	4.00	2.00	2.00
21	1.00	6.00	9.00	4.00	2.00	2.00	2.00
22	1.00	5.00	5.00	5.00	4.00	2.00	1.00
23	2.00	3.00	2.00	4.00	2.00	2.00	2.00
24	1.00	7.00	15.00	6.00	6.00	1.00	1.00
25	2.00	6.00	6.00	5.00	3.00	1.00	2.00
26	1.00	6.00	13.00	6.00	6.00	1.00	1.00
27	2.00	5.00	4.00	5.00	5.00	1.00	1.00
28	2.00	4.00	2.00	3.00	2.00	2.00	2.00
29	1.00	4.00	4.00	5.00	3.00	1.00	2.00
30	1.00	3.00	3.00	7.00	5.00	1.00	2.00

Group Discussion

1. "Because cross-tabulation has certain basic limitations, this technique should not be used extensively in commercial marketing research." Discuss as a small group.

2. "Why waste time doing basic data analysis? Why not just conduct sophisticated multivariate data analysis (see Chapter 15)?" Discuss.

Hewlett-Packard Running Case

Review the Hewlett-Packard (HP) case, Case 1.1, and questionnaire given toward the end of the book. Go to the Web site for this book and download the HP data file.

1. Calculate the frequency distribution for each variable in the data file. Examine the distribution to get a feel for the data.

2. Cross-tabulate the recoded questions q4 (overall satisfaction with HP), q5 (would recommend HP), and q6 (likelihood of choosing HP) with the recoded demographic characteristics. Interpret the results.

3. Cross-tabulate the recoded questions on price sensitivity (q9_5per and q9_10per) with the recoded demographic characteristics. Interpret the results.

ONLINE VIDEO CASE 16.1

MARRIOTT: Marketing Research Leads to Expanded Offerings

Visit **www.pearsonhighered.com/malhotra** to read the video case and view the accompanying video. Marriott: Marketing Research Leads to Expanded Offerings highlights Marriott's discovery from focus groups and survey research that it could have many types of hotels serving different market segments, and that these market segments, although all providing the same basic needs, would not compete with each other. The case can be used as a springboard for students to design a short survey regarding a comparison in consumer perceptions about the various Marriott brands in the chain—in light of the chapter's objectives, discuss various hypotheses the researcher can test and what frequency distributions and cross-tabulations can be performed in light of those hypotheses. Specific marketing research questions on this and the previous chapters are posed in the video case.

Data Analysis: Hypothesis Testing Related to Differences

Source: AP Image/Oscar Sosa.

LEARNING OBJECTIVES

After reading this chapter, the student should be able to:

1. Understand the role of the *t* distribution in testing hypotheses that are related to differences.

2. Explain how to test the hypothesis related to one sample.

3. Describe how hypothesis testing changes when there are two independent samples rather than one, and when testing for differences in proportions rather than means.

4. Discuss how to test a hypothesis for paired samples.

5. Explain the analysis of variance procedure for testing a hypothesis related to more than two samples.

6. Illustrate the application of hypothesis testing to social media.

" While groups such as users or nonusers of a brand are similar in many ways, making statistical comparisons between such groups on their attitude toward a brand can be very revealing. **"**

Jennifer Garvey
Director, Marketing Services, Verizon Information Services, Dallas–Ft. Worth, Texas

Loyalty Versus Promiscuity and Convenience Versus Price

As of 2011, grocery-store shoppers have actually been able to save money by spending more. How is this possible? Through the Internet, consumers now have access to a rewards and rebate program offered by grocery stores and other merchants. Programs, such as Microrebate Investing, move a percentage of a loyal consumer's purchases directly into an investment account. These programs are designed for customers at all income levels, with no prequalifications to membership. This is only one of many ways in which supermarkets and grocery stores are attempting to build customer loyalty.

A recent study examined the differences between 138 loyal shoppers (LS) and 110 promiscuous (disloyal) shoppers (PS) of a major supermarket. Both groups of shoppers were asked to indicate the importance of 15 shopping attributes on a 7-point scale (1 = not important, 7 = very important). Based on the two-independent-samples t-tests, which are used to test the hypothesis of differences between means of two samples, significant differences were identified on 5 of the 15 attributes, as indicated in the following below.

Although the promiscuous shoppers were motivated by the low prices, the loyal shoppers gave significantly greater importance to convenience (access, parking, and opening hours) and displays and decor. Thus, even supermarkets such as Winn-Dixie (www.winn-dixie.com) that offer lower prices, albeit with a more limited product selection, cannot compete on the basis of price alone. To attract loyal shoppers, they must offer convenience, good aisle displays, and attractive internal decor.[1]

Attribute	Mean Importance Rating		Significance Level
	PS	LS	
Low prices	6.30	6.14	0.044
Convenient access	6.24	6.49	0.045
Convenient parking	6.17	6.63	0.030
Convenient opening hours	5.99	6.46	0.001
Attractive displays and decor	4.67	5.14	0.026

Overview

Chapter 16 described basic data analysis, including frequency distributions, cross-tabulation, and the general procedure for hypothesis testing including tests for association. As explained in that chapter, hypothesis-testing procedures are classified as tests of associations or tests of differences. This chapter presents tests for examining hypotheses related to differences, as in the opening vignette.

The parametric tests presented in this chapter assume that the data are at least interval scaled. We first discuss the case for difference in means for one sample followed by hypothesis testing for two samples. We then make the extension to more than two samples and also examine hypothesis testing associated with differences in proportions. Figure 17.1 briefly explains the focus of the chapter, the relation of this chapter to the previous ones, and the steps of the marketing research process on which this chapter concentrates. Figure 17.2 provides an overview of the topics discussed in this chapter and how they flow from one to the next.

Help for running the SPSS and Excel programs used in this chapter is provided in four ways: (1) detailed step-by-step instructions are given later in the chapter, (2) you can download (from the Web site for this book) computerized demonstration movies illustrating these step-by-step instructions, (3) you can download screen captures with notes illustrating these step-by-step instructions, and (4) you can refer to the Study Guide and Technology Manual, a supplement that accompanies this book.

Hypothesis Testing Related to Differences

Chapter 16 considered hypothesis testing related to associations. These hypotheses are of the form that two variables are associated with or related to each other. For example, the values of homes purchased are related to the buyers' incomes. Here the focus is on hypothesis testing related to differences. These hypotheses are of the form that two variables are different from each other, for example, that people living in the suburbs have higher incomes than people living in

FIGURE 17.1

Relationship of Hypothesis Testing Related to Differences to the Previous Chapters and the Marketing Research Process

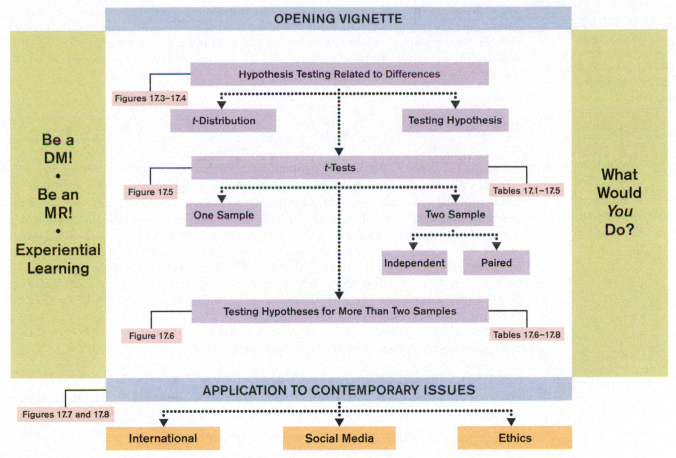

FIGURE 17.2

Hypothesis Testing Related to Differences: An Overview

the downtown areas. A classification of hypothesis-testing procedures for examining differences is presented in Figure 17.3. These procedures are related to examining differences in means or proportions.

First, we focus on hypothesis-testing procedures examining differences in means. These procedures also are called **parametric tests**, because they assume that the variables of interest are measured on at least an interval scale, for example, that the average household spends more than $100 per month on cellular phone services. Here, the monthly expenditure on cellular phone services is measured on a ratio scale. The most popular parametric test is the *t*-test conducted for examining hypotheses about means. The *t*-test can be conducted on the means of one sample or two samples of observations. In the case of two samples, the samples can be independent or paired. The opening vignette provided an application of a *t*-test for the difference in means of two independent samples—loyal shoppers and promiscuous shoppers. All *t*-tests are based on the *t* distribution.

The *t* Distribution

Parametric tests provide inferences for making statements about the means of parent populations. A **t-test** is commonly used for this purpose. This test is based on the *Student's t* statistic.

parametric tests
Hypothesis-testing procedures that assume the variables of interest are measured on at least an interval scale.

t-test
A univariate hypothesis test using the *t* distribution, which is used when the standard deviation is unknown and the sample size is small.

FIGURE 17.3

Hypothesis Tests Related to Differences

t statistic
A statistic that assumes the variable has a symmetric bell-shaped distribution and the mean is known (or assumed to be known) and the population variance is estimated from the sample.

The **t statistic** is calculated by assuming that the variable is normally distributed, the mean is known, and the population variance is estimated from the sample. Assume that the random variable X is normally distributed, with mean μ and unknown population variance σ^2, which is estimated by the sample variance s^2. Recall that the standard deviation of the sample mean, $\overline{X}$, is estimated as

$$s_{\overline{x}} = s/\sqrt{n}$$

Thus,

$$t = (\overline{X} - \mu)/s_{\overline{x}}$$

is t distributed with $n - 1$ degrees of freedom.

t distribution
A symmetric bell-shaped distribution that is useful for small-sample ($n < 30$) testing.

The **t distribution** is similar to the normal distribution in appearance. Both distributions are bell shaped and symmetric. However, the t distribution has more area in the tails and less in the center than the normal distribution. This is because population variance σ^2 is unknown and is estimated by the sample variance s^2. Given the uncertainty in the value of s^2, the observed values of t are more variable than those of z. Thus, we must go a larger number of standard deviations from zero to encompass a certain percentage of values from the t distribution than is the case with the normal distribution. As the number of degrees of freedom increases, however, the t distribution approaches the normal distribution. In fact, for large samples of 120 or more the t distribution and the normal distribution are virtually indistinguishable. Table 4 in the Appendix of Statistical Tables shows selected percentiles of the t distribution. Although normality is assumed, the t-test is quite robust to departures from normality.

Hypothesis Testing Based on the t Statistic

For the special case when the t statistic is used, the general procedure for hypothesis testing discussed in the previous chapter is applied as follows (see Figure 17.4).

1. Formulate the null (H_0) and the alternative (H_1) hypotheses.
2. Select the appropriate formula for the t statistic.

FIGURE 17.4

Conducting t-Tests

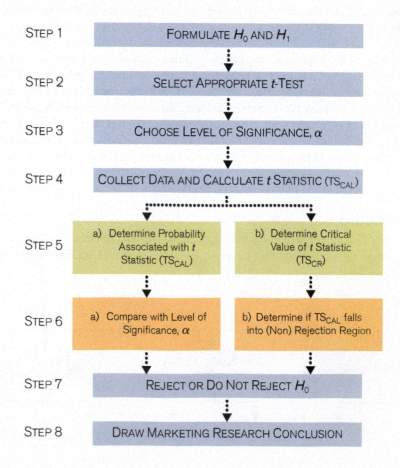

3. Select a significance level, α, for testing H_0. Typically, the 0.05 level is selected.
4. Take one or two samples and compute the mean and standard deviation for each sample. Calculate the t statistic assuming H_0 is true. Calculate the degrees of freedom.
5. Estimate the probability of getting a more extreme value of the statistic from Table 4 in the Appendix of Statistical Tables. Alternatively, calculate the critical value of the t statistic. Note that in determining the critical value of the test statistic the area to the right of the critical value is either α or $\alpha/2$. It is α for a one-tailed test and $\alpha/2$ for a two-tailed test.
6. Compare the probability computed in step 5 with the significance level selected in step 3. (Alternatively, compare the calculated t statistic in step 4 with the critical value determined in step 5.)
7. Make the statistical decision to reject or not reject the null hypotheses. If the probability computed in step 5 is smaller than the significance level selected in step 3, reject H_0. If the probability is larger, do not reject H_0. (Alternatively, if the absolute value of the calculated t statistic in step 4 is larger than the absolute value of the critical value determined in step 5, reject H_0. If the absolute calculated value is smaller than the absolute critical value, do not reject H_0). Failure to reject H_0 does not necessarily imply that H_0 is true. It only means that the true state is not significantly different from that assumed by H_0.[2]
8. Express the conclusion reached by the t-test in terms of the marketing research problem.

The general procedure for conducting t-tests is illustrated in the following sections, beginning with the one-sample case.

One-Sample *t*-Test

In marketing research, the researcher often is interested in making statements about a single variable against a known or given standard. The following are examples of such statements:

- The market share for the new product will exceed 15 percent.
- At least 65 percent of customers will like the new package design.
- The average monthly household expenditure on groceries exceeds $500.
- The new service plan will be preferred by at least 70 percent of the customers.

These statements can be translated into null hypotheses that can be tested using a one-sample test, such as the z-test or the t-test. In the case of a t-test for a single mean, the researcher is interested in testing whether the population mean conforms to a given hypothesis (H_0). In the opening vignette, the hypothesis that the mean rating of each attribute for the overall sample (loyal shoppers and promiscuous shoppers combined) exceeded 5.0 would be tested using the one-sample t-test.

Test for a Single Mean

Suppose a new machine attachment would be introduced if it receives a mean of greater than 7 on a 10-point scale. A sample of 20 purchase engineers is shown the attachment and asked to evaluate it. The results indicate a mean rating of 7.9 with a standard deviation of 1.6. A significance level of $\alpha = 0.05$ is selected. Should the part be introduced?

$$H_0: \mu \leq 7.0$$

$$H_1: \mu > 7.0$$

$$t = (\overline{X} - \mu)/s_{\overline{x}}$$

$$s_{\overline{x}} = s/\sqrt{n}$$

$$s_{\overline{x}} = 1.6/\sqrt{20} = 1.6/4.472 = 0.358$$

$$t = (7.9 - 7.0)/0.358 = 0.9/0.358 = 2.514$$

The degrees of freedom for the t statistic to test a hypothesis about one mean are $n - 1$. In this case, $n - 1 = 20 - 1$, or 19. From Table 4 in the Appendix of Statistical Tables, the probability of getting a more extreme value than 2.514 is less than 0.05; actually, it is less than 0.025.

(Alternatively, the critical t value for 19 degrees of freedom and a significance level of 0.05 is 1.7291, which is less than the calculated value.) Therefore, the null hypothesis is rejected, favoring the introduction of the part.

Note that if the population standard deviation was assumed to be known as 1.5, rather than estimated from the sample, a **z-test** would be appropriate. In this case, the value of the z statistic would be:

$$z = (\overline{X} - \mu)/\sigma_{\overline{x}}$$

where

$$\sigma_{\overline{x}} = 1.5/\sqrt{20} = 1.5/4.472 = 0.335$$

and

$$z = (7.9 - 7.0)/0.335 = 0.9/0.335 = 2.687$$

From Table 2 in the Appendix of Statistical Tables, the probability of getting a more extreme value of z than 2.687 is 0.0036, which is less than 0.05. (Alternatively, the critical z value for a one-tailed test and a significance level of 0.05 is 1.645, which is less than the calculated value.) Therefore, the null hypothesis is rejected, and we can reach the same conclusion arrived at earlier by the t-test.

The one-sample t-test is further illustrated using the data of Table 17.1. This table contains data from two samples, each consisting of 10 respondents. Sample 1 consists of teenagers (ages 13 to 19), whereas sample 2 consists of adults 20 years old or older. The respondents were asked to indicate their preferences for Disney theme parks, immediately before and immediately after their visits, using a 10-point scale. This table gives the data for only

z-test
A univariate hypothesis test using the standard normal distribution.

SPSS Data File

Excel Data File

TABLE 17.1 Preference for Disney Before and After Visiting the Resort

Respondent Number	Sample	Preference for Disney	
		Before	After
1	1.00	7.00	9.00
2	1.00	6.00	8.00
3	1.00	5.00	8.00
4	1.00	6.00	9.00
5	1.00	4.00	7.00
6	1.00	6.00	8.00
7	1.00	5.00	7.00
8	1.00	4.00	7.00
9	1.00	7.00	9.00
10	1.00	5.00	7.00
11	2.00	3.00	7.00
12	2.00	4.00	8.00
13	2.00	4.00	7.00
14	2.00	3.00	6.00
15	2.00	6.00	8.00
16	2.00	5.00	8.00
17	2.00	4.00	9.00
18	2.00	3.00	6.00
19	2.00	3.00	7.00
20	2.00	5.00	9.00

20 respondents, because we want to show the calculations of the basic statistics by hand. These hand calculations are shown to provide a better idea of the basic concepts. In practice, the sample size is much larger. The analysis of such large data sets is illustrated later in the chapter in the Experiential Learning exercise, which analyzes the data for 146 respondents in a survey for Musial University.

The null hypothesis for Table 17.1, based on a previous survey, is that the mean preference for sample 1 before entering the theme park (PREFERENCE 11) will be 5.0. It is possible that the preference for Disney parks could have increased or decreased since the last survey. Hence, the hypotheses are as follows:

$$H_0: \mu = 5.0$$

$$H_1: \mu \neq 5.0$$

We show the calculations for a one-sample t-test by hand. It can be seen that the mean preference of sample one before entering the park is 5.5 with a standard deviation of 1.08. These calculations are as follows:

$$\overline{X}_1 = (7 + 6 + 5 + 6 + 4 + 6 + 5 + 4 + 7 + 5)/10$$

$$= 55/10$$

$$= 5.5$$

$$\Sigma(X_i - \overline{X}_1)^2 = (7 - 5.5)^2 + (6 - 5.5)^2 + (5 - 5.5)^2 + (6 - 5.5)^2$$

$$+ (4 - 5.5)^2 + (6 - 5.5)^2 + (5 - 5.5)^2$$

$$+ (4 - 5.5)^2 + (7 - 5.5)^2 + (5 - 5.5)^2$$

$$= 2.25 + 0.25 + 0.25 + 0.25 + 2.25 + 0.25 + 0.25$$

$$+ 2.25 + 2.25 + 0.25$$

$$= 10.50$$

$$s_{x_1}^2 = 10.50/(10 - 1)$$

$$s_{x_1} = \sqrt{(10.5)/(10 - 1)}$$

$$= 1.08$$

Therefore,

$$t = (\overline{X} - \mu)/s_{\overline{x}}$$

$$s_{\overline{x}} = s/\sqrt{n}$$

$$s_{\overline{x}} = 1.08/\sqrt{10} = 1.08/3.16 = 0.342$$

$$t = (5.5 - 5.0)/0.342 = 0.5/0.342 = 1.46$$

With 9 degrees of freedom, the probability of getting a more extreme value of t exceeds 0.10 (see Table 4 in the Appendix of Statistical Tables). Hence, the null hypothesis cannot be rejected. In other words, the mean preference of sample one before entering the theme park is no different from 5.0. Thus, based on the results, the preference of teenagers has not changed since the last survey. This one-sample t-test was also conducted using a statistical program. The results are described in Table 17.2. The corresponding SPSS and Excel outputs with explanatory remarks can be downloaded from the Web site for this book.

Test for a Single Proportion

Such hypotheses relate to the proportion or percentage pertaining to a single population. Examples might be "the proportion of brand-loyal users of Coca-Cola exceeds 0.2" or "70 percent of the households eat out at least once a week." The procedure for testing a hypothesis associated with a proportion for one sample was illustrated in Chapter 16 in the section titled "A General Procedure for Hypothesis Testing."

TABLE 17.2 One-Sample *t*-Test: Teenagers' Preference Before Visiting

Variable	Number of Cases	Mean	Standard Deviation	Standard Error of Mean
Preference Before Visiting Test Value = 5	10	5.5000	1.080	0.342

| Mean Difference | 95% Confidence Interval | | *t* Value | Degrees of Freedom | Two-Tailed Significance |
	Lower	Upper			
0.50	−0.273	1.273	1.46	9	0.177

Two-Sample *t*-Test

As can be seen from Figure 17.3, the two samples can be either independent or paired. Furthermore, the hypotheses and the related tests could pertain to examining differences in means or proportions.

Two Independent Samples

independent samples
Two samples that are not experimentally related. The measurement of one sample has no effect on the values of the other sample.

Samples drawn randomly from different populations are termed **independent samples**. Several hypotheses in marketing relate to parameters from two different populations:

- The populations of users and nonusers of a brand differ in terms of their perceptions of the brand.
- The high-income consumers spend more on entertainment than low-income consumers.
- The proportion of brand-loyal users in segment I is more than the proportion in segment II.
- The proportion of households with an Internet connection in the United States exceeds that in Germany.

In each of the foregoing hypotheses, we have two different populations: users and nonusers, high-income and low-income consumers, segment I and segment II, and the United States and Germany. Samples drawn randomly from these populations will be independent samples. In the opening vignette, the loyal shoppers (LS) and the promiscuous shoppers (PS) constituted two independent samples. For the purpose of analysis, data pertaining to different groups of respondents (e.g., males and females) are generally treated as independent samples even though the data may pertain to the same survey. As in the case for one sample, the hypotheses can relate to means or proportions. The first two hypotheses in the introduction to this section relate to means, whereas the latter two relate to proportions.

MEANS   In the case of means for two independent samples, the hypotheses take the following form:

$$H_0: \mu_1 = \mu_2$$

$$H_1: \mu_1 \neq \mu_2$$

In the opening vignette, the hypotheses tested for the importance of each attribute by the loyal shoppers (LS) and the promiscuous shoppers (PS) were:

$$H_0: \mu_{LS} = \mu_{PS}$$

$$H_1: \mu_{LS} \neq \mu_{PS}$$

The two populations are sampled and the means and variances computed based on samples of sizes n_1 and n_2. If both populations are found to have the same variance, a pooled variance estimate is computed from the two sample variances as follows:

$$s^2 = \frac{\sum_{i=1}^{n_1}(X_{i_1} - \overline{X}_1)^2 + \sum_{i=1}^{n_2}(X_{i_2} - \overline{X}_2)^2}{n_1 + n_2 - 2}$$

or

$$s^2 = \frac{(n_1 - 1)s_1^2 + (n_2 - 1)s_2^2}{n_1 + n_2 - 2}$$

The standard deviation of the test statistic can be estimated as

$$s_{\bar{x}_1 - \bar{x}_2} = \sqrt{s^2 \left(\frac{1}{n_1} + \frac{1}{n_2} \right)}$$

The appropriate value of t can be calculated as

$$t = \frac{(\overline{X}_1 - \overline{X}_2) - (\mu_1 - \mu_2)}{s_{\bar{x}_1 - \bar{x}_2}}$$

The degrees of freedom in this case are $(n_1 + n_2 - 2)$.

If the two populations have unequal variances, an exact t cannot be computed for the difference in sample means. For example, consumers in the United States have well-developed preferences for brands, whereas such preference formation seems to be weak for consumers in developing countries. Thus, preferences for shampoo brands in the United States are expected to exhibit lower variance as compared to preferences in the developing country of Sierra Leone in West Africa. In these cases, an approximation to t is computed. The number of degrees of freedom in this case is usually not an integer, but a reasonably accurate probability can be obtained by rounding to the nearest integer.[3] In this case, the standard deviation of the test statistic can be estimated as follows:

$$s_{\bar{x}_1 - \bar{x}_2} = \sqrt{\left(\frac{s_1^2}{n_1} + \frac{s_2^2}{n_2} \right)}$$

An **F-test** of sample variance can be performed if it is not known whether the two populations have equal variance. In this case, the hypotheses are

$$H_0: \sigma_1^2 = \sigma_2^2$$
$$H_1: \sigma_1^2 \neq \sigma_2^2$$

F-test
A statistical test of the equality of the variances of two populations.

The **F statistic** is computed from the sample variances as follows:

$$F_{(n_1-1),(n_2-1)} = \frac{s_1^2}{s_2^2}$$

F statistic
A statistic that is calculated as the ratio of two sample variances, with the larger sample variance in the numerator.

where

s_1^2 = sample variance for sample 1, the larger sample variance

s_2^2 = sample variance for sample 2, the smaller sample variance

n_1 = size of sample 1

n_2 = size of sample 2

$n_1 - 1$ = degrees of freedom for sample 1

$n_2 - 1$ = degrees of freedom for sample 2

As can be seen, the critical value of the **F distribution** depends on two sets of degrees of freedom—those in the numerator and those in the denominator. The critical values of F for various degrees of freedom for the numerator and denominator are given in Table 5 of the Appendix of Statistical Tables. If the probability of F is greater than the significance level α, H_0 is not rejected and t based on the pooled variance estimate can be used. However, if the probability of F is less than or equal to α, H_0 is rejected and t based on a separate variance estimate is used.

F distribution
A frequency distribution that depends upon two sets of degrees of freedom: the degrees of freedom in the numerator and the degrees of freedom in the denominator.

Using the data of Table 17.1, we can examine whether the teenagers have a different preference (PREFERENCE 11) than adults (PREFERENCE 21) before entering the park. A two-independent-samples t-test is conducted. Because the difference could be in either direction, a two-tailed test is used.

First, we show the calculations by hand. It can be seen that sample one has a mean of 5.5 with a standard deviation of 1.080 or a variance of $(1.080)^2 = 1.166$. These calculations were illustrated earlier for the one-sample test. Similar calculations will show that sample two has a mean of 4.0 and a standard deviation of 1.054 or a variance of 1.111.

$$\overline{X}_2 = (3 + 4 + 4 + 3 + 6 + 5 + 4 + 3 + 3 + 5)/10$$

$$= 40/10$$

$$= 4.0$$

$$\Sigma(X_i - \overline{X}_2)^2 = (3 - 4)^2 + (4 - 4)^2 + (4 - 4)^2 + (3 - 4)^2 + (6 - 4)^2$$

$$+ (5 - 4)^2 + (4 - 4)^2 + (3 - 4)^2 + (3 - 4)^2 + (5 - 4)^2$$

$$= 1 + 0 + 0 + 1 + 4 + 1 + 0 + 1 + 1 + 1$$

$$= 10$$

Therefore,

$$s^2_{x_2} = 10/(10 - 1)$$

$$= 1.111$$

The value of the F statistic for testing the equality of variances is

$$F_{9,9} = (1.166/1.111) = 1.05$$

Note that the F-test of sample variances has a probability that exceeds 0.05. Alternatively, the critical vale of $F_{9,9}$ is 3.18 (see Table 5 in the Appendix of Statistical Tables). Accordingly, the null hypothesis of equal variances cannot be rejected, and the t-test based on the pooled variance estimate should be used.

The pooled variance estimate can be calculated as

$$s^2 = \frac{(10 - 1)1.166 + (10 - 1)1.111}{10 + 10 - 2}$$

$$= 1.139$$

Thus,

$$s_{\overline{x}_1 - \overline{x}_2} = \sqrt{1.139\left(\frac{1}{10} + \frac{1}{10}\right)}$$

$$= 0.477$$

Under the null hypothesis, the value of the t statistic is

$$t = (5.5 - 4.0)/0.477$$

$$= 3.14$$

The t value is 3.14, and with $20 - 2 = 18$ degrees of freedom this gives us a probability of 0.006, which is less than the significance level of $0.05/2 = 0.025$. Alternatively, the critical value of t is 2.1009 (see Table 4 in the Appendix of Statistical Tables). Note that in determining the critical value of the test statistic (TS_{CR}), the area to the right of the critical value is $\alpha/2$ for the two-tail test being conducted. Because the calculated value of t exceeds the critical value, the null hypothesis of equal means is rejected. Thus, the conclusion is that the teenagers and adults differ in their preferences for Disney theme parks before entering the park. This two-sample t-test also was conducted using statistical software, and the results are presented in Table 17.3; the corresponding SPSS and Excel outputs with explanatory notes can be downloaded from the Web site. Table 17.3 also shows the t-test using separate variance estimates, because most computer programs automatically conduct the t-test both ways.

TABLE 17.3 *t*-Test for Independent Samples: Preference Before Visiting

Variable Sample	Number of Cases	Mean	Standard Deviation	Standard Error of Mean
Teenagers	10	5.5000	1.080	0.342
Adults	10	4.0000	1.054	0.333

SPSS Output File

Mean Difference = 1.5000
Test for Equality of Variances: $F = 1.05$; $P = 0.472$

t-Test for Equality of Means

Variances	*t* Value	Degrees of Freedom	Two-Tailed Significance	Standard Error of Difference	95% CI for Difference
Equal	3.14	18.00	0.006	0.477	(0.497, 2.503)
Unequal	3.14	17.99	0.006	0.477	(0.497, 2.503)

Excel Output File

Suppose we wanted to determine whether teenagers have a higher preference for Disney parks as compared to adults. In this case, a one-tailed rather than a two-tailed test should be used. The hypotheses are as follows:

$$H_0: \mu_1 \leq \mu_2$$
$$H_1: \mu_1 > \mu_2$$

The *t* statistic is calculated in exactly the same way as in the two-tailed test. In determining the critical value of the test statistic (TS_{CR}), however, the area to the right of the critical value is α for a one-tailed test (see Figure 17.5). In this case, the critical value of *t* is 1.7341, leading to a similar conclusion as arrived at earlier.

A two-tailed test is more conservative than the corresponding one-tailed test. If a hypothesis is rejected using a two-tailed test, then it will also be rejected using the corresponding one-tailed test. As explained in Chapter 16, the area to the right of the critical value is α for a one-tail test and $\alpha/2$ for a two-tail test. In other words, the absolute value of the critical value is larger for a two-tailed test than it is for a one-tailed test. As another application of the *t*-test, consider the following example.

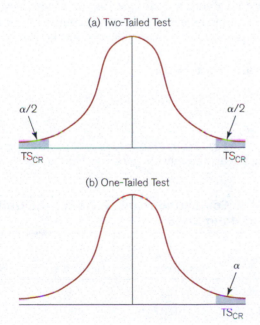

(a) Two-Tailed Test

(b) One-Tailed Test

FIGURE 17.5

Calculating the Critical Value of the Test Statistic: TS$_{CR}$ for Two-Tailed and One-Tailed Tests

Research in Action

Gen Xers Versus Baby Boomers in a Quest for Luxury

The American Express Platinum Luxury Survey was conducted among a random cross-section of 770 wealthy U.S. consumers:

- 270 consumers with a household income over $200,000 of any age group
- 250 Baby Boomers with a household income of $125,000 to $199,999 (born between 1946–1964, average age of 50 years)
- 250 Gen Xers with a household income of $125,000 to $199,999 (born between 1964–1976, average age of 34 years)

The survey was administered through several channels, including one-on-one interviews at luxury stores. The survey found that Gen Xers' annual spending far exceeds that of Baby Boomers in a number of luxury-good categories, including:

- 60 percent more than Baby Boomers on fragrance, cosmetics, and beauty products ($3,235 vs. $2,017)
- 47 percent more on fashion accessories ($6,066 vs. $4,116)
- 36 percent more on men's and women's clothing ($23,027 vs. $16,924)
- 32 percent more on wines and liquors ($3,922 vs. $2,966)
- 33 percent more than Boomers for entertainment ($3,629 vs. $2,722)
- 17 percent more for personal/health services ($3,324 vs. $2,838)

Two-sample t-tests indicated that all of these differences were statistically significant at the 0.05 level. The conclusion was that luxurious high-end products, such as those marketed by Gucci, Louis Vuitton, Hermes, Cartier, Christian Dior, and so on, should be targeted at Gen Xers, while at the same time maintaining relationships through marketing campaigns or continual quality service with the Baby Boomers.[4]

Source: © Cultura/Alamy.

In this example, we tested the difference between means. A similar test is available for testing the difference between proportions for two independent samples.

PROPORTIONS A case involving proportions for two independent samples is illustrated in Table 17.4, which gives the number of users and nonusers of jeans in the United States and Hong Kong. Is the proportion of users the same in the United States and Hong Kong samples?

The null and alternative hypotheses are

$$H_0: \pi_1 = \pi_2$$

$$H_1: \pi_1 \neq \pi_2$$

A z-test is used as in testing the proportion for one sample. This is a large-sample problem. The samples from each population must be large so that the binomial distribution of sample

TABLE 17.4 Comparing Jeans Users for the United States and Hong Kong

Sample	Usage of Jeans		Row Totals
	Users	Nonusers	
United States	160	40	200
Hong Kong	120	80	200
Column totals	**280**	**120**	

proportions can be approximated by the normal distribution. As a rule of thumb, both np and $n(1 - p)$ must be greater than 10 for each sample. In this case, the test statistic is given by

$$z = \frac{p_1 - p_2}{s_{p_1 - p_2}}$$

In the test statistic, the numerator is the difference between the proportions in the two samples, p_1 and p_2. The denominator is the standard error of the difference in the two proportions and is given by

$$s_{p_1 - p_2} = \sqrt{p(1 - p)\left[\frac{1}{n_1} + \frac{1}{n_2}\right]}$$

where

$$p = \frac{n_1 p_1 + n_2 p_2}{n_1 + n_2}$$

A significance level of $\alpha = 0.05$ is selected. Given the data of Table 17.4, the test statistic can be calculated as:

$$p_1 = 160/200 = 0.8$$

$$p_2 = 120/200 = 0.6$$

$$p_1 - p_2 = 0.8 - 0.6 = 0.20$$

$$p = (200 \times 0.8 + 200 \times 0.6)/(200 + 200) = 0.7$$

$$s_{p_1 - p_2} = \sqrt{0.7 \times 0.3\left[\frac{1}{200} + \frac{1}{200}\right]} = 0.04583$$

$$z = 0.2/0.4583 = 4.36$$

Given a two-tailed test, the area to the right of the critical value is $\alpha/2$, or 0.025. Hence, the critical value of the test statistic is 1.96. Because the calculated value exceeds the critical value, the null hypothesis is rejected. Thus, the proportion of users (0.80 for the United States and 0.60 for Hong Kong) is significantly different for the two samples.

As an alternative to the parametric z-test considered earlier, one could also use the cross-tabulation procedure to conduct a chi-square test, especially if the samples are not large. In this case, we will have a 2×2 table. One variable will be used to denote the sample and will assume the value 1 for sample one and the value of 2 for sample two. The other variable will be the dichotomous variable of interest. The t-test in this case is equivalent to a chi-square test for independence in a 2×2 contingency table. The relationship is

$$\chi^2_{.95(1)} = t^2_{.05(n_1 + n_2 - 2)}$$

For large samples, the t distribution approaches the normal distribution, thus the t-test and the z-test are equivalent.

Paired Samples

In many marketing research applications, the observations for the two groups are not selected from independent samples. Rather, the observations relate to **paired samples** in that the two sets of observations relate to the same respondents. Examples of hypotheses related to paired samples include the following:

- Shoppers consider brand name to be more important than price when purchasing fashion clothing.
- Households spend more money on pizza than on hamburgers.
- The proportion of households who subscribe to a daily newspaper exceeds the proportion subscribing to magazines.
- The proportion of a bank's customers who have a checking account exceeds the proportion who have a savings account.

paired samples
In hypothesis testing, the observations are paired so that the two sets of observations relate to the same respondents.

Each of the foregoing hypotheses relates to the same set of people. Furthermore, the first two hypotheses relate to means, whereas the latter two relate to proportions.

MEANS A sample of respondents can rate two competing brands, indicate the relative importance of two attributes of a product, or evaluate a brand at two different times. The difference in these cases is examined by a **paired-samples *t*-test**. In the opening vignette, the hypothesis that the loyal shoppers (LS) consider convenient parking more important than low prices would be tested by using a paired-samples *t*-test. To compute *t* for paired samples, the paired-difference variable (D) is formed and its mean and variance calculated. Then, the *t* statistic is computed. The degrees of freedom are $n - 1$, where n is the number of pairs. The relevant formulas are as follows:

paired-samples *t*-test
A test for differences in the means of paired samples.

$$H_0: \mu_D = 0$$

$$H_1: \mu_D \neq 0$$

$$t_{n-1} = \frac{\overline{D} - \mu_D}{s_{\overline{D}}}$$

where

$$\overline{D} = \frac{\sum_{i=1}^{n} D_i}{n}$$

$$s_D = \sqrt{\frac{\sum_{i=1}^{n}(D_i - \overline{D})^2}{n - 1}}$$

$$s_{\overline{D}} = \frac{s_D}{\sqrt{n}}$$

For the data given in Table 17.1, a paired *t*-test could be used to determine if there is a difference in the preference before (PREFERENCE 11) and after visiting the Disney theme park (PREFERENCE 12) for respondents in sample one. First, the hand calculations are shown. The mean difference between the variables is 2.4, with a standard deviation of 0.516 and a standard error of 0.163. These calculations are as follows:

$$\overline{D} = ((9 - 7) + (8 - 6) + (8 - 5) + (9 - 6) + (7 - 4)$$

$$+ (8 - 6) + (7 - 5) + (7 - 4) + (9 - 7) + (7 - 5))/10$$

$$= (2 + 2 + 3 + 3 + 3 + 2 + 2 + 3 + 2 + 2)/10$$

$$= 2.4$$

$$s_D^2 = ((2 - 2.4)^2 + (2 - 2.4)^2 + (3 - 2.4)^2 + (3 - 2.4)^2$$

$$+ (3 - 2.4)^2 + (2 - 2.4)^2 + (2 - 2.4)^2 + (3 - 2.4)^2$$

$$+ (2 - 2.4)^2 + (2 - 2.4)^2)/(10 - 1)$$

$$= (0.16 + 0.16 + 0.36 + 0.36 + 0.36$$

$$+ 0.16 + 0.16 + 0.36 + 0.16 + 0.16)/9$$

$$= 0.2667$$

TABLE 17.5 *t*-Tests for Paired Samples: Teenagers

Variable	Number of Pairs	Correlation	Two-Tailed Significance	Mean	Standard Deviation	Standard Error of Mean
Preference Before Visiting				5.5000	1.080	0.342
	10	0.881	0.001			
Preference After Visiting				7.9000	0.876	0.277

Paired Differences

Mean	Standard Deviation	Standard Error of Mean	*t* Value	Degrees of Freedom	Two-Tailed Significance	95% Confidence Interval
22.4000	0.516	0.163	−14.70	9	0.000	(−2.769, −2.031)

Thus,

$$s_D = \sqrt{0.2667}$$
$$= 0.516$$

and

$$s_{\overline{D}} = \frac{0.516}{\sqrt{10}}$$
$$= 0.516/3.162$$
$$= 0.163$$

This results in a *t* value of

$$2.4/0.163$$
$$= 14.7$$

With $10 - 1 = 9$ degrees of freedom, this has a probability of less than 0.001. Alternatively, the critical value of *t* for the two-tailed test is 2.2622 (see Table 4 in the Appendix of Statistical Tables), which is less than the calculated value of 14.7. Hence, the null hypothesis is rejected. Therefore, the preferences of teenagers before and after visiting the Disney theme parks are significantly different. This paired-samples *t*-test also was conducted using statistical software, and the resulting output is shown in Table 17.5. The corresponding SPSS and Excel outputs with explanatory notes can be downloaded from the Web site for this book. A one-tailed test would have the same value for the *t* statistic, but the level of significance will be α, rather than $\alpha/2$ (see Figure 17.5). Thus, if we wanted to test whether the preferences after visiting the theme park were significantly greater than before the visit, a one-tailed test would also lead to the rejection of the null hypothesis

$$H_0: \mu_D \le 0$$
$$H_1: \mu_D > 0$$

where

$$D = \text{preference after the visit} - \text{preference before the visit}$$

Note that the computer program tested the difference as Before − After, whereas the hand calculations were based on the difference as After − Before; hence, the negative mean difference and the negative *t* value in the output given in Table 17.5. Another application is provided in the context of determining the effectiveness of advertising.

Research in Action

Rockport Rocks the Shoe Market with Comfort Appeal

In 2011, Rockport's advertising slogan was "Choose to Walk," touting the lightweight and walking comfort of its shoes. This slogan was rendered differently for men and women, however. The TV commercials, as well as the print ads, were carefully tested before they were released to the media. A group of 200 men were asked to respond to a series of 10 scales designed to measure attitude toward Rockport shoes. They were then exposed to the TV commercial as part of an entertaining program. After the program, attitude toward Rockport shoes was again measured using the same 10 scales (see the one-group pretest–posttest design in Chapter 8). A paired *t*-test indicated a significant increase in attitude after exposure to the commercial. Similar testing was done for commercials and print ads geared to women. The TV commercials and the print ads not only fared well in the test, but also were successful in achieving sales growth.[5]

Source: 0571/Avantis/ZUMA Press/Newscom.

PROPORTIONS   The difference in proportions for paired samples can be tested by the chi-square test explained in Chapter 16. In this case, each of the paired variables has two categories resulting in a 2 × 2 table.

Be a DM!	Be an MR!
Nike: Independent and Paired (*t*-Tests)	
As the marketing director for Nike, how would you improve Nike's image and competitive position?	Visit www.nike.com and search the Internet—including social media—as well as your library's online databases to obtain information on the factors consumers use to evaluate competing brands of athletic shoes. The users and nonusers of Nike evaluated the brand on five factors using Likert-type scales. How would you analyze these data using two independent samples and paired-samples *t*-tests?

Social Media

Testing Hypotheses for More Than Two Samples

First, we focus on means followed by proportions for more than two samples. We briefly describe the more general analysis of variance procedure but our emphasis is on one-way analysis of variance.

Means for More than Two Samples

analysis of variance (ANOVA)
A statistical technique for examining the differences among means for two or more populations.

Procedures for examining differences between more than two population means are called **analysis of variance (ANOVA)**. The null hypothesis is that all means are equal. Marketing researchers often are interested in examining the differences in the mean values of more than two groups. For example:

- Do the various segments differ in terms of their volumes of product consumption?
- Do the brand evaluations of groups exposed to different commercials vary?
- Do retailers, wholesalers, and agents differ in their attitudes toward the firm's distribution policies?
- Do the users, nonusers, and former users of a brand differ in their attitudes toward the brand?

The answers to these and similar questions can be determined by conducting ANOVA, as described in Figure 17.6 and explained in this section. Suppose the researcher was interested in examining whether heavy users, medium users, light users, and nonusers of shampoo differed in their preferences for Pert shampoo, measured on a 9-point Likert scale. The null hypothesis that the four groups were not different in their preference for Pert could be tested using ANOVA. When conducting ANOVA, it is necessary to distinguish between dependent and independent variables.

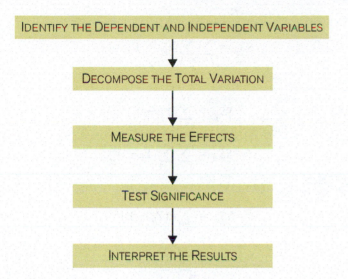

FIGURE 17.6
Conducting One-Way ANOVA

IDENTIFY THE DEPENDENT AND INDEPENDENT VARIABLES   In its simplest form, ANOVA must have a dependent variable (preference for Pert shampoo) that is metric (measured using an interval or ratio scale, see Chapter 9) and one or more independent variables. The independent variables must be categorical (nonmetric), for example, age and income categories. The general ANOVA framework can handle more than one categorical independent variable that define the various groups. **One-way analysis of variance** involves only one categorical variable, or a single **factor** that defines the different samples or groups. These groups also are called **treatment** conditions. Thus, the different independent samples are treated as categories of a single independent variable. The differences in preference of heavy users, medium users, light users, and nonusers would be examined by one-way analysis of variance. In this case, heavy users, medium users, light users, and nonusers of shampoo would constitute different samples or groups and would be treated as categories of a single independent variable called "shampoo usage."

In the opening vignette, suppose the respondents were classified into three groups: loyal shoppers (LS2—loyal to only one supermarket), multiloyal shoppers (MS2—loyal to two or three supermarkets), and promiscuous shoppers (PS2—nonloyal shoppers). The differences in the mean importance ratings attached to each attribute by the LS2, MS2, and PS2 groups would be tested using one-way ANOVA.

In one-way ANOVA, the dependent variable is denoted by Y and the independent variable by X. X is a categorical variable having c categories. There are n observations on Y for each category of X. Thus, the sample size in each category of X is n, and the total sample size $N = n \times c$. Although the sample sizes in the categories of X (the group sizes) are assumed to be equal for the sake of simplicity, this is not a requirement.

DECOMPOSE THE TOTAL VARIATION   In examining the differences among means, one-way ANOVA involves the **decomposition of the total variation** observed in the dependent variable (see Figure 17.6). This variation is measured by the sums of squares corrected for the mean (SS). Analysis of variance is so-named because it examines the variability or variation in the sample (dependent variable) and, based on the variability, determines whether there is reason to believe that the population means differ.

The total variation in Y, denoted by SS_y, can be decomposed into two components:

$$SS_y = SS_{between} + SS_{within}$$

where the subscripts *between* and *within* refer to the categories of X. $SS_{between}$ is the variation in Y related to the variation in the means of the categories of X. It represents variation between the categories of X. In other words, $SS_{between}$ is the portion of the sum of squares in Y related to the independent variable or factor X. For this reason, $SS_{between}$ also is denoted as SS_x. SS_{within} is the variation in Y related to the variation within each category of X. SS_{within} is not accounted for by X. Therefore, it is referred to as SS_{error}. The total variation in Y can be decomposed as:

$$SS_y = SS_x + SS_{error}$$

one-way analysis of variance
An ANOVA technique in which there is only one factor.

factors
Categorical independent variables. All the independent variables must be categorical (nonmetric) to use ANOVA.

treatment
In ANOVA, a particular combination of factor levels or categories.

decomposition of the total variation
In one-way ANOVA, separation of the variation observed in the dependent variable into the variation due to the independent variables plus the variation due to error.

SS_y
The total variation in Y.

$SS_{between}$
Also denoted as SS_x, the variation in Y related to the variation in the means of the categories of X. This represents variation between the categories of X, or the portion of the sum of squares in Y related to X.

SS_{within}
Also referred to as SS_{error}, the variation in Y due to the variation within each of the categories of X. This variation is not accounted for by X.

where

$$SS_y = \sum_{j=1}^{c} \sum_{i=1}^{n} (Y_{ij} - \overline{Y})^2$$

or

$$SS_y = \sum_{i=1}^{N} (Y_i - \overline{Y})^2$$

$$SS_x = \sum_{j=1}^{c} \sum_{i=1}^{n} (\overline{Y}_j - \overline{Y})^2$$

or

$$SS_x = \sum_{j=1}^{c} n(\overline{Y}_j - \overline{Y})^2$$

$$SS_{error} = \sum_{j=1}^{c} \sum_{i=1}^{n} (Y_{ij} - \overline{Y}_j)^2$$

where

Y_i = individual observation

$\overline{Y}_j$ = mean for category j

$\overline{Y}$ = mean over the whole sample, or grand mean

Y_{ij} = ith observation in the jth category

c = number of categories of X

n = number of observations in each category

$N = n \times c$, the total sample size

MEASURE THE EFFECTS   The effects of X on Y are measured by SSx. Because SSx is related to the variation in the means of the categories of X, the relative magnitude of SSx increases as the differences among the means of Y in the categories of X increase. The relative magnitude of SSx also increases as the variations in Y within the categories of X decrease. The strength of the effects of X on Y are measured as follows:

$$\eta^2 = SS_x/SS_y = (SS_y - SS_{error})/SS_y$$

The value of eta^2, η^2, varies between 0 and 1. It assumes a value of 0 when all the category means are equal, indicating that X has no effect on Y. The value of η^2 will be 1 when there is no variability within each category of X but there is some variability between categories. Thus, **eta^2**, η^2, is a measure of the variation in Y that is explained by the independent variable X. Not only can we measure the effects of X on Y, but we can also test for their significance.

eta^2 (η^2)
Statistic that measures the strength of the effects of X (independent variable or factor) on Y (dependent variable); value ranges between 0 and 1.

TEST THE SIGNIFICANCE   In one-way ANOVA, the interest lies in testing the null hypothesis that the category means are equal in the population (see Figure 17.6). In other words,

$$H_0: \mu_1 = \mu_2 = \mu_3 = ... = \mu_c$$

Under the null hypothesis, SS_x and SS_{error} come from the same source of variation. In such a case, the estimate of the population variance of Y can be based on either between-category variation or within-category variation. In other words,

the estimate of the population variance of Y

$$= SS_x/(c - 1)$$

$$= \textbf{Mean square} \text{ due to } X$$

$$= MS_x$$

mean square
The sum of squares divided by the appropriate degrees of freedom.

or

$$= SS_{error}/(N - c)$$

$$= \text{Mean square due to error}$$

$$= MS_{error}$$

The **significance of the overall effect** in terms of the null hypothesis may be tested by the F statistic based on the ratio between these two estimates:

$$F = \frac{SS_x/(c - 1)}{SS_{error}/(N - c)} = \frac{MS_x}{MS_{error}}$$

This statistic follows the F distribution, with $(c - 1)$ and $(N - c)$ degrees of freedom (df). A table of the F distribution is given as Table 5 in the Appendix of Statistical Tables at the end of the book. As mentioned earlier, the F distribution is a probability distribution of the ratios of sample variances. It is characterized by degrees of freedom for the numerator and degrees of freedom for the denominator.[6]

INTERPRET THE RESULTS If the null hypothesis of equal category means is not rejected, then the independent variable does not have a significant effect on the dependent variable. However, if the null hypothesis is rejected, then the effect of the independent variable is significant. In other words, the mean value of the dependent variable will be different for different categories of the independent variable. A comparison of the category mean values will indicate the nature of the effect of the independent variable.

Illustrative Applications of One-Way Analysis of Variance

These concepts are first illustrated with an example showing calculations done by hand followed by calculations using computer analysis. Suppose that a major supermarket is attempting to determine the effect of in-store advertising (X) on sales (Y). In-store advertising is varied at three levels: high, medium, and low. Fifteen stores are randomly selected, and five stores are randomly assigned to each treatment condition. The experiment lasts for 4 weeks. Sales are monitored, normalized to account for extraneous factors (i.e., store size, traffic, and so on), and converted to a 0-to-10 scale. The data obtained (Y_{ij}) are reported in Table 17.6. Again, the sample size ($n = 15$ stores) is limited so that the hand calculations do not become unwieldy.

The null hypothesis is that the category means are equal:

$$H_0: \mu_1 = \mu_2 = \mu_3$$

To test the null hypothesis, the various means and sums of squares are computed as follows:

Category means: $\overline{Y}_j$ 45/5   25/5   20/5
                              = 9   = 5   = 4

Grand mean: $\overline{Y}$ $= (45 + 25 + 20)/15 = 6$

$$SS_y = (10 - 6)^2 + (9 - 6)^2 + (10 - 6)^2 + (8 - 6)^2 + (8 - 6)^2$$
$$+ (6 - 6)^2 + (4 - 6)^2 + (7 - 6)^2 + (3 - 6)^2 + (5 - 6)^2$$
$$+ (5 - 6)^2 + (6 - 6)^2 + (5 - 6)^2 + (2 - 6)^2 + (2 - 6)^2$$
$$= 16 + 9 + 16 + 4 + 4$$
$$+ 0 + 4 + 1 + 9 + 1$$
$$+ 1 + 0 + 1 + 16 + 16$$
$$= 98$$

TABLE 17.6 Effect of In-Store Promotion on Sales

| Store No. | Level of In-Store Promotion | | |
| | Normalized Sales | | |
	High	Medium	Low
1	10	6	5
2	9	4	6
3	10	7	5
4	8	3	2
5	8	5	2

SPSS Data File

Excel Data File

$$SS_x = 5(9 - 6)^2 + 5(5 - 6)^2 + 5(4 - 6)^2$$
$$= 45 + 5 + 20$$
$$= 70$$

$$SS_{error} = (10 - 9)^2 + (9 - 9)^2 + (10 - 9)^2 + (8 - 9)^2 + (8 - 9)^2$$
$$+ (6 - 5)^2 + (4 - 5)^2 + (7 - 5)^2 + (3 - 5)^2 + (5 - 5)^2$$
$$+ (5 - 4)^2 + (6 - 4)^2 + (5 - 4)^2 + (2 - 4)^2 + (2 - 4)^2$$
$$= 1 + 0 + 1 + 1 + 1 + 1 + 1 + 4 + 4 + 0$$
$$+ 1 + 4 + 1 + 4 + 4$$
$$= 28$$

It can be verified that

$$SS_y = SS_x + SS_{error}$$

as follows:

$$98 = 70 + 28$$

The strength of the effects of X on Y are measured as follows:

$$\eta^2 = SS_x/SS_y$$
$$= 70/98$$
$$= 0.714$$

In other words, 71.4 percent of the variation in sales (Y) is accounted for by in-store advertising (X), indicating a strong effect. The null hypothesis can now be tested.

$$F = \frac{SS_x/(c - 1)}{SS_{error}/(N - c)} = \frac{MS_x}{MS_{error}}$$

$$F = \frac{70/(3 - 1)}{28/(15 - 3)}$$

$$= 15.0$$

From Table 5 in the Appendix of Statistical Tables, we see that for 2 and 12 degrees of freedom and $\alpha = 0.05$, the critical value of F is 3.89. Because the calculated value of F is greater than the critical value, the null hypothesis is rejected. Therefore, we can conclude that the population means for the three levels of in-store advertising are indeed different. The relative magnitudes of the means for the three categories indicate that a high level of in-store advertising leads to significantly higher sales. This one-way ANOVA was also conducted using statistical software, and the output is shown in Table 17.7. The corresponding SPSS and Excel outputs with explanatory notes can be downloaded from the Web site for this book.

Proportions for More Than Two Samples

To test differences in proportions for more than two samples, one could also use the cross-tabulation procedure to conduct a chi-square test (see Chapter 16). In this case, we will have a $2 \times c$ table. One variable will be used to denote the sample and will assume the value of 1 for sample one, the value of 2 for sample two, and the value of c for sample c. The other variable will be the dichotomous variable of interest. The various hypothesis-testing procedures for examining differences in means and proportions are summarized in Table 17.8.

TABLE 17.7 One-Way Analysis of Variance

Source of Variation	Sum of Squares	Degrees of Freedom	Mean Square	F	Significance of F
Main effects	70.00	2	35.00	15.00	.001
In-store promotion	70.00	2	35.00	15.00	.001
Explained (between groups)	70.00	2	35.00	15.00	.001
Residual (within groups)	28.00	12	2.33		
Total	**98.00**	**14**	**7.00**		

SPSS Output File

Excel Output File

Research in Action

One-Way Analysis of Variance Favors "Ready to Work" Story

Levi Strauss & Company was battling competition from designer labels and private-label brands. Designers such as Ralph Lauren Polo, Calvin Klein, Guess?, and Tommy Hilfiger, as well as traditional competitors such as Gap, had launched substantial marketing and advertising campaigns. At the same time, JC Penney Company and Sears, Roebuck & Company had strong national branding efforts in place for their own private-label jeans.

In response to such stiff competition, Levi Strauss developed three alternative image themes: "Levi's. They go on"; "They're not Levi's jeans until we say they are"; and "Ready to work." The three themes were tested. Three groups of 150 respondents each were recruited. Each group was asked to evaluate one theme by rating it on a 10-point scale. A one-way ANOVA was conducted to examine the differences in the ratings provided by the three groups. "Ready to work" received significantly higher ratings than the other two alternatives. Thus, this campaign was chosen for roll-out on the national media. As of 2011, Levi Strauss is one of the largest makers of brand-name clothing globally, selling jeans and sportswear under the Levi's, Dockers, and Levi Strauss Signature names in more than 110 countries.[7]

Source: AP Photo/Paul Sakuma.

TABLE 17.8 A Summary of Hypothesis Testing

Sample	Test/Comments
One sample	
Means	t-test, if variance is unknown
	z-test, if variance is known
Proportions	z-test
Two independent samples	
Means	Two-group t-test
	F-test for equality of variances
Proportions	z-test
	Chi-square test
Paired samples	
Means	Paired t-test
Proportions	Chi-square test
More than two samples	
Means	One-way analysis of variance
Proportions	Chi-square test

Be a DM!	Be an MR!
Who Are the Experts, Novices, and Nonusers of Home Computers?	
As the marketing director for Dell, how would you segment the home computer market?	Visit www.dell.com and search the Internet—including social media—as well as your library's online databases to obtain information on computer usage in U.S. households. As a marketing research analyst working for Dell, how would you determine whether the three home-computer usage segments (experts, novices, and nonusers) differ in terms of 10 psychographic characteristics, each measured on a 7-point scale?

Summary Illustration Using the Opening Vignette

Hypotheses about means of one or two populations are commonly examined by using a *t*-test. Different forms of the *t*-test are suitable for testing hypotheses based on one sample, two independent samples, or paired samples. In the opening vignette, the hypothesis that the mean rating of each attribute for the overall sample (loyal shoppers, LS, and promiscuous shoppers, PS) exceeded 5.0 would be tested using the one-sample *t*-test. The hypotheses related to differences in the mean importance ratings attached to each attribute by the LS and the PS would be tested using the two-independent-samples *t*-test. The hypothesis that the LS consider convenient parking to be more important than low prices would be tested by using a paired-samples *t*-test. Similar tests could be used for testing differences in proportions.

One-way ANOVA involves tests of differences in the means of more than two independent samples. The samples are treated as categories of a single independent variable. The null hypothesis of equal means is tested by an *F* statistic, which is the ratio of the mean square related to the independent variable to the mean square related to error. In the opening vignette, suppose the respondents were classified into three groups: loyal shoppers (LS2—loyal to only one supermarket), multiloyal shoppers (MS2—loyal to two or three supermarkets), and promiscuous shoppers (PS2—nonloyal shoppers). The differences in the mean importance ratings attached to each attribute by the LS2, MS2, and PS2 groups would be tested using one-way ANOVA. The differences in the proportion of females among the LS2, MS2, and PS2 could be tested using the cross-tabulation procedure to conduct a chi-square test (see Chapter 16). Figures 17.7 (page 496) and 17.8 (page 497) provide concept maps for conducting *t*-tests and one-way ANOVA, respectively. In these figures, the major concepts are connected by bold arrows using descriptors. Thus, in Figure 17.7, hypothesis testing requires the researcher to formulate H_0 and H_1. Each major concept is described by minor concepts that are connected to that major concept by lines with descriptors. Thus, the formulation of H_0 and H_1 is guided by the norm that H_0 reflects status quo, whereas an effect is expected with H_1. The rest of the figure can be interpreted similarly.

Marketing Research and Social Media

When quantitative data are collected from social media, such as by conducting surveys, all the tests of hypotheses discussed in this chapter can be implemented following the usual procedures. Even in the case of qualitative data, it may be possible to conduct some of these tests if the data are coded appropriately. We illustrate an application of analysis of variance in examining the relationship between social media presence and financial success.

Research in Action

When It Comes to Social Media, Don't Be a Wallflower

Wetpaint, in conjunction with Altimeter Group, conducted a study to examine the relationship between social media presence and financial success. The study showed that the brands most engaged in social media are also experiencing higher financial success rates than those of their non-engaged peers. The study focused on 100 companies from the 2008 Business Week/ Interbrand Best Global Brands survey and their use of the many social media platforms like Facebook, Twitter, blogs, wikis, and forums.

Financial success was measured in terms of percentage revenue growth, percentage gross margin growth, and net margin growth and was treated as the dependent variable. The independent variables were the level and depth of engagement of the companies in social media. Companies were grouped according to their level and depth of engagement into Mavens, Butterflies, Selectives, and Wallflowers and compared as follows:

- Mavens are brands engaged in seven or more channels and have high engagement scores.

- Butterflies are similarly engaged in seven or more channels but have lower-than-average engagement scores.
- Selectives are brands that are engaged in six or fewer channels and have higher-than-average engagement scores.
- Wallflowers are the brands that are engaged in six or fewer channels and have below-average engagement scores.

The researchers segregated the companies into their respective groups and analyzed their respective revenues/ margins, and compared the groups' aggregate averages for each financial metric using analysis of variance. The differences were significant, with Mavens performing the best and Wallflowers the worst in terms of revenue and profit. Thus, when it comes to social media, businesses need to emphasize quality, not just quantity. It is important to keep your Web content fresh while replying to comments as well as building your network and updating your profile status. Don't just check the sites regularly and mechanically: Engage your consumer audience.[8]

Source: "The World's Most Valuable Brands. Who's Most Engaged?," from http://engagementdb.com/Report, accessed October 4, 2010. Used with permission from wetpaint.com.

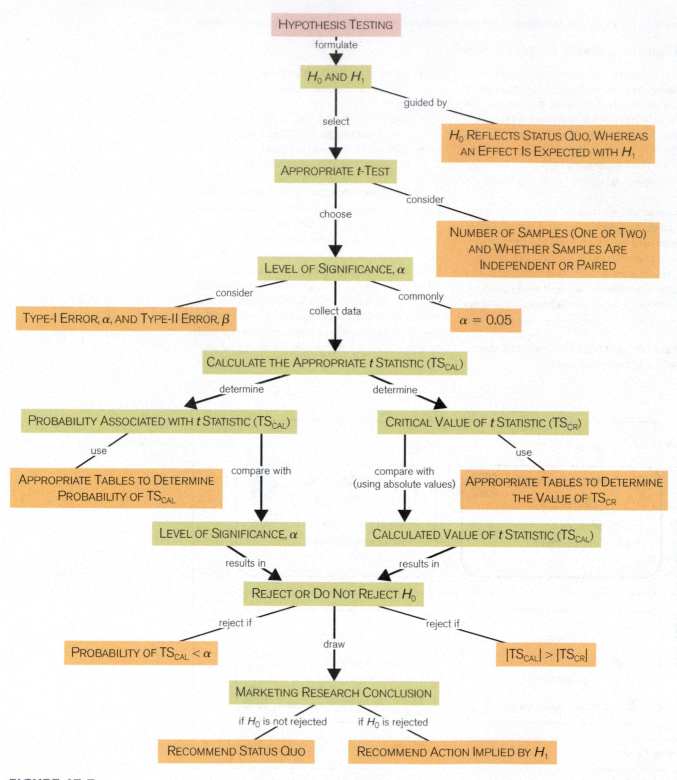

FIGURE 17.7

A Concept Map for Conducting *t*-Tests

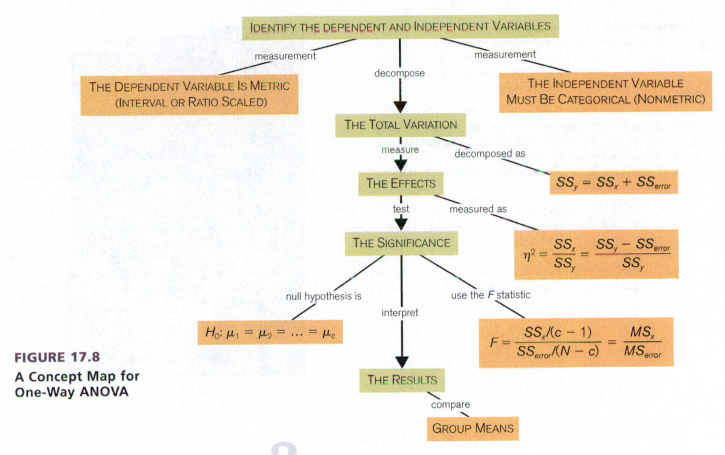

FIGURE 17.8

A Concept Map for One-Way ANOVA

WHAT WOULD YOU DO?

Marriott: Luring Business Travelers

The Situation

Marriott International, Inc. (www.marriott.com) is a leading worldwide hospitality company. Its origins can be traced to a small root-beer stand opened in Washington, D.C., in 1927 by J. Willard and Alice S. Marriott. As of 2011, Marriott International has more than 3,000 lodging properties located in the United States and 67 other countries and territories. Among Marriott's most frequent visitors are its business-travel customers. For many years, business travelers have faced a fundamental problem in finding a comfortable and convenient way to accomplish their jobs in hotel rooms that lack a functional workspace. Although many of the business travelers were not very productive, they did hone important skills, such as writing legibly on top of a comforter, stretching arms beyond maximum length to reach hidden outlets behind or underneath furniture, and squinting to make documents readable by bedside lamplight.

Marriott recognized these unmet needs of its business travelers and wanted to do something about it. Susan Hodapp, brand director for Marriott Hotels, Resorts and Suites, commissioned a survey to determine business travelers' preferences for hotels and the factors that are important in their hotel selection process. Part of the questionnaire focused on the features of the hotel room. Each respondent rated the relative importance of the following factors on a 7-point scale (1 = not at all important, 7 = extremely important): Room décor, room lighting, room furniture, voice and data access in the room, and price of the room per night.

The Marketing Research Decision

1. Marriott would like to determine what features of a hotel room are most important in business travelers' choice of a hotel. What analysis should be conducted?
   a. Two-independent-samples *t*-test: Means
   b. Two-independent-samples *t*-test: Proportions
   c. Paired-samples *t*-test: Means
   d. Paired-samples *t*-test: Proportions
   e. One-way ANOVA

2. Discuss how the type of data analysis you recommend to Susan Hodapp would enable her to understand business travelers' preferences for hotel rooms.

The Marketing Management Decision

1. To lure business travelers, Marriott should focus on:
   a. Room décor
   b. Room lighting
   c. Room furniture
   d. Voice and data access in the room
   e. Price of the room per night

2. Discuss how the management-decision action that you recommend to Susan Hodapp is influenced by the type of data analysis you suggested earlier and by the findings of that analysis.

(continued)

What Susan Hodapp Did

The survey revealed various features business travelers wanted most in their rooms. In response, Marriott introduced its "Room That Works" program, creating a modern-day Renaissance of workspace design. Today, many guest rooms are furnished with upgraded workstations with standard features such as:

- Roomy, oversized desks with plenty of space to spread out papers
- Lighting fixtures that not only produce adequate work-area light, but also feature desk-level outlets and data ports for laptops or other productivity devices
- An ergonomic, adjustable chair that swivels
- Multiple-line telephones with call-waiting feature so guests can use the Internet and receive calls simultaneously

Hodapp said she felt the company's customers wanted added flexibility in a workstation. "Our guests have a compressed time frame to get things done, so we wanted them to be able to modify the work environment for personalized comfort," she said. Therefore, Marriott's workstations feature desks on casters and an arm that swings out of the guestroom desk for additional workspace. Customer satisfaction among the business travelers has increased significantly since the workstations were introduced.[9]

Source: © Kazimierz Jurewicz/Alamy.

Software Applications

The major program for conducting *t*-tests in SPSS is *T* TEST. This program can be used to conduct *t*-tests on a single sample, independent, or paired samples. The available parametric tests in Excel and other spreadsheets include the *T*-TEST, paired two sample for means; *T*-TEST, two independent samples assuming equal variances; *T*-TEST, two independent samples assuming unequal variances; *z*-TEST, two samples for means; and *F*-TEST: two samples for variances (see Exhibit 17.1). Parametric tests available in Minitab under the STAT > BASIC STATISTICS function are *z*-TEST mean, *T*-TEST of the mean, and two-sample *T*-TEST. In SAS, the program *T* TEST can be used.

SPSS and Excel also have programs for conducting analysis of variance. In addition to the basic analysis that we have considered, these programs can also perform more complex analysis. Minitab and SAS also offer programs. Exhibit 17.2 contains a description of the relevant programs for conducting analysis of variance. Refer to the user manuals for these packages for more details.

EXHIBIT 17.1
Computer Programs for *t*-Tests

SPSS

The major program for conducting *t*-tests in SPSS is *T* TEST. This program can be used to conduct *t*-tests on a single sample, independent, or paired samples.

Excel

The available parametric tests in EXCEL and other spreadsheets include the *T*-TEST paired sample for means; *T*-TEST: two independent samples assuming equal variances; *T*-TEST: two independent samples assuming unequal variances; *z*-TEST: two samples for means; and *F*-TEST: two samples for variances.

Minitab

Parametric tests available in MINITAB under the STAT > BASIC STATISTICS function are *z*-TEST mean, *T*-TEST of the mean, and two-sample *T*-TEST.

SAS

In SAS, the program *T* TEST can be used to conduct *t*-tests on independent as well as paired samples.

EXHIBIT 17.2
Computer Programs for One-Way ANOVA

SPSS

One-way ANOVA can be efficiently performed using the program, ONE-WAY ANOVA.

Excel

One-way ANOVA can be accessed from DATA > DATA ANALYSIS > ANOVA: SINGLE FACTOR.

Minitab

ANOVA can be accessed from the STAT > ANOVA function. This function performs one-way ANOVA and can also handle more complex designs. In order to compute the mean and standard deviation, the cross-tabulation function must be used. To obtain F and p values, use the balanced ANOVA.

SAS

The main program for performing analysis of variance is ANOVA. This program can handle data from a wide variety of experimental designs. One-Way ANOVA can be efficiently performed using ONE-WAY ANOVA within the ANOVA task.

SPSS and Excel Computerized Demonstration Movies

We have developed computerized demonstration movies that give step-by-step instructions for running all the SPSS and Excel programs that are discussed in this book. These demonstration movies can be downloaded from the Web site for this book. The instructions for running these demonstration movies are given in Exhibit 15.2.

SPSS and Excel Screen Captures with Notes

The step-by-step instructions for running the various SPSS and Excel programs discussed in this book are also illustrated in screen captures with appropriate notes. These screen captures can be downloaded from the Web site for this book.

SPSS Windows

The major program for conducting t-tests in SPSS is T TEST. This program can be used to conduct t-tests on one sample or independent or paired samples. One-way ANOVA can be efficiently performed using the program One-Way ANOVA. To select these procedures using SPSS for Windows, click:

> Analyze > Compare Means > Means . . .
> Analyze > Compare Means > One-Sample *T test* . . .
> Analyze > Compare Means > Independent-Samples *T test* . . .
> Analyze > Compare Means > Paired-Samples *T test* . . .
> Analyze > Compare Means > One-Way ANOVA . . .

Detailed Steps: Overview

Detailed step-by-step instructions for running the SPSS programs for the data analysis presented in this chapter can be downloaded from the Web site for this book in two forms: (1) computerized demonstration movies, and (2) screen captures. In addition, these steps are illustrated in the following sections. These steps are given for PASW STATISTICS 18 and IBM SPSS STATISTICS 19; they are essentially the same in both these versions. The steps in the earlier versions are about the same with minor differences in the labeling of some of the boxes. The demonstration movies, and screen captures for the earlier versions, have also been posted on the Web site.

Detailed Steps: One-Sample *t*-Test

Provided here are the detailed steps for running a one-sample test on the data of Table 17.1. The null hypothesis is that the mean preference for sample one before entering the theme park is 5.0.

1. Select DATA from the SPSS menu bar.
2. Click SELECT CASES.
3. Check IF CONDITION IS SATISFIED. Then click the IF button.
4. Move SAMPLE [sample] into the SELECT CASES: IF box. Click "=" and then click "1."
5. Click CONTINUE.
6. Check FILTER OUT UNSELECTED CASES.
7. Click OK.
8. Select ANALYZE from the SPSS menu bar.
9. Click COMPARE MEANS and then ONE-SAMPLE *T TEST*.
10. Move Preference Before Visiting [pref1] into the TEST VARIABLE(S) box.
11. Type "5" in the TEST VALUE box.
12. Click OK.

Detailed Steps: Two-Independent-Samples *t*-Test

Next are the detailed steps for running a two-independent-samples *t*-test on the data of Table 17.1. The null hypothesis is that the mean preference for adults and teenagers before visiting Disney theme parks is the same. First, make sure all cases will be included in the analysis.

> Menu Bar
> > DATA
> > > Select CASES.
> > > > Select ALL CASES.
> > > > > Click OK.

Perform the analysis as follows:

1. Select ANALYZE from the SPSS menu bar.
2. Click COMPARE MEANS and then INDEPENDENT-SAMPLES *T TEST*.
3. Move "Preference Before Visiting [pref1]" into the TEST VARIABLE(S) box.
4. Move "Sample [sample]" into the GROUPING VARIABLE box.
5. Click DEFINE GROUPS.
6. Type "1" in the GROUP 1 box and "2" in the GROUP 2 box.
7. Click CONTINUE.
8. Click OK.

Detailed Steps: Paired-Samples *t*-Test

Next are the detailed steps for running a paired-samples *t*-test on the data of Table 17.1. The null hypothesis is that there is no difference in the mean preference of teenagers before and after visiting Disney theme parks.

1. Select DATA from the SPSS menu bar.
2. Click SELECT CASES.
3. Check IF CONDITION IS SATISFIED. Then click the IF button.
4. Move "SAMPLE[sample]" into the SELECT CASES: IF box. Click "=" and then click "1."
5. Click CONTINUE.
6. Check FILTER OUT UNSELECTED CASES.
7. Click OK.
8. Select ANALYZE from the SPSS menu bar.
9. Click COMPARE MEANS and then PAIRED-SAMPLES T TEST.

10. Select "Preference Before Visiting [pref1]" and then select "Preference After Visiting [pref2]." Move these variables into the PAIRED VARIABLES: box.
11. Click OK.

Detailed Steps: One-Way ANOVA

The following are the detailed steps for running a one-way ANOVA on the data of Table 17.6. The null hypothesis is that there is no difference in mean normalized sales for the three levels of in-store promotion.

1. Select ANALYZE from the SPSS menu bar.
2. Click COMPARE MEANS and then ONE-WAY ANOVA.
3. Move "Normalized Sales [sales]" into the DEPENDENT LIST box.
4. Move "In-Store Promotion [promotio]" into the FACTOR box.
5. Click OPTIONS.
6. Click Descriptive.
7. Click CONTINUE.
8. Click OK.

Experiential Learning

Testing Differences

Go to the textbook Web site and download the survey used in interviewing nonreturning students at Musial University (MU), an urban public university in the midsized city of Musial. Although the actual name of the university has been disguised, the research project and the accompanying data are real. The administrators at MU were interested in obtaining the perspectives of "dropout" or "stopout" students so that the administrators at MU could enhance the programs, facilities, and services at MU. Download the actual survey used in this study (Musial Retention Survey.doc) as well as the relevant SPSS system file (Musial Retention Data.sav).

- Read the survey Musial Retention Survey.doc.
- Open SPSS and the SPSS system file Musial Retention Data.sav.
- At the bottom of the SPSS window, click on the tab VARIABLE VIEW.
- Enter LABELS.

Enter abbreviated forms of the names for the questions. For example, Q1 could be "enrolled elsewhere," Q2 could be "educational plans," and so forth. Do this for Q3, Q4, and Q5a through Q5bb. Enter these names directly into each corresponding cell in the LABEL column.

- Enter VALUES for the LABELS.

Enter labels for the possible values for each question. For example, for Q1, a value of "1" should receive a label of "Yes," a value of "2" should receive a label of "No," and so forth. Do this for all questions. For Q5a through Q5bb, the value of "1" should receive a label of "Strongly Disagree," and the value of "10" should receive a label of "Strongly Agree." Enter these names directly into each corresponding cell in the "Values" column by first clicking each cell (initially with "None" entered), then clicking the gray box with three dots that appears in the cell. In the Values window, enter the value (e.g., "1"), enter the label (e.g., "Yes"), and then click the ADD button before clicking the OK button that closes the Values window for the cell.

- Clean the data for all questions except the ID question.

As was done in the Data Prep Experiential Learning Exercise of Chapter 15, "−9" must be recoded to SYSMIS. An alternative method for doing this would be to enter "−9" into each cell in the column MISSING after clicking the VARIABLE VIEW tab at the bottom of the SPSS window. Likewise, the range "11 to highest" must be recoded to SYSMIS.

t-tests

Conduct three *t*-tests comparing the subgroups of Q1 (those enrolled at another institution this semester vs. those who are not) on the following dependent variables:

Q5j: MU encourages students to participate in extracurricular activities.
Q5k: MU offers good recreational facilities to students.
Q5l: The social environment at MU is great.

(What is your null hypothesis (H_0) and alternative hypothesis (H_1) for each of these t-tests?)

In SPSS, take the following steps to examine the means and standard deviations for these three variables:

ANALYZE
  COMPARE MEANS
    MEANS
      MEANS window
        DEPENDENT LIST, enter q5.j[q5.j], q5.k[q5.k], q5.l[q5.l].
          LIST, enter Q1[Q1].
          Click OK.

In SPSS, take the following steps to conduct *t*-tests comparing the subgroups of Q1 on the three dependent variables q5.j, q5.k, and q5.l:

ANALYZE
  COMPARE MEANS

SPSS Data File

(continued)

INDEPENDENT-SAMPLES T TEST
INDEPENDENT-SAMPLES T TEST window
TEST VARIABLE(S), enter q5.j[q5.j], q5.k[q5.k], q5.l[q5.l].
GROUPING VARIABLE, enter Q1[Q1].
DEFINE GROUPS
GROUP 1 = 1
GROUP 2 = 2
Click CONTINUE.
Click OK.

Examine your results by assuming the variance among the groups is equal, and viewing the corresponding cells for each of the three variables under the columns labeled "t" and "Sig (2-tailed)."

One-Way ANOVA

Compare the subgroups of Q2 "educational plans for the future" on the dependent variable of Q5n "I would have very much enjoyed having a football team at MU." First, collapse some of the categories to avoid splintering the subgroups for Q2 with too few cases to allow statistically meaningful comparisons. Do this in the following way:

Recode Grouping Variable Q2:
TRANSFORM
RECODE INTO DIFFERENT VARIABLES
RECODE INTO DIFFERENT VARIABLES window
Select Q2 and move it to NUMERIC VARIABLE -> OUTPUT VARIABLE: window.
Under OUTPUT VARIABLE, type Q2new in the NAME box.
Select OLD AND NEW VALUE.
Under OLD VALUE
RANGE
1 through 2
Under NEW VALUE
COPY OLD VALUE
Then select ADD.
Under OLD VALUE
VALUE
3
Under NEW VALUE
NEW VALUE
2
Then select ADD.
Under OLD VALUE

RANGE
4 through 5
Under NEW VALUE
NEW VALUE
3
Select ADD, then CONTINUE.
Click CHANGE and then OK on the RECODE INTO DIFFERENT VARIABLES.

Check the results of this recoding in the following way:

ANALYZE
DESCRIPTIVE STATISTICS
FREQUENCIES
Q2new
Click OK.

Note: You should have subgroups of 70 (plan to reenter MU), 46 (attending another school), and 25 (no plans).

One-Way ANOVA

Compare the sentiments for a football program (which MU does not currently have) across the three subgroups of Q2 regarding educational plans for the future. *(What are the H_0 and H_1 for your ANOVA analysis?)*

ANALYZE
COMPARE MEANS
ONE-WAY ANOVA
ONE-WAY ANOVA window
DEPENDENT LIST
I would have very much enjoyed a football team at MU [q5.n]
FACTOR
Q2new
Click OK.

Epilogue

Download Musial Retention Report.ppt to get a glimpse of what was presented to the MU administrators in a PowerPoint presentation. The most illuminating finding for the MU administrators was that almost 50 percent of the nonreturning students declared an intention to return to MU before the end of the year. This was far more than any of the administrators had expected. (This result can be seen in the frequency distribution for Q2.)

Excel

We give an overview of the detailed steps involved in conducting these analyses using Excel. Then we provide detailed step-by-step instructions for conducting one-sample *t*-test, two-independent-samples *t*-test, paired-samples *t*-test, and one-way ANOVA.

Detailed Steps: Overview

Detailed step-by-step instructions for running the Excel programs for the data analysis presented in this chapter can be downloaded from the Web site for this book in two forms: (1) computerized demonstration movies, and (2) screen captures. In addition, these steps are illustrated in the following sections. These steps are given for Excel 2007 and Excel 2010;

they are essentially the same in both these versions. The steps in the earlier versions are about the same with minor differences in how "Data Analysis" is accessed and the labeling of some of the boxes. The demonstration movies, and screen captures for the earlier versions, have also been posted on the Web site.

Detailed Steps: One-Sample *t*-Test

The following are detailed steps for running a one-sample test on the data of Table 17.1. The null hypothesis is that the mean preference for sample one before entering the theme park is 5.0.

1. Add a column with the name "Dummy" beside PREF2 and fill the first 10 rows with "5".
2. Select DATA tab.
3. In the ANALYSIS tab, select DATA ANALYSIS.
4. DATA ANALYSIS window pops up.
5. Select *t*-TEST: PAIRED TWO SAMPLE FOR MEANS in DATA ANALYSIS window.
6. Click OK.
7. *t*-TEST: PAIRED TWO SAMPLE FOR MEANS window appears on the screen.
8. *t*-TEST: PAIRED TWO SAMPLE FOR MEANS window has two parts:
   a. INPUT
   b. OUTPUT OPTIONS
9. INPUT portion asks for two inputs:
   a. Click in the VARIABLE 1 RANGE box. Select (highlight) the first 10 rows of data under PREF1. $C$2:$C$11 should appear on VARIABLE 1 RANGE.
   b. Click in the VARIABLE 2 RANGE box. Select (highlight) the first 10 rows of data under Dummy. $E$2:$E$11 should appear on VARIABLE 2 RANGE.
   c. Leave HYPOTHESIZED MEAN DIFFERENCE and LABELS blank.
   d. Default value of ALPHA is 0.05 is seen on the ALPHA box. Let the ALPHA value be like that.
10. In the OUTPUT OPTIONS pop-up window, select NEW WORKBOOK Options.
11. Click OK.

Detailed Steps: Two-Independent-Samples *t*-Test

The following are detailed steps for running a two-independent-samples *t*-test on the data of Table 17.1. The null hypothesis is that the mean preference for adults and teenagers before visiting Disney theme parks is the same.

1. Select DATA tab.
2. In the ANALYSIS group, select DATA ANALYSIS.
3. DATA ANALYSIS window pops up.
4. Select *t*-TEST: TWO-SAMPLE ASSUMING EQUAL VARIANCES in the DATA ANALYSIS window.
5. Click OK.
6. *t*-TEST: TWO-SAMPLE ASSUMING EQUAL VARIANCES window pops up.
7. *t*-TEST: TWO-SAMPLE ASSUMING EQUAL VARIANCES window has two parts:
   a. INPUT
   b. OUTPUT OPTIONS
8. INPUT portion asks for two inputs:
   a. Click in the VARIABLE 1 RANGE box. Select (highlight) the first 10 rows of data under PREF1. $C$2:$C$11 should appear on VARIABLE 1 RANGE.
   b. Click in the VARIABLE 2 RANGE box. Select (highlight) the last 10 rows of data under PREF1. $C$12:$C$21 should appear on VARIABLE 2 RANGE.
   c. Leave HYPOTHESIZED MEAN DIFFERENCE and LABELS blank.
   d. Default value of ALPHA is 0.05 is seen on the ALPHA box. Let the ALPHA value be like that.
9. In the OUTPUT OPTIONS pop-up window, select NEW WORKBOOK Options.
10. Click OK.

Detailed Steps: Paired-Samples *t*-Test

The following are detailed steps for running a paired-samples *t*-test on the data of Table 17.1. The null hypothesis is that there is no difference in the mean preference of teenagers before and after visiting Disney theme parks.

1. Select DATA tab.
2. In the ANALYSIS tab, select DATA ANALYSIS.
3. DATA ANALYSIS window pops up.
4. Select *t*-TEST: PAIRED TWO SAMPLE FOR MEANS in the DATA ANALYSIS window.
5. Click OK.
6. *t*-TEST: PAIRED TWO SAMPLE FOR MEANS window pops up.
7. *t*-TEST: PAIRED TWO SAMPLE FOR MEANS window has two parts:
   a. INPUT
   b. OUTPUT OPTIONS
8. INPUT portion asks for two inputs:
   a. Click in the VARIABLE 1 RANGE box. Select (highlight) the first 10 rows of data under PREF1. $C$2:$C$11 should appear on VARIABLE 1 RANGE.
   b. Click in the VARIABLE 2 RANGE box. Select (highlight) the first 10 rows of data under PREF2. $D$2:$D$11 should appear on VARIABLE 2 RANGE.
   c. Leave HYPOTHESIZED MEAN DIFFERENCE and LABELS blank.
   d. Default value of ALPHA is 0.05 is seen on the ALPHA box. Let the ALPHA value be like that.
9. In the Output portion of pop-up window, select NEW WORKBOOK.
10. Click OK.

Detailed Steps: One-Way ANOVA

The following are the detailed steps for running a one-way ANOVA on the data of Table 17.6. The null hypothesis is that there is no difference in mean normalized sales for the three levels of in-store promotion.

1. Select DATA tab.
2. In the ANALYSIS tab, select DATA ANALYSIS.
3. DATA ANALYSIS Window pops up.
4. Select ANOVA: SINGLE FACTOR from DATA ANALYSIS Window.
5. Click OK.
6. ANOVA: SINGLE FACTOR window pops up.
7. ANOVA: SINGLE FACTOR window has two portions:
   a. INPUT
   b. OUTPUT OPTIONS
8. INPUT portion asks for two inputs:
   a. Click in the INPUT RANGE box. Select (highlight) all the data under the columns High, Medium, Low at the same time. $B$2:$D$6 should appear in the INPUT RANGE.
   b. Click on COLUMNS beside GROUPED BY.
   c. LABELS IN FIRST ROW should not be checked.
   d. Leave ALPHA at default value of 0.05.
9. In OUTPUT OPTIONS pop-up window, select NEW WORKBOOK Option.
10. Click OK.

Summary

Hypotheses related to differences in the population means and, in some cases, proportions can be tested using the t distribution. Different forms of the t-test are suitable for testing hypotheses based on one sample, two independent samples, or paired samples.

One-way ANOVA involves a single metric dependent variable and a single independent categorical variable. Interest lies in testing the null hypothesis that the category means are equal in the population. The total variation in the dependent variable is decomposed into two components: variation related to the independent variable and variation related to error. The variation is measured in terms of the sums of squares corrected for the mean (SS). The mean square is obtained by dividing the SS by the corresponding degrees of freedom. The null hypothesis of equal means is tested by an F statistic, which is the ratio of the mean square related to the independent variable to the mean square related to error.

Key Terms and Concepts

Parametric tests   475
t-test   475
t statistic   476
t distribution   476
z-test   478
Independent samples   480
F-test   481
F statistic   481

F distribution   481
Paired samples   485
Paired-samples t-test   486
Analysis of variance (ANOVA)   488
One-way analysis of variance   489
Factor   489
Treatment   489
Decomposition of the total variation   489

SS_y 489
$SS_{between}$ (SS_x)   489
SS_{within} (SS_{error})   489
Eta^2 (η^2)   490
Mean square   490
Significance of the overall
    effect   491

Suggested Cases and Video Cases

Running Case with Real Data

1.1 Hewlett-Packard

Comprehensive Cases with Real Data

3.1 Bank of America   3.2 McDonald's   3.3 Boeing

Comprehensive Brief Harvard Business School Cases

4.1 TruEarth Healthy Foods: Market Research for a New Product Introduction (4065)
4.2 The Springfield Nor'easters: Maximizing Revenues in the Minor Leagues (2510)
4.3 Metabical: Positioning and Communications Strategy for a New Weight-Loss Drug (4240)
4.4 Saxonville Sausage Company (2085)

Online Video Case

17.1 Marriott

Live Research: Conducting a Marketing Research Project

1. Differences between groups are of interest in most projects. These can be examined by using an independent-samples *t*-test for two groups or one-way ANOVA for more than two groups.

2. Often each respondent evaluates many stimuli. For example, each respondent might evaluate different brands or provide importance ratings for different attributes. In such cases, differences between pairs of stimuli can be examined using the paired-samples *t*-test.

Acronym

The major characteristics of *t*-tests can be summarized by the acronym *T TEST*:

T   distribution is similar to the normal distribution

T   est of difference: Means or proportions

E   stimate of variance from the sample

S   ingle sample

T   wo samples: independent or paired

Review Questions

1. Present a classification of hypothesis-testing procedures.
2. Describe the general procedure for conducting a *t*-test.
3. Give the formula for the *t* statistic when examining a hypothesis related to a single mean.
4. Give the formula for the *t* statistic when examining a hypothesis related to a single proportion.
5. Give the formula for the *t* statistic when examining a hypothesis related to means of two independent samples.
6. Give the formula for the *t* statistic when examining a hypothesis related to means of paired samples.
7. What is the relationship between analysis of variance and the *t*-test?
8. What is total variation? How is it decomposed in a one-way analysis of variance?
9. What is the null hypothesis in one-way ANOVA? What basic statistic is used to test the null hypothesis in one-way ANOVA? How is this statistic computed?

Applied Problems

1. In each of the following situations, indicate the statistical analysis you would conduct and the appropriate test or test statistic that should be used.
   a. Consumer preferences for Dove soap were obtained on an 11-point Likert scale. The same consumers were then shown a commercial about Dove. After the commercial, preferences for Dove were again measured. Has the commercial been successful in inducing a change in preferences?
   b. Respondents in a survey of 1,000 households were asked to indicate their frequency of domestic air travel on an interval scale. They were also classified "as being in high-, medium-, or low-income categories. Is the frequency of domestic air travel related to income level?
   c. In a telephone survey using a representative sample of 3,000 households, the respondents were asked to indicate their preference for fast-food restaurants using a 7-point Likert-type scale. The sample was divided into small and large households based on a median split of the household size. Does preference for fast-food restaurants vary by household size?

2. The current advertising campaign for a major automobile brand would be changed if fewer than 70 percent of the consumers like it.
   a. Formulate the null and alternative hypotheses.
   b. Which statistical test would you use? Why?
   c. A random sample of 300 consumers was surveyed, and 204 respondents indicated that they liked the campaign. Should the campaign be changed? Why or why not?

3. A major computer manufacturer is having an end-of-season sale on computers. The number of computers sold during this sale at a sample of 10 stores was 800, 1,100, 0, 400, 700, 800, 1,000, 500, 800, and 300.
   a. Is there evidence that an average of more than 500 computers per store were sold during this sale? Use $\alpha = 0.05$.
   b. What assumption is necessary to perform this test?

4. After receiving complaints from readers, your campus newspaper decides to redesign its front page. Two new formats, B and C, are developed and tested against the current format, A. A total of 75 students are randomly selected, and 25 students are randomly assigned to each of three format conditions. The students are asked to evaluate the effectiveness of the format on an 11-point scale (1= poor, 11 = excellent).
   a. State the null hypothesis.
   b. What statistical test should you use?
   c. What are the degrees of freedom that are associated with the test statistic?

5. A marketing researcher wants to test the hypothesis that, within the population, there is no difference in the importance attached to shopping by consumers living in the northern, southern, eastern, and western United States. A study is conducted and analysis of variance is used to analyze the data. The results obtained are presented in the following table.

Source	df	Sum of Squares	Mean Squares	F Ratio	F Probability
Between groups	3	70.212	23.404	1.12	0.3
Within groups	996	20812.416	20.896		

   a. Is there sufficient evidence to reject the null hypothesis?
   b. What conclusion can be drawn from the table?

c. If the average importance was computed for each group, would you expect the sample means to be similar or different?
d. What was the total sample size in this study?

6. In a pilot study examining the effectiveness of three commercials (A, B, and C), 10 consumers were assigned to view each commercial and rate it on a 9-point Likert scale. The data obtained are shown in the following table. These data should be analyzed by doing hand calculations (i.e., without using the computer).

	Commercial	
A	B	C
4	7	8
5	4	7
3	6	7
4	5	6
3	4	8
4	6	7
4	5	8
3	5	8
5	4	5
5	4	6

   a. Calculate the category means and the grand mean.
   b. Calculate SS_y, SS_x, and SS_{error}.
   c. Calculate η^2.
   d. Calculate the value of F.
   e. Are the three commercials equally effective?

7. Conduct the following analyses for the Internet usage data given in Applied Problem number 7 in Chapter 16.
   a. Test the hypothesis that the mean familiarity with the Internet exceeds 4.0.
   b. Is the Internet usage different for males as compared to females? Formulate the null and alternative hypotheses, and conduct the test.
   c. Is the proportion of respondents using the Internet for shopping the same for males and females? Formulate the null and alternative hypotheses, and conduct the test.
   d. Do the respondents differ in their attitude toward the Internet and attitude toward technology? Formulate the null and alternative hypotheses, and conduct the test.

8. In a pretest, respondents were asked to express their preference for an outdoor lifestyle (V1) using a 7-point scale (1 = not at all preferred, 7 = greatly preferred). They were also asked to indicate the importance of the following variables on a 7-point scale (1 = not at all important, 7 = very important).

V1	V2	V3	V4	V5	V6	V7	V8
7.00	3.00	6.00	4.00	5.00	2.00	1.00	1.00
1.00	1.00	1.00	2.00	1.00	2.00	1.00	1.00
6.00	2.00	5.00	4.00	4.00	5.00	1.00	1.00
4.00	3.00	4.00	6.00	3.00	2.00	1.00	1.00
1.00	2.00	2.00	3.00	1.00	2.00	1.00	1.00
6.00	3.00	5.00	4.00	6.00	2.00	1.00	1.00
5.00	3.00	4.00	3.00	4.00	5.00	1.00	1.00
6.00	4.00	5.00	4.00	5.00	1.00	1.00	1.00
3.00	3.00	2.00	2.00	2.00	2.00	1.00	1.00
2.00	4.00	2.00	6.00	2.00	2.00	1.00	1.00
6.00	4.00	5.00	3.00	5.00	5.00	1.00	2.00
2.00	3.00	1.00	4.00	2.00	1.00	1.00	2.00
7.00	2.00	6.00	4.00	5.00	6.00	1.00	2.00
4.00	6.00	4.00	5.00	3.00	3.00	1.00	2.00
1.00	3.00	1.00	2.00	1.00	4.00	1.00	2.00
6.00	6.00	6.00	3.00	4.00	5.00	2.00	2.00
5.00	5.00	6.00	4.00	4.00	6.00	2.00	2.00
7.00	7.00	4.00	4.00	7.00	7.00	2.00	2.00
2.00	6.00	3.00	7.00	4.00	3.00	2.00	2.00
3.00	7.00	3.00	6.00	4.00	4.00	2.00	2.00
1.00	5.00	2.00	6.00	3.00	3.00	2.00	3.00
5.00	6.00	4.00	7.00	5.00	6.00	2.00	3.00
2.00	4.00	1.00	5.00	4.00	4.00	2.00	3.00
4.00	7.00	4.00	7.00	4.00	6.00	2.00	3.00
6.00	7.00	4.00	2.00	1.00	7.00	2.00	3.00
3.00	6.00	4.00	6.00	4.00	4.00	2.00	3.00
4.00	7.00	7.00	4.00	2.00	5.00	2.00	3.00
3.00	7.00	2.00	6.00	4.00	3.00	2.00	3.00
4.00	6.00	3.00	7.00	2.00	7.00	2.00	3.00
5.00	6.00	2.00	6.00	7.00	2.00	2.00	3.00

SPSS Data File

Excel Data File

V2 = enjoying nature
V3 = relating to the weather
V4 = living in harmony with the environment
V5 = exercising regularly
V6 = meeting other people

The gender of the respondent (V7) was coded as
1 = female and 2 = male. The location of residence
(V8) was coded as 1 = midtown/downtown,
2 = suburbs, and 3 = countryside. The data obtained
are given in the previous table.

Using a statistical package of your choice, answer the
following questions. In each case, formulate the null and
the alternative hypotheses and conduct the appropriate
statistical test(s).

  a. Does the mean preference for an outdoor lifestyle
     exceed 3.0?
  b. Does the mean importance of enjoying nature
     exceed 3.5?
  c. Does the mean preference for an outdoor lifestyle
     differ for males and females?
  d. Does the importance attached to V2 through V6 differ
     for males and females?
  e. Do the respondents attach more importance to enjoying
     nature than they do to relating to the weather?
  f. Do the respondents attach more importance to
     relating to the weather than they do to meeting other
     people?
  g. Do the respondents attach more importance to living in
     harmony with the environment than they do to
     exercising regularly?

Group Discussion

1. "The *t*-tests are so simple to conduct that they should be
   used more often in analyzing marketing research data."
   Discuss as a small group.

2. Which procedure is more useful in marketing research—
   t-test or analysis of variance? Discuss as a small group.

Hewlett-Packard Running Case

Review the Hewlett-Packard (HP) case, Case 1.1, and questionnaire given toward the end of the book. Go to the Web site for
this book and download the HP data file.

1. The mean response on which of the evaluations
   of HP (q8_1 to q8_13) exceeds 5 (the midpoint of
   the scale)?
2. Are the two overall satisfaction groups derived based
   on the recoding of q4 as specified in Chapter 15

different in terms of each of the evaluations of HP
(q8_1 to q8_13)?
3. Are the two likely to recommend groups derived based on
   the recoding of q5 as specified in Chapter 15 different in
   terms of each of the evaluations of HP (q8_1 to q8_13)?
4. Are the two likelihood of choosing HP groups derived
   based on the recoding of q6 as specified in Chapter 15
   different in terms of each of the evaluations of HP (q8_1
   to q8_13)?

5. Is the mean of responses to q8_1 (Make ordering a computer system easy) and q8_2 (Let customers order computer systems customized to their specifications) different?

6. Is the mean of responses to q8_9 ("Bundle" its computers with appropriate software) and q8_10 ("Bundle" its computers with Internet access) different?

7. Is the mean of responses to q8_6 (Have computers that run programs quickly) and q8_7 (Have high-quality computers with no technical problems) different?

8. Are the three price-sensitive groups based on q9_5per as derived in Chapter 15 different in terms of each of the evaluations of HP (q8_1 to q8_13)? Interpret the results.

9. Are the three price-sensitive groups based on q9_19per as derived in Chapter 15 different in terms of each of the evaluations of HP (q8_1 to q8_13)? Interpret the results.

10. Do the demographic groups as recoded in Chapter 15 (recoded q11, q12, q13) and q14 differ in terms of overall satisfaction with HP computers (q4)? Interpret the results.

11. Do the demographic groups as recoded in Chapter 15 (recoded q11, q12, q13) and q14 differ in terms of likelihood of recommending HP computers (q5)? Interpret the results.

12. Do the demographic groups as recoded in Chapter 15 (recoded q11, q12, q13) and q14 differ in terms of likelihood of choosing HP computers (q6)? Interpret the results.

ONLINE VIDEO CASE 17.1

MARRIOTT: Marketing Research Leads to Expanded Offerings

Visit **www.pearsonhighered.com/malhotra** to read the video case and view the accompanying video. Marriott: Marketing Research Leads to Expanded Offerings suggests that differentiation among Marriott's brands is not based on service and pricing alone—marketing research has revealed other attributes that are important, including convenient locations and luxury-class rooms. The case can be used as a springboard for students to design a short survey regarding what attributes consumers deem important in hotels—in light of the chapter's objectives, discuss how the survey questionnaire and the data analysis strategy can be designed so that parametric tests of hypotheses can be performed. Specific marketing research questions on this and the previous chapters are posed in the video case.

18 Data Analysis: Correlation and Regression

Source: © Victor Fraile/Alamy.

LEARNING OBJECTIVES

After reading this chapter, the student should be able to:

1. Explain product moment correlation and how it provides a foundation for regression analysis.

2. Understand the nature and methods of bivariate regression analysis, and how the general model can be described.

3. Describe the estimation of parameters, standardized regression coefficient, significance testing, and prediction accuracy in bivariate regression.

4. Discuss how multiple regression differs from bivariate regression.

5. Explain the meaning of partial regression coefficients.

6. **Social Media** Illustrate the application of correlation and regression to social media.

" As marketing research professionals, we continually examine the relationship between consumers' perceptions and ultimate purchase decisions. Consequently, correlation and regression techniques serve as the foundation for many of the most commonly used analytical tools in marketing research. **"**

Jamie Baker-Prewitt, Ph.D.
Vice President, Marketing and Decision Support Sciences, Burke, Inc., Cincinnati, Ohio

Regression Models Model the Marketing Strategy of Adidas

Adidas AG (www.adidas.com) is the second largest sportswear manufacturer in the world. It is globally recognized by its official logo of three parallel stripes and had revenues of Euro 11.99 billion in 2010. The company wanted to be a leader in how it brings products to market, in what its products do for the athletes, and in how it services them. Adidas is a sports-performance brand.

Adidas realized that preference for athletic shoes has strong positive correlations with sports-related variables, such as interest in sports, attitude toward sports personalities, attendance at sports events, and time spent watching sports on television. Research by the company revealed that consumers with a greater interest in sports, a more favorable attitude toward sports personalities, or higher attendance at sports events exhibited a stronger preference for brand-name athletic shoes. A multiple regression model with preference for athletic shoes as the dependent variable and interest in sports, attitude toward sports personalities, attendance at sports events, and time spent watching sports on television as the independent variables had a very good fit. The model fit was determined by strength of association (a measure of how strongly the dependent variable and the independent variables are related) and the accuracy of predicted values of the dependent variable. The coefficient (partial regression coefficient) associated with each independent variable was positive and significant, indicating that higher values on each independent variable were associated with stronger preference for athletic shoes. Thus, the model had the following form:

Estimated preference for athletic shoes = $a + b_1$ (interest in sports) + b_2 (attitude toward sports personalities) + b_3 (attendance at sports events) + b_4 (time spent watching sports on television)

Where a = constant, and b_1, b_2, b_3, and b_4 are positive partial regression coefficients.

Armed with such information, Adidas attempted to boost the visibility of its brand with star athletes. It featured Muhammad Ali; Ali's daughter, Laila, also a world champion boxer; soccer icons David Beckham and Zinedine Zidane; Thai tennis star Paradorn Srichaphan; long-distance runner Haile Gebrselassie; and NBA all-star Tracy McGrady. As of 2011, Adidas had the tagline of "Experience the spirit of sport." Regression models have played a key role in the development of Adidas' marketing strategy.[1]

Overview

This chapter first describes the concept of the product moment correlation, or the correlation coefficient. The product moment correlation is a measure of the strength of association between two metric variables. It lays the conceptual foundation for regression analysis. Regression analysis is widely used for explaining variation in a dependent variable in terms of a set of independent variables. In marketing, the dependent variable could be market share, sales, or brand preference, and the independent variables could be marketing management variables, such as advertising, price, distribution, product quality, and demographic and lifestyles variables. This was illustrated in the opening vignette, where the regression model had preference for athletic shoes as the dependent variable and sports-related lifestyle variables as the independent variables.

A simple bivariate case is presented to introduce regression analysis. The chapter describes estimation, standardization of the regression coefficients, testing and examination of the strength and significance of association between variables, prediction accuracy, and the assumptions underlying the regression model. Next, the multiple regression model is presented, with an emphasis on the interpretation of parameters, strength of association, significance tests, and examination of residuals. Figure 18.1 briefly explains the focus of the chapter, the relationship of this chapter to the previous ones, and the steps of the marketing research process on which this chapter concentrates. Figure 18.2 provides an overview of the different topics discussed in this chapter and how they flow from one to the next.

Help for running the SPSS and Excel programs used in this chapter is provided in four ways: (1) detailed step-by-step instructions are given later in the chapter, (2) you can download (from the Web site for this book) computerized demonstration movies illustrating these step-by-step instructions, (3) you can download screen captures with notes illustrating these step-by-step instructions, and (4) you can refer to the Study Guide and Technology Manual, a supplement that accompanies this book.

Fundamental to regression analysis is an understanding of the product moment correlation.

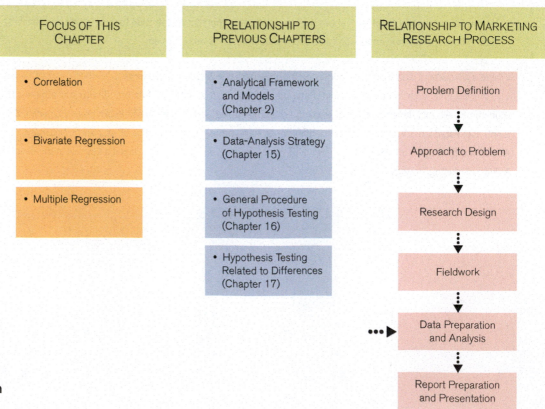

FIGURE 18.1

Relationship of Correlation and Regression to the Previous Chapters and the Marketing Research Process

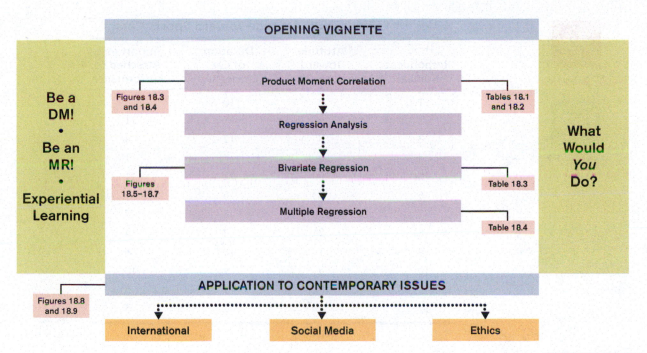

FIGURE 18.2

Correlation and Regression: An Overview

Product Moment Correlation

In marketing research, researchers often are interested in summarizing the strength of association between two metric variables, as in the following situations:

- How strongly are sales related to advertising expenditures?
- Is there an association between market share and size of the sales force?
- Are consumers' perceptions of quality related to their perceptions of price?

In situations like these, the **product moment correlation** is used. The product moment correlation, which is denoted by r, is the most widely used statistic that summarizes the strength and direction of association between two metric (interval- or ratio-scaled) variables, say X and Y. It is used to determine whether a linear or straight-line relationship exists between X and Y, as well as the degree to which the variation in one variable, X, is related to the variation in another variable, Y. Because it was originally proposed by Karl Pearson, it also is known as the *Pearson correlation coefficient*. Other terms used to refer to the product moment correlation are *simple correlation*, *bivariate correlation*, or merely the *correlation coefficient*.

In the opening vignette, preference for athletic shoes showed strong positive correlations with sports-related variables, such as interest in sports, attitude toward sports personalities, attendance at sports events, and time spent watching sports on television. From a sample of n observations, X and Y, the product moment correlation, r, can be calculated as:

product moment correlation (r)
A statistic summarizing the strength and direction of linear association between two metric variables.

$$r = \frac{\sum_{i=1}^{n}(X_i - \overline{X})(Y_i - \overline{Y})}{\sqrt{\sum_{i=1}^{n}(X_i - \overline{X})^2 \sum_{i=1}^{n}(Y_i - \overline{Y})^2}}$$

Division of the numerator and denominator by $(n - 1)$ gives

$$r = \frac{\sum_{i=1}^{n}\dfrac{(X_i - \overline{X})(Y_i - \overline{Y})}{n - 1}}{\sqrt{\sum_{i=1}^{n}\dfrac{(X_i - \overline{X})^2}{n - 1} \sum_{i=1}^{n}\dfrac{(Y_i - \overline{Y})^2}{n - 1}}}$$

$$= \frac{COV_{xy}}{s_x s_y}$$

SPSS Data File

Excel Data File

TABLE 18.1 Explaining Attitude Toward Sports Cars

Respondent Number	Attitude Toward Sports Cars	Duration of Car Ownership	Importance Attached to Performance
1	6	10	3
2	9	12	11
3	8	12	4
4	3	4	1
5	10	12	11
6	4	6	1
7	5	8	7
8	2	2	4
9	11	18	8
10	9	9	10
11	10	17	8
12	2	2	5

covariance

A systematic relationship between two variables in which a change in one implies a corresponding change in the other (COV_{xy}).

In these equations, $\overline{X}$ and $\overline{Y}$ denote the sample means and s_x and s_y the standard deviations. COV_{xy}, the **covariance** between X and Y, measures the extent to which X and Y are related. The covariance can be either positive or negative. Division by $s_x s_y$ achieves standardization, so that r varies between -1.0 and $+1.0$. Note that the correlation coefficient is an absolute number and is not expressed in any unit of measurement. The correlation coefficient between two variables will be the same regardless of their underlying units of measurement.

As an example, suppose a researcher wants to explain attitudes toward sports cars (attitude) in terms of the number of years the respondent has owned a sports car (duration). The attitude is measured on an 11-point scale (1 = do not like sports cars, 11 = very much like sports cars), and the duration of car ownership is measured in terms of the number of years the respondent has owned one or more sports cars. In a pretest of 12 respondents, the data shown in Table 18.1 were obtained.

This table gives the data for only 12 respondents, because we want to show the calculations of the basic statistics by hand. We think that it is important to show these hand calculations so that you can get a better idea of the basic concepts. In practice, the sample size is much larger. We illustrate the analysis of such large data sets later in the chapter in an Experiential Learning exercise that analyzes the data for 146 respondents in a survey for Musial University.

The correlation coefficient between attitude and duration based on the data of Table 18.1 is calculated as follows:

$$\overline{X} = (10 + 12 + 12 + 4 + 12 + 6 + 8 + 2 + 18 + 9 + 17 + 2)/12$$

$$= 9.33$$

$$\overline{Y} = (6 + 9 + 8 + 3 + 10 + 4 + 5 + 2 + 11 + 9 + 10 + 2)/12$$

$$= 6.58$$

$$\sum_{i=1}^{n} (X_i - \overline{X})(Y_i - \overline{Y}) = (10 - 9.33)(6 - 6.58) + (12 - 9.33)(9 - 6.58)$$
$$+ (12 - 9.33)(8 - 6.58) + (4 - 9.33)(3 - 6.58)$$
$$+ (12 - 9.33)(10 - 6.58) + (6 - 9.33)(4 - 6.58)$$
$$+ (8 - 9.33)(5 - 6.58) + (2 - 9.33)(2 - 6.58)$$
$$+ (18 - 9.33)(11 - 6.58) + (9 - 9.33)(9 - 6.58)$$
$$+ (17 - 9.33)(10 - 6.58) + (2 - 9.33)(2 - 6.58)$$

$$= -0.3886 + 6.4614 + 3.7914 + 19.0814$$
$$+ 9.1314 + 8.5914 + 2.1014 + 33.5714$$
$$+ 38.3214 - 0.7986 + 26.2314 + 33.5714$$
$$= 179.6668$$

$$\sum_{i=1}^{n} (X_i - \bar{X})^2 = (10 - 9.33)^2 + (12 - 9.33)^2 + (12 - 9.33)^2 + (4 - 9.33)^2$$
$$+ (12 - 9.33)^2 + (6 - 9.33)^2 + (8 - 9.33)^2 + (2 - 9.33)^2$$
$$+ (18 - 9.33)^2 + (9 - 9.33)^2 + (17 - 9.33)^2 + (2 - 9.33)^2$$
$$= 0.4489 + 7.1289 + 7.1289 + 28.4089$$
$$+ 7.1289 + 11.0889 + 1.7689 + 53.7289$$
$$+ 75.1689 + 0.1089 + 58.8289 + 53.7289$$
$$= 304.6668$$

$$\sum_{i=1}^{n} (Y_i - \bar{Y})^2 = (6 - 6.58)^2 + (9 - 6.58)^2 + (8 - 6.58)^2 + (3 - 6.58)^2$$
$$+ (10 - 6.58)^2 + (4 - 6.58)^2 + (5 - 6.58)^2 + (2 - 6.58)^2$$
$$+ (11 - 6.58)^2 + (9 - 6.58)^2 + (10 - 6.58)^2 + (2 - 6.58)^2$$
$$= 0.3364 + 5.8564 + 2.0164 + 12.8164$$
$$+ 11.6964 + 6.6564 + 2.4964 + 20.9764$$
$$+ 19.5364 + 5.8564 + 11.6964 + 20.9764$$
$$= 120.9168$$

Thus,

$$r = \frac{179.6668}{\sqrt{(304.6668)(120.9168)}}$$

or

$$r = \frac{179.6668}{(17.4547)(10.9962)}$$

$$= 0.9361$$

These calculations are summarized in Table 18.2. The product moment correlation can also be calculated using SPSS and Excel, and the corresponding outputs with explanatory notes can be downloaded from the Web site for this book. In this example, the value of r, 0.9361, is close to 1.0.

This means that the number of years a respondent has owned a sports car is strongly associated with the respondent's attitude toward sports cars. Thus, the length of time a person has owned a sports car is positively related to degree of favorableness of the attitude toward sports cars. Furthermore, the positive sign of r implies a positive relationship; the longer the duration of sports car ownership, the more favorable the attitude, and vice versa. For example, if John has owned a sports car much longer than Paul, John is likely to have a much more favorable attitude toward sports cars than Paul. Over many years of ownership, John sees his sports car as a treasured possession. In contrast, Paul has only recently purchased a sports car and has yet to develop such strong feelings toward it. This can be seen from a plot of Y (attitude toward sports cars) against X (duration of sports car ownership) given in Figure 18.3. The points seem to be arranged in a band running from the bottom left to the top right.

TABLE 18.2 Calculation of the Product Moment Correlation

Number	Attitude (Y)	Duration (X)	$(X_i - \bar{X})$	$(X_i - \bar{X})^2$	$(Y_i - \bar{Y})$	$(Y_i - \bar{Y})^2$	$(X_i - \bar{X})(Y_i - \bar{Y})$
1	6	10	0.667	0.4489	−0.583	0.3364	−0.3886
2	9	12	2.667	7.1289	2.417	5.8564	6.4614
3	8	12	2.667	7.1289	1.417	2.0164	3.7914
4	3	4	−5.333	28.4089	−3.583	12.8164	19.0814
5	10	12	2.667	7.1289	3.417	11.6964	9.1314
6	4	6	−3.333	11.0889	−2.583	6.6564	8.5914
7	5	8	−1.333	1.7689	−1.583	2.4964	2.1014
8	2	2	−7.333	53.7289	−4.583	20.9764	3.5714
9	11	18	8.667	75.1689	7.417	19.5364	38.3214
10	9	9	−0.333	0.1089	2.417	5.8564	−0.7986
11	10	17	7.667	58.8289	3.417	11.6964	26.2314
12	2	2	−7.333	53.7289	−4.583	20.9764	33.5714
Mean	6.583	9.333					
Sum				304.6668		120.9168	179.6668

Using the above values the product moment correlation can be calculated as

$$r = \frac{\sum\limits_{i=1}^{n}(X_i - \bar{X})(Y_i - \bar{Y})}{\sqrt{\sum\limits_{i=1}^{n}(X_i - \bar{X})^2 \sum\limits_{i=1}^{n}(Y_i - \bar{Y})^2}}$$

or

$$r = \frac{179.6668}{\sqrt{(304.6668)(120.9168)}} = \frac{179.6668}{(17.4547)(10.9962)} = 0.9361$$

FIGURE 18.3

Plot of Attitude with Duration of Sports Car Ownership

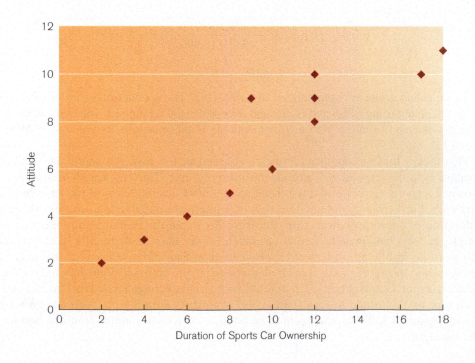

Because r indicates the degree to which variation in one variable is related to variation in another, it can also be expressed in terms of the decomposition of the total variation (see the explanation in Chapter 17). In other words,

$$r^2 = \frac{\text{Explained variation}}{\text{Total variation}}$$

$$= \frac{SS_x}{SS_y}$$

$$= \frac{\text{Total variation} - \text{Error variation}}{\text{Total variation}}$$

$$= \frac{SS_y - SS_{error}}{SS_y}$$

Therefore, r^2 measures the proportion of variation in one variable that is explained by the other. Both r and r^2 are symmetric measures of association. In other words, the correlation of X with Y is the same as the correlation of Y with X. It does not matter which variable is considered the dependent variable and which the independent. The product moment coefficient measures the strength of the linear relationship and is not designed to measure nonlinear relationships. Thus $r = 0$ merely indicates that there is no linear relationship between X and Y. It does not mean that X and Y are unrelated. A nonlinear relationship between them could exist that is not captured by r (see Figure 18.4).

When it is computed for a population rather than a sample, the product moment correlation is denoted by ρ, the Greek letter rho. The coefficient r is an estimator of ρ. Note that the calculation of r assumes that X and Y are metric variables whose distributions have the same shape. If these assumptions are not met, r is deflated and underestimates ρ. In marketing research, data obtained by using rating scales with a small number of categories might not be strictly interval. This tends to deflate r, resulting in an underestimation of ρ.

The statistical significance of the relationship between two variables measured by using r can be conveniently tested. The hypotheses are:

$$H_0: \rho = 0$$

$$H_1: \rho \neq 0$$

The test statistic is:

$$t = r \left[\frac{n - 2}{1 - r^2} \right]^{1/2}$$

which has a t distribution with $n - 2$ degrees of freedom. For the correlation coefficient calculated based on the data given in Table 18.1,

$$t = 0.9361 \left[\frac{12 - 2}{1 - (0.9361)^2} \right]^{1/2}$$

or

$$t = 0.9361 \left[\frac{10}{0.1237} \right]^{1/2}$$

or

$$t = 0.9381 [80.8407]^{1/2}$$

$$= 0.9361 \times 8.991$$

$$= 8.414$$

and the degrees of freedom are $12 - 2 = 10$. From the t distribution table (Table 4 in the Appendix of Statistical Tables), the critical value of t for a two-tailed test and $\alpha = 0.05$ is 2.2281.

FIGURE 18.4

A Nonlinear Relationship for Which *r* = 0

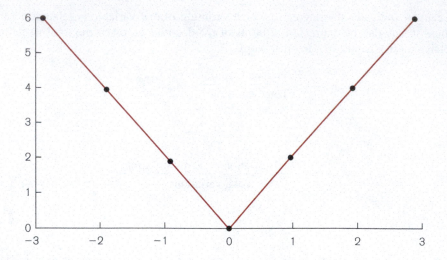

Hence, the null hypothesis of no relationship between *X* and *Y* is rejected. This, along with the positive sign of *r*, indicates that attitude toward sports cars is positively related to the duration of sports car ownership. Moreover, the high value of *r* indicates that this relationship is strong. The usefulness of the product moment correlation, *r*, in assessing linear relationships is illustrated by the following example.

Research in Action

It's a Small World

A global study analyzed the ratings of 186 countries on seven dimensions of quality of life (QOL): favorable cost of living (COL), culture (CUL), economy (ECON), freedom (FREE), infrastructure (INFRA), health (HEA), and environment (ENV). The simple correlations between these dimensions are as follows:

	COL	CUL	ECON	FREE	INFRA	HEA	ENV
COL	1.0						
CUL	−.03	1.0					
ECON	.27*	.66*	1.0				
FREE	−.05	.57*	.46*	1.0			
INFRA	−.26*	.76*	.85*	.55*	1.0		
HEA	−.03	.78*	.59*	.47*	.70*	1.0	
ENV	−.05	.04	−.02	.10	−.01	−.07	1.0

*Indicates correlation is statistically significant at $\alpha = .05$

The magnitude of the correlation indicates the extent to which the two QOL dimensions are interrelated. The highest correlation of .85 is observed between INFRA and ECON, indicating that infrastructure and economic development are highly interrelated. In contrast, there is no relationship between infrastructure and environment ($r = -.01$). Based on ratings on the QOL dimensions, the 186 countries were classified into 12 clusters or groups. The 10th cluster, which consisted of 19 developed countries, including the United States, Canada, the United Kingdom, Japan, France, Germany, and the Scandinavian countries, represented the highest QOL.

Country policy makers can use this information to identify possible rival countries, to direct investment, and to form alliances with countries having complementary resources, cultures, and economic development.[2]

The product moment provides a conceptual foundation for bivariate as well as multiple regression analysis.

Regression Analysis

Regression analysis is a powerful and flexible procedure for analyzing associative relationships between a metric-dependent variable and one or more metric-independent variables. It can be used in the following ways:

1. Determine whether the independent variables explain a significant variation in the dependent variable: whether a relationship exists.
2. Determine how much of the variation in the dependent variable can be explained by the independent variables: strength of the relationship.
3. Determine the structure or form of the relationship: the mathematical equation relating the independent and dependent variables.
4. Predict the values of the dependent variable.
5. Control for other independent variables when evaluating the contributions of a specific variable or set of variables.

Although the independent variables can explain the variation in the dependent variable, this does not necessarily imply causation. The use of the terms *dependent* or *criterion* variables and *independent* or *predictor* variables in regression analysis arises from the mathematical relationship between the variables. These terms do not imply that the criterion variable is dependent on the independent variables in a causal sense, because at least two of the three criteria for causation discussed in Chapter 8 (time order of occurrence of variables and absence of other causal factors) might not be satisfied. Regression analysis is concerned with the nature and degree of association between variables and does not imply or assume any causality. We will discuss bivariate regression first, followed by multiple regression.

regression analysis
A statistical procedure for analyzing associative relationships between a metric-dependent variable and one or more metric-independent variables.

Bivariate Regression

Bivariate regression is a procedure for deriving a mathematical relationship, in the form of an equation, between a single metric dependent or criterion variable and a single metric independent or predictor variable. The analysis is similar in many ways to determining the simple correlation between two variables. However, because an equation has to be derived, one variable must be identified as the dependent variable and the other as the independent variable. For example, the growth rate of the U.S. economy has a positive correlation with the level of consumer spending. Thus, a **bivariate regression model** could be constructed with growth rate of the U.S. economy as the dependent variable and the level of consumer spending as the independent variable. The examples of simple correlation given earlier can be translated into the regression context:

- Can variation in sales be explained in terms of variation in advertising expenditures? What is the structure and form of this relationship, and can it be modeled mathematically by an equation describing a straight line?
- Can the variation in market share be accounted for by the size of the sales force?
- Are consumers' perceptions of quality determined by their perceptions of price?

bivariate regression
A procedure for deriving a mathematical relationship, in the form of an equation, between a single metric dependent variable and a single metric independent variable.

bivariate regression model
An equation used to explain regression analysis in which one independent variable is regressed onto a single dependent variable.

Conducting Bivariate Regression Analysis

The steps involved in conducting bivariate regression analysis are described in Figure 18.5. Suppose the researcher wants to explain attitudes toward sports cars in terms of the duration of car ownership (see Table 18.1). In deriving such relationships, it often is useful to first examine a scatter diagram.

Scatter Diagram

A **scatter diagram**, or *scattergram*, is a plot of the values of two variables for all the cases or observations. It is customary to plot the dependent variable on the vertical axis and the independent variable on the horizontal axis. A scatter diagram is useful for determining the form of the relationship between the variables. It also can alert the researcher to any patterns or problems in the data. Any unusual combinations of the two variables can be easily identified. A plot of Y (attitude toward sports cars) against X (duration of car ownership) was given in Figure 18.3. The points seem to be arranged in a band running from the bottom left to the top right.

scatter diagram (scattergram)
A plot of the values of two variables for all the cases or observations.

FIGURE 18.5
Conducting Bivariate Regression Analysis

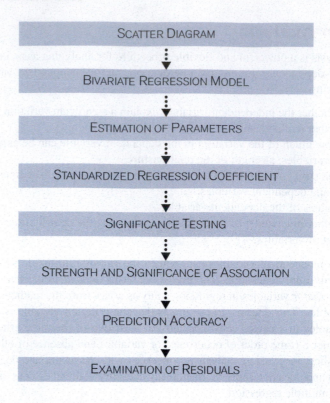

One can see the pattern: as one variable increases, so does the other. It appears from this scattergram that the relationship between X and Y is linear and that it could be well described by a straight line. By fitting the best straight line to the data, the equation of the line gives the estimate of the underlying relationship in the data. How should the straight line be fitted to best describe the data?

least-squares procedure
A technique for fitting a straight line to a scattergram by minimizing the sum of squares of the vertical distances of all the points from the line.

The most commonly used technique for fitting a straight line to a scattergram is the **least-squares procedure**. This technique determines the best-fitting line by minimizing the sum of squares of the vertical distances of all the points from the line. The best-fitting line is called the *regression line*. Any point that does not fall on the regression line is not fully accounted for. The vertical distance from the point to the line is the error, e_j (see Figure 18.6). The distances of all the points from the line are squared and added together to arrive at the sum of the squared errors, which is a measure of total error.

The equation for the total error is $\sum e_j^2$

FIGURE 18.6
Bivariate Regression

In fitting the line, the least-squares procedure minimizes the **sum of squared errors**. If Y is plotted on the vertical axis and X on the horizontal axis, as in Figure 18.6, the best-fitting line is called the regression of Y on X, because the sum of the squares of the vertical distances is minimized. The scatter diagram indicates whether the relationship between Y and X can be modeled as a straight line, and, consequently, whether the bivariate regression model is appropriate.

sum of squared errors
The sum of the squared vertical differences between the actual data point and the predicted one on the regression line.

Bivariate Regression Model

In the bivariate regression model, the general form of a straight line is:

$$Y = \beta_0 + \beta_1 X$$

where

Y = dependent or criterion variable

X = independent or predictor variable

β_0 = intercept of the line

β_1 = slope of the line

This equation is very similar to the equation of a straight line with which you are familiar: $y = mx + b$, with $b = \beta_0$, and $m = \beta_1$. This model implies a deterministic relationship, in that Y is completely determined by X. The value of Y can be perfectly predicted if β_0 and β_1 are known. In marketing research, however, very few relationships are deterministic. Thus, the regression procedure adds an error term to account for the probabilistic or stochastic nature of the relationship. The basic regression equation becomes:

$$Y_i = \beta_0 + \beta_1 X + e_i$$

where e_i is the error term associated with the ith observation.[3] Estimation of the regression parameters, β_0 and β_1, is relatively simple.

Estimation of Parameters

In most cases, β_0 and β_1 are unknown and are estimated from the sample observations using the equation

$$\hat{Y}_i = a + bX_i$$

where $\hat{Y}_i$ is the **estimated or predicted value** of Y_i, and a and b are estimators of β_0 and β_1, respectively. The constant b is usually referred to as the *nonstandardized regression coefficient*. It is the slope of the regression line, and it indicates the expected change in Y when X is changed by one unit. The formulas for calculating a and b are simple. The slope, b, can be computed in terms of the covariance between X and Y (COV_{xy}) and the variance of X as:

estimated or predicted value
The value $\hat{Y}_i = a + bX_i$ where $\hat{Y}_i$ is the estimated or predicted value of Y_i, and a and b are estimators of β_0 and β_1, respectively.

$$b = \frac{COV_{xy}}{s_x^2}$$

$$= \frac{\sum_{i=1}^{n}(X_i - \overline{X})(Y_i - \overline{Y})}{\sum_{i=1}^{n}(X_i - \overline{X})^2}$$

$$= \frac{\sum_{i=1}^{n}X_i Y_i - n\overline{X}\overline{Y}}{\sum_{i=1}^{n}X_i^2 - n\overline{X}^2}$$

The intercept, a, can then be calculated using:

$$a = \overline{Y} - b\overline{X}$$

For the data in Table 18.1, the estimation of parameters for the regression of attitude (Y) on duration (X) can be illustrated as follows:

$$\sum_{i=1}^{12} X_i Y_i = (10)(6) + (12)(9) + (12)(8) + (4)(3) + (12)(10) + (6)(4)$$
$$+ (8)(5) + (2)(2) + (18)(11) + (9)(9) + (17)(10) + (2)(2)$$
$$= 917$$

$$\sum_{i=1}^{12} X_i^2 = 10^2 + 12^2 + 12^2 + 4^2 + 12^2 + 6^2$$
$$+ 8^2 + 2^2 + 18^2 + 9^2 + 17^2 + 2^2$$
$$= 1350$$

Recall from earlier calculations of the simple correlation that

$$\bar{X} = 9.333$$
$$\bar{Y} = 6.583$$

Given $n = 12$, b can be calculated as:

$$b = \frac{917 - (12)(9.333)(6.583)}{1350 - (12)(9.333)^2}$$

or

$$b = \frac{917 - 737.270}{1350 - 1045.259}$$
$$= \frac{179.73}{304.741}$$
$$= 0.5897$$
$$a = \bar{Y} - b\bar{X}$$
$$= 6.583 - (0.5897)(9.333)$$
$$= 6.583 - 5.504$$
$$= 1.079$$

Note that these coefficients have been estimated on the raw (untransformed) data. Should standardization of the data be considered desirable, the calculation of the standardized coefficients also is straightforward.

Using software and the data shown in Table 18.1, the regression of attitude on duration of car ownership yielded the results shown in Table 18.3. The corresponding SPSS and Excel outputs with explanatory notes can be downloaded from the Web site for this book. The intercept, a, equals 1.0793, and the slope, b, equals 0.5897, as shown earlier by hand calculations. Therefore, the estimated equation is:

$$\text{Attitude}(\hat{Y}) = 1.0793 + 0.5897(\text{Duration of car ownership})$$

Standardized Regression Coefficient

standardization

The process by which the raw data are transformed into new variables that have a mean of 0 and a variance of 1.

beta coefficient (beta weight)

Denotes the standardized regression coefficient.

Standardization is the process by which the raw data are transformed into new variables that have a mean of 0 and a variance of 1. This process is similar to the calculation of z values discussed earlier (Chapters 13, 16, and 17). To standardize a variable, simply subtract the mean and divide the difference by the standard deviation. When the data (both the independent and the dependent variable) are standardized, the intercept assumes a value of 0. The term **beta coefficient**, or *beta weight*, is used to denote the standardized regression coefficient. Standardization is

TABLE 18.3 Bivariate Regression

Multiple R	.9361
R^2	.8762
Adjusted R^2	.8639
Standard Error	1.2233

SPSS Output File

Excel Output File

Analysis of Variance

	df	Sum of Squares	Mean Square
Regression	1	105.9522	105.9522
Residual	10	14.9644	1.4964
$F = 70.8027$		Significance of $F = .0000$	

Variables in the Equation

Variable	b	SE_b	Beta (B)	T	Sig. T
Duration	.5897	.0701	.9361	8.414	.0000
(Constant)	1.0793	.7434		1.452	.1772

sometimes desirable because it is easier to compare the beta coefficients than it is to compare the raw coefficients. In this case, the slope obtained by the regression of Y on X, B_{yx}, is the same as the slope obtained by the regression of X on Y, B_{xy}. Moreover, each of these regression coefficients is equal to the simple correlation between X and Y.

$$B_{yx} = B_{xy} = r_{xy}$$

Thus, instead of running product moment correlations in the opening vignette, we could have alternatively run four separate bivariate regressions on the standardized data, with preference for athletic shoes as the dependent variable. Each of the independent variables, in turn, would serve as the independent, or predictor, variable: interest in sports, attitude toward sports personalities, attendance at sports events, and time spent watching sports on television.

A simple relationship exists between the standardized and nonstandardized regression coefficients:

$$B_{yx} = b_{yx}(s_x/s_y)$$

Attitude toward sports cars can be explained by the duration of sports car ownership using bivariate regression.

Source: testing/Shutterstock.

To illustrate the calculation of the beta coefficient by hand for the bivariate regression of Table 18.1, recall from the hand calculations for the correlation coefficient that

$$\sum_{i=1}^{n} (Y_i - \bar{Y})^2 = 120.9168$$

Therefore,

$$s_y = \sqrt{\frac{120.9168}{(12 - 1)}}$$

$$= 3.3155$$

and,

$$\sum_{i=1}^{n} (X_i - \bar{X})^2 = 304.6668$$

Therefore,

$$s_x = \sqrt{\frac{304.6668}{(12 - 1)}}$$

$$= 5.2628$$

Therefore,

$$B_{yx} = (0.5897)(5.2628)/(3.3155)$$

$$= 0.9361$$

For the regression results given in Table 18.3, the value of the beta coefficient also is estimated as 0.9361. Note that this is also the value of r calculated earlier in this chapter.

Once the parameters have been estimated, they can be tested for significance.

Significance Testing

The statistical significance of the linear relationship between X and Y can be tested by examining the hypotheses:

$$H_0 : \beta_1 = 0$$

$$H_1 : \beta_1 \neq 0$$

The null hypothesis implies that there is no linear relationship between X and Y. The alternative hypothesis is that there is a relationship, positive or negative, between X and Y. For example, the relationship between income and the number of times people dine out in a month can be statistically tested by bivariate regression. The null hypothesis would be that income has no relationship with the number of times people dine out in a month. The alternative hypothesis would be that income has a positive relationship with the number of times people dine out in a month. If the null hypothesis is not rejected, then it can be concluded that there is no relationship between X and Y, even though the regression coefficient might not be exactly zero. Typically, a two-tailed test is done. A t statistic with $n - 2$ degrees of freedom can be used, where

$$t = \frac{b}{SE_b}$$

standard error
Denotes the standard deviation of b.

SE_b denotes the standard deviation of b and is called the **standard error**.[4] The t distribution was discussed in Chapter 17.

The standard error or standard deviation of b is estimated as 0.07008, and the value of the t statistic is $t = 0.5897/0.07008 = 8.414$, with $n - 2 = 10$ degrees of freedom (see Table 18.3). From Table 4 in the Appendix of Statistical Tables, we see that the critical value of t with 10 degrees of freedom and $\alpha = 0.05$ is 2.228 for a two-tailed test. Because the calculated value of t is larger than the critical value, the null hypothesis is rejected. Hence, a significant linear relationship exists between attitude toward sports cars and duration of car ownership. The positive sign of the slope coefficient indicates that this relationship is positive. In other words, those who have owned sports cars for a longer time have more favorable attitudes toward sports cars, indicating a stronger liking for these cars.

Strength and Significance of Association

A related inference involves determining the strength and significance of the association between Y and X. The strength of association is measured by the **coefficient of determination**, r^2. In bivariate regression, r^2 is the square of the simple correlation coefficient obtained by correlating the two variables. The coefficient r^2 varies between 0 and 1. It signifies the proportion of the total variation in Y that is accounted for by the variation in X. The decomposition of the total variation in Y is similar to that for analysis of variance (see Chapter 17).

coefficient of determination
The proportion of variance in one variable associated with the variability in a second variable.

As shown in Figure 18.7, the total variation, SS_y, can be decomposed into the variation accounted for by the regression line, SS_{reg}, and the error or residual variation, SS_{error} or SS_{res}, as follows:

$$SS_y = SS_{reg} + SS_{res}$$

where

$$SS_y = \sum_{i=1}^{n} (Y_i - \bar{Y})^2$$

$$SS_{reg} = \sum_{i=1}^{n} (\hat{Y}_i - \bar{Y})^2$$

$$SS_{res} = \sum_{i=1}^{n} (Y_i - \hat{Y}_i)^2$$

The strength of association may then be calculated as follows:

$$r^2 = \frac{SS_{reg}}{SS_y}$$

$$= \frac{SS_y - SS_{res}}{SS_y}$$

To illustrate the calculations of r^2, consider again the effect of the duration of car ownership on attitude toward sports cars. Recall from earlier hand calculations of the simple correlation coefficient that:

$$SS_y = \sum_{i=1}^{n} (Y_i - \bar{Y})^2$$

$$= 120.9168$$

The predicted values ($\hat{Y}$) can be calculated using the regression equation:

$$\text{Attitude } (\hat{Y}) = 1.0793 + 0.5897(\text{Duration of car ownership})$$

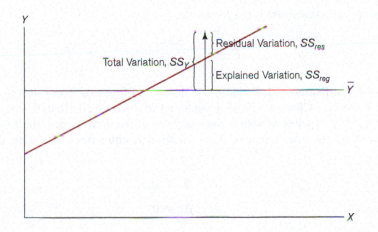

FIGURE 18.7

Decomposition of the Total Variation in Bivariate Regression

For the first observation in Table 18.1, this value is:

$$(\hat{Y}) = 1.0793 + 0.5897 \times 10 = 6.9763$$

For each successive observation, the predicted values are, in order, 8.1557, 8.1557, 3.4381, 8.1557, 4.6175, 5.7969, 2.2587, 11.6939, 6.3866, 11.1042, and 2.2587. Therefore,

$$
\begin{aligned}
SS_{reg} = \sum_{i=1}^{n}(\hat{Y}_i - \bar{Y})^2 = & \ (6.9763 - 6.5833)^2 + (8.1557 - 6.5833)^2 \\
& + (8.1557 - 6.5833)^2 + (3.4381 - 6.5833)^2 \\
& + (8.1557 - 6.5833)^2 + (4.6175 - 6.5833)^2 \\
& + (5.7969 - 6.5833)^2 + (2.2587 - 6.5833)^2 \\
& + (11.6939 - 6.5833)^2 + (6.3866 - 6.5833)^2 \\
& + (11.1042 - 6.5833)^2 + (2.2587 - 6.5833)^2 \\
= & \ 0.1544 + 2.4724 + 2.4724 + 9.8922 + 2.4724 \\
& + 3.8643 + 0.6184 + 18.7021 + 26.1182 \\
& + 0.0387 + 20.4385 + 18.7021 \\
= & \ 105.9522
\end{aligned}
$$

$$
\begin{aligned}
SS_{res} = \sum_{i=1}^{n}(Y_i - \hat{Y}_i)^2 = & \ (6 - 6.9763)^2 + (9 - 8.1557)^2 + (8 - 8.1557)^2 \\
& + (3 - 3.4381)^2 + (10 - 8.1557)^2 + (4 - 4.6175)^2 \\
& + (5 - 5.7969)^2 + (2 - 2.2587)^2 + (11 - 11.6939)^2 \\
& + (9 - 6.3866)^2 + (10 - 11.1042)^2 + (2 - 2.2587)^2 \\
= & \ 14.9644
\end{aligned}
$$

It can be seen that $SS_y = SS_{reg} + SS_{res}$. Furthermore,

$$
\begin{aligned}
r^2 = & \ SS_{reg}/SS_y \\
= & \ 105.9524/120.9168 \\
= & \ 0.8762
\end{aligned}
$$

Another, equivalent test for examining the significance of the linear relationship between X and Y (significance of b) is the test for the significance of the coefficient of determination. The hypotheses in this case are:

$$H_0 : R_{pop}^2 = 0$$

$$H_1 : R_{pop}^2 > 0$$

The appropriate test statistic is the F statistic:

$$F = \frac{SS_{reg}}{SS_{res}/(n-2)}$$

which has an F distribution with 1 and $n - 2$ degrees of freedom. The F-test is a generalized form of the t-test (see Chapter 17). If a random variable is t distributed with n degrees of freedom, then t^2 is F distributed with 1 and n degrees of freedom. Hence, the F-test for testing the significance of the coefficient of determination is equivalent to testing the following hypotheses:

$$H_0 : \beta_1 = 0$$

$$H_1 : \beta_1 \neq 0$$

or

$$H_0: \rho = 0$$

$$H_1: \rho \neq 0$$

From Table 18.3, it can be seen that:

$$r^2 = 105.9522/(105.9522 + 14.9644)$$

$$= 0.8762$$

which is the same as the value calculated earlier by hand. The value of the F statistic is:

$$F = 105.9522/(14.9644/10)$$

$$= 70.8027$$

with 1 and 10 degrees of freedom. The calculated F statistic exceeds the critical value of 4.96 determined from Table 5 in the Appendix of Statistical Tables. Therefore, the relationship is significant at $\alpha = 0.05$, corroborating the results of the t-test. If the relationship between X and Y is significant, it is meaningful to predict the values of Y based on the values of X and to estimate prediction accuracy.

Prediction Accuracy

To estimate the accuracy of predicted values, $\hat{Y}$, it is useful to calculate the **standard error of estimate (SEE)**. This statistic is the standard deviation of the actual Y values from the predicted $\hat{Y}$ values. The larger the SEE is, the poorer the fit of the regression. From Table 18.3, it can be seen that SEE is 1.2233. The SEE can be used for constructing confidence intervals around predicted values of Y (see Chapter 13).

standard error of estimate (SEE)
The standard deviation of the actual Y values from the predicted $\hat{Y}$ values.

Assumptions

The regression model makes a number of assumptions in estimating the parameters and in significance testing, as shown in Figure 18.6:

1. The error term is normally distributed. For each fixed value of X, the distribution of Y is normal.
2. The means of all these normal distributions of Y, given X, lie on a straight line with slope b.
3. The mean of the error term is 0.
4. The variance of the error term is constant. This variance does not depend on the values assumed by X.
5. The error terms are uncorrelated. In other words, the observations have been drawn independently.

Insights into the extent to which these assumptions have been met can be gained by an examination of residuals, which is covered in the next section on multiple regression.

The following example illustrates how regression analysis can result in findings with great managerial relevance.

Research in Action

Avoiding Dissatisfaction to Enhance Overall Satisfaction

A large health maintenance organization (HMO) collects data regularly as part of its ongoing patient satisfaction measurement program. In a recent study, data on patient satisfaction, quality of interaction, and related variables were obtained from 4,517 patients who subscribed to 501 primary care physicians (PCPs) affiliated with the HMO. The survey was conducted by telephone. To estimate the impact of the quality of interaction with the PCP on patient satisfaction, the researchers conducted a series of regression analyses.

The dependent variable was patient satisfaction, and the independent variable was the quality of PCP interaction. Three regressions were run: for satisfied patients, for dissatisfied patients, and for all patients. The estimates of the regression coefficient for these three regressions were 1.04, 3.73, and 2.02, respectively. As can be seen, the value of the coefficient was the highest for dissatisfied patients, indicating that dissatisfied patients are differentially more sensitive to the quality of PCP

(continued)

Source: RNewsFoto/Subaru of America Inc/Associated Press.

interaction. The implication is that, in order to enhance overall patient satisfaction, health care providers should accord greater attention to those aspects of PCP interaction that lead to dissatisfaction than to those that lead to satisfaction. The 2010 Health Insurance Plan Satisfaction Study conducted by J.D. Power and Associates surveyed 33,000 U.S. health plan members from 133 health plans in 17 regions in the United States. The results showed that after improving slightly in 2009, overall health plan member satisfaction has declined significantly in 2010, from an overall index score of 712 (on a 1,000-point scale) in 2009 to 701 in 2010. Thus, there is much room for improvement.[5]

Be an MR!	Be a DM!
Associating Ford Advertising and Sales	

Social Media

Visit www.ford.com and search the Internet—including social media—as well as your library's online databases to obtain information on the relationship between advertising and sales for automobile manufacturers. Formulate a bivariate regression model explaining the relationship between advertising and sales in the automobile industry.

As the marketing director for Ford Motor Company, how would you determine your advertising expenditures?

Multiple Regression

multiple regression

A statistical technique that simultaneously develops a mathematical relationship between two or more independent variables and an interval-scaled dependent variable.

multiple regression model

An equation used to explain the results of multiple regression analysis.

Multiple regression involves a single dependent variable and two or more independent variables. Just as bivariate regression attempts to fit a best line to the data, regression with two independent variables tries to fit a best plane to the data. To extend the bivariate regression example considered earlier, the growth rate of the U.S. economy has a positive correlation with the level of consumer spending and a negative correlation with the level of interest rates. Thus, a **multiple regression model** could be constructed with growth rate of the U.S. economy as the dependent variable and the level of consumer spending and the level of interest rates as the independent variables. The concept is similar in regression with more than two independent variables. The questions raised in the context of bivariate regression can also be answered by multiple regression by considering additional independent variables:

- Can variation in sales be explained in terms of variation in advertising expenditures, prices, and level of distribution?
- Can variation in market shares be accounted for by the size of the sales force, advertising expenditures, and sales promotion budgets?
- Are consumers' perceptions of quality determined by their perceptions of prices, brand image, and brand attributes?

Additional questions can also be answered by multiple regression:

- How much of the variation in sales can be explained by advertising expenditures, prices, and level of distribution?
- What is the contribution of advertising expenditures in explaining the variation in sales when the levels of prices and distribution are controlled?
- What levels of sales may be expected given the levels of advertising expenditures, prices, and level of distribution?

The general form of the multiple regression model is as follows:

$$Y = \beta_0 + \beta_1 X_1 + \beta_2 X_2 + \beta_3 X_3 + \ldots + \beta_k X_k + e$$

which is estimated by the following equation:

$$\hat{Y} = a + b_1 X_1 + b_2 X_2 + b_3 X_3 + \ldots + b_k X_k$$

As before, the coefficient a represents the intercept, but the bs are now the partial regression coefficients. The least-squares criterion estimates the parameters in such a way as to minimize the total error, SS_{res}. This process also maximizes the correlation between the actual values of Y and the predicted values . All the assumptions made in bivariate regression also apply in multiple regression.

Conducting Multiple Regression Analysis

The steps involved in conducting multiple regression analysis are similar to those for bivariate regression analysis. The discussion focuses on partial regression coefficients, strength of association, and significance testing.

Partial Regression Coefficients

To understand the meaning of a partial regression coefficient, let us consider again the multiple regression model with growth rate of the U.S. economy as the dependent variable and the level of consumer spending and the level of interest rates as the independent variables. In this case, there are two independent variables, so that:

$$\hat{Y} = a + b_1X_1 + b_2X_2$$

First, note that the relative magnitude of the partial regression coefficient of an independent variable is, in general, different from that of its bivariate regression coefficient. In other words, the partial regression coefficient, b_1, will be different from the regression coefficient, b, obtained by regressing Y on only X_1. This happens because X_1 and X_2 are usually correlated. In bivariate regression, X_2 was not considered, and any variation in Y that was shared by X_1 and X_2 was attributed to X_1. However, in the case of multiple independent variables, this is no longer true. Thus, in modeling the growth rate of the U.S. economy, the (partial) regression coefficient for the level of consumer spending in the multiple regression model will differ from that of the bivariate regression model.

The interpretation of the **partial regression coefficient**, b_1, is that it represents the expected change in Y when X_1 is changed by one unit but X_2 is held constant or otherwise controlled. Thus, the partial regression coefficient for the level of consumer spending will be different in multiple regression than the coefficient in bivariate regression. Likewise, b_2 represents the expected change in Y for a unit change in X_2, when X_1 is held constant. Thus, calling b_1 and b_2 partial regression coefficients is appropriate. It can also be seen that the combined effects of X_1 and X_2 on Y are additive. In other words, if X_1 and X_2 are each changed by one unit, the expected change in Y would be $(b_1 + b_2)$.

Extension to the case of k variables is straightforward. The partial regression coefficient, b_1, represents the expected change in Y when X_1 is changed by one unit and X_2 through X_k are held constant. It can also be interpreted as the bivariate regression coefficient, b, for the regression of Y on the residuals of X_1, when the effect of X_2 through X_k has been removed from X_1.

In the opening vignette, a multiple regression model was estimated with preference for athletic shoes as the dependent variable and interest in sports, attitude toward sports personalities, attendance at sports events, and time spent watching sports on television as the independent variables. The partial regression coefficient associated with each independent variable was positive and significant, indicating that higher values on each independent variable were associated with stronger preference for athletic shoes. The partial regression coefficient for interest in sports would represent the expected change in preference for athletic shoes when interest in sports is changed by one unit and attitude toward sports personalities, attendance at sports events, and time spent watching sports on television are held constant.

The beta coefficients are the partial regression coefficients obtained when all the variables $(Y, X_1, X_2, \ldots X_k)$ have been standardized to a mean of 0 and a variance of 1 before estimating the regression equation. The relationship of the standardized to the nonstandardized coefficients remains the same as before:

$$B_1 = b_1(s_{x_1}/s_y)$$

$$\vdots$$

$$B_k = b_k(s_{x_k}/s_y)$$

partial regression coefficient Denotes the change in the predicted value of Y when X_1 is changed by one unit but the other independent variables, X_2 to X_k, are held constant.

The intercept and the partial regression coefficients are estimated by solving a system of simultaneous equations derived by differentiating and equating the partial derivatives to 0. Because the various computer programs automatically estimate these coefficients, the details are not presented here. However, it is worth noting that the equations cannot be solved if (1) the sample size, n, is smaller than or equal to the number of independent variables, k, or (2) one independent variable is perfectly correlated with another.

Suppose that in explaining the attitude toward sports cars, we now introduce a second variable, the importance of performance. The data for the 12 pretest respondents on attitude toward sports cars, duration of sports car ownership, and importance attached to performance are given in Table 18.1. The results of multiple regression analysis are depicted in Table 18.4.

The corresponding SPSS and Excel outputs with explanatory notes can be downloaded from the Web site for this book. The partial regression coefficient for duration (X_1) is now 0.4811, which is different from what it was in the bivariate case. The corresponding beta coefficient is 0.7636. The partial regression coefficient for importance attached to performance (X_2) is 0.2887, with a beta coefficient of 0.3138. The estimated regression equation is:

$$\hat{Y} = 0.3373 + 0.4811X_1 + 0.2887X_2$$

or

$$\text{Attitude} = 0.3373 + 0.4811(\text{Duration}) + 0.2887(\text{Importance})$$

This equation can be used for a variety of purposes, including predicting attitudes toward sports cars, given knowledge of the respondents' duration of sports car ownership and the importance they attach to performance.

Strength of Association

The strength of the relationship stipulated by the regression equation can be determined by using the appropriate measures of association. The total variation is decomposed as in the bivariate case:

$$SS_y = SS_{reg} + SS_{res}$$

where

$$SS_y = \sum_{i=1}^{n} (Y_i - \bar{Y})^2$$

$$SS_{reg} = \sum_{i=1}^{n} (\hat{Y}_i - \bar{Y})^2$$

$$SS_{res} = \sum_{i=1}^{n} (Y_i - \hat{Y}_i)^2$$

SPSS Output File

Excel Output File

TABLE 18.4 Multiple Regression

Multiple R	.9721
R^2	.9450
Adjusted R^2	.9330
Standard Error	.8597

Analysis of Variance

	df	Sum of Squares	Mean Square
Regression	2	114.2643	57.1321
Residual	9	6.6524	.7392
$F = 77.2936$		Significance of $F = .0000$	

Variables in the Equation

Variable	b	SE_b	Beta (B)	T	Sig. T
Importance	.2887	.08608	.3138	3.353	.0085
Duration	.4811	.05895	.7636	8.160	.0000
(Constant)	.3373	.56736		.595	.5668

The strength of association is measured by the square of the multiple correlation coefficient, R^2, which also is called the **coefficient of multiple determination**:

$$R^2 = \frac{SS_{reg}}{SS_y}$$

The multiple correlation coefficient, R, can also be viewed as the simple correlation coefficient, r, between Y and $\hat{Y}$. Several points about the characteristics of R^2 are worth noting. The coefficient of multiple determination, R^2, cannot be less than the highest bivariate, r^2, of any individual independent variable with the dependent variable. R^2 will be larger when the correlations between the independent variables are low. If the independent variables are statistically independent (uncorrelated), then R^2 will be the sum of bivariate r^2 of each independent variable with the dependent variable. R^2 cannot decrease as more independent variables are added to the regression equation. However, diminishing returns do set in, so that after the first few variables the additional independent variables do not make much of a contribution. For this reason, R^2 is adjusted for the number of independent variables and the sample size by using the following formula:

$$\textbf{Adjusted } R^2 = R^2 - \frac{k(1 - R^2)}{n - k - 1}$$

For the regression results given in Table 18.4, the value of R^2 is:

$$R^2 = 114.2643/(114.2643 + 6.6524)$$

$$= 114.2643/120.9167$$

$$= .9450$$

This is higher than the r^2 value of 0.8762 obtained in the bivariate case. The r^2 in the bivariate case is the square of the simple (product moment) correlation between attitude toward sports cars and duration of sports car ownership. The R^2 obtained in multiple regression also is higher than the square of the simple correlation between attitude and importance attached to performance (which can be estimated as 0.5379). The adjusted R^2 is estimated as:

$$\text{Adjusted } R^2 = 0.9450 - 2(1.0 - 0.9450)/(12 - 2 - 1)$$

$$= 0.9450 - 0.0120$$

$$= 0.9330$$

Note that the value of adjusted R^2 is close to R^2 and both are higher than r^2 for the bivariate case. This suggests that the addition of the second independent variable—importance attached to performance—makes a contribution in explaining the variation in attitude toward sports cars. Of course, R^2 should be significant, and higher values of R^2 are more desirable than lower values. However, in commercial marketing research, values of R^2 as high as 0.9 or higher are uncommon. Values of R^2 in the 0.5 to 0.8 range may be reasonable in many commercial marketing research projects.

Significance Testing

Significance testing involves testing the significance of the overall regression equation as well as specific partial regression coefficients. The null hypothesis for the overall test is that the coefficient of multiple determination in the population, R^2_{pop}, is zero.

$$H_0 : R^2_{pop} = 0$$

This is equivalent to the following null hypothesis:

$$H_0 : \beta_1 = \beta_2 = \beta_3 = \ldots = \beta_k = 0$$

coefficient of multiple determination
In multiple regression, the strength of association is measured by the square of the multiple correlation coefficient, R^2, which is called the coefficient of multiple determination.

adjusted R^2
The value of R^2 adjusted for the number of independent variables and the sample size.

The overall test can be conducted by using an F statistic:

$$F = \frac{SS_{reg}/k}{SS_{res}/(n-k-1)}$$

$$= \frac{R^2/k}{(1-R^2)/(n-k-1)}$$

which has an F distribution with k and $(n-k-1)$ degrees of freedom. For the multiple regression results given in Table 18.4,

$$F = \frac{114.2643/2}{6.6524/9} = 77.2936$$

which is significant at $\alpha = 0.05$.

   If the overall null hypothesis is rejected, one or more population partial regression coefficients have a value different from 0. To determine which specific coefficients (b_is) are nonzero, additional tests are necessary. Testing for the significance of the b_is can be done in a manner similar to that in the bivariate case by using t-tests. The significance of the partial coefficient for importance attached to performance can be tested by the following equation:

$$t = \frac{b}{SE_b}$$

$$= 0.2887/0.08608$$

$$= 3.353$$

which has a t distribution with $n-k-1$ degrees of freedom. This coefficient is significant at $\alpha = 0.05$. The significance of the coefficient for duration of sports car ownership is tested in a similar way and found to be significant. Therefore, both the duration of sports car ownership and the importance attached to performance are important in explaining attitude toward sports cars. However, if any of the regression coefficients are not significant, they should be treated as zero.

   Some software programs provide an equivalent F-test, often called the **partial F-test**. This involves a decomposition of the total regression sum of squares, SS_{reg}, into components related to each independent variable.

Examination of Residuals

A **residual** is the difference between the observed value of Y_i and the value predicted by the regression equation, $\hat{Y}_i$. Residuals are used in the calculation of several statistics associated with regression. Scattergrams of the residuals, in which the residuals are plotted against the predicted values, $\hat{Y}_i$; time; respondents; or predictor variables, provide useful insights in examining the appropriateness of the underlying assumptions and the regression model fitted. For example, the assumption of a normally distributed error term can be examined by constructing a histogram of the residuals. A visual check reveals whether the distribution is normal. Additionally, if the pattern of residuals is not random, then some of the underlying assumptions are being violated. In particular, we suggest the following simplified but effective procedure for examining residuals:

1. Examine the histogram of standardized residuals. Compare the frequency of residuals to the normal distribution. If the difference is small, then the normality assumption can reasonably be met.
2. Examine the normal probability plot of standardized residuals. The normal probability plot shows the observed standardized residuals compared to expected standardized residuals from a normal distribution. If the observed residuals are normally distributed, they will fall on the 45-degree line.
3. Examine the plot of standardized residuals versus standardized predicted values. This plot should be random with no discernible pattern. This will provide an indication on the assumptions of linearity and constant variance for the error term.
4. Look at the table of residual statistics and identify any standardized predicted values or standardized residuals that are more than plus or minus three standard deviations. Values larger than this might indicate the presence of outliers in the data.

partial F-test
This is an F-test that involves a decomposition of the total regression sum of squares, SS_{reg}, into components related to each independent variable.

residual
The difference between the observed value of Y_i and the value predicted by the regression equation, $\hat{Y}_i$.

SPSS Output File

The plots and the table can be requested when the regression is run, for example, when using SPSS. Go the student Web site for this book and retrieve the file named Chapter 18 Multiple Regression.spo. This is the SPSS output file for multiple regression on the data of Table 18.1, and it includes the three plots that we have recommended. From the histogram, it can be seen that five residuals are positive, whereas seven residuals are negative. By comparing the frequency distribution with the normal distribution that is plotted in the same output, we can see that the assumption of normality is probably not met but that the departure from normality might not be severe. Of course, one can do a more formal statistical test for normality if that is warranted. All the standardized residuals are within plus or minus two standard deviations. Furthermore, many of the residuals are relatively small, which means that most of the model predictions are quite good.

The normal probability plot shows that the residuals are quite close to the 45-degree line shown in the graph. When we look at the plot of the standardized residuals against the standardized predicted values, no systematic pattern can be discerned in the spread of the residuals. Finally, the table of residual statistics indicates that all the standardized predicted values and all the standardized residuals are within plus or minus two standard deviations. Hence, we can conclude that multiple regression on the data of Table 18.1 does not appear to result in gross violations of the assumptions. This suggests that the relationship we are trying to predict is linear and that the error terms are more or less normally distributed.

Regression is a robust statistical procedure, and substantial violations of the assumptions are needed to cause serious problems. We further illustrate the application of multiple regression with an example.

Research in Action

Wendy's: Improving Likelihood of Patronage

Wendy's (www.wendys.com), part of the Wendy's/Arby's group (www.wendysarbys.com) with revenues of $3.42 billion in 2010, had more than 6,500 restaurants worldwide as of 2010. In an online survey, respondents were asked to rate their likelihood of patronizing popular fast-food restaurants and to rate those restaurants on various factors using 5-point Likert-type scales. A multiple regression analysis was conducted. Likelihood to patronize was the dependent variable. The independent variables were the evaluations of the restaurant on the various factors that influence patronage. The fit of the regression model was good, and the coefficients for the following variables were significant at the 0.05 level:

Menu selection
Quality
Service
Value
Convenience of location

Based on this analysis, Wendy's started making improvements on all the significant factors. For example, menu selection was improved by adding the Steakhouse Double-Melt Cheeseburger, which consists of two patties of fresh, never frozen, beef packed with a melted middle. In addition, it expanded its well-known Frosty, which is a cool, creamy chocolate or vanilla treat, by serving it with ice-cold root beer, Coca-Cola, and other drinks. On July 9, 2010, Wendy's raised the bar on salads by introducing four new fresh salads: Spicy Chicken Caesar salad, BLT Cobb salad, Apple Pecan Chicken salad, and Baja salad. Improvements were also made on the other factors. These changes have resulted in increased sales.[6]

Source: © Michael Neelon(misc)/Alamy.

Be a DM!

Be an MR!

Brand Evaluation and Preference for Dell

As the marketing director for Dell's laptop computers, how would you improve the brand's image and competitive positioning?

Visit www.dell.com and search the Internet—including social media—as well as your library's online databases to obtain information on the factors consumers use to evaluate competing brands of laptop computers. Formulate a multiple regression model explaining consumer preferences for laptop computer brands as a function of the brand evaluations on the consumer choice criteria factors used to evaluate competing brands.

Social Media

Summary Illustration Using the Opening Vignette

The product moment correlation coefficient measures the linear association between two metric variables. In the opening vignette, preference for athletic shoes showed strong positive correlations with sports-related variables, such as interest in sports, attitude toward sports personalities, attendance at sports events, and time spent watching sports on television.

Bivariate regression derives a mathematical equation in the form of a straight line between a single metric criterion variable and a single metric predictor variable. Instead of running product moment correlations, we could have alternatively run four separate bivariate regressions on the standardized data with preference for athletic shoes as the dependent variable. Each of the independent variables, in turn, would serve as the predictor variable: interest in sports, attitude toward sports personalities, attendance at sports events, and time spent watching sports on television.

Multiple regression involves a single dependent variable and two or more independent variables. The partial regression coefficient represents the expected change in the dependent variable when one of the independent variables is changed by one unit and the other independent variables are held constant. A multiple regression model—with preference for athletic shoes as the dependent variable, and interest in sports, attitude toward sports personalities, attendance at sports events, and time spent watching sports on television as the independent variables—had very good strength of association. The partial regression coefficient associated with each independent variable was positive and significant, indicating that higher values on each independent variable were associated with stronger preference for athletic shoes. The partial regression coefficient for interest in sports would represent the expected change in preference for athletic shoes when interest in sports is changed by one unit and attitude toward sports personalities, attendance at sports events, and time spent watching sports on television are held constant. Figures 18.8 and 18.9 provide concept maps for conducting product moment correlation and bivariate regression, respectively. In these figures, the major concepts are connected by bold arrows using descriptors. Thus, in Figure 18.8, product moment correlation is calculated using metric (interval- or ratio-scaled) data, X and Y. Each major concept is described by minor concepts that are connected to that major concept by lines with

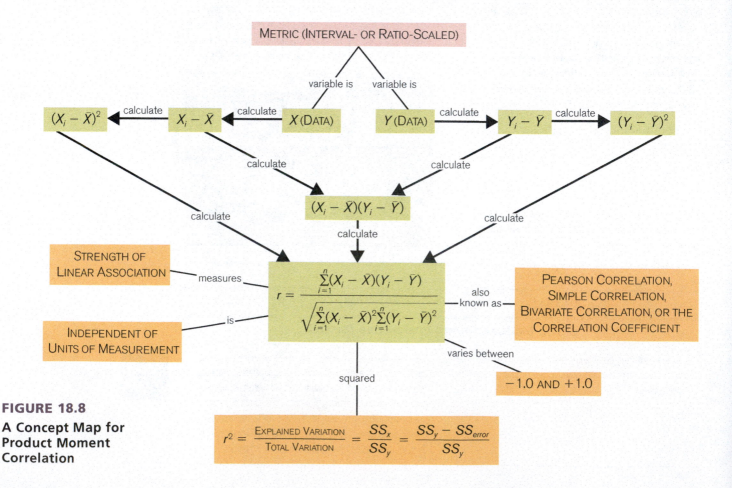

FIGURE 18.8

A Concept Map for Product Moment Correlation

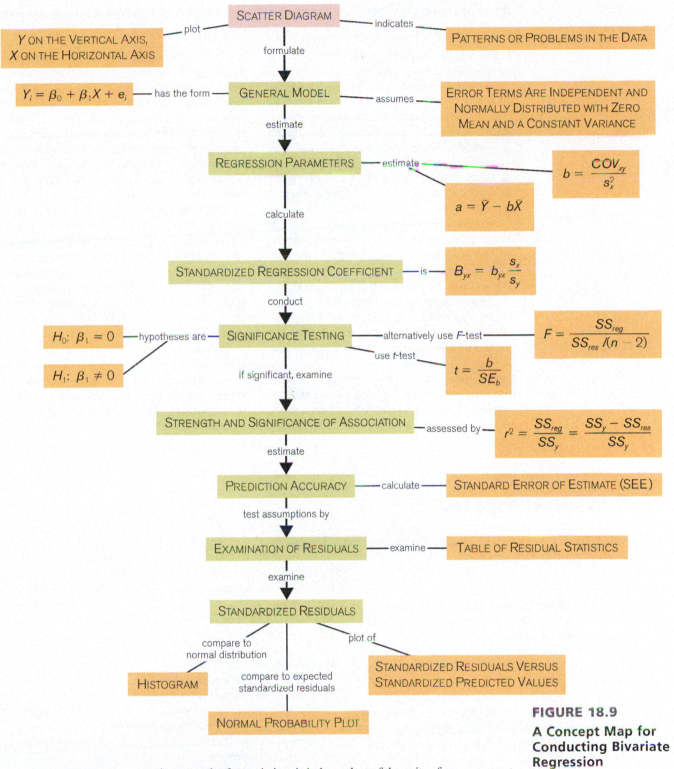

FIGURE 18.9

A Concept Map for Conducting Bivariate Regression

descriptors. Thus, r measures the strength of association, is independent of the units of measurement, etc. The rest of the figure can be interpreted similarly.

Marketing Research and Social Media

When quantitative data are collected from social media, such as by conducting surveys, correlation and regression procedures discussed in this chapter can be implemented as usual. Even in the case of qualitative data, it may be possible to conduct some correlation and regression analysis if the data are coded appropriately. We illustrate an application of correlation analysis in comparing Twitter sentiments results to those obtained from public opinion polls.

Research in Action

Twitter Sentiments Yields Results Similar to Public Opinion Polls

A Carnegie Mellon study of computer analysis of sentiments expressed in a billion Twitter messages during 2008–2009 yielded measures of consumer confidence and of presidential job approval similar to those of well-established public opinion polls. In the study, Noah Smith and his colleagues at Carnegie Mellon collected a billion microblog messages—averaging about 11 words each—posted to Twitter during 2008 and 2009. They used simple text analysis techniques to identify messages that pertained to the economy or to politics and then found words within the text that indicated whether the writer expressed positive or negative sentiments.

Results regarding consumer confidence were compared with the Index of Consumer Sentiment (ICS) from Reuters/University of Michigan Surveys of Consumers and the Gallup Organization's Economic Confidence Index. Political sentiments regarding President Obama were compared with Gallup's daily tracking poll on presidential job approval, and views regarding the 2008 U.S. presidential election were compared with a compilation of 46 different polls prepared by Pollster.com. The ICS, Gallup, and Pollster.com measurements were all obtained from telephone surveys using traditional survey techniques.

The Twitter-derived sentiment measurements were much more volatile day-to-day than the polling data, but when the researchers "smoothed" the results by averaging them over a period of days, the results often correlated closely with the polling data.

Consumer confidence, for instance, followed the same general slide through 2008 and the same rebound in February/March of 2009 as was seen in the poll data. The researchers noted that the ICS and Gallup data had a correlation of 0.86 over the period; the Twitter-derived sentiments had between 0.72 and 0.79 correlation with the Gallup data, depending on the number of days averaged to smooth the data. Likewise, both the Twitter-derived sentiments and the traditional polls reflected declining approval of President Obama's job performance during 2009, with a 0.72 correlation between them.

However, the researchers found that their sentiment analysis did not correlate as well with election polling during 2008. For instance, increased mentions of "Obama" tended to correlate with rises in Barack Obama's polling numbers, but increased mentions of "McCain" also correlated with rises in Obama's popularity. Improved computational methods for understanding natural language, particularly the unusual lexicon of microblogs, will be necessary before Twitter feeds can be reliably mined to predict elections, the researchers concluded.

The findings suggest that analyzing the text found in streams of tweets could become an inexpensive and rapid way of gauging public opinion on at least some subjects. However, tools for extracting public opinion from social media text are still crude and social media remain in their infancy, indicating the need to exercise caution when using the results.[7]

WHAT WOULD YOU DO?

The West Michigan Whitecaps: Fanning Fan Loyalty

The Situation

The West Michigan Whitecaps (www.whitecaps-baseball.com or westmichigan.whitecaps.milb.com/index.jsp?sid=t582), a minor league baseball team in Grand Rapids, wondered what it should do to develop fan loyalty. How could the team best keep it, make it grow, and take advantage of it? In order to find out, Whitecap's president Lew Chamberlin hired Message Factors (www.messagefactors.com), a Memphis, Tennessee–based research firm, to help the Whitecaps determine how to effectively maintain fan loyalty on a limited budget. Message Factors developed a study that used a proprietary value analysis technique that would examine the relationship between the overall perceived value and specific satisfaction attributes in order to determine loyalty drivers. The analysis technique determined four things: (1) the basics—what customers expect of the company; (2) value issues—what customers value about the company; (3) irritations—what customers do not like about the company; and (4) unimportants—what customers do not care about.

Qualitative research was conducted to identify a set of 71 attributes that influenced fan loyalty. Next, a questionnaire was designed that incorporated the 71 attributes. This questionnaire was then administered to 1,010 fans at Whitecaps games. From this, the marketing research company was able to find the information it sought. The basics were determined to be values such as stadium safety, restroom cleanliness, and variety in the food items available. The Whitecaps want to not only meet these basic expectations, but also to surpass them to guarantee that fans will return and be loyal. The value issues are the ones that can really help the team build loyalty. These

included things such as helpful box office personnel, convenience of purchasing tickets, easy parking, and autograph opportunities. Some irritations were identified, such as the high price, low quality, and lack of variety of souvenirs. However, the research also showed that fans do not really expect to be pleased with these areas of sports attendance. It was also determined that there were no unimportant aspects.

The Marketing Research Decision

1. In order to determine the relative importance of value drivers, what type of data analysis should Message Factors conduct?
   a. Mean importance of helpful box office personnel, convenience of purchasing tickets, ease of parking, and autograph opportunities
   b. Cross-tabulation of overall value with helpful box office personnel, convenience of purchasing tickets, ease of parking, and autograph opportunities
   c. Product moment correlations of overall value with helpful box office personnel, convenience of purchasing tickets, ease of parking, and autograph opportunities
   d. Multiple regression with overall value as the dependent variable and helpful box office personnel, convenience of purchasing tickets, ease of parking, and autograph opportunities as the independent variables
   e. All of the above

2. Discuss the role of the type of data analysis you recommend in enabling Lew Chamberlin to determine the relative importance of the four value drivers.

The Marketing Management Decision

1. In order to enhance the value of Whitecaps games for the fans, what should Lew Chamberlin do?
   a. Train box office and other personnel to be helpful.
   b. Increase the convenience of purchasing tickets.
   c. Increase the convenience of parking.
   d. Provide fans with opportunities for autographs.
   e. All of the above.

2. Discuss how the marketing management-decision action that you recommend to Lew Chamberlin is influenced by the type of data analysis that you suggested earlier and by the findings of that analysis.

What Lew Chamberlin Did

Data analysis revealed that the Whitecaps had performed well on the basics, so it was able to shift its focus to improving in the value areas. Analysis also showed that the personnel variable was a very high contributor to value perception. The Whitecaps were rated as average in this area, as were its competitors, so this is a key area that provides the Whitecaps with an opportunity to be better than and overtake the competition. Lew Chamberlin also improved ease of ticket purchasing and provided fans with opportunities for autographs after the game. The next season, the Whitecaps raised ticket prices by 25 percent and still got a 100-percent renewal. Lew Chamberlin had figured out how to enhance fan loyalty![8]

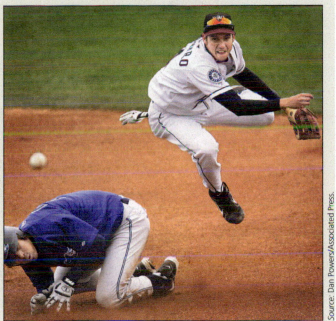

Source: Dan Powers/Associated Press.

Software Applications

The computer programs available for conducting correlation analysis are described in Exhibit 18.1. In SPSS, for computing product moment correlations select ANALYZE > CORRELATE > BIVARIATE. Correlations can be determined in Excel by using the DATA > DATA ANALYSIS > CORRELATION function. In Minitab, correlation can be computed using the STAT > BASIC STATISTICS > CORRELATION function. In SAS, the correlation analysis can be conducted by selecting ANALYZE > MULTIVARIATE > CORRELATIONS.

As described in Exhibit 18.2, the statistical packages contain several programs for performing regression analysis, calculating the associated statistics, performing tests for significance, and plotting the residuals. In SPSS, the main program is REGRESSION. To run bivariate and multiple regressions click ANALYZE > REGRESSION > LINEAR. In Excel, REGRESSION can

EXHIBIT 18.1
Computer Programs for Correlations

SPSS
The CORRELATE > BIVARIATE program computes product moment correlations with significance levels. Univariate statistics, covariance, and cross-product deviations may also be requested. Significance levels are included in the output.

Excel
Correlations can be determined in Excel by using the DATA > DATA ANALYSIS > CORRELATION function. Use the Correlation Worksheet Function when a correlation coefficient for two cell ranges is needed.

Minitab
Correlation can be computed using STAT > BASIC STATISTICS > CORRELATION function. It calculates product moment correlations using all the columns.

SAS
For a point-and-click approach for performing metric correlations, use the ANALYZE task within SAS Enterprise Guide. The MULTIVARIATE > CORRELATIONS task offers Pearson product moment correlations, as well as some other measures.

EXHIBIT 18.2
Computer Programs for Regression

SPSS
REGRESSION > LINEAR calculates bivariate and multiple regression equations, associated statistics, and plots. It allows for an easy examination of residuals. Regression statistics can be requested with PLOT, which produces simple scattergrams and some other types of plots.

Excel
REGRESSION can be accessed from the DATA > DATA ANALYSIS menu. Depending on the features selected, the output can consist of a summary output table, including an ANOVA table, a standard error of Y estimate, coefficients, standard error of coefficients, R^2 values, and the number of observations. In addition, the function computes a residual output table, residual plot, line fit plot, normal probability plot, and a two-column probability data-output table.

Minitab
Regression analysis, under the STAT > REGRESSION function, can perform simple and multiple analysis. The output includes a linear regression equation, table of coefficients, R^2, R^2 adjusted, analysis of variance table, and a table of fits and residuals that provide unusual observations. Other available features include fitted line plot and residual plots.

SAS
For a point-and-click approach for performing regression analysis, use the ANALYZE task within SAS Enterprise Guide. The REGRESSION > LINEAR task calculates bivariate and multiple regression equations, associated statistics, and plots. It allows for an easy examination of residuals.

be accessed from the DATA > DATA ANALYSIS menu. In Minitab, REGRESSION ANALYSIS, under the STAT > REGRESSION function, can perform bivariate and multiple regression analyses. In SAS, the most general way to run regressions is to select ANALYZE > REGRESSION > LINEAR, similar to SPSS.

SPSS and Excel Computerized Demonstration Movies

We have developed computerized demonstration movies that give step-by-step instructions for running all the SPSS and Excel programs that are discussed in this book. These demonstration movies can be downloaded from the Web site for this book. The instructions for running these demonstration movies are given in Exhibit 15.2.

SPSS and Excel Screen Captures with Notes

The step-by-step instructions for running the various SPSS and Excel programs discussed in this book are also illustrated in screen captures with appropriate notes. These screen captures can be downloaded from the Web site for this book.

SPSS Windows

The CORRELATE program computes product moment correlations with significance levels. Univariate statistics, covariance, and cross-product deviations can also be requested. Significance levels are included in the output. To select this procedures using SPSS for Windows click:

Analyze > Correlate > Bivariate . . .

Scatterplots can be obtained by selecting:

Graphs > Legacy Dialogs >Scatter/Dot > Simple Scatter > Define

REGRESSION calculates bivariate and multiple regression equations, associated statistics, and plots. It allows for an easy examination of residuals. This procedure can be run by selecting:

Analyze > Regression > Linear . . .

Detailed Steps: Overview

Detailed step-by-step instructions for running the SPSS programs for the data analysis presented in this chapter can be downloaded from the Web site for this book in two forms: (1) computerized demonstration movies, and (2) screen captures. In addition, these steps are illustrated in the following sections. These steps are given for PASW STATISTICS 18 and IBM SPSS STATISTICS 19; they are essentially the same in both these versions. The steps in the earlier versions are about the same with minor differences in the labeling of some of the boxes. The demonstration movies, and screen captures for the earlier versions, have also been posted on the Web site.

Detailed Steps: Correlation

The following are the detailed steps for running a correlation between attitude toward sports cars and duration of sports car ownership given in Table 18.1. A positive correlation is to be expected.

1. Select ANALYZE from the SPSS menu bar.
2. Click CORRELATE and then BIVARIATE.
3. Move "Attitude Towards Sports Cars[attitude]" and "Duration of Car Ownership[duration]" into the VARIABLES: box.
4. Check PEARSON under CORRELATION COEFFICIENTS.
5. Check ONE-TAILED under TEST OF SIGNIFICANCE.
6. Check FLAG SIGNIFICANT CORRELATIONS.
7. Click OK.

Detailed Steps: Bivariate and Multiple Regression

The following are the detailed steps for running a bivariate regression with attitude toward sports cars as the dependent variable and duration of sports car ownership as the independent variable using the data of Table 18.1.

1. Select ANALYZE from the SPSS menu bar.
2. Click REGRESSION and then LINEAR.
3. Move "Attitude Towards Sports Cars[attitude]" into the DEPENDENT box.
4. Move "Duration of Car Ownership[duration]" into the INDEPENDENT(S) box.
5. Select ENTER in the METHOD box (default option).
6. Click STATISTICS and check ESTIMATES under REGRESSION COEFFICIENTS.
7. Check MODEL FIT.
8. Click CONTINUE.
9. Click PLOTS.
10. In the LINEAR REGRESSION:PLOTS box, move *ZRESID into the Y: box and *ZPRED into the X: box.
11. Check HISTOGRAM and NORMAL PROBABILITY PLOT in the STANDARDIZED RESIDUALS PLOTS.
12. Click CONTINUE.
13. Click OK.

The steps for running multiple regression are similar, except for step 4. In step 4, move "Duration of Car Ownership" and "Importance Attached to Performance[importan]" into the INDEPENDENT(S) box.

Experiential Learning

Correlation and Regression

Go to the textbook Web site and download the survey used in interviewing recently nonreturning students at Musial University (MU), a public urban university in the midsized city of Musial. The administrators at MU were interested in obtaining the perspectives of "dropout" or "stopout" students so that MU could enhance its programs, facilities, and services. Although the actual name of the university has been disguised, the research project and the accompanying data are real. Download the actual survey used in this study: Musial Retention Survey.doc, as well as the SPSS system file: Musial Retention Data.sav.

1. Read Musial Retention Survey.doc.
2. Open SPSS and read-in your data from Musial Retention Data.sav.
3. Try to understand the associations for having no football program at MU.

SPSS Data File

(continued)

Focus on question Q5n ("I would have very much enjoyed having a football team at MU.") and the correlations with these variables: Q5k, good recreation facilities; Q5l, great social environment; Q5o, attended many sporting events; Q5x, rich learning environment; Q5aa, felt my progress mattered to MU administrators; and Q5bb, felt I mattered to other students.

Create a correlation table composed of Pearson product moment correlations for the seven variables Q5n, Q5k, Q5l, Q5o, Q5x, Q5aa, and Q5bb. Review the output.
(What are the H_0 and H_1 for each of these binary relationships?)

> ANALYZE
> > CORRELATE
> > > BIVARIATE
> > > > BIVARIATE CORRELATIONS window
> > > > > Select I would have . . . [q5n], q5.k[q5.k], q5.l[q5.l], q5.o[q5.o], q5.x[q5.x], q5.aa[q5.aa], and q5.bb[q5.bb].
> > > > > > Click OK.

Using Q5x as the dependent variable ("The MU learning environment is a rich one."), conduct a multiple regression analysis composed of five independent variables: Q5k, good recreation facilities; Q5l, great social environment; Q5r, convenient location; Q5s, good advising center; and Q5bb, felt I mattered to other students.
(What are the H_0 and H_1 for your regression model?)

> ANALYZE
> > REGRESSION
> > > LINEAR
> > > > DEPENDENT box of the LINEAR REGRESION window
> > > > > Enter q5.x[q5.x] ("...learning environment is a rich one.").
> > > > INDEPENDENT(S) box of the LINEAR REGRESION window
> > > > > Enter all five variables q5.k[q5.k], q5.l[q5.l], q5.r[q5.r], q5.s[q5.s], and q5.bb[q5.bb].

Make sure the Method selected is ENTER (default).
Click the STATISTICS button.
> Select DESCRIPTIVES in addition to the default selections.
> Click CONTINUE.
Click the OPTIONS button.
Under MISSING VALUES select REPLACE WITH MEAN.
> (In this way, you will make sure any missing values receive a mean value.)

> Click CONTINUE.
> > Click OK.
> > > Review your SPSS output.
Run the Correlation analysis for the five variables chosen for the previous regression analysis.

> ANALYZE
> > CORRELATE
> > > BIVARIATE
> > > > BIVARIATE CORRELATIONS window
> > > > > Select q5.x[q5.x], q5.k[q5.k], q5.l[q5.l], q5.r[q5.r], q5.s[q5.s], and q5.bb[q5.bb]
> > > > > > Click OK.

Compare the binary correlation coefficients of q5.x[q5.x] with q5.k[q5.k], q5.l[q5.l], q5.r[q5.r], q5.s[q5.s], and q5.bb[q5.bb] in the Correlations portion with the Beta values under the Standardized Coefficients column of the Coefficients table for your multiple regression analysis. What did you find? Why is this so?

Extra

As you can sense, many analyses can be conducted with this data set. Have fun doing cross-tabulations, *t*-tests, and other analyses.

Epilogue

Download Musial Retention Report.ppt to glimpse what was presented to the MU administrators in a formal presentation session.

Excel

We give an overview of the detailed steps involved in conducting these analyses using Excel. Then we provide detailed step-by-step instructions for estimating correlation, as well as bivariate and multiple regression.

Detailed Steps: Overview

Detailed step-by-step instructions for running the Excel programs for the data analysis presented in this chapter can be downloaded from the Web site for this book in two forms: (1) computerized demonstration movies, and (2) screen captures. In addition, these steps are illustrated in the following sections. These steps are given for Excel 2007 and Excel 2010; they are essentially the same in both these versions. The steps in the earlier versions are about the same with minor differences in how "Data Analysis" is accessed and the labeling of some of the boxes. The demonstration movies, and screen captures for the earlier versions, have also been posted on the Web site.

Detailed Steps: Correlation

The following are the detailed steps for running a correlation between attitude toward sports cars and duration of sports car ownership given in Table 18.1.

1. Select DATA tab.
2. In the ANALYSIS tab, select DATA ANALYSIS.

3. DATA ANALYSIS window pops up.
4. Select CORRELATION from the DATA ANALYSIS window.
5. Click OK.
6. The CORRELATION pop-up window appears on the screen.
7. The CORRELATION window has two portions:
    a. INPUT
    b. OUTPUT OPTIONS
8. The INPUT portion asks for the following inputs:
    a. Click in the INPUT RANGE box. Select (highlight) all rows of data under ATTITUDE and DURATION. $B$2:$C$13 should appear on INPUT RANGE.
    b. Click on COLUMNS beside GROUPED BY.
    c. Leave LABELS IN FIRST ROW as blank.
9. In the OUTPUT OPTIONS pop-up window, select NEW WORKBOOK Option.
10. Click OK.

Detailed Steps: Bivariate and Multiple Regression

The following are the detailed steps for running a bivariate regression with attitude toward sports cars as the dependent variable and duration of sports car ownership as the independent variable using the data in Table 18.1.

1. Select DATA tab.
2. In the ANALYSIS tab, select DATA ANALYSIS
3. DATA ANALYSIS window pops up.
4. Select REGRESSION from the DATA ANALYSIS window.
5. Click OK.
6. The REGRESSION pop-up window appears on the screen.
7. The REGRESSION window has four portions:
    a. INPUT
    b. OUTPUT OPTIONS
    c. RESIDUALS
    d. NORMAL PROBABILITY
8. The INPUT portion asks for the following:
    a. Click in the INPUT Y RANGE box. Select (highlight) all the rows of data under ATTITUDE. $B$2:$B$13 should appear in INPUT Y RANGE box.
    b. Click in the INPUT X RANGE box. Select (highlight) all the rows of data under DURATION. $C$2:$C$13 should appear in INPUT X RANGE box.
    c. Leave LABELS and CONSTANT IS ZERO as blanks. CONFIDENCE LEVEL should be 95% (default).
9. In the OUTPUT OPTIONS, select NEW WORKBOOK option.
10. Under RESIDUALS check RESIDUAL PLOTS.
11. Under NORMAL PROBABILITY check NORMAL PROBABILITY PLOTS.
12. Click OK.

The steps for running multiple regression are similar, except for step 8b. In step 8b, click in the INPUT X RANGE box. Select (highlight) all the rows of data under Duration and Importance. $C$2:$D$13 should appear on INPUT X RANGE.

Summary

The product moment correlation coefficient, r, measures the linear association between two metric (interval- or ratio-scaled) variables. Its square, r^2, measures the proportion of variation in one variable explained by the other.

Bivariate regression derives a mathematical equation between a single metric criterion variable and a single metric predictor variable. The equation is derived in the form of a straight line by using the least-squares procedure. When the regression is run on standardized data, the intercept assumes a value of 0, and the regression coefficients are called beta weights. The strength of association is measured by the coefficient of determination, r^2, which is obtained by computing a ratio of SS_{reg} to SS_y. Scattergrams of the residuals are useful for examining the appropriateness of the underlying assumptions and the fit of the regression model.

Multiple regression involves a single dependent variable and two or more independent variables. The partial regression coefficient, b_1, represents the expected change in Y when X_1 is changed by one unit and X_2 through X_k are held constant. The strength of association is measured by the coefficient of multiple determination, R^2. The significance of the overall regression equation may be tested by the overall F-test. Individual partial regression coefficients can be tested for significance using the t-test.

Key Terms and Concepts

Product moment correlation (r)   513
Covariance   514
Regression analysis   519
Bivariate regression   519
Bivariate regression model   519
Scatter diagram (scattergram)   519
Least-squares procedure   520

Sum of squared errors   521
Estimated or predicted value   521
Standardization   522
Beta coefficient (beta weight)   522
Standard error   524
Coefficient of determination   525
Standard error of estimate (SEE)   527

Multiple regression   528
Multiple regression model   528
Partial regression coefficient   529
Coefficient of multiple determination   531
Adjusted R^2 531
Partial F-test   532
Residual   532

Suggested Cases and Video Cases

Running Case with Real Data

1.1 Hewlett-Packard

Comprehensive Cases with Real Data

3.1 Bank of America   3.2 McDonald's   3.3 Boeing

Comprehensive Brief Harvard Business School Cases

4.1 TruEarth Healthy Foods: Market Research for a New Product Introduction (4065)
4.2 The Springfield Nor'easters: Maximizing Revenues in the Minor Leagues (2510)
4.3 Metabical: Positioning and Communications Strategy for a New Weight-Loss Drug (4240)
4.4 Saxonville Sausage Company (2085)

Online Video Case

18.1 Marriott

Live Research: Conducting a Marketing Research Project

1. It is desirable to calculate product moment correlations between all interval-scaled variables. This gives an idea of the correlations between variables.

2. Students should also be encouraged to run several bivariate regressions and to compare these results with the corresponding product moment correlations.

3. Multiple regressions should be run when examining the association between a single dependent variable and several independent variables.

Acronym

The main features of regression analysis may be summarized by the acronym REGRESSION:

R esidual analysis is useful

E stimation of parameters: solution of simultaneous equations

G eneral model is linear

R^2 strength of association

E rror terms are independent and $N(0, \sigma^2)$

S tandardized regression coefficients

S tandard error of estimate: prediction accuracy

I ndividual coefficients and overall F-tests

O ptimal: minimizes total error

N onstandardized regression coefficients

Review Questions

1. What is the product moment correlation coefficient? Does a product moment correlation of zero between two variables imply that the variables are not related?
2. Give an example of a bivariate regression model and identify the dependent and the independent variables.
3. What are the main uses of regression analysis?
4. What is the least-squares procedure?
5. Explain the meaning of standardized regression coefficients.
6. How is the strength of association measured in bivariate regression? In multiple regression?

7. What is meant by prediction accuracy?
8. What is the standard error of estimate?
9. What assumptions underlie the error term?
10. What is multiple regression? How does it differ from bivariate regression?
11. Explain the meaning of a partial regression coefficient. Why is it called such?
12. State the null hypothesis in testing the significance of the overall multiple regression equation. How is this null hypothesis tested?

Applied Problems

1. A major supermarket chain wants to determine the effect of promotion on relative competitiveness. Data were obtained from 15 states on the promotional expenses relative to a major competitor (competitor expenses = 100) and on sales relative to this competitor (competitor sales = 100).

Store No.	Relative Promotional Expense	Relative Sales
1	95	98
2	92	94
3	103	110
4	115	125
5	77	82
6	79	84
7	105	112
8	94	99
9	85	93
10	101	107
11	106	114
12	120	132
13	118	129
14	75	79
15	99	105

You are assigned the task of telling the manager whether there is any relationship between relative promotional expense and relative sales.

a. Plot the relative sales (y-axis) against the relative promotional expense (x-axis), and interpret this diagram.

b. Which measure would you use to determine whether there is a relationship between the two variables? Explain.
c. Run a bivariate regression analysis of relative sales on relative promotional expense.
d. Interpret the regression coefficients.
e. Is the regression relationship significant?
f. If the company matched the competitor in terms of promotional expense (if the relative promotional expense was 100), what would the company's relative sales be?
g. Interpret the resulting r^2.

2. To understand the role of quality and price in influencing the patronage of drugstores, 14 major stores in a large metropolitan area were rated in terms of preference to shop, quality of merchandise, and fair pricing. All the ratings were obtained on an 11-point scale, with higher numbers indicating more positive ratings.

State No.	Preference	Quality	Price
1	6	5	3
2	9	6	11
3	8	6	4
4	3	2	1
5	10	6	11
6	4	3	1
7	5	4	7
8	2	1	4
9	11	9	8
10	9	5	10
11	10	8	8
12	2	1	5
13	9	8	5
14	5	3	2

SPSS Data File

Excel Data File

a. Run a multiple regression analysis explaining store preference in terms of quality of merchandise and pricing.
b. Interpret the partial regression coefficients.
c. Determine the significance of the overall regression.
d. Determine the significance of the partial regression coefficients.

3. Imagine that you have come across a magazine article reporting the following relationship between annual expenditure on prepared dinners (*PD*) and annual income (*INC*):

$$PD = 23.4 + 0.003\ INC$$

The coefficient of the *INC* variable is reported as significant.

a. Does this relationship seem plausible? Is it possible to have a coefficient that is small in magnitude and yet significant?
b. From the information given, can you tell how good the estimated model is?
c. What are the expected expenditures on *PD*s of a family earning $30,000?
d. If a family earning $40,000 spent $130 annually on *PD*s, what is the residual?
e. What is the meaning of a negative residual?

4. Conduct the following analyses for the Internet usage data given in Applied Problem number 7, in Chapter 16.

a. Find the simple correlations between the following sets of variables: Internet usage and attitude toward Internet, Internet usage and attitude toward technology, and attitude toward Internet and attitude toward technology. Interpret the results.
b. Run a bivariate regression with Internet usage as the dependent variable and attitude toward Internet as the independent variable. Interpret the results.
c. Run a bivariate regression with Internet usage as the dependent variable and attitude toward technology as the independent variable. Interpret the results.
d. Run a multiple regression with Internet usage as the dependent variable and attitude toward Internet and attitude toward technology as the independent variables. Interpret the results.

5. Conduct the following analyses for the preference of the outdoor-lifestyle data given in Applied Problem number 8, of Chapter 17. Recall that:

V1 = preference for an outdoor lifestyle
V2 = enjoying nature
V3 = relating to the weather
V4 = living in harmony with the environment
V5 = exercising regularly
V6 = meeting other people

a. Calculate the simple correlations between V1 to V6 and interpret the results.
b. Run a bivariate regression with preference for an outdoor lifestyle (V1) as the dependent variable and

the importance of enjoying nature (V2) as the independent variable. Interpret the results.
c. Run a multiple regression with preference for an outdoor lifestyle as the dependent variable and V2 to V6 as the independent variables. Interpret the results. Compare the coefficients for V2 obtained in the bivariate and the multiple regressions.

6. In a pretest, data were obtained from 20 respondents on preferences for sneakers on a 7-point scale where 1= not at all preferred and 7 = greatly preferred (V1). The respondents also provided their evaluations of the sneakers on comfort (V2), style (V3), and durability (V4), also on 7-point scales where 1= poor and 7 = excellent. The resulting data follow.

V1	V2	V3	V4
6.00	6.00	3.00	5.00
2.00	3.00	2.00	4.00
7.00	5.00	6.00	7.00
4.00	6.00	4.00	5.00
1.00	3.00	2.00	2.00
6.00	5.00	6.00	7.00
5.00	6.00	7.00	5.00
7.00	3.00	5.00	4.00
2.00	4.00	6.00	3.00
3.00	5.00	3.00	6.00
1.00	3.00	2.00	3.00
5.00	4.00	5.00	4.00
2.00	2.00	1.00	5.00
4.00	5.00	4.00	6.00
6.00	5.00	4.00	7.00
3.00	3.00	4.00	2.00
4.00	4.00	3.00	2.00
3.00	4.00	3.00	2.00
4.00	4.00	3.00	2.00
2.00	3.00	2.00	4.00

SPSS Data File

Excel Data File

a. Calculate the simple correlations between V1 to V4 and interpret the results.
b. Run a bivariate regression with preference for sneakers (V1) as the dependent variable and evaluation on comfort (V2) as the independent variable. Interpret the results.
c. Run a bivariate regression with preference for sneakers (V1) as the dependent variable and evaluation on style (V3) as the independent variable. Interpret the results.
d. Run a bivariate regression with preference for sneakers (V1) as the dependent variable and evaluation on durability (V4) as the independent variable. Interpret the results.
e. Run a multiple regression with preference for sneakers (V1) as the dependent variable and V2 to V4 as the independent variables. Interpret the results. Compare the coefficients for V2, V3, and V4 obtained in the bivariate and the multiple regressions.

Group Discussion

1. As a small group, discuss the following statement: "Regression is such a basic technique that it should always be used in analyzing data."

2. As a small group, discuss the relationship between bivariate correlation, bivariate regression, and multiple regression.

Hewlett-Packard Running Case

Review the Hewlett-Packard (HP) case, Case 1.1, and questionnaire given toward the end of the book. Go to the Web site for this book and download the HP data file.

1. Can the overall satisfaction (q4) be explained in terms of all the 13 evaluations of HP (q8_1 to q8_13) when the independent variables are considered simultaneously? Interpret the results.

2. Can the likelihood of choosing HP (q6) be explained in terms of all the 13 evaluations of HP (q8_1 to q8_13) when the independent variables are considered simultaneously? Interpret the results.

3. Can price sensitivity of q9a (q9_5per) be explained in terms of all the 13 evaluations of HP (q8_1 to q8_13) when the independent variables are considered simultaneously? Interpret the results.

4. Can price sensitivity of q9b (q9_10 per) be explained in terms of all the 13 evaluations of HP (q8_1 to q8_13) when the independent variables are considered simultaneously? Interpret the results.

ONLINE VIDEO CASE 18.1

MARRIOTT: Marketing Research Leads to Expanded Offerings

Visit www.pearsonhighered.com/malhotra to read the video case and view the accompanying video. Marriott: Marketing Research Leads to Expanded Offerings specifies that analysis of internal secondary data identified a substantial number of travelers who stayed in Marriott hotels for more than a few nights. Additionally, focus groups and surveys revealed that these extended-stay travelers have different needs, such as adequate business meeting space, a kitchenette, and suite space for variety. The case can be used as a springboard for students to design a short survey regarding the consumer needs that hotels can and should fulfill—in light of the chapter's objectives, discuss how the survey questionnaire and the data analysis strategy can be designed so that bivariate regression and multiple regression analyses can be performed. Specific marketing research questions on this and the previous chapters are posed in the video case.

19

Report Preparation and Presentation

Source: Jiang Xintong/Xinhua/PhotoshotNewscom.

LEARNING OBJECTIVES

After reading this chapter, the student should be able to:

1. Understand the process that should be followed in preparing and presenting the final report.

2. Explain the guidelines available for writing a report that includes graphs and tables.

3. Describe how an oral presentation should be made and some of the principles involved.

4. Discuss the importance of follow-up with the client, and the assistance that should be given

to the client in implementing and evaluating the research project.

5. Explain how the report preparation and presentation process differs in international marketing research.

6. **Social Media** Describe how social media facilitate and enhance report preparation and presentation.

7. Discuss the ethical issues related to the interpretation and reporting of the research process and findings.

" In any report or presentation, get right to the point in why these results matter to the firm. The tendency for beginners is to present all the answers and all the data, whether relevant or not. The role of the analyst is to boil, filter, and distill, so the audience receives the pure distillation. **"**

Jerry Thomas
President/CEO, Decision Analyst, Inc., Arlington, Texas

Research Reports Make United's Friendly Skies Even More Friendly

United Airlines (www.united.com) is the largest airline in the world following its merger with Continental Airlines on October 1, 2010. The airline puts a premium on customer satisfaction. For its in-flight customer satisfaction tracking program, United surveys passengers on some 900 flights per month using a 4-page scannable questionnaire. It administers 192,000 questionnaires in nine languages to people traveling to 40 different countries. The survey covers passenger satisfaction with the entire air travel process: reservations, airport service, flight attendants, meal service, and the aircraft itself.

The marketing research department at United prepares a monthly report summarizing the customer satisfaction data for about 100 people worldwide, including airport, country, and regional managers; executive management; and others at United's headquarters. The report is thorough and includes all of the following: title page, table of contents, executive summary, problem definition, approach, research design, data analysis, results, and conclusions and recommendations. Several tables and graphs are included to enhance the clarity of the findings. The report findings also are available online.

After issuing the monthly report, the marketing research department handles several requests from internal customers (i.e., various departments within United Airlines) for additional analysis. For example, the marketing department might request a breakdown of customer satisfaction rating by demographic characteristics for a specific route (city pair), such as Chicago to Los Angeles. Because the data can be linked to operational data, such as arrival and departure times and number of passengers, United's researchers can dig deep to answer questions from internal customers. Alex Maggi, United's senior staff analyst for market research, says:

> We have often used the data to identify the reasons why some ratings might differ from one airport to another or one segment to another, by looking at customer mix, by linking survey data to operational data. For example, we can take ratings for a given flight and link them to the on-time performance of the flight in that market and we can show that when on-time performance went down so did the ratings in specific categories.

This monthly report on customer satisfaction and the follow-up activities that it generates have helped United Airlines to become much more customer focused, thereby improving its competitive positioning and making its friendly skies even more friendly.[1]

Overview

Report preparation and presentation constitutes the sixth and final step of the marketing research project. It follows problem definition, developing an approach, research design formulation, fieldwork, and data preparation and analysis. This chapter describes the importance of this final step as well as a process for report preparation and presentation. Figure 19.1 briefly explains the focus of the chapter, the relation of this chapter to the previous ones, and the steps of the marketing research process on which this chapter concentrates. As illustrated in the opening vignette, well-prepared marketing research reports and associated follow-up activities add substantial value to the marketing research process.

This chapter provides guidelines for report preparation, including report writing and preparing tables and graphs. Oral presentation of the report is discussed. Research follow-up, including assisting the client and evaluating the research process, is described. The chapter also discusses special considerations for report preparation and presentation in international marketing research, use of social media, and ethics. Figure 19.2 provides an overview of the topics discussed in this chapter and how they flow from one to the next.

Importance of the Report and Presentation

report
A written and/or oral presentation of the research process, results, recommendations, and/or conclusions to a specific audience.

A **report** is a written and/or oral presentation of the research process, results, recommendations, and/or conclusions to a specific audience. The written report and the oral presentation are the tangible products of the research effort, and the report serves as a historical record of the project. If inadequate attention is paid to this step, the value of the project to management will be greatly diminished. The involvement of many marketing managers in the project is limited to the written report and the oral presentation. These managers evaluate the quality of the entire project based on the quality of the report and presentation. Management's decision to undertake marketing research in the future or to use the particular research supplier again will be influenced by the perceived usefulness of the report and the presentation. For these reasons, report preparation and presentation assume great importance.

FIGURE 19.1

Relationship of Report Preparation and Presentation to the Previous Chapters and the Marketing Research Process

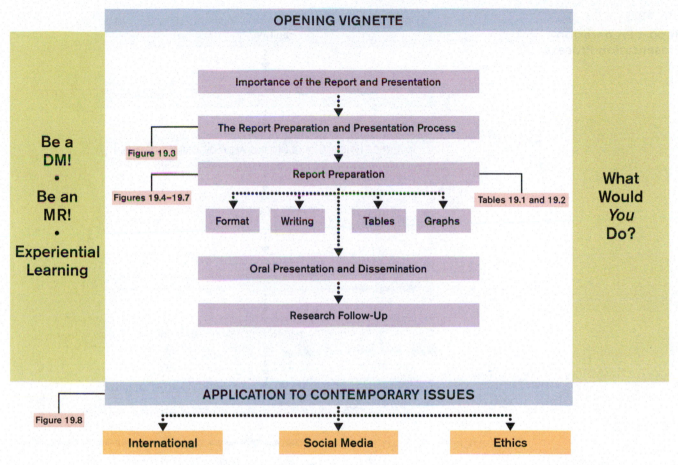

FIGURE 19.2
Report Preparation and Presentation: An Overview

The Report Preparation and Presentation Process

Figure 19.3 illustrates the report preparation and presentation process. The process begins with interpreting the results of data analysis in light of the marketing research problem, approach, research design, and fieldwork.

Instead of merely summarizing the statistical results, the researcher should present the findings in such a way that they can be used directly as input into decision making. Wherever appropriate, conclusions should be drawn and recommendations that management can act upon should be made. Before writing the report, the researcher should discuss the major findings, conclusions, and recommendations with the client's key decision makers. These discussions play a major role in ensuring that the report meets the client's needs and is ultimately accepted. These discussions should confirm specific dates for the delivery of the written report and other data.

The entire marketing research project should be summarized in a single written report or in several reports addressed to different readers. For example, a report prepared for top management should emphasize the strategic aspects of the research project rather than the operating details. The reverse is true for a report prepared for operating managers. Generally, an oral presentation supplements these written documents. After the presentation, the client should be given an opportunity to reflect on the report and the project. After that, the researcher should take the necessary follow-up actions. Such actions are found in the opening vignette, in which United's marketing research department handles several requests for additional data analysis. The researcher should assist the client in understanding the report, implementing the findings, undertaking further research, and evaluating the research process in retrospect. The importance of the researcher being intimately involved in the report preparation and presentation process is highlighted by the following example.

FIGURE 19.3

The Report Preparation and Presentation Process

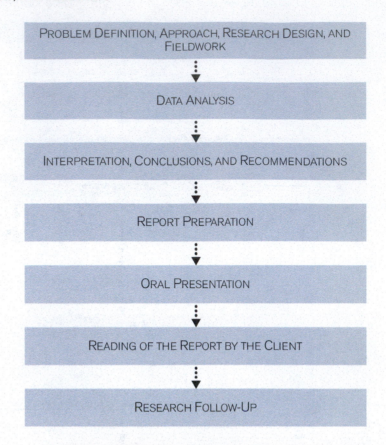

PROBLEM DEFINITION, APPROACH, RESEARCH DESIGN, AND FIELDWORK

DATA ANALYSIS

INTERPRETATION, CONCLUSIONS, AND RECOMMENDATIONS

REPORT PREPARATION

ORAL PRESENTATION

READING OF THE REPORT BY THE CLIENT

RESEARCH FOLLOW-UP

Research in Action

Focus Group Moderators' Ghostwriters Can Shortchange Clients

Thomas Greenbaum, president of Groups Plus Inc. (www.groupsplus.com) of Wilton, Connecticut, a marketing research company focusing on qualitative research, notes a disturbing trend in recent years in the focus-group service sector. Greenbaum asserts that some moderators of focus groups misrepresent their work to clients because their reports are written by ghostwriters who did not participate in the focus-group sessions.

According to Greenbaum, perhaps more than half of moderators use ghostwriters to develop their reports for clients. Often, junior researchers learning the business or part-time employees write these ghostwritten reports. Greenbaum criticizes such ghostwriting because those who merely listen to audiotapes or view videotapes of focus-group sessions cannot always accurately report the nonverbal reactions of focus-group participants. Greenbaum calls upon moderators to be forthright with clients about the authorship of focus-group reports. He also calls upon clients to be more demanding of their contracted research suppliers.

"Although some people in the industry defend ghostwriting by saying they always review the reports before they are sent to the client, or perhaps even write certain key sections, this practice must be looked at carefully by clients who use focus-group research," Greenbaum says. "If the clients know in advance that their reports will be written by someone else, it is clearly less of a problem, but they still do not get the best effort from their research consultants."[2]

Source: Grantpix, Index Stock Imagery/Newscom.

Report Preparation

Researchers differ in the way they prepare a research report. The personality, background, expertise, and responsibility of the researcher, along with the decision maker (DM) to whom the report is addressed, interact to give each report a unique character. In short or repetitive projects, an extensive formal written report of the type described here might not be prepared. Nonetheless, the guidelines for formatting and writing reports and designing tables and graphs generally should be followed.

Report Format

Report formats are likely to vary with the researcher or the marketing research firm conducting the project, the client for whom the project is being conducted, and the nature of the project itself. Hence, the following is intended as a guideline from which the researcher can develop a format for the research project at hand. Most formal research reports, as in the opening vignette, include most of the following elements.

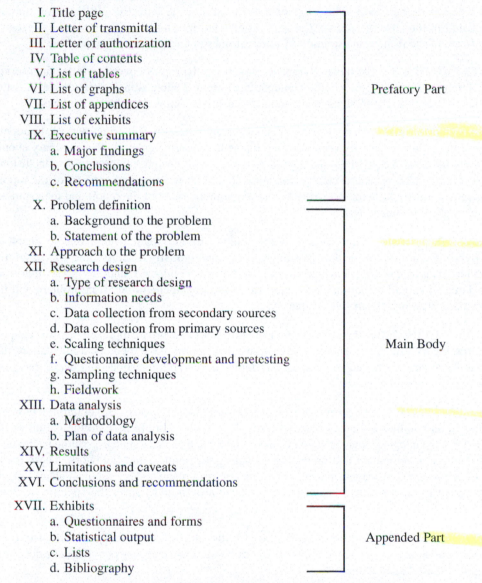

I. Title page
II. Letter of transmittal
III. Letter of authorization
IV. Table of contents
V. List of tables
VI. List of graphs
VII. List of appendices
VIII. List of exhibits
IX. Executive summary
   a. Major findings
   b. Conclusions
   c. Recommendations

Prefatory Part

X. Problem definition
   a. Background to the problem
   b. Statement of the problem
XI. Approach to the problem
XII. Research design
   a. Type of research design
   b. Information needs
   c. Data collection from secondary sources
   d. Data collection from primary sources
   e. Scaling techniques
   f. Questionnaire development and pretesting
   g. Sampling techniques
   h. Fieldwork
XIII. Data analysis
   a. Methodology
   b. Plan of data analysis
XIV. Results
XV. Limitations and caveats
XVI. Conclusions and recommendations

Main Body

XVII. Exhibits
   a. Questionnaires and forms
   b. Statistical output
   c. Lists
   d. Bibliography

Appended Part

Sections I to IX constitute the prefatory part, sections X through XVI the main body, and section XVII the appended part of the report. This format closely follows the earlier steps of the marketing research process. The format should be flexible, however, so that it can accommodate the unique features of a specific project. For instance, the results might be presented in several chapters of the report. For example, in a national survey data analysis might be conducted for the overall sample, and the data for each of the four geographic regions might be analyzed separately. In this case, the results can be presented in five chapters instead of one.

TITLE PAGE The title page should include the title of the report, information (name, address, Web site URL, e-mail address, and telephone numbers) about the researcher or organization conducting the research, the name of the client for whom the report was prepared, and the date of release. The title should also indicate the nature of the project.

LETTER OF TRANSMITTAL A formal report generally contains a **letter of transmittal** that delivers the report to the client and summarizes the researcher's overall experience with the

letter of transmittal
A letter that delivers the report to the client and summarizes the researcher's overall experience with the project without mentioning the findings.

project. The letter should also identify the need for further action on the part of the client, such as implementation of the findings or further research that should be undertaken.

LETTER OF AUTHORIZATION   The client writes a letter of authorization to the researcher before work on the project begins. It authorizes the researcher to proceed with the project and specifies its scope and the terms of the contract. Often, it is sufficient to refer to the letter of authorization in the letter of transmittal. Sometimes, however, it is necessary to include a copy of the letter of authorization in the report. The letter of transmittal and the letter of authorization may be eliminated in the case of recurring projects conducted internally by the marketing research department of the firm, as in the case of United Airlines in the opening vignette.

TABLE OF CONTENTS   The table of contents should list the topics covered and the appropriate page numbers. In most reports, only the major headings and subheadings are included. A list of tables, list of graphs, list of appendices, and list of exhibits follow the table of contents.

EXECUTIVE SUMMARY   The executive summary is an extremely important part of the report, because this often is the only portion of the report that executives read. The summary should concisely describe the problem, the approach, the research design, major results, conclusions, and recommendations. The executive summary should be written after the rest of the report, because it is much easier for the writer to read through the body of the report and then summarize the most important points.

PROBLEM DEFINITION   This section of the report provides background on the problem, highlights discussions with the decision makers and industry experts, and discusses the secondary data analysis, the qualitative research that was conducted, and the factors that were considered. It should contain a clear statement of the management-decision problem and the marketing research problem (see Chapter 2).

APPROACH TO THE PROBLEM   This section should discuss the broad approach that was adopted in addressing the problem. It should also contain a description of the theoretical foundations that guided the research, any analytical models formulated, research questions and hypotheses, and identify the information needed.

RESEARCH DESIGN   The section on research design should specify the details of how the research was conducted (see Chapters 3 through 13). This should include the nature of the research design adopted, data collection from secondary and primary sources, scaling techniques, questionnaire development and pretesting, sampling techniques, and fieldwork. These topics should be presented in a nontechnical, easy-to-understand manner. The technical details should be included in an appendix. This section of the report should justify the specific methods selected.

DATA ANALYSIS   This section should describe the plan of data analysis and justify the data-analysis strategy and techniques used. The techniques used for analysis should be described in simple, nontechnical terms.

RESULTS   This section is normally the longest part of the report and can comprise several chapters. Often, the results are presented not only at the aggregate level, but also at the subgroup (market segment, geographical area, etc.) level. The results should be organized in a coherent and logical way. The presentation of the results should be geared directly to the components of the marketing research problem and the information needs that were identified. The details should be presented in tables and graphs and the main findings discussed in the text.

LIMITATIONS AND CAVEATS   All marketing research projects have limitations caused by time, budget, and other organizational constraints. Furthermore, the research design adopted might be limited in terms of the various types of errors (see Chapter 3) that might be serious enough to warrant discussion. This section should be written with great care and a balanced perspective. On the one hand, the researcher must make sure that management does not overly rely on the results or use them for unintended purposes, such as projecting them to unintended populations. On the other hand, this section should not erode their confidence in the research or unduly minimize its importance.

CONCLUSIONS AND RECOMMENDATIONS Presenting a mere summary of the statistical results is not sufficient. The researcher should interpret the results in light of the problem being addressed to arrive at major conclusions. Based on the results and conclusions, the researcher might make recommendations to the decision makers. Sometimes marketing researchers are not asked to make recommendations because they research only one area but do not understand the bigger picture at the client firm. If recommendations are made, they should be feasible, practical, actionable, and directly usable as inputs into managerial decision making. Conclusions and recommendations should be discussed with the client before finalizing them. It is very important that the report of a conclusive research project (see Chapter 3) be written in such a way that the findings can be used as input into managerial decision making. Otherwise the report is unlikely to get due attention from management, as illustrated by the following example.

Research in Action

Does Management Read Marketing Research Reports?

Every profession has its nagging doubts. Teachers sometimes wonder if their students are really learning anything; police officers occasionally question whether they are actually reducing crime. Once in a while, marketing researchers have a sneaking suspicion that no one is reading their reports.

Determined to resolve this doubt, one marketing researcher inserted a very undignified photo of himself from a recent office party in the middle of his report. Weeks went by as the report was passed through brand and category management with no response. Finally, the senior vice president of advertising called to ask if he needed a vacation. Evidently, this senior vice president was the only one who had read the report in detail.

Who is responsible when research reports are ignored—the research department or management? According to a study recently released by the Advertising Research Foundation and the American Marketing Association, most marketing managers truly believe that marketing research can be valuable. They also claim that most of what they read is not delivering the kind of information they need to make business decisions. Thus, the responsibility of writing readable reports lies with marketing researchers.[3]

Source: © AsiaLifestyle/Alamy

Report Writing

A report should be written for specific readers—the marketing managers who will use the results. The report should take into account the readers' technical sophistication and interest in the project, as well as the circumstances under which they will read the report and how they will use it.

Technical jargon should be avoided. The researcher often is required to cater to the needs of several audiences with different levels of technical sophistication and interest in the project. Such conflicting needs can be met by including different sections in the report for different readers or separate reports entirely.

The report should be easy to follow. It should be structured logically and written clearly. An excellent check on the clarity of a report is to have two or three people who are unfamiliar with the project read it and offer critical comments. Several revisions of the report might be needed before the final document emerges.

Objectivity is a virtue that should guide report writing. The report should accurately present the methodology, results, and conclusions of the project without slanting the findings to conform to management's expectations.

It is important to reinforce key information in the text with tables, graphs, pictures, maps, and other visual devices. Visual aids can greatly facilitate communication and add to the clarity and impact of the report. The appearance of a report also is important. The report should be professionally reproduced with quality paper, typing, and binding. Guidelines for tabular and graphical presentation are discussed next.

Be an MR!	Be a DM!
Gallup on Reports	
Visit www.gallup.com and search for recent reports posted on this Web site. What can you learn about report writing from these reports? Critically evaluate, from a researcher's perspective, the format of one of the reports posted at www.gallup.com.	As the marketing manager for whom the report was meant, how useful do you find the report you considered?

Guidelines for Tables

Statistical tables are a vital part of the report and deserve special attention (see the opening vignette). We illustrate the guidelines for tables using the data for Hewlett-Packard sales reported in Tables 19.1 and 19.2. The numbers in parentheses in the following paragraphs refer to the numbered sections of the table.

TITLE AND NUMBER   Every table should have a number (1a) and title (1b). The title should be brief, yet clearly describe the information provided. Arabic numbers are used to identify tables so that they can be referred to easily in the text.

ARRANGEMENT OF DATA ITEMS   Data should be arranged in a table to emphasize the most significant aspect of the data. For example, when the data pertain to time, the items should be arranged by appropriate time period. When order of magnitude is most important, the data items should be arranged in that order (2a). If ease of locating items is critical, an alphabetical arrangement is most appropriate.

BASIS OF MEASUREMENT   The basis or unit of measurement should be clearly stated (3a).

leaders

Dots or hyphens that are used in a table to lead the eye horizontally, impart uniformity, and improve readability.

LEADERS, RULINGS, SPACES   **Leaders**—dots or hyphens used to lead the eye horizontally—impart uniformity and improve readability (4a). Instead of horizontal or vertical rules, use white spaces (4b) to set off data items. Skipping lines after different sections of the data can also assist the eye. Horizontal rules (4c) often are used after the headings.

EXPLANATIONS AND COMMENTS: HEADINGS, STUBS, AND FOOTNOTES   Explanations and comments clarifying the table can be provided in the form of captions, stubs, and footnotes. Designations placed over the vertical columns are called *headings* (5a). Designations placed in the left-hand column are called **stubs** (5b). Information that cannot be incorporated into the table should be explained by footnotes (5c). Letters or symbols should be used for footnotes rather than numbers. The footnotes should come after the main table but before the source note.

stubs

Designations placed in the left-hand column of a table.

SOURCES OF THE DATA   If the data contained in the table are secondary, the source of data should be cited (6a).

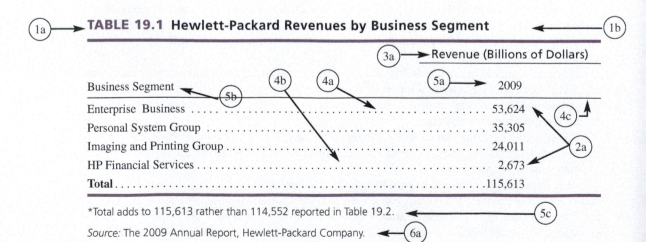

TABLE 19.1 Hewlett-Packard Revenues by Business Segment

Business Segment	Revenue (Billions of Dollars)
	2009
Enterprise Business	53,624
Personal System Group	35,305
Imaging and Printing Group	24,011
HP Financial Services	2,673
Total	115,613

*Total adds to 115,613 rather than 114,552 reported in Table 19.2.

Source: The 2009 Annual Report, Hewlett-Packard Company.

TABLE 19.2 Hewlett-Packard Net Revenue: 2005–2009

Year	Net Revenue (Millions of Dollars)
2005	86,696
2006	91,658
2007	104,286
2008	118,364
2009	114,552

Source: The 2009 Annual Report, Hewlett-Packard Company.

Guidelines for Graphs

As a general rule, graphic aids should be used whenever practical, as in the opening vignette. Graphical display of information can effectively complement the text and tables to enhance clarity of communication and impact. As the saying goes, a picture is worth a thousand words. The guidelines for preparing graphs are similar to those for tables. Therefore, this section focuses on the different types of graphical aids. Several of these are illustrated using the data from Table 19.1 and other data for Hewlett-Packard (HP) reported in Table 19.2.[4]

GEOGRAPHIC AND OTHER MAPS Geographic and other maps, such as product positioning maps, can communicate relative location and other comparative information. Geographic maps can pertain to countries, states, counties, sales territories, and other divisions. For example, suppose the researcher wanted to display the percentage of HP revenues by business segment for each state in the United States. This information could be effectively communicated in a map in which each state was divided into four areas, proportionate to the percentage sales for each of HP's major product lines: enterprise business, personal systems, imaging and printing, and financial services. Each area could be displayed in a different color or pattern.

PIE CHARTS In a **pie chart**, also called a *round chart*, the area of each section, as a percentage of the total area of the circle, reflects the percentage associated with the value of a specific variable. A pie chart is not useful for displaying relationships over time or relationships among several variables. As a general guideline, a pie chart should not require more than seven sections. Figure 19.4 shows a pie chart for HP revenues by business segment for 2009, as presented in Table 19.1.

pie chart
A round chart divided into sections.

LINE CHARTS A **line chart** connects a series of data points using continuous lines. This is an attractive way of illustrating trends and changes over time. Figure 19.5 shows a line chart for HP revenues from 2005 to 2009 based on Table 19.2. Several series can be compared on the same chart, and forecasts, interpolations, and extrapolations can be shown. If several series are displayed simultaneously, each line should have a distinctive color or form.

line chart
A chart that connects a series of data points using continuous lines.

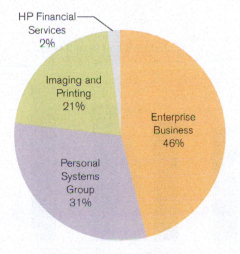

FIGURE 19.4

Pie Chart of 2009 HP Revenues by Business Segment

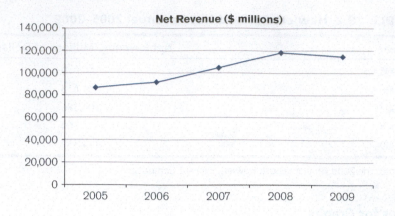

FIGURE 19.5

Line Chart of HP Revenue from 2005 to 2009

pictograph

A graphical depiction that makes use of small pictures or symbols to display the data.

bar chart

A chart that displays data in bars positioned horizontally or vertically.

histogram

A vertical bar chart in which the height of the bars represents the relative or cumulative frequency of occurrence.

PICTOGRAPHS A **pictograph** uses small pictures or symbols to display the data. Figure 19.6 presents a pictograph for HP revenues from 2005 to 2009. As can be seen from Figure 19.6, pictographs do not depict results precisely. Therefore, caution should be exercised when using them.

HISTOGRAMS AND BAR CHARTS A **bar chart** displays data in various bars that can be positioned horizontally or vertically. Bar charts can be used to present absolute and relative magnitudes, differences, and changes. The **histogram** is a vertical bar chart where the height of the bars represents the relative or cumulative frequency of occurrence of a specific variable (see Figure 19.7).

SCHEMATIC FIGURES AND FLOWCHARTS Schematic figures and flowcharts take on a number of different forms. They can be used to display the steps or components of a process, as in Figure 19.3, or they can be used as classification diagrams. Examples of classification charts for classifying secondary data were provided in Chapter 4 (Figures 4.3 and 4.4).

FIGURE 19.6

Pictograph of HP Revenues

2009	$$$$$$$$$$$$
2008	$$$$$$$$$$$$
2007	$$$$$$$$$$$
2006	$$$$$$$$$$
2005	$$$$$$$$$

FIGURE 19.7

Histogram of HP Revenues

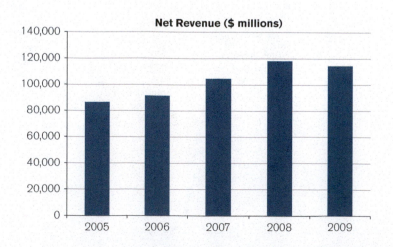

Research in Action

Graphing the Impact of Ethical Brands

Growing concerns about pollution, global warming, and exploitation of workers in Third World countries have driven consumers to use their wallets to make their voices heard. A marketing research study by the GfK Group (www.gfk.com) showed that companies that do not make corporate social responsibility core to their daily operations will be left behind.

A five-country study on consumer perspectives of ethical brands included 5,000 respondents from the United Kingdom, the United States, France, Germany, and Spain. The study found that consumers are choosing to buy only from companies that they believe to be ethical. Companies' ethical credentials have become defining brand attributes, and many customers are willing to pay a premium for an "ethical guarantee." Nearly one-third (31%) of respondents claimed they would pay a 5- to 10-percent premium for an ethical product over a conventional one, and 43 percent stated that they thought that ethical brands made businesses more accountable for their actions. Also, 56 percent of respondents thought that ethical brands should be promoted more heavily. The study also revealed that a striking number of consumers believe that business ethics have declined in the last 5 years (ranging from 64% in Germany to 43% in Spain). To maximize the impact, several graphs were used to highlight the results, as illustrated in the accompanying figure.

Information such as this has caught the ear of several major firms, particularly L'Oreal (www.loreal.com). To improve its image as a socially responsible company, L'Oreal bought The Body Shop (www.thebodyshop.com), the second "most ethical brand" in the United Kingdom. As of 2011, the Body Shop stopped animal testing and has dedicated itself for the good of the society.[5]

Business Ethics over the Past 5 Years—in This Country

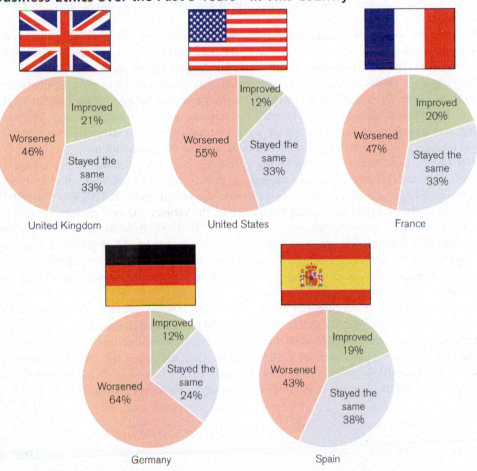

Reporting Coca-Cola

Visit www.coca-cola.com and search for the company's latest annual report. Critically evaluate the use of graphs in Coca-Cola's latest annual report. What additional graphs would you construct?

As the vice president of marketing, how useful do you find the graphs in Coca-Cola's latest annual report?

Oral Presentation and Dissemination

The researcher should present the entire marketing research project to the management of the client firm. This presentation will help management understand and accept the written report. Any preliminary questions that the management might have can be addressed in the presentation. Because many executives form their first and lasting impressions about the project based on the presentation, its importance cannot be overemphasized.

The key to an effective presentation is preparation. A written script or detailed outline should be prepared following the format of the written report. The presentation must be geared to the audience. For this purpose, the researcher should determine their backgrounds, interests, and involvement in the project, as well as the extent to which they are likely to be affected by it. For example, a presentation prepared for the advertising department should put more emphasis on advertising decisions, including budget, media, copy, and execution details. The presentation should be rehearsed several times before it is made to management.

Visual aids, such as tables and graphs, should be displayed with a variety of media. It is important to maintain eye contact and interact with the audience during the presentation. Sufficient opportunity should be provided for questions, both during and after the presentation. The presentation should be made interesting and convincing with the use of appropriate stories, examples, experiences, and quotations. Filler words such as "uh," "y'know," and "all right" should not be used.

The **"tell 'em" principle** is effective for structuring a presentation. This principle states: (1) tell 'em what you're going to tell 'em, (2) tell 'em, and (3) tell 'em what you've told 'em. Another useful guideline is the **"KISS 'em" principle,** which stands for: *K*eep *I*t *S*imple and *S*traightforward.

Body language also is important. It helps speakers to convey their ideas more emphatically. Body language can reinforce the issue or the point the speaker is trying to communicate to the audience. The speaker should vary the volume, pitch, voice quality, articulation, and rate while speaking. The presentation should terminate with a strong closing. To stress its importance, a top-level manager in the client's organization should sponsor the presentation.

TNS (www.tnsglobal.com), a marketing research firm and a Kantar Group company, conducted a research project to measure the relative effectiveness of television, print, and radio as advertising media for a client firm. It also assessed the effectiveness of 10 TV commercials, radio commercials, and print ads. Given the nature of the project, the oral presentation of the report was particularly important in communicating the findings. In addition to a PowerPoint presentation, TNS used a DVD player (for playing TV commercials), a CD player (for playing radio commercials), and a storyboard (for showing print ads). The presentation was made to the client's top corporate officers, consisting of the president, all vice presidents, and all assistant vice presidents at one of their monthly meetings.[6]

The dissemination of the research results should go beyond the oral presentation. The marketing research report, or at least sections of it, should be widely distributed to key executives within the client firm and be made available on demand, as by online distribution. This was illustrated in the opening vignette in which United Airlines makes the monthly customer satisfaction report available online. After dissemination, key executives in the client firm should be given time to read the report in detail before follow-up activities are initiated.

"tell 'em" principle
An effective guideline for structuring a presentation. This principle states: (1) tell 'em what you're going to tell 'em, (2) tell 'em, and (3) tell 'em what you've told 'em.

"KISS 'em" principle
A principle of report presentation that states Keep It Simple and Straightforward.

Research in Action

Important Presentation Realities

How many minutes should a research team that worked on a months-long consumer attitudes research project be given to brief the CEO of a *Fortune* 500 company, such as the Ford Motor Company? One hour? 30 minutes? Both of these estimates are far above what is actually done. According to Mary Klupp, a veteran researcher with the Ford Motor Company and director of Global Consumer Insights for Ford Financial, researchers would be granted a maximum of 12 minutes. Other senior executives would give researchers a 15-minute time block.[7] The CEO's likely expectations from any research briefing are as follows:

- Remind me what this is about again.
- In our last communication, what did we agree you, the researcher, should do?

- What were the most important numbers (results) I need to know? (Give them to me in percentages, so that I will be able to make comparisons with other information I already have in that form.)
- How confident are you in making the recommendations based on this research?
- What decision should I make based on these research results?
- What will be the impact on sales/profits or our workforce?

To answer these questions effectively, the researcher needs to apply powerful thinking about how the results of extensive analysis can be linked to the issues facing the CEO. This will lead to the greatest benefit of research in that the CEO can greatly increase the likelihood of executing the right decisions or of capitalizing on valuable opportunities.

Research Follow-Up

The researcher's task does not end with the oral presentation. Two other tasks remain. First, the researcher should help the client understand and implement the findings and take any follow-up actions. Second, while it is still fresh in her or his mind, the researcher should evaluate the entire marketing research project.

Assisting the Client

After the client has read the report in detail, questions might arise. The client might not understand parts of the report, particularly those dealing with technical matters. The researcher should provide any help that is needed, as is routinely done by the marketing research department of United Airlines in the opening vignette. Sometimes the researcher helps implement the findings. Often, the client retains the researcher to help select a new product or advertising agency, to develop a pricing policy, segment the market, or take other marketing actions. An important reason for client follow-up is to discuss further research projects. For example, the researcher and management might agree to repeat the study after 2 years. Finally, the researcher should help the client firm make the information generated in the marketing research project a part of the firm's marketing (management) information system (MIS) or decision support system (DSS), as discussed in Chapter 1.

Evaluating the Research Project

Although marketing research is scientific, it also involves creativity, intuition, and expertise. Hence, every marketing research project provides an opportunity for learning, and the researcher should critically evaluate the entire project to obtain new insights and knowledge. The key question to ask is: Could this project have been conducted more effectively or efficiently? This question, of course, raises several more specific questions. Could the problem have been defined differently so as to enhance the value of the project to the client or reduce the costs? Would a different approach have yielded better results? Was the research design the best? What about the mode of data collection? Should mall intercepts have been used instead of telephone interviews? Was the sampling plan the most appropriate? Were the sources of possible design error correctly anticipated and kept under control, at least in a qualitative sense? If not, what changes could have been made? How could the selection, training, and supervision of field-workers have been altered to improve data collection? Was the data-analysis strategy effective in yielding information useful for decision making? Were the conclusions and recommendations appropriate and useful to the client? Was the report adequately written and presented? Was the project completed within the time and budget allocated? If not, what went wrong? The insights gained from such an evaluation will benefit the researcher and subsequent projects.

Technology and Reporting

Marketing research reports can be published or posted directly to the Web. Normally, these reports are not located in publicly accessible areas but in locations that are protected by passwords or on corporate intranets. The various word-processing, spreadsheet, and presentation packages have the capability to produce material in a format that can be posted directly to the Web, thus facilitating the process. Specialized software is also available.

Logi Report by LogiXML (www.logixml.com) is a free report development system that lets you create and deliver rich, Web-based reports to end-users. It is wizard-driven and uses a full library of reusable elements, requiring little or no coding on the part of the report developer. The Web-based reports it produces are easy and intuitive for end-users. It has several useful features from drill-down and drill-through to charting, from data grouping to export functionality, and more. Two upgrades are available for purchase: Logi Info and Logi Ad Hoc. Logi Info offers full-featured managed reporting, analysis, and dashboard solution. Logi Ad Hoc empowers end-users to create and share their own reports without waiting for developers.

Publishing marketing research reports on the Web offers a number of advantages. Reports posted online can incorporate all kinds of multimedia, including graphs, pictures, animation, audio, and full-motion video. The dissemination is immediate, and an authorized person anywhere in the world can access the reports online. The reports can be searched electronically to identify material of specific interest. For example, a Coca-Cola manager in Brazil can electronically locate the portions of the report that pertain to South America. Storage and future retrieval is efficient and effortless. It is easy to integrate these reports to become a part of the decision support system.

Experiential Learning

Brevity in Report Writing and Presentation

SPSS Data File

Ipsos Group SA is a leading global marketing research company. Go to www.ipsos-na.com, review the list of press releases in the archives, and choose a press release with data that can be rendered into a brief report. Use Excel to create a set of charts for your report and import the charts into PowerPoint. Some of the press releases already include PowerPoint slides; others include charts that can be readily imported into PowerPoint.

Can you make a compelling business presentation in 3 minutes? Select a topic from Ipsos' press release archive. Then, develop a 3-minute presentation using no more than five PowerPoint slides to explain (1) why this research finding matters to a firm in an industry of your choosing and (2) what this firm can do to take advantage of this finding.

Alternatively, you can create your report and presentation by using your analysis skills and SPSS program to include a set of Excel charts from one of the following sources:

- Chapter 10's McCann Erickson Experiential Learning Exercise
- Chapter 16's Kit Kat taste test
- Chapter 17's Musial University retention study results

Share your final presentation with a group of fellow students in a formal setting.

1. What was the most challenging part of preparing, rehearsing, and making this presentation?

2. What will you do differently in your next presentation as a result of what you have learned in this experiential learning exercise?

Summary Illustration Using the Opening Vignette

Report preparation and presentation is the last, but not the least, step in the marketing research project. A formal report should be prepared and an oral presentation made. As in the case of United Airlines' customer satisfaction survey, the report should be thorough and include a table of contents, executive summary, problem definition, approach, research design, data analysis, results, and conclusions and recommendations. Several tables and graphs should be prepared to enhance the clarity of the findings. The report, or at least some portion of it, might need to be widely disseminated, for example, by making the findings available online as United Airlines did. After management has read the report, the researcher should conduct a follow-up. The researcher should provide assistance to management and

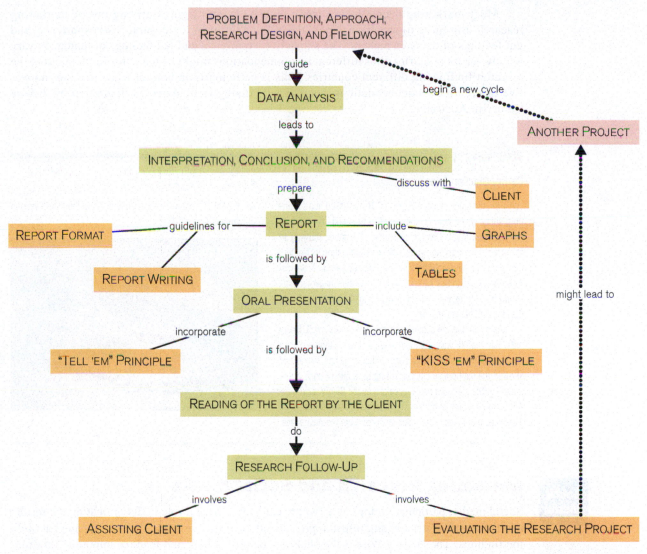

FIGURE 19.8

A Concept Map for Report Preparation and Presentation

conduct a thorough evaluation of the marketing research project, as illustrated by the numerous requests that the marketing research department of United Airlines handles following each report. Figure 19.8 provides a concept map for report preparation and presentation. In this figure, the major concepts are connected by bold arrows using descriptors. Thus, problem definition, approach, research design, and fieldwork guide data analysis, which leads to interpretation, conclusions, and recommendations. Each major concept is described by minor concepts that are connected to that major concept by lines with descriptors. Thus, the conclusions and recommendations should be discussed with the client. The rest of the figure can be interpreted similarly.

International Marketing Research

The guidelines presented earlier in this chapter apply to international marketing research as well, although report preparation can be complicated by the need to prepare reports for management in different countries and in different languages. In such a case, the researcher should prepare different versions of the report, each geared to specific readers. The reports should be comparable, although the formats might differ. The guidelines for oral presentation also are similar to those given earlier, with the added proviso that the presenter should be sensitive to cultural norms. For example, telling jokes, which is frequently done in the United States, is not appropriate in all cultures.

Most marketing decisions are made from facts and figures arising out of marketing research. But these figures have to pass the test and limits of logic, subjective experience, and gut feelings of decision makers. The subjective experience and gut feelings of managers vary widely across countries, thus different recommendations might be made for implementing the research findings in different countries. This is particularly important when making innovative or creative recommendations, such as advertising campaigns, as illustrated by Toyota Camry in Australia.

Research in Action

Camry Chicken Fries Ford

"Why did the chicken cross the road?" Toyota asked in a continuing series of TV commercials aired in Australia. The answer: "To sell more Toyota Camrys, of course." The spots, showing an animated chicken trying to cross the road and getting its feathers blown off by a passing Camry, were created by Saatchi & Saatchi Advertising. When Bob Miller, Toyota's general manager for marketing, tried to explain the ad to Toyota management in Japan, they thought he was insane.

Maybe so, but the commercials did unbelievably well. Hoary old joke that it was, the gag helped Toyota topple Ford's dominance in Australia. As part of a continuing series, the next ad showed the featherless chicken sitting on a pile of eggs in the middle of the road and hatching chicks as the Camry sped past. Although such use of humor would not have made sense to the Japanese, it solicited a favorable response from the Australians.

As of 2011, Toyota was successfully pushing the hybrid version of Camry in Australia.[8]

Source: Răăo New.

Marketing Research and Social Media

Social media, particularly blogs and Twitter, can play a crucial role in disseminating the results and the report of a marketing research project and the decisions made by the company based on the findings. The Nielsen Wire is the Nielsen Company's blog and features important information from its mass of publications and research units, covering the latest daily updates in consumer behavior and media, and marketing trends. The Nielsen Company also does a fine job of using its Twitter platform, posting its latest studies, global news, and insights pertaining to the latest research done by the company. Likewise, Google makes extensive use of social media to inform the public of its new initiatives and other information about the company. Google bought over a blog platform known as Blogspot (www.blogger.com) to allow individuals and companies to disseminate information to others at little to no cost at all. Google itself has a blog (www.googleblog.blogspot.com), which it uses to keep its consumers updated with information, insights, and updates to their technology. It also integrates the Google culture into the blogging world. Likewise, blogs can also provide an avenue for a company to obtain consumer reaction to the research findings as well as their feedback on the decisions made and actions taken by the company based on the research findings.

Social media research results can be effectively presented using charts and graphs such as the Twitter trends' statistics graph. Social media community members' stories can often be effective illustrations of statistical findings when used in reports or executive presentations. These points are illustrated by the Motrin example.

Research in Action

Who Cried in the End? Johnson & Johnson and Not the Moms!

Johnson & Johnson is a well-known *Fortune* 500 company. Its products include St. Joseph aspirin, Band Aid, Baby Powder, Tylenol, and last but not least, Motrin. Of the many pain-relieving products, Motrin is one that eases the aches that mothers will experience from holding their babies in carriers such as slings and wraps. However, this product caused a huge outrage within the community of moms.

A commercial on YouTube posted by Johnson & Johnson stated:

"They say that babies who are carried close to their mothers' bodies cry less than others."

and then asked

"Do moms that wear their babies cry more than those who don't?"

As many as 27,000 views of the Motrin's commercial were generated in just 21 hours. Mothers who saw the Motrin ad were infuriated and felt that they were judged for being moms. They expressed their disagreement with the commercial by coming together on Twitter. At first this seemed like a minor issue; however, when the Twitter trends' statistics graph was generated, it proved otherwise. The chart that follows clearly illustrated the trends of Motrin compared to other popular tweets mentioning brands like Apple and Microsoft. The immediate, obvious surge in the number of mentions for Motrin above and beyond the latter two brands emerged after the rage over the Motrin ad, a stark contrast from its previously unnoticeable mentions.

In this case, moms who were angry came together on Twitter to discuss, comment, and later had the intention to even boycott Motrin for coming up with such an offensive commercial. Examples of a few comments and "voices" are reproduced here.

The power of Twitter trends' statistics graph, backed by qualitative comments, was so convincing that Motrin removed the commercial as soon as it could. This shows that companies should listen to their consumers and pay attention to information about their brand that is found on social media.[9]

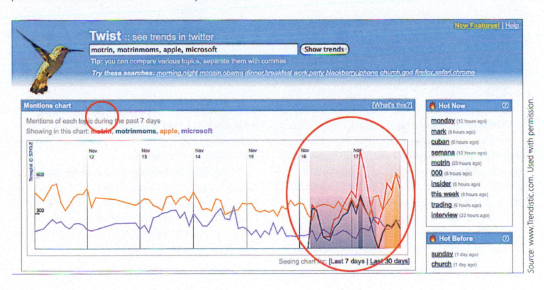

Source: www.Trendistic.com. Used with permission.

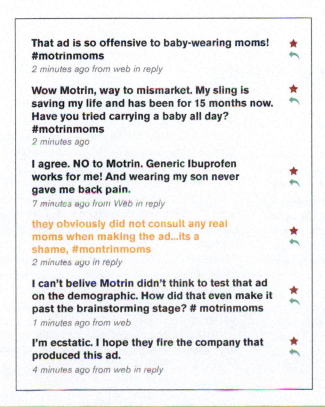

Ethics in Marketing Research

Several ethical issues also arise during report preparation and presentation. These issues include ignoring pertinent data when drawing conclusions or making recommendations, not reporting relevant information (such as low response rates), deliberately misusing statistics, falsifying figures, altering research results, and misinterpreting the results with the objective of supporting a personal or corporate viewpoint. These issues should be addressed in a satisfactory manner, and the researchers should prepare reports that accurately and fully document the details of all the procedures and findings.

Like researchers, clients also have the responsibility for full and accurate disclosure of the research findings and are obligated to employ these findings honorably. For example, a client who distorts the research findings to make a more favorable claim in advertising can negatively affect the public. Ethical issues also arise when client firms, such as tobacco companies, use marketing research findings to formulate questionable marketing programs.

Research in Action

Tobacco Industry Is a "Smoking Gun"

It is well known that tobacco smoking is responsible for 30 percent of all cancer deaths in the United States. It also is a leading cause of heart disease and is associated with colds, gastric ulcers, chronic bronchitis, emphysema, and other diseases. Should tobacco companies be ethically responsible for this situation? Is it ethical for these companies to employ marketing research to create glamorous images for cigarettes that have a strong appeal to the target market?

Based on the findings of extensive research, it is estimated that advertising by the tobacco industry plays a part in creating more than 3,000 teenage smokers each day in the United States. Advertising for Camel cigarettes through the Old Joe (Joe Camel) cartoon advertisements increased Camel's share of the illegal children's cigarette market segment from 0.5 percent to 32.8 percent, representing sales estimated at $500 million per year.

These detrimental effects were not limited to the United States. Not only was the tobacco industry enticing children to smoke, but it also targeted other less-informed populations, such as those living in Third World countries. This raises the question of whether tobacco companies employed these tactics in an effort to replace those U.S. smokers who quit or die.[10]

WHAT WOULD YOU DO?

Subaru of America, Inc.: A Report on Reporting

The Situation

Yoshio Hasunuma, CEO of Subaru (www.subaru.com), knows that customer loyalty is a big part of the automotive industry today, and Subaru has long been aware of this fact. In the past, Subaru relied heavily on traditional, paper-based customer response surveys. Short, follow-up Purchase Experience Surveys and Service Experience Surveys were mailed to customers within 7 to 14 days after purchase. These surveys entailed both multiple-choice questions and open-ended questions. The response rates from the mailings ranged from 30 to 45 percent. After all the data were collected from the mailings, dealerships received a Subaru Owner Loyalty Indicator (SOLI) rating quarterly report. These reports provided valuable information to the dealer, but they received this information only four times a year. Upon receipt of the comments from their customers, it was usually too late to resolve any of their problems.

The solution for Yoshio Hasunuma was the Internet, which would provide faster, more flexible service and information to dealers, field staff, and the management team. Subaru hired the Data Recognition Corp. (DRC) (www.datarecognitioncorp.com), based in Minneapolis, to design the program and provide ongoing service. The process begins by scanning the responses from customer survey forms using optical character recognition. Customer comments are captured and categorized. Next, all survey information is electronically added to the appropriate dealer's database using a customized program developed by DRC. The entire process is managed by DRC; this means Subaru can concentrate on selling cars.

The Web-based reports give field managers an opportunity to see what is happening at their assigned dealerships. They can access up-to-the-minute reports on a specific dealership before meeting with the dealer. This works well because the managers are able to access this information from anywhere as long as they can tap into the Internet.

Dealers are able to use the site to stay apprised of customer satisfaction. They can see their quality scores and check on a particular salesperson's performance. Dealers are able to take immediate action because of this new technology. This allows for better management and, in the long run, better performance from all employees.

As dealers became more comfortable with the Web format, they began to request more detailed and timely reports. Due to this request, Subaru has recently begun to develop a series of reports called Just in Time Reports. These reports provide immediate access to current performance rankings in addition to the quarterly rankings. This has become another tool to help Subaru boost sales and performance. This new technology and refocused goals on customer measurement and loyalty will help propel Subaru ahead of its competition.

The Marketing Research Decision

1. Although Subaru management finds the reports to be very useful, the dealers have a slightly different opinion. To improve the usefulness of the report to the dealers, the report should be modified to:
   a. Put more stress on the problem definition
   b. Describe the research design extensively
   c. Explain data analysis in more detail
   d. Emphasize the limitations and caveats
   e. Contain more graphs

2. Discuss the role of the type of report you recommend for enabling Yoshio Hasunuma to make the dealer sales effort more effective.

The Marketing Management Decision

1. To make the dealer sales effort more effective, Yoshio Hasunuma should (check as many as are applicable):
   a. Build closer online relationship with consumers
   b. Build closer online relationship with dealers
   c. Boost Internet leads for dealers
   d. Make greater use of the Internet for reporting research findings to dealers
   e. Boost dealers' online presence

2. Discuss how the management-decision action that you recommend to Yoshio Hasunuma is influenced by the type of report that you suggested earlier.

What Yoshio Hasunuma Did

Subaru of America has launched an e-business program that the automaker hopes will build a closer online relationship with customers while providing Subaru dealers with enhanced e-business features for their own sites. The program, developed in partnership with The Cobalt Group (www.cobalt.com), is designed to boost Internet leads and sales for dealers and to create a consistent online presence for Subaru's 500 dealers. This collaborative effort puts dealers at the center of the sales and value equation. The system includes features that let local dealers customize their sites with regard to online pricing flexibility to interactive hours. Since the emergence of the new Subaru dealer Internet program, dealers have seen a boost in their online traffic and are receiving better leads with more informative quote requests. As of 2011, Subaru was marketing its automobiles as "Top Safety Picks."[11]

Source: PRNewsFoto/Walser Automotive Group.

Software Applications

The major statistical packages have procedures for constructing tables and graphs and for preparing reports. In SPSS, GRAPHS can be accessed from the menu bar. Also, a separate program called REPORTING can be used to present results in the desired format. Excel has extensive charting capabilities that can be accessed through the INSERT tab on the menu bar. Excel through Microsoft Office provides a direct link to Word and PowerPoint for report preparation and presentation. Minitab also has the capability to create graphs and charts and to edit them for use in reports or professional presentations. Graphs can be created using GRAPH > PLOT, or GRAPH > CHART, or GRAPH > HISTOGRAM. Editing can be done using EDIT > EDIT LAST COMMAND DIALOG. Results from SAS Learning Edition can be used to create a customized report that can be printed, exported, and shared with other applications. The OLAP Analyzer within SAS Learning Edition enables you to access and analyze data that is stored in an OLAP cube.

Summary

Report preparation and presentation is the final step in the marketing research project. This process begins with interpretation of data-analysis results and leads to conclusions and recommendations. Next, the formal report is written and an oral presentation made. After management has read the report, the researcher should conduct a follow-up, assisting management and undertaking a thorough evaluation of the marketing research project.

In international marketing research, report preparation can be complicated by the need to prepare reports for management in different countries and in different languages. The use of social media and available software can greatly facilitate and enhance report preparation, presentation, and dissemination. Social media community members' stories can often be effective illustrations of statistical findings in reports or presentations. Several ethical issues are pertinent, particularly those related to the interpretation and reporting of the research process and findings to the client and to the subsequent ways the client uses these results.

Key Terms and Concepts

Report   548
Letter of transmittal   551
Leaders   554
Stubs   554

Pie chart   555
Line chart   555
Pictograph   556
Bar chart   556

Histogram   556
"Tell 'em" principle   558
"KISS 'em" principle   558

Suggested Cases and Video Cases

Running Case with Real Data

1.1 Hewlett-Packard

Comprehensive Critical Thinking Cases

2.1 American Idol   2.2 Baskin-Robbins   2.3 Akron Children's Hospital

Comprehensive Cases with Real Data

3.1 Bank of America   3.2 McDonald's   3.3 Boeing

Comprehensive Brief Harvard Business School Cases

4.1 TruEarth Healthy Foods: Market Research for a New Product Introduction (4065)
4.2 The Springfield Nor'easters: Maximizing Revenues in the Minor Leagues (2510)
4.3 Metabical: Positioning and Communications Strategy for a New Weight-Loss Drug (4240)
4.4 Saxonville Sausage Company (2085)

Online Video Case

19.1 Marriott

Live Research: Conducting a Marketing Research Project

1. The individual parts of the report can be assigned to teams, with each team writing a specific part. Each team also prepares the PowerPoint slides for that part.
2. The project coordinators should be responsible for compiling the final report and the presentation.
3. Make liberal use of graphs.
4. A presentation of the project should be made to the client, with each team presenting its portion.

5. If each team has worked on the entire report, compile the final report by combining the best parts of the various team reports. This task can be handled by the project coordinators under the supervision of the instructor. The team to make the client presentation can be selected by the instructor based on class presentations by individual teams.

Acronyms

The guidelines for constructing tables can be described by the acronym TABLES:

T itle and number

A rrangement of data items

B asis of measurement

L eaders, rulings, spaces

E xplanations and comments: headings, stubs, and footnotes

S ources of data

GRAPHS can be used as an acronym for guidelines for constructing graphs:

G eographic and other maps

R ound or pie chart

A ssembly or line charts

P ictographs

H istograms and bar charts

S chematic figures and flowcharts

The guidelines for making a presentation can be summarized by the acronym PRESENTATION:

P reparation

R ehearse your presentation

E ye contact

S tories, experiences, examples, and quotations

E quipment: multimedia

N o filler words

T ell 'em principle

A udience analysis

T erminate with a strong closing

I nteract with the audience

O utline or script should be prepared

N umber-one level manager should sponsor it

Review Questions

1. Describe the process of report preparation.
2. Describe a commonly used format for writing marketing research reports.
3. Describe the following parts of a report: title page, table of contents, executive summary, problem definition, research design, data analysis, and conclusions and recommendations.
4. Why is the "Limitations and Caveats" section included in the report?
5. Discuss the importance of objectivity in writing a marketing research report.
6. Describe the guidelines for report writing.
7. How should the data items be arranged in a table?
8. What is a pie chart? For what type of information is it suitable? For what type of information is it not suitable?
9. Describe a line chart. What kind of information is commonly displayed using this type of chart?
10. Describe the role of pictographs. What is the relationship between bar charts and histograms?
11. What is the purpose of an oral presentation? What guidelines should be followed in an oral presentation?
12. Describe the "tell 'em" and "KISS 'em" principles.
13. Describe the evaluation of a marketing research project in retrospect.
14. **Social Media** How can social media be used to enhance report preparation and presentation?

Applied Problems

1. The following passage is taken from a marketing research report prepared for a group of printers and lithographers without much formal business education who run a small family-owned business.

   > To measure the image of the printing industry, two different scaling techniques were employed. The first was a series of semantic differential scales. The second consisted of a set of Likert scales. The use of two different techniques for measurement could be justified based on the need to assess the convergent validity of the findings. Data obtained using both these techniques were treated as interval-scaled. Pearson product moment correlations were computed between the sets of ratings. The resulting correlations were high, indicating a high level of convergent validity.

   Rewrite this paragraph so that it is suitable for inclusion in the report for this audience.

2. Graphically illustrate the consumer decision-making process described in the following paragraph:

    The consumer first becomes aware of the need. Then the consumer simultaneously searches for information from several sources: retailers, advertising, word of mouth, independent publications, social media, and the Internet at large. Next, the consumer develops a criterion for evaluating the available brands in the marketplace. Based on this evaluation, the consumer selects the most preferred brand.

3. For the data given in Tables 19.1 and 19.2, use a graphics package or a spreadsheet, such as Excel, to construct the following graphs:
   a. Pie chart
   b. Line chart
   c. Bar chart

4. Visit www.gallup.com to identify a recent report prepared by this company. How does the format of this report compare to the one in the book?

Group Discussion

1. As a small group, discuss the following statement: "All the graphical aids are really very similar; it doesn't matter which ones you use."
2. "Writing a report that is concise yet complete is virtually impossible, because these two objectives are conflicting." Discuss.
3. "Writing, presenting, and reading reports is an acquired talent." Discuss.

Hewlett-Packard Running Case

Review the Hewlett-Packard (HP) case, Case 1.1, and questionnaire given toward the end of the book.

1. **Social Media** Write a report for HP management summarizing the results of your analyses. Prepare a set of charts using Excel. How can you make use of social media in enhancing your report?
2. What recommendations do you have for the management?
3. Can you make a compelling business presentation in 10 minutes? Develop a 10-minute presentation for HP management using no more than 10 PowerPoint slides.
4. Share your final presentation with a group of fellow students (representing HP management) in a formal setting.
5. What was the most challenging part of preparing, rehearsing, and making this presentation?
6. What will you do differently in your next presentation as a result of what you have learned in this experiential learning exercise?

ONLINE VIDEO CASE 19.1

MARRIOTT: Marketing Research Leads to Expanded Offerings

Visit **www.pearsonhighered.com/malhotra** to read the video case and view the accompanying video. Marriott: Marketing Research Leads to Expanded Offerings highlights Marriott's success in using marketing research to develop a segmentation strategy of targeting different customers with different needs by providing different products and options. The case can be used as a springboard for students to design and conduct a short survey and present their results (with graphs and tables) regarding comparisons in consumer perceptions about Marriott and three competing hotel chains. Specific marketing research questions on this and the previous chapters are posed in the video case.

CASE 1.1   HEWLETT-PACKARD (HP)

Using Marketing Research to Gain a Competitive Edge

SPSS Data File   Excel Data File

The Hewlett-Packard Company (HP) is known worldwide for its printers, personal computers, and related services. With Headquarters in Palo Alto, California, it has a global presence in the fields of computing, printing, and digital imaging. It markets products such as printers, cameras, and ink cartridges to households and small businesses. It also provides software and services (www.hp.com). The company once catered primarily to engineering and medical markets but spun off that line of business as Agilent Technologies in 1999.

Founded by Stanford graduates William Hewlett and David Packard in Palo Alto in 1934, Hewlett and Packard started HP with an investment of $538. The company incorporated 15 years later and went public in 1957. Not until the 1960s and 1970s did HP recognize the market for information technology products. As a consequence of meeting this need, HP introduced the computer industry to Silicon Valley. At the time, products from Silicon Valley were limited to calculators, converters, and semiconverters. In the 1980s, HP began to develop industrial laser printers for desktops and prospered.

In the 1990s, HP expanded its computer-product line, which initially had been targeted at university, research, and business customers, to consumers. Later in the decade, HP launched hpshopping.com as an independent subsidiary to sell online, direct to consumers; the store was rebranded "HP Home & Home Office Store" in 2005. HP also grew through acquisitions, buying Apollo Computer in 1989, Convex Computer in 1995, and Compaq in 2002. Compaq itself had bought Tandem Computers in 1997 (which had been started by ex–HP employees) and Digital Equipment Corporation in 1998. Following this strategy, HP became a major player in desktops, laptops, and servers for many different markets.

HP posted $91.7 billion in annual revenue in 2006 compared to $91.4 billion for IBM, making it the world's largest technology vendor in terms of sales. In October 2006, HP gained the number one ranking in worldwide personal computer shipments, surpassing rival Dell. The gap between HP and Dell widened substantially at the end of 2006, with HP taking a near 3.5 percent market share lead. In 2007 the revenue was $104 billion, making HP the first IT company in history to report revenues exceeding $100 billion. HP posted $114.6 billion in annual revenue in 2009 and $127.16 billion in 2010, continuing its growth trajectory.

As of 2011, HP is a global technology company. It generates net revenue and earns its profits from the sale of products, technologies, solutions, and services to consumers, businesses, and governments. HP's portfolio includes personal computers, handheld computing devices, home and business imaging and printing devices, publishing systems, storage and servers, a wide array of information technology services, and software solutions. HP has a dynamic, powerful team of 150,000 employees with capabilities in 170 countries doing business in more than 40 currencies and more than 10 languages.

According to Computer Industry Almanac Inc., in 2005, in the first 30 years of the PC industry worldwide—from 1975 to 2004—cumulative PC sales have surpassed 1.4 billion units, reaching nearly 130 million units in 1990, and more than 1.6 billion units in 2005. As seen from Table 1, the leading PC companies have changed considerably in the last 20 years. Apple and IBM were the worldwide leaders in PC unit sales until the early 1990s. Since 1994, Compaq, Dell, or HP has been the leader in PC unit sales.

Marketing Issue and Marketing Research

HP identified that the technical trials that customers often face crop up at the most unexpected and inconvenient times in the daily course of business. Equipment and applications are going to break down, most often right when a critical project is due or while the customer is

TABLE 1   Worldwide Unit Sales of PCs: 1991 to 2010

Worldwide Sales	1991–1995 (Sales in Millions)	1996–2000 (Sales in Millions)	2001–2005 (Sales in Millions)	2006–2010 (Sales in Millions)*
Dell	5.4	42.1	133	246
HP and Compaq	21.3	95.0	130	205
IBM and Lenovo	18.0	43.5	64.8	107
Acer	1.7	9.5	28.8	79
NEC and PB	9.3	25.7	26.5	38
Apple	16.2	17.6	17.2	33
Toshiba	4.6	15.9	24.2	41
Gateway	3.8	18.0	16.5	32
Total PC Sales	**201**	**492**	**810**	**1,300**

*Estimated

on the road. The customer's first line of action is usually to call in to the support help desk or perhaps research the problem online. HP Services addresses the customer's pain points in these situations by understanding the critical role support plays and how quickly the customer needs resolution. HP's award-winning support organization is dedicated to getting the customer up and running as quickly as possible and preventing future problems so companies can continue to meet their business deliverables. In fact, the HP Services customer support organization is becoming increasingly recognized as a leader, ahead of IBM and Dell.

As early as 2004, the industry acknowledged HP's commitment to customer satisfaction with more than seven honors and awards. HP earned the highest overall rating from its customers in a Computerworld/InterUnity Group Inc. survey of nearly 1,200 information technology managers and professionals. In this study, customers gave HP the top satisfaction marks in six of eight categories, including meeting customer expectations, contributing to customer profitability, product quality, product reliability, and licensing policies. Customer satisfaction has continued to rate high through 2011.

Given its commitment to customer service and satisfaction, HP conducted a survey of recent purchasers of HP PCs and notebooks. HP wants to understand how its consumers use their HP computers. It also wants to understand the level of satisfaction that consumers are deriving from HP's products. HP wants to estimate the probability that customers will be repeat buyers and whether current customers will recommend HP to their friends and family. Finally, HP wants to determine if there is any correlation on any of these identified usage factors and the underlying demographic characteristics of its customers. The questionnaire that was used is provided here; the associated data collected can be downloaded from the Web site for this book.

References

1. www.hp.com, accessed January 3, 2011.
2. Wikipedia, "Hewlett-Packard Company," http://en.wikipedia.org/wiki/Hewlett-packard, accessed March 11, 2011.
3. B. Bergstein, "HP Extends Lead over Dell in PC Market," *International Business Times* (January 17, 2007), www.ibtimes.com/articles/20070117add-pc-shipments.htm, accessed May 19, 2008.
4. Computer Industry Almanac, Inc., "1.3B Cumulative PC Sales over Next 5 Years: Dell and HP Will Each Sell Over 200M PCs in Next 5 Years" (June 12, 2006), www.c-i-a.com/pr0606.htm, accessed June 10, 2007.
5. Hewlett-Packard, "HP Surveys Nation's Small Businesses to Learn What Fuels the Engines of Today's Economy," HP News Release (2007), www.hp.com/hpinfo/newsroom/press/2005/050427a.html, accessed June 19, 2007.

Note: This case was prepared for class discussion purposes only and does not represent the views of HP or its affiliates. The problem scenario is hypothetical and the name of the actual company has been disguised. **However, the data provided are real and were collected in an actual survey by a prominent marketing research firm, whose name is also disguised.** Some questions have been deleted, and data for other questions are not provided because of proprietary concerns.

HEWLETT-PACKARD (HP) PERSONAL COMPUTERS INTERNET INTERVIEW

Thank you for your interest in our study.

Burke is an independent marketing research firm that has been commissioned by HP Computers to get the honest opinions of recent purchasers of HP personal computer systems. You will be asked to offer your views about HP and describe your Internet usage.

This survey should only take a few minutes of your time. By completing this survey, you will be automatically entered into a drawing for $100 gift certificates that can be used at a variety of major online retailers. If you don't complete the survey, you may qualify for the drawing by writing to the address contained on the email inviting you to participate in this project.

Unless you give us your permission at the end of the survey to release your name to HP along with your responses, your individual responses will be kept confidential.

INTERNET USAGE

Q1 Approximately how many total hours per week do you spend online? This would be the total from all the locations you might use.

Less than 1 hour -1
1 to 5 hours -2
6 to 10 hours -3
11 to 20 hours -4
21 to 40 hours -5
41 hours or more -6

Q2 Following is a list of things people can do online. Please indicate which of these you have ever done on the Internet. *(Rotate responses.)*

Don't Know = 0

Ask First		Yes	No
_____	Communicated with others via newsgroups or chat rooms	-1	-2
_____	Looked for a job	-1	-2
_____	Planned or booked trips	-1	-2
_____	Downloaded a picture or graphic	-1	-2
_____	Downloaded sounds or audio clips	-1	-2
_____	Looked up information about a TV show or movie	-1	-2
_____	Downloaded a video clip	-1	-2

Q3 What other type of things do you use the Internet for?

_____

HP SATISFACTION AND LOYALTY

Q4 Overall, how satisfied are you with your HP computer system?

Very satisfied -1
Somewhat satisfied -2
Somewhat dissatisfied -3
or Very dissatisfied -4

Q5 How likely would you be to recommend HP to a friend or relative?

Definitely would recommend -1
Probably would -2
Might or might not -3
Probably would not -4
or Definitely would not recommend -5

Q6 If you could make your computer purchase decision again, how likely would you be to choose HP?

Definitely would -1
Probably would -2
Might or might not -3
Probably would not -4
or Definitely would not -5

Q7 Deleted (Open ended)

COMPUTER MANUFACTURER IMPORTANCE/PERFORMANCE RATINGS

Q8 The following set of statements refers to personal computer manufacturers. For each statement, please first indicate to what extent you agree that **HP Computers** meets that requirement.

To do this, please use a scale from 1 to 9, where a "1" means you **do not agree at all** with the statement, and a "9" means you **agree completely**. Of course, you may use any number between 1 and 9 that best describes how much you agree or disagree with the statement. Don't Know = 0

How much do you agree that **HP Computers** does *(insert statement)*?

(Rotate statements.)

<u>Ask First</u>   <u>Rating</u>

_____ Make ordering a computer system easy   _____
_____ Let customers order computer systems customized to their specifications   _____
_____ Deliver its products quickly   _____
_____ Price its products competitively   _____
_____ Feature attractively designed computer system components   _____
_____ Have computers that run programs quickly   _____
_____ Have high-quality computers with no technical problems   _____
_____ Have high-quality peripherals (e.g., monitor, keyboard, mouse, speakers, disk drives)   _____
_____ "Bundle" its computers with appropriate software   _____
_____ "Bundle" its computers with Internet access   _____
_____ Allow users to easily assemble components   _____
_____ Have computer systems that users can readily upgrade   _____
_____ Offer easily accessible technical support   _____

Q9A If the price of the HP computer system you purchased had been 5% higher, and all other personal computer prices had been the same, how likely would you have been to have purchased your HP computer system?

Definitely would have purchased -1
Probably would have purchased -2
Might or might not have purchased -3
Probably would not have purchased -4
or Definitely would not have purchased -5

Q9B If the price of the HP computer system you purchased had been 10% higher, and all other personal computer prices had been the same, how likely would you have been to have purchased your HP computer system?

Definitely would have purchased -1
Probably would have purchased -2
Might or might not have purchased -3
Probably would not have purchased -4
or Definitely would not have purchased -5

EARLY ADOPTER ATTRIBUTES

Q10 Following is a series of statements that people may use to describe themselves. Please indicate how much you agree or disagree that they describe you. To do this, please use a scale of 1 to 7 where a "1" means you **disagree completely** and a "7" means you **agree completely**. Of course, you may use any number between 1 and 7.

Don't Know = 0

The first/next statement is *(insert statement)*. What number from 1 to 7 best indicates how much you agree or disagree that this statement describes you?

<u>Ask First</u>   <u>Rating</u>

Market Maven Items

_____ I like introducing new brands and products to my friends   _____
_____ I like helping people by providing them with information about many kinds of products   _____
_____ People ask me for information about products, places to shop, or sales   _____
_____ My friends think of me as a good source of information when it comes to new products or sales   _____

Innovativeness

_____ I like to take a chance   _____
_____ Buying a new product that has not yet been proven is usually a waste of time and money   _____
_____ If people would quit wasting their time experimenting, we would get a lot more accomplished   _____
_____ I like to try new and different things   _____
_____ I often try new brands before my friends and neighbors do   _____
_____ I like to experiment with new ways of doing things   _____

Opinion Leadership

_____   When it comes to computer-related products, my friends are very likely to ask my opinion   _____

_____   I am often used as a source of advice about computer-related products by friends and neighbors   _____

_____   I often tell my friends what I think about computer-related products   _____

DEMOGRAPHICS

Q11   These next questions are about you and your household and will just be used to divide our interviews into groups.

What was the last grade of school you completed?

Some High School or less -1
High School Graduate -2
Some College/Technical School -3
College Graduate or higher -4

Q12   Which of the following best describes your age?

18 to 19 -1
20 to 24 -2
25 to 29 -3
30 to 34 -4
35 to 39 -5
40 to 44 -6
45 to 49 -7
50 to 54 -8
55 to 59 -9
60 to 64 -10
65 to 69 -11
70 to 74 -12
75 to 79 -13
80 or older -14

Q13   Which of the following best describes your household's total yearly income before taxes?

Under $20,000 -1
$20,000 – $29,999 -2
$30,000 – $49,999 -3
$50,000 – $74,999 -4
$75,000 – $99,999 -5
$100,000 or over -6
No Answer -0

Q14   Are you . . . ?

Male -1
Female -2

This completes all the questions.
Thank you very much for your assistance with this interview!

COMPREHENSIVE CRITICAL THINKING CASES

CASE 2.1   AMERICAN IDOL

A Big Hit for Marketing Research?

"This could be more of a challenge than we previously thought," Melissa Marcello told her business associate Julie Litzenberger. After nodding in agreement, Litzenberger put down her cup of coffee at the Vienna, Virginia, Starbucks coffee shop near her firm's headquarters.[1]

Both Marcello and Litzenberger were far along their career paths as researchers in the winter of 2010 when they met at Starbucks. Marcello was CEO of research agency Pursuant, Inc. (www.pursuantresearch.com), and Litzenberger led the public relations division at marketing communications agency Sage Communications (www.sagecommunications.com). Both were based in the Washington, D.C., area.

Litzenberger took the last bite of her cinnamon scone before sipping her latte. She nodded again to Marcello across the table for two before answering. "Research studies that are the most successful in moving the needle are the studies where the research firm uses scientific and credible methods, poses the right questions, and provides the client company with the insights needed to sufficiently reduce risk in decision making," Litzenberger said. "In short, improving decision making is what effective marketing research is about."

Over the years, Marcello and Litzenberger had witnessed prospective client companies voicing resistance to pursuing marketing research. Skeptics of professional marketing research sometimes would say that they "already knew enough about customers to make decisions." Other times, skeptics would assail the sampling methods of studies in an attempt to dismiss the results. And in other instances, skeptics would merely claim that finding the answers to such questions about customers would be too expensive to obtain. In sum, professionally done marketing research was presented as being impractical.

Marcello and Litzenberger were attempting to overcome a challenge in client development. Specifically, they were attempting to obtain evidence to confront skeptics of professionally done marketing research without comprising the privacy of previous clients with whom they had worked. It was inappropriate for them to share the results of previous studies with anyone other than the clients who had contracted them for those studies.

While considering dozens of ideas over the past 3 weeks of project-development brainstorming sessions, Marcello and Litzenberger were now focused on one project for demonstrating the usefulness of marketing research to prospective clients. The research question was: "What still needs to be known about the viewers and voters for contestants of the popular TV show *American Idol?*"

American Idol (www.americanidol.com) is an annual televised singing competition, which began its first season in 2002. The program has always sought to discover the best young singer in the United States. Each year, a series of nationwide auditions are followed by a series of telecasts featuring the singers who advance to the next week's show based on public voting. Throughout the show's history, three judges have critiqued the singing of surviving contestants each week, and good-guy Ryan Seacrest has hosted the show each year. Judges for the tenth season (2011) were Randy Jackson, Jennifer Lopez, and Steven Tyler.

American Idol experienced personnel and creative changes amid declining viewership in 2010. The 2010 season finale had approximately 24 million viewers watching Lee DeWyze and Crystal Bowersox compared to the previous year, which had approximately 29 million viewers. Ratings for the Wednesday results show in 2010 slipped 14 percent in the all-important category of adults ages 18 to 49, who are most coveted by advertisers. Despite these issues, there was lack of third-party research to gain more insight into who the viewers actually were or their motivations for voting for *American Idol* contestants.

"Are we kidding ourselves?" Marcello challenged Litzenberger. "Who would care about a study investigating *American Idol* viewers?"

"How about the sponsors of the show?" Litzenberger quickly countered. "Pepsi Cola passed on sponsoring the show during its development, but Coca-Cola decided to take a risk and invested $10 million to become a sponsor in *American Idol's* first season. That's a lot of cola and that was a lot of risk to take in the volatile world of broadcast television!"

"You're right," Marcello said. "I later read in *USA Today* that Kelly Clarkson might have been voted the first American Idol, but Coke was the real winner. So maybe Pepsi was the real loser. Coke and Ford now spend tens of millions each year not only to be sponsors, but also to have tie-in promotions, such as you might find at www.cokemusic.com."

"But just how durable is the show's concept?" Litzenberger asked after finishing her latte. "What if we find that voters are mostly preteen girls? What if we find that adults don't vote for the contestants or adults don't have confidence in the judges' opinions?"

"The news media should find such answers more delicious than that slice of pumpkin bread I am spying in that glass case over there by the cash register," Marcello said. "Journalists will almost always cover what they regard as relevant and quantifiable trends in popular culture."

Litzenberger leaned forward. "So how do you propose that we do such a study?"

"We've devoted hours to this question at my firm for better than a week. Here's our best thinking on it as of today," Marcello said. "We could place about six questions on Opinion Research Corporation's CARAVAN (www.opinionresearch.com) national omnibus telephone survey to find out more about who, among adults 18 or older living in the United States, watched and voted in the 2011 season of *American Idol.* Such an omnibus survey could be done by telephone during 3 days in late April 2011."

"OK, but what about sampling?" Litzenberger said. "You know we might get attacked on this. It could be really expensive, too. Can we afford it?"

"If we do it this way, we can afford it," Marcello said. "It will run about $1,000 per question. We'll have the Opinion Research Corporation ask our questions along with those of other sponsoring companies to a randomly selected national sample of 1,045 adults comprised about evenly of men and women. With a total sample size of more than 1,000, we will be able to say with 95-percent certainty that the results would be accurate to within ±3.0 percent. This exceeds acceptable standards for a survey about media preferences."

"So if only 10 percent of our sample reported voting for *American Idol* contestants, we would be able to say with 95-percent confidence that the actual percentage of the adult population who voted was somewhere between 7 and 13 percent?" Litzenberger asked.

"You've got it," Marcello affirmed. "Of course, it could be a lower or a much higher percentage. Nobody really knows now. Anybody who says otherwise is merely speculating."

Silence now overcame these two researchers as they reflected on the future courses of action they could take. They could drop the whole idea of demonstrating the usefulness of marketing research. They could pursue this *American Idol* study. If so, what questions should be asked to respondents and why? Should they could continue to consider other ideas for such a study and pursue it later. What should they do? Why?

Critical Thinking Questions

1. Marcello and Litzenberger felt it was important to conduct this study because _____.
   (State the relevant background information used to justify their work.)
2. The main purpose of Marcello and Litzenberger's study was _____.
   (State as accurately as possible the purpose for doing the study.)
3. The key questions Marcello and Litzenberger are addressing are _____.
   (Identify the key questions in the minds of the case's protagonists.)
4. The methods used to answer their key questions were _____.
   (Describe the general approach used and include details that assist in evaluating the quality of the results; for example, sample size, etc.)
5. The most important information in this article is _____.
   (Identify the facts, observations, and/or data Marcello and Litzenberger are using to support their conclusions. Be quantitative.)
6. The results can be put into context by comparing them to _____.
   (Place the quantitative results into an easily understood context by expressing as percentages or by comparing them to an intuitively understood value—for example, twice the size of a football field.)
7. The main inferences/conclusions in this article are _____.
   (Identify the key conclusions the case protagonists present in the article.)
8. If we take this line of reasoning seriously, the implications are _____.
   (What consequences are likely to follow if people take Marcello and Litzenberger's reasoning seriously?)

Technical Questions
Chapter 1
9. What steps of the six-step marketing research process are evident in this case?
10. What is the role of marketing research in marketing decision making suggested by this case?

Chapter 2
11. Define the management-decision problem confronting Melissa Marcello and Julie Litzenberger and a corresponding marketing research problem and show the linkages between the two.

Chapter 3
12. If Marcello and Litzenberger decide to conduct this study, what research design should they adopt? Relate the different phases of the research design to specific aspects of the marketing research problem.

Chapters 4 and 5
13. What kind of secondary and syndicated data would be helpful in addressing the questions raised by Marcello and Litzenberger? What is the role played by such data?

Chapter 6
14. Discuss the role of qualitative research in gaining a better understanding of why people view *American Idol*.

Chapter 7
15. Is the telephone survey the most appropriate method in this case? If not, which survey method would you recommend?

Chapter 8
16. Why did Marcello and Litzenberger not consider doing an experiment? What aspects of *American Idol* viewers should be researched by conducting an experiment?

Chapters 9 and 10
17. Discuss the role of measurement and scaling in assessing the audience response to *American Idol*.

Chapter 11
18. Critically evaluate the wording of the following question: "Who is your favorite *American Idol*?"

Chapter 12
19. Describe the sampling process employed by Opinion Research Corporation's CARAVAN. (Hint: Visit www.opinionresearch.com.)

Chapter 13
20. Is the sample size appropriate? Why or why not?

Chapter 14
21. If you were the supervisor in charge of the CARAVAN telephone interviewers, what challenges would you face?

Chapter 19
22. As part of the management team at Fox that produces *American Idol*, how would you evaluate the report produced by Marcello and Litzenberger? How will the proposed study help you make decisions about the show?

References

1. www.americanidol.com, accessed January 5, 2011.
2. J. F. Scott Collins, "'American Idol' in Disarray," *Los Angeles Times* (July 31, 2010), www.latimes.com/entertainment/news/tv/la-et-idol-future-20100731,0,1548813.story, accessed August 1, 2010.
3. Adapted from Melissa Marcello and Julie Litzenberger, "Fascinating Findings," *Quirk's Marketing Research Review*, 21(3) (March 2007): 58–62.

Note: The contribution of Professor Mark Peterson in developing this case is gratefully acknowledged.

CASE 2.2   BASKIN-ROBBINS

Can It Bask in the Good 'Ole Days?

It was early December and Baskin-Robbins Brand Officer Ken Kimmel had just returned from lunch. To his surprise, his walk from the parking lot to the Randolph, Massachusetts, headquarters building had quickly turned into a sprint. Kimmel was trying to avoid the chilly effects of a Nor'easter that was whipping most of New England with arctic winds.

Like the nasty weather Kimmel just escaped, the frozen-food retailing industry had become more hostile to Baskin-Robbins (www.baskinrobbins.com) in recent years. New entrants, such as Cold Stone Creamery founded in 1988, had popularized the in-store experience with customers watching their ice cream creations being made before their eyes on cold stone slabs. For years, Baskin-Robbins had turned their back to Cold Stone Creamery's gains, in a similar way the Baskin-Robbins counter staff turned their back on customers to make a banana split. Cold Stone Creamery's sales were now almost 75 percent of Baskin-Robbins' sales.

In response, the Baskin-Robbins executive group along with Kimmel had recently moved to redesign stores, but it was not easy convincing the thousands of franchisees who ran the Baskin-Robbins stores to change. A store redesign could run up to $50,000 and was funded mostly by the franchisees. One aspect of the redesign resulted in lowering the ice cream cases to make it easier for children to look down into the ice cream bins.

Another change being considered was changing the Baskin-Robbins logo to coincide with the redesign of store interiors. The logo appears on napkins, cone wrappers, spoons, cups, uniforms, and signs at each Baskin-Robbins store. The estimated cost for making such a change was $5 million for Baskin-Robbins headquarters. Individual franchisees would have to invest about $10,000 for the logo change to be made inside the stores.

Later that afternoon, Kimmel's brand group was deep in discussion about whether to change the brand symbol of Baskin-Robbins at the same time stores would be redesigned.

"The context has changed since the mid-1980s," visiting retailing consultant Zack Wheatly said. "Customers are more demanding about the hospitality experience. They earn more money and they can buy comparable ice creams to Baskin-Robbins in grocery stores now."

Kimmel sensed it was time to mention recent strategy decisions by the Baskin-Robbins executive group.

"While our competitors are pushing this mix-in experience—a higher-priced theater experience—Baskin-Robbins has decided to focus on delivering a great value for our consumers in an accessible kind of environment," Kimmel responded. "The executive group has decided that we are going to focus on our new products as opposed to the theater of the business. As part of this new emphasis, we have recently begun highlighting innovations such as our own frozen coffee beverage—the Cappuccino Blast—and a fruit-based beverage—Bold Breezes. Carrying frozen custard is also on the horizon."

Marsha Davis, Kimmel's research director, took her turn in the conversation. "Is Baskin-Robbins such an established brand that the logo for Baskin-Robbins should not be overhauled?" Davis asked.

"I know what you are suggesting," Wheatly replied. "Conventional wisdom in this industry would say that one shouldn't tinker with an established brand."

"We have discussed this among ourselves here at headquarters with the CEO and other senior executives, and we have also invested in hearing from consultants in retailing communications," Kimmel said. "They think the decision to change the logo should be taken only after extensive deliberation and direct research with customers."

"Right," Wheatly said. "Analysts in the quick-service restaurant industry have reported in the trade journals that the new entrants have continued to grow faster than Baskin-Robbins—especially in the key metric of same-store sales compared the previous year. What did the qualitative research say about the proposed new logos?"

Davis paused, dug in her briefcase, and removed the glossy printed versions of the old logo and the leading candidate among the proposed new logos. She put them both on the table facing the others.

"We talked with four focus groups in Chicago, LA, and New York and they agreed that the Baskin-Robbins brand represented irresistible treats, smiles, and fun," Davis said. "They also liked this proposed logo that the senior executive group liked."

"So where do we go from here?" Kimmel asked.

"Because your management wants to make a change to the logo only if it is necessary, you should study your customers' attitude toward the new logo, so that you can explain whether a logo change is warranted," Wheatly said.

Everyone stopped talking to reflect on what was just said. After about 10 seconds, Kimmel raised an open hand to the group.

"Wait. This is beginning to remind me of the New Coke introduction," Kimmel said after some reflection. "Customers' subjective attachment to the old Coke was ignored, then. We need to ask about the old logo, too. Also, I know the senior executives want a clear margin of preference for the new logo. If the new logo is not preferred 2:1 in a head-to-head competition with the old one, we need to drop it."

Wheatly picked up the line of thought.

"OK, and now that you mention it, we also need to present the drawings of the new redesigned stores and have the customers respond to the old and new logos after understanding what our new stores will be like," Wheatly said.

"So restating our problem, I guess it sounds this way," Davis said. "Because management wants to make a change to the logo only if it is absolutely necessary, we should study our customers' attitudes toward the old logo and toward the new logo after showing them the drawings of the redesigned stores. Only then can we explain whether customers prefer the new logo 2:1 over the old logo."

The words seem to hang in the air in the conference room at Baskin-Robbins headquarters. The statement of the marketing research problem was sounding much improved to Kimmel. But he also had the following thoughts: (1) Given that Baskin-Robbins had moved to redesign store interiors, should the brand logo be changed to signal something new is happening at Baskin-Robbins? (2) If the logo is changed, would there be synergy between the logo change and the redesigned interiors? Synergistic results could be dramatic. A new look, a new menu, and a new strategy focused on delivering "irresistible treats, smiles, and fun" in an accessible way and at a reasonable price could check the momentum rival brands have developed by focusing on a high-end, in-store experience. Considering these elements, the strategic importance of the Baskin-Robbins' research project became more clear in Kimmel's mind.

But had they missed anything in their process of developing the statement of the research problem? Were they focused upon the right issue now? Should they continue to consider other logos for such a study? Should they just go ahead with the new logo because focus group participants had liked the new logo and the senior executives had, as well? What should they do? Why?

Critical Thinking Questions

1. Baskin-Robbins Brand Officer Ken Kimmel felt it was important to conduct this study because _____.
   (State the relevant background information for justification.)
2. The main purpose of the Baskin-Robbins study was _____.
   (State as accurately as possible their reason for doing the study.)
3. The key questions the Baskin-Robbins brand team is addressing are _____.
   (Identify the key questions in the minds of the case protagonists.)
4. The methods used by Kimmel and his team to identify the marketing research problem were _____.
   (Describe the general approach used and include details that assist in evaluating the quality of the results.)
5. The most important understanding about Baskin-Robbins as an organization that led the firm to consider a new logo as part of problem definition was _____.
   (Identify the facts, observations, and/or data Kimmel and his team are using to support their conclusions. Be quantitative.)
6. The series of marketing research problem statements can be put into context by comparing each to _____.
   (Place the marketing research problem statements into other readily understood contexts.)
7. The main inferences/conclusions in this case pertaining to problem definition are _____.
   (Identify the key conclusions implied by the case.)
8. If we take this line of reasoning seriously, the implications for many other firms seeking to define the marketing research problem related to rebranding are _____.
   (What consequences are likely to follow if people take the brand team's reasoning seriously and apply them to other firms?)

Technical Questions

Chapter 1

9. What is the role of marketing research in deciding whether to change the logo in this case?

Chapter 2

10. Define the management-decision problem confronting the Baskin-Robbins executive group, along with Kimmel, and a corresponding marketing research problem and show the linkages between the two.
11. What specific research question and hypothesis are suggested in this case?

Chapter 3

12. If Kimmel decides to conduct a study to address the marketing research problem, what research design should be adopted? Relate the different phases of the research design to specific aspects of the marketing research problem.

Chapters 4 and 5

13. What kind of secondary and syndicated data would be helpful in addressing the issue of changing the brand logo? What is the role played by such data?

Chapter 6

14. Discuss the role of qualitative research in gaining a better understanding of the influence of the brand image on consumer selection of an ice cream brand.

Chapter 7

15. Do you think that Kimmel should commission a survey in this case? If yes, which survey method would you recommend and why?

Chapter 8

16. Can an experiment be conducted to address the issue of changing the brand logo? If yes, what experimental design would you recommend and why?

Chapters 9 and 10

17. Discuss the role of measurement and scaling in assessing the consumer response to the old and new logos. Which scaling technique(s) would you recommend and why?

Chapter 11

18. After showing the respondent the old and the new logos, the following question is asked: "Do you like the new logo better than the old logo?" Critically evaluate the wording of this question.

Chapter 12

19. If mall-intercept interviews are to be conducted to determine consumers' preferences for ice cream brands, design a suitable sampling process.

Chapter 13

20. What should be the sample size and how it should be determined?

Chapter 14

21. If you were the supervisor in charge of mall-intercept interviewing, what challenges would you face in training the interviewers?

Chapter 19

22. How should the executive group, along with Kimmel, evaluate the marketing research report? How will the findings of marketing research help them make decisions about changing the brand logo?

References

1. www.baskinrobbins.com, accessed February 15, 2011.
2. Sherri Daye Scott, "Remaining Relevant," *QSR* (February 2006): 26–30.
3. David Colker, "Ice Cream Battle Getting Hotter," *Los Angeles Times* (November 5, 2005): C1.

Note: The contribution of Professor Mark Peterson in developing this case is gratefully acknowledged.

CASE 2.3 KID STUFF?

Determining the Best Positioning Strategy for Akron Children's Hospital

"I'm not sure we are getting anywhere in this meeting," Aaron Powell thought to himself as he pushed his chair away from the conference room table and slowly stood up to stretch his legs after an hour had already gone past.

Powell, Akron Children's Hospital's (ACH; www. akronchildrens.org) marketing director, stood to gaze out the conference room windows onto the two ribbons of train tracks that curled near the hospital on the north side of this midsized city in Northeast Ohio. He was thinking about how rival hospitals, such as Akron City Hospital, Akron General Medical Center, and St. Thomas Hospital, had recently hired marketing directors like himself. The urgency to advance Akron Children's Hospital's marketing effort was going to intensify in the next year.

Powell's meeting was going into its second hour. In addition to Powell, the meeting's participants were Mark Norton, the hospital operations officer (Powell's boss), and Janet Jones from the Cleveland-based Marcus Thomas communications and research agency (www. marcusthomasllc.com). One staff member from finance was there, along with the soon-to-be-retiring public relations director for the hospital. In the past, both of these staffers would support whatever Norton proposed or liked. It now looked like Powell and Jones were on the other side of a divide about how to approach positioning Akron Children's Hospital in next year's advertising campaign. To make matters worse, Powell and Jones appeared to be outnumbered, and the tension in the room was palpable.

"Let me read the research problem statement all of us revised in the first hour of our meeting," Jones said. "Akron Children's Hospital board wants the hospital to become the preferred hospital in the high-growth areas of the region. Accordingly, we are studying positioning possibilities, so that the board can select the best positioning for next year's communications campaign intended to boost the number of patient cases 10 percent in the following year."

"That's it. That's what we want," Norton said. "But I don't think we have to pursue a research project with a survey that just may lead us to reinvent the wheel—and for $60,000, too."

"What wheel is that?" Powell asked, turning away from the window to face Norton.

"Aaron, you know as well as I do that this hospital is all about children. It's even in our name," Norton said. "Emphasize the kids. Whatever we do in the media should feature the kids. Just do some focus groups that will allow Marcus Thomas to get some ideas for their advertising about kids and our hospital. That should only cost about $20,000. But honestly, I am not sure we even need that."

"Mark, remember that McDonald's tends to emphasize kids, too, but adults are featured in their advertising most of the time," Powell said. "Marcus Thomas needs to cover the entire range of issues families consider when choosing a hospital for their kid. If we miss something important, one of the other hospitals in Akron might claim they are the better hospital when it comes to this."

"Aaron is making a good point," Jones said. "Right now, we don't know which positioning would help Akron Children's the most."

"So describe which paths we can pursue now," Norton said.

"Plan A—do focus groups only, as you suggested," Jones said. "Plan B—do focus groups with a follow-on survey. Plan C—do a survey with follow-on focus groups. And plan D—do no research."

"Tell me more about each of these," Norton said.

"In plan A, Marcus Thomas would conduct four focus groups, with an average of 10 respondents per group," Jones said. "We'll ask participants to discuss their experiences while at a hospital. Participants will be required to be the primary decision makers for health care decisions within the family and have a child—newborns to 18 years old—with an acute condition and who had spent at least 3 consecutive days in a hospital. Because most health care decision makers within a family tend to be women, most of the participants will be female between 25 and 54 years old with one or more children ranging from newborns to 18 years old."

"Cost?" Norton asked.

"About $20,000," Powell said.

Jones continued. "In plan B, we'll do plan A, plus a field survey to follow-up on the issues we identify in the focus groups. First, we'll ask about unaided and aided awareness of hospitals in the region. Then, based on what we learn in the focus groups, we will identify the concepts of three positioning strategies and ask survey respondents which one they prefer most and which one they prefer next most. We'll be able to statistically determine the degree of preference among the positioning alternatives."

"The three strategies might be, one, Akron Children's Hospital has doctors who listen to you," Powell said. "Or, two, we know how to meet the unique needs of children, or, three, we use the latest advances in treating children."

"Cost?" Norton asked again.

"About $60,000," Powell said.

"What about plan C? Why does that make sense?" Norton asked.

"We can identify the best positioning strategy by conducting a survey. The salient aspects of this positioning strategy to the consumers can then be explored via focus groups. The cost will be the same as plan B; that is, $60,000," responded Jones.

"And plan D—no research. Turn our creative staff loose and hang on for the ride," Jones said with a wry smile.

Norton returned the smile and looked around the room. "Doesn't your firm do the advertising for the Ohio Lottery?" Norton asked. "With plan D, we might do better by playing the Ohio Lottery!"

Sensing the humor, everyone in the room laughed together. Finally, tension seemed to begin dissipating.

Norton nodded slowly. Powell nodded, too. However, the questions Powell was thinking about still remained. Which of the plans would Akron Children's Hospital pursue—plan A, plan B, plan C, or plan D? If money was invested, would it be a worthwhile investment? Would the idea of research being a "cost" (with no apparent return) persist in the minds of Norton and the other staff members long after this meeting? What could be done now to help Norton and the other executives view research as an investment (with an implied return)?

Critical Thinking Questions

1. Akron Children's Hospital Marketing Director Aaron Powell felt it was important to conduct this study because _____. (State the relevant background information for justification.)

2. The main purpose of the Akron Children's Hospital study was _____. (State as accurately as possible the reason for doing the study.)

3. The key questions the Akron Children's Hospital employees address in the case are _____. (Identify the key questions in the minds of the case protagonists.)

4. The methods used by Powell and his team to answer the marketing research problem were _____.
   (Describe the general approach used and include details that assist in evaluating the quality of the results.)
5. The most important understanding about Akron Children's Hospital as an organization that led the firm to consider the research about its positioning was _____.
   (Identify the facts, observations, and/or data Powell and his team are using to support their conclusions.)
6. The research design decision can be put into context by _____.
   (Place the research design decision into other readily understood contexts.)
7. The main inferences/conclusions in this case are _____.
   (Identify the key conclusions implied by the case.)
8. If we take this line of reasoning seriously, the implications for many other firms are _____.
   (What consequences are likely to follow if people take the team's reasoning seriously and apply it to other firms?)

Technical Questions

Chapter 1

9. What is the role of marketing research in determining the best positioning strategy for Akron Children's Hospital?

Chapter 2

10. Define the management-decision problem confronting Akron Children's Hospital and a corresponding marketing research problem and show the linkages between the two.

Chapter 3

11. In this case, how do Norton and the finance people differ from the marketers (Powell and Jones) in their views about the roles of exploratory and conclusive designs?
12. In your opinion, what would be the best sequence for using exploratory and conclusive research in this case?

Chapters 4 and 5

13. What kind of secondary and syndicated data would be helpful in determining a positioning strategy for Akron Children's Hospital? What is the role played by such data?

Chapter 6

14. Discuss the role of qualitative research in gaining a better understanding of how households select a hospital for their children when in need of health care for acute cases.

Chapter 7

15. Do you think that Norton should commission a survey in this case? If yes, which survey method would you recommend and why?

Chapter 8

16. Can an experiment be conducted to address the issue of the best positioning strategy? If yes, what experimental design would you recommend and why?

Chapters 9 and 10

17. Discuss the role of measurement and scaling in assessing households' preferences for hospitals for their children when in need of health care for acute cases.

Chapter 11

18. Design a questionnaire to measure consumer preferences for children's hospitals.

Chapter 12

19. If a mail survey is to be conducted to determine households' preferences for children's hospitals, design a suitable sampling process.

Chapter 13

20. What should the sample size be and how should it be determined?

Chapter 14

21. If you were the supervisor in charge, what challenges would you face in training the interviewers for the survey of Chapter 7?

Chapter 19

22. How should Norton evaluate the marketing research report? How will the findings of marketing research help Akron Children's Hospital select an appropriate positioning strategy?

References

1. www.akronchildrens.org, accessed March 15, 2011.

2. Adapted from Robin Segbers, "Adding a Human Touch," *Quirk's Marketing Research Review* (June 2006): 30–34.

Note: The contribution of Professor Mark Peterson in developing this case is gratefully acknowledged.

COMPREHENSIVE CASES WITH REAL DATA

CASE 3.1   BANK OF AMERICA

Leading the American Way

SPSS Data File   Excel Data File

Bank of America, headquartered in Charlotte, North Carolina, is the largest bank holding company in the United States, by assets, and the second largest bank by market capitalization. BankAmerica began as the American Bank of Italy, which was founded in 1904 by Amadeo Giannini, and Bank of America still operates under Federal Charter 13044, which was granted to Giannini on March 1, 1927. The bank has its roots in two former banks: NationsBank and the San Francisco–based BankAmerica. The two merged in 1998 and assumed the name Bank of America. At the time, the merger was the largest bank acquisition in history. Bank of America acquired Countrywide Financial in 2008, giving the bank a substantial market share of the mortgage business. Bank of America acquired Merrill Lynch & Co. in 2009. This acquisition made Bank of America the largest financial services company in the world.

Bank of America caters its services to individual consumers, small and midsize businesses, and large corporations with a full range of banking, investment, asset management, and other financial products and services. As of 2011, Bank of America serves clients in more than 150 countries and has relationships with 99 percent of the U.S. *Fortune* 500 companies and 83 percent of the *Fortune* Global 500 companies. This publicly traded corporation provides a diversified range of financial and risk-management products and services both domestically and internationally through four market segments: Global Consumer & Small Business Banking, Global Corporate & Investment Banking, Global Wealth & Investment Management, and International.

Global Consumer and Small Business Banking

Global Consumer and Small Business Banking (GC&SBB) is the largest division in the company; it deals primarily with consumer banking and credit card issuance. The acquisition of FleetBoston and MBNA significantly expanded its size and range of services, generating about 50 percent of the company's total revenue in 2007. It competes directly with the retail banking divisions of Citigroup and JPMorgan Chase. As of 2011, the GC&SBB organization includes more than 6,100 retail branches and more than 18,700 ATMs across the United States.

Global Corporate and Investment Banking

The bank's investment banking activities operate under the Merrill Lynch subsidiary and provide mergers and acquisitions advisory, underwriting, capital markets, as well as sales and trading in fixed income and equities markets. Its strongest groups include Leveraged Finance, Syndicated Loans, and Mortgage Backed Securities. It has one of the largest research teams on Wall Street.

Global Wealth and Investment Management

Global Wealth and Investment Management (GWIM) manages assets of institutions and individuals. It is among the 10 largest U.S. wealth managers (ranked by private banking assets under management in accounts of $1 million or more as of June 30, 2010). GWIM has five primary lines of business: Premier Banking & Investments (including Banc of America Investment Services, Inc.), The Private Bank, Family Wealth Advisors, Columbia Management Group, and Banc of America Specialist.

Bank of America has recently spent $675 million building its U.S. investment banking business and is looking to become one of the top five investment banks worldwide. Bank of America already has excellent relationships with the corporate and financial institutions world. These relationships, as well as a balance sheet that most banks would kill for, are the foundations for a lofty ambition.

International Operations

Bank of America's Global Corporate and Investment Banking spans the globe with divisions in the United States, Europe, and Asia. The U.S. headquarters are located in New York, European headquarters are based in London, UK and Asia's headquarters are based in Hong Kong.

Bank of America generates 90 percent of its revenues in its domestic market and continues to buy businesses in the United States. The core of Bank of America's strategy is to be the number one bank in its domestic market. It has achieved this through key acquisitions. As a result of its mergers and acquisitions, Bank of America is now the largest issuer of credit, debit, and prepaid cards in the world based on total purchase volume, as well as the largest consumer and small business bank in the United States.

Competition

On a national and international level, Bank of America's main competition consists of Citigroup, Wells Fargo, and JPMorgan Chase & Company. However, Bank of America also encounters fierce competition from regional and local banks all over the country.

Marketing Issue and Marketing Research

With Bank of America representing so many customers, it needed to provide a wider range of services to meet their needs. Bank of America's Innovation and Development Team (I&D Team) realized that the customers wanted different things when it came to banking other than the "traditionally designed bank branch." Therefore, Bank of America conducted a study to understand its consumers, their lifestyles, and potential for customer segmentation in terms of investment products and service needs. The questionnaire used follows and the data file is provided on the Web site for this book. The outputs and the analyses of this study should help Bank of America carve its growth plan and its successful implementation.

Questions

Chapter 1

1. Discuss the role that marketing research can play in helping Bank of America formulate sound marketing strategies.

Chapter 2

2. Management would like to further expand Bank of America's market share in the consumer market. Define the management-decision problem.

3. Define an appropriate marketing research problem based on the management-decision problem you have identified.

Chapter 3

4. Formulate an appropriate research design for investigating the marketing research problem that you have defined in Chapter 2.

Chapter 4

5. Use the Internet to determine the market shares of the major banks for the last calendar year.

Chapter 5

6. What type of syndicated data will be useful to Bank of America?

Chapter 6

7. Discuss the role of focus groups versus depth interviews in helping Bank of America expand its market share.

Chapter 7

8. If a survey is to be conducted to determine consumer preferences for banks, which survey method should be used and why?

Chapter 8

9. Discuss the role of preexperimental versus true experimental designs in helping Bank of America expand its product offerings.

Chapter 9

10. Illustrate the use of paired comparison and constant sum scales in measuring consumer preferences for banks. Should any of these scales be used?

Chapter 10

11. Develop a multi-item scale for measuring attitudes toward Bank of America.

Chapter 11

12. Critically evaluate the questionnaire developed for the Bank of America survey.

Chapter 12

13. What sampling plan should be adopted for the survey of Chapter 7?

Chapter 13

14. How should the sample size be determined?

Chapter 14

15. How would you supervise and evaluate field workers for conducting the survey of Chapter 7?

Chapter 15

16. Many of the importance items have more than 10 percent of the values missing. Identify these items. How would you address these missing values?
17. Recode the following demographic characteristics into the categories specified:
    a. Age (Q9): 27–57 = 1, 58–68 = 2, 69–75 = 3, 76–90 = 4
    b. Marital status (Q11): now married = 1, all other, i.e., now not married = 2
    c. Number of dependent children (Q12): 3–10 = 3

d. Education (Q14): Combine some high school, high school graduate, and vocational or technical school into a single category, and also combine law school graduate, dental/medical school graduate, and doctorate into a single category.
18. Recode the advantage of using primary provider (Q5) into two categories: 1–3 = 1 (small advantage) and 4–5 = 2 (big advantage).
19. Recode overall satisfaction with service provider (Q6_a) into three categories: 2–4 = 1, 5 = 2, 6 = 3.

Chapter 16

20. Calculate an overall rating score for the primary financial provider by summing the ratings of all the 13 items in Q6 (Q6_a through Q6_m). Obtain a frequency distribution and summary statistics. Interpret the results.
21. Are the decision-making approaches (Q8) related to any of the demographic characteristics (Q9 through Q15, as recoded in Chapter 15)?
22. Is the recoded advantage of using primary provider (recoded Q5) related to any of the recoded demographic characteristics?

Chapter 17

23. Is the recoded advantage of using primary provider (recoded Q5) related to any of the importance variables (Q1_a through Q1_l)?
24. Is the recoded advantage of using primary provider (recoded Q5) related to any of the ratings of the primary financial provider (Q6_a through Q6_m)?
25. Is "the performance of investments with this provider" (Q1_a) more important than "online services offered" (Q1_e)? Formulate the null and alternative hypotheses and conduct an appropriate test.
26. Is the likelihood of "recommend your primary provider to someone you know" (Q2) lower than the likelihood of "continue to use your primary provider at least at the same level as up to now" (Q3)? Formulate the null and alternative hypotheses and conduct an appropriate test.
27. Can the decision-making approaches (Q8) explain any of the importance variables (Q1_a through Q1_l)?
28. Is there a relationship between the importance variables considered individually (Q1_a through Q1_l) and the recoded demographic characteristics (Q9 through Q15)?

Chapter 18

29. Can the likelihood of "recommend your primary provider to someone you know" (Q2) be explained by the ratings of the primary financial provider (Q6_a through Q6_m) when these ratings are considered simultaneously?
30. Can the likelihood of "continue to use your primary provider at least at the same level as up to now" (Q3) be explained by the ratings of the primary financial provider (Q6_a through Q6_m) when these ratings are considered simultaneously?

Chapter 19

31. Write a report for Bank of America based on all the analyses that you have conducted. What do you recommend Bank of America do in order to continue to grow?

References

1. www.bankofamerica.com, accessed February 3, 2011.
2. http://en.wikipedia.org/wiki/Bank_of_America, accessed January 4, 2011.
3. Associated Press, "Bank of America to Acquire Countrywide Deal for Country's Largest Mortgage Lender Valued at $4.1 Billion"

(January 11, 2008), www.msnbc.msn.com/id/22606833, accessed May 19, 2008.
4. S. Thomke, "How Bank of America Turned Branches into Service-Development Laboratories," http://hbswk.hbs.edu/item/3459.html, accessed May 31, 2007.

Note: This case was prepared for class discussion purposes only and does not represent the views of Bank of America or its affiliates. The problem scenario is hypothetical and the name of the actual company has been disguised. **However, the data provided are real and were collected in an actual survey by a prominent marketing research firm, whose name is also disguised.** Some questions have been deleted, while the data for other questions are not provided because of proprietary reasons.

ANNUAL FINANCIAL SERVICES SURVEY

Introduction

This survey asks some questions about financial services, i.e., about investments and banking. The **primary financial services provider** (company) is where you have the **largest** portion of your household's investments and savings/checking assets. Your cooperation in answering these questions is greatly appreciated.

Part A. Financial Services Provider

1. If you were selecting a **primary financial provider (company) today**, how important would each of the following be to you? **(X ONE box for EACH.)**

	Extremely Important	Very Important	Somewhat Important	Somewhat Unimportant	Not Important at All
a. Performance of investments with this provider	5 ☐	4 ☐	3 ☐	2 ☐	1 ☐
b. Fees or commissions charged	5 ☐	4 ☐	3 ☐	2 ☐	1 ☐
c. Depth of products and services to meet the range of your investment needs	5 ☐	4 ☐	3 ☐	2 ☐	1 ☐
d. Ability to resolve problems	5 ☐	4 ☐	3 ☐	2 ☐	1 ☐
e. Online services offered	5 ☐	4 ☐	3 ☐	2 ☐	1 ☐
f. Multiple providers' products to choose from	5 ☐	4 ☐	3 ☐	2 ☐	1 ☐
g. Quality of advice	5 ☐	4 ☐	3 ☐	2 ☐	1 ☐
h. Knowledge of representatives or advisors you deal with	5 ☐	4 ☐	3 ☐	2 ☐	1 ☐
i. Representative knowing your overall situation and needs	5 ☐	4 ☐	3 ☐	2 ☐	1 ☐
j. Access to other professional resources	5 ☐	4 ☐	3 ☐	2 ☐	1 ☐
k. Degree to which my provider knows me	5 ☐	4 ☐	3 ☐	2 ☐	1 ☐
l. Quality of service	5 ☐	4 ☐	3 ☐	2 ☐	1 ☐

	Extremely Likely	Very Likely	Somewhat Likely	Somewhat Unlikely	Very Unlikely
2. How **likely** are you to recommend your primary provider to someone you know? **(X ONE box.)**	5 ☐	4 ☐	3 ☐	2 ☐	1 ☐
3. How **likely** is it that you will continue to use your primary provider at least at the same level as up to now? **(X ONE box.)**	5 ☐	4 ☐	3 ☐	2 ☐	1 ☐
4. How **likely** is it that you or your household will **drop** or **replace** your primary provider? **(X ONE box.)**	5 ☐	4 ☐	3 ☐	2 ☐	1 ☐
	Very Big	**Big**	**Some**	**Slight**	**None**
5. How would you rate the **advantage** to you of using your primary provider rather than other financial services providers? **(X ONE box.)**	5 ☐	4 ☐	3 ☐	2 ☐	1 ☐

6. How would you rate the following elements of your **primary financial provider (company)?** If it is not applicable, select "**NA.**" **(X ONE box for EACH statement.)**

	Excellent	Very Good	Good	Fair	Poor	NA
a. Overall satisfaction with primary provider	6 ☐	5 ☐	4 ☐	3 ☐	2 ☐	1 ☐
b. Performance of investments with this provider	6 ☐	5 ☐	4 ☐	3 ☐	2 ☐	1 ☐
c. Fees or commissions charged	6 ☐	5 ☐	4 ☐	3 ☐	2 ☐	1 ☐
d. Depth of products and services to meet the range of your investments needs	6 ☐	5 ☐	4 ☐	3 ☐	2 ☐	1 ☐
e. Ability to resolve problems	6 ☐	5 ☐	4 ☐	3 ☐	2 ☐	1 ☐
f. Online services offered	6 ☐	5 ☐	4 ☐	3 ☐	2 ☐	1 ☐
g. Multiple providers' products to choose from	6 ☐	5 ☐	4 ☐	3 ☐	2 ☐	1 ☐
h. Quality of advice	6 ☐	5 ☐	4 ☐	3 ☐	2 ☐	1 ☐
i. Knowledge of representatives or advisors you deal with	6 ☐	5 ☐	4 ☐	3 ☐	2 ☐	1 ☐
j. Representative knowing your overall situation and needs	6 ☐	5 ☐	4 ☐	3 ☐	2 ☐	1 ☐
k. Access to other professional resources	6 ☐	5 ☐	4 ☐	3 ☐	2 ☐	1 ☐
l. Degree to which my provider knows me	6 ☐	5 ☐	4 ☐	3 ☐	2 ☐	1 ☐
m. Quality of service	6 ☐	5 ☐	4 ☐	3 ☐	2 ☐	1 ☐

7. During the past 12 months, have you or anyone in your household switched some assets (other than checking account assets) from one investment/savings **provider** to another? (Do NOT include switching money from one individual investment such as a stock or bond to another stock or bond within the same brokerage or investment company.) Please **exclude** assets in a 401(k), 403(b), 457 or similar defined contribution retirement accounts.

   1 ☐ Yes   2 ☐ No

8. The following are some different approaches you and/or your household might take regarding advice and investment decision-making. Please read each one and then answer the question below.

   1. Using a variety of online or offline information sources, you make your own investment decisions without the assistance of an investment professional or advisor.
   2. Using a variety of online or offline information sources, you make most of your own investment decisions but use an investment professional or advisor for specialized needs only (e.g., alternative investments or tax advice).
   3. You regularly consult with an investment professional or advisor and you may also get additional information yourself, but you make most of the final decisions.
   4. You rely upon an investment professional or advisor to make most or all your investment decisions.

For the majority of your assets, which ONE of the above (1–4) BEST describes your preferred approach? **(Write in a number from 1–4.)**

Number: _____

Part B. Demographic Characteristics

Your answers to the following questions will be used to help us interpret the information you have provided.

9. What is your age?

   Age: _____ years

10. Are you . . .?

   1 ☐ Male   2 ☐ Female

11. What is your current marital status? **(X ONE box.)**

   1 ☐ Now married   3 ☐ Divorced   5 ☐ Single, never married

   2 ☐ Widowed   4 ☐ Separated   6 ☐ Living together, not married

12. How many people in your household are dependent children? **(Write In)**

   # _____

13. How many other dependents are you supporting (e.g., parents, grandparents)? **(Write In)**

\# _____

14. For the following type of financial transaction, please indicate who is primarily responsible, or if the responsibilities are shared. **(X ONE box for each.)**

	Male Head of Household	Female Head of Household	Shared Equally	Other
Investment decision making	1 ☐	2 ☐	3 ☐	4 ☐

15. What is the highest level of education you have completed? **(X ONE box.)**

01 ☐ Some high school

02 ☐ High school graduate

03 ☐ Vocational or technical school/apprenticeship

04 ☐ Some college

05 ☐ College graduate

06 ☐ Some graduate school

07 ☐ Master's degree

08 ☐ Law school graduate

09 ☐ Dental/medical school graduate

10 ☐ Doctorate

16. What is your retirement status? **(X ONE box.)**

1 ☐ Retired   2 ☐ Semi-Retired   3 ☐ Not Retired

CASE 3.2 MCDONALD'S

The World's Number One Fast-Food Company!

SPSS Data File Excel Data File

McDonald's (www.mcdonalds.com) history began when its founder, Ray Kroc, opened the first restaurant in 1955 in Des Plaines, Illinois. The strong foundation that he built and the dedication of its talented executives have enabled McDonald's to prosper. As of 2011, McDonald's is the world's number one fast-food company by sales, with more than 32,000 flagship restaurants serving burgers and fries in more than 117 countries. The popular chain is well known for its Big Macs, Quarter Pounders, and Chicken McNuggets.

Most of its outlets are freestanding units. However, McDonald's also has many quick-service kiosk units located in airports and retail areas. Each unit gets its food and packaging from approved suppliers and uses standardized procedures to ensure that a Big Mac purchased in Pittsburgh tastes the same as one bought in Beijing. About 75 percent of its restaurants are run by franchisees with 2010 revenues amounting to $24.07 billion. Table 1 gives the company's sales and market share in recent years.

McDonald's has always been a family restaurant. The family focus is a positioning strategy that is reflected in everything the corporation does. McDonald's knows that by targeting families, it hits one of the most attractive, loyal consumer groups available. It gets into the parents' wallets via the kids' minds. A survey of American schoolchildren found that 96 percent could recognize Ronald McDonald. Santa Claus is the only fictional character with a higher degree of popularity. The effect of McDonald's on the nation's culture, economy, and diet is hard to exaggerate.

McDonald's has not only become the number one restaurant for the children, but the 1-minute service promise, the slogan "I'm lovin' it," and introducing a "forever young" brand has also enabled it to gain a significant market share among youths and busy adults. McDonald's intends to add new features to its restaurants. For example, the "linger zone" would offer a place for customers to relax by offering armchairs, sofas, and wireless connections. The "grab and go" zone would offer tall counters with bar stools for those on the go who would like to eat alone. The restaurants would also have plasma televisions televising the news and weather reports. The "flexible" zone with booths with cushions and flexible seating would target families. For each of these zones, different music would target each customer group.

In recent years, McDonald's has extended into a café-style setting, called *McCafe*, to compete with the popularity of Starbucks and coffee shops in general. McDonald's is now another place for the coffee lovers to get their cup of coffee. Recently, *Consumer Reports* magazine ranked McDonald's coffee ahead of Starbucks, saying it tastes better and costs less. McDonald's coffee has "surprisingly high" appeal, with 35 percent of consumers surveyed saying that McDonald's brew got better in the past year.

McDonald's U.S. restaurants are uniting behind this new brand message and energy. They are focused on bringing the "I'm lovin' it" theme to life not only in its advertising, but also for every customer who visits its restaurants. This world-class marketing strategy is the latest element of McDonald's overall plan to continue stimulating customers through persuasive food choices, great service and restaurant operations, value, and exciting new restaurant decors. Still running in 2011, "I'm lovin' it" is a key part of McDonald's business strategy to connect with customers in highly pertinent, culturally important ways around the world. To quote Bill Lamar, senior vice president and chief marketing officer of McDonald's USA: "It will rekindle the emotional bond our customers have with McDonald's through a campaign that depicts how people live, what they love about life and what they love about McDonald's."

With the successful expansion of McDonald's into many international markets, the company has become a symbol of globalization and the spread of the American way of life. The business is managed as distinct geographic segments: United States; Europe; Asia/Pacific, Middle East, and Africa (APMEA); Latin America; and Canada. The U.S. and Europe segments each account for approximately 35 percent of total revenues, while France, Germany, and the United Kingdom, collectively, account for approximately 60 percent of Europe's revenues. APMEA accounts for 14 percent of the total revenues, Latin America for 8 percent, and Canada for 5 percent of the total revenue. The remaining 3 percent come from other sources.

As shown in Table 2, the global fast-food market is projected to grow at 5.3 percent per year through 2013. This has intensified the competition. In order to maintain and fortify its leadership position in the competitive fast-food industry, McDonald's conducted a survey. McDonald's wanted to study customer demographics and awareness of different competing fast-food chains; the satisfaction responses of consumers in

TABLE 2 Global Fast-Food Market Value Forecast: $ Billion, 2008–2013

Year	$ Billion	% Growth
2008	$154.7	6.6%
2009	164.3	6.2
2010	173.1	5.3
2011	182.1	5.2
2012	191.0	4.9
2013	200.0	4.7
CAGR, 2008–2013		5.3

Source: Datamonitor.

TABLE 1 McDonald's Revenues and Market Share 2004–2009

	2004	2005	2006	2007	2008	2009
Revenues (USD billions)	$18.59	$19.12	$20.90	$22.79	$23.52	$22.74
Global market share (%)	15.53%	14.97%	15.40%	15.69%	15.21%	13.84%

terms of family orientation, comfort, price, quick service, healthy foods, cleanliness, and so on; and patronage preferences in terms of eat-in or drive-through. The questionnaire used follows and the data obtained are provided. Based on the data collected and analysis of this study, McDonald's intends to improve its service and brand orientation.

Questions

Chapter 1

1. Discuss the role that marketing research can play in helping a fast-food restaurant such as McDonald's formulate sound marketing strategies.

Chapter 2

2. McDonald's is considering further expansion in the United States. Define the management-decision problem.
3. Define an appropriate marketing research problem based on the management-decision problem you have identified.

Chapter 3

4. Formulate an appropriate research design for investigating the marketing research problem you have defined in Chapter 2.

Chapter 4

5. Use the Internet to determine the market shares of the major national fast-food chains for the last calendar year.

Chapter 5

6. What type of syndicated data will be useful to McDonald's?

Chapter 6

7. Discuss the role of qualitative research in helping McDonald's expand further in the United States.

Chapter 7

8. McDonald's has developed a new fish sandwich with a distinctive Cajun taste. It would like to determine consumers' response to this new sandwich before introducing it in the marketplace. If a survey is to be conducted to determine consumer preferences, which survey method should be used and why?

Chapter 8

9. Discuss the role of experimentation in helping McDonald's determine its optimal level of advertising expenditures.

Chapter 9

10. Illustrate the use of primary type of scales in measuring consumer preferences for fast-food restaurants.

Chapter 10

11. Illustrate the use of Likert, semantic differential, and Stapel scales in measuring consumer preferences for fast-food restaurants.

Chapter 11

12. Develop a questionnaire for assessing consumer preferences for fast-food restaurants.

Chapters 12 and 13

13. What sampling plan should be adopted for the survey of Chapter 7? How should the sample size be determined?

Chapter 14

14. How should the field-workers be selected and trained to conduct the fieldwork for the survey in Chapter 7?

Chapter 15

15. How should the missing values be treated for the following demographic variables: education (D5), income (D6), employment status (D7), and marital status (D8)?
16. Recode payment method (D1) by combining Debit card, Check, and Other into one category.
17. Recode number of people living at home (D3A) as follows: for adults age 18+, four or more should be combined into one category labeled 4+; for each of the three remaining age groups (under 5, 6–11, and 12–17), two or more should be combined into a single category labeled 2+.
18. Recode education (D5) by combining the lowest two categories and labeling it completed high school or less.
19. Recode income (D6) by combining the highest three categories and labeling it $100,000 or more.
20. Recode employment status (D7) by combining homemaker, retired, and unemployed into a single category.
21. Classify respondents into light, medium, and heavy users of fast food based on a frequency distribution of S3A: In the past four weeks, approximately how many times have you, yourself, eaten food from a fast-food restaurant? Use the following classification: 1–4 times = light, 5–8 times = medium, 9 or more times = heavy.

Chapter 16

22. Run a frequency distribution for all variables except respondent ID (respoind). Why is this analysis useful?
23. Cross-tabulate fast-food consumption classification (recoded S3A, see Chapter 15 questions) with the demographic characteristics (some recoded as specified in Chapter 15): age (S1), gender (S2), payment method (D1), number of people living at home (D3A), education (D5), income (D6), employment (D7), marital status (D8), and region. Interpret the results.
24. Cross-tabulate payment method (recoded D1) with the remaining demographic characteristics (some recoded as specified in Chapter 15): age (S1), gender (S2), number of people living at home (D3A), education (D5), income (D6), employment (D7), marital status (D8), and region. Interpret the results.
25. Cross-tabulate eating there more often, less often, or about the same as a year or so ago (q8_1, q8_7, q8_26, q8_36, q8_39) with the demographic characteristics (some recoded as specified in Chapter 15): age (S1), gender (S2), payment method (D1), number of people living at home (D3A), education (D5), income (D6), employment (D7), marital status (D8), and region. Interpret the results.

Chapter 17

26. Do the ratings on the psychographic statements (q14_1, q14_2, q14_3, q14_4, q14_5, q14_6, and q14_7) differ for males and females?
27. Do the respondents agree more with "I have been making an effort to look for fast-food choices that have better nutritional value than the foods I have chosen in the past" (q14_6) than they do with "I consider the amount of fat in the foods my kids eat at fast-food restaurants" (q14_5)?
28. Do the restaurant ratings (q9_1, q9_7, q9_26, q9_36, q9_39) differ for the various demographic characteristics (some recoded as specified in Chapter 15): age (S1), gender (S2), payment method (D1), number of people living at home (D3A), education (D5), income (D6), employment (D7), marital status (D8), and region? Interpret the results.
29. Do the four groups defined by "the extent to which you find it difficult to make up your mind about which fast-food restaurant

to go to" (q13) differ in their restaurant ratings (q9_1, q9_7, q9_26, q9_36, q9_39)?

and q14_7) when the statements are considered simultaneously?

Chapter 18

30. Can each of the restaurant ratings (q9_1, q9_7, q9_26, q9_36, q9_39) be explained in terms of the ratings on the psychographic statement (q14_1, q14_2, q14_3, q14_4, q14_5, q14_6,

Chapter 19

31. Write a report for McDonald's management summarizing the results of your analyses. What recommendations do you have for the management?

References

1. www.mcdonalds.com, accessed February 12, 2011.
2. "McDonald's Offers Ethics with Those Fries," *BusinessWeek* (2007), http://businessweek.com/globalbiz/content/jan2007/

gb20070109_958716.htm?link_ position=link3, accessed June 18, 2007.

Note: This case was prepared for class discussion purposes only and does not represent the views of McDonald's or its affiliates. The problem scenario is hypothetical and the name of the actual company has been disguised. **However, the data provided are real and were collected in an actual survey by a prominent marketing research firm, whose name is also disguised.** Some questions have been deleted, while the data for other questions are not provided because of proprietary reasons.

Online MCDONALD'S Commitment Study Questionnaire

April 1, 2011

RID _____

Thank you for participating in our survey.

S1. To begin, which of the following categories includes your age? (CHOOSE ONE RESPONSE ONLY.)

    1 Under 18   **[TERMINATE QS1]**
    2 18–24
    3 25–29
    4 30–34
    5 35–39
    6 40–45
    7 46 or older   **[TERMINATE QS1]**
    – Refused   **[TERMINATE QS1]**

S2. Are you…? (CHOOSE ONE RESPONSE ONLY.)

    1 Male
    2 Female

S3. OMITTED

S3A. In the past 4 weeks, approximately how many times have you, yourself, eaten food from a fast-food restaurant? **[ACCEPT WHOLE NUMBERS ONLY, DO NOT ACCEPT RANGE.] [RANGE: 0–99]**

_____
    & DK/refused **[TERMINATE QS3A]**
    [TERMINATE QS3A IF ZERO]

  1. OMITTED
  2. OMITTED
  3. OMITTED
3a. You have indicated that you have heard of these restaurants. When was the last time, if ever, that you, yourself, have eaten from each one? (PLEASE SELECT ONE TIME FRAME FOR EACH RESTAURANT.) **[FORMAT AS GRID: INCLUDE RESPONSES FROM Q1.]**

    1 Within the past 4 weeks
    2 More than 4 weeks to within the past 3 months
    3 More than 3 months ago
    4 Never

  4. OMITTED
  5. OMITTED
  6. OMITTED
  7. OMITTED

8. For each of the restaurants listed below, please indicate whether you, yourself, are eating from there more often, less often, or about the same frequency as a year or so ago. **[SHOW ONLY THOSE Q3a = 1 or 2]**

	More often	About the same	Less often
Insert brands	1	2	3

9. I'd like you to rate the restaurants you, yourself, have eaten from in the past 3 months using a 10-point scale, where "10" means you think it is perfect, and "1" means you think it is terrible. Now taking into account everything that you look for in a fast-food restaurant, how would you rate each of the following? **[SHOW Q3a = 1 or 2]**

Terrible (1)	2	3	4	5	6	7	8	9	Perfect (10)
○	○	○	○	○	○	○	○	○	○

10. OMITTED
11. OMITTED
12. OMITTED
13. Sometimes it is difficult for people to make up their minds about which fast-food restaurant to go to on a given visit. Think about when you go to a fast-food restaurant. In general, which of the following statements best describes the extent to which you find it difficult to make up your mind about which fast-food restaurant to go to? (CHOOSE ONE RESPONSE ONLY.)

   1 I **always know** exactly which fast-food restaurant I am going to go to
   2 I **usually know** exactly which fast-food restaurant I am going to go to
   3 I'm **usually undecided** about which fast-food restaurant I am going to go to
   4 I'm **always undecided** about which fast-food restaurant I am going to go to

14. Below is a list of statements that may or may not be used to describe you in general. Using the scale of Agree completely, Agree somewhat, Neither agree nor disagree, Disagree somewhat, and Disagree completely, please indicate how strongly you agree or disagree with each statement. (CHOOSE ONE RESPONSE FOR EACH STATEMENT.)

Disagree Completely	Disagree Somewhat	Neither Agree nor Disagree	Agree Somewhat	Agree Completely	N/A
○	○	○	○	○	○

   1 I try to stay current on the latest health and nutrition information.
   2 I read nutritional labels on most products I buy.
   3 I am making more of an effort to find out about the nutritional content of the foods I eat at fast-food restaurants.
   4 I consider the amount of fat in the foods I eat at fast-food restaurants.
   5 I consider the amount of fat in the foods my kids eat at fast-food restaurants.
   6 I have been making an effort to look for fast-food choices that have better nutritional value than the foods I have chosen in the past.
   7 I am eating at fast-food restaurants less often out of concern for the high fat content in the foods at fast-food restaurants.

   These last few questions are for classification purposes only.

D1. Which of the following methods do you most often use when purchasing from fast-food restaurants? Do you pay . . .? (CHOOSE ONE RESPONSE ONLY.)

   1. Cash
   2. Credit card
   3. Debit card
   4. Check
   5. Other

D2. OMITTED

D3. OMITTED

D3A. How many people in each of the following age groups live in your home? (PLEASE ENTER A NUMBER FOR EACH AGE RANGE. ENTER "0" IF THERE IS NO ONE IN THAT RANGE IN YOUR HOUSEHOLD.)

   A. Adults age 18+ **[RANGE: 1–15]**
   B. Children under age 5 **[RANGE: 0–9]**
   C. Children age 6–11 **[RANGE: 0–9]**
   D. Children age 12–17 **[RANGE: 0–9]**

D4. OMITTED

D5. Which of the following best represents the last level of education that you, yourself, completed? (CHOOSE ONE RESPONSE ONLY.)

   1 Some high school or less
   2 Completed high school
   3 Some college
   4 Completed college
   5 Post graduate
   – Prefer not to answer

D6. Which of the following best describes your family's annual household income before taxes? (CHOOSE ONE RESPONSE ONLY.)

   1 Under $25,000
   2 $25,000 but under $50,000
   3 $50,000 but under $75,000
   4 $75,000 but under $100,000
   5 $100,000 but under $150,000
   6 $150,000 but under $200,000
   7 $200,000 or more
   – Prefer not to answer

D7. Which of the following best describes your employment status? (CHOOSE ONE RESPONSE ONLY.)

   1 Full-time
   2 Part-time
   3 Retired
   4 Student
   5 Homemaker
   6 Unemployed
   – Prefer not to answer

D8. Are you...?

   1 Single, Separated, Divorced, Widowed
   0 Married/Living as Married
   – Prefer not to answer

Thank you for taking the time to participate in our research!

	Q1
Arby's	1
Atlanta Bread Company	2
A&W	3
Baja Fresh	4
Blimpie	5
Boston Chicken/Market	6
Burger King	7
Captain D's	8
Carl's Jr.	9
Checkers Drive-In	10
Chick-Fil-A	11
Chipotle Mexican Grill	12
Church's	13
Del Taco	14
Domino's Pizza	15
El Pollo Loco	16
Grandy's	17

(Continued)

	Q1
Green Burrito	18
Hardee's	19
In-N-Out Burger	20
Jack in the Box	21
KFC/Kentucky Fried Chicken	22
La Salsa	23
Little Caesars	24
Long John Silver's	25
McDonald's	26
Panda Express	27
Panera Bread	28
Papa John's	41
Pick Up Stix	29
Pizza Hut	30
Popeyes	31
Quiznos	32
Rally's	33
Rubio's	34
Sonic	35
Subway	36
Taco Bell	37
Taco Bueno	38
McDonald's	39
Whataburger	40
OMITTED—OTHER SPECIFY	
None	42

CASE 3.3 BOEING

Taking Flight

SPSS Data File   Excel Data File

The Boeing Company (www.boeing.com), together with its sub-sidiaries, is an aerospace company that operates in six principal segments. The first five are collectively known as Integrated Defense Systems (IDS) and include Commercial Airplanes, Aircraft and Weapon Systems, Network Systems, Support Systems, and Launch and Orbital Systems. The sixth principal segment is Boeing Capital Corporation (BCC). The Commercial Airplanes operations principally involve development, production, and marketing of commercial jet aircraft and providing related support services, primarily to the commercial airline industry worldwide. W. James McNerney, Jr., was the CEO as of 2011, and the company is a leader in the global defense and aerospace market. The company's revenues in recent years are provided in Table 1.

In April 2004, Boeing announced its first new plane in 10 years, the 787 Dreamliner, a powerful but fuel-stingy midsize aircraft. This aircraft is capable of transporting passengers on long-haul routes that now are the province of jumbo jets. With spacious interiors, large luggage cabinets, and huge windows, it promises to be a change maker. The 787 was the result of considerable marketing research, which is an ongoing process at Boeing. Nicole Piasecki, vice president of the Marketing and Business Strategy division, claimed that Boeing had researched the market for more than 40 years. It has studied passengers, airlines, airports, and the dynamics of air travel on a global scale. Internal and external secondary sources of data were analyzed first and then primary research was conducted.

To understand the needs of its customers—airlines—the company went beyond just determining the airlines' needs; it also tried to comprehend the needs of airline passengers, as well as those of the aircraft's financiers. Based on its research, Boeing concluded that the declining emphasis on hub-and-spoke travel will generate the greatest growth in smaller mid-market airplanes and lesser growth in jumbo jets. Growth in air travel has been met by an increase in new nonstop markets and by frequency growth instead of an increase in airplane capacity/size. Based on these findings, the company developed the 787 Dreamliner.

On July 18, 2010, the 787 Dreamliner made its international debut, landing at the Farnborough Airport, United Kingdom, in support of the Farnborough International Airshow. Built by an international team, this aircraft provides airlines around the globe with a new level of efficiency in operations, with a 20-percent reduction in fuel use when compared to similar-sized airplanes. It also brings a new level of passenger comfort to travelers, including bigger windows and more personal space as well as an environment designed to help them arrive at their destinations feeling refreshed.

The Dreamliner should revive Boeing's somewhat tired product line and stem Airbus's market-share depredations. More than 3,000 midsize aircraft, including the Boeing 757 and 767 and Airbus A300, A310, and A330 models, will be reaching the end of their operating lives by 2025 or so, along with various Lockheed and Douglas models. The sales opportunity is huge. Yet, the Boeing sales force must be more effective than ever before in the company's history.

Mr. McNerney wants to put a very strong marketing and sales organization in place to take advantage of the opportunities that lie ahead for the 787 Dreamliner. His years of experience have shown him that salesperson loyalty is very important, because of the long-term nature of contracts with the major air carriers of the world. Being driven by fundamentals, McNerney wants to understand what drives a salesperson's loyalty toward the place of work. He hopes that this research effort will inform him on how to develop his business-to-business sales force in the future through improved selection, training, and leadership of Boeing salespersons. He commissioned TNS, one of the leading custom marketing research firms, to undertake the research. The research firm of TNS adopted the following methodology.

Methodology

The project began with an exploratory phase that involved a thorough analysis of secondary data. Both academic and trade sources were examined. This was followed by eight focus groups with B2B field salespersons from a variety of industries. The findings of the exploratory phase were used to design a descriptive survey. A telephone survey was administered to a cross-section of business-to-business salespersons ages 18 to 65 in the United States and in the Canadian metropolitan areas of Toronto and Montreal using a list obtained from Sales and Marketing Executives International (SMEI). This age qualification enabled the company to reach the population of potential adult workers in the specified regions, avoiding most retirees. The final sample size comprised 1,000 adults in the United States and Canada. This sample size ensured a sampling error of less than 3 percentage points. Expecting a cooperation rate of 33.3 percent, the sample frame consisted of 3,000 people from the SMEI list.

All U.S. telephone interviews were handled from TNS's office in Atlanta, using trained interviewers and computer-assisted telephone interviewing (CATI). Interviewing of the Montreal and Toronto metropolitan areas was conducted locally by a Canadian affiliate of the company to best facilitate regional French and English dialects.

In terms of the survey duration, TNS's experience has shown that a 30-minute telephone interview is not desirable. The completion rate suffers, because people judge it to be too long a period of time to cooperate and either refuse to participate or to complete the full interview. Therefore, the duration of the telephone interview was limited to 10 minutes. The questionnaire used is presented at the end of the case. The data obtained were analyzed. A formal report was prepared and presented to Boeing.

TABLE 1 Boeing Revenues, 2000–2010

Year	Revenue in U.S. Dollar Billions
2000	$51.3
2001	58.2
2002	53.8
2003	50.3
2004	51.4
2005	53.6
2006	61.5
2007	66.4
2008	60.9
2009	68.3
2010	64.3

Building a Loyal Sales Force

As McNerney pondered the report from TNS, he still wondered what would be the best way to build the loyalty of his current sales force. He would also like to recruit a new breed of loyal salespeople. The potential for the 787 Dreamliner is high. Having a loyal sales force would be a key to realizing it.

Questions

Chapter 1

1. Discuss the role that marketing research can play in helping McNerney build a strong Boeing sales force.
2. Discuss the role that marketing research can play in enabling strong sales for the 787 Dreamliner.

Chapter 2

3. McNerney wants the 787 Dreamliner to be a strong success. Define the management-decision problem.
4. Define the corresponding marketing research problem.
5. Develop two research questions with two hypotheses corresponding to each.

Chapter 3

6. Do you think that the research design adopted by TNS was appropriate? Why or why not?

Chapters 4 and 5

7. Search the Internet to determine the demand by a major airline for new planes in the next 5 years.
8. Search the Internet to determine the total number of passengers that traveled by air in the past year.
9. What type of internal database will help Boeing in forecasting the demand for new planes by its customers?

Chapter 6

10. Discuss the role of qualitative research in helping Boeing develop and market the 787 Dreamliner.
11. Which qualitative research technique should be used to determine air passengers' attitudes and preferences for various types of aircraft?

Chapter 7

12. If a survey is to be conducted to determine air passengers' attitudes and preferences for various types of aircraft, which survey method should be used and why?
13. If a survey is to be conducted to determine commercial airlines' attitudes and preferences for various types of aircraft, which survey method should be used and why?
14. Was the telephone survey conducted by TNS the most appropriate method for determining the drivers of sales force loyalty toward the place of work? If not, which survey method would you recommend?

Chapter 8

15. Discuss the role of causal research in developing an advertising campaign for the 787 Dreamliner.

Chapter 9

16. Develop ordinal and interval scales for measuring preference of commercial airlines for Boeing 757, 767, and 787 and Airbus A300, A310, and A330 models.

Chapter 10

17. Develop Likert, semantic differential, and Stapel scales for measuring the importance that commercial airlines attach to the fuel efficiency of a plane.
18. Which type of scale would you use for measuring commercial airlines' image of Boeing? Develop such a scale.

Chapter 11

19. Critically evaluate the questionnaire given in this case. What improvements do you suggest?

Chapter 12

20. Describe the sampling plan adopted in this case. Do you think it is appropriate?

Chapter 13

21. Do you think that the sample size was appropriate in this case? Present statistical reasoning to support your answer.

Chapter 14

22. This case made use of telephone surveys. How would you customize the fieldwork process mentioned in the book to the case of telephone interviews?

Chapter 15

23. Carry out consistency checks for the data file for this case. Do you identify any problems with the data?
24. Develop a codebook for questions D1 to D12 of the questionnaire for this case.

Chapter 16

25. Run a frequency distribution including descriptive statistics for all the variables. Interpret the results.
26. Recode question 3 ("How loyal would you say that you are personally to the place you work?") into a new variable with two categories (1 to 6 = 1, low loyalty; 7 = 2, high loyalty). Recode question 4 ("How much loyalty would you say the place you work for has to you?") into a new variable with three categories (1 to 3 = 1, no loyalty; 4 to 5 = 2, some loyalty; 6 to 7 = 3, high loyalty). Are these two categorical variables associated? Interpret your results.
27. Do salespeople who exhibit low or high loyalty to a place of work (recoded question 3) differ in terms of each of the demographic characteristics, D1 to D12? In other words, is salesperson loyalty associated with any of the 12 demographic characteristics? Note that age (D10) is recorded as the year of birth. Instead of D10, use the age variable. Divide the sample into four roughly equal age groups based on age.
28. Sum all the items (a through o) of question 2 to form an overall satisfaction scale. Obtain a frequency distribution and summary statistics for this overall satisfaction scale. Interpret the results.

Chapter 17

29. Do salespeople who exhibit low or high loyalty to a place of work (recoded question 3) differ in terms of each of the items of question 1 (a through h)?
30. Do salespeople who exhibit low or high loyalty to a place of work (recoded question 3) differ in terms of each of the satisfaction items of question 2 (a through o)? Identify the five items that exhibit the greatest difference between the two groups.

31. Do the no-loyalty, some-loyalty, or high-loyalty groups of question 4 (recoded question 4) differ in terms of each of the satisfaction items of question 2 (a through o)?

Chapter 18

32. What is the correlation between the two original loyalty measures of questions 3 and 4? What can be said of the causal relationship between the two original measures of loyalty?

33. Conduct a multiple regression using the loyalty to the place of work (original question 3) as the dependent variable. The five independent variables will be the five items of question 2 that exhibited the greatest difference in the t-tests of Chapter 17. Interpret the results.

34. Conduct a multiple regression using the loyalty to the place of work (original question 3) as the dependent variable and items a through f of question 2 as the independent variables. Interpret the results.

Chapter 19

35. What do McNerney and his staff need to know about business-to-business salesperson loyalty? Create a one-page, single-spaced summary of these results.

References

1. www.boeing.com, accessed May 19, 2011.
2. "Boeing 787 Dreamliner Makes International Debut," http://boeing.mediaroom.com/index.php?s=43&item=1317, accessed November 12, 2010.
3. Stanley Holmes, "Boeing Straightens Up and Flies Right," *BusinessWeek* (April 27, 2008), http://businessweek.com/bwdaily/dnflash/apr2006/nf20060427_0379_db016.htm?cha, accessed May 11, 2008.

Note: This case was prepared for class discussion purposes only and does not represent the views of Boeing or its affiliates. The problem scenario is hypothetical and the name of the actual company has been disguised. **However, the data provided are real and were collected in an actual survey by a prominent marketing research firm, whose name is also disguised.** Some questions have been deleted, while the data for other questions are not provided because of proprietary reasons.

SURVEY OF NORTH AMERICAN B2B SALESPERSONS

Hello, I am _____ from TNS, a national public opinion research firm. We are conducting a very important survey about job satisfaction for B2B salespersons. For your help today, we will send you an executive summary of the results of our study. This will allow you to understand how your perspectives compare with other B2B salespersons. This survey should take no more than 10 minutes.

Screener Questions

(CATI Programmer: Please note that all screener questions and responses must be included in the programming so that individual responses can be tabulated for respondents that qualify.)

S1. Are you currently employed full-time, employed part-time, or are you not employed?

a. Full-time	SKIP TO Q.1
b. Part-time	SKIP TO Q.1
c. Employed on a temporary basis	SKIP TO Q.1
d. Employed on a contract basis	SKIP TO Q.1
e. Not employed	CONTINUE
f. Retired	CONTINUE
g. Don't know/refused	DO NOT READ

S2. Do you plan to enter (or reenter) the workforce within the next year, the next 1 to 5 years, the next 6 to 10 years, longer than 10 years, or not at all?

a. Within the next year	CONTINUE
b. 1 to 5 years	CONTINUE
c. 6 to 10 years	CONTINUE
d. >10 years	CONTINUE
e. Not at all	THANK AND TERMINATE

(ASK EVERYONE)

1. I would like you to think about how work fits into your life personally, whether or not you are currently working. I am going to read you some statements about working and your career. Using a scale from 1 to 7—where 1 means *"completely disagree"* and 7 means *"completely agree,"* I'd like you to consider each statement. First (READ STATEMENT). (RANDOMIZE LIST)

a. I am just starting out in the work world.
b. I am moving up the ladder in my work, but I haven't reached my peak yet.
c. I am at the peak of my working potential.
d. I am in a holding pattern when it comes to work, not really moving ahead but not falling behind.
e. I am now past the peak of my work life and am slowing down.
f. I expect to retire from work in the next 5 years.

g. I am on a break from working at the moment but expect to return to work within the next 12 months.

h. I am not working at the moment and do not expect to return for at least a year.

(ASKED OF THOSE WHO ANSWERED "a," "b," "c," or "d" TO S1.)

2. Please rate each of the following aspects of your work in terms of how satisfied you feel with each. Please use a scale of 1 to 7, with 1 meaning you *"disagree very much"* with that aspect and 7 meaning you *"very much agree"* with that aspect of your work. (RANDOMIZE LIST)

a. Management really knows its job.

b. My customers are fair.

c. I'm really doing something worthwhile in my job.

d. My work is challenging.

e. I have plenty of freedom on my job to use my own judgment.

f. I'm satisfied with the way employee benefits are handled around here.

g. My opportunities for advancement are reasonable.

h. I am highly paid.

i. My job is interesting.

j. The workspace given is adequate.

k. Compared with other companies, employee benefits here are good.

l. The people I work with get along well together.

m. I'm allowed to work from home, if I desire.

n. Management here is really interested in the welfare of employees.

(ASKED OF THOSE WHO ANSWERED "a," "b," "c," or "d" TO S1.)

3. We hear a lot these days about company loyalty or the degree to which employees feel loyal and committed to their employer. How loyal would you say that you are personally to the place you work using a scale of 1 to 7, where 1 means *"not at all loyal"* and 7 means *"extremely loyal"*?

1 2 3 4 5 6 7

(ASKED OF THOSE WHO ANSWERED "a," "b," "c," or "d" TO S1.)

4. Now using the same scale where 1 means *"not at all loyal"* and 7 means *"extremely loyal,"* how much loyalty would you say the place you work for has to *you*?

1 2 3 4 5 6 7

Demographics

D1. Gender

a. Male

b. Female

D2. What is the highest level of education you have completed?

a. Some high school or less

b. High school graduate

c. Some college

d. College graduate

e. Post-graduate degree

f. Don't know/refused   DO NOT READ

D3. What is your current marital status?

a. Single

b. Married

c. Living with someone as if married

d. Separated

e. Divorced

f. Widowed

g. Don't know/refused   DO NOT READ

D4. How would you classify yourself?

a. American Indian or Alaskan Native

b. Asian

c. Black or African American

d. White

e. Other [specify: _____]

f. Don't know/refused   DO NOT READ

D5. Do you consider yourself to be of Hispanic origin?

    a. Yes
    b. No
    c. Don't know/refused   DO NOT READ

D6. How many children under the age of 6 are currently living at home with you?

    a. Under age 6 _____

D7. How long have you been working in your current position?

    a. Less than 1 year
    b. 1 to less than 5 years
    c. 5 to less than 10 years
    d. 10 to less than 20 years
    e. 20 to less than 30 years
    f. 30 years or more
    g. Don't know/refused   DO NOT READ

D8. Do you plan to change jobs in the next 5 years?

    a. Yes
    b. No
    c. Don't know/refused   DO NOT READ

    (ASK EVERYONE)

D9. How many jobs have you had in the past 5 years?

    a. 0
    b. 1
    c. 2
    d. 3
    e. 4
    f. 5
    g. 6 to 9
    h. 10 or more
    i. Don't know/refused   DO NOT READ

D10. In what year were you born?

    a. _____
    b. Refused   DO NOT READ

D11. How many people in your household contribute their income to the household?

    a. 0
    b. 1
    c. 2
    d. 3 or more
    e. Don't know/refused   DO NOT READ

D12. I'm going to read to you a list of income categories. Please stop me when I get to the category that best describes the total combined household income before taxes of all members of your household.

    a. Under $25,000
    b. $25,000 to less than $40,000
    c. $40,000 to less than $50,000
    d. $50,000 to less than $60,000
    e. $60,000 to less than $75,000
    f. $75,000 to less than $100,000
    g. $100,000 to less than $150,000
    h. $150,000 or more
    i. Don't know/refused   DO NOT READ

D13. State _____

Thank you for completing The Survey of North American B2B Salespersons. If you would like an e-mail copy of the executive summary, please provide your e-mail address now. You should receive your copy in the next 90 days from TNS.

COMPREHENSIVE BRIEF HARVARD BUSINESS SCHOOL CASES

The Harvard cases are not printed in the book. Students can purchase these cases directly from Harvard Business Online at harvardbusinessonline. hbsp.harvard.edu. or web.hbr.org/store/index.php. However, we give the marketing research questions for each chapter for each case.

CASE 4.1   TRUEARTH HEALTHY FOODS

Market Research for a New Product Introduction (4065)

Comprehensive Questions

Chapter 1

1. Discuss the role that marketing research can play in helping TruEarth Healthy Foods formulate sound marketing strategies.
2. Discuss the role that marketing research can play in helping TruEarth Healthy Foods determine whether it should introduce a refrigerated pizza developed using a new whole grain pizza crust.

Chapter 2

3. Define the management-decision problem facing TruEarth Healthy Foods with respect to refrigerated pizza.
4. Define an appropriate marketing research problem based on the management-decision problem you have identified.
5. Develop two research questions, each with an associated hypothesis.

Chapter 3

6. What type of research design was adopted in determining consumer purchase intent for the new refrigerated pizza?
7. Critically evaluate the research design that was adopted in determining consumer purchase intent for the new refrigerated pizza.

Chapter 4

8. Use the Internet to determine the market shares of the major firms catering to the refrigerated pizza market for the last calendar year.
9. What type of internal secondary data will be useful to TruEarth?

Chapter 5

10. What type of syndicated data will be useful to TruEarth?

Chapter 6

11. Discuss the role of qualitative research in helping TruEarth penetrate the frozen pizza market in the United States.
12. **Social Media** How can TruEarth make use of social media to conduct qualitative research to understand consumer response to refrigerated pizza?

Chapter 7

13. Do you think that the mall-intercept survey conducted by TruEarth to test the refrigerated pizza idea was the best survey method in this case? Why or why not? Defend your reasoning.
14. Do you think that the observation method can be used in this case? If yes, what observation method would you recommend and what insights you hope to gain?

Chapter 8

15. In what way could TruEarth make use of experimentation? What specific experimental design would you recommend?

Chapter 9

16. Illustrate the use of the primary scales for measuring consumer preferences for refrigerated pizza.

Chapter 10

17. Develop Likert, semantic differential, and Stapel scales for measuring consumer preferences for refrigerated pizza.

Chapter 11

18. Develop a questionnaire for measuring consumer preferences for a refrigerated pizza developed using a new whole grain pizza crust.

Chapter 12

19. What sampling plan was adopted for the mall-intercept survey of Chapter 7? How could this sampling plan be improved?

Chapter 13

20. What was the sample size used in the mall-intercept survey? Do you think this sample size was adequate?
21. How should the sample size be determined for the mall-intercept survey?

Chapter 14

22. How would you conduct the training and supervision of the field-workers for the mall-intercept survey of Chapter 7?

Chapters 15 to 18

23. According to TruEarth's Isabel Eckstein, product for the whole family, convenient, easy to prepare, fresh taste, variety, quality of ingredients, and healthiness of ingredients are all independent variables that affect the preference for pizza (see Exhibit 6). Assume that in a survey of frozen/refrigerated pizza brands, each of the independent variables is measured on a 7-point scale, with 1 = poor and 7 = excellent. Preference for pizza brand is also measured on a 7-point scale, with 1 = not at all preferred and 7 = greatly preferred. Each respondent rates TruEarth and three frozen/refrigerated pizza brands on all the independent variables as well as preference. What statistical technique(s) would you use to answer the following questions?

a. Is preference related to each of the independent variables considered individually? What is the nature of the relationship you expect?

b. Is preference related to all the independent variables considered simultaneously?

c. Do the respondents evaluate the pizza brands more favorably on fresh taste than they do on variety?

d. The sample is divided into two groups: regular customers of TruEarth and customers of other brands. Do these two groups differ in terms of their ratings of TruEarth on quality of ingredients?

e. Are the two groups of question d different in terms of income measured as high, medium, and low?

f. The sample is divided in three groups: heavy, medium, and light users of pizzas (of all kinds). Do the three groups differ in terms of preference for TruEarth?

g. About 13 percent of the respondents have missing values on one or more variables. How would you treat the missing values?

h. A question asked the respondents to check as many of the seven pizza brands that they had purchased in the past year. How should the data for this question be coded?

24. What can TruEarth learn about how consumers view pizza from Exhibit 6?

25. How do the pizza concept test results (Exhibits 7 and 8) compare with the findings for pasta (Exhibits 3 and 4)?

26. How do you interpret Exhibits 9 and 10 to evaluate interest in pizza?

Chapter 19

27. What is your recommendation to TruEarth? Should the company launch the pizza?

28. What charts and graphs would you use in preparing a report for TruEarth?

29. Prepare a 10-minute presentation for TruEarth using no more than 10 PowerPoint slides.

Application Questions

30. If marketing research to determine consumer preferences for refrigerated pizza was to be conducted in Latin America, how would the research process differ?

31. **Social Media** Discuss how TruEarth can make use of social media to understand consumer perceptions and preferences for refrigerated and other kinds of pizzas.

32. Discuss the ethical issues involved in researching consumer preferences for refrigerated pizza.

CASE 4.2 THE SPRINGFIELD NOR'EASTERS

Maximizing Revenues in the Minor Leagues (2510)

Comprehensive Questions

Chapter 1

1. Discuss the role that marketing research can play in helping the Springfield Nor'easters formulate sound marketing strategies.
2. Discuss the role that marketing research can play in helping the Springfield Nor'easters to maximize revenues in the minor leagues.

Chapter 2

3. Define the management-decision problem facing the Springfield Nor'easters.
4. Define an appropriate marketing research problem based on the management-decision problem you have identified.
5. Develop a graphical model explaining how consumers decide to attend a spectator sport.

Chapter 3

6. What type of research design was adopted by Larry Buckingham?
7. Critically evaluate the research design adopted by Larry Buckingham.

Chapter 4

8. Use the Internet to determine the amount of money spent by households in attending spectator sport events for the last calendar year.
9. What type of internal secondary data will be useful to the Springfield Nor'easters?

Chapter 5

10. What type of syndicated data will be useful to the Springfield Nor'easters?

Chapter 6

11. Discuss the role of qualitative research in helping the Springfield Nor'easters understand the entertainment and spectator sports needs of households.
12. **Social Media** How can the Springfield Nor'easters make use of social media to conduct qualitative research to understand the spectator sports needs of households?

Chapter 7

13. Do you think that the online (Web-based) survey conducted by the Springfield Nor'easters was the best survey method in this case? Why or why not? Defend your reasoning.
14. Do you think that the observation method can be used in this case? If yes, what observation method would you recommend and what insights you hope to gain?

Chapter 8

15. In what way could the Springfield Nor'easters make use of experimentation? What specific experimental design would you recommend?

Chapter 9

16. Illustrate the use of the primary scales for measuring consumer intentions for spectator sports.

Chapter 10

17. Develop Likert, semantic differential, and Stapel scales for measuring consumer intentions for spectator sports.

Chapter 11

18. Critically evaluate the questionnaire developed by Larry Buckingham as given in Exhibit 5.

Chapter 12

19. What sampling plan was adopted for the online survey of Chapter 7? Was this plan appropriate? What sampling plan would you recommend?

Chapter 13

20. What was the sample size used in the online survey? Do you think this sample size was adequate?
21. How should the sample size be determined for the survey?

Chapter 14

22. Discuss the fieldworker process for the online survey of Chapter 7? How does this process compare to that given in the book?

Chapters 15 to 18

23. According to the Springfield Nor'easters' Larry Buckingham, interest in sports, attitude toward sports personalities, time spent watching sports on television, ticket prices, winning record of the teams in the previous season, and accessibility of the stadium/parking are all independent variables that affect the intention to attend a spectator sport event (game). Assume that in a survey, each of the independent variables is measured on a 7-point scale, with 1 = poor and 7 = excellent. Intention to attend a spectator sport event (game) is also measured on a 7-point scale, with 1 = not at all likely and 7 = very likely. Each respondent rates the Springfield Nor'easters, minor league hockey team, college football, little league baseball, and girl's softball on all the independent variables as well as intention to attend. What statistical technique(s) would you use to answer the following questions?

   a. Is intention related to each of the independent variables considered individually? What is the nature of the relationship you expect?
   b. Is intention related to all the independent variables considered simultaneously?
   c. Do the respondents evaluate the spectator sports more favorably on ticket prices than they do on accessibility/parking?
   d. The sample is divided into two groups: regular attendees of spectator sports and occasional/nonattendees. Do these two groups differ in terms of intentions to attend the Springfield Nor'easters games?
   e. Are the two groups of question d different in terms of income measured as high, medium, and low?
   f. The sample is divided in four groups: heavy, medium, light, and nonattendees of spectator sports. Do the four groups differ in terms of intentions for the Springfield Nor'easters?

g. About 8 percent of the respondents have missing values on one or more variables. How would you treat the missing values?

h. A question asked the respondents to check as many of the four spectator sports that they had attended in the past 3 years (see Exhibit 4). How should the data for this question be coded?

Chapter 19

24. What is your recommendation to the Springfield Nor'easters?

25. What charts and graphs would you use in preparing a report for the Springfield Nor'easters?

26. Prepare a 10-minute presentation for the Springfield Nor'easters using no more than 10 PowerPoint slides.

Application Questions

27. If marketing research to determine consumer intentions for spectator sports was to be conducted in western Europe, how would the research process differ?

28. **Social Media** Discuss how the Springfield Nor'easters can make use of social media to obtain relevant information on attitudes and attendance of spectator sports.

29. Discuss the ethical issues involved in researching consumer intentions for spectator sports.

CASE 4.3   METABICAL

Positioning and Communications Strategy for a New Weight-Loss Drug (4240)

Comprehensive Questions

Chapter 1

1. Discuss the role that marketing research can play in helping Cambridge Sciences Pharmaceuticals (CSP) formulate sound marketing strategies.
2. Discuss the role that marketing research can play in helping CSP determine a positioning and communications strategy for its new prescription weight-loss drug, Metabical.

Chapter 2

3. Define the management-decision problem facing CSP.
4. Define an appropriate marketing research problem based on the management-decision problem you have identified.
5. Develop two research questions, each with an associated hypothesis.

Chapter 3

6. What type of research design was adopted as reported in the section titled "Market Research" (pages 4 and 5 of the case)?

Chapter 4

7. Search the Internet to determine the percentage of U.S. adults who are overweight ($25 \leq$ BMI <30), obese ($30 \leq$ BMI < 40), and severely obese (BMI > 40) in the last calendar year. What was the U.S. adult population in the last calendar year? Thus, you are updating the first table of Exhibit 1.
8. What type of internal secondary data will be useful to CSP?

Chapter 5

9. What type of syndicated data will be useful to CSP?

Chapter 6

10. Discuss the role of qualitative research in helping CSP penetrate the prescription weight-loss drug market in the United States.
11. **Social Media** How can CSP make use of social media to conduct qualitative research to understand the motivations, beliefs, and attitudes of individuals toward losing weight?

Chapter 7

12. Exhibit 2 of the case reports the results of the "2007 Marketing Survey." What do you think is the best method for conducting such a survey? Defend your reasoning.
13. Do you think that the observation method can be used in this case? If yes, what observation method would you recommend and what insights you hope to gain?

Chapter 8

14. In what way could CSP make use of experimentation? What specific experimental design would you recommend?

Chapter 9

15. Illustrate the use of the primary scales for measuring consumer preferences for prescription weight-loss drugs.

Chapter 10

16. Develop Likert, semantic differential, and Stapel scales for measuring consumer preferences for prescription weight-loss drugs.

Chapter 11

17. Develop a questionnaire for measuring consumer preferences for prescription weight-loss drugs.

Chapter 12

18. What sampling plan should be adopted for the survey of Chapter 7 (Exhibit 2)?

Chapter 13

19. What was the sample size used in the survey of Chapter 7 (Exhibit 2)? Do you think this sample size was adequate?
20. How should the sample size be determined for the survey?

Chapter 14

21. How would you conduct the training and supervision of the field-workers for the survey of Chapter 7?

Chapters 15 to 18

22. According to CSP's Barbara Printup, effectiveness in losing weight, side effects, price, ease of completing the course, and image of the manufacturer are all independent variables that affect the preference for a prescription weight-loss drug. Assume that in a survey of prescription weight-loss drugs, each of the independent variables is measured on a 7-point scale, with 1 = poor and 7 = excellent. Preference for prescription weight-loss drugs is also measured on a 7-point scale, with 1 = not at all preferred and 7 = greatly preferred. Each respondent rates CSP and three competing prescription weight-loss drugs on all the independent variables as well as preference. What statistical technique(s) would you use to answer the following questions:

   a. Is preference related to each of the independent variables considered individually? What is the nature of the relationship you expect?
   b. Is preference related to all the independent variables considered simultaneously?
   c. Do the respondents evaluate the prescription weight-loss drugs more favorably on effectiveness in losing weight than they do on side effects?
   d. The sample is divided into two groups: users of prescription weight-loss drugs and nonusers. Do these two groups differ in terms of their preference for CSP's Metabical?
   e. Are the two groups of question d different in terms of income measured as high, medium, and low?
   f. The sample is divided in three groups: heavy, medium, and light/nonusers of prescription weight-loss drugs. Do the three groups differ in terms of preference for CSP's Metabical?
   g. About 18 percent of the respondents have missing values on one or more variables. How would you treat the missing values?
   h. A question asked the respondents to check as many of the eight prescription weight-loss drugs that they had used in the past 2 years. How should the data for this question be coded?

23. Based on the information given in the case, what should be the target market for Metabical?

Chapter 19

24. What is your recommendation to CSP?
25. What charts and graphs would you use in preparing a report for CSP?
26. Prepare a 10-minute presentation for CSP using no more than 10 PowerPoint slides.

Application Questions

27. If marketing research to determine consumer preferences for prescription weight-loss drugs was to be conducted in Southeast Asia, how would the research process differ?
28. **Social Media** Discuss how CSP can make use of social media to gain an understanding of how consumers view prescription weight-loss drugs.
29. Discuss the ethical issues involved in researching consumer preferences for pre scription weight-loss drugs.

CASE 4.4   SAXONVILLE SAUSAGE COMPANY (2085)

Comprehensive Questions

Chapter 1

1. Discuss the role that marketing research can play in helping Saxonville Sausage Company formulate sound marketing strategies.
2. Discuss the role that marketing research can play in helping Saxonville Sausage Company determine whether it should introduce a national Italian sausage brand.

Chapter 2

3. Define the management-decision problem facing Saxonville Sausage.
4. Define an appropriate marketing research problem based on the management-decision problem you have identified.
5. Develop two research questions, each with an associated hypothesis.

Chapter 3

6. What type of research design was adopted? What information was obtained?

Chapter 4

7. Use the Internet to determine the market (dollars sales) of Italian and other sausages for the last calendar year.
8. What type of internal secondary data was used by Saxonville Sausage?

Chapter 5

9. What type of syndicated data will be useful to Saxonville Sausage?

Chapter 6

10. Discuss the role of qualitative research in helping Saxonville Sausage penetrate the Italian sausage market in the United States.
11. **Social Media** How can Saxonville Sausage make use of social media to conduct qualitative research to gain an understanding of attitudes toward Italian sausages?

Chapter 7

12. Which survey method would be the most appropriate for conducting the quantitative testing reported in step four (Exhibit 11)? Defend your reasoning.
13. Do you think that the observation method can be used in this case? If yes, what observation method would you recommend and what insights you hope to gain?

Chapter 8

14. In what way could Saxonville Sausage make use of experimentation? What specific experimental design would you recommend?

Chapter 9

15. Illustrate the use of the primary scales for measuring consumer preferences for Italian sausage.

Chapter 10

16. Develop Likert, semantic differential, and Stapel scales for measuring consumer preferences for Italian sausage.

Chapter 11

17. Develop a questionnaire for measuring consumer preferences for Italian sausage.

Chapter 12

18. What sampling plan should be adopted for the quantitative testing (step four) survey of Chapter 7?

Chapter 13

19. What was the sample size used in the quantitative testing (step four) survey? Do you think this sample size was adequate?
20. How should the sample size be determined for the survey?

Chapter 14

21. How would you conduct the training and supervision of the field-workers for the quantitative testing (step four) survey of Chapter 7?

Chapters 15 to 18

22. According to Saxonville Sausage's Laura Bishop, director of market research, easy to do, family-pleasing, quality, price, texture, and aroma are all independent variables that affect the preference for an Italian sausage brand. Assume that in a survey of Italian sausage brands, each of the independent variables is measured on a 7-point scale, with 1 = poor and 7 = excellent. Preference for an Italian sausage brand is also measured on a 7-point scale, with 1 = not at all preferred and 7 = greatly preferred. Each respondent rates Saxonville Sausage and three competing brands on all the independent variables as well as preference. What statistical technique(s) would you use to answer the following questions?

    a. Is preference related to each of the independent variables considered individually? What is the nature of the relationship you expect?
    b. Is preference related to all the independent variables considered simultaneously?
    c. Do the respondents evaluate the Italian sausage brands more favorable on quality than they do on price?
    d. The sample is divided into two groups: regular customers of Saxonville Sausage and customers of other brands. Do these two groups differ in terms of their ratings of Saxonville Sausage on quality?
    e. Are the two groups of question d different in terms of income measured as high, medium, and low?
    f. The sample is divided in three groups: heavy, medium, and light users of Italian sausages. Do the three groups differ in terms of preference for Saxonville Sausage?
    g. About 15 percent of the respondents have missing values on one or more variables. How would you treat the missing values?
    h. A question asked the respondents to check as many of the eight Italian sausage brands that they had purchased in the past year. How should the data for this question be coded?

Chapter 19

23. What is your recommendation to Saxonville Sausage? Which positioning concept should the company implement?

24. What charts and graphs would you use in preparing a report for Saxonville Sausage?

25. Prepare a 10-minute presentation for Saxonville Sausage using no more than 10 PowerPoint slides.

Application Questions

26. If marketing research to determine consumer preferences for Italian Sausages was to be conducted in Italy, how would the research process differ?

27. **Social Media** Discuss how Saxonville Sausage can make use of social media to obtain relevant information on consumers' values, beliefs, attitudes, and preferences for Italian sausages.

28. Discuss the ethical issues involved in researching consumer preferences for Italian sausages.

ONLINE VIDEO CASES

Online Video cases referenced at the end of each chapter are located at www.pearsonhighered.com/malhotra and include the case, questions, and the accompanying streaming video. The list of video cases is as follows, with the first number referring to the chapter number:

Online Video Case 1.1   Burke: Learning and Growing Through Marketing Research

Online Video Case 2.1   Accenture: The Accent Is in the Name

Online Video Case 3.1   National Football League: The King of Professional Sports

Online Video Case 4.1   The Mayo Clinic: Staying Healthy with Marketing Research

Online Video Case 5.1   eGO: Reinventing Wheels

Online Video Case 6.1   Nike: Associating Athletes, Performance, and the Brand

Online Video Case 7.1   Starbucks: Staying Local While Going Global Through Marketing Research

Online Video Case 8.1   AFLAC: Marketing Research Quacks a Duck

Online Video Case 9.1   Procter & Gamble: Using Marketing Research to Build Brands

Online Video Case 10.1   Nivea: Marketing Research Leads to Consistency in Marketing

Online Video Case 11.1   Dunkin' Donuts: Dunking the Competition

Online Video Case 12.1   Motorola: Projecting the Moto Lifestyle

Online Video Case 13.1   Subaru: "Mr. Survey" Monitors Customer Satisfaction

Online Video Case 14.1   Intel: Building Blocks Inside Out

Online Video Case 15.1   Marriott: Marketing Research Leads to Expanded Offerings

Online Video Case 16.1   Marriott: Marketing Research Leads to Expanded Offerings

Online Video Case 17.1   Marriott: Marketing Research Leads to Expanded Offerings

Online Video Case 18.1   Marriott: Marketing Research Leads to Expanded Offerings

Online Video Case 19.1   Marriott: Marketing Research Leads to Expanded Offerings

APPENDIX

Statistical Tables

TABLE 1 Simple Random Numbers

Line/Col.	(1)	(2)	(3)	(4)	(5)	(6)	(7)	(8)	(9)	(10)	(11)	(12)	(13)	(14)
1	10480	15011	01536	02011	81647	91646	69179	14194	62590	36207	20969	99570	91291	90700
2	22368	46573	25595	85393	30995	89198	27982	53402	93965	34095	52666	19174	39615	99505
3	24130	48390	22527	97265	76393	64809	15179	24830	49340	32081	30680	19655	63348	58629
4	42167	93093	06243	61680	07856	16376	39440	53537	71341	57004	00849	74917	97758	16379
5	37570	39975	81837	16656	06121	91782	60468	81305	49684	60072	14110	06927	01263	54613
6	77921	06907	11008	42751	27756	53498	18602	70659	90655	15053	21916	81825	44394	42880
7	99562	72905	56420	69994	98872	31016	71194	18738	44013	48840	63213	21069	10634	12952
8	96301	91977	05463	07972	18876	20922	94595	56869	69014	60045	18425	84903	42508	32307
9	89579	14342	63661	10281	17453	18103	57740	84378	25331	12568	58678	44947	05585	56941
10	85475	36857	53342	53988	53060	59533	38867	62300	08158	17983	16439	11458	18593	64952
11	28918	69578	88231	33276	70997	79936	56865	05859	90106	31595	01547	85590	91610	78188
12	63553	40961	48235	03427	49626	69445	18663	72695	52180	20847	12234	90511	33703	90322
13	09429	93969	52636	92737	88974	33488	36320	17617	30015	08272	84115	27156	30613	74952
14	10365	61129	87529	85689	48237	52267	67689	93394	01511	26358	85104	20285	29975	89868
15	07119	97336	71048	08178	77233	13916	47564	81056	97735	85977	29372	74461	28551	90707
16	51085	12765	51821	51259	77452	16308	60756	92144	49442	53900	70960	63990	75601	40719
17	02368	21382	52404	60268	89368	19885	55322	44819	01188	65255	64835	44919	05944	55157
18	01011	54092	33362	94904	31273	04146	18594	29852	71685	85030	51132	01915	92747	64951
19	52162	53916	46369	58586	23216	14513	83149	98736	23495	64350	94738	17752	35156	35749
20	07056	97628	33787	09998	42698	06691	76988	13602	51851	46104	88916	19509	25625	58104
21	48663	91245	85828	14346	09172	30163	90229	04734	59193	22178	30421	61666	99904	32812
22	54164	58492	22421	74103	47070	25306	76468	26384	58151	06646	21524	15227	96909	44592
23	32639	32363	05597	24200	13363	38005	94342	28728	35806	06912	17012	64161	18296	22851
24	29334	27001	87637	87308	58731	00256	45834	15398	46557	41135	10307	07684	36188	18510
25	02488	33062	28834	07351	19731	92420	60952	61280	50001	67658	32586	86679	50720	94953
26	81525	72295	04839	96423	24878	82651	66566	14778	76797	14780	13300	87074	79666	95725
27	29676	20591	68086	26432	46901	20849	89768	81536	86645	12659	92259	57102	80428	25280
28	00742	57392	39064	66432	84673	40027	32832	61362	98947	96067	64760	64584	96096	98253
29	05366	04213	25669	26422	44407	44048	37937	63904	45766	66134	75470	66520	34693	90449
30	91921	26418	64117	94305	26766	25940	39972	22209	71500	64568	91402	42416	07844	69618
31	00582	04711	87917	77341	42206	35126	74087	99547	81817	42607	43808	76655	62028	76630
32	00725	69884	62797	56170	86324	88072	76222	36086	84637	93161	76038	65855	77919	88006
33	69011	65795	95876	55293	18988	27354	26575	08625	40801	59920	29841	80150	12777	48501
34	25976	57948	29888	88604	67917	48708	18912	82271	65424	69774	33611	54262	85963	03547
35	09763	83473	73577	12908	30883	18317	28290	35797	05998	41688	34952	37888	38917	88050
36	91567	42595	27958	30134	04024	86385	29880	99730	55536	84855	29088	09250	79656	73211
37	17955	56349	90999	49127	20044	59931	06115	20542	18059	02008	73708	83517	36103	42791
38	46503	18584	18845	49618	02304	51038	20655	58727	28168	15475	56942	53389	20562	87338

(Continued)

TABLE 1 (Continued)

Line/Col.	(1)	(2)	(3)	(4)	(5)	(6)	(7)	(8)	(9)	(10)	(11)	(12)	(13)	(14)
39	92157	89634	94824	78171	84610	82834	09922	25417	44137	48413	25555	21246	35509	20468
40	14577	62765	35605	81263	39667	47358	56873	56307	61607	49518	89656	20103	77490	18062
41	98427	07523	33362	64270	01638	92477	66969	98420	04880	45585	46565	04102	46880	45709
42	34914	63976	88720	82765	34476	17032	87589	40836	32427	70002	70663	88863	77775	69348
43	70060	28277	39475	46473	23219	53416	94970	25832	69975	94884	19661	72828	00102	66794
44	53976	54914	06990	67245	68350	82948	11398	42878	80287	88267	47363	46634	06541	97809
45	76072	29515	40980	07391	58745	25774	22987	80059	39911	96189	41151	14222	60697	59583
46	90725	52210	83974	29992	65831	38857	50490	83765	55657	14361	31720	57375	56228	41546
47	64364	67412	33339	31926	14883	24413	59744	92351	97473	89286	35931	04110	23726	51900
48	08962	00358	31662	25388	61642	34072	81249	35648	56891	69352	48373	45578	78547	81788
49	95012	68379	93526	70765	10592	04542	76463	54328	02349	17247	28865	14777	62730	92277
50	15664	10493	20492	38301	91132	21999	59516	81652	27195	48223	46751	22923	32261	85653
51	16408	81899	04153	53381	79401	21438	83035	92350	36693	31238	59649	91754	72772	02338
52	18629	81953	05520	91962	04739	13092	97662	24822	94730	06496	35090	04822	86774	98289
53	73115	35101	47498	87637	99016	71060	88824	71013	18735	20286	23153	72924	35165	43040
54	57491	16703	23167	49323	45021	33132	12544	41035	80780	45393	44812	12515	98931	91202
55	30405	83946	23792	14422	15059	45799	22716	19792	09983	74353	68668	30429	70735	25499
56	16631	35006	85900	98275	32388	52390	16815	69293	82732	38480	73817	32523	41961	44437
57	96773	20206	42559	78985	05300	22164	24369	54224	35083	19687	11052	91491	60383	19746
58	38935	64202	14349	82674	66523	44133	00697	35552	35970	19124	63318	29686	03387	59846
59	31624	76384	17403	53363	44167	64486	64758	75366	76554	31601	12614	33072	60332	92325
60	78919	19474	23632	27889	47914	02584	37680	20801	72152	39339	34806	08930	85001	87820
61	03931	33309	57047	74211	63445	17361	62825	39908	05607	91284	68833	25570	38818	46920
62	74426	33278	43972	10119	89917	15665	52872	73823	73144	88662	88970	74492	51805	99378
63	09066	00903	20795	95452	92648	45454	69552	88815	16553	51125	79375	97596	16296	66092
64	42238	12426	87025	14267	20979	04508	64535	31355	86064	29472	47689	05974	52468	16834
65	16153	08002	26504	41744	81959	65642	74240	56302	00033	67107	77510	70625	28725	34191
66	21457	40742	29820	96783	29400	21840	15035	34537	33310	06116	95240	15957	16572	06004
67	21581	57802	02050	89728	17937	37621	47075	42080	97403	48626	68995	43805	33386	21597
68	55612	78095	83197	33732	05810	24813	86902	60397	16489	03264	88525	42786	05269	92532
69	44657	66999	99324	51281	84463	60563	79312	93454	68876	25471	93911	25650	12682	73572
70	91340	84979	46949	81973	37949	61023	43997	15263	80644	43942	89203	71795	99533	50501
71	91227	21199	31935	27022	84067	05462	35216	14486	29891	68607	41867	14951	91696	85065
72	50001	38140	66321	19924	72163	09538	12151	06878	91903	18749	34405	56087	82790	70925
73	65390	05224	72958	28609	81406	39147	25549	48542	42627	45233	57202	94617	23772	07896
74	27504	96131	83944	41575	10573	03619	64482	73923	36152	05184	94142	25299	94387	34925
75	37169	94851	39117	89632	00959	16487	65536	49071	39782	17095	02330	74301	00275	48280
76	11508	70225	51111	38351	19444	66499	71945	05422	13442	78675	84031	66938	93654	59894
77	37449	30362	06694	54690	04052	53115	62757	95348	78662	11163	81651	50245	34971	52974
78	46515	70331	85922	38329	57015	15765	97161	17869	45349	61796	66345	81073	49106	79860
79	30986	81223	42416	58353	21532	30502	32305	86482	05174	07901	54339	58861	74818	46942
80	63798	64995	46583	09785	44160	78128	83991	42865	92520	83531	80377	35909	81250	54238
81	82486	84846	99254	67632	43218	50076	21361	64816	51202	88124	41870	52689	51275	83556
82	21885	32906	92431	09060	64297	51674	64126	62570	26123	05155	59194	52799	28225	85762

(Continued)

608 APPENDIX

TABLE 1 (Continued)

Line/Col.	(1)	(2)	(3)	(4)	(5)	(6)	(7)	(8)	(9)	(10)	(11)	(12)	(13)	(14)
83	60336	98782	07408	53458	13564	59089	26445	29789	85205	41001	12535	12133	14645	23541
84	43937	46891	24010	25560	86355	33941	25786	54990	71899	15475	95434	98227	21824	19535
85	97656	63175	89303	16275	07100	92063	21942	18611	47348	20203	18534	03862	78095	50136
86	03299	01221	05418	38982	55758	92237	26759	86367	21216	98442	08303	56613	91511	75928
87	79626	06486	03574	17668	07785	76020	79924	25651	83325	88428	85076	72811	22717	50585
88	85636	68335	47539	03129	65651	11977	02510	26113	99447	68645	34327	15152	55230	93448
89	18039	14367	61337	06177	12143	46609	32989	74014	64708	00533	35398	58408	13261	47908
90	08362	15656	60627	36478	65648	16764	53412	09013	07832	41574	17639	82163	60859	75567
91	79556	29068	04142	16268	15387	12856	66227	38358	22478	73373	88732	09443	82558	05250
92	92608	82674	27072	32534	17075	27698	98204	63863	11951	34648	88022	56148	34925	57031
93	23982	25835	40055	67006	12293	02753	14827	23235	35071	99704	37543	11601	35503	85171
94	09915	96306	05908	97901	28395	14186	00821	80703	70426	75647	76310	88717	37890	40129
95	59037	33300	26695	62247	69927	76123	50842	43834	86654	70959	79725	93872	28117	19233
96	42488	78077	69882	61657	34136	79180	97526	43092	04098	73571	80799	76536	71255	64239
97	46764	86273	63003	93017	31204	36692	40202	35275	57306	55543	53203	18098	47625	88684
98	03237	45430	55417	63282	90816	17349	88298	90183	36600	78406	06216	95787	42579	90730
99	86591	81482	52667	61582	14972	90053	89534	76036	49199	43716	97548	04379	46370	28672
100	38534	01715	94964	87288	65680	43772	39560	12918	80537	62738	19636	51132	25739	56947

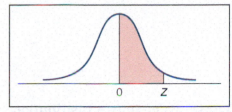

TABLE 2 Area Under the Normal Curve

Z	.00	.01	.02	.03	.04	.05	.06	.07	.08	.09
0.0	.0000	.0040	.0080	.0120	.0160	.0199	.0239	.0279	.0319	.0359
0.1	.0398	.0438	.0478	.0517	.0557	.0596	.0636	.0675	.0714	.0753
0.2	.0793	.0832	.0871	.0910	.0948	.0987	.1026	.1064	.1103	.1141
0.3	.1179	.1217	.1255	.1293	.1331	.1368	.1406	.1443	.1480	.1517
0.4	.1554	.1591	.1628	.1664	.1700	.1736	.1772	.1808	.1844	.1879
0.5	.1915	.1950	.1985	.2019	.2054	.2088	.2123	.2157	.2190	.2224
0.6	.2257	.2291	.2324	.2357	.2389	.2422	.2454	.2486	.2518	.2549
0.7	.2580	.2612	.2642	.2673	.2704	.2734	.2764	.2794	.2823	.2852
0.8	.2881	.2910	.2939	.2967	.2995	.3023	.3051	.3078	.3106	.3133
0.9	.3159	.3186	.3212	.3238	.3264	.3289	.3315	.3340	.3365	.3389
1.0	.3413	.3438	.3461	.3485	.3508	.3531	.3554	.3577	.3599	.3621
1.1	.3643	.3665	.3686	.3708	.3729	.3749	.3770	.3790	.3810	.3830
1.2	.3849	.3869	.3888	.3907	.3925	.3944	.3962	.3980	.3997	.4015
1.3	.4032	.4049	.4066	.4082	.4099	.4115	.4131	.4147	.4162	.4177
1.4	.4192	.4207	.4222	.4236	.4251	.4265	.4279	.4292	.4306	.4319
1.5	.4332	.4345	.4357	.4370	.4382	.4394	.4406	.4418	.4429	.4441
1.6	.4452	.4463	.4474	.4484	.4495	.4505	.4515	.4525	.4535	.4545
1.7	.4554	.4564	.4573	.4582	.4591	.4599	.4608	.4616	.4625	.4633
1.8	.4641	.4649	.4656	.4664	.4671	.4678	.4686	.4693	.4699	.4706
1.9	.4713	.4719	.4726	.4732	.4738	.4744	.4750	.4756	.4761	.4767
2.0	.4772	.4778	.4783	.4788	.4793	.4798	.4803	.4808	.4812	.4817
2.1	.4821	.4826	.4830	.4834	.4838	.4842	.4846	.4850	.4854	.4857
2.2	.4861	.4864	.4868	.4871	.4875	.4878	.4881	.4884	.4887	.4890
2.3	.4893	.4896	.4898	.4901	.4904	.4906	.4909	.4911	.4913	.4916
2.4	.4918	.4920	.4922	.4925	.4927	.4929	.4931	.4932	.4934	.4936
2.5	.4938	.4940	.4941	.4943	.4945	.4946	.4948	.4949	.4951	.4952
2.6	.4953	.4955	.4956	.4957	.4959	.4960	.4961	.4962	.4963	.4964
2.7	.4965	.4966	.4967	.4968	.4969	.4970	.4971	.4972	.4973	.4974
2.8	.4974	.4975	.4976	.4977	.4977	.4978	.4979	.4979	.4980	.4981
2.9	.4981	.4982	.4982	.4983	.4984	.4984	.4985	.4985	.4986	.4986
3.0	.49865	.49869	.49874	.49878	.49882	.49886	.49889	.49893	.49897	.49900
3.1	.49903	.49906	.49910	.49913	.49916	.49918	.49921	.49924	.49926	.49929
3.2	.49931	.49934	.49936	.49938	.49940	.49942	.49944	.49946	.49948	.49950
3.3	.49952	.49953	.49955	.49957	.49958	.49960	.49961	.49962	.49964	.49965
3.4	.49966	.49968	.49969	.49970	.49971	.49972	.49973	.49974	.49975	.49976
3.5	.49977	.49978	.49978	.49979	.49980	.49981	.49981	.49982	.49983	.49983
3.6	.49984	.49985	.49985	.49986	.49986	.49987	.49987	.49988	.49988	.49989
3.7	.49989	.49990	.49990	.49990	.49991	.49991	.49992	.49992	.49992	.49992
3.8	.49993	.49993	.49993	.49994	.49994	.49994	.49994	.49995	.49995	.49995
3.9	.49995	.49995	.49996	.49996	.49996	.49996	.49996	.49996	.49997	.49997

Entry represents area under the standard normal distribution from the mean to Z.

TABLE 3 Chi-Square Distribution

Degrees of Freedom	Upper-Tail Areas (α)											
	.995	.99	.975	.95	.90	.75	.25	.10	.05	.025	.01	.005
1			0.001	0.004	0.016	0.102	1.323	2.706	3.841	5.024	6.635	7.879
2	0.010	0.020	0.051	0.103	0.211	0.575	2.773	4.605	5.991	7.378	9.210	10.597
3	0.072	0.115	0.216	0.352	0.584	1.213	4.108	6.251	7.815	9.348	11.345	12.838
4	0.207	0.297	0.484	0.711	1.064	1.923	5.385	7.779	9.488	11.143	13.277	14.860
5	0.412	0.554	0.831	1.145	1.610	2.675	6.626	9.236	11.071	12.833	15.086	16.750
6	0.676	0.872	1.237	1.635	2.204	3.455	7.841	10.645	12.592	14.449	16.812	18.548
7	0.989	1.239	1.690	2.167	2.833	4.255	9.037	12.017	14.067	16.013	18.475	20.278
8	1.344	1.646	2.180	2.733	3.490	5.071	10.219	13.362	15.507	17.535	20.090	21.955
9	1.735	2.088	2.700	3.325	4.168	5.899	11.389	14.684	16.919	19.023	21.666	23.589
10	2.156	2.558	3.247	3.940	4.865	6.737	12.549	15.987	18.307	20.483	23.209	25.188
11	2.603	3.053	3.816	4.575	5.578	7.584	13.701	17.275	19.675	21.920	24.725	26.757
12	3.074	3.571	4.404	5.226	6.304	8.438	14.845	18.549	21.026	23.337	26.217	28.299
13	3.565	4.107	5.009	5.892	7.042	9.299	15.984	19.812	22.362	24.736	27.688	29.819
14	4.075	4.660	5.629	6.571	7.790	10.165	17.117	21.064	23.685	26.119	29.141	31.319
15	4.601	5.229	6.262	7.261	8.547	11.037	18.245	22.307	24.996	27.488	30.578	32.801
16	5.142	5.812	6.908	7.962	9.312	11.912	19.369	23.542	26.296	28.845	32.000	34.267
17	5.697	6.408	7.564	8.672	10.085	12.792	20.489	24.769	27.587	30.191	33.409	35.718
18	6.265	7.015	8.231	9.390	10.865	13.675	21.605	25.989	28.869	31.526	34.805	37.156
19	6.844	7.633	8.907	10.117	11.651	14.562	22.718	27.204	30.144	32.852	36.191	38.582
20	7.434	8.260	9.591	10.851	12.443	15.452	23.828	28.412	31.410	34.170	37.566	39.997
21	8.034	8.897	10.283	11.591	13.240	16.344	24.935	29.615	32.671	35.479	38.932	41.401
22	8.643	9.542	10.982	12.338	14.042	17.240	26.039	30.813	33.924	36.781	40.289	42.796
23	9.260	10.196	11.689	13.091	14.848	18.137	27.141	32.007	35.172	38.076	41.638	44.181
24	9.886	10.856	12.401	13.848	15.659	19.037	28.241	33.196	36.415	39.364	42.980	45.559
25	10.520	11.524	13.120	14.611	16.473	19.939	29.339	34.382	37.652	40.646	44.314	46.928
26	11.160	12.198	13.844	15.379	17.292	20.843	30.435	35.563	38.885	41.923	45.642	48.290
27	11.808	12.879	14.573	16.151	18.114	21.749	31.528	36.741	40.113	43.194	46.963	49.645
28	12.461	13.565	15.308	16.928	18.939	22.657	32.620	37.916	41.337	44.461	48.278	50.993
29	13.121	14.257	16.047	17.708	19.768	23.567	33.711	39.087	42.557	45.722	49.588	52.336
30	13.787	14.954	16.791	18.493	20.599	24.478	34.800	40.256	43.773	46.979	50.892	53.672
31	14.458	15.655	17.539	19.281	21.434	25.390	35.887	41.422	44.985	48.232	52.191	55.003
32	15.134	16.362	18.291	20.072	22.271	26.304	36.973	42.585	46.194	49.480	53.486	56.328
33	15.815	17.074	19.047	20.867	23.110	27.219	38.058	43.745	47.400	50.725	54.776	57.648
34	16.501	17.789	19.806	21.664	23.952	28.136	39.141	44.903	48.602	51.966	56.061	58.964
35	17.192	18.509	20.569	22.465	24.797	29.054	40.223	46.059	49.802	53.203	57.342	60.275
36	17.887	19.233	21.336	23.269	25.643	29.973	41.304	47.212	50.998	54.437	58.619	61.581
37	18.586	19.960	22.106	24.075	26.492	30.893	42.383	48.363	52.192	55.668	59.892	62.883
38	19.289	20.691	22.878	24.884	27.343	31.815	43.462	49.513	53.384	56.896	61.162	64.181

(Continued)

TABLE 3 (Continued)

Degrees of Freedom	Upper-Tail Areas (α)											
	.995	.99	.975	.95	.90	.75	.25	.10	.05	.025	.01	.005
39	19.996	21.426	23.654	25.695	28.196	32.737	44.539	50.660	54.572	58.120	62.428	65.476
40	20.707	22.164	24.433	26.509	29.051	33.660	45.616	51.805	55.758	59.342	63.691	66.766
41	21.421	22.906	25.215	27.326	29.907	34.585	46.692	52.949	56.942	60.561	64.950	68.053
42	22.138	23.650	25.999	28.144	30.765	35.510	47.766	54.090	58.124	61.777	66.206	69.336
43	22.859	24.398	26.785	28.965	31.625	36.436	48.840	55.230	59.304	62.990	67.459	70.616
44	23.584	25.148	27.575	29.787	32.487	37.363	49.913	56.369	60.481	64.201	68.710	71.893
45	24.311	25.901	28.366	30.612	33.350	38.291	50.985	57.505	61.656	65.410	69.957	73.166
46	25.041	26.657	29.160	31.439	34.215	39.220	52.056	58.641	62.830	66.617	71.201	74.437
47	25.775	27.416	29.956	32.268	35.081	40.149	53.127	59.774	64.001	67.821	72.443	75.704
48	26.511	28.177	30.755	33.098	35.949	41.079	54.196	60.907	65.171	69.023	73.683	76.969
49	27.249	28.941	31.555	33.930	36.818	42.010	55.265	62.038	66.339	70.222	74.919	78.231
50	27.991	29.707	32.357	34.764	37.689	42.942	56.334	63.167	67.505	71.420	76.154	79.490
51	28.735	30.475	33.162	35.600	38.560	43.874	57.401	64.295	68.669	72.616	77.386	80.747
52	29.481	31.246	33.968	36.437	39.433	44.808	58.468	65.422	69.832	73.810	78.616	82.001
53	30.230	32.018	34.776	37.276	40.308	45.741	59.534	66.548	70.993	75.002	79.843	83.253
54	30.981	32.793	35.586	38.116	41.183	46.676	60.600	67.673	72.153	76.192	81.069	84.502
55	31.735	33.570	36.398	38.958	42.060	47.610	61.665	68.796	73.311	77.380	82.292	85.749
56	32.490	34.350	37.212	39.801	42.937	48.546	62.729	69.919	74.468	78.567	83.513	86.994
57	33.248	35.131	38.027	40.646	43.816	49.482	63.793	71.040	75.624	79.752	84.733	88.236
58	34.008	35.913	38.844	41.492	44.696	50.419	64.857	72.160	76.778	80.936	85.950	89.477
59	34.770	36.698	39.662	42.339	45.577	51.356	65.919	73.279	77.931	82.117	87.166	90.715
60	35.534	37.485	40.482	43.188	46.459	52.294	66.981	74.397	79.082	83.298	88.379	91.952

For a particular number of degrees of freedom, entry represents the critical value of X^2 corresponding to a specified upper-tail area, α.
For larger values of degrees of freedom (df) the expression $z = \sqrt{2X^2} - \sqrt{2(df) - 1}$ may be used and the resulting upper-tail area can be obtained from the table of the standardized normal distribution.

TABLE 4 t Distribution

Degrees of Freedom	Upper-Tail Areas (α)					
	.25	.10	.05	.025	.01	.005
1	1.0000	3.0777	6.3138	12.7062	31.8207	63.6574
2	0.8165	1.8856	2.9200	4.3027	6.9646	9.9248
3	0.7649	1.6377	2.3534	3.1824	4.5407	5.8409
4	0.7407	1.5332	2.1318	2.7764	3.7469	4.6041
5	0.7267	1.4759	2.0150	2.5706	3.3649	4.0322
6	0.7176	1.4398	1.9432	2.4469	3.1427	3.7074
7	0.7111	1.4149	1.8946	2.3646	2.9980	3.4995
8	0.7064	1.3968	1.8595	2.3060	2.8965	3.3554
9	0.7027	1.3830	1.8331	2.2622	2.8214	3.2498
10	0.6998	1.3722	1.8125	2.2281	2.7638	3.1693
11	0.6974	1.3634	1.7959	2.2010	2.7181	3.1058
12	0.6955	1.3562	1.7823	2.1788	2.6810	3.0545
13	0.6938	1.3502	1.7709	2.1604	2.6503	3.0123
14	0.6924	1.3450	1.7613	2.1448	2.6245	2.9768
15	0.6912	1.3406	1.7531	2.1315	2.6025	2.9467
16	0.6901	1.3368	1.7459	2.1199	2.5835	2.9208
17	0.6892	1.3334	1.7396	2.1098	2.5669	2.8982
18	0.6884	1.3304	1.7341	2.1009	2.5524	2.8784
19	0.6876	1.3277	1.7291	2.0930	2.5395	2.8609
20	0.6870	1.3253	1.7247	2.0860	2.5280	2.8453
21	0.6864	1.3232	1.7207	2.0796	2.5177	2.8314
22	0.6858	1.3212	1.7171	2.0739	2.5083	2.8188
23	0.6853	1.3195	1.7139	2.0687	2.4999	2.8073
24	0.6848	1.3178	1.7109	2.0639	2.4922	2.7969
25	0.6844	1.3163	1.7081	2.0595	2.4851	2.7874
26	0.6840	1.3150	1.7056	2.0555	2.4786	2.7787
27	0.6837	1.3137	1.7033	2.0518	2.4727	2.7707
28	0.6834	1.3125	1.7011	2.0484	2.4671	2.7633
29	0.6830	1.3114	1.6991	2.0452	2.4620	2.7564
30	0.6828	1.3104	1.6973	2.0423	2.4573	2.7500
31	0.6825	1.3095	1.6955	2.0395	2.4528	2.7440
32	0.6822	1.3086	1.6939	2.0369	2.4487	2.7385
33	0.6820	1.3077	1.6924	2.0345	2.4448	2.7333
34	0.6818	1.3070	1.6909	2.0322	2.4411	2.7284
35	0.6816	1.3062	1.6896	2.0301	2.4377	2.7238
36	0.6814	1.3055	1.6883	2.0281	2.4345	2.7195
37	0.6812	1.3049	1.6871	2.0262	2.4314	2.7154
38	0.6810	1.3042	1.6860	2.0244	2.4286	2.7116

(Continued)

TABLE 4 (Continued)

Degrees of Freedom	Upper-Tail Areas (α)					
	.25	.10	.05	.025	.01	.005
39	0.6808	1.3036	1.6849	2.0227	2.4258	2.7079
40	0.6807	1.3031	1.6839	2.0211	2.4233	2.7045
41	0.6805	1.3025	1.6829	2.0195	2.4208	2.7012
42	0.6804	1.3020	1.6820	2.0181	2.4185	2.6981
43	0.6802	1.3016	1.6811	2.0167	2.4163	2.6951
44	0.6801	1.3011	1.6802	2.0154	2.4141	2.6923
45	0.6800	1.3006	1.6794	2.0141	2.4121	2.6896
46	0.6799	1.3002	1.6787	2.0129	2.4102	2.6870
47	0.6797	1.2998	1.6779	2.0117	2.4083	2.6846
48	0.6796	1.2994	1.6772	2.0106	2.4066	2.6822
49	0.6795	1.2991	1.6766	2.0096	2.4049	2.6800
50	0.6794	1.2987	1.6759	2.0086	2.4033	2.6778
51	0.6793	1.2984	1.6753	2.0076	2.4017	2.6757
52	0.6792	1.2980	1.6747	2.0066	2.4002	2.6737
53	0.6791	1.2977	1.6741	2.0057	2.3988	2.6718
54	0.6791	1.2974	1.6736	2.0049	2.3974	2.6700
55	0.6790	1.2971	1.6730	2.0040	2.3961	2.6682
56	0.6789	1.2969	1.6725	2.0032	2.3948	2.6665
57	0.6788	1.2966	1.6720	2.0025	2.3936	2.6649
58	0.6787	1.2963	1.6716	2.0017	2.3924	2.6633
59	0.6787	1.2961	1.6711	2.0010	2.3912	2.6618
60	0.6786	1.2958	1.6706	2.0003	2.3901	2.6603
61	0.6785	1.2956	1.6702	1.9996	2.3890	2.6589
62	0.6785	1.2954	1.6698	1.9990	2.3880	2.6575
63	0.6784	1.2951	1.6694	1.9983	2.3870	2.6561
64	0.6783	1.2949	1.6690	1.9977	2.3860	2.6549
65	0.6783	1.2947	1.6686	1.9971	2.3851	2.6536
66	0.6782	1.2945	1.6683	1.9966	2.3842	2.6524
67	0.6782	1.2943	1.6679	1.9960	2.3833	2.6512
68	0.6781	1.2941	1.6676	1.9955	2.3824	2.6501
69	0.6781	1.2939	1.6672	1.9949	2.3816	2.6490
70	0.6780	1.2938	1.6669	1.9944	2.3808	2.6479
71	0.6780	1.2936	1.6666	1.9939	2.3800	2.6469
72	0.6779	1.2934	1.6663	1.9935	2.3793	2.6459
73	0.6779	1.2933	1.6660	1.9930	2.3785	2.6449
74	0.6778	1.2931	1.6657	1.9925	2.3778	2.6439
75	0.6778	1.2929	1.6654	1.9921	2.3771	2.6430
76	0.6777	1.2928	1.6652	1.9917	2.3764	2.6421
77	0.6777	1.2926	1.6649	1.9913	2.3758	2.6412
78	0.6776	1.2925	1.6646	1.9908	2.3751	2.6403
79	0.6776	1.2924	1.6644	1.9905	2.3745	2.6395
80	0.6776	1.2922	1.6641	1.9901	2.3739	2.6387
81	0.6775	1.2921	1.6639	1.9897	2.3733	2.6379
82	0.6775	1.2920	1.6636	1.9893	2.3727	2.6371

(Continued)

TABLE 4 (Continued)

Degrees of Freedom	Upper-Tail Areas (α)					
	.25	.10	.05	.025	.01	.005
83	0.6775	1.2918	1.6634	1.9890	2.3721	2.6364
84	0.6774	1.2917	1.6632	1.9886	2.3716	2.6356
85	0.6774	1.2916	1.6630	1.9883	2.3710	2.6349
86	0.6774	1.2915	1.6628	1.9879	2.3705	2.6342
87	0.6773	1.2914	1.6626	1.9876	2.3700	2.6335
88	0.6773	1.2912	1.6624	1.9873	2.3695	2.6329
89	0.6773	1.2911	1.6622	1.9870	2.3690	2.6322
90	0.6772	1.2910	1.6620	1.9867	2.3685	2.6316
91	0.6772	1.2909	1.6618	1.9864	2.3680	2.6309
92	0.6772	1.2908	1.6616	1.9861	2.3676	2.6303
93	0.6771	1.2907	1.6614	1.9858	2.3671	2.6297
94	0.6771	1.2906	1.6612	1.9855	2.3667	2.6291
95	0.6771	1.2905	1.6611	1.9853	2.3662	2.6286
96	0.6771	1.2904	1.6609	1.9850	2.3658	2.6280
97	0.6770	1.2903	1.6607	1.9847	2.3654	2.6275
98	0.6770	1.2902	1.6606	1.9845	2.3650	2.6269
99	0.6770	1.2902	1.6604	1.9842	2.3646	2.6264
100	0.6770	1.2901	1.6602	1.9840	2.3642	2.6259
110	0.6767	1.2893	1.6588	1.9818	2.3607	2.6213
120	0.6765	1.2886	1.6577	1.9799	2.3578	2.6174
130	0.6764	1.2881	1.6567	1.9784	2.3554	2.6142
140	0.6762	1.2876	1.6558	1.9771	2.3533	2.6114
150	0.6761	1.2872	1.6551	1.9759	2.3515	2.6090
∞	0.6745	1.2816	1.6449	1.9600	2.3263	2.5758

For a particular number of degrees of freedom, entry represents the critical value of t corresponding to a specified upper-tail area, α.

TABLE 5 F Distribution

$\alpha = .05$

$F_{(\alpha, df_1, df_2)}$

Denominator df_2	Numerator df_1																		
	1	2	3	4	5	6	7	8	9	10	12	15	20	24	30	40	60	120	∞
1	161.4	199.5	215.7	224.6	230.2	234.0	236.8	238.9	240.5	241.9	243.9	245.9	248.0	249.1	250.1	251.1	252.2	253.3	254.3
2	18.51	19.00	19.16	19.25	19.30	19.33	19.35	19.37	19.38	19.40	19.41	19.43	19.45	19.45	19.46	19.47	19.48	19.49	19.50
3	10.13	9.55	9.28	9.12	9.01	8.94	8.89	8.85	8.81	8.79	8.74	8.70	8.66	8.64	8.62	8.59	8.57	8.55	8.53
4	7.71	6.94	6.59	6.39	6.26	6.16	6.09	6.04	6.00	5.96	5.91	5.86	5.80	5.77	5.75	5.72	5.69	5.66	5.63
5	6.61	5.79	5.41	5.19	5.05	4.95	4.88	4.82	4.77	4.74	4.68	4.62	4.56	4.53	4.50	4.46	4.43	4.40	4.36
6	5.99	5.14	4.76	4.53	4.39	4.28	4.21	4.15	4.10	4.06	4.00	3.94	3.87	3.84	3.81	3.77	3.74	3.70	3.67
7	5.59	4.74	4.35	4.12	3.97	3.87	3.79	3.73	3.68	3.64	3.57	3.51	3.44	3.41	3.38	3.34	3.30	3.27	3.23
8	5.32	4.46	4.07	3.84	3.69	3.58	3.50	3.44	3.39	3.35	3.28	3.22	3.15	3.12	3.08	3.04	3.01	2.97	2.93
9	5.12	4.26	3.86	3.63	3.48	3.37	3.29	3.23	3.18	3.14	3.07	3.01	2.94	2.90	2.86	2.83	2.79	2.75	2.71
10	4.96	4.10	3.71	3.48	3.33	3.22	3.14	3.07	3.02	2.98	2.91	2.85	2.77	2.74	2.70	2.66	2.62	2.58	2.54
11	4.84	3.98	3.59	3.36	3.20	3.09	3.01	2.95	2.90	2.85	2.79	2.72	2.65	2.61	2.57	2.53	2.49	2.45	2.40
12	4.75	3.89	3.49	3.26	3.11	3.00	2.91	2.85	2.80	2.75	2.69	2.62	2.54	2.51	2.47	2.43	2.38	2.34	2.30
13	4.67	3.81	3.41	3.18	3.03	2.92	2.83	2.77	2.71	2.67	2.60	2.53	2.46	2.42	2.38	2.34	2.30	2.25	2.21
14	4.60	3.74	3.34	3.11	2.96	2.85	2.76	2.70	2.65	2.60	2.53	2.46	2.39	2.35	2.31	2.27	2.22	2.18	2.13
15	4.54	3.68	3.29	3.06	2.90	2.79	2.71	2.64	2.59	2.54	2.48	2.40	2.33	2.29	2.25	2.20	2.16	2.11	2.07
16	4.49	3.63	3.24	3.01	2.85	2.74	2.66	2.59	2.54	2.49	2.42	2.35	2.28	2.24	2.19	2.15	2.11	2.06	2.01
17	4.45	3.59	3.20	2.96	2.81	2.70	2.61	2.55	2.49	2.45	2.38	2.31	2.23	2.19	2.15	2.10	2.06	2.01	1.96
18	4.41	3.55	3.16	2.93	2.77	2.66	2.58	2.51	2.46	2.41	2.34	2.27	2.19	2.15	2.11	2.06	2.02	1.97	1.92
19	4.38	3.52	3.13	2.90	2.74	2.63	2.54	2.48	2.42	2.38	2.31	2.23	2.16	2.11	2.07	2.03	1.98	1.93	1.88
20	4.35	3.49	3.10	2.87	2.71	2.60	2.51	2.45	2.39	2.35	2.28	2.20	2.12	2.08	2.04	1.99	1.95	1.90	1.84
21	4.32	3.47	3.07	2.84	2.68	2.57	2.49	2.42	2.37	2.32	2.25	2.18	2.10	2.05	2.01	1.96	1.92	1.87	1.81
22	4.30	3.44	3.05	2.82	2.66	2.55	2.46	2.40	2.34	2.30	2.23	2.15	2.07	2.03	1.98	1.94	1.89	1.84	1.78
23	4.28	3.42	3.03	2.80	2.64	2.53	2.44	2.37	2.32	2.27	2.20	2.13	2.05	2.01	1.96	1.91	1.86	1.81	1.76
24	4.26	3.40	3.01	2.78	2.62	2.51	2.42	2.36	2.30	2.25	2.18	2.11	2.03	1.98	1.94	1.89	1.84	1.79	1.73
25	4.24	3.39	2.99	2.76	2.60	2.49	2.40	2.34	2.28	2.24	2.16	2.09	2.01	1.96	1.92	1.87	1.82	1.77	1.71
26	4.23	3.37	2.98	2.74	2.59	2.47	2.39	2.32	2.27	2.22	2.15	2.07	1.99	1.95	1.90	1.85	1.80	1.75	1.69
27	4.21	3.35	2.96	2.73	2.57	2.46	2.37	2.31	2.25	2.20	2.13	2.06	1.97	1.93	1.88	1.84	1.79	1.73	1.67
28	4.20	3.34	2.95	2.71	2.56	2.45	2.36	2.29	2.24	2.19	2.12	2.04	1.96	1.91	1.87	1.82	1.77	1.71	1.65
29	4.18	3.33	2.93	2.70	2.55	2.43	2.35	2.28	2.22	2.18	2.10	2.03	1.94	1.90	1.85	1.81	1.75	1.70	1.64
30	4.17	3.32	2.92	2.69	2.53	2.42	2.33	2.27	2.21	2.16	2.09	2.01	1.93	1.89	1.84	1.79	1.74	1.68	1.62
40	4.08	3.23	2.84	2.61	2.45	2.34	2.25	2.18	2.12	2.08	2.00	1.92	1.84	1.79	1.74	1.69	1.64	1.58	1.51
60	4.00	3.15	2.76	2.53	2.37	2.25	2.17	2.10	2.04	1.99	1.92	1.84	1.75	1.70	1.65	1.59	1.53	1.47	1.39
120	3.92	3.07	2.68	2.45	2.29	2.17	2.09	2.02	1.96	1.91	1.83	1.75	1.66	1.61	1.55	1.50	1.43	1.35	1.25
∞	3.84	3.00	2.60	2.37	2.21	2.10	2.01	1.94	1.88	1.83	1.75	1.67	1.57	1.52	1.46	1.39	1.32	1.25	1.00

(Continued)

TABLE 5 (Continued)

$\alpha = .025$

Numerator df_1

Denominator df_2	1	2	3	4	5	6	7	8	9	10	12	15	20	24	30	40	60	120	∞
1	647.8	799.5	864.2	899.6	921.8	937.1	948.2	956.7	963.3	968.6	976.7	984.9	993.1	997.2	1001	1006	1010	1014	1018
2	38.51	39.00	39.17	39.25	39.30	39.33	39.36	39.37	39.39	39.40	39.41	39.43	39.45	39.46	39.46	39.47	39.48	39.49	39.50
3	17.44	16.04	15.44	15.10	14.88	14.73	14.62	14.54	14.47	14.42	14.34	14.25	14.17	14.12	14.08	14.04	13.99	13.95	13.90
4	12.22	10.65	9.98	9.60	9.36	9.20	9.07	8.98	8.90	8.84	8.75	8.66	8.56	8.51	8.46	8.41	8.36	8.31	8.26
5	10.01	8.43	7.76	7.39	7.15	6.98	6.85	6.76	6.68	6.62	6.52	6.43	6.33	6.28	6.23	6.18	6.12	6.07	6.02
6	8.81	7.26	6.60	6.23	5.99	5.82	5.70	5.60	5.52	5.46	5.37	5.27	5.17	5.12	5.07	5.01	4.96	4.90	4.85
7	8.07	6.54	5.89	5.52	5.29	5.12	4.99	4.90	4.82	4.76	4.67	4.57	4.47	4.42	4.36	4.31	4.25	4.20	4.14
8	7.57	6.06	5.42	5.05	4.82	4.65	4.53	4.43	4.36	4.30	4.20	4.10	4.00	3.95	3.89	3.84	3.78	3.73	3.67
9	7.21	5.71	5.08	4.72	4.48	4.32	4.20	4.10	4.03	3.96	3.87	3.77	3.67	3.61	3.56	3.51	3.45	3.39	3.33
10	6.94	5.46	4.83	4.47	4.24	4.07	3.95	3.85	3.78	3.72	3.62	3.52	3.42	3.37	3.31	3.26	3.20	3.14	3.08
11	6.72	5.26	4.63	4.28	4.04	3.88	3.76	3.66	3.59	3.53	3.43	3.33	3.23	3.17	3.12	3.06	3.00	2.94	2.88
12	6.55	5.10	4.47	4.12	3.89	3.73	3.61	3.51	3.44	3.37	3.28	3.18	3.07	3.02	2.96	2.91	2.85	2.79	2.72
13	6.41	4.97	4.35	4.00	3.77	3.60	3.48	3.39	3.31	3.25	3.15	3.05	2.95	2.89	2.84	2.78	2.72	2.66	2.60
14	6.30	4.86	4.24	3.89	3.66	3.50	3.38	3.29	3.21	3.15	3.05	2.95	2.84	2.79	2.73	2.67	2.61	2.55	2.49
15	6.20	4.77	4.15	3.80	3.58	3.41	3.29	3.20	3.12	3.06	2.96	2.86	2.76	2.70	2.64	2.59	2.52	2.46	2.40
16	6.12	4.69	4.08	3.73	3.50	3.34	3.22	3.12	3.05	2.99	2.89	2.79	2.68	2.63	2.57	2.51	2.45	2.38	2.32
17	6.04	4.62	4.01	3.66	3.44	3.28	3.16	3.06	2.98	2.92	2.82	2.72	2.62	2.56	2.50	2.44	2.38	2.32	2.25
18	5.98	4.56	3.95	3.61	3.38	3.22	3.10	3.01	2.93	2.87	2.77	2.67	2.56	2.50	2.44	2.38	2.32	2.26	2.19
19	5.92	4.51	3.90	3.56	3.33	3.17	3.05	2.96	2.88	2.82	2.72	2.62	2.51	2.45	2.39	2.33	2.27	2.20	2.13
20	5.87	4.46	3.86	3.51	3.29	3.13	3.01	2.91	2.84	2.77	2.68	2.57	2.46	2.41	2.35	2.29	2.22	2.16	2.09
21	5.83	4.42	3.82	3.48	3.25	3.09	2.97	2.87	2.80	2.73	2.64	2.53	2.42	2.37	2.31	2.25	2.18	2.11	2.04
22	5.79	4.38	3.78	3.44	3.22	3.05	2.93	2.84	2.76	2.70	2.60	2.50	2.39	2.33	2.27	2.21	2.14	2.08	2.00
23	5.75	4.35	3.75	3.41	3.18	3.02	2.90	2.81	2.73	2.67	2.57	2.47	2.36	2.30	2.24	2.18	2.11	2.04	1.97
24	5.72	4.32	3.72	3.38	3.15	2.99	2.87	2.78	2.70	2.64	2.54	2.44	2.33	2.27	2.21	2.15	2.08	2.01	1.94
25	5.69	4.29	3.69	3.35	3.13	2.97	2.85	2.75	2.68	2.61	2.51	2.41	2.30	2.24	2.18	2.12	2.05	1.98	1.91
26	5.66	4.27	3.67	3.33	3.10	2.94	2.82	2.73	2.65	2.59	2.49	2.39	2.28	2.22	2.16	2.09	2.03	1.95	1.88
27	5.63	4.24	3.65	3.31	3.08	2.92	2.80	2.71	2.63	2.57	2.47	2.36	2.25	2.19	2.13	2.07	2.00	1.93	1.85
28	5.61	4.22	3.63	3.29	3.06	2.90	2.78	2.69	2.61	2.55	2.45	2.34	2.23	2.17	2.11	2.05	1.98	1.91	1.83
29	5.59	4.20	3.61	3.27	3.04	2.88	2.76	2.67	2.59	2.53	2.43	2.32	2.21	2.15	2.09	2.03	1.96	1.89	1.81
30	5.57	4.18	3.59	3.25	3.03	2.87	2.75	2.65	2.57	2.51	2.41	2.31	2.20	2.14	2.07	2.01	1.94	1.87	1.79
40	5.42	4.05	3.46	3.13	2.90	2.74	2.62	2.53	2.45	2.39	2.29	2.18	2.07	2.01	1.94	1.88	1.80	1.72	1.64
60	5.29	3.93	3.34	3.01	2.79	2.63	2.51	2.41	2.33	2.27	2.17	2.06	1.94	1.88	1.82	1.74	1.67	1.58	1.48
120	5.15	3.80	3.23	2.89	2.67	2.52	2.39	2.30	2.22	2.16	2.05	1.94	1.82	1.76	1.69	1.61	1.53	1.43	1.31
∞	5.02	3.69	3.12	2.79	2.57	2.41	2.29	2.19	2.11	2.05	1.94	1.83	1.71	1.64	1.57	1.48	1.39	1.27	1.00

TABLE 5 (Continued)

$\alpha = .01$

$F_{(\alpha, df_1, df_2)}$

		Numerator df_1																	
Denominator df_2	1	2	3	4	5	6	7	8	9	10	12	15	20	24	30	40	60	120	∞
1	4052	4999.5	5403	5625	5764	5859	5928	5982	6022	6056	6106	6157	6209	6235	6261	6287	6313	6339	6366
2	98.50	99.00	99.17	99.25	99.30	99.33	99.36	99.37	99.39	99.40	99.42	99.43	99.45	99.46	99.47	99.47	99.48	99.49	99.50
3	34.12	30.82	29.46	28.71	28.24	27.91	27.67	27.49	27.35	27.23	27.05	26.87	26.69	26.60	26.50	26.41	26.32	26.22	26.13
4	21.20	18.00	16.69	15.98	15.52	15.21	14.98	14.80	14.66	14.55	14.37	14.20	14.02	13.93	13.84	13.75	13.65	13.56	13.46
5	16.26	13.27	12.06	11.39	10.97	10.67	10.46	10.29	10.16	10.05	9.89	9.72	9.55	9.47	9.38	9.29	9.20	9.11	9.02
6	13.75	10.92	9.78	9.15	8.75	8.47	8.26	8.10	7.98	7.87	7.72	7.56	7.40	7.31	7.23	7.14	7.06	6.97	6.88
7	12.25	9.55	8.45	7.85	7.46	7.19	6.99	6.84	6.72	6.62	6.47	6.31	6.16	6.07	5.99	5.91	5.82	5.74	5.65
8	11.26	8.65	7.59	7.01	6.63	6.37	6.18	6.03	5.91	5.81	5.67	5.52	5.36	5.28	5.20	5.12	5.03	4.95	4.86
9	10.56	8.02	6.99	6.42	6.06	5.80	5.61	5.47	5.35	5.26	5.11	4.96	4.81	4.73	4.65	4.57	4.48	4.40	4.31
10	10.04	7.56	6.55	5.99	5.64	5.39	5.20	5.06	4.94	4.85	4.71	4.56	4.41	4.33	4.25	4.17	4.08	4.00	3.91
11	9.65	7.21	6.22	5.67	5.32	5.07	4.89	4.74	4.63	4.54	4.40	4.25	4.10	4.02	3.94	3.86	3.78	3.69	3.60
12	9.33	6.93	5.95	5.41	5.06	4.82	4.64	4.50	4.39	4.30	4.16	4.01	3.86	3.78	3.70	3.62	3.54	3.45	3.36
13	9.07	6.70	5.74	5.21	4.86	4.62	4.44	4.30	4.19	4.10	3.96	3.82	3.66	3.59	3.51	3.43	3.34	3.25	3.17
14	8.86	6.51	5.56	5.04	4.69	4.46	4.28	4.14	4.03	3.94	3.80	3.66	3.51	3.43	3.35	3.27	3.18	3.09	3.00
15	8.68	6.36	5.42	4.89	4.56	4.32	4.14	4.00	3.89	3.80	3.67	3.52	3.37	3.29	3.21	3.13	3.05	2.96	2.87
16	8.53	6.23	5.29	4.77	4.44	4.20	4.03	3.89	3.78	3.69	3.55	3.41	3.26	3.18	3.10	3.02	2.93	2.84	2.75
17	8.40	6.11	5.18	4.67	4.34	4.10	3.93	3.79	3.68	3.59	3.46	3.31	3.16	3.08	3.00	2.92	2.83	2.75	2.65
18	8.29	6.01	5.09	4.58	4.25	4.01	3.84	3.71	3.60	3.51	3.37	3.23	3.08	3.00	2.92	2.84	2.75	2.66	2.57
19	8.18	5.93	5.01	4.50	4.17	3.94	3.77	3.63	3.52	3.43	3.30	3.15	3.00	2.92	2.84	2.76	2.67	2.58	2.49
20	8.10	5.85	4.94	4.43	4.10	3.87	3.70	3.56	3.46	3.37	3.23	3.09	2.94	2.86	2.78	2.69	2.61	2.52	2.42
21	8.02	5.78	4.87	4.37	4.04	3.81	3.64	3.51	3.40	3.31	3.17	3.03	2.88	2.80	2.72	2.64	2.55	2.46	2.36
22	7.95	5.72	4.82	4.31	3.99	3.76	3.59	3.45	3.35	3.26	3.12	2.98	2.83	2.75	2.67	2.58	2.50	2.40	2.31
23	7.88	5.66	4.76	4.26	3.94	3.71	3.54	3.41	3.30	3.21	3.07	2.93	2.78	2.70	2.62	2.54	2.45	2.35	2.26
24	7.82	5.61	4.72	4.22	3.90	3.67	3.50	3.36	3.26	3.17	3.03	2.89	2.74	2.66	2.58	2.49	2.40	2.31	2.21
25	7.77	5.57	4.68	4.18	3.85	3.63	3.46	3.32	3.22	3.13	2.99	2.85	2.70	2.62	2.54	2.45	2.36	2.27	2.17
26	7.72	5.53	4.64	4.14	3.82	3.59	3.42	3.29	3.18	3.09	2.96	2.81	2.66	2.58	2.50	2.42	2.33	2.23	2.13
27	7.68	5.49	4.60	4.11	3.78	3.56	3.39	3.26	3.15	3.06	2.93	2.78	2.63	2.55	2.47	2.38	2.29	2.20	2.10
28	7.64	5.45	4.57	4.07	3.75	3.53	3.36	3.23	3.12	3.03	2.90	2.75	2.60	2.52	2.44	2.35	2.26	2.17	2.06
29	7.60	5.42	4.54	4.04	3.73	3.50	3.33	3.20	3.09	3.00	2.87	2.73	2.57	2.49	2.41	2.33	2.23	2.14	2.03
30	7.56	5.39	4.51	4.02	3.70	3.47	3.30	3.17	3.07	2.98	2.84	2.70	2.55	2.47	2.39	2.30	2.21	2.11	2.01
40	7.31	5.18	4.31	3.83	3.51	3.29	3.12	2.99	2.89	2.80	2.66	2.52	2.37	2.29	2.20	2.11	2.02	1.92	1.80
60	7.08	4.98	4.13	3.65	3.34	3.12	2.95	2.82	2.72	2.63	2.50	2.35	2.20	2.12	2.03	1.94	1.84	1.73	1.60
120	6.85	4.79	3.95	3.48	3.17	2.96	2.79	2.66	2.56	2.47	2.34	2.19	2.03	1.95	1.86	1.76	1.66	1.53	1.38
∞	6.63	4.61	3.78	3.32	3.02	2.80	2.64	2.51	2.41	2.32	2.18	2.04	1.88	1.79	1.70	1.59	1.47	1.32	1.00

For a particular combination of numerator and denominator degrees of freedom, entry represents the critical values of F corresponding to a specified upper-tail area, α.

Endnotes

Chapter 1

1. www.reebok.com, accessed February 15, 2011; Rachael S. Davis, "Reebok: The Brand That Fits," *Textile World,* 157(6) (December 2007): 56–57; Thomas J. Ryan, "Reebok Launches Running-Focused Ad Campaign," *SGB,* 40(5) (May 2007): 14; Mei Fong, "Yao Gives Reebok an Assist in China," *The Wall Street Journal* (September 28, 2007): B1–B2.

2. www.southerncompany.com, accessed February 5, 2011; Robert Swanekamp, "Southern Company Emphasizes Employee Development," *Power,* 144(6) (November–December, 2000): 25.

3. About McDonald's, *McDonald's Corporation,* from www.mcdonalds.com/corp/about.html, accessed January 6, 2011; T. L. Stanley, "Seinfeld, McD's, Brach's Help Build Bee Movie Buzz," *Brandweek,* 48(38) (October 2007): 6; Kenneth Hein, "Brisk Sales—With a Side of Trans-Fat," *Brandweek,* 48(25) (June 2007): S42–S43; Kate MacArthur, "Fast-Food Rethinks Marketing," *Advertising Age* (Midwest region edition), 74(26) (June 30, 2003): SR2.

4. www.sony.com, accessed March 3, 2011; Greg Tarr, "Sony Slates $100M Ad Campaign," *TWICE: This Week in Consumer Electronics,* 22(13) (June 2007): 31–33; Normandy Madden, "Global Highlight: Sony's 'Live Color Wall,'" *Advertising Age,* 78(47) (November 2007): 22; http://news.sel.sony.com/en/press_room/corporate_news/release/26912.html, accessed February 15, 2011.

5. John W. Huppertz, "Passion vs. Dispassion," *Marketing Research: A Magazine of Management and Applications,* 15(2) (Summer 2003): 16; Naresh K. Malhotra, "Shifting Perspective on the Shifting Paradigm in Marketing Research," *Journal of the Academy of Marketing Science,* 20 (Fall 1992): 379–387; William Perreault, "The Shifting Paradigm in Marketing Research," *Journal of the Academy of Marketing Science,* 20 (Fall 1992): 367–375.

6. Jack Honomichl, "Top 25 Global Research Organizations," *Marketing News* (August 30, 2010): 16.

7. "Higher Education Market Research and Strategic Planning," www.forwardanalytics.com/industrial_research/Higher_Education_Market_Research.html, accessed December 16, 2007; Ralph W. Giacobbe and Madhav N. Segal, "Rethinking Marketing Research Education: A Conceptual, Analytical, and Empirical Investigation," *Journal of Marketing Education,* 16 (Spring 1994): 43–58.

8. Paul Gillin, *Secrets of Social Media Marketing* (Fresno, CA: Quill Driver Books, 2009).

9. Jack Honomichl, "Top 25 Global Research Organizations," *Marketing News* (August 30, 2010): 16.

10. www.pg.com, accessed January 20, 2011; Anonymous, "Cracking China: In a New Book, Procter & Gamble Tells How It Brought Consumerism to an Untapped Market," http://findarticles.com/p/articles/mi_m4070/is_199/ai_n6104076, accessed December 16, 2007; Normandy Madden, "China Warms Up to P&G," *Advertising Age,* 74(14) (April 7, 2003): S5; "P&G Viewed China as a National Market and Is Conquering It," *The Wall Street Journal* (September 12, 1995): A1.

11. Starbucks Facebook page, www.facebook.com/home.php?#!/Starbucks?v=wall&ref=ts, accessed October 8, 2010; My Starbucks Idea, http://mystarbucksidea.force.com, accessed October 8, 2010; "Seattle's Best Coffee Introduces New Specialty Iced Drinks to Help Beat the Summer Heat," http://news.starbucks.com/article_display.cfm?article_id=394, accessed October 8, 2010.

12. J. Garcia de Madariaga and C. Valor, "Stakeholders Management Systems: Empirical Insights from Relationship Marketing and Market Orientation Perspectives," *Journal of Business Ethics,* 71 (2007): 425–439; Anonymous, "The Market Research Industry and Research Ethics," http://media.wiley.com/product_data/excerpt/81/04717552/0471755281.pdf, accessed December 16, 2007; Scott J. Vitell, Joseph G. P. Paolillo, and James L. Thomas, "The Perceived Role of Ethics and Social Responsibility: A Study of Marketing Professionals," *Business Ethics Quarterly,* 13(1) (January 2003): 63; Diane K. Bowers, "The Strategic Role of the Telemarketing Sales Rule in the Research Industry," *Marketing Research: A Magazine of Management and Applications,* 11(1) (Spring 1999): 34–35.

13. http://shop.samsonite.com/info/About_Samsonite, accessed October 11, 2010.

Chapter 2

1. Based on www.subaru.com, accessed January 12, 2011; Auto Business News, "Subaru of America Reports 2009 Sales," *Auto Business News.* Electronic News Publishing (January 6, 2010); Karl Greenberg, "Subaru Is Driven by New Marketing, New Direction, Lance Armstrong," *Brandweek,* 44(8) (February 24, 2003): 12.

2. www.nike.com, accessed January 14, 2011; Hoover's, A D&B Company, "Nike Inc," http://premium.hoovers.gate.lib.buffalo.edu/subscribe/co/factsheet.xhtml?ID=rcthcfhfshkyjc, accessed May 31, 2007; D. Pluchino, "Coke, Pepsi, Nike, and Adidas Are Tops in Video Game Market Research Study According to Phoenix Marketing International" (November 9, 2006), www.gamesindustry.biz/content_page.php?aid=21000, accessed May 31, 2007; Decision Analyst, "Favourite Brands," www.decisionanalyst.com/publ_data/2005/FavoriteBrand.asp, accessed May 31, 2007.

3. www2.ncl.com, accessed January 22, 2011; David Eisen, "CRUISE: Holland America's Take on Freestyle," *Travel Agent,* 331(9) (November 2007): 101; Johanna Jainchill, "NCL Breaks Out a Few More Marketing Initiatives for Ad Campaign," *Travel Weekly,* 66(23) (June 2007): 34; Andrew Scott, "Norwegian Cruise Lines Rebrands with $100 Million Campaign," http://promomagazine.com/othertactics/news/norwegian_rebrands_092106, accessed December 17, 2007; Anonymous, "Norwegian Cruise Line," *Incentive,* 177(11) (November 2003): 89; David Goetzl, "Luxury Cruise Lines Woo Boomers to Sea," *Advertising Age,* 70(11) (March 15, 1999): 26; "It's Different Out Here—Norwegian Cruises," *Adweek* (special planning section) (August 5, 1996): 7.

4. www.pgeverydaysolutions.com/pgeds/pg-brandsaver-new-products.jsp, accessed October 11, 2010.

5. www.gillettevenus.com/en_US/satin_care/index.jsp, accessed January 5, 2011; Pamela Edwards, "Calendar Girl," *Essence,* 36(10) (February 2006): 45–49; Anonymous, "Vanity Fares Market Profile on: Health and Beauty Market,"

www.checkout.ie/MarketProfile.asp?ID=187, accessed December 17, 2007; Anonymous, "Gillette Passion for Shaving," *Retail World*, 56(15) (August 4–August 15, 2003): 30; "A Woman's Touch," *Discount Merchandiser*, 39(5) (May 1999): 104; Sean Mehegan, "Gillette Big on Body Wash," *Brandweek*, 38(5) (February 3, 1997): 5.

6. Wayne C. Booth, Gregory G. Colomb, and Joseph M. Williams, *The Craft of Research* (Chicago: University of Chicago Press, 1995).

7. J. Neff, "*Pampers Steps Up Digital, Social-Media Efforts*," http://adage.com/article?article_id=143963, accessed June 15, 2010; E. Byron, "Diaper Gripes Grow Louder for P&G," *The Wall Street Journal* (May 14, 2010); Jennifer Pellet, "Lessons FROM Brand Leaders," *Chief Executive*, 221 (October 2006): 26; Patricia Sellers, "P&G: Teaching an Old Dog New Tricks," *Fortune* (May 31, 2004): 167–180.

8. www.lee.com, accessed January 11, 2011; Bob Garfield, "Boring and Banal: That's a Pretty Good Fit for Lee," *Advertising Age* (Midwest region edition), 77(37) (September 2006): 45; David Lipke, "Lee Poised for New Marketing Blitz. 'Get What Fits' Campaign to Launch in August on Television, Radio and in Print," *DNR* (New York), 36(31) (July 2006): 4; Sandra O'Loughlin, "Lee Jeans Launching One True Fit in Move to Extend Market Share," *Brandweek*, 44(2) (January 13, 2003): 4; Sandra O'Loughlin, "Buddy Lee Takes Show on the Road," *Brandweek*, 44(33) (September 15, 2003): 12.

9. California Milk Processor Board, *News & Events—Mootopian Summer*, www.gotmilk.com/#/news-and-events/87, accessed July 7, 2010; Anonymous, "On a Mission for Milk—Interactive Campaign Challenges Consumers to 'Get the Glass,'" *PR Newswire* (New York), (March 2007); Jeff Manning, "Got Milk? A Decade of Lessons Pours In," *Brandweek*, 44(22) (June 2, 2003): 24; Hillary Chura and Stephanie Thompson, "Bozell Moving Beyond Mustaches in Milk Ads," *Advertising Age*, 70(43) (October 18, 1999): 81.

10. www.heinz.com, accessed January 20, 2011; Tania Mason, "Heinz Backs Its Best Varieties," *Marketing* (March 27, 2003): 17; Judann Dagnoli, "Why Heinz Went Sour in Brazil," *Advertising Age* (December 5, 1988): 61–62.

11. www.dell.com, accessed January 9, 2011; Mei Lin Fung, "You Can Learn From 'Dell Hell.' Dell Did," www.customerthink .com/article/you_can_learn_dell_hell_dell_did, accessed March 11, 2008; Dominque Hind, "Dell's Journey to Listening— IdeaStorm," http://dominiquehind.wordpress.com/2008/09/27/ dells-journey-to-listening-ideastorm, accessed September 27, 2008.

12. Anonymous, "Closing the Gap Between the Ethical and Profitable," *Marketing Week* (October 16, 2003): 32; Ishmael P. Akaah, "Influence of Deontological and Teleological Factors on Research Ethics Evaluations," *Journal of Business Research*, 39(2) (June 1997): 71–80; G. R. Laczniak and P. E. Murphy, *Ethical Marketing Decisions, the Higher Road* (Boston: Allyn and Bacon, 1993). For hypotheses development in an ethical context, see Scott J. Vitell and Encarnacion Ramos Hidalgo, "The Impact of Corporate Ethical Values and Enforcement of Ethical Codes on the Perceived Importance of Ethics in Business: A Comparison of U.S. and Spanish Managers," *Journal of Business Ethics* 64 (2006): 31–43.

13. www.kelloggcompany.com, accessed February 12, 2011; Maja Beckstrom, "Snack Attack Battle Plan: Here Are a Few Ideas for Improving the Quality of the Between-Meal Calories Kids Consume," *Knight Ridder Tribune Business News* (March 2007): 1; Anonymous, "Kellogg's Broadens Special K Range with Oats
& Honey Variant," www.talkingretail.com/products/7334/ Kelloggs-broadens-Special-K-ra.ehtml, accessed December 18, 2007; www.kelloggs.com, accessed January 10, 2008.

Chapter 3

1. www.spiegel.com, accessed January 22, 2011; Anonymous, "Spiegel Brands Inc. Implements Guided Self-Service Solution from Spoken Communications, Inc. Guided Speech IVR Is Far More Effective and Efficient Than IVR Alone," *PR Newswire* (New York) (August 2007); Karyn Monget with contributions from David Moin, "Penney's, Spiegel Make Lingerie Moves," *WWD* (New York), 192(73) (October 2006): 14; Sandra O'Loughlin, "Struggling Spiegel Group Dresses Up Eddie Bauer," *Brandweek*, 44(31) (September 1, 2003): 10; Mercedes Cardona, "Eddie Bauer Banks on Basics for Season," *Advertising Age*, 74(47) (November 24, 2003): 10.

2. www.bankofamerica.com, accessed January 12, 20011; Valerie Bauerlein, "Bank of America CEO in Spotlight After Deal," *The Wall Street Journal* (August 27, 2007): A1, A9.

3. Adapted from www.jergens.com, accessed January 17, 2011; Anonymous, "Sara Lee Hunts Household and Body Care Marketer," *Marketing Week* (October 2007); Lisa I. Fried, "Retailers Cleaning Up with Body Washes, Gift Sets— Drugstore Chains," *Drug Store News*, http://findarticles. com/p/articles/mi_m3374/is_n17_v18/ai_18804351, accessed December 19, 2007.

4. Adapted from www.tylenol.com, accessed March 4, 2011; Rance Crain, "Hold the Love, J&J—We'd Rather Have Honesty in Our Tylenol Ads," *Advertising Age*, 78(47) (November 2007): 15; www.colorcom.com/consult.html http://philadelphia. bizjournals.com/philadelphia/stories/2005/03/14/tidbits 1.html; "Tylenol Is Different," www.tylenol.com/page. jhtml?id=tylenol/painex/subonly.inc, accessed June 21, 2007.

5. www.windows.com, accessed January 5, 2011; Anonymous, "Not Everyone Is Drinking Microsoft's Vista Kool-Aid," *Brandweek* (October 2007); Ina Fried, "Microsoft Readying Vista Marketing Blitz," *CNET News.com*, www.news.com/ Microsoft-readying-Vista-marketing-blitz/2100–1012_3– 6047217.html, accessed December 19, 2007.

6. www.thecro.com/?q=be_100best, accessed January 11, 2011; http://kelloggs.investoreports.com/kellogg_ar_2006/html/kellogg_ ar_2006_2.php, accessed July 27, 2007; www.thetimes100. co.uk/downloads/kellogg/kellogg_9_full.pdf, accessed July 27, 2007; http://kelloggs.investoreports.com/kellogg_ar_2006/ html/kellogg_ar_2006_7.php, accessed July 27, 2007.

7. Adapted from "P&G's Cell Phone Strategy in Japan: The Way to 'Double Billion-Dollar-Brand' Products" (January 29, 2007), http://business.nikkeibp.co.jp/article/eng/20070129/117847, accessed August 27, 2007; Anonymous, "Japan Units of P&G, Unilever Seek to Reclaim Market Share," *Nikkei Report* (July 2007); Catherine Becker, "Hair and Cosmetic Products in the Japanese Market," *Marketing and Research Today*, 25(1) (February 1997): 31–37.

8. Kimberly Smith, "How a New Product Launch via Facebook Resulted in Immediate Sales," www.generatormarketing.ie/ New_product_llaunch_Facebook.php, accessed July 20, 2010.

9. Susan Bardi Kleiser, Eugene Sivadas, James J. Kellaris, and Robert F. Dahlstrom, "Ethical Ideologies: Efficient Assessment and Influence on Ethical Judgments of Marketing Practices," *Psychology & Marketing*, 20(1) (January 2003): 1; Betsy

Peterson, "Ethics Revisited," *Marketing Research: A Magazine of Management & Applications*, 8(4) (Winter 1996): 47– 48. For research design in an ethical context, see Grace T-R Lin and Jerry Lin, "Ethical Customer Value Creation: Drivers and Barriers," *Journal of Business Ethics,* 67 (2006): 93–105.

10. B. Gilbreath, "NASCAR Marketing Dept: Be Careful What You Wish For," www.marketingwithmeaning.com/2010/03/09/nascar-marketing-dept-be-careful-what-you-wish-for, accessed June 15, 2010; Barry Janoff, "Can Nascar Be Numero Uno with Hispanic Fans, Marketers?" *Brandweek*, 48(29) (August 2007): 10; Barry Janoff, "Daytona 500 Marketing on Track," *Brandweek*, 48(7) (February 2007): 14; Leigh Somerville, "In the Driver's Seat: NASCAR Seeks Diversification," *The Business Journal*, 5(49) (August 8, 2003): 11.

Chapter 4

1. www.vindy.com, accessed January 4, 2011; Lucia Moses, "Papers Get Bigger Piece of Ad Pie," *Editor & Publisher*, 136(44) (December 8, 2003): 5; Anonymous, "Secondary Source Materials," *Database*, 21(5) (October–November 1998): 20; Joe Nicholson, "Report for the Vindicator," *Editor & Publisher*, 132(38) (September 18, 1999): 38.

2. "News Releases—Frost Introduces Text Messaging to Frost Mobile Banking Services," www.frostbank.com/SiteCollection Documents/About%20Frost/News%20Releases/FrostIntroduces TextMessaging_web_May172010.pdf, accessed July 26, 2010; John F. Waldron, "Pat Frost Out to Build Stronger Connections South of the Border," *San Antonio Business Journal*, 16(30) (August 16, 2002): B25; Bill Stoneman, "Banking on Customers," *American Demographics*, 19(2) (February 1997): 36–41.

3. Joseph S. Rabianski, "Primary and Secondary Data: Concepts, Concerns, Errors, and Issues," *The Appraisal Journal*, 71(1) (January 2003): 43–55; John Chapman, "Cast a Critical Eye: Small Area Estimates and Projections Sometimes Can Be Dramatically Different," *American Demographics*, 9 (February 1987): 30. See also Charles Blankson and Stavros P. Kalafatis, "Positioning Strategies of International and Multicultural-Oriented Service Brands," *Journal of Services Marketing*, 21(6) (2007): 435–450.

4. Based on www.ge.com, accessed February 2, 2011; Beth Snyder Bulik, "Is There an Expensive Washing Machine in Your Future?" *Advertising Age*, 78(44) (November 5, 2007): 10; Gary H. Anthes, "Portal Powers GE Sales," *Computerworld*, 37(22) (June 2, 2003): 31; Pamela L. Moore, "GE Catches Online Fever," *BusinessWeek*, 3694 (August 14, 2000): 122; Andy Cohen, "General Electric," *Sales & Marketing Management* 149(11) (October 1997): 57.

5. "About synerG—Overview," http://synerg.org, accessed August 23, 2010; www.news-record.com/apps/pbcs.dll/article? AID=/20060928/NEWSREC0101/60928005/-1/NEWSREC0201, accessed January 27, 2008.

6. Based on www.att.com, accessed January 14, 20011; Society of Competitive Intelligence Professionals, "What Is Competitive Intelligence?" www.scip.org/ci, accessed January 27, 2011; Jim Underwood, *Competitive Intelligence* (Oxford, UK: Capstone Publishing, 2002), pp. 56–59.

7. T. Crampton, "How Taobao Beats eBay In China," www.thomascrampton.com/china/taobao-china-ecommerce, accessed July 27, 2010; O. Malik, "eBay's China Syndrome" (2006), http://gigaom.com/2006/07/24/ebays-china-syndrome, accessed January 10, 2008; W. Mulligan, "Online Auction Market

in China: eBay/EachNet vs. Yahoo!/Taobao" (2006), http://china.seekingalpha.com/article/14162, accessed January 10, 2008; "eBay Changes Its Strategy in China: Giant eBay Loses Ground to Taobao," www.icmr.icfai.org/Business%20Updates/micro%20casestudies/Business%20Strategy/MCBS0010.htm, accessed January 10, 2008; www.chinataiwan.org/web/webportal/W5023951/Ushaotian/A463003.html, accessed January 10, 2008.

8. IBM Retail Twitter page, http://twitter.com/ibmretail, accessed October 8, 2010; IBM Communications Twitter page, http://twitter.com/IBM_NEWS, accessed October 8, 2010; World Retail Congress Mission Statement, www.worldretail congress.com/page.cfm/Link=286/t=m/goSection=2, accessed October 8, 2010.

9. www.census.gov/privacy/data_protection/federal_law.html, accessed October 14, 2010.

10. Corporate Information, http://companyinfo.tommy.com/#/company_profile/company_overview, accessed July 22, 2010; Mark Ritson, "Hilfiger Has Learned the Hard Way," *Marketing* (May 17, 2006): 19; Tara Croft, "Tommy Hilfiger Seeks Targets," *The Daily Deal* (May 9, 2003); http://tommyhilfiger .com, accessed January 9, 2008.

Chapter 5

1. Based on Joseph Carroll, "'Business Casual' Most Common Work Attire: Women More Likely Than Men to Wear Formal Business Clothing on the Job," *Gallup Poll Briefing* (October 4, 2007): 1–5; Anonymous, "Casual Monday-Through-Friday," *Adweek*, 48(40) (November 5, 2007): 60; Cyndee Miller, "A Casual Affair: Clothesmakers Respond to Dress-Down Trend with New Lines, Consumer Education Programs," *Marketing News*, 29(6) (March 13, 1995): 1–2.

2. www.synovate.com, accessed March 30, 2011.

3. www.gallup-robinson.com, accessed January 15, 2011; www.wzzm13.com/news/news_article.aspx? storyid=64189, accessed January 15, 2008; www.imediaconnection.com/content/10165.asp, accessed January 15, 2008; www.daimler chrysler.com/Projects/c2c/channel/documents/991609_dcx_200 7_ir_ releases_70214_cg_e.pdf, accessed January 15, 2008.

4. www.allpar.com/cars/chrysler/200.html?ktrack=kcplink, accessed October 15, 2010.

5. www.nielsen.com, accessed March 11, 2011; Anonymous, "Nielsen Takes First Step in Measuring Multi-Format TV Audiences," *Faultline*, 179 (November 8, 2006): 7–9; Rick Wartzman, "Nielsen Ratings Spark a Battle over Just Who Speaks Spanish," *Wall Street Journal* (February 25, 2000): B1.

6. M. Grenville, "Stats and Research: More Texts Than Calls in USA," www.160characters.org/news. php?action=view&nid= 2738, accessed October 15, 2010.

7. www.symphonyiri.com, accessed January 10, 2011; Mike Duff, "Supercenters, Super-Results: Format Dominates Food-Sector," *Retailing Today,* 46(9) (June 4, 2007): 12–14.

8. www.Nielsen.com, accessed January 10, 2011.

9. www.gfkrt.com/usa, accessed February 4, 2011.

10. www.v8juice.com, accessed March 3, 2011; Anonymous, "Campbell Soup," *Wall Street Journal* (Eastern edition), 250(120) (November 20, 2007): B6; Lori Dahm, "V8 v. Fusion: A Healthy History," *Beverage Industry*, 97(10) (October 2006): 36; Joanne Lipman, "Single-Source Ad Research Heralds Detailed Look at Household Habits," *Wall Street Journal* (February 16, 1988): 39.

11. Paul Hannon, "European Consumers Lift Spending," *Wall Street Journal* (Eastern edition), 249(128) (June 2, 2007): A8;

"Electrolux Q2 Profits Higher on Better Product Mix; Beats Market Forecasts," update July 17, 2007, www.forbes.com/afxnewslimited/feeds/afx/2007/07/17/afx3919960.html, accessed August 28, 2007; David Smith, "A Deficit of Consumer Loyalty," *Management Today* (July 1996): 22; "Europeans More Active as Consumers," *Marketing News* (October 6, 1991): 17.

12. Aberdeen Group, "Nielsen Online's BuzzMetrics Customers Approach, and Many Attain, Best-in-Class Status," http://en-us.nielsen.com/content/dam/nielsen/en_us/documents/pdf/White%20Papers%20and%20Reports/Buzz%20Metrics%20Research%20Brief%20(Aberdeen).pdf, accessed January 5, 2011.

13. S. Baragona, "McDonald's Faces Possible Lawsuit over Fast-Food Marketing to Kids," http://www1.voanews.com/english/news/usa/McDonalds-Faces-Possible-Lawsuit-Over-Fast-Food-Marketing-to-Kids-97067449.html, accessed July 25, 2010; Barbara Mueller, "Just Where Does Corporate Responsibility End and Consumer Responsibility Begin? The Case of Marketing Food to Kids Around the Globe," *International Journal of Advertising*, 26(4) (2007): 561–564; Rob Gray, "Perils of Sending Brands to School," *Marketing* (April 22, 1999): 30–31; Kevin Heubusch, "Is It Ok to Sell to Kids?" *American Demographics*, 19(1) (January 1997): 55.

14. www.bostonmarket.com, accessed January 23, 2011; Michael Sanson, "What's It Going to Take to Fix Boston Market?" *Restaurant Hospitality*, 91(9) (September 2007):6; www.bostonmarket.com/newsroom/index.jsp?page=press Releases&subPage=2003/060403, accessed January 15, 2008; www.bostonmarket.com/newsroom/index.jsp?page=pressReleases&subPage=2003/012003, accessed January 15, 2008.

Chapter 6

1. www.gillettevenus.com, accessed January 15, 2011; http://retail.seekingalpha.com/article/43498, accessed August 7, 2007; William Symonds, "Can Gillette Regain Its Edge?" *Business Week*, 3867 (January 26, 2004): 46; Charles Forelle, "Gillette to Launch Vibrating Razor," *Wall Street Journal* (Eastern edition), 243(11) (January 16, 2004): A8; Anonymous, "RB to Launch 'Bladeless' Female Razor," *Marketing Week* (November 6, 2003): 9.

2. Rosaline Barbour, *Doing Focus Groups* (Thousand Oaks: Sage Publications, 2008); Judith Langer, "'On' and 'Offline' Focus Groups: Claims, Questions," *Marketing News*, 34(12) (June 5, 2000): H38; Richard Cook, "Focus Groups Have to Evolve if They Are to Survive," *Campaign-London* (July 9, 1999): 14; Howard Furmansky, "Debunking the Myths About Focus Groups," *Marketing News*, 31(13) (June 23, 1997): 22.

3. David Stewart, *Focus Group: Theory and Practice,* 2nd ed. (Thousand Oaks: Sage Publications, 2006); Elizabeth Dinan, "Focus Group Firm Uses Web for Efficiency, Size," *Mass High Tech*, 21(51) (December 22, 2003): 3; Lynn Vincent, "Seven Deadly Sins of Focus Groups," *Bank Marketing*, 31(5) (May 1999): 36–39; John M. Hess and R. L. King, eds., "Group Interviewing," *New Science of Planning* (Chicago: American Marketing Association, 1968), p. 4.

4. Del Monte Foods, "Canine Assistants—It's Good to Give Milk-Bone," www.milkbone.com/canineassistants, accessed January 3, 2011; www.markettools.com/resources/files/CS_DelMonte.pdf, accessed July 14, 2007.

5. www.intel.com, accessed March 3, 2011; "'We've Picked up the Pace': Intel CEO Otellini Forecasts Profit Growth Outpacing Revenue in 2007, '08," Market Watch from Dow Jones, www.marketwatch.com/news/story/intel-ceo-sees-profit-gains/story.aspx?guid= %7B8B1D5398–2B83–49AA-94D7– 33E34B FA2F6D%7D, accessed January 23, 2008; "The Times 100—Case Studies for Intel" (March 24, 2007), www.thetimes100.co.uk/case_ study.php?cID=85&csID=227&pID=1, accessed June 17, 2007; Intel in Healthcare, "Intel in Healthcare Overview," http://download.intel.com/healthcare/pdf/Intel_in_Healthcare_Brochure.pdf, accessed May 30, 2007.

6. www.mars.com, accessed March 5, 2011; Mike Beirne, "Mars Attacks! Preps Flood of SKUs as Hershey Reels," *Brandweek*, 48(42) (November 19, 2007): 12; Mike Beirne, "Mars Gets Hot and Spicy for Hispanic Consumers," *Brandweek*, 44(21) (May 26, 2003): 10; Kennedy Carol, "The Chocolate Wars: Inside the Secret Worlds of Mars and Hershey," *Director*, 52(9) (April 1999): 80; Judann Pollack, "Mars Says Milky Way Lite Eating Up the Competition," *Advertising Age*, 67(40) (September 30, 1996): 28.

7. Porsche Cars North America, Inc., "About Porsche," www.porsche.com/usa/aboutporsche, accessed January 7, 2011; Kevin Wilson, "Panoply of Porsches Past," *AutoWeek*, 57(49) (December 3, 2007): 48–50; Alex Taylor, III, "Porsche Risky Recipe," *Fortune*, 147(3) (February 17, 2003): 91; Chris Reiter, "Porsche to Offer Cheaper Version of Hot SUV," *Wall Street Journal* (Eastern edition), 242(42) (August 28, 2003): D2; Alex Taylor, III, "Porsche Slices Up Its Buyers," *Fortune*, 131(1) (January 16, 1995): 24.

8. Anonymous, "Fear of Flying," *The Economist*, 383 (8542) Special section (June 16, 2007): 3–5; Jill Dunning, "Fear of Flying: White-Knuckle Ride," *Director*, 57(4) (November 2003): 51; "Fear of Flying, *The Economist*, 339(7966) (May 18, 1996): 30.

9. www.iberia.com, accessed October 18, 2010; Jens Flottau, "Bullish on Iberia," *Aviation Week & Space Technology*, 167(4) (July 23, 2007): 42; Anonymous, "Airlines Brief: Iberia," *Wall Street Journal* (February 3, 2003): C11; John Pollack, "Iberia Eyes Americas," *Advertising Age* (Midwest Region Edition) (April 27, 1992): 114.

10. www.womma.org/casestudy/examples/generate-buzz/passenger-and-jcpenney-create, accessed July 27, 2010.

11. L. Rohter, "Obama Attacks McCain in a Bid to Attract Hispanic Voters," *New York Times* (September 18, 2008); Scott D. Wells and Elizabeth A. Dudash, "Wha'd'ya Know? Examining Young Voters' Political Information and Efficacy in the 2004 Election," *American Behavioral Scientist*, 50(9) (May 2007): 1280–1289; Joan Obra, "Political Mudslinging Makes Money for Media Companies," *Knight Ridder Tribune Business News* (August 20, 2003): 1; S. Banker, "The Ethics of Political Marketing Practices, The Rhetorical Perspective," *Journal of Business Ethics*, 11 (1992): 843–848. For the role of qualitative research in ethics research, see Chong Ju Choi, Tarek I. Eldomiaty, and Sae Won Kim, "Consumer Trust, Social Marketing and Ethics of Welfare Exchange," *Journal of Business Ethics* 74 (2007): 17–23.

12. www.ibm.com, accessed January 18, 2011; www-3.ibm.com/software/swnews/swnews.nsf/n/ jmae5n7sjh?OpenDocument&Site=default, accessed January 18, 2008; J. Nicholas Hoover, "Lotus' Leap," *InformationWeek*, 1123 (January 29, 2007): 29–31.

Chapter 7

1. Based on www.pg.com and www.olay.com, accessed February 4, 2011; Louise Jack, "P&G Rebrands Laundry Products to Encourage People to Rewear Clothes," *Marketing Week,* 30(46) (November 15, 2007): 8; "1993 Edison Best New Products Awards Winners," *Marketing News* (April 25, 1994): E5.

2. www.pizzahut.com, accessed March 12, 2011; Anonymous, "Pizza Hut," *Nation's Restaurant News,* 41(41) (October 15, 2007): 36; Chad Ruben, "Pizza Hut Explores Customer Satisfaction," *Marketing News*, 30(7) (March 25, 1997): 15.

3. Based on www.altamontemall.com, accessed January 12, 2011; www.prnewswire.com/cgi-bin/stories.pl? ACCT=104&STORY= /www/story/09–14–1999/0001021344&EDATE, accessed June 21, 2007.

4. Based on www.campbellfoodservice.com, accessed March 19, 2011; Anonymous, "Soup's On," *Restaurants & Institutions*, 115(17) (September 15, 2005): 63–68; Stephanie Thompson, "Campbell Can Latest Soup Effort," *Advertising Age*, 71(32) (July 31, 2000): 1–2; "Campbell Soup's Stockpot Makes Appointments to Its Sales Teams," *Nation's Restaurant News*, 33(5) (February 1, 1999): 48; "1996 Saw Record Number of New Products," *Quirk's Marketing Research*, 11(2) (February 1997): 27–30.

5. "Accessibility in Windows 7," www.microsoft.com/enable/ products/windows7/default.aspx, accessed July 17, 2010; "Accessibility Technology in Computing," www.microsoft .com/enable/research/default.aspx, accessed March 27, 2010.

6. Anonymous, "Starbucks Soars in China," *Asia Times Online Chinese Business* (June 15, 2006), www.atimes.com/atimes/ China_Business/HF15Cb06.html, accessed June 20, 2007.

7. www.steelcase.com, accessed March 7, 2011; Anonymous, "Flexible Furniture for Flexible Space," *Building Design & Construction,* 48(3) (March 2007): 42–45; Anne Marie Moss, "The Office of the Future," *FDM, Furniture Design & Manufacturing*, 69(8) (August 1997): 36–42; "Ignore Your Customers," *Fortune* (May 1, 1995): 121–122, 124, 126.

8. www.porticoresearch.com, accessed January 5, 2011; Barbara Benson, "Market Researcher Wins Clients with Documentaries," *Crain's New York Business*, 17(17) (April 23, 2001): 31. See also Lorne McMillan and Brends Ng, "Ethnography Within Consumer Research—A Critical Case Study of Consumer Film Festivals," *International Journal of Market Research*, 49(6) (2007): 707–714.

9. www.gfk.com/group/press_information/press_releases/006688/ index.en.html, accessed October 20, 2010.

10. www.slideshare.net/jedsundwall/social-media-survey-results, accessed October 7, 2010.

11. Thomas R. Shaw, "The Moral Intensity of Privacy: An Empirical Study of Webmasters' Attitudes," *Journal of Business Ethics*, 46(4) (September 2003): 301; Lou E. Pelton, Jhinuk Chowdhury and Scott J. Vitell, Jr., "A Framework for the Examination of Relational Ethics: An Interactionist Perspective," *Journal of Business Ethics*, 19(3) (Part 2) (April 1999): 241–253; Marla Royne Stafford and Thomas F. Stafford, "Participant Observation and the Pursuit of Truth: Methodological and Ethical Considerations," *Journal of the Market Research Society*, 35 (January 1993): 63–76.

12. www.wired.com, accessed January 23, 2011; "What Are Cookies and How Does Hotwire Use Them?" www.hotwire.com/ helpcenter/my-account/security-privacy/cookies.jsp, accessed July 3, 2010. For the use of surveys in ethics research see John Cherry, "The Impact of Normative Influence and Locus of Control on Ethical Judgments and Intentions: A Cross-Cultural Comparison," *Journal of Business Ethics,* 68 (2006): 113–132.

13. www.microsoft.com, accessed March 25, 2011; www.microsoft. com/business/en-us/solutions/cloudservices/default.aspx, accessed July 27, 2010; Anonymous, "Microsoft Enters Small-Business VoIP Market," *TelecomWeb News Break* (October 3, 2007): 2; Renee Boucher Ferguson, "Automating the Back Office: Netledger, Microsoft Aim Updates at Smaller Firms," *eWeek* (August 4, 2003): 1.

Chapter 8

1. www.muzak.com, accessed January 7, 2011; "Target Customers with In-Store Marketing Messages from Muzak Voice," http:// voice.muzak.com/solutions/in_store, accessed October 15, 2010; James J. Farrell, "Merchandising Music," *Clergy Journal*, 79(4) (February 2003): 14; Colleen Bazdarich, "A Buying Mood? Maybe It's the Muzak," *Business 2.0*, 3(3) (March 2002): 100.

2. www.popai.org, accessed March 3, 2011; Deborah Vence, "Point of Purchase Displays," *Marketing News,* 41(18) (August 1, 2007): 8; Matthew Valentine, "And the Overall Winner Is . . . the P-O-P Sector," *In-Store Marketing* (November 2003): 15; Rachel Miller, "In-Store Impact on Impulse Shoppers," *Marketing* (November 21, 2002): 27–28; Ken Gofton, "POP Moves Up the Charts," *Marketing* (POP & Field Marketing Supplement) (April 17, 1997): xi.

3. http://en.wikipedia.org/wiki/Coupon, accessed October 23, 2011; Harper Roehm and Michelle Roehm, "The Relationship Between FSI Advertising Style and Coupon Redemption," *Marketing Letters*, 18(4) (October 2007): 237–247; Robert W. Shoemaker and Vikas Tibrewala, "Relating Coupon Redemption Rates to Past Purchasing of the Brand," *Journal of Advertising Research*, 25 (October–November 1985): 40–47.

4. Other forms of test marketing are controlled and minimarket tests, simulated test marketing, electronic test marketing, virtual test marketing, and Web-enabled test marketing. For details, see Naresh K. Malhotra, *Marketing Research: An Applied Orientation,* 6th ed. (Upper Saddle River, NJ: Prentice Hall, 2007).

5. Marius Oiaga, "Pepsi Teams Up with Microsoft for Global Football Campaign," http://news.softpedia. com/news/Pepsi-Teams-Up-with-Microsoft-for-Global-Football-campaign-139999.shtml, accessed October 23, 2010.

6. Jon Gibs and Sean Bruich, "Nielsen/Facebook Report: The Value of Social Media Ad Impressions," http://blog.nielsen.com/ nielsenwire/online_mobile/nielsenfacebook-ad-report, accessed October 5, 2010.

7. www.levis.com, accessed January 22, 2011; Anonymous, "Levi's 'Copper Jeans,'" *Creativity*, 15(5) (May 2007): 119; Fara Warner, "Levi's Fashions a New Strategy," *Fast Company,* 64 (November 2002): 48.

Chapter 9

1. www.olympic.org, accessed January 24, 2011; John Consoli, "Olympians Might Not Be the Idols They Once Were," *Adweek*, 47(8) (February 20, 2006): 7; James P. Sterba, "Winter Olympics 2002: Annie and Wyatt, Where Are You?—Or Why the Gun-Happy U.S. Keeps Missing the Mark in the Olympic Biathlon," *Wall Street Journal* (February 14, 2002): A6; "Olympics Big with Teens Around the World," *Quirk's Marketing Research* (March 1996), www.quirks.com, accessed January 9, 2004.

2. Based on Bruce Sylvester, "Americans Fall Prey to Weight-Loss Supplement 'Hype,'" www.healthfinder.gov/news/ newsstory.asp?docID=535687, accessed August 21, 2007.

3. www.fifa.com, accessed March 9, 2011.

4. "U.S. Retail Industry Overview," www.plunkettresearch.com/ Industries/Retailing/RetailingStatistics/tabid/268/Default.aspx, accessed October 25, 2010; Chittum Ryan and Vauhini Vara,

"A Mall Grows in San Francisco," *Wall Street Journal*
(Eastern edition), 248(80) (October 4, 2006): B1, B14; "The
Malling of America," *Quirk's Marketing Research Review*
(May 1990): 15.

5. www.nissan-global.com, accessed January 16, 2011; "Nissan
Leaf Electric Vehicle Plugs into Portugal's First Charging
Station," http://newsroom.nissan-europe.com/EU/en-gb/
Media/Media. aspx?mediaid=15366, accessed July 27, 2010;
Michele Martin, "Why Nissan Cars Are Sporty in the U.S. but
Sensible in Europe," *Campaign-London* (July 4, 1997): 21.

6. Paul Gillin, *Secrets of Social Media Marketing* (Fresno, CA:
Quill Driver Books, 2009); "Nabisco (Kraft Foods) 100
Calorie Packs Product List," www.100caloriesnacks.net/
nabisco-kraft-foods-100-calorie-packs-product-list, accessed
January 5, 2011.

7. James R. Heichelbech, "Ethics 101 Unabridged," *Marketing
Research*, 15(1) (Spring 2003): 45; Cheryl MacLellan and John
Dobson, "Women, Ethics, and MBAs," *Journal of Business
Ethics*, 16(11) (August 1997): 1201–1209; Ishmael Akaah,
"Differences in Research Ethics Judgments Between Male and
Female Marketing Professionals," *Journal of Business Ethics*, 8
(1989): 375–381. For the use of primary scales in an ethical
context, see Pat Auger, Timothy M. Devinney, and Jordan J.
Louviere, "Using Best-Worst Scaling Methodology to
Investigate Consumer Ethical Beliefs Across Countries," *Journal
of Business Ethics* 70 (2007): 299–326.

8. www.newbalance.com, accessed March 5, 2011; Judy Leand,
"New Balance Targets Dedicated Runners with NBx," *SGB*,
40(3) (March 2007): 10; Hilary Cassidy, "New Balance Ages
Up; IMG Skates Off with Disson," *Brandweek*, 42(2)
(January 8, 2001): 8.

Chapter 10

1. http://en.wikipedia.org/wiki/82nd_Academy_Awards, accessed
October 25, 2010; Richard Schickel, "Martin Scorsese," *Time*,
169(20) (May 14, 2007): 132; John Lippman, "Hollywood
Research Official Resigns—Rivals Seen Seeking Turf in
Movie-Tracking Surveys Long Controlled by NRG," *Wall Street
Journal* (September 23, 2002): B6; Shannon Dortch, "Going to
the Movies," *American Demographics*, 18(12) (December
1996): 4–7; Joe Rapolla, "Music Finds an Audience If You
Know How to Look," *Marketing News*, 29(18) (August 28,
1995): 17.

2. www.mcdonalds.com, accessed March 7, 2011; Anonymous,
"Those Who Get It—and Those Who Just Don't," *Advertising
Age*, 78(24) (June 11, 2007): 21; Kate Macarthur, "McD's Taps
Timberlake for 'I'm Lovin' It' Tie-In," *Advertising Age*, 74(31)
(August 4, 2003): 3; William Murphy and Sidney Tang,
"Continuous Likability Measurement," *Marketing Research: A
Magazine of Management & Applications*, 10(2) (Summer
1998): 28–35; Ian Fenwick and Marshal D. Rice, "Reliability of
Continuous Measurement Copy-Testing Methods," *Journal of
Advertising Research*, 31(1) (February–March 1991): 23–29.

3. "Domestic Models Outperform Imports in Vehicle Appeal for
the First Time in 13 Years," http://businesscenter.jdpower.
com/news/pressrelease.aspx?ID=2010121, accessed
October 25, 2010.

4. Naresh K. Malhotra, "A Scale to Measure Self-Concepts, Person
Concepts and Product Concepts," *Journal of Marketing
Research*, 18 (November 1981): 456–464. See also Lawrence C.
Soley, "Semantic Differential Scales in Advertising Research: A
Critical Appraisal," *American Academy of Advertising*

Conference Proceedings (2006): 10–19; Julie H. Yu, Gerald
Albaum, and Michael Swenson, "Is a Central Tendency Error
Inherent in the Use of Semantic Differential Scales in Different
Cultures?" *International Journal of Market Research*, 45
(Second Quarter 2003): 213.

5. Zumbo Yan Liu and D. Bruno, "The Impact of Outliers on
Cronbach's Coefficient Alpha Estimate of Reliability: Visual
Analogue Scales," *Educational & Psychological Measurement*,
67(4) (August 2007): 620–634; Adam Duhachek, Anne T.
Coughlan, and Dawn Iacobucci, "Results on the Standard Error
of the Coefficient Alpha Index of Reliability," *Marketing
Science,* 24(2) (Spring 2005): 294–301; William M. Rogers,
Neal Schmitt, and Morelle E. Mullins, "Correction of
Unreliability of Multifactor Measures: Comparison of Alpha and
Parallel Forms Approaches," *Organizational Research Methods*,
5(2) (April 2002): 184–199; Kevin E. Voss, Donald E. Stem, Jr.,
and Stergios Fotopoulos, "A Comment on the Relationship
Between Coefficient Alpha and Scale Characteristics,"
Marketing Letters, 11(2) (May 2000): 177; Robert A. Peterson,
"A Meta-Analysis of Chronbach's Coefficient Alpha," *Journal of
Consumer Research*, 21 (September 1994): 381–391.

6. www.mccannerickson.com, accessed March 21, 2011; Mark
Peterson and Naresh K. Malhotra, "Measuring the Appraisal of
Ad-Based Affect with Ad Promises," *Journal of Business
Research*, 42 (1998): 227–239.

7. www.mastercard.com/us/company/en/insights/pdfs/2008/
MCWW_WCoC-Report_2008.pdf, accessed May 1, 2011;
MasterCard Worldwide, "New MasterCard Worldwide Research
Explores Strategic Role of Cities in Driving Global Commerce,"
News Release (June 18, 2007), www.mastercard.com/
us/company/en/newsroom/pr_wcoc.html, accessed
July 15, 2007.

8. Naresh K. Malhotra, *Marketing Research: An Applied
Orientation*, 6th ed. (Upper Saddle River, NJ: Prentice Hall,
2010).

9. Paul Gillin, *Secrets of Social Media Marketing* (Fresno, CA:
Quill Driver Books, 2009).

10. Joan Marie McMahon and Robert J. Harvey, "Psychometric
Properties of the Reidenbach–Robin Multidimensional Ethics
Scale," *Journal of Business Ethics,* 72(1) (April 2007): 27–39;
Saul Klein, "Marketing Norms Measurement: An International
Validation and Comparison," *Journal of Business Ethics*, 18(1)
(January 1999): 65–72; Anusorn Singhapakdi, Scott J. Vitell,
Kumar C. Rallapalli, and Kenneth L. Kraft, "The Perceived Role
of Ethics and Social Responsibility: A Scale Development,"
Journal of Business Ethics, 15(11) (November 1996):
1131–1140; R. Eric Reidenbach and Donald P. Robin, "A
Response to 'On Measuring Ethical Judgments,'" *Journal of
Business Ethics*, 14 (February 1995): 159–162.

11. www.monster.com, accessed April 2, 2011; Jemima Bokaie,
"Monster Awards £77m Global Ad Task to BBDO," *Marketing*
(September 12, 2007): 2; Andrea L. Stape, "Job-Search Site
Monster Gets Ready to Make Noise," *Knight Ridder Tribune
Business News* (August 28, 2003): 1; John R. Rossiter, "The
C-OAR-SE Procedure for Scale Development in Marketing,"
International Journal of Research in Marketing, 19(4)
(December 2002): 305.

Chapter 11

1. Based on www.worldvision.org, accessed January 4, 2011; Maja
Pawinska, "World Vision Raises Profile Among Scots," *PR Week*
(May 23, 2003): 13; Greg Gattuso, Elaine Santoro, and

George R. Reis, "Notebooks Open Hearts of Sponsors," *Fund Raising Management*, 27(10) (December 1966): 10–11.

2. Based on wwwfamilyroomllc.com, accessed February 15, 2011; Anonymous, "Toons' Study Finds Kids Call the Shots in Buying Decisions," *Businessline* (February 12, 2003): 1; Paul Miller, "Tapping the Teen Market," *Catalog Age*, 20(8) (July 2003): 31.

3. Based on Timothy R. Graeff, "Reducing Uninformed Responses: The Effects of Product-Class Familiarity and Measuring Brand Knowledge on Surveys," *Psychology & Marketing*, 24(8) (August 2007): 681–702; Janet M. Kelly and David Swindell, "The Case for the Inexperienced User: Rethinking Filter Questions in Citizen Satisfaction Surveys," *American Review of Public Administration*, 33(1) (March 2003): 91–109; Kenneth C. Schneider and James C. Johnson, "Link Between Response-Inducing Strategies and Uninformed Response," *Marketing Intelligence & Planning*, 12(1) (1994): 29–36; Del I. Hawkins and Kenneth A. Coney, "Uninformed Response Error in Survey Research," *Journal of Marketing Research* (August 1981): 373.

4. www.healthychoice.com, accessed March 5, 2011; Steven Gray, "ConAgra Says Healthy Choice Can Be Tasty, Too," *Wall Street Journal* (Eastern edition), 248(44) (August 22, 2006): B2; Sonia Reyes, "Healthy Choice for Ice Cream," *Brandweek*, 44(1) (January 6, 2003): 3; "Edison, American Marketing Association, Best New Product Awards," *Marketing News*, 31(6) (March 17, 1997): E5.

5. www.aa.com, accessed January 6, 2011; "America Airlines Comprehensively Manages Customer and Employee Feedback with Key Survey," www.KeySurvey.com, accessed June 1, 2007.

6. Based on www.kelloggs.com, accessed January 10, 2011; Sonia R. Reyes, "Kellogg's Goes Bananas for Healthier Corn Flakes," *Brandweek*, 45(1) (January 5, 2004): 4; Judann Pollack and Beth Snyder, "Kellogg's Shifts Two JWT Brands to Burnett in Rift," *Advertising Age*, 70(5) (February 1, 1999): 3, 44; "Edison, American Marketing Association, Best New Product Awards," *Marketing News*, 31(6) (March 17, 1997): E5.

7. Rating a brand on specific attributes early in a survey can affect responses to a later overall brand evaluation. For example, see Larry M. Bartels, "Question Order and Declining Faith in Elections," *Public Opinion Quarterly*, 66(1) (Spring 2002): 67–79; Barbara A. Bickart, "Carryover and Backfire Effects in Marketing Research," *Journal of Marketing Research*, 30 (February 1993): 52–62.

8. Elizabeth Dean, Rachel Caspar, Georgina McAvinchey, Leticia Reed, and Rosanna Quiroz, "Developing a Low-Cost Technique for Parallel Cross-Cultural Instrument Development: The Question Appraisal System (QAS-04)," *International Journal of Social Research Methodology*, 10(3) (July 2007): 227–241; Robert A. Peterson, *Constructing Effective Questionnaires* (Thousand Oaks, CA: Sage, 2000); Elizabeth Martin and Anne E. Polivka, "Diagnostics for Redesigning Survey Questionnaires," *Public Opinion Quarterly*, 59(4) (Winter 1995): 547–567; A. Diamantopoulos, Bodo B. Schlegelmilch, and Nina Reynolds, "Pretesting in Questionnaire Design: The Impact of Respondent Characteristics on Error Detection," *Journal of the Market Research Society*, 36 (October 1994): 295–314.

9. Based on Christina Passariello, Sarah Nassauer, and Hanting Tang, "European Jewelers Engage in Global Battle for Brides," *Wall Street Journal* (Eastern edition), 250(28) (August 3, 2007): B1–B2; Peter Coolsen, "Opinion Surveys Uncover Cultural Preferences," *Nonprofit World* 17(2) (March–April 1999): 17–18; Edgar P. Hibbert and Jonathan Liu, *International Market Research—A Financial Perspective* (Oxford: Blackwell Publishers Inc., 1996).

10. Paul Gillin, *Secrets of Social Media Marketing* (Fresno, CA: Quill Driver Books, 2009).

11. Howard J. Gershon and Gary E. Buerstatte, "The E in Marketing: Ethics in the Age of Misbehavior," *Journal of Healthcare Management*, 48(5) (September–October 2003): 292; Thomas Donalson and Thomas Dunfee, "When Ethics Travel: The Promise and Peril of Global Business Ethics," *California Management Review*, 41(4) (Summer 1999): 45–63; R. W. Armstrong, "An Empirical Investigation of International Marketing Ethics: Problems Encountered by Australian Firms," *Journal of Business Ethics*, 11 (1992): 161–171. For questionnaire design in the context of ethics research, see Ian Phau and Garick Kea, "Attitudes of University Students Toward Business Ethics: A Cross-National Investigation of Australia, Singapore and Hong Kong," *Journal of Business Ethics*, 72 (2007): 61–75.

12. www.delta.com, accessed March 9, 2011; Anonymous, "Survey Shows: Customers Still Must Come First," *Aviation Week & Space Technology*, 165(1) (July 3, 2006): 58; Joseph Rydholm, "A Global Perspective," *Quirks Marketing Research Review* (November 2000), www.quirks.com/articles/article.asp?arg_ArticleId=623, accessed January 18, 2008.

Chapter 12

1. Based on www.pg.com, accessed February 11, 2011; Martin Croft, "Men's Toiletries Come of Age," *Marketing Week*, 22(16) (May 20, 1999): 40–41; "Edison, American Marketing Association, Best New Product Awards," *Marketing News*, 31(6) (March 17, 1997): E5.

2. www.census.gov, accessed January 23, 2011; Brenda S. Farrell, "2010 Census: Planning and Testing Activities Are Making Progress," *GAO Reports* (March 1, 2006): 1–22; Anonymous, "Gearing Up for 2010," *Forecast* 23(2) (February 2003): 11; Carol O. Rogers, "Census 2000 Update," *Indiana Business Review*, 75(1) (Spring 2000): 12; "Just a Traditional Census," *U.S. News & World Report* (July 29, 1991): 10.

3. For the effect of sample frame error on research results, see Gregory B. Murphy, "The Effects of Organizational Sampling Frame Selection," *Journal of Business Venturing*, 17(3) (May 2002): 237; Seymour Sudman and Edward Blair, "Sampling in the Twenty-First Century," *Journal of the Academy of Marketing Science*, 27(2) (Spring 1999): 269–277.

4. Miao Wang, Jiaxin Wang, and Jinlin Zhao, "An Empirical Study of the Effect of Customer Participation on Service Quality," *Journal of Quality Assurance in Hospitality & Tourism*, 8(1) (2007): 49–73; Todd Pack, "Orlando, Fla., Survey Finds Only a Quarter of Tourists Changing Plans," *Knight Ridder Tribune Business News* (April 1, 2003): 1; "Florida Travel Habits Subject of Phone Survey," *Quirk's Marketing Research Review* (May 1987): 10, 11, 31, 56, 60.

5. Based on www.starbucks.com, accessed March 4, 2011; Anonymous, "Coffee News: An Anniversary Promo; Two Cold Coffee Concoctions," *BusinessWorld* (July 10, 2003): 1; "Edison, American Marketing Association, Best New Product Awards," *Marketing News*, 31(6) (March 17, 1997): E11.

6. Alexis A. Palmer, Patti A. Freeman, and Ramon B. Zabriskie, "Family Deepening: A Qualitative Inquiry into the Experience of Families Who Participate in Service Expeditions," *Journal of Leisure Research*, 39(3) (Third quarter, 2007): 438–458; Penny Maher, Peter Higgs, and Nick Crofts, "Risk Behaviours of

Young Indo-Chinese Injecting Drug Users in Sydney and Melbourne," *Australian and New Zealand Journal of Public Health*, 25(1) (February 2001): 50–54; Raymond F. Barker, "A Demographic Profile of Marketing Research Interviewers," *Journal of the Market Research Society* (July 1987): 279–292.

7. www.gm.com, accessed April 6, 2011; Ken Thomas, "New GM Poll Shows Americans Want Energy Independence," www.detnews.com/2005/autoinsider/0506/30/0auto-233063.htm, accessed April 10, 2008; John Gartner, "GM Resurrects the Electric Car," www.wired.com/cars/futuretransport/news/2007/01/72424, accessed April 10, 2008.

8. When the sampling interval, *i*, is not a whole number, the easiest solution is to use as the interval the nearest whole number below or above *i*. If rounding has too great an effect on the sample size, add or delete the extra cases.

9. www.tennis.com, accessed January 8, 2011; Lisa Granatstein, "Tennis Moves to Net Readers," *Mediaweek*, 8(44) (November 23, 1998): 32; "Readership Survey Serves Tennis Magazine's Marketing Needs," *Quirk's Marketing Research Review* (May 1988): 75–76.

10. Based on www.bmwusa.com, accessed March 7, 2011; Anonymous, "Company Spotlight: BMW," *MarketWatch: Automotive* 6(12) (December 2007): 14–20; David Chris Reiter, "BMW Reports Increase in Net, Driven by New 5 Series Sedan," *Wall Street Journal* (November 7, 2003): B2; "Edison, American Marketing Association, Best New Product Awards," *Marketing News*, 31(6) (March 17, 1997): E4.

11. Based on www.chanel.com, accessed March 3, 2011; http://uma.chanel.com/home.php, accessed September 4, 2007; Laurel Wentz and Emma Hall, "Kidman to Appear in Chanel No. 5 Ads," *Advertising Age*, 75(3) (January 19, 2004): 17; Barbara Busch, "The Scent of Advertising," *Global Cosmetic Industry*, 171(6) (June 2003): 24; "Edison, American Marketing Association, Best New Product Awards," *Marketing News*, 31(6) (March 17, 1997): E4.

12. For the use of different nonprobability and probability sampling techniques in cross-cultural research, see N. L. Reynolds, A. C. Simintiras, and A. Diamantopoulos, "Theoretical Justification of Sampling Choices in International Marketing Research: Key Issues and Guidelines for Researchers," *Journal of International Business Studies*, 34(1) (January 2003): 80–89; Humphrey Taylor, "The Very Different Methods Used to Conduct Telephone Surveys of the Public," *Journal of the Market Research Society*, 39(3) (July 1997): 421–432; Saeed Samiee and Insik Jeong, "Cross-Cultural Research in Advertising: An Assessment of Methodologies," *Journal of the Academy of Marketing Science*, 22 (Summer 1994): 205–215.

13. Julie Anne Lee, Ellen Garbarino, and Dawn Lerman, "How Cultural Differences in Uncertainty Avoidance Affect Product Perceptions," *International Marketing Review* 24(3) (2007): 330–349; B. J. Verhage, U. Yavas, R. T. Green, and E. Borak, "The Perceived Risk Brand Loyalty Relationship: An International Perspective," *Journal of Global Marketing*, 3(3) (1990): 7–22.

14. Paul Gillin, *Secrets of Social Media Marketing* (Fresno, CA: Quill Driver Books, 2009).

15. Daulatram B. Lund, "An Empirical Examination of Marketing Professional's Ethical Behavior in Differing Situations," *Journal of Business Ethics*, 24(4) (April 2000): 331–342; William A. Weeks, Carlos W. Moore, Joseph A. McKinney, and Justin G. Longenecker, "The Effects of Gender and Career Stage on Ethical Judgment," *Journal of Business Ethics*, 20(4) (Part 2)
(July 1999): 301–313; Marshall Schminke and Maureen L. Ambrose, "Asymmetric Perceptions of Ethical Frameworks of Men and Women in Business and Nonbusiness Settings," *Journal of Business Ethics*, 16(7) (May 1997): 719–729; I. P. Akaah, "Differences in Research Ethics Judgments Between Male and Female Marketing Professionals," *Journal of Business Ethics*, 8 (1989): 375–381. For sampling in the context of ethics research, see William E. Shafer, Kyoko Fukukawa, and Grace M. Lee, "Values and the Perceived Importance of Ethics and Social Responsibility: The US Versus China," *Journal of Business Ethics*, 70 (2007): 265–284.

16. www.mtv.com, accessed April 23, 2011; Lars Brandle, "MTV Adopts Gold Standard," *Billboard* 119(50) (December 15, 2007): 19; Catherine Belton, Brian Bremner, Kerry Capell, Manjeet Kripalani, Tom Lowry, and Dexter Roberts, "MTV's World," *BusinessWeek*, 3770 (February 18, 2002): 81; Gordon Masson, "MTV Availability Reaches 100 Million Mark in Europe," *Billboard*, 113(29) (July 21, 2001): 10–11.

Chapter 13

1. Based on www.chicagotribune.com, accessed January 4, 2011; "Study Finds Canadians Switching on to Internet, Tuning out TV and Radio" (July 31, 2007), www.cbc.ca, accessed August 9, 2007; Suzanne Vranica and Charles Goldsmith, "Nielsen Adapts Its Methods as TV Evolves," *Wall Street Journal* (September 29, 2003): B1; Phillip E. Pfeifer, "The Economic Selection of Sample Sizes for List Testing," *Journal of Interactive Marketing*, 12(3) (Summer 1998): 5–20; "The 'Infocritical' Eye," *Marketing Research: A Magazine of Management & Applications*, 9(1) (Spring 1997): 37–39.

2. A discussion of the sampling distribution can be found in any basic statistics textbook. For example, see Mark L. Berenson, David M. Levine, Timothy Krehbiel, and David F. Stephan, *Basic Business Statistics: Concepts and Applications*, 12th ed. (Upper Saddle River, NJ: Prentice Hall, 2010).

3. www.theacsi.org, accessed March 6, 2011; Doug Olenick, "Customer Satisfaction Index: Majaps Brands Up, PCs Down," *TWICE: This Week in Consumer Electronics,* 22(17) (August 20, 2007): 16; Barbara Everitt Bryant and Jaesung Cha, "Crossing the Threshold: Some Customers Are Harder to Please Than Others, So Analyze Satisfaction Scores Carefully," *Marketing Research: A Magazine of Management & Applications*, 8(4) (winter 1996): 21–28.

4. www.hp.com/go/smallbusinessweek2005, accessed October 28, 2010.

5. Based on www.lancome.com, accessed January 7, 2011; Alexandra Jardine, "L'Oreal Puts Brands Under One Roof," *Marketing* (May 27, 1999): 4; "Edison, American Marketing Association, Best New Product Awards," *Marketing News*, 31(6) (March 17, 1997): E6.

6. www.nokia.com, accessed March 21, 2011; "A First Look at 2007 Handset Sales," *Wireless Business Forecast* (May 3, 2007): 5; Hoovers, "Nokia Corporation (2007)," www.hoovers.com/nokia/—ID_41820—/free-co-factsheet.xhtml, accessed June 20, 2007; "What Mobile Gamers Say They Want," *Wireless Business Forecast* (January 12, 2007): 3.

7. Paul Gillin, *Secrets of Social Media Marketing* (Fresno, CA: Quill Driver Books, 2009).

8. Mark Halperin and Amy Sullivan, "How America Decides," *Time,* 170(25) (December 17, 2007): 38–41; Vicki G. Morwitz and Carol Pluzinski, "Do Polls Reflect Opinions or Do Opinions Reflect Polls? The Impact of Political Polling on Voters'

Expectations, Preferences, and Behavior," *Journal of Consumer Research*, 23(1) (June 1996): 53–67. For sample size determination in the context of ethics research, see Sarah Steenhaut and Patrick van Kenhove, "An Empirical Investigation of the Relationship Among a Consumer's Personal Values, Ethical Ideology and Ethical Beliefs," *Journal of Business Ethics,* 64 (2006): 137–155.

9. Based on www.pg.com, accessed April 21; 2011; Vanessa L. Facenda, "P&G Sees Valuable Assets in $86M Charmin Relaunch," *Brandweek,* 48(37) (October 15, 2007): 5; Jack Neff, "P&G Brings Potty to Parties," *Advertising Age* (Midwest region edition), 74(7) (February 17, 2003): 22.

Chapter 14

1. Based on www.gallup.com, accessed January 4, 2008; Leah Nathans Spiro, "Gallup, the Pollster, Wants to Be Known for Its Consulting," *New York Times* (July 21, 2003): C6; Gale D. Muller and Jane Miller, "Interviewers Make the Difference," *Marketing Research: A Magazine of Management & Applications*, 8(1) (Spring 1996): 8–9.

2. Teresa Whitacre, "Behavioral Interviewing—Find Your STAR," *Quality Progress,* 40(6) (June 2007): 72–73; Ted Samson, "Interviewing 101—For Managers," *InfoWorld*, 22(13) (March 27, 2000): 101; Peggy Lawless, "Empathic Interviewing Equals Insightful Results," *Marketing News*, 33(1) (January 4, 1999): 20; Bud Phillips, "The Four Faces of Interviewers," *Journal of Data Collection*, 23 (Winter 1983): 35–40.

3. www.whirlpool.com, accessed January 22, 2011; "Household Appliance: Washers and Dryers—US," *MarketResearch.com* (August 1, 2006–February 24, 2007), www.market research.com/product/ display.asp? productid=1337663 &SID=41184446–377143908–336506586&kw=whirlpool, accessed January 18, 2008; William Perreault and Jerome McCarthy, *Basic Marketing,* 15th ed. (New York: McGraw-Hill, 2005).

4. Based on www.oralb.com, accessed January 4, 2011.

5. Based on "New Treats from Mars Chocolate North America Combine Sweet & Savory Flavors," www.mars.com/ global/news-and-media/press-releases/news-releases.aspx? SiteId=94&Id=1917, accessed October 28, 2010.

6. http://ec.europa.eu/trade/creating-opportunities/bilateral-relations/countries/united-states, accessed January 5, 2011; Janet Guyon, "Brand America," *Fortune*, 148(9) (October 27, 2003): 179; Laurel Wentz, "Poll: Europe Favors U.S. Products," *Advertising Age* (September 23, 1991): 16.

7. Society for New Communications Research, "Division: Academic, Category: Online Reputation Management, Georgia Institute of Technology," Report, 2009.

8. www.nissanusa.com, accessed March 11, 2011; Jonathan Welsh, "Me and My Car," *Wall Street Journal* (Eastern edition), 250(121) (November 21, 2007): D4; Michael McCarthy, "Nissan Xterra Discover Extra Success," *USA Today Online* (February 26, 2001), www.usatoday.com/money/index/2001–02–26-ad-track-nissan .htm#more, accessed January 28, 2008.

Chapter 15

1. www.sears.com, accessed April 5, 2011; "New CRM System Speeds Sears Campaign Process: DMA2010," www.dmnews .com/new-crm-system-speeds-sears-campaign-process-dma 2010/article/180834, accessed October 29, 2010; Kathy Shwiff and Brian Coyle, "Sears, Vying for Restoration, Signs Confidentiality Pact," *Wall Street Journal* (Eastern edition),

250(137) (December 11, 2007): A23; Deena M. Amato-McCoy, "Sears Combines Retail Reporting and Customer Databases on a Single Platform," *Stores*, 84(11) (November 2002): 26; Cyndee Miller, "Redux Deluxe: Sears Comeback an Event Most Marketers Would Kill for," *Marketing News*, 30(15) (July 15, 1996): 1, 14.

2. Piotr Chelminski and Robin A. Coulter, "The Effects of Cultural Individualism and Self-Confidence on Propensity to Voice: From Theory to Measurement to Practice," *Journal of International Marketing,* 15(4) (2007): 94–118; Jagdip Singh and Robert E. Wilkes, "When Consumers Complain: A Path Analysis of the Key Antecedents of Consumer Complaint Response Estimates," *Journal of the Academy of Marketing Science*, 24 (Fall 1996): 350–365.

3. See the SPSS, Excel, SAS, and Minitab manuals available for microcomputers and mainframes.

4. www.apple.com, accessed March 3, 2011; "Apple Presents iPhone 4," www.apple.com/pr/library/2010/06/07iphone.html, accessed August 15, 2010; S. Chaudhuri, "Why Apple's iPhone Is Not the Next iPod," www.fastcompany.com/articles/2007/ 05/apple-iphone-not-next-ipod.html, accessed June 21, 2007.

5. Based on www.acer.com, accessed April 25, 2011; "Acer Launches New S1 Line of Ultra-Thin, Space-Saving Displays with Advanced Eco-Friendly Technology and Packaging," http://us.acer.com/acer/news_detail.do?LanguageISOCtx Param=en&sp=page13&ctx2.c2att1=25&kcond9.c2att193=2489 6&CountryISOCtxParam=US&ctx1g.c2att92=453&ctx1.att 21k=1&CRC=114449110, accessed October 30, 2010; Carla Thornton, "Acer Gets Glossy; Lenovo Perfects Its Tablet," *PC World,* 25(10) (October 2007): 72; Geoffrey James "U.S. Computer Market: Where East Meets West," *Upside*, 8(12) (December 1996): 78–81.

6. Society for New Communications Research, "Division: Academic, Category: Online Reputation Management, Georgia Institute of Technology," Report, 2009.

7. Daniel P. Lorence, "The Perils of Data Misreporting," *Association for Computing Machinery. Communications of the ACM*, 46(11) (November 2003): 85; Frederick Greenman and John Sherman, "Business School Ethics: An Overlooked Topic," *Business & Society Review* 104(2) (Summer 1999): 171–177; Cheryl MacLellan and John Dobson, "Women, Ethics, and MBAs," *Journal of Business Ethics*, 16(11) (August 1997): 1201–1209; G. M. Zinkhan, M. Bisesi, and M. J. Saxton, "MBAs' Changing Attitudes Toward Marketing Dilemmas: 1981–1987," *Journal of Business Ethics*, 8(1989): 963–974. For data preparation in the context of ethics research, see Scott Vitell, Jatinder Singh, and Joseph Paolillo, "Consumers' Ethical Beliefs: The Roles of Money, Religiosity and Attitude Toward Business," *Journal of Business Ethics*, 73(4) (August 2007): 369–379.

8. Based on bananarepublic.gap.com, accessed May 3, 2011; Vicki M. Young, "Calhoun Drops Interim Status at Banana Republic," *WWD: Women's Wear Daily,* 194(78) (October 12, 2007): 2; Alice Z. Cuneo, "Calhoun Takes Up Challenge to Revamp Banana Republic," *Advertising Age*, 74(24) (June 16, 2003): 22.

Chapter 16

1. Based on "Consumers Use over $3.5 Billion in Coupons," www.newsamerica.com/ourcompany/ Documents/ Inmar%20Press%20Release.pdf, accessed September 3, 2010; http://couponing.about.com/od/localcoupons/a/2006

couponusage.htm, accessed September 3, 2010; Susan K. Harmon and C. Jeanne Hill, "Gender and Coupon Use," *The Journal of Product and Brand Management*, 12(2/3) (2003): 166; Jack Neff, "Internet Enabling Coupon Fraud Biz," *Advertising Age*, 74(42) (October 20, 2003): 3–4; "Coupons, In-Store Promotions Motivate Consumer Purchasing," *Marketing News* (October 9, 1995): 6.

2. Anonymous, "MDs Seek PR Prescriptions," *Advertising Age*, 77(12) (March 20, 2006): 22; Daniel D. Butler and Avery M. Abernethy, "Yellow Pages Advertising by Physicians," *Journal of Health Care Marketing*, 16 (Spring 1996): 45–50.

3. For our purposes, no distinction will be made between formal hypothesis testing and statistical inference by means of confidence intervals.

4. Technically, a null hypothesis cannot be accepted. It can be either rejected or not rejected. This distinction, however, is inconsequential in applied research.

5. www.ichotelsgroup.com/h/d/hi/1/en/home, accessed January 10, 2011; and "Holiday Inn Brand Experience," www.holidayinn. com/hotels/us/en/global/3/exp/exp_home?cm_sp=IMMerch-_-HI2_US_en-_-Experience_NewHolidayInn#BrandExperience, accessed September 3, 2010.

6. Abbey Klaassen, "Ads for the People, by the People," *Advertising Age,* 77(9) (February 27, 2006): 1–59; Robin T. Peterson and Douglas T. Ross, "A Content Analysis of the Portrayal of Mature Individuals in Television Commercials," *Journal of Business Ethics*, 16 (1997): 425–433.

7. www.cmswire.com/cms/web-engagement/wem-lessons-case-studies-on-social-media-monitoring—007702.php, http://moremoney.blogs.money.cnn.com/2009/07/09/musicians-damaged-luggage-complaint-is-smash-youtube-hit, and http://blog.nielsen.com/nielsenwire/consumer/global-advertising-consumers-trust-real-friends-and-virtual-strangers-the-most, accessed August 24, 2010.

8. "General Mills and Curves International Partnership Delivers New Weight Management Food Brand" (May 8, 2007), www.midatlanticcurves.com/curves_cereal.htm, accessed September 5, 2007.

Chapter 17

1. Based on Ogenyi Omar and Sudaporn Sawmong, "Customer Satisfaction and Loyalty to British Supermarkets," *Journal of Food Products Marketing,* 13(2) (2007): 19–32; Peter J. McGoldrick and Elisabeth Andre, "Consumer Misbehavior: Promiscuity or Loyalty in Grocery Shopping," *Journal of Retailing and Consumer Services*, 4(2) (1997): 73–81.

2. Technically, a null hypothesis cannot be accepted. It can be either rejected or not rejected. This distinction, however, is inconsequential in applied research.

3. The condition when the variances cannot be assumed to be equal is known as the "Behrens–Fisher problem." Controversy exists as to the best procedure in this case.

4. American Express, "American Express Platinum Luxury Survey Shows Wealthy Gen X Consumers Are Mighty in Luxury Buying Power, Spending More Than Baby Boomer Population," http://home3.americanexpress.com/corp/pc/ 2005/genx_lux.asp, accessed August 1, 2007.

5. Based on Judy Leand, "Rockport Launches Torsion Comfort Footwear," *SGB,* 40(2) (February 2007): 14; Carol Krol, "Rockport Updates Image with Comfort Philosophy," *Advertising Age* (August 11, 1997): 6.

6. The *F*-test is a generalized form of the *t*-test. If a random variable is *t* distributed with *n* degrees of freedom, then t^2 is *F* distributed with 1 and *n* degrees of freedom. Where there are two factor levels or treatments, ANOVA is equivalent to the two-sided *t*-test.

7. Based on "Global Workplaces," www.levistrauss.com/about/global-workplaces, accessed September 22, 2010; Anonymous, "Levi's Accelerates Comeback with 14% Increase in Profit," *Wall Street Journal* (Eastern edition), 250(8) (July 11, 2007): B5; Sandra O'Loughlin, "Levi Strauss, Sears Have It Their Way at Burger King," *Brandweek*, 45(25) (June 21, 2004): 5; Soo Youn, Soo, "Levi's New Signature Jeans Brand Seeks to Cure Company's Blues," *Knight Ridder Tribune Business News* (May 20, 2004): 1.

8. ENGAGEMENTdb, "The World's Most Valuable Brands. Who's Most Engaged?" http://engagementdb.com/Report, accessed October 4, 2010.

9. www.marriott.com, accessed March 27, 2011; Glenn Haussman, "Desks Become Important Aspect in Laptop Culture" (June 18, 1999), www.hotelinteractive.com/news/articleView.asp?articleID=46, accessed January 8, 2008.

Chapter 18

1. Based on www.adidas-group.com, accessed March 5, 2011; "The Adidas-group," www.adidas-group.com/en/News/archive/2006/default.asp, accessed July 11, 2007; Alfred Hille, "Sporting Heritage to Boost Adidas Profile," *Media* (February 27, 2004): 5; "Adidas: Earning Its Stripes in the U.S," *BusinessWeek Online* (October 13, 2003).

2. Mark Peterson and Naresh K. Malhotra, "Comparative Marketing Measures of Societal Quality of Life: Substantive Dimensions in 186 Countries," *Journal of Macromarketing*, 17(1) (Spring 1997): 25–38. See also Raj Thomson, "There's No Place Like Home, Well Very Few," *Human Resources Magazine,* 12(2) (June–July 2007): 16–17.

3. In a strict sense, the regression model requires that errors of measurement be associated only with the criterion variable and that the predictor variables be measured without error.

4. Technically, the numerator is $b - \beta$. However, since it has been hypothesized that $\beta = 0$, it can be omitted from the formula.

5. "2010 Health Insurance Plan Satisfaction Study," www.jdpower.com, accessed September 12, 2010; Bryan K. Brenner, "Adopt a Marketing Model to Increase Client Satisfaction," *Journal of Financial Service Professionals,* 61(3) (May 2007): 8–10; Vikas Mittal, William T. Ross, Jr., and Patrick M. Baldasare, "The Asymmetric Impact of Negative and Positive Attribute-Level Performance on Overall Satisfaction and Repurchase Intentions," *Journal of Marketing*, 62(1) (January 1998): 33–47; Vikas Mittal and Patrick M. Baldasare, "Eliminate the Negative: Managers Should Optimize Rather Than Maximize Performance to Enhance Patient Satisfaction," *Journal of Health Care Marketing*, 16(3) (Fall 1996): 24–31.

6. www.wendys.com, accessed March 22, 2011; "Wendy's Unveils Expansion Plans, Sports New Image," *BusinessWorld* (May 21, 2007): 1; Hoover Inc., "Sample Survey McDonald's Survey," (June 5, 2007), www.questionpro.com/akira/showSurvey Library.do?surveyID=189596, accessed June 7, 2007.

7. "Carnegie Mellon Study of Twitter Sentiments Yields Results Similar to Public Opinion Polls," www.cmu.edu/news/archive/2010/May/may11_twitterpolls.shtml, accessed October 4, 2010.

8. "Front Office Staff—West Michigan Whitecaps About," http://web.minorleaguebaseball.com/about/ page.jsp?ymd=20090206&content_id=506266&vkey=about_t582&fext=.jsp&sid=t582,

accessed November 4, 2010; Tom Logue, "Minor League, Major Loyalty: Michigan Baseball Team Surveys Its Fans," *Quirk's Marketing Research Review* (October 2000), www.quirks .com/articles/search.aspx? searchID=11015695, accessed April 22, 2008.

Chapter 19

1. www.united.com, accessed August 11, 2011; "United Airlines Enhances Easy Check-In Self-Service Units," *Airline Industry Information* (December 5, 2003): 1; Steve Raabe, "United Airlines Passengers Report Improvement in Customer Service," *Knight Ridder Tribune Business News* (December 20, 2002): 1; Joseph Rydholm, "Surveying the Friendly Skies," *Quirk's Marketing Research Review* (May 1996): 11, 33–35.

2. Michele D. Newhouse, "Writing Robust Reports," *Association Management*, 55(3) (March 2003): 83; Thomas L. Greenbaum, "Note to Clients: Hands Off Moderator Report," *Marketing News*, 31(13) (June 23, 1997): 22; Thomas L. Greenbaum, "Using 'Ghosts' to Write Reports Hurts Viability of Focus Group," *Marketing News*, 27(19) (September 13, 1993): 25.

3. Gillian Christie, "Golden Rules of Writing Well," *Chartered Accountants Journal*, 86(11) (December 2007): 60–61; Naomi R. Henderson, "In Defense of Clients," *Marketing Research: A Magazine of Management and Applications*, 15(2) (Summer 2003): 38; Jeannine Bergers Everett, "Value-Added Research Begins Where the Marketplace Meets Management," *Marketing Research: A Magazine of Management and Applications*, 9(1) (Spring 1997): 33–36.

4. www.hp.com, accessed March 22, 2011; Hewlett Packard, "HP Surveys Nation's Small Businesses to Learn What Fuels the Engines of Today's Economy," HP news release, www.hp. com/hpinfo/newsroom/press/2005/050427a.html, accessed June 19, 2007; Brian Bergstein, "HP Extends Lead over Dell in PC Market," *International Business Times,* www.ibtimes.com/ articles/20070117/add-pc-shipments.htm, accessed July 17, 2007.

5. www.thebodyshop.com, accessed March 15, 2011; "What Is Business Ethics?" www.wisegeek.com/what-is-business-ethics.htm, accessed January 7, 2011; Gfk, "Consumers Changing the Ethical Business Agenda" (2007), www.gfk.com/imperia/md/content/businessgrafics/pd_ethical_br ands_international_efin_neu.pdf, accessed May 31, 2007.

6. Information provided by TNS.

7. Personal communication from Mary Klupp.

8. www.toyota.com.au, accessed March 3, 2011; Sonja Koremans, "Auto Brands Flock to Sydney Motor Show," *B&T Weekly,* 57(2632) (October 12, 2007): 4; "Toyota Grabs Biggest Market Share in Australia in February," *Jiji Press English News Service* (March 6, 2003): 1; Lee Geoffrey, "Aussies Chicken Fries Ford," *Advertising Age* (January 18, 1993): 124.

9. A. Kapin, "Motrin's Pain: Viral Video Disaster," www.fastcompany.com/blog/allyson-kapin/radical-tech/motrins-pain-viral-video-disaster, accessed July 23, 2010; C. L. Owens, "Johnson & Johnson—Presentation Transcript," www.slideshare.net/guest901f5569/johnson-johnson-2591972, accessed July 23, 2010; and M. Roumen, "The Motrin Case: The Voice Of The Crowd," www.viralblog.com/social-media/ the-motrin-case-the-voice-of-the-crowd, accessed July 23, 2010.

10. Anonymous, "States to Sue Reynolds American Over Cigarette Ad," *Wall Street Journal* (Eastern edition), 250(132) (December 5, 2007): B4; Lindsey Tanner, "Tobacco Firms Put on Pressure," *Marketing News*, 36(19) (September 16, 2002): 44; Elise Truly Sautter and Nancy A. Oretskin, "Tobacco Targeting: The Ethical Complexity of Marketing to Minorities," *Journal of Business Ethics*, 16(10) (July 1997): 1011–1017; Kenman L. Wong, "Tobacco Advertising and Children: The Limits of First Amendment Protection," *Journal of Business Ethics*, 15(10) (October 1996): 1051–1064; S. Rapp, "Cigarettes: A Question of Ethics," *Marketing* (November 5, 1992): 17. See also Waymond Rodgers and Susana Gago, "Biblical Scriptures Underlying Six Ethical Models Influencing Organizational Practices," *Journal of Business Ethics,* 64 (2006): 125–136.

11. www.subaru.com, accessed March 27, 2011; Anonymous, "Subaru Sheds Rally Car Image," *Precision Marketing* (London) (October 2007): 5; Anonymous, "Subaru Uses Smart Television Spots by DDB to Help Launch the New 2008 Model Year Lineup—New Cars and Clever Creative Target Specific, Well-Defined Audiences," *PR Newswire* (New York) (August 2007); Terry Box, "Subaru's Expansion Route Includes Solo Dealerships, Sporty Vehicles," *Knight Ridder Tribune Business News* (August 16, 2003): 1.

Index

Note: Page numbers with *t* indicate tables; those with *f* indicate figures.

Subject Index